LONDON RECOLLECTED

THE VILLAGE LONDON SERIES

Other titles already published are:

VILLAGE LONDON Volume I

VILLAGE LONDON Volume II

LONDON RECOLLECTED Volume I

LONDON RECOLLECTED Volume II

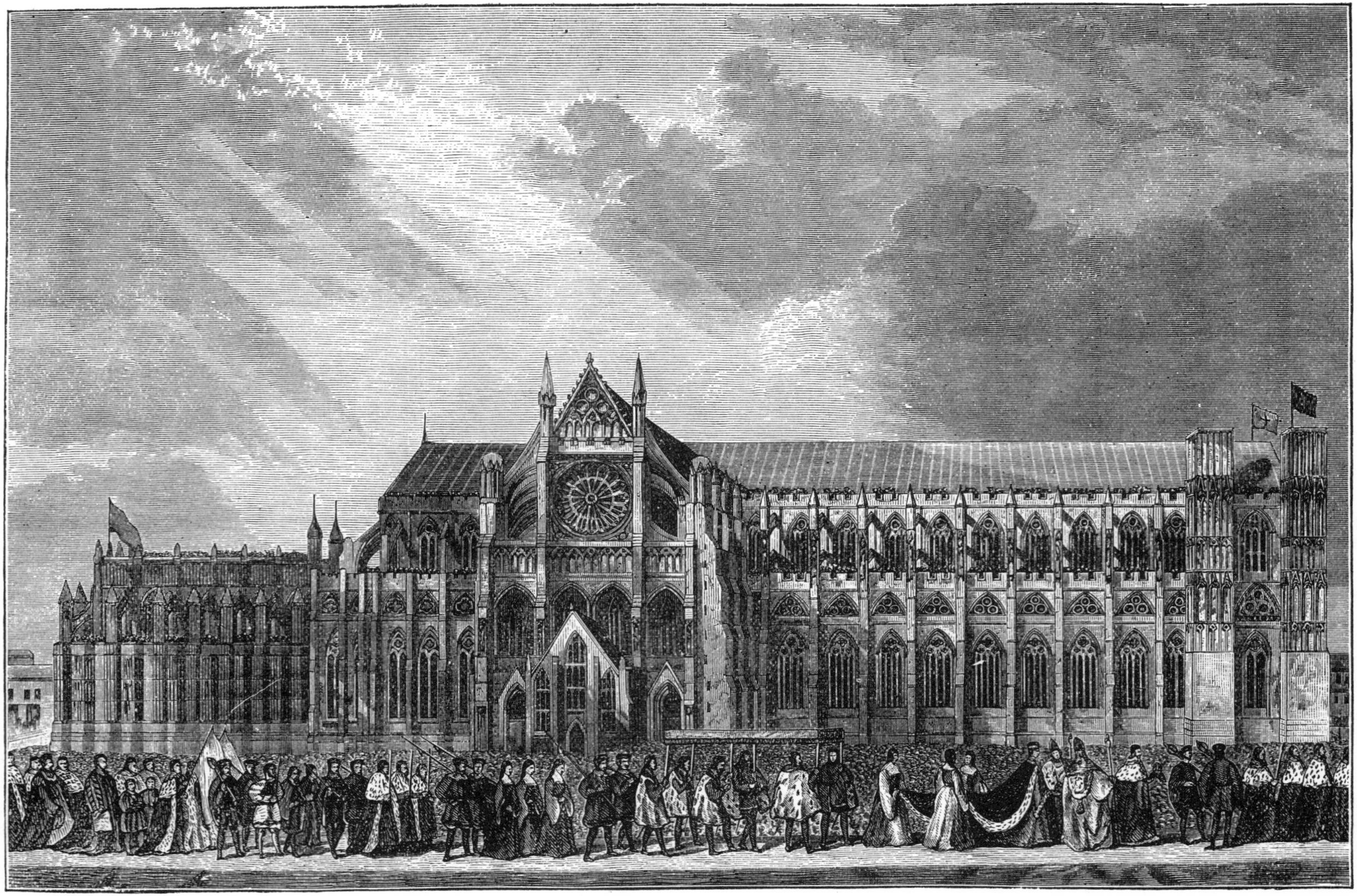

THE CORONATION PROCESSION OF ANNE BOLEYN TO WESTMINSTER ABBEY.
(From a Drawing by David Roberts in the Tyrrell Collection.)

LONDON RECOLLECTED

ITS HISTORY, LORE AND LEGEND

by
EDWARD WALFORD

VOLUME III

THE ALDERMAN PRESS
London

First published in 1872-8 by Cassell, Petter, Galpin & Co.
under the title *Old and New London.*

British Library Cataloguing in Publication Data.

Walford, Edward.
[Old and new London] London Recollected : its
history, lore and legend.
Vol. 3.
1. London (England) ——— History
I. Walford, Edward
942.1 DA677

ISBN 0-946619-03-4

Published by The Alderman Press, 1986
1/7 Church Street, London N9 9DR

Printed in Great Britain by
St. Edmundsbury Press, Bury St. Edmunds, Suffolk.
and bound by Dorstel Press Limited.

CONTENTS.

WESTMINSTER AND THE WESTERN SUBURBS.

CHAPTER VIII.

LINCOLN'S INN.

CHAPTER IX.

THE STRAND—INTRODUCTORY AND HISTORICAL.

CHAPTER X.

THE STRAND.—SOUTHERN TRIBUTARIES.

CHAPTER XI.

THE STRAND.—SOUTHERN TRIBUTARIES (*continued*).

CHAPTER XII.

THE STRAND.—SOUTHERN TRIBUTARIES (*continued*).

CHAPTER XIII.

THE STRAND.—SOUTHERN TRIBUTARIES (*continued*).

CHAPTER XIV.

ST. MARY-LE-STRAND, THE MAYPOLE, &c.

CHAPTER XV.

SOMERSET HOUSE AND KING'S COLLEGE.

CHAPTER XVI.

THE SAVOY.

CHAPTER XVII.

THE STRAND.—SOUTHERN TRIBUTARIES (*continued*).

CHAPTER XVIII.

THE STRAND.—NORTHERN TRIBUTARIES.

CHAPTER XIX.

CHARING CROSS, THE RAILWAY STATIONS, AND OLD HUNGERFORD MARKET.

CHAPTER XX.

NORTHUMBERLAND HOUSE AND ITS ASSOCIATIONS.

CHAPTER XXI.

TRAFALGAR SQUARE, THE NATIONAL GALLERIES, &c.

CHAPTER XXII.

ST. MARTIN'S-IN-THE-FIELDS.

CHAPTER XXIII.

LEICESTER SQUARE AND ITS NEIGHBOURHOOD.

CHAPTER XXIV.

SOHO.

CHAPTER XXV.

SOHO SQUARE AND ITS NEIGHBOURHOOD.

CHAPTER XXVI.

ST. GILES'S-IN-THE-FIELDS.

CHAPTER XXVII.

THE PARISH OF ST. GILES'S-IN-THE-FIELDS (*continued*).

CHAPTER XXVIII.

DRURY LANE THEATRE.

CHAPTER XXIX.

COVENT GARDEN THEATRE.

CHAPTER XXX.

COVENT GARDEN.—GENERAL DESCRIPTION.

CHAPTER XXXI.

COVENT GARDEN (*continued*).

CHAPTER XXXII.

COVENT GARDEN AND ITS NEIGHBOURHOOD (*continued*).

CHAPTER XXXIII.

COVENT GARDEN AND ITS NEIGHBOURHOOD (*continued*).

CHAPTER XXXIV.

COVENT GARDEN AND ITS NEIGHBOURHOOD (*continued*).

CHAPTER XXXV.

COVENT GARDEN AND ITS NEIGHBOURHOOD (*continued*).

PAGE

CHAPTER XXXVI.

COVENT GARDEN AND ITS NEIGHBOURHOOD (*continued*).

CHAPTER XXXVII.

THE RIVER THAMES.

CHAPTER XXXVIII.

THE RIVER THAMES (*continued*).

CHAPTER XXXIX.

THE RIVER THAMES (*continued*).

CHAPTER XL.

THE VICTORIA EMBANKMENT.

CHAPTER XLI.

SCOTLAND YARD AND THE METROPOLITAN POLICE.

CHAPTER XLII.

WHITEHALL.—HISTORICAL REMARKS.

CHAPTER XLIII.

WHITEHALL AND ITS HISTORICAL ASSOCIATIONS (*continued*).

CHAPTER XLIV.

WHITEHALL AND ITS HISTORICAL ASSOCIATIONS (*continued*).

CHAPTER XLV.

WHITEHALL.—THE BUILDINGS DESCRIBED.

CHAPTER XLVI.

WHITEHALL AND ITS HISTORICAL REMINISCENCES (*continued*).

CHAPTER XLVII.

WHITEHALL.—ITS PRECINCT, GARDENS, &c.

CHAPTER XLVIII.

WHITEHALL.—THE WESTERN SIDE.

CHAPTER XLIX.

WESTMINSTER ABBEY.—ITS EARLY HISTORY.

CHAPTER L.

WESTMINSTER ABBEY.—HISTORICAL CEREMONIES, &c.

CHAPTER LI.

WESTMINSTER ABBEY.—A SURVEY OF THE BUILDING.

CHAPTER LII.

WESTMINSTER ABBEY.—THE CHOIR, TRANSEPTS, &c.

PAGE

CHAPTER LIII.

WESTMINSTER ABBEY.—THE CHAPELS AND ROYAL TOMBS.

CHAPTER LIV.

WESTMINSTER ABBEY.—THE CHAPTER HOUSE, CLOISTERS, DEANERY, &c.

CHAPTER LV.

WESTMINSTER SCHOOL.

CHAPTER LVI.

WESTMINSTER SCHOOL (*continued*).

CHAPTER LVII.

THE SANCTUARY AND THE ALMONRY.

CHAPTER LVIII.

THE ROYAL PALACE OF WESTMINSTER.

CHAPTER LIX.

THE NEW PALACE, WESTMINSTER.

CHAPTER LX.

HISTORICAL REMINISCENCES OF THE HOUSES OF PARLIAMENT.

CHAPTER LXI.

NEW PALACE YARD AND WESTMINSTER HALL.

CHAPTER LXII.

WESTMINSTER HALL.—INCIDENTS IN ITS PAST HISTORY.

CHAPTER LXIII.

THE OLD LAW COURTS AND OLD PALACE YARD.

CHAPTER LXIV.

WESTMINSTER.—ST. MARGARET'S CHURCH.

probably erected for the benefit of such traders as were not qualified to carry on their business in the City, and may possibly have been of the reign of Henry VIII.

"These," says Mr. J. Wykeham Archer, in his "Vestiges of Old London," "appear to have preceded the buildings of Butcher's Row, which, with Middle Row, extended from Temple Bar to St. Mary-le-Strand, the houses on the south side of Holywell Street forming their western extremity." The old house with its bulk-shop, which adjoined Temple Bar, and which had remained a surviving vestige of the sweeping measures of Alderman Pickett in the beginning of the century, stood in its original condition down to 1846, when it was modernised by the removal of the heavy pents which surmounted its ground-floor. The house bore on its front a notice to the effect that it was "established in the reign of Henry VIII.," and was occupied by "Short and Son, late Creed, Fishmongers." An engraving of it, in one of its last stages, will be found in the above-mentioned work of Mr. Archer, who explains the term "bulk-shop" as a word of Flemish origin, signifying a stall before a shop, and also associated with the idea of strength or substance. Thus deprived of its pents, it became finally the bookshop of Messrs. Reeves and Turner. The house was a mere timber frame, filled up with lath and plaster. It was pulled down in 1865 to make room for the new Law Courts.

It will be remembered that Shakespeare speaks of misery making men acquainted with "strange bedfellows." It is probable that in these words he is alluding to his experiences, where he must often have seen the heavy canopies of these parts projecting over the pathways, with their wood or leaden coverings turned up at the edge like some old-fashioned beaver, the ends being sunk a little so as to let the rain pass off. "The bulk-shops," writes Mr. J. W. Archer, "besides their connection with the thrift of olden time, have associations which invest them with a degree of poetic interest, arising from the practice of erratic and destitute authors appropriating their ledges for the purpose of a dormitory, in common with other homeless wanderers and belated roysterers. . . . The gifted but wayward poet, Savage, is said to have frequently had recourse to such shelter during his moody night wanderings; and Nat Lee, as we know, expired upon a 'bulk' in Clare Market, when overcome by wine in returning from an orgie at the 'Bear and Harrow,' in Butcher's Row, to his lodgings in Duke Street. In a pleasanter vein it is related of an inferior bard, Derrick, that, being discovered by Floyd, another poor author in each sense of the term, on one of these ledges, and being suddenly awakened, he started up, exclaiming, 'My dear Floyd, I am sorry to see you in this destitute state; will you go home with me to my lodging?'"

Close to Butcher's Row, at the date to which we refer, we should have come upon a stone cross, or rather its remains, for Strype, in his edition of "Stow's London," in 1755, speaks of it as "now headless," a decapitation which it probably owed to an effort of Puritan zeal in the days of the Great Rebellion. It is probable that at the time of the demolition of Butcher's Row all vestiges of the mutilated cross were swept away.

In Malcolm's "Anecdotes of London," published early in the present century, he says, "A stranger who had visited London in 1790 would, on his return in 1804, be astonished to find a spacious area (with the church nearly in the centre) on the site of Butcher's Row, and some other passages, undeserving of the name of streets, which were composed of those wretched fabrics overhanging their foundations—the bane of ancient London—where the plague, with all its attendant horrors, frowned destruction on the miserable inhabitants, reserving its forces for the attacks of each returning summer."

Passing on, we reach the churchyard of St. Clement Danes, so called, as antiquaries affirm, "because Harold, a Danish king, and other Danes, were buried there." One story commonly told is to the effect that to avenge an insult to his own mother, Hardicanute ordered his half-brother's body to be torn out of its grave and thrown into the Thames, and that, being cast ashore, a fisherman took it up and gave it decent burial in this place, which was consecrated to receive it. Another account states that in the reign of Ethelred, the Danes having pillaged the fair abbey of Chertsey, were here met on their return, and slain by the Londoners. And there is yet a third version, which is told by Lord Burleigh (who lived in this parish), on the authority of Fleetwood, the antiquary, to the effect that when the Danes were driven out of England, a few were left behind, being married to English women; and that these were ordered by the king to dwell "between the Isle of Thorney, which is now called Westminster, and Caer Lud, now Ludgate, and that there they built a church.

In "A Survey of St. Clement Danes," made in 1732, we are told, "The old church was built 730 years ago, and between 1608 and 1633 the repairs cost £1,586."

The body of the old church was taken down in 1680, and the present fabric was built in 1682 by

Edward Pearce, under the direction of Sir C. Wren, who superintended the work gratuitously, as recorded on a marble slab in the north aisle. The present tower and steeple were added in 1719, and underwent extensive repairs and restorations in 1839. The tower contains a peal of ten bells, of a particularly musical sound, cast in 1693. The clock strikes the hours twice; "the hour being first struck on a large bell, and then repeated on a smaller one, so that when the first has been miscounted, the second may be more correctly observed." (Thomson's "Time and Timekeepers.") Besides the clock, there is a set of chimes which play the "Old Hundredth" Psalm. The bells also chime the tunes of "Hanover," and the "Lass o' Gowrie," at nine, twelve, and five o'clock, daily; indeed, the chimes of St. Clement's Church may still be heard as Falstaff describes having heard them with Justice Shallow.

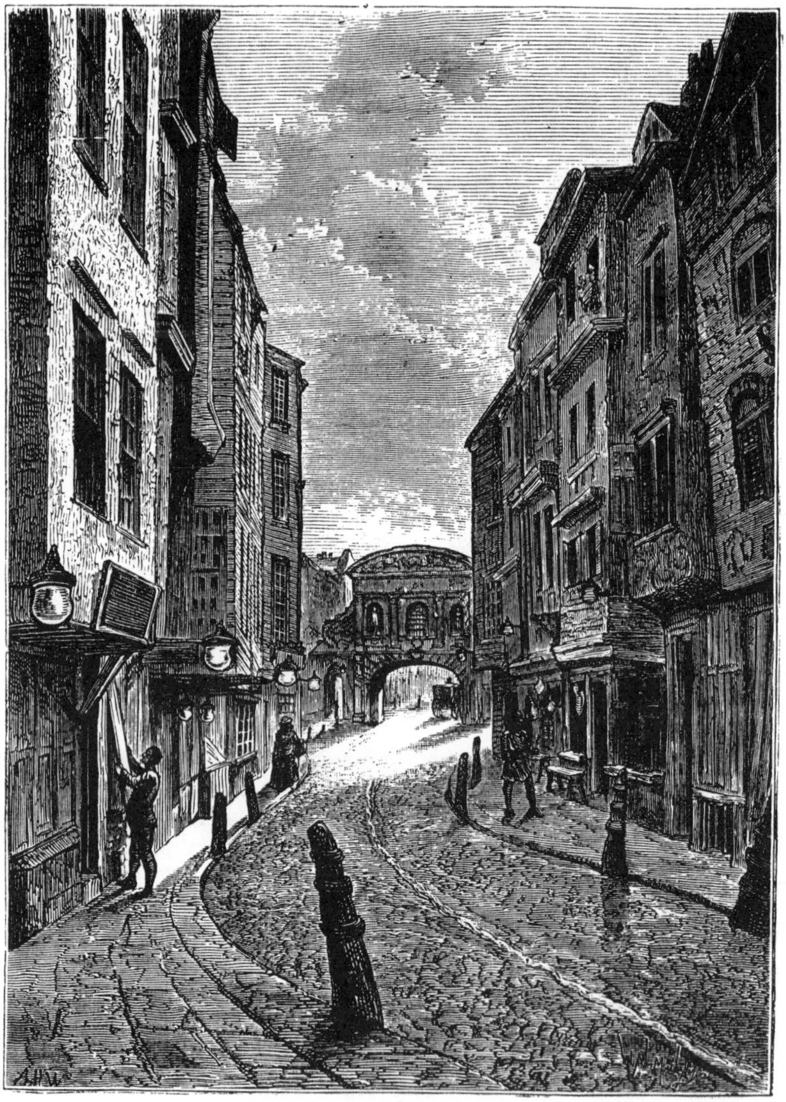

BUTCHER'S ROW IN 1800. (*See page* 11.)

The present Church of St. Clement Danes stands a little to the south of the ancient church or chapel of St. Clement, which had existed from the Conquest till long after the Reformation, occupying a part of what then was a rather large churchyard. It probably covers, as nearly as possible, the grave of Harold Harefoot, the mound over which was levelled by order of his vindictive and besotted brother. The church has always kept a marked position among those of the metropolis; and as it stands at once close to the City boundaries and on the high road to Westminster, all public processions, from the days of the Plantagenets to those of Victoria, have passed the building. When the Princess Alexandra of Denmark passed by it, on the 10th of March, 1863, the address presented to her by the parishioners on that occasion must have suggested to her mind a pleasing contrast to the traditionary feuds of eight hundred years ago

OLD HOUSES FORMERLY STANDING IN BUTCHER'S ROW, ABOUT 1800. (*See page* 11.)

between the country she had left and that to which she had come.

The present structure, like its predecessor, is dedicated to St. Clement, the patron saint of felt-workers, and also of sailors; and the symbolic anchor of St. Clement is still to be seen on nearly all the public buildings in the parish. The church is built of a white stone, both beautiful and durable; the architecture is of the Corinthian order. Fronting the Strand was formerly a spacious circular portico, supported by Ionic pillars. The interior of the edifice is commodious and handsome of its kind, and the roof inside is "camerated," and highly ornamented. The pulpit and altar are richly carved in the Tuscan style, and the top of the communion-table is of ancient and valuable marble, supposed to have belonged to the old church. The organ is one of Father Smith's. The lofty tower and steeple, 116 feet high, which were added to the church in 1719, exhibit in succession Ionic, Corinthian, and Composite tiers of architecture.

In the north gallery of this church there is a pew which is more revered and respected than the "squire's pew" in many a country parish church.

Men of all parties and creeds cordially agree in this feeling. The lover of old times and old principles reveres the spot, and the admirer of what is new respects it while criticising the man who has made it famous and historical. Over a century has passed away since the death of Dr. Samuel Johnson, but in spite of all the changes that have since come over the world, there still stands here the simple memorial of his former presence as a worshipper within these walls. A plain plate of brass, fixed to the back of the pew, reminds us that here the great essayist and lexicographer used to kneel in worship. "Westminster Abbey can show his grave, and St. Paul's his monument; but here is preserved the memory of the sacred place where the rugged but sensitive man used for many a long year to ask for strength and grace." It has been remarked that "Boswell shows us Johnson in his chambers, in the club, and in the streets; but his own confessions enable us to understand him at church." And the remark is true. While listening to him on a Saturday night, at the "Mitre," or the "Turk's Head," we mark his rude and even fierce replies, his vehement prejudices, his domineering and despotic intellect, we should scarcely deem him a man of deep religious feelings. But when the bells of St. Clement's were heard next morning in the Inner Temple Lane, the porter regularly opened the gates to let out the well-known scholastic, large-wigged "Mr." Johnson. The man knew that, in spite of his wig, he was not a member of the Temple; but some notion of his rising fame had reached even the porters, and his rough generosity had won their respect. On by the posts of Fleet Street, touching each as he goes along, rolls rather than walks, "Mr. Johnson, the dictionary-maker." He seems more solemn than usual, and the sound of the church bells deepens his passiveness into melancholy. How is this? one who did not know the man might ask. Who was more merry than he last night at the "Mitre?" how ready were his quotations! how apt his illustrations! how overpowering his arguments! He seems quite another man to-day. No, he is just the same man, but in another mood. He enters the church as though anxious to avoid notice, and shows that with him, at least, the service is a reality. He tells us that he strove, like many another brave and good man, honestly to solve the great problem, "how to purify and fortify his soul, and hold real communion with the Highest," and that he did this in St. Clement's Church. That pew in the north gallery, as the brass plate tells us, was the actual scene and arena of this struggle. Here he sat after his good resolution to go to church every Sunday, and to read the Scriptures; and hither he repaired in the last year of his life, at the age of seventy-five, to return thanks to God for his recovery from an illness of a hundred-and-twenty-nine days. The following is the inscription to which reference is made above:—

"In this pew and beside this pillar, for many years attended divine service the celebrated Dr. Samuel Johnson, the philosopher, the poet, the great lexicographer, the profound moralist, and chief writer of his time. Born 1709, died 1784. In the remembrance and honour of noble faculties, nobly employed, some inhabitants of the parish of St. Clement Danes have placed this slight memorial, A.D. 1851."

The parish is so well endowed with charities that the paupers of other neighbourhoods used to flock into it at the commencement of winter, for the sake of all they could get, and the vestry were obliged to limit their gifts to those who had resided for the space of a year.

There were almshouses for poor women in the upper and lower churchyard, at the time of the parish survey in 1732. "In the upper churchyard are six almshouses, with six rooms, and twelve poor women in each house, who are allowed 2s. per week; and in the lower churchyard are five rooms for poor women, each of whom has 2s. 6d. per week; they have also coals at Christmas, if they can make interest to get them."

The vaults beneath the church were crowded to excess. On the receipt of an Order in Council for closing them in 1858, the coffins were all placed together in one part of the vault and hermetically sealed, the whole being enclosed with a strong brick wall. Mr. Diprose tells us that towards the close of the last century "the vaults were discovered to be on fire, and continued burning for some days, many bodies being consumed."

In the church lie buried some few individuals whose names the world would not wish to forget; among others, Thomas Rymer, who compiled the "Fœdera," and the dramatic poets, Nathaniel Lee and Thomas Otway, and Bishop Berkeley, the philosopher, and friend of Pope, who attributed to him "every virtue under heaven." Sir John Roe, who died in Ben Jonson's arms, of the plague, 1606; Dr. Kitchener, and the Oxberrys, father and son, are also buried here. Among other monuments are those of Hippocrates de Otthen, who was physician to the Emperor of Germany, and was sent over to England at the request of Queen Elizabeth (in whose service, and in that of the Earl of Leicester, he was long employed), and of John Arundel, Bishop of Exeter, who died in 1503.

In this church was solemnised, two centuries

ago, that marriage of Sir Thomas Grosvenor with Miss Davies, the wealthy heiress of Ebury Manor, which brought into the family of the Duke of Westminster their property in Pimlico and what is now Belgravia.

The registers of St. Clement's commence with the year 1558, and are kept in far better order than in most parishes. They record the deaths of some hundreds of parishioners in 1665, the year of the Great Plague, which made great havoc in the close streets near Temple Bar, and also in Milford Lane.

One of the earliest entries of baptism is as follows:—"June 6, 1563, Master Robert Cicill, the sonne of ye L. highe Threasurer of England." Some nineteen years afterwards, the subject of this entry earned "honorable mention" for the gracious courtesy and politeness of his manners towards his inferiors.

DR. JOHNSON'S PEW IN ST. CLEMENT'S. (*See page* 14.)

The neighbourhood of St. Clement Danes Church appears to have borne anything but a good reputation so far back as three centuries ago, by reason of "the unthrifts of the Inns of Chancery," who made so much disturbance in the streets by night that the inhabitants, we read, were fain to keep watches for the sake of mutual protection. Thus, "in 1582," says honest John Stow, "the Recorder himself, with six more of the honest inhabitants, stood by St. Clement's Church to see the lanthorn hung out, and to observe if he could meet with any of these outrageous dealers. About seven of the clock at night they saw young Mr. Robert Cecil, the Lord Treasurer's son, who was afterwards Secretary of State to the Queen, pass by the church. As he passed, he gave them a civil salute, at which they said, 'Lo! you may see how a nobleman's son can use himself and how he putteth off his cap to poor men; our Lord bless him.' This passage," adds Stow, "the Recorder wrote in a letter to his father, adding, 'Your lordship hath cause to thank God for so virtuous a child.'" We may draw an obvious inference from the story of Mr. Robert Cecil's conduct in this instance as to the usual habits of the fast young noblemen of Elizabeth's time.

CHAPTER III.

ST. CLEMENT DANES (*continued*):—THE LAW COURTS.

"Where do stand forth the laws of state sublime."—*Sophocles.*

Early Courts of Law—Inns of Court—Want of a Central Building—New Law Courts Projected—Selection of Architect—Discussion about the Site—Plan and Design of the New Building—Temple Bar Memorial—Old Buildings Swept away—The Old Fish Shop—Holloway's—Shire Lane and its Inhabitants—Sir C. Sedley—The Well of St. Clement's—Bell Yard—Plough Alley—Boswell Court: a Relic of Old Times—Clement's Lane: its Decline and Fall—A Grand Clearance.

It is scarcely necessary to remind our readers that in theory it is the sovereign who sits in his (or her) right in England to administer justice to all, and hence the place in which the law is administered in this country has always been styled a "Court." And, as in early times, when law was rude and simple, the king used often to sit in his own court to administer justice, it was the custom for the seat of law to be within the palace of royalty. Hence, very naturally, when, in the Saxon and Norman times, the king's palace was at Westminster, it was a matter of course that the courts of law should grow up around the very person of the sovereign, though occasionally they were moved wherever the king travelled and took up his abode; in this case they were said to be held *in banco regis*, that is, in the presence of the king himself.

A great impetus to the concentration of the courts of law in the metropolis was doubtless given by Henry VIII.; for, whereas down to his day courts of arbitration had been held from time immemorial to decide cheaply and simply small matters in dispute in the several baronies, such as questions between landlord and tenant, between master and man, he ordered these and other like cases to be brought up to London, and, as Mr. Froude tells us in his "History of England," "country people found themselves compelled to take journeys to the metropolis, and to sue or be sued at his Courts at Westminster."

Gradually, however, as the English law shaped itself into a system and a science, which demanded a legal education in those who actually followed it as a profession, other "courts" of law arose nearer to the Inns of Court and the abodes of the gentlemen of the long robe; and down almost to this day, one portion of both law and equity had been administered in the rooms adjoining Westminster Hall, and another in other courts at Lincoln's Inn. But this division and distribution of the head-quarters and fountains of English justice between two localities, a mile at least apart, had long been a matter of complaint among most practical Englishmen; and from time to time, especially during the present century, there had arisen murmurs "not loud, but deep," on account of the loss of time involved to both judges and counsel by this unhappy local severance. And it can be no matter of surprise that, from time to time, various proposals were made to concentrate in a single spot the scattered forces of the law. With a view to carrying out this national undertaking—as far back as the year 1841, as we learn from the evidence printed by order of the House of Commons—the late Sir Charles Barry designed a large building of Grecian architecture, which he intended to have placed in Lincoln's Inn Fields. It was to have contained a great Central Hall, about equal to Westminster Hall in size, around which twelve smaller courts should cluster; the entire group of buildings, if it had been carried into effect at that time, would have covered a third of the area within the rails of Lincoln's Inn Fields, and have been surrounded by a belt of plantations, in order to keep up the delusion of rurality. Funds, however, were most fortunately wanting; and great objections were made to the plan of blocking up so large an open space, where open spaces were so rare; in fact, persons who lived about Fleet Street, the Strand, and Holborn, had long considered this open area, though enclosed, as their "country walk," and seriously asserted that to all intents and purposes they had been in the country when they had completed their early morning tour round "the Fields."

At length, when the patience of the lawyers and of the rest of the public had been nearly worn out, and when attention had been frequently called to the subject in Parliament, Her Majesty was pleased in 1858 to order a Royal Commission to be issued, "for the purpose of inquiring into and reporting on the expediency of bringing into one place, or at all events into one neighbourhood, all the superior Courts of Law and Equity, the Divorce and Probate Court, and those of the Admiralty, Bankruptcy, &c., as well as of suggesting means for providing a fit site, and erecting a building suited to the purpose in hand." The Commission accordingly recommended the selection of the site on the northern side of the Strand, between Temple Bar and St. Clement's Church. In 1861 a Bill was introduced in order to carry this recommendation into effect; but it was thrown out by a narrow majority, and the question slumbered until 1865, when the urgency of some such provision for the due administration of the law had again made itself practically felt. Two Acts of Parliament were passed in consequence, to carry out the recommendations already mentioned. The one Act empowered the Commissioners of Works and Public Buildings to acquire the site which had been recommended, and the other provided the funds necessary for the cost of the building itself, partly by a contribution of £1,000,000 of unclaimed interest on stock standing to the credit of suitors in the Court of Chancery, and partly by a small tax to be imposed on litigants in the other courts.

Another body of Commissioners was next appointed, consisting of forty eminent members of the legal profession, including Lords Cranworth, Hatherley, Cairns, and Penzance, Vice-Chancellors Stuart, Malins, and others, in order to advise the Treasury in its choice of an architect and plans for the new "Palace of Justice." The next step was to nominate a smaller body, consisting of five individuals of high standing—Mr. Gladstone, Sir W. Stirling-Maxwell, Lord Chief Justice Cockburn, Sir Roundell Palmer (afterwards Lord Selborne), and Mr. William Cowper (later Lord Mount-Temple), along with two professional architects—Mr. John Shaw and Mr. G. Pownall, who were to act as "Judges of Designs;" and a competition among the best architects of the day was invited. Eleven designs were sent in, and these were exhibited to the public, in 1868, in a temporary building put up in New Square, Lincoln's Inn; and in the end the design of Mr. G. E. Street, R.A., was accepted—not, however, until after a very strong feeling had been shown in favour of that of Mr. E. M. Barry, a son of the architect of the Houses of Parliament.

Even after the architect, however, had been chosen, a further delay arose, as a large number of the public, and some of the competitors—Mr. Street himself among the rest—expressed an opinion that a space between the Strand and the Thames Embankment, to the east of Somerset House, would be a preferable site to that already chosen, and which had been prepared and cleared by the removal, in 1866–8, of no less than thirty close, foul, and filthy courts, yards, lanes, and alleys. And at last, after all the above-mentioned delays had come to an end, the first brick of the "Law Courts of the future"—the great central National Palace of Justice—was actually laid, on the last day of April, 1874, at the north-east corner of the chosen ground, at the junction of Bell Yard and Carey Street. The site, which had then been cleared for several years, comprised the surface of nearly eight acres, extending from Bell Yard on the east to Clement's Inn on the west, and from Carey Street on the north to the Strand and Pickett Street on the south. The substratum of solid concrete, which had been laid two or three years previously, covered about six acres and a half of this space, the remainder now forming what is known as St. Clement's Gardens, separating the Courts from Clement's Inn, and pleasantly laid out.

The buildings themselves are thus minutely described in the *Times* of May 19th, 1874:—

"They are of Gothic design, and, viewed by non-professional eyes, might be set down as somewhat irregular examples of the Decorated or Second Pointed style. But their architect has embodied in his designs so much of modern improvements, and has so thoroughly studied the adaptation of the architecture of the Edwardian period to the requirements of our age, that we fancy he would prefer to call the structure a specimen of the 'Victorian style.' The whole building forms, approximately at least, a somewhat irregular square, the Strand front being 483 feet in length, while the depth from the Strand to Carey Street is about 460 feet. The southern, northern, and western fronts will be of Portland stone, while the eastern front will present a combination of Portland stone interspersed with red bricks, as will be the case with the interior courts and quadrangles. The entire pile of buildings will be divided into two blocks—the eastern and lesser one, which will be erected, under the contract, in three years; and the larger block to the west, which it will take six or seven years to complete. Each front is to be relieved by dwarf towers, arches, and other features; and there will be two high towers, one at the south-east angle, and one at the eastern end of Carey Street. The former will be 170 feet in height, or nearly four times the height of Temple Bar.

"The whole edifice will be three, four, and five storeys in height in different parts; and its lofty pitched roofs will be relieved by the insertion of gables, dormers, and pinnacles, in great variety. The general height of the building up to the ridge of the roof will be about 90 or 95 feet; and over the rest will rise the Central Hall, in the main or western block, to which the rest of the building will be subordinate. This Central Hall will be about 140 feet to the top of its roof, or 90 feet measured inside up to the crown of the stone-vaulted ceiling. Underneath it will be a large lower chamber, which, if it were underground, might be termed a crypt.

"The ground plan, as it stands at present, shows that the architect has given accommodation to no less than 18 distinct courts, each with its own entrance and staircase, with separate approaches and doors for the judges, the jury, the witnesses, the Bar, and the public, together with rooms for clerks, secretaries, and registrars, and also waiting-rooms.

"On the western side, towards Clement's Inn, there will be left a large, open space. This will probably be used as gardens, and there will be a flight of broad stone steps, leading up into the western end of Carey Street. It will be possible, if required, to erect here a western block of buildings, corresponding with that on the eastern side.

"The cost of the building, if the estimates allowed by the Commissioners should not be exceeded, will be three-quarters of a million. The structure will absorb no less than 62,000 tons of Portland and 18,000 tons of other stone, and also about 35,000,000 of red and white bricks. It will be remembered, in conclusion, that, about two years ago, Mr. Street proposed the removal of St. Clement's Church to a site on the vacant space on the west side of the new building—a proposal which met with the approval not only of Mr. Lowe, but also of the then Lord Chancellor. The Metropolitan Board of Works, however, declined to entertain the idea, although the Government offered to provide the site free of cost."

Mr. Street, in a printed minute, dated May, 1869, thus sums up the chief "æsthetical advantages," of the Carey Street site:—

"The elevation above the river is considerable. The entrances to the Central Hall will be exactly on the same level as the courtyard in front of the western entrance of St. Paul's Cathedral, and the floor of the Central Hall will be 22 feet higher here than it would be on the Embankment. To this extent, therefore, it will in all distant views rise higher and be better seen than on the lower site. And I think that the position will be an important one, crowning the hill opposite St. Paul's, and supplying what the views of London at present much want,—namely, some very marked architectural feature in the long expanse of building between St. Paul's and Westminster."

The stately pile was opened by the Queen on the 11th of December, 1882, but the gifted architect who had designed it was no longer living to rejoice in the completion of his *magnum opus*.

It is unquestionably true that any great public good can only be achieved at the cost of much private inconvenience; and the New Law Courts cannot claim to be any exception to this general rule. No sensible man can doubt that the destruction of so many filthy slums must ultimately prove a gain to the community at large; yet it is also undeniable that the first effect of the work of demolition was to render 4,000 persons homeless, and subsequently to drive three-fourths

THE OLD FISH SHOP BY TEMPLE BAR, 1846. (*See page* 11.)

of them into other courts and alleys not far away, which, being previously well filled, were speedily, from the overcrowding consequent upon so enormous an influx, rendered as unhealthy as the squalid dens from which the immigrants had been routed. It is also true that a liberal compensation was awarded by Government, even in cases were no legal claim could have been made, and that the utmost kindness and forbearance was shown by the Commissioners and officials entrusted to administer that compensation; but it may be doubted whether, in the case of this class, who live from hand to mouth, the unwonted possession of so large a sum was not rather the reverse of a benefit. We are told that about £20 was paid to each weekly tenant, and this being in many instances squandered in the course of a few days, the recipient appeared, with drunken imprecations, before the distributors to demand more.

SERLE'S PLACE. *From a Drawing taken shortly before its Demolition.* (*See page* 21.)

Many ingenious plans have been mooted, by philosophers and philanthropists of all ages, for the effectual cleansing of certain Augean stables; but the summary one of pulling down the building, and turning its 4,000 denizens adrift to seek shelter where best they may, is a bold stroke, which has at least the advantage of novelty, if even it savour a little of the line of policy familiarly known as "robbing Peter to pay Paul."

And now, having given some slight idea of the appearance which these eight acres—once suggestive of "the abomination of desolation"—present now that Mr. Street's stately fabric rises from their surface, let us take a brief retrospective view of them as they were not only in their last stage of decay, but in their palmy days, when St. Clement Danes was a favourite abode of "the quality."

The truth of the old proverb, "Threatened folk live long," was proved by our old acquaintance Temple Bar, which remained *in statu quo* down to the year 1878. The stones, having lain in a builder's yard for about ten years, were set up in 1888-9, at an entrance to Sir H. Meux's Park, at Theobalds, in Hertfordshire. Of this relic of the past we have already given, in a previous volume, a full and exhaustive history, which leaves nothing to be added or desired further than that since its removal its site has been marked by a column, set up at the cost of the Corporation of London. The pedestal of the "memorial" is adorned with appropriate bas-reliefs, above which on either side are statues of the Queen and the Prince of Wales, and the whole is surmounted by a bronze griffin supporting a shield bearing the city arms. The memorial, the object of much hostile criticism, was erected from the designs of Sir Horace Jones, the statues being the work of Sir J. E. Boehm, R.A.

It would be equally tedious and unnecessary to give a minute description of all the lanes, courts, and alleys which have been swept away in the process of clearing these eight acres, many of them being remarkable only for the generally unwholesome atmosphere, both moral and physical, which pervaded them; we must, therefore, be contented to particularise such among them as are sufficiently interesting, from historical associations, to make their memories and names worth preserving.

On the north side of the old gateway stood, a few years ago, a quaint, narrow wooden house with projecting gables, and a physiognomy all its own. Here generations of fishmongers had plied their scaly trade, and here a certain Mr. Crockford, erst dealer in shell-fish, and subsequently gambling-house keeper and millionaire, laid the foundation of his fortune. During his life-time he refused to allow the old house in the Strand to be altered; but after his death, which occurred in 1844, the gable roof and pent-house were removed. The fishmonger's shop afterwards became that of a hairdresser, and finally, reversing the old saying about "coming to vile uses at last," it passed—as we have stated—into the hands of the well-known second-hand booksellers, Messrs. Reeves and Turner, who owned it when it was doomed to come down to make room for the New Law Courts, in 1865 (see page 11).

A few steps farther on, between Temple Bar and the entrance of St. Clement's Lane, nearly opposite to Messrs. Twining's bank, stood the house of Messrs. Holloway, the great wholesale manufacturers of the pills which bear their name. It is said that for many years the firm spent upwards of ten thousand pounds a year for advertisements in the town, country, and foreign newspapers.

As near as possible on the site of the shop of Messrs. Holloway stood, formerly, an old house with gable roof and an ornamental front, engraved in Smith's "Antiquities of Westminster." It was famous as being the reputed residence of the Duc de Sully, when ambassador here, before he could be accommodated at Arundel House.* At that time it is said to have been inhabited by Christopher Harley, Count de Beaumont, ambassador from France in 1605. In another house, a few steps still further westward, the *Daily Telegraph* (the first of the penny daily papers) was originally published, by its founder, Colonel Sleigh.

Returning to Temple Bar, we now make our way northwards, following the eastern side of the new block of buildings, and—with some latent suspicion that we may even meet with foul play from the ghosts of its former inhabitants—up Shire or Shere Lane, from which many of Addison's and other papers in the *Advertiser* are dated.

The western side of Shire Lane was in the parish of St. Clement Danes; and therefore the meetings of the "Kit Cat" Club at the "Trumpet," which were noticed in the early part of this work, belong properly, and strictly speaking, to this place; but it will be sufficient here to note the fact, and to refer our readers to the description previously given for fuller details on the subject. We may mention, however, that it was a thoroughfare for foot-passengers only, very narrow and filthy, and well deserving the character given of it in the *Quarterly Review* (No. 143), as "a vile, squalid place, noisy and noxious, nearly inaccessible to

* With reference to this assertion, Malcolm states that such a report arose from the fact of one of the houses in that narrow street bearing on its front the *fleur-de-lys* of France, and suggests that this was put there, not to commemorate Sully's arrival, but in compliment to our Henry V., the conqueror of France.

both light and air, and swarming with a population of a most disreputable character." On the left side especially the houses were of "bad repute;" and Mr. Diprose, in his "Walk round St. Clement Danes," informs us that many years ago there existed a communication from one of them with a house on the north side of the Strand, a few doors from Temple Bar, through which thieves used to escape after ill-using their victims. Higher up on the same side were three houses which were made into one by connecting passages, almost like a rabbit warren; this was known by the name of "Cadgers' Hall," being the *rendezvous* of beggars. A few doors higher up still was another double house, called the "Retreat," through which, we are told, there was a way for thieves to pass through into Crown Court, and so into the Strand. It is worthy of record that this lane retained its old character to the last, a man being prosecuted for a robbery committed in it as late as the year 1865.

Shire Lane must have achieved an undesirable reputation at an early stage of its existence, as even in the reign of James I. it was called "Rogues' Lane," and in our own day the very name of Shire Lane had, in 1845, become such an abomination that it was ordered to be henceforth known as Upper, Middle, and Lower Serle's Place. This change of name appears to have had, to some extent, a salutary effect, as we are told by Mr. Diprose that "portions of this lane have of late years much improved in character, particularly the upper end, where Isaac Bickerstaff lived."

In Shire Lane, in the year 1639, the delightful song writer, and oracle of the licentious wits of his day, Sir Charles Sedley, first saw the light. He was baptised in the old church of St. Clement's.

Ship Yard adjoined Shire Lane on the left. "The houses in it," says Mr. Diprose, "were built very high and close together, the upper part projecting over the lower, thus admitting very little air or light." Some of them also were of great age and unhealthy, the entire locality being made up of such "courts" without any roadway. This locality was a colony of thieves; and Mr. Diprose tells us, on the authority of a "very old inhabitant" of it, that the latter remembered a time when capital punishment was constantly inflicted for robbery, and when an execution at Newgate seldom took place without someone from this spot being amongst the number. "At the back of this court," adds the same writer, "there stood formerly a block of houses, from four to five storeys in height, which were let out to vagrants, thieves, sharpers, smashers, and other abandoned characters. Throughout the vaults of this rookery there existed a continuous communication or passage, so that easy access could be obtained from one to the other, facilitating escape or concealment in the event of pursuit, which, from the nature of the nefarious traffic in practice, very often occurred. The end house of this block of buildings was selected for the manufactory of counterfeit coin, and passed by the name of the 'Smashing Lumber.' The ingenuity employed in the construction of the apartments may be mentioned. In the first place, every room had its secret trap or panel, that a free entrance or exit might be quickly effected from one place to the other; and from the upper storey, which was the workshop or factory, there was a shaft or well constructed, in direct communication with the cellar before noticed. The whole of the coining apparatus and the *employés* could be conveyed away as by a touch of magic, being lowered in a basket by means of a pulley. This secret gang must have had a prosperous run for many years, and the master of it, after amassing a large sum, wisely disappeared at the right moment; for not long after the introduction of the new police, and the appointment of detectives, this den was discovered and abolished."

We are told, in the "Life and Times of Sir Christopher Hatton," by Nicholas, that "an inn near Temple Bar, called 'The Ship,'" was granted to him; and Chambers tells us, in his "Book of Days," that "Ship Yard denotes the sign of the 'Ship,' a house established in honour of Sir Francis Drake, and having for its sign the bark in which he circumnavigated the world."

It is difficult to associate the neighbourhood of Shire Lane with pilgrims, clear springs, and running brooks, but we read in the *Times* of May 1st, 1874:—"Another relic of old London has lately passed away; the holy well of St. Clement, on the north of St. Clement Danes Church, has been filled in and covered over with earth and rubble, in order to form part of the foundation of the Law Courts of the future. It is said that penitents and pilgrims used to visit this well as early as the reign of Ethelred, and it was known from time immemorial as 'St. Clement's Well.' Charles Knight, in his 'London,' published in 1841, mentions the well as 'now covered over with a pump,' and he adds that 'the well still remains flowing as steadily and as freshly as ever.' It has often been supposed that this well supplied the old Roman bath in Strand Lane, but this is a mistake, the water which feeds that bath springing up out of the London clay below on the spot with perfect regularity."

Round this holy well, in the early Christian era,

newly-baptised converts clad in white robes were wont to assemble to commemorate Ascension Day and Whitsuntide; and in later times, after the murder of Thomas à Becket had made Canterbury the constant resort of pilgrims from all parts of England, the holy well of St. Clement was a favourite halting-place of the pious cavalcades for rest and refreshment.

In the "Beauties of England and Wales" (Middlesex, vol. x., published in 1815), Mr. Nightingale says, "A pump now covers St. Clement's Well. Fitzstephen, in his description of London, in the reign of Henry II., informs us that "round the City again, and towards the north, arise certain excellent springs at a small distance, whose waters are sweet, salubrious, and clear, and whose runnels murmur o'er the shining stones. Among these, Holywell, Clerkenwell, and St. Clement's Well may be esteemed the principal, as being much the most frequented, both by the scholars from the school (Westminster), and the youth from the City, when in a summer's evening they are disposed to take an airing. This well was also much resorted to on account of its being supposed of peculiar efficacy in the cure of cutaneous and other disorders, and was consequently a place of importance to devotees. The estimation of its efficacy and sanctity have long ceased."

Bell Yard, occupied principally by law publishers at the northern extremity, and towards the Strand by a medley of small, uninviting-looking shops, was more than a century ago the abode of Fortescue, who lived in a house at the upper end of the yard, which is further honoured by being described by Fortescue's friend, Pope, as "that filthy old place, Bell Yard." Several of the small passages in this vicinity are worthy of no more particular mention than is contained in Seymour's "History of the Parishes of London and Westminster," written in 1734.

"A little above St. Clement's Well, of note for its excellent spring water, is Plough Alley, which, with three turnings, goes into a street by the Plough stables, which fronts the playhouse by Lincoln's Inn Grange, in Little Lincoln's Inn Fields. More towards Clare Market is Horseshoe Court, a pretty handsome place, with a freestone pavement, having a prospect into St. Clement's Inn Gardens. And opposite to this court is Yates' Court, not over good nor large. Between Temple Bar and the turning into St. Clement's Inn, on the north side of the Butcher's Row, are several courts, most of which are but small. The first is Ship Yard, a thoroughfare into Little Shear Lane, with a pretty broad passage; on the east side is an open place going into a small court called Chair Court, with a fair freestone pavement. Next to Ship Yard are these courts: Swan Court, very small; Star Court, indifferent, good, and large, with an open air; White Hart Court, long but narrow; Lock Alley, long, but small; Windmill Court very small and inconsiderable: Crown Court hath an open air about the midst, and leadeth into Little Shear Lane. Bear and Harrow Court is so called from such a sign, belonging to a noted eating-house, at the entrance into it. This court (or rather alley, from its length and narrowness) runs into Boswell Court."

It is a common mistake to suppose that Boswell Court owed its name to the biographer of Dr. Johnson. Its age and its name are at least as old as the times of the Tudors, in whose day, and in those of the Stuarts, as we are told, it was the abode of "the quality." "Here lived," says Mr. Diprose, "Lady Raleigh, the widow of the unfortunate Sir Walter." Another distinguished resident was Sir Edward Lyttleton, successively Solicitor-General, and Lord Chief Justice of England, in 1639. From Boswell House, Gilbert Talbot wrote a letter of "London gossip" to his father, the Earl of Shrewsbury, in the reign of Elizabeth, a letter which is printed in Lodge's "Illustrations." Among the other eminent inhabitants of this court was Lady Fanshawe, as we learn from her "Memoirs," where she says, "In his" (her husband's) "absence, I took house in Boswell Court, near Temple Bar, for two years, immediately moving all my goods thereto."

Ascending northwards towards Carey Street was a flight of steps which led into New Boswell Court, a dreary-looking enclosure, although described by Hatton in 1708 as "a pleasant place." At the side of these steps might be seen to the very last a curious relic of other days, a watchman's box, the last box of the old "Charlies," which was drawn up from the pavement during the day-time.

This ancient order of watchmen was instituted about the middle of the thirteenth century, and carried on its functions, growing yearly more feeble and inefficient, until, in 1829, the "Charlies," as they were termed in the slang of the day, found themselves superseded by the new police, organised by Sir Robert Peel. These midnight guardians of the peace—and it may be observed *en passant* that the only qualifications necessary for the post would appear to have been extreme old age, and general incapacity—suffered many things at the hands of the young "bucks" and "bloods" of the Regency. A watchman found dozing in his box in the intervals of going his rounds to utter his monotonous cry, was apt to be overturned, box and all, and left to kick and struggle helplessly, like a turtle on its back, until assistance arrived. Or he would be kindly offered a dram to keep him awake, and this dram being drugged, quickly sank him in deeper sleep than before, in which state "Charley" and his box, being transferred to a truck, were forthwith trundled into another quarter of the town, and left to awake at leisure.

Old Boswell Court, from having been the chief abode of the "quality," gradually came to be let out in chambers and apartments. The houses were mostly of red brick with carved doorways. The house at the southern end was, for the last twenty years prior to its demolition, the printing and publishing office of Messrs. Kelly's "Post Office Directories" of London and of the several counties of England.

The old entrance to St. Clement's Lane from the Strand was through an open gateway flanked by massive pillars of stone. This archway was erected by the Corporation of London, as a tribute of respect for Alderman Pickett, through whose exertions the thoroughfare of the Strand was widened, at an expense of more than a quarter of a million sterling. The new thoroughfare was named Pickett Street, after the public benefactor, but the name never became popular, and soon passed away, the houses being reckoned as part of the Strand. A little beyond the gateway the lane bore off to the left, and led to the back of King's College Hospital, merging in Gilbert (now Twining) Street, and thence being continued through Portsmouth Street into the south-west corner of Lincoln's Inn Fields. The line of this lane—what is left of it—runs north from the north-west end of the Law Courts, and it will no doubt soon be superseded by a wider thoroughfare, for as these pages go to press, the dark and obscure outlets by which it still communicates with Clare Market and its neighbourhood are being swept away.

Among the other residents in this lane was Sir John Trevor (a cousin of the infamous Judge Jeffreys), at one time Speaker of the House of Commons, and twice Master of the Rolls; the same who was expelled from the House for bribery, though he had the good sense to warn James II. against his arbitrary conduct. He died here in May, 1717, and was buried in the Rolls Chapel on the east side of Chancery Lane. Another distinguished inhabitant was Oliver Cromwell, in his early days. The Lords Paget also had their town mansion here, as appears by the parish registers.

In the course of time, however, the lane, "from being the polished abode of wit, genius, and fashion, was converted by the ruthless hand of Time into a huge overcrowded den, where blasphemy, rags, gin, hollow-eyed poverty, and stinted industry, were all fearfully huddled together. Where noble dames once moved with costly and flowing trains, a short time since women in rags rocked to sleep the children of misery, to whom hunger gave a fearful vitality; and where courtiers used to exchange the bow of recognition, fearful and brutal collisions between man and man took place. Upon the once polished floor, now broken and filthy, where stately revelry held its court, human beings lay stretched in that association which extreme misery only knows; and the once elegant boudoir of some dead duchess was inhabited by seven or eight wretched human beings. Doors stood ajar with the gaping look of poverty and desolation, where the loud resounding knocks of some tall, gold-laced menial were once heard; and where the flaxen-haired daughters of wealth once sported, neglected children in filth and rags dozed out their wretched existence.

"In this sun-forsaken, dreary region lived, among the rest, a very large colony of the poorest and wildest of the Irish, attracted in the first instance, no doubt, by its nearness to the Catholic chapel in Lincoln's Inn Fields; but these, though equally poor, dirty, and drunken with the tenants of the adjoining courts, were never actually absorbed by their English neighbours. To the last they remained *ipsis Hibernis Hiberniores*, and when the rookery was broken up they migrated, if we are rightly informed, to Drury Lane and the Seven Dials.

"As a proof that the locality was as demoralised as it was poor, we may add that when wholesale executions occurred at Newgate or Tyburn, as they did occasionally occur 'when George III. was king,' it was rare indeed for this locality not to have its representative amongst those unhappy wretches who paid the last penalty of the law."

It has been very appositely observed that "Charles Dickens might well have placed the scenes of his quaintest stories of low Cockney life in the midst of this doomed quarter of London, which was the haunt of gaiety and pleasure in the reign of Charles II., and is associated with the memories of the 'bloods' and the 'bucks' of the Restoration, and the wits of the days of Queen Anne."

Mr. Diprose—who, as an old inhabitant of the parish, is well qualified to speak on the subject —gives a list of the courts, alleys, and streets which were quietly removed and effaced, in order to furnish a site for the Palace of Justice.

They are as follows, nearly thirty in all:—Bailey's Court, Bear and Harrow Court, Bell Yard, Old and New Boswell Courts, Boswell Yard, Brick Court, Chair Court, Clement's Court, Clement's Inn Foregate, Clement's Lane, Cromwell Place, Crown Court, Crown Place, Hemlock Court, Great and Little Horseshoe Courts, New Court, Pickett Place, Plough Court, Robin Hood Court, Upper, Lower, and Middle Serle's Place, Ship Yard, Ship and Anchor Court, Shire Lane, and Star Court, all of them more or less dirty and overcrowded.

Besides these, however, there have disappeared a considerable part of the Strand (Pickett Street), Carey Street, Yates' Court, and St. Clement's Lane, nearly all of which have histories still attaching to them, although all traces of them have disappeared, and their place knows them no more.

The demolition of so many small tenements, in order to make a site for the Palace of Justice, did not have so great an influence as might have been supposed upon the people living in the parish of St. Clement's, which continued to swarm with a poor population. Previously it stood at about 16,000, and immediately after this clearance it was about 15,000, a great number of the inhabitants of the old lanes and alleys having removed only into the neighbourhood of Clare Market, which, even before the influx, was almost equally close and filthy, and sadly overcrowded.

BOSWELL COURT. (*From a Sketch taken shortly before its Demolition.*)

In the reign of Queen Anne Clement's Lane was the Bond Street of London, and several of its houses were the haunts of those royal and noble intrigues which figure so largely in the anecdote-memoirs of the time. "Here," says Mr. Diprose, "Steele used to show his gaudy attire, Bolingbroke his stately presence, and Pope that decrepit form which was yet the tabernacle of a noble soul within. Here Swift, with downcast head and scowling visage, used to growl to himself as the mighty satirist made and unmade cabinets; and the gentle Addison here turned some of those polished periods which have called forth the envy and admiration of after ages."

THEATRE, PORTUGAL STREET. (*See page* 27.)

We will conclude this chapter with a few words quoted from an article in *Cassell's Magazine* in 1870, styled, "A Walk Round St. Clement Danes":—

"Gone now are the glories of St. Clement Danes. Gone are the sedan chairs and coaches that once had here their favourite and (it is said) their earliest stands. Gone are the 'Thames watermen,' whom our fathers and grandfathers knew so well, resplendent in their scarlet coats and badges, but who were driven out by the penny steamers. Gone, too, are the 'smashers,' and the 'Charlies;' gone, too, is that little court to the north of St. Clement's Church, of which we have already seen what Winter had to say with reference to the concoction of the fiendish Gunpowder Plot. Gone, too, now are the once fair gardens of Essex House and Norfolk House; gone are the wild beasts which once were kept in Holywell Street; gone is the last of those stocks which once held in awe the roguish apprentices and youthful roughs of the parish; gone is the 'Denzil Street gang,' and the 'Alphabet' public-house, whilom so well known to the theatrical profession; gone is the far-famed Norfolk Giant, who once kept the 'Craven Head' in wretched Drury Lane; and gone is 'Joe Miller;' gone, too, are his 'jests,' and possibly his grave.

"But in the place of these and other relics of past ages we shall shortly see rising on the now bare site a stately building, the like of which Londoners have not seen reared in modern days, save only at the river-side at Westminster—a palace in which it is our earnest prayer, as Englishmen, that Justice may long sit to hold evenly the scales of law."

CHAPTER IV.

ST. CLEMENT DANES (*continued*).—A WALK ROUND THE PARISH.

"Sacer est locus; ite profani."—*Virgil.*

Carey Street—Its Reminiscences—Residences of Benjamin Franklin, Sir William Blackstone, and Mrs. Chapone—The "Grange" Inn—The "Plough" Tavern and Gully the Prize-fighter—The "Seven Stars"—Serle's Court, now called New Square—Ravenscroft's Wig-shop—Serle's Coffee House—Portugal Row—Playhouse Street—The Duke's Theatre—Origin of the Sergeant's Guard at the Theatre Royal—Curious Playbills of the Last Century—Portugal Street—King's College Hospital—Burial-place of Joe Miller—Enon Chapel and the Modern "Golgotha"—The "Old Black Jack."

Leaving the Palace of Justice upon our left hand, we will now continue our way westwards from the top of what was once Shire Lane, but which, as before mentioned, gradually developed into Serle's Place.

At right angles to Serle Street, and running from east to west, is Carey Street, the south side of which was demolished to form the north side of the New Courts of Law. These houses, at the time of their demolition, were almost all tenanted by solicitors and law-stationers. Although, as compared with the rest of the neighbourhood, markedly wanting in memories of the past, Carey Street has its reminiscences. The heroic Lady Fanshawe tells us, in her "Memoirs," that in 1655-6 she and her family spent a twelvemonth in it, as tenants of a house belonging to Sir George Carey, from whom apparently the street was named. It is said by Mr. Diprose that at No. 19 Benjamin Franklin is supposed to have lived whilst working as a journeyman printer in the neighbourhood. Sir William Blackstone lived in this street in 1761; and the celebrated Mrs. Chapone, authoress of "Letters on the Improvement of the Mind," and an ardent disciple of Richardson, also resided here until her husband's death.

It is difficult to imagine any levity of conduct in a street once inhabited by this most decorous lady; indeed, Carey Street, to its credit be it spoken, seems, in spite of its surroundings, to have been

"Content to dwell in decencies for ever,"

which is perhaps the reason why its name is scarcely mentioned by Stow, Pennant, Northouck, or Malcolm, or even by such modern writers as Peter Cunningham and John Timbs. If there be truth in the old adage, "Happy are the people whose history is a blank," the denizens of Carey Street are much to be congratulated.

Though the street was dull and sober in outward appearance, yet it may probably have been the scene of more than one gay frolic in other days. The "Grange" Inn—removed in 1853 to make room for King's College Hospital—with its picturesque yard and offices, was much patronised in its day by the actors of the Duke's Theatre hard by, and of other places of the same kind. It is mentioned by Sir W. Davenant, in his "Playhouse to Let." The "Plough" Tavern, also in this street,—kept at one time by Mr. John Gully, the prize-fighter, afterwards M.P. for Pontefract—was an ancient hostelry of good repute, as among those who made it their head-quarters in London was the antiquary, Browne Willis. Another inn in the street was the "Seven Stars," formerly the "Leg and Seven Stars," a corruption of the "League and Seven Stars," denoting the Seven United Provinces.

Little is known of the family of Serle, after whom this street is named, except what Mr. P. Cunningham tells us in his "Handbook of London," namely, that it was called after a Mr. Henry Serle, one of the benchers of Lincoln's Inn, who died about 1690, having bought some property in this parish from the executors of Sir John Birkenhead, the writer of "Mercurius Aulicus," during the Great Rebellion.

The early name of New Square, Lincoln's Inn Fields, which lies on the north side of Carey Street, was Serle's Court; and the arms of Serle were quartered with those of the Inn over the gateway, which still leads into Carey Street, and was formerly known as Serle's Gate.

New Square is so called on account of its comparatively recent erection (about 1725). Seymour, in his "Survey of London and Westminster" (1735), speaks of the centre of the Court being "spacious and nicely kept, and covered with gravel, raised low, the middle to cast off the rain when it falls. In the middle of the court," he adds, "is a curious stone pillar artificially wrought, on which is a dial-clock, with four boys who used to spout water out of Triton shells, and at the bottom is a basin, that receives the said streams of water falling down from the shells, all incompassed with handsome iron bars." The garden in the centre was not railed in until about the year 1844. In 1867 a temporary building was erected in it for the purpose of exhibiting the various architectural designs for the New Law Courts.

In Serle Street was the old shop of Messrs. Ravenscroft, the famous wig-makers, which had been for a century a rendezvous of legal celebrities. Here might be seen on the walls of the shop a series of portraits of big-wigged lawyers, from Judge Blackstone downwards, and a book of legal autographs was kept in the shop with an almost religious veneration.

At the corner of Serle Street and Portugal Street stood the celebrated coffee-house, so long known to law and to literature as "Serle's." The entrance, flanked with two massive doorposts of a classical design, remained to the last unaltered from what it must have been in the days of Akenside and his friend and patron, Jeremiah Dyson, who used to make this his head-quarters. Addison frequented it in order to study the humours of the young barristers who met there of an evening, and it is not difficult to imagine him seated in a quiet nook, and watching all that is said and done. He thus mentions the house in No. 49 of the *Spectator:* "I do not know that I meet in any of my walks objects which move both my spleen and laughter so effectually as those young fellows at the Grecian, Squire's, Searle's, and all other coffee-houses adjacent to the law, who rise early for no other purpose but to publish their laziness."

The author of "London Poems" writes very graphically in allusion to this neighbourhood—

"Beneath the shade of Temple Bar
 Walk shabby wits who serve the state;
Steele, with mad laughter steeped in war,
 And Addison with smile sedate,
And Swift, the bilious English Rabelais,
 Plods westward shabbily,
On my Lord Bolingbroke alone to wait."

The whole of the space bounded by Carey Street, Serle Street, and Portugal Street, has recently been cleared, and a block of buildings used as the Bankruptcy Court has been erected on the site.

But it is time that we took up our walking-sticks and pursued our journey a little further to the north and north-west, and entered Portugal Street.

In spite of the levelling of the burying-ground on its southern side, and the erection of King's College Hospital on its site, it must be owned that Portugal Street has a dull and dingy look, as if it had met with misfortune. The blank dead wall presented by the back of the museum of the Royal College of Surgeons on the northern side contributes to this effect, and the few shops which it contains are mostly those of law-stationers and printers. Its very name, suggestive of the unhappy wife of Charles II., would seem to have cast a blight on it; and we are told that it inherited the name when the south side of Lincoln's Inn Fields ceased to be called Portugal Row. Yet, in olden days, it must have been lively and gay; for did not the "Lincoln's Inn Theatre" once cover the site of the museum just named? and was not the "Duke's Playhouse" hard by?

In Strype's time the street was without a name; and that venerable antiquary, with good reason, proposed to call it "Playhouse Street," though his suggestion fell on dull and heedless ears.

"On the back side of Portugal Row," says a writer in 1734, "is a street which runneth to Lincoln's Inn Gate, which used to pass without a name; but since the place is increased by the new buildings in Little Lincoln's Inn Fields, and the settling of the playhouse, it may have a name given it, and not improperly, Playhouse Street. Fronting the playhouse is a street which goeth to Plough Stables, which also had no name, unless one may call it Grange Street, from the 'Grange' Inn, a place of good note; nigh to which is the parish roundhouse, on the back side of which is a churchyard also belonging to the parish."

We have said that in this street there were formerly two theatres; but in reality there have been three, as "honest John Timbs" is careful to remind us. He writes, "The first theatre here (named the Duke's Theatre, from the Duke of York, its great patron, and the opera, from its musical performances), was originally a tennis-court. It was altered for Sir William Davenant, and opened in 1662 with his operatic *Siege of Rhodes*, when regular scenery was first introduced upon our stage." Here Pepys, in 1662, saw acted *Romeo and Juliet* (for the first time), *Hamlet*, and *Macbeth*, adding, on the last occasion, that he saw "a mighty company of citizens, ordinary 'prentices, and mean people in the pit." Here, too, as he tells us, he first saw, and sat next to, "pretty, witty" Nell Gwynne, when King Charles and Lady Castlemaine were there to see Lord Orrery's *Mustapha* performed. It is said also, that in this theatre female characters were first played by women, among whom the most famous were Elizabeth Davenant, Mary Saunderson (afterwards Mrs. Betterton), Mary (or Moll) Davis, Mrs. Long, and Mrs. Barry. Davenant having acted musical pieces before the Restoration, Pepys frequently calls this theatre "the Opera," though, in fact, tragedies and comedies only were performed there. It should be added that among the principal actors here was Thomas Betterton, "the rival of Burbage and Garrick, and the last survivor of the old school of English actors." Sir William Davenant made this theatre his head-quarters, if not his home. Early in 1671-2 the players of the Duke's Theatre removed to Dorset Gardens; and the King's Company, being burnt out from Drury Lane, made use of it for about a year, when it was again turned into a tennis-court. The rest of its history shall be told in the words of Mr. Timbs:—"It was refitted and reopened in 1695, with Congreve's comedy of *Love for Love*, which was then played for the first time. This second theatre was taken down and a new house built for Christopher Rich, and opened by John Rich in 1714. . . . . Here Quin played his best parts; and from a *fracas* in which he was embroiled originated the Sergeant's Guard at the Theatre Royal. The first English opera was performed here in 1717-18; here was originally used the stage motto, *Veluti in Speculum;* and here in 1727-28 the *Beggar's Opera* was produced and acted for sixty-two nights, "making Gay rich and Rich gay." In 1732 Rich removed to Covent Garden, which he had lately built, and the Portugal Street house was let by turns for Italian operas, oratorios, balls, concerts, and exhibitions."

In 1735 Mr. Gifford, who had opened another place of amusement in Goodman's Fields, took this theatre, lately vacant by the withdrawal of Rich and his company to Covent Garden, but gave it up at the end of two years, when it was closed. Having undergone several vicissitudes, it became at length the pottery and china warehouse of Messrs. Spode and Copeland. It was here that in 1735 Macklin killed Mr. Hannam; and Nightingale, in the tenth volume of the "Beauties of England and Wales," gives the following strange account of its last performance: "The shutting up of this structure has been whimsically accounted for by vulgar tradition. Upon a representation of the pantomime of *Harlequin and Dr. Faustus*, when a tribe of demons, necessary for the piece, were assembled, a supernumerary devil was observed, who, not approving of going out in a complaisant manner at the door, to show a *devil's trick*, flew up to the ceiling, made his way through the tiling, and tore away one-fourth of the house; which circumstance so affrighted the manager, that the proprietor had not courage to open the house ever afterwards."

With regard to the *Beggar's Opera* we find the following remonstrance in the *Gentleman's Magazine*, September 15th, 1773:—"This day Sir John Fielding informed the bench of justices that he had last year written to Mr. Garrick concerning the impropriety of performing the *Beggar's Opera*, which never has been represented on the stage without creating an additional number of real thieves; he begged, therefore, the gentlemen present would join with him in requesting Mr. Garrick to desist from performing that opera on Saturday evening. The bench immediately consented to the proposal; and a polite card was dispatched to Mr. Garrick for that purpose. To which Mr. Garrick returned for answer, that his company was so imperfect and divided (many of his performers being yet in the country), that it would be impossible for him to open with any other piece; but added, that he would in future do everything in his power to oblige them."

Here is the copy of a playbill of this theatre a century and a half ago:—

"The Sixth day, 1720, for the benefit of the author, by the company of comedians, at the Theatre in Little Lincoln's Inn Fields, this present Saturday, being the 16th of January, will be presented a new farce of three acts, call'd *The Half-pay Officers.* A principal part to be perform'd by Peg Fryar, it being the 6th time of her performance on any stage since the reign of King Charles II. To which will be added the new farce of two acts, call'd *Hob's Wedding*, being the sequel of the *Country Wake.* With entertainments of dancing by Mrs. Fryar, particularly the Bashful Maid, and an Irish Trot. Boxes, 5s. Pit, 3s. Gallery, 2s. N.B.—The author's tickets, which could not come in on the third night, will be taken to-day."

This performance was patronised by royalty, as we find that on Monday, the 11th January, 1720, "His Royal Highness the Prince came to the New Playhouse in Little Lincoln's Inn Fields, and saw a new farce of three acts, call'd *The Half-pay Officers*, with another new farce of two acts, call'd *Hob's Wedding.*"

To this we cannot resist appending a playbill culled from Mr. Diprose's "Anecdotes of the Stage and Players":—

By his Majesty's Company of Comedians.
Kilkenny Theatre Royal.
(Positively the last night, because the Company go to-morrow to Waterford.)
On Saturday, May 14, 1793,
Will be performed by desire and command of several respectable people in this learned Matrapolish, for the benefit of Mr. Kearnes, the manager,
The Tragedy of
HAMLET, PRINCE OF DENMARK.
Originally written and composed by the celebrated Dan Hyes, of Limerick, and insarted in Shakespeare's works.

Hamlet, by Mr. Kearnes (being his first appearance in that character, and who, between the acts, will perform several solos on the patent bag-pipes, which play two tunes at the same time). Ophelia, by Mrs. Prior, who will introduce several favourite airs in character, particularly "The Lass of Richmond Hill," and "We'll be unhappy together," from the Rev. Mr. Dibdin's oddities. The parts of the King and Queen, by directions of the Rev. Father O'Callaghan, will be omitted, as too immoral for any stage. Polonius, the comical politician, by a young gentleman, being his first appearance in public. The Ghost, the Grave-digger, and Laertes, by Mr. Sampson, the great London comedian. The characters to be dressed in Roman shapes. To which will be added, an interlude, in which will be introduced several slight-of-hand tricks, by the celebrated surveyor Hunt. The whole to conclude with the farce of

MAHOMET THE IMPOSTER.

Mahomet, by Mr. Kearnes.

Tickets to be had of Mr. Kearnes, at the sign of the "Goat's Beard," in Castle Street.

The value of the tickets, as usual, will be taken out (if required) in candles, bacon, soap, butter, cheese, potatoes, &c.—as Mr. Kearnes wishes, in every particular, to accommodate the public. N.B.—No smoking allowed.—No person whatsoever will be admitted into the boxes without shoes or stockings.

In 1726, George I. paid a visit to the theatre in Lincoln's Inn Fields, and the event is thus recorded in one of the newspapers of the day:—

"March 18.—Last night His Majesty went to the Theatre Royal in Lincoln's Inn Fields, to see the play of the *Country Wife*, and the entertainment of *Apollo and Daphne*, in which was performed a particular flying on that occasion, of a Cupid descending, and presenting His Majesty with a book of the entertainment, and then ascended—at which new piece of machinery the audience seemed much pleased."

The after history of the place is curious. Having been used first as a barrack and then as an auction room, it was bought by Messrs. Copeland and Spode, as a repository for their china-ware; and finally the premises were taken down in 1848, or the following year, to make room for the enlargement of the museum of the College of Surgeons, which was finished in 1854.

By the rate-books of St. Clement Danes for 1668 we find Portugal Street to have been the residence of many distinguished personages in the seventeenth century. The Earl of Rochester lived "in the house next to the Duke's Theatre," from whence he gives notice to a correspondent, "If you write to me, direct to Lincoln's Inn Fields, the house next to the Duke Playhouse, in Portugal Row, there lives your humble servant,—ROCHESTER."

John Timbs tells us that Portugal Street was the last place where the stocks were set up in London, those of St. Clement Danes, which had formerly stood in the Strand, near Temple Bar, having remained here until about the year 1820. He adds that they were on the north side, facing the hospital. He also reminds us that even in recent days the street enjoyed "a sort of cant notoriety," from the fact of the Insolvent Debtors' Court being in it.

On the south side of Portugal Street, near the centre of the few small courts that have not been swept away, stands King's College Hospital, which owes its existence mainly to the exertions of Dr. R. B. Todd. It forms a plain, substantial, and unpretending block of buildings, four storeys in height, and is hardly old enough as yet to have a history, having been founded only as far back as the year 1839. It grew naturally out of the wants of the Medical Department of King's College in the Strand, of which we shall have more to say in another chapter. It stands on the site of the old workhouse of St. Clement Danes, and of one of the burial-grounds already mentioned. Its design was twofold: to offer the medical students of the college the advantage of witnessing medical and surgical practice, and receiving clinical instruction from their own professors; and secondly, to afford medical and surgical aid to a poor neighbourhood, at a distance from any other hospital. The architect was Mr. T. Bellamy. The patients relieved by the hospital in 1840 were about 4,000, a number which, in a quarter of a century, was multiplied nearly tenfold. New buildings on an extensive scale were added in 1852, and more recently the building has been still further enlarged. The medical staff of the College comprises four "consulting" physicians, seven physicians, besides "assistant" physicians, a "consulting" surgeon, three surgeons with "assistants," a surgeon-dentist, &c.; and the syllabus of its lectures embraces about twenty different subjects. It will accommodate about two hundred patients. The medical students attending hospital practice within its walls average upwards of three hundred. It is under a committee of management, and is but slenderly endowed. The hospital has appended to it a medical library, several museums, a chemical laboratory, and other appliances. The usual course extends over four years, though some few students complete it in three. Though so recently established, it can already boast of a long list of distinguished names among its professors and lecturers.

A part of the buildings of this hospital stands on ground which, up to about the year 1850, was one of the burial-places belonging to the parish. It was about the third of an acre in extent, and called the "Green Ground," as if in mockery. From a report of a parochial committee in 1848, we learn that upwards of 5,500 bodies had been interred within it in the previous quarter of a century. The scenes witnessed here were of the most offensive character. In it was interred, among other lesser celebrities, Joe Miller, the author of the "Jest Book" which bears his name, who died in 1738. A monument was erected to his memory, with an inscription, said to be by Stephen Duck, who began life as a thresher, but afterwards entered the Church, and wrote some poems, which incurred the satire of Dean Swift. This monument, having become decayed and almost illegible, was renewed in 1816, and is to be seen leaning up against the wall of one of the offices of the hospital. The inscription on it ran as follows :—

"Here lie the remains of honest Joe Miller,
Who was a tender husband, a sincere friend,
A facetious companion, and an excellent comedian.
He departed this life the 15th day of August, 1738, aged 54 years."

OLD HOUSES IN WYCH STREET, 1876. (*See page* 34.)

"If humour, wit, and honesty could save
The humorous, witty, honest from the grave,
His grave had not so soon its tenant found,
With honesty, and wit, and humour crowned !
Or could esteem and love preserve our health,
And guard us longer from the stroke of death,
The stroke of death on him had later fell,
Whom all mankind esteemed and loved so well."

Of "Joe Miller" little is known except what may be gathered from his tombstone. He was famous in his day as an actor for his excellent personations of some of the characters in the comedies of Congreve, and as a gleaner and compiler of other men's witticisms he has enjoyed a reputation for wit and humour which in all probability he never deserved. Allibone's "Dictionary of Authors" tells us that "his 'Jest Book' was originally published in 1739 as the compilation of his friend, Elijah Jenkins, but the real editor (and author, as it is asserted) was John Mottley, the author of a 'Life of Peter the Great.' The book itself appears to have gained a sudden celebrity, second only to that of 'Ingoldsby Legends' and 'Pickwick,' three separate editions of it having appeared in 1739, and seven editions being disposed of in as many years."

Mr. Peter Cunningham, in his "Handbook of London," published in 1850, speaks of Joe Miller's headstone as standing in the old burying-ground "half concealed in summer by a clump of sunflowers," and draws the special attention of his readers to "the 'Grange' public-house, with its old and picturesque inn-yard." It may be remembered that Sir William Davenant, in his "Playhouse to Let," mentions this hostelry in a way which implies that it was a haunt of players. "Let him enter and send his train to our house-inn, the 'Grange.'" But alas! for the progress of modern improvements, the "Grange" and its yard are gone. It was taken down in 1853, and its site is now covered by a part of the hospital.

But far worse than the graveyard alluded to above, was another place of burial within the limits of this parish, long known as Enon Chapel, but afterwards converted into a chapel of ease to St. Clement's, and called Clare Market Chapel. The building stood till 1889 at the eastern entrance to Clement's Inn, the access to it being through a gateway leading into a narrow and extremely dingy court, which opens out into Carey Street. It was converted from secular to religious uses in 1823, by a Dissenting congregation, of whom Mr. Diprose writes—

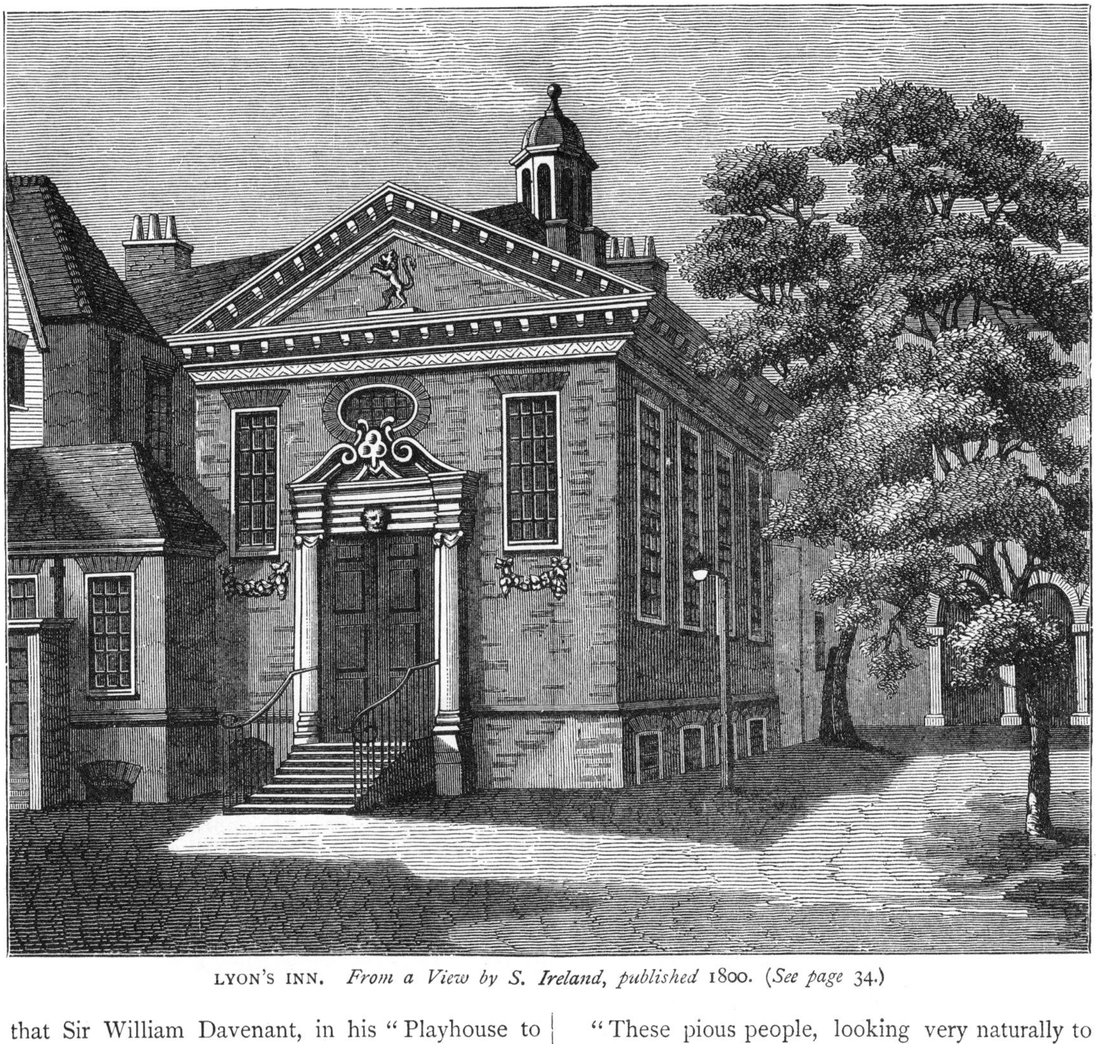

LYON'S INN. *From a View by S. Ireland, published* 1800. (*See page* 34.)

"These pious people, looking very naturally to ways and means, turned the vaults beneath their meeting-house into a burial-place, which soon became filled with coffins up to the very rafters, so that there was only the wooden flooring between the living youth and the festering dead, for a Sunday-school was held in the chapel as well as the congregational meeting. This state of things was allowed to continue till 1844, when a new sewer having to be carried under the building, the Commissioners of Sewers discovered the loathsome charnel-house, and had the place closed, but left the bodies to lie there and rot, heedless of all consequences. The upper premises then became tenanted by a set of teetotallers, who, amongst other uses, turned it into a dancing-room, where the thoughtless and giddy went to 'foot it' away over the mouldering remains of sad mortality, part of the bygone generation turning to dust beneath the dancers' feet." This loathsome abomination ceased in 1847-8, when a surgeon, Mr. G. A. Walker, gained possession of the chapel with the intention of removing the remains from the vault, or "dust-hole," as it was usually called, to a more appropriate place. The work of exhumation was then commenced, and a pyramid of human bones was exposed to view, separated from piles of coffin wood in various stages of decay. This "Golgotha" was visited by about 6,000 persons, previous to its removal, and some idea may be formed of the horrid appearance of the scene, when it is stated that the quantity of remains comprised four upheaved van loads. The whole mass of bodies was decently interred by Mr. Walker, at his own cost, in one pit in the cemetery at Norwood, the coffin-wood being piled up and burnt. It is indeed strange to think that such foul abuses were not swept away until the reign of Victoria.

Was it in jest and scorn, or in a fit of royal pleasantry, that the little thoroughfare which joins the west end of Portugal Street to the south-west angle of Lincoln's Inn Fields was called Portsmouth Street? At all events it is not a little strange that this should have been the case when the Queen of Charles II. was Catharine of *Portugal*, and one of his court favourites the Duchess of *Portsmouth*. It is a short, narrow, and not very interesting street, though it still contains one or two of the few surviving wooden houses of the Stuart times. Mr. Peter Cunningham tells us that the "Old Black Jack," in this street, demolished in 1896, a famous hostelry of Joe Miller, was long known as the "Jump," on account of the fact that another of its frequenters, "Jack Sheppard," that hero of our town-bred urchins, once jumped out of its first-floor window, to escape the emissaries of Jonathan Wild. John Timbs tells us that here used to meet, until the year 1816, the members of a club known as the "Honourable Society of Jackers."

CHAPTER V.

THE STRAND (NORTHERN TRIBUTARIES).—CLEMENT'S INN, NEW INN, LYON'S INN, ETC.

"He must to the Inns of Court. I was of Clement's once myself, where they talk of Mad Shallow still."—2 *Henry IV.*, Act iii. 2.

Curious Legend about St. Clement's Lane—Clement's Inn—New Inn—Stanhope Street—Birthplace of Grimaldi—Holywell Street—The "Old Drury" Tavern—Ancient Shop-Signs—"Bookseller's Row"—Wych Street—New Inn—The "White Lion" and Jack Sheppard—The "Angel" Inn and Bishop Hooper—"Saddling the Spit"—Lyon's Inn—The "Spotted Dog"—The Globe Theatre—The Opera Comique—The Olympic Theatre.

Turning southwards down what used to be a portion of St. Clement's Lane, and which lies between King's College Hospital and New Inn, it occurs to us that the narrow, dark, and irregular alleys in the neighbourhood of Clare Market and Wych Street, encumbered as they were with low projecting eaves, arched doorways, and bulkheads, must have afforded every facility, a century ago, or even less, for the unforeseen attacks of footpads and for the escape of the offenders; and even now it is almost as true as it was a century ago, that in the words of a writer in the *Builder*, "the whole nest of streets and passages behind the south side of Lincoln's Inn Fields requires re-arrangement and improvement. There is a legend hereabout that years ago a young man from the country, bearing a black bag, started one winter night from Portugal Street to get into the Strand, and that he has been wandering round and about ever since, constantly returning with a disconsolate aspect to his original starting-point. On foggy nights his form may be descried in Clare Market. Anyhow, no one has yet heard that he ever reached the Strand."

Fortescue, a celebrated man of letters in the fifteenth century, was of the fanciful opinion that the name Inns of Court arose from these places being the inns or hotels where young noblemen and others belonging to the Court temporarily resided; for many persons of rank sent their sons here to pursue a course of study, without designing them to follow the profession of the law.

Clement's Inn, the west boundary of the New Law Courts, was so named, as we are told by Stow, "Because it standeth near to Clement's Church, but nearer to the fair fountain called Clement's Well." It is stated by Dugdale to have been an Inn of Chancery in the reign of Edward II.; but Pennant speaks of it as dating back only as far as the reign of Edward IV.

The following is quoted from Sir George Buc, an old writer, whose style at least is quaint and amusing:—"Clement's Inne was a messuage belonging to the parish of St. Clement Dane, the deuise whereof is an anchor without a stocke, with a capital C couchant upon it; and this is grauen in stone over the gate of St. Clement's Inne. It seemeth to be a hieroglyphike, or rebus (as some conjecture), figuring herein. St. Clement, who having been Pope, and so reputed head of the Church (and the Church being resembled to a shippe), both his name and office are expressed in this deuise of the 'C' and anchor."

The entrance to Clement's Inn from the thoroughfare on the north side of the church of St. Clement Danes was formerly through a tall archway, supported by lofty columns, which, however, has been demolished to make room for the New Law Courts. Our readers will scarcely need to be reminded that St. Clement's Inn is the one which Shakespeare has made immortal as the home of "Master Shallow" in his Templar days, as may be seen by the motto prefixed to this chapter.

Clement's Inn is said by Seymour in his "Survey" to have descended to the Earls of Clare from Sir William Hollis, Lord Mayor of London in 1539.

In the garden of this inn used to be a celebrated bronze figure of a negro supporting a sundial, said to have been brought from Italy early in the eighteenth century by Lord Clare, by whom it was presented to the Inn. Dickens, however, in the "Uncommercial Traveller," gives quite another version of the origin of this figure, which has recently been removed to the Inner Temple Gardens. The inn has now been rebuilt, and the Hall is no longer to be found.

New Inn, which adjoins Clement's Inn, is said by tradition to have been removed to Wych Street from Seacole Lane, before which time there was here a common hostelry or inn, known by the sign of the "Blessed Virgin."

"To this inn," says Seymour, with his usual accuracy, in his "Survey of London and Westminster" (1735), "are pleasant walks and gardens. The north-easterly part joints to Clement's Inn, from which it is separated by a handsome iron gate, shut up a nights, which was placed here anno 1723."

Pennant, writing in 1805, says of it—"New Inn, where the students of the Strand Inn nestled after they were routed thence by the Duke of Somerset. In New Inn the great Sir Thomas More received the early part of his education before he removed to Lincoln's Inn." The armorial bearings of this Inn are *Vert, a flower-pot argent.* It became an Inn of Chancery in 1485.

Stanhope Street, in this immediate neighbourhood, is worthy of a passing note as having been the birthplace of the famous clown, Grimaldi, who here first saw the light of day, Dec. 18, 1778. He seems to have been born in the purple of the theatre. His father was of Italian extraction; his mother, according to Mr. Diprose, was a Miss Rebecca Brooker, who had been from infancy a dancer at Drury Lane, and subsequently played "old woman" at Sadler's Wells. From "Pink's History of Clerkenwell" we learn that "Joe Grimaldi" made his first appearance at "the Wells" in 1781 in the character of a monkey, became part proprietor of the house in 1818, and finally quitted it in 1832. He died, somewhat suddenly, at his house in Southampton Street, Pentonville Road, at the end of May, 1837, and was buried in the churchyard of St. James's, Pentonville, by the side of his friend Charles Dibdin.

There is but little in the way of antiquarian lore or of recent anecdote to be told concerning Holywell Street, which no doubt received its name—not, we fear, much in keeping with its real character—from the "holy well" already mentioned near St. Clement's Church. Leigh Hunt, in his "London Journal," passes it by with discreet silence. Allen, in his "History of London," dismisses it in a line, styling it a "narrow, inconvenient avenue of old, ill-formed houses;" and Mr. Peter Cunningham "a narrow, dirty lane, chiefly occupied by old clothesmen and the vendors of low publications."

It appears from honest Strype that in his day it was tenanted by "divers salesmen and piecebrokers," and was commonly called "the Back Side of St. Clement's." Mr. Timbs says that the "holy well" which gave to it its name was "under the 'Old Dog' Tavern" (No. 24); but this is clearly a mistake. He adds that the "salesmen and piecebrokers of Strype's day have nearly deserted it, and that it is now the head-quarters of old bookstalls." A few lofty-gabled and deep-bayed fronts still remain upon some of the houses, especially on the southern side. It is only fair to add that during the last few years the character of the street has shown some improvement, owing to the enforcement of Lord Campbell's Act against the sale of bad books and prints, for which formerly this thoroughfare was a notorious market. At the corner of one of the houses on the south side, near the centre of the street, there remained until quite recently a grotesque carving—a lion's head—probably the last of such ornaments in the metropolis.

Holywell Street, we may be pardoned for adding here, was formerly used as the emporium of the mercers, who had their appropriate signs. Of these one still remains, the "Half Moon," a carved projecting sign; another—the "Indian Queen," painted by one of the members of the first association of the Royal Academy, one Catton—might be seen down to a recent period. The "Golden Ball" in this street was a noted house for silk remnants, and continued in repute to the end of the last century. As the mercery trade declined in Holywell Street, the traffic in frippery and old clothes took its place, but this has now practically disappeared.

A few houses in this street are still occupied by booksellers of a certain class—those who deal in a questionable kind of literature; and in the interest of the more respectable inhabitants, it has been proposed more than once to alter the name to "Booksellers' Row," but the street continues to be known as Holywell Street. It is only right to add that in the street at the present time are many highly respectable second-hand book-shops. The removal of all the buildings on the south side, from St. Clement's Church to St. Mary's-le-Strand, so as to widen this part of the street, is now (1897) under consideration.

Wych Street—our pathway as we walk from St. Clement's Church towards Drury Lane—derives its name from the Via de Aldwych, whereof it originally formed a part, a lane leading from the north side of the Strand to Broad Street, St. Giles's. It still contains, especially on the south side, some of those curious old wooden-fronted and gabled houses which are equally picturesque and inconvenient. Like Holywell Street, of late years this thoroughfare gained a notoriety for the sale of books and prints of an immoral class, but of this traffic few signs are now to be seen. In bygone days, however, it was tenanted by a very different class of persons; although in 1734, according to a statement quoted by Mr. Diprose, this street was "much taken up by upholsterers for the sale of bedding and second-hand household goods."

On the north side of Wych Street, nearly about the centre, is the entrance to New Inn, through which in the day-time there is a thoroughfare into the dismal region of Clare Market. In a narrow court of this street the notorious Jack Sheppard served his apprenticeship to Mr. Wood, the carpenter; and in White Lion Passage stood the "hostelrie" of the "White Lion," the scene of many of the events in the career of that prince of "cracksmen," who used nightly to meet in the taproom his professional friends and acquaintances, and with whose feats and various adventures the pen of Mr. Harrison Ainsworth has made us so familiar. The house was pulled down in 1880.

The site of the old "White Lion" was at the corner of one of the courts on the northern side, and was latterly occupied as a carpenter's shop.

Speaking of Wych Street as it was in the days of Jack Sheppard, we may say of the Via de Aldwych, as the writer of "Haunted London" says of Holborn Hill—

> "The street curves quaint,
> And cumbrous sign-boards creak on left and right."

From the "Angel" Inn, at the bottom of Wych Street, Bishop Hooper was taken in 1554 to Gloucester to be burnt at the stake. Something more than two centuries later, the "Angel" Inn figured in a curious advertisement which appeared in the *Public Advertiser*, March 28, 1769:—

> "To be sold, a Black Girl, 11 years of age; extremely handy; works at her needle tolerably, and speaks English well. Inquire of Mr. Owen, at the 'Angel' Inn, behind St. Clement's Church, in the Strand."

It is said by Allen, in his "History of London," that the "Great Fire" of 1666 was not the first of its kind which laid London waste, for that "in 1136 a great fire happened within the City, which destroyed all the way westward to St. Clement Danes," but he does not mention the precise spot where this fire ended at the west.

We have seen that the parish of St. Clement Danes was not considered remarkable for decency and order in the reign of Queen Elizabeth; but, in spite of the rank, wit, and fashion which distinguished it a century and a half later, we find that it even then bore no better character; and the Clement's Lane of the First and Second Georges was no bad precursor to the Wych Street of our own day. The *London Spy* of that date observes, half in earnest and half in jest, that it "is deemed an excellent air for breeding attorneys in, the chief subject of all conversation turning here upon verdicts, costs, damages, writs of inquiry, &c."

According to the same authority, published in 1725, there was formerly in the parish of St. Clement's the custom of "saddling the spit," which, the writer adds, "is now laid aside, for reasons well known at Westminster Hall." It would seem that whatever this custom may have been—and as far as we have been able to discover, history preserves a discreet silence as to its nature—it was a rough and boisterous one, "more honoured in the breach than in the observance."

Lyon's Inn, now demolished, was an old Inn of Chancery, belonging in former days to the Inner Temple. It faced Newcastle Street, on its eastern side, between Wych Street and Holywell Street; one entrance led to it from the latter, and also another through Horne Court, next door to an inn known as the "Spotted Dog." Mr. Diprose, in his "Account of St. Clement Danes," tells us that this same "Spotted Dog" had been a hostelry for some 230 years at least before its demolition in 1864, for the purpose of carrying out a building speculation of the "Strand Hotel Company," a speculation which ended in failure. It is said—but we know not with what amount of truth—that the once holy well, which gave its name to the street, was under the "Spotted Dog."

Howes, in his "Annals," in continuation of Stow, quaintly tell us that it was "a guest inn or hostelerie held at the sign of the 'Lyon,' and purchased by gentlemen professors and students in the law in the reign of King Henry VIII., and converted to an Inn of Chancery." Sir Edward Coke was a student there in 1578.

This Inn, never of much importance, had fallen utterly into disrepute before the beginning of this century, and become the resort of gamblers and swindlers. Here lived Mr. Weare, who was murdered near Edgware by Thurtell, in 1824. The latter in defence pleaded in extenuation that Weare had cheated him at cards out of £300.

Each of the three Inns alluded to in this chapter was governed by a Principal or Treasurer, and a number of "Ancients," corresponding to Benchers; and Seymour tells us, in his "Survey," that there were "mootings" in each Inn in every term.

The property of "Lyons Inn" was sold about the year 1863, and on its site now stand two theatres, the "Globe," as if in memory of Shakespeare's theatre, and the "Opera Comique."

The Globe Theatre, which covers its western portion, was built and opened in 1868. It has a narrow frontage in Newcastle Street. On this site the Architectural Association had its first home. The theatre was built from the instructions of Mr. Sefton Parry, the proprietor, and will seat 1,500 persons. The auditorium is effectively decorated in relief, and has a domed ceiling, with a sunlight in the centre. The site having been excavated very considerably for the proposed hotel, the floor of the pit has been made many feet below the line of the street, and is approached by a steep flight of steps from Wych Street. In Wych Street also are the entrances to the gallery stairs, and that to the "royal box." The ordinary boxes are entered from Newcastle Street, and are on a level with the street, so that stairs are avoided. Here, too, enter the occupants of the stalls. The seats are all fairly commodious, and conveniently placed, so that all that is passing on the stage can be distinctly seen and heard from any part of the house. The house opened with Mr. H. J. Byron's comedy of "Cyril's Success," which in itself proved a great success from a financial point of view.

The principal front of the "Opera Comique" is in the Strand, and observant passengers who know the narrowness of the area between the Strand and Holywell Street will find it difficult to imagine how, even in London, where now-a-days theatres are edged in among houses anyhow, an "Opera Comique" can have been formed there. This frontage, however, is, in truth, nothing but the entrance to a passage which leads across Holywell Street to a theatre that has been built between that and Wych Street. The building, which is very small, backs on the "Globe," and is to a considerable extent underground, as will be understood when we mention that a long flight of stairs in Wych Street leads down to the stage level, and that the pit, of course, is lower than that again. The theatre was opened in 1870, and has seen several changes of lessees. It is nicely decorated, and commodiously arranged. Its greatest prosperity has been in the production of those comic operas with which the names of Messrs. Gilbert and Sullivan are popularly associated, notably "H.M.S. Pinafore," and "The Pirates of Penzance."

The Olympic Theatre, at the end of Wych Street, occupies the site of old Craven House, which was taken down in 1803, the ground being purchased by Mr. Philip Astley, of the "Amphitheatre" over Westminster Bridge, who constructed what was called at the time "a house of public exhibition of horsemanship and droll," which he styled "the Olympic Pavilion." It was opened as such in 1806, but the speculation does not appear to have been successful. In 1813 the lease was sold to Robert Elliston, who introduced pieces of sufficient merit to attract the fashionable dwellers in the West-end, and by that means raised the theatre to something like successful popularity. The building was destroyed by fire in 1849, but rebuilt and opened again in the same year. It was pulled down in 1890, and rebuilt in the following year. Madame Vestris had the management of the "Olympic" from 1832 to 1839, and many eminent actors and actresses appeared upon its boards. The pieces brought out at this theatre were principally melodramas of the superior kind. For many years Robson, one of the most gifted modern comedians, attracted thousands here to witness his wonderful delineations of the tears and laughter, the joys and sorrows, of human life in its humbler aspects. Mr. Horace Wigan was for some time manager here; Mr. Benjamin Webster has likewise had the management, and since then Miss Ada Cavendish and others have taken it in hand.

OLD CRAVEN HOUSE, 1800. (*See page* 35.)

CHAPTER VI.

THE STRAND (NORTHERN TRIBUTARIES).—DRURY LANE AND CLARE MARKET.

"O may thy virtue guard thee through the roads
Of Drury's mazy courts and dark abodes!"—*Gay's* "*Trivia.*"

"Paltry and proud as drabs in Drury Lane."—*Pope.*

The Hundred of Drury—Drury House, afterwards called Craven House—The "Queen of Bohemia"—Drury Lane—Eminent Inhabitants—Residence of Nell Gwynne—The "Cock and Magpie"—The "Craven Head" and the Norfolk Giant—Disreputable Character of Drury Lane in the Past Century—Pepys' Visit to the "Cockpit"—Puritan Observances—The Theatre in Vere Street—"Spiriting Away" an Infant—Princes Street—Clare Market—John Henley, the Demagogue—Clare House—Killigrew's Theatre—Mrs. Bracegirdle's Benevolence—The "Bull's Head" and the Artists' Club—The "Spiller's Head" Tavern—Clare Market Chapel—Denzil Street—Holles Street.

"On the borders of St. Giles-in-the-Fields," says the *London Spy*, "is situated that ancient and venerable spot the Hundred of Drury, which, I hear, is the property of two or three parishes more." The character of this region may be inferred from the words which follow: "There are reckoned to be one hundred and seven 'pleasure-houses' within and about this settlement; and a Roman Catholic priest, who has lodged here many years, assures me that to his knowledge the Societies for the Reformation of Morals have taken as much pains, and expended as large sums to reclaim this new Sodom, as would have fitted out a force sufficient to have conquered the Spanish West Indies."

Pennant remarks it as a singular occurrence that this lane, "of late times so notorious for intrigue," should receive its name from a word which, in the language of Chaucer, had an amorous signification:

"Of bataile and of chevalrie,
Of ladies' love and *druerie*,
Anon I wot you tell."

Drury House, from which the lane originally took its name, stood at the west end of Wych Street. It was built by Sir William Drury, who is reported to have been not only the head of a great family, but Knight of the Garter. He held a command in the Irish wars in the reign of Elizabeth, and showed great ability as an officer. He unfortunately fell in a duel with a Sir John Burroughes, about a foolish quarrel for precedency. The house deserves to be remembered as the place where the rash friends of the Queen's favourite, the Earl of Essex devised those wild schemes which led to the ruin of himself and his adherents. The "Account of St. Clement's in 1734," to which we have so often referred, speaks of it as "a very large house, or which may rather be termed several houses. The entrance," adds the writer, "is through a pair of gates, which leadeth into a large yard for the reception of coaches." At the back of the house was a handsome garden. "In the following century," says Allen, in his "History of London," "it was possessed by the heroic Lord Craven, who rebuilt it. It was lately a large brick pile, concealed by other buildings, and turned into a public-house bearing the sign of the 'Queen of Bohemia,' the earl's admired mistress, whose battles he fought, animated at once by love and duty. When on the death of her husband he could aspire to her hand, he is supposed to have succeeded; at all events history says that they were privately married, and that he built for her the fine seat at Hampstead Marshal, in Berkshire, afterwards destroyed by fire."

THE "COCK AND MAGPIE," DRURY LANE. *From an Original Sketch in* 1840. (*See page* 38.)

The services rendered by Lord Craven to London, his native city, are worthy of being recorded here. He was so indefatigable in preventing the ravages of fire, that it is said "his horse would smell the outbreak of a fire, and neigh to give the alarm." He and Monk, Duke of Albemarle, stayed in London throughout the visitation of the Great Plague in 1665, and at the hazard of their own lives preserved order in the midst of the horrors of the time. Allen adds that there used to be in Craven Buildings a very good fresco portrait of this hero in armour, mounted on a white horse, and with his truncheon in hand, and on each side an earl's and a baron's coronet, with the letters "W. C." (William Craven). This painting, though several times re-coloured in oils, has long since perished; but an engraving of it is preserved in Smith's "Antiquities of London."

It deserves to be recorded of Sir Robert Drury that he for some time entertained, as a welcome and honoured guest, at his mansion in Drury Lane, the amiable and learned Dr. John Donne, afterwards Dean of St. Paul's, when he was young and poor, having contracted marriage with a young lady of high connections, against the will, or at all events without the consent, of her relatives. It is added that he not only gave him and his wife the free use of apartments, but also was "a cherisher of his studies, and such a friend as sympathised with him and his in all their joys and sorrows." Such friends, no doubt, were rare then; as rare, perhaps, as now-a-days; but it is a pleasure to record such an act of genuine friendship.

The exact date of the removal of Lord Craven's family from Drury Lane to their subsequent residence at Bayswater, where now is Craven Hill, is not known; but it must have been just before the close of the seventeenth century. Craven House itself was taken down early in the present century, and the site is now occupied by the Olympic Theatre, as stated in the last chapter.

Drury Lane was once the "Via de Aldwych," a name still preserved in Wych Street, as already mentioned. Then the great family of the Druries built in it a town house, and the Earls of Craven and Clare followed. It became a Belgravia. Here lived Archibald, the famous and ill-fated Marquis of Argyle. Here, too, close to Cradle Alley, Arthur Annesley, Earl of Anglesey, and Lord Privy Seal under Charles II., had his town house. Here, too, in the heyday of her glory, lived Nell Gwynne, the "pretty Nelly" whom Pepys saw "standing at her lodgings' door in her smock sleeves and bodice, a mighty pretty creature." Here also resided John Lacy, the comedian, and Sir William Alexander, the poet, afterwards Earl of Stirling.

At the same period was residing here a relative of the staid Mr. Evelyn, who, after recording in his "Diary" that he attended the marriage of his niece to the eldest son of Mr. Attorney Montagu, at Southampton Chapel, and eulogising the magnificence of the entertainment, adds, "the bride was bedded at my sister's lodgings in Drury Lane."

It was in Drury Lane, not very far from the steps of the Olympic Theatre, that Lord Mohun made his unsuccessful attempt to carry off the beautiful and much-wooed actress, Mrs. Bracegirdle, as we shall presently show.

By the time of Steele, Drury Lane had changed its character, and its narrow, close, and filthy courts were rising into existence.

All that is now left of Drury Lane is its memory of past glories. The shades of the persons above mentioned, as well as those of the pretty Mrs. Bracegirdle, the fiery Lord Mohun, and of the quarrelsome Carlo Fantom, the Croatian, who challenged his man and killed him, "because the noise of his spurs pleased him not," haunt it still. On the west side is a small burial-ground, unknown to Stow or Strype, to most of the map-makers, and to Peter Cunningham. It lies between Russell Street and Long Acre. For many years it had exhibited a most desolate and miserable aspect; indeed, it had become a sort of "no man's land." During the year 1874, however, the authorities of St. Martin's-in-the-Fields, to whom the ground belongs, at some considerable expense had the graveyard levelled and converted into a garden with walks and shrubberies. A neat brick wall separates the grounds from the public street, and on one side a brick building has been erected, to be used as a mortuary.

Towards the lower end of Drury Lane, nearly opposite to Drury or Craven House, is a quaint old gabled house, with its pents still remaining. A quarter of a century ago it was known as the "Cock and Magpie," but more recently as "Stockley's Cheap Bookshop." It is said that the region to the north, leading up towards St. Giles's, was once known as "Cock and Pie Fields;" but antiquaries are divided on the question as to whether they were so called from the house, or the house from them. Whichever may be the case, it is certain that the "Cock and Magpie" as a sign, is but a travesty of a chivalric legend, which Douce thus explains:—"In the days of ancient chivalry it was the practice to make solemn vows or engagements for the performance of any considerable enterprise. This was usually performed during some great feast or entertainment, at which a roasted peacock, being served up by ladies in a dish of gold or silver, was presented to the knight, who then made his particular vow with great solemnity. When this custom had fallen into disuse, the peacock nevertheless continued to be a favourite dish, and was introduced on the table in a pie, the head, with gilded beak, being proudly elevated above the crust, and the splendid tail expanded.

Other birds of smaller value were afterwards introduced in the same manner; and the recollection of the old peacock vows might occasion the less serious, or even the burlesque, imitation of swearing, not only by the bird itself, but also by the pie: hence, probably, came the oath 'By cock and pie,' for the use of which no very great antiquity can be found." From "Cock o' pie" to "Cock and magpie" the transition was easy and obvious.

Opposite to the above is the "Craven Head" Tavern, which, from 1851 to 1855, was kept by Mr. Robert Hales, the "Norfolk Giant." He was born in 1820, near Yarmouth, where his father was a small farmer, and was one of nine children, all far above the ordinary stature. He was exhibited by Barnum, in America, in 1848, and was one of the curiosities of London in the year of the first Great Exhibition. In the April of that year he was presented to the Queen, who gave him a watch and chain, and also to other crowned heads. He stood upwards of eight feet in height. His death occurred in 1863, at the age of forty-eight.

Drury Court is a narrow little street, leading down from Drury Lane to St. Mary's Church in the Strand. Its eastern side is composed of a range of houses which have stood apparently more than two centuries and a half.

It will be remembered that in the *Tatler* (No. 46) Steele gives a picture of the morality of Drury Lane, describing it as a district divided into particular "ladyships," analogous to "lordships" in other parts, "over which matrons of known ability preside." Its character, too, as well in the present as in the past century, is delicately hinted at by Gay, in the lines quoted from "Trivia," at the head of this chapter. The "Dog," a low public-house in this street, was known as the robbers' den; and nothing can confirm more clearly the character of the immediate neighbourhood, to which we have referred, than the fact that Drury Lane was the scene of the "Harlot's Progress," by Hogarth.

In Drury Lane was one of the several "cock-pits," or places reserved for cock-fighting, which a century ago or earlier were to be found scattered about London. Mr. John Timbs tells us that one of our oldest theatres was called the "Cock-pit," namely, the "Phœnix" in Drury Lane, and that the site of it was still to be traced in the name of Pit or Pitt Place, an abridgment of "Cock-pit" Place. Samuel Pepys thus describes in his "Diary" a visit to one of these places, not far from Drury Lane:—"December 21. To Shoe Lane to a cock-fighting at a new pit: but Lord! to see the strange variety of people, from Parliament men, to the poorest 'prentices, bakers, brewers, butchers, draymen, and what not; and all these fellows, one with another, cursing and betting. Strange that such poor people, that look as if they had not bread to put in their mouths, shall bet three or four pounds at a time, and lose it, and yet bet as much the next battle, so that one of them will lose £10 or £20 at a meeting! I soon had enough of it."

From Stubs's "Anatomie of Abuses," published in 1585, it is evident that in the good old Tudor times Sunday was the day of all the week especially set apart for this amusement. As early as the reign of Henry II., according to Fitzstephen, cock-fighting was the sport of school-boys in and around London on Shrove Tuesday; and from that time, though occasionally forbidden by some of our sovereigns, it continued to exist among us, as we shall see hereafter.

At the beginning of the eighteenth century it would seem that Drury Lane had succeeded to a part at least of the reputation of Grub Street, as the residence of poor poets and hack rhymsters, as witness the words of Pope, in his "Dunciad"—

> "Cries he who high in Drury Lane,
> Lulled by soft zephyrs through the broken pane,
> Rhymes ere he wakes, and prints before Term ends,
> Obliged by hunger, and request of friends."

And in like spirit wrote Oliver Goldsmith—

> "Where the 'Red Lion,' staring o'er the way,
> Invites each passing stranger that can pay;
> Where Calvert's butt and Parson's black champagne
> Regale the drabs and bloods of Drury Lane,
> There, in a lonely room, from bailiffs snug,
> The Muse found Scroggins, stretch'd beneath a rug."

"Their Majesties' servants," as might have been expected, fared but ill during the austere tyranny of the Puritan faction. At the Restoration the survivors of the old actors naturally formed themselves into a company, and Downes tells us that they acted at the Tennis-court, in Vere Street, Clare Market, till a new theatre was built; and Guest is of opinion that both before and after that event they performed at the Cockpit in Drury Lane. The theatre in Vere Street was opened November 8th, 1660, by Killigrew and Davenant, under a patent which allowed women to act the female parts, a practice till then unknown in England.

It was at this theatre that an unknown young lady was performing the character of Roxana, in the *Siege of Rhodes*, who fell a victim to Aubrey de Vere, the last (and most unworthy) Earl of Oxford of the ancient line. This scion of a noble house, finding that he could secure his prey in no other way, brought to her lodging a sham clergyman and a sham marriage certificate; and she learnt to her cost, when it was too late, that she had no pretension whatever to style herself Countess of Oxford.

It is clear that although the Puritans disapproved of plays *pur et simple*, they tolerated mixed entertainments of a musical kind. Such an entertainment, we know from Evelyn, was given after the death of Oliver Cromwell, for he writes, in May, 1659:—"I went to see a new opera after the Italian way in recitative music and scenes. . . . It was prodigious that in a time of such public consternation such a 'vanity' should be kept up or permitted." That this entertainment was something different from a tragedy or comedy is clear from another entry by Evelyn in his "Diary," in January, 1661:—"After divers years since I had seen any play, I went to see acted *The Scornful Lady*, at a new theatre in Lincoln's Inn Fields."

Mr. Peter Cunningham tells us that Laguerre, whose "sprawling saints" are immortalised by Pope, was a member of a club of *virtuosi* who used to meet at a house in Drury Lane, and that he painted on its walls a Bacchanalian procession, which he presented to its members. But apparently the *habitat* of this club was unknown to him.

It was in a low lodging-house in Lincoln Court, one of the gloomiest purlieus on the eastern side of the upper part of Drury Lane, that in 1861 was discovered the infant son of a Mr. and Mrs. Hill—relatives of the Burdett family—which had been "spirited away" from its mother's charge at Rugby by its father. The story is thus told by a writer in *Cassell's Magazine* of May 24th, 1873:—

"The boy's own father, after falsifying the register of its birth, took it to London, and handed it over to some women whom he met in the street. The police were soon put upon the track of the culprits, who were shown to have received the missing infant from its unnatural parent. The papers took up the matter, which became a 'nine days' wonder,' and in a little time the child was discovered in Lincoln Court, Drury Lane, a place tenanted by the lowest class of Irish. It was in a sadly dirty state, and such clothing as it had on its back was not the same which it wore on leaving Rugby; but in spite of dirt and rags, there was something about the child which marked it off from the beggars' brats among whom it was playing, and its *distingué* looks led to its recovery. Ultimately the father was acquitted of the charge on which he was arraigned. Both he and Mrs. Hill, however, died shortly afterwards. This court was pulled down in 1880, to make room for model lodging-houses.

The following brief extract from a daily paper in the year of grace 1874 tells its own sad story:—"On Saturday, Mr. Langham held an inquest on the body of Miss Eliza Merrit, aged fifty-six, who it was said, was the daughter of a Church of England rector, and after struggling amid ill health to earn a living as a governess and by needlework, had ultimately, as the evidence showed, died of want, alone, in a small back room in Drury Lane!"

Drury Lane is rapidly losing its look of dingy antiquity. A few years ago some large blocks of dwellings for the working classes were built on the eastern side, and as these pages go to press (1897) a considerable portion of the western side is being rebuilt.

It should be added here that this street—or, at all events, a part of it—at one time was called Prince's Street; "but the old name triumphed," says Mr. Peter Cunningham, "and Prince's Street was confined to a new row of tenements branching off to the east, and still distinguished by that name."

The thoroughfare known as Clare Market, leading eastwards into Lincoln's Inn Fields, was so called in honour of the Earl of Clare, who lived "in a princely mansion" adjacent. His name is inscribed as a parishioner of St. Clement Danes in the rate-books of 1617. In Howell's "Londinopolis" of 1657 we read:—"Then is there, towards Drury Lane, a new market, called Clare Market; then is there a street and palace of the same name, built by the Earl of Clare, who lived there in a princely mansion, having a house, a street, and a market both for flesh and fish, all bearing his name." It is thus mentioned by Strype:—"Clare Market very considerable and well served with provisions, both flesh and fish; for, besides the butchers in the shambles, it is much resorted unto by the country butchers and higglers. The market-days are Wednesdays and Saturdays. The toll belongs to the Duke of Newcastle (Pelham-Holles) as ground landlord thereof."

"This market," says Nightingale, in the tenth volume of the "Beauties of England and Wales," "stands on what was originally called Clement's Inn Fields. In the year 1657 a Bill was passed for preventing the increase of buildings, in which was a clause permitting the Earl of Clare to erect the market, which bore his title, in these fields, to be held on Tuesdays, Thursdays, and Saturdays. The earl, it seems, also erected a chapel of ease to St. Clement's, which is said to have been converted to dwelling-houses. That these lands were before in the possession of Holles we have already shown under Clement's Inn. Charles I., in 1640, granted his license to Thomas York, his executors, &c., to erect as many buildings as they thought proper upon St. Clement's Inn Fields, the inheritance of the Earl of Clare, 'to be built on each side of the causeway, leading from Gibbon's Bowling Alley, at the coming-out of Lincoln's Inn Fields, to the Rein Deer Yard, that leadeth unto Drury Lane, not to exceed, on either side, the number of 120 feet in length or front, and 60 feet in breadth, to be of stone or brick.'* Charles I. issued another license in 1642, permitting Gervase Holles, Esq., to erect fifteen houses, a chapel, and to make several streets of the width of thirty, thirty-four, and forty feet. These streets still retain the names and titles of their founders, in Clare Street, Denzil Street, Holles Street, &c." Rein Deer Yard was, probably, what is now called Bear Yard, and Gibbon's Bowling Alley was covered by the first theatre erected by Sir William Davenant, whence he afterwards removed to Portugal Street. Here, during the administration of Sir Robert Walpole, in the reign of George II., John Henley, a disappointed demagogue, stood on a tub and vented his factious ebullitions, which he distinguished by the name of oratory. He is alluded to by Pope, in his "Epistle to Arbuthnot," but not in very quotable terms. Possessing some abilities, he was also obnoxious to Government by the publication of the "Hyp Doctor," and other papers on the politics of the times. A contemporary writer speaks of him as—

"Preacher at once and zany of the age."

On Henley's death in 1756, his demise was thus announced in the *Gentleman's Magazine*:—"Rev. Orator Henley, aged 64."

We learn from the "Harleian Miscellany" that the City had a long lawsuit with Lord Clare for this property, but that at last the City yielded. It appears, also, from the same source, that the success of his lordship in obtaining a charter for his market led to one important result, namely, the establishment of other markets round about the metropolis, some of which are now things of the past, such as Hungerford, Brooke, and Bloomsbury Markets, and that in Petty France, in Westminster, and St. James's and Newport Markets, which are still in existence.

Of the house of Holles, Lord Clare, whose family names are so perpetuated in this vicinity, no remains are left, nor is the precise site of it known. It was a large and stately mansion, shut in with a high wall, and its grounds joined on to the eastern side of those of Craven House. Clare Street is mentioned in Strype's edition of Stow as "a good open place fronting the market," while Clare Market bears the reputation of being "a street well inhabited by tradesmen." No engraving of old Clare House is known to exist, nor is any detailed description of the house to be found. All that we know is that the Earl of Clare, as we are told by Howell, lived in his "palace" here in a "princely manner," to which, we fear, the present aspect of the place presents a very marked contrast.

With the Earl of Clare, and other aristocratic denizens of St. Clement Danes, have passed away "the butchers in the shambles, and country butchers," who used to supply these wealthy households. The merchandise at present exposed for sale in Clare Market consists principally of dried fish, inferior vegetables, and other humble viands, suited to the pockets of the poor inhabitants of the narrow courts and alleys around.

The celebrated actress, Mrs. Bracegirdle, we are told, was in the habit of going often into Clare Market, and of giving money to such poor basket-women as were out of employ, thereby calling down many blessings on her head.

As Clare Market lay between two great theatres, its butchers and hucksters, as remarked by Mr. Timbs, were the arbiters of the galleries, and the leaders of theatrical rows, as well as the musicians at the marriages of actresses, and the chief mourners at players' funerals. In one of the many public-houses which, as was natural, abounded here, Hogarth, in the days of his apprenticeship, was a frequent boon-companion of Joe Miller.

In Gibbon's Court, Clare Market, was a small theatre, in which Killigrew's company performed for a short time. Pepys speaks of it as a handsome building, "the finest, I believe, that ever was in England." This, however, must have been an exaggeration. It soon passed away, and its remains were long used as slaughter-houses and carpenters' shops. The butchers of Clare Market are now nearly extinct; but Mr. P. Cunningham tells us that so lately as 1850 from 350 to 400 sheep, and from 50 to 200 oxen, were slaughtered there. He adds, "In a yard distinct from the more public portion of the market is the place where the Jews slaughter their cattle, according to a ceremony prescribed by the laws of their religion."

When Cromwell revived the prohibition of his predecessor against the erection of new buildings in and near London, imposing even a fine on its violation, an exception, we are told, was made in favour of the new buildings then scarcely finished, in Clare Market. In consequence of this exemption, unfortunately for the healthiness of the locality, they were not made "of brick or stone," or "upright, and without projecting their upper storeys into the street."

The "Artists' Club," of which Hogarth was a

* Malcolm's "London," vol. iii., p. 292.

member, used to meet at the "Bull's Head" Tavern in this market. Here also was the "Spiller's Head" Inn, named after James Spiller, a well-known actor, where was held a club principally consisting of artists, authors, and actors connected with the Lincoln's Inn Fields Theatre. It was founded about the year 1690, under the auspices of Colley Cibber, Tom D'Urfey, and many noted characters. Of Spiller, Mr. Diprose tells us, "he was an immense favourite with the butchers of Clare Market, one of whom was so charmed with his performances that he took down the sign of the "Bull and Butcher," and put up "Spiller's Head." The success or failure both of actors and pieces appears in those days to have greatly depended on the verdict of the butchers of Clare Market, whose approval was sometimes recorded by managers in their advertisements!

HALL OF THE ROYAL COLLEGE OF SURGEONS. (*See page* 46.)

To the pen of one of these low patrons of the drama is assigned the following graceful elegy upon the death of James Spiller in 1729:—

"Down with your marrow-bones and cleavers all,
And on your marrow-bones ye butchers fall;
For prayers from you who never prayed before
Perhaps poor Jemmy may to life restore."

In 1701 there appeared at a place of entertainment in Islington, called "Miles's Music House," afterwards known as "Sadler's Wells Theatre," "a strange sort of monster that does everything like a monkey, mimics man like a jackanapes, but is not a jackanapes; jumps upon tables and into windows on all fours like a cat, but is not a cat; does all things like a beast, but is not a beast; does nothing like a man, but is a man! He has given such wonderful content to the butchers of Clare Market," says a contemporary writer, "that the house is every day as full as the Bear Gardens, and draws the City wives and 'prentices out of London much more than a man hanged in chains."

Something has of late years been done to improve Clare Market, and at present (1897) the "house-breaker" and the builder are hard at work. Gilbert Street has nearly disappeared, and recently a clearance scheme was adopted which is estimated to cost three-quarters of a million.

Adjoining Clare Market are Holles and Denzil Streets, the latter "so called," as we are told by a mural tablet on one of its houses, "by Gilbert, Earl of Clare, in memory of his uncle Denzil, Lord Holles, who died in 1679, a great honour to his

IN LINCOLN'S INN FIELDS.

NEWCASTLE HOUSE. SIR JOHN SOANE'S HOUSE.

DUKE OF ANCASTER'S HOUSE.

name, and the exact paturne of his father's great meritt, John, Earl of Clare." This Lord Holles, it will be remembered, was one of the five members of the House of Commons whose person Charles I. made an ineffectual effort to seize.

Holles Street, which runs into Stanhope Street, was built in 1647, and was called, like its neighbour Denzil Street, after Holles, Earl of Clare.

Of Vere Street, which runs northwards parallel to Stanhope Street, we know little except what Mr. Peter Cunningham has told us, namely, that in 1688 it numbered among its inhabitants Sir Thomas Lyttelton and also the poet Ogilby, who here disposed of his books by a lottery; and that in it stood Gibbon's Tennis Court, subsequently converted into a theatre by Killigrew. Of these two places, however, nothing now remains, and the street is dull and dreary.

CHAPTER VII.

LINCOLN'S INN FIELDS.

"Laudaturque domus longos quæ prospicit agros."—*Horace.*

Formation of Lincoln's Inn Fields—Dimensions of the Square—Inigo Jones's Plan—Noble Families resident here—The Poet Gay's Estimate of the Place—"Mumpers" and "Rufflers"—Used as Training-grounds for Horses—Bad Reputation of the Fields in Former Times—Execution of Lord William Russell—The Tennis Court—The Royal College of Surgeons—Sardinian Chapel—The Sardinian Ambassador's Residence—The "Devil's Gap"—Institution for the Remedy of Organic Defects, &c.—Society for Promoting Christian Knowledge—Newcastle House—The Soane Museum—Inns of Court Hotel—Whetstone Park—Milton's Residence—Great and Little Turnstiles—Proposal to erect the Courts of Law in Lincoln's Inn Fields.

THIS open space, which happily still serves to supply fresh air to the residents of the crowded courts of Drury Lane and Clare Market, affords in its central enclosure one of the largest and finest public gardens in London, and in point of antiquity is perhaps the oldest. In 1659, we find from Charles Knight's "History of London," James Cooper, Robert Henley, and Francis Finch, Esquires, and other owners of "certain parcels of ground in the fields, commonly called Lincoln's Inn Fields, were exempted from all forfeitures and penalties which they might incur in regard to any new buildings they might erect on three sides of the same fields, previously to the 1st of October in that year, provided that they paid for the public service one year's full value for every such house within one month of its erection; and provided that they should convey the 'residue of the said fields' to the Society of Lincoln's Inn, for laying the same into walks for common use and benefit, whereby the annoyances which formerly have been in the same fields will be taken away, and passengers there for the future better secured."

It has often been stated, and repeated until generally accepted as true, that the square of Lincoln's Inn Fields was designedly laid out so as to be exactly of the size of the base of the Great Pyramid. "This," remarks Horace Walpole, "would have been much admired in an age when the keep of Kenilworth Castle was erected in the form of a horse-fetter and the Escurial in the shape of St. Lawrence's gridiron;" but a reference to Colonel Howard-Vyse's work "On the Pyramids" will show that the fanciful idea is untrue, the Fields measuring 821 feet by 625, while the Great Pyramid covers a space of 764 feet square.

The "square" was formed in the seventeenth century by no less a person than Inigo Jones, to whom, along with other gentlemen and one or two members of the Court, a special commission was issued by James I., for the purpose of having the ground laid out and improved under his direction. Several of the houses on the west and south sides are of his design. "The expense of laying out the grounds," as we learn from Northouck, "was levied on the surrounding parishes and Inns of Court." The west side was originally known as Arch Row, the south as Portugal Row, and the north as Newman's Row; but the names dropped out of use at the close of the last century.

The original plan for "laying out and planting" these fields, drawn by the hand of Inigo Jones, is still to be seen in Lord Pembroke's collection at Wilton House. The chief feature in it is Lindsey (afterwards Ancaster) House, in the centre of the west side, now divided into two houses and cut up into chambers for lawyers. It is unchanged in all its external features, except that the balustrade along the front of the roof has lost the handsome vases by which it was formerly surmounted.

Among the noble families who lived in this spot was that of the Berties, Earls of Lindsey and afterwards Dukes of Ancaster; but they seem to have migrated to Chelsea in the reign of Charles II. In this square at various dates lived also the great Lord Somers; Digby, Earl of Bristol; Montague, Earl of Sandwich; the Countess of Middlesex, and the Duke of Newcastle; and in the present century Lords Kenyon and Erskine, Sir John Soane, and Mr. Spencer Perceval. A century ago Lord Northington, Lord Chancellor, lived in a house on the south side of the square, on the site of the Royal College of Surgeons. At the birth of her first son, Charles Beauclerk, afterwards the first Duke of St. Albans, Nell Gwynne was living in lodgings in Lincoln's Inn Fields, being up to that time regularly engaged at the theatre close by.

It is to be feared that although Lincoln's Inn Fields is said to be the largest and handsomest square, not only in London, but in Europe, it has not borne a very good character in olden times. At all events Gay speaks of the Fields in his "Trivia" as the head-quarters of beggars by day and of robbers at night:—

"Where Lincoln's Inn's wide space is railed around,
Cross not with venturous step; there oft is found
The lurking thief, who, while the daylight shone,
Made the walls echo with his begging tone.
That crutch, which late compassion mov'd, shall wound
Thy bleeding head, and fell thee to the ground.
Though thou art tempted by the linkman's call,
Yet trust him not along the lonely wall;
In the midway he'll quench the flaming brand,
And share the booty with the pilfering band."

Blount tells us, in his "Law Dictionary," that he used to see idle fellows here playing at "the Wheel of Fortune;" and it is clear, from more than one contemporary allusion in comedies, that the square was the regular haunt of cripples, with crutches, who lived by mendicancy, which they carried on in the most barefaced, if not intimidating, manner. Here, too, according to Peter Cunningham, "the astrologer Lilly, when a servant at Mr. Wright's, at the corner house, over against Strand Bridge, spent his idle hours in 'bowling,' along with Wat the cobbler, Dick the blacksmith, and such like."

We occasionally find in the literature of the seventeenth century allusions to the "Mumpers" and "Rufflers" of Lincoln's Inn Fields. These were, according to Mr. John Timbs, names given to the troops of idle vagrants by whom the "Fields" were infested; and readers of the *Spectator* will hardly need to be reminded of "Scarecrow," the beggar of that place, who, having disabled himself in his right leg, asks alms all day, in order to get a warm supper at night. The "Rufflers," if we may accept the statement of the same authority, were "wretches who assumed the characters of maimed soldiers," who had suffered in the battles of the Great Rebellion, and found a ready prey in the people of fashion and quality as they drove by.

The "railing" to which Gay alludes in his poem, it should be here remarked, was only a series of wooden posts and rails, the iron rails not having been put up until the year 1735, when the money for so enclosing and adorning the Fields was raised by a rate on the inhabitants. The plan of the railing, its gates, and its ornaments, was submitted to and approved by the Duke of Newcastle, the minister of George II., who was one of the residents of the square. We are told that before Lincoln's Inn Fields were so railed in they were used as a training-ground by horse-breakers, and that many robberies were committed in its neighbourhood. And Ireland, in his "Inns of Court," tells us a story which shows us that they were surrounded by a rough and lawless set of people: "Sir John Jekyll having been very active in bringing into Parliament a Bill to raise the price of gin, became very obnoxious to the poor, and, when walking one day in the Fields at the time of breaking the horses, the populace threw him down and trampled on him, from which his life was in great danger."

Peter Cunningham, in his "Handbook of London," tells another story which shows that the bad reputation of these Fields at the time of their enclosure was of more than half a century in standing: "Through these fields," he writes, "in the reign of Charles II., Thomas Sadler, a well-known thief, attended by his confederates, made his mock procession at night with the mace and purse of Lord Chancellor Finch, which they had stolen from the Lord Chancellor's closet in Great Queen Street, and were carrying off to their lodging in Knightrider Street. One of the confederates walked before Sadler, with the mace of the Lord Chancellor exposed on his shoulder; while another, equally prominent, followed after him carrying the Chancellor's purse. For this theft Sadler was executed at Tyburn." And to go back a little further still. "Here," he adds, "even in the place where they had used to meet and confer on their traitorous practices, were Ballard, Babington, and their accomplices beheaded, to the number of fourteen." Here, too, in 1683, a far worthier man, whom it is almost a sin to mention in such company, Lord William Russell, laid his noble head on the block, Dr. Tillotson standing by his side. The reader of Burnet's "History of his Own Time," will not forget his description of the scene of Lord William Russell's execution in this square. He writes, "Tillotson and I went with him in the coach to the place of execution. Some of the crowd that filled the streets wept, while others insulted. He was singing psalms a great part of the way, and said he hoped to sing better ones soon. As he observed the great crowd of people all the way, he said to us, 'I hope I shall quickly see a much better assembly.' When he came to the scaffold, he walked about it four or five times; then he turned to the sheriffs and delivered his papers. . . . He prayed by himself, then Tillotson prayed with him. After that he prayed again by himself, then undressed himself, and laid his head on the block without the least change of countenance; and it was cut off at two strokes." The death of this patriotic nobleman must for ever remain as a blot of deep dye on the memories of those who commanded his execution.

We learn incidentally that early in the last century Betterton and his company were playing at the "Tennis Court,"* in Lincoln's Inn Fields, when it was first proposed to him by Vanbrugh and Congreve, as builder and writer, to join in starting a new theatre in the Haymarket.

On the south side of the square, the Hall of the Royal College of Surgeons is the principal ornament. The building was erected, or rather rebuilt, in 1835–6, under the superintendence of the late Sir Charles Barry. The College of Surgeons was chartered in the year 1800, since which time many valuable advantages have been conferred upon the society by the Legislature. The front of the hall consists of a noble portico, with fluted columns, whilst along the top of the edifice is a bold entablature, with enriched cornice. To the left of the entrance-hall are two or three spacious rooms for the use of the secretary and other officials, and on the right a doorway gives access to the museum, which forms perhaps the chief feature of the building. This occupies three large and lofty rooms, lighted from the top, and each surrounded by two galleries, in which are displayed, as well as in cases on the ground-floor, the valuable collection of objects of which the museum consists. The basis of this collection was originally formed by John Hunter, whose museum was situated in Leicester Square. It was purchased from his widow at his death, by the Government, for the sum of £15,000, and presented to the College of Surgeons. "The main object which he had in view in forming it," says the writer of an admirable account of Hunter and his museum in the *Penny Cyclopædia*, was to illustrate, as far as possible, the whole subject of life by preparations of the bodies in which the phenomena are presented. The principal and most valuable part of the collection, forming the physiological series, consisted of dissections of the organs of plants and animals, classed according to their different vital functions, and in each arranged so as to present every variety of form, beginning from the most simple, and passing upwards to the most complex. They were disposed in two main divisions: the first, illustrative of the functions which minister to the necessities of the individual; the second, of those which provide for the continuance of the species. . . . The pathological part of the museum contained about 2,500 specimens, arranged in three principal departments: the first illustrating the processes of common diseases, and the actions of restoration; the second, the effects of specific diseases; and the third, the effects of various diseases, arranged according to their locality in the body. Appended to these was a collection of about 700 calculi and other inorganic concretions." This, it may be added, has been considerably augmented by subsequent purchases, and also by gifts to the college; so that it may now be fairly said to form the richest collection of the kind in existence.

Among the objects of curiosity preserved here are the skeletons of several human beings and animals, which during the time of their existence had obtained some celebrity. Among them may be mentioned Jonathan Wild, the notorious thief-catcher; Mlle. Crachani, a Sicilian dwarf, who at the age of ten years was just twenty inches high; Charles Byrne, or O'Brien, the Irish giant, who at his death measured eight feet four inches; and also the gigantic elephant "Chunee," which was formerly exhibited on the stage at Covent Garden Theatre, and afterwards in the menagerie at Exeter Change, where, in 1824, "in consequence of the return of an annual paroxysm producing such ungovernable violence as to endanger the breaking down of the den," its destruction caused so much sympathy at the time. Its death was effected by shooting, but not until the animal had received upwards of 100 musket and rifle shots. The skeleton of this animal is twelve feet four inches high.

In the first room of the museum is a very life-like marble statue of John Hunter, the founder of the collection, by H. Weekes, Esq., R.A., erected by public subscription in 1864. The library of the institution is a noble room extending over the entrance-hall and adjoining offices, and contains a few portraits of eminent surgeons. The council room has a few portraits hanging upon its walls, and also a cartoon of Holbein's great picture of the "Grant of the Charter to the Barber-Surgeons," of which the original is in the council room of the Barbers' Company in Monkwell Street. The lectures to students, of which there are three courses

* Pepys writes, Nov. 20, 1660, "Mr. Shepley and I to the new play-house near Lincoln's Inn Fields, which was formerly Gibbon's Tennis Court. . . . Here I saw for the first time one Moone (Mohun), who is said to be the best actor in the world, lately come over with the king; and, indeed, it is the finest play house, I believe, that ever was in England."

during the year, take place in the theatre, a lofty but somewhat contracted-looking place, with wainscoted walls, crimson seats, and a square-panelled ceiling, in the centre of which is a lantern or skylight. The museum, it should be added, is not intended as a place of exhibition, but a place of study. Members of both Houses of Parliament, the dignitaries of the church and law, members of learned and scientific bodies, physicians, surgeons, &c., have not only the privilege of visiting it personally, but of introducing visitors.

On the western side of Lincoln's Inn Fields, a little south of Lindsey House, is a heavy and gloomy archway (said, however, to be the work of Inigo Jones), which leads into Duke Street. On the south side of this, close to the archway, stands the Sardinian Chapel, the oldest Roman Catholic chapel in London. It was originally attached to the residence of the Sardinian Ambassador, and dates as a building from the year 1648. It is well known that during the reigns of the later Tudors and the Stuarts, the Roman Catholics in England were forbidden to hear mass, or have chapels of their own for the performance of their worship. They therefore resorted in large numbers to the chapels of the foreign ambassadors, where their attendance was at first connived at, and afterwards gradually tolerated and allowed. The ambassador's residence stood in Lincoln's Inn Fields, and originally the only way into it lay through the house. In the Gordon Riots, in 1780, this house and the chapel were attacked and partially destroyed, as being the chief resort of the Roman Catholic nobility and gentry, and of the Bishop or Vicar Apostolic of the London district, who lived in a small house in seclusion in Castle Street, Holborn. After the suppression of the riots, the chapel was rebuilt and enlarged westwards, by adding to it the ground formerly occupied by the ambassador's stables. During the first twenty years of the present century this chapel formed the centre of the Roman Catholic worship and of the charities of that Church; but it was superseded by the erection of St. Mary's, Moorfields, in 1820, and subsequently by the erection of other Roman Catholic Churches in Islington, Clerkenwell, Soho, &c. It formerly had a fine choir, and still shows in its fine ecclesiastical plate and pictures some remains of its former importance. It has now gradually come to be a chapel for the Catholics of its immediate neighbourhood, many of whom are foreigners. A body of Franciscans, we are told, was established in connection with the Sardinian Chapel, near Lincoln's Inn Fields, in the reign of James II

As late as the reign of George II. there was on this side of the square an archway with a tenement attached to it, known in common parlance as "the Devil's Gap." It was taken down in 1756, in consequence of the dilapidated state into which it had fallen. Its last permanent tenant, some century before, as we learn from the *London Gazette* of that year, was an attorney or money-lender, Jonathan Crouch, a man who, in the days of Civil War, squeezed the life-blood out of his victims, regardless whether they were Puritans or Royalists. He over-reached himself in an effort to secure a rich and youthful heiress as a wife for his son; and his melancholy end in a death-struggle with the rival for the young lady's hand forms one of the most sensational tales in Waters' "Traditions of London." The affair caused an intense excitement at the time, and it is said that the house, or rather den, of Crouch in the Devil's Gap could not find a tenant for many a year afterwards.

On the same side of the square was, early in the present century, the "Institution for the Remedy of Organic Defects and Impediments of Speech," established by Mr. Thelwall, who, having been in early life a somewhat revolutionary reformer, later turned his attention to philanthropy, and taught elocution with success. All remembrance, however, of the institution and its founder, has long since passed away.

At the northern end of the west side, at the corner of Great Queen Street, over the pathway of which one end of it is carried on arches, the visitor will be sure to note a large and handsome mansion which for the last half-century formed the headquarters of the Society for Promoting Christian Knowledge. It was originally built by the Marquis of Powis* in 1686, no doubt on account of its nearness to the Sardinian Chapel, as the family were at that time Roman Catholics. It afterwards became the residence of the Duke of Newcastle, the Prime Minister of George II.'s reign, after whom it was called Newcastle House till 1879.

Nearly in the centre of the north side of the square stands the museum founded in 1837, by a bequest of Sir John Soane, and called after his name. The son of a common bricklayer in a Berkshire village, he rose into celebrity as an architect, and designed, among other buildings, the Bank of England, and most of the terraces in the Regent's Park. He was also clerk of the works

* The marquis was outlawed by William and Mary for his fidelity to James II., whose exile he shared, and by whom after his abdication, he was created Duke of Powis. He was the father of the foundress of the Convent of Augustinian nuns at Bruges, and also of the Countess of Nithsdale, who so nobly effected the escape of her husband from the Tower of London while under sentence of death.

at St. James's Palace, and architect generally to the Houses of Parliament, and other public buildings. He was subsequently elected Professor of Architecture to the Royal Academy. All his life long he had been a collector of books, statues, pictures, coins, medals, and other curiosities mostly Tuesday, Wednesday, Thursday, and Friday in March, April, May, June, July, and August; at other times the curator must be specially applied to for tickets. Students can obtain from the curator, or from any of the trustees, permission to copy any of the pictures and other works of art.

LINCOLN'S INN GATE, CHANCERY LANE. (*See page* 52.)

antique, with which he stored the house where he lived and died. The museum, filled from top to bottom with a beautifully arranged collection of models of art in every phase and form, small as it is, may be said to be almost as useful to the art student as is the Louvre at Paris. And yet, standing in the centre of London, it is but little known, though open to the public gratuitously. It is open always to students in painting, sculpture, and architecture; and to the general public every

In 1833 Sir John Soane obtained an Act of Parliament for settling and preserving his museum, library, and works of art "for the benefit of the public, and for establishing a sufficient endowment for the due maintenance of the same." The building may be distinguished from the others in the row in which it stands from the peculiar semi-Gothic style in which it is erected. Between the windows of the ground and of the first floor are fragments of Gothic corbels from ancient buildings, erected, probably, about the close of the twelfth century. Upon each side of the gallery of the second floor are copies in terra-cotta from the Caryatides in front of the Temple of Poseidon at Athens.

The walls of the entrance-hall are coloured to imitate porphyry, and decorated with casts in plaster after the antique, medallion reliefs, and other sculptures. The dining-room and library, which may be considered as one room, being separated only by

LINCOLN'S INN CHAPEL. (*See page* 54.)

two projecting piers formed into book-cases, is the first apartment entered. The ceiling is formed into compartments, enriched by paintings by the late Henry Howard, R.A. Over the chimney-piece is a portrait of Sir John Soane, painted by Sir Thomas Lawrence, in 1829, almost the last picture painted by that distinguished artist; and beneath this is a highly-finished model in plaster of the Board of Trade and Privy Council Offices, &c., at Whitehall, being a design for completing the buildings north and south of Downing Street, made by Sir John Soane in 1826. This room contains a large number of plaster models of ancient Greek and Roman buildings, such as the Parthenon, the Pantheon, and the Tower of the Winds; and there is also a large model in cork of part of the ancient city of Pompeii.

The next room contains a considerable collection of marble fragments of Greek and Roman sculpture, of antique bronzes, and some curious natural productions. In what is called the Monument Court, the walls of which are enriched with various fragments of ancient buildings and pieces of sculpture, is an architectural group about thirty feet high, comprising works of various forms and nations.

One of the principal apartments in the basement of the building is called the Sepulchral Chamber; and in the centre of it is the splendid ancient Egyptian sarcophagus discovered by the traveller Belzoni in 1817, in a royal tomb in a valley near Thebes. It was purchased by Sir John Soane for the sum of £2,000. The pictures are chiefly in the rooms on the first and second floors, and among them will be seen several by Hogarth, Turner, and Sir Charles Eastlake, and a large number of architectural designs by Sir John Soane himself.

Near the above building stands a palatial

edifice, known as the Inns of Court Hotel. It remained for many years in an unfinished state. In 1874 its appearance was thus graphically described by a writer in one of the illustrated newspapers :—"It is windowless, doorless, and the sky can be seen through the skeleton bones of its untiled roof. It is blackening from exposure to our grimy, smoke-laden atmosphere ; and, for all its bigness of form and solidity of structure, already declining and decaying like a phthisical youth without ever having reached maturity or consummation. It is the monument—after the manner of the broken columns emblematic of mortality, so frequently to be found in cemeteries—of a rage that once existed for monster hotels. The rage is gone—here are its ruins." It was, however, at length taken in hand again, and has been since 1876 one of the busiest and most elegant hotels in London.

Parallel to the northern side of the "Fields," and lying between them and Holborn, is a row of buildings, formerly occupied as houses, and dignified by the name of "Whetstone Park," but afterwards converted into stables. Two hundred years or more ago it was a place of very bad reputation, and was attacked by the London apprentices in 1602. The loose character of Whetstone Park and its inhabitants is a frequent subject of allusion in the plays of Dryden and Shadwell, and occasionally in Butler's "Hudibras" and Ned Ward's *London Spy*. But Whetstone Park is not without at least one distinguished inmate. At all events we read in Philips's "Life of Milton" that the author of "Paradise Lost" "left his great house in Barbican, and betook himself to a smaller (in Holborn) among them that open backward into Lincoln's Inn Fields. Here he lived a private life, still prosecuting his studies and curious search into knowledge."

At each end of this park are narrow foot-entrances leading into Holborn, called the Great and Little Turnstiles, names which testify to the rurality of Lincoln's Inn Fields, when turnstiles were put up to let pedestrians pass through, whilst they checked the straying of the cattle that fed there. Mr. John Timbs says that Turnstile Alley, when first built, was "designed as a change for the sale of Welsh flannels;" but afterwards both of these narrow thoroughfares became the homes and haunts of booksellers and publishers. One of these booksellers, Cartwright, was also known in his day as a player, and he left his plays and his pictures to Alleyn's College of "God's Gift" at Dulwich.

The new law buildings belonging to the Society of Lincoln's Inn harmonise finely with the associations of the neighbourhood ; and these, with the low wall of Lincoln's Inn Gardens, occupy the eastern side of the square. Before speaking of these buildings, we may add that this fine open space was very nearly being lost to the public a few years since, for in 1843 the late Sir Charles Barry designed a magnificent structure for the New Courts of Law—which even then were in contemplation—to occupy the centre of Lincoln's Inn Fields. Nearly two hundred years before, a question had been mooted whether it would not be possible to establish an Academy of Painting, the head-quarters of which should have covered the self-same spot. Happily Providence preserved the square on each occasion of danger, and in 1895 the gardens in the centre were acquired by the London County Council and dedicated to the public. At the south-east corner is a handsome four-sided granite fountain, reared in 1889 to commemorate Mr. Philip Twells, a member of Lincoln's Inn, who sat in Parliament for the City of London.

It has always been a matter of complaint that the access to so noble a square on all sides should have been so wretched as it is. It has no direct street leading into it from either Holborn or the Strand, though at the north-east and north-west corners there are the narrow footways known as the Great and Little Turnstiles. From Long Acre it is approached by way of Great Queen Street. At the south-east corner, Serle Street serves as an outlet to Carey Street, and this, with Portsmouth Street at the south-west corner, leads into Chancery Lane, and so on to Fleet Street. Northouck, as far back as 1785, suggested that the "situation" of Covent Garden Market furnished a hint for continuing Great Russell Street in a straight line uniformly to the south-west corner, instead of through Prince's (now Kemble) Street, and Duke Street. But little has yet been done in the way of forming adequate approaches to this fine square.

CHAPTER VIII.

LINCOLN'S INN.

"The walks of Lincoln's Inn
Under the elms."—*Ben Jonson.*

Fortescue's definition of "Inns of Court"—The "Revels"—Regulation of the Growth of Beards—"Mootings"—Lincoln's Inn a mansion of Henry de Lacy, Earl of Lincoln—Description of the Buildings—The Thurloe Papers—Ben Jonson as a Bricklayer—Humorous Translation of Inscription on "Foundation stone"—Sir Matthew Hale—The Gardens—History of Lincoln's Inn—Sir Thomas More—Illustrious Members of Lincoln's Inn.

As distinguished from the Inns of Chancery, such as Barnard's and Staple Inns, Lincoln's Inn is an "Inn of Court;" in other words, as defined by Waterhouse, the learned commentator on Fortescue, "one of the Hospitia Majora, such as receive not gudgeons and smelts, but the polypuses and leviathans, the behemoths and the giants of the law." How far this remark may be true, and how far an exaggeration, we must leave it to the lawyers of this and other Courts to determine. Fortescue speaks in glowing terms of the Inns of Court in his own time; and, as a member of Lincoln's Inn, he may be presumed to draw his expressions from what he had seen on this spot. He says: "Of the Inns of Court there are four in number. In the least frequented there are about 200 students. In these greater Inns a student cannot well be maintained under £28 a year [equivalent to at least £500 now]. For this reason the students are sons of persons of quality, those of an inferior rank not being able to bear the expenses. There is both in the Inns of Court and the Inns of Chancery a sort of academy or gymnasium, where they learn singing and all kinds of music, and such other accomplishments and diversions (which are called revels) as are suitable to their quality and usually practised at court. Out of term the greater part apply themselves to the study of the law. All vice is discouraged and banished. The greatest nobility of the kingdom often place their children in those Inns of Court, not so much to make the law their study, but to form their manners and to preserve them from the contagion of vice."

Possibly, however, the garrulous old writer has taken rather too *couleur de rose* a view of the domestic virtue taught and practised in his favourite Inns of Court. One subject, however, the celebration of "Revels" at certain seasons of the year within their walls, comes too frequently under the notice of the student of English history to be passed by unnoticed here. The idea of the actual existence of such "Revels" is so much out of keeping with our practical and prosaic age of stuff and silk gowns, and barristers' wigs and the gravity of a judge, that it cannot fail to prove attractive alike to writers and readers. It is to be feared that the popular notion concerning them is drawn by far too exclusively from the lines of Gray, which are not true to fact:—

"The grave Lord Keeper led the brawls,
The seals and maces danced before him."

It would have been far more true to have spoken of the "Revels" as plays performed by the youthful students of each Inn of Court, in the presence of the grave and reverend seigniors of the same.

These "Revels," together with almost every other harmless diversion of the kind, with much that was characteristic of our national manners and habits, would seem to have passed out of use during the time of the Puritan tyranny, which is usually styled the Commonwealth. The plays of Æschylus and Sophocles and of William Shakespeare were alike profane and unholy things in the eyes of these sour-visaged "Saints of the Lord," who tore down the Maypoles in our streets and broke the painted windows that adorned our churches, and which the Reformers had spared. It may, however, be said in their excuse that these "Revels," while they lasted, were got up with great extravagance, and that many a parent suffered for his son's outlay on such "private theatricals." But then, though distasteful to the pockets of paterfamilias, it may be said that they must have been "good for trade."

"Lincoln's Inn," says Charles Knight, in his *Cyclopædia of London*, was never behind the Temple in its masques and Christmas revels; nor were the exercises of dancing and singing merely permitted, but even insisted on, at this Inn; for by an order made on February 6th, in the 7th of James I., it appears that "the under-barristers were by decimation *put out of commons* for example's sake, because the whole Bar were offended by their not dancing on the Candlemas Day preceding, according to the ancient order of the Society, when the Judges were present; and a threat was added, that if the like fault were repeated they should be fined or disbarred."

Very careful provision would seem to have been made by the council or benchers of the

Inn with regard to such minute matters as the apparel of its members, who were bound to dress soberly and to avoid gay colours. On the matter of beards, too, it would seem that they exercised a degree of control which savoured of austerity. For instance, it is on record that the student who wore a beard should pay double for his daily commons and dinner in hall. In the first year of Queen Elizabeth it was ordered "that no fellow of the house should wear a beard of above a fortnight's growth under penalty of loss of commons, and, in case of obstinacy, of final expulsion." Such, however, was the love of long beards, that it triumphed over these sumptuary restrictions, and in November, 1562, all previous orders on the subject were repealed or withdrawn. The long rapier, an appendage of fashion of a still more obnoxious character than the long beard, did not fare equally well. When Elizabeth, whose orders were paramount, ordered watches to be set at each gate of the City to take the measure of every gentleman's sword, and to see that it did not exceed three feet, members of the Inns of Court were obliged to conform, like other citizens, to this standard; and they were further obliged to lay aside their rapiers on entering their several dining-halls, and to content themselves with the daggers which they wore behind.

The life of a law student at the time of which we speak, when, as at Oxford and Cambridge, the students really lived in their "chambers" instead of in lodgings at a distance, and kept up a real bond of fellowship and social intercourse by the common use of a hall and a chapel, must have presented an immense contrast to the usage of our own day. Even down to so late a period as the close of Elizabeth's reign, we are told, the members of Lincoln's Inn resorted once every year in the summer to Kentish Town, where they dined together and indulged in sports, just as now-a-days the employés of some printing establishment drive off to Richmond or the Crystal Palace to celebrate their "wayz-goose." The only remnant of the old social customs which once prevailed is to be found in the fact that there is a dinner served daily in the hall during term-time for those who care to partake of it. But this must have been a reality, and only a part of the daily routine of existence at the time when the collegiate system was not as yet wholly banished from the Inns of Court, when men really lived in their chambers and spent their lives in their Inn, at all events until they took on themselves the responsibility of a wife and a domestic establishment. Nor was their legal education neglected even at the dinner-table; for at each mess it was a rule that there was to be a "moot" daily. We all of us speak of a "moot-point," but few, perhaps, understand its meaning. The junior member of each mess had to propound to the rest at his table some knotty question of law, which was discussed by each in turn during the dinner. This excellent custom, however, still kept up as it is by members of many religious orders in the Roman Catholic Church, has long since disappeared from the Hall of Lincoln's Inn, although there is extant and probably unrepealed a standing order of the reign of Edward VI., to the effect that every junior at each mess during dinner should "put to the rest a short case of one point which was to be argued thoroughly."

It is obvious that while the lawyer must have an especial, he cannot feel that he has an exclusive, interest in the early history of the Inns of Court, which form so considerable a part of the antiquities of the metropolis. The buildings of Lincoln's Inn for instance, though consecrated to the legal profession for the past five or six hundred years, if they could speak of their earlier years, would tell us of Knights Templars, and of the proud house of De Lacy, Earls of Lincoln, and of more than one bishop who held the Great Seal in the days of the Plantagenets.

If our imagination could carry us back to the thirteenth century, we should notice, as we walked up what now is Chancery Lane, but then was known as New Street, leading from the Temple Bar up to "Old Bourne," the palace of the Bishops of Chichester, the mansion of Henry de Lacy, Earl of Lincoln, and the beautiful church of the Knights Templars, resplendent with the solemn services which were daily celebrated within it. It is from this Earl of Lincoln that what is now "Lincoln's Inn" derives its name; and it is the opinion of the learned antiquary, Francis Thynne, that it was constituted a regular Inn of Court not long after that nobleman's death in 1312. Those of the buildings which still remain, however, are not older than the Tudor times, the old gateway and the hall having been both erected in the reign of Henry VII. The frontage of these old buildings facing Chancery Lane is about 500 feet in length. The gatehouse is a fine specimen of late red brickwork of a Gothic type, and is now almost the only example of that sort of work to be found in London. The principal gateway, and the two flanking towers on either side, still stand in the same condition as when they were first erected, except that their red colour has been dulled by three centuries and a half of dust and smoke; but the windows for the most part have been modernised, much to the loss of picturesque effect. Over the gateway are still to be seen three shields of arms in as many square compartments. The first are those of Lacy, Earl of Lincoln; those in the centre are the royal arms of England; and the third and last are the bearings of the actual builder of the gate, Sir Thomas Lovel, Knight. Beneath these is the date A.D. 1518. These heraldic sculptures were repaired and redecorated in 1815.

It was rumoured some years ago that this gateway was to be removed at no distant date, in accordance with a plan for rebuilding the suites of chambers on one uniform plan; but happily little has been heard more recently of this "improvement." We should be sorry to lose the venerable but somewhat gloomy edifice, on account of the many illustrious personages with whom its memory is associated, and who must have passed beneath its portals on their way to "chambers"—Sir Thomas More, Lord Keeper Egerton, Dr. Donne, Sir Henry Spelman, Sir Matthew Hale, Sir John Durham, Attorney-General Noy, Rushworth, Lord Thurlow, Lord Shaftesbury, Lord Mansfield, Lord Eldon, and Lord Erskine.

Some of the brick buildings adjoining the gateway in Chancery Lane are of a later date than the entrance itself; and it is in all probability to this portion of the structure that quaint old Fuller alludes when he writes of Ben Jonson, that "he helped in the building of the new structure in Lincoln's Inn, and having a trowel in one hand, he had a book in his pocket."

Mr. Peter Cunningham tells us that in the south angle of the great court leading out of Chancery Lane, formerly called the Gatehouse Court, but now Old Buildings, in No. 24, in the apartments on the ground-floor on the left-hand side, Thurloe, the secretary to Oliver Cromwell, had chambers from 1645 to 1659. Cromwell himself must often have darkened by his presence this doorway; and here, by the merest accident, long after Thurloe's death, his papers and correspondence with the Lord Protector and other members of the Roundhead party were discovered, having lain for years concealed behind a false ceiling. Mr. John Timbs, in his "Romance of London," relates a curious anecdote concerning these chambers, to the effect that one evening Oliver Cromwell came thither to talk over with Thurloe a plot for seizing the person of Prince Charles, then at Bruges, and his brothers the Dukes of York and Gloucester, when, finding Thurloe's clerk asleep at his desk, he drew his dagger to kill him, thinking (as was really the case) that he had been overheard, and was with difficulty stopped by his secretary from carrying out his design. The young clerk found means to warn the royal party of their danger, and the plot fell through. If this story be really true, it may safely be asserted that in this very set of chambers English royalty has been saved.

The "Thurloe Papers," it may be added on the self-same authority, were disposed of by the discoverer to Lord Chancellor Somers, who caused them to be bound up in sixty-seven volumes in folio, and they form the principal part of the collections afterwards published by Dr. Birch, and known by the name of the "Thurloe State Papers."

The old hall, as seen through the archway leading into the court from Chancery Lane, with its high-pitched roof externally, has all the appearance of a monastic building, from its buttresses and pointed windows. It is situated in the first court opposite the entrance gate; it was erected in the twenty-second year of King Henry VII., so that it is nearly of the same date with the gateway; its appearance, however, is very different from the dull red brick of the entrance, being covered with an exterior coating of white plaster or stucco. It has undergone alterations at various dates, and in 1819 it was lengthened by ten or twelve feet, and the present unsightly modern ceiling was substituted for the fine open roof of oak, which was removed or concealed. The hall is about 70 feet by 30, and 32 feet high. "It was divided," says Mr. Spilsbury, the Librarian of Lincoln's Inn, "in 1853, by permission of the benchers, in order to form two courts, the one for the Lord Chancellor, and the other for the Lords Justices of Appeal, until suitable accommodation can be provided by the country for the administration of justice." In 1874 the partition was removed. At the upper end used to be a picture of Paul before Felix, painted for the society by Hogarth, who was paid £200 for the work, as may be seen from his framed autograph letter acknowledging the receipt of the money. This picture, together with a statue of Lord Eldon by Westmacott, has been removed to the new hall. The heraldic achievements in stained glass with which the windows were formerly enriched, as well as those of the panels of the walls, have also been removed to the new hall, where, too, are several other fine-art treasures.

Here were held all the "Revels" of the society, in which the benchers themselves indulged. Dancing was especially enjoined, and was thought to conduce to the end of making gentlemen more fit for their books at other times. One of the latest "Revels," at which King Charles II. was present, is noticed both by Evelyn and Pepys in their respective diaries. On a second visit of that monarch to Lincoln's Inn, on the 27th of February, 1671, he was accompanied by his brother, the Duke of York, Prince Rupert, the Duke of Monmouth, and others of the nobility. These illustrious and distinguished personages were admitted members of the Honourable Society, and entered their names in the Admittance Book, where their signatures are preserved." Hogarth's picture, mentioned above, it may be interesting here to remark, was painted at the instigation of Lord Mansfield, as the best way of expending a legacy of £200 left to the benchers.

The chapel possesses features of peculiar interest. It has been the opinion of some antiquaries that it is a restoration or reconstruction of a much earlier edifice; but there is evidence which proves conclusively that the present building was erected in the reign of James I., and that the old chapel was standing at the time of the consecration of the new one. It was built from the designs of Inigo Jones, and consecrated in 1623. Ben Jonson is said to have assisted with his trowel in the building of this chapel, as well as of the outer wall already mentioned. Its size is 60 by 40 feet, and it is about 44 feet high. The windows are filled with stained glass of very brilliant colours, and the carved work of the oaken seats is of very chaste design, and superior execution, as specimens of the style prevailing in the reign of James I. The crypt under the chapel, now dwarfed by the gradual raising of

ESSEX WATER GATE, ESSEX STREET, STRAND. (*See page* 68.)

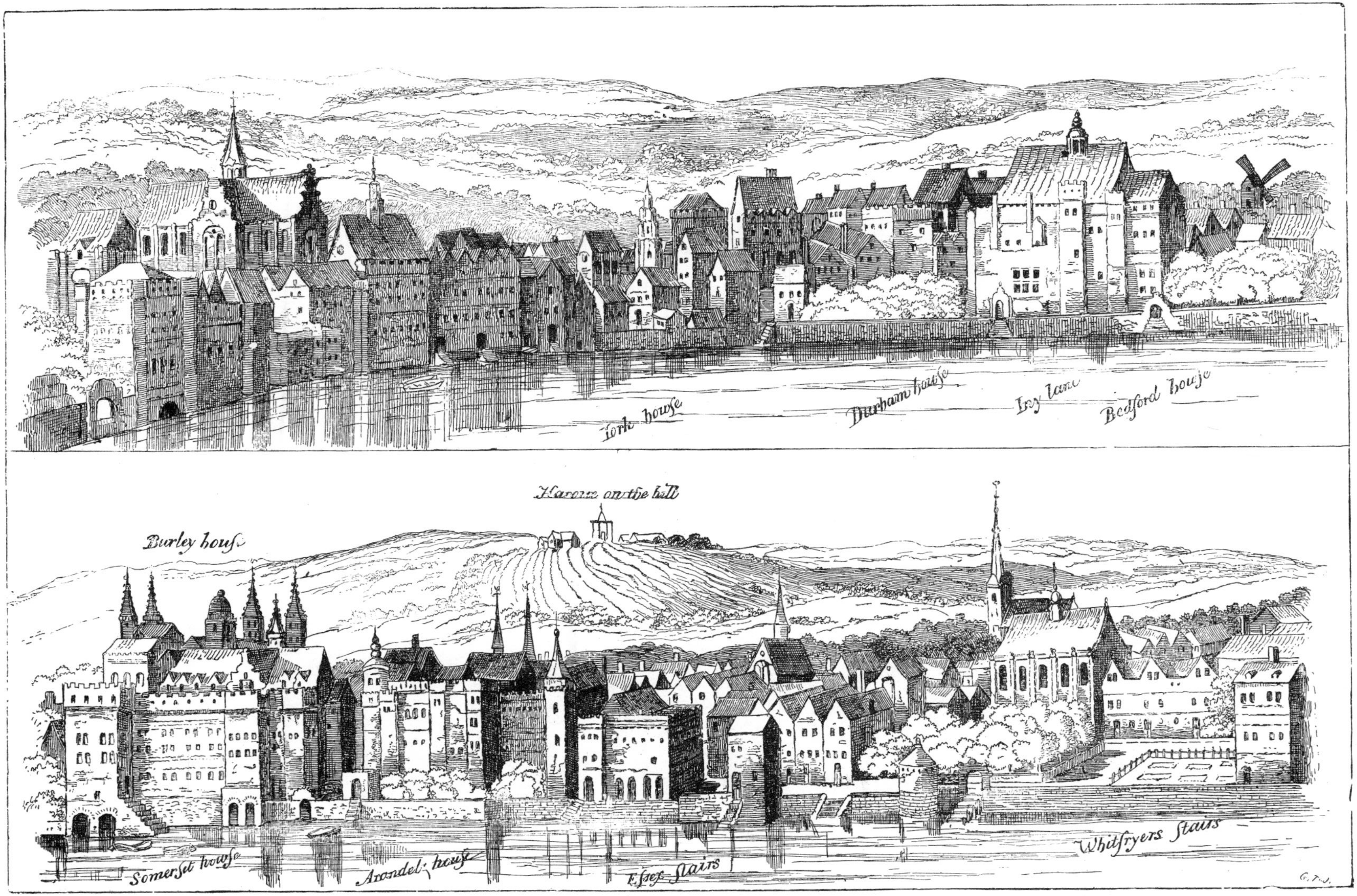

THE STRAND FROM THE THAMES, SIXTEENTH CENTURY.

the ground, was built, like the cloisters in the Temple, as a place for the students and lawyers "to walk in and talk and confer their learnings." Mr. Peter Cunningham reminds us that the round nave of the Temple Church was formerly used for a like purpose, and Butler and Pepys both allude to the custom. This crypt was long reserved as a burial-place for the benchers of the Inn. In it sleeps Secretary Thurloe, and near him repose Alexander Brome, the Cavalier song-writer, and William Prynne, already mentioned, who wrote against the unloveliness of love-locks, and the inscription on whose grave was already blotted out when Wood wrote his "Athenæ Oxonienses." The chapel was enlarged in 1882–83.

The present noble hall and library, built of red brick, with stone dressings, by the late Mr. Philip Hardwick, R.A., was commenced in 1843. The first stone of the hall was laid on the 20th of April in that year by Sir James Lewis Knight-Bruce, the treasurer of the society. It bears the following inscription:—

" Stet lapis, arboribus nudo defixus in horto,
Fundamen pulchræ tempus in omne domûs.
Aula vetus lites et legum ænigmata servet,
Ipsa novo exorior nobilitanda coquo.
XXIJ. CAL. MAIJ, MDCCCXLIIJ."

The inscription was humorously translated by the late Sir George Rose as follows:—

" The trees of yore
Are seen no more :
Unshaded now the garden lies.
May the red bricks,
Which here we fix,
Be lasting as our equities.
The olden dome
With musty tome
Of law and litigation suits :
In this we look
For a better 'cook' *
Than he who wrote the 'Institutes.'"

The library was originally 80 feet long, but in 1873 it received an addition of 50 feet to its length. The present dimensions are 130 feet by 40 feet, and 44 feet high. The original foundation of this library is of earlier date than any now existing in the metropolis, namely, 1497. At the time of the removal of the books to the present building, in 1845, the number of volumes was about 18,000. It has since gone on increasing, so that the library now contains about 40,000 volumes, on law, jurisprudence, history, and other cognate and collateral studies. In addition to the collection of law books, admitted to be the most complete in this country, the shelves of the library are well furnished with books in historical and various other classes of literature. The Reports of Cases in England are extant in a regular series from the reign of Edward II., from whose time to that of Henry VIII. they were taken by the prothonotaries, or chief scribes of the court, at the expense of the Crown, and published annually, whence they are known under the denomination of the "Year Book." Here also is an unique copy of the fourth volume of "Prynne's Records," purchased in 1849 at the sale at Stowe for £335. Here likewise is preserved the collection of legal MSS. and books bequeathed to the Inn by Sir Matthew Hale, "a treasure," he says in his will, "that is not fit for every man's view." The formation of this library was commenced as early as the reign of Henry VII., and the acquisition of books received a great impulse by an order issued in the early part of the reign of James I., to the effect that every person called to the Bar should contribute to it 13s. 4d., and every bencher on his election 20s. In the Council Room of the society is the portrait of Sir Matthew Hale, by Wright.

Stone Buildings—so called from the material of which they are built—lie at the north-eastern extremity of Lincoln's Inn. The range of buildings forms part of a design made in 1780 for rebuilding the whole Inn. The structure is commodious and imposing when viewed from the gardens, or even from Lincoln's Inn Fields. Part of the eastern side of Lincoln's Inn, abutting upon Chancery Lane, was rebuilt in 1880–81. The new buildings are of red brick, with stone dressings.

The houses in New Square were built in the reign of Charles II. In the open space in the centre of the square there was formerly a Corinthian column, bearing a vertical sun-dial. The houses, which form three sides of the square—as stated, indeed, in a previous chapter—were formerly called Serle's Court, having been erected in 1682 by Henry Serle, one of the benchers of Lincoln's Inn. They are of brick, and are wholly occupied as chambers, many of the most eminent members of the Bar and legal profession holding them. It may be worth while to record here the fact that Sir Samuel Romilly had chambers at Nos. 2 and 6, Sir William Grant at No. 3, and at No. 11 Lord Selborne, whilst as yet only Sir Roundell Palmer. The site upon which New Square is built was originally called Fickett's Field, or Little Lincoln's Inn Field. The garden in the centre was railed and planted in 1845; and in 1867 was erected, within the enclosure, the temporary building for the exhibition of the designs for the New Law Courts.

The gardens of Lincoln's Inn, though not

* Alluding to Coke's "Institutes," a legal work of high reputation.

washed like those of the Temple, by the "silver" Thames, and though not possessing equal historical associations with the spot where the White and Red Rose were chosen as the badges of two rival and royal houses, were not and indeed are not without a beauty of their own; and the fine elms which they contain are an ornament to the neighbourhood. They were famous of old, however, but have been much curtailed by the erection of the new hall and library at the south-western angle. There is a fine and broad terrace walk; but "the walk under the elms," celebrated by Ben Jonson, has disappeared. In these gardens, as we learn from the *Tatler* (No. 100), old Isaac Bickerstaffe delighted to walk, being privileged to do so by his friends amongst the benchers, who had grown old along there with himself. In the time of the old Earls of Lincoln the gardens are said to have been most fruitful, supplying apples, nuts, and cherries in great abundance, as well as flowers and "kitchen herbs," the produce of which, over and above what was needed for his lordship's household, brought in to the steward of the estate a large sum annually.

The readers of Pepys' "Diary" will scarcely need to be reminded here of the following entry, as it has been so often quoted before:—"27 June, 1663. To Lincoln's Inn, and there walked up and down to see the new garden which they are making, and will be very pretty, and so to walk under the chapel by agreement."

As to the past history of Lincoln's Inn, a part of its site was occupied in ancient times by the church and house of a body of "preaching friars," who came to England in 1221, and received much encouragement and great support in London. Hubert de Burgh, the powerful Earl of Kent, who died in 1252, and was buried in their church, left to them his house in Westminster, which was nothing less than the ancient White Hall, afterwards York House, of which we shall have to speak presently. The friars sold it to the Archbishop of York, who left it an heirloom to his successors in the see.

In 1250 the friars of this order held a grand convocation at their house, when no less than 500 churchmen were present. On the first day of their meeting, Henry III. attended their chapter, and sat with them at their table to a dinner which his royal self had provided. Afterwards the queen did the same, and her example was followed by the Bishop of London, the Abbots of Westminster, St. Albans, Waltham, and others. Here the friars continued until 1276, when the Mayor and other influential citizens of London gave them a piece of ground near Baynard's Castle, between Ludgate and the Thames, to build a new monastery and church, which was afterwards known as the "Black Friars." The old house appears to have been the property of William de Haverill, the King's Treasurer, and on his attainder for treason, to have been given by the Crown to Ralph de Nevill, Bishop of Chichester, and Lord Chancellor, who built there a large house which he occupied till his death in 1244. The memory of the bishop is retained in the name of a small court between the Inn and Chancery Lane, still called "Chichester Rents." Having passed through one intermediate owner, it became the residence of Henry de Lacy, Earl of Lincoln, to whom Edward I. made a present also of the old friars' house. The two thus joined together formed a residence for the earl; and hence the place was styled his "Inn," meaning his lodging or house. It is said that the earl introduced law students into his "Inn" as early as the year 1310; but this is at best doubtful. Nor is it clear, nor do historians or antiquaries tell us, how the Bishops of Chichester again became the owners of the "Inn." Such, however, apparently was the case, for they held it until the beginning of the sixteenth century, when Robert Sherborne, bishop of that see, conveyed it to an Essex gentlemen named Sulyard, whose family conveyed it, in 1579, to William Kingsmith and the rest of the benchers for the modest sum of £520.

As the title-deeds of Lincoln's Inn do not go further back than December, 1535, its early history is naturally involved in no little obscurity. The tradition of its establishment in the reign of Edward III., is highly probable, although no evidence of a documentary nature can be adduced to prove it. The first mention of the four Inns of Court—of which Lincoln's Inn beyond a doubt was one—occurs in the writings of Fortescue, who wrote in the latter half of the fifteenth century. According to the received opinion, Lincoln's Inn had flourished for a century and a half before Fortescue wrote; but certainly we meet with no record of any distinguished student within its walls at that date. From a record of the same age with Fortescue, namely, the "Black Book" of the Inn itself, we find that, whether it was the oldest of the four Inns of Court or not, at all events it was the first which instituted a settled order of government, and made provision for the needs of legal education. This Black Book commences in 1423, and gives the name of Fortescue himself as one of its governors or benchers. In 1440 the governors began to be formally sworn on taking office, and the students on admission were also required to take an oath of obedience to that body. In 1464 the Society of Lincoln's Inn made an important step of progress in their organisation of legal education, by appointing a "reader" to give readings in the law to the students during the vacation of the courts. The first reader whose name is recorded is William Huddersfield. The persons chosen as readers were the most eminent lawyers of the day under the degree of serjeant. A reader in 1475, and again in 1481, was Sir Thomas Lovel, who built the gatehouse of the Inn. The name of John More, the autumn reader for 1489, introduces us to an episode in the history of the Inn. In 1464 John More was raised from the office of butler to that of steward. In 1470 his long and faithful services in those two capacities were rewarded by his admission to be a member of the society, and in 1489, and again in 1495, he held the high and honourable office of reader. His son John succeeded the father in the office of butler, and enjoyed the like promotion. The son of this latter John More was the illustrious Sir Thomas More, the chancellor and martyr. Oı Sir Thomas More's conduct upon the woolsack it was said, in the punning style of the day:—

"When More some years had Chancellor been,
No *more* suits did remain;
The same shall never *more* be seen,
Till More be there again."

Allen, in his "History of London," remarks of this Inn that "it ranks next to the Temple, which it equals in the number of eminent lawyers that it has produced." Of these it may be sufficient to mention Sir John Fortescue, one of the "fathers of the English law," who held the Great Seal under Henry VI.; that virtuous chancellor, Sir Thomas More; the learned antiquary, Sir Henry Spelman; the great Sir Matthew Hale, and Lord Chancellor Egerton. Prynne, the well-known victim of Star Chamber tyranny, was also a member of this society. For an alleged libel in the "Histrio-Mastix" he was condemned by that court to pay a fine of £5,000, to lose his ears, to stand in the pillory, and to be imprisoned for life. Nor did the odious sentence end there, for the Chamber, "assuming an authority co-extensive with its vindictiveness," ordered Prynne to be expelled from the University of Oxford and also from the Society of Lincoln's Inn.

The Inns of Court have deservedly been styled "the noblest nurseries of humanity and liberty in the kingdom." They are four in number, viz., the Inner Temple, the Middle Temple, Lincoln's Inn, and Gray's Inn. They are called Inns of *Court*, because they were anciently held in the Aula Regia, or Court of the King's Palace. They are governed by a self-elected body of benchers, consisting of the most distinguished and successful members of the Bar. The distinction between barristers and solicitors is still maintained; but it is provided that a student who, at any time before his admission to an Inn of Court, had been in practice as a solicitor for not less than five consecutive years, but who had ceased to be a solicitor prior to his admission as a student, may be examined for Call to the Bar without keeping any Terms, and upon passing the examination may be at once called.

At what time students were first admitted into Lincoln's Inn seems to be a doubtful point. Malcolm, on the authority of an old heraldic MS. which styles the Inn "an ancient ally unto the Middle Temple," observes that "there is no mention of any flourishing estate of the students and professors of the common law resident in this college till the reign of Henry VI., when it appears by the rolls and remembrance of that house the same then began to be famous."

Since the year 1581, when the first appointment of preacher to the society appears to have been made, many of the most eloquent and distinguished divines of the Church of England have filled the office, amongst whom have been Archbishop Tillotson, Dr. Donne, Thomas Gataker, and Dr. Hurd; Bishops Warburton, Heber, and Maltby; and Archbishop Thomson. In fact, the Preachership of Lincoln's Inn has often been regarded as a "stepping-stone to a bishopric."

Among the most illustrious students, benchers, treasurers, and members of this Inn have been Sir Robert Atkins, Lord Chief Baron of the Exchequer, *temp.* William III.; Sir John Fortescue; Anthony, first Earl of Shaftesbury; Lord Southampton; Archbishop Tillotson; Sir Arthur Plantagenet, natural son of Edward IV.; Sir Joseph Jekyll; Sir Thomas Egerton, Lord Keeper of the Great Seal, *temp.* Elizabeth; Sir Thomas More, Chancellor of England, already mentioned; the Earl of Hardwicke; Lord Talbot; Sir Robert Walpole; Sir Matthew Hale, whose gift to the library is noticed above; Lord Mansfield; Lord Walsingham; Dr. Warburton, Bishop of Gloucester; Lord Camden; Lord Henley; William Pitt; Addington, afterwards Lord Sidmouth; Lord Ellenborough, the Chief Justice; the Right Hon. Spencer Perceval; Lord Dunfermline; and at least seven Lord Chancellors of our own day, Brougham, Cottenham, Campbell, Selborne, Hatherley, Cranworth, and Herschell.

CHAPTER IX.

THE STRAND—INTRODUCTORY AND HISTORICAL.

"Come, Fortescue, sincere, experienced friend,
Thy briefs, thy deeds, and e'en thy fees suspend;
Come, let us leave the Temple's silent walls;
My business to my distant lodging calls;
Through the long Strand together let us stray,
With thee conversing, I forget the way."—*Gay.*

Condition of the Strand in the Days of the Plantagenets and Tudors—Rules for Hackney Coaches—Taylor, the "Water Poet"—Origin of the Name of the Strand—Graphic Sketch of the Strand Five Centuries ago—New Paving Act—State Pageants—Temple Bar in Danger.

During the reign of Henry VIII. an active stir had commenced for the reparation of streets and highways in and about the metropolis, and the necessity for such improvement is fully shown by the words of the royal statute which was then enacted for the purpose. In granting permission to lay out a new road in the Weald of Kent, which formed an important thoroughfare to London, we are told that "many other common ways in the said Weald be so deep and so noyous, by wearing and course of water and other occasions, that people cannot have their carriages or passages by horses, upon or by the same, but to their great pains, peril, or jeopardy." Nor in approaching London was the case improved, in several instances at least; for the suburban districts, as yet only villages separated from the City by fields, gardens, and a sprinkling of cottages, were connected with the City by a highway, often left in grievous disrepair through the negligence of the inhabitants. Such was the case even with that great artery of the metropolis—the Strand—of which we are about to treat.

Frequented though it was, and necessary for the comfort of the City, yet this highway, in the thirty-fourth and thirty-fifth years of Henry VIII., is described as a road "full of pits and sloughs, very perilous and noisome." There is extant somewhere or other in the Rolls of Parliament, a complaint of the high-road between the Temple "and the village of Charing" being so deep in mire as to be almost impassable. In fact it had earned a thoroughly bad character. It was described in the statute above quoted as "very noyous and foul, and in many places thereof very jeopardous to all people passing and repassing, as well on horseback as on foot, both in winter and in summer, by night and by day." By this route, however, Cardinal Wolsey, when residing in Chancery Lane, used to ride down to Westminster Hall, in all the magnificence which befitted a "Prince of the Church," as already described in the first volume of this work (page 81).

In speaking, however, of the disgraceful condition of the high-road between London and Westminster in the days of the Plantagenets, we are in danger, perhaps, of forgetting the fact that at that time the traffic along it consisted mainly of foot passengers, or riders on horseback, carriages being then almost as unknown as hansom cabs or omnibuses. Elizabeth, as we know, rode usually on a pillion, even on state occasions; and fifty years after her, we are told, there were only thirty vehicles on wheels in the whole of London. No wonder, therefore, that many of our old thoroughfares are still narrow in the extreme.

In the present admirably-paved state of the streets of the metropolis, the following statement relative to the Strand, Charing Cross, and Parliament Street, must appear strange:—"In 1353, the road from London to Westminster had become so dangerous for the transit of passengers or carriage of goods, as to demand the interference of Government. A mandate was therefore directed, in the name of the king and council, dated Westminster, Nov. 20, to John de Bedeforde, of London, appointing him the commissioner for the paving of the road in question. This instrument recites, that the highway leading from the gate called Temple Bar, London, to the door of Westminster Abbey, by the frequent passage of carts, horses, merchandise, and provisions, to the Staple at Westminster, ever since its establishment, had become so deep and muddy, and the pavement so much injured and broken, that unless soon repaired, great perils must be incurred by the passage both of men and of carriages. In order to remedy this evil, therefore, it was ordained that the foot-pavement adjoining to the houses on the line of the road should be newly laid, at the expense of the owners of the nearest houses; and that money should be levied by tolls on goods sold at the Staple, to defray the charge of paving the road between the kennels on each side."

In 1625 there were *twenty* hackney coaches in London; but they multiplied so rapidly, that in ten years afterwards Government took the alarm at their general use, and endeavoured to limit it, upon the plea that these carriages "disturbed the ears of king, queen, and nobles, jostled horse and foot passengers, tore up the streets and pavements, and increased the price of hay and horse provender." It was therefore ordered "that no hackney or hired coaches be used or suffered in London, Westminster, or the suburbs thereof, except they be to travel at least three miles out of the same; and also, that no person shall go in a coach in the said streets, except the owner of the coach shall constantly keep up four able horses for our (the king's) service when required." But the time had gone by when such despotic edicts were in force; and Cromwell himself, we are told, was destined soon after to drive four-in-hand, in Jehu fashion, through this forbidden territory, and be capsized for his pains.

Scarcely had this innovation been commenced in London, when Taylor, the "Water Poet," who plied a scull upon the Thames, exclaimed, "They have undone my poor trade!" Speaking of the coaches, he adds, "This infernal swarm of trade spillers have so overrun the land, that we can get no living on the water; for I dare truly affirm, that every day in any term, especially if the court be at Whitehall, they do rob us of our livings, and carry five hundred and sixty fares daily from us." Alluding also to the confusion produced by this startling civic revolution, he adds, "I pray you look into the streets, and the chambers or lodgings in Fleet Street or the Strand, how they are pestered with them (coaches), especially after a mask or a play at the court, where even the very earth quakes and trembles, the casements shatter, tatter, and clatter, and such a confused noise is made, so that a man can neither sleep, speak, hear, write, nor eat his dinner or supper quiet for them."

The scene occasionally presented by the Strand through its entire length, if we may believe such an eyewitness as John Evelyn, was very gay and brilliant. He writes in his Diary, "May 29, 1660. This day his majestie, Charles II., came to London, after a sad and long exile and calamitous suffering both of the king and church, being seventeen years. This was also his birthday, and with a triumph above 20,000 horse and foot, brandishing their swords and shouting with inexpressible joy; the ways strew'd with flowers, the bells ringing, the streets hung with tapestry, fountains running with wine; the mayor, aldermen, and all the companies in their liveries, chains of gold, and banners; lords and nobles clad in cloth of silver, gold, and velvet; the windowes and balconies well set with ladies; trumpets, music, and myriads of people flocking even so far as from Rochester, so as they were seven hours in passing the City, even from two till ten at night. I stood in the Strand and beheld it, and bless'd God. And all this was done without one drop of bloodshed, and by that very army which rebelled against him; but it was the Lord's doings, for such a restoration was never mentioned in any history, ancient or modern, since the return of the Jews from the Babylonish captivity; nor so joyful a day and so bright ever seen in this nation, this happening when to expect or effect it was past all human policy."

To pass on to a somewhat later date, we are told by Malcolm that when, in 1689, the number of hackney carriages in London was limited by Act of Parliament to 400, the inhabitants of the Strand and Fleet Street petitioned against any increase in their numbers, on the ground that "they prevented the quality from getting to their shops!"

During the time of Queen Elizabeth, considerable improvement had been effected by the filling up of the gaps or blanks left between the dwellings that had already been built along the Strand; and by the end of her long reign, both sides of this line of route had been nearly covered with the mansions of the nobility, so that Westminster may be said at that time to have been joined on to London. The still rural character, however, of the districts abutting on the north side, at the time when the Strand was only an unpaved road, may be gathered from the existence to our own day of such names as the Convent (Covent) Garden, Long Acre, St. Martin's-in-the-Fields, and Lincoln's Inn Fields, most of which were open country at the date of the earliest existing map of the metropolis.

The name of the Strand is clearly of Saxon and not of Norman origin; and, if we may trust a writer in the *Penny Cyclopædia*, it is mentioned by name in the Saxon Chronicle. And as a proof of the statement it is recorded that upon the Strand Earl Godwin and his son Harold drew up their land forces in the insurrection which they headed against Edward the Confessor, in A.D. 1052.

We find this thoroughfare sometimes spoken of as "the High Street of Westminster, commonly called the Strand," as, for instance, in the lease by which Sir Wm. Cecil agrees to take his property in this neighbourhood for a term of years from the Earl of Bedford. The lease is printed *in extenso* in the thirtieth volume of the "Archæologia."

The following graphic sketch, which we take from *All the Year Round*, carries us back to the Strand of five hundred years ago:—

"Beyond the Bars is the river-side road, called 'Strand Street.' It was sorely in need of paving until lately, when a tax for its repair was levied on all goods carried along it to the Staple at Westminster. Here, many lords, spiritual and temporal, have goodly Inns, of which you can see but two or three: the Bishop of Exeter's close on the left; the Bishop of Bath's beyond it; and the Bishop of Chester's, with the old stone cross before it. At that cross the Judges have sometimes sat to try pleas. The palace which you can just see to the left is the Savoy, so called from Peter, Count of Savoy, who built it in the reign of our Henry III., whose Queen was the Count's niece. Now the Duke of Lancaster is the owner thereof, and John, the captive King of France, lodged there not long since. The bridge over the lane in the centre of the road is called 'Strand Bridge.' On the right of St. Clement Danes Church you see the wells of St. Clement and Holy Well; and, beyond them, the vineyard and convent garden of the Abbey of Westminster, skirted by the woods of Long Acre. The church among the fields in the distance is St. Martin's."

MILFORD LANE IN 1820. (*See page* 70.)

Between the Strand and the river-side there are four or five great and noble families whose names and histories are interwoven with the vicinity. Nearest to Temple Bar, the Devereuxes, Earls of Essex; next the Howards, of the ducal family of Norfolk; then the Protector Somerset; the Cecils, Earls of Salisbury and Exeter; and Villiers, Duke of Buckingham; to say nothing of the proud line of Percy, Dukes of Northumberland, who up to 1874 kept up their town residence at Charing Cross. About one and all of these in succession we shall have plenty to say in the next few pages.

Mr. A. Wood, in his "Ecclesiastical Antiquities of London," tells us that "the Abbot of Westminster had a garden on the banks of the Thames, where Westminster and London join, near St. Clement Danes. It was called the 'Frère Pye Garden,' and stood opposite to the palaces of the Bishops of Durham and Carlisle." The site is fixed by its garden, which is now Covent Garden.

The town house of the Duke of Beaufort in the reign of Charles II. stood here, on the site of what now are known as Beaufort Buildings; but the family removed thence to Beaufort House at Chelsea in 1682. Then there was Essex House, and the Inn of the Bishops of Norwich (afterwards York House), which as far back as the reign of Edward III. spread out their embattled fronts towards the Strand, while their extensive gardens, terraces, and water-stairs sloped down to the river. Spelman says that in the troublous times of the Tudors most of the houses of the prelates in the Strand were taken from them by courtiers "without any recompense."

Among the characteristic features of the Strand at this period were the bridges that spanned the various water-courses flowing from the meadows and open fields on the north, and crossing this thoroughfare in their way to the Thames. One or two of these bridges were kept in remembrance down to comparatively recent times in the names of Ivy Bridge Lane and Strand Bridge Lane, of the latter of which—now simply Strand Lane—we shall have to speak presently, in connection with the old Roman bath which is situated there. Then there was the stone cross, of which old Stow speaks as being situated in front of the spot now occupied by St. Mary's Church, and which in its turn gave place to the famous Maypole, thus alluded to in the "Dunciad," and of which we shall speak hereafter:—

"Amidst the area wide they took their stand,
Where the tall Maypole once o'erlook'd the Strand;
But now, as Anne and Piety ordain,
A church collects the saints of Drury Lane."

Stow states that the Liberty of the Duchy of Lancaster extended from Temple Bar to the east side of Cecil Street, near what is now the Adelphi, and from the stocks just outside Temple Bar to "a stone cross, now headless," over against the Maypole in the Strand, and along by Exeter Change and Burleigh Street.

The foot-pavement of this quarter of the town, as well as of other parts of Westminster, would seem to have been in a deplorable state as recently as the year 1762, when a new paving Act was passed. Until that time, it appears, every inhabitant did before his own house just what was right in his own eyes, without rule or plan. The consequence was that some parts of the footway were paved admirably, some indifferently, and some were left unpaved—mere pools of mud and water—according to the wealth or caprice of each resident. A proof of the general filth of this part of the Strand may be found in the *London Chronicle* of the time, where we read, *apropos* of the new measure of reform, "All sorts of dirt and ashes, oyster-shells, the offals of fish, poultry, and other kinds of meat, will now no longer be suffered to be thrown loose into the streets, but must be kept until the dustman comes round; nor will the annoyances erected by coachmakers be permitted; and when a house is pulled down the rubbish must be carried to the proper place, and not left on the footway."

In the description of the Strand given by him in 1807, Pennant complains of the street as being in some places too narrow for the incredible number of persons and carriages passing through it.

The Strand has witnessed in its day some strange and curious sights. For instance, we read that Queen Elizabeth, when she rode into the City, sat on a pillion behind her Lord Chancellor, wagons and the newly-invented "carriages" being in disfavour with her Majesty. Among the numerous pageants which the thoroughfare of the Strand has witnessed may be mentioned the procession of Queen Elizabeth in state to St. Paul's, to return thanks for the victories over the Spanish Armada. Queen Anne passed this way in state to St. Paul's on several occasions, to commemorate victories over France and Spain. In 1704 there was a state visit to the City to celebrate the victory of Blenheim; and in like manner have been commemorated the victories of Ramillies and other important triumphs. Then there was the religious ceremonial when George III. and his consort went in state to St. Paul's to offer a nation's thanks for its king's recovery; the solemn conveyance of captured banners and the great naval procession to St. Paul's, headed by the King, in 1797; the funeral procession of Lord Nelson in 1806, and that of the Duke of Wellington in 1852; and the visits of Queen Victoria, when she went in state to dine at Guildhall, and to open the new Exchange, in 1872 to return thanks for the recovery of the Prince of Wales, and in 1887 on the occasion of her Jubilee.

But probably none of these pageants ever presented a scene so striking as when the gates of Temple Bar were opened at the approach of the second Charles on his restoration, and the King, brought back to his own again, rode gallantly through the City to Whitehall. The houses of the Strand were adorned with the richest tapestry, and window, balcony, and scaffold were crowded with all that was beautiful and loyal. The streets were lined with members of the City companies in their liveries, and the loud music of the trained-bands, and the din of the bells from a hundred steeples, were drowned in the cheers of the enthusiastic populace. This event appears all the more impressive when contrasted with the rueful spectacle presented by Temple Bar just eighty years later, when the heads of the most devoted followers of the house of Stuart were exposed over its gates, as if in bitter derision of the monarchs of the exiled Stuart line whose effigies adorned its niches.

Temple Bar—almost the last relic of the geographical sovereignty of London—had for many years previous to its removal, as already recorded by us (see page 20 *ante*), been in an utterly hopeless and forlorn condition; in fact, it was latterly propped up and supported by wooden beams, otherwise it would probably have fallen. Its demolition was first suggested rather more than a century ago, as is clear from the following lines which were written on the report of its proposed removal as far back as 1788 :—

"THE METROPOLITAN PROPHECY.

"If that gate is pulled down, 'twixt the Court and the City,
You'll blend in one mass prudent, worthless, and witty;
If you league cit and lordling, as brother and brother,
You'll break Order's chain, and they'll war with each other.
Like the great wall of China, it keeps out the Tartars
From making irruptions where industry barters.
Like Samson's wild foxes they'll fire your houses,
And madden your spinsters, and cozen your spouses;
They'll destroy in one sweep both the mart and the forum,
Which your fathers held dear and their fathers before 'em."

But it is time to pass from these general remarks to a more detailed account of the thoroughfare of which we treat.

CHAPTER X.

THE STRAND :—SOUTHERN TRIBUTARIES.

"Westward the tide of Empire makes its way."

Thanet Place—The old "Rose" Tavern—Palsgrave Place—The "Palsgrave's Head"—Andrew Marvell—The London and Westminster Joint-Stock Bank—Messrs. Strahan, Paul, and Bates—Messrs. Twining and Co.'s Bank and Tea-warehouse—"George's Hotel"—Devereux Court—"Tom's Coffee House"—The "Grecian"—Eldon Chambers.

EXTENDING from Fleet Street as far as the present Essex Street was formerly an Outer Temple, which, with the Inner and Middle Temples, constituted the residences of the Knights Templars. This space is now for the most part occupied by a large block of offices which perpetuates the name, at the back of the fine new Law Courts branch of Lloyds Bank, and by Thanet Place and Devereux Court.

Thanet Place stands as nearly as possible on the site of the old "Rose Tavern," a place of rendezvous for lawyers and wits in the last century. It was named after the Earls of Thanet, to whom it belonged, and from whom the property passed, in 1780, by purchase to one John Cooke, a bookseller in Paternoster Row. The "Rose Tavern" is described by Strype as being in his day a "well-customed house, with good convenience of rooms and a good garden;" and T. Fairchild, in his "City Gardener," in 1722, tells us that in this garden was "a vine that covers an arbour where the sun very rarely comes, and has had ripe grapes upon it." It makes our mouths water as we pass along the street on a hot summer afternoon, with the thermometer at 83° in the shade, to hear of grapes growing in the open air close to our left hand even a century and a half ago. The "painted room" at this tavern is mentioned in Horace Walpole's "Letters," but it has long since passed out of memory.

Palsgrave Place was a narrow paved court, about half-way between Temple Bar and Essex Street, named after the Palsgrave Frederick, King of Bohemia, who in 1612 married the Princess Elizabeth, daughter of James I. Close by was the tavern known as the "Palsgrave's Head," where Prior and Montague make the "country mouse and city mouse" bilk the hackney coachman :—

"But now at Piccadilly they arrive,
And taking coach towards Temple Bar they drive;
But at St. Clement's Church cut out the back,
And slipping through the 'Palsgrave' bilk't poor hack."

Some of the taverns of the seventeenth century appear to have been established over the shops in this locality; for in 1679, according to Mr. Diprose's "Account of St. Clement Danes," "a goldsmith named Crutch carried on business under this tavern, and most of the shops were marked by signs. William Faithorne, an engraver of merit, lived 'at the sign of the Ship, next to the Drake, opposite to the Palsgrave's Head Tavern, without Temple Bar.'" Another house of entertainment or tavern in this neighbourhood, much frequented by members of Parliament and City gallants of the seventeenth century, was "Heycock's Ordinary." Here usually dined Andrew Marvell, some time member for Hull, and famous in his day as a wit and satirist; and here, according to the above authority, he administered a severe castigation to certain members of the House, known to be in the pay of the Crown, which ensured the subserviency of their votes. "Having ate heartily of boiled beef, with some roasted pigeons and asparagus, he drank his pint of port, and on the coming in of the reckoning took a piece of money out of his pocket, held it between his finger and thumb, and addressing his venal associates, said, 'Gentlemen, who would lett himself out for hire while he can have such a dinner for half-a-crown?'"

Another "scene," in which Andrew Marvell appears as the principal character, may possibly have taken place here. The anecdote has been often related, but will bear repetition:—"The borough of Hull, in the reign of Charles II., chose Andrew Marvell, a young gentleman of little or no fortune, and maintained him in London for the service of the public. His understanding, integrity, and spirit were dreadful to the then infamous administration. Persuaded that he would be theirs for properly asking, they sent his old schoolfellow, the Lord Treasurer Danby, to renew acquaintance with him in his garret. At parting, the Lord Treasurer, out of pure affection, slipped into his hand an order upon the Treasury for £1,000, and then went to his chariot. Marvell, looking at the paper, called out after the Treasurer, 'My lord, I request another moment.' They went up again to the garret, and Jack, the servant-boy, was called. 'Jack, child, what had I for dinner yesterday?' 'Don't you remember, sir? You had the little shoulder of mutton that you ordered me to bring from a woman in the market.' 'Very right, child. What have I for dinner to-day?' 'Don't you know, sir, that you bid me lay the bladebone to broil?' ''Tis so; very right, child; go away.' 'My lord, do you hear that? Andrew Marvell's dinner is provided. There's your piece of paper; I want it not. I know the sort of kindness you intended. I live here to serve my constituents. The ministry may seek men for their purpose; I am not one.'"

The house No. 217, Strand, now a branch of the London and Westminster Joint-Stock Bank, but which till lately was occupied as a bank by Messrs. Strahan (originally Snow), Paul, and Bates, has a history approaching in venerable antiquity to that of its neighbour (now rebuilt), Child's Bank. The name of the firm was originally Snow and Walton, who carried on business here as pawnbrokers during the Commonwealth, their house bearing the sign of the "Golden Anchor." Their ledgers went back as far as the year 1672. There was a book in the possession of the late members of the firm, showing that they were established as bankers in the reign of Charles II., when their accounts were kept in decimals. The firm came to a disgraceful and disastrous end in 1855, the leading partners of it being tried criminally and convicted of misappropriating the moneys of their customers, for which they were sentenced to various terms of imprisonment, a climax which offers a striking contrast to the reputation enjoyed by the original owner and founder of the house, a wealthy goldsmith named Snow, whose memory is thus immortalised by Gay:—

"Disdain not, Snow, my humble verse to hear;
Stick thy black pen awhile behind thy ear.
O thou whose penetrative wisdom found
The South Sea rocks and shelves when thousands drown'd,
When Credit sank and Commerce gasping lay,
Thou stood'st, nor sent one bill unpaid away;
When not a guinea clinked on Martin's boards,
And Atwel's self was drained of all his hoards,
Thou stood'st—an Indian king in size and hue—
Thy unexhausted store was our Peru."

Adjoining the above house, and opposite to the spot where formerly stood Butcher's Row, are the banking-house and tea-warehouse of Messrs. Twining and Co. The latter was founded about the year 1710 by the great-great-grandfather of the present partners, Mr. Thomas Twining, whose portrait, painted by Hogarth, "Kit-cat size," hangs in the back parlour of the establishment. The house, or houses—for they really are two, though made one practically by internal communication—stand between the Strand and the east side of Devereux Court. The original depôt for the sale of the then scarce and fashionable beverage, tea, stood at the south-west angle of the present premises, on the site of what had been "Tom's Coffee House," directly opposite the "Grecian." A peep into the old books of the firm shows that in the reign of Queen Anne tea was sold by the few houses then in the trade at various prices between twenty and thirty shillings per pound, and that ladies of fashion used to flock to Messrs. Twining's house in Devereux Court, in order to sip the enlivening beverage in very small china cups, for which they paid their shillings, much as now-a-days they sit in their carriages eating ices at the door of Gunter's in Berkeley Square on hot days in June. The bank was gradually engrafted by Messrs. Twining on the old business, after it had been carried on for more than a century from sire to son, and may be said, as a separate institution, to date from the commercial panic of 1825. It is, perhaps, worthy of note that a member of this family, which has been so long and so honourably connected with commerce, was that elegant and accomplished scholar, the Rev. Thomas Twining, the translator of Aristotle's "Poetics" in the days of our grandfathers.

Separated from the above-mentioned establishment by the entrance to Devereux Court is "George's Hotel," which stands on the site of what was once "George's Coffee House"—one which, though not equal in reputation to "Tom's" or the "Grecian," had associations of its own. It is mentioned by Foote in his "Life of Murray," as a place where the wits of the town in 1751 would assemble in the evening; and among its frequenters was the poet Shenstone—he of the "Leasowes"—who tells us that for a subscription of a shilling he could read all the lesser pamphlets of the day. It ceased to be known as a coffee-house about the year 1842, and has since been used as an hotel.

When the new sewers were being constructed in the Strand, a little to the east of St. Clement's Church, in 1802, the workmen found a stone bridge of a single arch, strongly built, and covered to some depth with rubbish and soil. A doubt arises as to whether this could have been an arch turned over a gully or ditch at a time when the fields along the north side of the Strand were furrowed with water-courses, or whether it was actually the *Pons Novi Templi* passed by the lords and others who went from London to attend the Parliament at Westminster in the reign of Edward III., and the repair of which that monarch called upon the Templars to effect. In the absence of architectural details, or at least a sketch of the bridge, we shall not attempt to decide so knotty a point.

Devereux Court, into which we now pass, is famous as having been the *locale* of two of the most celebrated coffee-houses—"Tom's" and the "Grecian." It takes its name from Robert Devereux, Earl of Essex, the Parliamentary general, who was born in Essex House (part of which stood upon this spot), and of whom we shall have more to say presently.

Of "Tom's" coffee-house we know that Akenside was a frequenter in the winter evenings, and that Pope here addresses a letter to Fortescue, the "counsel learned in the law." Another of its frequenters was Dr. Birch, the antiquary.

The "Grecian," again, was much frequented by a goodly company of wits and poets, including Addison, Steele, and Goldsmith, and derived its name from having been kept originally by a Greek from the Levant. As far back as 1664–5, says Mr. Diprose, "he advertised his Turkey coffee-berry, chocolate, sherbet, and tea, good and cheap; and announced his readiness to give gratuitous instruction in the art of preparing the said liquors." And Steele, in the first number of the *Tatler*, supplies us with an idea of the character of this house, when he tells the public that he "shall date all gallantry from 'White's,' all poetry from 'Wills's,' all foreign and domestic news from 'St. James's,' and all learned articles from the 'Grecian.'" The existence of the rival coffee-houses gave a high literary character to Devereux Court in the seventeenth and eighteenth centuries. The face of the "Spectator" himself was very well known at the "Grecian," "adjacent to the law," and the house was frequented by the Irish and Lancashire Templars, and also by Fellows of the Royal Society. It was Foote's morning lounge, and in a snug and cozy corner here Goldsmith occasionally "wound up his shoemaker's holiday with supper."

In the *Spectator* (No. 49) Addison describes his feelings at seeing the young Templars lounge at the "Grecian" early in the morning, either dressed for Westminster, and with the assumed air of men with heavy business engagements, or else in gay caps and slippers, as though wishing to display their indolence.

Dr. King relates how two hot-blooded young gentlemen quarrelled one evening at the "Grecian" upon the appropriate subject of the accent of a certain Greek word, and not being able to adjust the matter amicably, stepped out into the court and settled it with their swords, the one falling by the other's hand. The topographer of Leeds, Ralph Thoresby, describes how on one occasion, after a meeting of the Royal Society, he came back to the "Grecian," and spent the rest of the evening there in the company of Sir Isaac Newton.

At the "Grecian" Akenside spent such of his winter evenings as he could spare from "Tom's," as we learn from Sir John Hawkins's "Life of Johnson," "entangled in disputes and altercations, chiefly on subjects of literature and politics, that fixed on his character the stamp of haughtiness and self-conceit, and drew him into disagreeable situations." The "Grecian" ceased to be a coffee-house or tavern about the year 1842, and shortly afterwards it was converted into "chambers." A part of the building, however, now known as "Eldon Chambers," is used as a refreshment-bar. High up, on the front of this house, is a bust of Lord Essex, and beneath it the inscription, "This is Devereux Court, 1676."

LONDON, FROM THE TOP OF ARUNDEL HOUSE. *From an Etching by Hollar.* (*See page* 71.)

CHAPTER XI.

THE STRAND:—SOUTHERN TRIBUTARIES (*continued*).

"The glories of our birth and state
Are shadows, not substantial things."—*Shirley.*

Exeter House—Attacked by the Populace—Seized by Lord Paget, and Bequeathed to Robert, Earl of Essex—Paterson, the Auctioneer—Essex Street—"Sam's" Club at the "Essex Head"—Anecdote of the Young Pretender—The Robin Hood Society—Charles Dibdin—The Unitarian Chapel—Earliest Inhabitants of Essex Street.

THE site now covered by Essex Street and Devereux Court was, as stated above, originally a portion of the Outer Temple, and, as Dugdale supposes, belonged at one time to the "Prior and Canons of the Holy Sepulchre." In the reign of Edward III. it passed into the hands of the Bishops of Exeter, whose town residence was built here. It was called Exeter House, and they occupied it till the time of Henry VI. In 1326, as readers of English history are aware, Queen Isabella, "the she-wolf of France," consort of Edward II., landed from France to chase the Spensers from the side of her husband, and advanced upon London. The king and his evil counsellors fled to the frontiers of Wales; but Walter Stapleton, then Bishop of Exeter, Lord Treasurer of England, held out stoutly for his sovereign in his house, and as custos of London, demanded from the Lord Mayor the keys of the City to prevent any uprising in the disaffected City. And then a scene occurred which would require the pen of a Macaulay to paint in adequate colours. "The watchful populace," says Mr. Diprose, "fearing the Mayor's submission, and roused by Isabella's proclamation, which had been hung on the new cross in Cheapside, rose in arms and took the keys. They ran to Exeter House, then newly erected, fired the gates, and plundered or burnt all the plate, money, jewels, and goods that it contained. The bishop rode to the north door of St. Paul's to take sanctuary; but there the mob tore him from off his horse, stripped him of his armour, and dragging him to Cheapside, proclaimed him a traitor and an enemy of their liberties, and lopping off his head set it on a pole." Bishop Stapleton's remains were buried under a heap of rubbish or sand hard by his own gateway.

At the Reformation the house was seized on by Lord Paget, who called it after his name. The great Earl of Leicester was its next occupant. He changed it to "Leicester House," and bequeathed it to his son-in-law, the unfortunate favourite of Queen Elizabeth, Robert, Earl of Essex, from whom it derived the name under which it was known

ARUNDEL HOUSE (TO THE SOUTH). (*From an Etching by Hollar.*)

ARUNDEL HOUSE (TO THE NORTH). *From an Etching by Hollar.* (*See page* 71.)

for many years, and the memory of which is still retained in Essex Street. It will be remembered that it was from this house that he made, towards the end of Elizabeth's reign, his frantic and imprudent sally, in the vain hope of exciting the citizens of London to take up arms against their sovereign. Finding that his star at court was sensibly waning after the death of Lord Burleigh, and the estrangement of his sovereign, he listened to the advice of those who would have had Raleigh, Cecil, and Cobham banished from the Queen's councils. To strengthen his interest in antagonism to the Queen and the Court, he threw open the gates of Essex House to all discontented persons, and especially to those of the Puritan party. In February, 1601, he took part in an overt act of rebellion, assembling his friends, to whom he stated that his life was threatened by Raleigh and Cobham. "In consequence of this news, Lords Sandys and Monteagle, the Earls of Rutland and Southampton, with nearly 300 other gentlemen, assembled at Essex House, where it was divulged that Essex had resolved at once to rid himself of his enemies by forcing his way to the Queen, and informing her of his danger from those who had so long abused their influence with her Majesty. Having shut up within his gates the Lord Keeper, the Lord Chief Justice, and others whom the Queen, aware of what was passing, had sent to inquire into the cause of the tumult, Essex proceeded with his friends to the City, where, crying aloud, 'For the Queen! for the Queen! a plot is laid against my life!' he tried to enlist the citizens in his favour. But notwithstanding his popularity no one took up arms: the cause of the tumult was either unknown or mistaken. At length the Earl endeavoured to return home, but he was met by a party of soldiers near Ludgate, where a tumult ensued, in which he was twice shot through the hat. At last he reached Essex House; but after a short defence he was compelled to surrender, and along with Lord Southampton was committed to the Tower. . . . . He was tried for high treason in Westminster Hall on the 15th of the same month, and executed on the 25th on Tower Hill." His son, the next Earl, the celebrated Parliamentary general, was born here; and in the Cavalier songs of the day the house is often alluded to as "Cuckold's Hall." It was here, according to Whitelocke, that the Earl, after the battle of Newbury, received a deputation from the House of Commons and the citizens of London with the Speaker and the Lord Mayor at their head.

Spenser thus speaks of Essex House in his "Prothalamium:"—

"Next whereunto there stands a stately place,
Where oft I gaynèd gifts and goodly grace
Of that great Lord which therein wont to dwell,
Whose want too well now feeds my friendless case."

It is said that Sir N. Throgmorton was poisoned here; and within its walls was lodged, in 1613, the Count Palatine of the Rhine, when he came to London as the accepted suitor of "the Lady Elizabeth," daughter of James I.

It appears that in or about 1640 the great mansion of Essex House was divided, the one half being let by Lord Essex on a long lease to William Seymour, Earl of Hertford, whose name is so well known to history in connection with that of Lady Arabella Stuart. Twenty years later we find Lord Southampton, the Lord Treasurer of Charles II., living here; and the house was tenanted by Sir Orlando Bridgman, the Lord Keeper in 1669, when it is described by Pepys as "large but ugly." Strype tells us that after this it was purchased by a builder, who appears to have converted the site into a good speculation, the houses which he erected in its place being soon occupied by "the quality." Old Essex House was partly demolished about the year 1682, and Essex Street rose on the site of its ruins about two years later.

The other half of the original edifice long retained its name of Essex House, and it is worthy of note that it served as a receptacle for the Cottonian Library in the reigns of Anne and George I. It appears that this part of the house was afterwards inhabited by an auctioneer. It was at Essex House, according to Horace Walpole, that this auctioneer, named Paterson, in 1761, first offered for public sale subjects in painted glass—the art of producing which appears to have been lost—imported by him from Flanders.

It must be owned that the architecture of Essex Street, with its unsightly square-headed archway at the lower end, leading by a flight of stone steps to the Embankment, is by no means attractive or tasteful; but in this respect it resembles its precursor, Essex House, which is described by Pepys as a "large but ugly" mansion. The property was divided and let, as stated above, and ultimately the house was pulled down and the materials sold, towards the middle of the reign of George III., from which the present houses date. The arch and the steps at the end of the street are said by John Timbs to have formed the water-gate of old Essex House; if so, we can only say that it presented a sorry contrast to the work of Inigo Jones half a mile further west. In a view of the "Frost Fair" on the Thames in the reign of Charles II., where the royal party are walking on to the ice at the Temple stairs, to witness the sport, this heavy archway is seen in the background, and through it can be descried the gardens and terraces and the eaves of Essex House.

At the "Essex Head" in this street, rebuilt the year before he died (1783), Dr. Johnson established a club called "Sam's," for the benefit of the landlord, one Samuel Greaves, who had been an old servant of his friends, the Thrales. It was not so select as the Literary Club, but cheaper. Johnson, in writing to Sir Joshua Reynolds, and asking him to join it, says, "The terms are lax and the expenses light; we meet thrice a week, and he who misses forfeits twopence." The rules of this club, as drawn up by Dr. Johnson himself, will be found at length in Boswell's "Life;" and our readers may be amused to learn that the "forfeit" for non-attendance being found too low, was raised to three-pence!

It was in Essex Street that Dr. King, as we learn from his "Anecdotes of His Own Time," was privately presented by Lady Primrose, "in her dressing-room," to Prince Charles Edward Stuart, "the Young Pretender," during his short, secret, and stolen visit to London, between the 5th and the 11th of September, 1750. The house of this same lady, in this street, some three years before, curiously enough, had afforded a temporary home to Flora Macdonald, after her release from the mild imprisonment to which she had been subjected by the Government.

In the year 1613 the Robin Hood Society was established at the house of Sir Hugh Middleton in this street. It was removed to the "Robin Hood" Tavern in Butcher Row, when it was presided over by a baker. "Here," Mr. Diprose tells us, "Burke displayed those oratorical powers which afterwards became so transcendent. When, becoming reconciled to the Pitt administration, he went over to the Tory benches, exclaiming, 'I quit the camp,' Sheridan instantly rose and observed, 'As the honourable gentleman had quitted them as a deserter, he hoped he would not return as a spy;' and when the king settled a pension on Burke, Sheridan remarked that 'it was no wonder that Mr. Burke should come to the House of Commons for his bread, when he formerly went to a baker for his eloquence'—meaning the Robin Hood Club." Poor Oliver Goldsmith was a member of this club. The meetings were held on Monday nights, when questions were proposed on which any one present might speak if he did not exceed seven minutes. When these were finished, the "baker," who presided with a hammer in his hand, summed up the arguments.

In 1788 Charles Dibdin, being "tired of dramatic uncertainties," made a start on his own account by turning some rooms in this street into a theatre of his own, from which, however, he soon afterwards moved to a more fashionable neighbourhood further west.

On the west side of Essex Street is a building formerly a Unitarian chapel, in which during the last hundred years have ministered in succession Theophilus Lindsey, Dr. Disney, Thomas Belsham, and Thomas Madge; it is now the head-quarters of the denomination.

Of the founder of this Unitarian chapel it may be well here to add a few particulars. His name was Theophilus Lindsey, and he was a godson of the Earl of Huntingdon, in whose family his mother had resided. He took his degree at St. John's College, Cambridge, and was presented by a connection of the Huntingdon family, whilst quite a young man, with the chapel in Spital Square. He afterwards became chaplain to Algernon, Duke of Somerset, and after the duke's death was continued in the same post by the Duchess, who sent him abroad with her grandson, the Duke of Northumberland, as tutor. Having held for a few years a living in Dorsetshire, he exchanged it, by the interest of his old friend Lord Huntingdon, for that of Catterick in Yorkshire, where he was promised a bishopric in Ireland on the appointment of Viscount Townshend as Lord Lieutenant. In 1773, on account of scruples which he had long cherished, he resigned his Yorkshire living and became a convert to Unitarianism. He preached his first sermon at Essex House in 1774, and the new chapel was opened shortly after, Franklin, with many other eminent men, being present. He acted as pastor of it for twenty years, during the latter part being assisted by Dr. Disney, who had also seceded from the Church of England. He died in 1808. Whether we agree or disagree with the creed he adopted, we must admire the man who in a selfish and thoughtless age could sacrifice his worldly prospects to his conscience. The chapel was built on part of the site of the property of Essex House. In the forecourt, facing Essex Street, a monument was erected in 1880 in honour of the first twelve originators of Sunday Schools, from the time of Cardinal Borromeo in 1580 to that of Theophilus Lindsey and Robert Raikes in 1780.

Among the earliest inhabitants of Essex Street were Chamberlain (the author of several works on banks of credit, on land, security, &c.) and Arthur Maynwaring. Here also lived Dr. George Fordyce, a noted epicurean of the eighteenth century. In Jeaffreson's "Book about Doctors," we are told that "during twenty years he dined daily at 'Dolly's' chop-house, and at his meat he always took a jug of strong ale, a quarter of a pint of brandy, and a bottle of port. Having imbibed these refreshing stimulants, he walked back to his house, and gave a lecture to his pupils."

The late Lord Cholmondeley, who died in 1770, and who was not unknown as an antiquary, used to say that one day, when visiting a house in this street, he found, scratched to all appearance with a diamond, on a weather-stained piece of glass in a top room, the following letters, "I . C . U . S . X . & E . R ," which he interpreted, "I see you, Essex, and Elizabeth Regina." If he was right in his interpretation, it would seem probable that some inquisitive occupant of this room, overlooking Essex House, had seen the Queen flirting with the Earl, and, like Captain Cuttle, had on the spot "made a note" of it.

CHAPTER XII.

THE STRAND :—SOUTHERN TRIBUTARIES (*continued*).

"All the blood of the Howards."—*Pope.*

Milford Lane—The Chapel of the Holy Ghost—The *Illustrated London News*—Messrs. Woodfall and Kinder's—Arundel House—The Arundel Collection—Lord Seymour's Dalliance with the Princess Elizabeth—The Duc de Sully at Arundel House—"Old Parr"—Distinguished Inhabitants of Arundel Street—The "Crown and Anchor" Tavern—The Whittington Club—The Temple Club—Messrs. W. H. Smith and Son's News Agency—An Early News Mart—Strand Lane—The Old Roman Bath—Jacob Tonson.

It may reasonably be supposed that just on the west of Temple Bar the ground five or six centuries ago was marshy and low, and that a brook ran thence into the Thames. This, too, is rendered probable by the name of Milford Lane, which leads down from St. Clement's Church to the river-side; and the supposition is confirmed by the fact that in 1802 the remains of a bridge of stone, eleven feet in length, and covered by rubbish, was found on digging between Temple Bar and the east end of St. Clement's Church, as stated already in a previous chapter. It is suggested by Mr. T. C. Noble, in his "Memorials of Temple Bar," that this was probably the very bridge mentioned in the reign of Edward III. as built by the Templars of that day by command of the king. Towards its lower end the lane winds round to the east, meeting the steps at the bottom of Essex Street. This part of the parish appears to have been always inhabited by the poorer and less "respectable" classes; and it suffered accordingly most severely from the Plague in 1665.

Stow remarks that he could not account for the origin of the name of Milford Lane; but no doubt it comes from a *ford*—not over the Thames, as Mr. Timbs suggests, but across the little stream which ran there across and under the Strand into the Thames, near which was a *mill.* Mr. Timbs tells us that the former is shown in a print of the reign of James I., and that he has seen a "token" of the Windmill, near Temple Bar; but this may possibly have been an inn. It is a narrow, crooked, and ill-built thoroughfare, and now contains more stables and warehouses than private dwellings. Yet it was once well tenanted. In it lived Sir Richard Baker, the author of the "Chronicles," which, as most readers of the *Spectator* will remember, was the favourite work of Sir Roger de Coverley. The rectors of St. Clement Danes for many generations dwelt about half-way down the lane. It would not now be regarded as a desirable situation.

An unwelcome notoriety has been given to this lane in a poem by Henry Saville, commonly attributed to the witty Earl of Dorset, and beginning—

"In Milford Lane, near to St. Clement's steeple;"

and Gay also mentions it in his "Trivia," in the following terms :—

"Behold that narrow street which steep descends,
Whose building to the slimy shore extends.
Here Arundel's famed structure rear'd its frame,
The street alone retains an empty name;
There Essex' stately pile adorn'd the shore,
There Cecil, Bedford, Villiers—now no more."

The lane, it should be mentioned here, when it really was a lane, acted as a boundary between the property of Lord Essex on the east, and that of the Earl of Arundel on the west.

Tradition assures us that in the Strand, between Essex Street and Milford Lane, was formerly a chapel dedicated to the Holy Ghost; but no prints of it have been preserved, nor is it known when or by whom it was founded, or when it passed away. Mr. Newton, in his "London in the Olden Time," conjectures that it was originally a chapel belonging to the Knights Templars, and that in after time it became the chapel of the Bishop of Exeter's Inn.

He identifies its site, as nearly as possible, with the Unitarian chapel in Essex Street already mentioned.

At the top of the lane, on the eastern side, there stood down to about the year 1850 some picturesque wooden houses, with gables and ornamental fronts; but these were pulled down to make room for the erection of Milford House, in which since that date the *Illustrated London News* has been printed. It is published at the corner of Milford Lane and the Strand, on the other side of the way. This paper—the first of our "illustrated" journals—was started by the late Mr. Herbert Ingram, a native of Boston, in 1841, and by his energy and ability soon grew into a splendid property; but it needs no description here. We should, however, record in this place his melancholy death by drowning in 1860, on one of the American inland lakes. At the opposite corner house was published in 1858 its short-lived rival, the *Illustrated News of the World.*

At the bottom of this lane stood till 1888 the printing-office of Woodfall and Kinder. It was Mr. Woodfall's grandfather who printed the famous "Letters of Junius." "The business," says Mr. John Timbs, "was first established about the year 1720, in Grocers' Hall Court, and in Angel Court, Skinner Street, George Woodfall printed his edition of 'Junius'—the first book printed there."

Between Milford Lane and Strand Lane—a narrow and rather winding thoroughfare leading to the Embankment a few yards to the east of Somerset House—the entire space, about three hundred yards in length and the same in breadth, formed the site of the town residence of the Howards, Earls of Arundel and Dukes of Norfolk. It was a dull, heavy structure, as may be seen from Hollar's prints; but its gardens and terraces were as extensive as befitted the dignity of so noble a house and family. The outlines and extent of the estate, as it was in the days of the Stuarts, may be easily gathered from the names subsequently given to the streets which were laid out upon its site, perpetuating the names of Norfolk, Arundel, Howard, and Surrey—names so familiar to the readers of English history under the Tudors, and also to the students of art and antiquity. Hollar's prints, however, do not give a very attractive view of it, for though it covered a considerable space, the buildings themselves were low and mean.

But it did not belong to the Howards in very ancient days, having been before the Reformation the "Inn" or house of the Bishops of Bath and Wells, and known also as Hampton House. In the reign of Henry VIII., or of his successor Edward VI., it was seized and appropriated by royalty, and from royal hands it passed by an easy transition into the hands of Lord Thomas Seymour of Sudley, High Admiral of England, brother of the Protector Somerset, who called it Seymour Place. On the execution of Lord Seymour for treason, the dead lord's house was bought, together with its gardens and lands adjoining, by Henry Fitzalan, Earl of Arundel; and, Strype tells us, for the incredibly small sum of little more than forty pounds. This Lord Arundel, at his death in 1579, was succeeded in his title by his grandson, Philip Howard, son of the Duke of Norfolk who had been beheaded for taking part with Mary, Queen of Scots; and, though Philip Howard died in exile and attainted, his son Thomas contrived to obtain from James I. a reversal of the attainder and a restoration of his coronet.

Under this Earl of Arundel, the house which stood here became not merely a depôt, but the very home and centre of art and art treasures, as the repository of that collection long known as the "Arundelian Marbles," and "of which," to use the words of Mr. Peter Cunningham, "the very ruins are now ornaments to several private cabinets." We learn that the collection, when in its entire state, comprised no less than 37 statues, 128 busts, and 250 inscribed marbles, besides sarcophagi, altars, gems, and fragments of ancient art, all antique, and obtained with great care and discriminating skill in Italy. Besides these, "there really belonged to the collection a variety of other art-treasures which the Earl had purchased in Italy, but which he never could obtain leave to transport to England." However faulty he may be represented by Lord Clarendon, his judgment as a connoisseur in the fine arts will always remain undisputed. Views of the galleries in Arundel House are to be seen in the backgrounds of Van Somer's portraits of the Earl and Countess.

During the Cromwellian wars, Arundel House and its contents, of which, especially at that time, any nobleman might well have been proud, were given back to the Earl of Arundel's grandson, Henry Howard, sixth Duke of Norfolk, who, at the recommendation of John Evelyn and John Selden, the author of "Marmora Arundeliana," gave the marbles to the University of Oxford, which they still adorn, and the library to the Royal Society, which held its meetings for some time at Arundel House.

The Compleat Gentleman, a publication of the seventeenth century, informs the world, and with some truth, that to the Earl's "liberal charges and magnificence this angle of the world oweth the first

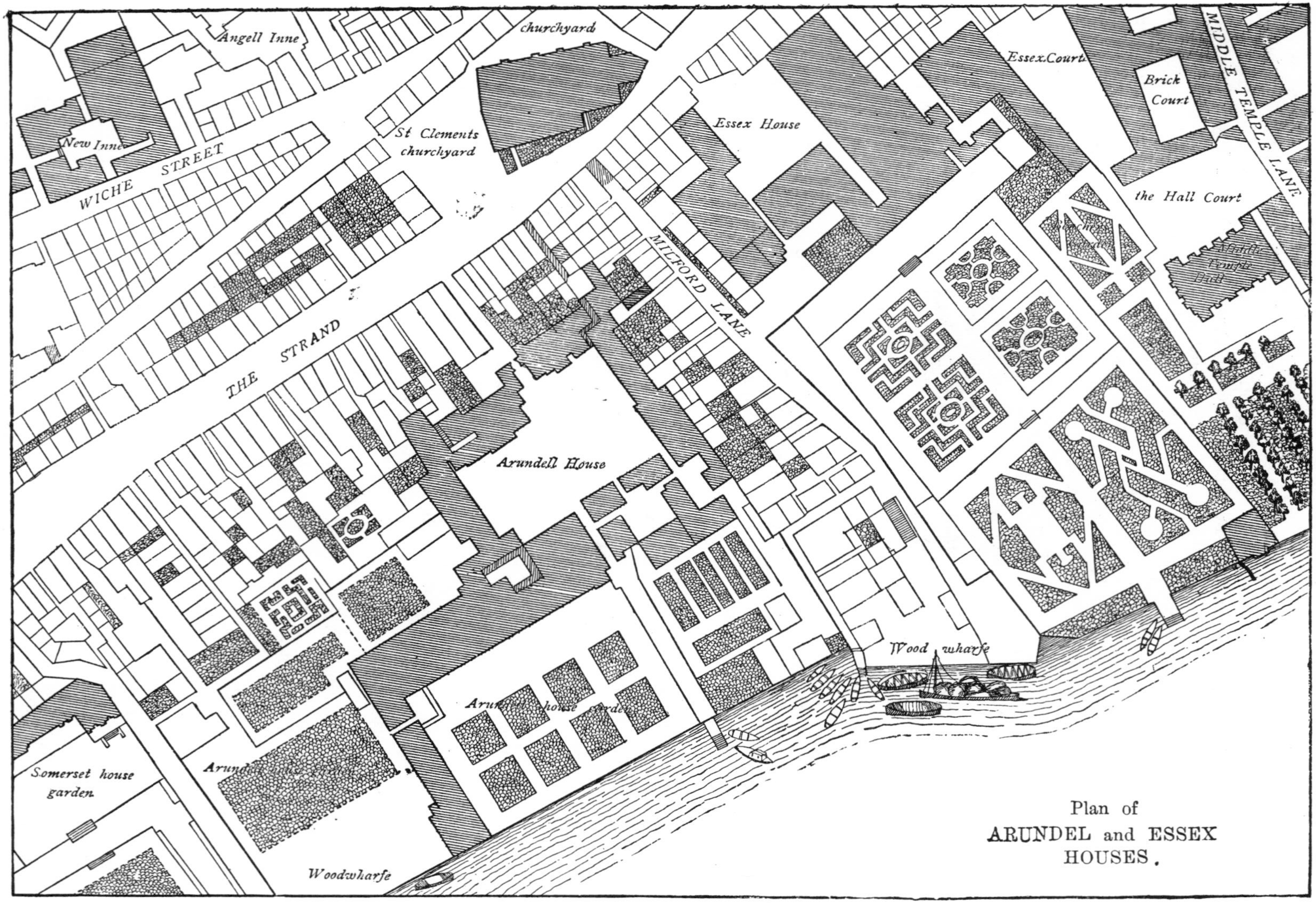

PLAN OF ARUNDEL AND ESSEX HOUSES. (*From an original Etching by* **Hollar**, *published in Ogilby and Morgan's Twenty-Sheet Plan of London.*)

sight of Greek and Roman statues, with whose admired presence he began to honour the gardens and galleries of Arundel House, and hath ever since continued to transplant old Greece to England." It may be mentioned here that the remainder of the Earl of Arundel's collection was kept for many years at Tart House, the residence of Howard, the unfortunate Lord Stafford, in Pimlico, and was ultimately sold in 1720.

"This place," says Pennant, "was one of the scenes of Lord Seymour's indecent dalliance with the Princess Elizabeth, afterwards queen. At first he certainly was not ill received, notwithstanding he had just espoused the unhappy Catherine Parr. Ambition, not lust, actuated this wretched man; his designs on Elizabeth, and consequently on the crown, spurred him on. The instrument of his design was one Thomas Parry, cofferer to the princess, to whom he offered for her Grace's accommodation the use of his house and all its furniture during her stay in London. The queen's death, and her own suspicions on her death-bed, gave just cause for the worst surmises. Seymour's execution, which soon followed, put an end to his projects, and saved Elizabeth and the nation from a tyrant possibly worse than him from whom they had but a few years before been released." The whole of Seymour's infamous conduct respecting the unhappy Queen Dowager is fully detailed in Lord Burleigh's State papers.

JACOB TONSON. (*See page* 79.)

Arundel House came to the Duke of Norfolk from the Earl of Arundel by the marriage which united in one line the Fitzalans and the Howards. While tenanted by the Howards, the mansion is described as "a large and old-built house, with a spacious yard for stabling towards the Strand, and with a gate to enclose it, where there was the porter's lodge, and as large a garden towards the Thames."

The house was at one time occupied by the Duc de Sully, who in spite of its humble appearance on the outside, tells us that it was one of the finest and most convenient in London, on account of the number of rooms and apartments on the ground-floor. At Arundel House, too, in its best and palmy days, John Evelyn and his family were frequent visitors. He tells us in his "Diary," under date July, 1662, that he was forced to take home his son John, "who had been much brought up amongst Mr. Howard's children here, for feare of their perverting him to the Catholic religion."

Arundel House, too, is in other ways connected with history. To it the Earl invited Hollar, the artist, who engraved some of his finest plates while enjoying its princely hospitality—among others his (now very scarce) "View of London from the Roof of Arundel House." There also lived for a short time Lord William Howard, the "Belted Will" of border fame. And there also, in November, 1635, died Thomas Parr, known to the world as "Old Parr," having been invited to come thither from his home in Shropshire, in order to become domesticated in the Earl's household, and to be introduced to Charles I., when upwards of a century and a half old. He did not, however, long survive the change; high feeding and the close air of London in a few months brought him to his grave, at the age of 152 years and nine months. His body, as we learn from the *Philosophical Transactions*, was dissected at the king's command by Harvey, who attributed the old man's death to peripneumonia, brought on by the impurity of a London atmosphere and sudden change in his diet.

Taylor, the water poet, gives us the following description of Old Parr, when he saw him in London:—

"His limbs their strength have left,
His teeth all gone but one, his sight bereft,
His sinews shrunk, his blood most chill and cold—
Small solace!—imperfections manifold.
Yet still his spirits possess his mortal trunk,
Nor are his senses in his ruins shrunk;
But that his hearing's quick, his stomach good,
He'll feed well, sleep well, well digest his food.
He will speak merrily, laugh, and be merry,
Drink ale, and now and then a cup of sherry;
Loves company and understanding talk,
And (on both sides held up) will often walk.
And though old age his face with wrinkles fill,
He hath been handsome, and is comely still;
Well fac'd; and though his beard not oft corrected,
Yet neat it grows, not like a beard neglected.
From head to heel his body hath all over
A quick-set, thick-set, natural, hairy cover."

Thomas Parr, according to the inscription on his tomb in Westminster Abbey, was born in Shropshire in 1483; and it is added, "he lived in the reign of ten princes, viz., Edward IV., Edward V., Richard III., Henry VII., Henry VIII., Edward VI., Mary, Elizabeth, James I., and Charles I.; aged 152 years, and was buried here Nov. 15, 1635. He lived at Alberbury, in Shropshire; had an illegitimate child born to him when over 100 years old; and married his second wife, Catherine Milton, at the age of 120. By her he had one child, and after his second marriage he was employed in threshing, and other husbandry work. King Charles, on seeing him, said, 'You have lived longer than other men; now what have you done more than other men?' 'Sir,' he replied, 'I did penance when I was a hundred years old.'" There is a portrait of Old Parr, said to be by Rubens.

"When Arundel House was pulled down," in the seventeenth century, we are told by Allen, "there was a design to build a mansion-house for the family out of the accumulated rents on that part of the gardens which faced the river, and an Act of Parliament was obtained for the purpose; but the design was never carried out." He adds that it was to Arundel House that the Royal Society removed from Gresham College, after the Fire of London, being invited thither by Henry, Duke of Norfolk. They returned to their old home in 1674, soon after which the house was sentenced to be taken down. The Duke, as we are informed by Pennant, had presented his valuable library to the society.

It would seem, from Gay's "Trivia," that for a long time after the demolition of Arundel House the eastern part of the Strand lay forsaken and neglected, though perhaps there may be some little amount of poetic exaggeration in the following lines:—

"Where Arundel's famed structure reared its frame,
The street alone retains an empty name;
Where Titian's glowing paint the canvas warm'd,
And Raphael's fair design in canvas charm'd,
Now hangs the bellman's song, and pasted there
The coloured prints of Overton appear.
Where statues breathed the work of Phidias' hands,
A wooden pump or lonely watch-house stands."

Arundel Street, however, built in 1678 on part of the site of Arundel House, has had in its time some distinguished inhabitants. Amongst others were Simon Harecourt, afterwards Lord Chancellor; Rymer, the antiquary, and author of the celebrated "Fœdera;" John Anstis, Garter King-at-Arms; and the well-known actress, Mrs. Porter.

At the upper end of this street, on the site of the Temple Club, formerly stood the noted "Crown and Anchor" Tavern—so named, no doubt, from the anchor of St. Clement already alluded to—the head-quarters of the Westminster Reformers in the days of Fox and "Old Glory," Sir Francis Burdett. Here, too, were held many of the meetings of the Catholic Association before the passing of the Roman Catholic Relief Act in 1829. The tavern stood as nearly as possible on the site of the buildings in which the Academy of Ancient Music was first instituted in the reign of Queen Anne. The premises extended a considerable way down the street, and at the back of them was a large and spacious room, upwards of eighty feet long, which was used as a banqueting apartment. Upon the occasion of Fox's birthday, in 1798, a great banquet was given here, at which 2,000 Reformers sat down to drink the toast of "The People the Source of Power."

Here the portly form of Dr. Johnson, in company with his friend Boswell, might often be seen; and during the Westminster elections in the last century it became one of the principal houses where the candidates of both sides were wont to address the constituents. It was at the "Crown and Anchor" that Daniel O'Connell first assailed that "venerable champion of civil and religious liberty," Henry Brougham; and it was here, too, that Cobbett fell foul of Sir Francis Burdett, who, we are told, "at once angrily responded by stating that Cobbett owed him a thousand pounds. Cobbett acknowledged receiving the money, but stated that it was a gift, and consequently not a debt." The "King of Clubs" was instituted here early in the present century; its members met every Saturday. One of the chief members was Richard Sharpe, a West India merchant and a well-known Parliamentary speaker during Addington's and Percival's administrations.

The coffee-room of the "Crown and Anchor" had for many years hanging upon its walls a picture which caused some stir among the parishioners of St. Clement Danes early in the last century. It appears that in 1725 the parish was thrown into a state of commotion by an order from Dr. Gibson, then Bishop of London, for the removal of an altar-piece lately painted by Kent, which had cost no small sum, and was supposed to be really a satire on the reigning house of Hanover, by containing scarcely disguised portraits of the wife and children of "The Pretender." The painting, of course, at once became famous, and Hogarth engraved an exact fac-simile of it, as may be seen in Nichol's "Biographical Anecdotes" of that painter. The original, after being removed from the church, was hung up in the coffee-room of this tavern, from which it was subsequently removed into the parish vestry-room.

In 1846 the Whittington Club was instituted at the "Crown and Anchor," under the auspices of Douglas Jerrold and several other gentlemen connected with literature and art. The "Whittington Club and Metropolitan Athenæum," for such was its ambitious name, was founded as a cheap club for men and women of the middle or upper-middle classes, and "with a view to throw open to them those increased physical comforts and facilities for moral and intellectual education, which are the most attractive characteristics of modern London life, but which, in the absence of individual wealth, associated members can alone command." Accordingly, in addition to the usual conveniences in the way of dining, &c., courses of lectures, and classes in chemistry, music, modern languages, and literature, &c., were established, together with weekly re-unions, in which dancing had a place. The subscription was low, £1 1s. or £2 2s. yearly, according to the residence of the member in country or in town; and 10s. 6d. for ladies.

The Whittington Club was named after Richard Whittington, the former "Lord Mayor of great London," and in one of its large rooms hung a picture of "Dick Whittington listening to the sound of Bow Bells," by Newenham, which was given to the club by its founder. The original premises of the "Crown and Anchor" were burnt down in 1854, but they were subsequently rebuilt on the former plan. The Whittington Club, however, languished, and at last came to an end in 1873. The building then underwent considerable alteration, and at the end of the same year was re-opened as the Temple Club. The house, which was erected at a cost of more than £20,000, contained above thirty rooms; what was formerly the hall, a magnificent apartment, capable of seating 1,000 persons, became the dining-room. One of the principal objects which the founders had in view was to "create the nucleus of a community whose members, uninfluenced by any political bias and unconfined to any literary or scientific pursuit, might enjoy a neutral ground whereon to reciprocate their ideas with regard to art, literature, and science." The Temple Club in 1881, when it was broken up, numbered about 2,000 members.

At the opposite corner of Arundel Street, with its principal entrance in the Strand, is that great emporium of modern intelligence, the news-agency of Messrs. Smith and Son, which is, perhaps, the most extraordinary house of business in London, not alone from the rapidity and dexterity of its operations, but the facility and certainty with which business is transacted to such an enormous extent in so short a time. The building is lofty, and covers a large space of ground, and is complete in every department. On the ground-floor is a noble and spacious hall, forming almost the extent of the entire premises, and is surrounded by two galleries. The bustle is at its height at an early hour in the morning, when vehicles are bringing in the morning papers from the different printing-offices: these are at once folded into oblong packages, wrapped in brown paper covers already addressed, and dispatched in light red carts to the various railway stations for transmission to different parts of the world. Thousands of newspapers are transmitted to their destination in the course of the week from this establishment, and a large staff of clerks are engaged, besides men and boys employed in the packing departments. In addition to this extensive wholesale newspaper business, Messrs. W. H. Smith and Son have established a circulating library upon a most extensive scale; and they also have in their railway bookstalls an exceedingly valuable monopoly. Printing, advertising, and bookbinding likewise form important items in this vast commercial establishment, and so admirable are the arrangements that each department is complete in itself, and conducted as a separate business; the whole giving employment to many hundreds of hands.

From the *Bookseller* we learn that Mr. W. H. Smith, grandfather of the present proprietor, and founder of this gigantic establishment, was born in the year 1792, and "at a very early age undertook the management of a newspaper business at the West-end of the town, removing in a few years to the site of the present premises. At the early part of this century newspapers required two days to go to Manchester, Liverpool, and other great towns far distant from London, for they were only conveyed by the night coaches, which took from twenty to thirty hours to reach their various destinations, so that Monday's newspapers could not be received before Wednesday morning. To obviate this inconvenient delay Mr. Smith started express carts and saddle-horses, so as to overtake the early morning coaches, and thus the day's paper was delivered by the morrow, making a saving of twenty-four hours in the transmission. For some time this admirable project scarcely paid its way, and it seemed almost a failure; but the perseverance of its projector was such that he boldly pursued his course under all its difficulties, and eventually won his way, acquiring the largest newspaper agency trade in London, to which he then devoted himself wholly and solely, giving up entirely the stationery business with which he had previously incorporated it. As time changes all things, so coach travelling was superseded by railway locomotion, and Mr. Smith was not slow in adapting the conduct of his business to suit this wonderful alteration. In 1852 Mr. Smith retired into private life, and for above six years he resided at Bournemouth, doing all the good he could in his new neighbourhood, for his activity was such that he could not be idle. He died in 1865." The son of this gentleman, and his successor as head of the establishment, was Mr. William Henry Smith. He was Financial Secretary of the Treasury from 1874 to 1877, and First Lord of the Admiralty from 1877 to 1880. In 1880 he became First Lord of the Treasury, and Leader of the House of Commons in 1886, dying in 1891, when a peerage was conferred upon his widow.

A rough idea may be formed of the extent of the agency at work in the circulation of newspapers and other publications of a serial kind, one-third of which it is calculated pass through the hands of Messrs. Smith, when we give our readers the following statement, courteously furnished by Mr. Wellsman, the editor of "The Newspaper Press Directory":—There are now (1897) published in the United Kingdom 2,396 newspapers distributed as follows:—England—London, 494; provinces, 1,377—1871; Wales, 102; Scotland, 232; Ireland, 171; British Isles, 20. Of these there are—172 daily papers published in England; 7 ditto in Wales; 19 ditto in Scotland; 18 ditto in Ireland; 2 ditto in the British Isles. On reference to the first edition of this useful Directory for 1846, we find the following interesting facts—viz., that in that year there were published in the United Kingdom 551 journals; of these 14 were issued daily, viz., 12 in England and 2 in Ireland; but in 1897 there are now established and circulated 2,396 papers, of which no less than 218 are issued daily, showing that the press of the country has more than quadrupled during the last fifty-one years. The increase in daily papers has been still more remarkable; the daily issues standing at 218 against 14 in 1846. The magazines now in course of publication, including the quarterly reviews, number 2,184, of which 537 are of a decidedly religious character, representing the Church of England, Wesleyans, Methodists, Baptists, Independents, Roman Catholics, and other Christian communities.

It is not a little singular that a century and a half ago the chief news-mart stood not far from this very place. In proof of this assertion we would quote the following passage from the *London Spy* published in 1725:—"Now I am in this neighbourhood I know it will be expected that some notice should be taken of Mr. William, the faithful messenger of the Muses, who is constantly administering to the public the advices foreign and domestick, and is early every morning ranging his papers in order, . . . according to their seniority and credit respectively, upon the counter." The list of these, with which the writer favours us, is strange and well worth a passing note:—The *Daily Courant* he posts first, as superior in credit to any other, excepting the *Gazette*, for the affairs abroad. After him the *Daily Journal* and *Daily Post*, as the two intelligencers at home. The *Post Boy* takes the right hand of the *Flying Post* and *Postman*, and the weekly journals and pamphlets are piled in the window on one side. Those paying no stamp duties are not permitted to herd among the friends of the Revenue. But this is not all. The Strand, if second, has been for a century second only to Fleet Street in literary interest of this particular kind. At No. 132 an enterprising citizen named Wright established, in 1740, the first of those circulating libraries which, for about a century and a half, have afforded so large a market for our novelists. Mr. John Timbs tells us that he was so far successful that he shortly had four rivals in Holborn, Fleet Street, and in his own more immediate neighbourhood; but some of these must have failed, if it be true, as stated by him, that in 1770 there were only four circulating libraries in the entire metropolis. Another literary celebrity, connected with the Strand, was the friend of Pope, old Jacob Tonson, of whom we give a portrait on page 73, and of whom we shall have more to say at the close of the chapter.

A narrow and rather winding lane a few yards to the east of Somerset House, and just opposite to St. Mary's Church, led in former times to the water-side. It was called Strand Lane, and the pier or small landing-place at the bottom of it was known as "Strand Bridge." In it was a row of old tenements formerly known as Golden Buildings, but the name has disappeared. On its western side stood the "Strand Inn." The "landing-place on the bank of the Thames" at this spot is mentioned by Stow, and no doubt was constantly used by the inmates of the Inn. Occasionally, however, it afforded accommodation to other persons; and in the *Spectator*, No. 454, we read how Addison "landed with ten sail of apricot boats at Strand Bridge, after having put in at Nine Elms and taken in melons, consigned by Mr. Cuffe of that place to Sarah Sewell and Company, at their stall in Covent Garden."

Mr. Newton, in his "London in the Olden Time," says that the bottom of Strand Lane appears to have been an ancient landing-place, communicating directly with Lambeth, and with the Via de Aldewych, which led toward the north-west country.

It is just worth noting here that the term "Strand Bridge" was applied by Stow and others to a bridge *in* the Strand, by which the roadway just to the west of the Maypole was carried over a brook. In the present century, too, it was the name originally designed for Sir John Rennie's noble structure subsequently known as Waterloo Bridge.

It is thought by antiquaries that Strand Lane, which is somewhat tortuous, follows pretty nearly the line of a little brook or rivulet which carried off the water from the higher grounds about Catherine Street and Drury Lane, passing under the thoroughfare of the Strand, which, as Stow observes, was carried over it by a bridge. On the left-hand side of this lane, in passing from the Strand, may be noticed a somewhat rural-looking cottage, on which hangs a notice that within is "The old Roman Bath." It will thus be seen that passengers along the Strand in the present day are within some fifty or sixty feet of one of the oldest structures in London, one of its few real and genuine remains which date from the era of the Roman occupation of England, and possibly even as far back as the reigns of Titus or Vespasian, if not of Julius Cæsar himself.

The piece of land in which the bath is situated formed part of the property of a very ancient family, the Danvers (or D'Anvers), of Swithland, in Leicestershire; and although the existence of the bath was evidently unknown to Stow, Maitland, Pennant, and Malcolm, from the absence of any mention of it in their pages, yet, from time immemorial, in the neighbourhood, the fact of its being a Roman bath has been received with implicit credence.

There is apparently a dim tradition existing, to the effect that the bath had been closed up for a long period, and then re-discovered. Of this old bath Mr. Newton observes in his "London in the Olden Time," that it is "without doubt a veritable Roman structure, as an inspection of the old walls will prove." A descent of four or five steps leads to a lofty vaulted passage, on the left of which is a doorway leading into a vaulted chamber, about sixteen feet in length, the same in height, and about nine feet in width, in the floor of which is the bath itself. This is about thirteen feet long, six broad, and four feet six inches deep. Mr. Charles Knight, in his "London," tells us that "the spring is said to be connected with the neighbouring holy well, which gives name to Holywell Street, and their respective position makes the statement probable.* Through the beautiful clear water . . . . appear the sides and bottom of the bath."

The walls of this extremely interesting building are formed of layers of brick, of that peculiar flat and neat-looking aspect which certainly seems to imply the impress of Roman hands, divided only by thin layers of stucco; whilst the pavement consists of a layer of similar brick covered with stucco, and rests upon a mass of stucco and rubble. The bricks are nine inches and a half long, four inches and a half broad, and an inch and three-quarters thick. At the farther end of the bath is a small projecting strip or ledge of white marble, and beneath it a hollow in the wall slanting down to one corner. These are beyond doubt the remains of a flight of steps which once led down into the water. Mr. Charles Knight adds :—" Immediately opposite the steps was a door connected with a vaulted passage, still existing below; and towards the back of three houses in Surrey Street, and continuing from thence upwards in the direction of

OLD ROMAN BATH, STRAND LANE. (*See page* 77.)

* See, however, *ante*, p. 21.

the Strand. These vaults have some remarkable features; among others, there is a low arch of a very peculiar form, the rounded top projecting gradually forward beyond the line of its sides, in the house immediately behind the bath." The bath is perpetually supplied from the spring, and discharges at the rate of ten tons per day. The water in this through the sandy bottom, and its flow is pretty even, both winter and summer. There are no pipes which supply it; and as it has in no way been affected by the excavations for the Law Courts, nor for the Underground Railway, which runs along the Embankment, it is plainly natural, and not artificial, and sparkles as clear as crystal.

GOLDEN BUILDINGS. *(See page 77.)*

old Roman bath, which is beautifully clear and extremely cold, is now used solely for drinking; there is, however, another bath-room on the right of the passage by which we entered, which is used as a plunging bath, and is open all the year round. This new bath, the proprietor tells us, "was built by the Earl of Essex, in the reign of Queen Elizabeth, 1588." The source of the water which supplies this bath is unknown. It bubbles up

It may as well be mentioned here, though we have not travelled quite as far westward yet, that at No. 141 in the Strand, between St. Mary's Church and the corner of Wellington Street, on a site now covered by part of Somerset House, was the book-shop of Jacob Tonson, the friend and publisher of Pope, &c. Hither he removed from Gray's Inn Gateway in 1712, and the shop was known by the sign of the "Shakespeare's Head."

It is described as being "over against Catherine Street."

The subsequent history of the house occupied by Tonson is thus told by Mr. Peter Cunningham:—"The house (No. 141), since rebuilt, was afterwards occupied by Andrew Millar, the publisher, and friend of Thomson, Fielding, Hume, and Robertson; and, after Millar's death, by Thomas Cadell, his apprentice, the friend and publisher of Gibbon. Thomson's 'Seasons,' Fielding's 'Tom Jones,' and the 'Histories' of Hume, Robertson, and Gibbon, were first published at this house. Millar was a Scotchman, and, true to his country and countrymen, distinguished his house by substituting Buchanan's head for that of Shakspeare as its sign. Could any one save a Scotchman have been guilty of such a deed of Vandalism?"

The name of Jacob Tonson is familiar to every reader, not only of Pope, but of Horace Walpole, as the secretary of the "Kit-Cat" Club. The son of a barber-surgeon in Holborn, he was born about the year 1656. At fourteen years of age he was bound apprentice to a bookseller, and on reaching manhood joined with his brother Richard in partnership. He published extensively for Addison, Dryden, and Pope; and his edition of Clarke's "Cæsar," which issued from his shop in 1712, is said to have been the largest and most expensive work which up to that time had been published in England. It was this Jacob Tonson who had the portraits of the members of the "Kit-Cat" Club painted for him in a uniform size, which still retains the name. On retiring from business he lived chiefly at Barn Elms, in the village of Barnes, where his house was for many years a centre of literary society. He died in 1736, but his memory survives, having been kept alive on the title-pages of many great works in the eighteenth century, and by the pen of Mr. Charles Knight, in his "Shadows of the London Booksellers." In a dialogue between Tonson and Congreve, published in 1714, in a volume of poems by Rowe, there is a pleasant description of Tonson before he was spoiled by grand associates:—

> "While, in your early days of reputation,
> You for blue garters had not such a passion;
> While yet you did not live, as now your trade is,
> To drink with noble lords, and toast their ladies,
> Thou, Jacob Tonson, were, to my conceiving,
> The cheerfullest, best, honest fellow living."

CHAPTER XIII.

THE STRAND:—SOUTHERN TRIBUTARIES (*continued*).

"Interdum rapere occupat."—*Horace.*

Sir Thomas Lyttelton and Bishop Burnet—Norfolk Street—Royal Farmers' and General Insurance Company—St. John's House—Conservative Land Society—Eminent Residents in Norfolk Street—Surrey Street—Office for Licensing Hackney Coaches—Voltaire and Will Congreve—Howard Street—Attempted Abduction of Mrs. Bracegirdle, the Actress—Murder of Mr. Mountfort.

BETWEEN Arundel and Norfolk Streets were two houses which were only demolished in 1896, to provide a site for Horrex's Hotel. Sir Thomas Lyttelton, Speaker of the House of Commons in 1698, lived in one, and next door to him the father of Bishop Burnet. "Here Burnet and Sir Thomas spent much of their time together; and it was the custom of the latter, when he had any great business to transact in Parliament, to talk it over previously with Burnet, who was to act the part of 'devil's advocate,' by bringing forward against it every conceivable argument, true or false." Burnet's house continued to be in the family until the end of the last or early in the present century, when it was possessed by a bookseller named Burnet, a collateral descendant of the bishop.

Norfolk Street, the next street westward from Arundel Street, was built in 1682, on a part of the site of Arundel House and grounds. Most of the houses in this street have of late been used as private hotels; but there are one or two which call for special mention. At No. 3 are the offices of the Royal Farmers' and General Insurance Company.

About half way down on the western side is St. John's House, the home of a sisterhood of ladies belonging to the English Church, who devote their lives to the work of nursing the sick poor, and of training up a body of nurses really fitted for that work. It was founded in 1848, under the modest title of "The Training Institution for Nurses in Hospitals, Families, and the Poor," beginning its work in St. John's, a poor district of St. Pancras. In 1852 the sisterhood removed to Queen Square, Westminster, in order that the sisters might have the double advantage of the religious services of the Abbey and of a more special training in the wards of the Westminster Hospital.

In 1854 the sisterhood supplied some of the nurses who accompanied Miss Nightingale to the Crimea, whither twenty more of their number were dispatched in the following year. In 1856 the sisters removed to Norfolk Street, having entered on the work of nursing the patients in King's College Hospital. The sisters wear a distinctive dress, with a small cross and medal. Besides King's College Hospital, the sisters of St. John's House nurse the patients in Charing Cross Hospital, and those of the Galignani English Hospital at Paris. They also dispense annually about 4,000 diets, which are supplied for the use of convalescent patients by the members of the Order of St. John. In this invaluable institution everything is carried out on the voluntary principle, and although it is styled a "sisterhood," under a superioress, the members are not tied down by any "vows of poverty, monastic obedience, or celibacy;" there is "no cloistered seclusion, but a full, free, and willing devotion to the great cause of Christian charity."

Among the notabilities who have resided in Norfolk Street may be named Dr. Birch, the historian of the Royal Society, and John Hamilton Mortimer, the painter, styled "the English Salvator Rosa." A "Supper at Mortimer's" forms the subject of a chapter in those chatty volumes entitled "Wine and Walnuts," published in 1823. Sir Roger de Coverley is stated by Addison to have put up in this street, before he went to live in Soho Square. Mr. Dowling, a gentleman well known in sporting circles, and some time editor of *Bell's Life*, lived for many years in this street; as also did Sam Ireland, the father of the author of the Shakespearian forgeries; Albany Wallis, the friend and executor of Garrick; Mountfort, the actor; Mr. William Shippen, the incorruptible M.P.—the only man, according to Sir Robert Walpole, who was proof against a bribe; Penn, the founder of Pennsylvania; Peter the Great; and Samuel Taylor Coleridge, who from 1814 to 1816 lived at No. 42, on the east side, in a house which was removed in 1896 to make way for Horrex's Hotel, a large building of white stone with Aberdeen granite pilasters, fronting both the Strand and Norfolk Street. The street has been largely rebuilt during the last few years, and now contains several handsome blocks of offices, such as Hastings House, Amberley House, and Mowbray House.

We learn from Sir John Hawkins's "Life of Doctor Johnson" that the house occupied by Penn was at the south-western angle of the street, close to the river-side, and he chose the house as one out of which he could slip by water in case of any emergency. It would appear that this house was actually that occupied by Peter the Great, if the following notice in the *Postman* of January 13, 1698, be correct:—"On Monday night the Czar of Muscovy arrived from Holland, and went directly to the house prepared for him in Norfolk Street, near the water-side." While staying here he was visited by King William III. and by very many other members of the Court and aristocracy.

Surrey Street, built about the same time, is described by Strype as "replenished with good buildings." He draws especial attention to the two houses at the bottom, which "front the Thames," with pleasant, though small, gardens "towards the river," that on the east side belonging to "the Hon. Charles Howard, Esq., brother to Henry, Duke of Norfolk." Towards the Strand, he also tells us that there was a fine large and curious house built by a Mr. Nevinson Fox. In this street, during the last century, was the head office for the licensing of hackney coaches, but this building being burnt down, the office was transferred to Great Queen Street, Lincoln's Inn Fields.

Voltaire, as we learn from his life, when in London, paid a visit to Will Congreve, who was living in this street, and who also died in it. "On this and on other occasions," says Peter Cunningham, "Congreve affected to be thought a man of fashion rather than of wit, on which Voltaire remarked, with his usual cynicism, that 'if he had been only a gentleman, he should not have come thither to visit him.'" Another celebrated literary character, who lived in Surrey Street, was George Sale, the translator of the Koran; his death took place here in 1736.

Howard Street, which runs at right angles across the centre of Norfolk Street, from Arundel Street to Surrey Street, and like neighbouring streets, has been largely rebuilt of late years, has never been remarkable for distinguished residents. It was, however, before it had been built twenty years, the scene of a terrible tragedy, the remembrance of which still survives. In it Will Mountfort, one of "his Majesty's servants"—in other words, a player—was murdered on the night of December 9th, 1692. The story is one of interest, and involves some celebrated characters. We tell the tale as told to us by Mr. Peter Cunningham in his "Handbook of London:"—

"A gallant of the town, a Captain Richard Hill, had conceived what Cibber calls a 'tendre,' or passion for Mrs. Bracegirdle, the beautiful actress. He is said to have offered her his hand, and to have been refused. His passion at last became ungovernable, and he at once determined on carrying her off by force. For this purpose he borrowed a suit of night linen of Mrs. Radd, the landlady in whose house in Buckingham Court he lodged, induced his friend Lord Mohun to assist him in his attempt, dodged the fair actress for a whole day at the theatre, stationed a coach near the 'Horseshoe' Tavern, in Drury Lane, to carry her off in, and hired six soldiers to force her into it as she returned from supping with Mr. Page, in Princes Street (off Drury Lane), to her own lodging in the house of a Mrs. Dorothy Brown, in this street. As the beautiful actress came down Drury Lane, about ten at night, accompanied by her mother and brother, and escorted by her friend, Mr. Page, one of the soldiers seized her in his arms, and endeavoured to force her into the coach. Page resisting the attempt, Hill drew his sword, and struck a blow at Page's head, which fell, however, only on his hand. The lady's screams drew a rabble about her, and Hill, finding his endeavours ineffectual, bid the soldiers let her go. Lord Mohun, who was in the coach all this time, now stepped out of it, and with his friend Hill, insisted on seeing the lady home, Mr. Page accompanying them, and remaining with Mrs. Bracegirdle for some time after for her better security.

"Disappointed in their object, Lord Mohun and Captain Hill remained in the street, Hill with his sword drawn, and vowing revenge, as he had done before, to Mrs. Bracegirdle on her way home. Here they sent to the 'Horseshoe' Tavern in Drury Lane, for a bottle of canary, of which they drank in the middle of the street. In the meantime Mrs. Bracegirdle sent her servant to her friend Mr. Mountfort's house in Norfolk Street adjoining, to know if he was at home. The servant returned with an answer that he was not, and was sent again by her mistress to desire Mrs. Mountfort to send to her husband to take care of himself: 'in regard my Lord Mohun and Captain Hill, who (she feared) had no good intention toward him, did wait in the street.

"Mountfort was sought for in several places without success, but Mohun and Hill had not waited long before he turned the corner of Norfolk Street, with, it is said by one witness (Captain Hill's servant), his sword over his arm. It appears in the evidence before the coroner, that he had heard while in Norfolk Street (if not before) of the attempt to carry off Mrs. Bracegirdle, and was also aware that Lord Mohun and Hill were in the street; for Mrs. Brown, the landlady of the house in which Mrs. Bracegirdle lodged, solicited him to keep away. Every precaution was, however, ineffectual. He addressed Lord Mohun (who embraced him, it would appear, very tenderly), and said how sorry he was to find that he (Lord Mohun) would justify the rudeness of Captain Hill, or keep company with such a pitiful fellow, or words to the like effect. 'And then,' says Thomas Leak, the Captain's servant, 'the Captain came forward and said he would justify himself, and went toward the middle of the street, and Mr. Mountfort followed him and drew.' Ann Jones, a servant (it would appear, in Mrs. Bracegirdle's house), declared in evidence that Hill came behind Mountfort and gave him a box on the ear, and bade him draw. It is said they fought. Mountfort certainly fell, with a desperate wound on the right side of the belly, near the short rib, of which he died the next day, assuring Mr. Page, while lying on the floor in his own parlour, as Page declares in evidence, that Hill ran him through the body before he could draw the sword. Lord Mohun affirmed they fought, and that he saw a piece of Mountfort's sword lying on the ground. As Mountfort fell, Hill ran off, and the Duchy watch coming up, Lord Mohun surrendered himself, with his sword still in the scabbard.

"The scene of this sad tragedy was that part of Howard Street lying between Norfolk Street and Surrey Street. Mountfort's house was two doors from the south-west corner. Mountfort was a handsome man, and Hill is said to have attributed his rejection by Mrs. Bracegirdle to her love for Mountfort, an unlikely passion it is thought, as Mountfort was a married man, with a good-looking wife of his own, afterwards Mrs. Verbruggen, and a celebrated actress withal. Mountfort (only thirty-three when he died) lies buried in the adjoining church of St. Clement Danes."

Mrs. Bracegirdle continued to inhabit her old quarters for very many years. "Above forty years since," says Davies, "I saw at Mrs. Bracegirdle's house in Howard Street a picture of Mrs. Barry, by Sir G. Kneller, in the same apartments with the portraits of Betterton and Congreve." The seconder of Captain Hill in this discreditable affair was the Lord Mohun, whose name we shall have occasion to mention again hereafter, when we come to speak of Hyde Park, as having fallen in a duel with the Duke of Hamilton.

Mrs. Bracegirdle, born in 1663, was known as one of the most attractive and fascinating of our earliest actresses, and it is said that every one of her male audience became her lover, or at all events her admirer. Her virtue was remarkable, being "as impregnable as the rock of Gibraltar." She is called by Dr. Doran "that Diana of the stage before whom Congreve and Lord Lovelace, at the head of a troop of bodkined fops, worshipped in vain."

This troop of fops, it may be added, would sometimes include the Dukes of Devonshire and Dorset and the Earl of Halifax; amongst whom it is said that the latter remarked at a coffee-house one day, "Come, you are always praising the lady's virtue: why then do you not reward the lady who will not sell it?" then and there offering to head a subscription list with £200, *pour encourager les autres.* "Four times that amount was raised," says Dr. Doran, "and with it the nobles, with their swords in their hands, waited on Mrs. Bracegirdle"—no doubt in Howard Street—"who accepted the testimonial."

Mrs. Bracegirdle was very kind to the poor, and especially to the poorer members of her profession. She is described by Aston as "of a lovely height, with dark brown hair and eyebrows, black sparkling eyes, and a fresh blushing complexion; and whenever she exerted herself, had an involuntary flushing in her breast, neck, and face, having continually a cheerful aspect and a fine set of even white teeth, and never making an exit without leaving the audience in imitation of her pleasant countenance." Colley Cibber tells us that "she inspired the best authors to write for her; and two of them (Rowe and Congreve), when they gave her a lover in a play, seemed palpably to plead their own passions, and make their private court to her in fictitious characters."

But there is a reverse to this exquisite medal. In Spence's "Anecdotes," and in Bellchambers' edition of "Colley Cibber," it is asserted or assumed that this chaste lady was really Congreve's mistress; and Dr. Young seems to hint the same thing, when he says that "Congreve was very intimate with Mrs. Bracegirdle, and lived in the same street with her, his house being very near hers, until his acquaintance with the young Duchess of Marlborough."

This scandal would seem to have been confirmed by the voice of contemporary testimony. Lord Macaulay calls her, however, a "cold, vain, interested coquette, who perfectly understood how much the influence of her own charms was increased by the fame of a severity which cost her nothing, and who could venture to flirt with a succession of admirers in the just confidence that the flame which she might kindle in them would not thaw her own ice." It was probably in a good-natured banter at the lady's real proclivities that Nicholas Rowe, in one of his short poems, exhorts Lord Scarsdale to

"All publicly espouse the dame,
And say, Confound the town."

Thackeray confirms the above account of the attempted seizure of Mrs. Bracegirdle, which, he says, occurred "opposite to my Lord Craven's house in Drury Lane, by the door of which she was to pass on her way from the theatre." He adds, "Mr. Page called for help; the population of Drury Lane rose; it was impossible to effect the capture; and so, bidding the soldiers to go about their business, and the coach to drive off, Hill let go of his prey sulkily, and he waited for other opportunities of revenge." As to her acting, if we may credit C. Dibdin, "she equally delighted in melting tenderness and playful coquetry; . . . . . and even at an advanced age, when she played Angelica in *Love for Love*, for Betterton's benefit, she retained all her powers of pleasing." She died in 1748.

At one time, as our readers will remember, when it had been resolved to erect the long-expected buildings for the New Law Courts of the future, even after the site between St. Clement's Church and Carey Street had been cleared, it was in contemplation to build them on the ground which lies between Howard Street and the Thames Embankment; and Mr. G. E. Street, the architect to whom this work had been entrusted, put forth in print his reasons, both æsthetic and practical, for preferring the site between the Strand and the river. But into these it is not necessary that we should now enter, as the subject has long since passed out of the range of discussion.

It may, however, be said that in the long run the proposal of the Embankment site was negatived by the Art Commissioners, and that the Legislature in 1873 fixed definitely and conclusively that the Law Courts of the future were to stand, as indeed they do now, between the Strand and Carey Street. In fact, the building and opening of them settled the question for ever. Howard Street, Norfolk Street, Surrey Street, Arundel Street, and Essex Street will therefore, so far as they are concerned, be allowed to remain *in statu quo.*

COURT OF OLD SOMERSET HOUSE, FROM THE NORTH. (*See page* 92.)

CHAPTER XIV.

ST. MARY-LE-STRAND, THE MAYPOLE, &c.

"Fairly we marched on, till our approach
Within the spacious passage of the Strand
Objected to our sight a summer broach
Yclep'd a Maypole, which, in all our land,
No city, town, nor street can parallel;
Nor can the lofty spire of Clerkenwell—
Although we have the advantage of a rock—
Perch up more high his turning weather-cock."

Building of St. Mary-le-Strand Church—Singular Accident—The Young Pretender here renounces the Roman Catholic Faith—Strand Bridge—Strand Theatre—The Original Church of St. Mary-le-Strand—Setting up the Maypole—Anne Clarges, Wife of the First Duke of Albemarle—Maypole Alley—Sir Isaac Newton purchases the Maypole—An Ancient Cross—Chester, or Strand Inn.

It is said by all the antiquaries who have written on the subject of London topography, that the present church of St. Mary-le-Strand covers the site of the spot on which in the olden time was set up the Maypole which the sour-visaged Puritans pulled down as dangerous to the morals of youth. It was called "St. Mary's as a matter of course, because its predecessor, which stood on the south side of the Strand, and was demolished by the Protector Somerset, was dedicated to St. Mary the Virgin." It is said that the Protector was at the time so all-powerful in matters of state, that he was never forced to make to the parishioners any compensation for the robbery of which he was guilty, though from his time down to the year 1723 they were churchless, and in order to be decently baptised, married, or buried, they were forced to have recourse to the ministers of neighbouring parishes.

In accordance with an Act passed in the reign of Queen Anne, for building fifty new churches in and around the metropolis, this site was fixed on for the first of these sacred edifices, which must have been much needed, on account of the growth of the population westward of St. Clement Danes. The first stone of it was laid in 1714, but it was not till nine years later, as we have said, that it was actually consecrated. Gibbs was the architect, and in his own account of St. Mary's Church says it was the first building he was employed upon after his

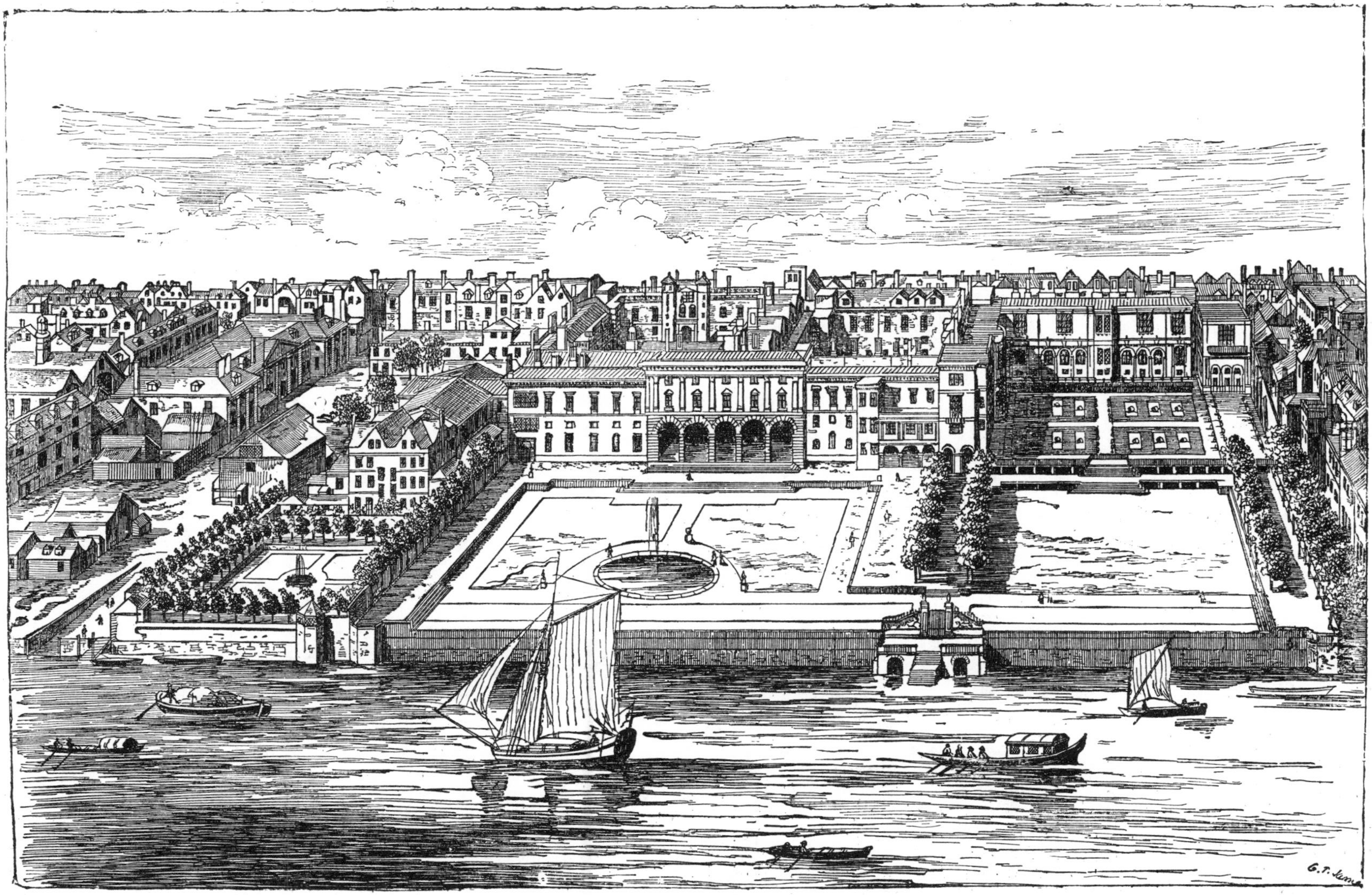

SOMERSET HOUSE IN 1755. (*See page* 93.)

arrival from Italy; and few structures, perhaps, have been more severely criticised. The building is fine of its kind, but not extensive, and stands, as it were, in the centre of the roadway of the Strand, in a line with the houses which form the southern side of Holywell Street, and from which it is separated by the entrance to Newcastle Street. The entrance, at the west end, is by a circular flight of steps which lead to a portico of Ionic columns, covered with a dome, which is crowned with an elegant vase. The columns are continued along the body of the church, with pilasters of the same order at the corners; and between the columns are niches, handsomely ornamented. Over the dome is a pediment, supported by Corinthian columns, which are also continued round the body of the church, over those of the Ionic order beneath, between which are the windows placed over the niches. A handsome balustrade is carried round the top, and its summit is adorned with vases. The steeple at the west end is ornamented with composite columns and capitals. There was at first no steeple designed for the church; only a small campanile, or turret, for a bell, was to have been over the west end of it; but at the distance of eighty feet from the west front it was intended to have erected a column, 250 feet high, in honour of Queen Anne, on the top of which her statue was to be placed. The design for the column was approved by the commissioners, and a great quantity of stone was brought to the place for laying the foundation of it; but the idea of erecting that monument was abandoned upon the Queen's death, and the present steeple was erected instead of the campanile, as at first proposed. Internally the church has a sumptuous appearance. The side walls display two ranges of pilasters, one above the other; the ceiling is slightly arched, and is divided into compartments, covered with decorations in stucco, and richly coloured; and the altar at the east end, which is placed within a very large and striking-looking recess, has above it three large windows filled with stained glass, with subjects of the Annunciation, the Passion, &c. The church underwent restoration in 1862, but in 1888 it was closed as unsafe, though reopened in 1889.

A sad accident happened at this spot during the procession of royalty to St. Paul's on the proclamation of peace in 1802. Just as the heralds came abreast of the building, a man who was standing on the roof of the church happened to lay his hand on one of the stone arms upon the parapet, knocked it down upon the crowd below, and so killed three persons.

If we may believe the statement of David Hume, it was in this church that Charles Edward Stuart, "the Young Pretender," as he is more generally styled, formally renounced the Roman Catholic faith, and professed the religion of the Church of England, doubtless for political rather than religious motives.

The author of "Walks through London" says that "at the digging the foundation for the St. Mary-le-Strand Church, the virgin earth was discovered at the depth of nineteen feet; a proof that the ground in this neighbourhood originally was not much higher than the Thames. This village was, therefore, truly denominated the Strand, from its situation on the bank of the river. Where Catherine Street now stands a stream of water ran into the Thames. Over this, in the Strand, was a bridge called Strand Bridge."

Nearly opposite to St. Mary's Church is the Strand Theatre. The house is small, and at one time was commonly known as the "Bandbox." It was originally built for the exhibition of a panorama, but was altered to a theatre in 1831. We will reserve a detailed description of this house for a future chapter.

The original Church of St. Mary-le-Strand was built under the dedication of "The Nativity of our Lady and the Innocents," and in consequence of a religious sisterhood attached to it. It was sometimes styled also "St. Ursula of the Strand." It was formerly in the patronage of the Bishops of Worcester, possibly because built or endowed by one of those prelates, whose town-house adjoined it, while the Inns of the Bishops of Lichfield and Coventry, Llandaff, and Chester were not far off. The old Church of St. Mary occupied the site of the eastern part of the present Somerset House. In the reign of James I. a windmill, and also a watch-house stood on the site of the present church; and Stow observes that on this spot there was "a stone building or conduit over a spring."

The Maypole, to which we have already referred as formerly standing on the site of the church of St. Mary-le-Strand, was called by the Puritans one of the "last remnants of vile heathenism, round which people in holiday times used to dance, quite ignorant of its original intent and meaning." Each May morning, as our readers are doubtless aware, it was customary to deck these poles with wreaths of flowers, round which the people danced pretty nearly the whole day. A severe blow was given to these merry-makings by the Puritans, and in 1644 a Parliamentary ordinance swept them all away, including this very famous one, which, according to old Stow, stood 100 feet high. On the

Restoration, however, a new and loftier one was set up amid much ceremony and rejoicing. From a tract printed at the time, entitled "The Citie's Loyaltie Displayed," we learn that this Maypole was 134 feet high, and was erected upon the cost of the parishioners there adjacent, and the gracious consent of his sacred Majesty, with the illustrious Prince the Duke of York. "This tree was a most choice and remarkable piece; 'twas made below bridge and brought in two parts up to Scotland Yard, near the king's palace, and from thence it was conveyed, April 14, 1661, to the Strand, to be erected. It was brought with a streamer flourishing before it, drums beating all the way, and other sorts of musick. It was supposed to be so long that landsmen could not possibly raise it. Prince James, Duke of York, Lord High Admiral of England, commanded twelve seamen off aboard ship to come and officiate the business; whereupon they came, and brought their cables, pullies, and other tackling, and six great anchors. After these were brought three crowns, borne by three men bareheaded, and a streamer displaying all the way before them, drums beating and other musick playing, numerous multitudes of people thronging the streets, with great shouts and acclamations, all day long. The Maypole then being joined together and looped about with bands of iron, the crown and cane, with the king's arms richly gilded, was placed on the head of it; a large hoop, like a balcony, was about the middle of it. Then, amid sounds of trumpets and drums, and loud cheerings, and the shouts of the people, the Maypole, 'far more glorious, bigger, and higher than ever any one that stood before it,' was raised upright, which highly did please the Merrie Monarch and the illustrious Prince, Duke of York; and the little children did much rejoice, and ancient people did clap their hands, saying golden days began to appear." A party of morris-dancers now came forward, "finely decked with purple scarfs, in their half-shirts, with a tabor and a pipe, the ancient music, and danced round about the Maypole."

The setting up of this Maypole is said to have been the deed of a blacksmith, John Clarges, who lived hard by, and whose daughter Anne had been so fortunate in her matrimonial career as to secure for her husband no less a celebrated person than General Monk, Duke of Albemarle, at a time when courtiers and noble lords and princes did not always look to the highest rank for their wives. With her is connected a story which may best be told, perhaps, by a brief outline of a certain *cause célèbre* in which her name figures prominently:—

"During the trial of an action for trespass between William Sherwin, plaintiff, and Sir Walter Clarges, Baronet, defendant, at the bar of King's Bench, in November, 1700, the following circumstance occurred:—The plaintiff, as heir and representative of Thomas Monk, Esq., elder brother of George, Duke of Albemarle, claimed the manor of Sutton, in Yorkshire, and other lands in Newton, Eaton Bridge, and Shipton, as heir-at-law to the said duke, against the defendant, to whom they had been left by his only son and successor, Christopher, the second duke, who died without issue in 1688."

In the course of the trial some very curious particulars were disclosed with respect to the family of Anne Clarges, the wife of George, the first Duke of Albemarle. "It appeared that she was daughter of John Clarges, a farrier in the Savoy, who was farrier to the duke, then Colonel Monk. She was married in 1632, in the church of St. Lawrence Pountney, to Thomas Ratford, son of another man of the same name, who had been a farrier and a servant in the employment of Prince Charles, and resident in the Mews (no doubt the King's Mews at Charing Cross). She had a daughter who was born in 1634, and who died at four years old. She lived with her husband at the 'Three Spanish Gipsies,' in the New Exchange, in the Strand, and sold such things as washballs, powder, and gloves, and also taught girls plain work. About 1647 she was acting as sempstress to Colonel Monk, and used to carry him his linen. In 1648 her father and mother died, and in the following year she and her husband 'fell out and parted,' but no certificate from any parish register could be produced to prove his burial. However, in 1652, she was married at the church of St. George, Southwark, to General George Monk, and was delivered in the following year of a son, Christopher, who, as stated above, became, or at all events was called, the second duke, and who died in 1688. Several witnesses were brought forward to swear that they had seen Thomas Ratford, her Grace's first husband, alive as lately as January, 1669–70, many years after her marriage with the first duke and the birth of the second. In opposition to this evidence, it was alleged that all along, during the lives of Dukes George and Christopher, this matter was never questioned; that the latter was universally received as the son of the former; and further, that the matter had been thrice already tried at the bar of the King's Bench, and the defendant had gained three verdicts. A witness swore that he owed Ratford five or six pounds, which he had never demanded; and a man who had married a cousin of the Duke of

Albemarle had been told by his wife that Ratford died five or six years before the duke married. In summing up, Lord Chief Justice Holt told the jury, 'If you are certain that Duke Christopher was born while Thomas Ratford was living, you must find for the plaintiff. If you believe that he was born after Ratford was dead, or that nothing appears what became of him after Duke George married his wife, you must find for the defendant.' In the end a verdict was given for the defendant, who was only son to Sir Thomas Clarges, Knight, brother of the duchess, and who was created a baronet in 1674."

Newcastle Street, at the north-east corner of the church of St. Mary-le-Strand, was formerly called Maypole Alley, but early in the last century was changed to its present name, after John Holles, Duke of Newcastle, the then owner of the property, and the name has been transferred to another place not far off. At the junction of Drury Lane and Wych Street, on the north side, close to the Olympic Theatre, is a narrow court, which is still known as Maypole Alley, near which stood the forge of John Clarges, the blacksmith, alluded to above as having set up the Maypole at the time of the Restoration.

As all earthly glories are doomed in time to fade, so this gaily-bedecked Maypole, after standing for upwards of fifty years, had become so decayed in the ground, that it was deemed necessary to replace it by a new one. Accordingly, it was removed in 1713, and a new one erected in its place a little further to the west, nearly opposite to Somerset House, where now stands a drinking fountain. It was set up on the 4th of July in that year, with great joy and festivity, but it was destined to be short-lived. When this latter Maypole was taken down in its turn, Sir Isaac Newton, who lived near Leicester Fields, bought it from the parishioners, and sent it as a present to his friend, the Rev. Mr. Pound, at Wanstead in Essex, who obtained leave from his squire, Lord Castlemaine, to erect it in Wanstead Park, for the support of what then was the largest telescope in Europe, being 125 feet in length. It was constructed by Huygens, and presented by him to the Royal Society, of which he was a member. It had not long stood in the park, when one morning some amusing verses were found affixed to the Maypole, alluding to its change of position and employment. They are given by Pennant as follows:—

"Once I adorned the Strand,
But now have found
My way to Pound
On Baron Newton's land;
Where my aspiring head aloft is reared,
T' observe the motions of th' ethereal Lord.
Here sometimes raised a machine by my side,
Through which is seen the sparkling milky tide;
Here oft I'm scented with a balmy dew,
A pleasant blessing which the Strand ne'er knew.
There stood I only to receive abuse,
But here converted to a nobler use;
So that with me all passengers will say,
'I'm better far than when the Pole of May.'"

Of the old cross in the Strand, Mr. Newton tells us, in his "London in the Olden Time," that it was mutilated at the time of the Reformation, and that it stood for some years headless, and was eventually taken down in the reign of Charles II. He identifies its site with that of the Maypole, already mentioned.

Allen, in his "History of London," says that "opposite to Chester Inn" (which, by the way, appears to have been the same building that was afterwards called "Strand Inn," and which stood where now is the east end of Somerset House) "stood an ancient cross, at which the judges occasionally used to sit to administer justice outside the City walls."

The origin of the judges administering justice in public is of very remote antiquity, as is evident from the frequent allusion to the custom made in Holy Scripture, where judges are spoken of as sitting "in the gate;" and the reason of so public a situation being chosen, says Herbert, in his "Inns of Court," was on two accounts: "that their proceedings might be generally seen, and that none might go out of the common way to seek for justice."

"Strand Inn" was one of those Inns of Court belonging to the Middle Temple so ruthlessly pulled down in the reign of Edward VI., by the Protector Somerset, for the building of Somerset House, when the students settled at New Inn, in Wych Street, another of the Inns of Chancery. Pennant records the tradition that it was in this place that Occleve, the poet of the reign of Henry V., studied law.

Mr. Newton tells us, in his "London in the Olden Time," that "Strand Inn" having ceased to be occupied as an episcopal residence, "a part of it became separated, and let off to students of the law, in whose occupation it was known both as 'Chester Inn' and 'Strand Inn.'" He adds that when seized on by the Protector Somerset, he "for some time kept his court there." On its west side was another large house, called the "Bishop of Worcester's Inn," of which we know nothing except it was a long time the residence of the Bishops of that see, and no print or view of it has come down to our times.

CHAPTER XV.

SOMERSET HOUSE AND KING'S COLLEGE.

"Before my gate a street's broad channel goes,
Which still with waves of crowding people flows;
And every day there passes by my side,
Up to its western reach, the London tide,
The spring-time of the term. My front looks down
On all the pride and business of the town."—*Cowley.*

Old Somerset House—Rapacity of the Protector Somerset—John of Padua, Architect of the Original Building—Downfall and Execution of the Protector—Somerset House assigned to the Princess Elizabeth—Afterwards the Residence of the Queens of England—Its Name changed to Denmark House—Additions made by Inigo Jones—Banishment of the Capuchin Fathers, and Desecration of the Chapel—The Services in the Chapel restored, and Pepys' Account of them—Catherine of Braganza—Attempt to implicate the Royal Household with the Murder of Sir Edmundbury Godfrey—The Cemetery—Description of the Old Buildings—Their Demolition—Building of New Somerset House—Amusing Tradition relative to Somerset House—King's College.

THE building so familiar to Londoners, old and young, by the name of Somerset House, occupies the space formerly covered by four or five buildings of note in their day, of some of which we have already spoken. It appears from Stow that in order to make a level space of ground to hold the fair new palace which he purposed to erect—"that large and goodly house now called Somerset House"—the Protector Somerset pulled down, and "without any recompense," the Inns, as they were called, of the Bishops of Chester, Llandaff, Lichfield and Coventry, and Worcester, with all the tenements adjoining, and also the old parish church of St. Mary's.

The original Somerset House, it is almost needless to remark, took its name from the Duke of Somerset, the Lord Protector of the reign of the boy-king, Edward VI.; but the present building is of much more recent date. By the attainder of Somerset it reverted to the Crown, and it was frequently tenanted by Queen Elizabeth. Anne of Denmark, the wife of James I., and Catherine of Braganza, the neglected queen of Charles II., both in succession held their courts within its walls. At length it came to be appropriated by usage as a residence to the queens-dowager, and was frequently appointed as a temporary residence for such of the ambassadors of foreign princes as the later Stuarts and the earlier Brunswick sovereigns cared especially to honour.

Mr. A. Wood, in his "Ecclesiastical Antiquities of London and its Suburbs," is of opinion that the Protector Somerset already possessed some property on the site of Somerset House when he began the great work of pulling down his neighbours' houses around their ears and his own. But be this true or not, he seems to have known, or at all events to have made, little distinction between *meum* and *tuum*, and when he had once resolved on his end—namely, to build a palace on this central site, at a bend commanding the view of the river from London Bridge to the Abbey at Westminster—he was not likely to be at much loss as to the means to be employed. Wide space and materials were all that he needed, and these he soon obtained in a manner such as we should now probably distinguish by the term "by hook or by crook." And further, in order to complete the undertaking in a thoroughly substantial and, as it would now be called, "first-class" style, he pulled down also the charnel-house of Old St. Paul's and the chapel over it, together with a structure in "Pardon Churchyard, near the Charterhouse, throwing the dead into Finsbury Fields," and the steeple, tower, and part of the church of the Priory of St. John of Jerusalem at Clerkenwell. With these materials he commenced his work, unblessed by either the Church, or the people, or the poor.

Bishop Burnet, alluding to the Protector's rapacity, admits that "many bishops and cathedrals had resigned many manors to him for obtaining his favour," though he adds, "this was not done without leave obtained from the king." He also accuses the Protector of selling chantry lands to his friends at easy rates, for which it was concluded he had great presents. The rise of Somerset House exposed its owner to the reflection that "when the king was engaged in such wars, and when London was much disordered by the plague that had been in it for some months, he was then bringing architects from Italy, and designing such a palace as had not been seen in England."

Pennant tells us that the architect employed by the Protector Somerset in the erection of Somerset House was the celebrated John of Padua, the architect of Longleat, in Wiltshire, who is said, in Walpole's "Anecdotes of Painting," to have held, under Henry VIII., the post of "Devizer of His Majesty's Buildings."

Whether the Protector Somerset ever resided in the palace he had thus been at so much trouble in building, there is some room to doubt. The building itself was commenced in 1546-7, and as soon after as the month of October, 1548, at which time the works were still going on, he was deprived of the Protectorship and committed to the Tower.

He was, however, pardoned after two years' imprisonment, and restored to the Council; but in the following year he was again committed to the Tower on charges of high treason, and was beheaded on Tower Hill in January, 1552. One of the grounds of dissatisfaction at first exhibited against him appears to have been "his ambition and seeking of his own glory, as appeared by his building of most sumptuous and costly buildings, most probably, however, at the expense of her kinsman, Lord Hunsdon, to whom she had given the use of it. Such, at all events, was the opinion of Pennant.

Stow tells us that the queen of James I. made this house her palace, and that she entertained the king with a feast within its walls on Shrove Tuesday, 1616, when the latter was so delighted at her reception of him that he ordered it to be

SOMERSET HOUSE AND STAIRS.
As they appeared before they were pulled down in 1776. (*See page* 93.)

and specially in the time of the king's wars, and the king's soldiers unpaid." On the attainder of the Duke of Somerset his palace was, of course, forfeited to the Crown, and his nephew, King Edward, appears to have assigned it to his sister, the Princess Elizabeth, for her use whenever she visited her sister's court. But when she came to the throne, she preferred the regions of Whitehall and St. James's, and fashion followed in the wake of royalty westwards. At this period the building is spoken of as "Somerset Place, beyond Strand Bridge." On Elizabeth's succession to the throne some partial restoration of Somerset's property was probably made, for Somerset Place became the residence of the Dowager Duchess.

Elizabeth seems to have lived here occasionally, called Denmark House in her honour. The palace was greatly improved and beautified by the queen, who added much to it in the way of new buildings, Inigo Jones being called in to furnish the designs. She also brought a supply of water to it by pipes laid on from Hyde Park. In 1626 it was settled for life on Henrietta Maria, the queen of Charles I., for whom it had been stipulated on her marriage that she should be allowed the free practice of her religion, having been born and brought up a pious Catholic. Accordingly it was fitted up for the reception of herself and her household, including, of course, a body of priests to say mass daily, and to celebrate the offices of the Church. The priests in attendance on the queen were Capuchins. They had succeeded to the

Oratorians, who had been expelled by the influence of Buckingham (Steenie) with his royal master. The foundation-stone of the chapel was laid by the queen, the work being carried out under the direction of Inigo Jones. The first stone was laid with great ceremony. From six in the morning there was a succession of masses daily till nearly noon, and as it was difficult to approach the sacraments elsewhere, except clandestinely, the confessionals were thronged constantly. On Sundays and festivals there was a controversial lecture at noon, and soon after followed vespers, sung by the Capuchins and musicians in the galleries. When vespers were over, there was a sermon on the gospel of the day, and lastly, compline. The chapel seems to have been also turned to account constantly in other ways. There were frequent "conferences" for the edification of Catholics and the instruction of Protestants, and on three days in each week the Catholic doctrine was taught catechetically in English and in French. The consequence was that there were frequent conversions to the ancient faith, and the name of the chapel began to offend the ruling powers. Accordingly, when the queen was absent in Holland, it was resolved by the authorities to make an assault upon the place. The Capuchin fathers were silenced and driven out, then imprisoned, and at length banished; their dwelling itself was pulled down, and the chapel desecrated, in spite of its being the

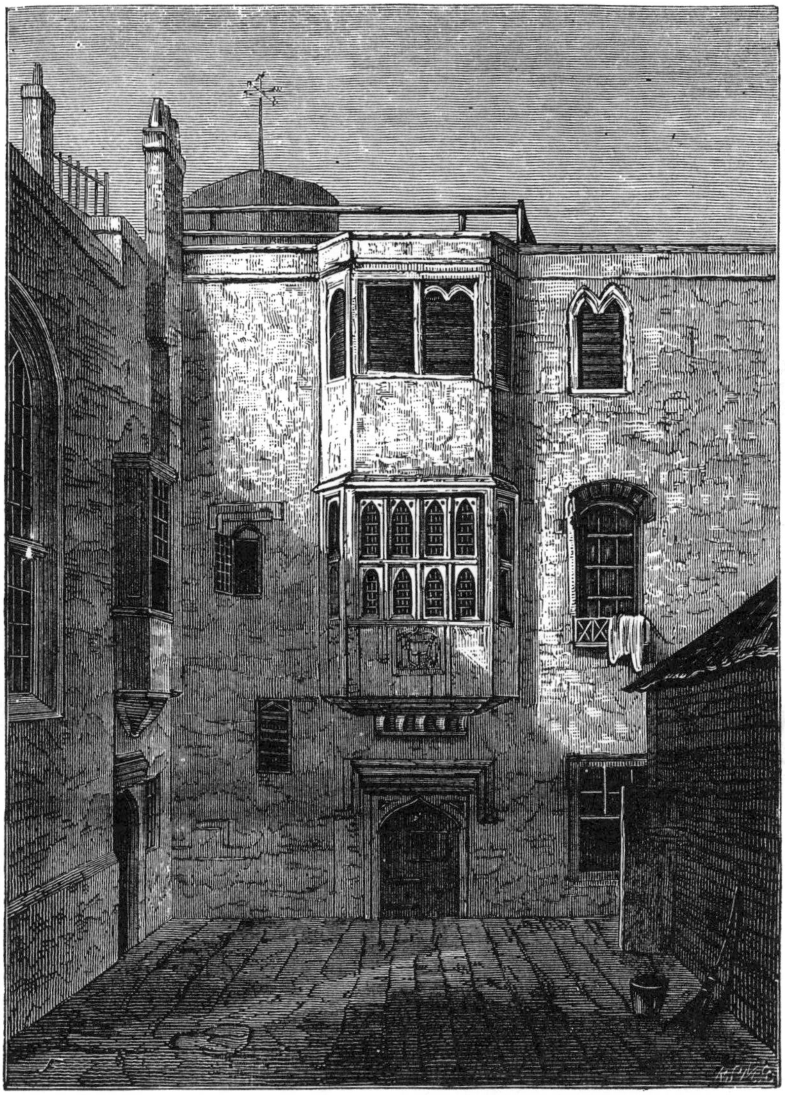

THE SAVOY. *From a Drawing by J. P. Neale, published in* 1815. (*See page* 96.)

property of the queen. The Capuchins were brought back, and the chapel was repaired, when Henrietta Maria returned to England, a widowed queen, after her son's restoration.

Here, in September, 1660, died the Duke of Gloucester, from the small-pox; and hence his body was taken by water "down Somerset Stairs," as Pepys tells us, to Westminster, to be buried in the Abbey.

Pepys, in his "Diary," gives an account of a service held in the chapel of Somerset House in 1663-4. "On the 24th, being Ash Wednesday, to the Queen's chapel, where I staid and saw mass, till a man came and bade me go out or kneel down; so I did go out; and thence to Somerset House, and there into the chapel, where Mons. D'Espagne, a Frenchman, used to preach." In October he again visits Somerset House, and saw the queen's new rooms, "which are most stately and nobly furnished!" In January, 1664-5, he went there again, and was shown the queen's mother's chamber and closet, "most beautiful places for furniture and pictures." In consequence, however, of the plague in the June following, the Court prepared to leave Whitehall and Somerset House. The Queen went to France, and there died in 1669. On the death of Charles II. in 1685, Somerset House became the residence of Catherine of Braganza, who lived here until her return to Portugal in 1692. It had previously belonged to her as Queen Consort, and during the ultra-Protestant *furore*, which exhibited itself for some years prior to the Revolution, attempts were made to implicate her household in the pretended Popish Plot of the time, and to connect the mysterious murder of Sir Edmundbury Godfrey in 1678 with persons in her service.

There is so much doubt and uncertainty mixed up with the story of the murder of Sir Edmundbury Godfrey, that it is almost impossible to winnow the truth from the falsehood, owing to the perjuries of Titus Oates and his confederate, Bedloe, the discharged servant of the Lord Belasyse. But it appears clear that the worthy justice of the peace was inveigled to a spot close to "the Watergate at Somerset House," under the pretence of his presence being wanted to allay a quarrel, and that he was strangled on the spot with a twisted handkerchief. His dead body, it would seem, was afterwards carried to Primrose Hill, at that time a retired and lonely spot, where a sword was run through it. For their presumed share in this murder three persons were hung at Tyburn in 1679. An attempt was made by Oates and Bedloe to implicate the Jesuits in the plot, and even the Queen, who then resided at Somerset House; but Charles, with his usual wit, refused to listen to the charge, telling Burnet that though "she was a weak woman, and had some disagreeable humours, she was not capable of a wicked thing."

We have already said that, under the Stuarts, Somerset House was frequently appointed for the reception of ambassadors whom the sovereign and the court delighted to honour. The last foreigner of importance who lodged there was the Venetian ambassador, who made a public entry into it in 1763, shortly before the building was pulled down.

From the time of the departure of Catherine of Braganza, Somerset House ceases to possess any interest in its strictly palatial character. It continued as an appurtenance of successive queens down to the year 1775, when Parliament was recommended, in a message from the Crown, to settle upon Queen Charlotte the house in which she then resided, "formerly called Buckingham House, but then known by the name of the Queen's House," in which case Somerset House, already settled upon her, should be given up and appropriated "to such uses as shall be found most useful to the public."

Mr. Wood, in his "Ecclesiastical Antiquities," tells us that in the reign of James II., Dr. Smith, one of the four vicars-apostolic who acted as Catholic bishops in England, was consecrated at Somerset House. There was also in the grounds of Somerset House a small cemetery, in which the Catholic members of the Queen's household were buried. In 1638 Father Richard Blount, who had "reconciled" Anne of Denmark, the consort of James I., to the Roman Church, was buried here by the Queen's permission. The value of such a permission at that time may be inferred from the fact that, owing to the severity of the penal laws, Catholics were for the most part obliged to be buried in Protestant cemeteries, with rites distasteful to themselves; and they were only too glad when the priest who attended them in their last illness could bless a little mould which was put into their coffin, and perform the usual ceremonies in secret, and even at a distance from their bodies.

A map and ground-plan of old Somerset, or Denmark House in 1706, shows that it consisted of one large and principal quadrangle, called "the Upper Court," facing the Strand. Its out-buildings were very extensive, and still more so its terraced gardens, facing the Thames, with stairs at either end. In the southern front of the quadrangle named above were the Guard Chamber, with a waiting-room, the Privy Chamber, the Presence Chamber, from the west end of which a flight of stone steps led down into the garden. On the western side, from the Strand nearly to the river-side, there ran along Duchy Lane (now absorbed in Wellington Street South) a row of coach-houses, stables, and store-yards. To the south-east angle of the chief quadrangle there was a passage down the "Back Stairs" to a second, or lower court, two storeys lower than the upper court. Here were the more private apartments of the queen—the "Coffee Room," "Back Stair Room," "Oratory," dressing-room, bed-chamber, and "Withdrawing Room," the two last-named facing the gardens and commanding a fine view of the reach of the river. Still further to the east, extending across what now is part of King's College, as far as Strand Passage, or Lane, were a variety of other buildings, occupied by the members of the Court, called the French Buildings, connected with the Yellow Room, the Cross Gallery, the Long Gallery, and leading to a "pleasance" which opened into the garden. A print in the *Gentleman's Magazine*, showing some of these last-named buildings before they were pulled down, together with the new building of Sir William Chambers on the north, leads us to suppose that, though interesting as a specimen of the style of Edward VI., their removal was no great loss from an architectural point of view.

The gardens were laid out in the square and monotonous style of the period, so well described by Pope—

> "Grove nods to grove, each alley has its brother,
> And half the garden just reflects the other."

This was literally true here, for in front of both the greater and the lesser quadrangle there were square gardens, with straight gravel walks on each side, and three avenues of trees; a handsome flight of stone steps, with iron gates; and on either side some handsome statues of Tritons and Nereids. Along the river ran a raised terrace, with a heavy dwarf wall. In a print of the river front of Somerset House, dated 1706, there appears moored a little way off the stairs a sort of house-barge, under which is written "The Folly," and a queer-shaped wherry, approaching the form of a gondola.

"I am extremely pleased," observes Stow, "with the front of the first court of Somerset House, next the Strand, as it affords us a view of the first dawning of taste in England, this being the only fabric that I know which deviates from the Gothic, or imitates the manner of the ancients." How amused would Pugin or Sir Gilbert Scott be to read this statement! and also the sentiment which follows:—"Here are columns, arches, and cornices that appear to have some meaning; if proportions are neglected, if beauty is not understood, if there is in it a strange mixture of barbarism and splendour, the mistakes admit of great alleviations." In all probability the architect was an Englishman, and this his first attempt to refine on the work of his predecessors.

It is currently believed that James Stuart, the elder "Pretender," was at one time secreted in old Somerset House; and there is an allusion to this belief in the *Town Spy*, published in 1725:—"The Pretender's residing at Somerset House in the year of Peace was blabbed out by one of the Duke d'Aum—nt's postilions."

The demolition of the old building was commenced as soon as an Act could be passed, and Sir William Chambers was appointed architect of the new buildings. They were commenced in 1776, and in 1779 one of the fronts was completed. The site occupies an area of upwards of 800 feet by 500. The front towards the Strand consists of a rustic basement of nine arches, supporting Corinthian columns, and an attic in the centre, and a balustrade at each extremity. Emblematic figures of Ocean and of the eight principal rivers of England in alto-relievo adorn the keystones of the arches. Medallions of George III., Queen Charlotte, and the Prince of Wales were formerly placed over the three central windows of the first floor. The attic is divided into separate portions by statues of Justice, Truth, Valour, and Moderation; and the summit is crowned with the British arms, supported by emblematical figures of Fame and the genius of England. The chief feature of the river front of Somerset House is its broad terrace, about 600 feet in length, raised on rustic arches, and ornamented with emblematic figures of the Thames. The centre of the large quadrangle opposite the chief entrance from the Strand is occupied by a gigantic piece of bronze work, executed by Bacon. The principal figure is a fanciful and almost allegorical representation of Father Thames.

The building affords at present accommodation during the working hours of the day to upwards of 900 Government officials, belonging to the Audit Office, the Inland Revenue Office, the Office of the Registrar-General, and the offices connected with Doctors' Commons. In the north front the annual exhibition of the Royal Academy was held from 1780 down to about the year 1837, when it was transferred to the National Gallery in Trafalgar Square. The use of apartments in Somerset House for the meetings of the society was also granted in 1780. The Royal Society removed from Somerset House to Burlington House, Piccadilly, in 1856. The Society of Antiquaries, and also the Royal Astronomical and the Geological Societies, have also at various times occupied apartments in Somerset House.

"The royal patronage of the arts," writes Malcolm, in 1806, "is most conspicuous in this grand building, which contains the apartments of the Royal Society, the Society of Antiquaries, and the Royal Academy of Painting. The two former assemble on the east side of the vestibule or entrance, and the latter on the west."

The Society of Antiquaries dates its origin from the year 1751. Malcolm tells us that previous to that time several unsuccessful, or at least interrupted, attempts had been made, in the reigns of Elizabeth, James, and Charles I., to establish such a society, but nothing effective was done until the reign of George II., who granted a charter, styling himself the founder and patron of the Society of Antiquaries, appointing Martin Folkes, Esq., as its president, and limiting the society's permanent income to £1,000 a year. The president must be assisted by a council of twenty members, half of whom are elected annually, along with himself, and the officers and members of the society are required to possess an accurate knowledge of the history and antiquities of their own and foreign nations, and to be "loyal and virtuous members of the community." The Archbishop of Canterbury, the Lord Chancellor, the Lord Privy Seal, and the Secretaries of State for the time being, are visitors of the society. The number of fellows is not limited by their charter. At their meetings descriptions and dissertations are read, and illustrative drawings are exhibited. Their transactions as a body are under the control of an elective director in the arrangement of communications to be published. Their official publication, in a handsome quarto form, is known as the "Archæologia."

Pennant writes, in 1806: "The Royal Society and the Society of Antiquaries both hold their meetings here; and here also are annually exhibited the works of the British painters and sculptors."

Mr. John Timbs, in his "Romance of London," tells us an amusing traditionary story relative to this place:—"A little above the entrance-door to the Office of Stamps and Taxes is let into the wall a white watch-face. Of this it is told that when the wall was being built a workman fell from the scaffolding, and was saved from being killed only by the ribbon of his watch, which caught upon a piece of projecting ornament. In thankful remembrance of his wonderful preservation, he is said, and is believed to this day, to have inserted his watch in the face of the wall." A very pretty story, indeed, if it was only true. But, unfortunately for the age of poetry, Mr. Timbs lets us into the real secret of the watch, which is essentially prosaic. "It was placed," he says, "in its present position, many years ago, by the Royal Society, as a meridian mark for a portable transit instrument in one of the windows of the anteroom;" and the late Admiral W. H. Smyth, the eminent hydrographer to the Admiralty, would often tell his friends that, having assisted in mounting the instrument, he well remembered the watch being inserted in the wall. We fear, therefore, that the poetic view must be dismissed.

Running parallel with the buildings forming the west side of the quadrangle, and having its frontage towards Lancaster Place, a new wing was built in 1857, from the designs of Mr. Pennethorne, in a style of architecture corresponding with the rest of the building. Here are the offices of the Inland Revenue Department, and in the basement several rooms are set apart for the printing of postage and other stamps, postal wrappers, envelopes, &c.

The vaults were once used for keeping some of the public records, now collected into one repository in Fetter Lane. Most of the wills formerly kept in Doctors' Commons are now housed here.

The whole of the east wing was left incomplete by Sir William Chambers, but in 1829 this part of the edifice was finished from the designs of Sir Robert Smirke, R.A., and it now forms King's College, which was founded by royal charter in the previous year. The entrance is a neat, though confined semi-circular archway from the Strand, over which stand the Royal Arms, supported by figures symbolical of Wisdom and Holiness, with the motto, "Sancte et Sapienter." The building extends from the Strand to the Thames, and occupies a considerable area of ground. The interior, which is very capacious, is well calculated for its intended objects. The centre of the principal floor is occupied by the chapel, under which is the hall for examinations, &c., and a new triangular wing, one storey high, built in a line with Somerset House, and fronting the Thames Embankment, adjoining the residence of the Principal, has been erected for the purposes of the college.

The government of King's College is vested in a Council, which reports annually to the Court of Governors and Proprietors, as the official title of the corporation runs. Forty-two members compose this council, nine of whom are the official governors; one is the treasurer, eight are life governors, and the other twenty-four, of whom six go out every year, are elected by the Court of Proprietors, from a list prepared by the Governors.

There are certain endowments, which are specially appropriated to certain prizes, scholarships, and professorships, classical and scientific; but the College possesses no endowment applicable to general purposes, and the whole of the expenditure required for the ordinary every-day work of the College, with the exception of a small parliamentary grant, has to be defrayed out of the fees paid by the students. The general education of the College is carried on in eight distinct departments—viz., the theological department; the department of general literature; the department of engineering; the medical department; the evening classes; the Civil Service department; the department for ladies, carried on in Kensington Square; and finally, the school. This last is in the hands of a head master, subject to consultation with the Principal, who has the general supervision of the whole College. There are five Divinity professors, namely, the Revs. R. J. Knowling (who is also Vice-Principal and Chaplain), Dr. Stanley Leathes, A. I. M'Caul, C. Hole, H. C. Shuttleworth, W. E. Collins, and Harold Smith. It should be added that the education given here is strictly in accordance with the principles of the Church of England. The grant was withdrawn by the last Liberal Government, but restored by the present Ministry.

The students of King's College are divided into two classes—the "matriculated" and the "occasional." The former are those who are admitted to the full prescribed course of study, while the latter, through inability to attend the whole course, devote themselves to the pursuit of one particular subject, as at the two great universities of England. The Principals of King's College in the forty years which have passed since its foundation have been distinguished theologians, Bishops Otter, Lonsdale, and Barry, Canon Jelf, and Dr. Wace.

CHAPTER XVI.

THE SAVOY.

"There is a power
And magic in the ruined battlement,
To which the palace of the present hour
Must yield its pomp, and wait till ages are its dower."

Early History of the Savoy Palace—John, the French King, lodged here—The Savoy attacked by the Citizens of London, and by Wat Tyler—Converted into a Hospital by Henry VII.—Assembly of the Commissioners for the Revision of the Liturgy—A Colony of Jesuits established in the Savoy—The Chapel of St. Mary—Distinguished Persons buried here—Funeral of the Earl of Bedford—The "Worshipful Company of Upholders."

A LITTLE to the west of Somerset House, on ground sloping rather steeply down to the riverside, stood what was originally the Palace, and afterwards the Hospital, of the Savoy. It was built by that all-powerful noble, Simon de Montfort, Earl of Leicester, in 1245; but in the thirtieth year of Henry III. it was granted by the king to Peter of Savoy (from whom it took its name), uncle of his queen, Eleanor of Provence, according to Pennant, "on condition of yielding yearly at the Exchequer three barbed arrows for all services." This Peter of Savoy, Earl of Savoy and of Richmond, was son of Thomas, Earl of Savoy, brother of Boniface, Archbishop of Canterbury.

From the Earl of Savoy the place passed, probably by gift, to the Brethren de Monte Jovis, that is, of the Great St. Bernard in Savoy, who had a priory at Hornchurch, in Essex; and, according to Stow, Queen Eleanor purchased the site from this fraternity and gave it to her second son, Edmund, Earl of Lancaster. This gift was confirmed by letters patent by the earl's elder brother, King Edward I., in his twenty-first year, and "from that time the Savoy was reputed and taken as parcel of the earldom and honour of Lancaster."

John, the French king, was lodged here in 1357, when brought to England as a captive by the Black Prince, after the battle of Poictiers, and here he was often visited by Edward III. and his queen. At this time it bore the reputation of being "the fairest manor in England." Six years later he returned of his own accord, and again took up his final residence at the Savoy. In Stow's "Chronicles," under the date of 1364, we find the following passage:—"The 9th day of April, died John, King of France, at the Savoy; his corpse was honourably conveyed to St. Denis, in France."

In 1377 the Savoy stood a narrow chance of being demolished by the citizens of London, who had flocked thither, "evidently bent on mischief," after the support which John of Gaunt gave to Wickliffe at a synod held in St. Paul's Cathedral. The Bishop of London, on hearing of the riot, hurried to the Savoy, and averted the danger that threatened it. But this quelling of the tumult appears to have been only temporary, for the palace of the Savoy was fired, pillaged, and almost demolished with gunpowder by a lawless mob of rebels, led by Wat Tyler, in 1381, "for the malice which they bore to John of Gaunt and his principles." And there is no doubt that they did their work thoroughly, for not only was the hall blown up and the houses destroyed, but the rebels had a narrow escape from perishing in their ruins. The leaders of the party, it appears, were so conscientious in their anger, that they gave orders that none of their men should turn anything found to their own use, but that gold, silver, and all other spoil, should be burnt. Finding, therefore, certain boxes, which they thought might contain such loot, they threw them into the flames, with the result above stated. Others of these hypocritical ruffians perished at the same time. "To the number of thirty-two," we are told, "the rebels entered a cellar of the Savoy, where they drank so much of sweet wines, that they were not able to come out in time, but were shut in with wood and stones, that walled up the doors, where they were heard crying and calling seven days after, but none came to help them out until they were dead."

Reverting to the king's hands after this, we next find it beautifully restored and rebuilt by Henry VII., who dedicated it to St. John, in 1509, as a hospital for the reception of a hundred poor people. In spite of a report made by the Royal Commissioners in the fifth year of Edward VI., to the effect that there was "no default and no disorder" to be found in its inmates, it was dissolved two years later, its revenues being seized upon by royalty. The hospital was re-founded and re-endowed by Queen Mary soon after her accession, when "the ladies of the court and maids of honour . . . . stored it anew with beds, bedding, and other furniture in a very ample manner."

The hospital, however, fared but badly under Elizabeth. It escaped, indeed, the royal claws, but it was most unfortunate in its master, who "embezzled its revenues exceedingly, and sold away divers chantries belonging to it." Happily, he was deprived.

For a number of years the Savoy Chapel served for both the neighbouring parishioners of St. Mary-le-Strand as well as for inmates of the "precinct of the Savoy."

THE SAVOY IN 1650. (*From a very scarce Etching by Hollar.*)

In the time of the plague appearing, the liberty of the Duchy of Lancaster was looked upon as "some security to the Court," to keep the unwelcome visitor from making its way thither from the City; and it was accordingly entrusted to the care of bailiffs, who were charged to ward it off. And thus Stow tells us that in the year 1577, when the plague was in the City, and the Court was removed in consequence to Windsor, the Earl of Leicester appointed a bailiff to take charge of the district, and to see that it was kept closed against infection, threatening to pluck his coat from off his back in case of his neglect. We read that the

Recorder Fleetwood, an active and a good man, lent his help to the bailiff in surveying the duchy, "passing constantly with all the constables between the Bars and the Tilt Yard, in both the liberties, to see the houses shut in." It is to be hoped that this primitive quarantine arrangement was successful in its results.

The place, too, is not without its literary associations, for Chaucer wrote some of his poems in the Savoy.

It was here that the "Confession of Faith" by the Independents was drawn up, in the time of Cromwell and his Directory.

The Savoy is also famous in connection with the history of the Church of England, having been the place in which Charles II., after the Restoration, ordered the assemblies of the Commissioners for the Revision of the Liturgy to be held. Twelve of the chief bishops of the time, with nine assisting clergymen, took part in its proceedings on behalf of the Established Church, while the Nonconformist party were represented by Baxter, Calamy, Reynolds, and other leaders of the Dissenters. The meeting is known to history as the Savoy Conference, and its results were to confirm the High Church party in the Catholic or sacramental view of the Prayer Book (which was enforced by the Act of Uniformity), and to disallow the Presbyterian scruples.

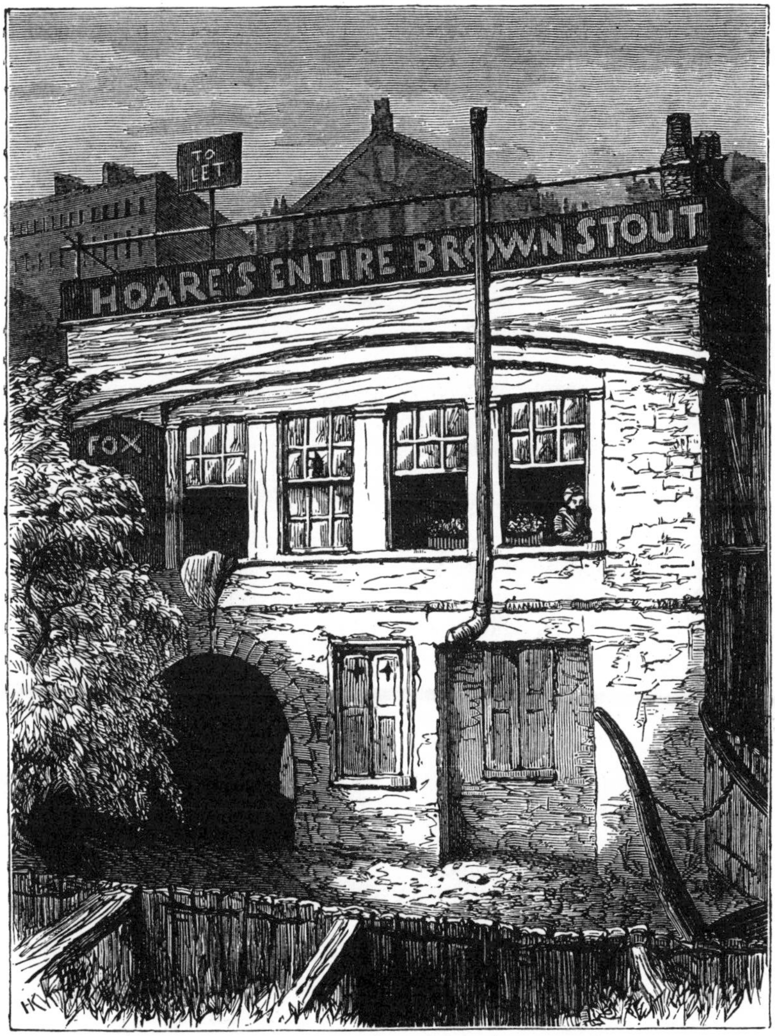

THE "FOX-UNDER-THE-HILL," 1860. (*See page* 101.)

Mr. Peter Cunningham reminds us that "at this time Fuller, author of the 'Worthies,' was Lecturer at the Savoy, and that the poet Cowley was a candidate at court for the office of Master."

The Savoy has not been exempt from sundry

vicissitudes in respect to the religion of its tenants, and at one time has given shelter to exiled Roman Catholics, and at another to Protestants driven from France by the revocation of the Edict of Nantes.

It is recorded by Roman Catholic historians that in the reign of James II. a colony of Jesuits was established in the Savoy under one F. Palmer, as rector. He opened schools which numbered some four hundred pupils, half Catholics and half Protestants; and adjoining the schools was a printing-press. Rules were provided for these schools and published in print. It was declared therein that the intention of them was to teach youth virtue and learning; that those that came thither should be taught gratis, and to be at no further charge than of buying of their own pens, ink, paper, and books; that these schools should be common to all, of what condition soever, and none to be excluded when they should be thought fit to begin to learn Latin and wrote sufficiently well. "In these schools to be taught Greek and Latin, poetry and rhetoric. And whether Catholics or Protestants came to these schools, yet in teaching no distinction to be made, yet all to be taught with equal diligence and care; and neither by masters or scholars any tampering or meddling to persuade any one from the profession of his own religion. But few there were but did believe —nay, could not believe otherwise than that this pretended charitable project was for the advantages hereby to be compassed for the promoting the Roman religion. These schools were soon dissolved upon the ceasing of the Government of King James; and the clock that was made for the use of the Savoy School was afterwards bought and set up upon a gentleman's house in Low Layton, as was said. In this Savoy were placed by William III. many families of poor French Protestants, and where they that had skill in trade and manufacture wrought to get something for their livelihood; however, they were opposed and complained of by many of the tradesmen of London as hindering and prejudicing them. Here also was, and is, a church for them. The late Bishop of London came hither himself sometimes, and passionately desired their good, and maintained many of their proselytes. The poor French here inhabiting with their families had many of them three shillings allowance weekly, and some four. To countenance them more, to this church came many of the said king's privy councillors, secretaries of state, and other great officers of the kingdom; and through them and their contributions, the church was chiefly able to subsist. They use the Liturgy of the Church of England turned into French, and their ministers are episcopally ordained."

Strype, writing in 1755, thus describes the then existing state of the Savoy :—

"This Savoy House is very great, and at this present a very ruinous building. In the midst of its buildings is a very spacious hall, the walls three feet broad at least, of stone without and brick and stone inward. The ceiling is very curiously built with wood, and having knobs in due places hanging down, and images of angels holding before their breasts coats of arms, but hardly discoverable; for one is a cross gules between four stars, or else mullets. It is covered with lead, but in divers places perished, where it lies open to the weather. This large hall is now divided into several large apartments. A cooper hath a part of it for the stowing of his hoops and for his work; other parts of it serve as two marshalseas for keeping prisoners—as deserters, men pressed for military service, Dutch recruits, &c. Towards the east end of this hall is a fair cupola with glass windows, but all broken, which makes it probable the hall was as long again, since cupolas are wont to be built about the middle of great halls.

"In the Savoy, of how ruinous soever is, are divers good houses. First, the king's printing-press, for proclamations, Acts of Parliament, gazettes, and such-like public papers; next, a prison; thirdly, a parish church and three or four other churches and places for religious assemblies, viz., for Dutch, for High Germans, and Lutherans, and lastly, for Protestant Dissenters and Quakers. Here are also harbours for many refugees and poor people."

The old hall, as stated above, had the usual louvre in the centre of the roof; this roof was of fine timber, with pendants supposed to have resembled those in Crosby Hall. Images of angels at the corbels bore on their breasts shields with coats of arms, as in the roof at Westminster Hall.

According to a map or ground-plan of the Savoy in 1736, the part between the present chapel and the river was a prison, between which and the Lutheran Church were "barracks" and some "gardens," since used as a Lutheran burying-ground. Nearer still to the river, with which it was connected by a "water-gate," was the chapel of the German Calvinists, so that two different sets of doctrines were being taught by German preachers almost within earshot of each other. To the east stood the ancient hospital of St. John, then used as "barracks," divided from the Lutheran

Church by some "officers' houses" and "the Friery." Between this and the Strand again were gardens, and two houses, the one occupied by "Nutt, the printer," and the other marked "Vaillant, bookseller, his warehouse."

Nearly where now are Wellington Street South and Lancaster Buildings, were a "French Church," a small close known as "Green Tree Court," and sundry dwellings, some of them marked as "Dutchy Houses."

Prints of the remains of the Savoy in 1793 and 1798 show a few of the walls of the Hospital of St. John the Baptist still standing. They were, apparently, of the Tudor, or latest Gothic style, as was also the "prison," which has a fine Perpendicular entrance, and oriel window above it. At the foot of the print is a statement to the effect that "this part of the Savoy is now occupied by the army as a place of confinement for their deserters and transports."

Henry VII. helped to rebuild the Savoy, as a hospital for a hundred distressed people. This building was in the form of a cross, and Pennant adds that its walls were entire down to his time (1806). The Records of the Duchy of Lancaster were formerly kept in a building close by, in Lancaster Place.

A considerable part of the old Savoy was standing at the beginning of the present century; but it was demolished to form the approach to Waterloo Bridge.

The present "Chapel of St. Mary in the Hospital, or of St. John the Baptist in the Savoy"—for it rejoices in the double name—is of early sixteenth century date. Its interior was burnt in 1864, but subsequently restored in the ancient style, at the cost of Her Majesty the Queen, under the superintendence of Mr. Sydney Smirke. It is small, but well-proportioned, consisting of a nave without aisles or chancel.

It has a rich reredos over the altar, which faces the north, having niches with domed canopies at either extremity. The window over the altar is of five lights, with vertical mullions of the Perpendicular or Tudor style. There are two sedilia, with a piscina between them and the east, or rather, north wall; the oak roof is coved at the sides, and divided with quatrefoil panels, showing the emblems of the Passion, the sacred monogram, the Lamb and Flag, the pelican in her piety, the types of St. John the Baptist, and sundry heraldic ornaments. It is richly painted throughout, and the prevailing colour is blue. Among the "memorial" windows that have been inserted is one to the Prince Consort, placed here by the Queen, in her capacity as Duchess of Lancaster and patroness of the living.

In the Savoy Chapel were buried many famous personages; among others, Gavin Douglas, the poet-Bishop of Dunkeld, son of Archibald "Bell the Cat," Earl of Angus. The reader of Scott's "Marmion" will remember how, at the wedding of De Wilton and Clare—

> "A bishop at the altar stood—
> A noble lord of Douglas blood;"

and he will be glad to learn that in the Savoy he "sleeps the sleep that knows not waking." Here, too, was buried, at his own request, Christopher Davenport, better known as Franciscus à Sanctâ Clarâ, who translated from the Portuguese the "Chronicles of the Franciscan Order," and who "reconciled Anne, Duchess of York, to the church which her husband had joined."

Among the persons who have either been buried or had monuments erected to them here are Mrs. Killigrew, the actress, daughter of Dr. Killigrew, one of the Masters of the Savoy; George, third Earl of Cumberland, of the old line of Clifford; Richard Lander, the African traveller; George Wither, the poet and satirist; and the Earl of Feversham, who commanded King James's troops at Sedgemoor. In the burial-ground attached to the church is the tomb of William Hilton, many years Keeper of the Royal Academy.

The precinct of the Savoy was made into a parish by Bishop Grindal, in the reign of Elizabeth, when the Protector Somerset demolished the old Church of St. Mary, to make room for his new palace, and it is probably the smallest parish in the metropolis or its suburbs west of Temple Bar.

A very distinguished man became the Master of the Savoy in the reign of James I. We refer to Antonio de Dominis, ex-Archbishop of Spalatro, who, adopting strong anti-papal tenets, came to England, where he published a learned treatise, "De Republicâ Ecclesiasticâ," and was ultimately made Dean of Windsor. He was a Master also of Natural Philosophy. He does not, however, lie buried here, as late in life he went to Rome, in order to make his peace with the Church which he had left.

Machyn, in his "Diary," records the burial, in 1554, of the Earl of Bedford, Lord Privy Seal, who died "at his house beside the Savoy," and was carried thence to his home at Chenies for interment. His funeral procession, as it started hence, must have been a splendid sight. He was carried with three crosses before him, and many clerks and priests in attendance, "till they came to the hill above St. James's, when some turned back.

All were mounted on horseback. First, there rode one in black bearing a silver cross; then came priests in surplices; then came the standard; then the gentlemen and chief officers; then the heralds, with the helmet, mantle, and crest, the armour and insignia; then came the funeral car with painted banners; then the saddle-horse; then the mourners, chief of them Lord Russell's son; then the Lord Treasurer, the Master of the Horse, and various members of the nobility, all clad in black. Everywhere on the course of the procession the clergy came forth to meet it, and alms were distributed among the poor."

In speaking of the parish of St. Mary-in-the-Savoy, the *London Spy*, published in 1725, says that it was the head-quarters of "the Worshipful Company of Upholders," meaning the undertakers; and the writer adds a graduated scale of fees paid by those black-coated and keen-eyed gentry to coachmen, footmen, and other persons in positions where news travels quickly, for ready information as to the deaths, actual or approaching, of titled and wealthy personages.

A number of dingy coal-wharves was all that, during the first half of the present century, and, indeed, until the formation of the Thames Embankment, stood by the river-side to mark the site of a palace which had been the residence of John of Gaunt, Duke of Lancaster, and of the poet Chaucer. Some lofty buildings, including an hotel and the Medical Examination Hall, have been erected on their site, and between the Savoy and the Embankment now is a garden, where shrubs and flowers delight the eye of the weary Londoner.

CHAPTER XVII.

THE STRAND:—SOUTHERN TRIBUTARIES (*continued*).

"Here Essex' stately pile adorned the shore;
There Cecil's, Bedford's, Villiers'—now no more."—*Gay.*

Beaufort Buildings—Fielding, the Novelist—Worcester House—Carey House—The "Fox-under-the-Hill"—Beaufort House—Salisbury House—The Middle Exchange—Cecil Street—The Arundel Club—Ivy Bridge Lane—Durham House—The New Exchange—The Duchess of Tyrconnel, the "White Milliner"—A Singular Tragedy and Curious *Dénouement*—Coutts's Bank—The Adelphi—Garrick's House—The "Shades"—The Society of Arts—Buckingham Street—York Stairs—Buckingham Water Gate—Villiers Street.

PROCEEDING still westward on our pilgrimage along the Strand, we next arrive at Beaufort Buildings, where in the last century resided Fielding, the novelist, of whom an interesting anecdote is told in the *Gentleman's Magazine* for 1786:—"Some parochial taxes for his house in Beaufort Buildings being unpaid, and for which he had been demanded again and again, or, in the vulgar phrase, dunned *de die in diem*, he was at last given to understand by the collector, who had an esteem for him, that he could delay the payment no longer. In this dilemma the author of 'Tom Jones' called a council of his thoughts to whom he should apply for a temporary accommodation, on the pledge of the embryos of his own brain. Jacob Tonson was his usual resource on these occasions. To him, therefore, he addressed himself, and mortgaged the coming sheets of some work then in hand. He received the cash—some ten or twelve guineas. Full freighted with this sum, he was returning home, when lo! fate, in the guise of friendship, had determined to intercept him in his passage, and to prevent him reaching his destination with his pecuniary cargo. When within a few doors of his own house he met an old college chum, whom he had not seen for many years, and finding he had been unfortunate in life, gave him all the money he had just received. On reaching home he was informed that the collector had called twice for the taxes. Fielding's reply was laconic, but memorable:—'Friendship has called for the money and had it; let the collector call again!" The reader will be glad to hear that a second application to Jacob Tonson enabled him to satisfy the parish demands." At the corner house, No. 96, Strand, now occupied by Eugene Rimmel, the perfumer, formerly lived another of the same profession, Charles Lillie, whom Steele has commemorated in the pages of the *Tatler*, and whose name is also embalmed in the *Spectator*.

On the site of Beaufort Buildings, between the Savoy and Durham Place, stood Worcester House, the town mansion of the Earls of Worcester, and previously the residence of the Bishops of Carlisle. Its gardens extended to the river-side. The great Earl of Clarendon occupied this house before his own mansion was built, paying for it the annual rent of £500.

In the Strand, near the Savoy, was a house known as Carey and afterwards as Stafford House.

It is casually mentioned by Pepys as "a house now of entertainment, next my Lady Ashly's, where I have heretofore heard Common Prayer read." Dryden, too, in his "Wild Gallant," speaks with evident delight of "the sack at Cary House with the apricot flavour." We must also mention another house of some repute which stood close by this spot down to a recent date, namely, the tavern known as the "Fox-under-the-Hill," the entrance to which was at No. 75 in the Strand. This inn was shut up after the erection of the Victoria Embankment, and, along with the rest of the dilapidated tenements between the Savoy, the Adelphi, and the Embankment Garden, has since been swept away. We have preserved a representation of the old inn on page 97.

Concerning the old house of the Earls of Worcester, afterwards called Beaufort House, honest John Stow tells a story to the effect that "there being a very large walnut-tree growing in the garden, which much obstructed the eastern prospect of Salisbury House, near adjoining, it was proposed to the Earl of Worcester's gardener, by the Earl of Salisbury or his agent, that if he could prevail with his lord to cut down the said tree, he should have £100. The offer was told to the Earl of Worcester, who ordered him to do it and to take the £100; both which were performed to the great satisfaction of the Earl of Salisbury, as he thought; but, there being no great kindness between the two earls, the Earl of Worcester soon caused to be built in the place of the walnut-tree a large house of brick, which took away all his prospect." The house was burnt down in 1695.

The building adjoining, Salisbury House, gave place to Cecil Street and Salisbury Street, the latter of which, before the construction of the Thames Embankment, led to Salisbury Stairs. Salisbury House—or, as it was sometimes called, Cecil House—was built by Robert Cecil, first Earl of Salisbury, a son of the great Lord Burghley, and was a "large and stately" mansion. In 1678 a great part of it was pulled down, and Cecil and Salisbury Streets were built on its site. A portion of Cecil House, consisting of one large room, was subsequently fitted up with shops on both sides, and opened as "the Middle Exchange." This building extended to the river, where there was a flight of steps for the use of passengers by water. The place seems to have borne anything but a good reputation—being called the "Whore's nest"—and in the end going to ruin it was pulled down, with the remains of great Salisbury House, about the year 1696. Upon the site was built Cecil Street, of which Strype speaks as a "fair street with very good houses, fit for persons of repute," so that it is to be hoped that the former tenants of the "nest" were put to flight.

Of Cecil Street we have little or nothing to remark, as its annals appear to be a blank of late years, except that in the last century it was inhabited by the Lord Grey, the Archbishop of York, and Dr. Wollaston, and both it and Salisbury Street are now nothing but approaches to the Hôtel Cecil.

At the bottom of Salisbury Street, on the left hand, in a house swept away to make way for the hotel, had been established, since 1865, the Arundel Club, so called from its original abode in Arundel Street, and now housed in Adelphi Terrace. It consists mainly of literary men and artists. One of its possessions is a fine portrait of Marinarni, many years scene-painter at Drury Lane, painted by the late Mr. Clarkson Stanfield, R.A., and presented to the club by his son, Mr. G. C. Stanfield.

The next turning westwards of Salisbury Street, down to what once was the river-side, was called Ivy Lane, leading to Ivy Bridge, or Pier—the same which in our own memories was used as the landing-stage of the halfpenny steamboats that used to ply between the Strand and London Bridge, but was discontinued shortly after the disastrous explosion of the *Cricket* at the "Fox" pier (so called after the "Fox-under-the-Hill" tavern), in August, 1847. The place is mentioned by both Stow and Strype. The former says that the lane "parted the Liberty of the Duchy (of Lancaster) and the city of Westminster on the south side," and that the "bridge" had been lately taken down. Strype adds that the road was very bad and almost impassable.

Near this spot, Pennant tells us, the former Earls of Rutland had "a house at which several of that noble family breathed their last." He does not, however, say anything which can enable us to identify its situation.

Adjoining Ivy Bridge Lane on the west was Durham House, the "Inn" of the Bishops of Durham, one of the most interesting of the old Strand palaces. According to Pennant, its original founder was Anthony de Beck, Patriarch of Jerusalem and Bishop of Durham in the reign of Edward I. It was rebuilt by Thomas Hatfield, soon after his nomination to that see, in 1345; he was Secretary of State to Edward III., and lived here till he was old. Even from the rough sketch of it in Aggas's map, Durham House would seem to have been an "Inn" of some importance; but from Hollar we gather a more correct idea of its appearance, when viewed from the river. It is described by Norden as "high and stately, supported with lofty marble pillars;" but it would appear to have been dull and heavy, as well as grand, like many of its neighbours on the banks of the river. Henry VIII. obtained this house by way of exchange from Cuthbert Tonstall, the bishop whose name is so well known in English history. It is to be hoped that in this case the "exchange" was not really a "robbery." Durham House, after it passed out of the hands of the Church into those of royalty, became celebrated as a gay scene of chivalric entertainment on many occasions. In the year 1540, for example, as Stow informs us, a magnificent tournament was held at Westminster. It had been proclaimed in France, Flanders, Scotland, and Spain, for all comers that would undertake the challenge of England, which were Sir John Dudley, Sir Thomas Seymour, Sir Thomas Poynings, and Sir George Carew, Knights, and Anthony Kingston and Richard Cromwell, Esquires. The old chronicler then gives a vivid picture of the tournament in detail, and adds, "That day, after the jousts performed, the challengers rode into Durham House, where they kept open household, and feasted the king and queen, with their ladies and all the court." On one day the Lord Mayor of London and the aldermen, with their wives, were entertained with a display of jousting, and there was a merry dance in the evening.

IVY BRIDGE LANE, 1860. (*See page* 101.)

YORK STAIRS AND THE WATER TOWER. *From a Print dated* 1780. (*See page* 108.)

Young Edward, on reaching the throne, gave Durham House to his sister, the Princess Elizabeth, and she in her turn, when she became queen, bestowed it on Sir Walter Raleigh. On his attainder, however, the property was restored to the Bishops of Durham, but soon after sold to the Earl of Pembroke. In Edward's reign a royal mint was established at Durham House, under the direction of the Lord High Admiral Seymour. It was at Durham House that, in May, 1553, the Duke of Northumberland, who then inhabited it, beheld the accomplishment of the first act of his plan for placing his niece, Lady Jane Grey, upon the throne—namely, her marriage with his son, Lord Guildford Dudley. Two months later, and within four days of the death of the king, the Lady Jane was conducted from Durham House to the Tower with great pomp and ceremony, and openly proclaimed queen. The result is but too well known to every reader of English history.

In the reign of James I. the thatched stables of the mansion, fronting the Strand, were pulled down, and a large building, called the "New Exchange," erected in their place. It was opened in 1609 in the presence of the king, the queen, and Prince Henry, when his Majesty bestowed upon it the name of "Britain's Burse." A rich banquet was served on the occasion, at the expense of Lord Salisbury.

The New Exchange consisted of a basement, in which were cellars; the ground-floor, level with the street, a public walk; and an upper storey, in which were stalls or shops occupied by milliners and sempstresses, and other trades that supply dresses. The building did not attain any great success till after the Restoration, when it became quite a fashionable resort, and so popular that there is scarcely a dramatist of the time of Charles II. who is without a reference to this gay place. The shops, or stalls, had their respective signs, one of which, the "Three Spanish Gipsies," was kept by Thomas Radford and his wife, the daughter of John Clarges, a farrier in the Savoy. The farrier's daughter, as we have stated in a previous chapter, ultimately became Duchess of Albemarle. She died within a few days of the duke, and was buried by his side in Henry VII.'s Chapel, at Westminster Abbey.

But she was by no means the only duchess associated with the New Exchange. The Duchess of Tyrconnel, wife of Richard Talbot, Lord Deputy of Ireland under James II., after the abdication of the one and the death of the other, is said to have supported herself for a short time in one of the trades of the place; and she is commemorated by Horace Walpole with his usual piquancy. Pennant speaks of her as "a female suspected to have been his duchess," adding that she "supported herself here for a few days, till she was known and, otherwise provided for, by the trade of the place, for she had delicacy enough to wish not to be detected." She sat in a white mask and a white dress, and was known as the "White Milliner." This anecdote was dramatised by Douglas Jerrold, and produced at Covent Garden Theatre in 1840, as "The White Milliner." She died in 1730 in the Convent of the Poor Clares in Dublin.

It was here, too, that a certain Mr. Gerard was walking one day, meditating how he should best carry into execution a certain plot in which he was engaged—the assassination of no less a person than Oliver Cromwell—when he was insulted by Don Pantaleon, brother of the Portuguese ambassador, and resented it so warmly that the latter, in revenge, the next day sent a set of ruffians to murder him. His murderers mistook their victim, and killed another man. The *dénouement* is curious, as well as tragical. Don Pantaleon was tried, found guilty, and condemned. On the scaffold he met the very man whom he had intended to destroy, Mr. Gerard, whose plot in the interim had been discovered, and the two suffered in company.

The New Exchange was a long building running parallel with the Strand, and its site is now occupied by the houses Nos. 54 to 64, the bank of Messrs. Coutts being the centre. It stands on the court garden front of Durham House, and, next to Drummond's, is the oldest of the West-end banks. It was founded by one George Middleton, and originally stood in St. Martin's Lane, not far from St. Martin's Church, but was removed to its present site by Mr. Thomas Coutts, an enterprising Scotchman, the story of whose rise is thus narrated:—His father was a merchant at Edinburgh, who had four sons, the two youngest of whom, James and Thomas, were brought up in the paternal counting-house. James, at the age of twenty-five, came to London, and first settled in St. Mary Axe, as a Scotch merchant, but from that business, however, he subsequently retired to become a banker. He took a house in the Strand, the same in which the firm still exists; and he was joined here, some years after, by his brother Thomas, as a partner. On the death of James soon afterwards, Thomas continued to carry on the banking business, and with such an energetic spirit, that he soon gained many friends, and found himself on the sure road to success. Mr. Lawson, in his "History of Banking," tells a story concerning Mr. Coutts' shrewdness and enterprise which will bear repeating:—"In the early part of his career Mr. Coutts, anxious to secure the cordial co-operation of the heads of the various banking-houses in London, was in the habit of frequently inviting them to dinner. On one of these occasions, the manager of a City bank, in retailing the news of the day, accidentally remarked that a certain nobleman had applied to his firm for the loan of £30,000, and had been refused. Mr. Coutts listened, and said nothing; but the moment his guests had retired, about ten o'clock in the evening, he started off to the house of the nobleman mentioned, and requested the honour of an interview with his lordship the next day. On the following morning the nobleman called at the bank. Mr. Coutts received him with the greatest politeness, and taking thirty one-thousand pound notes from a drawer presented them to his lordship. The latter, very agreeably surprised, exclaimed, 'But what security am I to give you?' 'I shall be satisfied with your lordship's note of hand,' was the reply. The 'I.O.U.' was instantly given, with the remark, 'I find I shall only require for the present £10,000; I therefore return you £20,000, with which you will be pleased to open an account in my name.' This generous—or, as it may more truly be called, exceedingly well-calculated—act of Mr. Coutts was not lost upon the nobleman, who, in addition to paying in within a few months £200,000 to his account, the produce of the sale of an estate, recommended several high personages to patronise the bank in the Strand. Among new clients who opened accounts there was King George III." Most members of the king's family, the late Duke of Wellington, &c., banked here, and so did Dr. Johnson and Sir Walter Scott.

Mr. Coutts had not only many friends, but even real admirers, among the nobility, and he is said to have been an object of attraction to not a few designing matrons, who had marriageable daughters. But all these aristocratic matrimonial speculations were somewhat rudely dispelled and frustrated, and Mr. Coutts in the end "took unto himself a wife," in the person of one Elizabeth Starkey, a domestic in his brother's service. The union, it is affirmed, was productive of great happiness to the banker, and he was blessed with three daughters, each of whom became married to men of title—namely, the Marquis of Bute, the Earl of Guildford, and Sir Francis Burdett, Bart. After the death of his first wife, Mr. Coutts gave his hand to Miss Harriet Mellon, the celebrated actress. On this second marriage, both Mr. and Mrs. Coutts were made the constant subjects of unworthy ridicule, which, however, had no other effect than that of strengthening the confidence of the husband in his wife, a confidence which was displayed in a remarkable manner in the will made by Mr. Coutts shortly before his death, which happened in 1821. By this will he left the whole of his fortune, amounting to some £900,000, to his widow, "for her sole use and benefit, and at her absolute disposal, without the deduction of a single legacy to any other person." Mrs. Coutts subsequently (1827) married the Duke of St. Albans; but under the marriage settlement wisely reserved to herself the whole control of the immense fortune left to her by her first husband. On her death, in 1837, she bequeathed her vast property to the favourite granddaughter of Mr. Coutts, Miss Angela Burdett, the youngest daughter of Sir Francis Burdett, the estimable and beneficent lady, founder of so many churches, schools, and other buildings for ameliorating the condition of the working classes, on whom the Queen has been pleased to confer the title of Baroness, and who is now well known as Lady Burdett Coutts.

The partners in "Coutts and Co." (1897) are Messrs. William M. Coulthurst, G. J. Marjoribanks, Hugh L. Antrobus, W. Rolle Malcolm, the Hon. H. Dudley Ryder, J. H. Dudley Ryder, F. J. W. Farquhar, Lord Archibald Campbell, the Hon. W. F. D. Smith, and the Baroness Burdett Coutts. It is supposed that Messrs. Coutts' is the largest private bank, and has the most extensive connection among the nobility and landed gentry of any existing firm.

We learn from Mr. Peter Cunningham's "Hand-Book of London," that the interior of the house occupied by Messrs. Coutts is very handsome and well decorated, containing, *inter alia*, some "good marble chimney-pieces of the Bacon and Cipriani school." He adds: "The dining-room is hung with Chinese subjects on paper, sent to Mr. Coutts by Lord Macartney, whilst on his embassy to China, in 1792-5. In another room is a collection of portraits of the early friends of the wealthy banker, including the portrait of Armstrong, the early poet, by Sir Joshua Reynolds. The strong rooms and vaults of the house will repay an endeavour to obtain a sight of them. Here, in a succession of cloister-like avenues, are stored, in boxes of all shapes, sizes, and colours, the patents, title-deeds, plate, &c., of many of the nobility and gentry; and the order in which the place is kept is perfectly wondrous."

The estate of Durham Yard, having become an unprofitable heap of ruin, was purchased by Messrs. Adam, four brothers, architects by profession, who built upon it, in 1768, parallel with the river, the noble terrace known as the Adelphi, and also two or three streets running at right angles with it, and communicating with the Strand, in which they have preserved their respective Christian names, as well as family name—as Adam Street, John Street, Robert Street, &c.

The following account of the brothers Adam we take from "Pilgrimages in London:"—

"Robert Adam was the eldest brother; he had travelled much, had visited Palmyra and Baalbec, and in all his architectural works there is a peculiar style, which displays itself in the ornamental portions of the Adelphi buildings—the introduction of an exuberance of delicate ornament. Scotchmen are proverbially fond of their country, and the immense building speculations into which the Messrs. Adam had entered afforded them an opportunity of giving employment to their countrymen, as well as of obtaining their services, when engaged in Scotland, at a lower rate of wages than was demanded by English bricklayers and labourers. Some hundreds were, therefore, imported from Scotland, and came attended by half-a-dozen bagpipes, for the purpose, as was asserted, of keeping up the national feeling. These pipers played daily while the embankments were formed and the foundations laid; and as the sweet chords of the classic lyre of Orpheus are said to have moved inanimate objects, so arose the Adelphi to the squeak of the Scotch bagpipes. But the charms of music to soothe the savage breast were, in this instance, vainly tried, as the workmen soon discovered that they were paid less than the London market price of their labour, and they consequently very speedily relinquished what they called "the curse of Adam," for more pay and less work, as an extra hour had been stipulated for. What was to be done? The undertaking could not be allowed to stand still, but it was impossible to comply with the advance of wages and the diminution of time demanded. In this state of things Ireland was thought of, and a similar bargain to that which had been made in Scotland was made there, with the exception of the bagpipers whose national melodies had produced so little harmony. It was this importation from Ireland, I believe, that first opened the channel for the export of labourers and hodmen to England, and which stream of emigration has flowed regularly from the same source down to the present hour. But as nothing of importance long remains secret, the Irishmen, although satisfied to abide by their bargain of hard work and small pay, felt displeased that they had been deprived of the music enjoyed by their predecessors, and vented their humour in a coarse joke, upon which I have remarked that Scotchmen of all ranks are, even to the present moment, peculiarly sensitive; for Pat, with a knowing wink of his eye, asserted that if his employers had deprived him of the drone of the bagpipes by day, their honours had given him instead, both day and night, the lively amusement of the fiddle."

We ought not, and indeed we cannot forget to record here the fact that in the centre house of Adelphi Terrace died, in 1779, no less a man of note than David Garrick, within a few hundred yards from the scene of his professional triumphs. He had been an inmate of it for the last seven years of his life. The house, marked by one of the tablets of the Society of Arts, is now occupied by the Institute of Naval Architects. In the same street lived Topham Beauclerk, the wit, politician, and friend of Johnson.

The author of "Haunted London" tells us an interesting story connected with this part of the Strand. "When the Adelphi was building, Garrick applied for the western corner house of Adam Street on behalf of his friend, Andrew Beckett, the bookseller, and obtained it, promising the brothers, if the request were granted, to make the shop, as old Jacob Tonson's shop once was, the rendezvous of the first people in London." At Osborne's Hotel in the Adelphi, the King and Queen of the Sandwich Islands resided during their visit to this country in 1824. They both died during their sojourn in London in July of that year, and were buried in the vaults under St. Martin's Church.

Garrick died in the back room of the first floor of his house in the Adelphi. The ceiling of the drawing-room, if we may believe Mr. J. T. Smith, the author of "A Book for a Rainy Day," was painted by Zocchi, the subject being "Venus attired by the Graces;" and the chimney-piece of the same room is said to have cost £800.

Mr. Timbs remarks that "the Adelphi arches, many of which are used for cellars and coal-wharves, remind us, in their grim vastness, of the Etruscan cloaca of ancient Rome. Beneath the 'dark arches,' as they were (and are) called, the most abandoned characters used to lurk; outcasts and vagrants came there to sleep; and many a street-thief escaped from his pursuers in those subterranean haunts, before the introduction of gas-lights and a vigilant police. Even now tramps prowl in a ghastly manner down the dim-lit passages." The piers on which the Adelphi arches rest having shown symptoms of insecurity, the whole of the structure was gradually underpinned, and otherwise strengthened, in the years 1872–4.

The 'Shades"—or, as the place was called in slang terms, the "Darkies"—was in former days one of the places of bad reputation with which the neighbourhood abounded; but the name and the reality have both passed away.

In John Street, at No. 18, is the building designed and erected for the Society of Arts. This society has a history of its own, and has not been without its influence on the world of art and science in England. It originated, in 1753, through the public spirit of William Shipley, a drawing-master, and brother to the then Bishop of St. Asaph. Mr. Shipley first obtained the approval and concurrence of Lord Folkestone, Lord Romney, the Bishop of Worcester, Dr. Isaac Maddox, and a few other friends, and in 1754 the first meeting was held at Rawthmell's Coffee House. Its meetings were afterwards held in Crane Court, Fleet Street; next in Craig's Court, Charing Cross; and subsequently in a house in the Strand, opposite Beaufort Buildings. In 1774 the Society took up its quarters in the building it now occupies. The object of the society was the encouragement of art in connection with manufacture, &c. In 1755 the society met at Peel's Coffee House. The Royal Academy is said to have sprung from the Society of Arts, and in 1776 the latter proposed to the Academy—which had been instituted in 1768—that they should paint the great council-room at the Adelphi, and be remunerated by the public exhibition of their works therein. The Academy, with Sir Joshua Reynolds at its head, refused this proposal; but in the following year James Barry, who had signed the refusal with the rest, volunteered to decorate the room without any remuneration at all. His offer was accepted, and the result was the production of six great pictures, which occupied him seven years in painting. The subjects are so connected as to illustrate this great maxim of moral truth: "That the attainment of happiness, individual as well as public, depends on the cultivation of the human faculties."

There are here a few other pictures and minor works of art and ingenuity, and they are open to the inspection of the public, free of charge, from ten till four, every week-day except Wednesday and Saturday. It is worthy of note that in 1844 Sir William Fothergill Cooke, who was at that time a member of the Council, and Vice-President of the Society of Arts, originated at a council-meeting his scheme for an International Exhibition of Industry, which was eventually carried out in 1851. In the same street, No. 14, are the headquarters of the Royal National Lifeboat Institution, founded in 1824.

Buckingham Street, our next turning in passing westward along the Strand, and Villiers Street, a thoroughfare running parallel with it, mark the site of York House, a building so named from having been the town residence of the Archbishop of that see, after the fall of Wolsey and the loss of their former and more magnificent palace at Whitehall, which has passed irrevocably into the hands of the Crown. It had been in ancient times the house or "inn," as it was termed, of the Bishops of Norwich, who, however, exchanged it for an abbey in Norfolk in the early part of the reign of Henry VIII. The next owner, Charles Brandon, Duke of Suffolk, obtained it in exchange for his own residence, Southwark House, across the river. In the reign of Queen Mary it was purchased by Heath, Archbishop of York, who called it York House; but the name did not long continue, as his successor, Archbishop Matthew, under James I., exchanged it with the Crown for certain manors in the far North. It was afterwards inhabited by Lord Chancellor Egerton, also by Sir Nicholas Bacon, the philosopher's father, as Keeper of the Great Seal; and subsequently by Bacon himself, on his attaining the dignity of Lord Chancellor, and it was here that he was deprived of the "Great Seal," on his degradation. York House then passed, as we have said, into the hands of the Crown, and was granted a few years later to George Villiers, Duke of Buckingham, who rebuilt it in a style of great magnificence. In the year after the execution of Charles I. the Parliament bestowed it on General Fairfax, whose daughter and heiress marrying Villiers, the second Duke of Buckingham of that line, it reverted to its rightful owner, who resided here for several years after the Restoration. He was, however, a man whose taste and extravagances led him into pecuniary difficulties, and to pay his debts he sold it for building purposes, bargaining, however, that his name and titles should be kept in memory by the streets built upon it, and which were called, respectively, George, Villiers, Duke, and Buckingham Streets. These are all that now remain to tell the antiquary of the nineteenth century the story of George Villiers, Duke of Buckingham, his rise at Court, and his fall.

His mansion never lost its name of York House, and the water-gate at the foot of Buckingham Street continued to be known as "York Stairs." The water-gate is the only vestige now remaining of this once splendid mansion.

On the side next the river appear the arms of the House of Villiers, and on the north side is their family motto, "Fidei Coticula Crux" (the Cross is the Touchstone of Faith).

At York House, within a few yards of the spot

where he first saw the light, Bacon kept his sixtieth birthday. How much he loved the place may be gathered from his answer to the Duke of Lennox, who had urged him to sell his mansion. "In this you will pardon me: York House is the house where my father died, and where I drew my first breath; and there I will yield my last breath, if it so please God and the King." He did not, however, return to the house after his imprisonment in the Tower.

The old mansion was pulled down, as we have de Bologna's "Cain and Abel." The "superstitious" pictures were sold by order of the Parliament in 1645, and the house was given by Cromwell to General Fairfax, by the marriage of whose daughter and heiress with George, second Duke of Buckingham, as we have already said, it was re-conveyed to the Villiers family. The duke resided here for a time, but in 1672 he sold the estate for £30,000.

Not far from the gate stood formerly a high and not very shapely tower of wood, erected in 1690–5,

BUCKINGHAM GATE IN 1830.

already noticed, by the Duke of Buckingham, who erected in its place a modern fashionable residence, the state apartments of which were fitted up with large mirrors, and other costly pieces of luxury. Between the house and the river he carried a long terrace with an embattled wall, in the middle of which was the water-gate above mentioned. After the duke's death, in the year 1628, York House was let on lease to the Earl of Northumberland. "Here was," says Mr. Timbs, "a fine collection of paintings, among which is supposed to have been the lost portrait of Prince Charles, by Velasquez." Here also was the collection of sculptures which belonged to Rubens, and in the garden was John for supplying the Strand and its neighbourhood with the water of the then silvery Thames. Happily both the tower and the water-works, and also the water so supplied, have long been things of the past. In a print published in 1780, representing York Stairs and the Water-gate, the wooden tower of the water-works close by is shown. It was an octangular structure about seventy feet high, with small round loopholes as windows, to light the interior.

The two houses at the bottom of Buckingham Street, facing the river, have each an association of its own with the past. That on the west side was the residence of Samuel Pepys, from whose amusing

"Diary" we have drawn so largely; but it has been entirely remodelled, if not rebuilt, since his time. At the last house, on the opposite side of the street, lived Peter the Great during part of his stay in this country. And among the other celebrated persons who have made Buckingham Street their home, for a time at least, are the witty Earl of Dorset, Robert Harley, Earl of Oxford, John Henderson, the actor, and William Etty, the painter. The latter lived at No. 14, occupying chambers Sir Richard Steele for the first two or three years after the loss of his wife in 1721.

Mr. Timbs identifies the site of the house in which Bacon was born with that of No. 31, in the Strand, at the west corner of Villiers Street. It was for many years the shop of Messrs. Roake and Varty, and contained a portion of the old ceiling of the house once inhabited by Bacon. The house was pulled down in 1863 to form the approach to the railway station.

EXETER CHANGE IN 1826. (*See page* 116.)

and a studio at the top of the house, from 1826 down to a few months before his death in 1849. In the lower rooms of the same house Mr. Clarkson Stanfield had chambers, when commencing his career as a scene-painter, and before he became known by his noble sea-pieces. At Hampton Court there is a very good view of Buckingham Street, taken from the river, about the year 1756, which shows the houses of Peter the Great and Pepys.

In Villiers Street John Evelyn was living in 1683–4, as he tells us in his "Diary." "I took a house in Villiers Street, York Buildings, for the winter, having many important causes to dispatch, and for the education of my daughters." Here, too, as Mr. Peter Cunningham reminds us, lived

"In former times," writes Allen, in his "History of London," "the banks of the Thames, from Whitehall to Somerset House, were ornamented with numerous palaces of the nobility, many consisting of two and three courts, and fitted up in the most sumptuous manner. Even as late as the time of Edward VI. elegant gardens, protected by lofty walls, embellished the margin of our great river, from Privy Bridge to Baynard's Hall. The gardens appended to the sumptuous buildings of the Savoy, and York, Paget, and Arundel Palaces." Each intervening spot was still guarded by a wall, and frequently laid out in decorative walks, a most pleasing contrast to the present state of the same district. On the Strand side of the original

Somerset Place the lapse of two centuries has worked wonders in improvement. There was no continued street here till about the year 1553. The side next the Thames then consisted of distinct mansions, screened from the vulgar eye by cheerless extensions of massive brick wall. The north side was formed by a thin row of detached houses, each of which possessed a garden, and all beyond was country. St. Giles's was a distant country hamlet.

It was on account of these numerous palatial residences, no doubt, and not on account of the magnificence of its shops, that Middleton, the dramatist, styles the Strand "luxurious." These, it would seem, were, for the most part, far from being "luxurious," consisting mainly of fishmongers' stalls and sheds, against the erection of which the authorities were often forced to protest, and sometimes to take even stronger measures. For instance, Howes writes: "For divers years of late certain fishmongers have erected and set up fish-stalls in the middle of the street in the Strand, almost over against Denmark House; all which were broken down by special commission this month of May, 1630, lest in a short space they might grow from stalls into sheds, and then to dwelling-houses."

It has been often remarked that out of the mansions which lay crowded between the Strand and the Thames, a very large number appear to have belonged to prelates of the Church in proportion to those of the titled aristocracy—the Howards and the Cecils. And if a reason is asked, it may be found in the "Table Talk" of John Selden, who observes that "anciently the noblemen lay within the City for safety and security, but the bishops' houses were by the water-side, because they were held to be sacred persons whom nobody would hurt." In consequence, we are told by Mr. Peter Cunningham as many as nine bishops possessed inns or hostelries in this district previous to the Reformation.

As an instance of the insecurity of life—for the laity, at least—in the neighbourhood of the Strand, in the reign of George I., we take the following from a newspaper of the year 1720:—"Last night a gentlewoman returning late from the Court at St. James's, was stopped a little before she came to her lodgings, in Cecil Street, in the Strand, by one Captain Fitzgerald, who would have taken her out of her chair by force; but upon her making an outcry, the chairmen were about to pull out the poles, in order to secure her from his violence; which seeing, the captain drew his sword, and sheathed it in the body of an unfortunate watchman, just come to their assistance, who instantly dropped down dead. The captain was secured for that night in St. Martin's Roundhouse, and the next day committed to the Gatehouse."

CHAPTER XVIII.

THE STRAND:—NORTHERN TRIBUTARIES.

"Where Catherine Street descends into the Strand."—*Gay.*

Catherine Street—Derivation of its Name—The *Morning Chronicle* and Mr. John Black—Wimbledon House—D'Oyley's Warehouse—Exeter Street—Exeter Arcade—The Strand Music Hall—The Gaiety—The *Morning Post*—Exeter House, and Visit of Queen Elizabeth to Lord Burleigh—Exeter Change—The Menagerie—The Elephant "Chunee"—The Lyceum Theatre—The Beef-steak Club—Exeter Hall—The Adelphi Theatre—Maiden Lane and its Noted Residents—Southampton Street—The "Bedford Head"—The Corps of Commissionaires—Bedford House—The *Lancet* and Mr. T. Wakley—General Monk and the Duchess of Albemarle—Newspapers published in the Strand.

THAT the Strand, especially that part of it which lay nearest to the two royal theatres, bore no good reputation in the days of our great-grandfathers, may be gathered from Gay's "Trivia." The poet, who speaks of the dangers of the "mazy" purlieus of Drury Lane, gives an equally bad character to the inhabitants of Catherine Street, in spite of the derivation of its name from the Greek word denoting "purity." The street, it may be added, is now chiefly devoted to second-class coffee-rooms and eating-houses, and the offices of various newspapers. About half-way down the street, on the eastern side, at No. 22, is the office of the *Echo*, a newspaper which is worthy of record here, since the publication of its first number, in 1868, marked an era in the history of the cheap press, as being the first halfpenny daily paper started in London.

In Catherine Street were published the *Court Gazette* and *Court Journal*, the *Naval and Military Gazette*, the *Racing Times*, the *London Herald*, the *Illustrated Times*, and also the *Literary Gazette* in the last days of its existence. The *Era* also was published here for many years. The upper part of the thoroughfare was formerly called Brydges Street, but the two were made into one and called Catherine Street by the authority of the Board of Works in 1872.

Before going further westward we may notice

that at No. 332, Strand, opposite Somerset House, now the office of the *Weekly Times*, was published for many years prior to its decease in 1861, at the age of more than a century, the *Morning Chronicle*. This was the organ of the Whig party in the days of Fox, and afterwards in those of Lord Grey, Lord Melbourne, and Lord John Russell; and under the successive editorships of Mr. J. Perry and Mr. John Black it obtained a leading position such as that now held by the *Times*. Among the contributors of literary and political articles who, during the hundred years of its existence, were frequent visitors to the editor's inner room, were Richard Brinsley Sheridan, Professor Porson, Jekyll, the wit and M.P., David Ricardo, James Mill, the historian, Lords Erskine and Durham, Albany Fonblanque, Horace Smith, Mr. Poulett Thomson (afterwards Lord Sydenham), Harry Brougham, Lord (then "plain John") Campbell, Joseph Hume, Mr. J. R. M'Culloch, Sir John Bowring, Mr. Charles Buller, and Mr. N. W. Senior. The supposed ghost of Sir Philip Francis also haunted the editorial sanctum, and it will not be forgotten that it was as a reporter on the staff of the *Morning Chronicle* that Charles Dickens earned some of the first five-pound notes which afterwards flowed into his pocket so freely.

The following story will serve to illustrate at once the character of Mr. Black (who died in 1855) and the position of the *Chronicle* in its palmy days:—Mr. Black was a great favourite with Lord Melbourne when the latter was Prime Minister. His lordship esteemed him not only for his great learning, his wonderful memory, his apt illustration of every topic of discourse by an apparently inexhaustible fund of anecdote derived from the most recondite sources, but for his simplicity and *bonhomie*. John Black was a modern Diogenes in everything but his ill-nature. On one occasion Lord Melbourne said to him, "Mr. Black, you are the only person who comes to see me who forgets who I am." The editor opened his eyes with astonishment. "You forget that I am Prime Minister." Mr. Black was about to apologise, but the Premier continued, "Everybody else takes especial care to remember it, but I wish they would forget it; they only remember it to ask me for places and favours. Now, Mr. Black," added his lordship, "you never ask me for anything, and I wish you would; for, seriously, I should be most happy to do anything in my power to serve you." "I am truly obliged," said Mr. Black, "but I don't want anything; I am editor of the *Morning Chronicle*. I like my business, and I live happily on my income." "Then, by Heaven," said the peer, "I envy you; and you're the only man I ever did."

On the west side of Catherine Street, and covering the ground now occupied by the Gaiety Theatre and Restaurant and the adjacent buildings, formerly stood Wimbledon House, a noble mansion built at the close of the sixteenth or early in the seventeenth century by Sir Edward Cecil, third son of Thomas, Earl of Exeter. He was an eminent military character in the reigns of James I. and Charles I., by the latter of whom he was created Viscount Wimbledon; but, as he died without issue, the title ceased at his death. This mansion was burnt down, as we learn from John Stow, in 1628, the next day after its noble owner's country seat at Wimbledon had been accidentally destroyed by an explosion of gunpowder. Strange to say, the name of Wimbledon House is entirely forgotten in this neighbourhood, its memory not being perpetuated even by a court or an alley. *Sic transit gloria!*

Part of the site of Wimbledon House was afterwards occupied by "D'Oyley's warehouse," a shop which has never been outdone in name and fame even in these days of monster establishments. The following account of it we take from the *European Magazine*:—"There have been few shops in the metropolis that have acquired more celebrity than D'Oyley's warehouse. . . . We have been told that the original founder of the house was a French refugee, who sought an asylum in this country after the revocation of the Edict of Nantes, and formed a connection in the weaving branch of business with some persons in Spitalfields, whose manufactures, most judiciously fostered by the Government and patriotically encouraged by the nobility, were just then reaching that eminence which they afterwards attained. D'Oyley himself was a man of great ingenuity, and having the best assistance he invented, fabricated, and introduced a variety of stuffs, some of which were new, and all of them such as had never been seen in England. He combined the different articles silken and woollen, and spread them into such an infinite number of forms and patterns, that his shop quickly became the mart of taste, and his goods, when first issued, came to be the height of fashion." To this gentleman it is that the *Spectator* alludes in one of its papers, when it says that "if D'Oyley had not by his ingenious inventions enabled us to dress our wives and daughters in cheap stuffs, we should not have had the means to have carried on the war." In another paper (No. 319) the gentleman who was so fond of striking bold strokes in dress characteristically observes: "A few months after I brought up the *modish* jacket, or the coat with close sleeves, I struck the first in a plain doiley; but that failing, I struck it a second time in blue camlet, which was also one of Doiley's stuffs." In Vanbrugh's *Provoked Wife*, in the scene in Spring Gardens, Lady Fanciful says to Mademoiselle, pointing to Lady Brute and Belinda, "I fear those doiley stuffs are not worn for want of better clothes." "The warehouse was almost equally famous, even in very early times, not only for articles to suit the ladies, but also as the grand emporium for gentlemen's night-gowns and night-caps. . . . In the former part of the eighteenth century, all the beaux who used to stick to the custom of breakfasting at coffee-houses appendant to the Inns of Court, made their morning strolls in their elegant *déshabille*, which was carelessly confined around the waist by a band or sash of yellow, red, green, or blue, according to the taste of the wearer; these were also exclusively of D'Oyley's manufacture. This idle fashion of lounging during the morning in such a dress was not quite extinct in 1760-70, for we remember about that period to have seen some of those early birds in their night-gowns, caps, &c., at Wills's Coffee House near Lincoln's Inn Gate, in Searle Street, about that period." D'Oyley's warehouse, however, was celebrated not for this article alone, but in general for its woollen manufactures. Steele, it may be remembered, speaks in the *Guardian* (No. 102) of his "Doily suit," and Dryden in one place mentions "Doyly petticoats;" but if we may believe Gay's "Trivia," these articles were more elegant than useful in winter, and but a sorry protection against the cold.

It was only at some date between 1848 and 1852 that the name of "D'Oyley's Warehouse (A. Walker & Co., 346, the Strand)" disappeared from the annual issues of Messrs. Kelly's *Post Office Directory*. The site of this famous warehouse is now the printing and publishing offices of the *Morning Post* newspaper.

Exeter Street has witnessed some of those early struggles which either make or mar the lives of literary men. It is well known to every reader of Boswell that it was in this street that Dr. Johnson, on his first arrival in London, lodged and dined at a staymaker's, paying for his keep the large sum of fourpence-halfpenny per day; and that he was living here when he and his friend Garrick "were compelled to borrow five pounds on their joint note from Mr. Wilcox, the bookseller."

Running obliquely from the bottom of Catherine Street to Wellington Street was formerly a small arcade, built by the late Marquis of Exeter—a lineal descendant of the great Lord Burleigh, whose family still own the property—with the view of resuscitating the glories of old Exeter 'Change. He entrusted the work to Mr. Sydney Smirke, the well-known architect, who designed a polygonal compartment at each end of the arcade, which comprised ten neat shops with dwellings over them. There were "polychromic arabesque decorations, imitation bronze gates, and other ornamentations; and the street fronts, of fine red brick, with stone dressings, were in good Jacobean style." But the place, as a business speculation, was a total failure; the public gave the arcade "the cold shoulder;" the shops were mostly tenantless, and an air of solitariness and desertion seemed to take possession of it. The site was in the end considered eligible as part of the design for a large music hall, fronting the Strand; and within the year 1863, after a short and struggling career, the arcade disappeared. The Strand Music Hall, which rose upon its site, does not appear to have been much more successful than its predecessor, for in a very short time the company, under whose auspices the music hall was erected, collapsed, and the building underwent another transformation. An elegant and fashionable theatre—the "Gaiety"—with a commodious and well-appointed restaurant adjoining, has taken its place.

The "Gaiety," which was opened in 1868, will seat 2,000 persons. It was built from the designs of Mr. C. J. Phillips, and in the Gothic style of architecture. The entrance in the Strand leads by a few steps to the level of the stalls, and by a spacious staircase to the balcony or grand tier, and the upper boxes. Another entrance in Exeter Street, designed as a private entrance for the Royal Family, is available as an exit way in case of a sudden panic, there being a stone staircase from the doorway to the highest part of the theatre, with communications on every level. The entrances to the pit and gallery are in Catherine Street, and the stage entrance is in Wellington Street. The columns supporting the various tiers of boxes, &c., are carried up to a sufficient height above the gallery, and from the cap springs a series of pointed arches, supporting cornice and coved ceiling, in the centre of which is a sun-light burner. There is a depth of some twenty feet below the stage, for sinking large scenes, and a height of fifty feet above. The original decoration of the interior was striking and effective, a very noticeable feature being the frieze over the proscenium, which was designed and painted by Mr. H. S. Marks. It represents a king and queen of mediæval times, with surrounding courtiers, watching a "mask" which is being performed before them. The "Gaiety" deserves the credit, be it great or small, of having been the first to acclimatize in London what is known as the *Opera Bouffe* of Paris. The pieces played on the night of the opening were the operetta of *The Two Harlequins* and a comedy drama, entitled *On the Cards*, in the last of which pieces the veteran Mr. Alfred Wigan displayed some admirable acting. The opening night closed with the extravaganza of *Robert the Devil*. The entertainment given at the "Gaiety" consists of burlesque, farce, operetta, &c., and among the names associated with the house are those of Miss Nellie Farren, Mr. Edward Terry, and the late Fred Leslie. A sumptuous restaurant was attached to the theatre at first starting; but it was afterwards separated, owing to the stringency of a clause in the Licensing Act.

In Wellington Street has been printed and published, for more than half a century, the *Morning Post*, the first number of which appeared on the 2nd of November, 1772, thirteen years before the establishment of the *Times*. The paper was originally published at No. 14, Fleet Street; but it was removed to the Strand, and subsequently to Wellington Street, where it is now housed in handsome new offices. Its earliest editor was the Rev. Henry Bate Dudley, at once a man about the town of fashion, an Essex rector, a Cambridgeshire magistrate, and a political and dramatic writer. At one time he held a deanery in Ireland. Whilst editor of the *Morning Post* he inserted an article which happened to give offence to a Captain Stoney, and, on refusing to give up the writer's name, he received a challenge, which he accepted. The parties adjourned to the "Adelphi" Tavern, in the Strand, hard by, and called for a private room and a brace of pistols. These having failed, the combatants resorted to swords, and, both being wounded, they were separated with some difficulty. Dudley (who, having made the acquaintance of the Prince Regent, in after life was created a baronet) soon after this quarrelled with the proprietors of the *Post*, and established the *Morning Herald* as its rival. In 1776 a pirated edition of the *Post* was brought out, but soon suppressed by an affidavit sworn at Bow Street that the paper established in 1772 was "the original *Morning Post*."

Among the contributors to the *Post* during the first half century of its existence were Charles Lamb, Robert Southey, Sir J. Mackintosh, William Wordsworth, Arthur Young, and S. T. Coleridge. Lord Byron alludes to this latter fact in the third canto of "Don Juan:"—

> "Or Coleridge, long before his flighty pen
> Lent to the *Morning Post* its aristocracy."

The connection of Coleridge with the paper dated from 1797, when he began to supply "political pieces," and three years later, as he tells us himself, he was "solicited to undertake the literary and political departments" of the paper. He ceased to write for the *Post* regularly in 1802. More recently the paper numbered among its contributors William Jerdan, Thomas Moore, W. Mackworth Praed, and Mr. James Stephen, afterwards M.P., the father of Sir James Stephen. On account of the firm adherence of its managers to the side of George IV., in the trial of Queen Caroline, the office was more than once attacked by the Radical party; and its windows were broken with brickbats by the mob because the editor refused to illuminate his windows to celebrate the release of Sir Francis Burdett from the Tower. Lord Byron, in more than one passage of his poems, mentions the *Morning Post* by name, and on one occasion he records the fact that the literature of the Prince Regent at his breakfast table at Carlton House consisted of "Death warrants and the *Morning Post*." Elsewhere he couples it with the then brilliant and high-standing papers, the *Courier* and the *Chronicle*, and it is worth noting that one editor of Byron commences his list of "testimonies in favour of Don Juan" with an extract from "the most courtly, decorous, and high-spirited of papers, the *Morning Post*." In June, 1881, the *Morning Post* followed the example of most of its daily contemporaries, and reduced its price to a penny!

On the site of Exeter House, and of its successor, the "Exeter 'Change" of the age of our grandfathers, antiquaries tell us that there once stood the rectory-house belonging to St. Clement Danes' parish, "with a garden and a close for the parson's horse." Such, at all events, was the case until a certain Sir Thomas Palmer, during the reign of Edward VI., came into possession of the living, which he lost by forfeiture for treason. Sir Thomas pulled down the house, and "rebuilt the same of brick and timber very large and spacious." Sir. T. Palmer is called "a creature of the Duke of Somerset," his mansion "a magnificent house of brick and timber." In the first year of Mary it reverted to the Crown, in which it remained vested until it was granted by Elizabeth to Sir William Cecil, her Lord Treasurer, who enlarged and partly rebuilt it, and called it Burleigh or Cecil House. According to Pennant, Burleigh House was "a noble pile, built with brick, and adorned with four square turrets." As appears from ancient plans, it faced the Strand, its gardens extending "from the west side of the garden walk of Wimbledon House (nearly where now runs Wellington Street) to the green lane westwards, which now is Southampton Street."

Cecil, when he became Lord Burleigh, was honoured in this house by a visit from Queen Elizabeth, who, knowing him to be a martyr to the gout, would allow him to sit in her presence. This was, of course, a great concession from such an imperious queen, even to such a favourite; and when he would apologise for the weak state of his legs, her Majesty would playfully remark, "My lord, we make use of you not for the badness of your legs, but for the goodness of your head." Allen remarks, in his "History of London," that "in all probability when she came to Burleigh House, the queen wore that pyramidical head-dress, built of wire, lace, ribbons, and jewels, which shot up to so great a height, and made part of the fashion of the day; for, when the principal esquire in attendance ushered her into the house, he suggested to her Majesty to stoop. 'For your master's sake, I will stoop,' she replied haughtily, 'but not for the King of Spain.'" Lord Burleigh spent most of his days between this house and his country residence at Theobalds, in Hertfordshire. "At his house in London," we learn from the "Desiderata Curiosa," "he kept ordinarily in household fourscore persons besides . . . . such as attended him at court. The charge of his housekeeping in London amounted to thirty pounds a week," a very large sum indeed in those days,

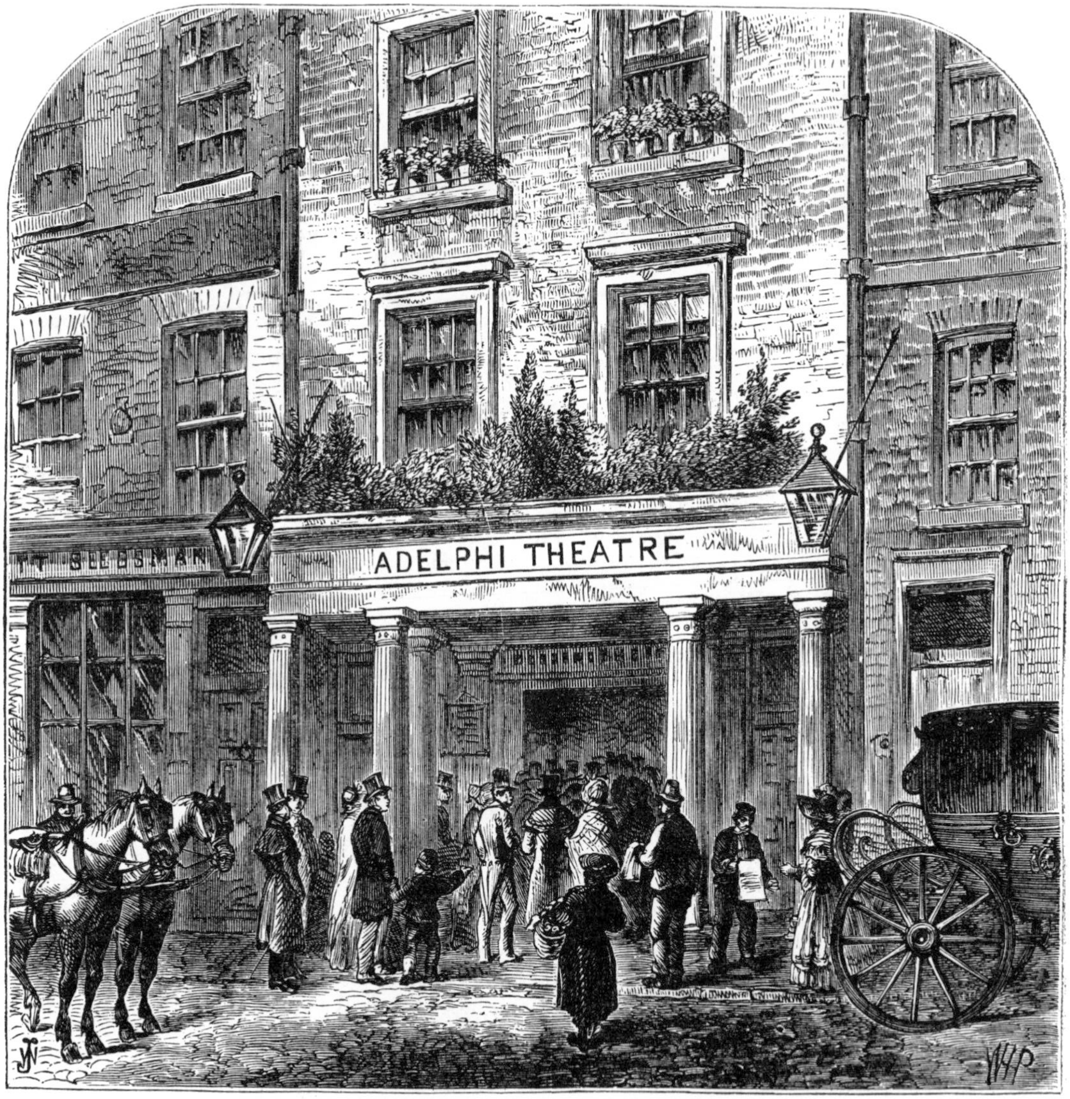

THE OLD ADELPHI THEATRE, 1860. (*See page* 119.)

"and the whole sum yearly £1,560, and this in his absence; and in term time, or when his lordship lay at London, his charges increased ten or twelve pounds more. Besides keeping these houses he bought great quantities of corn in times of dearth, to furnish markets about his house at under prices, to pull down the price so as to relieve the poor. He also gave, for the releasing of prisoners in many of his latter years, thirty and even forty pounds in a term. And for twenty years together he gave yearly in beef, bread, and money at Christmas to the poor of Westminster, St. Martin's, St. Clement's, and Theobalds, thirty-five, and sometimes forty pounds per annum. He also gave yearly to twenty poor men lodging at the Savoy, twenty suits of apparel: so as his certain alms, besides extraordinaries, was cast up to be £500 yearly, one year with another."

Lord Burleigh died here in 1598. The house afterwards passed into the hands of his son Thomas, who, being created Earl of Exeter, gave it that name, which it retained almost to our own days. After the Fire of London it was occupied for some few years by the members of Doctors' Commons, and the various courts of the Arches, the Admiralty, &c., were carried on here. At last, being deserted by the family, it was divided, the lower part being turned into shops of various descriptions, while the upper part, containing a menagerie of wild beasts and reptiles, became known as "Exeter 'Change."

TURNER'S HOUSE IN MAIDEN LANE. *From an Original Sketch.* (*See page* 119.)

Exeter 'Change, when it arose on the ruins of Exeter House, was in no sense externally beautiful, being designed wholly and solely for business purposes. It consisted of three spacious floors, which contained apartments on each side fitted up as shops for milliners, sempstresses, hosiers, &c., and has been from time to time the home of many interesting exhibitions. It appears to have passed through several phases of existence during the last two centuries. It is said by Malcolm to have been built, as it stood till lately, about the time of William and Mary, by a Dr. Barbon, "a speculator in houses," who mortgaged it to the Duke of Devonshire and Sir Francis Child. In 1708 the lower storey comprised forty-eight shops, mostly occupied by milliners, while the upper storey was tenanted by the "Company of Upholsterers." In 1714, one John Gumley, of whom little is known beyond his name, rented the upper part of the building as a warehouse for pier-glasses, &c.; and it is worthy of note that Sir Richard Steele devotes part of one of his papers in the *Tatler* to what looks much like what Mr. Sneer, in *The Critic*, would have called a "puff direct" in his favour. In 1721 it was used by a Mr. Cany as an exhibition room for the display of a wonderful bed, eighteen feet in height, for the sight of which—still more wonderful—visitors paid half-a-crown! In 1732 the body of the poet Gay lay in state here before its interment in Westminster Abbey. In 1764, Malcolm tells us "the great room was opened as an improvement on modern statute halls," and in 1772 the eccentric Lord Baltimore's body here lay in state before its removal in a hearse to Epsom. For some years after this it appears to have been used as a warehouse for storing the printed volumes of the Rolls and Journals of the House of Lords. After this it became "Pidcock's Exhibition of Wild Beasts," and as such it long continued a most popular place of resort, being constantly visited by "country cousins." The beasts were in cages and dens upstairs, the lower part being made a thoroughfare lined with shops on either side, like the Lowther and Burlington Arcades of our own day.

Thornton, in his "Survey of London and Westminster," in 1786, describes it as "erected for the purposes of trade, and consisting of two floors, the lower being laid out in small shops ranged on each side of a long gallery, and the upper one used for auctions and other temporary purposes."

In the early part of the present century the front of Exeter 'Change, projecting as it did over the pavement of the Strand, and daubed all over with pictures of monsters and wild beasts between its Corinthian pillars, must have presented a grotesque appearance not easily to be forgotten by the "country cousins" who came in shoals to see it; and its attractions were heightened in the eyes of the children by Mr. Pidcock's sham Yeoman of the Guard, stationed outside (like the Beef-eaters at the Tower), to invite the passers-by to step in and see the lions, tigers, elephants, and monkeys.

It appears that the wild beasts, which formed such an attraction to the Londoners and their "country cousins" at the commencement of the present century, had not become domesticated in Exeter 'Change so early as 1773. At all events, Northouck, in his "History of London," published in that year, is silent on the subject, and speaks of it only as an old-fashioned building erected for the purposes of trade, and consisting of a long room with a row of shops on each side, and a large room above, "now used for auctions." The 'Change itself projected into the street so as greatly to narrow it; and Northouck remarks that in his opinion it ought to be taken down, the street being greatly contracted by its projection, and by "the sheds stuck round it on the outside;" and his opinion will be confirmed on referring to our engraving of its frontage (see page 109).

The menagerie was successively occupied by Pidcock, Polito, and Cross; and some half a century ago the sight-lover had to pay half-a-crown to see a few animals confined in small dens and cages in rooms of various size, the walls painted with exotic scenery, in order to favour the illusion; whereas now the finest collection of living animals in Europe may be seen in a beautiful garden for a shilling, and on Mondays for sixpence! The roar of the lions and tigers of Exeter 'Change could be distinctly heard in the street, and often frightened horses in the roadway. During Cross's tenancy, in 1826, the elephant "Chunee," which had been shown here since 1809, became ungovernable, as it is said, through the return of an annual paroxysm, and so greatly endangered the safety of the menagerie that it was deemed advisable to put the animal to death. For this purpose a file of soldiers was engaged, and 152 bullets were fired before it fell. The elephant weighed nearly five tons, stood eleven feet in height, and was valued at £1,000. The skin, which weighed 17 cwt., was sold to a tanner for £50; the bones weighed 876 lbs.; and the entire skeleton, sold for £100, is now in the museum of the Royal College of Surgeons in Lincoln's Inn Fields. "Chunee" had achieved some theatrical distinction: he had performed in the spectacle of *Blue Beard*, at Covent Garden; and he had kept up an intimate acquaintance with Edmund Kean, whom he would fondle with his trunk, in return for a few loaves of bread.

Mr. J. T. Smith, in his "Book for a Rainy Day," tells us how he went late at night to the menagerie, accompanied by his friend, Sir J. Winter Lake, when they had the gratification of taking a pot of "Barclay's Entire," in company with Chunee, whom they had met shortly before, being led by its keeper between ropes along the narrow part of the Strand.

The greatness of the Exeter 'Change departed with Chunee; the animals were removed to the King's Mews, in 1828, and two years afterwards Exeter 'Change was entirely taken down. Previous to the opening of the Zoological Gardens in the Regent's Park, Exeter 'Change and the Tower were the only two places in the metropolis where wild beasts could be seen alive, except in travelling menageries; and it was to those two places that "country cousins" were taken on their first arrival in London, so that to "see the lions" passed into a proverb.

The Lyceum Theatre, on the western side of what is now known as Wellington Street, stands on part of the site of old Exeter House, according to Newton's "London in the Olden Time." The ground whereon the theatre stands was purchased about the year 1765, when the Society of Artists was incorporated, by James Payne, the architect of Salisbury House, and on it he built an academy or exhibition room, to anticipate the royal establishment then in contemplation; and here several exhibitions took place. The apartments consisted of a large saloon, with a sky-light, and lesser rooms adjoining. Upon the insolvency of the society this place was deserted, and sold by auction to proprietors, who converted the back part of it into a theatre, and here Mr. Dibdin and Dr. Arnold exhibited their musical talents for some time. It was afterwards taken by a Mr. Porter for the exhibition of his "Grand National Paintings of the 'Siege of Seringapatam,' 'The Siege of Acre,' 'The Battle of Lodi,' 'The Battle of Agincourt,' &c." The place was subsequently used for a variety of miscellaneous entertainments. Here, in 1802, was first shown Madame Tussaud's exhibition of wax-work figures, on her arrival in England from France. The theatre was rebuilt in 1816, but destroyed by fire in 1830. It was again rebuilt, and opened with English Opera in 1834; but although success at first appeared certain, the losses of the lessee subsequently became so great that the theatre was closed in the following year. In 1841 the theatre was taken by the English Opera Company, under the management of Mr. Balfe; equestrian performances were introduced in 1844; and in the same year it was re-opened with a dramatic company, under the management of Mrs. Keeley. The Lyceum has since been under the management of, or had among its members, several theatrical celebrities, by none of whom has more been done to elevate its reputation than by Sir Henry Irving, whose Shaksperian revivals must ever be memorable in theatrical annals.

Behind the scenes of this theatre are some rooms in which a society of roysterers known as "The Sublime Society of Beef-steaks," used to meet on Saturdays, from November to the end of June, to partake of a dinner of beef-steaks. "They abhor," writes Mr. Peter Cunningham in 1851, "the notion of being thought a club; they dedicate their hours to 'Beef and Liberty,' and enjoy a hearty English dinner with hearty English appetites. The room in which they dine, a little Escurial in itself, is most appropriately fitted up—the doors, wainscoting, and roof of good old English oak, being ornamented with gridirons, as thickly as Henry VII.'s chapel with the portcullis of its founder. Everything here assumes the shape, or is distinguished by the representation of their favourite implement—the gridiron. The cook is seen at his office, through the bars of a spacious gridiron, and the original gridiron of the society (the survivor of two terrific fires), holds a conspicuous position in the centre of the ceiling. Every member has the right of inviting a friend, and pickles are not allowed till after the third helping. The 'Steaks' had their origin in a convivial gathering, founded in 1735 by John Rich, the patentee of Covent Garden Theatre, and George Lambert, the scene-painter."

Among the members of this defunct association were George, Prince of Wales, and his brothers, the Dukes of York and Sussex, Richard Brinsley Sheridan, Lord Sandwich, Paul Whitehead, David Garrick, Sir F. Burdett, Harry Brougham, John Wilkes, the Duke of Argyle, Alderman Wood, the Duke of Leinster, and Lord Saltoun. The club had its president and vice-president, its "bishop," or chaplain, who said grace, and its "boots," as the steward or burser was called; and our readers may be amused at learning that the Dukes of Sussex and Leinster in their turn discharged the duties of "boots." Its evening for meeting was Saturday, and its festivals were of a somewhat bacchanalian character; the standing dish of "beef-steaks," from which it derived its name, being washed down by the best of ale and wine, to say nothing of stronger liquors. The wine, as it passed round the table, was always accompanied by songs; and the

"Laureate of the Steaks" was the celebrated wit, Charles Morris, who in early life had been in the Life Guards, and who lived to be ninety before he resigned his office and his life. One of his effusions, composed for this club, has the following stanza:—

"Like Briton's island lies our steak,
A sea of gravy bounds it;
Shalots, confus'dly scattered, make
The rockwork that surrounds it.
Your isle's best emblem these behold,
Remember ancient story:
Be, like your grandsires, first and bold,
And live and die with glory."

This song rendered Morris so great a favourite with the Prince that he adopted him into the circle of his intimate friends, and made him his constant guest both at Carlton House and at the Pavilion at Brighton. He was succeeded in his "Laureateship of the Steaks" by Mr. C. Hallett.

When the club was broken up in 1869, the pictures of former members, which adorned the walls of the room where they assembled for dinner (mostly copies, however, not originals), were sold for only about £70. The plate, however, brought very high prices; the forks and table-spoons, all bearing the emblem of the club—viz., a gridiron—fetched about a sovereign apiece; but the grand competition was for a punch-ladle, with a handle in the shape of a gridiron, and inlaid with a Queen Anne guinea, which realised £14 5s., and for the ribbon and badge of the president, a gridiron of silver, made in 1735, and knocked down at £23. Other articles fetched equally fancy prices, as souvenirs of a bygone institution. Thus a cheese-toaster brought £12 6s., a *couteau de chasse*, the reputed work of B. Cellini, the gift of Dr. Askew, £84; a brown jug of stone ware, silver mounted, £7; a pair of halberts, £3 10s.; an Oriental punch-bowl, presented by Lord Saltoun, £17 15s. Some wine-glasses, engraved with the gridiron, realised from 27 to 34 shillings a pair; while the pewter dishes, plates, and quart pots fetched nearly the price of silver. The chairs, which had been occupied by so many distinguished members, including that of the president, were knocked down at various prices between £7 and £14 apiece. The actual gridiron, which had for years been the centre of so much veneration and homage, plain as it was, fetched five guineas and a half. Almost all the articles, in addition to being stamped with the gridiron, were labelled "Beef and Liberty." The marble bust of Wilkes, which formerly had adorned the dining-room, fell under the auctioneer's hammer for twenty-two guineas. For the above particulars we are indebted to "The Life and Death of the Sublime Society," by "Brother" W. Arnold, published by Messrs. Bradbury, Evans, and Co.

At a short distance westward of the Lyceum Theatre stands the building known to the religious and musical world as Exeter Hall. It was erected in the years 1830–31, by Mr. G. Deering, in the Græco-Corinthian style of architecture, but has since been much improved. In 1880 the Hall became the property of the Young Men's Christian Association; and in March, 1881, it was re-opened, after having undergone extensive alterations and enlargement, the cost of which, together with the purchase-money for the building, amounted to nearly £50,000. The edifice is intended as a place for holding public meetings, the most noted of which are those annual religious gatherings known as "May Meetings." Besides these, the Hall is occasionally used for the meetings of charitable and other institutions; and also for choral assemblies. Here for many years took place the concerts of the Sacred Harmonic Society, which consisted principally of oratorios, by some well-known composer, and occasionally of purely church music, such as the anthems sung in divine worship.

Oratorios, like the sacred plays, are of ancient date, and, according to a writer in *Chambers's Cyclopædia*, were so called from the chapel or *oratory*, the place where these compositions were first performed. St. Filippo Neri, born in 1515, has been considered as the founder of the oratorio. He engaged poets and composers to produce dialogues, on subjects from Scriptural and legendary history, in verse, and set to music, which were performed in his chapel or oratory on Sundays and Church festivals. The subjects were "Job and his Friends," "The Prodigal Son," "The Angel Gabriel with the Virgin," and "The Mystery of the Incarnation." By far the greatest master of oratorio was Handel, who perfected that species of music, and was the first to introduce it into England. On the occasion of the first public performance of an oratorio in London, in the year 1732, it was so complete a novelty that it was deemed necessary to give the following explanation in advertising it:—"By His Majesty's command, at the King's Theatre in the Haymarket, on Tuesday, the 2nd of May, will be performed the sacred story of 'Esther,' an oratorio in English, composed by Handel, and to be performed by a great number of voices and instruments.—N.B. There will be no acting on the stage, but the house will be fitted up in a decent manner for the audience." The oratorio of "Esther" had been privately given, some years previously, in the chapel at Canons, the seat of the "princely" Duke of Chandos. The two crowning works of Handel were "Israel in Egypt" and "The Messiah." The former is considered to rank highest of all compositions of the oratorio class; but the latter has attained an even more universal popularity, and from the time when it was first brought out down to the present day, it has been performed for the benefit of nearly every charitable institution in the kingdom. In Handel's time the orchestra was but very imperfectly developed; and since that period it was customary in London to have oratorios performed twice a week during Lent in the various theatres, but these performances were given up on the institution of the oratorios at Exeter Hall. At various halls in London, and at musical festivals elsewhere, oratorios are now performed on a large scale, and with a power and a perfection previously unknown. The greatest oratorio performances, however, are now those of the Handel Triennial Festivals at the Crystal Palace. At the first of these festivals, in 1862, the chorus amounted to 3,120 voices, and there was an orchestra of 505 performers; at the present time even these numbers are exceeded.

About half-way between Exeter Hall and Charing Cross are the Vaudeville and the Adelphi Theatres. The former, which was erected in the year 1870, from the designs of Mr. C. J. Phillips, is a neat building internally, but has very little pretension to architectural display in its exterior. It will seat about 1,000 persons, and was built for the performance of comedy, burlesque, and farce. The pieces produced on the opening night were *Love or Money*, a comedy by Mr. A. Halliday, and a burlesque, entitled *Don Carlos, or the Infant in Arms*.

The Adelphi Theatre stands opposite Adam Street, and is the second building of the kind that has stood here. Mr. John Scott, colour-maker, of the Strand, was the original architect, and it was built in 1806 under his superintendence. The old theatre was pulled down in the summer of 1858, and the first stone of the present edifice was laid by Mr. Benjamin Webster, in his Masonic capacity. The Adelphi has been principally celebrated for melodramas. Terry's Theatre, also in the Strand, was built for Mr. Edward Terry; the Tivoli Music-hall, at the Charing Cross end, dates from 1890.

Parallel with the Strand at this part, and to the south of Covent Garden Market, is Maiden Lane, sometimes, though erroneously, supposed to have been so called from a sisterhood of nuns, attached to the abbey, whose sheltered "Convent Garden" it bounded on the southern side. In early rate-books of St. Paul's, Covent Garden, it is spoken of as Maiden Lane, behind the "Bull" Inn. Bull Inn Court, no doubt, marks the site of the inn here mentioned. In Maiden Lane Voltaire lodged during his visit to London in 1726, and in it lived Andrew Marvell, of whom we have already made mention as an honest member of Parliament, and whose name we shall again have occasion to record as a satirist, when we come to Charing Cross. Here, too, at one time, lived Archbishop Sancroft, the nonjuror, before he had taken his seat on the episcopal bench. No. 20 (now removed) was a tavern called the "Cyder Cellars," a house which gained some notoriety in its day. It was a favourite haunt of Professor Porson, and afterwards became a "School of Arms." "Proctor, the sculptor," says Mr. Peter Cunningham, "died in reduced circumstances, in a house in Maiden Lane, opposite the 'Cyder Cellars.'" Here also, at No. 26, on the north side, was born, in May, 1775, no less an artist than Joseph Mallord William Turner, his father being at that time a hair-dresser and a householder. Here the great painter early began to draw from Nature, and a front room in the old house in Maiden Lane is said to have been his first studio. The house has been lately rebuilt. The Roman Catholic church of Corpus Christi occupies the south-east corner of Maiden Lane.

Southampton Street was so called in compliment to Lady Rachel Russell, daughter of Thomas Wriothesley, Earl of Southampton, and wife of William, Lord Russell, the patriot. At No. 27 in this street Garrick resided before his removal to the Adelphi. Mrs. Oldfield, the actress, also lived in Southampton Street. Tavistock Street was the stable-yard to Bedford House; and where Tavistock and York Streets meet was "the horse-pond."

In Southampton Street was a celebrated eating-house, known as "The Bedford Head," which is several times mentioned by Pope and Walpole. Its exact site is not known, but it is recorded that the steps of its back door were on the south side of Denmark Court. Pope writes in his "Satires:"—

> "Let me extol a cat on oysters fed,
> I'll have a party at the 'Bedford Head.'"

And again, in his "Sober Advice," he expresses himself in terms which would seem to imply that the house was well known for its good fare:—

> "When sharp with hunger, scorn you to be fed,
> Except on pea-chicks at the 'Bedford Head?'"

And this is confirmed by the fact that Paul Whitehead ordered for himself and a party of gay roisterers a "great supper" at the "Bedford Head," as Horace Walpole tells his correspondent, Sir Horace Mann, under date November, 1741. There is now a "Bedford Head" in Maiden Lane, but it is a new tavern, and does not inherit the traditions of the former house.

In Exchange Court, on the north side, between Nos. 419 and 420, Strand, near Bedford Street, are the head-quarters of the Corps of Commissionaires, a set of men who, having served in the army, the navy, or the police, and having good characters and being in the receipt of pensions, are willing to earn a livelihood by going on messages, delivering circulars, or being detailed off on private business. Some are permanently and others temporarily employed. They are all amenable to the authority of an adjutant, and wear a uniform. They have a mess-room, reading-room, &c., and also a military band. They were first organised in the year 1859; and at the present time their strength is about 2,000 men, of whom the great majority are employed in various parts of London.

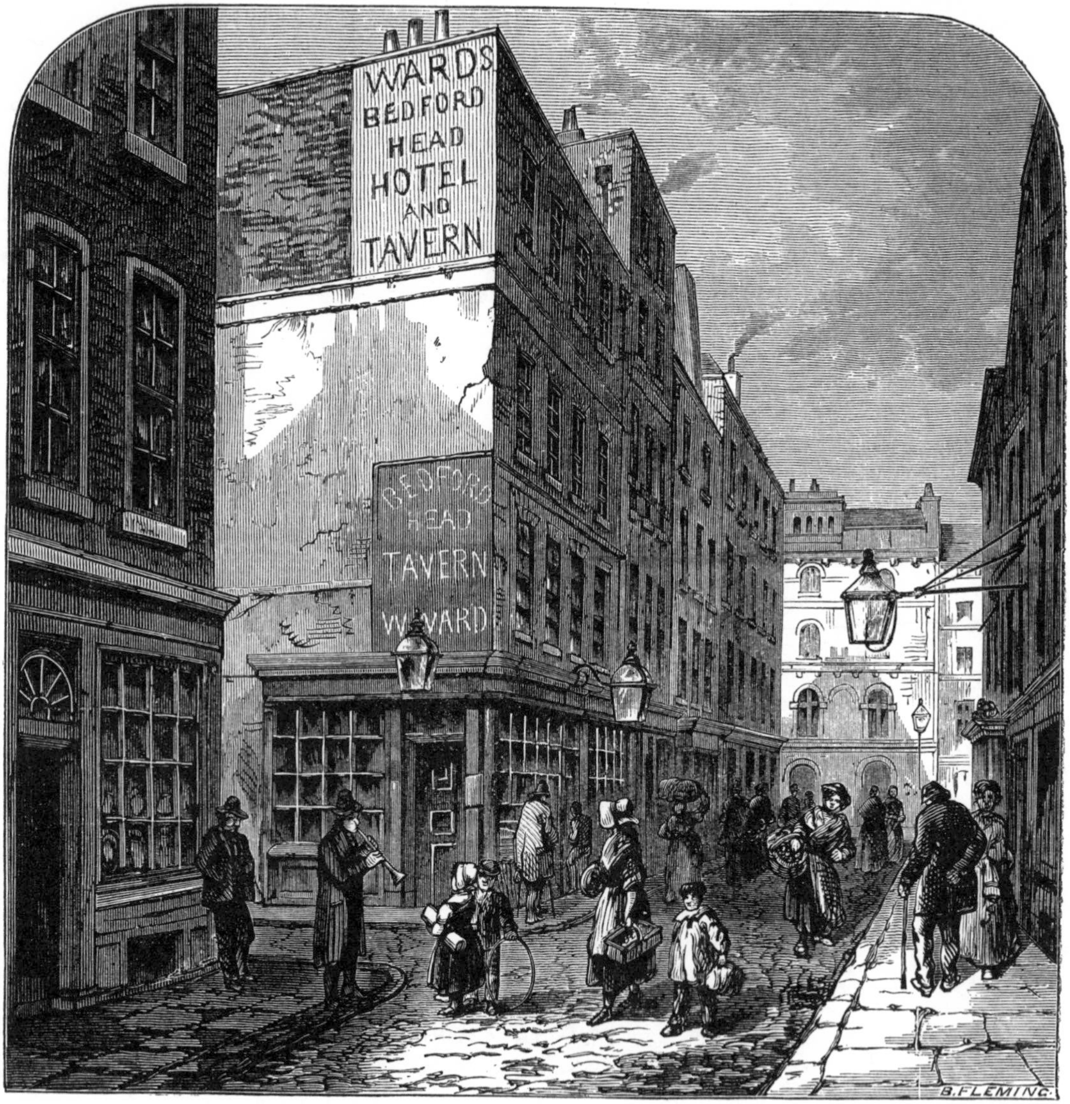

THE OLD "BEDFORD HEAD."

On what is now Southampton Street stood the ancient mansion of the Earls and Dukes of Bedford. It is described by Strype as having been "a large but old-built house, with a great yard before it for the reception of carriages; with a spacious garden, having a terrace-walk adjoining to the brick wall next the garden, behind which were coach-houses and stables, with a conveyance into Charles Street, through a large gate." This house and garden being demolished in 1704, the site was covered by Tavistock, Southampton, and some other streets.

Before the Russell family built the town-house in the Strand they occupied, for a time, the Bishop of Carlisle's "inn," over against their newly-erected mansion, the site of which was afterwards built upon and called "Carlisle Rents." Stow speaks of it in 1598 as "Russell or Bedford House." In 1704 they removed to Bedford House, Bloomsbury, of which we shall speak hereafter.

At the corner of Bedford Street is now the publishing office of the *Lancet*. This journal was established in 1823 by Mr. Thomas Wakley, who, as we learn from the "Autobiographical Recollections of J. F. Clarke, M.R.C.S.," for many years on the staff of the *Lancet*, was the son of a village farmer in Devonshire. As a boy he was of a restless disposition, and anxious to go to sea. He was apprenticed to an apothecary at Taunton, but finished his indentures with two other gentlemen, one at Henley-on-Thames, and the other at Beaminster. He became a student at the united hospitals of Guy's and St. Thomas's, where Sir Astley Cooper was then the popular lecturer on surgery. He passed the College of Surgeons in 1817, and from thence till 1823 he kept a shop in the Strand, at the east corner of Norfolk Street. His old schoolfellow, Mr. Collard—the venerable head of the firm of pianoforte manufacturers of that name—assisted him in the first seven or eight numbers of his new journal. After a time the *Lancet* was printed at the office of Mills, Jowett, and Mills, in Bolt Court, Fleet Street. *Cobbett's Register* was printed at the same establishment, and Wakley, to some extent, made the style of Cobbett his model. At this time it was no uncommon occurrence for four persons to meet in a little room in Mills's office. Three of them made themselves famous—William Cobbett, William Lawrence, and Thomas Wakley; the fourth was a barrister of the name of Keen, who used to join the party on printing nights, probably with a view of determining whether the productions which were about to appear were libellous. The sanctum was seldom violated. The printer's boy was the only person admitted, and he in after life described the room as the scene of the utmost merriment. He could hear as he ascended the stairs the boisterous laugh of Cobbett above the rest; the loud, cheerful, good-humoured ring of Wakley; and on entering the room, could see the quiet, sneering smile of Lawrence; and hear the suppressed giggle of the lawyer. Lawrence left the *Lancet* when he achieved power, and his place was supplied by Wardrop—witty, and able, and unscrupulous. The *Lancet* soon got into hot water, and the insertion of an

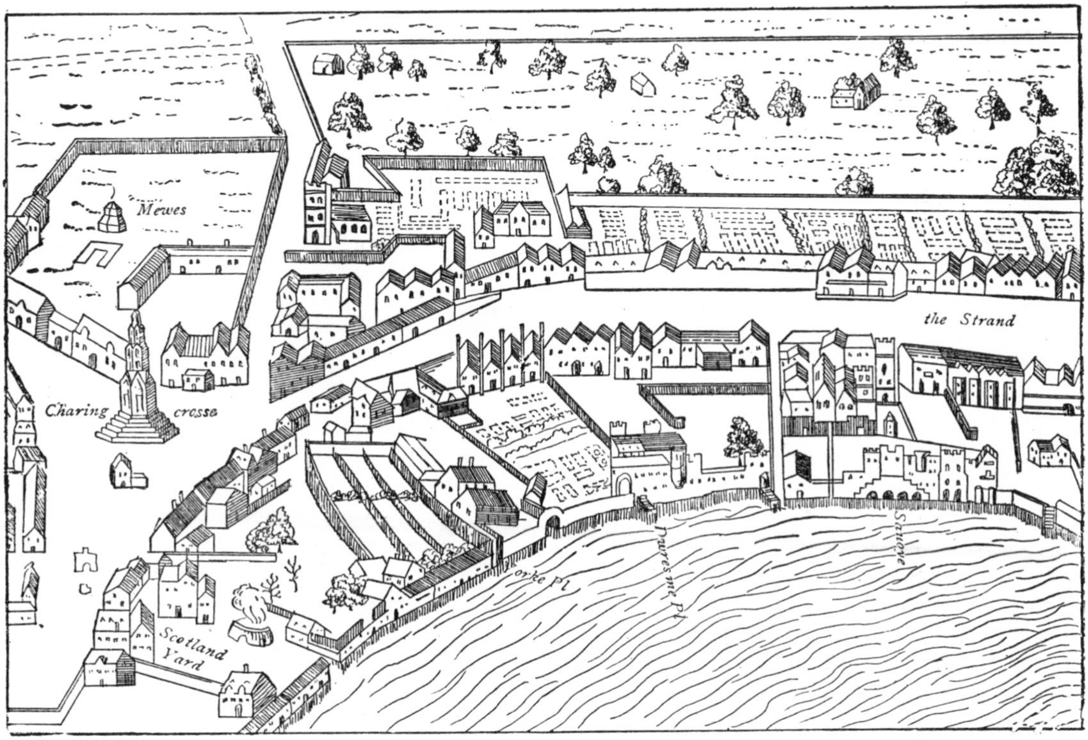

THE STRAND IN 1560. (*From the Map of Ralph Aggas.*)

account of a defective operation for the stone, by Mr. Bransby Cooper, the nephew of Sir Astley, led to the latter bringing against it an action for libel, which created a great sensation at the time. In addition to the report, leading articles of an exciting kind, and squibs and epigrams—some in the worst taste—were inserted. The following is given as a specimen:—

"When Cooper's 'nevvy' cut for stone,
His toils were long and heavy;
The patient quicker parts has shown,
He soon cut Cooper's nevvy."

Mr. Wakley defended himself on his trial, and the verdict for the plaintiff, £100 damages, was considered to be in his favour. Outside Westminster Hall there was a large crowd who cheered him vociferously, and the *Sun* newspaper kept up its type till twelve o'clock at night in order to record the verdict. The reporter of the case, the late Mr. Lambert, was expelled the hospitals, and a board was placed in the hall of Guy's, cautioning all students against reporting for the *Lancet*. This restriction, however, is no longer in force, and the bitterness of the contest is almost forgotten.

Among the many scenes enacted in the Strand, we may be pardoned for mentioning one in which some of the personages whom we have already mentioned were concerned, including General Monk and the Duchess of Albemarle. On the news of Monk being called upon to concert the first measures towards the restoration of royalty, in February, 1659, Pepys tells us, in his "Diary," that the Strand was one blaze of bonfires, and that he himself counted no less than "fourteen between St. Dunstan's Church, Fleet Street, and the Strand Bridge," near Somerset House. A day or two afterwards he records a very different sight—"Two soldiers hanged in the Strand for their late mutiny at Somerset House."

Pepys has the following entry in his "Diary," under date 4th November, 1666:—"The Duke of Albemarle is grown a drunken sot, and drinks with nobody but Troutbecke, whom nobody else will keep company with. Of whom he" (Mr. Cooling) "told me this story: That once the Duke of Albemarle in his drink taking notice, as of a wonder, that Nan Hyde should ever come to be Duchess of York. 'Nay,' says Troutbecke, 'never wonder at that, for if you will give me another bottle of wine, I will tell you as great, if not greater, miracle. And what was that but that our dirty Besse' (meaning his duchess) 'should come to be Duchess of Albemarle.'"

Aubrey says that the mother of this low-born and low-bred duchess was one of "five women barbers" belonging to the locality, thus celebrated in a ballad of the day:—

"Did ever you hear the like,
Or ever hear the fame,
Of five women barbers
That lived in Drury Lane?"

As Aubrey published his "Lives" as early as 1679, he is probably to be trusted on a fact which would be within his own knowledge. And he identifies the site of the blacksmith's forge with "the corner shop, the first turning on y[e] right, as you come out of the Strand into Drury Lane;" and Mr. John Timbs adds, that "it is believed to be that at the right-hand corner of Drury Court, now (1850) a butcher's."

In spite of her low birth and vulgar habits, however, the Duchess of Albemarle is credited with having had a considerable hand in bringing about the Restoration. She was a great loyalist, and Monk, though not afraid of an enemy in the field, was terribly afraid of her and of her tongue; so that it is not improbable that in his case "the grey mare was the better horse," and that it was at her suggestion that he put himself at the head of the movement for bringing King Charles "to his own again." And yet this was the woman of whom Pepys could write in his "Diary:"—"4th April, 1667. I find the Duke of Albemarle at dinner with sorry company—some of his officers of the army—dirty dishes and a nasty wife at table, and bad meat, of which I made but an ill dinner."

The Duchess of Albemarle seems to have been anything rather than attractive personally, but Pepys seems to have regarded her with positive aversion. He never has a good word to say for her, and calls her a "plain and homely dowdy," and a very "ill-looked woman." Could ill-nature well go further?

Next to Fleet Street, the thoroughfare of the Strand has been during the present century the chief home of that Muse who presides over the newspaper press. Here, or else in the streets leading out of it, have been published not only the *Morning Chronicle*, the *Post*, and the *Daily Telegraph*, and the *Illustrated London News*, as mentioned already, but the *Sun*, the *Globe*, *Bell's Life in London*, the *Observer*, the *Leader*, the *Press*, the *Economist*, the *Court Journal*, the *Spectator*, the *Examiner*, the *Field*, the *Queen*, and the *Graphic*, besides a host of other inferior journals, the list of which "were long to tell," and whose obituaries are well-nigh forgotten. It may be worth recording that in 1835, the year prior to the reduction of the Newspaper Duty, the gross amount of duty on newspapers in the United Kingdom was £553,197.

The reduction of the Newspaper Duty took effect on the 15th of September, 1836. In the half-year ending April 5, 1836, the number of newspapers stamped in Great Britain was 14,874,652, and the net amount of duty received was £196,909. In the half-year ending April 5, 1837, the number of newspapers stamped in Great Britain was 21,362,148, and the net amount of duty received was £88,502; showing an increase in the number in the last half-year, as compared with the corresponding half-year before the reduction, of 6,487,496, and a loss of revenue of £108,317. Of the above number of stamps taken out in the half-year ending April 5, 1837, 11,547,241 stamps were issued since 1st of January, 1837, when the distinctive die came into use; whereas only 14,784,652 were issued in the six months ending April, 1836.

Before quitting the literary associations of the Strand, we may note that the first publisher of Samuel Rogers was Mr. Cadell, in the Strand. It was in 1786 that the former first appeared in print with his "Ode to Superstition." The author called and left his MS. in Cadell's shop with a short note containing a bank-note to cover any possible loss that might arise from publication. Mr. Rogers lived down to the end of 1855.

CHAPTER XIX.

CHARING CROSS, THE RAILWAY STATIONS, AND OLD HUNGERFORD MARKET.

"Erect a rich and stately carved cross,
Whereon her statue shall with glory shine;
And henceforth see you call it Charing Cross."—*Peele, "King Edward I."*

Derivation of the Name of Charing—Description of the Original Cross—Lines on its Downfall—Sir Thomas Wyatt's Encounter with Queen Mary's Troops—A Cunning Royalist—The Statue of Charles I.—Andrew Marvell's Satire—The Story of the Sword—Execution of the Regicides—Curious Exhibitions at Charing Cross—The Royal Mews—The Charing Cross Hospital—Westminster Ophthalmic Hospital—Toole's Theatre—The "Golden Cross"—Charing Cross Railway Station and Hotel—The New Eleanor Cross—The Railway Bridge—Old Hungerford Market—Hungerford Bridge—The Lowther Arcade—Adelaide Gallery—Craven Street—Northumberland Street.

Charing Cross, as every Londoner knows, is the name given to the open space at the western end of the Strand, from which Whitehall, Cockspur Street, and St. Martin's Lane branch off in different directions; but of late years a considerable portion of it has been absorbed in what is now called Trafalgar Square. The name is most probably derived from the old village of Charing, which stood here, a sort of halting-place in bygone times for travellers between the cities of London and Westminster; though some fanciful writers have sought its derivation in the words *chère reine*, alluding to the cross which was here set up by Edward I. in memory of his "dear Queen" Eleanor. The latter, as every reader of a child's History of England knows, accompanied Edward I. to the Holy Land, where, on his "being wounded by a certain Moor with a poisoned dagger, and rather growing worse than better by the applications of his physicians, she administered a new and unheard-of remedy. Full of affection and duty, she daily licked the wound which the force of the poison prevented from closing, and sucked out the deadly matter. By dint of this, or, to speak more truly, by the power of conjugal affection, she so drew out the noxious matter, that the wound healing, the king perfectly recovered, and she received not the least harm." It is well known that wherever her bier rested, as at Waltham, Tottenham, and other places, her sorrowful husband erected a cross, or, as Tom Hood whimsically said, in his usual punning vein, *apropos* of the cross at Tottenham:—

"A royal game of fox and goose,
To play for such a loss;
Wherever she put down her *orts*,
There he—set up a *cross!*"

The original cross was of wood, wholly or to a great extent; but it was built in stone by Richard, and, after his death, by a son or brother, Roger de Crundale. The material used was Caen stone, and the steps were of fine smooth marble. It appears to have been of an octagonal form, and, in an upper stage, ornamented with eight figures. On Aggas' map is shown a small house occupying the spot where the equestrian statue of Charles I. now stands. This may possibly have been an erection known as the Hermitage, described otherwise as "a small chapel dedicated to St. Catharine, which stood over against the cross."

"This cross," says Stow, "builded of stone, was of old time a fair piece of work, there made by command of Edward I." Mr. Newton, in his "London in the Olden Time," tells us that it "appears to have been more elegant than any of the other eight crosses erected to Queen Eleanor's memory. It was of Caen stone, beautifully wrought with many figures, and raised upon steps of marble." He also subsequently styles it a "superb piece of architecture." The cross itself was sentenced by the Parliament to be taken down in 1643, but its actual demolition was not carried out till some four years later, namely, in the summer of 1647. Lilly, in his "Observations on the Life of King Charles I.," published in 1715, says that part of the stones of which it was composed were em-

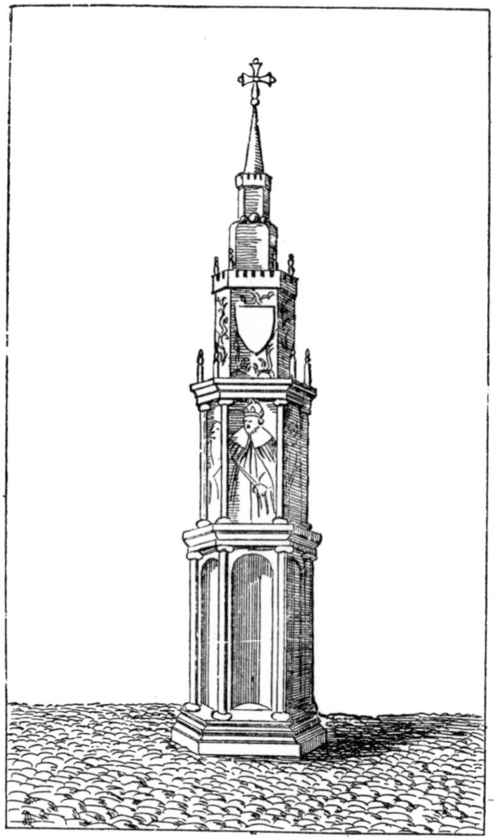

OLD CHARING CROSS.
From a Copy of a very old Print published by N. Smith in 1792.

ployed in paving the front of Whitehall, whilst other stones were made into knife-hafts and other articles, which, when polished, looked like marble.

The following lines on the downfall of the cross itself, which are quoted from "Percy's Reliques," are interesting and amusing :—

"Undone, undone the lawyers are ;
They wander about the towne ;
Nor can find the way to Westminster,
Now Charing Cross is downe :
At the end of the Strand they made a stand,
Swearing they are at a loss,
And, chaffing, say, that's not the way—
They must go by Charing Cross.

"The Parliament to vote it down
Conceived it very fitting,
For fear it should fall and kill them all,
In the house as they were sitting.
They were told, God wot, it had a plot,
Which made them so hard-hearted,
To give command it should not stand,
But be taken down and carted.

"Men talk of plots ; this might have been worse,
For anything I know,
Than that Tomkins and Chaloner
Were hanged for long agoe.
Our Parliament did that prevent,
And wisely them defended ;
For plots they will discover still
Before they were intended.

"But neither man, woman, nor child
Will say, I'm confident,
They ever heard it speak one word
Against the Parliament.
An informer swore it letters bore,
Or else it had been free ;
I'll take, in troth, my Bible oath,
It could neither write nor read.

"The committee said, that verily
To Popery it was bent ;
For aught I know it might be so,
For to church it never went.*
What with excise, and such device,
The kingdom doth begin
To think you'll leave ne'er a cross
Without doors nor within.

"Methinks the Common Council should
Of it have taken pity,
'Cause, good old cross, it always stood
So firmly to the City.
Since crosses you so much disdain,
Faith, if I were as you,
For fear the king should rule again,
I'd pull down Tyburn too."

Mr. Wood, in his "Ecclesiastical Antiquities of London," gives the site of the ancient Hospital of St. Mary of Rounceval (de Roscidâ valle), at the angle of Whitehall and the Strand, so that no doubt it formed a part of Northumberland House. Dugdale, in his "Monasticon," tells us that the original hospital at Charing Cross was founded for the benefit of "lunatic and distracted people," but that the date of its foundation is not known.

In the year 1554, Charing Cross became the scene of an encounter between the troops of Queen Mary and a band of rebels headed by Sir Thomas Wyatt, who, having taken up arms against the Queen, was advancing against the City. The episode is thus described by the honest chronicler, John Stow :—

"The same night (February 6th), about five of

* An allusion to the absence of Catholics from the Protestant worship.

the clock, a trumpeter went about, and warned all horsemen and men-at-arms to be at St. James's Field; and all footmen also to be there by six of the clock next morning. The Queen's scout, on his return to the court, declared Wyatt's being at Brentford, which sudden news made all in the court wonderfully afraid. Drums went through London at four of the clock in the morning, commanding all soldiers to armour, and so to Charing Cross. Wyatt, hearing that the Earl of Pembroke was come into the field, stayed at Knightsbridge until day, when his men rested, being very weary with the travel of the night and day before, and also partly feebled and faint, having received small sustenance since their coming out of Southwark. There was no small ado in London, and likewise the Tower made great preparation of defence. By ten of the clock, the Earl of Pembroke had set his troop of horsemen on the hill in the highway above St. James's, his footmen were set in two battles somewhat lower, and nearer Charing Cross, at the lane turning down by the brick wall from Islington-ward (St. Martin's Lane), where he had also certain other horsemen, and he had planted his ordnance upon a hill-side in the meantime. Wyatt and his company planted his ordnance upon a hill beyond St. James's, almost over against the Park Corner; and himself, after a few words spoken to his soldiers, came down the old lane on foot, hard by the court gate at St. James's, with four or five ancients, his men marching in good array. The Earl of Pembroke's horsemen hovered all the while without moving, until all was passed by saving the tail; upon which they did set, and cut off; the other marched forward in array, and never stayed or returned to the aid of their tail. The great ordnance shot off freshly on both sides. Wyatt's ordnance overshot the troop of horsemen. The Queen's whole battle of footmen standing still, Wyatt passed along by the wall towards Charing Cross, where the said horsemen that were there set upon part of them, but were soon forced back. At Charing Cross there stood Sir John Gage, Lord Chamberlain, with the guard and a number of others, almost a thousand; the which, upon Wyatt's coming, shot at his company, but at the last fled to the court gates, while certain pursued, and forced with shot to shut the court gate against them. In this repulse, the Lord Chamberlain and others were so amazed that they many cryed treason in the court, and had thought that the Earl of Pembroke, who was assaulting the tail of his enemies, had gone (over) to Wyatt, taking his part against the Queen." The upshot of the affair, however, was that Wyatt surrendered.

Of late years the working classes of London have claimed a right to hold large meetings in Trafalgar Square, but a riot having on one occasion taken place in connection with a Socialistic demonstration, all meetings were for a time prohibited.

The bronze equestrian statue of Charles I. at Charing Cross is generally reckoned one of the best of our public statues, and certainly is admirably placed. It was modelled by Hubert Le Sueur, a Frenchman who came to England about the year 1630, and the statue was cast by a commission from the Earl of Arundel, in 1639, "on a spot of ground hard by Covent Garden Church." It was erected just before the beginning of the serious troubles between Charles and the Parliament. A writer in *Chambers's Journal* thus sums up its history:—"When the hapless monarch was consigned to the block, his statue became as unpopular as himself; accordingly, it was taken down by order of the revolutionary Parliament, and was sold to one Rivers, a brazier, who lived at the Dial near Holborn Conduit, with strict injunctions that it should be broken up. But Rivers was either a royalist or a sly-boots; he kept the statue intact, buried it underground, and drove a brisk trade in knives and forks, with bronze handles, which he pretended were made out of the obnoxious statue. He clearly must have made a good thing out of the knives and forks which he manufactured in bronze for sale, since 'the Royalists no doubt eagerly bought them as relics of their unfortunate and lamented sovereign, whilst the Puritans and Roundheads would be equally glad to secure them as trophies of the downfall of a despot.' Long after the season of turmoil, when Charles II. and the Royalists were in power and in fashion, the bronze statue came again forth into light, and was set up in 1674 on its present position. The stone pedestal, sculptured with the royal arms, trophies, &c., was long regarded as the work of Grinling Gibbons; but, if we may believe Mr. John Timbs, a written account is extant, proving it to be by Joshua Marshall, master-mason to the Crown. On the 29th of May—the anniversary of the restoration of Charles II.—the statue was formerly decorated with boughs of oak. The poet Waller praised the king and the statue with most courtly panegyric, but Andrew Marvell contrived to make a good deal of fun out of both, and in the following way:—Sir Robert Vyner, Lord Mayor of London, about that time had put up an equestrian statue of Charles II. at the Stocks Market, on the spot where the Mansion House now stands; and as Marvell had not much more love for the one than for the other monarch, he wrote a clever satiric dialogue purporting to be held between the two rival horses. Each horse reviled the king who bestrode the other horse—the one attacking the profligacy of Charles II., the other the despotic conduct of Charles I. The Charing Cross steed making an attack on the Stocks Market monarch, said, amongst other bitter things, that it was wondrous

> "That he should be styled 'Defender of Faith,'
> Who believes not a word that the word of God saith."

And added, in allusion to the current belief that Charles II. had professed himself a Roman Catholic:—

> "Though changed his religion, I hope he's so civil
> Not to think his own father is gone to the devil."

It has been said, but we know not with how much of truth, that the sculptor, on finding that he had omitted to put girths to the saddle and trappings of the horse, till it was too late to remedy the defect, put an end to his existence. The omission is stated to have been pointed out by a countryman. Horace Walpole observes of it that "the commanding grace of the figure and the exquisite form of the horse, are striking even to the most unpractised eye."

THE KING'S MEWS. (*From a View by Wale, about* 1750.)

The statue of Charles was once furnished with a sword. The story of the base theft of the weapon, which we have taken from Chambers' "Book of Days," is a strange one, as our readers will see for themselves:—In *Notes and Queries* for 1850, Mr. Planché asked, "When did the real sword which, but a few years back, hung at the side of the equestrian statue of King Charles at Charing

CHARING CROSS FROM NORTHUMBERLAND HOUSE IN 1750.

Cross, disappear? That the sword was a real one of that period, I state upon the authority of my learned friend, Sir Samuel Meyrick, who had ascertained the fact, and who pointed out to me its loss." To this query Mr. Street replied, "The sword disappeared about the time of the coronation of her present Majesty, when some scaffolding was erected around the statue, which afforded great facilities for removing the rapier—for such it was; and I always understood that it found its way into the so-called museum of the notorious Captain D——, where, in company with the wand of the Great Wizard of the North, and other well-known articles, it was carefully labelled and numbered, and a little account appended relating the circumstances of its acquisition and removal." The editor of *Notes and Queries* pointedly added to this communication, "The age of chivalry is certainly past, otherwise the idea of disarming a statue would never have entered the head of any man of arms even in his most frolicsome mood." We may conclude then that the present sword of this remarkable statue is a modern substitute. The pedestal upon which this statue stands is very ornamental. The plinth, formerly of Portland stone, was renewed in granite and slightly raised in 1856; the restoration being made under the superintendence of Sir Gilbert Scott.

The cross was also used for other practical purposes; at its foot royal proclamations were read, and in general any matter of public interest was proclaimed. To this fact Swift alludes:—

> "And all that passes *inter nos*
> May be proclaimed at Charing Cross."

Here, also, occasionally culprits stood in the pillory, as being the most public place in the west of the metropolis. Amongst those who so suffered here was the bookseller, Edmund Curll, who lost his ears on the occasion. His memory is embalmed in the "Dunciad" of Pope, as the author of sundry pieces which deserved anything but immortality. He died in 1748.

We may remark here that some of the regicides, including General Harrison, Peters, and Cook, were executed on the very site where the cross had stood; and Wood, in his "Athenæ Oxonienses," adds that Harrison was put to death with his face looking towards the Banqueting House at Whitehall. Pepys, in his "Diary," thus records the event:—"Oct. 30, 1660. I went out to Charing Cross to see Major-General Harrison hanged, drawn, and quartered; which was done there, he looking as cheerful as any man could do in that condition. He was presently cut down, and his head and heart shown to the people, at which there was great shouts of joy. . . . Thus it was my chance to see the king beheaded at Whitehall, and to see the first blood shed in revenge for the king at Charing Cross." The fanatic Harrison, we may here observe, was the son of a butcher at Newcastle-under-Lyne, appointed by Cromwell to convey Charles I. from Windsor to Whitehall, in order to stand his trial, on which he sat also as one of the judges.

The two regicides Cook and Peters suffered together; and the body of Harrison having hung the due time, was cut down, and the process of quartering commenced, when, at the suggestion of Colonel Turner, Peters was brought forward that he might be witness of the horrible mutilation. The hangman, rubbing his bloody hands, asked him how he liked it. "I am not terrified; do your worst," was the reply; and a few minutes later his strangled body was quivering beneath the knife of the executioner. If the accounts of the last moments of the daring men who suffered at this time be true, it will be seen that, whatever crimes might be laid to their charge, the guilt of cowardice could not be imputed to the regicides.

Charing Cross was one of the places most frequented by shows and exhibitions in the days of Charles II. and James II. In August, 1664, Samuel Pepys writes in his "Diary:" "At Charing Cross, I there saw the great Dutchman that is come over, under whose arm I went with my hat on, and could not reach higher than his eyebrows with the tips of my fingers."

It was at the "Admiral Duncan" tavern, Charing Cross, that, in March, 1824, the men of Cumberland and Westmoreland in the metropolis met together, and resolved to found the Annual North Country Wrestling Matches, which have ever since that time been celebrated year by year on Good Friday, and which we shall mention more fully hereafter.

We are reminded by the author of "Haunted London" that, in 1666–67, an Italian puppet-player set up his booth at Charing Cross, and probably introduced "Punch" into England. He paid a small rent to the overseers of St. Martin's parish, and is called in their book, "Punchinello." "In 1668," adds Mr. Cunningham, "a Mr. Devone erected a small playhouse in the same place." In the Harleian MSS. there is still extant a song in rather rugged verse, written to ridicule the long delay in setting up the king's statue; it is curious as containing an early allusion to "Punch:"—

> "What can the mystery be that Charing Cross
> These five months continues still blinded with board?
> Dear Wheeler impart: we are all at a loss,
> Unless Punchinello is to be restored."

Milton, we are told, lodged at one Thomson's,

next door to the "Bull's Head Tavern," at Charing Cross, close to the opening into Spring Gardens, during the time that he was writing his "Angliæ Defensio."

Thornton, in his "Survey of London and Westminster," published in 1785, tells us that on the north side of Charing Cross there is a large square, on one side of which is a handsome building, used as stabling for his Majesty's horses, and generally known as the "Mews," or "Meuse." The word is derived, as every antiquary knows, from the "mew" of the young of the falcon and hawk tribe. It appears that, as early as the year 1377, this place was used for the purposes of the king's hawks and falconers, the sport of falconry being then one of the most favourite pastimes of the aristocracy, and the Chief Falconer being one of the most important members of the Royal Household. This office, which is hereditary, was granted by Charles II. to Charles, Duke of St. Albans, his son by "Mrs. Gwynne," and "the heirs male of his body;" and it still continues attached to the title. At one time it would seem that the king's stables were at Lomesbury, or, as it is now styled, Bloomsbury; but these stables being burnt down in 1537, King Harry ordered the hawks to be removed, and the "Mews" altered and enlarged for the reception of his steeds; so from that day down to the reign of George IV. the royal stables stood here, and the word "mews," in London at least, has become equivalent to a range of stabling.

It would appear, from such books of London topography as we have been able to consult, that the old building of Henry VIII.'s time having become decayed, a new and handsome edifice was begun in 1732, by George II. It was built in the classical style, with central columns and a pediment, and adorned with cupolas and lanterns; but the effect of this architectural display was spoiled by the narrow space in front, and on either side of it, and by the small and mean buildings with which it was hemmed in. It stood as nearly as possible on the site of the front of the present National Gallery, as is clear from a print in Thornton's "Survey of London and Westminster."

Charing Cross Hospital, which stands a little to the east of St. Martin's Church at the junction of Agar Street and King William Street, was built from the designs of Mr. Decimus Burton. It is one of the twelve general hospitals of the metropolis, and was founded in 1818. The general hospitals, as distinguished from the special hospitals or dispensaries, are "institutions for administering medical and surgical relief to patients within the building (in-patients), or attending at specified times (out-patients), and suffering under any illness or disease, except such as are incurable and contagious." The present hospital was erected in 1831. By this institution not only are patients treated both as out-patients and in-patients, but such as require it are attended at their homes, particularly midwifery cases, and children suffering under contagious disorders. In-patients with letters are admitted on Mondays at twelve; cases of accident at all times immediately. The present yearly average number of patients is about 25,000, and the hospital is almost entirely dependent upon voluntary contributions. Close by, in Chandos Street, is the Eye Hospital, or, to give it its full title, "The Royal Westminster Ophthalmic Hospital." This institution is most cosmopolitan in the bounty which it distributes.

Toole's Theatre, in King William Street, once known as the Charing Cross Theatre, was reopened by Mr. J. L. Toole, after enlargement, in 1882, and finally closed in 1896, the noise from it being found detrimental to the patients of the Charing Cross Hospital. It was formerly used as a chapel and residence by the Fathers of the London Oratory of St. Philip Neri (1848–56), before their removal to Brompton. In 1850 Dr. Newman delivered here his celebrated "Lectures on Anglican Difficulties."

The "Golden Cross," previous to the days of railroads, was a busy and important coaching hotel; in fact, it was called "The Bull and Mouth of the West." Of late years it has degenerated into a railway parcel-office. The author of "Haunted London" tells us that, "till late in the last century, a lofty sign-post, and a long water-trough, such as still adorn country towns, stood before the gate of this inn." It may be well to note here that the old "Golden Cross" Inn, at the door of which Charles Dickens represents Mr. Pickwick to have had the memorable encounter with the philosophic cabman, stood several yards to the west of its present position, and was removed to make way for the laying out of Trafalgar Square.

Re-crossing the Strand at this point, we come to Charing Cross Railway Station and Hotel; and here we may pause to say a few words about the metropolitan railways. The vast strides that have been made in railway communication in the metropolis within the last few years, have been such as almost to encircle London and its suburbs with three distinct lines. The havoc that has been made during this time by the railways which have entered and intersected the metropolis is far greater than could have been imagined; and to describe it we cannot do better than quote the words of a writer in one of the principal illustrated newspapers :—

"First," he says, "the hideous hoarding—and once raised, a hoarding seems the most difficult thing in the world to level: London has become a very city of hoardings; then the task of destroying houses, or of snapping off odd bits of streets, and leaving maimed and melancholy fragments—unsightly, untenantable, forlorn *débris;* then the shapeless scraps of land, unneeded by the railway, and unavailable for other purposes; wretched enclosures, where rubbish may be shot, broken crockery heaped, with the usual refuse of cabbage-stalks, rusty, battered saucepans, dead animals, oyster-shells, and cast boots and shoes—odd ones, always, pairs never come together in these waste territories. Of the abominable bridges that cross the roads at ugly angles; of the viaducts that provide dry arches for the congregation and accommodation of street Arabs and gutter children; of the cucumber frames that supply light and air to the underground traffic; of the colossal sheds of stations, notably those that mar the river's banks, that soar and project like Brobdingnag poke-bonnets—we have no need to remind the reader. These are only to be classed as ruins, inasmuch as they are productive of and occasion ruins, and are themselves ruinous to all chance of the good-looking of London. But that, perhaps, is past praying for. Still, admitting the plainness of our city, we need not surely take pains to make its disadvantages in point of aspect more and more self-assertive and offensive. By discretion and consideration in the matter of mien and attire, even the ugliest can avoid at any rate advertising lack of comeliness and charm.

"But there are other modern ruins than those wrought by railway enterprise and experiment. In various parts of the town may be traced 'our failures' in regard to change and improvement: inchoate works that seem to be the grave-stones of abortive speculation and buried capital. Close to Charing Cross Railway Bridge—itself founded, we may observe, on the ruin of a graceful suspension bridge, of quite modern construction—groups of piles may be discerned, denoting where much treasure has been sunken. These and certain devastations in Scotland Yard are the only evidences that remain of a remarkable scheme, abandoned, or very long in abeyance, for connecting Whitehall and the Waterloo Road by means of a pneumatic railway tube passing under the river. The project may be stone dead or only fast asleep for a term: it has produced a modern ruin, however, not in the least picturesque in its aspect."

At Charing Cross we have two railway stations within a stone's-throw of each other: one is the West-end terminus of the South-Eastern Railway, and the other is a station on the Metropolitan District Railway. The former, which was built about the year 1863, occupies the site of what was once Hungerford Market, and, with the vast building forming the booking-offices and hotel, covers a large space of ground. In the centre of the enclosure facing the Strand, and in front of the hotel and entrance to the railway station, there is a very handsome and elaborate cross, in the decorated Gothic style of the thirteenth and fourteenth centuries, erected in 1863. It is built on or near the spot whereon, if tradition be correct, formerly stood the cross erected by Edward I., to which we have already alluded above. It is said to be a reproduction, as near as possible, of the old one; it is from the designs of Mr. E. M. Barry, R.A., based on the scanty guidance of two or three scarce and indistinct prints. The height from the base to the summit is about seventy feet, and it cost between £1,700 and £1,800. It is of Portland and Mansfield stone, and Aberdeen granite, and the sculptor was Mr. Thomas Earp. Unfortunately, it is dwarfed and obscured by the huge hotel under whose shadow it nestles. It is thus described in the "Curiosities of London:"—"In the upper story are eight crowned statues of Queen Eleanor, four representing her as queen, with the royal insignia, and the other four with the attributes of a Christian woman. At the feet of the statues are eight kneeling figures of angels. The shields in the lower stage are copied from those existing on the crosses at Waltham and Northampton, and on the queen's tomb, displaying the royal arms of England with those of Leon, Castile, and Ponthieu. The diaper above the tracery, in the lowest stage of the monument, is composed of octagonal patterns, richly undercut, representing alternately the Castle of Castile and the lion rampant of Leon; the pillar and couch of the effigy have a similar design. The carving generally of the crockets, capitals, canopies, diapers, gurgoyles, &c., agrees with the best remains of the English art of the thirteenth century."

The bridge by which the lines of railway are carried over the Thames consists of nine spans—six of 154 feet, and three of 100 feet—and is supported by cylinders sunk into the bed of the river, and by the piers and abutments of the old suspension-bridge, the site of which it occupies. The superstructure of each of the 154-feet openings consists of two main-girders, to the outer side of which are suspended cross-girders for carrying the roadway platform. The cross-girders extend beyond the main-girders, and form a series of cantilevers on the outer side, for supporting a foot-path seven feet in width, by which foot-passengers can now pass over toll free. The superstructure of the three 100-feet openings is fan-shaped, and forms the connection of the bridge with the railway station. A beautiful view of the Thames Embankment is obtained from the north end of Charing Cross bridge. Looking eastward, the water-gate, built by Inigo Jones for Villiers, Duke of Buckingham, alluded to in an earlier chapter, appears half hid behind an artificial mound covered with foliage; whilst westward we have a magnificent view of the Houses of Parliament, Westminster Abbey, Lambeth Palace, and other historical buildings.

The Charing Cross station of the Metropolitan District Railway is at the bottom of Villiers Street, and near the stairs leading to the footway over the bridge. The railway, which passes under the roadway of the Embankment, affords a communication between the City and the extreme western suburbs, Richmond, Ealing, &c., by way of Westminster and South Kensington.

The site of Hungerford Market, which existed from the close of the seventeenth century down to 1862, when it was pulled down to make room for the Charing Cross Hotel and Railway Station, was formerly the property of a family of the same name, whose landed estates were at Farley Castle, on the borders of Wiltshire and Somersetshire, not many miles from Bath, and whose tragic fortunes have often been told, but by no one more eloquently than by Sir Bernard Burke, in his "Vicissitudes of Families." Sir Edward Hungerford, who was made a Knight of the Order of the Bath at the coronation of Charles II., had here a magnificent mansion, which, on the break-up of Durham Yard, was cut up and converted into small tenements, which together formed a market, being connected by a covered piazza of not very attractive appearance. Over the market was a large room called "the French Church," from having been used as a place of worship by the Protestant refugees expelled from that country on the revocation of the Edict of Nantes. This building afterwards became a charity-school for the parish of St. Martin's-in-the-Fields, but at the beginning of the present century was in a very dilapidated state. It was subsequently converted into a tavern and music-hall. On the north side of the building stood a very poor bust of Charles II., marking the date of the erection.

The greatness of the Hungerford family ceased with Sir Edward Hungerford, who, by his excessive extravagance, squandered a princely fortune, and died a poor Knight of Windsor in the year 1711, at the advanced age of 115. The town house of the Hungerford family was destroyed by fire during his life, and the circumstance is thus mentioned by Pepys in his "Diary:"—"April 26, 1669.—A great fire happened in Durham Yard last night, burning the house of one Lady Hungerford, who was to come to town to it this night; and so the house is burned, new furnished, by carelessness of the girl, sent to take off a candle from a bunch of candles, which she did by burning it off, and left the rest, as is supposed, on fire. The king and court were here, it seems, and stopped the fire by blowing up the next house." Sir Edward obtained permission to hold a market three days a week on the site of his former mansion, and this was the origin of the Hungerford Market.

The market was rebuilt early in the present century, in a very heavy Italian style of architecture, by Mr. Fowler, the architect of Covent Garden Market. The upper part of the market consisted of three avenues, with shops on each side, the whole roofed into one mass. The business done in the sale of fish was very considerable, and there were also shops or stalls for the sale of fruit, vegetables, and butchers' meat.

The failure of Hungerford Market as a commercial speculation was but the perpetuation of the unhappy fate which seems always to have overhung the fortunes of that name. More than three centuries and a half ago, in 1523, a member of the Hungerford family—Dame Agnes, or Alice, Hungerford—was hung at Tyburn for the murder of her step-son; and some curious details concerning the household stuff remaining at her husband's house at Charing Cross may be found in the thirty-eighth volume of the "Archæologia." The Sir Edward Hungerford of 150 years later, known in history as "the spendthrift," gave 500 guineas for a wig in which to figure at a court ball at St. James's; and to satisfy his fondness for play, he sold no less than twenty-eight manors. It was this Sir Edward who pulled down the town mansion of the Hungerfords. The glory, or shame, of Sir Edward was not forgotten in the market-house which arose on its site, for in a niche on its northern side was placed a bust of that gentleman in a large wig, probably intended to immortalise the extravagant purchase which we have recorded above.

"On my way towards the rotten old Hungerford Stairs," writes Mr. J. T. Smith, in 1829, "my organ of inquisitiveness was arrested by two carvings in stone of a wheatsheaf and sickles, let into the sides of the houses at the north end, leading to the 'Swan.' A waterman said that the southern end of the market was used for the sale of corn; but probably the truer reason is to be found in the fact that that device was the crest of the Hungerfords."

In the row of houses fronting the old market, and forming part of the Strand, at No. 18, where his father was a bookseller, the elder Charles Mathews first saw the light, in 1776. The shop, at that time, was the favourite resort of the leading Nonconformist ministers of the time, including Rowland Hill, Dr. Adam Clarke, &c.

Hungerford Bridge, the approach to which was through the market, was constructed in 1845 upon the suspension principle, and was the work of the late Mr. Brunel. The centre span was, perhaps, the largest of any existing work of the kind, being no less than 676 feet, whilst the total length of the bridge was 1,352 feet. The chains to which the suspending-rods were fastened were double on each side of the bridge; the two piers were of ornamental brickwork, whilst the clear height of the bridge above high water in the centre was 32 feet, and at the sides 28 feet, thus giving a rise of four feet. The span of the centre division of the bridge was the only part worthy of any particular notice. The bridge, which is said to have cost £100,000, opened up a communication between Hungerford Market and the worst part of Lambeth. On its removal, to make room for the present railway bridge, it was transferred to Clifton, near Bristol, where it now spans the waters of the Avon.

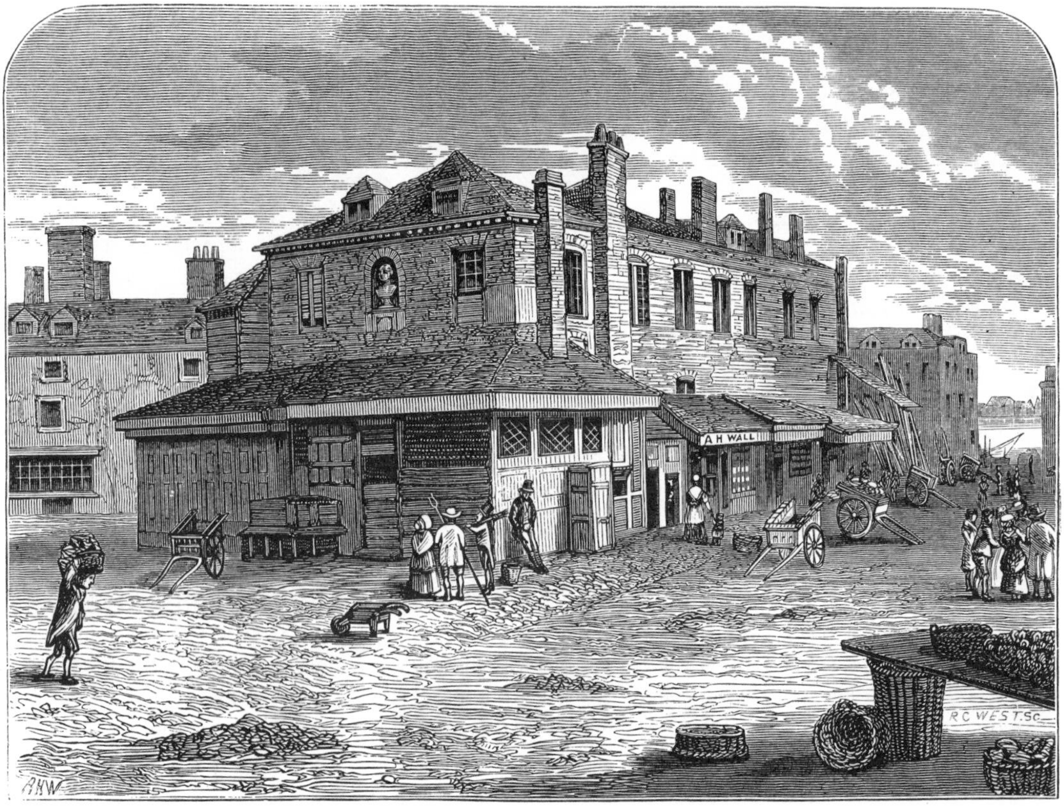

OLD HUNGERFORD MARKET. *(From a View published in* 1805.)

Nearly opposite the railway station, and running diagonally towards Adelaide Street, is the Lowther Arcade. It is nearly 250 feet in length, and has shops on either side for the sale of fancy goods. As the admission is free, and the place is considered one of the "sights" of London, it is continually thronged with children and their attendants, buying toys at the French, German, and Swiss shops. The Lowther Bazaar, which flourished for a time at the period of the Great Exhibition in 1851, was on the other side of the Strand. Besides stalls for the sale of fancy articles, it had many other objects of interest for the amusement of visitors.

Adjoining the Lowther Arcade, with its entrance in Adelaide Street, is the Adelaide Gallery, originally intended as a place of amusement and instruction combined. It was first opened in the year 1830, and named after Queen Adelaide, the consort of William IV. Its varied fortunes, from the day when it was opened as a temple of science, down to its transformation into a casino, are thus cleverly sketched by the late Mr. Albert Smith in his little book on "London Life and Character:"—

"Some time back—dates are dry things, so we need not care about the precise year—there existed in the neighbourhood of the Lowther Arcade an establishment called the Adelaide Gallery. It was at first devoted to the diffusion of knowledge. Clever professors were there, teaching elaborate sciences in lectures of twenty minutes each; fearful engines revolved, and hissed, and quivered, as the fettered steam that formed their entrails grumbled sullenly in its bondage; mice led gasping sub-aqueous lives in diving-bells; clock-work steamers ticked round and round a basin perpetually, to prove the efficacy of invisible paddles; and on all sides were clever machines which stray visitors were puzzled to class either as coffee-mills, water-wheels, roasting-jacks, or musical instruments. There were artful snares laid for giving galvanic shocks to the unwary; steam-guns that turned bullets into bad sixpences against the target; and dark microscopic rooms for shaking the principles of teetotalers, by showing the wriggling abominations in a drop of the water which they were supposed daily to gulp down.

"Then came a transition stage in the existence of the Adelaide Gallery, at first stealthily brought about. The oxy-hydrogen light was slily applied to the comic magic-lantern; and laughing gas was made instead of carbonic acid. By degrees music stole in; then wizards; and lastly, talented vocal foreigners from Ethiopia and the Pyrenees. Science was driven to her wit's end for a livelihood, but she still endeavoured to appear respectable. The names of new attractions were covertly put into the bills, sneaking under the original engines and machines in smaller type. But, between the two stools of philosophy and fun, Science shared the usual fate attendant upon such a position—she broke down altogether. Her grave votaries were disgusted with the comic songs, and the admirers of the banjo were bored with the lectures. So neither went to see her; poor Science declined into the *Gazette*, and fled to America.

"But during all this time a mania for dancing had been gradually coming on, and at last burst forth. Not even the propensity of St. Vitus, when, in the Middle Ages, a red slipper placed on the highway was sufficient to collect and set going a host of dancing maniacs in his popular *pas*, could have kept pace with the movement. New dances were called for, and new music for them. The

HUNGERFORD MARKET, FROM THE BRIDGE, IN 1850. (*See page* 131.)

supply was equal to the demand; the domestic 'Paine's First Set,' of Quadrille's childhood, was laid aside for Herz; then for Musard; and then for Jullien, Weippert, Coote, and others. Clever people had always defined the earth to be one large ball, and there was every chance of its practically proving the truth of the statement.

"Travellers also began to tell bright legends of Terpsichore's palaces in her own land—of the Chaumière, with its bosquets and Montagnes Russes; of the *guinguettes* beyond the barriers of Paris; of the Chateau Rouge; and lastly, of the glittering Bal Mabille, with its palm-tree lights and trellises of bronze vines—its ruling spirits, whose names became great facts in Paris—*grande brune* Mogador, the graceful Frisette and Rigolette, the inimitable student Brididi—*le moulin perpetuel*, as he was called in Quartier Latin—whom no one could approach in his wonderful gyrations; and, finally, the veteran Chicard. And at last all the steam-engines and water-works were cleared away, and the Adelaide Gallery was devoted entirely to the goddess of the 'twinkling feet,' and called a casino. Imagine a long and very high room—so high that there are two rows of museum-like galleries running round the walls, between the floor and ceiling. At one end is a capital orchestra, and beneath it a refreshment room; the entrance staircases are at the other." It was altered into the Marionette Theatre in 1852, and is now one of the refreshment rooms of Messrs. Gatti.

In Craven Street, the next turning westwards after passing the railway station, No. 7, on the west side, as the passer-by is informed by a tablet affixed to the front, was at one time the abode of Benjamin Franklin. It was afterwards used as the head-quarters of the "Society for the Relief of Persons Imprisoned for Small Debts." The abolition, however, of imprisonment for debt in ordinary cases has rendered the work of this society unnecessary. The society was mainly established by the influence of the celebrated Dr. Dodd. It is stated, as a proof of the hardship of the former laws in respect of debtors, that in fifteen months from its commencement, the society was enabled to discharge no less than 986 persons, many of whom were confined only for their fees, and who together had dependent on them as many as 566 wives and 2,389 children. "The objects of this charity," says an old prospectus, "are those, whether men or women, whose debts do not exceed ten pounds; those have the preference who are infirm or have large families."

Craven Street, as we learn from the rate-books of St. Martin's, was known until 1742 as "Spur Alley." It is the property of the Earl of Craven, who gave it his name. According to one account, Grinling Gibbons, whose exquisite wood-carving adorns St. Paul's, was a native of this street, but the fact is disputed. Here, too, lived the Rev. Mr. Hackman, who shot Miss Ray in Covent Garden, as we shall relate hereafter. And here, too, lived and died James Smith, one of the two brothers to whose wit we owe the "Rejected Addresses." In his day, as in our own, the street was largely tenanted by solicitors as offices, a fact which served as the basis of a double epigram; for a friend, noticing the fact, and also the pleasant view of the Thames at the bottom of the street, expressed himself thus—

"Fly, honesty, fly, to some safer retreat,
For there's *craft* in the river, and *craft* in the street."

In answer to which James Smith remarked, off-hand, that there was no necessity to make any such rapid exodus, and why?—

"For the lawyers are *just* at the top of the street,
And the barges are *just* at the bottom."

It was in "Green's Lane in the Strand, near to Hungerford Market," that Sir Edmundbury Godfrey was living at the time when he was murdered: he was a wool merchant, and his wharf was at the bottom of Northumberland Street.

Northumberland Street, which runs down from the Strand, a few doors to the west of Charing Cross Railway Station, was formerly known as Hartshorne Lane. Here lived Ben Jonson in his schoolboy days, going first to a private school near St. Martin's Church, and afterwards to Westminster School. In Northumberland Street was published the *Pall Mall Gazette* for many years after its first appearance in 1864. In Northumberland Court, hard by, Nelson lodged when a young lieutenant.

It is worthy of note that the house next door to Northumberland House, eastwards (now absorbed in the Grand Hotel), was for many years the official residence of the Secretary of State. Sir Harry Vane, as we know, lived here, as also did several of his predecessors and successors in that office.

In concluding our notice of the Strand, we may be pardoned for adding that we love to think of it as it appeared years ago, when it was an open highway, with here and there a great man's house with gardens to the water-side. The scene has now indeed changed, both in the appearance of the great thoroughfare, and in the people by whom it is frequented, so that we are tempted to exclaim with Charles Lamb, "I often shed tears in the motley Strand, for fulness of joy at such multitude of life."

CHAPTER XX.

NORTHUMBERLAND HOUSE AND ITS ASSOCIATIONS.

"Descendunt statuæ, restemque sequuntur."—*Juvenal.*

Situation and Early Owners—Passes into the Hands of the Howards—Called Northampton House—Name changed to Suffolk House—Again altered to Northumberland House—The "Proud" Duke of Somerset—Sir Hugh Smithson, afterwards Duke of Northumberland—Description of the Building—Anecdote about the Percy Lion—The Gardens—Sale and Demolition of the House.—Northumberland Avenue.

After having stood for nearly three hundred years, a most conspicuous feature of London, and the most notable house in the most characteristic of streets, the old town mansion of the Percies was levelled with the ground, in the autumn of the year of grace, 1874, in order to form a new thoroughfare from Charing Cross to the Victoria Embankment. Thus one more landmark of old London, one more witness of the life of the past, has been effaced.

Northumberland House, it is true, could not lay claim to much architectural beauty; and it had been so much altered and rebuilt at various times, that it had no very high pretensions to notice on account of its antiquity; yet few places were more familiar to the Londoner and his "country cousins," few fronts gave more character to their neighbourhood. It was a dull, plain building, full of a certain dignity, indeed, but of the unloveliest fashion of a period when men built houses more for living in than being looked at. "The progress of wealth and of luxury," says a writer in the *Standard*, shortly before its demolition, "has long since dimmed the splendours of what was once the proudest of the London houses of the English nobility. The march of fashion westward had left it isolated amidst an uncongenial neighbourhood of small shops. Commerce had overtaken and overwhelmed it, so that it stood out somewhat abruptly in the full stream of London life, making it too violent a contrast with the surrounding houses, and destroying whatever of felicity there might have been in the situation. In the days when the Strand was but a road between London and Westminster, lined with private houses of the great and noble on either side, and with gardens going down to the river, it might have been an abode fit even for the proud Earls of Northumberland, to whom it descended. But with the Thames Embankment on one side, and Trafalgar Square on the other, with omnibuses perpetually passing its front door, Northumberland House was a standing anachronism, if not an impediment, which was destined to succumb to the influence of time and the Metropolitan Board of Works."

The Percies, it is true, did not build the house, nor was it their first abode in London. Stow mentions two others occupied by this family, before they obtained possession of their Strand tenement, as of many other fair property, by marriage. The first was in the parish of St. Anne's, close to Aldersgate, which in Strype's days had become degraded into a tavern. It was inhabited by Henry Percy (Hotspur) before it was forfeited to Henry IV., who bestowed it upon his wife, Queen Jane, as her "wardrobe." Another Northumberland House was in the parish of St. Katherine Colman, on the south side of Fenchurch Street, the memory of which still survives in Northumberland Alley. This belonged to Henry, the third Earl of Northumberland, in the reign of Henry VI.; and after his time it became converted into a gambling-house, and its gardens into bowling-alleys. A third Northumberland House, occupied by Henry, the ninth earl, was in the Blackfriars, in a house abutting on the property of William Shakespeare.

The Northumberland House which forms the subject of this chapter, was, at the time of its removal, at the close of 1874, the very last relic of all the noble mansions and palaces which, in the seventeenth century, adorned the river-front of the Strand. It may therefore be well to enter into a more elaborate description of it.

It stood, if the antiquary, Pennant, was rightly informed, on the site of a certain chapel, or hospital, of St. Mary, which had been founded in the reign of Henry III., by William, Earl of Pembroke, on a piece of ground which he had given to the priory of Rouncivalle, in Navarre. In the reign of Henry V. the hospital was suppressed, as belonging to an alien monastery, with all the other houses of the kind in the kingdom, but was again restored by Edward IV., to be finally dissolved at the Reformation.

By Henry VIII. the house was granted to a private individual, who is styled Sir Thomas Cawerden, but of whom little or nothing is known. It afterwards belonged to Sir Robert Brett, and from his hands it appears to have passed into those of Henry Howard, Earl of Northampton, who, in the time of James I., built here a house, calling it after his own name. He left it to his kinsman, the Earl of Suffolk, known to history as Lord High Treasurer; and by the marriage of Algernon Percy,

Earl of Northumberland, with Elizabeth, daughter and heiress of Thomas, Earl of Suffolk, it passed into the hands of the Percies, Earls, and afterwards Dukes, of Northumberland.

From a paper privately printed by the Duke of Northumberland, in 1866, we learn that the site of this house and garden was purchased, with other property, in the beginning of the seventeenth century, from Sir Robert Brett, by Henry Howard, Earl of Northampton, the second son of Henry, Earl of Surrey, "the poet." On this site, the Earl of Northampton built a "sumptuous palace," having for his architects Benard Jansen, a foreigner of some repute in the time of James I., and also Gerard Christmas. The house, which was of brick, was finished in the year 1605, and was then called "Northampton House." The initials of Gerard Christmas were preserved in the letters C. Æ, (Christmas Ædificavit), which used to be in large capitals over the old stone gateway, which was pulled down and replaced by a new front towards the Strand, in the reign of George II. The house at that time consisted of three sides of a quadrangle, the centre fronting the Strand, and open towards the garden and river. The Earl of Northampton died here in 1614. By his will, dated the 14th of June, 1614, he devised this house and garden, with the river-side property, to his nephew, Thomas Howard, first Earl of Suffolk, the second son of Thomas, fourth Duke of Norfolk. This was the Earl of Suffolk who, as Lord Thomas Howard, "being in that memorable engagement of the Spanish Armada, was, at sea, knighted for his good services therein." He was created Earl of Suffolk, and appointed Lord High Treasurer by James I. He completed the quadrangle by building the front towards the garden and the river.* It was then called "Suffolk House;" and it may be mentioned as a proof of the ease with which names are changed in London, that Howell, in his "Londinopolis," speaks of it as "that most stately palace of Suffolk or Northampton House." To this house Suckling refers in his ballad on the marriage of Roger Boyle, Lord Broghill, with the Lady Margaret Howard, daughter of the Earl of Suffolk. The Earl of Suffolk died here in 1626, when the property passed to his son Theophilus, second Earl of Suffolk, and then to his grandson James, third Earl of Suffolk, whose sister, the Lady Elizabeth Howard, married, in 1642, Algernon Percy, Earl of Northumberland. On this marriage the property was, by an indenture dated a few days previously, conveyed by the Earl of Suffolk and his trustees to the trustees of the Earl of Northumberland. The principal apartments were then on the Strand side, but the Earl of Northumberland reconstructed the garden or river front, under the direction of Inigo Jones, and that front then comprised the principal apartments; it is mentioned by Evelyn as being "the new front," when he visited the house in 1658. The house was afterwards called "Northumberland House."

This Earl of Northumberland was the earl who was so celebrated in the times of Charles I. and the Commonwealth, and to whom the care of the royal children was committed by the Parliament. It was in the spring of 1660, after he had taken up his quarters at Whitehall, that "General Monk was invited, with the Earl of Manchester, Hollis, Sir William Waller, Lewis, and other eminent persons, to Northumberland House," by Earl Algernon, and here (says Lord Clarendon), "in secret conference with them, some of those measures were concerted which led to the speedy restoration of the Monarchy."

The *menu* of the noble family at Northumberland House about this time was curious, if we may judge from an entry in the Earl of Northumberland's Household Book, where we find allowed for "my Lord and Ladie's table," "ij. pecys of salt fische, vj. pecys of salt fische, vj. becormed herryng, iiij. white herryng, or a dish of sproots (sprats)." Surely, a deep draught of Canary or Malvoisie would be needed to wash down so dry a repast!

The Earl of Northumberland last-mentioned died in the year 1688. Joceline, his son and successor, was the last of the old male line, and on his death, in 1670, without sons, Northumberland House became the property of his only daughter, the Lady Elizabeth Percy,† the celebrated heiress of that day, who married the "proud" Duke of Somerset, for, it is said, her third husband. Her first husband, whom she married when only fourteen years of age, was Henry Cavendish, Earl

* This nobleman also built Audley End, in Essex, now the seat of Lord Braybrooke. Evelyn, in his description of this place ("the goodly palace built by Howard, Earl of Suffolk, once Lord Treasurer"), which he visited in 1654, refers to the pavilions, where, "instead of railes and balusters, there is a bordure of capital letters, as was lately also at Suffolk House, near Charing Cross, built by the said Lord Treasurer."

† Lady Elizabeth Percy was, in her own right, Baroness Percy. On the death of her father, in 1670, the honours created by Queen Mary ceased. Charles II. created, in 1674, his natural son, by the Duchess of Cleveland, George Fitz Roy, Earl, and afterwards Duke of Northumberland; but that nobleman dying in 1716 those dignities expired. In the meantime one James Percy, a trunk-maker, claimed the honours of the Percy family, and so annoyed the House of Lords that their lordships at last sentenced him to wear a paper in Westminster Hall, declaring him "a false and impudent pretender to the earldom of Northumberland."—*Burke's Peerage.*

of Ogle (son and heir of Henry, Duke of Newcastle), who assumed the name of Percy. According to Sir Bernard Burke, her ladyship "appears to have been only contracted to Thomas Thynne, Esq., of Longleate, who was assassinated in February, 1681–2;" but she married, in 1682, Charles Seymour, Duke of Somerset, who also assumed, by preliminary engagement, the surname and arms of Percy, "but from that stipulation he was released when her grace attained majority." At Northumberland House the Duke and Duchess lived "in great state and magnificence."

With reference to this nobleman a story is told, which may bear repetition here, to the effect that he was in the habit of driving up to town from his residence at Petworth, in Sussex, in imitation of royalty, in a coach and six. On one occasion, when sitting in his easy chair, after his second or third marriage, the duchess entered the room, and was about to salute him with a kiss. This so wounded the dignity of his Grace, that he is reported to have severely reprimanded the duchess, telling her that even his first wife, the noble heiress of the Percies, would not have thought of taking such liberties with him.

On the death of his Grace, in 1748, the property passed to his son Algernon, who, on the death of his mother, in 1722, had been summoned to Parliament as Baron Percy. His Grace greatly improved the north, or Strand front, and built the gallery, or great room, forming the western wing to the south front. In the cornice or balustrading on the top of the south front he caused to be inserted the letters and date, "A. S. P. N. (Algernon Seymour Princeps Northumbriæ), A.D. 1749." As there was already a Somerset House, the mansion, during the time it was the residence of the Dukes of Northumberland, was still called "Northumberland House." His Grace was created Baron Warkworth of Warkworth Castle, Northumberland, and Earl of Northumberland, in 1749, with remainder, in default of male issue, to Sir Hugh Smithson, Bart., a country gentleman of Stanwick, in Yorkshire, who had married his only daughter, the Lady Elizabeth Seymour.

It was at Northumberland House, about this time, that Oliver Goldsmith, "our gentle poet," when waiting upon the Earl of Northumberland, mistook the earl's servant for the earl, and only discovered his error after the delivery of a neatly-ordered address, after which the poor author precipitately fled. His Grace died in 1750, when the property passed to his said daughter, whose husband was afterwards created Duke of Northumberland. This nobleman faced the quadrangle with stone, and added to the gallery wing, built by the Duke of Somerset. He also restored the Strand front and other parts which had been damaged by a great fire there in 1780. From Hugh, first Duke of Northumberland, the property passed to his son Hugh, second duke, and then to his grandsons, Hugh, Algernon, and George, the third, fourth, and fifth dukes successively.

"The noble family of Northumberland," says a writer in the *Builder*, "have always been famed for their hospitality and humanity. The name of Smithson has obtained fame and an adjectival form in the United States, where the munificence of an Englishman (who claimed some kind of connection with the noble family of Northumberland) has given that country the opportunity of raising a noble institution for the advancement and popularisation of science."

Besides the principal quadrangle, which was to the north, and which the visitor entered at the porter's lodge from the Strand, the building had two wings running down at right angles from the main body of the house towards the river; that on the eastern side being devoted to the accommodation of the domestics, with stabling beyond; whilst the western wing contained the Grand Ball Room, in which royalty must often have been present, at various dates, from the days of Horace Walpole to our own time.

Along the Strand front, as we learn from Evelyn's memoirs, instead of the customary ornamental railings, there ran "a border of capital letters;" and that this was the case is corroborated by an entry in the burial register of St. Martin's Church, where a young man named Appleyard was buried in May, 1618, "slain by a stone falling from my Lord Treasurer's house."

According to a drawing by Hollar in the Pepysian Library at Cambridge (we give a facsimile of it on page 6), Northumberland, or, as it was then called, Suffolk House, is represented as a square, dull, and heavy-looking building, with lofty towers at the four angles, ending in domes of irregular shape. The house is apparently three storeys high, and has a high pitched roof. Each side is pierced with nine heavy-looking windows. The print represents it as it appeared in the early part of the reign of Charles I. The gardens between the house and the Thames are filled with a grove of trees, and alongside the river is a dull, long wall, with stairs leading down to the water.

Evelyn thus records in his "Diary," under date 1658:—"I went to see the Earl of Northumberland's pictures at Suffolk House, whereof that of the 'Venetian Senators'" (better known by its other name of the "Cornaro Family"), "was one of the best of Titian's; and another of Andrea del Sarto, viz. 'a Madonna, Christ, St. John, and an Old Woman,' &c.; a 'St. Catharina' of Da Vinci, with divers portraits of [by] Vandyke; a 'Nativity' of Georgioni; the 'Last of our Blessed Kings' (Charles I.), and the 'Duke of York,' by Lely; a 'Rosarie' by the famous Jesuits of Bruxelles, and severall more. The new front towards the gardens is tolerable, were it not drown'd by a too massie and clomsie pair of stayres of stone, without any neate invention."

There is a fine picture of Northumberland House by Canaletti, showing the small houses and other tenements opposite to it, and the Strand with the sign-boards in front of the houses. A copy of the picture is given on page 139.

"There is a tradition," says Mr. Nightingale, in the "Beauties of England," "that when the Earl of Northampton erected his mansion at the village of Charing, he was ridiculed for having chosen a situation so far distant from his town residence; and, indeed, if we cast our eye over the maps of London, published about that period, we shall not be surprised at the remark."

From 1605, when the house was finished by the Earl of Northampton, almost down to the time of its demolition, so many changes were made in the building at different periods, that, in fact, with the exception of the front, little of the old house remained. Great alterations were made at Northumberland House in the years 1748–1752, which were begun by Algernon, Duke of Somerset, and completed by his son-in-law and daughter, the Earl and Countess of Northumberland. Northumberland House more than once suffered very severely from fire. The following is an account of one that occurred on Saturday, March 18th, 1780:—"It broke out about five in the morning, and raged till eight, in which time it burnt from the east end, where it began, to the west. Among the apartments consumed are those of Dr. Percy, Dean of Carlisle. We are happy to inform our readers that the greatest part of the doctor's invaluable library is fortunately preserved." It was here that the poetical doctor, whilst residing as chaplain, was visited by his brother poet, Oliver Goldsmith.

In the year 1749 the whole building was repaired and altered, the blue lion (the crest of the Percies) being placed in the position in which he was to be

STAIRCASE IN NORTHUMBERLAND HOUSE. *From an Original Sketch.* (*See page* 140.)

NORTHUMBERLAND HOUSE. (*From the View by Canaletti.*)

seen for 125 years. There is an apocryphal legend in connection with that noble brute, that he was at first placed with his head towards Carlton House and St. James's Palace, but afterwards, on the occasion of some slight received by one of the Dukes of Northumberland, turned round with its face to the Corporation of London. The quarrel being made up after the accession of the Prince Regent as George IV., the lion returned to his original bearings. It was on this occasion, we believe, that "the first gentleman in Europe" remarked that "the king knows nothing and remembers nothing of the quarrels of the Prince of Wales."

Pennant, writing in 1806, observes, "It is unfortunate that nothing can be more confined than the situation of this great house. The noble front is pent up by a very narrow part of the Strand, and behind by a mean cluster of houses, coal-wharves, and other offensive objects, as far as the banks of the Thames." He congratulates himself, however, on the probability of seeing, in a little time, these nuisances removed, and a terrace arising in their stead, rivalling that of Somerset House. What would the zealous old antiquary have said had he lived to our day, and seen the materials of the palace of the proud house of Percy sold as old building materials under the auctioneer's hammer?

As to its interior, it was a grand, but dull and gloomy house, containing a large number of rooms. Everything in it, pictures, furniture, &c., were massive and costly in the extreme; but the want of light caused it to lack that air of cheerfulness which is so characteristic of the modern Italian style.

The central part of the Strand front, which, in a tablet on the top, bore the date when some alterations in that part of the building were made about the year 1752, might be considered as the most valuable remnant of the original pile. The lion, by which it was surmounted, was cast in lead, and was about twelve feet in length. The vestibule of the interior was eighty-two feet long, and more than twelve in breadth, ornamented with Doric columns. Each end communicated with a staircase, leading to the principal apartments facing the garden and the Thames. They consisted of several spacious rooms fitted up in the most elegant manner, embellished with paintings, among which might be found the well-known "Cornaro Family," by Titian, a work well worthy of its reputation, and for which Algernon, Earl of Northumberland, is stated to have given Vandyck 1,000 guineas; and a wonderful vase, which now has a story of its own; "St. Sebastian Bound," by Guercino; "The Adoration of the Shepherds," by Bassano; and others by well-known masters. The great feature of the house was the ball-room, or grand gallery, upwards of 100 feet in length, in which were placed large and very fine copies by Mengs, after Raphael's "School of Athens," in the Vatican, of the size of the originals; also the "Assembly of the Gods," and the "Marriage of Cupid and Psyche," in the Farnesina; the "Triumph of Bacchus and Ariadne," from Caracci's picture in the Farnese Palace; and "Apollo driving the Chariot of the Sun," from Reni's fresco in the Villa Rospigliosi, at Rome. These celebrated works, and the decoration of the noble apartment, constituted it one of the landmarks of high art in the metropolis. The grand staircase consisted of a centre flight of thirteen moulded vein marble steps, and two flights of sixteen steps, with centre landing twenty-two feet by six feet, two circular plinths, and a handsome and richly-gilt ormolu scroll balustrade, with moulded Spanish mahogany hand-rail. The mansion contained nearly 150 rooms appropriated for the private uses of the family.

Previously to 1851, those few who obtained admission to the fine apartments of this grand old mansion, did so with considerable difficulty, and few therefore had any idea of what was behind the familiar front; but in that year, when multitudes visited London and the Great Exhibition, the house was thrown open to the public, and thousands availed themselves of the privilege to walk across the courtyard and up the handsome marble staircase, into the noble ball-room and picture-gallery, and inspect the rich treasures which the house contained.

The gardens on the river-front occupied a larger space than might have been suspected, but had long been left unkempt and neglected, forming a little wilderness in close proximity to the busiest thoroughfare in London. Their aspect, when at last the light of publicity was thrown upon them, was somewhat sad and ghastly, the old hawthorns and hazels looking like Dryads of old suddenly exposed to the gaze of an irreverent troop of Satyrs. With their departure, under the ruthless decree of the Board of Works, has disappeared one more green spot from the heart of London.

We may add, that in the privately-printed documents referred to above, the last owner of this noble mansion appeared to have given his sanction for its removal with great reluctance, if we may judge from the tenor of the concluding paragraph, which runs thus:—"The Duke of Northumberland is naturally desirous that this great historical house, commenced by a Howard, continued by a Percy, and completed by a Seymour, which has been the residence of his ancestors for more than two centuries and a half, should continue to be the residence of his descendants; but the Metropolitan Board of Works are desirous that this house, which, with its garden, is one of the landmarks of London, and is probably the oldest residential house in the metropolis, should be destroyed." Arrangements for its sale to the Metropolitan Board of Works, in order to open an entrance to the Thames Embankment, were completed in 1873, the purchase-money agreed upon being £500,000. The sale was concluded definitely in June, 1874. In the following month the lion, which had stood for a century and a quarter, keeping watch and ward over the great entrance, was taken down and removed to Sion House at Isleworth; and the work of demolition was soon afterwards commenced.

In September, 1874, the fine old mansion underwent its final phase of degradation, its materials being brought under the hammer of the auctioneer. The lots consisted of 3,000,000 bricks, the grand marble staircase, the elaborate ornamentation of the hall, dining, and reception rooms, the state decorations which adorned the hall and corridors, &c. The aggregate sum realised by the sale amounted to but little more than £6,500, and of this the grand staircase alone fetched £360.

On the site of Northumberland House and its gardens three monster hotels, called the Grand, the Victoria, and the Métropole, have been erected. The fronts of the hotels open upon a broad roadway, connecting Charing Cross with the Embankment, and known as Northumberland Avenue. In this thoroughfare are the Royal Colonial Institute and the offices of the Society for Promoting Christian Knowledge. The former of these institutions, established in 1868, furnishes a point of contact for those connected with the Colonies and India.

CHAPTER XXI.

TRAFALGAR SQUARE, THE NATIONAL GALLERIES, &c.

"England expects that every man
This day will do his duty."—*Old Song.*

Formation of Trafalgar Square—The "King's Mews"—Mr. Cross's Menagerie—A State Coach-house—The Royal Humane Society—The Nelson Monument—Sir E. Landseer's Lions—Statues of George IV., Havelock, Napier, and General Gordon—Proposal for planting Trafalgar Square as a Garden—The Royal College of Physicians—Dr. Harvey's Benefaction—Anecdote of Dr. Baillie—Dr. Radcliffe and Sir Godfrey Kneller—History of the Foundation of the College of Physicians—Cockspur Street—O'Brien, the Irish Giant—Statue of George III.—Society of Painters in Water-colours—The National Gallery—Its Formation and Subsequent Additions—Agitation for an Academy of Painting—Sir Godfrey Kneller's Drawing Academy—Sir James Thornhill's Propositions rejected—Establishment of the Royal Academy—Sir Joshua Reynolds, Benjamin West, Sir Thomas Lawrence, Sir Martin A. Shee, Sir Charles L. Eastlake, Sir Francis Grant, Lord Leighton, Sir John Millais, and Sir E. J. Poynter—The National Portrait Gallery.

THE large and open space known as Trafalgar Square, occupying as it does a commanding position, as it looks down Parliament Street towards the Abbey and the Houses of Parliament, was pronounced by the great Sir Robert Peel, perhaps with a little exaggeration, the finest site in Europe. Its formation was commenced about the year 1830, on a spot of ground that up to that time was covered with a knot of filthy and disreputable abodes. In 1829, it appears, a variety of improvements were made immediately around St. Martin's Church. Amongst others, a whole labyrinth of close courts and small alleys was then cleared away—a district including places known as the Bermudas, the Caribbee or Cribbe Islands, and Porridge Island, notorious for its cook-shops; whilst, nearer Charing Cross, several wretched buildings were swept away, with the same object in view. The savoury delights of "Porridge Island" as a provocation to the appetite more than once formed the subject of banter between Dr. Johnson and Mrs. Thrale, at Streatham.

There had previously been an open space or square on this spot, but of more contracted dimensions. On its north side, where now stands the National Gallery, was the large building called the "King's Mews," to which we have alluded in a previous chapter. It was from this place, during the civil wars of the houses of York and Lancaster, that the Lincolnshire rebels, under Robert Rydsdale, took Lord Rivers and his son John, carried them away, and beheaded them at Northampton. Early in the present century the "Mews" was occupied by Mr. Cross's collection of wild animals, which were removed hither on the breaking-up of Exeter 'Change; here also the first exhibitions of machinery were held, and the public records were for a long time preserved—or, at least, such of them as were not eaten by rats. It may be added that Chaucer was not only Clerk of the King's Works, but also "Clerk of the Mews at Charing."

On the east side of the square was a mean-looking building, with folding doors, used as a state coach-house in the time of George II. Here at the present time are the offices of the Humane Society. This benevolent institution, which was founded by Dr. Hawes in the year 1774, has been instrumental in saving thousands of lives from drowning, more especially in the Thames and in the ornamental waters in the public parks. We shall have to speak of its operations hereafter, when we come to describe the Serpentine.

In the centre of the open space, facing the statue of King Charles, and looking down Whitehall to the Abbey and Houses of Parliament, stands the statue of Lord Nelson, upon the summit of a column which the nation raised, it must be owned, with a tardy generosity, in 1840–3, in honour of her greatest naval hero. The fluted column itself, with capital cast in gun-metal, which is 176 feet high, and in the Corinthian style, was designed by Mr. William Railton, architect; whilst the colossal statue of the great naval hero is the work of the late Mr. E. H. Baily, R.A., and is admired for its fine proportions. The square pedestal is thirty-six feet in height, and is of beautiful proportion, the four sides containing, in basso-relievo, representations of Nelson's four great battles, cast in gun-metal taken from the enemy in his various engagements—namely, the Battle of the Nile, by Woodington; the Battle of St. Vincent, by Watson; the Battle of Copenhagen, by Ternouth; and the Death of Nelson, by Carew. These four works are fine examples of English sculpture, and, with the statue, cost above £28,000. The four gigantic lions at the angles of the base were at first assigned to the sculptor, Mr. Lough, but were subsequently executed by the late Sir Edwin Landseer. The attempt to add the laurels of a sculptor to those of a painter can hardly be said to have been a successful one. For many years the lions were not forthcoming, and the guardians of the pillar were still in the artist's studio at St. John's Wood Road. They were so constantly promised that at last the public patience was sorely tried, and Sir Edwin's embryo lions began to furnish a standing jest to the newspaper writers. At length, in the year 1868, they were set up; but many a cruel joke was uttered at their expense: amongst others it was said that the old lion on the top of Northumberland House would not acknowledge them as brethren.

On the north side of the enclosure, between the column and the National Gallery, are two fountains, supplied by a well near Charing Cross, upwards of 380 feet deep, sunk by Messrs. Easton and Amos, for the Government, for the purpose of supplying these fountains, Buckingham Palace, and several of the Government offices in Whitehall. The fountains are of Peterhead granite, but are by no means striking objects. They were an afterthought, being added in 1845, from a design by the late Sir Charles Barry.

In the north-east corner of Trafalgar Square is the bronze equestrian statue of George IV., by Sir F. Chantrey, which was placed in its present position in 1845. It is considered a very fine work of art, and cost 9,000 guineas. At the south-east corner of the Square is the bronze statue erected in 1861, to the memory of Major-General Sir Henry Havelock, from the design of Behnes; and at the south-west corner is another bronze statue, of Sir Charles Napier, by Adams, erected in 1857; while in 1888 a statue of General Gordon, by Thornycroft, was erected in the centre of the Square facing the Nelson column.

Upon the demolition of Northumberland House, mentioned in the preceding chapter, the Duke of Northumberland offered to lay out some of the purchase-money which he received for his late residence in beautifying Trafalgar Square. *Apropos* of this intention, it may be observed that this was not the first time that such a plan had been contemplated, as in the "British Almanack and Companion," published in 1838 by Charles Knight, the following notice occurs:—"How the area of Trafalgar Square will be laid out or decorated we cannot yet say. At present a strong opposition is manifesting itself to the plan of its being made an enclosed garden, under the pretence that the people will thereby be deprived of an open promenade. This, however," observes Mr. Knight, "does not exactly follow, for the public might be admitted into the garden under the same regulations as those under which they are now admitted into St. James's Park."

In 1879 the work of "beautifying" Trafalgar Square, by planting it with trees, was carried out; the trees being continued on either side of Northumberland Avenue, to those on the Embankment.

At the north-west corner of the Square, with its frontage in Pall Mall East, is the Royal College of Physicians. This elegant and commodious building was erected in 1825, from the designs of the late Sir Robert Smirke. The principal front of the structure is composed of a hexastyle projecting portico of the Ionic order, which supports a well-proportioned pediment. The front is elongated by two antæ in one each side of the portico, which is repeated, with a break between them, in the eastern front; it has also a distinguishing centre-piece of two slightly-projecting antæ and an elevated attic, with a balustrade in each wing.

The building is divided into two storeys, and the windows are decorated with architraves and sub-cornices. The columns are beautifully wrought, and impart to the edifice at once a pleasing and grand appearance. Within, the apartments are of airy and noble proportions. A door on the left of the entrance-hall leads into the dining-room, which is lighted by six windows overlooking Trafalgar Square. The room is handsomely decorated, and has over the fireplace a fine portrait of Dr. Harvey. During the time of the Civil War, when the property of the College at Amen Corner was condemned as part of the possessions of the Church, and actually put up to auction, Dr. Harvey became the purchaser, and shortly afterwards settled it in perpetuity upon the College. From the entrance-hall a staircase leads towards the gallery or landing, whence are entered the library and Censor's room. This latter apartment has its oak-panelled walls adorned with pictures and busts. Here Candidates for diplomas used to undergo their examinations, at three separate meetings of the Censors' board, the *vivâ voce* part of each such examination being carried on in Latin. These examinations are strict, and afford good security to the public that none but those who have had a liberal and learned education can hope for success, and that the order of English physicians shall always consist of men who will do honour to their profession by their general abilities and high qualifications. Among the busts that adorn the Censor's room, is one of Dr. Baillie, of whom the following anecdote is told in Charles Knight's "London:"—"This learned doctor was occasionally very irritable, and indisposed to attend to the details of an uninteresting story. After listening with torture to a prosing account from a lady who ailed so little that she was going to an opera that evening, he had happily escaped from the room, when he was urgently requested to step up stairs again; it was to ask him whether on her return from the opera she might eat some oysters. 'Yes, ma'am,' said Baillie, 'shells and all!'"

The library, a splendid room—long, broad, and high—is lighted by three beautiful lanterns in the ceiling, and the walls consist of two storeys, marked at intervals by flat oaken pillars below, and clusters of flat and round imitation-marble pillars above. In the lower storey the shelves round the walls are filled with books, mostly the gift of the Marquis of Dorchester, who left his valuable library to the College. In the gallery which extends round the upper part of the room, the walls are fitted up with bookcases, hidden by crimson curtains, containing preparations, amongst which are some of the nerves and blood-vessels constructed by Hunter. From the gallery a narrow staircase leads up to a small theatre or lecture-room, where are some interesting busts and portraits, and among the latter a fine one of Hunter. Among the portraits in the library is one of Dr. Radcliffe, the founder of the magnificent institution at Oxford which bears his name, and whose executors gave £2,000 towards the erection of this building. It was painted by Sir Godfrey Kneller. An anecdote in which both the painter and the doctor are concerned we give as it is related:—"They lived next to each other in Bow Street, Covent Garden, and the painter having beautiful pleasure-grounds, a door was opened for the accommodation of his friend and neighbour. In consequence of some annoyance, Sir Godfrey threatened to close up the door; to which Radcliffe replied that he might do anything with it, if he would not paint it. 'Did my very good friend Dr. Radcliffe say so?' cried Sir Godfrey. 'Go you back to him, and after presenting my service to him, tell him that I can take anything from him but physic.'"

The eminent society of which we are speaking was established in 1523, under a charter from Henry VIII., which authorised its council to forbid any one to practise as a physician within seven miles of London without having been admitted a licentiate or fellow of this College. Nor can any one become a fellow without having taken a degree in the faculty of medicine at Oxford or Cambridge, or be admitted a licentiate without a previous study at an English university, or obtaining a diploma from Edinburgh, Glasgow, or Dublin, and passing an examination before the Censors of the College.

The first building which served as a "college" for the society was a mansion in Knightrider Street, given to them by Dr. Linacre, physician to King Henry VIII. They afterwards removed to a house which they purchased in Amen Corner, Paternoster Row, where Dr. Harvey built a library and a public hall, which he granted for ever to the College, and endowed it with his estate, which he resigned to them in his lifetime. Part of this estate is assigned for an annual oration in commemoration of their munificent benefactor, and to provide a dinner for the members of the College. This building was burned down in the Great Fire of 1666, after which the society purchased a piece of ground on the west side of Warwick Lane, and raised a considerable sum in 1674 for the erection of a new college. Sir John Cutler offering to subscribe a large donation, a committee was appointed to wait upon him to thank him for his liberality; and in 1668 statues in honour of the king and the liberal donor were ordered to be executed at the expense of the College. In 1689, the buildings being completed, the Fellows borrowed a sum of money of Sir John to defray the expenses; but, upon his death, to their great surprise, his executors demanded upwards of £7,000 of them; as in his books he had made them debtors, not only for the sum he had lent them, but also for the sum he had given them, and all the accumulated interest. The executors at length accepted £2,000, and the College expunged the inscription of the old miser's liberality from under his statue, that remained in a niche in the western front of the theatre, which was standing in Warwick Lane down to a very recent period.*

The majority of the leading physicians and of their opulent patients now reside more to the westward of the metropolis than they did in the reign of Charles II., when the fellows assembled in that goodly building of brick and stone which Dr. Garth describes in his "Dispensary" as a place—

> "Where stands a dome majestic to the sight,
> And sumptuous arches bear its oval height;
> A golden globe, placed high with artful skill,
> Seems to the distant sight a gilded pill."

* See Vol. I., p. 216, and Vol. II., p. 431.

Accordingly they removed their establishment to the substantial and elegant structure in Pall Mall East here described.

Cockspur Street, the thoroughfare uniting Charing Cross with Pall Mall East, skirts the south side of the Union Club, which joins on to the Royal College of Physicians, and of which we will say more in our chapter on the Club-land of Pall Mall. In this street died, in 1783, O'Brien, the famous Irish giant, whom we have already mentioned in our account of the College of Surgeons in Lincoln's Inn Fields. At the junction of this street with Pall Mall stands the equestrian statue of George III., by Wyatt, which, though it has been considered, in an equestrian sense, one of the best "seats" for a horseman in London, has been much derided on account of the stiff "pig-tail" so characteristic of that monarch. When it was cast, in 1835 or 1836, permission was obtained for its erection on the triangular spot of waste ground on which it stands—not a bad place to show off a statue to advantage. But some of the tenants of the adjoining houses, finding that in their leases it was covenanted that the open space should not be occupied, raised objections which were held valid

GARDEN FRONT OF NORTHUMBERLAND HOUSE. *From an Original Sketch.* (*See page* 140.)

by the then Vice-Chancellor. His ruling, however, was set aside on appeal to the Lord Chancellor, and so the statue was set up.

Returning along Pall Mall East we have on our left, next to the United University Club House, the building devoted to the uses of the Royal Society of Painters in Water-Colours, of which Sir John Gilbert, R.A., is president. The exhibition of the works of members of this society takes place twice in the year, in spring and winter, and the public are admitted on payment of a shilling.

the main front is too much cut up in petty detail, and some have even humorously nicknamed it "The National Cruet-stand"—an idea which has evidently been suggested by the pepperbox-shaped cupolas with which it is crowned.

The National Collection of Paintings originated in the year 1824, in the purchase of the Angerstein gallery of thirty-eight pictures, for which a sum of £57,000 was voted by Government. The owner of these pictures, Mr. Julius Angerstein, was an opulent banker, and secured his collection abroad,

SIR JOSHUA REYNOLDS. (*See page* 148.)

We now arrive at the National Gallery, and ascend the steps leading to the portico, where we certainly obtain one of the finest views in London. Looking across Trafalgar Square, its fountains sparkling (occasionally) in the sunlight, the scene embraces the open vista of Whitehall and Parliament Street, which is closed by the towers and pinnacles of the Houses of Parliament and the venerable walls of the Abbey.

From its first conception to the present time no building, perhaps, has been the subject of more lively criticism than that which now serves as the chief depository of the pictures belonging to the nation. The edifice is hardly a fine one in itself, nor is it considered in any sense adequate to its national object. Most persons agree that

chiefly during the war against the Great Napoleon. The nucleus of a National Gallery having been thus formed, several bequests and presentations of valuable paintings were afterwards made to the nation by public-spirited individuals, and extensive purchases have also been at different times effected by the Government, mainly on the recommendation of the President of the Royal Academy. Sir George Beaumont, an amateur artist of great taste and skill, presented to the country, in 1826, fifteen choice pictures, chiefly by the ancient masters. In the same year the Rev. William Holwell Carr, who is stated to have expended a fortune in acquiring it, bequeathed to the nation the whole of his collection, amounting to about thirty in number, and all of a high class. This was followed, in 1838, by a bequest from Lord Farnborough of fifteen paintings, comprising specimens of the Dutch, Flemish, and Italian schools. Eighteen more pictures were presented by Lieut.-Colonel Ollney. George IV., William IV., and the Duke of Northumberland are also to be included amongst the liberal contributors to the national collection. The Governors of the British Institution likewise presented several valuable paintings. To these were added the collections made by Mr. Vernon and Mr. Wynn Ellis; and last, though not least, there is the Turner collection, which was presented to the nation by the greatest of our modern landscape painters.

These pictures—at least, such of them as were national property—were at first shown to the public in a small, dingy, ill-lighted house on the south side of Pall Mall, until 1833, when it was proposed to erect a special building for them. The site chosen was that hitherto occupied by the Royal Mews, and the present building was erected. The new building was completed in 1838, from the designs of Mr. Wilkins, the architect; but it was scarcely occupied before it was discovered to be much too small. In preparing his design, Mr. Wilkins was sorely hampered with conditions. The edifice was not to intercept the view of the portico of St. Martin's Church; it must not infringe on the barrack space in the rear; the public must have one right of way through it, and the Guards another; the old columns of Carlton House were to be used up; and the true faith in architecture insisted on having porticoes, dome, and cupolas; moreover, the building, by no means too large for a National Gallery, was to be shared with the Royal Academy. With such instructions Mr. Wilkins prepared his plans and estimates. The building was to cost £50,000, but, as in most other instances, perhaps, the architect was not to be bound by his estimate. The entire cost reached, we believe, some £25,000 in addition.

Notwithstanding the limited space in the new building, the pictures belonging to the nation were brought thither and deposited in the eastern wing, whilst the other portion of it was handed over to the Royal Academy, of which institution we will here say a few words.

It is stated by several writers that the establishment of an academy for painting was agitated as far back as the time of Charles II.; and when the subject was revived at a subsequent date, its projectors and patrons appear to have intended to erect the necessary buildings for its accommodation in the centre of Lincoln's Inn Fields. Happily, however, the idea was never carried out, and that square was still preserved as an open space.

For long years the sentiment had prevailed in England that art was no affair of the State, had no sort of interest for the governing power of the country, or, indeed, for the general public; and it was, of course, left to those persons to whom an academy of art was in any way a matter of necessity or importance to found such an institution for themselves. For the benefit of his brother artists, therefore, Sir Godfrey Kneller instituted a private drawing-academy in London, in the year 1711; but certain forms and ceremonies having been introduced into the academy which were objectionable to several members, divisions and jealousies arose in the general body; and finally, the president and his followers, finding themselves caricatured and opposed, locked out their opponents, and closed the academy.

Sir James Thornhill, who had headed the most important of the parties into which the institution had become divided, and who held the appointment of historical painter to George I., then submitted to the Government of the day a plan for the foundation of a Royal Academy which should encourage and educate the young artists of England; and the site proposed by him was at the upper end of the King's Mews, Charing Cross. The Government, however, declined to find the means for carrying out the design, and the proposition accordingly fell to the ground.

Not altogether daunted by this ill success, Sir James Thornhill determined to do what he could on his own responsibility, and without the aid of the Treasury. He therefore opened a drawing-academy at his house in James Street, Covent Garden, and gave tickets to all who desired admission. It is to be feared that Sir James's generosity was somewhat abused. At all events, dissensions arose in his academy, as in Kneller's, and a rival school was founded, where, according to Hogarth, a "female figure was introduced, to make it more inviting to subscribers." This, however, did not last long; and, on the death of Sir James, his academy was also closed.

It is mentioned casually in a London newspaper of October 12, 1723, as an article of information, that "the Academy of Painting and Sculpture opened on Monday last, as usual, in St. Martin's Lane." We may, however, search in vain through the diaries of Pepys and Evelyn, and through the letters of Horace Walpole, for information as to the members and the character of this academy. Malcolm, whose industry in hunting up old and curious facts is above praise, tells us, in his "Londinium Redivivum," that an academy for students in painting was held in Queen Street for some years previous to 1724, in which year, a difference arising on some question of art, its members parted company. One part of them seceded with Vanderbank, who opened an academy in what had been a Presbyterian meeting-house, in the same neighbourhood; "but this," adds Malcolm, "soon came to nothing." Sir James Thornhill, the head of the other party, built at the back of his house, near Covent Garden Theatre, a room for this purpose; and this subsisted till his death, in 1734, when his son-in-law, Hogarth, becoming possessed of the models, lent them to a society of artists, who took a house for their accommodation in St. Martin's Lane. The members of this society afterwards met at the "Turk's Head," in Gerrard Street; and in 1760 they were bold enough to make their first exhibition of paintings, at "the great room of the Society for the Encouragement of Arts, Manufactures, and Commerce, opposite Beaufort Buildings." Encouraged by success, they next year again exhibited, under the title of "A Society of Artists associated for the Relief of the Distressed and Decayed of their own Body, their Widows and Children." Their exhibitions were continued afterwards for several years—first in Spring Gardens, and then in Pall Mall, where they were visited, on June 1, 1767, by George III. and his queen, who presented the association with a purse of a hundred pounds. This gift being made known in the journals of the day, set the tide of fashion in the right direction, and ensured the success of "the Exhibition," as it soon became to be called *par excellence*.

The first formal meeting of the Royal Academy was held in Pall Mall, on the 14th of December, 1768. Mr. Chambers, the architect, who had been appointed treasurer, read a report to the artists assembled, relating the steps that had been taken to found the Academy. It set forth that on the previous 28th of November, Messrs. Chambers, Cotes, Moser, and West had had the honour of presenting a memorial to the Crown, signed by twenty-two artists, soliciting the royal assistance and protection in establishing a new society for promoting the arts of design. The objects of the society were stated to be "the establishing a well-regulated school or academy of design, for the use of students in the arts, and an annual exhibition open to all artists of distinguished merit, where they may offer their performances to public inspection, and acquire that degree of reputation and encouragement which they shall be deemed to deserve." Statements of the intentions of the memorialists were afterwards drawn up and submitted to the king, who, on the 10th of December, signified his approbation, ordered that the plan should be carried into execution, and with his own hand signed Mr. Chambers' plan—"the Instrument," as it was then and has ever since that time been called. Mr. Chambers then read the "Instrument" to the meeting, after which the artists present signed an obligation, or declaration, promising to observe all the laws and regulations contained in that document, and all future laws that might be made for the better government of the society, and to employ their utmost endeavours to promote the honour and interest of the establishment so long as they should continue members of it. The Academy thus obtained its constitution, and assumed such form of legal existence as it has ever since possessed.

The rules declared that the Academy should consist of forty members only, who should be called Academicians; they were to be at the time of their admission, painters, sculptors, or architects of reputation in their professions, of high moral character, not under twenty-five years of age, resident in Great Britain, and not members of any other society of artists established in London.

Of the forty members who were to constitute the Academy, the "Instrument," as signed by the king, named thirty-six only; and of these, while many were artists of fame, there were many others whose names, but for their registry upon the list of original Academicians, would probably never have been known to posterity in any way. Having named the original members, the "Instrument" proceeded to lay down the rules for the further government of the institution; to prescribe the manner of electing future members, a council and president, a secretary and keeper (the treasurer was to be nominated by his Majesty, "as the king is graciously pleased to pay all deficiencies"), the appointment of different professors, the establishment of schools, and a library for the free use of students, and of an annual exhibition of works of art to be "open to all artists of distinguished merit." New laws were to be framed from time to time, but to have no force until "ratified by the consent of the general assembly and the approbation of the king." At the end of the Instrument the king wrote: "I approve of this plan; let it be put in execution"—adding his signature, "George R."

Thus the plan was matured, and the Royal Academy was instituted, under the patronage of King George III. The success of the institution was further secured by the fortunate appointment of Sir Joshua Reynolds, whose grasp of the first principles of art has never been excelled, as its first president.

The members of the Royal Academy used to

give large dinners to the nobility and gentry and the exhibitors, at the "Freemasons' Tavern," on the king's birthday; but subsequently the exhibitors were left out of the list of invited guests. In 1770 they celebrated the king's birthday in the following manner, by the aid of their own pencils, as we learn from the *London Chronicle* of June 5th in that year:—"Yesterday being the anniversary of his Majesty's birthday, the Royal Academicians gave an elegant entertainment at their house in Pall Mall; and in the evening the whole front of the Royal Academy was illuminated with transparent paintings, as usual, executed by the Academicians." The designs were fanciful in the extreme, and the paintings on this occasion, it may interest our readers to learn, were by Cipriani, Dance, Richards, Baker, and Benjamin West (afterwards president).

A few short notices of the distinguished men who have successively occupied the presidential chair of the Royal Academy may not be out of place here.

Sir Joshua Reynolds, the first on the list, was a native of Plympton, near Plymouth, in Devonshire, where he was born in the year 1723. At the age of seventeen he became a pupil of Hudson, but after two years' study he returned to Plymouth. He subsequently paid visits to Italy with Keppel, and afterwards settling in London, founded the Literary Club, in conjunction with Johnson, in the year 1764. He was a man highly cultivated and scholar-like, and had immense power in grasping the principles of art; in fact, he may be put down as the real originator of the English school of painting. Among his principal pictures may be mentioned, "Garrick between Tragedy and Comedy," "Mrs. Siddons as the Tragic Muse," "The Infant Hercules," "Sheridan," &c. Sir Joshua was appointed principal painter to the king in 1784, became partially blind in 1789, and died in 1792.

Benjamin West, his successor, who was born at Springfield, in Pennsylvania, in 1738, was somewhat heavy and formal in his style of painting. He visited Rome in 1760, and three years later arrived in England, where he became the *protégé* of George III. He was appointed historical painter to the king in 1772, and occupied the presidential chair from 1792 down to his death in 1820.

Sir Thomas Lawrence, the next president in succession, was a native of Bristol, where he first saw the light in the year 1769. He became a student at the Royal Academy in 1787. Courtly, graceful, with perhaps more beauty than Sir Joshua Reynolds, but not half his power, Thomas Lawrence soon became a rising man in the art world, and in 1792 was appointed to the post of painter to George III. He was knighted by the Prince Regent in 1815, and succeeded to the presidential chair of the Royal Academy in 1820. For many years Sir Thomas Lawrence derived from his works an income approaching the large sum of £15,000 per annum; but so eagerly did he contest the possession of any rare and valuable art productions when occasion offered, that even this princely income was not enough for him; and true as it is that the value of the collection which he had formed was estimated, after his decease, at £50,000, he nevertheless died in straitened circumstances. His death occurred in the year 1830, and his memory was honoured by a tomb in St. Paul's Cathedral.

Sir Martin Archer Shee, who will be remembered as the author of "Rhymes on Art," and similar works, was born in Dublin, in 1770. He came to London at the age of eighteen, and in the following year exhibited at the Royal Academy. He became a Royal Academician in 1800, and received the honour of knighthood on his appointment to the presidential chair, in 1830. He died at Brighton, in 1850.

Sir Charles Locke Eastlake, the successor of the above, was a native of Plymouth, and was born in 1793. He became a student of the Royal Academy in 1808, and in early life paid visits to Italy in company with Sir C. Barry and Brockendon. He was appointed Secretary to the Commission of Fine Arts in 1841, and Librarian to the Royal Academy in the following year. He was afterwards chosen Keeper of the National Gallery, and subsequently became Director. Sir Charles Eastlake died at Pisa, in 1865.

Sir Francis Grant, the next President, was the fourth son of Mr. Francis Grant, of Kilgraston, Perthshire. He was born in 1803, became an Associate in 1842, and attained full honours in 1851. He died in 1878, and was succeeded by Sir Frederic (afterwards Lord) Leighton, a son of the late Mr. Frederick Leighton, of Scarborough. Born in 1830, he was admitted an Associate in 1864, elected a Royal Academician in 1868, and died in 1896. Sir John Everett Millais, Bart., who followed him in the Chair, only lived to occupy it a few months, and he in turn was succeeded by Sir E. J. Poynter the Director of the National Gallery.

The inconvenience caused by the building in Trafalgar Square having to afford shelter to both the National Gallery and the Royal Academy taxed the energy of Parliament for years to find a remedy. In 1848 Lord John Russell, Sir Robert Peel, Mr.

Hume, and others forming *one* Committee of the House of Commons, "after careful deliberation, unanimously concurred in the opinion" that the present National Gallery should be enlarged and improved. Two years later Lord John Russell, Sir Robert Peel, Mr. Hume, and others, forming *another* Committee, reported that they could "not recommend that any expenditure should be at present incurred for the purpose of increasing the accommodation of a National Gallery on the present site," and were "not prepared to state that the preservation of the pictures and convenient access for the purpose of study and improvement of taste would not be better secured in a gallery further removed from the smoke and dust of London."

The result of this very negative report was to induce architects and others, year after year, to inflict on the public their views of the vexed question. At one time, indeed, the House of Commons voted £167,000, and the Prince Consort added to that sum the surplus of the Exhibition of 1851, with which was bought the land opposite and outside Hyde Park, at Kensington Gore, the site for which the Government had previously commenced negotiations with the same object, though they had failed to secure it at the time. The House of Commons, however, rejected the plan for removing the National Gallery to this site; and the then notion of rebuilding the Gallery seems now to be finally abandoned. Part of the difficulty has been got over by the removal of the Royal Academy to Burlington House, of which we shall have more to say hereafter, when we come to Piccadilly. The Vernon and Sheepshanks galleries, too, which form part of the national collection, have been removed westward, and found more suitable quarters in the saloons of the South Kensington Museum. Moreover, great enlargements and improvements have been made in the Gallery from time to time, and no expense has been spared to render it fireproof.

To the National Gallery has been added, on the east and north sides, the National Portrait Gallery,* for the reception of the national collection of portraits, which were at one time exhibited at the South Kensington Museum, and afterwards at the Bethnal Green branch of that institution. The site was provided by the Government; the building, begun in 1890 and completed in 1896, was reared at the expense of Mr. W. H. Alexander, who in 1888 undertook to devote a sum of £80,000 to the purpose. Mr. Evan Christian was the architect, and after his decease the supervision of the work was entrusted to Mr. J. H. Christian. The structure is not a particularly effective one, which may be due in part to the general harmony with the older Gallery which the architect appears to have felt himself obliged to maintain; but the east wing, with the main entrance facing St. Martin's Place, is not without elegance, plain and heavy as is the north façade, fronting the Charing Cross Road.

The more ancient portraits of the collection are arranged in chronological order on the top floor. The portraits in the east wing of the upper floor, and most of those on the first floor, are disposed in groups—artists, statesmen, actors, &c. In the east wing of the lower floor are some specimens of the sculptor's art, and in the gallery of the upper basement are large pictures of the Houses of Parliament in session. Among the modern portraits is a fine series from the brush of Mr. G. F. Watts, R.A., the generous gift of the artist.

* *See also* Vol. IV., pp. 32–33.

CHAPTER XXII.

ST. MARTIN'S-IN-THE-FIELDS.

"Why, how now, Babell, whither wilt thou build?
I see old Holbourne, Charing Crosse, the Strand,
Are going to St. Giles's-in-the-Field."—*Tom Freeman's Epigrams* (1614).

St. Martin's-in-the-Fields in the Sixteenth and Seventeenth Centuries—The Church built by Henry VIII.—The Church rebuilt—Description of the Edifice—Burial of Sir Edmundbury Godfrey—Notabilities interred in the Churchyard—The Parish Rate-books—Curious Stories about St. Martin's Church—The Royal Society of Literature—Anthropological Institute—National Society for aiding the Sick and Wounded in War—Archbishop Tenison's Library and School—An Ancient Chapel or Oratory—Historic and Artistic Associations of St. Martin's Lane.

If we could throw ourselves mentally back three centuries, and could take a view of the district lying between St. James's Palace and the villages of Charing and St. Giles's, as it appeared about the year 1560, we should see little more than an open tract of fields. At that time there were only three, or, at the most, four houses towards the eastern end of Pall Mall, and a little further a small church, which has long since disappeared. Still nearer to the Palace, about the centre of what is now St. James's Square, was a well, enclosed in four low walls. The Hay Market and Hedge Lane, as late as the reign of Charles II., were literally lanes, fringed on either side with hedges; and all to the north was open country. In the ancient plans of London the Hay Market is quite clear of buildings, and Windmill Street, when first built, derived its name from a windmill standing in a field on its west side, with a small rural stable in the rear of it.

The parish of St. Martin was originally taken out of that of St. Margaret; and yet so rapid was its growth, that in 1786 it had come to be "one of the most populous within the bills of mortality," being estimated to contain more than 5,000 houses, although the parishes of St. Paul's, Covent Garden; St. Anne's, Soho; St. James's, Piccadilly; and St. George's, Hanover Square, had all been in turn carved out of it.

In very early times it is said that a chapel dedicated to St. Martin was erected near Charing Cross, "for the convenience of the officers of Westminster Abbey and Palace, on their way to Covent Garden;" and this, no doubt, was the original "St. Martin's-in-the-Fields." But this is only a tradition. More trustworthy is the statement that St. Martin's was built by order and at the cost of Henry VIII., who disliked to see the funerals of his liege subjects passing through or past Whitehall, much as Louis XIV. of France resolved to build the Château at Versailles because he could not help seeing the towers of St. Denis from the terrace at Saint-Germain.

The church is so called after the chivalrous Hungarian, St. Martin, who was Bishop of Tours in the fourth century, and in whose honour it is dedicated. It received its surname, "in the fields," like its sister church of St. Giles, from its situation outside the City proper, when it was first taken into the bills of mortality, in order to distinguish it from other churches eastwards under the same dedication.

THE FIRST ROYAL ACADEMY; ABOUT 1740. (*See page* 147.)

That there was a church on or near this spot as far back as the times of our Norman kings is shown by a dispute, in the year 1222, between William, Abbot of Westminster, and Eustace, Bishop of London, in which the former claimed for it exemption from the bishop's authority—a claim which was decided by the Archbishop of Canterbury in favour of the abbot. This would appear to confirm the tradition that originally it was a chapel for the use of the monks of Westminster, when they visited the convent whose

OLD COCKSPUR STREET.

garden abutted on it to the east. Be this, however, as it may, the endowments of St. Martin's Chapel fell, along with the monks to whom it belonged, under the ruthless paw of Henry VIII., who is said, as already remarked, to have erected in its stead a small parochial church. In 1607 this church was enlarged, at the cost of Prince Henry, son of King James I.

While the Strand was inhabited by the highest titled families, it is no matter of wonder that St. Martin's-in-the-Fields should have been a somewhat fashionable parish in the early Georgian era. In 1721 the church was pulled down, and the present edifice was erected in its place. It was built by Gibbs, the architect of the Radcliffe Library at Oxford, and cost nearly £60,000. George I. took a great interest in the building of the church, and is said to have been so delighted at its completion that he gave £100 to be distributed among the workmen employed on it, and £1,500 more to purchase an organ. The organ, however, was long ago replaced by another.

The portico, of lofty Corinthian columns, is much admired, as, indeed, is the entire west front, to which an ascent is gained up a long flight of steps. In the pediment are seen the royal arms in bas-relief, beneath which is a Latin inscription relating to the foundation of the church. The steeple is stately and elegant, and very lofty, and in the tower is an excellent peal of twelve bells.

"The church of St. Martin," says Mr. Gwynn, "is esteemed one of the best in this city, though far from being so fine as it is usually represented to be. The absurd rustication of the windows, and the heavy sills and trusses under them, are unpardonable blemishes, and very improperly introduced into this composition of the Corinthian order, as it takes away the delicacy which should be preserved in this kind of building. The steeple itself is good, but it is so constructed that it seems to stand upon the roof of the church, there being no appearance of its continuation from the foundation, and consequently it seems to want support; an error of which Gibbs is not alone guilty, but which is very elegantly and judiciously avoided in the turrets in front of St. Paul's; indeed, the spire of the steeple of St. Martin's Church being formed by internal sweeps, makes the angles too acute, which always produces an ill effect. Upon the whole, St. Martin's Church is composed on a grand style of one order, and the portico is truly noble."

Mr. Malton says, "We have in the exterior of this church an excellent example of Roman architecture in its highest style of improvement, without the tawdry and meretricious ornaments with which the Romans frequently disfigured their sacred edifices. It is also the most successful attempt to unite the light and picturesque beauty of the modern steeple to the sober grandeur and square solidity of the Grecian temple. The insulated columns in the recesses at the extremity of the flanks of this church are striking and bold, and once had the merit of novelty, though it is now, by frequent imitation, become less remarkable."

Vast vaults extend from the portico to the east end of the structure: they are light and dry, and contain great numbers of bodies, deposited within separate apartments, and on the floor of the open space. These vaults, however, have for many years been closed up, interments being no longer permitted. The roof of the church is supported by eight pillars, and also by four pilasters and entablatures, which support the ceilings over the aisles. The vaulting of the nave is elaborately ornamented with stucco-work, and the sacrarium commences with a semi-circle and terminates in a recess. The interior decorations are very fine. Mr. Gibbs, the architect, in speaking of the elliptical ceiling, says he found by experience that it is "much better for the voice than the semi-circular, though not so beautiful. It is divided into panels, enriched with fret-work by Signors Artari and Bagutti, the best fret-workers that ever came to England." Slender Corinthian columns, raised on high pedestals, rising to the front of the galleries, serve to support both them and the roof, which, on the sides, rests upon them in a very ornamental arch-work. The east end is richly adorned with fret-work and gilding; and over the altar is a large Venetian window, filled with stained glass.

An allusion to the worshippers in the new church occurs in the "London Spy," published in 1725. "The inhabitants are now supplied with a decent tabernacle, which can produce as handsome a show of white hands, diamond rings, pretty snuff-boxes, and gilt prayer-books, as any cathedral whatever. Here the fair penitents pray in their patches, sue for pardon in their paint, and see their heaven in man." St. Martin's was the royal parish, and in its registers were recorded the births of the princes and princesses born in Westminster, previous to the formation of St. James's parish.

In the vestry-room, on the south-east side of the church, is an admirably-executed model of St. Martin's Church. The vestry walls are adorned with portraits of most of the vicars since the year 1670, many of whom attained high distinction in the Church. There are also half-length portraits of George I., and of Mr. Gibbs, the architect, and one of the unfortunate Sir Edmundbury Godfrey. In one of the windows is a painting of St. Martin dividing his mantle with a beggar, in illustration of the ancient legend.

In the churchyard, which is now covered with flat stones, was buried, "with great solemnity," after having lain in state at Bridewell Hospital for two days, the body of Sir Edmundbury Godfrey. "The pall was supported by eight knights, all justices of the peace; and in the procession were all the city aldermen, together with seventy-two clergymen, in full canonicals, who walked in couples before the body, and a great multitude followed after." The clergyman who preached the sermon on the occasion was supported on either side by a brother divine. A tablet to the memory of Sir Edmundbury Godfrey was erected in the east cloister of Westminster Abbey.

The story of the murder of Sir Edmundbury Godfrey has been often told; but as it belongs specially to the spot which we are now visiting, it shall be told here once more, in the words of Pennant:—"The infamous witnesses against his supposed murderers declared that he was waylaid, and inveigled into the palace under pretence of keeping the peace between two servants who were fighting in the yard: that he was there strangled, his neck broke, and his own sword run through his body; that he was kept four days before they ventured to remove him; at length his corpse was first carried in a sedan-chair to Soho, and then on a horse to Primrose Hill, between Kilburn and Hampstead. There it certainly was found, transfixed with the sword, and his money in his pocket, and his rings on his fingers. The murder, therefore, was not by robbers, but the effect of private revenge. But it is not probable that it was committed within these walls; for the assassins would never have hazarded a discovery by carrying the corpse three miles, when they could have so safely disposed of it into the Thames. The abandoned characters of the evidences, Prance and Bedloe, (the former of whom had been treated with most horrid cruelties to compel him to confess what he declared he never was guilty of), together with the absurd and irreconcilable testimony they gave on the trial, has made unprejudiced times to doubt the whole. That he was murdered there is no doubt; he had been an active magistrate, and had made many enemies. The marks of strangling round his throat, and his broken neck, evince the impossibility of his having put an end to his own existence, as some have insinuated. But the innocence of the three poor convicts would not avail, the torrent of prejudice prevailing against them; and they were executed, denying the facts in the moment of death. One was a Protestant, the other two Roman Catholics, and belonging to the Chapel; so probably were fixed on by the instigators of the accusation in order to involve the queen in the uncharitable suspicion."

This tragedy became at the time the subject of several medals. On one is the bust of Sir Edmundbury and two hands strangling him; on the reverse the Pope giving his benediction to a man strangling another on the ground. On a second, with the same bust, is the representation of the carrying the magistrate on horseback to Primrose Hill. A third makes him walking with his broken neck, and sword buried in his body; and on the reverse St. Denis with his head in his hand, with this inscription:—

"Godfrey walks up-hill after he was dead;
Denis walks down-hill carrying his head."

The churchyard contains also the bones of the notorious highwayman, Jack Sheppard. Here, too, lies buried the once famous sculptor, Roubiliac; also the witty, but somewhat licentious, dramatist, Farquhar, author of the *Beau's Stratagem*. Here likewise lies John Hunter, the distinguished anatomist, of whom we have spoken in our account of the museum of the Royal College of Surgeons; as also does the illustrious philosopher, Robert Boyle. Here, too, were buried Sir Theodore Mayerne, Court physician, and the friend of Vandyke; and also Nell Gwynne, whose funeral sermon was preached by Dr. Tenison, incumbent of the parish, and afterwards Archbishop of Canterbury.

The flat pavement on the southern side of the church, facing the "Golden Cross," is called "the Watermen's Burying-ground," from the number of old Thames watermen who were brought thither to their last long rest from Hungerford, York, and Whitehall Stairs.

The rate-books of this parish, which (says Mr. Cunningham) are arranged sheet by sheet, after the manner of a Post Office directory, contain the name of every householder in the parish, from the levying of the first poor-law rate, in the reign of Elizabeth, down to the present time, and the church registers are admirably kept. The rate-books help us to identify the dwellings of very many distinguished persons in the last century.

A curious story about this church is told by Evelyn in his "Diary," under date Good Friday, 1687. "Dr. Tenison preached at St. Martin's. . . . During the service a man came into neere the middle of the church with his sword drawne, with severall others in that posture: in this jealous time it put the congregation into greate confusion;

but it appeared to be one who fled for sanctuary, being pursued by bayliffs."

Mr. Malcolm records an event of a somewhat similar nature which occurred in this church on the 10th of September, 1729. During evening prayers a gentleman abruptly entered, and fired two pistols at the Rev. Mr. Taylor, who was repeating the service; one of the bullets grazed the surplice, but the other entered the body of Mr. Williams, farrier, of Bedfordbury, who was sitting in a pew near the minister. The congregation fled in alarm from the church, but a sturdy carman resolutely proceeded to secure the offender, which he could not effect without a severe encounter, and much bruising him, particularly on the head. On his examination it was found that this man, named Roger Campaznol, was the son of the Governor of Brest, in France; that having been cheated by his landlord, a Huguenot, resident near the Seven Dials, of £138, his mind became deranged, so that he was unable to distinguish the victim of his revenge. After his committal to Newgate he made two or three attempts to commit suicide.

In St. Martin's Place, near the church, were the offices of the Royal Society of Literature, and of the Anthropological Institute of Great Britain and Ireland. The Royal Society of Literature was instituted in 1820, and received the royal charter in 1826. It originated in an accidental conversation between Dr. Burgess—afterwards Bishop of St. David's and of Salisbury—and an eminent personage connected with the royal household, in October, 1820, respecting the various institutions which adorn the British nation. It was agreed that a society seemed to be wanting for the encouragement and promotion of general literature; and that if a society somewhat resembling the French Academy of *Belles Lettres* could be established it might be productive of great advantage to the cause of knowledge. The suggestion was communicated to Sir Benjamin Bloomfield, and by him was mentioned to the king, to whom he had been private secretary during the regency. His Majesty having expressed his approbation, a general outline of the institution was, by command, submitted to the royal perusal. The Bishop of St. David's was shortly afterwards summoned to Carlton House for the purpose of devising the best mode of giving effect to the undertaking, and was entrusted with a full commission to arrange the plan of the society. He accordingly invited a few of his personal friends to assist him, and for some time they had frequent conferences on the subject. Their first meeting took place on the 10th of November, and the title proposed for the Society was "Royal Society of Literature for the Encouragement of Indigent Merit, and the Promotion of General Literature;" but at a subsequent meeting the objectionable words in this title were expunged, and the title then stood "Royal Society for the Encouragement of Literature." In order to give signs of public life in the Society, a part of the proposed plan was immediately acted on—namely, the offer of prizes for the following subjects:—

1. For the King's Premium, one hundred guineas: "On the age, writings, and genius of Homer; and on the state of religion, society, learning, and the arts during that period. Collected from the writings of Homer."

2. For the Society's Premium, fifty guineas: "Dartmoor; a poem."

3. For the Society's Premium, twenty-five guineas: "On the History of the Greek Language, and the present language of Greece, especially in the Ionian Islands; and on the difference between ancient and modern Greek." This premium was subsequently increased to fifty guineas, and another of the like sum was proposed for the best poem on "The Fall of Constantinople in the Fifteenth Century."

The first prize awarded by the Society was for the second premium, for which five candidates appeared. Their productions were referred to a sub-committee, who adjudged the prize to the writer of the poem bearing the motto "Come, bright Improvement," which was found to be written by Felicia Hemans.

Among the first members of the Society were the king, two of the royal dukes, several of the bishops, and many other distinguished persons. In its early stages the Society met with some opposition in different quarters; but by the middle of the year 1823, the constitution and regulations were completed and submitted to the king, and were finally approved of under the royal sign-manual. Stability and importance were given to the Society by a royal charter granted in the sixth year of George IV. in these terms:—"To our right trusty and well-beloved Thomas, by Divine permission Bishop of Salisbury,* and others of our loving subjects who have, under our royal patronage, formed themselves into a Society for the advancement of literature, by the publication of unedited remains of ancient literature, and of such works as may be of great intrinsic value, but not of that popular character which usually claims the attention of publishers; by the promotion of discoveries in literature; by endeavouring to fix the

* He had recently been translated to this see from St. David's.

standard, as far as practicable, and to preserve the purity of the English language, by the critical improvement of English lexicography; by the reading at public meetings of interesting papers on history, philosophy, poetry, philology, and the arts, and the publication of such of those papers as shall be approved of; by the assigning of honorary rewards to works of great literary merit, and to important discoveries in literature; and by establishing a correspondence with learned men in foreign countries for the purpose of literary inquiry and information."

In 1826 George IV. made to the Society a grant of the Crown land opposite St. Martin's Church, and the leading and official members voluntarily subscribed £4,300 as a building-fund, with which they erected their original place of meeting. In 1828 the Society adopted the publications of the Egyptian Society, and has since contributed some important researches on the antiquities of Egypt. In rewarding literary men the royal founder enabled the Society to act with princely liberality, by placing at its disposal 1,100 guineas a year, "to be bestowed on the Associates for life, to be elected by the officers and council, each to receive 100 guineas per annum; and the remaining 100 guineas to be expended on two gold medals, to be bestowed annually upon individuals whose literary merits entitled them to the honour."

In connection with the above gift of 1,100 guineas by the king, Mr. Harford, in his "Life of Dr. Burgess, Bishop of Salisbury" (1840), relates the following anecdote:—"It is a curious fact, which his majesty, George IV., himself mentioned with a smile to the present Dean of Salisbury (Dr. Pearson) that the Bishop, from a misconception of his meaning, at their first interview, committed the king as an *annual* subscriber of £1,000—a sum which he had intended only as a donation to the Society at its outset, while his annual subscription was to have been limited to £100. As, however, his lordship, in his zeal, had immediately proclaimed the king's munificence, and Fame, through the medium of the press, had almost as quickly trumpeted it with her hundred tongues throughout the country, there was no retreat; and the king not only cheerfully acquiesced, but amused himself with the incident." On the death of George IV., in 1830, this gratifying bequest ceased.

A valuable library has been formed, and greatly enriched by the lexicographical and antiquarian publications presented by Mr. Todd, and by papers furnished by many eminent writers. In 1886 the Society removed to Delahay Street, Westminster; it is now located in Hanover Square.

Admission to the Royal Society of Literature is obtained by a certificate, signed by three members, and an election by ballot. Ordinary members pay three guineas on admission, and two guineas annually, or compound by a payment of twenty guineas. At the meetings of this Society papers are read by learned men, English and foreigners. The Society, however, incurred considerable ridicule by having admitted a certain M. Cosprons, a few years since, to read a paper, as a French *savant*, under the assumed title of "M. le Duc de Rousillon." The mistake was soon found out, and the "illustrious" *soi-disant* duke was never asked to read a second paper.

The Anthropological Institute of Great Britain and Ireland, whose rooms were in the same building as the above Society, was established in 1863 for the purpose of promoting the study of anthropology in a strictly scientific manner; it also is now located in Hanover Square. There is an interesting museum, and the publications of the Society are presented to the members. Sir John Lubbock was for long President of this Society, an office now occupied by Dr. Macalister.

In St. Martin's Place were likewise the offices of the Friend of the Clergy Corporation, an institution, under the patronage of the Prince of Wales, "for allowing pensions, not exceeding £40 per annum, to the widows and orphan unmarried daughters of clergymen of the Established Church, and for affording temporary assistance to necessitous clergymen and their families."

St. Martin's Place is worthy of note as having been, during the Franco-Prussian War, the head-quarters of the National Society for Aiding the Sick and Wounded, which was founded at a meeting of the English Langue of the Order of St. John held here in July, 1870. During the year and a half of that terrible struggle this Society sent abroad to Germany and France, in nearly equal proportions, money and stores—such as lint, bandages, wine, and surgical appliances—to the value of about half a million, earning thereby the hearty thanks of both the belligerent nations. After the termination of the European struggle the Society resolved not to disband itself, but to continue *en permanence*, so as to be ready for action in case of the outbreak of another war. Its offices, however, are now in Duke Street, Adelphi.

In what used to be Castle Street, behind the National Gallery, a library was founded by Dr. Tenison—afterwards Archbishop of Canterbury—in 1685, for the use of his school, over which it was placed. In 1697, the doctor, who was then vicar of St. Martin's, gave £1,000 towards a fund for the maintenance of his school, and afterwards, by the consent of Dr. Patrick, Bishop of Ely, another sum of £500 which had been left to them jointly, in trust, to be disposed of in charitable uses; these two sums, together with the leasehold messuages, for the term of forty years, he vested in trustees, for the support of his school and library. Out of the profits of these investments the librarian and masters had an annual salary for teaching thirty boys, sons of the inhabitants of St. Martin's parish.

This institution was at first situated in Castle Street, at the back of the Mews, which, as we have already shown, afterwards gave place to the National Gallery. Here it stood down to the year 1872, when it was removed to give room for the enlargement of the National Gallery.

The original design of the founder was to supply the clergy and studious persons of Westminster with a place of retirement and study. "He told me," says Evelyn ("Diary," Feb. 15, 1684), "there were thirty or forty young men in orders in his parish, either governors to young gentlemen, or chaplains to noblemen, who, being reproved by him on occasion for frequenting taverns or coffee-houses, told him they would study or employ their time better if they had books. This put the pious Doctor on this design." On the 23rd Evelyn again writes, "Afterwards I went with Sir Christopher Wren to Dr. Tenison, when we made the drawing and estimate of the expense of the library to be begun the next spring near the Mews."

The library was not by any means confined to theological subjects, but comprised works of general literature. Amongst the 5,000 volumes of the ordinary staple from which libraries were formed a century and a half ago, were some MSS. of great interest. The library contained a beautiful Sarum Missal of the thirteenth century, and a magnificently illuminated Psalter of a little earlier period. But the gems of the collection, perhaps, were the "Psychomachia of Prudentius," and the "Versarium of Fortunatus," both very rare. The library was dispersed on the removal of the school in 1872.

By a series of misfortunes this institution, it appears, had been reduced, of late years, to the last stage of decay. Its slender endowment was almost entirely lost in the South Sea Bubble, and

WEST VIEW OF THE OLD CHURCH OF ST. MARTIN'S-IN-THE-FIELDS; PULLED DOWN IN 1721.
(*From a Print published by J. T. Smith in* 1808.)

ST. MARTIN'S LANE. 1820. (*See page* 158.)

its resources failed altogether on the expiration of a lease, the remainder of which was taken by the Commissioners of Woods and Forests for the improvement of Charing Cross. There were in the end no means of providing salaries for the officers or for any of the expenses incidental to the maintenance of a library, and the fate of an institution which ought to be interesting to all lovers of literature came to be regarded with apprehension and anxiety.

For many years the trustees permitted a society of subscribing members to hold its meetings, to play at chess, and read newspapers in the reading-room; and thus a sort of club or mechanics' institute came to hold its meetings in Archbishop Tenison's Library, and a list of lectures was posted outside the door. A portion even of the shelves of the old library had been appropriated to the books of the new society; and if clergymen and "studious persons," more especially intended by the founder, had resorted to Tenison's Library for purposes of study, they would soon have given up the attempt in despair. A late eminent bookseller bore the following testimony as to the state of the original library a few years previous to its sale by the auctioneer in 1872:—"The books and manuscripts in the library are many of them of great curiosity, rarity, and value, but have suffered injury from dust and neglect; were they properly cleaned and repaired, and the room made comfortable to readers, it would, in my opinion, be much frequented, and accessions be made to the library in the way of books presented." The original intention of the founder having thus been withheld, the interest of the parishioners and others in this library gradually decreased, and it at length became scarcely at all frequented on its own account. The place had altogether a forlorn and miserable appearance; its volumes buried in dust and exposed to the vicissitudes of heat and damp, so that one would be painfully reminded of the day when, under the auspices of the three illustrious men mentioned above, the building was planned, and of the goodly show which Strype tells us the books with their "gilt backs" made in his time.

The Rev. P. Hale, the librarian, some time ago issued a "Plea for Archbishop Tenison's Library," in which he remarked:—"It seems to be a moral law that every institution, in spite of the care and munificence of its founder, should fall short of his aim, in order to give room for the vigilance and charity of his successor."

Notwithstanding the above plea for the preservation of the library, sufficient public interest in it does not appear to have been awakened, and the books and manuscripts were consequently sold and dispersed, the proceeds of the sale being devoted to the erection of the new Archbishop Tenison's School, in Leicester Square.

The clearance effected for the extension of the National Gallery, the erection of the National Portrait Gallery, and the formation of the Charing Cross Road, has greatly improved the aspect of St. Martin's Place. The Charing Cross Road is a handsome thoroughfare which runs northwards through the heart of St. Giles's-in-the-Fields to the point of junction between Oxford Street and New Oxford Street, whence it is continued in a northerly direction by Tottenham Court Road. At its southern end, curving round into St. Martin's Lane, of which we shall speak presently, is the St. Martin's Town Hall and Library. Adjoining this is the Garrick Theatre, built for Mr. John Hare. Farther up are some large blocks of industrial dwellings and a Welsh Presbyterian Chapel; and about half-way between St. Martin's Place and Oxford Street the road intersects the Shaftesbury Avenue at the spot now known as Cambridge Circus, but formerly, when it was but the meeting-place of a number of narrow streets, as the Five Dials.

On the west side of St. Martin's Lane, near Long Acre, is Aldridge's Horse Repository—a middle-class "Tattersall's"—established in 1753.

Newton tells us, in his "London in the Olden Time," that nearly at the end of the Strand a country lane, without habitations, ran northwards between the fields up to St. Giles's hospital. "A small chapel or oratory," he adds, "we know not of what antiquity, stood in the thirteenth century by the east side of this lane in the fields, about a hundred yards from the highway of the Strand." He considers it probable that this chapel was served by the monks of St. Peter's Abbey, to whom the land about the neighbourhood belonged, and who "bestowed their benedictions on, and collected halfpennies from the pilgrims and travellers passing to and from the north country and the City of Westminster."

This country road, which first obtained the name of St. Martin's Lane about the reign of Charles I., was bounded on the eastern side by the wall of the Convent Garden, and opened into the "Cock and Pie Fields," so called from a house of that name where cakes and ale were sold.

At the bottom of St. Martin's Lane was a nest or rookery of narrow lanes and streets, which rejoiced in slang names, such as "Porridge Island," "The Bermudas," and the "Straits of the Strand," of which mention has already been made. The names constantly imported into the comedies of the time by Ben Jonson and other authors. From the allusions to them which occur, it is clear that they were occupied by a low lot, who indulged in gin, ale, and fighting. Porridge Island, especially, was filled with second-rate cook-shops. In the *World*, of November, 1753, we find an allusion to "a fine gentleman whose lodgings no one is acquainted with," as having his dinner "served up under cover of a pewter plate from the cook-shops in Porridge Island." Part of this rookery was swept away about 1830, and in 1880–81 a further improvement was made by the erection of large blocks of model lodging-houses, occupying nearly all the space between Bedford Street and Bedfordbury.

Many of the houses in St. Martin's Lane have historic and artistic associations, which carry us back to the days of George II. Thus, for instance, Mr. Peter Cunningham informs us that "in a great room on the west side, nearly opposite old 'Slaughter's,' N. Home, the painter, exhibited in 1775 his celebrated 'Conjurer,' intended as a satire on the way in which Sir Joshua Reynolds composed his pictures; and in Cecil Court, in the following year, was born Abraham Raimbach, the engraver."

Smith, too, tells us in his "Nollekens," that the house No. 96, on the west side, "has a large staircase, curiously painted, of figures viewing a procession, which was executed for the famous Dr. Misaubin, about the year 1732, by a painter named Clermont, a Frenchman. Behind the house there is a large room, the inside of which is given by Hogarth in his 'Rake's Progress,' where he has introduced portraits of the doctor and his Irish wife."

St. Martin's Lane, if we except a few houses on the eastern side, at the end near to St. Martin's Church, was built between the years 1610 and 1615. Up to that time it was apparently a really green country lane, known as West Church Lane, with scarcely a single cottage all the way up to St. Giles's. A little before that date we read that Sir Hugh Platt, the most scientific horticulturist of his age, had a garden in St. Martin's Lane. Among its most distinguished inhabitants in its early days were Sir John Suckling, the poet, Sir Kenelm Digby, and D. Mytens, the painter. Here, too, lived at one time the celebrated Earl of Shaftesbury, Dr. (afterwards Archbishop) Thomas Tenison, whilst he was the Vicar of St. Martin's, and the Whig poet, Ambrose Philips. In this street, too, nearly opposite where now are May's Buildings, lived Sir Joshua Reynolds when he first came as a young man to London; and Sir James Thornhill, who established at the back of his house the artists' school, out of which it is scarcely an exaggeration to say that the Royal Academy took its beginning. Fuseli and Roubilliac, too, in their day had studios here; and those artists who did not actually live in the lane, used to frequent it of an evening, repairing as visitors to "Slaughter's Coffee-house," their accustomed haunt. Here Hogarth was a constant visitor, stepping round from his quarters hard by in Leicester Square; and many of the larger houses, if they have not been tenanted by artists, have been the haunts and homes of extensive picture-dealers.

Allan Cunningham tells us that Roubilliac's first studio was in Peter's Court in this lane, a favourite haunt of artists; "the room," he adds, "has been since pulled down and rebuilt, and its site is now occupied as a meeting-house by the Society of Friends." Roubilliac afterwards removed to a larger studio on the western side of the street, where he died in 1762.

"At the south-west corner of this lane," writes Stow, "there was one house wherein sometimes were distraught and lunatic people; of what antiquity founded, or by whom, I have not heard; neither of its suppression. But it is said that some time a king of England, not liking such a kind of people to remain so near his palace, caused them to be removed further off to Bethlehem, without Bishopsgate; and to that hospital the said house by Charing Cross doth yet remain." The upper part of St. Martin's Lane was originally termed the Terrace, implying probably that it consisted of a number of larger and more imposing edifices built at one time.

Ben Jonson was born in Hartshorn Lane, near Northumberland House, Charing Cross. We learn this from Fuller, who says, "Though I cannot, with all my industrious inquiry, find him in his cradle, yet I can fetch him from his long coats. When a little child he lived in Hartshorn Lane, Charing Cross, when his mother married a bricklayer for her second husband. He was first bred in a private school in St. Martin's Court, then in Westminster School."

Such was St. Martin's Lane in the olden days, before it had become the resort of loose characters, among whom, in the words of Ben Jonson, "the quarrelling lesson was read, and the seconds were bottled ale and tobacco." For, to speak the truth, St. Martin's parish would seem to have been remarkable for tipplers. At all events, that trustworthy authority, the "London Spy," hints that "the malt duty is nowhere better promoted than in this part of the town."

It is to be feared that the narrow gorge by

which to the present day exit is made from St. Martin's Lane into Trafalgar Square, is a standing proof that two hundred years ago the "commissioners for reforming the buildings, ways, and streets, and for regulating the hackney coaches in London," did not do their duty quite as efficiently as our present Metropolitan Board of Works. At all events, John Evelyn tells us, in his "Diary," under date May 25th, 1662, that he and his brother commissioners went from Scotland Yard to the neighbourhood of St. Martin's Church, in order "to view how St. Martin's Lane might be made more passable into the Strand." We fear that, although more than two centuries have passed away since that time, the work has yet to be satisfactorily achieved.

CHAPTER XXIII.

LEICESTER SQUARE AND ITS NEIGHBOURHOOD.

"He made the desert smile."

Leicester Fields—Formation of the Square—Famous Duels fought here—Leicester House—Anecdote of George III.'s Childhood—Sir Ashton Lever's Museum—Saville House—Miss Linwood's Exhibition of Needlework—Destruction of Saville House—Residence of Sir Joshua Reynolds—Hogarth's House—The "Pic-nic Club"—John Hunter's Museum—The Alhambra—Burford's Panorama—The Church of Notre Dame de France—Wyld's "Great Globe"—Downfall of the Statue of George I.—Renovation of the Square by Baron A. Grant—Residence of Sir Isaac Newton—Cranbourn Street and Cranbourn Alley.

THERE are, perhaps, few places in the metropolis remaining at the present day that combine the characteristics of "Old and New London"—rolled into one as it were—to a greater extent than Leicester Square. It dates from the time of the second Charles, to whose reign we are indebted for many of those open spaces in the metropolis which tend so necessarily towards its salubrity. Down to the very last days of the Protectorate, Leicester Fields—as the place was then, and even more recently, termed—was entirely unbuilt upon. The north side of the Leicester Square of to-day was the only place occupied in the vicinity, and this was taken up by Leicester House and its gardens, at the back of which was a large open common, which was used for many years as a place for military exercise.

The history of the square, in fact, begins with Leicester House, which was built between 1632 and 1636, by Robert Sidney, Earl of Leicester, whose voluminous correspondence, preserved among the "Sidney Papers," is a history, in little, of his time, and of whose sons, Philip and Algernon Sidney, Leicester Fields hold many memories.

In Aggas' map there are no houses either north or west of the mews enclosure. St. Martin's Lane is represented with hedgerows, and the site of Leicester Square is a drying-ground for clothes. A woman is laying out sundry garments on the grass, and in the next field are cattle, and a milk-maid carrying her pail. Stow, in his "Survey" of 1598, says of the mews—"And this is the farthest building west on the north side of that High Street." From Faithorne's map, compiled between 1643 and 1647, and published in 1658, we know that, just before the Restoration, St. Martin's was literally "in the fields," a windmill and a few scattered houses stood where Windmill Street now is, and Leicester House was still in grounds not surrounded by buildings.

Of Aggas' map of London, so far as it concerns this region, Mr. Tom Taylor remarks:—"There is so much in the map which brings Shakespeare to mind, that one is surprised not to find the Globe, and the Red Bull, the Fortune, and the Curtain playhouses as conspicuous as the 'Bull and Bear' Gardens."

In this map all the country to the north of Charing Cross and west of Chancery Lane is still entirely devoted to country life and uses, and the Hospital for Lepers, dedicated to St. Giles, stood in the fields, with nothing between it and the spot where now stands Leicester Square. The line of St. Martin's Lane was, however, occupied by buildings on both sides as far as St. Giles's Church. Soon after the Restoration increasing prosperity led to a rapid increase of dwellings. The parish of St. Martin had so enlarged its population that "numerous inhabitants were deprived of an opportunity of publicly celebrating the divine offices," and the result of an application to Parliament was that a separate parish was formed, and a new parish church was built, dedicated to St. Anne, mother of the Virgin. Around this (in what is now known as Dean Street, Soho) buildings clustered, and within fifty years the parish contained 1,337 houses, according to Maitland. He adds the following information about the prosperity of the parish:—"There are of persons that keep coaches seventy-three," and there "is a workhouse for the reception of the poor;" and then he goes on:—"The fields in these parts being lately converted into buildings, I have not discovered anything of antiquity in this parish;" many parts so greatly abound with French that it is an "easy matter for a stranger to fancy himself in France." This is a characteristic of the parish that has not altered. Strype, in 1720, speaks of the "chapels in these parts for the use of the French nation, where our Liturgy turned into French is used, French ministers that are refugees episcopally ordained officiating; several whereof are hereabouts seen walking in the canonical habit of the English clergy. Abundance of French people, many whereof are voluntary exiles for their religion, live in these streets and lanes, following honest trades, and some gentry of the same nation."

From John Overton's map, published in 1706, it is easy to see how the buildings surrounding Leicester Square lay at that time. The grass in the centre is marked as enclosed. Cranbourn Street and Bear Lane give access by the north-east corner, and "Dirty Lane," or Green Street, by the south-east. Panton Street, *viâ* "Slug Street," opens the south-west corner, but the north-west side is completely closed. Later maps show the communication by way of Sidney Alley, a narrow footway; but the route by which carriages from the west now drive to Drury Lane or Covent Garden was then blocked by a line of houses. Though we cannot trace the building of the square with any accuracy, we have a slight sketch of it by Strype in 1720, which could not have been more than some forty or fifty years after its completion. He says it is "a very handsome square, railed about and gravelled within. The buildings are very good, and well inhabited, and frequented by the gentry. The north and west rows of buildings, which are in St. Anne's parish, are the best; and especially on the north, where is Leicester House, the seat of the Earl of Leicester, being a large building with a fair court before it for the reception of coaches, and a fine garden behind it; the south and east sides being in the parish of St. Martin's."

Rocque's map of 1737 shows how rapidly buildings spread north and west. Leicester House was no longer in the country, as up to Oxford Street the ground was filled with houses. The *Country Journal of Craftsmen*, under the date of April 16, 1737, contains the following statement:—"Leicester field is going to be fitted up in a very elegant manner: a new wall and rails to be erected all round, and a basin in the middle, after the manner of Lincoln's Inn Fields." Northouck, in 1773, writes:—"This is a handsome square, the inner part of which is enclosed by iron rails, and adorned with grass plats and gravel walks. In the centre is an equestrian statue of his present Majesty, gilt." This statue was really of George I., modelled by C. Buchard for the Duke of Chandos, and brought hither from Canons, having been purchased by the inhabitants of the square. It was finely gilt, and in 1812 was re-gilt. Of its later history we shall have more to say presently.

Between the Restoration and the Revolution, Leicester Field, as it was then called, had become surrounded by houses and streets, and had assumed nearly its present dimensions. Before the end of the seventeenth century the centre, as shown above, had been railed round, and was as famous for duels as the ground behind Montague House in later times. Here it was that the famous duel occurred, in 1699, between Captains French and Coote, in which Coote was slain on the spot at night, and French and Lord Warwick wounded. In it, too, was implicated Lord Mohun, of duelling notoriety, but who, by all accounts, on this occasion did his best to arrange the difference between the two hot-headed Irishmen. Thackeray has described in "Esmond" how Lord Mohun and Lord Castlewood, with their respective friends, went to the Duke's playhouse and saw Mrs. Bracegirdle in *Love in a Wood*, then to the "Greyhound" in Charing Cross to sup, where the two lords quarrelled, according to previous arrangement, and it was agreed to take chairs and go to Leicester Field. Colonel Westbury, second to Lord Castlewood, asked, with a low bow to my Lord of Warwick and Holland, second to Lord Mohun, whether he should have the honour of exchanging a pass or two with his lordship. "It is an honour to me," said my Lord of Warwick and Holland, "to be matched with a gentleman who has been at Mons and Namur." Captain Macartney, the second second, if we may so say, of Lord Mohun, asked permission to give a lesson to Harry Esmond, who was then fresh from Cambridge, and destined for holy orders. Chairs were called, and the word was given for Leicester Field, where the gentlemen were set down opposite the "Standard" Tavern. It was moonlight, and the town was abed, and only a few lights shone in the windows of the houses, but the night was bright enough for the purpose of the disputants. All six entered the square, the chairmen standing without the railing and keeping the gate, lest any persons should disturb the meeting. After Harry had been engaged for some two minutes, a cry from the chairmen, who were smoking their pipes, and leaning over the railing as they watched the dim combat within, announced that some catastrophe had occurred. Lord Castlewood had received a mortal wound, and he was carried to the house of Mr. Aimes, surgeon, in Long Acre, where he died.

Besides Leicester House, there were now other great houses in the square. To the west of it stood a mansion belonging to Lord Ailesbury, inhabited in the year 1698 by Lord Carmarthen, the eccentric son of the Duke of Leeds, an enthusiastic amateur sailor and shipbuilder, as well as drinker and rough customer, to whom William III. confided the care of the Czar Peter. In Lord Carmarthen the latter found a congenial spirit, and his great delight while in England was to sail all day with him in his yacht, the *Peregrine*, and drink brandy spiced with pepper with him all night in Norfolk Street, or Leicester Field. Before going to the theatre, it is recorded that the Czar, besides a pint of brandy and a bottle of sherry, "floored eight bottles of sack after dinner." To the Czar, in January, 1712, succeeded, as a great foreign visitor, Prince Eugene, "a little, ugly, yellow wizened man, with one shoulder higher than the other." He was the hero of the populace, for the English people were eager to carry on the war, and the Prince was against the impending peace which the new Tory Government were just about to patch up. On the 14th of March the Prince left London, having entirely failed in his warlike mission; and the same month brought the Mohocks, "a race of rogues," Swift writes to Stella, "that play the devil about the town every night and slit people's noses—young Davenant telling us at Court how he was set upon by them, and how they ran his chair through with a sword. It is not safe being in the streets at night for them. The Bishop of Salisbury's (Burnet's) son is said to be of the gang. They are all Whigs." Thus writes the great Tory champion of the Whig bishop's son. He, too, had his abode in Leicester Field in 1712, the year of his greatest literary activity.

STATUE OF GEORGE I. AND HOGARTH'S HOUSE, 1790.

As we have already mentioned, Leicester House was the first element of the "square," and as buildings gradually grew up around, it formed the boundary on the north side. The house itself stood well back, having a spacious courtyard in front as well as an extensive garden in the rear. Northouck describes the house in 1773 as "a large brick building, with a wide courtyard before." There is extant a drawing of Leicester House by George Virtue, taken in 1748, showing the sentries at the

LEICESTER SQUARE, ABOUT 1750.

gates of Saville and Leicester Houses. Leicester House was of brick, with two storeys, and an attic, and a range of nine windows in front. In 1788 the house was taken down, and maps of 1799, such as Horwood's and Edward Waters', show the building along the north side entirely completed. The enclosure had two rows of trees round it, and was laid out with cross walks; various maps exhibit different arrangements of trees and walks.

Leicester House was the abode of the Sidneys—that noble family of which, in the sixteenth century, Sir Henry Sidney, "the wisest, greatest, and justest Lord-Deputy Ireland ever had," and his more famous son Philip, were the great ornaments. In the year 1632, Sir Henry's son, Robert, then Earl of Leicester, built Leicester House, having derived the ownership of the Lammas-land of St. Giles's through the grant of Henry VIII. to his ancestor, Lord Lisle. This Lammas-land was the tract of ground lying between Charing Cross and Oxford Road, or St. Giles's Road, and over it the citizens of Westminster had right of common, though the fee-simple was in St. Giles's, St. James's, and other hospitals. Before another century had elapsed those common rights had passed away, before that determined progress from east to west, which building in London has made in generation after generation.

At Leicester House the Sidneys dwelt all through the troublous times of the Commonwealth to the end of the century, their leading spirit being the unhappy Algernon Sidney, the pure patriot and impracticable politician who was persecuted both by Cromwell and Charles II. until he died on the scaffold after the iniquitous trial for the Rye House Plot, in 1683. It was not till near the close of the eighteenth century that the Sidney property of Leicester Fields passed to the Tulk family for £90,000, which went to pay off the incumbrances on Penshurst; and from the representatives of the Tulks their rights over the enclosure now called the square were in the year 1874 acquired by Mr. Albert Grant for £13,000, and made over to the Board of Works in trust for the public.

Leicester House was for a short time the residence of the Princess Elizabeth, only daughter of James I., the titular Queen of Bohemia, to whom Lord Craven devoted his life and labours, and who, in 1662, here ended her unfortunate life. Besides the Queen of Bohemia—the "Queen of Hearts," as she was called by all who came under the magic of her influence—Leicester House was inhabited in the last century by other royal and noble personages. In 1668 we find lodging in Leicester House the French ambassador, Charles Colbert, Marquis de Croisay. Pepys tells us in his "Diary," under date October 21st, 1668, that he paid a visit to the French ambassador, Colbert, at Leicester House. Evelyn records a dinner he ate at Leicester House with the grave and gay Anne, Countess of Sunderland, when she sent for Richardson, the famous fire-eater, to exhibit his prowess before them. In 1708, the house was let to the Imperial ambassador, who, in 1712, there received Prince Eugene as his guest, when "on a secret mission to prevent peace from being arranged between Great Britain and France," as we have already noticed.

At Leicester House, in the year 1721, was born William, Duke of Cumberland, the hero of Culloden. There, between 1717 and 1760, lived the Princes of Wales, when a Prince of Wales was always at deadly feud with the head of his house. George II., whilst Prince of Wales, there fed his grudge against his father, which Mr. Taylor, in his "History of Leicester Square," tells us had its deepest root in the sympathy with his hapless mother, Sophia Dorothea, doomed to life-long imprisonment at Zell, on a charge of an intrigue with Count Philip Königsmark, the younger brother of the man who contrived the assassination of Thomas Thynne, of Longleat, of which we shall have more to say hereafter. In his day life in Leicester House was as dull as ditch-water, and not much purer; and when he succeeded to the throne in 1727, Frederick Prince of Wales (though he lived for a short time in Norfolk House, in St. James's Square, where George III. was born in 1738) became the tenant of Leicester House the year after Sir Robert Walpole's downfall in 1742, and that mansion became again, as Pennant happily called it, "the pouting place of princes" till the somewhat sudden death of Frederick, in 1751. The king never visited his son during his illness, and received the news when playing cards with the Countess Walmoden with the cool expression, "*Fritz ist todt.*"

An amusing story relating to the childhood of George III. is told in connection with Leicester House. A foreigner, named Goupée, an artist of some note in his day, and a favourite with Frederick Prince of Wales, was a frequent visitor there. One day the prince said to him, "Come, sit down, Goupée, and paint me a picture on such a subject. But Goupée perceiving Prince George (afterwards King George III.) a prisoner behind a chair, took the liberty humbly to represent to his royal patron, how impossible it was for him to sit down to execute his royal highness's commands with spirit, while the prince was standing, and under his royal displeasure. "Come out, George, then," said the good-natured prince, "Goupée has released you."

When Goupée was eighty-four years of age, and very poor, he had to nurse and maintain a mad woman, who was the object of his delight when young; he therefore often put himself in the king's sight at Kensington, where he lived. At length the king stopped his coach, and called to him. "How do you do, Goupée?" said the king, and after a few other questions asked him if he had enough to live upon. "Little enough, indeed," replied Goupée; "and as I once took your majesty out of prison, I hope you will not let me go to one." His majesty ordered him a pension of a guinea a week, but he did not live to enjoy it more than a few months.

Here, as we are reminded by Peter Cunningham, the Princess of Wales was waited upon by the wife of the unfortunate Earl of Cromartie, who was so deeply involved in the fatal Scottish rising of 1745. She came leading in her hand her four little children, the sight of whom ought to have roused a feeling of sympathy in a maternal heart. "The princess saw her," says Gray, in one of his letters, "but made her no other answer than by bringing in her own children and by placing them by her."

On the 26th of October, 1760, George III. was proclaimed king before Saville House, in Leicester Square; and on the 29th it was crowded with the mob, assembled to see the courtiers thronging to Leicester House to kiss the hand of the new king. The Dowager Princess of Wales continued to live in Leicester House till 1766, when she removed to Carlton House; and about the same time occurred the last incident connected with royalty in Leicester Fields—the death, at Saville House, of Prince Frederick William, the youngest brother of the king, aged sixteen. While tenanted by the Royal family, the evenings at Leicester House were often enlivened by private theatricals, in which it is recorded that the future king of England and his brothers acted their childish parts with ability and spirit.

Leicester House subsequently became occupied by private persons, and was at one time used by Sir Ashton Lever as a Museum of Natural History. In 1784 Sir Ashton presented a petition to the House of Commons, praying to be allowed to dispose of his museum by a lottery, as Alderman Boydell had done with his gallery. On this occasion it was stated by his manager that it had been brought to London in the year 1775; that it had occupied twelve years in forming, and contained upwards of 26,000 articles; that the money taken for admission amounted, from February, 1775, to February, 1784, to about £13,000, out of which £660 had been paid for house-rent and taxes. Sir Ashton proposed that his whole museum should go together, and that there should be 40,000 tickets at one guinea each, but of this number only 8,000 tickets were sold. However, the proprietor allowed the lottery to take place, and although he held 28,000 tickets, he lost his museum, which was won by a Mr. Parkinson, who held only two. The house was pulled down shortly afterwards, and the site is now bounded on the west by Leicester Place, a wide thoroughfare leading to Lisle Street. New Lisle Street was built in 1791 on the site of the gardens of Leicester House.

Adjoining Leicester House, on the west, stood, until very recently, a large mansion, called Saville House, formerly the residence of the patriotic Sir George Saville, who was many years Knight of the Shire for the County of York, a relative of the Earls and Marquises of Halifax, and who introduced the Catholic Relief Bill, which led to the Gordon riots in 1780. Saville House, it is well known, occupied nearly the centre of the northern side of the square. It has been, however, as Mr. Timbs remarks in his "Romance of London," frequently confounded with Leicester House, which it adjoined. The latter house, however, stood at the north-eastern extremity, and to this mansion was added Saville House, a communication being made between the two houses for the children of Frederick, Prince of Wales. Saville House was likewise called Ailesbury House, and here Thomas, third Earl of Ailesbury, entertained Peter the Great, when he visited England in the year 1698; and here, too, in all probability, the Czar enjoyed his pet tipple with his boon companion, the Marquis of Carmarthen, as we have already stated. The house passed into the Saville family through the marriage of Lord Ailesbury's son and successor, Charles, third and last Earl of Ailesbury of that creation, who married Lady Ann Saville, eldest daughter and co-heir of Sir William Saville, second Marquis of Halifax. At any rate, Sir George Saville, Bart., M.P., who owned the house in 1780, was the male heir of the Savilles and of the Marquis of Halifax, and the inheritor of the baronetcy. The house, in the Gordon riots, was stripped of its valuable furniture, books, and pictures, which the rioters burnt in the square; and the iron rails were torn from the front of the house and used by the mob as weapons.

Saville House was rebuilt early in the present century, and soon became a sort of "Noah's Ark," for exhibition purposes. Here Miss Linwood exhibited her needlework, from the year 1800 until her death in 1845; and here, too, the National Political Union held its reform meetings, recalling the storms of the previous century. Then came a succession of prodigies of nature and art. Amongst the latter were a large moving panorama of the Mississippi River, and a series of views of New Zealand; concerts and balls, and exhibitions of too questionable a shape for us to detail. "Through some sixty years of the showman's art, flaring by night and by day, Saville House lasted unharmed until the catastrophe of 1865, when the royal baby-house and the cheap pleasure-haunt were burnt in the short space of two hours."

Part of the house, on being refitted after the Gordon riots, was occupied by a carpet manufacturer, and subsequently by Messrs. Stagg and Mantle, drapers and silk mercers; and also by Messrs. Bickers and Bush, extensive booksellers. The eastern wing of it was for many years the show-room of Miss Linwood's exhibition of needlework, as mentioned above, which enjoyed a popularity second only to that of Madame Tussaud's exhibition of wax-work in Marylebone. This exhibition gave a new name to Saville House, it being known for nearly half a century as the Linwood Gallery. It comprised about sixty copies of the best and finest pictures of the English and foreign schools of art, all executed by the most delicate handicraft with the needle, the tapestry "possessing all the correct drawing, just colouring, and light and shade of the original pictures from which they are copied." The entrance to this exhibition was up a flight of stone steps, leading to a large room.

After enjoying half a century of popularity, the exhibition came to an end in 1844, and the pictures were sold by auction, realising only a comparative trifle. No less than 3,000 guineas had been refused for the chief work, viz., "Salvator Mundi," after Carlo Dolci, and Miss Linwood bequeathed it to the Queen; but so reduced was the value of these works at her death, that when Messrs. Christie and Manson sold the collection by auction, all the pictures, except a few which were reserved, did not realise more than £1,000. The rooms which they occupied were then turned into a concert and ball-room, and made use of for entertainments of a very questionable character; but they were burnt down in February, 1865, the Prince of Wales being among the spectators of the conflagration. The house was presently rebuilt, and in the early part of 1881 was opened for the exhibition of a panorama illustrative of the Charge of Balaclava. The painting, which covered about 1,500 square yards of canvas, was the work of M. Poilpot and Mr. Stephen Jacobs. A part of the building was used as a "Fine Art Gallery."

Underneath Saville House were some extensive apartments, to which access was obtained by a flight of a few steps from the square. The chief room, often called the "theatre," was used for various exhibitions from time to time, including "Miller's Mechanical and Picturesque Representations," consisting of seven views of cities, "the figures of which," says a prospectus in 1814, "are impressed with movements peculiar to each, so as to imitate the operations of nature." The passage leading to this theatre, Mr. Britton tells us, in 1815, "has been lately opened as one of those singular establishments called bazaars."

On the site of this place of entertainment now stands the Empire Theatre, which was opened in the year 1885.

A large house, No. 47, on the western side of the square, was for many years the residence of Sir Joshua Reynolds. Here duchesses and marchionesses, ladies and fair daughters of the aristocracy sat to the monarch of the world of art, to be immortalised by his brush. Here Burke and Foote, Goldsmith and Dr. Johnson, Garrick and Boswell, and most of the celebrated men of the last century, were in the habit of assembling, and of dining almost every week at the hospitable board of the great portrait painter. His house here, we are told, was magnificently proportioned; it possessed one of the finest staircases in London; it was fitted up with exquisite taste, and it was the rendezvous of the literary world. Here Sir Joshua worked with the greatest assiduity until the last, and only ended his laborious toil, which was, however, to him a labour of love, with his life.

Of Sir Joshua Reynolds (who died here in 1792) it would be presumptuous to say a word of praise, beyond quoting the words of Edmund Burke:—"Sir Joshua Reynolds was, on very many accounts, one of the most memorable men of his time. He was the first Englishman who added the praise of his elegant arts to the other glories of his country. In taste, in grace, in facility, in happy invention, and in the richness and harmony of colouring, he was equal to the great masters of the renowned ages. In portrait-painting he was beyond them, for he communicated to that description of the art in which English artists are the most engaged a variety, a fancy, and a dignity derived from the higher branches which even those who professed them in a superior manner did not always preserve, when they delineated individual nature. In painting portraits, he appeared not to be raised upon that platform, but to descend to it from a higher sphere. His paintings illustrate his lessons, and his lessons seem to be derived from his paintings. He possessed the theory as perfectly as the practice of his art. To be such a painter, he was a profound and penetrating philosopher. In full affluence of foreign and domestic fame, admired by the expert in art, and by the learned in science, courted by the great, caressed by sovereign powers, and celebrated by distinguished poets, his native humility, modesty, and candour never forsook him, even on surprise or provocation; nor was the least degree of arrogance or assumption visible to the most scrutinising eye in any part of his conduct or discourse. His talents of every kind, powerful from nature, and not meanly cultivated by letters, his social virtues in all the relations and all the habitudes of life, rendered him the centre of a very great and unparalleled variety of agreeable societies, which will be dissipated by his death. He had too much merit not to excite some jealousy, too much innocence to provoke any enmity. The loss of no man of his time can be felt with more sincere, general, and unmixed sorrow."

Sir Joshua Reynolds' handsome house was next held by the Earl of Inchiquin; then by a society known as the Western Literary and Scientific Institution; it was subsequently taken by Messrs. Puttick and Simpson, the eminent auctioneers, who removed hither from Piccadilly. The actual apartment used as their auction-room was Sir Joshua's studio.

Allan Cunningham, in his "Lives of Painters," gives us the following peep into Sir Joshua Reynolds' painting-room a century ago, and an insight into his regular habits:—

"His study was octagonal, some twenty feet long by sixteen broad, and about fifteen feet high. The window was small and square, and the sill nine feet from the floor. His sitters' chair moved on castors, and stood above the floor about a foot and a half. He held his palettes by the handle, and the sticks of his brushes were eighteen inches long. He wrought standing, and with great celerity; he rose early, breakfasted at nine, entered his study at ten, examined designs or touched unfinished portraits till eleven brought a sitter, painted till four, then dressed, and gave the evening to company."

The first London residence of Sir Thomas Lawrence, the pupil and successor of Sir Joshua Reynolds as the fashionable portrait painter of the day, was over a confectioner's shop, at No. 4 in the square, a house which was subsequently incorporated in Saville House when the latter building was enlarged.

Bell (afterwards the far-famed Sir Charles Bell) lived in Leicester Square, in the house where Mr. Speaker Onslow had resided. He, in turn, was succeeded by Cruikshank, Sir Joshua Reynolds' medical attendant, the same who succeeded to Hunter's Medical School.

At the south-eastern corner of the square stood the house in which the inimitable George Hogarth lived and worked for many years. It was in 1733 that Hogarth settled here with his young wife, whom he had carried off from the house of her father, Sir James Thornhill, three years before. The house bore the sign of the "Golden Head," and in it most of Hogarth's finest works were engraved and sold; and there, after his death, his widow lived till 1789. In April, 1790, "the pictures and prints of the late Mrs. Hogarth" were sold by auction by Mr. Greenwood, at the "Golden Head," Leicester Square. Though the catalogue contained numerous pictures by Hogarth's own hand, by Sir James Thornhill, and a variety of portraits of the artist, his wife, sister, and other relatives, the entire sale realised only £255. It must raise a smile to read that on this occasion a "parcel of Academy figures and studies by Mr. Hogarth" fetched only eleven shillings and sixpence! After this sale the connection of the Hogarths with Leicester Square ceased.

With reference to the sign of the "Golden Head," Nichols, in his second edition of "Biographical Anecdotes of William Hogarth," says, "Hogarth made one essay in sculpture. He wanted a sign to distinguish his house in Leicester Fields, and thinking none more proper than the "Golden Head," he, out of a mass of cork made up of several thicknesses compacted together, carved a bust of Vandyck, which he gilt and placed over his door. It is long since decayed, and was succeeded by a head in plaster, which has also perished; and is supplied by a head of Sir Isaac Newton" (since taken down). "Hogarth also modelled another resemblance of Vandyck in clay, which is likewise destroyed." Hogarth's house, or, at all events, part of it, was afterwards converted into the "Sablonnière Hotel," which was kept by an Italian named Pagliano, and largely frequented by foreigners. The building was pulled down in 1870, and on its site was erected the new school-house of Archbishop Tenison, which was removed thither from its old quarters at the back of the National Gallery, to which we have referred in the preceding chapter.

At some public rooms in this square, kept by a foreigner, M. de Texier, as Lord William Lennox tells us, the first "Pic-nic Club" was organised in London, by the aid of Lady Albinia Cumberland, and Colonel (afterwards Sir Charles) Greville. Individuals of either sex belonged to it, and took their chances in a strange lottery, being bound to supply whatever dish, or other eatable or drinkable, they might draw. To this concerts and amateur dramatic entertainments were added; but the club did not prosper, being probably "in advance of the time," and much opposed by parents of the old-fashioned, straight-laced school. It was also attacked by the caricaturists, who, by driving the ladies away, succeeded in slaying it outright. There was a rival Pic-nic Society at the Pantheon in Oxford Street, but it shared a like fate.

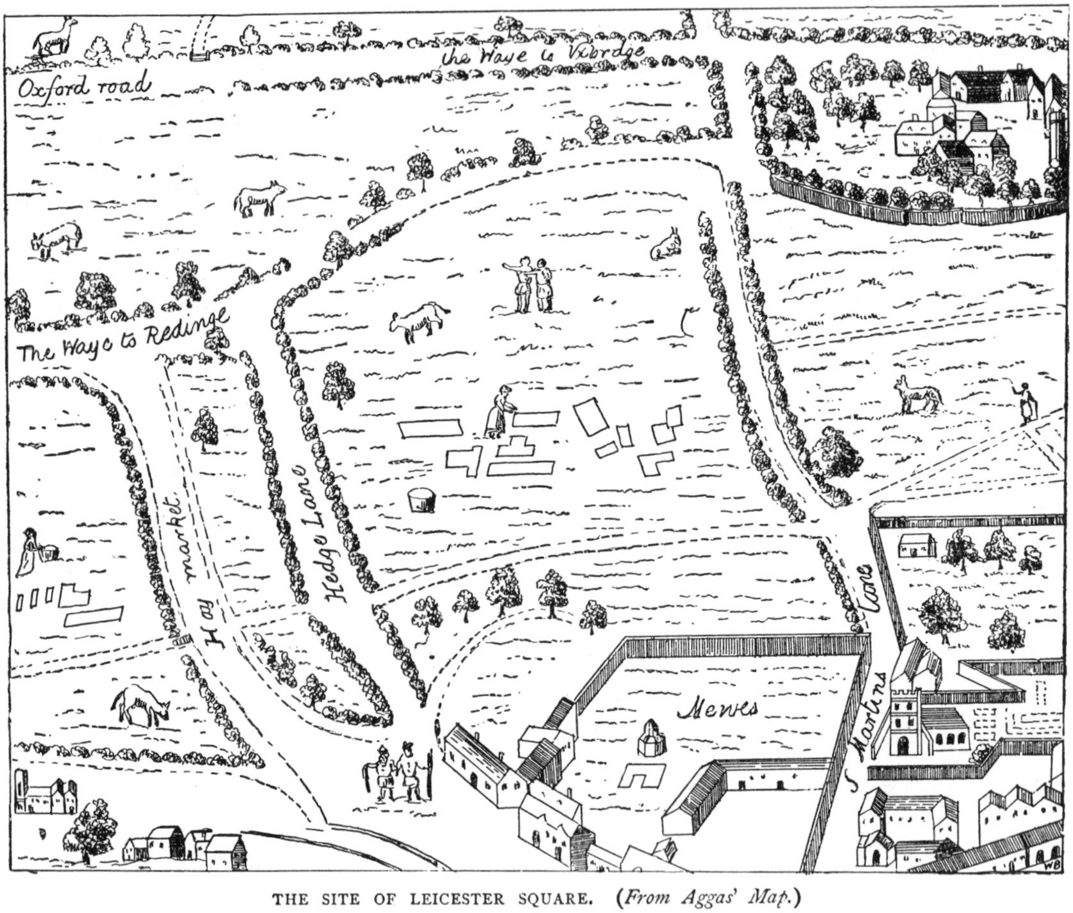

THE SITE OF LEICESTER SQUARE. (*From Aggas' Map.*)

Almost in the centre of the eastern side, nearly on the site of the Alhambra, stood the Anatomical Museum of John Hunter, the celebrated surgeon, where was formed the nucleus of the Hunterian Museum, now at the College of Surgeons, Lincoln's Inn Fields. It was in 1783 that John Hunter became owner of No. 28, immediately south of the present Alhambra, and at the back of it, on ground leading to Castle Street, he built his famous Museum of Comparative Anatomy. In 1785 the erection was complete, and one of the first acquisitions of its owner was the skeleton of O'Brien, the Irish giant, which may still be seen, as we have already said, in the College of Surgeons. Foote tells us that Hunter held, on Sunday evenings, during the winter months, regular receptions of his friends or public medical levées, for which he sent out cards of invitation; he "regaled them with tea and coffee," and "treated them with medical occurrences." Having raised the science of surgery to a height never believed to be possible, and thus benefited the whole human race, Hunter died of disease of the heart, aggravated by an angry discussion in the Board-room of St. George's Hospital, in the sixty-fourth year of his age, "without an equal in the world in his combined character of surgeon and naturalist." He was buried in St. Martin's Church, and his widow would gladly have raised a monument to his memory in Westminster Abbey, but he died poor, and she could not pay the fees. Thus he remained without a statue till Mr. A. Grant selected him as a fit subject for one of the busts in Leicester Square. In 1897 No. 28 came into the builder's hands.

The building now known as the Alhambra Palace of Varieties is a place of amusement where ballet and variety "turns" form the chief features of attraction. It was built in the Moorish or Arabesque style, and opened about 1852–3 as a place of popular instruction, somewhat after the plan of the Polytechnic, and bore at first the name of the "Royal Panopticon of Science and Art." It was burlesque and other pieces requiring scenic effect, Architecturally, it is one of the most elegant places of entertainment of the kind in London. The façade of the building is flat, with lofty minarets at the corners; and the dome in the centre, together with the coloured decoration, make it a striking

THE PANOPTICON, IN 1854.

got up under the auspices of several philanthropic individuals as a joint-stock undertaking. But the speculation did not answer, and after a few years the company broke up. The building was closed for a time, and then re-opened under the name by which it is at present known. It is at once a theatre and a music-hall. It consists of a spacious auditorium, with three tiers of galleries, and a stage particularly adapted for the representation of object. The chief feature of the interior is the rotunda. The great organ, built for the Panopticon, was purchased for St. Paul's Cathedral, but has since been removed to Clifton. The theatre was burnt down in 1882, and rebuilt in 1883-4. In 1897 it was extended to the Charing Cross Road.

In Orange Court, Leicester Fields, the artist, Opie, was living, when discovered by Wyatt.

In this square, towards the close of the last century, Charles Dibdin built and opened a theatre of his own under the name of "Sans Souci."

J. T. Smith tells us, in his "Book for a Rainy Day," that "for many years the back parlour of the 'Feathers' public-house—which stood on the side of Leicester Fields, and which was so called in compliment to its neighbour Frederick, Prince of Wales, who inhabited Leicester House—had been frequented by artists, and several well-known amateurs. Among the former were Stuart, the Athenian traveller; Scott, the marine painter; old Oram, of the Board of Works; Luke Sullivan, the miniature-painter, who engraved Hogarth's picture of 'The March to Finchley,' now in the Foundling Hospital; Captain Grose, the author of 'Antiquities of England,' 'History of Armour,' &c.; Mr. Hearne, the draughtsman of many of England's antiquities, Nathaniel Smith, my father, &c. The amateurs were Henderson, the actor; Mr. Morris, a silver-smith; Mr. John Ireland, then a watchmaker in Maiden Lane, and since editor of Boydell's edition of Dr. Trusler's work, 'Hogarth Moralised;' and Mr. Baker, of St. Paul's Churchyard, whose collection of Bartolozzi's works was unequalled. When this house, the sign of the 'Feathers,' was taken down, to make way for Dibdin's theatre, several of its frequenters adjourned to the 'Coach and Horses' in Castle Street, Leicester Fields; but in consequence of their not proving customers sufficiently expensive for that establishment, the landlord one evening venturing to light them out with a farthing candle, they betook themselves to Gerard Street, and thence to the 'Blue Posts' in Dean Street, where the association dwindled to three members, and died a natural death."

The building known as the "Panorama" stood in the north-east corner of the square, and was an exhibition of ancient reputation. Here Burford's celebrated panoramas were exhibited for several years. Part of the building was subsequently used as a "penny news-room," and as a sort of Red Republicans' Club; but it was finally converted into a Roman Catholic church, dedicated to "Notre Dame de France," under the ministration of the Marist Fathers. The mission was established here in conjunction with *Les Sœurs de Charité Françaises*, or the establishment of the Sisters of Charity in Leicester Place. Some idea of the benefits resulting from this combined force may be gathered from the address of Cardinal Manning at the consecration of the mission in April, 1874. After referring to the manner in which the structure had been raised and embellished, and to the resources for the mission, he said, "With such a church on one side of Leicester Place, and the many establishments of the Sisters of Charity on the other, not only the street itself, but the entire foreign colony around it, enjoys advantages which any other portion of London might envy. We have said 'establishments,' for though there are only eight Sisters of Charity at Leicester Place, they carry on a hospital, a dispensary, a girls' school, an infants' school, a *crèche*, a patronage for young girls, a system of out-door relief, and, with the assistance of a master, a boys' school. Since the foundation of the hospital and the dispensary in 1867, relief has been given to 1,400 in-patients, and 19,000 out-patients; while in relief to the poor souls, 20,000 pounds weight of bread are distributed each year by those 'ministering angels' in human form. In this *crèche* they have an average of twenty-five babies of poor mothers who have to go out and work for their daily bread; in their infant school eighty lisping little ones; in their girls' school seventy pupils; and in their boys' school thirty-six. The patronage numbers from fifty to sixty young girls on its books. If we reflect for a moment on the heterogeneous elements of which the French population of Soho is composed, the work undertaken by the Marist Fathers and the Sisters of Charity will at once appear to be "simply appalling." Other charitable institutions in the square are the Dental Hospital of London and St. John's Hospital for Diseases of the Skin.

We have already referred to the central enclosure of Leicester Square in the early stages of its existence, and it now remains to add that shortly after the commencement of the nineteenth century its glory began to fade. The square gradually became deserted by the gentry who had previously resided within its limits, and in 1851 the area was occupied by a large domed building, in which was exhibited Wyld's "Great Globe." This representation of the world we live in was sixty-five feet in diameter, and comprised a surface of some ten thousand square feet. Galleries encircled the interior of the building at different heights from the ground, by which means visitors were enabled to walk round and inspect every portion of the globe, an attendant, staff in hand, pointing out its principal features; lectures were likewise delivered at intervals during the day. In addition to the "Great Globe," Mr. Wyld introduced, in 1854, a well-executed model of the Crimea, and as this had the positions of the different armies of the Allies and of the Russians correctly laid down from day to day, according as news arrived in England from the seat of war, it was soon the chief object of interest to the thousands who flocked to Leicester Square every day. In 1859 a curious Oriental

Museum was exhibited here, illustrative of life in Turkey, Armenia, and Albania, with life-like models of the interiors of palaces, harems, bazaars, offices of State, and courts of justice, with priests, soldiers, and janissaries, &c., much after the fashion of Madame Tussaud's.

On the removal of Wyld's "Great Globe," after occupying the square for about ten years, the enclosure became exposed once more in all its hideous nakedness. From that time down to the middle of the year 1874, its condition was simply a disgrace to the metropolis. Overgrown with rank and fetid vegetation, it was a public nuisance, both in an æsthetic and in a sanitary point of view; covered with the *débris* of tin pots and kettles, cast-off shoes, old clothes, and dead cats and dogs, it was an eye-sore to every one forced to pass by it. As for the "golden horse and its rider," the effigy of George I., which had been set up in the centre of the enclosure when Leicester House was the "pouting place of princes," besides having suffered all the inclemencies of the weather for years, it had become the subject of every species of practical joke by almost every *gamin* in London. The horse is said to have been modelled after that of Le Sueur at Charing Cross; whilst the statue of George I. was considered a great work of art in its day, and was one of the sights of London, until after a quarter of a century of humiliations, after being the standing butt of ribald caricaturists, and the easy mark of witlings, it gradually fell to pieces. The effigy of his Majesty was the first to be assailed. His arms were first cut off; then his legs followed suit, and afterwards his head; when the iconoclasts, who had doomed him to destruction, at last dismounted him, propping up the mutilated torso against the remains of the once caracolling charger on which the statue had been mounted, and which was in nearly or quite as dilapidated a plight. It would be almost impossible to tell all the pranks that were played upon this ill-starred monument, and how *Punch* and his comic contemporaries made fun of it, whilst the more serious organs waxed indignant as they dilated on the unmerited insults to which it was subjected. One night a party of jovial spirits actually whitewashed it all over, and daubed it ignominiously with large black spots; it was soon after destroyed.

The disgraceful state of Leicester Square became such that it attracted the attention of Parliament, and innumerable were the discussions that took place upon it, with, however, little amelioration in its actual condition. In the year 1869 it was reported that the enterprising proprietors were about to sell the land for building purposes, but upon a communication being sent to the Board of Works, informing them of the fact, it was resolved that the Board would "do all in its power" to prevent the open space from being swallowed up by bricks and mortar. The owners of the fee-simple in the land had all along, in a sort of dog-in-the-manger spirit, not only refused to reclaim the square themselves, but had resisted every effort, or refused every offer of other more beneficent persons, who were willing and eager to undertake a work which it should have been their first duty to accomplish. At length, after an immense amount of litigation, it was finally settled by a decision of the Master of the Rolls, in December, 1873, "that the vacant space in Leicester Square is not to be built over, but will be retained as open ground, for the purposes of ornament and recreation." A "defence committee" was established, and owing to their initiative Mr. Albert Grant was led to make an offer of purchasing the square. Early in 1874 that gentleman set measures on foot which finally resulted in his obtaining possession of the square, on the payment of a large sum for purchase-money to the proprietors. He had determined to present it, as a people's garden, to the citizens of the metropolis; and the purchase having been effected, steps were immediately taken to carry out the intentions of the donor. In laying out the ground, nothing pretentious was attempted. The central space was converted into an ornamental garden, and adorned with statuary, &c. The principal ornament of the new square is a white marble fountain, surmounted by a statue of Shakespeare, also in white marble, the figure being an exact reproduction by Signor Fontana of the statue designed by Kent, and executed by Scheemakers, on the Westminster Abbey cenotaph. The water spouts from jets round the pedestal, and from the beaks of dolphins at each of its corners, into a marble basin. Flower-beds surround this central mass, and the enclosure—so long a squalid and unsightly waste—is now a gay and pleasant garden of flowering shrubs, green plots, inlaid with bright flower-beds and broad gravelled paths. In each angle of the garden is a bust of white marble on a granite pedestal. To the south-east stands Hogarth, by Durham; to the south-west, Newton, by Weekes; to the north-east, John Hunter, by Woolner; and to the north-west, Reynolds, by Marshall.

The ceremony of transferring the ground to the Metropolitan Board of Works for the enjoyment of the public, took place on the 9th of July, 1874. The sum expended by Mr. Grant in purchasing the property and laying out the grounds, &c., amounted to about £30,000.

Close by Leicester Fields in St. Martin's Street, on the east side, lived, in 1710, after his removal from Jermyn Street, Sir Isaac Newton, Master of the Mint and President of the Royal Society, then, perhaps, better known by those titles than by his astronomical works. Though still dingy and dreary, in spite of its having been partly rebuilt, St. Martin's Street in 1710 was good enough for envoys and high officials, and thither Newton drew all that was scientific to his entertainments, while the wits of the day were attracted by the philosopher's clever and charming niece, Catherine Barton, who kept house for him for sixteen years, from 1710 to 1727. In this famous house in St. Martin's Street afterwards lived Dr. Charles Burney, the author of the "History of Music" and other works, the father of a still more famous daughter, Frances, authoress of "Evelina," the petted friend of all the blues and wits of her generation, and the writer of a diary second only to Boswell's "Life of Johnson" for its vivid pictures of the life and manners of the time of George III. In this house Dr. Burney lived between 1770 and 1789, when he removed to Chelsea Hospital. The house, which adjoins the Orange Street chapel, has been put to various uses since Dr. Burney's days, and is now known as Newton Hall. It is easily to be identified, since it bears one of the tablets of the Society of Arts.

It was here that the antiquary, Dr. Stukely, called one day, by appointment. The servant who opened the door said that Sir Isaac was in his study. No one was permitted to disturb him there; but, as it was near his dinner-time, the visitor sat down to wait for him. In a short time a boiled chicken under a cover was brought in for dinner. An hour passed, and Sir Isaac did not appear. The doctor then ate the fowl, and, covering up the empty dish, desired the servant to get another dressed for his master. Before that was ready, the great man came down. He apologised for his delay, and added, "Give me but leave to take my short dinner, and I shall be at your service. I am fatigued and faint." Saying this, he lifted up the cover, and without emotion, turned about to Stukely with a smile, "See," he said, "what we studious people are! I forgot that I had dined."

In the last century, as now, the neighbourhood of Leicester Fields was the favourite resort of foreigners. Green Street, Bear Street, Castle Street, and Panton Street, formed a district called, as was a purlieu in Westminster too, near the Sanctuary, "Petty France." The dwellers in Leicester Fields' slums, and in the adjoining district of Soho, it would seem, were mainly Catholics, frequenting the Sardinian ambassadors' chapel in Duke Street, Lincoln's Inn Fields. The French hairdressers and perfumers lived mostly under the Piazza in Covent Garden, in Bow Street, and in Long Acre; and very few contrived to live east of Temple Bar.

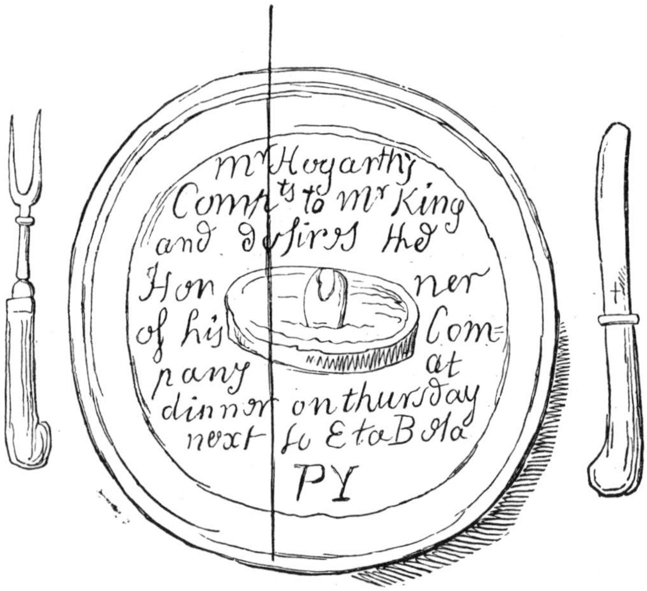

AN INVITATION CARD BY HOGARTH.

Cranbourn Street, or, as it was formerly called, Cranbourn Alley, which runs out of Leicester Square at the north-east angle, dates from about 1677, when it was simply a footway for passengers, and named after the family of Cecil, Earl of Salisbury, whose second title was, and is, Viscount Cranbourne. The alley was formed into a street by the pulling down of the whole of one side in 1843-44, thus forming a continuous roadway from Coventry Street, along the top of the Square, into Long Acre. In this alley, Hogarth was apprenticed to a goldsmith named Gamble, in order to learn the art of silver-plate engraving. Mr. Peter Cunningham remarks that "a shop-bill engraved for Gamble by his eminent pupil is the envy of every collector of Hogarth's works." At one time Cranbourn Alley was a celebrated mart for cheap articles in the way of straw bonnets and millinery. To such an extent was this the case, that a Cranbourn Alley article then bore the same meaning which we now are in the habit of affixing to "Brummagem" goods.

Cranbourn Alley, it would seem, was in 1725 a place where the street-songs, broadsides, &c., of the day were hawked and cried. "I never pass through Cranbourn Alley," writes the witty author of the "London Spy," "but I am astonish'd at the remissness and lenity of the magistrates in suffering the Pretender's interest to be carry'd on and promoted in so publick and shameful a manner as it there is. Here a fellow stands eternally bawling out his Pye-Corner Pastorals, in behalf of 'Dear Jemmy, lovely Jemmy,' &c. I have been credibly inform'd that this man has actually in his pocket a commission under the Pretender's great seal, constituting him his Ballad Singer in Ordinary in Great Britain." Of course this is badinage; but no doubt the Jacobite ballad-monger was one of the institutions of the alley, though close to the gates of Denmark House.

A famous shop in old Cranbourn Alley was the silversmith's, Hamlet's—a long, low shop, whose windows seemed to have no end, and not to have been dusted for centuries, with dim vistas of dish-covers, coffee-biggins, and centre-pieces. Hamlet's stock-in-trade is said to have been worth millions. Seven watchmen kept guard over it every night, and half the aristocracy were in his debt. Royalty itself had gone credit for plate and jewellery at Hamlet's. The proprietor of the establishment in the end took to building, and came to grief. His shop is now no more, and his name in the neighbourhood almost forgotten. "Very curious is it to mark," says a well-known writer, "how old trades and old types of inhabitants linger about localities. They were obliged to pull old Cranbourne Street and Cranbourn Alley quite down before they could get rid of the silversmiths, and even now they are seen sprouting forth again round about the familiar haunt."

On the north side of Cranbourn Street, at the Leicester Square end, is Daly's Theatre, a well-appointed house which was built in 1893 for the American company which was the means of introducing Miss Ada Rehan to the notice of theatrical London.

CHAPTER XXIV.

SOHO.

"The lights are fled, the garlands dead."—*Old Song.*

The Situation and Etymology of Soho—Historical Reminiscences—Newport Market—French Refugees—Gerrard Street—The Toxophilite Society—Dryden's House—Edmund Burke—The "Turk's Head" Tavern, and the Literary Club—The "Literary Society"—Macclesfield or Gerard House—The Prince of Wales's Shooting-ground—L'Hôtel de l'Étoile—St. Anne's Church—The Burial-place of Lord Camelford—Vicissitudes of the King of Corsica—The Parish Watch-house and "Sir Harry Dimsdale."

It has been often remarked—but at the same time, we think, not altogether truthfully—that the past history and character of London cannot be read—like that of Paris, Rome, or Athens—from the appearance of its public buildings and principal thoroughfares. Thus, for instance, Mr. T. Raikes says, in his "Journal," in 1844—"What a difference there is between Paris and London! You may walk through the latter from Hyde Park Corner to Wapping, and, with the exception of a few old churches, the Tower, and the Monument, you see nothing that calls to mind the ancient history of the country. In Paris every street is a *memoria technica* of some anecdote in former times. The one is all poetry, the other is all prose. The Faubourg St. Honoré is now become the residence of the aristocracy in Paris. It is what the Quai des Tournelles and the Quai d'Anjou were in the times of Charles IX., Henri III., and Henri IV.; what the Palais Royal and the Marais were in the times of Louis XIII. and Louis XIV.; what the Faubourg St. Germain was in the times of Louis XV., XVI., and the Restoration. These different migrations of the nobility have left in their former quarters the traces of past splendour, which time has hitherto respected, but which the barbarism of the present age is eager to destroy. One exception to this feeling may be cited. The beautiful old Hôtel Lambert, in the Rue St. Louis, which I visited with Glengall a few years ago, has been purchased by Prince Czartoryski, who has repaired and restored it to its original freshness. Liberty and equality are fine words, but they will leave no monuments behind them, except railroads, barracks, and model prisons."

But, at all events, there is one portion of our metropolis to which this remark will not apply; for we fancy that no city in Europe can more thoroughly tell the story of its own past history, than can Soho testify to the glories of other days, which still surround its decaying and decayed houses as with a halo.

The name Soho, as it is uncertain in its derivation, so also is it loosely applicable to a neighbourhood which it would be impossible to define accurately. It is enough to describe it roughly as lying between St. Martin's and St. Giles'-in-the-Fields, Leicester Square and Oxford Street; but its limits on the western side are very vague. It lies mostly in the district of St. Anne's, which was formed out of the parish of St. Martin's-in-the-Fields, towards the end of the seventeenth century. Pegge mentions the tradition that the name of "Soho"—the watchword at the battle of Sedgemoor, in 1685—was given to a "square" that at that time existed here, called King's Square, in memory of the Duke of Monmouth, whose mansion was upon the south side. Mr. Peter Cunningham, however, negatives this assertion, for he tells us that he has found the name of "Soho" in the rate-books of St. Martin's parish as early as the year 1632. At any rate, people were described as living at the "brick kilns near Soho" as far back as 1636—nearly half a century before the famous battle of Sedgemoor.

GAMBLE'S SHOP-BILL. (*After Hogarth.*)

"The ruthless hand of historical truth," says a writer in the *Saturday Review*, "has of late years demolished many pretty stories, and has not spared the favourite legend of Soho. In the happy days when we believed in the immaculate purity of Anne Boleyn, when we derived Charing Cross from the *chère reine*, when we attributed the razing of Fotheringay to the filial piety of King James, and had a child-like faith generally in the honour and virtue of crowned heads, there were many tales to be repeated as constantly appropriate to the certain localities. Among them, and involving a singular perversion of facts, is the popular account of the name of this district. 'Soho' was the Duke of Monmouth's watchword at Sedgemoor, and was applied by his party to the square in which his town-house stood. So ran the tale. There is a sediment of truth in it. The Duke did live in a house on the south side of what was then called King's Square, and his memory was long cherished in that district and elsewhere. But the district was then called, as it is called still, 'Soho,' and King's Square was then, as it is still, in 'Soho.' Monmouth's watchword was derived from the name of the place where his house stood, not exactly from the name of the square, for it was then called generally King's Square, or else Soho Fields, and this name had been known, as Lord Macaulay points out, at least a year before Sedgemoor, and, as he might have pointed out, at least fifty years before that again. Where the name came from is a different question. It is easy to form conjectures about it, and to say it is derived either from the footpad's slang of the sixteenth century, when the fields were lonely at night, and divers persons were robbed in them, and so forth; or else from the cry of the huntsmen in calling off the harriers in the day when all to the west of Holborn and Drury Lane was open country. This sporting derivation of the name will appear the more probable if we remember what Stow says of these parts in 1562, 'The Lord Mayor, aldermen, and many worshipful persons rode to the conduit leads . . . according to the old custom, and then they went and hunted a hare before dinner and killed her; and thence went to dinner at the banqueting-house at the head of the conduit, where a great number were handsomely entertained by the chamberlain. After dinner they went to hunt the fox. There was a great cry for a mile, and at length the hounds killed him at the end of St. Giles', with great hollowing and blowing of horns at his death.' In reality, however, we do not know much about the matter, and had better let it alone; while for those who like associations of the kind, it will be enough to point out that Monmouth's house stood where there is now a hospital for women, and that the narrow alley called Bateman's Buildings is on part of the site. There is still an old-world air about the place. If you dive down into the streets and lanes, you see everywhere evidences of the greatness of former occupants. If a street-door is open, there is a

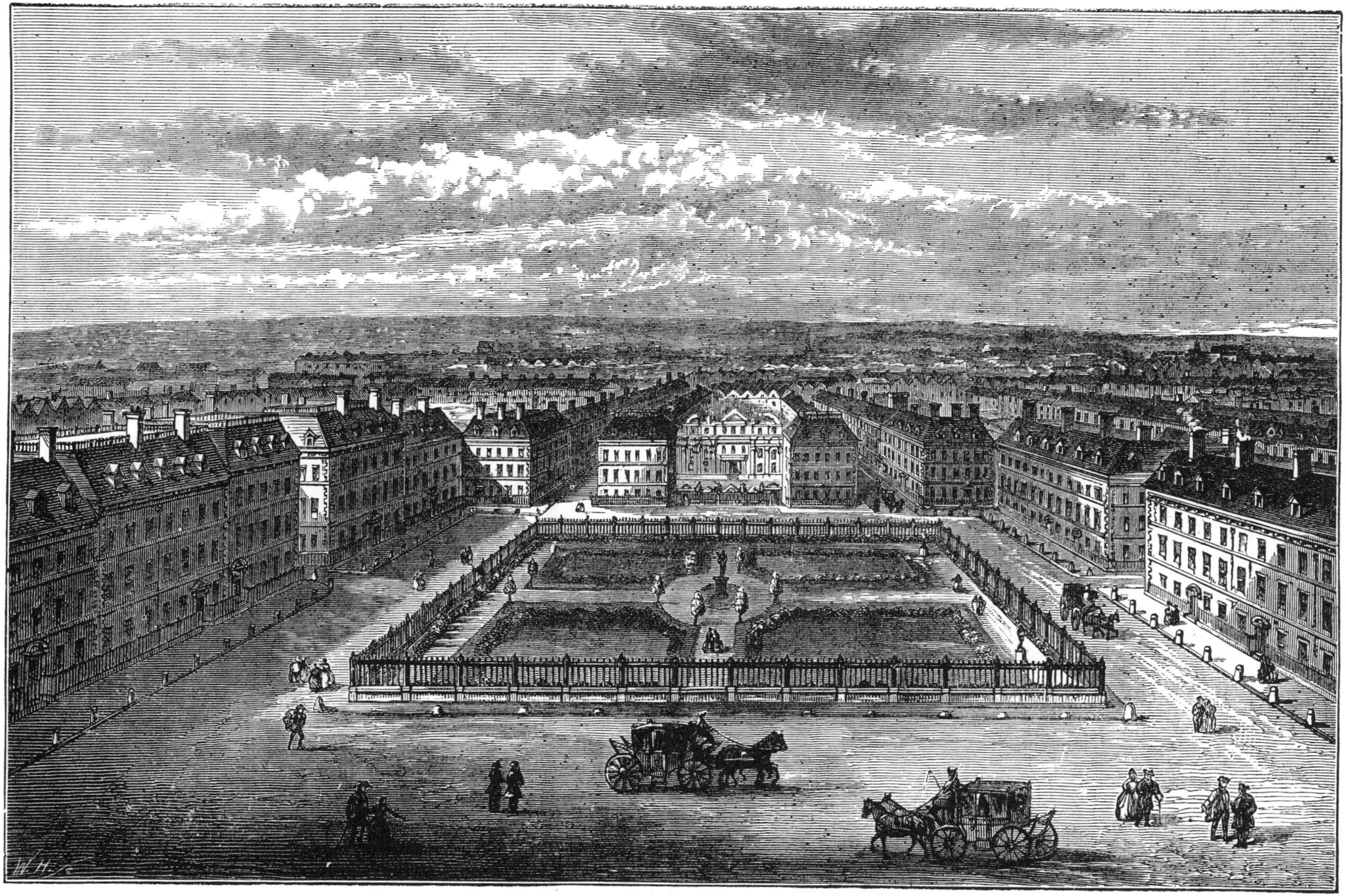

SOHO SQUARE, ABOUT 1700.

vision of carved oak-panelling, of fretted ceilings, of frescoed walls, of inlaid floors. Squalid as are some of the tenements, their inhabitants do not need to dream that they dwell in marble halls."

"Once on a time," continues the same writer, "even Seven Dials was fashionable; and is not a king buried in St. Giles's? for one Wright, an oil-man in Compton Street, had the body of Theodore of Corsica interred at his own expense, and Horace Walpole pointed the moral of the poor Fleet prisoner's tale in his well-known epitaph. Here and there, at the corners, a little bit of the quaint style now in vogue as Queen Anne's allures the unwary passenger into a noisome alley, and Soho can boast of fully as many smells as Cologne. The paradoxes, in which facts and statistics are so often connected, may receive another example from this densely populated and still more densely perfumed region, for it has been found that children survive the struggles of infancy better in Soho than in many a high and airy country parish. Paintings by Sir James Thornhill and Angelica Kauffmann are to be seen in some of the houses. Modern cast-iron railings may stand abashed before the finely-wrought work which encloses some of the filthiest areas. There are mantelpieces in marble, heavy with Corinthian columns, and elaborate entablatures in many an upper chamber let at so much a week. Visitors to the House of Mercy at the corner of Greek Street have an uncovenanted reward for their charity in seeing how the great Alderman Beckford was lodged when he did *not* make the speech now inscribed on his monument in Guildhall. Art still reigns in the house opposite, where the Royal Academy held its infant meetings; and it was close by, at the corner of Compton Street, that Johnson and Boswell, Reynolds and Burke, kept their literary evenings, and were derided by Goldsmith. The more purely scientific associations of the place are almost equally remarkable. In the south-west of the square, in the corner near Frith Street, Sir Joseph Banks and Mr. Payne Knight successively flourished, and the Linnæan Society had here its head-quarters before it was promoted to Burlington House. Since the whole of Soho was more or less fashionable, it is nothing remarkable to find Evelyn and Burnet and Dryden residing within its bounds; but there is some interest in the lying in state there of Sir Cloudesley Shovel, when his body, recovered from the sea at Scilly, was on its way to Westminster Abbey. No doubt an effigy surmounted the pall, and the illustrious foundling appeared in the Roman armour and the full-bottomed wig in which he reposes upon his monument. Half the sites of the curious scenes in Soho, half the residences of historical characters have, however, been left without identification. When the Society of Arts began some years ago to follow the French example, and to place little tablets on the houses in which great men lived or died, they did well; but of late, for some years, they have slackened their efforts, and the whole district deserves and still needs the signs of their activity. If they are not disposed to carry on the task, they should formally give it up. Here and there among the narrow streets and the crowded passages a shield of arms attached to the front of a house marks the former residence of a great noble, or the name of a corner suggests the scene of some great event; but for the most part the labyrinth is unexplored, and the sites are forgotten or altogether unknown."

In "Burns' Handbook of the Seasons," Soho is described as "an industrial district characterised by several special features of its own. The principal peculiarity which is most likely to arrest the attention of a stranger here is the display of antique furniture and archæological subjects to be seen in the warehouses of manufacturers, and in the *Dryasdust*-looking curiosity shops. It is worthy of notice that ancient furniture can be manufactured in this locality, of any age, from the tenth century to the nineteenth, and in all manner of styles, from the clumsy Dutch to those in fashion in the reign of Louis XIV. The curiosity shops in Soho are the means of drawing round them numbers of gentlemen, who are continually fishing for relics of a bygone age. Many men with mediæval idiosyncrasies have added to their stock of archæological stores from this antiquarian storehouse of modern-made furniture. Soho is also the emporium of musical-instrument makers; the square is full of pianoforte manufacturers: these lyres find their way into all parts of the civilised world, and tune the minds of millions of the human family to joy and sadness. This district is also a principal rendezvous for foreigners in London, many of whom here ply their avocations as artists and mechanics."

Although, as compared with Belgravia and Tyburnia, the district known as Soho may be called old, yet it has about it none of the poetry of a venerable antiquity. It is a dull, dingy, and dreary part of London, in spite of its proximity to Regent Street and Oxford Street, and it contains little that is picturesque to relieve the monotony of its appearance.

It was laid out for building in the reign of Charles II., and consists almost wholly of straight and narrow streets running at right angles to each other. In many of these streets, however, there are noble and substantial mansions, which were largely occupied by wealthy merchants and members of Parliament, and even by a few peers of the realm, down to the commencement of the present century.

Soho rejoices in a square; but that is of small dimensions and uninviting aspect; and it seems difficult to realise the fact that a century ago, when Mrs. Cornelys' masqued balls were in vogue, it was crowded night after night with the carriages of "the quality," and even of the highest ranks of the nobility; and that, so lately as the first years of her present Majesty's reign, the Duke of Marlborough occupied a residence in it during the Parliamentary session. It is now chiefly occupied by musical and medical publishers, and by other trades which do not depend much on the publicity of a thoroughfare.

We give on page 175 a rare and curious print of the square as it must have been about the year 1700. The view is that of the southern side, in the centre of which, within large iron gates and with a large square courtyard in front, stands Monmouth House. The gardens in the rear are square, and extend as far south as Compton Street; the entrance is flanked by two large houses, the only ones on that side. St. Anne's tower and spire not being built, there is nothing to break the monotony of the square and rectangular streets which cover the ground apparently nearly to Leicester Square. The statue is in the centre, and the whole of the enclosure is laid out after the regular Dutch type. In the original inscription to this print "Frith" Street is called "Thrift" Street, and "Greek" Street figures as "Grig" Street, while what is now Carlisle Street, running into the square from the west, rejoices in the name of "Merry Andrew" Street. The details of the square we shall give in the next chapter.

That the growth of a population and the building of houses in this neighbourhood was looked upon with no favour at Court, and that St. James's already was beginning to growl out its dislike in the direction of St. Giles's, is clear from a royal proclamation, dated in April, 1671, forbidding the erection of small cottages and other tenements in "the Windmill Fields, Dog Fields, and the fields adjoining 'So Hoe,'" on the ground that such buildings "do choak up the air of his Majesty's palaces and parks, and endanger the total loss of the waters which, by expensive conduits, are conveyed from those fields to our palace at White Hall." It is to be feared that this latter ground of alarm was not without foundation, for certainly it would be no longer possible to supply any of the royal residences with water from this neighbourhood; though Allen tells us that when the square was first laid out, "a fountain of four showers fell into a basin in the centre."

Commencing on the south side of this district, we find immediately behind Leicester Square a remarkable neighbourhood forming part of Soho, and comprising what used to be known as Newport Market, where Orator Henley held his mock preaching. The father of Horne Tooke was a poulterer here, or, as he is reported to have told his schoolfellows, "a Turkey merchant." In this queer locality a number of genuine French shops were, until recently, to be found much as they were during the emigration after the revocation of the Edict of Nantes. Many of them were cheap cafés and restaurants, like those near "the barrier" in Paris. Most of the French refugees who came to England settled here; and in a work published in 1688, entitled the "Happy Future of England," it is noticed that they had already filled 800 of the new-built and empty houses in London. Maitland, who wrote in 1739, observes that, "Many parts of the parish abound with French, so that it is an easy matter for a stranger to fancy himself in France."

Newport Market was so named from the town-house of the Earl of Newport, which stood close by at its north-west angle. It boasted of no attractiveness in the way of buildings, being neither more nor less than a narrow avenue of shops, occupied chiefly by butchers, the market being established for the sale of butcher's meat.

It had been more than once suggested that it would, perhaps, do much for the improvement of the western portion of the metropolis if the site of Newport Market could be used for some such purposes as for the erection of a block of Peabody buildings, and the suggestion was carried out in 1885-6, and now the aspect of the district has been entirely changed. Here originated the Newport Market Refuge and Industrial School, which has now been removed to Coburg Row, Westminster.

At the back of Leicester House, as we have already seen, were extensive lawns and gardens, where now stands Lisle Street, and "several noblemen residing in Gerrard Street were allowed to have private entrances into the gardens, where there was space for three pairs of targets." In these gardens, in 1781, Sir Ashton Lever, who has already been mentioned in connection with Saville House, in conjunction with Mr. Waring and other friends, started the Toxophilite Society, of which the then Prince of Wales shortly afterwards condescended to become patron. The butts, however, not having sufficient range, the members used to hold their fête-days at Canonbury Tower, at the Artillery Ground, Finsbury, or at Highbury Barn; holding, however, convivial gatherings in the evening in their own quarters here. For about twenty years this society continued to flourish, and its meetings were well supported; but its members dwindled sadly down during the long war against Napoleon, at the end of which they numbered but twenty-five. They afterwards hired a ground at Bayswater, and in 1834 obtained their present grounds in the Regent's Park, where we shall doubtless find the society again, in full plume and feather, when we reach that place.

Gerrard Street took its name from Gerard, Earl of Macclesfield, the owner of the site, and the building of the street was commenced about the year 1677.

In Gerrard Street, on the south side, "the fifth door on the left hand, coming from Newport Street," as he tells his friend Steward in a letter, lived John Dryden. We have Pope's authority, in "Spence's Anecdotes," for the assertion that he used commonly to write in the ground-room next the street. Mr. Peter Cunningham identifies this house with that which is now No. 43, and he quotes Dryden's own dedication of "Don Sebastian" to the Earl of Leicester, in which the poet styles himself "a poor inhabitant of your lordship's garden, whose best prospect is on the garden of Leicester House." Here Dryden died in the year 1700, and here, as John Timbs tells us, took place the disgraceful interference with the poet's funeral procession by a party of drunken Mohocks, headed by Lord Jeffries. The great Edmund Burke, too, in 1787, was a resident in Gerrard Street, at No. 37, which is now an hotel. Mr. J. T. Smith, who was living here at the same time, says of him, "Many a time when I had no inclination to go to bed at the dawn of day, I have looked down from my window to see whether the author of 'Sublime and Beautiful' had left his drawing-room, where I had seen the great orator many a night after he had left the House of Commons, seated at a table covered with papers, attended by an amanuensis who sat opposite to him."

But Burke and Dryden are not the only literary names on which Soho can pride itself. It was at the "Turk's Head," at the corner of Greek Street and Compton Street, and afterwards in Gerrard Street, that the Literary Club—sometimes also called "The Club"—was founded in 1764 by Dr. Johnson and Sir Joshua Reynolds. The "Turk's Head" had already a reputation of its own, having been a kind of head-quarters for the Loyal Association during the Scottish rising of 1745. "The members," says Mr. Peter Cunningham, "met one evening in every week, at seven, for supper, and generally continued their conversation till a late hour." Sir John Hawkins, Burke, and Goldsmith were among its original members, the latter being admitted in spite of Sir John Hawkins' objection to "Goldy" as a mere literary drudge. At its origin it was composed, or at all events intended to be composed, of representatives of intellectual power in various lines of excellence, Goldsmith gaining admission as "naturalist," on account of his "Animated Nature," whilst Reynolds was, of course, the painter, and Gibbon the historian. In 1772 the supper was changed to a dinner, and the number of members increased from twelve to twenty. In 1783 their landlord died; the original tavern was converted into a private house, and the club removed to Sackville Street. All elections took place by ballot. Johnson himself proposed Boswell, and the last member elected in Johnson's life was Dr. Burney. It was at first called "The Club," but at Garrick's death it was styled the "Literary Club." In 1780 the number of members was raised to forty. After several migrations in the neighbourhood of Dover Street and Sackville Street, in 1799 the club took up its quarters at the "Thatched House" tavern in St. James's Street.

After alluding to a speech of that gruff and sarcastic judge, Lord Chancellor Thurlow, in which his lordship called the "Thatched House" tavern an "alehouse," Mr. Timbs says that "from the time of Garrick's death the club was known as the 'Literary Club,' since which time, however, it has certainly lost its claim to this epithet. It was originally a club of authors by profession; it now numbers few except titled members, which was very far from being the intention of its founders. The name of the club is now 'The Johnson.'" He also states, in the first volume of his "Club Life in London," that "the centenary of the club was celebrated in 1864, at the Clarendon Hotel, the Dean of St. Paul's (then Dr. Milman) being in the chair. Among the members present were—His Excellency M. Sylvain Van de Weyer; Lords Stanhope, Clarendon, Brougham, Stanley, Cranworth, Kingsdown, Hatherley, and Harry Vane; the Bishops of London (Tait) and Oxford (Wilberforce); Sir Edmund Head, Mr. Spencer Walpole, Mr. Robert Lowe, Sir Henry Holland, Sir Charles Eastlake, Sir Roderick Murchison, Dr. Whewell, Professor Owen, Mr. George Grote, Mr. C. Austin, Mr. H. Reeve, and Mr. George Richmond."

In some of these statements, however, as it would seem from information to which we have had access, and which has been placed at our disposal, Mr. Timbs is not strictly accurate. Another association, known as the "Literary Society," has for many years run a parallel course to the "Literary Club," or, as it was formerly styled, "The Club," founded by Johnson and Reynolds. Though running parallel to each other, there is no rivalry or hostility between the two; for, indeed, many distinguished persons belong to both of them. The "Literary Society" is of comparatively recent origin, and one tradition says it is due to the disappointment of one or two of its originators at their non-admission into "The Club," where a single black ball has always excluded a candidate. Perhaps, however, the truer account of its origin may be found in the increase of men of literary, scientific, artistic, and administrative attainments of the grade of those who originally founded "The Literary Club." The latter name was not retained for long after Dr. Johnson's death, because it was too limited to express the real constitution of the association, though possibly it may be urged that the innovators may be held open to blame in choosing the present name of "The" Club, as laying claim to a singular and special excellence. There can be no doubt that generation after generation its members have been elected—not merely from among authors, but among painters, lawyers, statesmen, the only test being that of eminence in a man's own profession. In this way "The Club" has secured a series of "representative men," whose names, if given at length, would go far to justify the apparent conceit of the title. For instance, when Sir Charles Eastlake and Mr. George Richmond were chosen, it was held, no doubt, that they succeeded to the place once held in that circle by Sir Joshua Reynolds; that Grote, Hallam, and Milman were no unworthy successors of Edmund Gibbon; and possibly Professor Owen was at least as great a naturalist as Oliver Goldsmith.

"The Club" dined for many years, as stated by Mr. Timbs, at the "Thatched House" tavern, and afterwards at Grillon's, and at the "Clarendon Hotel." It may also be recorded as a matter of interest that at the centenary dinner Lord Brougham was the "father of the club," and that he came all the way from the south of France in order to be present on the occasion. Mr. John Timbs gives a list of seven absentees from that dinner, including Lords Russell and Carlisle; but one of the members who dined on that day at the "Clarendon" tells us expressly that "it was the only meeting within his memory which included all the then members." Lord Macaulay was very desirous to hold the dinner—not at the "Clarendon," but at the old house where the club had been commenced; but this was found to be impossible.

In 1864 the secretary was Dean Milman, who took a great pride in showing to friends the books and archives of the club, including a valuable collection of autographs. Among the other memorials in the possession of the club is the portrait of Sir Joshua Reynolds with his spectacles, which he painted with his own hand and presented to the society, and which is well known by an engraving.

The "Literary Society," the other association, dates, as we have said, from a far more recent period. Among its members we find the names of the Right Hon. Spencer H. Walpole (president), Lords Coleridge, Chelmsford, Dufferin, Houghton, Lawrence, Cairns, Stratford de Redcliffe, and Selborne; the Archbishop of York and the Bishop of Peterborough; the Dean of Westminster and Professor Partridge; General Sir Edward Sabine, Sir William Boxall, Sir Henry Rawlinson, Sir William Erle, Sir James W. Colvile, Sir John W. Lubbock, and Sir Travers Twiss; Mr. George Richmond, Mr. Henry Reeve, Lord Cranbrook, Sir E. Hamley, Captain Douglas Galton, the Right Hon. William Massey, Sir Charles T. Newton, Mr. J. A. Froude, Rear-Admiral Sherard Osborn, Mr. Kirkman D. Hodgson, and Mr. Matthew Arnold. It may be added that the "Literary Society" meets for dinner once a month on Mondays, at half-past seven, during the season, at Willis's Rooms, from November to July inclusive.

"Of the Literary Club," says Mrs. Piozzi, in her "Johnsoniana," "I have heard Dr. Johnson speak in the highest terms, and with a magnificent panegyric on each member, when it consisted of only a dozen or fourteen friends; but as soon as the necessity of enlarging it brought in new faces, and took off from his confidence in the company, he grew less fond of the meeting, and loudly proclaimed his carelessness as to who might be admitted, when it was become a mere dinner-club."

It was at the "Turk's Head," too, that a Society of Artists met in May, 1753; and another society, numbering among its members West, Chambers, Wilton, Sandby, and others, who, from the "Turk's Head," petitioned George III. to bestow his patronage on a Royal Academy of Art.

In Gerrard Street, just opposite to Macclesfield Street, stood, until recently, Macclesfield or Gerard House, the residence of Charles, first Lord Gerard, afterwards first Earl of Macclesfield. It was a poor, dull-looking structure, dating from about 1680. It was afterwards tenanted by Lord Mohun, the duellist, and also by Lyttelton. The house then became a lamp manufacturer's warehouse; the site is now occupied by offices of the National Telephone Company. To the last it retained many traces of its former magnificence, in the fine ceilings with carved cornices, mantelpieces, and one of the noblest staircases to be seen in London, down which gay ladies swept with their long trains in the days of my Lords Macclesfield and of the gay and profligate Lord Mohun.

was standing at the Restoration; and the site afterwards passed, probably by purchase, into the hands of Lord Gerard, who let out the ground around him on building leases.

Macclesfield Street, we may add, was in the last century popularly known by the abridged name of

DRYDEN'S HOUSE, GERRARD STREET. *From an Original Sketch.* (*See page* 178.)

Before quitting Gerrard Street, we may say that in this street the Linnæan Society held its meetings previous to its establishment in Soho Square.

The neighbourhood of Gerrard and Macclesfield Streets, as appears from a MS. in the British Museum, was originally an enclosure of ground made by Henry Prince of Wales, elder brother of Charles I., for the purpose of "the exercise of arms." Here, it appears, he built a house, which

"Maxfield" Street, but it has since recovered its orthography.

Princes Street, which crossed Gerrard Street at right angles, was built on part of the ground used as the prince's artillery yard. Here, in 1718, lived Halley, the astronomer.

The house in Windmill Street in which the Museum of John Hunter was formed and located before it was transferred to Leicester Square was converted into a foreign restaurant and dining hall, rejoicing in the name of L'Hôtel de l'Étoile.

We learn that as the parish of St. Martin's grew more and more populous, fresh streets being built to the north and west, the inhabitants of the newly-built district applied to the bishop and the legislature, by whose joint action a site of land in "Kemp's Field," as it then was called, was granted, though not without difficulty. In 1673, soon after the erection of the new church, it was made into a separate parish, a district cut off from St. Martin's being assigned to it. It was then "discharged from all manner of dependence on the mother church, and ordered to be called the parish church of St. Anne, within the liberty of Westminster." As, however, there was but a slender endowment, and no provision had been made for the completion of the tower and steeple, or for building a rectory house, commissioners were appointed to carry out this work; and in March, 1685, the church was consecrated by Dr. Compton, Bishop of London, "and dedicated," says Allen, "to 'the Mother of the Blessed Virgin.'" The parish commences at the eastern end of Oxford Street, including Soho Square and all the south side of Oxford Street as far as Wardour Street. Its eastern boundary is formed by Crown Street and West Street, and it extends southwards to about the centre of Leicester Square.

ST. ANNE'S, SOHO. (*From a Sketch taken in* 1840.)

Contrary to the usual custom, the chief front of this church is not to the west, but to the east, abutting on Dean Street. It is a very fair specimen internally of the classical style of the period, and calls for little remark or detail; but its spire may safely be said to rival that of St. George's, Bloomsbury, in ugliness. The name of the architect was Hakewill.

"The church was dedicated to St. Anne," says Allen, "out of compliment to the Princess Anne of Denmark. It is said to have been surmounted at first by a steeple of Danish architecture, which was 'the only specimen of the kind in London.'" But what the Danish style of art may have been in the early part of the eighteenth century, we are not informed.

In the vaults beneath this church is buried the eccentric and unhappy Lord Camelford, who fell in a duel which he fought at Kensington, in the year 1804. He was the only son of Thomas, first Lord Camelford, and was born in 1775. "This young nobleman," says his biographer in the *Gentleman's Magazine*, "was not only inclined to the more enlightened pursuits of literature, but his chemical researches, and his talents as a seaman, were worthy of the highest admiration. His lordship had an idea that his antagonist (Captain Best) was the best shot in England, and he was therefore extremely fearful lest his reputation should suffer, if he made any concession, however slight, to such a person."

It was Lord Camelford's eccentric wish, and, indeed, it was commanded by him in his will, that he should be buried in a lonely spot on an island in a lake in Switzerland; but as at the time of his death the European war was raging, it was impossible for his executors to carry out his instructions at once; and when the peace came, in 1815, he had been too long in his grave for his wishes to be remembered. So his body still lies in a gorgeous coffin, surmounted with his coronet, in the vaults under St. Anne's Church, which have for many years been sealed down and closed.

Among those who lie buried here is the Lady Grace Pierrepont, daughter of the Marquis of Dorchester. A letter published by Sir Henry Ellis in 1686 speaks of the Countess of Dorchester, Sedley's daughter, as furnishing a fine house in St. James's Square, and having just taken a seat (sitting) in the "newly-consecrated St. Anne's Church."

The church also contains the remains of royalty of a certain kind—namely, of a king of Corsica, whose unhappy career and end has been told by Sir Bernard Burke, in his "Vicissitudes of Families;" and before him by Horace Walpole and by Boswell. A tablet in the churchyard to his memory bears the following inscription:—

"Near this place is interred Theodore, King of Corsica, who died in this parish, December 11th, 1756, immediately after leaving the King's Bench Prison by the benefit of the Act of Insolvency; in consequence of which he registered his kingdom of Corsica for the benefit of his creditors.

> The grave, great teacher, to a level brings
> Heroes and beggars, galley-slaves and kings;
> But Theodore this moral learn'd ere dead;
> Fate pour'd its lesson on his living head—
> Bestow'd a kingdom and denied him bread."

It may interest our readers to know that this fallen monarch was buried at the cost of a small tradesman who had known him in the days of his prosperity, and that the tablet above-mentioned was erected by Horace Walpole, who also wrote the epitaph quoted above.

The King of Corsica was Stephen Theodore, Baron Neuhof of Prussia, and was born at Metz, in 1696. Mr. Cunningham styles him "an adventurer," and certainly in assuming royalty here he went a step further than most other pretenders. He was educated in France, under the care of the Duchess of Orleans. He entered the service of Charles XII. of Sweden, when his name and the distressed state of Corsica induced the inhabitants of the latter island to ask his protection, and in return to offer him their crown. In March, 1736, we are told, he arrived at Aleria in a ship, with two others very richly laden with provisions and ammunition. He was conducted to Corsica, and was elected king amid the acclamations of the people, and was crowned as Theodore I. At this time the Corsicans were in a state of comparative barbarism. Theodore coined money, and maintained an army of 15,000 men at his own cost. The Genoese, in envy and jealousy, published a manifesto filled with falsehoods, and set a price on his head. Finding his life attempted by his own people, he called an assembly, and made them a short speech, which so affected them that they called him their saviour and king. In 1743 he issued a "declaration" calling back to that island all Corsicans in foreign service, under the penalty of confiscation of their estates. His money being now exhausted, he was obliged to seek foreign succour, conferring the regency in his absence on twenty-eight of the nobles. Theodore now went from place to place begging assistance, and in constant fear of assassination. The English sent him to their fleet in the Mediterranean, instructing their admiral to re-establish him on his throne. The admiral, however, told Theodore that the Corsicans meant to oppose his landing. It appears that he was now, in his helpless condition, made the victim of foul play, for on returning soon after to London, money was lent to him by a scheme of the Genoese minister; for this debt he was arrested and sent to prison.

He was arrested by a *ruse*. He lived in a privileged place—probably the Sanctuary at Westminster—and his creditors seized him by making him believe that Lord Grenville wanted to see him on business of importance; he bit at the bait, thinking that he was to be reinstated at once. We may mention that while in England King Theodore distinguished himself, like his humble successor, the *soi-disant* Duc de Roussillon, by his fondness for the fair sex. He fell in love with Lady Lucy Stanhope, sister of the second earl, and even made her an offer of marriage; and another lady, a widow, he all but persuaded to share his shadowy crown.

Horace Walpole describes him as a "comely, middle-sized man, very reserved, and affecting much dignity." A life of him, Walpole tells us, was published, "too big to send but by messenger."

There is a fine portrait of Theodore, taken from life by order of the King of Naples, when under confinement in the castle at Gaeta.

Horace Walpole wrote a paper in the *World*, as he tells us, in order to promote a subscription for King Theodore during his imprisonment. His Majesty's character, however, as Walpole tells us, was so bad, that the sum raised was only fifty pounds; but "though it was much above his deserts, it was so much below his expectation that he sent a solicitor to threaten the printer with a prosecution for having taken so much liberty with his name; and that, too, after he had accepted the money." Well may Horace Walpole add, "I have done with countenancing kings."

It was at Soho that Theodore went "to the place which levels kings and beggars, an unnecessary journey for him," as Walpole says, "who had already fallen from the one to the other."

The story of his actual death is thus related by the gossiping pen of Horace Walpole, who met him at several parties in London in 1749:—"King Theodore recovered his liberty only by giving up his effects to his creditors under the Act of Insolvency; all the 'effects,' however, that he had to give up were his right, such as it was, to the throne of Corsica, which was registered accordingly in due form for the benefit of his creditors. As soon as Theodore was at liberty, he took a (sedan) chair and went to the Portuguese minister; but not finding him at home, and not having a sixpence to pay, he desired the chairmen to carry him to a tailor in Soho, whom he prevailed upon to harbour him; but he fell sick the next day, and died in three more."

"I would have served him if a king, even in jail, could he have been an honest man," said the individual who generously erected his monument.

It may be added that Boswell wrote an account of Theodore, strung together from anecdotes which he picked up from Walpole in Paris.

In the church or churchyard also lie Mr. William Hamilton, a Royal Academician of the last century; Sir John Macpherson; Mr. David Williams, who deserves to be remembered as the founder of the Literary Club; and William Hazlitt, the critic and essayist, over whom the grave closed in 1830.

Adjoining the south-east angle of St. Anne's Church is the parish mortuary. This building was formerly the "watch-house" in the days of the old "Charleys;" and here George Prince of Wales, in his youthful days, was more than once confronted with the ministers of parochial authority, on account of his share in some midnight brawl, but allowed to depart on unbuttoning his coat and showing the "star" on his breast beneath, whilst less well-born marauders were detained, to be brought before the "beak" the next day. Mr. J. T. Smith tells the following amusing anecdote concerning a scene witnessed by him at St. Anne's watch-house during one of those nocturnal rambles he occasionally indulged in whilst lodging in Gerrard Street:—

"Sir Harry Dinsdale, usually called Dimsdale, a short, feeble little man, was brought in to St. Anne's Watch-house, charged by two colossal guardians of the night with conduct most unruly. 'What have you, Sir Harry, to say to all this?' asked the Dogberry of St. Anne. The knight, who had been roughly handled, commenced like a true orator, in a low tone of voice, 'May it please ye, my magistrate, I am not drunk; it is *languor*. A parcel of the bloods of the Garden have treated me cruelly, because I would not treat them. This day, sir, I was sent for by Mr. Sheridan to make my speech upon the table at the Shakespeare Tavern, in *Common* Garden; he wrote the speech for me, and always gives me half-a-guinea when he sends for me to the tavern. You see I didn't go in my royal robes; I only put 'um on when I stand to be member.' Constable: 'Well, but, Sir Harry, why are you brought here?' One of the watchmen then observed, 'That though Sir Harry was but a little *shambling* fellow, he was so *upstroppolus*, and kicked him about at such a rate, that it was as much as he and his comrade could do to bring him along.' As there was no one to support the charge, Sir Harry was advised to go home, which, however, he swore he would not do at midnight without an escort. 'Do you know,' said he, "there's a parcel of *raps* now on the outside waiting for me.' The constable of the night gave orders for him to be protected to the public-house opposite the west end of St. Giles's Church, where he then lodged. Sir Harry, hearing a noise in the street, muttered, 'I shall catch it; I know I shall.' 'See the conquering hero comes' (*cries without*). 'Ay, they always use that tune when I gain my election at Garrett.'"

"Sir Harry Dimsdale," remarks Mr. J. T. Smith, "first came into notice on the death of 'Sir Geoffrey Dunstan,' a dealer in old wigs, who had been for many years returned 'member for Garrett,' on his becoming a candidate. He received mock knighthood, and was ever after known as 'Sir Harry.'" He exercised the itinerant trade of a muffin-man, in the afternoon; he had a little bell, which he held to his ear, smiling ironically at its tingling. His cry was—

> "Muffins! muffins! ladies, come buy *me!* pretty, handsome, blooming, smiling maids."

Flaxman, the sculptor, and Mrs. Mathews, of blue-stocking memory, equipped him as a hardware-man, and as such Mr. J. T. Smith made two etchings of him.

This parish has one point in which it differed two centuries ago, and, to a great extent, still differs, from the surrounding districts. To use the words of the "London Spy," in 1725, "King Charles II., of pious memory, was a great benefactor to this parish; for soon after the Plague of London he re-peopled it with ten thousand Protestant families from abroad, who prov'd the most implacable enemies the late French king ever had." The same satirist draws an amusing picture, evidently from life, of one of the "shabby-genteel" households of Soho in his day, where a shopkeeper maintained himself, his wife, and a grown-up daughter, on a limited income. He says, "They were extraordinary economists; brewed their own beer, washed at home; made a joint hold out two days, and a shift three; let three parts of their house ready furnished; and kept paying one quarter's rent under another. . . . The worst the world could say of them was that they liv'd above what they had; that the daughter was as proud a slut as ever clapp'd clog on shoe-leather; and that they entertained lodgers who were no better than they should be." What a picture Charles Dickens could have painted from this description!

CHAPTER XXV.

SOHO SQUARE AND ITS NEIGHBOURHOOD.

"Soho's busy Square."—*Wordsworth.*

Noted Residents in Soho—Appearance of the Square in Queen Anne's Reign—Proposal for the Restoration of the Square—Monmouth House—Lord Bateman—Carlisle House and the celebrated Mrs. Cornelys' Masquerades—St. Patrick's Chapel—Humorous Description of an Irish Wake—The White House and its Fashionable Patrons—Soho Bazaar—The Residence of Sir Joseph Banks—Origin of the Linnæan Society—Frith Street—Sir Samuel Romilly—Compton Street—Dean Street—The New Royalty Theatre—Greek Street—The House of Charity—Wardour Street—"The Mischief" in Oxford Street—Hog Lane (Charing Cross Road) and the Greek Chapel—Hogarth's "Noon."

Soho Square, as shown in the previous chapter, was originally called the King's Square, and dates from the reign of Charles II. Evelyn, as he tells us in his "Diary," visited at a house in this celebrated vicinity, and spent the winter of 1690 "at Soho, in the great Square." It must not be forgotten, of course, that Sir Roger de Coverley is described, in the beginning of the *Spectator*, as living, when he is in town, at Soho Square. Shadwell, too, in one of his comedies, written in 1691, uses terms which imply that it was a fashionable quarter of the town, for he represents an alderman's wife as having "forced" her husband out of Mark Lane "to live in Soho Square." And no doubt it was the centre of fashion when Grosvenor and Cavendish Squares were not yet in existence.

The building of the Square was only begun in 1681, and at that time it contained no more than nine inhabitants, among whom were the Duke of Monmouth, Colonel Ramsey, Mr. Pilcher, Mr. Broughton, Sir Henry Ingleby, and the Earl of Stamford, as the rate-books of St. Martin's attest.

Pennant says, though erroneously, that its original name was Monmouth Square, but that it came to be called after the king. Mr. Peter Cunningham, with his usual diligence, has sifted the question out by consulting the parish rate-books, ground leases, and other original documents, and so far as it is possible to prove a negative, he shows that it never was called Monmouth Square. It is possible, however that, from the Duke of Monmouth living in it, it may have been called "Monmouth's Square"—*i.e.*, the square in which Monmouth lived—and that this may have misled Pennant. The Duke of Monmouth lived in a large house with two wings on its southern side. It stood back, with a court before it.

This Duke of Monmouth was a natural son of Charles II., by Lucy Walters. His defeat at Sedgemoor, in 1685, and his subsequent execution, are matters of history.

Pennant mentions, as we have noticed before, a tradition to the effect that on the death of the Duke of Monmouth the name of the square was changed by his friends and admirers to Soho, that being the watchword of the day at the battle of Sedgemoor; but Mr. Cunningham has settled this question too in the negative, for he shows, by reference to contemporary documents, that whereas the battle of Sedgemoor was not fought till 1685, this district was called "Sohoe," or "Soho," nearly fifty years previously. For instance, the rate-books of St. Martin's, in 1636, speak of people living at "the Brick-kilns, near Soho;" and in 1650 the Commonwealth Survey describes "Shaver's Hall," or "Piccadilly Hall," as "lying between a roadway leading from Charing Cross to Knightes-bridge West, and a highway leading from Charing Cross towards So Hoe." In the face of such evidence, it would seem impossible not to set aside the derivation propounded by Pennant as wholly untenable. It is far more probable that the duke borrowed his "watchword of the day" at Sedgemoor from the neighbourhood in which his home was situated, just as Nelson might have chosen "Burnham" or "Merton" as his watchword at the Nile or Trafalgar. Mr. Peter Cunningham writes—"I never saw it called Monmouth Square in any map, letter, or printed book, or anywhere, indeed, but in Pennant. It was called King Square, certainly, but not Monmouth Square." This, it appears to us, settles the question.

Soho Square is described by Allen, in his "History of London," even so lately as 1839, as presenting a very pleasing and somewhat rural appearance, having in the centre a large area within a handsome iron railing, enclosing several trees and shrubs." We should, however, certainly venture to assert that the expressions are scarcely any longer applicable to the square. "In the centre," adds Allen, "is a pedestrian statue of Charles II., at the feet of which are figures emblematic of the rivers Thames, Trent, Severn, and Humber. They are now," he continues, "in a most wretchedly mutilated state, and the inscriptions on the base of the pedestal are quite illegible."

London was brightened in Queen Anne's reign by numbers of public conduits and fountains. Most of them have been removed or destroyed, but are now in some measure replaced by drinking-fountains, which are certainly of great benefit to thirsty wayfarers. We add a description of the ancient specimen in King's Square, Soho. In the centre was a fountain with four streams. In the middle of the basin was the statue of Charles II., in armour, on a pedestal, enriched with fruit and flowers; on the four sides of the base were figures representing the four chief rivers of the kingdom—Thames, Severn, Trent, and Humber; on the south side were figures of an old man and a young virgin, with a stream ascending; on the west lay the figure of a naked virgin (only nets wrapped about her) reposing on a fish, out of whose mouth flowed a stream of water; on the north, an old man recumbent on a coal-bed, and an urn in his hand whence issues a stream of water; on the east rested a very aged man, with water running from a vase, and his right hand laid upon a shell. The statue became so mutilated and disfigured, and the inscription quite effaced, that it was a difficult matter to distinguish whose it really was; some antiquaries, in fact, are of opinion that it was the effigy of the Duke of Monmouth. It stood originally in the middle of the basin of a fountain, which in its turn was filled up and converted into a somewhat unattractive flower-bed. In or about the year 1880 the centre of the square was "beautified," and the statue was removed.

At different times attempts have been made to obtain power to throw open this square to the general public, but it has been found to be impracticable. A meeting of the inhabitants was convened in 1874, and a committee formed. Mr. Albert Grant, to whom the public are indebted for the transformation of Leicester Square, as described in a preceding chapter, offered to lay out and develop the ground at an estimated cost of £7,000, and to endow it with an annual income of £150 in the names of a committee to be appointed by the inhabitants. But this, like other endeavours to secure the same end, came to nothing, and the use of the square is still confined to a privileged few. To the children of the thickly-populated streets around, the opening of the ground would be an incalculable boon.

Alderman Beckford, whom we have already mentioned as a resident of the square, made here a collection of works of art which subsequently were sold by public auction. This did not, however, deter him from beginning *de novo*, in order to decorate his new Wiltshire toy, Fonthill, which was destined in the end to share the same fate. Here also the shipwrecked remains of Sir Cloudesley Shovel lay in state in 1707. Bishop Burnet, the historian, lived in Soho Square before his removal to Clerkenwell, and here he had his curiosities, including the supposed "original Magna Charta," with part of the great seal remaining attached to it.

Monmouth House, as shown in an illustration on page 187, was a lofty brick building of three storeys, comprising a centre with slightly projecting wings. Each wing was adorned with three pilasters, with enriched capitals, rising to the level of the third storey, and each floor was lighted with large semi-circular-headed windows. The doorway in the centre was approached by a broad flight of steps, and protected by an ample porch supported by double columns on each side.

The house was built by Wren for the Duke of Monmouth, and after his death it was purchased by Lord Bateman, whose family occupied it for a time; but, as the stream of fashion was setting westwards, they travelled along with it, and, pulling down the mansion, let out the site on building leases. This would seem to be the fate of all the great houses in London sooner or later. The house, in 1717, was converted into auction-rooms, but was demolished in 1793; the Hospital for Women now occupies the site. The name of Lord Bateman is kept up by a row of houses called Bateman's Buildings, and by Bateman Street, connecting Dean Street with Greek Street. But the duke has not been so

KING THEODORE'S MONUMENT. (*See page* 182.)

lucky: for a time his name lived on in "Monmouth" Street, St. Giles's; but since it had obtained a bad name as the resort of Jew dealers in rags and old clothes, the thoroughfare was re-christened Dudley Street; the old clothes, however, have not passed away along with the unsavoury name. Of

MONMOUTH HOUSE, 1770.

this Lord Bateman, Horace Walpole tells the story that George I. created him an Irish peer to avoid making him a Knight of the Bath; "for," said his majesty, with the wit of Charles II., "I can make him a lord, but I cannot make him a gentleman." Before Lord Bateman's house was pulled down, it was let by him to various persons in the higher ranks of society. Among others, the French ambassador was residing in it in 1791–2.

In Carlisle Street we have perpetuated the name of the Howards, Earls of Carlisle (a branch of the ducal house of Norfolk), the head of whom was living, in the middle of the last century, in a house on the east side of the square. The mansion, which was built in the reign of James II., originally stood in the midst of a garden, the extent of which it would be difficult to define at the present time. The lower walls of the house were of red brick and on the lead-work of the cisterns was the date 1669. The mansion in its original condition must have had a magnificent appearance, with its marble-floored hall, its superbly decorated staircases, and its large and lofty rooms with enriched ceilings.

Towards the close of the last century it was tenanted by the celebrated Mrs. Cornelys, who turned it into a place of resort for masked balls and other fashionable amusements. Her assemblies were at one time the rage of the town, but she was in the end ruined by her extravagance. Hither "the quality" repaired in large numbers, although the morality of the place was rather questionable. Among the lady's chief patrons were the eccentric Duke of Queensberry ("Old Q.") and the notorious Duchess of Kingston, who appeared here in other characters, and especially on one occasion in that of Iphigenia, "in a state almost ready," as Horace Walpole slily remarks, "for the sacrifice." There is a scarce print of the duchess in this character, which shows rather a deficiency of dress. It was at one of Mrs. Cornelys' masquerades that the beautiful daughter of a peer wore the costume of an Indian princess, three black girls bearing her train, a canopy held over her head by two negro boys, and her dress covered with jewels worth £100,000. It was at another that Adam, in flesh-coloured tights and an apron of fig-leaves, was to be seen in company with the Duchess of Bolton as Diana. Death, in a white shroud, bearing his own coffin and epitaph; Lady Augusta Stuart as a Vestal; the Duke of Gloucester, in an old English habit, with a star on his cloak; and the Duke of Devonshire, "who was very fine, but in no particular character"—all these, and others, passed through her rooms; yet before many years had gone by Mrs. Cornelys was selling asses' milk at Knightsbridge, and in 1797 she died in the Fleet Prison, forming schemes to the very last for retrieving her broken fortunes. Attempts were unsuccessfully made to keep up the festivities of Carlisle House; but "Almack's" drew away the great, and the square gradually declined in the world—from fashion to philosophy, from artists to tradesmen, from shops to hospitals—until at length its lowest depth seems to have been reached.

Into the promenades at Mrs. Cornelys' house gentlemen were requested not to enter "with boots;" and in satire the manager of a rival amusement is said to have given this notice:—"THE NEW PARADISE.—No Gentlemen or Ladies to be admitted with nails in their shoes." Of the morality of Mrs. Cornelys and of Carlisle House, Northouck had no high opinion; but he throws the blame on their aristocratic patrons. He says, "Here the nobility of this kingdom long protected Mrs. Cornelys in entertaining their masquerade and gaming assemblies, in violation of the laws, and to the destruction of all sober principles."

It is clear, from the advertisements scattered up and down the files of the London newspapers, that, beginning with the winter of 1762–3, Mrs. Cornelys contrived to secure for some ten or twelve years the almost undivided patronage of the world of fashion, keeping the West End, and especially the neighbourhood of "Soho Fields," alive with a succession of balls, concerts, masquerades, "subscription music meetings," &c., and securing her interest with the families of "quality" by giving balls to their upper servants. Her advertisements are by themselves a study in the art of puffery, and occasionally throw light on the condition of life in London: as, for instance, when she "begs the chairmen and hackney-coach drivers not to quarrel, or to run their poles through each other's windows." On one occasion, when it was rumoured that the enterprising lady was about to open a sister institution in Bishopsgate Street, half the City was up in arms to oppose her on the ground of morality, and the lady was defeated. On several occasions as many as 800 persons of "quality" were present at her masquerades, the Duke of Gloucester, and even the King of Denmark, being of the number. At one time she was threatened with proceedings under the "Alien Act" by a rival in the same line of business; but by a judicious use of "soft sawder" she circumvented her opponents whilst appearing to give way to them, and thus she prolonged her lease of popularity. At length, however, by instituting a harmonic meeting, Mrs. Cornelys placed herself in an attitude of direct hostility to the Italian Opera House, whose managers applied to the magistrates to stop her entertainment. They were so far successful that Sir John Fielding ordered Guardini, the chief singer at Carlisle House, to be arrested. This was the first instalment of ill success which befell her; the next was the establishment of a rival house of entertainment at the Pantheon, in Oxford Street; and in spite of a desperate effort to prop up her falling fortunes by a new amusement, called a "Coterie"—the details of which have not come down to us—in July, 1772, there came a "smash," and in the November following the whole contents of Carlisle House, with its sumptuous decorations, were brought to the hammer. A graphic account of this sale will be found in the *Westminster Magazine* for January, 1773, under the title of "Cupid turned Auctioneer."

But the irrepressible Mrs. Cornelys was not destined to be crushed by a single failure. The "Circe" and "Sultana" of Soho gathered her aristocratic friends and patrons around her; and her name again appears, in 1774, as manager and conductress of a new series of concerts. These, however, would appear to have turned out profitless, for in August, 1775, Carlisle House was advertised for sale by Messrs. Christie "with or without its furniture." She still, however, seems to have fought on against fate, for as late as 1777 we find Mrs. Cornelys still organising masques at Carlisle House, though "the whole company did not exceed three hundred." The exact date of her last effort to amuse the fashionable world on this spot is unknown. In 1779, the establishment appears to have been under the management of a Mr. Hoffmann, who tried a variety of experiments in the way of "masked balls," and "benefit concerts," but with a like result. With the year 1780 we find a great change in the amusements of Carlisle House, for it was devoted to the meetings of a debating society, called the "School of Eloquence:" its meetings being presided over by a clergyman as "moderator;" on other evenings the rooms being devoted to "the reception of company previous to the 'masqued ridotto,'" at the Opera House. On Sunday evenings also there was a "public promenade," the admission to which was by a three-shilling ticket, which included refreshments of "tea, coffee, capillaire, orgeat, and lemonade." These various attractions were held out, but with inferior success, for several years, a Mr. William Wade officiating as master of the ceremonies. In vain did he open a "morning suite of rooms" supplied with the newspapers and periodicals of the day "*gratis* to subscribers;" in vain did he organise courses of "scientific lectures," and advertise concerts by the Polish dwarf, Count Borawlaski, with tickets at half-a-guinea, "entitling the purchaser to see and converse with that extraordinary personage." In 1785 the property was in Chancery, and the house sold under a decree of the court, and Mrs. Cornelys retired into private life at Knightsbridge, where we shall find her again.

What was once the music-room of Lord Carlisle's mansion, and afterwards the grand saloon of Mrs. Cornelys' establishment, was subsequently altered and turned into a Catholic chapel, known as "St. Patrick's, Soho," and largely frequented by the poor Irish of the neighbourhood. The property was purchased in 1792 by the exertions and influence of the celebrated Catholic preacher and controversialist, Dr. O'Leary, who died in 1802. In 1893 the chapel was rebuilt of red brick and Portland stone, in the Late Italian style, with a bell-tower a hundred and twenty-five feet high at the Sutton Street corner.

One of the treasures of St. Patrick's is a painting of the Crucifixion by Vandyke, said to be the finest specimen of a sacred painting by his hand in England, and equal to any in Belgium.

This chapel was formerly much frequented not only by the poor Irish who lived round Soho and St. Giles's, but also by Catholics of the wealthier class residing about Russell and Bedford Squares. It long divided with the Sardinian Chapel in Lincoln's Inn Fields the administration of the chief Roman Catholic charities; and the leading Roman Catholic bishops, Dr. Milner, Cardinal Wiseman, and Cardinal Manning have frequently advocated from its pulpit the cause of charity.

On the north side of the square is another imposing place of worship, the French Protestant Church of London, with a singularly effective façade of red brick and terra-cotta.

Prior to the foundation of St. Patrick's Mission in Sutton Street, mass was said at No. 13 in the Square, in the house of the Neapolitan ambassador, and also, though by stealth and secretly, at a small house in Denmark Street, where some French priests had taken up their abode on the commencement of troubles in France.

The Irish live in various parts of London, apart and amongst themselves, carrying with them the many virtues and vices of their native land, and never becoming absorbed in the nation to which, for years, they may be attached. Swindlers, thieves, and tramps may surround them, but do not in general affect them. Tim Malone still renews upon English ground his feuds with the O'Learys, commencing not within the memory of man; and some Bridget O'Rafferty pays Ellen O'Connor for evidence given by her grandfather against the rebels of '98. "It would be a curious investigation," says Mr. Diprose, in his "Book about London," "for the philosopher, how far the interest and progress of this most gallant and interesting nation have been affected by what, in the absence of a better definition, we shall designate the absence of merging power. Nor is it less curious, that whilst the Irish preserve their national characteristics as steadfastly as do the Jews, they have the quality of absorbing other nations, for we find that the English who settle in Ireland, not merely acquire the brogue, but become more Irish than the Irish themselves. *Ipsis Hibernis Hiberniores* is as true now as it was in the days of the poet Spenser. The 'Irish Hudibras' (1682) thus humorously describes an Irish wake:—

"'To their own sports (the masses ended)
The mourners now are recommended.
Some sit and chat, some laugh, some weep,
Some sing cronans, and some do sleep;
Some court, some scold, some blow, some puff,
Some take tobacco, some take snuff.
Some play the trump, some trot the hay,
Some at machan, some at noddy play;
Thus mixing up their grief and sorrow,
Yesterday buried, killed to-morrow.'"

The house occupying the northern angle of Sutton Street was celebrated in the last century, and the beginning of the present, as "the White House," and was a place of fashionable dissipation to which only the titled and wealthy classes had the privilege of admission. Its character may be inferred from the fact that it was one of the haunts of the then Prince of Wales, the old Duke of Queensberry, and the Marquis of Hertford; and the ruin of many a female heart may be dated from a visit within its walls. It is said by tradition that its apartments were known as the "Gold," "Silver," "Bronze" Rooms, &c., each being called from the prevailing character of its fittings, and that the walls of nearly every room were inlaid with mirrored panels.

Many of the rooms in this house, too, had a sensational name, as the "Commons," the "Painted Chamber," the "Grotto," the "Coal Hole," and the "Skeleton Room"—the latter so styled on account of a closet out of which a skeleton was made to step forth by the aid of machinery. The "White House," as a scene of profligacy, lived on into the present century, and having been empty for some years, was converted to business uses by the founders of the firm which at present occupies it—Messrs. Crosse and Blackwell, whose enormous premises extend to the Charing Cross Road, which they border for a considerable distance.

We shall not attempt to describe in detail the White House, which enjoyed such an unenviable reputation from the scenes which it witnessed in the days when George III. was King, and George Prince of Wales was living. It was not till 1837-8 that the White House underwent the transformation of which we have just spoken.

No. 21 in this square, which adjoined the "White House," and was afterwards Messrs. D'Almaine's musical repository, is now absorbed into the large warehouse of Messrs. Crosse and Blackwell. Though considerably modernised, it still retains one magnificently-carved mantelpiece and ornamental ceiling; and the grandly-proportioned rooms are the same as when the mansion was the town house of the Lords Fauconberg, and was thronged by beauty and fashion.

In the north-west corner of the square is the celebrated Soho Bazaar, one of the haunts most frequented by sight-seers, especially at Christmas, New Years's Day, and other gift-seasons. It was established in 1815, and for many years was a formidable rival to the Pantheon. It has been a fashionable lounge for ladies and children, and especially attractive to "country cousins." It has now an entrance in Oxford Street also, one of the houses on the south side of that roadway having been added to it. It is scarcely necessary to explain here that the word "bazaar" comes to us from the East, denoting a group of shops in which dealers in some one commodity or class ot commodities congregate in one place, much to the gain of both purchasers and sellers. Yet, as Mr. Chambers remarks, "a stranger may do well to bear in mind that in London . . . some approach is made to the system. For instance, coachmakers congregate in considerable numbers in Long Acre, watchmakers and jewellers in Clerkenwell, tanners and leather-dressers in Bermondsey, bird and birdcage sellers in Seven Dials, statuaries in the Euston Road, furniture-dealers and clothiers in Tottenham Court Road, hat-makers in Bermondsey and Southwark, dentists around St. Martin's Lane, and booksellers and publishers in Paternoster Row."

Soho Bazaar, to which belongs the distinction of having been the first of its kind in England, was established, according to Allen, by John Trotter, Esq. It was originally designed by Mr. Trotter as a *depôt* for the sale of articles in aid of the widows and orphans of those who had fallen in the long war against Napoleon; but the Government of the day did not entertain the proposal, and accordingly Mr. Trotter started the bazaar as a private speculation of his own. The institution was opened by Queen Charlotte, in 1816, and was extensively patronised by the royal family. The building, which does not present any architectural features, lies between Soho Square on the south, Oxford Street on the north, and Dean Street on the west, and consists of several rooms, conveniently fitted up with mahogany counters. The bazaar occupies two floors, and has counter accommodation for a large number of tenants. The rent of the counters, which are mostly for the sale of fancy goods, is very moderate. The bazaar has been frequently patronised by royalty; the Queen's eldest daughter, the Princess Victoria, at that time Crown Princess of Prussia, afterwards the Empress Frederick, honoured it with a visit in 1868.

Entering from Oxford Street, the visitor will find an assortment of bicycles of the latest patterns. Farther on are china articles, and stalls for sewing-machines. Up a small staircase to the left is an extensive picture-gallery. Other rooms close by are filled with a variety of fancy goods, or devoted to the purposes of photography. The two principal rooms in the building are about ninety feet long, and in them it is no exaggeration to say that the visitor may find a great variety of trades represented. Connected with the bazaar are spacious and well-appointed refreshment-rooms, and also offices for the registration of governesses and the hire of servants, &c. There is also a school in which the art of cycling is taught—for the bazaar, though intended as an emporium of fancy goods, has not been slow to adapt itself to changing conditions. The bazaar forms the subject of one of the whimsical descriptive ballads of James Catnatch, the founder of the business of which we shall have something to say in our next chapter.

During the latter part of the eighteenth and the earlier years of the present century, Soho Square attained some celebrity as the residence of the learned and accomplished philosopher, Sir Joseph Banks, so bitterly and caustically satirised by "Peter Pindar." He lived at No. 32, now the Hospital for Diseases of the Heart and Paralysis, and here he held his receptions, at which nearly every man eminent in science was a frequent attendant. Sir Joseph Banks, who was descended from an ancient Yorkshire family, was born in Argyle Street, in the parish of St. James's, Westminster, in 1743, and was educated at Harrow and Eton, whence he removed as a gentleman commoner to Christ Church, Oxford. His love of botany increased at the university, and there his mind warmly embraced all the other branches of natural history. In 1766 he was chosen into the Royal Society, and in that year went to Newfoundland, for the purpose of collecting plants. The Royal Society having made a proposition to the Government to effect a general voyage of discovery in those parts of the ocean which were still wholly unknown, or only partially discovered, and especially to observe the transit of Venus at Otaheite in 1769, Banks was appointed, in conjunction with Dr. Solander, naturalist to the expedition, which sailed from Plymouth Sound, under the command of Captain Cook, in August, 1768. After an absence of three years the expedition returned to England, the specimens which Banks had brought, at so much risk and expense, exciting much interest. In 1777, on the retirement of Sir John Pringle from the presidency of the Royal Society, Mr. Banks was elected to the vacant chair. In 1795 he was invested with the Order of the Bath, and he was afterwards sworn a member of the Privy Council, and chosen a member of the National Institute of France. His life was devoted to the prosecution of scientific researches, and the general diffusion of useful knowledge. In fact, he largely anticipated the Humboldts and Owens of a later day. Sir Joseph Banks died in June, 1820.

His house in Soho Square has also had other distinguished inhabitants; Sir J. E. Smith and Mr. Robert Brown, for example, both eminent naturalists. The Linnæan Society was founded in 1788, and held its meetings in Gerrard Street, until its establishment in Soho Square. Here it continued to flourish till its removal to Burlington House, Piccadilly, in 1855.

The Linnæan Society, it would appear, like many another great institution, had its origin in an accident. The late Sir John E. Smith, then a medical student, was breakfasting one day with Sir Joseph Banks, when the latter told him that he just had an offer of the memoranda and botanical collections of the great Linnæus for a thousand pounds, but that he had declined to buy them. Young Smith, whose zeal for botany was great, begged his father to advance to him the money, and at length persuaded him to do so, though not without difficulty. It may appear strange that Sweden should consent to part with the treasures of her far-famed naturalist; and indeed the king, Gustavus III., who had been absent in France, was much displeased, on his return, at hearing that a vessel had just sailed for England with these collections. He immediately dispatched a vessel to the Sound, to intercept it, but was too late. The herbarium, books, MSS., &c., arrived safely in London in 1784, packed in twenty-six cases, and cost the purchaser £1,088 5s. In the following year Smith was elected a Fellow of the Royal Society, and devoted himself more to botanical studies than to his profession as a physician. In 1792 he had the honour of being engaged to teach botany to Queen Charlotte and the princesses, and he was knighted by the Prince Regent in 1814. At his death, in 1828, the celebrated collection, with Sir J. E. Smith's additions, was purchased by the Linnæan Society, and still remains in their possession.

The house of Sir Joseph Banks was kept for many years by his sister, a learned lady, who had as great a passion for collecting coins as her brother had for botanical researches. Her appearance is thus described by the author of a "Book for a Rainy Day:"—"Her dress was that of the old school; her Barcelona quilted petticoat had a hole on either side, for the convenience of rummaging two immense pockets, stuffed with books of all sizes. This petticoat was covered with a deep stomachered gown, sometimes drawn through the pocket-holes, similar to those of many of the ladies of Bunbury's time, which he has produced in his picture. In this dress" (writes Mr. J. T. Smith) "I have frequently seen her walk, followed by a six-foot servant with a cane almost as tall as himself. Miss Banks, I may add, when she wanted to purchase a broadside in the streets, was more than once taken for a member of the ballad-singing confraternity. And yet this same lady, when she was in the prime of life, had been a fashionable whip, and driven a four-in-hand in the Park."

In the south-east corner of the square lived, for many years, the late Mr. Barnes, the responsible editor of the *Times;* and it was here that, when waited upon by some of the leading politicians of the time, he laid down the terms on which that paper would support the ministry of the Duke of Wellington, in 1828.

Among the other noted residents of Soho Square we may mention George II., when Prince of Wales; and also Field-Marshal Conway, Walpole's correspondent and friend.

In Frith Street, on the south side of the square, in the year 1757, was born one of our most celebrated advocates and philanthropists, Sir Samuel Romilly. He was descended from a Protestant family, who left France after the Revocation of the Edict of Nantes. His father was a jeweller, carrying on business in this street; and he was sent to the French Protestant School close by, where he received but an indifferent education; but as soon as he had left it he applied himself to self-culture, and his diligence in the acquisition of learning was largely rewarded in after life.

SIR SAMUEL ROMILLY.

Placed as a lad with a solicitor, whom he left for a merchant's office, which he also resigned, eventually he was articled to one of the sworn clerks of Chancery. At the expiration of his articles he qualified himself for the bar, but had to wait long and patiently ere he was rewarded with any practice. When briefs did at last fall to his lot, it very soon became manifest that they were held by a master, and the result was that a tide of prosperity set in, and "success came upon him like a flood." His income rose to about £9,000 a year, and in his diary he congratulated himself that he did not press his father to buy him a seat in the Six Clerks' Office. Romilly now rapidly rose to distinction in the Court of Chancery, where he was distinguished for his profound learning and forcible eloquence; and to him Lord Brougham has paid the following tribute:—"Romilly, by the force of his learning and talents, and the most spotless integrity, rose to the very height of professional ambition. He was beyond question or pretence of rivalry the first man in the courts in this country."

Romilly entered the House of Commons in 1806—the electors of Westminster having returned him to Parliament without the expenditure of a shilling on his part; a great thing in those days of bribery and corruption—and during the short administration of Mr. Grenville he was appointed Solicitor-General, and knighted. Nor was he distinguished professionally only; but during his political career he was listened to with rapt attention, and a passage in one of his speeches in favour of the abolition of the slave-trade received the singular honour of three distinct rounds of applause from the House.

THE SIGN OF THE "MISCHIEF." (*See page* 196).

But Romilly's grand claim to remembrance rests upon his humane efforts to mitigate the Draconic code of English law, in which nearly three hundred crimes, varying from murder to keeping company with a gipsy, were punishable with death. The first bill which he succeeded in getting passed was to repeal a statute of Elizabeth, which made it a capital offence to steal privately from the person of another. He next tried a bolder stroke, and introduced a bill to repeal several statutes which punished with death the crimes of stealing privately in a shop goods to the amount of five shillings; and of stealing to the amount of forty shillings in a dwelling-house; or in vessels in navigable rivers. But this bill was lost. Romilly, however, did not despair, but kept on agitating session after session, and cleared the way for the success which came when he was no more.

In his forty-first year Sir Samuel Romilly married Miss Garbett (a *protégée* of the Marquis of Lansdowne), a lady of rare talents and moral excellence. But after twenty years of happy married life, her health began to decline, and on the 29th of October, 1818, she died. This was a dreadful shock to Romilly, and produced such mental anguish, that delirium followed, and in an unwatched moment he sprang from his bed, cut his throat, and expired almost instantly—and this at a time when worldly honours were being heaped upon him! It is related that the following morning, when Lord Eldon took his seat on the bench and Romilly's place was vacant—iron man though he was—he exclaimed, "I cannot stay here!" and rising in great agitation, broke up the court. The bodies of husband and wife were buried in one grave, at Knill, in Herefordshire.

In Frith Street, too, at No. 6, Hazlitt, the essayist, died of cholera in 1830; he was buried, as we have stated, in St. Anne's Churchyard.

Compton Street was built in the reign of King Charles II., by Sir Francis Compton; and New Compton Street was first called Stiddolph Street, after Sir Richard Stiddolph, the owner of the land on which it was built. Both New Compton and Dean Streets were named after Bishop Compton, Dean of the Chapel Royal, who formerly held the living of St. Anne's, Soho. In Dean Street, on the west side, at No. 75 (now the warehouse of Messrs. Wilson, wholesale tin-plate workers, of Wardour Street), lived Sir James Thornhill, the painter, whose daughter married Hogarth. The house, which is still unaltered in its main features, has several handsome rooms, and a magnificent staircase; and the panels of the walls are adorned with a series of paintings by the hand of its former master.

At No. 33 in this street lived Harlowe, the painter of "The Trial of Queen Katherine." He died here in 1819, at an early age.

The small theatre in this street, now called the Royalty, was built in 1840, by Miss F. Kelly (an actress who had made herself a reputation in light comedy and domestic melodrama on the boards of Drury Lane and the Haymarket) as a school for acting, but she reaped little profit from the enterprise. It was for many years used chiefly for amateur theatricals, but afterwards became popular by its spirited performance of operetta and burlesque entertainments. Miss Kelly, who was the daughter of a retired military officer, was destined for the stage from her birth, and was familiar with the boards of Old Drury at ten years of age as a chorus-singer. Her *début* as an actress was at Glasgow, in 1807, she being then in her seventeenth year. She rose to great eminence in her profession, and was equally successful as a vocalist and an actress, succeeding to many of the parts which had been filled by the celebrated Madame Storace. For several years she was an extraordinary attraction at Drury Lane, and while performing one evening at that theatre, received a striking proof of the power of her charms. A pistol was fired at her from the pit, the ball passing directly over her head; and as the terrified lady fell insensible on the stage, it was at first thought she had been killed, and a scene of wild confusion ensued. The assailant was secured, and proved to be a lunatic who had for some time persecuted Miss Kelly with incoherent letters, expressive of his attachment. A similar attempt was made upon her life in Dublin, but happily with no greater success.

In the fiftieth year of her age, by which time she had acquired a handsome competence, it occurred to Miss Kelly to establish a school for acting, for which purpose she purchased an extensive freehold property in Dean Street, Soho, in the hope of improving the condition of dramatic art. The school was a success. A number of pupils hastened to enrol themselves under the banner of so accomplished a teacher, for few ever equalled Miss Kelly in the art of—

> "Making the laugher weep, the weeper smile;
> Catching all passion in her craft of wile."

Unfortunately her ambition did not stop here, but inspired her with the wild idea of building a new theatre on her own extensive premises. Encouraged by the lavish promises of support and subscriptions from her numerous patrons among the aristocracy, foremost of whom was the Duke of Devonshire, who especially interested himself in her hazardous undertaking, Miss Kelly converted the large yard and stabling attached to her house into the Theatre Royal, Dean Street, Soho, by which title, however, it was seldom known, generally passing under the name of "Miss Kelly's Theatre." The entrance to all parts of this toy playhouse was through Miss Kelly's private residence, a peculiarity of construction which had, at all events, the advantage of novelty.

Heralded by many a flourish of trumpets on the part of the newspapers, Miss Kelly opened her tiny theatre on the 25th of May, 1840, with a new piece by Mr. Morris Barnett, entitled *Summer and Winter*, in which the author and Miss Kelly sustained the principal parts, supported, as the announcement went, "by an efficient company." The result was as disastrous as it was speedy. The distinguished patronage, from which so much had been expected, proving more select than numerous, the theatre, after being open five nights, on two of which the actors outnumbered the audience, was closed abruptly. In November of the same year Miss Kelly announced herself *At Home*, at the Theatre Royal, Dean Street. The performance was monological, and similar to some entertainments which she had given a few years previously at the Strand, with but moderate success. The result was again a complete failure, and Miss Kelly retired into private life, a loser of more than £7,000 by her unlucky speculation.

In 1850 the little theatre, which had so long languished in obscurity, made a desperate rally, and presented itself to the public as the "New English Opera House," opening with, as the playbills announced, "a grand opera in three acts, entitled *The Last Crusade*, by Alexander Mitchell, the blind composer." This opera had been originally represented with great success at the Grand Ducal Theatre, Brunswick, but, possibly from the inefficiency of the company, proved a total failure at the Soho theatre, and the "New English Opera House" was speedily closed.

In 1861 it was entirely re-constructed, with great improvements, and re-opened on the 12th of November under the name of the "New Royalty," since which time it has enjoyed its fair share of success. In 1866 Miss M. Oliver assumed the management, and under herself and her successors the Royalty kept its *prestige*. It was re-built in 1882-83, when it came under the management of Miss Kate Santley.

Greek Street, which runs from north to south, parallel to Dean Street on the east, dates from the year 1680. Pennant considers that its name is a corruption of "Grig" Street, but it was more probably derived from a colony of merchants from the Levant, for whose use a Greek church was built hard by it in Crown Street.

What used to be the last house on the east side of Greek Street, at the south end, removed to make way for the new Palace Theatre, was occupied by Sir Thomas Lawrence for the first four years of the present century; and during the last century by Josiah Wedgwood. It had previously been a dissecting-room, for Soho Square and the adjoining streets were frequented by the faculty; but Wedgwood, on making it his show-room, named it "Portland House." Here he exhibited the magnificent service which he made for the Empress of Russia, and Queen Charlotte was among those who came hither to inspect it. A great artistic interest belonged to the premises, for, as Miss Meteyard remarks in her "Life of Wedgwood," "it was here that his fame culminated in the greatest of his works—the jasper tablets, the medallion portraits and busts, the cameos, and the Barberini Vase." Time, fire, and alterations, however, had so changed Portland House, that when it was demolished little of what was Wedgwood's Gallery remained except the outer walls; though not many years before it was pulled down the name of the great potter was to be seen here cut with a diamond on a window-pane.

Among the many charitable institutions to be found in Soho, none perhaps are more worthy of public support than one at the corner of the Square and of Greek Street, called "The House of Charity." It occupies the house which formerly belonged to Alderman Beckford, who lived here in princely splendour. The institution, which is under the patronage of the Archbishop of Canterbury, was founded in 1846; but the present building and fitting-up of the premises dates only from 1863, when they were taken at a cost of upwards of £3,000. "It is the only Home in London gratuitously afforded to such distressed persons as are of good character, upon a recommendation from some one who knows them. Thus many deserving persons are saved from the sufferings and privations which precede an application to the casual ward or nightly refuge, as well as from the degradation consequent upon their reception into such promiscuous places of resort. Among the various classes of distress relieved by this House are patients discharged from hospitals before they are sufficiently recovered to take situations; these find here a comfortable lodging and ample diet, and are generally successful in obtaining situations. Orphan or friendless girls who have unadvisedly come to London in search of employment, or have accidentally lost their places, meet here with protection, counsel, and, in general, with situations. Widows, who have been reduced to the necessity of seeking a subsistence for themselves, are here recommended to places of trust or domestic service. Emigrants, while breaking up their homes and converting their effects into money, wait here until they embark. Out-patients of hospitals, excluded, through want of room, or by regulations, from admission into them, are enabled to derive benefit, while here, by attending the hospitals for medical advice and treatment. In short, the House of Charity is," says the Council of the Institution in its report, "a home for every kind of friendlessness and destitution which is not the manifest offspring of vice and profligacy." On the other side of Greek Street is Lincoln House, now one of the centres of the West London Mission (Wesleyan), of which the headquarters are at St. James's Hall; and adjoining it is the Soho Club and Home for Working Girls.

Wardour Street, which runs from north to south, parallel to Dean Street on its western side, was named after the Lords Arundell of Wardour, one of whom married the daughter and heiress of one of those rare personages, successful gamesters—Colonel Thomas Panton, of St. Martin's-in-the-Fields, a gentleman whose name is still perpetuated in Panton Street, Haymarket.

Wardour Street, as a stone at the corner of Edward Street informs us, was built in 1686. Flaxman was living here in 1784 at No. 27. In this street also lived the once celebrated Tom Hudson, the comic song-writer and singer. He carried on business as a grocer, and every week he wrote a comic song, which he had printed upon his "tea-papers," and presented to his customers on the Saturday.

During the last half-century the name of this street has passed into a by-word and a proverb, as the head-quarters of curiosity-shops, antique and modern, genuine and fictitious. Leigh Hunt tells us in his "Town" that it was a favourite haunt of Charles Lamb, and that he had often heard the author of the "Essays of Elia" expatiate on the pleasure of strolling up Wardour Street on a summer afternoon.

The shops occupied by brokers and dealers in old furniture, pictures, prints, china, &c., are above a score in number, forming thus almost a bazaar or mart, and constituting a class apart from the rest of the locality. Here the late Lord Macaulay might be seen trudging home with a second-hand book, or packet of ballads, or broadsides; and here Mr. Gladstone himself, even when Prime Minister, would often take a stroll, picking up a specimen of old-fashioned china for the superb collection he once had in Carlton Terrace.

We read in old documents of "Old Soho, *alias* Wardour Street." To this street, no doubt, Pope really alluded when he wrote, in imitation of Horace:—

> "And when I flatter, let my dirty leaves
> Clothe spice, line trunks, or, fluttering in a row,
> Befringe the rails of Bedlam and Soho."

On the south side of Oxford Street, a few doors to the east of Charles Street, used to be an inn called "The Mischief." In its interior was kept and shown a curious sign which used to hang over the entrance, representing a man with a "load of mischief" on his back; the said load consisting of a shrewish-looking wife, a monkey or ape; and hard by are most suspicious-looking pawn-shops and gin-shops. The design, of which we give a copy on page 193, is worthy of Hogarth's pencil.

The narrow, winding lane running southwards from the corner of Oxford Street and Tottenham Court Road, long known as Crown Street, but in former times as Hog Lane, formed the boundary between the parishes of St. Giles and St. Anne, Soho. Its narrowness served to show its antiquity; and, no doubt, it derived its first name from the pigs that fed along its sides. In 1762 it came to be dignified by its more recent appellation from the "Rose and Crown" tavern. In 1887 it was absorbed in "Charing Cross Road." In it was the Greek church already spoken of, built for the use of "merchants from the Levant," in the time of Charles II. It does not appear, however, to have remained long in the hands of these oriental Christians, but to have been given up to the use of the French Protestants who settled in this neighbourhood in large force. As such it is immortalised by Hogarth.

The poor little chapel which belonged in succession to the Greeks and to the French refugees, stood on the western side of Crown Street, adjoining some almshouses, which are said to have been founded by Nell Gwynne.

In Hog Lane Hogarth has laid the scene of one of the best of his smaller pictures, "Noon." Mr. Peter Cunningham notes a curious fact with respect to this picture, namely, that it is "generally reversed in the engravings, and thus made untrue to the locality, which (he adds) Hogarth never was." The background of the picture gives us a view of the then newly-built church of St. Giles-in-the-Fields.

CHAPTER XXVI.

ST. GILES'S IN THE FIELDS.

"On Newgate steps Jack Chance was found,
And bred up near St. Giles's Pound."—*Old Song.*

St. Giles, the Patron Saint of Lepers—The Lepers' Hospital founded here—The Village of St. Giles in the Time of the Plantagenets, Tudors, and Stuarts—Executions at St. Giles's—The "Half-way House" on the Road to Tyburn—The Cage and the Pound—St. Giles's Church—Church Lane—Monmouth Court and the Catnatch Press—The Seven Dials—Shaved by a Woman—The Prince and the Beggars.

St. Giles, the patron saint of this and of so many other outlying parishes in English towns and cities, is said, by Alban Butler in his "Lives of the Saints," to have been of noble birth at Athens. He flourished in the seventh and eighth centuries, and combined with his piety a marked love of solitude. Quitting his own country he found a retreat in France, and passed many years of his life in the recesses of a forest in the neighbourhood of Nismes. It is said that the French king and a troop of hunters pursued a hind, which fled for protection to the saint. An arrow, intended for the hind, wounded the saint, who, however, continued his devotions, and refused all recompense for the injury done to his body. The hind, it appeared, had long nourished him with its milk, and had strayed into danger in one of the glades. This incident made Giles a great favourite with the king, but nothing could induce him to quit his forest for the atmosphere of a court. Towards the end of his life, however, he so far abandoned his solitude as to admit several disciples and found a monastery, which afterwards became a Benedictine abbey. The saint is commemorated in the Martyrologies of St. Bede and others, and St. Giles and the hind have often afforded a subject for the artist's pencil. St. Giles is the patron saint of lepers, and is styled in the calendar of the Roman Church "Abbot and Confessor."

It is very doubtful whether this manor and village, of which we now come to treat, was dedicated to St. Giles before the erection of the lepers' hospital by Queen Matilda, for there is no mention of it by any such name in "Domesday Book." The hospital consisted of a house or principal mansion, with an oratory and offices; but the "oratory" appears to have been only a chapel added on to the village church. "Private charity, however," says Newton, "augmented it in after times, and the brotherhood seem to have become subsequently possessed of other lands, as the Spital croft, consisting of sixteen acres, lying on the north side of the highway, opposite the great gate of the hospital, and also two estates called Newlands and Lelane, the exact situations of which, though probably contiguous, we are unable to point out."

According to existing records, the earliest notice of this district tells us that a hospital for lepers was founded here, about the year 1118, by Queen Matilda, the good wife of Henry I., and that it was attached as a "cell," or subordinate house, to a larger institution at Burton Lazars, in Leicestershire, then recently founded. Grants of royalty were confirmed by a bull of Pope Alexander VI (1240). The hospital here stood on land belonging to the Crown, and not very far from the present parish church. Its grounds were enclosed with a wall, and formed almost a triangle, embracing between seven and eight acres. On the north it was bounded by High Street, on the west by Crown Street, and on the east by Dudley (formerly Monmouth) Street. The conventual buildings do not appear to have been of any great size, and, so far as we know, there is no print of their extent. The foundation, however, as we happen to know, was for "forty lepers, one clerk, and one messenger, besides matrons, the master, and other members of the establishment." Mr. Newton tells us that the grant from the Crown expressly stipulated that the hospital should be built "on the spot where 'John, of good memory,' was chaplain;" and hence he argues that the village church formed part of the grant along with the ancient manor.

Carew, in his "Survey of Cornwall," says that leprosy was common in the far west in his own day (James I.), and attributes it to the "disorderly eating of sea-fish newly taken, and principally the livers of them, not well prepared, soused, pickled, or condited." St. James's, St. Giles's, and Burton Lazars, in Leicestershire, were the three oldest houses for lepers in the kingdom.

At the Reformation St. Giles's Hospital was dissolved, and granted by Henry VIII. to John Dudley, Viscount Lisle, whom the king graciously allowed to alienate it to John or Wymond Carew, in 1547. Belonging to the hospital was a Grange at Edmonton (Edelmston). At the time of this alienation (1547) Dr. Andrew Borde, "the first ot Merry Andrews," was the tenant of a messuage, with an orchard and garden, adjoining the said dissolved hospital. Mr. Parton identifies this with the site of the residence afterwards given to the rector by the Duchess of Dudley, and later known as Dudley Court. The hospital was endowed with lands at Feltham and Isleworth, and by an annual rent from St. Clement's parish. Lord Lisle fitted up the chief part of the building, and lived here two years. Mr. Parton publishes the list of masters and wardens of the hospital, with accounts, &c. Cotterell Garden, in St. Giles's parish, was confirmed to the hospital in 1186.

The hospital chapel and the parish church of St. Giles would appear to have been two distinct structures under a single roof, much like the arrangement still to be seen in St. Helen's Church, Bishopsgate. Before the high altar in the chapel burnt St. Giles's light. There was a second altar and chapel of St. Michael.

The chief part of the village of St. Giles, in the days of our Plantagenet kings, was composed of houses standing on the north of the highway which led westward from Holborn to Tyburn, and whose gardens stretched behind them to St. Blemund's Dyke. In Ralph Aggas' map it figures as a small village, or rather a small group of cottages, with their respective garden-plots nestling around the walls of the hospital. In 1541 an Act of Parliament was passed, ordering the "western road" of London, from "Holborne Bars" to St. Giles-in-the-Fields, to be paved, "as far as there was any habitation of both sides of the street." The village of St. Giles had its ancient stone cross, which seems to have stood near what is now the north end of Endell Street.

In 1413 there was in London a conspiracy of the sect called the Lollards. They met in the fields adjoining St. Giles's Hospital, headed by Sir John Oldcastle, who afterwards was executed on the spot, being hung in chains over a slow fire.

SEVEN DIALS, 1870. (*From an Original Sketch.*)

In the days of Elizabeth it was not so easy either for lepers or for ordinary people to find their way from St. Giles's to St. James's, as there were no continuous rows of houses in that south-west direction. But at the point where Tottenham Court Road now intersects Oxford Street, there was a notice, at the top of a narrow lane running across where is now Soho, "The Road to Reading." It led, however, by a somewhat singular bend, no further than the top of the Haymarket and a narrow lane parallel to it, which bore the rural name of Hedge Lane, not far from the corner of Leicester Fields.

The first era of building began a little before

VIEWS IN THE ROOKERY, ST. GILES'S, 1860.

1600, at which date Holborn and St. Giles's were nearly connected together. On the wall of the hospital being pulled down, houses began to be built on the east, west, and south sides of the church, and on both sides of St. Giles's Street new dwellings multiplied. Ten years later saw the commencement of Great Queen Street, and a continuation of the houses down both sides of Drury Lane. And so great was the increase that in 1623 no less than 897 houses were rated. Indeed, in Elizabeth's time, the parish was very largely built on, and distinguished by the rank of its inhabitants. (Both Elizabeth and James, it will be remembered, forbade building in the suburbs.) At the end of Charles II.'s reign there were more than 2,000; in Anne's, more than 3,000; in 1812, nearly 5,000 houses rated in the parish books.

A second great era of building came in with the Restoration. After the Revocation of the Edict of Nantes, large numbers of poor French emigrants took up their quarters about this part.

In this parish, unfortunately, the earlier volumes of the rate-books have perished, so that it is not possible to obtain such accurate information as to its inhabitants in the Tudor and Stuart times as we find in those of St. Martin's, and of St. Paul's, Covent Garden.

Although the parish of St. Giles is reckoned, as indeed it is, a poor and third-rate neighbourhood, and its very name has passed into a by-word as the very antipodes of fashionable St. James's, still it is richer in its materials for history than many districts inhabited by a class higher in the social scale. It is observed in "Haunted London" that "the story of St. Giles's parish should properly embrace the whole records of London vagrancy."

When criminals ceased to be executed at the Elms in Smithfield, or, as some say, at a much earlier date, a gallows was set up near the north-west corner of the wall of the hospital; and it soon became a regular custom to present every malefactor, as he passed the hospital gate in the fatal cart on his way to the gallows, with a glass of ale. When the hospital was dissolved, the custom was still kept up; and there is scarcely an execution at "Tyburn Tree," recorded in the "Newgate Calendar," in which the fact is not mentioned that the culprit called at a public-house *en route* for a parting draught.

The memory of this last drink given to criminals on their way was long preserved by Bowl Yard or Alley, on the south side of the High Street, over against Dyott Street, *alias* George Street; and Parton, in his "History of the Parish," published in 1822, makes mention of a public-house bearing the sign of "The Bowl," which stood between the end of St. Giles's, High Street, and Hog Lane.

"A like custom," writes Pennant, "obtained anciently at York, which gave rise to the saying, that the saddler of Bawtry was hanged for leaving his liquor: had he stopped, as was usual with other criminals, to drink his bowl of ale, his reprieve, which was actually on its way, would have arrived in time enough to have saved his life."

The "Bowl" would appear to have been succeeded by the "Angel," or to have had a rival in that inn. At all events, in 1873, the *City Press* reported that another memorial of ancient London was about to pass away, namely, the "Angel" Inn, at St. Giles's, the "half-way house" on the road to Tyburn—the house at which Jack Ketch and the criminal who was about to expiate his offence on the scaffold were wont to stop on their way to the gallows for a "last glass." The proprietor, however, was prevailed upon to stay the work of demolition for a time; but the house has since been rebuilt.

When Lord Cobham was executed at St. Giles's, it is said that a new gallows was put up for that special occasion. But Lord Cobham was not the only distinguished person who here paid the last penalty of the law. St. Giles's Pound is also memorable as the scene of the execution of some of the accomplices in Babington's plot against Queen Elizabeth, though Babington himself suffered at Lincoln's Inn Fields, "even in the place where they used to meet and conferre of their traytorous practices."

The Cage and the Pound originally stood close together in the middle of the High Street, but they were removed in 1656 to make room for alms-houses. The Pound, too, occupied, as we learn casually, a space of thirty feet near the same site, but it was removed about the same time to the corner of Tottenham Court Road, where it stood till 1765 on the site of the isolated block of houses opposite the entrance to Messrs. Meux's Brewery.

The immediate neighbourhood of this Pound bore none of the highest characters, if we may draw any inference on the subject from the words of a popular song by Mr. Thompson, an actor at Drury Lane Theatre, which we have prefixed as a motto to this chapter.

In the High Street, on the left-hand side going towards Tottenham Court Road, the late Mr. J. T. Smith remembered four large and handsome houses, "with grotesque masques on the key-stones above the first-floor windows." He also tells us that just where Oxford Street and Tottenham Court Road meet there was a large circular boundary-stone let into the pavement. "When," he adds, "the charity boys of St. Giles's parish walk the boundaries, those who have deserved flogging are whipped at this stone, in order that when they grow up they may remember the place, and be competent to give evidence should any dispute arise with the neighbouring parishes."

Mr. Smith also tells us, in his "Book for a Rainy Day," that he remembered a row of six small almshouses, surrounded by a dwarf brick wall, standing in the middle of High Street. They were pulled down about the year 1780, and rebuilt near the coal-yard at the north-east end of Drury Lane. There was formerly a vineyard here, as there was on the slope of the hill near to Hatton Garden.

It is remarkable that in almost every ancient town in England, the church of St. Giles stands either outside the walls, or, at all events, near its outlying parts, in allusion, doubtless, to the arrangements of the Israelites of old, who placed their lepers outside the camp.

St. Giles's Church stands on the south side of High Street, at the junction of Broad Street, and was erected between the years 1730 and 1734. It is a large and stately edifice, built entirely of Portland stone, and is vaulted beneath. The steeple, which rises to a height of about 160 feet, consists of a rustic pedestal, supporting a range of Doric pilasters; whilst above the clock is an octangular tower, with three-quarter Ionic columns, supporting a balustrade with vases, on which stands the spire, which is also octangular and belted. The interior of the church is bold and effective; the roof is supported by rows of Ionic pillars of Portland stone, and the semicircular-headed windows are mostly filled with coloured glass.

There was here a previous structure of red brick, consecrated by Laud, whilst Bishop of London, in 1623, and towards the building of which the poor "players of the Cockpit," so cruelly persecuted by the Puritan party, gave £20. This church was pulled down to make room for the present edifice, which was opened for worship in 1734. It had for its architect one Henry Flitcroft, the same who built the church of St. Olave, Southwark; and Mr. Peter Cunningham draws attention to the fact that it bears a close resemblance to that of St. Martin's-in-the-Fields. The first church of all on this spot appears to have had a round tower, not unlike those to be seen in the small parishes in the eastern parts of Norfolk and Suffolk.

Strype gives an account of several of the monuments in the church and churchyard, but we shall notice only a few. One of these was put up in 1611, by John Thornton to his wife, who died in childbed. He probably was the builder of Thornton's Alley, and that he was from the north country is more than probable from the legend round the family tomb:—

> "Full south this stone four foot doth lie,
> His father John and grandsire Harvey;
> Thornton of Thornton in Yorkshire bred,
> Where lives the fame of Thornton being dead."

Another stone in the churchyard records the death of one Eleanor Stewart, an old resident in the parish, who died in 1725, at the age, according to the inscription, of 123 and five months, an age which we bring here under the notice of those who deny centenarianism.

In the churchyard are tombs to the memory of Richard Pendrill, to whom Charles II. owed his escape after the fatal battle of Worcester, and of George Chapman, the earliest translator of Homer's "Iliad;" the latter is said to have been the work of Inigo Jones. The following bombastic epitaph on Pendrill's tomb will amuse our readers:—

> "Hold, passenger, here's shrouded in his hearse,
> Unparallel'd Pendrill through the universe;
> Like whom the Eastern star from heaven gave light
> To three lost kings, so he in such dark night
> To Britain's Monarch, toss'd by adverse war,
> On earth appear'd, a second Eastern star;
> A pole, a stem in her rebellious main,
> A pilot to her royal sovereign.
> Now to triumph in heaven's eternal sphere
> He's hence advanced for his just steerage here;
> Whilst Albion's chronicles with matchless fame
> Embalm the story of great Pendrill's name."

Chapman deserves more particular mention here, as the intimate friend of Ben Jonson, who thus speaks of his translation of Homer:—

> "Whose work could this be, Chapman, to refine
> Old Hesiod's ore, and give it thus, but thine,
> Who hadst before wrought in rich Homer's mine?
>
> "What treasure hast thou brought us, and what store
> Still, still dost thou arrive with at our shore,
> To make thy honour and our wealth the more?
>
> "If all the vulgar tongues that speak this day
> Were asked of thy discoveries, they must say,
> To the Greek coast thine only knew the way.
>
> "Such passage hast thou found, such returns made,
> As now of all men it is called the trade;
> And who make thither else, rob or invade."

He translated Hesiod's "Works and Days," as well as Homer, and was even better known as a play-writer; and was more than once imprisoned, along with Ben Jonson, for the freedom of his pen. Chapman and Fletcher, indeed, were Jonson's most intimate friends. He told Drummond of Hawthornden that he loved them both, and that "next to himself, they were the only poets who could make a masque." Chapman died in 1634, at the age of nearly eighty. The inscription was re-cut in 1891, but the tomb itself sadly needs repair.

Elsewhere is a stone which a few years ago had upon it some faint vestiges of what was once a coat of arms and some appearance of an inscription; but the most expert of heralds would fail to describe the one, and eyes, however penetrating, might be baffled to decipher the other. Yet this marked a grave without its dead—a mockery of the tomb—a cheating of the sexton; for hither were brought the decapitated remains of one who was among the brightest and most popular young noblemen of his time, and hence were they afterwards disinterred and privately conveyed to Dilston, in Northumberland, and deposited in the family vault, amid the ashes of his forefathers. Here, in fact, was first deposited the body of the amiable and unfortunate James Radcliffe, Earl of Derwentwater, whose fatal connection with the fortunes of the Pretender, and untimely death on Tower Hill, are matters of history, and reveal a sad tragedy, in which he was at once the hero and the victim. The body of the earl was again removed from its grave in Northumberland, and carried to Thorndon, Lord Petre's seat in Essex, for re-interment, in October, 1874.

In the church and in the churchyard adjoining repose several other persons known to history. Among them Lord Herbert of Cherbury; Shirley, the dramatic writer; Andrew Marvell, of whom we have already spoken; the notorious Countess of Shrewsbury; Sir Roger L'Estrange, the celebrated political writer; Michael Mohun, the actor; and Oliver Plunkett, the Roman Catholic Archbishop of Armagh, who was executed at Tyburn on the charge of high treason in 1681.

The only monument of interest in the church is to be seen in the first window in the north aisle. It is a recumbent figure of the Duchess of Dudley, who was created a duchess in her own right by Charles I., and who died in 1669. "This monument," Mr. P. Cunningham tells us, "was preserved when the church was rebuilt, as a piece of parochial gratitude to one whose benefactions to the parish in which she had resided had been both frequent and liberal." Among other matters, she had contributed very largely to the interior decoration of the church, but had the mortification of seeing her gifts condemned as Popish, cast out of the sacred edifice, and sold by order of the hypocritical Puritans. The duchess, who was also in other ways a benefactor to the parish of St. Giles, was buried at Stoneleigh, Warwickshire.

The gate at the entrance of the churchyard, which dates from the days of Charles II., is much admired. It is adorned with a bas-relief of the Day of Judgment. It formerly stood on the north side of the churchyard, but in 1865, being unsafe, it was taken down and carefully re-erected opposite the western entrance, in the idea that it would adorn the new street that was destined sooner or later to be opened from Tottenham Court Road to St. Martin's Lane.

Mr. J. T. Smith, in his "Book for a Rainy Day," speaks of this "Resurrection Gateway" as being of red and brown brick: he says of the carving above it that it was "borrowed, not from Michael Angelo, but from the workings of the brain of some ship-carver." Rowland Dobie, in his "History of St. Giles'," states that "the composition is, with various alterations, taken from Michael Angelo's 'Last Judgment.'" Mr. E. L. Blanchard, in his "London Guide Book," informs us that the carving is "an elaborate and curious specimen of bronze sculpture," and that it was "brought from Florence." But a better authority, Bishop Thorold, tells us, in his "Yearly Report on the parish, in 1865," that "*it is carved in oak, of the date of* 1658."

The lich-gate was erected from the designs of William Leverton, Esq., and cost altogether the sum of £185 14s. 6d., as may be seen in the parish records. Out of this sum "Love, the carver," received the miserable stipend of £27, showing the estimation in which sacred art was held under our Stuart kings. At the time of the removal of the gate, the tombstones were levelled in the churchyard, young trees were planted, the footway outside widened, and an ornamental railing placed by the kerb-stone instead of a dead wall.

Of all the dark and dismal thoroughfares in the parish of St. Giles's, or, indeed, in the great wilderness of London, few could be compared with that known as Church Lane, which ran between High Street and New Oxford Street. During the last half-century, while the metropolis has been undergoing the pressure of progress consequent upon the quick march of civilisation, what remained of the Church Lane of our early days was left with its little colony of Arabs as completely sequestered from London society as if it were part of Arabia Petræa. Few passed through Church Lane who were not members of its own select society. None else had any business there; and if they had, they would find it to their interest to get out of it as soon as possible. Its condition was a disgrace to the great city. It was pulled down in 1878–9.

The mansion house inhabited by Lord Lisle,

and afterwards by the Carews and the Duchess of Dudley, stood a little to the west of the church. It was demolished in order to build Denmark Street. Its site is marked by Lloyd's Court.

In Monmouth Court, off Little Earl Street, used to be, until its removal to Great St. Andrew Street, the printing and publishing office named after the late James Catnach, by whom it was founded in 1813. From it has been issued by far the largest store of ballads, songs, broadsides, "last dying speeches," &c., that has ever appeared in London, even in this most prolific age. Catnatch was a native of Alnwick, in Northumberland, and, coming to London when a lad to fight the battle of life, was apprenticed as a compositor in the office of the *Courier* newspaper. He deserves the credit of having been the first who, availing himself of larger capital and greater mechanical skill than his precursors and rivals, substituted white paper and real printer's ink for the execrable tea-paper, blotched with lamp-black and oil, which had marked the old broadside and ballad printing. He also first conceived and carried out the idea of publishing collections of songs by the yard, and giving for one penny (formerly the price of a single ballad) strings of poetry. He was the patron of much original talent among the bards of St. Giles's and Drury Lane; and in the quarter of a century which elapsed between the establishment of his press and his death, he had literally made a name in literature—of a particular kind. Among the events of the day which he turned to the best and most profitable account, were the trial of Queen Caroline, the Cato Street conspiracy, and the murder of Weare by Thurtell. On the last-named occasion, when the excitement about the execution was about to die out, he brought out a second penny broadside, headed "WE ARE alive again," which the public read as "WEARE." The public did not like the trick, and called it a "catch-penny;" hence arose the set phrase, which for a long time afterwards stuck to the issues of the Seven Dials' press, though they sold as well as ever. All sorts of stories are told to show the fertility of Catnatch's resources. He received such large sums in coppers, that he used to take them to the Bank of England in a hackney-coach; and when his neighbours in Seven Dials refused to take them, for fear of catching a fever which was said to have spread through their contact with low cadgers and hawkers, he boiled them *en masse* with a decoction of potash and vinegar, to make them bright, and his coppers recovered their popularity. He had also a knack of carving rough and rude illustrations on the backs of music-blocks, which he nailed on to pieces of wood. Probably through his connection with Northumberland, he next fortunately picked up some of the wood blocks of Thomas Bewick, which raised at once the character of his printing-press. His next step was to increase the quantity which he gave for a penny, embodying his generosity to the public in a phrase which soon was in everybody's mouth, "Songs, three yards a penny! Songs, beautiful songs!" He next employed his talents on cheap Christmas carols and broadsheets of a higher class; and having realised something more than a competency, retired, in 1839, to the neighbourhood of South Mimms, on the borders of Hertfordshire, where he died about two years afterwards. The business of the "Seven Dials' Printing Office" he left to his sister, Mrs. Ryle, by whom it was carried on for a time, in conjunction with a Mr. Paul. It is now managed by Mr. W. S. Fortey, who, as a boy, was employed by Mr. Catnatch. The press is still as busy as ever, and though rivals have arisen, it enjoys a literary *prestige* which will not soon pass away, if we may judge from the fact that it still turns out and sells yearly no less than a million of cheap fly-sheets of the various kinds mentioned above.

Some idea of the Catnatch literature may be formed from the two items here following, taken from the catalogue of a second-hand bookseller:—

"BROADSIDES.—A Collection of 9 Curious Old Broadsides and Christmas Carols, printed at Seven Dials and elsewhere. On rough folio paper, *and illustrated with quaint and rude woodcuts, in their original condition, with rough edges, neatly mounted on white paper and bound in half roxburghe.* Contents:—Letter written by Jesus Christ—6 Carols for Christmas—Messenger of Mortality, or Life and Death Contrasted—Massacre of the French King, by which the unfortunate Louis XVI. suffered on the scaffold, with a large woodcut of his execution.

"OLD SONGS AND BALLADS.—A Collection of 35 most Curious Old Songs and Ballads, printed at Seven Dials, on rough old straw paper, and *illustrated with quaint and rude woodcuts or engravings.* In their original condition with rough edges, *very neatly mounted on fine paper, and bound in half roxburghe.* This collection embraces a most varied series of old Ballads, commencing with the Wanton Wife of Bath, Woful Lamentation of Mrs. Jane Shore, Unhappy Lady of Hackney, Kentish Garland, Dorsetshire Garland, or Beggar's Wedding, Faithless Captain, and similar pieces. It next has 16 ballads with large engravings, illustrative of the pieces, bacchanalian, humorous, &c. &c.; and concludes with Liston's Drolleries (with a character portrait), the Paul Pry Songster (with woodcut of Liston as 'Paul Pry'), and the Harp of Ossian, &c."

The central space in this neighbourhood, called Seven Dials, was so named on account of the plan upon which the neighbourhood was laid out for building, seven streets being made to converge at a centre, where there was a pillar adorned with, or at all events, intended to be adorned with, seven dial faces. Till this column was put up, it was called "the Seven Streets," according to the "New View of London," which tells us that at the time of its publication (1708) only four of the seven streets had been actually built. The locality is ducer of the late lotteries, in imitation of those at Venice." Gay, in his "Trivia," sings :—

> "Here to seven streets Seven Dials count their day,
> And from each other catch the circling ray."

It appears that the dial-stone had but six faces, two of the seven streets opening into one angle.

THE GATEWAY OF ST. GILES'S, IN ITS ORIGINAL POSITION. (*See page* 202.)

built on what was formerly known as the Marshlands, and also as Cock and Pie Fields. These were surrounded by a ditch, which ran down to St. Martin's and so into the Thames, but was blotted out when the Seven Dials was built. Evelyn thus mentions the work in his "Diary," under date 5th October, 1694 :—"I went to see the building near St. Giles, where seven streets made a star, from a Doric pillar placed in the middle of a circular area, said to be built by Mr. Neale, intro-

The column and dials were removed in June, 1774, to search for a treasure supposed to be concealed beneath the base ; they were never replaced, but in 1822 were purchased of a stonemason, and the column was surmounted with a ducal coronet, and set up on Weybridge Green as a memorial to the late Duchess of York, who died at Oatlands, in 1820. The dial-stone formed a stepping-stone at the adjoining "Ship" inn. The angular direction of each street renders the spot rather embarrassing to a pedestrian who crosses this maze of buildings unexpectedly, and frequently causes him to diverge from the road that would lead him to his destination.

The business carried on in Seven Dials seems to be of a very heterogeneous character. It is the great haunt of bird and bird-cage sellers, also of the sellers of rabbits, cats, dogs, &c.; and as some of the houses, being of an old fashion, have broad ledges of lead over the shop windows, these are frequently found converted into miniature gardens, which help, in some degree, to counterbalance the squalor and misery still to be seen in some of the courts and lanes hard by. In certain of the streets close by not a few of the shops are devoted to the sale of old clothes, second-hand boots and shoes, &c.; ginger-beer, green-grocery, and theatrical stores. Cheap picture-frame makers also abound here. In many of the houses, in some of these streets, whole families seem to live and thrive in a single room. In Charles Knight's "London" we read that "cellars serving whole families for 'kitchen, and parlour, and bed-room, and all,' are to be found in other streets of London, but not so numerous and near to each other. Here they cluster like cells in a convent of the order of La Trappe, or like onions on a rope. It is curious and interesting to watch the habits of these human moles when they emerge, or half emerge, from their cavities. Their infants seem exempt from the dangers which haunt those of other people: at an age when most babies are not

QUEEN ANNE'S BATH. *(From a View taken in 1851.)*

trusted alone on a level floor, these urchins stand secure on the upmost round of a trap-ladder, studying the different conformations of the shoes of the passers-by. The mode of ingress of the adults is curious: they turn their backs to the entry, and, inserting first one foot and then the other, disappear by degrees. The process is not unlike (were such a thing conceivable) a sword sheathing itself. They appear a short-winded generation, often coming, like the otter, to the surface to breathe. In the twilight, which reigns at the bottom of their dens, you can sometimes discern the male busily cobbling shoes on one side of the entrance, and the female repairing all sorts of rent garments on the other. They seem to be free traders: at certain periods of the day tea-cups and saucers may be seen arranged on their boards; at others, plates and pewter pots. They have the appearance of being on the whole a contented race."

"On one occasion," says Mr. J. Smith, in his "Topography of London," "that I might indulge the humour of being shaved by a woman, I repaired to the Seven Dials, where, in Great St. Andrew's Street, a slender female performed the operation, whilst her husband, a strapping soldier in the Horse Guards, sat smoking his pipe. There was a famous woman in Swallow Street, who shaved; and I recollect a black woman in Butcher Row, a street formerly standing by the side of St. Clement's Church, near Temple Bar, who is said to have shaved with ease and dexterity. Mr. Batrick informs me that he has read of the five barberesses of Drury Lane, who shamefully maltreated a woman in the reign of Charles II."

Considering the class of the inhabitants, it is not surprising that many lodging-houses are to be met with here. Diprose, in his "Book about London," tells us that perhaps the most celebrated and notorious of those in St. Giles's was kept by "Mother Cummins."

It is related that Major Hanger accompanied George IV. to a beggars' carnival in St. Giles's. He had not been there long when the chairman, Sir Jeffery Dunstan, addressing the company, and pointing to the then Prince of Wales, said, "I call upon that ere gemman with a shirt for a song." The prince, as well as he could, got excused upon his friend promising to sing for him, and he chanted a ballad called "The Beggar's Wedding, or the Jovial Crew," with great applause. The major's health having been drank with nine times nine, and responded to by him, wishing them "good luck till they were tired of it," he departed with the prince, to afford the company time to fix their different routes for the ensuing day's business. At that period they used to have a general meeting in the course of the year, and each day they were divided into companies, each company having its particular walk; their earnings varied much, some getting as much as five shillings per day.

Monmouth (afterwards Dudley) Street, which will now be looked for in vain, is the street to which Daniel Burgess referred when preaching on the subject of a "robe of righteousness." "If any one of you, my brethren," he said, "would have a suit to last a twelvemonth, let him go to Monmouth Street; if for his lifetime, let him apply to the Court of Chancery; but if for eternity, let him put on the Saviour's robe of righteousness."

CHAPTER XXVII.

THE PARISH OF ST. GILES'S-IN-THE-FIELDS (*continued*).

"Rure ego viventem, tu dicis in urbe beatum."—*Horace.*

The Poor of St. Giles's—Curious Parish Regulations—"Old Simon," the Beggar—Denmark Street—Etymology of Brownlow and Belton Streets—Endell Street—Queen Anne's Bath—British Lying-in Hospital—Baths and Washhouses—French Protestant Episcopal Church—Bloomsbury Chapel—Bedford Chapel—Outbreak of the Plague of 1665 in St. Giles's—Lewknor's Lane, and its Character in the Reign of Queen Anne—Nell Gwynne's Reputed Birthplace—St. Giles's Almshouses—The Old Round House and Jack Sheppard's Escape—The Cockpit and Phœnix Theatres—The "White Lion" in Drury Lane—"The Flash Coves' Parliament"—Great Queen Street and its Fashionable Residents—The Gordon Riots—Opie's Popularity—James Hoole's Residence—The Freemasons' Hall and Tavern—The Wesleyan Chapel—The Marriage Register of David Garrick—Benjamin Franklin's Printing-press—Gate Street—The Great and Little Turnstiles—Tichborne Court—Religious Persecutions.

THE parish of St. Giles, with its nests of close and narrow alleys and courts inhabited by the lowest class of Irish costermongers, has passed into a byword as the synonym of filth and squalor. But now New Oxford Street and the Charing Cross Road have been carried through the worst part of its slums—"the Rookery" and Hog Lane—and though the work of improvement is not yet complete, much has been done to redeem the neighbourhood from reproach. Time was, as Peter Cunningham remarks, when "the parish could show its pound, its cage, its round-house and watch-house, its stocks, its whipping-post, and at one time its gallows," as our readers are already aware. The locality, nevertheless, is not without its historic or romantic interest, for "a redoubt with two flanks near St. Giles's Pound," and a small fort at the east end of Tyburn Road, are mentioned among the forts ordered to be raised round London by the Parliament in 1642.

According to the "London Spy" (1725), St. Giles's was in the days of the two first Georges a wealthy and populous parish, and one "said to furnish his Majesty's plantations in America with more souls than all the rest of the kingdom besides." It was also remarkable for producing the "Jack Ketches" of that day, as well as a fair proportion of the malefactors who suffered at Tyburn. The same authority quotes an old saying—

"St. Giles' breed,
Better hang than seed."

They were a noisy and riotous lot, fond of street brawls, equally "fat, ragged and saucy;" and the courts abounded in pedlars, fish-women, news-criers, and corn-cutters.

Parton, in his "History of St. Giles's," tells us that in remote times this parish "contained no greater proportion of poor than other parishes of a similar extent and population; the introduction of Irish mendicants, and other poor of that description, for which it afterwards became so noted, is not to be traced further back than the time of Queen Elizabeth." Strype, too, remarks that "when London began to increase in population, there was observed to be a confluence here out of the countries of such persons as were of the poorer sorts of trades and occupations; who, because they could not exercise them within the jurisdiction of the City, followed them within the suburbs; therefore the Queen, as well as forbidding the further erection of new buildings, ordered all persons within three miles of the gates of the City to forbear from letting or settling, or suffering any more than one family only to be placed in one house."

In 1637 it was ordered that, "to prevent the great influx of poor people into this parish, the beadles do present every fortnight, on the Sunday, the names of all *new-comers, under-setters, inmates, divided tenements, persons that have families in cellars*, and other abuses." "This," says Parton, "is the first mention of *cellars* as places of residence, and for which the parish afterwards became so noted that the expression of 'a cellar in St. Giles's' used to designate the lowest poverty, became afterwards proverbial, and is still used, though most of these subterranean dwellings are now gone."

Speaking of the beggars of St. Giles's, we should not omit to mention Simon Edy, who lived there in the middle of the last century. "Old Simon," as he was commonly named, lodged, with his dog, under a staircase in an old shattered building called "Rat's Castle," in Dyot Street.* He is thus described by Mr. J. T. Smith in his "Book for a Rainy Day:"—"He wore several hats, and suffered his beard to grow, which was of a dirty yellow-white. Upon his fingers were numerous brass rings. He had several waistcoats, and as many coats, increasing in size, so that he was enabled by the extent of the uppermost garment to cover the greater part of the bundles, containing rags of various colours, and distinct parcels with which he was girded about, consisting of books, canisters containing bread, cheese, and other articles of food; matches, a tinder-box, and meat for his dog; cuttings of curious events from old newspapers, scraps from Foxe's 'Book of Martyrs,' and three or four dogs'-eared and grease-thumbed numbers of the *Gentleman's Magazine*. From these and such-like productions he gained a great part of the information with which he sometimes entertained those persons who stopped to look at him." This eccentric character (perhaps the original of the "Simple Simon" of our nursery rhymes) stood for many years at the gate of St. Giles's Church, and a portrait of him is to be found in Mr. J. T. Smith's well-known book, "Sketches from the London Streets."

Denmark Street is described by Strype as "a fair, broad street, with good houses, and well inhabited by gentry." Near it is Lloyd's Court or Alley, to which Hogarth has given a celebrity by making it and the adjoining Hog Lane the scene of one of his series of sketches, "The Four Times of the Day." Lord Wharton's residence stood at the corner of this thoroughfare.

In Brownlow (now Betterton) Street died, in 1684, Michael Mohun, the actor. The street, and the adjoining one of Belton (now Endell) Street, derived their names from Sir John Brownlow, Bart., of Belton, whose name occurs constantly in the parish rate-books as a resident in the reign of Charles II. His town mansion and gardens stood on this site, but the former was pulled down before the year 1682. The noble estate of Belton, in Lincolnshire, passed by marriage to the Custs, the head of whom is now Earl Brownlow.

At No. 25, Endell Street (formerly Old Belton Street), in the rear of the premises occupied by Messrs. King, ironmongers, is an ancient bath, said

* This street, once so squalid, has been reconstructed.

by local tradition to have been used by Queen Anne, which for the most part has escaped the notice of antiquaries. It was fed by a fine spring of clear water, which was said to have medicinal qualities. Whether it was the favourite bagnio of Queen Anne or not, it certainly is a curious relic of other days, though shorn of its ancient glories. Descending a dark and narrow staircase, we find ourselves in a low apartment, about twelve or fourteen feet square, its walls inlaid with Dutch tiles, white, with blue patterns—clearly of the sixteenth century. It once had "a lofty French groined dome roof," but the upper part of the chamber is now cut off by a modern flooring, and formed into a blacksmith's forge.

In a "View of Old London" published in 1851, the bath is said to be "supplied direct from the spring, which is perpetually running; the water," adds the writer, "is always fresh, and is much used in the neighbourhood, where it is considered a good cure for rheumatism and other disorders. It is a powerful tonic, and evidently contains a considerable trace of iron." Some of the Dutch tiles have been taken away, and the lower part is now filled with lumber and rubbish instead of clear water, and the spring no longer flows; in this respect presenting a marked contrast to the "old Roman bath" of which we have spoken in our account of the Strand.*

There are one or two buildings in Endell Street deserving of mention, not only on account of their architectural merits, but for their beneficial effects on the humble class of the inhabitants for whom they are specially intended. The first of these is the British Lying-in Hospital, a picturesque Elizabethan structure, erected in 1849, with all the improvements of modern science. This institution was originally established in Brownlow Street, in 1749, but was removed in the above year to its new quarters. It is the oldest lying-in hospital in London. It is solely for affording medical and surgical treatment to married women, who are either admitted into the hospital as in-patients, or are attended at their own homes. Down to the year 1896 some 65,000 in-patients have received the benefits of this institution. The hospital is supported mainly by voluntary subscriptions and donations. The number of patients annually benefited is about 600, and the yearly receipts amount to about £1,500.

Then there are the Baths and Washhouses, a handsome edifice of Italian architecture, opened in 1852, not far from the site of Queen Anne's Bath; and close by are Christ Church, in the Early English style, erected in 1845, and the St. Giles Workhouse. The Protestant Swiss Church should also be mentioned.

In what used to be the southern part of Bloomsbury Street, now merged in Shaftesbury Avenue, are two chapels side by side. The first is the French Protestant Episcopal Church, built in the Early Pointed style, in 1845. This church was founded by Charles II., in the Savoy. Next is Bloomsbury Chapel, built by Sir Morton Peto for the Baptists. Adjoining this stood Bedford Chapel until, in 1896, it was pulled down. It was built, or at all events remodelled, in 1844, and here for some time the late Rev. J. C. M. Bellew officiated, and afterwards the Rev. Stopford Brooke.

St. Giles's Parish enjoys the distinction of having originated the Great Plague of 1665. It is on record that the first persons seized were members of a family living near the top of Drury Lane, where two men, said to have been Frenchmen, were attacked by it, and speedily carried off. The havoc caused by the plague in this parish alone, in the above-named year, amounted to 3,216 deaths, "its malignity," as Dr. Sydenham observes, "being mostly discovered among the poorer sort of people in St. Giles's." The parish registers and rate-books contain many curious entries relating to this sad year; amongst them, the receipt of £50 from Sir Edmundbury Godfrey, and of nearly £500 from Lord Craven, for visiting and relieving the poor.

What used to be Lewknor's Lane, opposite Short's Gardens, near the top of Drury Lane, derived its name from Sir Lewis Lewknor, who owned property here in the reign of James I. From an early date it bore a bad character, and in it Jonathan Wild kept "a house of ill-fame." Constant allusions to its residents occur in the plays of the time of Queen Anne; and Gay, in the *Beggar's Opera*, alludes to it as one of the three places in which ladies of easy virtue might be found. If we may judge from a passage in "Instructions how to find Mr. Curll's Authors," published in Swift's and Pope's Miscellanies, it was also the residence of hack-writers for the press. "At Mr. Summer's, a thief-catcher, in Lewknor's Lane, a man that wrote against the impiety of Mr. Rowe's plays." The thoroughfare (called Lutnor's Lane by Strype) was down to our own day, as it was two hundred years ago, "a very ordinary place." Immorality in the distant past is further indicated by Samuel Butler, who speaks—satirically, of course—of

"The nymphs of chaste Diana's train,
The same with those of Lewknor's Lane."

To which passage Sir Roger L'Estrange adds a note to the effect that it was a "rendezvous and

* See above, Chap. XII., p. 77.

nursery for lewd women, first resorted to by the Roundheads."

The Coal or Cole Yard, on the eastern side of Drury Lane, near its Holborn end, a row of miserable tenements, has of late years been rebuilt, and now rejoices in the name of Goldsmith Street. Here stood the old "Round House," in which highwaymen and other dangerous personages were confined until they could be brought before the sitting magistrates and formally committed to prison. In one of the cells, it is said, Jack Sheppard was ordered to be confined for a night, but before the morning he had made his escape. Other prisoners, however, remained here long enough to cut their names or initials on the walls and window-sills. The Coal Yard is also associated by tradition with another notorious person, for here, according to some, Nell Gwynne was born. The tradition is at best a doubtful one, for "pretty witty Nell" is also said to have first seen the light in Wales.

In Goldsmith Street are the Casual Wards of the St. Giles District Board of Works, which represents the united parishes of St. Giles-in-the-Fields and St. George, Bloomsbury, and in convenient contiguity is the Stone Yard, where those who have enjoyed the hospitality of the ratepayers during the night perform their allotted task before sallying forth to see what Fortune has in store for them. Here also are the Coroner's Court and Mortuary of the united parishes, and an industrial day school of the London School Board. The parish almshouses are in Smart's Buildings, close by.

A part of Oldwick Close, between Lincoln's Inn Fields and Drury Lane, was in possession of the celebrated Sir Kenelm Digby. In 1632 it was bounded on the western side by a ditch and a mud wall, intermixed with a few scattered buildings, among which was the Cockpit Theatre, erected about 1615, but pulled down by the mob in 1617, and all the apparel of the players torn to pieces. On its site arose a second theatre, called the Phœnix, but this again, after a few years, gave way to Drury Lane Theatre, of which we shall have more to say presently. In 1651 most of the property had passed into the possession of the ancient and worthy family of the Welds, of Lulworth Castle, Dorsetshire, the head of which, Mr. Humphrey Weld, built here a handsome residence, the site of which is marked by Wild (formerly Weld) Court and Little Wild Street.

In Parker Street, or Parker's Lane, which runs eastwards from Drury Lane to Little Queen Street, Holborn, were formerly situated the premises and stables of the Dutch ambassador. Here the London County Council has built a Municipal Lodging-house, which quickly became a very popular institution.

The "White Lion," in Drury Lane, in former years, was a place of resort late at night for "swells" of the upper class, and also for market-gardeners and other persons, who resorted to the neighbouring market. As may be imagined, it bore no very good reputation.

At the "Crown Coffee House," in this lane, was held, in former times, an evening assembly called "The Flash Coves' Parliament"—a loose sort of gathering of members of the bar, small tradesmen, and "men about town," each of whom bore the title of some member or other of the Upper House of Parliament: *e.g.*, one would be "Lord Brougham," another "the Duke of Wellington," another "Lord Grey," and so forth. This, however, has long since passed away.

Great Queen Street, which connects Drury Lane with Lincoln's Inn Fields, in a line with Long Acre, was so named in honour of Queen Elizabeth, and stands on the site of the common footpath which anciently separated the south part, or Aldewych Close (properly so called) from the northern division—latterly termed White Hart Close—which extended to Holborn. In the reign of Elizabeth this footpath appears to have become a roadway, but no houses were built on it up to that time. In a map of Westminster, by Norden, dated 1593, no houses are shown eastward of Drury Lane; but building must have commenced very shortly after this, for in Speed's Map of Westminster, in his "Great Britain," the commencement of Great Queen Street is indicated, together with a continuation of the houses on both sides of Drury Lane. In 1623 only fifteen houses appear to have existed on the south side of Great Queen Street, which was then open to the country, and the north side is of later date. Shortly after the Restoration, a new era of building having set in, the houses were finished on the south side of the street, from the designs, it is said, of Inigo Jones and his pupil Webbe. It was at one time called Henrietta Street, in compliment to Henrietta Maria, Queen of Charles I.

"According to one authority," says the author of "Haunted London," "Inigo Jones built Queen Street at the cost of the Jesuits, designing it for a square, and leaving in the middle a niche for the statue of Queen Henrietta. The 'stately and magnificent houses' begun on the north side, near Little Queen Street, were not continued. There were fleurs-de-luce placed on the walls in honour of the queen."

"Great Queen Street, in the time of the Stuarts," says Leigh Hunt, "was one of the grandest and most fashionable parts of the town. The famous Lord Herbert of Cherbury died there. Lord Bristol had a house in it, as also did Lord Chancellor Finch, and the Conway and Paulet families." Mr. Parton, the author of the topographical work on St. Giles's, mentions Paulet House, Cherbury House, and Conway House among the fine mansions still (1822) standing in this street.

The house of Lord Herbert of Cherbury—"the Sir Edward Herbert, the all-virtuous Herbert" of Ben Jonson—was a few doors from Great Wild Street. Here he wrote a part of his celebrated treatise, "De Veritate," and here he died, in 1648, aged seventy-seven, and was buried in St. Giles's Churchyard. The Lord Chancellor Finch mentioned above was the famous Royalist, Sir Heneage Finch, afterwards Earl of Nottingham, who died in 1682. He presided at Lord Stafford's trial, in 1680, and pronounced judgment on that unfortunate nobleman in a speech of great ability. He was the "Omri" of Dryden's "Absalom and Achitophel"—

> "To whom the double blessing does belong,
> With Moses' inspiration, Aaron's tongue."

Many other distinguished personages lived here about this time; "but," says Parton, "the appropriation of each house to its respective inhabitant is, however, a matter of uncertainty, no clue whatever being to be found among our parish records, nor, indeed, any mention made of them to guide our inquiries."

Sir Thomas Fairfax dated a printed proclamation from Great Queen Street, February 12th, 1648, and is supposed, on that account, to have lived in the street. George Digby, second Earl of Bristol, lived in Great Queen Street, says Evelyn (1671); his house was taken by the Commissioners of Trade and Plantations. The Duke of Buckingham, the Earl of Lauderdale, Sir John Finch, Waller the poet, and Colonel Titus (author of "Killing no Murder"), were among its new occupants. At Conway House, in this street, lived Lord Conway, an able soldier, defeated by the Scotch at Newburn. In the year 1733 the Earl of Rochford lived in Great Queen Street; here, too, about that time, lived Lady Dinely Goodyer, and Mrs. Kitty Clive the actress. It would be difficult, at this distant date, to fix upon the exact house in which any of these notabilities resided, for the practice of numbering was not in use till 1764; Burlington Street having been the first and Lincoln's Inn Fields the

OLD HOUSES IN GREAT QUEEN STREET, SOUTH SIDE, 1850.

MIDDLE ROW, ST. GILES'S, ABOUT 1838.

second place in London where it was adopted. Sir Martin Ffolkes, an eminent scholar and antiquary, was born in Great Queen Street in 1690. He was a great numismatist, and the first President of the Royal Society of Antiquaries. He died in 1784.

In 1780 the Gordon Riots may be said to have had their rise in Great Queen Street, the first meeting in favour of the petition presented by Lord George Gordon to Parliament, asking for the repeal of a measure of relief granted to the Roman Catholics, having been held in Coachmakers' Hall, in this street, on the 29th of May. On the rejection of the petition, on the 2nd of June, the mob burnt the Roman Catholic chapels in Duke Street, Lincoln's Inn Fields, and Welbeck Street. On the following days they proceeded to further excesses, and on the 6th of June the house of Mr. Justice Cox, in Great Queen Street, was burned, together with the houses of other magistrates who had become obnoxious. The rest of the story of the Gordon Riots is told in its proper place.

It is recorded that in 1735 Ryan the comedian, whose name was well known in connection with "Bartlemy Fair," was attacked in this street at midnight by a footpad, who fired a pistol in his face, severely wounding him in the jaw, and robbed him of his sword. He was hurt so badly that a performance was given at Covent Garden for his benefit, when the Prince of Wales sent him a purse of a hundred guineas.

No. 51 was until recently the office of Messrs. Kelly and Co., the well-known printers and publishers of the Post Office London and County Directories. Messrs. Kelly removed here from Old Boswell Court, on the demolition of that neighbourhood to clear a space for the new Law Courts; their offices are now at High Holborn.

In this street used to be one of those Homes for Homeless and Destitute Children which have done, of late years, such good service to the State. It was commenced in St. Giles's, in a loft over a cow-shed, about the year 1843, its originator being a Mr. Williams. It then gradually grew into a school, and was located for a time in Arthur Street, St. Giles's, whence it was removed hither in 1860. The premises which were occupied by the boys were formerly a carriage-maker's; they held from 120 to 130 boys, most of whom were gradually drafted off to the *Chichester* and *Arethusa* training-vessels, or to farm-work in the country, chiefly with a view to emigration, the rest being taught various trades and employments. A few years ago the head-quarters of this excellent charity were removed to Shaftesbury Avenue. In addition to the boys' refuge and working boys' home in the Avenue, there are a boys' home at Twickenham, a farm-school at Bisley, girls' homes at Sudbury and Ealing, and a sailors' home in East India Dock Road.

At No. 52 lived Sir Robert Strange, the eminent historical engraver, and adherent of Prince Charles Edward, "the Young Pretender." Strange died in 1792, and here his widow resided for some years afterwards.

Another artist of renown who resided in this street was Opie. He was living here in 1791, when his popularity was at its highest. In Opie's "Memoirs" we get a glimpse of the condition of Great Queen Street, when the roadway was sometimes blocked up with the carriages of his sitters. The great painter removed in 1792, and by the end of the century the street was no longer fashionable, the polite world having migrated westward.

At No. 56 in this street, in a large house, part of which is over the entrance to New Yard, lived James Hoole, the translator of Tasso, Metastasio, and Ariosto, who died in 1803. Born in London in 1727, he devoted his leisure hours to literary pursuits, especially to the study of the Italian language, of which he made himself a perfect master. He was the author of three original tragedies—*Cyrus*, *Timanthes*, and *Cleonice*—which were acted at Covent Garden, and also of some poems, and of a life of John Scott, of Amwell, the Quaker poet. With Hoole lived Hudson the painter, Sir Joshua Reynolds' master.

This house, now a steam pencil-factory, is the only one in the street which retains its original architectural features, all the rest having been either rebuilt or modernised. Worlidge, an artist of some celebrity, who was famous for his etchings in the manner of Rembrandt, died in this house in 1766. Richard Brinsley Sheridan lived in it for some years; many of the letters in Moore's "Life" are addressed to him here. How long Sheridan remained is not known, but it is related that he passed the day in seclusion at his house in Great Queen Street on the occasion of Garrick's funeral, in 1779. The "beautiful Perdita," Mrs. Robinson, the unfortunate favourite of George IV., appears to have lived in this same house shortly after her marriage in 1773; she describes the house in her "Memoirs" as "a large, old-fashioned mansion, the property of the widow of Mr. Worlidge."

Like the seven towns which claim to have given birth to Homer, Great Queen Street is claimed by some writers to have been the locality of the "scene" between Sir Godfrey Kneller and Dr. Radcliffe, which we have already described in our account of the Royal College of Physicians; *

* See Chap. XXI., p. 143.

others, however, fix the abodes of the great physician and Sir Godfrey in Bow Street, Covent Garden.

The most important buildings in Great Queen Street are the Freemasons' Hall and Tavern. These stand on the south side of the street, and present a noble and elegant appearance. The Hall was first built by an architect named Sandby—one of the original members of the Royal Academy—in 1775-6, as its name implies, for the purpose of furnishing one central place for the several lodges of Loyal Masons to hold their meetings and dinners, instead of borrowing, as up to that time had been the custom, the halls of the City companies. Freemasons' Hall, as we are told by Hunter, in his "History of London," was "dedicated" in May, 1776. The Tavern was built in 1786, by William Tyler.

The original Hall, at the back of the Tavern, was built at a cost of about £5,000, which was raised by a tontine. "It was the first house," says Elmes, "built in this country with the appropriate symbols of masonry, and with the suitable apartments for the holding of lodges, the initiating, passing, raising, and exalting of brethren." It was a noble room, although not so large as the present hall. Above the principal entrance was a gallery, with an organ; and at the opposite end was a coved recess, flanked by a pair of fluted Ionic columns, containing a marble statue of the late Duke of Sussex, executed for the Grand Lodge by Mr. E. H. Baily, R.A. Here very many public meetings—political, charitable, and religious—were held; but the last-named have mostly migrated to Exeter Hall, in the Strand.

Among the most important public meetings held at Freemasons' Tavern was one in June, 1824, at which Lords Liverpool, Brougham, Sir J. Mackintosh, Sir Robert Peel, Sir Humphry Davy, Mr. Huskisson, and Mr. Wilberforce, bore public testimony to the services of James Watt as the inventor of the steam-engine, and resolved that a national monument should be erected in his honour in Westminster Abbey. It was on this occasion that Peel frankly and generously acknowledged the debt of gratitude which was due to Watt from himself and his own family, as owing to him their prosperity and wealth. Here public dinners were given to John Philip Kemble, to James Hogg ("the Ettrick Shepherd"), and to many others who, either in the ranks of bravery, science, or literature, have won a name which shall last as long as the English language is spoken.

Of late years the Freemasons' Hall and Tavern have been considerably altered, and in part rebuilt, and now occupy a very much larger area than the original erection. The work was carried out, about the year 1866, under the direction of Mr. F. P. Cockerell, son of the late accomplished Professor of Architecture in the Royal Academy, and the illustrator of the Æginetan Marbles. The Grand Lodge buildings and the Freemasons' Tavern are now entirely separate establishments, although they join; the former, which stands on the west side of the Tavern, contains offices for all the Masonic charities, Grand Secretary's office, and lodge-rooms entirely for the use of the craft. These rooms, as it were, form the frontage of the large hall—a magnificent room, of noble proportions, which, from its internal fittings, may be truly termed the temple of Masonic rites. The room is beautifully decorated, and lit from above. Here have been held the balls and dinners of the Royal Scottish Humane, Artists', and other benevolent societies and institutions.

Mr. Timbs, in his "Curiosities of London," tells us how that St. Paul's, in 604, and St. Peter's, Westminster, in 605, were built by Freemasons; that Gundulph, Bishop of Rochester, who is said to have built the White Tower, governed the Freemasons. Peter of Colechurch, architect of Old London Bridge, was Grand Master. Henry VII., in a lodge of master Masons, founded his chapel at Westminster Abbey. Sir Thomas Gresham, who planned the Royal Exchange, was Grand Master; as was also Inigo Jones, the architect. Sir Christopher Wren, Grand Master, founded St. Paul's with his Lodge of Masons, and the trowel and mallet then used are preserved; and Covent Garden Theatre was founded, in 1808, by the Prince of Wales, in his capacity as Grand Master, assisted by the Grand Lodge. For some reason or other, however, Freemasonry has latterly been under the ban of the Roman Catholic Church.

Two doors eastward of Freemasons' Tavern is a Wesleyan Chapel; and it may be interesting to record here the fact, "not generally known," that at a place of worship on or near this spot on the 22nd of June, 1748, one "David Garrick, of St. Paul's, Covent Garden," was married by his friend, the celebrated Dr. Franklin, to "Eva Maria Violette, of St. James's, Westminster, a celebrated dancer." According, however, to her own statement to Mr. J. T. Smith, when within a few months of her death, Mrs. Garrick was married at the parish church of St. Giles's, and afterwards in the Chapel of the Portuguese Ambassador, in South Audley Street. She also said that she was born at Vienna, on the 29th of February, 1724. If so, at her death she must have been only three months short of entering on her hundredth year. She was buried beside her husband, in Poet's Corner, Westminster Abbey.

Although Mrs. Garrick's maiden name (apparently) is given in the above record of her marriage, there has always been a mystery about her birth. Lee Lewis asserted that she was a natural daughter of Lord Burlington. When Mrs. Garrick heard this, she replied with indignation, "Lee is a liar; Lord Burlington was not my father: but still, I am of noble birth." It was also said that Lord Burlington gave Garrick £10,000 to marry her. This, too, she denied, adding that she had only the interest on £6,000, which was paid to her by the Duke of Devonshire. She died at an advanced age, in October, 1822, in her arm-chair, in the front drawing-room of her house in the Adelphi, having survived her husband forty-three years. She had just ordered her servants to put out on chairs two or three dresses, in order to choose one in which to appear that evening at Drury Lane, it being a private view of Elliston's improvements for the coming season. Mr. J. T. Smith, who knew her personally, speaks thus of her in his "Book for a Rainy Day:"—"Perhaps no lady in public or private life held a more unexceptionable character. She was visited by persons of the first rank; even our late Queen Charlotte, who had honoured her with a visit at Hampton, found her peeling onions for pickling. The gracious queen commanded a knife to be brought, saying, 'I will peel some onions too.' The late King George IV. and King William IV., as well as other branches of the royal family, frequently honoured her with visits." In addressing her servants, however, she was in the habit of using more expletives than would now be thought ladylike in any circle, high or low.

Great Queen Street seems to have been a favourite locality for the residence of actors. Miss Pope, a celebrated actress of the last century, lived for forty years "two doors west of Freemasons' Tavern." She died at Hadley, in 1801. In a house on the south side, occupied before 1830 by Messrs. Allman, the booksellers, died Lewis, the comedian; and at No. 74, now part of Messrs. Wyman and Sons' premises, and known in these days as the "Lincoln's Inn Steam Printing Works," died, in 1826, Edward Prescott Holdway Knight, the comedian, commonly called "Little Knight." Within the walls of Messrs. Wymans' establishment (then Messrs. Cox and Co.'s) Laman Blanchard discharged the duties of a printer's reader side by side with his friend, Douglas Jerrold, who at that time (about the year 1825) was the editor of a periodical called *La Belle Assemblée;* and many other interesting literary traditions cling to the place.

Benjamin Franklin has been described by some writers to have worked at Messrs. Wymans' printing-office as a journeyman printer. This is an error, Franklin having been employed at Mr. Watts's, which was on the south side of Wild Court, a turning out of Great Wild Street, near the western end of Great Queen Street. The press which Franklin recognised as that at which he had worked as a journeyman pressman in London in the years 1723–6, stood in Messrs. Wymans' office, however, for many years. In course of time it was taken down, and passed into the hands of Messrs. Harrild and Sons, who in 1840 parted with it to Mr. J. V. Murray, of New York, on condition that he would secure for them in return a donation to the Printers' Pension Society of London—a highly-deserving institution (its object being the support of aged and decayed printers and widows of printers), and of which they were active members. By Mr. Murray the press was exhibited in Liverpool, and afterwards taken to America. So great was the interest excited by the exhibition of the press, that it was ultimately arranged to have a lecture delivered on "The Life of Benjamin Franklin" during its exhibition. This was accordingly done, and with such success as to enable the committee of the Printers' Pension Society to initiate the "Franklin Pension," amounting to ten guineas per year; and it is interesting to record that one of the early recipients of this small bounty was a very old servant of the firm in whose office he and the press had so long done duty together.

The following inscription is engraved upon the plate affixed to the front of the press:—

"Dr. Franklin's Remarks relative to this Press, made when he came to England as Agent of the Massachusetts, in the year 1768. The Doctor at this time visited the Printing-office of Mr. Watts, of Wild Street, Lincoln's Inn Fields, and, going up to this particular Press (afterwards in the possession of Messrs. Cox and Son, of Great Queen Street, of whom it was purchased), thus addressed the men who were working at it:—'Come, my friends, we will drink together. It is now forty years since I worked like you, at this Press, as a journeyman Printer." The Doctor then sent out for a gallon of Porter, and he drank with them—

'SUCCESS TO PRINTING.'

"From the above it will appear that it is 108 years since Dr. Franklin worked at this identical Press.

"June, 1833."

In 1863 the authorities of the South Kensington Museum of Patents, being engaged in collecting some early memorials relating to the art of printing, made application to Messrs. Wyman for the loan of a companion press to that above described, and which was then in daily use. After being photographed *in situ*, the press was removed to the Museum of Patents, it having been presented to the trustees by Mr. Wyman. This press, of which we here give an engraving, is a fac-simile of the

DUPLICATE OF FRANKLIN'S PRESS.

Franklin press, and there is strong reason to suppose that the celebrated American philosopher worked at it as well as at that which is now a venerated relic in the public museum of Philadelphia.

It may be added that at this printing-office in Great Queen Street, for nearly a century, was executed all the printing relating to our possessions in the East, for the once famous East India Company.

In Great Queen Street also is the Novelty Theatre, opened in 1882 under its present name, which, however, was afterwards changed to Folies Dramatiques, and this to the Jodrell Theatre. Its career has been a somewhat chequered one.

At the eastern end of Great Queen Street, where it debouches upon Lincoln's Inn Fields, now happily, as we have already had occasion to say, dedicated to the public use and enjoyment for ever, is Gate Street, the name of which is very significant of its origin, as being at the top of a lane out of which the horses would have strayed into the high road towards St. Giles's if it had not been for a gate. This thoroughfare leads to a narrow passage called Little Turnstile, which, with another known as the Great Turnstile, at the north-east corner of Lincoln's Inn Fields, opens up a communication between the "Fields" and High Holborn, the continuation of New Oxford Street.

The Great Turnstile, according to Strype, in 1720 was "a great thoroughfare, and a place inhabited by sempsters, shoemakers, and milliners, for which it is of considerable trade and well noted."

Of Whetstone Park, the connecting thoroughfare between the two Turnstiles, we have already spoken in our chapter on Lincoln's Inn Fields. We may, however, add that it was a resort of profligate persons some two centuries since, and that its character at that time is commemorated in the plays of Shadwell, Dryden, and Wycherley :—

> "Where ladies ply, as many tell us,
> Like brimstones in a Whetstone alehouse."

But, if we may believe Strype, its infamous and vicious inhabitants had been banished previous to the year 1720.

One of the small courts between Lincoln's Inn Fields and Holborn, near the eastern end of Whetstone Park, is called Tichborne Court; over the Holborn entrance were, until 1882, when the archway was rebuilt, the arms of the Tichbornes. This property came to the Tichborne family early in the seventeenth century, by the marriage of White Tichborne, Esq., of Aldershot (grandfather of the sixth baronet), with Ann, the daughter and heiress of Richard (or James) Supple, Esq, a member of the Vintners' Company.

THE ARMS OF TICHBORNE.

Among the more celebrated inhabitants of the parish of St. Giles's are, Andrew Marvell, whom we have already mentioned, and the profligate Countess of Shrewsbury, concerning whom Horace Walpole tells us that she held the horse of Villiers, Duke of Buckingham, while the latter killed her husband in a duel.

Among the old families in St. Giles's, Parton names the Spencers, or De Spencers, after whom the great ditch which ran along the southern side of the parish was called Spencer's Ditch or "Dig."

The name of this drain in more recent times was Cock and Pie Ditch.

The "History of St. Giles's-in-the-Fields," by Mr. Parton, contains a variety of curious and interesting matter, and we have drawn largely upon it in these pages. But we have not adopted all his out so minutely as to show each man's possession in the parish, and every garden-plot delineated, with flower-beds, parterres, and bordered walks, just as if the gardener of William III. or Queen Anne had been alive in the Wars of the Roses! Mr. Parton gives no authority for these details; and it is to be

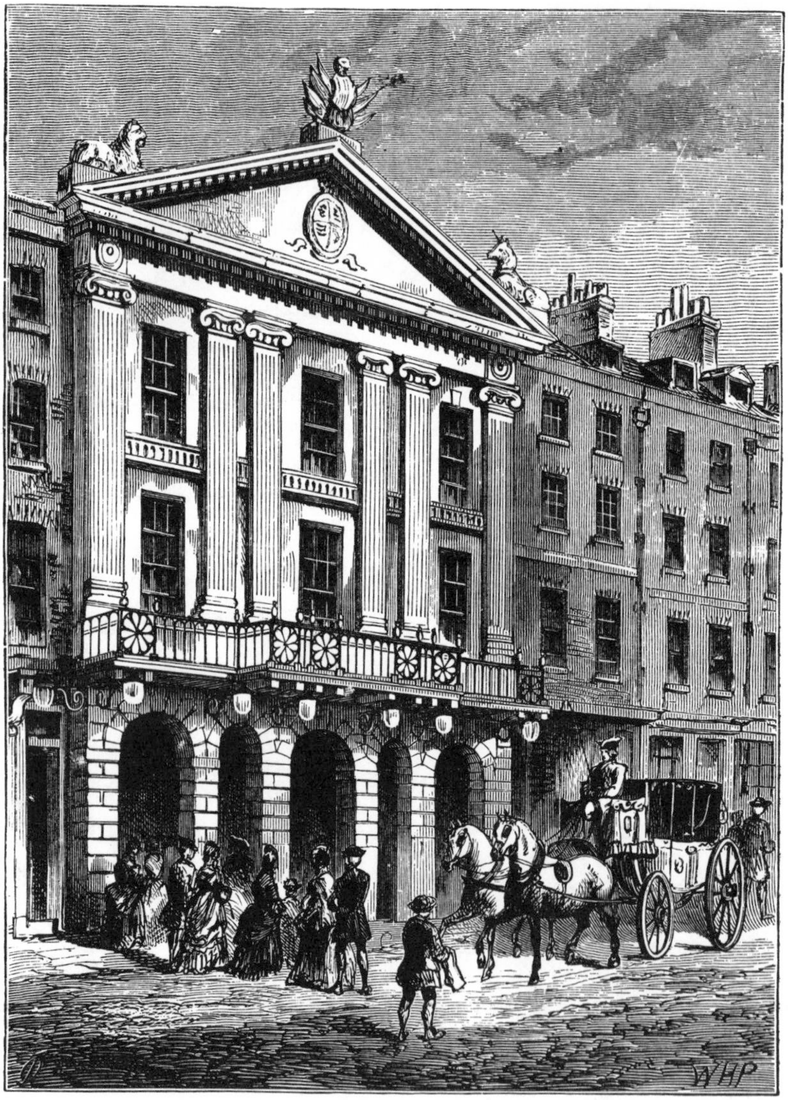

FRONT OF OLD DRURY LANE THEATRE.

statements, having our confidence in him as a topographer and historian a little shaken by the fact that he gives in it a plan or map of the parish as it was in the thirteenth century—in other words, two centuries and a half, at the least, earlier than the map of London by Ralph Aggas, which is the oldest authority known to antiquaries, and from which, it is clear, on a close inspection, that he has borrowed many of his details. It is, indeed, made feared that he allowed his antiquarian zeal to carry him in this one matter—like Herodotus of old—out of the domain of fact into the airy regions of fiction. In other respects, however, he would appear to have been a trusty chronicler, and his work from first to last is full of interest.

We may conclude our notice of St. Giles's with the following paragraph from a publication which does not often mislead, or misrepresent facts:—

DRURY LANE CELEBRITIES.

BETTERTON. GARRICK. MACKLIN.

MRS. PRITCHARD. MRS. ROBINSON.

"As lately as the year 1767," says a writer in the *Gentleman's Magazine*, "another mass-house was discovered in Hog Lane, near the Seven Dials," and the officiating priest was "condemned to perpetual imprisonment"—simply for saying mass and giving the communion to a sick person. After four years' imprisonment his sentence was "commuted into exile for life." At the end of the last century, if not early in the present, Dr. Archer, a well-known Roman Catholic divine, and the author of several volumes of sermons, said mass in the garret of a small public-house in St. Giles's, kept by an Irishman who was not ashamed of his religion. This sounds strange in our ears in the present state of general toleration and liberty; but more than a century before, in 1663, Pepys records the fact that "a priest was taken in his vestments officiating somewhere in Holborn the other day, and was committed [to prison] by Mr. Secretary Morris, according to law."

CHAPTER XXVIII.

DRURY LANE THEATRE.

"I sing of the singe of Miss Drury the First,
And the birth of Miss Drury the Second."—*Rejected Addresses.*

The Original Playhouse in Covent Garden—The Players Imprisoned in the Gate House—The Cockpit Theatre—Killigrew's Theatre in Drury Lane—Betterton's Early Triumphs—The Players first styled "His Majesty's Servants"—Testimonial to Mrs. Bracegirdle—Lovely "Nancy" Oldfield—Colley Cibber as Manager and Dramatist—Garrick at Drury Lane—Kitty Clive, the Comic Actress—A Batch of Fortunate Actresses—Edmund and Charles Kean—Mrs. Nisbet, Macready, and Madame Celeste—Anecdote of Madame Malibran—Michael Balfe, and the Statue erected to his Honour—Salaries of Celebrated Players—Changes and Vicissitudes of "Old Drury"—The New Theatre closed by Order of the Lord Chamberlain—Mrs. Siddons' *Début*—The Kembles—Sheridan's Habit of Procrastination—The Theatre again destroyed by Fire—Coolness of Sheridan—The "Rejected Addresses"—Mr. Whitbread and the Colonnade—Rebuilding and Opening of the New Theatre—Its subsequent Vicissitudes—Van Amburgh and his Wild Beasts—The Theatre opened as an Opera-house.

In speaking of Drury Lane Theatre there arises a frequent source of confusion in the fact that it had no especial name till the middle of the eighteenth century; being in the neighbourhood of Covent Garden, where the quality then resided, it was often styled "The Covent Garden Theatre." Thus Pepys, writing under date 1662: "To Lincoln's Inn Fields, and, it being too soon to go to dinner, I walked up and down, and looked upon the outside of the new theatre building in Covent Garden, which will be very fine." The late Mr. Richardson, of coffee-house celebrity, was in possession of a ticket inscribed, "For the Music at the Play House in Covent Garden, Tuesday, March 6, 1704"—nearly thirty years before Covent Garden Theatre, properly so called, was opened. It was also styled "The King's Theatre," and "The King's House;" Killigrew and his company being "His Majesty's Servants," while Davenant and his rival company were known by the name of "The Duke's Servants."

Guest writes, "I have not met with any play which is said on its title-page to have been acted in the Theatre Royal Drury Lane till after the division of the company in 1695; nor am I aware that the theatre is called 'Drury Lane' in any preface of the time. Even in 1704, *Love the Leveller* is said on its title-page to have been acted at the Theatre Royal in Brydges Street, Covent Garden. In 1719-20, an order from the Lord Chamberlain's office is addressed to 'The Managers of the Theatre in Drury Lane, in Covent Garden.'"

It is worthy of note that, although there were other theatres in London at an earlier date, there was, according to Guest, in the time of Shakespeare one at least outside the walls—namely, the Phœnix or Cockpit, on the eastern side of Drury Lane, the site of which was afterwards defined by Pitt Court—formerly Cockpit Alley. The company who acted there were styled "The Queen's Servants." In 1647, when an act was passed for the suppression of stage plays, the Cockpit was converted from the error of its ways into a school-room, but, in spite of the supremacy of the Puritans, its existence as a seat of learning was brief; it backslided, and again became a place of profane amusement, until in 1649, when the Puritan soldiers broke into the playhouse during a performance, routed the audience, and broke up the seats and stage. Nor was this all. Dr. Doran says that "the players, some of them the most accomplished of their day, were paraded through the streets in all their stage finery, and clapped into the Gate-house and other prisons, whence they were only too glad to escape, after much unseemly treatment, at the cost of all the theatrical property which they had carried on their backs." They had already experienced similar treatment in 1617, in a popular outbreak, when their clothes and properties were torn up by the mob, for what cause is not apparent.

Subsequently, after General Monk's arrival in London, the theatrical standard was raised again, and the drama commenced its new career at the Cockpit, with Rhodes for its "master"—managers being not then known—and Betterton as his pupil and apprentice.

Pepys thus writes in his "Diary," November 20th, 1660: "This morning I found my lord in bed late, he having been with the king, queen, and princesses at the Cockpit all night, where General Monk treated them, and after supper a play." It may be added that the original name of the "pit" in our theatres was the "cock-pit"—a word strongly corroborating the fact that our earliest places of such entertainment were used for lower sports before being applied to the purposes of the dramatic muse.

The principal actors at the Cockpit were Betterton and the beautiful youth, Edward Kynaston, who generally performed women's parts, before female actresses were permitted on the stage. Of Kynaston Pepys writes, Aug. 18: "Capt. Ferrers took me and Creed to the Cockpitt play—the first that I have had time to see since my coming from sea. *The Loyall Subject*, where one Kynaston, a boy, acted the duke's sister, but made the loveliest lady that ever I saw in my life." "Jan. 7. Tom and I and my wife to the theatre, and there saw *The Silent Woman.* Among other things here Kynaston, the boy, had the good turn to appear in three shapes: first as a poor woman, in ordinary clothes, to please 'Morose;' then in fine clothes, as a gallant, and in them was clearly the prettiest woman in the whole house; and lastly as a man, and then likewise did appear the handsomest man in the whole house."

Pepys tells us that the old actors were in possession of the Cockpit in August, 1660; also that he saw *The Cardinal* acted there, October 2, 1662; but the theatre was small, and seems to have soon been superseded. At all events, nothing further is known of its history. There is a chance allusion to it in *The Muse's Looking-glass* of Randolphe, wherein the following dialogue occurs:—

> "*Mrs. Flowerdew.* It was a zealous prayer
> I heard a brother make concerning playhouses.
> *Bird.* For charity, what is it?
> *F.* That the Globe,
> Wherein (quoth he) reigns a whole world of vice,
> Had been consum'd; the Phœnix burnt to ashes."

We hear very little of the other actors of the Cockpit, save that one Allen became a major in Charles's army, and acted as quartermaster-general at Oxford; and that two others, named Perkins and Sumner, finding their occupation gone, "kept house together at Clerkenwell, where they died some years before the Restoration."

Soon after the Restoration Thomas Killigrew, Page of Honour, and subsequently Master of the Revels, to Charles I., purchased from the Earl of Bedford a lease for forty-one years of a piece of ground situated in the two parishes of St. Martin's-in-the-Fields and St. Paul's, Covent Garden. On this site, until then known as the "Riding Yard," he erected, we are told, at a cost of £1,500, a theatre, the dimensions of which were 112 feet by 59 feet, and which was opened in 1663. The following is a copy of the first playbill issued:—

> "By His Majesty his company of Comedians, at the New Theatre in Drury Lane. This day, being Thursday, April 8th, 1663, will be acted a comedy called *The Humorous Lieutenant.* The King, Mr. Wintersell; Demetrius, Mr. Hart; Seleucus, Mr. Burt; Leontius, Major Mohun; Lieutenant, Mr. Clun; Celia, Mrs. Marshall. The Play will begin at Three o'clock exactly. Boxes, 4s.; Pit, 2s. 6d.; Middle Gallery, 1s. 6d.; Upper Gallery, 1s."

This comedy (by Beaumont and Fletcher) is mentioned in Pepys' "Diary," in the following terms:—"To the King's House, and there saw *The Humorous Lieutenant*—a silly play, I think—only the spirit in it that grows very tall, and then sinks again to nothing, having two heads breeding upon one, and then Knipp's singing, did please us. Here, in a box above, we spied Mrs. Pierce; and going out, they called us, and so we staid for them; and Knipp took us all in, and brought us to Nelly, a most pretty woman, who acted the great part, 'Cœlia,' to-day, very fine, and did it pretty well. I kissed her, and so did my wife; and a mighty pretty soul she is."

Of Killigrew it is recorded by Pepys that "when a boy he would go to the 'Red Bull,' and when the man cried to the boys, 'Who will go to be a devil, and he shall see the play for nothing?' then would he go in, and be a devil on the stage, and so get to see plays." It may here be remarked by way of parenthesis that the "Red Bull" which stood at the end of St. John Street, Clerkenwell, was, according to tradition, the playhouse before which Shakespeare held gentlemen's horses.

Dr. Doran writes:—"In December, 1661, there is a crowded house at the theatre in Lincoln's Inn Fields, to see young Mr. Betterton play the Dane's part in *Hamlet;* charming Mistress Saunderson acting 'Ophelia.' Old ladies and gentlemen flock in crowds to witness it, and the streets are fairly blocked with the lumbering carriages; among the carriage folk being Mrs. Palmer, destined to become, next year, Countess of Castlemaine." "It's beyond imagination," whispers Mr. Pepys to his neighbour, who answers only with a long-drawn "Hush!" "Mr. Betterton," rejoins Pepys, in the complacent tone of one qualified to judge, "is the best actor in the world, and Miss Saunderson is the best lady on the stage. It is a pity they are not married."

Fifty years after these early triumphs Mr. and Mrs. Betterton, having made their fortune as well as their fame, are living in Great Russell Street, Covent Garden, in a well-appointed house. In April, 1710, the former retired from the stage, fixing the 13th as his benefit-night at the Haymarket Theatre, then newly built. He died within forty-eight hours afterwards.

Actors were first known as "His Majesty's Servants" in 1603, having been previously styled "The Servants of the Lord Chamberlain." It may be mentioned here that as "His Majesty's Servants" the actors were entitled to wear, and did wear, the royal livery of scarlet. The last actor who wore it was Baddeley, who gave the annual "cake" to the green-room of Drury Lane. He was, we believe, the original "Moses" in *The School for Scandal.* A portrait of Baddeley, in his red waistcoat, used to be seen in poor old "Paddy" Green's collection at "Evans's." At this period dramatic entertainments began at one and terminated at three o'clock in the afternoon.

In 1663, as we see by the playbill before quoted, fashion had altered the hour of commencement to three p.m.; in 1667 it had crept on to four o'clock, until by degrees the evening came to be recognised as the most appropriate time for such amusements. Mohun and Hart had both held commissions in the army, and excelled in tragic and heroic parts. The former was a boon companion and favourite of Rochester. "Becky Marshal" is frequently mentioned by Pepys, and always with praise, as also is Mrs. Knipp, of whom Killigrew told him, "Knipp is like to make the best actor that ever come upon the stage, she understanding so well, that they are going to give her thirty pounds a year more."

Time and space alike, however, would be wanting to enumerate all the dramatic celebrities who have immortalised themselves upon the boards of "Old Drury;" their name is "Legion." As they pass in review before our imagination we can only briefly particularise a few of the most remarkable.

Here Thomas Betterton, who, as we have seen, served his apprenticeship at the Cockpit, and was long the chief attraction of the theatre in Lincoln's Inn Fields, took a farewell benefit in 1709, preliminary to the one before mentioned, being then in his seventy-fifth year. As admirable in his private as in his professional character; a devoted husband to a wife who, herself an actress, was as virtuous as she was beautiful; generous and charitable to excess to his poorer "brethren of the buskin;" the son of the cook of Charles I. fairly earned the universal esteem in which he was held, and which procured him a royal funeral in Westminster Abbey. Here Mrs. Bracegirdle, equally celebrated for her beauty and her coldness, drove troops of scented fops to distraction.

There seems little doubt of her attachment to the unfortunate Mountford, who acted "Alexander" to her "Statira," and who was murdered by Captain Hill, one of her many rejected suitors. Hill and Lord Mohun having made an abortive attempt to carry off Mrs. Bracegirdle, the former (as we have seen) vowed vengeance upon Mountford, whom he regarded as the cause of the lady's coldness. He accordingly laid wait for the actor in the street, and struck him. Mountford demanded "what that was for;" upon which (according to the dying man's deposition) Hill drew his sword and ran it through the actor's body.

At Drury Lane flourished the lovely "Nancy" Oldfield, who quitted the bar of the "Mitre" for the stage, and whose notorious intimacy with General Churchill, cousin of the great Duke of Marlborough, obtained for her a grave in Westminster Abbey. Persons of rank and distinction contended for the honour of bearing her pall, and her remains lay in state for three days in the Jerusalem Chamber!

Here, too, Barton Booth stimulated the rival parties of Whigs and Tories in Addison's famous tragedy of *Cato.* Of this piece Johnson remarks, in his "Life of Addison:" "The whole nation was at that time on fire with faction. The Whigs applauded every line in which liberty was mentioned as a satire on the Tories, and the Tories echoed every clap, to show that the satire was unfelt. The story of Bolingbroke is well known. He called Booth to his box, and gave him fifty guineas for defending the cause of liberty so well against a perpetual dictator."

Is not Drury Lane Theatre also intimately associated with the name of Colley Cibber, successful manager and dramatist, and for twenty-seven years Poet Laureate? His annual birthday and New Year odes, all religiously preserved in the *Gentleman's Magazine*, are so invariably bad that his friends asserted that he wrote them as so many jokes. The *London Magazine* for 1737 contains the following epigram:—

"ON SEEING TOBACCO-PIPES LIT WITH ONE OF THE LAUREATE'S ODES.

"While the soft song that warbles George's praise
From pipe to pipe the living flame conveys,
Critics who long have scorn'd must now admire;
For who can say his ode now wants its fire?"

Drury Lane at this time exhibited a perfect constellation of talent. Quin, Macklin, Garrick, Mrs. Clive, and Mrs. Pritchard, with others of subordinate merit, formed a company which has rarely been equalled. It must have been a cruel blow to Quin, long the favourite tragedian of the town, to see himself rivalled by Macklin, and subsequently surpassed by Garrick. In spite of the contempt with which he affected to regard the latter, he expressed his own secret misgivings in his first burst of indignation at the rapid success of the rising actor:—"If this young fellow be right, then *we* have all been wrong."

From 1747 to 1776 Drury Lane owned the sway of David Garrick, the English Roscius, of whom Horace Walpole says: "All the run is now after Garrick, a wine-merchant who is turned player. The Duke of Argyll says he is superior to Betterton." This, however, was not the opinion of the cynical Horace, although Alexander Pope's verdict on Garrick was, "That young man never had his equal as an actor, and he will never have a rival." And Dr. Johnson awarded him a still higher meed of praise in saying: "Here is a man who has advanced the dignity of his profession. Garrick has made a player a higher character."

Drury Lane made the fortune of the ugly, witty, and most popular comic actress, Kitty Clive, thus celebrated by Horace Walpole—

> "Here liv'd the laughter-loving dame—
> A matchless actress—Clive her name;
> The comic muse with her retir'd,
> And shed a tear when she expir'd."

To which Peter Pindar (Dr. Wolcot), who was a devoted admirer of Mrs. Jordan, retorted—

> "Know Comedy is hearty—all alive;
> Truth and thy trumpet seem not to agree;
> The sprightly lass no more expir'd with Clive
> Than Dame Humility will do with thee."

Here the silver-toned Mrs. Billington appeared in the opera of *Rosetta*. Haydn the composer, who admired this lady greatly, observed of Sir Joshua Reynolds' celebrated picture of her—where she is represented as "St. Cecilia" listening to the heavenly choir—"It is a very fine likeness, but there is a strange mistake in the picture. You have painted her listening to the angels; you ought to have represented the angels listening to her."

Old Drury witnessed the farewell performance of Miss Farren (Countess of Derby) in 1797, just before she exchanged the buskin for a coronet; witnessed, too, the first appearance of Harriet Mellon, in 1795, and her last, in February, 1815—for in the previous month she had wedded Mr. Coutts, the banker. In 1827, Mrs. Coutts having been then five years a widow, married the Duke of St. Albans, at that time in his twenty-seventh year. Drury Lane saw the rise of the long and devoted attachment of the Duke of Clarence to Mrs. Jordan, and the short-lived passion of George, Prince of Wales, for the lovely Mrs. Robinson, better known as "Perdita," the character in which she appeared on the evening when she captivated her royal admirer.

Here, in the present century, Edmund Kean ran his brilliant but erratic career, and his more estimable, although less highly gifted, son Charles made his *début* as "Young Norval." Here, in 1828, Joe Grimaldi, prince of clowns and of good fellows, took his farewell of the stage, where, the following year, Mrs. Nisbet (subsequently Lady Boothby), made her first curtsey to a London audience; and there for several years the imperious Macready rode roughshod over supers, brother-actors, and managers, until, after a personal assault upon the lessee, he transferred his services to the rival house. Neither must the name of Madame Celeste be omitted from the list; for, although it was not Drury Lane Theatre to which she owed her reputation as an actress, it was nevertheless there that she made her first appearance in London, in the ballad of *La Bayadere* in 1830. This lady may fairly be ranked among the wonders of her age, for in 1874 we find her performing the part of the Indian huntress in *The Green Bushes* with all the vigour and pathos and much of the freshness of her youth. During those four-and-forty years generations of great actresses had arisen, shone as stars for a score of years, and passed away into oblivion, marriage, or death; but Celeste still survived and flourished—half a century after her *début*—bidding defiance alike to old Time and new fashions, as if warranted, like Tennyson's brook, to "go on for ever."

The two first operas of Michael Balfe—*The Siege of Rochelle* and *The Maid of Artois*—were produced at Drury Lane in 1835-6. The gifted and ill-fated Madame Malibran sustained the principal part in *The Maid of Artois* a few months before her premature death. In Bunn's "History of the Stage" we are told an amusing anecdote of the famous vocalist in this character. She was supposed in the last act to be perishing with thirst in the desert; the scene was long and exhausting, the lady in delicate health. She therefore proposed to Bunn that he should somehow convey a pint of porter to her in the desert, promising him in that case an *encore* to the finale. "So," says Bunn, "I arranged that behind the pile of drifted sand on which she sinks exhausted a small aperture should be made in the stage, and through that aperture a pewter-pint of porter was conveyed to the parched lips of this rare child of song, which so revived her, after the terrible exertion of the scene, that she electrified the audience, and had strength to repeat the finale."

INTERIOR OF DRURY LANE THEATRE, 1804.

Bunn having paid Malibran £125 for each of fifteen performances in one month, she, after much persuasion, consented to sing for him throughout the next month for the sum of £1,000, but added, "For goodness' sake, do not let any one know I am singing on such terms!"

The name of Balfe, not the least eminent of British composers, is intimately associated with Drury Lane, from the time of the young Irishman's unassuming *début* in the orchestra to his subsequent triumphs as a successful composer of English, French, and Italian opera. The works of Michael Balfe are appreciated not only in England, but in France, Germany, and Italy. The statue erected to his honour in the vestibule of this temple, where so many of his triumphs have been achieved—a memorial to which numbers of the most distinguished patrons and professors of music, literature, and the drama, both native and foreign, added their quota—will be a lasting proof of the estimation in which he has been held both at home and abroad.

It is worth while to notice how the salaries of actors have been steadily rising during the last two centuries. We have Pepys' authority that Mrs.

"RICH'S GLORY." *After the Original Caricature.* (*See page* 227.)

Knipp, "who was like to make the best actor of her time," had her salary increased £30 a year. A century later Garrick, as head of his company, drew the highest salary—*i.e.*, £16 16s. a week. Yet fifty years, and Miss Farren, "the Oldfield of her day," is receiving £31 10s. a week, while scarcely a decade afterwards we find Edmund Kean drawing double that sum nightly.

It was remarked about fifty years ago by a well-known writer "that Malibran drew five times the salary of the Colonial Secretary, the President of America was not so well paid as Ellen Tree, or the Premier of Great Britain as Mr. Macready." What would he have said in 1874, when Madame Christine Nilsson received £200 a night at Drury Lane, and Madame Patti demanded and was paid £800 for singing six songs at the Liverpool Musical Festival?

"Old Drury," viewed simply as a building, has experienced many changes and vicissitudes. In 1672 it was burnt to the ground, and the company migrated to the theatre in Lincoln's Inn Fields, until the completion of a new building, designed by Sir Christopher Wren.

The new theatre was opened in 1674, with a prologue and epilogue by Dryden, who, as shown by Mr. R. P. Collier, in Vol. IV. of the Shakespeare Society's Papers, was joined with Killigrew, Mohun, &c., in the speculation of what was then colloquially termed "the New Play House."

In 1707 this theatre, of which Christopher Rich was then the patentee, was temporarily closed, by order of the Lord Chamberlain, in consequence of the violent quarrels between the proprietors and the actors. It subsequently passed into the hands of Willer, Dogget, Cibber, and Booth. In 1714 a life patent was granted to Sir R. Steele, which five years afterwards was revoked. In 1747, when Lacy and Garrick entered into partnership, the latter revived here the performance of Shakespeare's plays; the prologue on that occasion being written, as every Englishman knows, by Dr. Johnson.

In 1780, during the Gordon Riots, a "No Popery" mob got up a row in the theatre, to which they did considerable damage. The objects of their fury were "the papists and Frenchmen" whom Garrick had engaged to dance in a grand spectacular piece entitled *The Chinese Festival.* His Majesty George III., who happened to be present the night of the riot, seemed, it is said, rather amused than otherwise!

In 1775 the afterwards famous Mrs. Siddons, then in her twentieth year, made her first appearance at Drury Lane, in the character of "Portia," in *The Merchant of Venice.* She seems to have excited but little notice at this time, and retired to the provinces the following year. It was not until 1782, when her performance at the Bath Theatre had excited general admiration, that she obtained a re-engagement at Drury Lane—which she used often to call "the wilderness"—and where her brother, John Kemble, made his *début* as Hamlet, in 1783. In 1776, when Garrick retired from the profession, Messrs. Sheridan, Linley, and Ford became the proprietors of the theatre which he had rendered so justly celebrated. It was pulled down in 1791, and rebuilt, the company meanwhile performing at the Haymarket. In 1794 the new theatre—which was designed by Mr. Holland, and is said to have been a model of elegance and beauty—opened, with every prospect of a long and brilliant career. For some years subsequently the gifted Kemble family—John and Charles, with their unapproachable sister, Mrs. Siddons—were the principal attraction at Drury Lane, and the fortunes of the theatre were seriously affected by their withdrawal, in 1803.

We are told in the "Memoirs" of Sheridan that his translation of *The Death of Rolla*, under the title of *Pizarro*, brought him in £25,000 in five weeks. The *Era Almanack* mentions a curious instance of Sheridan's inveterate habit of procrastination:—"At the time the house was overflowing, on the first night's performance of *Pizarro*, all that was written of the play was actually rehearsing; and, incredible as it may appear, until the end of the fourth act, neither Mrs. Siddons, nor Charles Kemble, nor Barrymore, had all their speeches for the fifth. Mr. Sheridan was up-stairs in the prompter's-room, where he was writing the last part of the play while the earlier parts were acting, and every ten minutes he brought down as much of the dialogue as he had done, piecemeal, into the green-room, abusing himself and his negligence, and making a thousand winning and soothing apologies for having kept the performers so long in such painful suspense."

In 1809 Drury Lane Theatre was again destroyed by fire. Sheridan, at the time of the conflagration, was at the House of Commons, which voted an immediate adjournment when the disastrous news arrived; though Sheridan himself protested against such an interruption of public business on account of his own or any other private interests. He went thither, however, in all haste, and whilst seeing his own property in flames, sat down with his friend Barry in a coffee-house opposite, to a bottle of port, coolly remarking, in answer to some friendly expostulation, that it was "hard if a man could not drink a glass of wine by his own fire!"

The fire which burnt down "Old Drury" was

not altogether profitless to the world of poetry, though so heavy a blow to the dramatic muse, for it proved the immediate cause of the appearance of the "Rejected Addresses"—the joint production of Horace and James Smith—one of the most popular contributions to modern light literature. The history of the book was as follows:—In the month of August, 1812, there appeared in the daily newspapers an advertisement to the effect that the committee for rebuilding Drury Lane Theatre were anxious to promote a "free and fair competition" for an address to be spoken upon the re-opening of the theatre on the 10th of October ensuing, and that they had therefore announced to the public that they would be glad to receive such compositions, addressed to their secretary. Some hundred and twelve compositions were sent in—good, bad, and indifferent; and the two Smiths, seizing on the occasion, put together and published in a small volume twenty-one such imaginary addresses or prologues, imitating in the most delicate and graceful manner the styles of the chief writers of the day. The book, as soon as published, sold like wild-fire, and ran through very many editions before the end of the year, and soon established itself as an English classic. Among those writers who were thus travestied were Lord Byron, Scott, Crabbe, Wordsworth, Thomas Moore, Dr. Johnson, "Monk" Lewis, Fitzgerald, William Cobbett, and Samuel T. Coleridge. Of all the imitations, however, that of Sir Walter was universally pronounced the best; and as it contains a vivid description of the scene of conflagration, though in mock-heroic style, we may be pardoned for drawing upon it here rather largely.

First we have a picturesque description of London in darkness; next, we are thus introduced to the outbreak of the fire in the early morning—by a poetical licence, of course, since it happened, in fact, in the evening:—

"As Chaos, which, by heavenly doom,
Had slept in everlasting gloom,
Started with terror and surprise
When light first flashed upon her eyes:
So London's sons in nightcap woke,
In bedgown woke her dames;
For shouts were heard 'mid fire and smoke,
And twice ten thousand voices spoke—
'The Playhouse is in flames!'
And, lo! where Catherine Street extends,
A fiery tail its lustre lends
To every window-pane;
Blushes each spout in Martlet Court,
And Barbican, moth-eaten fort,
And Covent Garden kennels sport
A bright ensanguined drain."

Then follows the description of the arrival of the fire-engines, quite in the style of Sir Walter Scott in "Marmion" or "The Lady of the Lake:"—

"The summoned firemen woke at call,
And hied them to their stations all;
* * * * *
The engines thundered through the street,
Fire-hook, pipe, bucket, all complete,
And torches glared, and clattering feet
Along the pavement paced.
And one, the leader of the band,
From Charing Cross along the Strand,
Like stag by beagles hunted hard,
Ran till he stopped at Vinegar Yard.
The burning badge his shoulder bore,
The belt and oilskin cap he wore,
The cane he had his men to bang,
Showed foreman of the British gang.
His name was Higginbottom: now
'Tis meet that I should tell you how
The others came in view:
The Hand in Hand the race begun,
Then came the Phœnix and the Sun,
The Exchange, where old insurers run,
The Eagle, where the new."

And then we have the fire itself brought before us in all its sensational details:—

"A sadder scene was ne'er disclosed;
Without, within, in hideous show,
Devouring flames resistless glow,
And blazing rafters downwards go,
And never halloo, 'Heads below!'
Nor notice give at all.
The firemen, terrified, are slow
To bid the pumping torrent flow,
For fear the roof should fall.
Back, Robins, back! Crump, stand aloof!
Whitford, keep near the walls!
Huggins, regard your own behoof!
For, lo! the blazing, rocking roof
Down, down, in thunder, falls.
An awful pause succeeds the stroke,
And o'er the ruins volumed smoke,
Rolling around its pitchy shroud,
Concealed them from the astonished crowd.
At length the mist awhile was cleared,
When, lo! amidst the wreck upreared,
Gradual a moving head appeared,
And Eagle firemen knew
'Twas Joseph Muggins—name revered!—
The foreman of their crew.
Loud shouted all, in signs of woe,
'A Muggins! to the rescue, ho!'
And poured the hissing tide.
Meanwhile, Joe Muggins fought amain,
And strove and struggled, all in vain
For, rallying but to fall again,
He tottered, sunk, and died."

Last follows a picture, too often seen in other and lesser conflagrations, of the death of a gallant fireman, told with a mock-heroic power which never certainly has been surpassed.

Of the brothers Smith, the authors of these charming parodies, we have already spoken in our description of Craven Street, Strand. It will be therefore enough to add here the fact that, having shone as wits in London society for more than a quarter of a century, they died, James in 1839, and Horace ten years later. Lord Byron himself, in spite of being one of the authors so pleasantly satirised in the volume, called the "Rejected Addresses" by far the best thing of the kind since the "Rolliad." Slight and small as was the volume, it was reviewed at considerable length by Lord Jeffrey in the *Edinburgh Review*, while the *Quarterly* criticised it in company with forty of the "Addresses" which had really been "rejected" on the occasion, pronouncing it a model of "humour, good-humour, discrimination, and good taste." It may be of interest, and an encouragement to young authors, to learn that the copyright, which in the first instance Murray refused to buy for twenty, was sold by the brothers for upwards of a thousand pounds! The book has been republished in America, and is read with delight wherever the English language is known. The imitations of Wordsworth ("The Baby's Début"), Cobbett ("The Hampshire Farmer's Address"), Southey ("The Rebuilding"), Coleridge ("Play House Musings"), Crabbe ("The Theatre"), Lord Byron (the first stanzas of "Cui Bono?"), the songs entitled "Drury Lane Hustings" and "The Theatrical Alarm Bell" (imitations of the then editor of the *Morning Post*), and the travesties of *Macbeth*, *George Barnwell*, and *The Stranger*, were all written by James Smith; the rest, including the parody of Sir Walter Scott, by Horace.

The present edifice—the fourth erected on the site—modelled upon the plan of the great theatre at Bordeaux, by Mr. Wyatt, the architect, was opened in 1812, with a prologue written by Lord Byron. In 1831 the Doric portico in Catherine Street, and the colonnade in Little Russell Street, were added to the structure. It is not a little singular that the necessity of such a colonnade had been thus humorously brought under the notice of the Building Committee as far back as the year 1812, in one of the "Rejected Addresses," in the following lines, in imitation of S. T. Coleridge:—

"Oh, Mr. Whitbread! fie upon you, sir!
I think you should have built a colonnade.
When tender beauty, looking for her coach,
Protrudes her gloveless hand, perceives the shower,
And draws the tippet closer round her throat,
And ere she mount the step, the oozing mud
Sinks through her pale kid slipper.
On the morrow
She coughs at breakfast, and her gruff papa
Cries, 'There you go! this comes of playhouses!'
To build no portico is penny wise;
Heaven grant it prove not in the end pound foolish!"

The new building was pronounced by the imitators of Mr. Cobbett, in the "Rejected Addresses," "not a gimcrack palace, not a Solomon's temple, not a frost-work of Brobdingnag filagree, but a plain, honest, homely, industrious, wholesome, brown-brick playhouse"—a "large, comfortable house, thanks to Mr. Whitbread." The theatre, in 1818, was under a committee of noblemen and gentlemen, among whom were Lord Yarmouth (afterwards Marquis of Hertford) and Lord Byron, the latter of whom, however, soon after being appointed, left England, never to return.

For many years after that date the great national theatre ran an erratic and, for the most part, disastrous career, having been not inaptly compared to a syren luring adventurous lessees to ruin and bankruptcy. In the agony of desperation it has worn "motley," caught eagerly at every *bizarre* attraction, and been—

"Everything by turns, and nothing long;"

a monster concert-hall, a French hippodrome, and even an arena for the sports of Van Amburgh and his wild beasts, with spasmodic intervals of pantomime and legitimate drama. Sad to relate, we have it on the authority of Mr. Bunn, the lessee, that Van Amburgh was a greater success, in a pecuniary point of view, than Mr. Macready.

For several seasons it was the home of English opera, a class of entertainment which has never been appreciated as it deserves among our countrymen, though frequent attempts have been made to give it a position equal to that enjoyed by Italian opera. It may be observed here that Clara Novello, later the Countess Gugliucci, made a brilliant *début* at Drury Lane, in 1843, as "Sappho."

After the destruction by fire of Her Majesty's Theatre, in 1867, "Old Drury" rose greatly in the social scale, having been advanced to the dignity of the opposition opera-house to Covent Garden. This, however, was only a temporary arrangement until the new opera-house should be built. In 1879 the lesseeship of the theatre passed into the hands of Mr. (afterwards Sir) Augustus Harris, under whose management "Old Drury" has fully maintained its claim to be styled the "National Theatre." Sir Augustus, one of the greatest of theatrical managers, died in 1896.

Apart from the interest attaching to the theatre as a place of dramatic entertainment, some details of the present building may be placed on record here.

The general form of the edifice is that of a

parallelogram; its extent from north to south being 131 feet, and from east to west 237 feet, independently of the painting and scene-rooms, which are partially detached, extending 93 feet further eastward. The chief entrance is approached by a flight of steps, protected by a porch. The entrance-hall communicates, eastward, with the rotunda and the staircases to the boxes; on the north and south, with the pit-lobbies; and from the latter, by circuitous passages, with the pit itself. The rotunda and grand staircase form very beautiful portions of the theatre. The rotunda, 30 feet in diameter, is surrounded by a circular gallery, and crowned by an elegant dome. Here, among other statues of famous poets and actors, is the bust of Balfe already alluded to.

The auditory has a most imposing effect, and is built nearly in the form of a horse-shoe; it is 46 feet wide at the stage, 52 feet across the centre of the pit, and 48 feet from the front of the stage to the centre of the dress-circle. The height from the floor of the pit to the ceiling is 47 feet. There are three tiers of boxes, and an upper and lower gallery; and the house is calculated to accommodate upwards of 3,000 persons.

The proscenium, being as it were the portico of the stage, has less of imitative art in its decoration than the other parts of the house. On each side are two demi-columns of the Corinthian order, supporting a rich entablature, a coved ceiling, and, spanning the stage, an elliptical arch, the whole being very rich in gilding. Down to about the year 1860, when the theatre underwent extensive renovation, the proscenium bore above it the royal arms, together with the well-known classical motto "*Veluti in speculum.*" In its original state the interior of the theatre was circular, but it was altered to its present form during the management of Mr. Elliston, at a cost of not less than £21,000. The interior has several times been renovated and beautified at considerable expense, and now presents an aspect of uncommon splendour.

The stage is of great extent, being 96 feet from the orchestra to the back wall, and upwards of 77 feet in width from wall to wall. The manager's room, actress' dressing-rooms, and various other apartments, are on the north side of the stage; and on the south are the green-rooms, the prompter's-room, the actors' dressing-rooms, and a range of stabling for twenty horses. Above the auditory are the carpenters' shops and store-rooms; whilst the gas-fitters' and property-rooms are in the immediate vicinity of the stage. The painting-room is over the eastern extremity of the stage, and measures nearly 80 feet in length by 36 in height and width. An opening has been made through the original back wall of the stage, whereby the space below the painting-room can be made available for scenic effects, thus giving to the stage an entire depth of 125 feet, the largest of any stage in Europe.

CHAPTER XXIX.

COVENT GARDEN THEATRE.

"The houses twain
Of Covent Garden and of Drury Lane."—*Rejected Addresses.*

The Building of the Theatre—"Rich's Glory"—The First Performance at Covent Garden—Ladies at the Theatre—Receipts of the House—Performance of Handel's "Messiah"—Royalty flock to the Haymarket, and Horace Walpole's Remarks upon the Subject—First Appearance of "Peg" Woffington—Death of Rich, and Sale of Covent Garden Theatre—Charles Macklin, the Comedian and Centenarian—Stephen Kemble—Incledon—George Frederick Cooke—John Philip Kemble—"The Young Roscius"—The Theatre burnt in 1808—The Duke of Northumberland's Generosity to Kemble—The Theatre rebuilt and opened—The "O. P." Riots, succeeded by a run of uninterrupted Prosperity—Poetic Effusions upon Actresses wedded to Noblemen.

We have seen that "the new playhouse in Drury Lane" was frequently spoken of as "Covent Garden Theatre," and naturally enough, for the theatre in Bow Street was not built until the year 1731. The latter was a speculation of John Rich, the celebrated harlequin, and patentee of the theatre in Lincoln's Inn Fields, who removed hither with his company in 1732.

Hogarth's caricature of "Rich's Glory; or, His Triumphal Entry into Covent Garden," of which we give a copy on page 223, refers to this removal. The progress of the building was thus commented on in the *Daily Advertiser* for March 2, 1730:—"We hear the new theatre which is to be built in Covent Garden will be after the model of the opera-house in the Haymarket; and by the draught that has been approved of for the same, it's said it will exceed the opera-house in magnificence of structure."

The same paper for August 4, 1731, states:—"The new theatre building in Covent Garden for Mr. Rich is carrying on with such expedition and diligence (there being a great number of hands employed therein) that it's thought it will be completely finished and ready to receive his audience next winter. Several persons of distinction resort thither daily to view the said work, and seem much pleased at the performance."

The first performance at Covent Garden Theatre was advertised in the following manner:—

COVENT GARDEN THEATRE: FRONT IN 1850.

"By the Company of Comedians.—At the Theatre Royal in Covent Garden, on Thursday next, being the 7th day of December, 1732, will be revived a comedy called *The Way of the World*, written by Mr. Congreve. The cloathes, scenes, and decorations entirely new, and, on account of the great demand for places, the pit and boxes, by desire, will be laid together at 5s.; gallery, 2s; upper gallery, 1s.; and to prevent the scenes being crowded, the stage half-a-guinea. N.B.—All persons who want places are desired to send to the stage-door (the passage from Bow Street leading to it), where attendance will be given and places kept for the following night as usual."

It was doubtless *àpropos* of some such comedy as the one just mentioned that the *Guardian* remarks:—"As the playhouse affords us the most occasions of observing upon the behaviour of the face, it may be useful (for the direction of those who would be critics this way) to remark that the virgin ladies usually dispose themselves in front of the boxes, the young married women compose the second row, while the rear is generally made up of mothers of long standing, undesigning maids, and contented widows. Whoever will cast his eye upon them under this view, during the representation of a play, will find me so far in the right, that a *double entendre* strikes the first row into an affected gravity or careless indolence, the second will venture at a smile, but the third take the conceit entirely and express their mirth in a downright laugh."

Here, as Mr. Timbs reminds us, Rich and Lambert, in 1735, founded the Beefsteak Club; and here, in 1746, Garrick played for the season.

The site of the theatre was leased to Rich for a term of years by the Duke of Bedford, at a yearly rental of £100. It held before the curtain £200, which was at that time reckoned a good receipt. In Shakespeare's day £20 was considered profitable; and "in 1747," says Colley Cibber, in his "Apology," "Mrs. Rich said she was always contented if the receipts reached three figures." In 1750, further to increase the profits, seats were built on the stage sufficient to accommodate a large number of persons; but this arrangement was such an obstruction to the actors that it was abolished by

Garrick. At the time of the death of John Rich in 1761, the ground-rent had been raised from £100 to £300 per annum, and the property was estimated at £60,000. In 1792, when the Duke of Bedford, as ground-landlord, granted a new lease, it was at the rate of £940 a year.

It was at Covent Garden that Handel, in 1741, produced his great oratorio, the *Messiah*. The fashion of the day was against him, though he was supported by the court, the mob, and the poet of common sense, Alexander Pope, who records in his "Dunciad" how, on finding it impossible to hold his own against the Italian faction, Handel quietly withdrew to Ireland for a year or so, till the tide should turn in his favour. "Handel has set up an oratorio," writes Horace Walpole in 1742, "against the operas, and it succeeds." And well was Handel avenged. In a few years the Italian Opera House in the Haymarket went out of fashion, and the nobility set up their own rival house in Lincoln's Inn Fields. "What the Court then patronised," observes Charles Knight, "the aristocracy rejected." As usual, Horace Walpole has a cynical story to tell upon the subject. He writes thus to Mr. Conway, in 1761:—"The late royalties went to the Haymarket when it was the fashion to frequent the other opera in Lincoln's Inn Fields. Lord Chesterfield one night came into the latter, and was asked if he had been at the other house. 'Yes,' said he; 'but there was no one there but the king and queen; and as I thought they might be talking business, I came straight away.'"

INTERIOR OF COVENT GARDEN THEATRE IN 1804.

It was at Covent Garden that the fascinating Irish actress, Margaret Woffington, made her first appearance upon a London and her last upon any stage. Her choice of a character for her *début*, in 1738, excited the surprise of the public, being that of "Sir Harry Wildair;" but so captivating did she appear in it that Garrick, with whom it had been a favourite part, gave it up from that time. Her best *rôle* was that of "Rosalind," in *As You Like It*, to which, in 1757, she was speaking the epilogue with all the saucy piquancy peculiarly her own, when she was suddenly stricken with paralysis, and carried off the stage never to return to it. According to Dr. Doran, a bitter source of jealousy existed between "Peg" Woffington and the beautiful and notorious George Anne Bellamy, whose "Memoirs," written by herself with an astonishing absence of reserve, were formerly read and quoted by every lady of fashion. "The charming Bellamy," says Dr. Doran, "had procured from Paris two gorgeous dresses wherein to enact 'Statira' in the *Rival Queens*. 'Roxana' was played by Woffington, and she was so overcome by malice when she saw herself eclipsed by the dazzling glories of the resplendent Bellamy, that she rolled 'Statira' and her spangled sack in the dust, pommelling her the while with the handle of her stage dagger, as she declaimed, Alexander standing by:—

'Nor he, nor heaven shall shield thee from my justice !
Die, sorceress, die! and all my wrongs die with thee!'"

Rich lies buried in Hillingdon churchyard, near Uxbridge. A vignette of his tomb, and a fac-simile of his autograph, attached to an agreement with Charles Fleetwood respecting the receipts of Covent Garden Theatre, will be found in "Smith's Historical and Literary Curiosities."

A few years after the death of Rich the theatre, having been sold by his heirs for £60,000, was opened in 1767 by Messrs. Harris, Colman, Powell, and Rutherford. In 1774 Mr. Colman sold his share, and from this time the theatre was virtually under the management of Mr. Harris, who had by far the largest interest in the property. In 1787 it was almost wholly rebuilt, and was further altered and enlarged in 1792.

Covent Garden is rich in names famous in histrionic annals, each of which is a landmark to point out the progress of the drama during the last century and a half. Among the earliest of these is that of Charles Macklin, the comedian and centenarian, who frequently performed on its boards, and unless absent from London on engagements at Dublin, lived constantly almost under its shadow —mostly under its piazza; or hard by, in James Street, Hart Street, or Tavistock Row. Having once retired from the stage in middle life, in the hope of making a fortune by establishing a tavern and coffee-house in Hart Street, he returned to it after the failure of his scheme and his consequent bankruptcy, and for many years, whilst quite an old man, played leading parts with some of the fire of youth. His last appearance at Covent Garden was on May 7th, 1789, he being then eighty-nine years of age, when he attempted the part of "Shylock" for his "benefit," but was unable to proceed with the performance. But in spite of his loss of memory he still lived much abroad as usual, haunting the scene of his former triumphs, telling his stock of anecdotes over and over again, and, evening after evening, frequenting a public-house in Duke's Court, close by, where a large concourse would repair in order to hear the anecdotes of so aged and remarkable a person, who remembered the days of the dramatic giants of an earlier generation. "As the infirmities of age increased on him, he would wander feebly about the neighbourhood of Covent Garden, sometimes looking in at the theatre, though he went thither rather more from the force of habit than from any gratification that he could receive, except, perhaps, from the music between the acts. On these occasions the audience, it is said, would always venerate his age, and compassionate his condition; for on his entrance into the pit, however full the house might be, room was always made for him in his accustomed seat—the centre of the last row next to the orchestra; and when the performance was over he would walk home leisurely by himself across the square of Covent Garden to Tavistock Row, where he lived and where he died, a veritable centenarian, in 1797. His "Memoirs," which originally appeared in the *European Magazine*, but were subsequently re-published in a volume, furnish us with some curious information respecting society in London and the manners and habits of the gentry and professional classes a century ago.

Macklin does not say much for the morality of Covent Garden and its neighbourhood, or of the taverns and public-houses by which it was surrounded, or of the still lower public-houses near Clare Market, which were the resort of second-rate actors, and theatrical critics of Grub Street or Drury Lane, who "lived from hand to mouth." The ordinaries of the time, it appears, were charged from sixpence to a shilling a head—in the latter case being supplied with two courses, and attended by a superior sort of mixed company; though there were private rooms besides for wits of the higher order, and for such of the nobility as liked to frequent such places, where conviviality was often carried to excess. Macklin says also that the habits and manners of the dramatic as well as of other professions were very different from those which now prevail. The merchant, at that time, scarcely ever lived out of the City, his residence being always attached to his counting-house, and, indeed, his credit being in a great degree dependent on his observance of the established practice. According to Macklin, the first migration of the London merchants to the westward dates only from 1747, when a few of those who had already made large fortunes removed to Hatton Garden. The lawyers, too, he used to tell his hearers, used at that time to live mostly in their inns of court, or else about Westminster Hall; and in like manner the actors "did mostly congregate" around the two great theatres. Thus, as we know, Quin, Booth, and Wilks lived almost constantly in or about Bow

Street, Colley Cibber in Charles Street, Billy Howard in Henrietta Street, and Garrick, for a considerable portion of his life, in Southampton Street. The inferior players lodged in and about Vinegar Yard, Little Russell Street, and the lesser courts round the theatres; "so that," says Macklin, "we could all be mustered by beat of drum, could attend rehearsals without any inconvenience, and yet save coach-hire—no inconsiderable part, let me tell you, of a former player's annual expenses. I do not know how the change has been effected, but we are now all looking out for high ground—squares and genteel neighbourhoods—no matter how far distant from the theatre, which should be the great scene of business; as if, forsooth, local situations could give rhythm to the profession, or genteel neighbourhoods instinctively produce good manners." What he would have said on this subject if he had lived on into our own days may be easily inferred from these last remarks of the father of the theatrical world a century ago. But we must return from this digression to the theatre itself, from which we are in danger of wandering with the actors.

Stephen Kemble made his first appearance here, as "Othello," in 1783. Possessed, like all of his family, of considerable dramatic capabilities, his talents were unhappily obscured under a load of personal obesity, which had, however, the advantage of enabling him to enact the part of "Falstaff" (his best character) without stuffing! Charles Incledon—"The Ballad-singer—" as he loved to be termed—made his *début* as "Dermot," in *The Poor Soldier*, in 1790. His voice is said to have been the most melodious, as well as powerful, of his time; and his manner of singing such songs as "Black-eyed Susan," "The Soldier tired," and "The Storm," has never since been surpassed. In 1794 Charles Kemble, and in 1797 Mrs. Glover, made their first appearances here. In 1800 George Frederick Cooke achieved a great success as "Richard III." —a performance spoken of as "the best since Garrick." In 1803 John Philip Kemble purchased a sixth part of the property of the Covent Garden patent, transferring his own services, with those of his sister, Mrs. Siddons, and his brother Charles, from Drury Lane to Covent Garden. In 1804 "The Young Roscius," William Henry Betty, at twelve years of age was filling the theatre to overflowing, and a detachment of the Guards was posted outside, with a large body of constables inside, to preserve order amongst the thousands who had assembled hours before the opening of the doors. His salary was at first £50 a night, but, after three performances, was increased to £100; and at sixteen years of age he quitted the profession with a handsome fortune. Twelve years later he returned to the stage; but the performance of his maturer years was not considered to fulfil the promise of his youth; and disappointed at the coldness with which he was received, he again retired into private life. He died in August, 1874, aged eighty-two.

On the morning of the 30th of September, 1808, Covent Garden Theatre was totally destroyed by fire; a calamity which involved a fearful loss of human life—twenty-three firemen being killed by the unexpected fall of a part of the ruins. The splendid organ left by Handel, and the stock of wine belonging to the Beefsteak Club, shared the fate of the whole building. The loss of property was estimated at £150,000, of which £50,000 were covered by insurances.

John Kemble, who had invested his all in the share so recently purchased, met with universal sympathy, which, in some notable instances, did not confine itself to words. The Prince of Wales, afterwards George IV., presented him with £1,000; and the Duke of Northumberland with £10,000, which Kemble declined as a gift, but accepted as a loan, giving the duke his bond for the amount. On the 31st of December, 1808, the Prince of Wales laid the first stone of the new theatre, and the Duke of Northumberland sent Kemble back his bond, enclosed in a letter, saying that, "it being a day of rejoicing, he concluded there would be a bonfire, and he therefore requested that the enclosed obligation might be thrown in, to heighten the flames." The architect was Sir Robert Smirke, and the model selected, the Temple of Minerva in the Acropolis at Athens. The Doric portico in Bow Street, with its four fluted columns, and statues of Tragedy and Comedy, were by Flaxman, and the two long panels in the upper part, with representations in basso-relievo of ancient and modern drama, were by Flaxman and Rossi. Some £50,000 of the cost of the construction was received from the insurance offices, and the remaining £100,000 was raised by subscription shares of £500 each.

On the 18th of September, 1809, the splendid edifice was opened at "new prices," a proceeding which the management considered necessary on account of the enormous cost of the building. These new prices were by no means approved by the public, and led to the well-known "O.P." riots. On the opening night of the new theatre, a cry of "Old prices!" (afterwards diminished to "O.P.") burst from every part of the house. This continued and increased in violence till the 23rd, when rattles, drums, whistles, and cat-calls having completely drowned the voices of the actors, Mr. Kemble, the stage-manager, came forward and said "that a committee of gentlemen had undertaken to examine the finances of the concern, and that until they were prepared with their report the theatre would be closed." "Name them!" was shouted from all sides. Their names were declared. "All shareholders!" bawled a wag from the gallery. In a few days the theatre re-opened; the public paid no attention to the report of the referees, and the tumult was renewed for several weeks with even increased violence. The proprietors sent in hired bruisers to mill the refractory into subjection. This irritated most of their former friends, and amongst the rest the annotator, who accordingly wrote the song of "Heigh-ho, says Kemble," which was caught up by the ballad-singers, and sung under Mr. Kemble's house windows in Great Russell Street. In the end Kemble was obliged to give way, and after a humble apology, which was graciously accepted by a crowded audience, peace and the "old prices" were simultaneously restored.

For many years after this inauspicious commencement Covent Garden enjoyed a run of uninterrupted prosperity, the receipts between 1809 and 1821 averaging £80,000 each season. The largest annual amount taken at the theatre was in the year 1810-11, when the sum of £100,000 was received at the doors! The annual expenses during this period averaged £40,000—an outlay which required a skilful and liberal management to insure the large amounts just mentioned. It will be sufficient to mention the names of the principal performers at Covent Garden between 1809 and 1822 to show how powerful was the dramatic force there assembled:—In tragedy, Messrs. Kemble, Cooke, Macready, Young, &c. &c.; Mrs. Siddons, Miss O'Neill, &c. In comedy, Messrs. Liston, Munden, Charles Mathews, sen., W. Farren, &c.; Mesdames Jordan, Brunton, Foote, C. Kemble, &c. In opera, Messrs. Incledon, Braham, Pyne, and Mesdames Catalani, Bolton, Stephens, and Tree. "Kitty" Stephens made her first appearance here in 1812; Miss O'Neill, in 1814; Macready, in 1816; and Farren, in 1818. Several of these actresses and singers afterwards married noblemen; and the "Memoirs" of the late James Smith, published in 1840, contain various poetic effusions upon those ladies. We will quote a few, which will interest our readers:—

The first, in allusion to Miss Farren, Countess of Derby, runs thus:—

"Farren, Thalia's dear delight,
Can I forget the fatal night,
Of grief unstain'd by fiction,
(E'en now the recollection damps),
When Wroughton led thee to the lamps,
In graceful valediction?"

Another verse is in honour of Miss Brunton, Countess of Craven:—

"The Derby prize by Hymen won,
Again the god made bold to run
Beneath Thalia's steerage;
Sent forth a second earl to woo,
And captivating Brunton too,
Exalted to the peerage."

Of Miss Bolton, Lady Thurlow, whose celebrated part was "Polly" in *The Beggar's Opera*, the poet says—

"Thrice vanquished thus on Thespian soil,
Heart-whole from Cupid's toil
I caught a fleeting furlough:
Gay's Newgate *Opera* charmed me then,
But 'Polly' sang her requiem when
Fair Bolton turned to Thurlow."

Of Miss O'Neill, who made prize of a baronet in the matrimonial lottery, he writes:—

"These wounds some substitute might heal;
But what bold mortal bade O'Neill
Renounce her tragic station—
Taste, talent, beauty to trepan?
By Heaven! I wonder how the man
Escaped assassination!"

Appended to these verses is one from another pen, written some years later, immortalising the lady who afterwards became Countess of Essex:—

"Last of this dear, delightful list—
Most followed, wondered at, and missed
In Hymen's odds and evens—
Old Essex caged our nightingale,
And finished thy theatric tale,
Enchanting Kitty Stephens."

Miss Foote, although not celebrated in verse by the author of "The Rejected Addresses," was another actress of this period who was elevated from the stage to the peerage. She made her first appearance at Covent Garden, in 1814, as "Amanthis," in Mrs. Inchbald's comedy of *The Child of Nature;* and became Countess of Harrington in 1831. She died in 1867.

Among the many good stories and anecdotes relating to Drury Lane and Covent Garden Theatres to be found in abundance in the anecdote biography of the two last centuries, the following, relating as it does to Miss Farren, may be repeated here:—Lord Derby once applied in the green-room to Sheridan for the arrears of Lady Derby's (Miss Farren's) salary, averring that he would not leave the room until it was paid. "My dear lord," said Sheridan, "this is too bad; you have taken from us the brightest star in our little world, and now you quarrel with us for a little dust which she has left behind her."

Mrs. Siddons retired from the stage in 1812; her brother, John Kemble, followed her example in 1816, presenting his share of the theatre (one-sixth) to his brother Charles. In 1820 Mr. Harris, who owned seven-twelfths of the property, died, and from this time the fortunes of the theatre declined. Differences arose between Mr. Henry Harris (who had succeeded to his father's share) and Mr. Charles Kemble, resulting in legal proceedings.

In 1822 Mr. Henry Harris resigned his management, and the property was thrown into Chancery. Nevertheless, the Shakespearian play of *King John* was put upon the stage here in 1823, though Mr. Kemble was doubtful how far any attempt to improve the costume would succeed, being afraid lest he should be considered an "antiquary." But in this matter he listened to the advice of Mr. Planché, and the introduction of appropriate mail-armour and helmets of the thirteenth century was thoroughly appreciated by the public, "receipts of from £400 to £600 nightly soon reimbursed the management for the production; and a complete reformation of dramatic costume became from that moment inevitable upon the English stage."

In spite, however, of these and other undisputed successes, the theatre, in 1829, was seized by the parochial authorities, advertised for sale, and was only rescued by public subscriptions and voluntary contributions of the company. Charles Kemble's administration was not so fortunate as that of his brother, although the last three years of his management were brightened by the triumphs of his daughter, Miss Fanny Kemble, afterwards Mrs. Butler. Here was performed, in January, 1832, Lord Francis Egerton's tragedy of *Catharine of Cleves*. In 1833 Edmund Kean made his last appearance on these boards. In the same year the two great theatres of Drury Lane and Covent Garden were united under the management of Mr. Bunn, but the union was of short duration. In 1835 Covent Garden was leased to Mr. Osbaldistone, and the experiment tried of reducing the prices. Charles Kemble, Macready, and Miss Helen Faucit were the principal stars under this management, which only lasted two years, when the theatre passed into the hands of Macready. A Shakespearian revival now took place, and *The Tempest*, *Coriolanus*, *Henry V.*, and *King Lear* were produced in a style of gorgeous and appropriate magnificence. The profits were, however, by no means commensurate with the expenses, and within two years Mr. Macready retired from the management a considerable loser.

In 1839 Covent Garden Theatre was taken by Madame Vestris, the most fascinating actress of her time; Mr. Planché, as he tells us in his agreeable "Recollections," acting as superintendent of the decorative department, and introducing great reforms in the matter of costume, and acting also as "reader" of plays submitted to the manager by unknown authors; but in spite of the almost unrivalled attractions afforded by a company which, in addition to the talented lessee and her no less talented husband, Charles Mathews—including Messrs. Harley and Keeley, and Mesdames Nisbet, Humby, and Keeley, &c.—the speculation was a losing one, and was resigned at the end of the third season. About this time Dickens wrote for Covent Garden Theatre, by way of helping the manager, a farce about which the actors could not agree, and which he afterwards turned into his story of "The Lamplighter."

In April, 1842, Mr. Charles Kemble again essayed the direction of the theatre, which opened with the opera of *Norma*, Miss Adelaide Kemble being the prima donna; but Mr. C. Kemble, in spite of the prestige of his name, and his great success as an actor, was not destined to be fortunate as a manager, and the smallness of the receipts obliged him to withdraw the following November. The Christmas of the same year found the indomitable Mr. Bunn in possession, the entertainment offered being a curious olla-podrida, compounded of Shakespeare, English opera, and pantomime. Mr. Bunn's brief management ended in May, 1843, and the theatre was then let to the Anti-Corn-Law League, who used it for the purpose of a bazaar. Next, M. Jullien installed himself there for a season of winter promenade concerts, which were highly successful; and on March 4th, 1844, the first *bal-masqué* given in England during the present century took place at Covent Garden, under his auspices. During the spring of the same year *Antigone* was performed, the theatre being under the direction of M. Laurent. M. Jullien's concerts and *bal-masqué* again attracted large crowds during the season of 1845–6.

Mr. Planché, in his "Recollections," in contrasting Covent Garden with Drury Lane at this period, speaks of the former as "strong in comedy, and superior to its rival in spectacular entertainments." To a certain extent this remark held true long after it was made; and in proof of the latter part of the assertion, it may be said, without fear of contradiction, that Covent Garden was until recently celebrated for the gorgeousness and brilliancy of its pantomimes. In fact, so gorgeous were the spectacular entertainments here, that on one occasion we find Mr. Planché complaining to Mr. Kemble, the manager, that a thousand pounds were often lavished on a Christmas pantomime or an Easter spectacle, whilst the plays of Shakespeare were put upon the stage with "makeshift scenery, and old and second-rate dresses." *Apropos* of the degeneracy of the drama (proper), and of the rising taste for "spectacle," Byron writes—

"Gods! on those boards shall Folly rear her head,
Where Garrick trod and Kemble loves to tread."

It was at this time the project was formed of opening a rival opera-house to the one in the Haymarket; and in April, 1847, after undergoing important alterations and additions, Covent Garden Theatre commenced its new career as "The Royal Italian Opera House." The company consisted principally of seceders from Her Majesty's—hitherto the only Italian opera-house in London—and comprised the famous names of Giulia Grisi, Persiani, Mario, Tamburini, and even the great leader of the orchestra—Michael Costa himself. No wonder the alarmed lessee of Her Majesty's made strenuous efforts to prevent the threatened rivalry, in virtue of a privilege having been of old granted to the "King's Theatre" (the name by which it was known previously to her Majesty's accession) "for the exclusive production in perpetuity of Italian opera;" the same document containing a stipulation that "the patents of Drury Lane and Covent Garden should never be used for the purpose of Italian opera." That this exclusive right was no dead letter had been proved by Mr. Bunn in 1835, when the entire company of "The King's Theatre" had performed for one night only in *La Gazza Ladra* at Drury Lane—a performance immediately followed by a dignified protest from the Lord Chamberlain. A period of a dozen years, however, produces a change both of times and of Lords Chamberlains, and Mr. Lumley found out, as he tells us in his "Reminiscences," that he was under a government which discouraged monopolies of all kinds; and, his opposition notwithstanding, the Royal Italian Opera House, Covent Garden, was duly opened, "without let or hindrance."

BURNING OF COVENT GARDEN THEATRE IN 1856.

The *Era* of June 13th, 1847, remarks:—"It has been said that London cannot support two operatic companies; but while the house at the Haymarket was filled to overflowing by the presence of Jenny Lind, that at Covent Garden was crammed to suffocation by Grisi." Yet, although Grisi, so long the popular idol, still held her own, in spite of the Jenny Lind mania, and, supported by Alboni—who made a triumphant *début* during this year—insured a full house every night, the expenses were frightfully in excess of the receipts. Two years

COVENT GARDEN IN 1660.

sufficed to involve Mr. Delafield, the lessee, in bankruptcy, although he had commenced his speculation with £100,000. The reconstruction of the interior, by Albano, had cost £40,000; the vocal department, in 1848, cost £33,349, of which Alboni drew £4,000, and Grisi £3,106. The orchestra cost £10,048; the ballet, £8,105; gas and gasmen, £1,927; properties, £1,920; carpenters' work, £1,858; advertisements, £2,376; wardrobes, £3,100; printing, £982; bills of performance, £885; hairdressers, £100; salaries of officials, £2,118; law expenses, £2,100; and fireworks, £27! The whole expenditure in 1848 was £78,765; the aggregate receipts, including cloak-room, saloon, &c., £44,008.

A curious contrast to this lavish outlay is to be found in the modest charges of a play acted in the year 1511, on the Feast of St. Margaret, of which the expenses were as follow:—

	£	s.	d.
For Players	1	4	0
,, Musicians	0	5	6
,, John Hobbard, Priest, and Author of Play	0	2	8
,, Decorations, Dresses, and Play-books ...	0	1	0
,, Hire of Place of Performance	0	1	0
,, Furniture	0	1	4
,, Painting Three Phantoms and Three Devils	0	0	6
,, Fish, Bread, and Ale for Players ...	0	3	5
,, Four Chickens for the Hero	0	0	4
Sum total	£1	19	9

In 1850 Covent Garden passed into the hands of Mr. Gye. At the commencement of 1856 Mr. Gye let the theatre for a few weeks to Professor Anderson, the "Wizard of the North," whose short lease terminated on the 4th of March with a masked ball, for which Mr. Gye's reluctant consent had been extorted, after repeated refusals. It was not, as we have seen, the first or the second time that Covent Garden Theatre had been employed for the same purpose; but Mr. Gye's objections were in this instance unfortunately prophetic. The festivities were just concluding with the performance of the "National Anthem," at five a.m., there being then only about 200 of the vast crowd of revellers left in the building, when the alarm of fire was given, and in a few hours nothing remained of the splendid structure but a heap of smoking ruins. Happily no lives were lost, although little else was saved in the general destruction, except the façade, and Flaxman's statues and bassi-relievi. The origin of the fire was never ascertained. Such a catastrophe, occurring at a period when the preparations and engagements for the coming season were on the point of completion, was calculated to daunt the stoutest heart; but Mr. Gye's courage and fertility of resource were equal even to an emergency like this. He at once engaged the Lyceum for the season, made a manly appeal to the public to support him, and opened his temporary opera-house on the 15th of April to a brilliant and crowded audience. Early in the following year Mr. Gye obtained from the Duke of Bedford a lease of the site for a new theatre, at a rent of £850 for ninety years. This site included not only the ground on which the late theatre stood, but also that occupied by the "Piazza" Hotel, together with other tenements, the whole being equivalent to more than an acre. The funds for the new building were raised by loans; amongst the contributors being the Duke of Bedford, £15,000; Messrs. Lucas, £10,000; Colonel Meyrick, £5,000; Mr. Billings, £5,000; Mr. Maynard, £5,000; Sir E. Majoribanks and Mr. Antrobus, £5,000; besides Sir George Armytage, Mr. E. M. Barry, Mr. Turner, and others.

The yearly interest upon this large capital is necessarily considerable, and the securities contain a proviso that if the interest be in arrear over three months, or the premiums of fire insurance be not paid, the lessee is to be considered as a tenant at a rental of £4,000 per annum.

These preliminaries arranged, the work of rebuilding the theatre commenced, and progressed with extraordinary rapidity, and with every improvement in the way of lighting, ventilation, decoration, comfort, and precaution against fire which modern science and taste could suggest. In contemplating this, one of the largest and most magnificent theatres in Europe, it is difficult to realise that it was begun and completed within the short space of six months.

The edifice occupies a space of ground measuring 219 feet on the south side, next the Floral Hall, 210 feet on the Hart Street side, and 127 feet along the Bow Street end, where there is an enclosed portico projecting about 17 feet. The portico is about one-fifth larger than that of its predecessor, adorned by Corinthian columns 36 feet high, and by the figures and basso-relievos of Flaxman from the old building, which were cleverly adapted to the new theatre, and were insured by the Duke of Bedford for £1,000. The area of the stage, exclusive of the bow in advance of the proscenium, measures 90 feet by 88, and the cost of the stage-machinery and various appurtenances was nearly £2,500. There are eight main staircases, besides six minor ones, all of which are fireproof. In addition to the usual entrances there is a private one in Hart Street, with a staircase attached, leading to the royal box, and also a separate entrance and staircase leading to the box of the Duke of Bedford. The architect of this splendid structure was Mr. E. M. Barry; the contractors Messrs. Lucas; and the sum originally calculated, £60,000, but the estimate was greatly exceeded, and the actual cost has been computed at more than £70,000.

The new theatre is said to be of the same size as La Scala at Milan, which up to that time had the reputation of being the largest theatre in Europe, or perhaps in the world. The interior decorations are of a very chaste and elegant design.

It was opened on the 15th of May, 1858, by Mr. Harrison, in conjunction with Miss Louisa Pyne, with Meyerbeer's opera of *Les Huguenots*, which was performed to an overflowing audience, the numbers present on that occasion being 300 in excess of the estimate of a "full house;" and it was under their management that Balfe's celebrated opera of *Satanella* was produced with the greatest success. It was called by the critics of the time Balfe's "happy inspiration."

It would be a work of supererogation to mention the names of the great artists who within the last forty years have made their world-wide reputation upon these boards. Who of the present generation needs to be reminded of Adelina Patti, who rose upon the horizon of the musical world in 1861, and has reigned ever since queen of song and of hearts; of Pauline Lucca, equally fascinating and capricious; of the stately Titiens, always in splendid song, the only soprano that recalls to the connoisseur the singing of Pasta, Malibran, or Grisi; of Trebelli or Albani; of Nordica, Calvé, or Melba; of Santley, Faure, Nicolini, or Tamberlik; of the de Reszkes, Maurel, or Alvary?

For ten years after the opening of the new theatre in Covent Garden, the lessees of the rival opera-houses were fully occupied in endeavouring to solve the vexed question whether two such establishments simultaneously carried on, in opposition to one another, could be made to pay. In 1869 the belligerents, believing that the solution of the problem was to be found only in a coalition of forces, entered into partnership; but difficulties beset them from the very commencement, and the ultimate result was far from satisfactory, and, to begin with, Sir Michael Costa, the dignified *chef d'orchestre* at Covent Garden, declined to countenance the scheme, and withdrew his august services; Signors Arditi and Li Calsi being thereupon appointed to conduct by turns. Next, differences of opinion (to speak very mildly) arose among the "bright, particular stars" of the amalgamated companies, and terminated with the secession of Mdlles. Nilsson and Di Murska, and Signors Foli, Santley, Arditi, and others. Finally, the general public began to be dissatisfied, for a brisk competition between those who cater for its amusement is always an advantage, and monopoly of any sort invariably ends in mediocrity. Before the conclusion of the year 1870 the fusion had terminated in "confusion worse confounded;" Messrs. Mapleson and Gye had dissolved their brief partnership, and the season of 1871 saw them again in rivalry. But in the end the Covent Garden house triumphed, and its chief competitor has now given place to Mr. Beerbohm Tree's new theatre. A few years ago Covent Garden came into the hands of the late Sir Augustus Harris, the lessee of Drury Lane, under whose spirited management it enjoyed several brilliant seasons of opera, mainly German and modern Italian. A marked change has come over the taste of the English public in regard to opera, due mainly to the growing influence of Wagner, whose music-dramas are now appreciated hardly less in this country than in Germany.

Adjoining the theatre, on the southern side, is the Floral Hall, erected about the year 1860, somewhat on the plan of the original Crystal Palace in Hyde Park; but of this we shall have more to say in a subsequent chapter.

It may be interesting here to make a note of the fact recorded in Forster's "Life of Dickens," that when he was about twenty years old he applied to Mr. Bartley, the then manager of Covent Garden, for an engagement at that theatre, and that a day was fixed for him to make trial of his powers. When the day came he was laid up with a bad cold, and could not appear; his trial was therefore postponed till the next season. In the meantime he had made himself famous by his pen, and so he took to literature instead. Possibly to that "bad cold" we owe "Pickwick," "Nicholas Nickleby," and "Oliver Twist."

We have thus endeavoured to compress into a few pages an outline of the history of the two leading theatres, and, indeed, for many years, the only theatres of London. But the whole neighbourhood around Covent Garden teems with theatrical reminiscences, for which a volume, in reality, would scarcely suffice. We will, however, endeavour, in the following chapters, to skim lightly over the ground, yet carefully, and as exhaustively as possible, rambling about from street to street, as the bee flits from flower to flower, and sipping here and there from the stores of past history of the Stuart and Hanoverian ages.

CHAPTER XXX.

COVENT GARDEN:—GENERAL DESCRIPTION.

"Hail, market, hail, to all Megarians dear!"—*Aristophanes, "Acharnians."*

Extent of the District—Covent Garden in the Fourteenth Century—The Site passes into the hands of the Duke of Somerset, and afterwards the Earls of Bedford—Origin of the Market—Annals of Covent Garden—The Fashionable Days of Covent Garden—The Piazzas as a Promenade—History of the Market—The Sun-dial—The Hackney-coach Stands—The Mohocks and other Marauders.

THE region which we intend to embrace in this and the following chapter, extending, to speak roughly, from St. Martin's Lane on the west to Drury Lane on the east, and from Long Acre on the north to the Strand on the south—in other words, considerably less than half a mile the one way and a quarter of a mile the other—is remarkable as including in its circuit more of literary, and, indeed, of human interest, than any other spot in modern or ancient London. That interest belongs chiefly, if not wholly, to the last two centuries; and the memorials of it are scattered on every side of us in such thick profusion, that one can almost fancy we can see the *genius loci* standing there and pointing around him with his wand, and exclaiming, "Si monumentum requiris, circumspice;" like Sir Christopher Wren in the cathedral church of St. Paul. In the well-known words of the "Connoisseur," the neighbourhood of Covent Garden was in the last century—though it is no longer—"the acknowledged region of gallantry, wit, and criticism." And doubtless it was as a frequenter of this neighbourhood, and in love with the good literary society which its coffee-houses afforded, that Johnson assented with a "Why yes, sir," to Boswell's frank avowal that "the vicinity of the Strand was much better than Blackheath Park."

The latter half of the seventeenth century formed an important epoch in the growth of western London. We see from the Plan of London, published by Aggas in 1562, that it was then comparatively a small place, almost entirely confined to the limits of the City proper. But our capital "found itself so secure in the glorious government of Elizabeth," that by the year 1600 very considerable additions were made to the north of the long line of street now known as the Strand, and the gap between London proper and Westminster was nearly filled up.

Covent Garden—a corruption, we need hardly say, of "the Convent Garden"—was an enclosure belonging, as far back as the first quarter of the thirteenth century, to the abbots of Westminster, who it is supposed used the site as the burial-place for the convent, as being at a convenient distance for "burying their dead out of sight." Here were "fair spreading pastures" seven acres in extent, now all swallowed up in the general name of "Long Acre;" the present Long Acre, which was built in the reign of Charles I., being carried from the north-east towards the south-west—from the middle of St. Martin's Lane and the top of Drury Lane. It is said that where Long Acre runs there was once an avenue of stately elms, whose shade was grateful to the citizens of London when they walked out on holydays; and that there were country lanes with green fields on either side.

In the map of Ralph Aggas above alluded to, Covent Garden is shown as enclosed by a brick wall, which runs straight on the north side, parallel with these shady elms; whilst the southern side is bounded by the houses and small inclosures abutting upon the Strand highway. Nearly in the middle of the old garden there appear to be some small buildings, probably the dwellings of gardeners and other workmen, and the trees are scattered up and down the place so thick as to give it the appearance almost of a wilderness. "A large pond," writes Newton in his "London in the Olden Time," "is said to have existed near the middle of Covent Garden two centuries ago. It was fed partly by a running stream from the higher grounds, and partly by a local spring which still supplies a pump near the modern parish church. The overflow from this pond would pass by Ivy Bridge Lane down to the Thames."

Stow himself makes no mention of Covent Garden; but Strype tells us that it probably had the name of the Convent Garden, "because it was the garden and field of that large convent and monastery where Exeter House formerly stood." But here, no doubt, Strype is in error, for there are no traces of a "convent" or "monastery" on that site; and according to general tradition this convent garden belonged to the abbot and monks of Westminster, by whom it was used partly as their kitchen garden, supplying, no doubt, not only the wants of that religious community, but also the public markets, and so bringing in an income to the abbey, and partly as a burial-ground, as already stated. This supposition is confirmed by the fact that in digging for the foundations of the new market in 1829, a quantity of human bones was exhumed on the north side of the area.

Walter Savage Landor thus quaintly and pointedly describes the change which came over the Convent Garden of the monks of Westminster:—"The Convent becomes a playhouse; monks and nuns turn actors and actresses. The garden, formal and quiet, where a salad was cut for a lady abbess, and flowers were gathered to adorn images, becomes a market, noisy and full of life, distributing thousands of fruits and flowers to a vicious metropolis." It is to be feared, from the turn of his expressions here, that Landor did not remember that the Latin *conventus*, and its French equivalent, *couvent*, is strictly applied to the houses of religious men as well as women; if so, it is more probable that a salad cut on this spot was destined for the Abbot of St. Peter's, Westminster, and not for an abbess. But this is a matter of no great moment.

At the dissolution of the religious houses this property came into the hands of the Duke of Somerset, on whose attainder in 1552 it was given by the Crown to John Russell, Earl of Bedford, under the description of "Covent Garden, lying in the parish of St. Martin's-in-the-Fields next Charing Cross, with seven acres called Long Acre, of the yearly value of six pounds six shillings and eight pence."

It is probable that for a very long time after the Russells became possessed of this property, it still remained a garden, or at all events consisted of open fields; for in 1627, as Mr. P. Cunningham tells us, "only two persons were rated to the poor of the parish of St. Martin's-in-the-Fields under the head of 'Covent Garden.'"

"If we add an 'n' to 'Covent,' and say Convent Garden," observes a writer in the *City Press*, "we shall go back to the old days when nuns or friars studied their missals in the church orchard, and then we shall think of Henry VIII., and the Bedford family with their slice of consecrated ground. It was then, and long after, in the country, and was probably used for pasture until the growing population made it an object to possess a market." How the work prospered may be gathered in some measure from the fragmentary accounts which have reached us. The *Spectator* speaks of daily prayer at the Garden Church, and tells us how fine ladies, with black pages carrying their books, walked across the market to their pews. Even at the beginning of the century the arrangements were very primitive. "The middle walk consisted of odd, tumble-down shed shops, though the fruit, flowers, and vegetables were excellent. Crockery-ware was sold in several of them. There were two medical herb-shops, where you could purchase leeches; and snails, then employed to make broth for consumptive patients, were vended. Also a well-known itinerant bird-dealer had a stall, where he sold larks, canaries, owls, and, if you desired it, could get you a talking parrot, or manufacture you a love-bird, on the shortest notice. 'Quality folks' often walked in the centre avenue, but there was no accommodation for choice plants on the roof. The ducal proprietor improved the market into its present state; but of course far more might be done with the present site. Covent Garden was used for many years as a pasture-ground, and was subsequently let on a building lease. Then the square was planned, and Inigo Jones designed it. The piazza, which runs round a part of it, was also his work. The market originated casually. Vendors of vegetables and fruit from the neighbouring villages used the centre of the square as a market; and, in lapse of time, the market grew into a recognised institution. It was strangely unsightly, being but a rude combination of stalls and sheds. But in 1831 the present market buildings were erected at the Duke of Bedford's expense; and, a few years later, open-air accommodation was obtained on the roof, at the entrance, for the sale of plants, &c. The duke derives a considerable revenue from the rents and tolls. It is quite a problem to what the tolls amount. Those who occupy shops or stands by the week or year, and who sell the greater part of the produce brought in, merely pay their rents as for ordinary shops. Some of them, though held only from week to week, have continued in the same families through two or even three generations.

"The early morning at Covent Garden affords a curious sight. From 3.30 to 4.30 there is little bustle in the market, though business goes on rapidly. Early risers of both sexes—a class of 'higglers' who indorse the old proverb that 'the early bird catches the worm'—flock to the market. They form a medium between the grower and the small dealer, buying the whole stock from the former, and seeking to sell portions of it to the latter at a higher price. The crowd and bustle increase from five o'clock up to seven or eight. Porters, with baskets, offer their help to buyers. The piazzas become very lively with their clamour. Against every post and pillar are small tables, where coffee, tea, bread and butter may be purchased. Hawkers parade in every direction with cakes, buns, knives, and pocket-books for sale. Many customers seek for stimulants, and consume gin or hot spirits-and-water with avidity.

"In our climate piazzas were a novelty—we seldom need to exclude the sun—yet those in Covent Garden became popular. Long afterwards two piazzas were erected in Regent Street, and termed the 'Colonnade,' but they were not a success and have been removed. Those in Covent Garden, though much dishonoured, still (1870) remain; and are, perhaps, the only buildings in that style in England." Thus Byron says in "Beppo"—

ENTRANCE TO COVENT GARDEN MARKET, 1870.

"For, bating Covent Garden, I can hit on
No place that's called 'Piazza' in Great Britain."

The following is given by the same authority as a brief epitome of the annals of Covent Garden. We shall enlarge upon it as we proceed in our survey:—"The market buildings were commenced in 1632 by the Earl of Bedford. 1650, April 26. Col. Poyse was shot to death in the market. 1675, December 29. A proclamation issued against coffee-houses. 1679, January 8. To allow their continuance till June 24 following. The poet Dryden was assaulted in Covent Garden, on account of some verses in his 'Hind and Panther.' 1687, April 14. A soldier, William Grant, hanged in the market for running from his colours. 1636. This date is cut in a stone let into the brickwork of No. 23, King Street, of Evans's Hotel, we are told. It formed a prominent object in Hogarth's print, 'Morning.' And here lodged Sir William Alexander, Earl of Stirling, 1637; Thomas Killigrew, 1640; Denzil Hollis, 1644; and in 1647, Sir Harry Vane, and also Sir Kenelm Digby, 1662. Of Hollis this anecdote is told:—In a hot debate in Parliament, Ireton offended Hollis, upon which he persuaded him to walk out of the House, and told him he must fight to justify his words. Ireton pleaded that 'his conscience would not suffer him to fight a duel;' upon which Hollis pulled him by the nose, saying, 'If his conscience forbade his giving men satisfaction, it should also keep him from provoking them.' We are assured that nearly all the foundlings of St. Paul, Covent Garden, were laid at the door of Nathaniel, Lord Crewe, Bishop of Durham."

Covent Garden was made into a separate parish in 1645, and the patronage of it vested in the Russell family; the district which it comprises being cut off under the provisions of a special Act of Parliament from that of St. Martin's-in-the-Fields. The parish church was dedicated to St. Paul.

In the days of the first two Georges the parish was, if not the fashionable part of the town, at all events a fashionable district, and the residence of a great number of persons of title and high rank, as well as of men known in the world of art and literature. "A concourse of arts, literary characters and other men of genius frequented the numerous coffee-houses, wine and cider-cellars, &c., within the boundaries of Covent Garden," says Mr. Timbs, who adds the following formidable list of persons whose names are connected with the place:—Butler, Addison, Sir R. Steele, Otway, Dryden, Pope, Warburton, Cibber, Fielding, Churchill, Bolingbroke, and Dr. Johnson; Rich, Woodward, Booth, Wilkes, Garrick, and Macklin; Kitty Clive, "Peg" Woffington, Mrs. Pritchard, the Duchess of Bolton, Lady Derby, Lady Thurlow, and the Duchess of St. Alban's; Sir Peter Lely, Sir Godfrey Kneller, and Sir James Thornhill; Vandevelde, Zincke, Lambert, Hogarth, Hayman, Wilson, Dance, Meyer, and Samuel Foote. But even to this list it would be possible to make many additions.

COVENT GARDEN MARKET, LOOKING EASTWARD. (*From a Print of* 1786.)

Strange as it may appear, Covent Garden was for a long period fashionable as a residence and a promenade. From 1666 down to 1700 the following noble persons tenanted the Piazzas:—Lords Hollis, Brownlow, Lucas, Newport, Barkham; Crewe, Bishop of Durham, Duke of Richmond, Earl of Oxford, Sir Godfrey Kneller, Sir Edward Flood, Sir Kenelm Digby, Earl of Bedford, Hon. Colonel Russell, Bishop of St. David's, Marquis of Winchester, Earl of Sussex, and the Earl of Peterborough, in the house where the auctioneer Robins afterwards flourished.

Earl Ferrers, who was executed in 1760 for the murder of his steward, was living in Covent Garden in 1722. Even so lately as the reign of George II.

Covent Garden retained much of its fashionable character. At all events, in the March of 1730 the *Daily Advertiser* gravely tells its readers that "the Lady Mary Wortley Montague, who has been greatly indisposed at her house in Covent Garden for some time, is now perfectly recovered, and takes the benefit of the air in Hyde Park every morning, by advice of her physicians." The same journal for June 10, 1731, tells us that, "A few days ago the Right Hon. the Lady Mary Wortley Montague set out from her house in Covent Garden for Bath."

The Piazzas attracted many remarkable literary and scientific persons. In addition to Sir Godfrey Kneller, several gifted painters chose them for their studios—viz., John Zoffany, Aggas, Sir Peter Lely, Peter Roestraten, Mrs. S. P. Rose (a famous water-colourist), and John Mortimer Hamilton. Benjamin West, too, when he first came from America, resided in Covent Garden. The neighbouring streets also—King Street, Henrietta Street, &c.—were crowded with "persons of quality" and artists.

The area of Covent Garden, when as yet it had not been set aside for the worship of the goddess Pomona, was a fine open space, which served as a playground for the youths of London and Westminster, lying as it did half-way between each city. To this fact Gay alludes in his "Trivia," every line obviously being a sketch drawn from the life:—

"Where Covent Garden's famous temple stands,
That boasts the work of Jones' immortal hands,
Columns with plain magnificence appear,
And graceful porches lead along the square.
Here oft my course I bend, when, lo! from far
I spy the furies of the football war.
The 'prentice quits his shop to join the crew;
Increasing crowds the flying game pursue.
O whither shall I run? the throng draws nigh,
The ball now skims the street, now soars on high;
The dext'rous glazier strong returns the bound,
And jingling sashes on the penthouse sound."

But it is time to enter into a more detailed account of the district. The large square, with the fruit and vegetable market in its centre, which is known to every Londoner and to most Englishmen as "Covent Garden," was laid out during 1630-31 by Francis, fourth Earl of Bedford, from the designs of Inigo Jones. In all probability the Square was never completed, its sides being built at different times; and Peter Cunningham was of opinion that they may not have been even "designed in full." The Arcade or Piazza, however, ran along not only the north but the whole of the eastern side. That part to the south of Russell Street, however, was burnt down, and the Piazza was never replaced, probably from motives of economy.

The church of St. Paul, erected between the years 1631 and 1638, also from the design of Inigo Jones, formed, as it still forms, the western side of "the Garden," whilst its southern side for many years was formed by a blank wall which bounded the garden of Bedford House. Along this ran a row of trees, under the shade of which the market was originally held, and afterwards in a few temporary stalls and sheds.

The Square, or "Market-place," as it is often called in books and documents of the date of the Rebellion and of Charles II., seems to have grown gradually in importance as a place of business. Its inhabitants doubtless were proud of it, and foresaw that in the course of time it would prove a source of income and profit. Accordingly we find the parishioners of St. Paul's, in 1656, taxing themselves for painting the benches and seats there, and ten years later for planting a new row of trees; and between 1665 and 1668 the wealthier residents subscribed various sums towards setting up the column and dial mentioned below. It was not, however, until 1671 that the market was formally established under a charter granted by the king to the Earl of Bedford; and Mr. Cunningham tells us that eight years later, when the market was the first time actually rated to the poor, there were twenty-three salesmen amenable to the rate. For a contemporary description of the market as it was in 1689, we fortunately have Strype to refer to. He writes:—

"The south side of Covent Garden Square lieth open to Bedford Garden, where there is a small grotto of trees, most pleasant in the summer season; and on this side there is kept a market for fruits, herbs, roots, and flowers every Tuesday, Thursday, and Saturday; which is grown to a considerable account, and well served with choice goods, which makes it much resorted to." It would appear, however, from another passage in Strype, that at this time it was inferior as a market to the "Stocks' Market" in the City—of which we have already spoken*—afterwards transferred to the west side of Farringdon Street. In 1710, as we can see by a print published in that year, the market was still restricted to a few stalls and sheds on the south side.

Before the middle of the century, however, a great change had come over the place: the streets around being largely inhabited by well-to-do persons and their dependents, the market gradually increased; and the small hucksters and retail dealers began to erect sleeping apartments

* See Vol. I., p. 436; Vol. II., p. 497.

over their stalls to such an extent as to provoke a memorial from the inhabitants in vestry assembled to the Duke of Bedford, complaining of this encroachment as prejudicial to the tradesmen and fair dealers.

The prints of the square, at the time of which we write, show the inclosure as gravelled, and fenced in with rows of low posts and chains. In its centre was a fluted column of the Corinthian order, with a sun-dial on the top, which would appear by an inscription to have been erected in 1668. Thornton, in his "Survey of London and Westminster" (1786), speaks of the column as surrounded by *four* sun-dials, and informs us that the inner portion of the Square at that time was surrounded by light wooden rails.

The column, as we learn from another source, stood on a pedestal, which was raised upon six steps of black marble. The capital was very much enriched; it supported a square stone, *three* sides of which served as sun-dials. Upon this stone stood a globe, supported by four scrolls. It was removed in June, 1790.

Upon the steps of this column sat sundry old women who sold milk, porridge, barley-broth, &c., and to whom allusion is thus made in a *brochure* entitled "The Humours of Covent Garden," published in 1738:—

> "High in the midst of this most happy land
> A well-built marble pyramid does stand,
> By which spectators know the time o' th' day
> From beams reflecting of the solar ray;
> Its basis with ascending steps is grac'd,
> Around whose area cleanly matrons plac'd
> Vend their most wholesome food, by Nature good,
> To cheer the spirits and enrich the blood."

Mr. Peter Cunningham reminds us that the scene of Dryden's *Sir Martin Mar-all* is laid in this once fashionable quarter of the town, and that allusions to the Square, the Church, and the Piazza are of constant occurrence in the dramas of the reigns of Charles II., James II., William and Mary, and Anne. Thus the Piazza is the locality of a scene in *The Soldier's Fortune* of Otway, and also of one in *The Country Wife* of Wycherley.

There were plenty of stands for hackney coaches in and around Covent Garden at the commencement of the reign of George III., and Voltaire probably often used them in passing backwards and forwards between the theatres and his lodgings in Maiden Lane. The forms and shapes of these lumbering vehicles are familiar to all who know Kip's prints of the period referred to.

Such, then, in its main and leading features, was and is the district which will occupy our attention during the next two or three chapters, a district most interesting in a literary point of view, though the coffee-house and theatrical elements will be found, we fear, to predominate very much over that of domestic life. In fact, with the exception of certain actresses, and a few grand ladies of "the quality," the feminine element is "conspicuous by its absence," the coffee-houses of the last century being the equivalent of the clubs and club-land of the present.

The vicinity, however, it is only fair to state here, bore scarcely a higher repute on quite another score. At night it was simply unsafe for pedestrians. For was not Dryden waylaid and beaten by Mohocks or Mohawks at the corner of Rose Street and King Street? In spite of this fact, however, and although it is well known that certain parts of London, Hyde Park for instance, a century ago were very unsafe thoroughfares, on account of footpads and highway robbers, we may raise a smile of incredulity on the faces of some of our readers when we quote the following remarks from Shenstone, in the reign of George II.:—

"London is really dangerous at this time; the pickpockets, formerly content with mere filching, make no scruple to knock people down with bludgeons in Fleet Street and the Strand, and that at no later hour than eight o'clock at night; but in the Piazzas, Covent Garden, they come in large bodies, armed with couteaus, and attack whole parties, so that the danger of coming out of the playhouses is of some weight in the opposite scale when I am disposed to go to them oftener than I ought." And in like manner, and with the same meaning, Shadwell in one of his plays makes a character remark: "They were brave fellows indeed; for in those days a man could not go from the 'Rose' Tavern to the Piazza once but he must venture his life twice."

The Mohocks are well described in the *Spectator*, and in Swift's *Journal;* and Shadwell's comedy of *The Scourers* affords a striking picture of the dangerous state of the streets of London at night in the early part of the eighteenth century. In reference to this, Gay writes:—

> "Who has not heard the Scourers' midnight fame?
> Who has not trembled at the Mohocks' name?"

"These disorderly ruffians," observes Mr. Peter Cunningham, "seldom ventured within the City proper, where the watch was more efficient than in any other part; but took their stand about St. Clement Danes and Covent Garden, breaking the watchman's lantern and halberd, and frequently locking him up in his own stand-box." The curious reader may find much amusing information on this subject in the old ballad of "The Ranting

Rambler, or a Young Gentleman's Frolic through the City at night, and when he was taken by the Watch," printed in Mackay's "Songs of the London Prentices' and Traders;" and in Arthur Murphy's letters to David Garrick will be found a graphic sketch of one of the best of the race, known as "Tiger Roach," the bully of the "Bedford Coffee-house" in 1769.

It is satisfactory to know that, thanks to the police, both the Piazza and King Street are to be traversed now-a-days with less danger to life and limb.

CHAPTER XXXI.

COVENT GARDEN (*continued*).

"Thames Street gives cheeses, Covent Garden fruits;
Moorfields old books, and Monmouth Street old suits."—*Gay's Trivia.*

The Market described—The Covent Garden of the Past and Present contrasted—Best Time to view the Market—The Flower Market—The Piazza—The Irish Society of Fortune-hunters—Pepys in the Piazza—Theodore Hook and Sheridan—The Puppet Show—The "Bedford Coffee House"—The Floral Hall—The "Hummums"—"Evans's Hotel"—The Old Supper Room—The New Hall—Famous Residents in Covent Garden—Auction Rooms—Marriage à-la-Mode.

It is now, however, time to proceed to a more minute description of Covent Garden itself. The present market, which occupies all the centre of the square, consists of a central arcade and two side rows of shops, intersected in the centre by another thoroughfare at right angles. It was built, in 1830, by John, sixth Duke of Bedford, whose architect was Mr. William Fowler. The centre consists of an arch raised upon the entablature of two Tuscan columns, with a single-faced archivolt supported by two piers, which carry a lofty triangular pediment, the tympanum of which is embellished by the armorial bearings of the noble owner of the soil, his Grace the Duke of Bedford. On each side of this appropriate centre, which is high enough to admit a lofty loaded wagon into the central area, is a colonnade of the Tuscan order, projecting before the shops. The columns are of granite; and over the east end is the inscription, "JOHN, DUKE OF BEDFORD. Erected MDCCCXXX."

At each of the extreme angles of the four portions of this new market are raised quadrangular pavilions, which break the monotony of the composition in a very satisfactory and artistic manner, for they are at the same time useful and ornamental. The area of the market is about three acres, and it forms the principal mart of the metropolis for fruit, vegetables and flowers.

Those who wish to see the sight and smell the scent of fresh flowers in London in the summer should pay a visit to Covent Garden before, or, at the latest, soon after sunrise on Tuesday, Thursday, or Saturday; but the central arcade is a pretty sight at whatever time, and in whatever season, it may be visited.

"The contrast between the Covent Garden of fifty years ago and the present," says Mr. Diprose, in his "Book about London," "is as wide a one as can possibly exist. The old watchman—helpless for good, and the most corrupt of public officers—the turbulent and drunken old women, the porters quarrelling over their morning potations, the jaded and neglected horse dropping beneath the cart-load of half-rotten turnips, the London rakes—(fast men of those days)—making, not the night, but morning, hideous by their obscene blasphemies, and deeming it conduct becoming of gentlemen to interrupt honest industry and to scoff at early labour;—all this has gone, and so also are the terrible lessons that it inculcated. Order is now preserved as well as it can be amongst a rude assemblage of women and men whose battle for existence begins when the civilisation of the great city slumbers."

"There is no *rus in urbe*," writes Charles Kenny, "like Covent Garden Market. Here Nature empties forth her teeming lap filled with the choicest of produce. . . . It is the metropolitan congress of the vegetable kingdom, where every department of the 'growing' and 'blowing' world has its representatives—the useful and the ornamental, the needful and the superfluous, the esculent and the medicinal. It is a twofold temple, dedicated to Pomona and Flora, in which daily devotion is paid to the productive divinities. Here, as in a very temple, all classes and grades, all denominations and distinctions of men jostle each other in the humility of a common dependence on the same appetites, the same instincts, the same organs of taste, sight, and smell—the fashionable lady, who has left her brougham at the entrance, in quest of some pampered nursling of the conservatory, and the wan needlewoman bent on the purchase of a bunch of wallflowers, or a root of pale primroses to keep her paler cheeks in countenance; the artisan's wife, purveying for her husband's meal, and the comfortable housekeeper, primed with the discriminating lore of Mrs. Glass, making provisions for her winter's preserves; the bloated *gourmand*, in search of precocious peas, and the sickly hypochondriac eager to try the virtue of some healing herb.

"The priestesses who serve the temple form two distinct classes—those of Pomona and those of Flora—the basket-woman and the bouquet-girl. As to the former, hers is no finiking type of female beauty; the taper waist and slender neck would ill befit the rude labours she is devoted to. Her portly figure is rather architectural than sculptural in its graces; and with arms upraised, in support of the basket balanced on her head, she might serve as a model for the caryatids of a new temple to the deity she serves.

"He who would behold her in full activity must gratify his curiosity at some expense. He must voluntarily accomplish that which is enforced upon the vegetable visitor of the market—he must tear himself from his bed, foregoing the suavities of the morning's sleep to face the bleak air of dawning day: unless, indeed, he repair to the scene, as we have often done, as a sort of 'finish'—to use the language of antiquated fast men—after a round of evening parties, his temples throbbing with an unhallowed mixture of festive beverages, from the bland negus to the ice-bound fire of champagne punch; his senses jaded with a thousand artificial and violent delights; and, perhaps, a secret wound rankling at his heart—a wound that he has attempted to treat with light indifference, and to bury under a hecatomb of flirtations, but which now asserts itself with redoubled pangs, and mingles its reproaches to the many-voiced objurgations of conscience to sicken and disgust him with his existence. Under such circumstances is it that the most striking phase of Covent Garden—that which it presents on the morning of a market-day—will produce its fullest effect.

"Towards the afternoon another and very different phase of the market is presented. To the range of heavy-tilted carts and wagons has succeeded a line of brilliant and elegant equipages. The *utile* has given place to the *dulce*, and pleasure now shows itself almost as busy as need. Over this period of the day Flora more especially presides, and the bouquet-girl—her priestess—is in the height of her ministry. Her delicate fingers are now busily employed in tricking out the loveliness of Nature; for even her loveliest daughters must be drilled and trained ere they can make their *début* in the world of artifice they are called upon to adorn. Their slender stems need a wiry support to prop the head that else would droop in the oppressive atmosphere of the ball-room or the theatre. Art must draw fresh beauties from the contrast of each with the other; nor will the self-complacent ingenuity that paints the lily and gilds refined gold be satisfied till it has completed their toilet by investing them in a white robe of broidered paper.

"The clients of the bouquet-girl consist almost exclusively of the sighing herd of lovers. These, with the exception of an occasional wholesale order from the manager of a theatre with a view to some triumphant *début*, form the staple consumers of her wares. But among the whole tribe she has no such insatiate customer as he who is struggling in the toils of a *danseuse*. 'If music be the food of love,' bouquets are certainly the very air upon the regular supply of which hangs its existence; and on such air does the *danseuse*, chameleon-like, seem exclusively to live. They are the Alpha and Omega, the beginning and the end of her life—the symbols of her triumphs, public and domestic."

Covent Garden Market, it is true, is a limited arena, in comparison with its requirements, and consequently on market mornings the streets and avenues around, for half a mile, are thronged with merchants and traders, with heavy carts or wagons, from the elegantly painted light van to the hand-cart of the humble coster. "The apparent tumult of these occasions," says Mr. Diprose, in his "Book about London," "is all sober business, and the earnestness of all present is most remarkable to a stranger, who is apt to look upon the scene as one of the wildest uproar and confusion. The thousands of tons of vegetables and fruit are dispersed through every avenue and artery of the metropolis by nine o'clock, and the market is then apparently emptied; excepting the many choice fruits and early vegetables to be found in the beautiful arcade, when the peaceable folks arrive on the exquisite mission of discovering delicacies for some poor cast-down invalid friend; and it is in this long-continued arch that the bouquets are made for the evening exhibitions which do such terrible mischief in Cupid's calendar, at balls, theatre, opera, concert, and in the private boudoir of my 'ladye-love.'"

A visit to Covent Garden Market in the early morning in summer is a sight that should not be missed. Between the hours of one and five there is apparently little bustle in the market, though business goes on rapidly; and the scene presented is curious in the extreme. It is one of those phases of life in which Charles Dickens delighted, and which would require the pen of Swift, or Sterne, or Fielding, to describe adequately and picturesquely, as it deserves. It has been sketched slightly by several hands, but by none perhaps as effectively as it might be. Nor can this be a matter of wonder; for in order to get a view of the scene an effort is required which would be too great a tax on the energies of a hard-worked man of letters in London, and would involve an amount of self-denial beyond his powers. But at all events, it is freely granted that "this *market*" is the most popular, not only in England, but throughout the world. "When I had no money," writes Charles Dickens, "I took a turn in Covent Garden, and stared at the pine-apples."

"People who know Covent Garden only in its quiet afternoon aspect," says a writer in the *City Press*, describing things as they were five-and-twenty years or so ago, "can form no idea of the vile den it is at the busy hour of daybreak. Then the cabbages and peas that have been fermenting in the wagons for some hours past are tilted out on the flag-stones, and scrambled for by porters, who die early through exhaustion and excessive labour at unseemly hours. Then it is that the citizen's dinner is tossed to and fro, smoking with the temperature it has attained by close packing and long confinement, and is at last consigned to an unclean cart, for the district where its destiny is to be completed. The citizens are happily ignorant of the copper used in cooking, and the preliminary cooking vegetables are subjected to on their way to and from the market. We are fully cognisant of the fact that Spitalfields and Farringdon absorb some portion of the trade in vegetables; but Covent Garden is *the* market, *par excellence*, and it is a disgrace to the metropolis to be compelled to rely on the capabilities of a place which, spacious as it may be, is fitted at the very utmost to serve as a market for a town of 60,000 inhabitants."

POWELL'S PUPPET-SHOW. *From a Contemporary Print.* (*See page* 250.)

"The flower market of Covent Garden," observes a clever American writer, "is carried on in

COVENT GARDEN MARKET ABOUT 1820.

the open area opposite the church, and at the entrance of the grand row of shops which runs down the centre. The growers chiefly bring their productions into the market at or before midnight, and about one o'clock is the briskest period of the sale, the road being rendered almost impassable from the number of basket-women and others taking in their supply for the day of flowers in pots, as well as cut flowers. A more animated scene of the bustle of business, with the gay and varied hue of the flowers, and their delightful fragrance, it is scarcely possible to describe, than that which continues till about four or five o'clock, when the traders, having generally exhausted their stock, return home, and the dealers are on their way to supply their different walks and routes for the day. The peripatetic dealers having obtained their supply, the next who come in for their share are the various greengrocers of the metropolis, who take but a limited supply; whilst the remnants are left to salesmen for the day's demand of the market. The chief source of the costermonger's market is in the metropolis; and their supply being exhausted on other days but those of the market-days of Tuesday, Thursday, and Saturday, they replenish their stock from the nurserymen, who may be considered the manufacturers, in the neighbourhood of the metropolis, from whom the limited and humble flora of the metropolis is supplied. It is amusing likewise to contemplate the variety of persons who, at an early hour in the morning, are the visitants of the Market. There are the humble trader trafficking with the grower for his day's supply; the rake or the *roué*, and the unhappy companion of his night's frolic and dissipation, retiring to their unhallowed rest, whilst others are actively employed in the business of the day; the sot reeling home from his night's debauch, unfitted for the occupation which demands his exertion; the unfortunate, who, homeless, has wandered the streets, and contemplates luxuries in which he cannot indulge; and others induced to visit thus early this fac-simile, as it may be termed, of the most interesting of country enjoyments in the pursuit of health and pleasurable gratification. Such compose the motley group which we jostle against in an early visit to Covent Garden Market.

"The nature of the supply of flowers to the market of course depends upon the season; but it is surprising to what an extent *art* has beaten *nature* in the race for priority. In the midst of winter Covent Garden Market shows all the realities of advanced and advancing spring. In February we have primulas, mignonette, wall-flowers, violets, tulips, hyacinths, narcissuses, and other forced bulbs; in March, forced verbenas, camellias, epacrises, the heaths of Australia, lilacs, rhododendrons, azaleas, the honeysuckles of the American woods, and kalmias; in April these are more numerous, with a variety of hybrid heaths, acacias, forced roses, and pelargoniums; in May a greater variety of heaths are coming to perfection; and now also we have, in large and interesting variety, pelargoniums or geraniums, the standard flower of English ornament; mignonette, which has continued in perfection all through this artificial season, is now very abundant, and the beautiful China roses add a variety to the scene. In June the varieties of pelargoniums are in full perfection, and upwards of one hundred distinct sorts grace the show in the market; so great being the supply at this time of year that frequently from five to six hundred dozens are daily sent by growers. We have now the beautiful pendant fuchsias, many sorts of verbenas, cactuses, hydrangeas, cockscombs, balsams, stocks, heartsease; and pinks and picotees will soon be added to enliven the floral scene. Now, too, we have the pretty gardenia or Cape jasmine; and the sweet-scented lemon-plant. The flower-market is at the acme of its perfection, and the usual variety of supply continues, with little variation, till the autumnal months."

Some idea may be formed of the taste for flowers in London, and the extent of trade done in them, by reading a case of bankruptcy before Mr. Registrar Brougham, October 19th, 1871, at the hearing of which a proof was put in for £353 for flowers supplied in six months to one individual. Among the items were charges of 10s. 6d. for a moss-rose, and £150 for lilies of the valley and ferns.

A new building has been erected in the south-east corner of the market-place, in which the whole-sale business of the flower-market is mainly carried on. The structure possesses little or nothing in the way of architectural pretensions, and has its principal entrance in Wellington Street.

At Wilton House, near Salisbury, the seat of the Earl of Pembroke, there is a fine picture of Covent Garden, painted by Inigo Jones himself. It represents the place in its original state, with a tree standing in the middle. A companion picture by the same artist, as already stated, it may be added, gives a view of Lincoln's Inn Fields when first built upon.

The houses on the north and east sides of the market inclosure, as already mentioned, were so built as to form a covered pathway before the shop-fronts, which was commonly known as the Piazza. The name "piazza," as every scholar knows, means in the Italian simply "place," or "square;" but with us it denotes an open arcade of semi-cloistral appearance. Such an arcade, running round the north and part of the east side of the great Square of Covent Garden, came, we know not exactly how, to be called "The Piazza"—possibly an instance of the logical fallacy which puts the part for the whole—and thus the term in English has passed into quite a different signification; and so in Blount's "Glossographia" it is vaguely explained as "a market-place or chief street, such as that in Covent Garden."

The Piazza when first erected was a fashionable lounge, and generally regarded as a work of high artistic merit. Allusions are constantly made to it in the works of the dramatists of the time of the Stuarts and of the first half of the eighteenth century, as a place of appointments and assignations. Peter Cunningham tells us that the north side was called the Great, and the east the Little Piazza; and that so popular and fashionable did the place become, that for a century after its erection many of the female children baptised in the parish were christened "Piazza!"

Thornton, in his "Survey of London and Westminster," published in 1786, says of the Piazza, that if it had been carried around the Square, according to the plan of Inigo Jones, it would have rendered Covent Garden one of the finest squares in Europe. This is perhaps the language of exaggeration; but it certainly is much to be regretted that the design was not carried out in its entirety. Horace Walpole writes: "In the arcade there is nothing very remarkable; the pilasters are as errant and homely stripes as any plasterer could have made." On this Mr. Peter Cunningham very justly remarks: "This is very true now, though hardly true in Walpole's time, when the arcade remained as Inigo Jones had built it, with stone pilasters on a red-brick frontage. The pilasters, as we now see them, are lost in a mass of compo and white paint; the red bricks have been whitened over, and the pitched roof of red tile replaced with flat slates." It will be remembered by readers of the English drama, that in this same piazza Otway has laid one of the scenes in his play, *The Soldier of Fortune*.

In discoursing of this parish, the "London Spy" (1725) observes that "the vicissitude of all human affairs is pretty discernible in the lives of the gamesters who patrol the Piazza for about three hours generally in the afternoon." The writer adds sarcastically, with reference to the freaks of fortune often witnessed here, as now-a-days at Homburg or Baden, "I have known an inauspicious hand of cards or dice transmute a silver-hilted sword into a brass one. . . On the other hand, a pair of second-hand shoes has often here stepped at once into a chariot."

The same authority states that in this parish the Irish Society of Fortune-hunters are said to hold their quarterly meetings; but, as his account of their "transactions" on one of these occasions is clearly an exaggerated piece of satire, it is probable that the statement should be received *cum grano salis*. Little boys used to play a bat game—a sort of cricket—under the Piazza.

Pepys thus writes, in his "Diary," under date of January 2, 1664-5:—"To my Lord Brounker's by appointment, under the Piazza in Covent Garden, where I occasioned much mirth with a ballet [ballad] that I brought with me made from the seamen at sea to their ladies in town." This ballad, it would appear, was none other than the well-known song beginning—

"To all ye ladies now on land."

In the Piazza, close to the steps of Covent Garden Theatre, about 1704, lived Sir Godfrey Kneller, State-painter to five sovereigns of England in succession, and the painter of scores of the leaders of fashion, as well as of the portraits of the "Kit-cat Club."

Here too Wilson, "the English Claude," friend of Garrick and Dr. Arne, had rooms in his palmy days; poor unlucky Wilson, with his Bardolph nose and fondness for porter and skittles! Utter opposite of the courtly Reynolds, Wilson died neglected and forgotten in a little village in Denbighshire; still his fame among connoisseurs now is almost as great as that of the famous portrait-painter, and happy the possessor of one of his classic sunshiny landscapes.

The "Piazza" Hotel, which may now be looked for in vain, was long a favourite resort of Richard Brinsley Sheridan and his friends.

It was by an improvisation at the "Piazza" Tavern that Theodore Hook, when little more than a lad, made that favourable impression on Sheridan which led to his introduction to the gay West-end circles in which for many years he shone supreme as a wit and amateur singer.

Under the Piazza in Covent Garden, Powell, about 1710, set up his well-known Puppet Show, which had acquired great celebrity in the provinces at Bath, and which is immortalised in the *Spectator*. It was humorously announced by Steele that Powell would gratify the town with the performance of his drama on the story of the chaste Susannah, which would be graced by the addition of two new elders. In the fourteenth number of the *Spectator* is a bantering letter which purports to be written by the sexton of St. Paul's parish church, and in which the latter complains, "When I toll to prayers, I find my congregation take warning of my bell, morning and evening, to go to a puppet-show set forth by one Powell under the Piazza. By this means I have not only lost two of my best customers, whom I used to place, for sixpence a-piece, over against Mrs. Rachel Eyebright, but Mrs. Rachel herself has gone thither also. There now appear among us none but a few ordinary people, who come to church only to say their prayers, so that I have no work worth speaking of but on Sundays. I have placed my son at the Piazzas to acquaint the ladies that the bell rings for church, and that it stands on the other side of the garden; but they only laugh at the child. I desire that you would lay this before all the whole world, that I may not be made such a tool for the future, and that Punchinello may choose hours less canonical. As things are now, Mr. Powell has a full congregation, while we have a very thin house." So well known and popular was this place of amusement that Burnet asks, in "The Second Tale of a Tub," "What man or child that lives within the verge of Covent Garden, or what beau, belle, or visitant of Bath, knows not Mr. Powell?"

The "Bedford Coffee-house"—an establishment rendered famous in connection with the names of Garrick, Quin, Foote, Murphy, Sheridan, and other theatrical celebrities—stood at the north-east corner of the Piazza. "This coffee-house," observes a writer in the *Connoisseur* (in 1754), "affords every variety of character. This coffee-house is crowded every night with men of parts. Almost every one you meet is a polite scholar and a wit; jokes and *bon-mots* are echoed from box to box; every branch of literature is critically examined, and the merit of every production of the press, or performance at the theatres, weighed and determined. This school . . . . . has bred up many authors to the amazing entertainment and instruction of their readers." It appears to have been modelled on "Button's," but it never reached the fame of that coffee-house, frequented as it had been—even by the confession of its friends and supporters—by Addison, Steele, and Pope, in the previous generation. And yet the "Bedford" once attracted so much attention as a place of public resort as to have its history written. Nor is its history one of those "blanks" which, if the proverb be true, constitute the happiness of nations and peoples; for a search in the Library of the British Museum will convince even the most incredulous that the "Memoirs of the 'Bedford' Coffee House," which were first published in 1751, reached a second edition twelve years afterwards.

The "Bedford" was Foote's favourite coffee-house. In 1754, when it was in the height of its fame, Foote would sit there, in his usual corner, a king among the critics and wits, like Addison and Steele at "Button's." "The regular frequenters of the room," says Mr. John Timbs, "strove to get admitted to his party at supper; and others got as near as they could to the table, as the only wit flowed from Foote's tongue." Everybody who knew this celebrated wit came early, in the hope of being one of his party during supper; and those who were not acquaintances had the same curiosity in engaging the boxes near him. Foote, in return, was no niggard in his conversation, but, on the contrary, was as generous as he was affluent. He talked upon most subjects with great knowledge and fluency; and whenever a flash of wit, a joke, or a pun came in his way, he gave it in such a style of genuine humour as was always sure to circulate a laugh, and this laugh was his glory and triumph.

Another frequenter of the "Bedford" was Garrick. One day he was leaving the house with Foote, when the latter let fall a guinea, and exclaimed as he looked about for it, "Why, where on earth has it gone to?" "Gone to the d——l!" replied Garrick, still, however, continuing the search. "Well said, David," was the quick and witty answer of Foote; "let you alone for making a guinea go further than any one else in the world."

It will be remembered that here, too, at the shilling rubber meeting, arose the sharp squabble between Hogarth and Churchill, when Hogarth used some insulting language towards Churchill, who resented it in "The Epistle." "Never," says Horace Walpole, "did two angry men of their abilities throw mud at each other with less dexterity."

It was at the "Bedford Coffee-house" that the Beefsteak Club, of which we have already spoken in connection with the Lyceum Theatre, was for some time held under date of 1814. Mr. J. T. Smith, in his "Book for a Rainy Day," writes:—"Mr. John Nixon, of Basinghall Street, gave me the following information respecting the Beefsteak Club. Mr. Nixon, as secretary, had possession of the original book. Lambert's Club was first held in Covent Garden Theatre, in the upper room, called the 'Thunder and Lightning;' then in one even with the two-shilling gallery; next in an apartment even with the boxes; and afterwards in a lower room, where they remained until the fire. After that time, Mr. Harris insisted upon it, as the playhouse was a new building, that the Club should not be held there. They then went to the 'Bedford Coffee-house' next door. Upon the ceiling of the dining-room they placed Lambert's original gridiron, which had been saved from the fire. They had a kitchen, a cook, and a wine-cellar, &c, entirely independent of the 'Bedford Coffee-house.' The society held at Robins's room was called the 'Ad Libitum' Society, of which Mr. Nixon had the books, but it was quite unconnected with the Beefsteak Club." Previously to being called the "Bedford" the house had been held by Macklin, who then kept what Fielding calls a "Temple of Luxury."

In the north-east corner of the Piazza, and immediately adjoining the Opera House, with which it communicates, is the Floral Hall. This elegant building was intended as the realisation of a long-cherished scheme on the part of Mr. Gye, namely, to establish a vast central flower-market, for many years a growing desideratum in the metropolis. An opportunity was at last presented by the rebuilding of Covent Garden Theatre, after its destruction in 1856; and it was decided to carry out Mr. Gye's favourite plan, by erecting an arcade on the south side of the new Opera House. The ground-plan of the building may be described as resembling two sides of an unequal triangle, the principal entrance being by the side of the Opera House, in Bow Street, at the end of the longer side of the figure, while the other opens upon Covent Garden Market, on the side of the Piazza. The public footway of the Piazza is continued along the Covent Garden entrance, in the shape of a gallery roofed with glass and iron. The main arcades run in a direct line from the entrances, and are surmounted at the point of junction by a lofty dome of fifty feet span, which forms an imposing object in the view. This dome, as well as the roofs, are principally composed of wrought iron; the arches, columns, and piers are of cast iron; the frontage, both in Bow Street and the Piazza, is of iron and glass, of which the entire structure is principally composed, brickwork forming but a very small part of the composition. The utmost length of the arcade, from the Bow Street entrance to the west wall, is 227 feet; and the length of the shorter side, from Covent Garden Market to the wall of the theatre, nearly 100 feet. The total height, from the ground to the top of the arched dome, is rather over 90 feet. Each of the main arcades is 75 feet wide, and has a side-aisle between the main columns and the wall, 13 feet in width and 30 in height. The entrances are both elegant and simple, the doorways being so deeply recessed as, in conjunction with the richly-designed iron arches which give admission to the interior, to obviate the flat appearance which generally characterises buildings of glass and iron. The interior is fully equal in lightness and grace of design to the exterior. The columns which support the roof are of cast iron, with richly ornamented capitals, the latter perforated, in order to ventilate the basement beneath, with which the hollow columns communicate. The ground having been excavated beneath, the principal floor forms a basement of the same area as the building above it, and sixteen feet in height, the floor of the arcade being supported by cast-iron columns. This building was, as its name implies, designed for a flower-market, and was expected to prove a boon to the many florists and nurserymen scattered among the outskirts of London, but has never fulfilled the purpose for which it was erected. It was opened on the 7th of March, 1860, with a Volunteer ball, under royal patronage, and for a time was employed principally for promenade concerts; in it is now held the wholesale market for foreign fruit.

In the south-east corner of the market-place, and occupying that portion which was destroyed by fire, stood two hotels, known by the strange names of the "Old Hummums" and the "New Hummums." The name is a corruption of the Eastern word "Humoum." Mr. Wright, in his "History of Domestic Manners of England," says, "Among the customs introduced from Italy was the hot sweating bath, which, under the name of the hot-house, became widely known in England for a considerable time." Sweating in those hot-houses is spoken of by Ben Jonson; and in the old play of *The Puritan*, a character, speaking of some laborious undertaking, says, "Marry, it will take me much sweat; 'twere better to go to sixteen hot-houses." These "Hummums," however, when established in London, seem to have been mostly frequented by women of doubtful repute, and they became, as in the East, favourite rendezvous for gossip and company of not the most moral kind. They soon came to be used for the purposes of intrigue, and were eventually suppressed.

The "Old Hummums" was the scene of what Dr. Johnson pronounced the best accredited ghost-story that he had ever heard. The individual whose ghost was said to have appeared here in a supernatural manner was a Mr. Ford, a relation or connection of the learned doctor, and said to have been the riotous parson of Hogarth's "Midnight Modern Conversations." The "Old Hummums" was pulled down in 1881; and the site is now occupied by a large hotel, styled "The Hummums."

In the north-west corner of Covent Garden is a large house once known as Evans's Music-hall. It is a fine specimen of a London mansion of the olden time. It was built originally in the reign of Charles II., and was for a time the residence of Sir Kenelm Digby, as we learn from Aubrey's "Lives:"—"Since the restoration of Charles II., he (Sir Kenelm Digby) lived in the last faire house westward in the north portion of Covent Garden, where my Lord Denzill Holles lived since. He had a laboratory there. I think he dyed (died) in this house."

THE OLD ROOM AT "EVANS'S."

The mansion was subsequently altered, if not rebuilt, for the Earl of Orford, better known by the name of Admiral Russell, the same who, in 1692, defeated Admiral de Tourville, near La Hogue, and ruined the French fleet. From the Earl of Orford it passed to the Lords Archer. The house, which is said to have been the first family hotel established in London, is built of fine red brick, and down to about the year 1850, when considerable alterations were made in its appearance, the façade was thought to resemble the forecastle of a ship. The front of the house, still used as an hotel, is remarkable for its magnificent carved staircase, and for at least one elegantly painted ceiling, which remains in its original state.

At the end of the last, and during the early part of the present century, when used as a dinner and coffee-room only, it was called in the slang of the day, "The Star," from the number of men of rank by whom it was frequented. Indeed, it is said that

"MORNING." *From Hogarth's Print.* (*See page* 257.)

previous to the establishment of clubs, it was no unusual occurrence for nine dukes to dine there in one evening.

Part of the house was long used for the reception of the Savage Club, composed mainly of dramatists and dramatic authors.

"Evans's" is thus described by a writer in *Once a Week*, in 1867 :—"About twenty years ago the list of metropolitan concert-rooms was headed by 'the Cyder Cellars' and 'Evans's.' The entertainments to be found in such places were not very select; but while the former has disappeared altogether, the latter has been altered and purged. The surviving establishment, half supper-room and half music-hall, and one of the 'lions of London,' is situated at the western extremity of Covent Garden Piazza. It is subject to peculiar and stringent regulations. Ladies are not admitted, except on giving their names and addresses, and then only enjoy the privilege of watching the proceedings from behind a screen. The whole of the performances are sustained by the male sex, and an efficient choir of men and boys sing glees, ballads, madrigals, and selections from operas, the accompaniments being supplied on the piano and harmonium. . . The new hall, one of the most elaborately ornamented in London, was erected from designs by Mr. Finch Hill. Its proportions are certainly fine, and the decorations cost about £5,000. On the occasion of our last visit to 'Evans's,' we heard standard music, English, German, and Italian, performed with admirable spirit, precision, and delicacy. The performances commence at eight o'clock; and we recommend 'Evans's' to the notice of steady young men who admire a high class of music, see no harm in a good supper, but avoid theatres and the ordinary run of music-halls. The so-called *café* is a spacious room, supported by pillars, and hung round with portraits of actresses. Previous to the erection of the new hall, the chamber thus adorned was used as the singing-room."

The music-hall, to which the *café* formed a sort of vestibule, was built in 1856, and ran out at the rear of the house, occupying a plot of ground which was formerly the garden of Sir Kenelm Digby. At a later period the site contained a cottage in which the Kemble family occasionally resided, when in the full tide of their popularity. According to tradition it was in this cottage that their talented daughter, Miss Fanny Kemble, was born. The hall was about 70 feet in length, by about 33 feet in width and height. The carved ceiling, richly painted in panels, was supported on either side by a row of substantial columns with ornamental capitals, from which sprang bold and massive arches; these columns helped also to support the gallery, which extended along the two sides and one end of the hall, and in which were the private screened boxes alluded to above. The hall was well ventilated, well conducted, well served, and therefore well patronised, particularly between the hours of ten and twelve, when visitors were continually dropping in to enjoy a hot supper and listen at the same time to the charming melodies provided for their delectation.

After enjoying for many years a fair share of popularity. "Evans's Music-hall" was closed in 1880, and soon after the building was converted into a club-house to be occupied by the Falstaff Club. It is now known as Lockhart's Coffee Rooms.

Sir William Alexander, Earl of Stirling, the poet, resided in 1637 in a house in the north-west corner of Covent Garden; here also Thomas Killigrew, the wit, was living between the years 1637 and 1662. The site was afterwards occupied by Denzil Holles, Sir Harry Vane, Sir Kenelm Digby; Lord Crewe, Bishop of Durham; and Russell, Earl of Orford. The house was subsequently taken by Lord Archer, who married Sarah, the daughter of Mr. West, some time President of the Royal Society. Mr. West's library and collection of prints, coins, and medals, were sold in this house, and occupied the auctioneer six weeks in the disposal of them. After the above sale in 1773, the mansion was converted into a family hotel, by a person named Low, and is said to have been the first of the kind established in London. About 1790, a Mrs. Hudson became proprietor. Her advertisements were curious; one ends thus—"Accommodation, with stabling, for one hundred noblemen and horses." After one or two more changes in the proprietorship, the hotel came into the hands of Mr. W. C. Evans, of Covent Garden Theatre, whose name henceforth became so closely associated with it. In 1844 he retired, and Mr. John Green became proprietor and manager. This gentleman, who was well known in the musical profession as "Paddy Green," was a man of rather eccentric character; he died in December, 1874.

It was in the north-western angle of the Piazza that Sir Peter Lely resided for many years. It is well known that names were sometimes adopted from sign-boards. That of Rothschild, the "Red Shield," is an example. Another instance is to be found in Sir Peter Lely. "His grandfather," says Mr. Larwood, "was a perfumer, named Van der Vaas, and lived at the sign of the 'Lily'—possibly a 'vase' of lilies. When his son entered the English army, he discarded his Dutch name, and for the paternal sign adopted the more euphonious name of Lilly or Lely." He died at the age of sixty-three, in 1680.

To the above list of notables who have resided here must be added the name of Dr. Berkeley, the philosopher, Bishop of Cloyne. Zoffany's house was the same which afterwards became the auction-room of George Robins, and Peter Cunningham identified "the second house eastward from James Street" as the abode of Sir James Thornhill.

The auction-rooms of George Robins were for many years one of the celebrities of London. They were formerly known as "Langford's and Cox's," and formed part of the mansion originally tenanted by Sir Peter Lely; but more recently they were used by the owner of the Tavistock Hotel as breakfast-rooms. In these rooms, says Mr. Peter Cunningham, "Hogarth exhibited his 'Marriage à la Mode' gratis to the public." These are the same rooms which we have mentioned as subsequently tenanted by Richard Wilson, the landscape painter, if we may believe Mr. J. T. Smith, in his "Life of Nollekens."

It may be worth a passing note to record the fact that Covent Garden was the first place in London where a balcony or "belconey," as it was at first styled, was set up; it was said to be an invention of the Lord Arundel of the time.

CHAPTER XXXII.

COVENT GARDEN AND ITS NEIGHBOURHOOD (*continued*).

Ἀγορὰ 'ν Ἀθήναις χαῖρε.

Aristoph., "*Acharn.*"

St. Paul's Church first built—Destroyed by Fire and rebuilt—Dispute between the Earl of Bedford and the Vicar of St. Martin's-in-the-Fields—Horace Walpole's Criticism of the Building—Extracts from the Parish Register—Notabilities interred in the Churchyard—The Parish Rate-books and Church Registers—"King's" Coffee House—The Westminster Elections—The Duchess of Devonshire and Lady Duncannon's Patriotism—Fox "chaired" as the Man for the People—"Treasonable Practices" of the "Independent Electors"—Excitement consequent on the Westminster Elections—Morals of Covent Garden in the Seventeenth Century—Suicide of Mr. Damer—Arrest of the Muscovite Ambassador, and his Detention in the "Black Raven"—The "Finish"—The "Museum Minervæ"—The Marquis of Worcester and the Convent Garden—Noted Residents of Covent Garden—Tavistock Street—Tavistock Row—Charles Macklin's Residence—The Murder of Miss Ray.

THE parish church of St. Paul, Covent Garden, on the west side of the market, as we have said, was built by Inigo Jones, in 1633, at the expense of the ground-landlord, Francis, Earl of Bedford. It was consecrated by Juxon, Bishop of London, on the 27th of September, 1638; repaired, in 1727, by the Earl of Burlington; totally destroyed by fire on the 17th of September, 1795; and rebuilt (John Hardwick, architect) on the plan and in the proportions of the original building. The great delay between the period of erection and that of consecration was owing to a dispute between the Earl of Bedford and Bray, the Vicar of St. Martin's-in-the-Fields, on the right of presentation; the earl claiming it as his own, because he had built it at his own expense, and the vicar claiming it as his own, because, not being then parochial, it was nothing more than a chapel-of-ease to St. Martin's. The matter was heard by the King in Council on the 6th of April, 1638, and judgment given in favour of the earl.

The architecture of St. Paul's Church was not to the taste of Horace Walpole, who criticises it in his usual caustic style:—"The arcade of Covent Garden, and the church—two structures of which I want taste to see the beauties. In the arcade there is nothing remarkable; the pilasters are as errant and homely stripes as any plasterer would make. The barn roof over the portico of the church strikes my eyes with as little idea of dignity or beauty as it could do if it covered nothing but a barn. In justice to Inigo, one must own that the defect is not in the architect, but in the order: who ever saw a beautiful Tuscan building? Would the Romans have chosen that order for a temple? Mr. Onslow, the late Speaker, told me an anecdote that corroborates my opinion of this building. When the Earl of Bedford sent for Inigo, he told him he wanted a chapel for the parishioners of Covent Garden, but added he would not go to any considerable expense. 'In short,' said he, 'I would have it not much better than a barn.' 'Well, then,' replied Jones, 'you shall have the handsomest barn in England.' The expense of building was £4,500."

The parish register records the baptism of Lady Mary Wortley Montague, and the marriage (1764) of Lady Susan Strangways to O'Brien, the handsome actor.

In the churchyard hard by lie buried many eminent persons: amongst others, Robert Carr, Earl of Somerset, who died in 1645; Sir Henry Herbert (whose "office book," as "Master of the Revels," throws so much light on the history of our stage and drama in the time of Charles I.), brother to Lord Herbert of Cherbury and George Herbert, who died in 1673. Not far off rests Samuel Butler, the author of "Hudibras." Butler died in Rose Street, of consumption, on the 25th of September, 1680, and was buried, "according to his owne appointment," as Aubrey tells us in his "Lives," "in the churchyard of Covent Garden; sc. in the north part next the church at the east end. His feet touch the wall. His grave 2 yards distant from the pilaster of the dore (by his desire), 6 foot deepe. About 25 of his old acquaintance at his funerall: I myself being one." It is a "moot point" whether Samuel Butler was buried at the eastern or the western end of the north wall of the churchyard, the accounts of two individuals who might be presumed to be best acquainted with the exact spot where he lies being in conflict on this matter of detail. "Subsequently," says Mr. J. H. Jesse, "some persons unknown to fame erected a monument to the memory of the poet, in the churchyard, but apparently no trace of it now remains." Here, too, lies buried Sir Peter Lely, the painter, who died in the Piazza in 1680. His monument of white marble, which shared the fate of the church when destroyed by fire in 1795, was adorned with a bust of the great artist between two Cupids, as well as with fruit, foliage, and other devices, executed by Gibbons: the inscription alone has been preserved. Near him lie Dick Estcourt, the actor and wit, who died in 1711-12, and Edward Kynaston, the celebrated actor of female parts at the Restoration—a complete female stage-beauty, "that it has since been disputable among the judicious, whether any woman that succeeded him so sensibly touched the audience as he."* Here too rest William Wycherly, the dramatist, who died in Bow Street in 1715; Pierce Tempest, who drew the "Cries of London," known as "Tempest's Cries," and who died in 1717; and Grinling Gibbons, the sculptor and carver in wood, who died in 1721. Not far off are Mrs. Centlivre, author of *The Busybody* and *The Wonder*, and Robert Wilkes (the original "Sir Harry Wildair," celebrated by Steele for acting with the easy frankness of a gentleman), who died in 1731. Near him are James Worsdale, the painter, who carried Pope's letters to Curll and, dying in 1767, was buried in the churchyard, with an inscription (removed in 1848) of his own composing; also John Wolcot, the "Peter Pindar" of the reign of George III., whom he lashed, as well as his minister Pitt, with merciless vigour and persistency. He became the popular satirist of the day, and the fluency of his pen was equalled by its grossness and obscene vulgarity. Those who remember him when he lived in the neighbourhood say that he was a gross sensualist, in spite of his moral mission as a satirist, and that he whimsically lay in bed nearly all day because it was easier to exist when his body weighed only a few ounces than when he had to carry some fifteen stone about. He died in January, 1819, and deserves mention here on account of his eccentricities, of which it were much to be wished that they could be called harmless ones. But he was the enemy of others as well as of himself, and no one cares to say a good word on his behalf. Here also may or might be seen a curious epitaph upon Mr. Button, who kept the noted coffee-house in Russell Street:—

> "Odds fish, and fiery coals,
> Are graves become Button-holes!"

In St. Paul's Church is buried, in a nameless grave, a lady, who died in James Street, in this parish, in March, 1720, and who was described at the time simply as "the unknown." This mysterious person is described by Mr. J. Timbs, in his "Romance of London," as "middle-sized, with dark brown hair, and very beautiful features, and the mistress of every accomplishment of fashion. Her circumstances," he continues, "were affluent, and she possessed many rich trinkets set with diamonds. A Mr. John Ward, of Hackney, published several particulars of her in the newspapers, and amongst others said that a servant had been directed by her to deliver to him a letter after her death; but, as no servant appeared, he felt himself required to notice those circumstances, in order to acquaint her relations that her death occurred suddenly after a masquerade, where she declared that she had conversed with the king; and it was remembered that she had been seen in the private apartments of Queen Anne, though, after the queen's death, she lived in obscurity. 'The unknown' arrived in London in 1714 from Mansfield, in a carriage drawn by six horses. She frequently said that her brother was a nobleman, but that her elder brother dying unmarried, the title was extinct; adding that she had an uncle living from whom she had expectations. It was conjectured," adds Mr. Timbs, though he does not tell us why, "that she was the daughter of a Roman Catholic, who had consigned her to a convent." But the rumours "lacks confirmation."

Mr. J. H. Jesse, in his "London," pronounces St. Paul's Church as "unquestionably the most interesting spot in Covent Garden;" and possibly it might be so had not the old church been destroyed by fire at the end of the last century. "Few persons," he writes, "who are in the habit of passing by this heavy-looking building, are aware that, with the exception of Westminster Abbey, here lie the remains of more men of genius than, apparently, in any other church in London." He adds, however, that "except a small tablet to the memory of Macklin, the actor, it contains no

* Downe's "Roscius Anglicanus," 8vo. 1708.

monumental memorials of the dead;" a fact, we should have thought, which would have been very fatal to its claim to be the "most interesting spot" of the neighbourhood. We want to see these mute memorials with our eyes, and to read the names inscribed upon them, in order to realise, save in the faintest sense, the local and personal interest which clings to such places.

The rectory of St. Paul's, Covent Garden, is still in the patronage of the Duke of Bedford; and, curiously enough, the parish is entirely surrounded by that of St. Martin's-in-the-Fields, from which it was cut off.

The rate-books of this parish are kept carefully arranged in streets, like a Post-office Directory; and they contain the name of every householder from the first formation of the parish down to the present day. The church registers also are kept with scrupulous care.

Close under the portico of the church was a common kind of shed, "once well known," says Arthur Murphy, "to all gentlemen to whom beds are unknown," facetiously termed "King's Coffee House." "It was kept," writes Peter Cunningham, "by a person of the name of Tom King, and it forms a conspicuous feature in Hogarth's print of 'Morning.'" Of this print we give an engraving on page 253. The coffee-house has, however, long since been swept away.

As the hustings for the Westminster elections, from time immemorial to a recent date, have been fixed before the east end of St. Paul's Church, that side of Covent Garden has often witnessed the most exciting scenes. But never was witnessed, either there or elsewhere, an election more exciting than that of May, 1784, when the Tory party moved heaven and earth to exclude the Whig leader, Charles James Fox, from the representation of Westminster. As, day after day, the inhabitants of the metropolitan parishes had polled, and the numbers were nearly even, the task of beating up the outlying voters in the suburbs was undertaken with a heart and a will by Georgiana, Duchess of Devonshire, and her sister, Lady Duncannon. "These ladies," writes Sir N. W. Wraxall, "being furnished with lists of the outlying voters, drove in their carriages to their respective dwellings, sparing neither entreaties nor promises. In some instances even personal caresses were said to have been permitted in order to prevail on the sulky and inflexible; and there can be no doubt of common mechanics having been conveyed to the hustings by the Duchess in her own coach." The effect of such a powerful intervention soon showed itself. Fox was soon a hundred votes ahead of his opponent, Sir Cecil Wrey, and in spite of the counter efforts of the Countess of Salisbury, at the close of the poll he had a clear majority of 235. It was on this occasion that an Irish costermonger, if we may believe the story, came up to Her Grace of Devonshire, who was one of the leading beauties of the day, and respectfully and wittily entreated to be allowed to "light his pipe at her ladyship's eye." It is on record that Her Grace of Devonshire used regularly, on the occasion of an election, to hire a first-floor in Henrietta Street in order that she might witness the proceedings, and lend at least her countenance to the Whig party. From the hustings at Covent Garden a procession was formed, and Fox was "chaired," as the man of the people, through the chief streets of Westminster to Carlton House, the gates of which were thrown open to the excited multitude; the ostrich plumes carried in front of him denoting the patronage of the Whig cause by the Prince of Wales; while another flag was inscribed with the words, "Sacred to Female Patriotism," in allusion to the Duchess of Devonshire. The intense feelings excited on this occasion are thus summed up by a contemporary writer:—"All minor interests were swallowed up in this struggle, which held not only the capital, but also the nation, in suspense, while it rendered Covent Garden and its neighbourhood, during three successive weeks, a scene of outrage and even of blood."

The Westminster elections would seem generally to have been conducted with very bitter feelings on both sides. We are told by Wright, in a footnote to the letters of Horace Walpole, how the keeper of the "White Horse" in Piccadilly, being at a dinner among the "independent electors," taking notes in pencil, was beaten and cuffed by them, being supposed to be an informer against their treasonable practices. Among the more noteworthy persons who have figured upon the hustings here, have been Sir Francis Burdett ("Old Glory"), Sir John Hobhouse, Lord Cochrane, Mr. John Stuart Mill, and General Sir De Lacy Evans.

Down to the passing of the first Reform Bill the voting continued for fourteen days, during which the whole of London was kept in a state of violent excitement. Mr. H. C. Robinson, in his "Diary," speaks of a Westminster election as "a scene only ridiculous and disgusting. The vulgar abuse of the candidates from the vilest rabble," he adds, "is not rendered endurable by either wit or good temper."

"I saw," writes Cyrus Redding, "the election for Westminster, when Sheridan and Paull were rivals. Among other ridiculous things, a kind of stage was brought from Drury Lane Theatre, supported on men's shoulders; upon this there were four tailors busily at work, with a live goose and several huge cabbages; they came close up to the hustings, before Paull, amidst roars of laughing. The joke was, that Paull's father had been a tailor. A voter called out to Sheridan that he had long supported him, but should, after that, withdraw his countenance from him. 'Take it away at once—take it away at once,' cried Sheridan from the hustings; 'it is the most villainous-looking countenance I ever beheld!'"

MACKLIN'S HOUSE, TAVISTOCK ROW, 1870. (*See page* 260.)

As to the morals of Covent Garden in the seventeenth century, we may leave them to be inferred from the following couplet in the epilogue to Dryden's *Limberham*:—

"This town two bargains has not worth one farthing,
A Smithfield horse, and wife of Covent Garden."

And that the tastes of its inhabitants were alike loose and extravagant may be gathered from Wycherley, who speaks of "an ill-bred City dame, whose husband has been broke by living in Covent Garden."

In a tavern at Covent Garden, the husband of the exquisite sculptress, the Hon. Mrs. Damer, shot himself in 1776. Mr. Damer's suicide was hastened, and indeed provoked, by the refusal of his father, Lord Milton, to discharge his debts. Horace Walpole, after entering at length into this matter in a letter to Sir Horace Mann, in August, 1776, gives the following circumstantial account:—"On Thursday Mr. Damer supped at the 'Bedford Arms,' in Covent Garden, with four ladies and a blind fiddler. At three in the morning he dismissed his seraglio, ordering his Orpheus to come up again in half an hour. When he returned he found his master dead, and smelt gunpowder. He called: the master of the house came up; and they found Mr. Damer sitting in a sion, are not, it would seem, sufficient for happiness, and cannot check a pistol."

The following curious circumstance is mentioned in the "Life of Queen Anne," where, under date of 1708, we read that "the Muscovite Ambassador having had his audience of leave of the Queen,

DINING-ROOM OF THE GARRICK CLUB. (*See page* 263.)

chair dead, with one pistol beside him and another in his pocket. The ball had not gone through his head or made any report. On the table lay a scrap of paper with these words, 'The people of the house are not to blame for what has happened; it was my own act . . . .' What a catastrophe for a man at thirty-two, heir to two-and-twenty thousand a year!" Horace Walpole remarks, with his usual cynicism on this affair, that "Five thousand a year in present, and £22,000 in rever-

Mr. Morton, a laceman in Covent Garden, and some others of his creditors, caused him to be arrested, on the 21st of July, as he was riding in his coach. The bailiffs thrust themselves into the coach, took away his sword and cane, and carried him to a sponging-house, called the 'Black Raven.' Here the Ambassador sent to one of the Secretaries of State to acquaint him with his being insulted in that manner, but no secretaries could be found; and only Mr. Walpole, an under-secretary, came to him (as the Czar observes in his letter) to be witness to his disgrace; for, instead being discharg'd, he was compell'd to put in bail to the action. It seems the debt was but £50, and all the debts he ow'd did not amount to £300, which still renders the crime more unpardonable; and after all, no punishment adequate to the offence either way or (as 'tis said) could be inflicted on the offender by the laws of this kingdom. The Imperial, and Prussian, and other Foreign Ministers, looking upon themselves concern'd in this affair, demanded satisfaction for the outrage. Indeed, Morton and some others of the creditors, with the attorney and bailiffs, were summoned before the Council, and committed to custody for the present, and an information ordered to be preferred against them; but when the case came to be argued, the Court could not discover any law they had offended."

Among the notorieties of "the Garden" was the well-known night house called "The Finish." It stood on the south side of the market sheds, and was kept at the beginning of the present century by a Mrs. Butler. There, according to "Tom Cribb's Memorial to Congress," the "gentlemen of the road" used to divide their spoil in the grey dawn of the morning, when it was time for the night birds to fly to their roost. Hence Tommy Moore, who frequented this place, whimsically says that the "Congress" is—

"Some place that's like the 'Finish,' lads!
Where all your high pedestrian pads
That have been up and out all night
Running their rigs among the rattlers,
At morning meet, and, honour bright,
Agree to share the blunt and tatters."

One of the earliest records of the artistic fame of Covent Garden is that of Charles I. establishing, in the house of Sir Francis Kynaston, an academy called the "Museum Minervæ," for the instruction of gentlemen in arts and sciences, knowledge of metals, antiquities, painting, architecture, and foreign languages. Was this the first faint foreshadowing of the Royal Academy?

An amusing story in connection with Covent Garden—more especially with reference to the derivation of its name from Co*n*vent Garden—is told respecting the old Marquis of Worcester. His lordship being made prisoner, was committed to the custody of the Black-Rod, who then lived in Covent Garden; the noble Marquis, says the historiographer, demanded of Dr. Bayly and others in his company, "What they thought of fortune-tellers?" It was answered, "That some of them spoke shrewdly." Whereupon the Marquis said, "It was told me by some of them, before ever I was a Catholic, that I should die in a *Convent*, but I never believed them before now; yet I hope they will not bury me in a *Garden*."

Lady Muskerry, the Princess of Babylon of De Grammont's "Memoirs," was living here in 1676, according to Mr. P. Cunningham, in the north-west angle, at the corner of James Street. Nicholas Rowe, the dramatic poet, was residing in Covent Garden in 1716; and close by lived and died Thomas Southern, the author of *Oroonoko* and of the *Fatal Marriage*, whose remains are interred in the Church of St. Paul hard by. In Covent Garden there was, at all events, one auction-room for the sale of prints, &c., that of the elder Langford, the same who is introduced by Foote as "Mr. Puff" in his farce of *The Mirror*.

Of Tavistock Street, which adjoins the south side of Covent Garden, Mr. Walker writes thus in "The Original:"—"The standard of wealth is no less changed than the standard of society. Tavistock Street, Covent Garden, was once a street of fashionable shops, what Bond Street was till lately, and what Bond Street and Regent Street together are now. I remember hearing an old lady say that in her young days the crowd of handsome equipages in Tavistock Street was considered one of the sights of London. I have had the curiosity to stride it. It is about one hundred and sixty yards long, and, before the footways were widened, would have admitted three carriages abreast."

The only memory that Mr. Peter Cunningham recalls to us in his generally exhaustive "Handbook of London" concerning this street, is the fact that in it the celebrated singer, Leveridge, kept a public-house after retiring from the stage.

The house No. 4, in the corner of what used to be Tavistock Row, the same in which Miss Ray lived, was the last residence of Charles Macklin, the comedian and centenarian, who died here in July, 1797. And here, says Mr. Cunningham, "the elder Mathews was called upon to give the aged actor a taste of his boyish quality for the stage."

To Tavistock Row, now covered by the offices of the Strand District Board of Works, properly belongs the story of the murder of Miss Ray. Though referred to by Horace Walpole as "among the strangest that he had ever heard, and one which he could scarcely bring himself to believe," it has been often told, but by no one better than by Mr. John Timbs in his "Romance of London." It appears that the gay Earl of Sandwich, First Lord of the Admiralty under Lord North's administration, whilst passing through Covent Garden, espied one day a pretty milliner at No. 4, on the southern side, at the corner of Tavistock Street. Her name was Martha Ray; according to one account, her parents were labourers at Elstree, on the borders of Hertfordshire; though others say that they were staymakers in Holywell Street. Be this as it may, she had served her time as an apprentice with a mantua-maker in Clerkenwell Close; and when Lord Sandwich first saw her she was very young.* He removed her from the shop, had her education completed, and took her as his mistress, though he was old enough to be her father. In spite of his countess being alive, Lord Sandwich introduced her to his family circle at Hinchinbrooke, his seat in Huntingdonshire; and she charmed the county families around—especially the ladies, and even the bishop's wife—by her charming, yet modest, manners, and her beautiful voice. And we have the authority of Mr. Cradock for saying that in her situation she was a pattern of discretion; for when a lady of rank, between one of the acts of the oratorio, advanced to converse with her, she expressed her embarrassment; and Lord Sandwich, turning privately to a friend, said, "As you are well acquainted with that lady, I wish you would give her a hint that there is a boundary line in my family that I do not wish to see exceeded." She was already the mother of a young family by the earl, when she made the acquaintance of a certain Captain Hackman, an officer in a foot regiment, then quartered at Huntingdon, whom she soon inspired with the same passion as that which had brought Lord Sandwich to her feet. Hackman (whom Mr. Cradock met at Hinchinbrooke, the hospitable seat of Lord Sandwich) at once proposed marriage to her, but she told him that "she did not choose to carry a knapsack." Her new admirer therefore resolved to exchange the army for the Church, and became vicar of Wyverton, in Norfolk. Half inclined, probably, to marry Hackman, she appears now to have complained that no settlement had been made upon her, adding that she was anxious to relieve his lordship of expense, and to have even thought of taking an engagement as a singer at the Italian Opera, where she had an offer of £3,000 and a free benefit. Lord Sandwich, in some doubt as to the real mind of his mistress, now placed Miss Ray under the charge of a duenna; while Hackman grew jealous, and appears to have resolved to destroy either himself or Miss Ray, or both. On the evening of the 7th of April, 1779, Miss Ray went, with a female attendant, to Covent Garden Theatre, to see *Love in a Village*. She had declined to tell Mr. Hackman how she was engaged that evening; he appears, therefore, to have watched her movements, and saw her carriage drive by a coffee-house in Cockspur Street, where he had posted himself. As the carriage drove on, Hackman followed, at a quick pace, to the theatre. The ladies sat in a front box, and three gentlemen, all connected with the Admiralty, occasionally paid their compliments to them. Mr. Hackman, too, was sometimes in the lobby and sometimes in an upper side-box, and more than once called at the "Bedford Coffee-house" to take a glass of brandy and water, but still was unable, on returning to the theatre, to obtain an interview with Miss Ray. The upshot was that after the piece was over, when the crowd was beginning to pour out, Hackman rushed out of the door of the coffee-house, just opposite to that of the theatre, and as a gentleman was handing the lady into her carriage, drew forth a pistol and shot her through the head. He then drew another pistol to shoot himself; but the ball grazed without penetrating his head, and he then endeavoured to beat out his own brains with the butt-end of the pistol. In this attempt on his own life, however, he was prevented, and was carried off as a prisoner by the Bow Street "runners" to the Bridewell at Tothill Fields.

Horace Walpole gives us some additional particulars concerning the murder of Miss Ray in one of his letters to his acquaintance:—"Miss Ray, it appears, has been out of order, and abroad but twice all the winter. She went to the play on Wednesday night, for the second time, with Galli the singer. During the play the desperate lover was at the 'Bedford' Coffee-house, and behaved with great calmness, and drank a glass of capillaire. Towards the conclusion he sallied out into the Piazza, waiting till he saw his victim handed to her carriage by Mr. Macnamara, an Irish Templar, with whom she had been seen to coquet during the performance in the theatre. Hackman came behind her, pulled her by the gown, and, on her turning round, clapped the pistol to her forehead and shot her through the head. With another pistol he then attempted to shoot himself. . . . Now, is not the story full as strange as ever it was? Miss Ray has six children; the eldest son is fifteen; and she was at least three times as much."

The real fact, however, is that Miss Ray had borne to Lord Sandwich no less than nine children, five of whom were then living. One of these afterwards attained distinction, Mr. Basil Mon-

* Mr. Cradock, in his "Literary Memoirs," tells us that his lordship first saw her on going into a shop in this neighbourhood to buy a pair of gloves.

tague, Q.C., eminent both as a lawyer and as a man of letters, who died in 1851, and whose early success at the bar, it is said, was very greatly a result of his having contradicted the then Lord Chancellor on a point of law, and being told by his lordship next day that he was right in his view. But to return to Miss Ray's assassination. Hackman was tried at the Old Bailey for the murder, and the fact that he had two pistols instead of one compelled the jury to believe that it was not suicide only that he had contemplated as he sat that evening in the window of the hotel in Cockspur Street, but that his assassination of Miss Ray was a cool and deliberate act. Accordingly he was found guilty, sentenced to death and hanged at Tyburn, being accompanied in the coach by Lord Carlisle and by James Boswell, who, like George Selwyn, was fond of being present at executions.

A curious book, it may here be remarked before quitting the subject, arose out of this tragical story. In the following year was published an octavo volume pretending to contain the correspondence of Hackman and Miss Ray. It was entitled "Love and Madness; or a story too true, in a series of letters between parties whose names would perhaps be mentioned were they less known or less lamented." The book, appealing as it did to the sensational element in nature, soon ran through several editions. The real author of it was Sir Herbert Croft. Walpole, as if puzzled what to make of it, writes, "I doubt whether the letters are genuine; and yet, if fictitious, they are well executed, and enter into his character: hers appear less natural; and yet the editors were certainly more likely to be in possession of hers than of his. It is not probable that Lord Sandwich should have sent to the press what he found in her apartments; and no account is pretended to be given of how they came to light."

It was said that when Miss Ray's body was brought into the "Shakespeare" Tavern, George Selwyn put on a long black cloak, and sat in the room with the corpse, as a mourner; but the story "lacks confirmation."

CHAPTER XXXIII.

COVENT GARDEN AND ITS NEIGHBOURHOOD (*continued*).

Distinguished Inhabitants of James Street—Henrietta Street—Sir Robert Strange, the Historical Engraver—Duel between Sheridan and Mathews—Formation of the Society of Arts—King Street—D'Urfey's Allusion to the "Three Kings"—Hutchins' and Paterson's Auction Rooms—"The Essex Serpent"—Samuel Taylor Coleridge—The Garrick Club—Collection of Theatrical Portraits—Rose Street—Samuel Butler, the Author of "Hudibras"—Assault of Dryden—The "Pope's Head" and Curll the Bookseller—New Street—Dr. Johnson's Dinner—Artists in Long Acre—Wedgwood—Removal of Signboards—Bedford Street—An Old Tea Shop—Garrick in Southampton Street—The old Welsh Alehouse—Danby and Marvell—Voltaire—Turner—Quarrel between Hogarth and Churchill—The "Cider Cellars"—Chandos Street—Bedfordbury—Sir F. Kynaston and the Museum Minervæ.

CONTINUING our desultory tour, we next come to James Street, which runs out of Covent Garden on the north, and connects it with Long Acre: it shows the date of its erection by its name, being called after the Duke of York, afterwards James II. It is mentioned casually in the *Spectator*, No. 266, and has had at all events one distinguished inhabitant—Sir James Thornhill. In the *European Magazine* for 1804, the house is spoken of as situated on the eastern side of the street, with back offices and a painting-room abutting on Langford's (then Cock's) auction-rooms, in the Piazza; but since then the east side has been almost entirely rebuilt. Here, according to Mr. P. Cunningham, lived Sir Henry Herbert, the last Master of the Revels at the Stuart Court; and also the engraver, Charles Grignion. In other respects the street seems to have enjoyed but little celebrity in comparison with the neighbouring thoroughfares.

Henrietta Street, which connects the south-west corner of Covent Garden with Bedford Street, was built in 1637, and named after Henrietta Maria, queen of Charles I. Indeed, it may be said that all the streets around Covent Garden, except those named after the Russell family, bespeak by their names—all borrowed from our Stuart princes—the dates of their erection. Strafford, Lord Lieutenant of Ireland, was one of the earliest aristocratic inhabitants of this street. In 1640 Sir Robert Strange, the engraver, was living at the "Golden Head," in this street, when he published his proposals for engraving by subscription three historical prints. Two other interesting reminiscences belong to this street. It was at the "Castle" Tavern, in Henrietta Street, that Sheridan fought a duel with Mathews, his rival in the affections of Miss Linley; and at Rawthmell's Coffee-house that the Society of Arts was formed, in 1754.

King Street, the thoroughfare running parallel with Henrietta Street, and forming an outlet from the north-west corner of Covent Garden, was built at the same time as Henrietta Street. Lenthall, the Speaker of the House of Commons during the Commonwealth, lived in this street, in a house the site of which is now covered by the "Westminster Fire-office." Here was the residence of the three Indian kings mentioned in the *Tatler* and *Spectator*, and who lodged in the house of Mr. Arne, an upholsterer. This Mr. Arne was the father of the celebrated Dr. Arne, the composer. In after times an inn, called after these three Oriental sovereigns, would appear to have been established there; to it, probably, Tom D'Urfey alludes in his collection of songs, published in 1719:—

"Farewell, 'Three Kings,' where I have spent
Full many an idle hour;
Where oft I won, but never lost,
If it were in my power.
Farewell, my dearest Piccadill,
Notorious for great dinners;
Oh, what a tennis-court was there!
Alas! too good for sinners.
Now, God bless all that will be blest;
God bless the Inns of Court,
And God bless D'Avenant's Opera,
Which is the sport of sport."

From an early date King Street would appear to have been a favourite haunt for the auctioneers. Here were the sale-rooms of Hutchins, and of Paterson, to whose son Dr. Johnson stood as god-father, and for whom he wrote letters of recommendation to Sir Joshua Reynolds. In these two sale-rooms large collections of prints and pictures were constantly passing under the auctioneer's hammer; and among the crowds of purchasers were such men as Gough, the editor of Camden's "Britannia," with his formal-cut coat and waist-coat, and high boots, and carrying in his hand a "swish-whip" instead of a walking-stick; Dr. Lort, chaplain to the Duke of Devonshire, and the correspondent of "Old Cole," with his thick worsted stockings and "Busby" wig; Caleb Whiteford, witty and well dressed, after the fashion of the Garrick school; Dr. Gossett, Captain Baillie, Mr. Baker, Mr. Woodhouse, Mr. Musgrave, Mr. Pitt, and Mr. Woodhall—all of them keen-scented collectors of articles of *vertu*, and of prints by celebrated artists such as Hogarth, Cipriani, and Rowlandson.

In King Street there might still be seen, until a few years ago, "The Essex Serpent." Mr. Larwood suggests that this sign is an allusion to a fabulous monster recorded in a broadside of 1704, from which we learn that before Henry II. died a dragon of marvellous bigness was discovered at St. Osyth, in Essex. In the absence of any more probable hypothesis, we may accept this suggestion as plausible, if not as satisfactory.

In King Street also lived the philosophical poet, Samuel Taylor Coleridge, from 1799 down to 1802, whilst he was earning his livelihood as an unknown writer on political subjects for the *Morning Post.*

The Garrick Club was originally established in King Street, at No. 35, about the middle of the north side, in 1834; and here its fine gallery of theatrical and literary portraits remained until the opening of its new and permanent home in Garrick Street, in 1864.

Garrick Street is the name given to a wide and spacious thoroughfare which was driven about the year 1860 across the site of Rose Street and a nest of close and crowded alleys, between King Street and St. Martin's Lane. It takes its name from the Garrick Club, which occupies a noble building erected for its members by Mr. Marrable, and in which is to be seen the finest collection of theatrical portraits in the kingdom. It was first made by the elder Charles Mathews, at his residence in Kentish Town. It includes authentic likenesses of most of the theatrical celebrities of the past two centuries—Foote, Quin, Garrick, Nell Gwynne, Mrs. Billington, Nancy Dawson, Colley Cibber—some in costume, and others in private dress. The Club is allowed to be inspected on every Wednesday (except during September) by any one personally introduced by a member. Among the pictures, which cover nearly the whole of the walls of the various rooms set apart for the use of the members, may be specially mentioned the half-length portrait of Mrs. Oldfield, by Sir Godfrey Kneller; Mrs. Siddons, by Harlow; a fine picture of King; and Mr. and Mrs. Baddeley in *The Clandestine Marriage*, by Zoffany; Macklin as "Sir Pertinax Macsycophant," by De Wilde; Mathews, in five characters, by Harlow; Garrick between Tragedy and Comedy; Mrs. Bracegirdle; Mrs. Abington as "Lady Bab," by Hickey; the screen scene from the *School for Scandal*, as originally cast; Rich as harlequin (1753); King as "Touchstone," by Zoffany; C. Kemble and Fawcett in *Charles II.*, by Clint; Garrick as "Richard III.," by the elder Morland. Since the removal of the club to Garrick Street the number of pictures has been greatly augmented; among the more recent additions being a choice collection of water-colour full-length portraits of theatrical celebrities painted by Mr. John Leech. Upon the walls of the smoking-room there are a few large paintings by Clarkson Stanfield, Louis Haigh, David Roberts, and others. In the coffee-room there are some objects of interest to the curious, independent of the paintings upon the walls—namely, the jewels, &c., presented to Garrick and worn by him upon the stage. Among the busts, of which there are several in the Club, especially in the library, may be particularly noticed one of Thackeray; one of Mrs. Siddons and her brother; and one of Shakespeare, which was formerly bricked up in a wall, but was discovered and brought again to light during the demolition of the old Lincoln's Inn Theatre, in 1848.

Old Rose Street, which ran north and south from the western end of King Street, has been so altered within the last few years by the advancing spirit of clearance and ventilation that its original aspect has been almost entirely swept away. Previous to the year 1859, when many of its old and dilapidated tenements were pulled down in order to form the broad thoroughfare of Garrick Street, which now crosses it, here might be seen low gambling-houses; floors let out to numerous families with fearful broods of children; sundry variations of the magisterial permission "to be drunk on the premises;" strange, chaotic trades, to which no one skilled contribution imparted a distinctive character; and, by way of a moral drawn from the far-off pure air of open fields and farmyards, a London dairy, professing to be constantly supplied with fresh butter, cream, and new milk from the country: these were some of the special features of a thoroughfare which was marked by a tablet upon one of its houses bearing the superscription, "This is Red Rose Street, 1623." If the appearance of the street as above indicated, were all it could boast of, Rose Street might go down into dust without a word by way of epitaph. But there are circumstances connected with it which will render it immortal in our annals, when its very site shall have become a matter of doubt hundreds of years hence; for Samuel Butler, the author of "Hudibras," died here in 1680, of a complication of ailments and miseries, the most urgent of which was want.

We may here say that in this dark and narrow alley, too—for Rose Street is, or rather was, scarcely anything better—Dryden the poet was attacked by three hired assailants, and beaten, to use the expressive phrase, "within an inch of his life." This attack has become almost historical. Some of his biographers tell us that when the ferocious assault was made upon him he was going home to his house in Gerrard Street, from "Will's Coffee-house" in Russell Street, Covent Garden, which he was in the habit of frequently attending. This statement has given rise to much controversy, which the late Mr. Robert Bell, in the first volume of *Once a Week*, was at considerable pains to set at rest. The assault took place on the night of the 18th of December, 1679, so that the poet could not be making his way at the time to Gerrard Street, for that street, it is alleged, was not built till some two years later. Dryden is stated, on the authority of the rate-books of the parish, to have lived in Fleet Street from 1673 to 1682, when he removed to a house in Long Acre, exactly facing the dismal *embouchure* of Rose Street. Here he lived till 1686, when he went farther westward to the house 43, Gerrard Street, where he died on the 1st of May, 1700. "If these dates be correct," says the writer above referred to, "there would be no difficulty in determining where Dryden was living at the time; . . . for we find that while the rate-books of St. Bride's are quoted to show that in 1679 he was living in Fleet Street, the rate-books of St. Martin's are relied upon with equal confidence to prove that at the same time he was living in Long Acre. The biographers who have escaped the dilemma by sending him on to Gerrard Street at once may therefore turn out to be right, after all. Fleet Street, at all events, is put out of court. We know from the contemporary account of the circumstance that he was going from Covent Garden; and if he were going home, as must be inferred from the lateness of the hour, he could not have been going to Fleet Street, which would take him in the opposite direction, while the way both to Gerrard Street and Long Acre lay direct through this unsavoury Rose Avenue. To one or other of these places he must have been going. "Perhaps," the writer naïvely adds, "most readers will be of opinion that it is not very material which date is correct, or to what house he was wending his way at the time." The important event is the assault itself, and the circumstance that it occurred in Rose Street.

At the "Rose" Tavern, in or close to Rose Street, as Mr. John Timbs tells us, the "Treason Club" met, at the time of the Revolution, to consult with Lord Colchester, Mr. Thomas Wharton, and many others; and it was on this occasion resolved that the regiment under Lieutenant-Colonel Langdale's command should desert entire, as in fact it did in November, 1688.

In Rose Street lived the notorious bookseller, Edmund Curll, at the "Pope's Head," a sign which he had set up, not, certainly, out of affection for Alexander Pope, but rather from an opposite feeling. "After the quarrel which arose out of Curll's piratical publication of Pope's library correspondence," says Mr. Larwood, in his "History of Sign-

Boards," "Curll addressed, in May, 1735, a letter of thanks to the House of Lords, ending thus: 'I have engraved a new plate of Mr. Pope's head from Mr. Jervas's painting, and likewise intend to hang him up in effigy for a sign to all spectators of his falsehood and my veracity, which I will always

New Street, just by. Several of them had travelled. They expected to meet every day, but did not know one another's names. It used to cost the rest a shilling, for they drank wine; but I had a cut of meat for sixpence, and bread for a penny, and gave the waiter a penny; so that I was quite well served

INTERIOR OF ST. MARTIN'S HALL, 1850. (*See page* 269.)

maintain, under the Scotch motto, '*Nemo me impune lacesset.*'"

New Street, which forms the continuation from King Street to St. Martin's Lane, was a favourite resort of Dr. Johnson. His first lodgings were at the house of Mr. Norris, a staymaker, in Exeter Street, adjoining Catherine Street, in the Strand. "I dined," said he, "very well for eightpence, with very good company, at the 'Pine Apple,' in

—nay, better than the rest, for they gave the waiter nothing." In the reign of Charles II. New Street was very fashionably inhabited; for, as Mr. Peter Cunningham tells us, the Countess of Chesterfield, the lady with whom Van Dyck was in love, occupied a house on the south side in 1660. Flaxman, the famous sculptor, was living here in the years 1771 and 1772.

The neighbourhood to the east of St. Martin's

Lane up to Long Acre northwards a century ago formed the centre for artists of every class and their allies. The great Sir Joshua Reynolds, as we have seen in an earlier chapter, held his court in Leicester Square; the old Life Academy had been for years in a house at the top of a court in "the Lane," as it was at that time familiarly styled; and "in Long Acre itself were congregated the colour-makers, goldbeaters, artists' tool-makers, modellers, and journeymen of every kind," as Miss Meteyard tells us in her "Life of Wedgwood." Here, at the corner of Newport Street and of St. Martin's Lane, in a house with a double frontage into either thoroughfare, in 1768–74, were the show-rooms of Josiah Wedgwood's pottery-ware and porcelain, before he settled down in Greek Street, Soho, where we found him in a previous chapter. As Miss Meteyard remarks, "Newport Street and its neighbourhood have undergone, since then, so great an amount of alteration as to show at this day few, if any, vestiges of its old condition; but, judging by our present ideas relative to space, light, and accessibility, it must have been a gloomy and confined situation for such a shrine of the arts, and one so resorted to by the noblest in intellect and rank in the land." Although the house thus celebrated is no longer standing in its entirety, it may be of some interest to state, on the same authority, that whilst the ground-floor was a shop for the sale of ordinary goods, where "the public entered in and out at pleasure," the first-floor suite formed a gallery or repository into which only Mr. Wedgwood's wealthy and aristocratic patrons were admitted; and the second-floor formed the home of Mr. Wedgwood and his family when in town. Josiah himself thus describes the house in a letter to Bentley: "It is at the top of St. Martin's Lane, a corner house, 60 feet long; the streets are wide which lye to it, and carriages may come to it either from Westminster or the City without being incommoded with drays full of timber and coals, which are always pouring in from the various wharfs, and making stops in the Strand, very disagreeable and sometimes dangerous. The rent is . . . 100 guineas a year. My friends in town tell me that it is the best situation in London for my rooms."

Another fact relating to the neighbourhood of Covent Garden and St. Martin's Lane may as well be noticed here. It was the first in the West End of London to dispense with the old sign-boards which used to project over the pathways. A daily paper of November, 1762, tells us, as a piece of news, that "the signs in Duke Court, St. Martin's Lane, are all taken down, and affixed to the front of the houses." Thus the City of Westminster began the innovation by procuring an Act of Parliament with powers for that purpose. Other West-End parishes, including that of Marylebone, copied the example; the City of London in due course followed suit, and long before the end of the last century the picturesque signs were superseded by plain and prosaic numbers. Along with the signs, of course, went the sign-posts. Mr. J. Larwood tells us, in his "History of Sign-Boards," that this removal of the sign-posts, and the paving of the streets at the same time with Scotch granite, gave rise to the following epigram:—

"The Scottish new pavement deserves well our praise;
To the Scotch we're obliged, too, for mending our ways:
But this we can never forget, for they say
As that they have taken our posts all away."

Bedford Street, which runs northwards from the Strand to the west of the churchyard of St. Paul's, Covent Garden, can at all events boast of some ancient memories. Strype describes it as "a handsome, broad street, with very good houses," adding that since the Fire of London the latter are generally taken up by tradesmen of the better class, such as mercers, drapers, and lacemen; but these have given way to newspaper and publishing offices. The houses on the western side, Strype remarks, are better than those on the east. The upper part of the street dates from 1637; in the lower part is the West End branch of the Civil Service Stores, a handsome building of red brick faced with terra-cotta. In this street resided Quin the actor; Chief Justice Richardson; Sir Francis Kynaston, the poet; the Earl of Chesterfield; and Thomas Sheridan, the father of Richard Brinsley Sheridan. Whyte, in his "Miscellanea Nova," tells us how one day when there he looked out up Henrietta Street—opposite to which Mr. Sheridan lived—and saw Dr. Johnson walking "with a peculiar solemnity of deportment and an awkward sort of measured step, and laying his hands, as he went along, upon the top of each of the posts." No. 26 in this street, an old-established gold lace manufacturer's shop, retained its sign, "The Three Crowns," till the house was pulled down in 1875.

We find the following advertisement respecting the newly-introduced luxury of tea in the *Tatler* of March, 1710:—"The finest Imperial Tea, 18s.; Bohee, 12s., 16s., 20s., and 24s.; all sorts of Green, the lowest 12s. To be had of R. Tate, at the 'Star' in Bedford Court, near Bedford Street, Covent Garden." Tea had been introduced into England more than half a century before; but even at the date to which reference is here made it was evidently still a costly and rare article, if we may judge from the prices given in the above advertisement.

In consequence of the removal of house-signs (of which we have already spoken), the difficulty of finding out a house at night was greatly increased, and therefore other means were resorted to, as we learn from an advertisement of "Doctor James Tilbrough, a German doctor," who resided "over against the New Exchange in Bedford Street, at the sign of the Peacock, where you shall see at night two candles burning within one of the chambers before the balcony, and a lanthorn with a candle in it upon the balcony." We have mentioned in a preceding chapter that it is to Covent Garden that London is indebted for the introduction of "balconies."

Southampton Street is the name of the thoroughfare which connects the southern side of Covent Garden with the Strand. Garrick at one time lived in Southampton Street. Mr. Cradock, who knew him well, tells us several good stories about him. Garrick was a great mimic, and by his power of imitation could make Johnson seem extremely ridiculous. He could put on the doctor's rough and uncouth manners, and growl out four or five lines of Gray's "Bard," without, however, articulating the words. This he could do at his suppers to the entertainment of his friends, but not to the satisfaction of Dr. Johnson. Another anecdote, related likewise by Mr. Cradock, introduces Mrs. Garrick:—"My apartments," he tells us, "were at that time in Southampton Street, opposite to Mr. Garrick, who sometimes would divert a few friends with a ludicrous story at my expense, 'That I had stayed out so very late one night at the "Piazza" Coffee-house; and that at my return I had disturbed Mrs. Garrick and his whole neighbourhood; so much so, indeed, that he was afraid he must have called for the watch.' Part of this story might be correct; but Mrs. Garrick owned to whom it was indebted for its embellishments. The whole truth was, that the lady of the house where I lodged was built on a very large scale, and in her hurry to let me in, by some accident or other fell down in the passage, and could not readily be got up again; and I believe that, growing rather impatient, I possibly might call out very vociferously, till the lady could be safely removed; and that the husband, who was seriously disturbed, became angry, and absolutely declared that his wife at no future time should sit up so late for a lodger." From Southampton Street Garrick removed to his house in Adelphi Terrace, at the solicitation of his friend Lord Mansfield. The houses on the Terrace, from the beauty of their prospect, had been selected by his lordship for particular friends. The centre house was allotted to the great actor, but none of them, Mr. Cradock tells us, were quite suited to him, as his health was then declining, and the bleak situation was ill contrasted with the warm and sheltered apartments in Southampton Street which he had left. In Southampton Street lived and died old Gabriel Cibber, and here his son Colley Cibber was born.

Extending from Southampton Street to Bedford Street, about midway between the Strand and Henrietta Street, is Maiden Lane, on which we have already slightly touched in a previous chapter. We may add, however, that the well-known tavern here, called the "Old Welch Ale House," which stood on the site of the "Bedford Head," and which was pulled down in 1870, has risen, phœnix-like, in a new building, which has returned to its old designation, being now known as the "Bedford Head" hotel. It adjoins the site of the house of Andrew Marvell, poet and patriot, where he was lodging when Lord Danby climbed his stairs with a message and bribe from the king, but found him too honest and too proud to accept it. It is said that he was dining off the pickings of a mutton-bone when Lord Danby called, and that as soon as he was gone he was obliged to send to a friend to borrow a guinea. Two doors off, at an old French perruquier's, at the sign of the "White Peruke," Voltaire lodged when young, and when busy in publishing his "Henriade;" he was a constant visitor at the "Bedford," where his bust still adorns a room. Voltaire had been imprisoned in the Bastile for a libel, and after his release came over to London, where he procured many subscriptions towards publishing his poem. He remained here several years, becoming acquainted with Pope, Congreve, Young, and other celebrated literary men of his time; and tradition says that they frequently resorted to this tavern together of an evening. When J. M. W. Turner lived in this street (that is, before 1800) he would often spend an evening at the "Bedford." "In the parlour of the 'Bedford,'" says Mr. J. H. Jesse, in his "London," "met the 'Shilling Rubber Club,' of which Fielding, Hogarth, Goldsmith, and Churchill were members. It was at one of their meetings here that the quarrel arose between Hogarth and Churchill which induced the latter to satirise his friend, and the former to retaliate upon him with his unrivalled pencil. The 'Epistle to Hogarth' is comparatively forgotten; but Churchill will still live as 'Bruin' when his verse shall have passed into oblivion." The present tavern, which has resumed its ancient name, is adjoined on the west by a large block styled "Sussex Mansions," and let out as offices and for residential purposes.

Exactly opposite, on the south side, was a part of the premises of Messrs. Godfrey and Cooke, of Southampton Street, the oldest chemists and druggists in London, having been established in 1680. A hundred years ago, or a little more, Mr. Ambrose Godfrey, one of the firm, proposed to extinguish fires by a "new method of explosion and suffocation," thereby anticipating the "Fire Extincteur" of our own day. But these premises have now been absorbed into a handsome Catholic church, with schools and presbytery attached, solemnly opened by the late Cardinal Manning in the autumn of 1874.

On the south side, nearer to the west end of the street, was a house which in 1864 became a "School of Arms and of Athletic Exercises." It was previously a place notoriously of bad reputation as the "Cider Cellars"—a place of low and not very moral amusement for the fast young "swells" of the City and West End after the theatres were closed, and rivalling the "Coal Hole" and the "Judge and Jury" in their special characteristics of immorality. It had been devoted to the muse of song for a century and a half at the least. On the same side of the street is the Maiden Lane Synagogue, and also the back of the Adelphi Theatre, which stretches thus far from the Strand.

Maiden Lane is said by Mr. Isaac D'Israeli, in his "Curiosities of Literature," to have received its name from a statue of the Virgin Mary, "which in Catholic days adorned the corner of the street, as Bagford writes to Hearne," who also says that the frequent sign of "the Maidenhead" denoted "Our Lady's Head." But this may be a fanciful conjecture, as the sober and honest chronicler, John Stow, tells us that its original designation was "Ingene" or "Ing" Lane.

Chandos Street, which leads from Maiden Lane towards the lower end of St. Martin's Lane, was so called after Brydges, Lord Chandos, the ancestor of the "princely" Duke of Chandos. It was built in the reign of Charles I., and of late years has been largely rebuilt. It now contains the Medical School of Charing Cross Hospital, and one of the two frontages of the West End branch of the Civil Service Stores, the other being in Bedford Street. In the *Harleian Miscellany* we are told that at the corner of Chandos Street was the sign of a Balcony, "which country people were wont much to gaze on."

At the "Three Tuns," a bagnio in this street, the Honourable John Finch was stabbed, in a fit of jealousy, by a celebrated personage, Sally Pridden, whose portrait was painted by Sir Godfrey Kneller. She was called "Sally Salisbury," on account of a fancied resemblance to the then Countess of Salisbury. She died in Newgate whilst undergoing her sentence for the above deed of violence, "leaving behind her," says Caulfield, in his "Memoirs of Remarkable Persons," "the character of the most notorious woman that ever infested the Hundreds of Old Drury or Covent Garden either."

Bedfordbury is the name once given to a district containing a few small streets lying between St. Martin's Lane, on the West side, and Bedford Street, Covent Garden, on the east, but now confined to the narrow lane running southwards from New Street to Chandos Street. The district was built about the year 1635, and was once the residence of well-to-do families. It has, however, but few historical or literary associations; though Mr. Peter Cunningham records the fact that in 1636 Sir Francis Kynaston, the accomplished scholar and poet, was living hereabouts, "on the east side of the street towards Berrie," and he supposed that his name was perpetuated in Kynaston's Alley adjoining. All the eastern side of the lane was pulled down in 1880, and a block of model lodging-houses erected instead.

Of Sir Francis Kynaston some interesting details will be found in Faulkner's "History of Chelsea." It appears that during the prevalence of the plague in London, in 1636, Sir Francis, at that time Regent of the Museum Minervæ, presented to the king a petition requesting permission to remove his institute to Chelsea College, and the king granted his request. "The Museum Minervæ," adds Faulkner, "was an academy instituted in the eleventh year of King Charles I., and established at a house in or near Covent Garden, purchased for the purpose by Sir Francis Kynaston, and furnished by him with books, manuscripts, paintings, statues, musical and mathematical instruments, &c., and every requisite for a polite and liberal education. Only the nobility and gentry were admissible into the academy. Sir Francis Kynaston was chosen president or regent of the new institution, and professors were appointed to teach the various arts and sciences. The constitutions of the Museum Minervæ were published in London in 1626, in quarto." The authorities of Chelsea College, however, remonstrated against this royal concession, and so the grant never took effect. Sir Francis and his colleagues accordingly were obliged to content themselves with other quarters, at Little Chelsea. The subsequent history of the Museum

Minervæ we have not been able to trace; but it is worth mentioning here in connection with the borderland of Covent Garden and St. Martin's Lane, as in all probability it furnished some hints towards the first foundation—or, at all events, to the first rough outline—of the Royal Academy. It is supposed by Allibone that Sir Francis did not long survive the transaction here recorded, but died about the year 164-. He was the author of a Latin verse translation of Chaucer's "Troilus and Cressida," and of a poem entitled "Leoline and Sydanis, an Heroic Romance of the Adventures of two Amorous Princes," together with sundry affectionate addresses to his mistress under the name of "Cynthia." Sir Francis is mentioned in terms of appreciation in George Ellis's "Specimens of Early English Poets," and in the "Censura Literaria."

CHAPTER XXXIV.

COVENT GARDEN AND ITS NEIGHBOURHOOD (*continued*).

"Rus in urbe, urbs in rure."

Long Acre—Its Original Condition—The Head-quarters of Carriage-builders—Distinguished Residents—St. Martin's Hall—Mr. Hullah's Choral Classes—St. Martin's Hall destroyed by Fire and rebuilt—The Queen's Theatre—Messrs. Merryweather's Fire-engine Manufactory—Hanover Court, and Taylor the "Water-Poet"—Hart Street—Charles Macklin as a Tavern-keeper—Bow Street—The Police Office—Noted Residents—Fall of Grinling Gibbons' House—Dr. Radcliffe—The Poet Wycherley—The "Garrick's Head"—Exhibition of Sign-boards—The "Wrekin"—Wycherley's Dying Request to his Young Wife.

Having completed our desultory survey of the purlieus of Covent Garden lying westward as far as St. Martin's Lane, we once more turn our face towards the east, and wend our way through Long Acre. This fine thoroughfare, as already stated, was originally called "The Elms," and the "Elm Close;" then "The Seven Acres;" and in after times it got its present name from a long and narrow slip of ground belonging to the Abbot of Westminster, used as a pathway, which bordered the garden on the north. The pleasure-grounds behind the convent are said to have covered seven acres, and an avenue of tall elms is reported to have stood along the present line of road. Among the entries in the Council Books of the time of King Edward VI. mention is made of a grant from the king to the Earl of Bedford and his heirs male of "the Convent Garden" and of "the meadow-ground known as 'The Long Acre.'" It began to be built upon at the close of the sixteenth or early in the seventeenth century.

Probably from the time of Charles I., when coaches were first introduced into use in London, Long Acre became the head-quarters of carriage-builders, whose manufactories still exist there in considerable numbers, side by side with varnish-makers, coach-trimming makers, &c. Many of the other houses not so occupied were tenanted by persons of note; and others, again, by physicians and medical quacks. Stothard, the painter and Royal Academician, we are told, was the son of a carriage-maker in this street. John Dryden lived in it, on the north side, opposite to Rose Street; and Oliver Cromwell on the southern side, from 1637 to 1643.

Long Acre has had many other distinguished residents. Here lived the beautiful "Chloe" with whom Prior has made us so familiar in his poems. Instead, however, of being young, elegant, and beautiful, we learn that she was the commonplace wife of a cobbler, or, according to other accounts, of a soldier or an alehouse-keeper. But whoever and whatever she may have been, Pope tells us that "Prior used to bury himself here for whole days and nights together with the poor mean creature." Let us hope that she had merits of her own and qualities unknown to the world outside.

At a corner on the north side of Long Acre, where it meets Endell Street, with entrances in Wilson Street, Charles Street, and Long Acre, stood the Queen's Theatre. This building passed through the first two stages of its existence under the name of "St. Martin's Hall." The first edifice bearing that name was built, in the year 1847, by William Cubitt, from a design by the younger Westmacott, on a site which was presented to Mr. John Hullah by one of the civic companies. It was of the Elizabethan style of architecture, with a domed iron roof of immense space. The music-hall, which was capable of easily accommodating 3,000 persons, was opened in 1850 by Mr. Hullah, the founder of a new school of choral harmony. Here Mr. Hullah held his singing-classes; and oratorios and concerts, both instrumental and vocal, of a high order of excellence, were given under his direction. Here, too, Mr. Charles Dickens first appeared as a public lecturer, in April, 1858, on behalf of the Hospital for Sick Children, in Great Ormond Street, and a week or two later on his own account.

St. Martin's Hall was not only used for musical purposes, but also sometimes echoed to far less harmonious sounds when occupied by noisy and crowded meetings where political and social questions were agitated. On August 26, 1860, a fire broke out early in the morning in the coach-factory of Messrs. Kesterton, at the corner of Long Acre and Endell Street, closely adjoining St. Martin's Hall, and from the inflammable nature of the contents of the workshops the flames spread with a rapidity which defied the efforts of the engines. The fire was not long in reaching the roof of St. Martin's Hall, and this noble concert-room shared the fate of the adjacent building; not a vestige of it remained, and with it perished the fine organ by which it was adorned.

St. Martin's Hall was rebuilt, and reopened as a concert-hall in 1862, and musical and other entertainments were here held until 1867. Early in that year it was again engaged for a series of promenade concerts by Mr. Strange, lessee of the Alhambra; but its career as a concert-hall was drawing to a close. On the 24th of October, 1867, after undergoing considerable alterations, it was opened as a theatre by Mr. Alfred Wigan, under the title of "The Queen's," a name that had just before been discarded by the theatre near Tottenham Court Road, afterwards styled the "Prince of Wales's." From that period it changed hands several times, passing successively under the management of Messrs. Wigan, Liston, Young, and Clifton, and of Mrs. Seymour. Many well-known artists played at this theatre—Mr. J. L. Toole, Mr. Phelps, Miss Henrietta Hodson, and Mr. and Mrs. Rousby; the last-mentioned lady having made her *début* here in 1869, as "Fiordelisa" in *The Fool's Revenge*. *'Twixt Axe and Crown* and *Joan of Arc* were first produced here. After a short career, the Queen's Theatre was closed about 1875, and converted into "co-operative stores." It has now been converted into a paper warehouse.

Opposite this place, and occupying the corner of Long Acre and Bow Street, is the shop of Messrs. Merryweather, the celebrated fire-engine manufacturers. Their business dates from the

AN OLD COACHMAKER'S SHOP IN LONG ACRE (1870).

latter part of the seventeenth century; the firm being formerly known under the names of Hadley, Simpkin, and Lott. Until it was recently rebuilt, the house occupied by Messrs. Merryweather was supposed to be the only one either in Long Acre or in Bow Street standing in exactly the same condition as when first erected. The firm has in its possession several firemen's leather helmets, dating from 1720, if not earlier, and other curious relics of former times.

A little further westwards in Long Acre is Hanover Court, formerly Phœnix Alley, celebrated as having been once the home of Taylor the "water-poet," who died in it in 1653. He kept an alehouse here, and it is on record that, as one of the privileged watermen on the Thames, he signalised himself by his strenuous opposition to the introduction of coaches into London. The sign of the alehouse, it is said, was the "Crown," for which, on the establishment of the Commonwealth, he substituted his own head, with the following witty motto:–

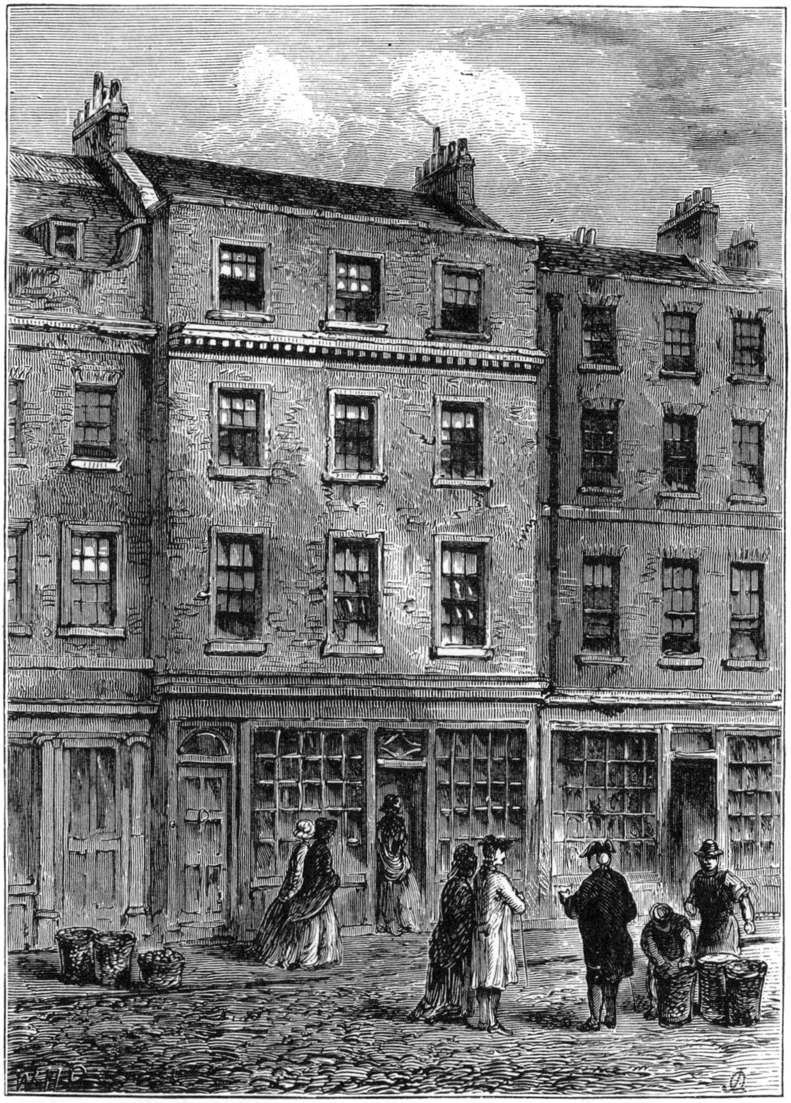

MR. DAVIES' SHOP, RUSSELL STREET. (*See page* 275.)

"There's many a head stands for a sign;
Then, gentle reader, why not mine?"

Hart Street, which runs parallel with Long Acre, between that thoroughfare and Covent Garden, was built about the year 1636–7, and derived its name from the "White Hart" Inn, which was still standing as late as the reign of George I. In it died Haines, the comic actor, in 1701. It was also at one time the abode of the celebrated Charles Macklin, who retired from the stage in middle life, under the idea of making his fortune here by establishing a tavern and coffee-house, in 1754. In the March of that year he opened a public ordinary, to be continued every day at four o'clock, price three shillings, "port, claret, or any other liquor included." An account of this dinner, given in Smith's "Historical and Literary Curiosities," presents us with an amusing picture of the manners of the day in coffee-houses and taverns. When the clock struck, a large bell suspended on the top of the house was rung for five minutes, and the dinner was ordered to be served. In ten minutes more it was put upon the table; the door was then closed, and no other guest was admitted. Macklin himself always brought in the first dish, in "a full dress suit," and with a napkin on his left arm; and when he had set it down he made a low bow and retired to a sideboard, surrounded by a bevy of waiters. For several months previous to opening he had trained his servants to communicate with him by signs, not a word being spoken by any of them while they remained in the room, for fear of interrupting the "feast of reason and the flow of soul." When the dinner was ended, and the wine set upon the table, Macklin quitted his situation, and, walking gravely up to his visitors, expressed a modest "hope that everything had been found agreeable and to their satisfaction," and then retired, making a low bow at the door. To this establishment Macklin afterwards added another, which he called "The British Inquisition," which, as stated in his advertisement, was to be on the plan of the ancient Greek, Roman, and modern French and Italian societies of liberal investigation. "Such subjects," he says in his announcement, "in arts, sciences, literature, criticism, philosophy, history, politics, and morality, as shall be found useful and entertaining to society, will there be lectured upon and freely debated. Particularly," it is added, "Mr. Macklin intends to lecture upon the comedy of the ancients, the use of their masks and flutes, their mimes and pantomimes, and the use and abuse of the stage. He will likewise lecture on the rise and progress of modern theatres, making a comparison between them and those of Greece and Rome, and between each other; he also proposes to lecture upon each of Shakespeare's plays." These discussions and discourses were to be held on the evenings of Monday and Friday, at seven o'clock; but the idea did not take. The whole establishment was a failure from the beginning; and in January, 1755, Charles Macklin became a bankrupt. After this failure he returned to the stage, doubtless a wiser man for his experience in business.

Bow Street, which forms the connecting link between Long Acre and Russell Street, and together with Endell Street and Wellington Street forms a direct communication between Oxford Street and the Strand, was built in 1637, being so called "as running in shape of a bent bow." Strype, who tells us this, also says that "the street is open and large, with very good houses, well inhabited, and resorted unto by gentry for lodgings, as are most of the other streets in this parish." This was in 1720. It ceased to be well inhabited about five years afterwards. The theatre (Covent Garden Theatre) on the west side we have described in a previous chapter. Bow Street Police Office, celebrated in the annals of crime, was established in 1749. It was formerly occupied by the novelist Fielding, who is said to have written "Tom Jones" within its walls. The office itself, as it appeared till quite recently was a mean and paltry structure, quite unworthy of being used as a temple of Justice. Its officials belong to history. The old Bow Street officers were called by fast men "Robin Redbreasts," on account of their wearing red vests; and though they were a set of brave and resolute men, they were too limited in numbers to be generally effective. Amongst the most vigilant and energetic we may mention Leadbitter, Ruthven, Goddard, and Keys. At night the only protection afforded to Londoners was a tribe of guardians who, though infinitely more in numbers, were far less useful in effect. These night guardians were generally aged and ineffective men, whose duty was to parade the streets; and the inhabitants, by rotation, had to sit up every night at the watch-house in Portugal Street, to take the charges—a pleasant task, after a man had been attending to his business all day!

Bow Street has long been celebrated all over the United Kingdom, and indeed throughout the world, as the head police-court of the metropolis, particularly since the time of Sir John Fielding, in the last century. Here are tried all extradition cases, which are taken by the chief magistrate, Sir John Bridge. The establishment consists of three magistrates, each attending two days in a week. All the magistrates belonging to this office are in the Commission of the Peace for the Counties of London, Middlesex, Surrey, Kent, Essex, and Herts. In 1880–81 a fine new building was erected on the east side of the street, to serve the purposes of both the Police Court and the Police Station. The edifice is in the Italian style of architecture, and covers a large space of ground. The old police-station was pulled down early in 1897.

Bow Street can boast of a series of illustrious names among its former inhabitants; for nearly opposite to the Police Office resided Edmund Waller the poet, from 1654 to 1656. Here, then, he was living when he wrote, in 1654, his famous panegyric upon Cromwell. William Longueville, the friend of Butler, too, lived close by. The witty Earl of Dorset resided in a house on the west side, in the years 1684 and 1685. Major Mohun, the famous actor, occupied a house on the east side, from 1671 to 1676 inclusive; Robert Harley, Earl of Oxford, the great Prime Minister of his day, was born in this street in 1661 ; and Grinling Gibbons, too, lived in a house on the east side (about the middle of the street), from 1678 to 1721, the period of his death. The house was distinguished by the name of "The King's Arms." In the *Postman* of the 24th of January, 1701, it is recorded that "on Thursday the house of Mr. Gibbons, the famous carver, in Bow Street, fell down; but by a special Providence none of the family were killed; but 'tis said that a young girl, which was playing in the court [King's Court ?], being missing, is supposed to be buried in the rubbish."

Among other illustrious inhabitants of this street must not be forgotten Sir Godfrey Kneller, and Dr. Radcliffe, the munificent founder of the museum at Oxford which bears his name. They lived next door to each other, and were great friends, though every now and then it would appear that they had their little quarrels, as we have shown in the anecdote narrated in a previous chapter.* On reading the anecdote we feel almost irresistibly compelled to ask, with Virgil, *Tantæne animis cœlestibus iræ?* It seems that on taking his degree at Oxford Dr. Radcliffe settled in Bow Street, at that time a fashionable suburb, and soon made in fees twenty guineas a day, "through his vigorous and decisive method of practice" (says Chambers, in his "Book of Days"), "as well as his pleasantry and ready wit; many, it is said, even feigning themselves ill in order to have the pleasure of a few minutes' conversation with the facetious doctor." Even at this time his books were so few in number that one day, on being asked where was his library, he pointed to a few phials, a skeleton, and a herbal, in one corner of his apartment, exclaiming with emphasis, "There, sir, is Radcliffe's Library." The answer has all the more point because late in life he became the owner of a very fine library, which he left to the University of Oxford. We shall have more to say about Dr. Radcliffe when we come to Kensington Palace. His fortune as a West-End physician was made in 1689, when he managed to restore to health King William just before he went to Ireland to fight the battle of the Boyne, and two years later, when he cured the young Duke of Gloucester of some fainting-fits which threatened to carry him off.

In this street, in lodgings "over against the 'Cock' Tavern," lived the dramatic poet Wycherley and his wife, the widow of the Earl of Drogheda, whom he gained by a chance introduction in a shop at Tunbridge Wells. Whilst residing here he had the honour of a visit from Charles II., who came to see him when ill, and presented him with money enough to pay the expenses of a visit to the south of France. It may perhaps be remembered that Wycherley had held a captain's commission in a regiment of which the Duke of Buckingham was colonel.

It was from the "Cock" Tavern that Sir John Coventry was on his way to his house in the neighbourhood of Pall Mall when he was severely wounded in the nose, as we shall relate when we come to speak of the neighbourhood of the Haymarket.

Mr. T. Raikes in his "Journal," under date 1842, writes:—"After dinner I went to the mock trials at the 'Garrick's Head,' in Bow Street. There is one man who imitates Brougham very well as a counsel; but the subject of debate was coarse, and the audience very vulgar."

In Bonnell Thornton's chambers in this street, "at the upper end, nearly opposite the Playhouse Passage," was held in 1762, an exhibition of sign-boards, by the "Society of Sign-Painters"—of whom, by the way, Hogarth was one. It was intended as a skit upon the exhibitions then newly introduced by the Society of Arts, Manufactures, and Commerce, and its catalogue included upwards of seventy paintings, some of them curious on account of the covered satire which they were intended to convey on political events and public characters. There was, for instance, much humour in placing "The Three Coffins" as a companion to "The Three Apothecaries' Gallipots," and "The Owl in the Ivy Bush" next to "King Charles in the Oak." The exhibition caused much smart and tart writing in the newspapers at the time, and the admission was fixed at a shilling. A full account of the exhibition will be found in the appendix to Mr. Larwood's "History of Sign-Boards."

Towards the close of the last century, when Rich was in the zenith of his managerial prosperity, and the new theatre in Covent Garden had

* See *ante*, page 143.

just commenced with the reproduction of *The Beggar's Opera* a series of what would now be called blazes of triumph, there was established in the immediate vicinity a rustic-looking hostel, to accommodate a refreshment-seeking crowd finding no unoccupied nook in the taverns adjacent. This hostel was "The Wrekin" in Broad Court, on the east side of Bow Street. The original landlord was one Powell, a native of Shropshire, and he chose for his sign the name of the high hill overshadowing the place of his birth. Hither came the actors of that date, and those who sought and valued their society of course followed in their train. The next proprietor was a gentleman named Harrold, of a good Herefordshire family, and who considerably raised the fortunes and the reputation of the house. For about half a century, under his management, "The Wrekin" was the chosen resort of the most prominent celebrities of the day; and as wine was the only refreshment supplied to those who entered the coffee-room, the visitors were exceedingly select. The Kembles—John and Charles—and the principal members of that powerful company then collected at the neighbouring theatre, would constantly avail themselves of this handy histrionic hostel to snatch a pleasant hour from the night, after the cessation of their professional duties. The tavern shared the vicissitudes of the theatre, on which it was in some degree dependent, and nearly every change of management at the one house was followed by a change in the direction of the other. Mr. Warner, the husband of the celebrated tragic actress Mrs. Warner, was at one time the landlord, and Mr. Hemming, an esteemed actor at the Haymarket and Adelphi Theatres, was another. Two famous clubs were here instituted, one called "The Rationals," and the other "The House of Uncommons." When Hemming left to become lessee of the "Café de l'Europe" in the Haymarket, he took the best of the visitors away with him. From 1842 "The Wrekin" began gradually to decline, and within the last few years its declension was so rapid that by the end of 1871 the ancient hostel was levelled with the ground, and its position occupied by a block of new houses manifestly let to respectable tenants.

Wycherley died in his house in Bow Street, in the year 1715, at the age of seventy-five. Of his death-bed we find an amusing anecdote in the "Letters" of Pope. "He had often told me, as, I doubt not, he told all his acquaintance, that he would marry as soon as his life was despaired of. Accordingly, a few days before his death, he underwent the ceremony, and joined together those two sacraments which, wise men say, should be the last we receive; for, if you observe, matrimony is placed after extreme unction in our catechism (*i.e.*, the Roman Catholic), as a kind of hint of the order of time in which they are to be taken. The old man then lay down, satisfied in the conscience of having by this one act paid his just debts, obliged a woman who (he was told) had merit, and shown an heroic resentment of the ill-usage of his next heir. Some hundred pounds which he had with the lady discharged those debts; a jointure of four hundred a year made her a recompense; and the nephew he left to comfort himself as well as he could with the miserable remains of a mortgaged estate. I saw our friend twice after this was done, less peevish in his sickness than he used to be in his health; neither much afraid of dying, nor (which in him had been more likely) much ashamed of marrying. The evening before he expired he called his young wife to the bedside, and earnestly entreated her not to deny him one request, the last he should make. Upon her assurances of consenting to it, he told her, 'My dear, it is only this, that you will never marry an old man again.' I cannot help remarking that sickness, which often destroys both wit and wisdom, yet seldom has power to remove that talent which we call humour. Mr. Wycherley showed his, even in this last compliment; though I think his request a little hard, for why should he bar her from doubling her jointure on the same easy terms?"

It seems strange at the present day to think of Bow Street as one of the most fashionable streets in London; but there can be no doubt that such must have been the character of this thoroughfare in the early part of the last century, for Dryden asserts as much in a casual manner when he writes:—

> "From fops, and wits, and cits, and Bow Street beaux."

CHAPTER XXXV.

COVENT GARDEN AND ITS NEIGHBOURHOOD (*continued*).

Russell Street—Tom Davies' Bookshop—The First Meeting of Boswell and Johnson—An Anecdote of Foote, the Actor—"Will's Coffee-house"—Dryden and Addison—Pope's Youthful Visits to "Will's"—"Button's Coffee-house"—The "Lion's Head"—"Tom's Coffee-house"—The "Shakespeare's Head"—The "Albion"—Distinguished Residents in Russell Street—"The Orpheus" Music-shop—The "Rose" Tavern—The "Harp" and "The City of Lushington"—Crown Court and the Scotch National Church—Richard Steele—Gradual Decline of "Button's Coffee-house."

QUITTING Bow Street, we now enter Russell Street, the thoroughfare connecting Covent Garden Market with Drury Lane. This street was built in 1634, and so called after the Russells, Earls and Dukes of Bedford, the ground-landlords. In 1720 "it was a fine broad street, well inhabited by tradesmen;" and much the same character may be accorded to it in the present day, excepting that that portion of it which skirts the northern side of Drury Lane Theatre is considerably narrowed. Russell Street is one which will always have a memory of a character sacred to all lovers of literature, because in it Boswell was first introduced to Dr. Samuel Johnson. The old bookshop of Tom Davies on the south side of the street, where Johnson first met the Scotchman who was destined to be his biographer, became in our own day the "Caledonian" Coffee-house; and its interest is not diminished by the fact that "Bozzy," as he himself informs us, never passed by it "without feeling reverence and regret." The meeting, to use Boswell's own words, was brought about in this manner:—"At last," he writes, "on Monday, the 16th of May, when I was sitting in Mr. Davies's back parlour, after having drunk tea with him and Mrs. Davies, Johnson unexpectedly came into the shop, and Mr. Davies having perceived him through the glass door of the room in which we were sitting, advancing towards us, he rumoured his awful approach to me, somewhat in the manner of an actor in the part of 'Horatio,' when he addresses 'Hamlet' on the appearance of his father's ghost—'Look, my lord! it comes!' I found that I had a very perfect idea of Johnson's figure from the portrait of him, painted by Sir Joshua Reynolds, soon after he had published his dictionary, in the attitude of sitting in his easy-chair in deep meditation. Mr. Davies mentioned my name, and respectfully introduced me to him. I was much agitated; and recollecting his prejudice against the Scotch, of which I had heard much, I said to Davies, 'Don't tell where I come from.' 'From Scotland,' cries Davies, roguishly. 'Mr. Johnson,' said I, 'I do indeed come from Scotland, but I cannot help it.' I am willing to flatter myself that I meant this as light pleasantry, to soothe and conciliate him, and not as an humiliating abasement at the expense of my country. But however that might be, this speech was somewhat unlucky, for, with that quickness of wit for which he was remarkable, he seized the expression 'come from Scotland,' which I used in the sense of being of that country; and as if I had said that I had come away from it, or left it, retorted, 'That, sir, I find, is what a good many of your country cannot help.' This stroke stunned me a good deal; and when we had sat down I felt myself not a little embarrassed, and apprehensive of what might come next."

In the "Literary Memoirs" of Mr. Cradock, who often met Johnson, Boswell, and Foote here, we find an anecdote of Foote in connection with the shop of Tom Davies which perhaps may not be unacceptable:—"Foote by accident met an inferior person in the street very like Dr. Arne, who, when full dressed, was sometimes rather a grotesque figure, and he contrived not only to obtain some old clothes of the doctor's, but likewise one of his cast-off wigs, and introduced the man on the stage to bring in music-books, as an attendant on the Commissary. The house was all astonishment, and many began even to doubt of the absolute identity. The doctor, of course, was most horribly annoyed; but Foote put money into his pocket, which was all he cared for. Soon after he proceeded so far as to order wooden figures to be made for a puppet-show, of which Dr. Johnson and Dr. Goldsmith were to be the leading characters. Goldsmith affected to laugh, though he seriously alluded to the circumstance in a letter to me; but the great Leviathan of literature was so incensed at the report as to purchase an immense oak cudgel, which he carried with him to Tom Davies's shop, and being there asked for what purpose that was intended, he sternly replied, 'For the castigation of vice upon the stage.'" This being immediately conveyed as it was meant to be, Foote, it is stated, was really intimidated, and the scheme, as to *them*, was given up.

"Will's" Coffee-house was situated on the north side, at the corner of Bow Street; "Button's" was "on the south side, about two doors from Covent Garden;" and "Tom's" on the north side. These coffee-houses have become such classic haunts, on account of their connection with the great names of the "Augustan" period of English literature, that we may be excused if we dwell on them somewhat in detail.

Of all the coffee-houses which in the seventeenth and eighteenth centuries supplied the place in society now occupied by the modern club, none holds a higher place in the literary history of London than "Will's." It stood at the junction of Russell Street and Bow Street, and Sir Walter Scott was of opinion that the original sign of the house was a "cow;" but this is doubted by Mr. Peter Cunningham. The room in which the wits of the day used to assemble, often under the presidency of no less a person than John Dryden, was on the first floor, the ground-rooms being then occupied as a haberdasher's shop. It took its familiar appellation from Will Urwin, by whom it was kept, and whose name is preserved to us in an advertisement offering a reward for the apprehension of a runaway servant in 1674. "It was Dryden," writes Pope, "who made 'Will's' Coffee-house the great resort of the wits of his time. After his death Addison transferred this pre-eminence to 'Button's,' who had been a servant of his own; they were opposite each other in Russell Street, Covent Garden. . . . Addison passed each day alike, and much in the same way as Dryden did. Dryden employed his mornings in writing, dined *en famille*, and then went to 'Will's;' only he came home earlier at nights."

Defoe, too, in his "Journey through England," bears the following testimony to the high repute in which "Will's" Coffee-house then stood with the aristocracy of birth as well as with that of letters:—"After the play, the best of the company go to 'Tom's' and 'Will's' Coffee-house, near adjoining, where there is playing at picket, and the best of conversation till midnight. Here you will see blue and green ribbons and stars sitting familiarly, and talking with the same freedom as if they had left their quality and degrees of distance at home." And it is clear that not only literature but politics formed a subject of constant discussion in that upper room, for doubtless it will be remarked that in his first number of the *Spectator* Addison says: "There is no place of general resort wherein I do not often make my appearance; sometimes I am seen thrusting my head into a round of politicians at 'Will's,' and listening with great attention to the narratives that are made in those little circular audiences."

The *entrée* to "Will's," it seems, was not more readily granted than admission to the "Athenæum" now-a-days would be to mere pretenders to literature, or to writers of every poem of the hour: thus, the *Spectator* speaks, with something of a sneer, of some luckless wight who "came to 'Will's' Coffee-house upon the merit of having writ a posie of a ring." The coffee-house, however, appears to have been used also—just like a club of our own day—as a place where two friends could meet quietly and discuss a subject—literary, religious, or political. Thus in "The Reasons of Mr. Bays' [*i.e.*, Dryden's] Changing his Religion," Mr. B. is represented as saying, "But, if you please to give me the meeting at 'Will's' Coffee-house about three in the afternoon, we'll remove into a private room, where, over a dish of tea, we may debate this important affair with all the solitude imaginable."

"At 'Will's' Coffee-house," says Dr. Johnson in Boswell's "Life," "Dryden had a particular chair to himself, which was set by the fire in winter, and was then called his winter chair; and was carried out for him to the balcony in summer, and was then called his summer chair. Cibber could tell no more than that he remembered him a decent old man, the arbiter of critical disputes at 'Will's.'"

The position held by the wits of "Will's" Coffee-house in the republic of letters may be pretty well inferred from the first number of the *Tatler*, in which Steele and Addison write—"All accounts of gallantry, pleasure, and entertainment shall be under the article of 'White's Chocolate-house;' poetry under that of 'Will's Coffee-house;' learning under the title of the 'Grecian;' foreign and domestic news you will have from 'St. James's Coffee-house.'" The same writer complains that "the place is very much altered since Mr. Dryden frequented it; where you used to see songs, epigrams and satires in the hands of every man you met. You have now only a pack of cards; and instead of the cavils about the turn of the expression, the elegance of the style, and the like, the learned now dispute only about the truth of the game." Hence probably the truth of such a couplet as this:—

"Rail on, ye triflers, who to 'Will's' repair,
For new lampoons, fresh cant, or modish air."

It was to "Will's" that Pope, when a mere child, induced his friends to carry him, in order that he might gaze on the great poet whose mantle he was destined in after life so worthily to wear. "Who does not wish," writes Dr. Johnson, "that Dryden could have known the value of the homage that was paid him, and foreseen the greatness of his young admirer?" In later years Pope became a constant frequenter of "Wills,'" though not till after the illustrious Dryden's death. "Pope had now," again writes Dr. Johnson, "declared himself a poet, and thinking himself entitled to poetical conversation, began at seventeen to frequent 'Will's,' a coffee-house on the north side of Russell Street, in Covent Garden, where the wits of that time used to assemble, and where Dryden had, when he lived, been accustomed to preside."

Malone tells us that "most of the criticisms which Dryden condescended to notice were made at his favourite haunt, 'Will's' Coffee-house." There were other personages, too, who used to repair to "Will's" to meet their friends. Thus, for instance, in Pepys' "Diary," under date October 2, 1660, we find the following entry:—"At 'Will's' I met Mr. Spicer, and with him to the abbey to see them at vespers."

THE LION'S HEAD AT "BUTTON'S."

On the opposite side of Russell Street to "Will's" was "Button's" Coffee-house, so called after the man who established it, in 1712—one Daniel Button, who had been a servant to Joseph Addison, or rather to his wife, the Countess of Warwick. If second, it was only second to "Will's" in its literary reputation, which dated from the appearance of Addison's *Cato*, and maintained it till his death, in 1719. It was here that Addison used to retreat "whenever he suffered any vexation from the countess;" and doubtless on other occasions also, for we know, from several independent sources of information, that he seldom let an evening pass by without looking in here along with his friends, Steele, Budgell, Philips, Carey, and Davenant. Here Pope, as he states, at one time used to meet Addison nearly every day; and here Ambrose Philips, as Dr. Johnson tells us, showed himself one of the *genus irritabile* by "hanging up a rod with which he threatened to chastise Pope." At "Button's" was the conventional office of the *Guardian*, whose editor erected at the entrance a lion's head with a large mouth (of which we give an engraving), to receive contributions from young and inexperienced authors.

SNUFF-BOX FROM "TOM'S" COFFEE-HOUSE. (*See p.* 278.)

Under the "lion's head" was inscribed the following couplet from Martial :—

"Curvantur magnis isti cervicibus ungues ;
Non nisi dilectâ pascitur iste ferâ."

Mr. P. Cunningham traces the movements of this formidable head from "Button's" to the "Shakespeare" Tavern, under Covent Garden Piazza, and thence to "Richardson's Hotel," in the same place, from which it was removed to Woburn Abbey, being bought by the Duke of Bedford.

The origin and purpose of the lion's head above named is thus related in the *Guardian* of July 9, 1713: "I have, I know not how, been drawn into tattle of myself, *more majorum* almost the length of a whole *Guardian*. I shall therefore fill up the remaining part of it with what still relates to my own person and my correspondents. Now I would have them all know that on the 20th instant it is my intention to erect a lion's head, in imitation of those I have described in Venice, through which all the private commonwealth is said to pass. This head is to open a most wide and voracious mouth, which shall take in such letters and papers as are conveyed to me by my correspondents, it being my resolution to have a particular regard to all such matters as come to my hands through the mouth of the lion. There will be under it a box, of which the key will be in my own custody, to receive such papers as are dropped into it. Whatever the lion swallows I shall digest for the use of the public. This head requires some time to finish, the workmen being resolved to give it several masterly touches, and to represent it as ravenous as possible. It will be set up in 'Button's' Coffee-house, in Covent Garden, who is directed to show the way to the lion's head, and to instruct any young author how to convey his works into the mouth of it with safety and secrecy."

"I think myself obliged to acquaint the public that the lion's head, of which I advertised them about a fortnight ago, is now erected at 'Button's' Coffee-house, in Russell Street, Covent Garden, where it opens its mouth at all hours for the reception of such intelligence as shall be thrown into it. It is reckoned an excellent piece of workmanship, and was designed by a great hand in imitation of the antique Egyptian lion, the face of it being compounded out of that of a lion and a wizard. The features are strong and well-furrowed. The whiskers are admired by all that have seen them. It is planted on the western side of the coffee-house, holding its paws under the chin, upon a box, which contains everything that he swallows. He is, indeed, a proper emblem of knowledge and action, being all head and paws." (*The Guardian*, No. 114, Wednesday, July 22, 1713.)

"Being obliged, at present, to attend a particular affair of my own, I do empower my printer to look into the arcana of the lion, and select out of them such as may be of public utility; and Mr. Button is hereby authorised and commanded to give my said printer free ingress and egress to the lion, without any hindrance, lest, or molestation whatsoever, until such time as he shall receive orders to the contrary. And, for so doing, this shall be his warrant." (*Guardian*, No. 142, August 24, 1713.)

Charles Johnson, famous for writing a play every year, was an attendant at "Button's" every day. He had, probably, thriven better in his vocation had he been somewhat leaner; he may be justly called a martyr to obesity, and may be said to have fallen a victim to the rotundity of his body. He kept a tavern in Bow Street, Covent Garden, and died about 1741. Though he was a man of inoffensive behaviour, yet he could not escape the satire of Pope, who, too ready to resent even any supposed offence, has, on some trivial pique, immortalised him in the "Dunciad."

In Russell Street, at No. 17, on the north side, was "Tom's" Coffee-house; but the house was pulled down in 1865, after having stood upwards of a century and a half. It was established about the year 1700, by a Mr. West, after whose Christian name it was called. It is mentioned in the "Journey through England," in 1714, as a place where "there was playing at piquet, and the best of conversation till midnight," and where "blue and green ribands with stars"—in other words, the bearers of the highest orders at Court—might be seen night after night "sitting and talking familiarly." Its balcony in the day-time was often crowded with members of the Upper House of Parliament, who came thither to drink tea and coffee and to be amused. In the early part of the reign of George III. there was established at "Tom's" a club, consisting of upwards of 600 members, including not only Garrick, Foote, Murphy, Dr. Dodd, George Colman, Goldsmith, Dr. Johnson, and William Bowyer, but the Duke of Montague, Sir George (afterwards Lord) Rodney, the great Lord Clive, the Earl of Anglesey, Lord Edward Bentinck, Earl Percy, and the Duke of Northumberland. Quoting Whitehead's "Legends of London," we might add that—

"These are the men that trod our public ways,
With brilliant wits that every fancy lov'd;
Congreve's wild, sportive flights of later days,
And graceful Addison whom all approv'd:
While graver Johnson's wisdom spoke like truth,
Burke's eloquence replied in tones sedate.
Here charming Goldsmith fluttered fresh as youth,
And Swift and Gay. But see, at Fame's broad gate
The dazzling crowds our kindly memory greet;
Their names this transient verse may not repeat."

"Tom's" continued to be used as a coffee-house down to 1814, when it passed into other uses; but many of the relics of the club still remain in private hands, including the books and lists of members and the snuff-box which was handed round among the company. This snuff-box, of which we give an engraving in page 277, is described by Mr. Timbs, in the *Illustrated London News* of 1865, as of large size and of tortoise-shell, and having on the lid in high relief, chased in silver, portraits of Charles I., Queen Anne, and the Royal Oak at Boscobel, with Charles II. hid in its branches.

At a tavern with the sign of the "Shakespeare's Head," in Russell Street, the Beefsteak Society, which we have already mentioned in our account of the Lyceum, used to meet before removing to that theatre. The sign is said by Mr. Larwood to have been "beautifully painted," and it was the work of George Lambert, scene-painter at Covent Garden Theatre.

In Russell Street was also another "Rose" Tavern, a noted place of debauchery in the Stuart times. Constant allusions to it occur in the comic writers of the age; Shadwell, for instance, in *The Scourers*, makes one of the characters observe, "Thou wilt never be his fellow . . . . oh! had you seen him scower as I did! oh! so delicately, so like a gentleman! how he cleared the 'Rose' Tavern." Mr. Larwood tells us that here, in 1712, was arranged the fatal duel between Lord Mohun and the Duke of Hamilton, of which we shall have to say more when we come to its actual scene, Hyde Park. How the character of "The Rose" for morality stood in the reign of Queen Anne, may be gathered from the following lines of the "Rake Reformed:"—

"Not far from thence appears a pendant sign,
Whose bush declares the product of the vine;
Where to the traveller's sight the full-blown 'Rose
Its dazzling beauties doth in gold disclose,
And painted beauties flock in tallied cloathes."

Hogarth has given a picture of one of the rooms in this house in his "Rake's Progress." "In 1766," adds Mr. Larwood, "the tavern was swallowed up in the enlargements of Drury Lane by Garrick; but the sign was preserved, and hung up against the front wall." An engraving of it is shown in Pennant's "London."

At the "Albion" Tavern in this street—the legitimate successor of the "Will's" and "Button's" of the last century—"the late-hour visitor," Mr. E. L. Blanchard tells us, "may occasionally see faces flitting past which have been familiar to him in association with the glare of the foot-lights; but the arrangements of that hotel are totally distinct from those of the old theatrical parlour which permitted a stranger to observe how 'Horatio' would eat a mutton chop, how 'Polonius' would crown the enjoyment of a Welsh rare-bit with a pipe, and how the thirsty 'Ghost' would evoke congenial spirits which really came when he did call for them. To mix in goodly theatrical company at the present day it is needful to be introduced to clubs like the Garrick, the Junior Garrick, or the Arundel. Such institutions have done much to alter the aspect of professional life after dark, and the marked change which has thus crept over the old haunts of the players is worth noting." The "Albion" will now be looked for in vain.

Among the temporary residents in Russell Street in olden time was John Evelyn. In his "Diary," under date September 10th, 1658, is the entry: "I came with my wife and family to London; tooke lodgings at the 3 Feathers in Russell Street, Covent Garden, for all the winter, my son being very unwell." Here, too, as he tells us, he was visited in the December following by "my Lord Count Arundel of Wardour."

Russell Street, during last century, and indeed during the earlier part of the present century, was largely inhabited by theatrical and other celebrities, of whom it would be impossible to give a full or complete list. Major Mohun; Betterton; Mrs. Barton Booth; Charles Lamb; Carr, Earl of Somerset, whose name is mixed up with the story of the poisoning of Sir Thomas Overbury; Armstrong, the poet; Joseph Taylor, one of the original performers of Shakespeare's plays—each and all of these individuals are enumerated by Mr. Peter Cunningham amongst those who have contributed to the memories of Russell Street.

In Russell Street, "next door to Isaac Bickerstaffe's Coffee-house," was the music-shop of a Mr. Peppard, which bore the appropriate sign of "The Orpheus;" and Gibbon tells us, in his "Memoirs," that, while a student at Magdalen College, Oxford, and when in doubt as to the claims of the rival Churches of England and Rome, he consulted the advice of a Mr. Lewis, a Roman Catholic bookseller in Russell Street, who recommended him to consult the priest, who received his formal abjuration of Protestantism, and admitted him into the bosom of "the one fold" in June, 1753.

In what used to be Little Russell Street formerly hung a sign of Shakespeare's head: it was painted by Clarkson, who received for it £500 Another sign—a whole-length portrait of the immortal bard, in the same street—was the work of a Royal Academician, Samuel Wale. But this had to be taken down, with many other signs, in obedience to the Act of Parliament, and was sold to a broker in Lower Grosvenor Street, at whose shop-door it stood for some years, neglected and despised, and at last was destroyed by exposure to the weather.

"The Harp," in this part of Russell Street, was long notorious as the resort of distinguished actors; and here used to be held, until only a few years ago, a society or club denominated "The City of Lushington," the members of which were presided over by a "Lord Mayor" and four "Aldermen," each of them being annually elected to those distinguished positions. Here Sims the elder flourished for many years. He was succeeded by his son, a tablet to whose memory may still be seen in the parlour of the aforesaid hostelry. In these words is he commemorated: "A tribute of respect to the memory of Sir William Sims, theatrical agent. Obiit Feb. 9th, 1841. Ætat. 54. He was for thirty-five years a distinguished member of this city, and thrice Lord Mayor. Many successful aspirants to histrionic fame are indebted to him for their advancement in the profession, and can look back with gratitude to his advice and assistance." This rattle-brained society of theatrical, commercial, mechanic, and other worthies, was most solemnly established, many years since, by the whimsical contrivance of a merry company of tipplers, that they might meet every night as citizens of "The City of Lushington," each having his own particular seat denoted as his ward, and each member, on admittance, having a particular ward assigned to him. "The uninitiated," says Mr. E. L. Blanchard, "may be advantageously told that certain burlesque ceremonies of municipal election are still continued at specified intervals, when nominal dignities are humorously conferred. The room retains all the original 'wards,' and the 'Edmund Kean corner' is scrupulously maintained as the post of honour." The title of this society,

"The City of Lushington," might lead our readers to infer that its proceedings were mixed up with a certain amount of levity and drunkenness; but this, we are credibly informed, was not the case in recent days, everything being conducted with the strictest propriety and decorum.

In Crown Court, close by, and opposite the stage entrance to Drury Lane Theatre, is the Scottish National Church, a place of worship which enjoyed great popularity under the ministry of the late Dr. Cumming, of prophetical notoriety.

At "Button's"—and, indeed, at most of the other coffee-houses—the leading company used to wear long, flowing flaxen wigs, and so did Sir Godfrey Kneller when he frequented it of an evening. John Timbs, in his "Club Life in London," tells us that "'Button's' continued in vogue until Addison's death and Steele's retirement into Wales, after which the house became gradually deserted; the coffee-drinkers went to the 'Bedford,' the dinner-parties to the 'Shakespeare.'"

Richard Steele, the celebrated wit, dramatic and essay writer, and one of the most frequent attendants at "Button's" in its palmy days, was the son of an English barrister who filled the post of secretary to the Duke of Ormond, and was born in Dublin in 1671. Through the influence of the Duke of Ormond he was sent to the Charterhouse School, in London, from whence he removed to Oxford. It was at the Charterhouse that he found Addison, a youth three years older than himself, and an intimacy was formed between them—one of the most memorable in literature. Steele commenced life by entering the army as a private soldier. His wit and brilliancy soon made him a favourite in the army, and he plunged into the fashionable vices and follies of the age, which enabled him to acquire that knowledge of life and character which proved so serviceable when he exchanged the sword for the pen. As a check on his irregular mode of life, and being thoroughly convinced of many things of which he had often repented, and which he more often repeated, he wrote for his own admonition a little work entitled "The Christian Hero;" but his gay companions did not relish this semi-religious work, and not being very deeply impressed by his own reasoning and pious examples, as a counterpoise he wrote a comedy, *The Funeral, or Grief à la Mode*, which was very successful. Steele had dedicated "The Christian Hero" to his colonel, Lord Cutts, who appointed him his secretary, and promised him a captain's command in the volunteers. It was not long, however, before Steele found that in exchanging the pen for the sword he had made a mistake; and he lost no time in following his more congenial pursuits. He wrote a number of plays, which were very successful; and through the popularity thus obtained he secured an appointment in the Stamp Office, London, which he resigned on being elected member for Stockbridge. His Parliamentary career, however, was not brilliant, for he was expelled the House for writing two alleged libels, called respectively "The Englishman" and "The Crisis," "which expulsion," says Lord Mahon, "was a fierce and most unwarrantable stretch of party violence."

The accession of George I. was a fortunate circumstance for Steele; for he not only received the honour of knighthood, but was appointed to a post of some importance at Hampton Court; and, what was far more congenial, was named Governor of the Royal Company of Comedians. And when the Rebellion of 1715 placed a number of forfeited estates at the disposal of the Government Steele was appointed a member of the Commission for Scotland. In this capacity, in 1717, he visited Edinburgh, and whilst there he is said on one occasion to have given a splendid entertainment to a multitude of decayed tradesmen and beggars collected from the streets!

Steele appears to have received fair remuneration for his literary work; and on the publication of his *Conscious Lovers*, in 1722, the king, to whom it was dedicated, gave him £500. But he was always poor, because always lavish, scheming, and unbusiness-like; yet nothing could depress the elasticity of his spirits. Being always engaged in some unsuccessful scheme or other, and with habits both benevolent and lavish, he wasted his regular income in anticipation of a greater, until absolute pecuniary distress was the result. Shortly before his death he retired into Wales, solely for the purpose of retrenching his affairs, so that he might pay his creditors. But it was too late, and before he could carry his honest intentions into effect death overtook him, and, enfeebled by dissipation and excess, he died, on September 1, 1729, at the age of fifty-eight.

It is as a witty and polished writer that Steele is best known, and especially as the originator of the *Tatler*, a paper in which Addison and some of the best writers of the time remarked on the politics of the age in which they lived. The *Spectator* and *Guardian* also received contributions from Steele's pen; and although the state of things which produced these works has passed away, yet these essays still rank as a worthy part of the standard literature of England.

After the death of Addison, the celebrity of

"Button's" Coffee-house declined, and a few years later we find its master in receipt of parish relief. His demise was thus announced in the *Daily Advertiser* at the time:—"On Sunday morning, died, after three days' illness, Mr. Button, who formerly kept 'Button's' Coffee-house, in Russell Street, Covent Garden, a very noted house for wits, being the place where the lyon produced the famous *Tatlers* and *Spectators*, written by the late Mr. Secretary Addison and Sir Richard Steele, Knt., which works will transmit their names with honour to posterity." Button lies buried, as already stated, among some of his illustrious guests, in St. Paul's Churchyard, close by.

CHAPTER XXXVI.

COVENT GARDEN AND ITS NEIGHBOURHOOD (*continued*).

καὶ δὴ καὶ ὁ τὰ συσσιτία εὑρὼν πολλῶν ἀγαθῶν αἴτιος.
Aristotle.

Club Life—Dickens's Love for Covent Garden—The "Sheridan Knowles" Tavern and the "Owls" Club—The "Whistling Oyster"—The "Shakespeare Head" Tavern—Johnson's Alamode Beef-shop—Wellington Street—Tavistock Street—Dramatic Sick Fund Association—Royal Dramatic College—A Batch of Newspaper Offices—Dr. Johnson and Dr. Perry—The Victoria Club—Royal General Theatrical Fund—Bohn's Library—The "Fleece" Inn and the "Turk's Head"—"Wright's" Coffee-house—Anecdote of Foote, the Actor—Discovery of Stone Coffins—Millar the Publisher and Fielding's "Amelia"—Sotheby and Wilkinson's Auction-rooms—Somerset House—Lancaster Place—The London Necropolis Company.

THE motto at the head of this chapter contains the opinion of one of the sages of antiquity upon the benefits which accrue to man as a "social" being through the instrumentality of the first deviser of what would now-a-days be called "Clubs" and "Club Life," but what the Athenians styled "Syssities," a system, that is, of common tables for citizens. The same institution, under a different name, flourished, so we are told, even among the hardy youth of Sparta; and in fact, as man is not merely a gregarious but also a social animal, we may lay it down as a principle that wherever a refined and polished society has prevailed, its life has been attended by some means or other for bringing men into each other's company to discuss questions of social, political, or literary interest. With these few remarks by way of preface, we pass to some further notice of the Club Life of Covent Garden and its neighbourhood.

The Club was the natural "outcome" of the coffee-houses, which, as we have stated in a previous volume, were first introduced in St. Michael's Alley, Cornhill, by a Turkey merchant in the time of the Commonwealth. In 1663 it was ordained by Act of Parliament that all coffee-houses should be licensed by the magistrates; and twelve years later, as Mr. Cunningham tells us, Charles II. issued a royal edict to close up the coffee-houses as "nurseries of sedition." The principle above quoted, however, asserted itself, and a few days afterwards the proclamation was cancelled.

Our modern celebrated clubs are founded upon eating and drinking, which are points wherein most men agree, and in which the learned and illiterate, the dull and the airy, the philosopher and the buffoon, can all of them bear a part. The Kit-Cat itself—of which we have already spoken in our account of Shire Lane—is said to have taken its original from the mutton pie. The Beef-steak and October Clubs were neither of them averse to eating and drinking, as is clear from their names.

Charles Dickens as a boy had an innate love for the neighbourhood of Covent Garden, as instinct with human life. With Johnson, he knew that "the full tide of life was in the Strand;" and if so, it can scarcely be wondered at that, precocious child, he loved to sit on the shore and watch its waves breaking on its northern bank. To be taken out for a walk into the real town, especially if it were anywhere about Covent Garden or the Strand, perfectly entranced him with pleasure. But most of all he had a "profound attraction of repulsion" to St. Giles's. If he could only induce any one soever to take him through Seven Dials he was supremely happy. "Good heaven!" he would exclaim, "what wild visions of prodigies of wickedness, want, and beggary, arose in my mind out of that place!" On the same authority we learn that George Colman's "Broad Grins" seized his fancy very much, and that he was so impressed by its description of Covent Garden in the piece called *The Elder Brother*, that he stole down to the Market by himself to compare it with the book. "He remembered," says Mr. J. Forster, "as he said in telling me this, snuffing up the flavour of the faded cabbage-leaves as if it were the very breath of comic fiction." But we must pass on from the domain of poetry into the prosaic region of fact.

In Brydges Street, Covent Garden (now absorbed into Catherine Street, of which it forms a continuation), facing the entrance to Drury Lane Theatre, was a tavern bearing the sign of "The Sheridan Knowles," who is supposed by Mr. Larwood to have been the last literary celebrity to whom such an honour was paid. There the club of "Owls" used at one time to hold its meetings. Sheridan Knowles was one of its especial patrons and frequenters; and as it embraced many authors, wits, and composers, its members, it may well be imagined, were not owls of the "moping" sort, whom Gray commemorates in his "Elegy." Every panel was inscribed with the name of some dead or living dramatist.

Now-a-days the carriages of the upper ten thousand have no difficulty in finding their way to Old Drury or Covent Garden Market. The access to Drury Lane Theatre, however, was remarkably bad in old times. Walker, writing in "The Original," in 1836, says:—"Within memory, the principal carriage approach to Old Drury Lane Theatre was through that part of Drury Lane which is now a flagged foot-passage, and called Drury Court, just opposite the new church in the Strand."

On the south side of Drury Lane Theatre, in a narrow court leading out of Catherine Street, called Vinegar Yard, was, until quite recently, a small tavern—or rather oyster and refreshment-rooms—dear to artists; and, if we may trust the *Daily Telegraph*, it enjoyed a reputation of much the same kind as that which in former days attached to "Button's" or "Will's" Coffee-houses. The house rejoiced in the fanciful name of "The Whistling Oyster," and its sign was a weirdly and grotesquely comical representation of a gigantic oyster whistling a tune, and with an intensely humorous twinkle beaming in its eye. The shop was first established by a Mr. Pearkes, in 1825. "It appears," said a writer in the *Daily Telegraph*, "that about the year 1840 the proprietor of the house in question, which had then, as it has now, a great name for the superior excellence of its delicate little 'natives,' heard a strange and unusual sound proceeding from one of the tubs in which the shell-fish lay piled in layers one over the other, placidly fattening upon oatmeal, and awaiting the inevitable advent of the remorseless knife. Mr. Pearkes, the landlord, listened, hardly at first believing his ears. There was, however, no doubt

THE SCOTCH NATIONAL CHURCH, CROWN COURT. (*See page* 280.)

about the matter. One of the oysters was distinctly whistling! or, at any rate, producing a sort of 'sifflement' with its shell. It was not difficult to detect this phenomenal bivalve, and in a very few minutes he was triumphantly picked out from and the creature, breathing in his own way by the due inspiration and expiration of water, forced a small jet through the tiny orifice each time that he drew his breath, and so made the strange noise that first caught the ear of his fortunate pro-

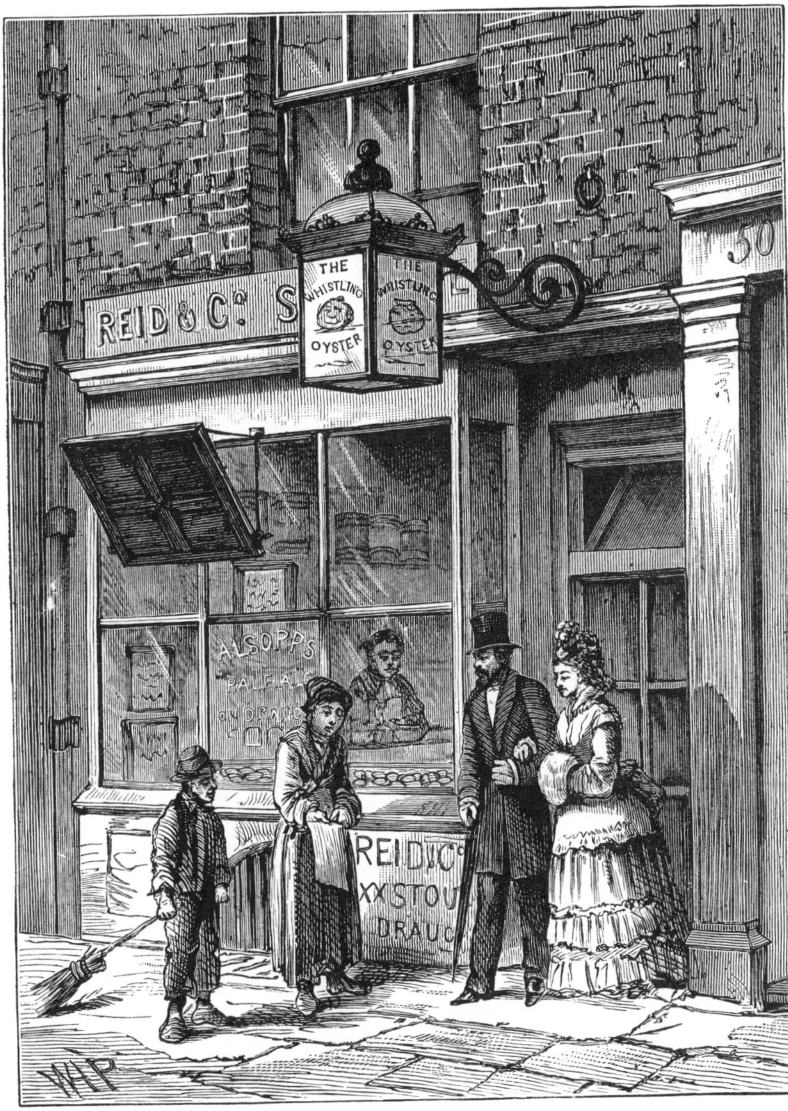

THE "WHISTLING OYSTER."

amongst his fellows, and put by himself in a spacious tub, with a bountiful supply of brine and meal. The news spread through the town, and for some days the fortunate Mr. Pearkes found his house besieged by curious crowds. That this Arion of oysters did really whistle, or do something very like whistling, is beyond all question. How he managed to do so is not upon record. Probably there existed somewhere in his shell a minute hole, such as those with which the stray oyster-shells upon the beach are usually riddled, prietor." As for the jokes and good sayings to which the creature gave rise during its brief span of life, they would fairly fill a large folio; and readers of *Punch* in its early volumes may even remember the famous picture of the "Whistling Oyster"—drawn, it is almost needless to add, from a purely imaginary point of view, and which those who have not been so fortunate as to have seen could behold reproduced in large upon the lamp which marked the door of the establishment in Vinegar Yard. Douglas Jerrold's suggestion was that the said oyster "had been crossed in love, and now whistled to keep up appearances, with an idea of showing that it didn't care." Thackeray used to declare that he was once actually in the shop when an American came in to see the phenomenon, as everybody else was doing, and, after hearing the talented mollusk go through its usual performance, strolled contemptuously out, declaring "it was nothing to an oyster he knew of in Massachusetts, which whistled 'Yankee Doodle' right through, and followed its master about the house like a dog." The subsequent fate of this interesting creature is a mystery —whether he was eaten alive, or ignominiously scalloped, or still more ignominiously handed over to the tender mercies of a cook in the neighbourhood to be served up in a bowl of oyster sauce as a relish to a hot beefsteak. In fact, like the "Lucy" of Wordsworth—

"None can tell
When th' oyster ceased to be."

But it is somewhat singular that so eccentric a creature should have existed in the middle of London, and in the middle of the nineteenth century, and that no history of his career should be on record: still more strange, we think, that he should have been set up over his master's shop as a sign, and yet that, with all its notoriety, it should have escaped the notice of Mr. Peter Cunningham, Mr. John Timbs, and even Mr. Larwood. The houses in Vinegar Yard have now been demolished.

If we may be allowed at this point to travel a little beyond the strict bounds of Covent Garden, it may be added that in Wych Street, Drury Lane, there was a "Shakespeare Head," the last haunt of the club of "Owls"—so called from the late hours they maintained. The tavern was kept at one time by Mr. Mark Lemon, afterwards the genial editor of *Punch*, assisted by his wife, formerly a singer of repute as Miss Romer. Mr. Larwood tells us that it was much frequented by actors, and that a club of *literati* used to meet on its first floor. Not far off hence was "Johnson's Alamode Beef-house," in Clare Court, close to Drury Lane, where Charles Dickens as a boy used to look in, whilst employed as a drudge at Hungerford Stairs, carrying his daily supply of bread, and "purchasing a small plate of alamode beef to eat with it," the waiter staring at the precocious boy eating his humble dinner, as if he had been a monster.

Wellington Street, strange to say, is not mentioned by Mr. P. Cunningham in his "Handbook of London," usually so exhaustive. It leads from Russell Street, in a straight line with Bow Street, across the Strand to Waterloo Bridge, and was newly made as an approach to that bridge in 1829-30. It follows as nearly as possible the line of what was once the boundary-wall separating the grounds of Exeter House from those of Wimbledon House, described in a previous chapter.

Tavistock Street, to which we have alluded in a former chapter, runs out of Wellington Street to the west, parallel with the Strand. In this street were originally the offices of the Dramatic, Equestrian, and Musical Sick Fund Association. This institution was founded in 1855, in order to assist members of these professions in sickness and in distress, and to help them to obtain employment. The offices of the Association are now in Adam Street, Adelphi. The office of the Royal Dramatic College was likewise in Tavistock Street. This institution was founded in 1858 for the relief of aged and infirm actors and actresses; but was eventually broken up, through want of support.

As we walk down the rather steep incline which leads across the Strand to Lancaster Place and Waterloo Bridge, we pass Exeter Street on the right and left of us. In this street, as we remarked in a previous chapter, Dr. Johnson lodged when he first came to town from Lichfield, and it was during his residence here that he first commenced his condensation of the speeches in Parliament for the *Gentleman's Magazine*. At the corner of Exeter Street was the office for the publication *Household Words*, and as such it was the constant haunt of Charles Dickens in his later years. Here was afterwards published the *Army and Navy Gazette*, founded and edited by Dr. W. H. Russell, and now located in York Street, Covent Garden. In Wellington Street used to be the publishing offices of a host of newspapers and magazines, and here one may still find those of the *Spectator*, the *Era*, the *Gardener's Chronicle*, and the *Morning Post* (already described). In this street, too, is the principal entrance to the Lyceum Theatre (see p. 117 *ante*). It must have been as nearly as possible on this spot that Dr. Johnson offended Dr. Percy, author of "Reliques of Ancient Poetry," by parodying the style of that charming and simple tale, "The Hermit of Warkworth," thus:—

"I put my hat upon my head,
And walked into the Strand,
And there I met an other man
With *his* hat in his hand."

"I must freely declare," says Nichols in his "Literary and Miscellaneous Memoirs," "with all my partiality for Johnson, that I think Dr. Percy had very great cause to take offence at a man who, by a ludicrous parody on a stanza of his 'Hermit,' had rendered him contemptible. It was urged that Johnson meant only to attack the metre; but he certainly turned the whole poem into ridicule. Mr. Garrick soon afterwards asked me," adds Nichols, "in a postscript to one of his letters, 'whether I had seen Johnson's criticism on the "Hermit?" it is already,' said he, 'over half the town.'"

On the eastern side of the street, occupying the corner of Exeter Street, is a handsome and substantial building of the Italian order, ambitiously styled "The Victoria Club." It has nothing, however, of royalty or aristocracy about it, and appears to have been designed mainly for betting-men. It was built about 1862; and some idea may be formed of the contrast between its members and the literary society which used to meet in the coffee-houses of the neighbourhood less than a century before it, when we add that, a few years after its foundation, the then highly intelligent committee and secretary were ignorant of its brief and unimportant history, and even of the name of its founder!

In Wellington Street used to be the offices of the Royal General Theatrical Fund. This institution was founded, in 1839, for the relief of "poor actors, actresses, singers, pantomimists, and dancers," to whom annuities are granted; aid is likewise afforded to the widows and orphans of members. It is now located in Catherine Street.

About half-way down Wellington Street, and opening into Catherine Street, is York Street. Here Mr. Henry G. Bohn, one of the most original and enterprising of modern publishers, carried on business from about the year 1835 down to 1866, when he retired, transferring his stock to Messrs. Bell and Daldy. He was one of the first publishers who tried the experiment of republishing standard works in a cheap form in "libraries" of various kinds. These amounted altogether to as many as 700 volumes, and the cost of their production could not have been very much short of £500,000. In York Street was the literary auction-room of Mr. Samuel Baker, in the middle of the last century, now represented by Messrs. Sotheby, Wilkinson, and Hodge, of whom we shall have to speak when we reach the southern part of Wellington Street. Here, too, was the "Fleece" Inn—a tavern, if we may believe Aubrey, "very unfortunate for homicides," three having happened within its walls in his time. It was afterwards turned into a private house, its former master having hanged himself! It is as well, perhaps, in this case that the timbers and walls of houses are not usually gifted with speech, or it would have been hard for its owner to find another tenant.

Another tavern in this street at one time enjoyed a different reputation to that of the "Fleece." This house bore the sign of the "Turk's Head," which was admirably painted by Cotton, and was much admired. The tavern had among its usual frequenters Bernard Lintot, the bookseller of the Strand, the rival of Tonson, and the "huge Lintot" of Pope's "Dunciad," who sang "Molly Mag" as none before or after him could sing it.

In York Street, about 1769-70, was a theatrical club which met of an evening at "Wright's Coffee-house." Foote, Holland, Powell, and many of the leading actors of the time were members; and Mr. Cradock, in his "Literary and Miscellaneous Memoirs," tells us how he went thither one evening with a young friend from the country, named Farmer, who had written on the subject of Shakespeare, and who particularly wanted to see Foote. The latter was a much kinder and more genial personage, as is clear from Cradock's narrative, than Dr. Johnson would have been if placed in a similar position. "Luckily an immediate opportunity occurred to me of introducing him, and of interesting the great satirist in his favour. Foote gravely and very handsomely said, 'I shall feel a particular pleasure in paying every attention to him as a friend of yours; he is a man of talents, and I am well acquainted with his excellent Essay on the Learning of Shakespeare;' and indeed he kept his word; for while Farmer stayed he did everything in his power to make himself agreeable and entertaining."

Foote was a man of great natural and ready wit, as would appear from the following anecdotes, which we owe to the same source:—"Mr. Howard happening to hint something about printing a second edition of his 'Thoughts and Maxims,' Foote replied directly, with a sneer, 'Right, sir, Second Thoughts are often best.' In like manner, when a gentleman, with whom he was more intimate, only quoted in jest some trifling circumstance about a game-leg, Foote maliciously replied, "Pray, sir, make no allusion to *my* weakest part; did I ever attack *your* head?' In fact, if the truth must be told, Foote at times spared neither friend nor foe. He had little regard for the feelings of others; if he thought of a witty thing that would create laughter, he said it. If Foote ever had a serious regard for any one, it was for Holland; yet at his death, or rather, indeed, after his funeral, he violated all decency concerning him. Holland was the son of a baker at Hampton, and on the stage was a close imitator of Garrick, who had such a respect for him that he played the 'Ghost' to his 'Hamlet' merely to serve him at his benefit. Holland died rather young, and Foote attended as one of the mourners. He was really grieved: and the friend from whom I had the account declared that his eyes were swollen with tears; yet when the gentleman said to him, afterwards, 'So, Foote, you have been attending the funeral of your dear friend Holland?' the latter instantly replied, 'Yes, we have shoved the little baker into his last oven!"

We have said that Covent Garden in all probability served not only as a monastic garden, but also as a burial-place for the members of the abbey of St. Peter's at Westminster. This supposition is confirmed by a fact mentioned by Mr. J. H. Jesse in his "London," that "stone coffins and other relics of the dead have from time to time been discovered behind the houses on the north side of York Street."

As we cross the Strand, we might have seen until quite recently, a door or two off, on the left, the shop which once was Tonson's, and afterwards passed to Millar, then to Alderman Cadell, and about which Sir N. W. Wraxall tells us a good story. Millar gave Fielding £800 for the copyright of his "Amelia"—a high price at that time. A literary friend having expressed an opinion that it was not worth anything like that amount, and that he had better get rid of it as soon as possible, Millar resorted to a capital "trick of the trade." At his first "trade sale" he said to his brother bibliopoles that he had several works to put up, for which he would be glad if they would bid, but that every copy of "Amelia" was already bespoke. "This manœuvre had its effect," says Wraxall; "all the booksellers were anxious to get their names put down for copies of it, and the edition, though a very large one, was immediately sold."

In that part of Wellington Street which joins the Strand to Waterloo Bridge, on the west side, on the site of part of the old Savoy, are the well-known rooms of Messrs. Sotheby, Wilkinson, and Hodge, auctioneers of literary property. The business was first established by Mr. Samuel Baker, in York Street, as stated above, in 1744. Thirty years later he was joined by Mr. G. Leigh, who appears to have conducted the business single-handed from 1777 down to 1780, when the name of Sotheby appears as his partner. In 1800 the firm was reinforced by the addition of Mr. Sotheby's son, and in 1804 the firm was styled "Leigh and S. Sotheby," their rooms being removed to "No. 145, the Strand." In 1816 the name of Leigh has disappeared from the title-pages of the sale catalogues, which mention the name of only "Mr. Sotheby." From 1818 down to 1828 Mr. Sotheby carried on the business in Wellington Street, since which time the establishment has gone on steadily progressing. Among the most celebrated sales which have been entrusted to this firm in the last and present centuries have been the libraries or other collections of Prince Talleyrand, Professor Porson, Bishop Horsley, Joseph Addison, W. S. Rose, John Gifford, E. Malone, Dr. Hawtrey, Sir William Tite, the first Emperor Napoleon, the Chevalier d'Eon, Dr. Charles Burney, the Marquis of Lansdowne, the Earl of Bute, Sir William Dolben, Mr. H. T. Hope, the Earl of Halifax, Sir M. Sykes, Mr. John Nichols, Sir S. Romilly, Sir W. Tite, Mr. J. G. Nichols, and Lord Crauford. It may interest our readers to learn that the volumes of catalogues of sales conducted by this firm are regularly deposited in the British Museum, where about 150 volumes, all carefully priced, may be seen, giving a history of literary properties sold from 1744 down to 1828, and several hundreds more carrying the same record down to nearly the present day.

The western frontage of Somerset House, nearly opposite to Messrs. Sotheby's auction-rooms, was erected in the year 1857, from the designs of Mr. Pennethorne, and is considered one of the most successful façades in modern London. In this wing of Somerset House are the offices of the Inland Revenue Department. On the opposite side of the street, standing somewhat back from the roadway, is a terrace of large houses, called Lancaster Place, as standing on ground belonging to the Duchy of Lancaster. They are mostly cut up into chambers for artists, engineers, and lawyers. One of them is used as the chief office of the London Necropolis Company, which owns the large cemetery near Woking station. In another, the late Mr. Samuel Carter Hall for many years edited the *Art Journal.*

Passing this terrace, we are at the northern end of Waterloo Bridge, at full liberty to find our way down the steps to the Embankment, where, strictly speaking, judging from the meaning of the term, we might have expected to find the "Strand" itself, and where we certainly should have found it in very "Old London"—say the London of a thousand years ago. Thence we pass on to the Thames itself, to which our next chapters shall be devoted.

CHAPTER XXXVII.

THE RIVER THAMES.

"Large, gentle, deep, majestic King of Floods."—*Thomson.*

The Pool—Importance of the Thames in the Olden Time—King James and the Corporation of London—Scenery of the Thames from London Bridge to Westminster—The 'Folly"—A Chinese Junk—The Ancient Church of St. Mary-the-Virgin—Lilly, the Astrologer—The Thames Police—The Royal Humane Society's Reception-room—Waterloo Bridge—The Last of the Savoy Palace—Carlisle House—The Adelphi Terrace—Rousseau and Garrick—Old Hungerford Bridge—Hungerford Stairs—Warren's Blacking Warehouse and Charles Dickens—The Thames Swimming Baths—Whitehall Stairs—Cowley's Funeral—Westminster Bridge—Wordsworth's Sonnet on the Scene from the Bridge at Sunrise.

We do not intend in this chapter to write a history of the Thames from its source to the sea; much less to become the biographer of the rivers that fall into it: that work has been already done by Dr. Charles Mackay, in his pleasant and chatty book, "The Thames and its Tributaries." It is our business and duty to show ourselves, like Theodore Hook, "familiar with the Thames from London Bridge up to Eel Pie Island"—perhaps even a little farther. Our discourse, therefore, will be only of the Thames at and near London; and for the present we shall keep "above bridge," simply contenting ourselves with the remark that, if the visitor from foreign lands would wish to form an adequate idea of the mercantile and commercial wealth of our great metropolis, he had better enter London not by the South-Eastern or the Chatham and Dover Railways, but by the silent highway of that noble river of which Englishmen are so proud. "The congregation of men, ships, and commerce of all nations in the 'Pool,' the din, the duskiness, the discord of order, activity, and industry, is finer," writes the author of "Babylon the Great," "than a bird's-eye view of London from the hills on the north or south, or than the royal gardens, the parks, and the palaces, that first present themselves to a stranger coming from the west. . . . This is indeed old Father Thames, in the overwhelming wonders of his wealth; and the ships and the warehouses that we see contain the stimulus and the reward of those men who have made England the queen and London the jewel of the world." Truly indeed did Cowper write—

> "Where has commerce such a mart,
> So rich, so throng'd, so drain'd, and so supplied
> As London—opulent, enlarg'd, and still
> Increasing London? Babylon of old
> No more the glory of the earth than she,
> A more accomplish'd world's chief glory now!"

The river, as the source of almost all the greatness and wealth of the metropolis, and also as one of its chief ornaments, deserves especial notice at our hands. But we are above, not below, London Bridge; so turning our backs on the warehouses which crowd the banks on either side from Wapping to the Tower, from Limehouse and Rotherhithe to Southwark Bridge, let us make our voyage westward, by the side of our new and magnificent embankment, imagining that, as we are treating at once of London "Old" and "New," we are sailing in our barge along the channel which so many great and historic personages, from kings and queens to prisoners of State, have traversed before us.

In London certainly the river has been from earliest times "the silent highway" between the Tower and Westminster. As the Court was usually either at the Old Palace of Westminster or at Whitehall, and most of the king's liege subjects lived in and around the City proper, a boat was naturally the usual conveyance of great people, whether lords of Parliament, courtiers, or ambassadors, into the presence of the sovereign, especially at a time when as yet the Strand was unpaved, and when wagons stuck in its miry wheel-ruts in the winter season.

As a proof of the importance of the Thames in old times as a thoroughfare from London to Westminster, it was ordered that the lanes and streets leading down to it were to be kept free from all impediments, so that persons going on horseback might experience no difficulty in reaching its banks.

A capital story, showing not only the value of the Thames, but the appreciation of that value by the citizens of London, is related concerning James I. and a certain Lord Mayor in his reign. "James being in want of some twenty thousand pounds, applied to the Corporation of London for the loan of that sum. The Corporation refused. The king, whose notions of the regal power were somewhat arbitrary, sent for the Lord Mayor and certain of the aldermen, and rated them severely for their disloyalty, insisting that they should raise the money forthwith 'by hook or by crook.' 'May it please your majesty,' said the Lord Mayor, 'we cannot lend you what we have not got.' 'You must get it,' replied the king, haughtily. 'We cannot, sire,' said the Lord Mayor. 'Then I'll compel you,' rejoined the king. 'But, sire, you

WESTMINSTER FROM THE GARDENS OF SOMERSET HOUSE, 1750. *(After a View by Canaletti.)*

cannot compel us,' retorted the Lord Mayor. 'No!' exclaimed James; 'then I'll ruin you and your city for ever. I'll remove my courts of law, my Court itself, and my Parliament to Winchester or to Oxford, and make a desert of Westminster; and then think what will become of you!' 'May it please your majesty,' meekly but firmly, 'you are at liberty to remove yourself and your courts wherever you please; but, sire, there will always be one consolation to the merchants of London: your majesty cannot take the Thames along with you.'"

The conservancy of the Thames was confirmed to the Lord Mayor and citizens of London by Henry IV., the same king whose dead body, by a strange fatality, is supposed to have been thrown into its waters. This jurisdiction was confirmed by Parliament, in 1487; and in 1538 the Common Council of London passed several regulations for the improvement of the navigation of the river, many of which are in force down to the present time, though some have been allowed to lapse, as out of date, and applicable only to a bygone state of things.*

Much of the scenery of the Thames in London and Westminster as it was at the commencement of the present century has been rescued from oblivion by the brothers Thomas and Paul Sandby, both Royal Academicians. Their elaborate drawings, taken from the terrace and gardens of Somerset House, exhibit on the Surrey side the landing-stairs of Kuper's Gardens, and on the Middlesex shore that part of the old Palace at Whitehall, then inhabited by the Duchess of Portsmouth, on the site of which afterwards the houses of Lord Farnborough and other noblemen were erected. There is also a scarce and valuable print showing the Thames at the Temple Gardens, executed and published, in 1671, under the auspices of Sir Heneage Finch, afterwards Earl of Nottingham, and reproduced in fac-simile, in 1770–71, at the charge of one of his descendants. It shows that the embanked front of the gardens was not straight, but broken by several recesses, in which are inserted stairs leading down to the water. A quantity of wherries moored at their foot proves how usual a mode of conveyance to all parts of London and Westminster the Thames was two centuries ago. The fac-simile of the print was not published, and

THE CHINESE JUNK. (*See page* 290.)

* See Vol. i., p. 442.

therefore it is to be found in only a few private collections. Spenser, too, gives us a "Distant View of the Temple" in the following lines:—

"Those bricky towers,
The which on Thamesis broad back do ride,
Where now the student lawyers have their bowers,
Where whilom wont the Templar Knights to bide,
Till they decayed through pride."

One of Sandby's prints of the river-front of Somerset House shows, moored off the stairs of Somerset House, a floating coffee-house, called "The Folly," the existence of which is known to few except curious antiquaries. This was a lounge of the rich gay wits and gallants of the days of Addison and Steele, and an appendage to the coffee and chocolate houses ashore of which we have spoken in our walks round Covent Garden. This floating coffee-house appears by degrees to have attracted a disreputable company, and at last died a natural death, or was suppressed as a nuisance. Being on the water, and not on *terra firma*, there are no title-deeds or other legal documents, or entries in the parish rate-books, to help us in our inquiry as to its fate. In its appearance it somewhat resembled the modern "house-boats" which serve as clubs for rowers at Oxford and at other places on the Thames.

"The Folly"—for such the structure alluded to was named—is said by Dr. C. Mackay to have been "as bulky as a man-of-war." "The Folly" was "divided into sundry rooms, with a platform and balustrade on the top." A view of it as it rode at anchor off Somerset House is given in Strype's edition of Stow; and the humours of it are drawn to the life in Ned Ward's "London Spy." "At first," says Sir John Hawkins, in a manuscript note in his "History of Music," "it was resorted to for refreshment by persons of fashion, and Queen Mary, with some of her courtiers, had once the curiosity to visit it; but it sank gradually into a receptacle for companies of loose and disorderly people, for the purposes of drinking and promiscuous dancing, and at length becoming scandalous, the building was suffered to go to decay, and the materials thereof became firewood."

In one of Tom D'Urfey's songs, called "A Touch of the Times," published in 1719, occurs the following allusion to "The Folly:"—

"When Drapers' smugg'd apprentices,
With Exchange girls most jolly,
After shop was shut up and all,
Could sail up to 'The Folly.'"

Mr. Larwood, in his "History of Sign-Boards," tells us that "The Folly" was not an unusual sign, and that it was generally applied to a very ambitious, extravagantly furnished, or highly ornamented house. "In such a sense," he remarks, "it was already used in Queen Elizabeth's reign:—

'Kirby Castle and Fisher's Folly,
Spinola's Pleasure and Megse's Glory.'

"'The Folly,' at first, was very well frequented, and the beauty and the fashion of the period used to go there on summer evenings, partake of refreshments on the platform, and enjoy the breeze on the river, then innocent of modern sewers and filth. Pepys paid it more than one visit, as he tells us in his 'Diary.' On one occasion it was honoured by a visit from Queen Mary and several members of her Court. Gradually, however, 'The Folly,' true to its name, 'took to evil courses; loose and disorderly ladies were admitted; and unrestrained drinking and dancing soon gave it an unenviable notoriety.' In this condition it was visited by 'Tom Brown,' who describes it with his usual coarse vigour, and remarks of it as follows:—'This whimsical piece of architecture was designed as a musical summer-house for the entertainment of the quality, where they might meet and ogle one another.'" He describes the company in very glowing colours, which it is not necessary to quote here, but tells us also that he found it such a confused scene of "folly" that, though not a very bashful person, he was at last compelled to return to his boat without drinking. At length the place became so scandalous that it had to be closed: it went to decay; and in the end, as we have already seen from Sir John Hawkins, "The Folly" was chopped up for firewood! *Sic transit gloria.*

Not very far from where "The Folly" was moored a century and a half ago, there was seen anchored in our own day a wonderful vessel which had crossed the Indian Ocean and sailed round the Cape of Good Hope, and so up the whole length of the Atlantic—a veritable "Chinese junk." It made the voyage, small as it was, without suffering wreck or disaster, and arrived in the Thames in 1848. For a time it lay off Blackwall, where it was visited by thousands—among others, by Charles Dickens. Afterwards, when the London "season" began, it was brought up just above Waterloo Bridge, and moored off the Strand. Dickens describes the impression of a visit to the junk as a total, entire change from England to the Celestial Empire. "Nothing," he writes, "is left but China. How the flowery region ever came into this latitude and longitude is the first thing one asks, and it is certainly not the least of the marvels. As Aladdin's palace was transported hither and thither by the rubbing of a lamp, so the crew of Chinamen aboard the Keying devoutly believed that their good ship would turn up quite safe at the desired port if they only tied red rags enough upon the mast, rudder, and cable. Somehow they did not succeed. Perhaps they ran short of rag; at any rate they had not enough on board to keep them above water; and to the bottom they would have undoubtedly gone if it had not been for the skill and coolness of half-a-dozen English sailors, who brought them over the ocean in safety. Well, if there be any one thing in the world that this extraordinary craft is not at all like, that thing is a ship of any kind. So narrow, so long, so grotesque, so low in the middle, so high at each end, like a china pen-tray; with no rigging, with nowhere to go aloft; with mats for sails, great warped cigars for masts, dragons and sea-monsters disporting themselves from stem to stern, and on the stern a gigantic cock of impossible aspect, defying the world (as well he may) to produce his equal—it would look more at home on the top of a public building, or at the top of a mountain, or in an avenue of trees, or down in a mine, than afloat on the water. As for the Chinese lounging on the deck, the most extravagant imagination would never dare to suppose them to be mariners. Imagine a ship's crew without a profile amongst them, in gauze pinafores and plaited hair, wearing stiff clogs a quarter of a foot thick in the sole, and lying at night in little scented boxes, like backgammon or chess pieces, or mother-of-pearl counters! But, by Jove! even this is nothing to your surprise when you get down into the cabin. There you get into a torture of perplexity; as, what became of all those lanterns hanging to the roof, when the junk was out at sea; whether they dangled there, banging and beating against each other, like so many jester's baubles; whether the idol Chin Tee, of the eighteen arms, enshrined in a celestial Punch's show, in the place of honour, ever tumbled out in heavy weather; whether the incense and the joss-stick still burnt before her, with a faint perfume and a little thread of smoke, while the mighty waves were roaring all around? Whether that preposterous tissue-paper umbrella in the corner was always spread, as being a convenient maritime instrument for walking about the decks with in a storm? Whether all the cool and shiny little chairs and tables were continually sliding about and bruising each other, and if not, why not? Whether anybody on the voyage ever read those two books printed in characters like bird-cages and fly-traps? Whether the mandarin passenger, He Sing, who had never been ten miles from home in his life before, lying sick on a bamboo couch in a private china closet of his own (where he is now perpetually writing autographs for inquisitive barbarians), ever began to doubt the potency of the Goddess of the Sea, whose counterfeit presentment, like a flowery monthly nurse, occupies the sailor's joss-house in the second gallery? Whether it is possible that the second mandarin, or the artist of the ship, Sam Sing, Esquire, R.A. of Canton, *can* ever go ashore without a walking-staff in cinnamon, agreeably to the usage of their likenesses in British tea-shops? Above all, whether the hoarse old ocean could ever have been seriously in earnest with this floating toy-shop; or had merely played with it in lightness of spirit roughly, but meaning no harm?—as the bull did with another kind of china-shop on St. Patrick's-day in the morning."

Close by the waterside, near where now stands Somerset House, formerly stood the ancient church of St. Mary the Virgin, the predecessor of the present church of St. Mary-le-Strand. It is stated by a writer in the *Sunday at Home* that no less a person than Thomas à Becket was once rector of the parish. But this statement "requires confirmation." Another well-known rector, in more recent times, was Dr. George Horneck, author of "The Crucified Jesus," and other popular religious treatises, who was so much beloved in London that it was said his parish stretched from Whitehall to Whitechapel.

At a corner house in the Strand, with the exact locality of which we are not acquainted, though Mr. P. Cunningham fixes it as "over against Strand Bridge," lived, in 1627, William Lilly the astrologer. He had just then privately married the widow of his master, one Gilbert Wright, in whose house he had been, up to that time, employed in menial work—cleaning the shoes and fetching tubs of water from the Thames; and having inherited her property seven years later, became the owner of house property in the neighbourhood, having, as he tells us in his autobiography, "purchased the moiety of thirteen houses in the Strand for £530." Lilly, who is the "Sidrophel" of Butler's "Hudibras," and who prophesied for the Parliament and for the king, according to the times, died in 1681, and was buried in Walton Church, Surrey, where there is a monument with a Latin inscription by the antiquary Elias Ashmole, who styles this consummate impostor "*Astrologus peritissimus.*"

For several years past, down to the close of 1873, might be seen moored off the bank of the river, nearly opposite Norfolk Street, the hull—we had almost said *hulk*—of a vessel which in its time had, we believe, "done the State some service" in foreign climes. This was an old 16-gun frigate named the *Royalist*, which, having grown too old to be of any further use in the navy, had been converted into a floating police station, as the inscription in large capital letters, "Thames Police Station," painted upon its side, informed the passer-by. At the above date this vessel was removed "below bridge," to do duty in a similar capacity off East Greenwich, in place of the *Investigator*. The Thames Police have now three stations, namely: One of the floating platforms by Waterloo Bridge, originally erected as a landing-stage for passengers; another at High Street, Wapping; and the third at Blackwall.

From the Report of the Commissioner of the Metropolitan Police issued in 1896, it appears that the total number of men employed in the Thames Police was 207, including a superintendent, 59 inspectors, and 147 constables. The men selected, it need hardly be stated, have a good knowledge of "river thieves" and of those who act in collusion with them, for during a recent year, by their vigilance and good management, upwards of 450 persons were apprehended for various offences. In case of fire, too, either on board vessels or in water-side premises, the assistance rendered by the Thames Police is invaluable.

During the recent year alluded to, the Thames Police were instrumental in rescuing twenty-three persons from drowning; these, with suicides prevented, make a goodly record of lives saved by them during the year. One case, showing the keen observation kept upon river craft, deserves to be kept in mind, though it took place more than twenty years ago. About midnight of the 25th of September, 1874, a boat's crew off Wapping discovered a sailing-barge so imbedded in the mud that the tide was flowing over the decks. They hastened on board, and found her fast filling, and five persons asleep in the cabin. To rouse them was the work of a few moments; but the tide flowed so rapidly that one of the constables was waist-deep in water before the last person was rescued. Had it not been for the vigilance and timely aid of the police these five lives would in all probability have been sacrificed. In cases of accident the Thames Police invariably render prompt assistance in conveying the sufferers to the nearest hospitals, and, when necessary, in giving information to their friends.

Some idea of the very disagreeable and painful duties performed by this able and useful body of men may be gathered from the fact that during each year the number of *deaths* which come under their cognisance amount to over a hundred. These include far more males than females, and are largely made up of "suicides" and "accidentally drowned;" there are usually a few, however, about which there appears to be some doubt as to how they came in the river, and these are therefore classed under the general heading of "found drowned." Nearly all these bodies pass through the hands of the police. In many cases photography is resorted to as a means of identification of the bodies.

The building on the western portion of the landing-stage whereon stands the Thames Police Station is used by the Royal Humane Society as a place for the reception of persons rescued from drowning. This has been placed at the disposal of the Society by the Thames Conservancy, free of charge; and all the necessary appliances have been provided for rescuing bodies from the river, by means of a properly-constructed boat, and for treating them when rescued. The maintenance of this receiving-house has caused a charge on the Society's funds to the extent of about £300 per annum, for the Society's men must be always in attendance, the apparatus and baths in readiness by night and by day, and a medical officer almost within call. During the century and a quarter which has elapsed since the Society was instituted, as we learn from a recent Annual Report, it has been the means of saving upwards of forty thousand persons from premature death. In the words of the Report, we may add that "no comment is necessary upon such a statement as this: it carries with it ample evidence of the beneficent work of the Society."

> "Death may usurp on Nature many hours,
> And yet the fire of life kindle again
> The overpressèd spirits. I have heard
> Of an Egyptian had nine hours lien dead,
> By good appliance was recovered."
>
> *Shakespeare: Pericles*, Act iii., sc. 1.

Waterloo Bridge, with the contemplation of which we now resume our voyage westward—the bridges lying eastward having been dealt with in the previous volumes of this work—was considered by Canova to be "the noblest bridge in the world," the great artist backing up his enthusiasm with the assertion that it was "alone worth coming from Rome to London to see." Indeed, the lightness, grace, and symmetry of the structure are such as to give the bridge a foremost rank in buildings of the kind; although it has been eclipsed in size by subsequent erections.

This grand and useful work, which M. Dupin, his celebrated French engineer, in his "Memoir" on the public works of England, called "a colossal monument worthy of Sesostris and the Cæsars," was produced by a joint-stock company. It was erected by the late Sir John Rennie, and, together with the approaches, cost about £1,000,000.

The Act for incorporating the Company, which was designated "The Strand Bridge Company," was passed in June, 1809. Under this authority they raised the sum of £500,000, in transferable shares of £100 each, and had authority to raise a further sum of £300,000, by the issue of new shares or by mortgage, if they should find it necessary. In July, 1813, the Company obtained another Act of Parliament, by which they were authorised to raise an additional sum of £200,000; and in the session of 1816 they obtained a third Act, which received the royal assent in July, and invested the Company with additional powers. By this Act the name of the bridge was changed from that of the "Strand Bridge" to "Waterloo," in honour of that great and decisive battle. It was very natural, considering the great and important victory which the Duke of Wellington had just gained over Buonaparte, that our countrymen during the Regency should have been somewhat profuse in applying the names "Wellington" and "Waterloo" to all and every sort of thing—Wellington streets, Wellington inns, and Wellington boots; Waterloo hotels, Waterloo academies, Waterloo coaches, and Waterloo bonnets—and that, when at a later date that class of conveyance was introduced, they should have adopted "Waterloo" as the designation of a line of omnibuses, and at last of a railway station.

The design, as executed, consists of nine semi-elliptical arches, with Grecian Doric columns in front of the piers, covered by an entablature and cornice, and surmounted by a balustrade. The roadway upon the summit of the arches is level, in a line with the Strand, and is carried by a gentle declivity on a series of brick arches, some of which are used as warehouses, over the roadway on the Surrey bank of the river, to the level of the roads about the Obelisk by the Surrey Theatre. The width of the river at Waterloo Bridge was 1,326 feet at high water before its curtailment by the Victoria Embankment; and the bridge consists of nine semi-elliptical arches, of 120 feet span, and thirty-five feet high, supported on piers thirty feet thick at the foundations, diminishing to twenty feet at the springing of the arches. They are eighty-seven feet in length, with points in the form of Gothic arches as cut-waters towards the stream. The first arch on the Middlesex side spans the Embankment. The dry or land arches on the Surrey side amount to forty, thirty-nine of which are semi-circular, sixteen feet in diameter, and one semi-elliptical, over the Belvedere Road, of twenty-six feet diameter. The entire length of the bridge and causeways is 2,426 feet, made up of 1,380 feet for the entire length of the bridge and abutments, 310 feet the length of the approach from the Strand, and 766 feet the length of the causeway on the land arches of the Surrey side.

The first stone of this fine bridge was laid on the 11th of October, 1811, and the foundations of which it was a part were built in coffer-dams formed by three concentric rows of piles. In building these majestic arches such care was taken by the able engineer under whose direction the bridge was built, that on removing the centres none of the arches sank more than an inch and a half; whereas, we are told, those of the celebrated bridge of Neuilly sank in several instances so much as to entirely destroy the original curvature of the arch.

When the allied sovereigns visited this country, in 1814, this bridge was in course of erection. The Emperor Alexander I. of Russia upon several occasions visited the works, and declared it would be the finest work in masonry in the world. It was opened with great pomp upon the second anniversary of the battle of Waterloo, June 18th, 1817, by the Prince Regent, accompanied by the royal dukes, Field-Marshal the Duke of Wellington, and attended by a brilliant staff of officers who were present at the battle of Waterloo. From the centre of the bridge there is a finer view of London on the banks of the Thames than can be seen elsewhere. Looking down the river, and immediately joining the bridge, close to the Embankment, rises the noble front of Somerset House—the finest object of the kind in London, not excepting the Houses of Parliament, which appear too low. A little further on, looking like a green oasis in the midst of a dark wilderness of bricks and mortar lie the pleasant gardens of the Temple. Lower down is the new Blackfriars Bridge, rising behind which, in unrivalled grandeur, are the dome and towers of St. Paul's Cathedral, and below this the Monument, the spires of other City churches, the Tower, shipping, &c. As a commercial speculation, Waterloo Bridge proved anything but profitable to the shareholders; but it must be some consolation to them that the works were so judiciously executed as to enable them to remain intact, notwithstanding the changes in the bed of the river. A toll of one halfpenny was formerly charged for foot-passengers over the bridge, and twopence for cabs, &c. An agitation was long kept up with the view of bringing about the abolition of the tolls, and at a meeting held in 1873 for the purpose of considering the matter it was stated that during the previous six years 5,000,000 persons annually passed over this bridge, producing an income of above £21,000 per annum. The bridge was subsequently bought by the Metropolitan Board of Works, and in 1878 the toll was abolished.

In order to form an approach from the Strand to Waterloo Bridge it was found necessary to remove very many interesting remains of ancient architecture—not only those belonging to the Savoy Palace on the west, but also several walls belonging to the palace of the Duke of Somerset, with buttresses and pointed windows with Gothic tracery. All memory of these old buildings has long since perished.

HUNGERFORD SUSPENSION BRIDGE, 1850. (*See page* 132.)

But it is time that we started on our voyage westward, noting on our way a few buildings which we did not describe minutely as we passed along the Strand.

"Next to the Savoy westward," writes the author of "London in the Olden Time," "was the palace of the Bishop of Carlisle, with grounds which extended to the lane running down to the river, called Ivy Bridge. Of the history of this house we know nothing, nor when nor by whom it was built. Aggas in his map represents a house of some extent as standing here, and Hollar gives an elevation of it. But this shared the fate of other Church property at the Reformation, being seized by Henry VIII., and given by him to the lucky courtier from Dorsetshire, John Russell, then Controller of the Royal Household—the ancestor, it need hardly be said here, and the founder of the fortunes of the ducal house of Bedford. Carlisle House was afterwards known as Worcester House." At the bottom of Ivy Bridge Lane was for many years the landing-stage for the "halfpenny" steamboats plying between this place and London Bridge, one of which blew up here in August, 1847.

The Adelphi Terrace, which we pass soon after leaving Waterloo Bridge, at one time formed a conspicuous feature as seen from the river, but is so far removed by the broad Embankment with its garden, and thrown into the shade by the lofty railway station close by, that it may now be passed almost unnoticed. Northouck, in writing of the new Adelphi Buildings, tells us that Mr. Lacy, the joint patentee with Garrick in Drury Lane, formed a plan for improving the whole north bank of the river upon a plan similar to that of the

OLD WESTMINSTER BRIDGE IN 1754. (*See page* 297.)

Adelphi Terrace, and that there exists a copper-plate engraving of his design, "engraved for private distribution." Of this noble terrace we have spoken in a previous chapter, but we may be pardoned for here adding a short anecdote concerning Garrick, who lived and died in the centre house: we give it on the authority of Mr. Cradock's "Literary and Miscellaneous Memoirs." "When Jean Jacques Rousseau was in England, Garrick paid him the compliment of playing two characters on purpose to oblige him; and as it was known that Rousseau would be present, the theatre was of course crowded to excess. Rousseau was highly gratified, but Mrs. Garrick declared that she had never spent a more unpleasant evening in her life, the recluse philosopher being so anxious to display himself, and hanging over the front of the box so much that she was obliged to hold him by the skirt of his coat to prevent him from falling over into the pit. After the performance, however, he paid a very handsome compliment to Garrick by saying, 'I have cried all through your tragedy, and laughed all through your comedy, without being at all able to understand your language.' At the end of the play Rousseau was entertained at supper at Garrick's house in the Adelphi, where many of the first literary characters of the time were invited to meet him."

Of the railway bridge which now crosses the river at this point we have already spoken in our account of the Charing Cross Railway, and a description of its predecessor, old Hungerford Suspension Bridge, will be found on page 132.

As we pass by Hungerford Bridge we can hardly help fancying that we can still see the building called "Hungerford Stairs," well known to the jolly Thames watermen of old, and of interest to English readers as one of the first abodes—we cannot call it home—of Charles Dickens, when a boy of ten. Here, at the blacking warehouse of one "Jonathan Warren, Number 80, Hungerford Stairs"—it is well to be particular—the future "Boz" was engaged, in 1822–4, as a sort of shop-drudge, at six shillings a week. He writes, in a sort of autobiographical sketch, published in his "Life," by John Forster:—

"The blacking-warehouse was the last house on the left-hand side of the way at old Hungerford Stairs. It was a crazy, break-down old house, abutting on the river, of course, and swarming with rats. Its wainscoted rooms, its rotten floors and staircases, and the old grey rats swarming down in the cellars and coming up the stairs at all times, and the dirt and decay of the place, rise up visibly before me, as if I were there again. The counting-house was on the first floor, looking over the coal-barges and the river. There was in it a recess where I used to sit and work. My work was to cover the pots of paste-blacking, first with a piece of oil-paper, and then with a piece of blue paper; to tie them round with a string, and then to clip the paper close and neat all round, until it looked as smart as a pot of ointment from an apothecary's shop. When a certain number of grosses of pots had attained this pitch of perfection I was to paste on each a printed label, and then go on again with more pots."

Such was the intellectual occupation to which, instead of school, his parents consigned the future novelist, whilst they were living, if not in comfort, at all events in decency, in Bayham Street, Camden Town, and afterwards in Gower Street North. "No words," says Charles Dickens, "can express the agony of my soul as I sank into this companionship, and felt my hopes of growing up to be a learned and distinguished man crushed in my breast."

At this time, he remembered (as his biographer, Mr. Forster, tells us) to have spent his dinner-hour in playing about on the coal-barges, or strolling about the back streets of the Adelphi, and exploring the recesses of its dark arches, in company with his youthful companions, "Poll" Green and Bob Fagin. One of his favourite localities was the little public-house, by the waterside, called "The Fox under the Hill,"* approached by an underground passage, and outside which, as he tells us in "Copperfield," he remembered having sat "eating something on a bench, and looking at some coal-heavers dancing before the house."

The blacking warehouse at Hungerford Stairs was removed afterwards to the corner of Chandos Street and Bedford Street, Covent Garden, and young Charles Dickens removed thither along with it, as part and parcel of the establishment. He tells us that so thoroughly did he dislike his drudgery there that, after quitting Hungerford, he never went back to look at the place where his servitude had began till old Hungerford Stairs were destroyed, and that for many a long year he could not bear to pass along Chandos Street, or to smell the cement that was used in the offensive trade.

Here at Hungerford Bridge—or to give it its more common designation at the present time, Charing Cross Bridge—floating swimming-baths were erected. These baths, which were planned on an extensive scale, contained many thousand gallons of filtered water, but the venture was not a success. Yet experiments have been made which have established beyond all doubt that

* See *ante*, p. 101.

the Thames water can be easily and effectually filtered. When filtered it is found to contain a very large proportion of sea-water; in fact, we have heard it said that at high tide it is almost entirely sea-water, though by no means so green as at Margate. But this statement we are inclined to question. Less than half a century ago the Thames, without undergoing the process of filtering, was pure enough for the Westminster boys both to row on it and to bathe in it; so that Gray might have addressed to the river under the royal towers of Westminster the noble lines in which he apostrophises it beneath the spires of Eton and Windsor:—

> "Say, Father Thames, for thou hast seen
> Full many a sprightly race
> Disporting on thy margent green
> The paths of pleasure trace;
> Who foremost now delight to cleave
> With pliant arm thy glassy wave?
> The captive linnet which enthral?
> What idle progeny succeed
> To chase the rolling circle's speed,
> Or urge the flying ball?"

Immediately after passing under Charing Cross Railway Bridge the Houses of Parliament and other edifices connected with Government come full into view. Close by the western side of the railway station, and extending to Scotland Yard, appeared, until their demolition towards the close of the year 1874, the gardens and grounds of Northumberland House, the historic mansion of the Percies, about which we have already spoken in a previous chapter. Now that Northumberland House is demolished, in order to form a broad and open thoroughfare from Charing Cross to the Victoria Embankment, we obtain a partial view of the National Gallery and also of the lofty Nelson Column in Trafalgar Square, with the steeple of St. Martin's Church close at hand; a cluster of buildings which leads us to exclaim, in the words of a modern poet—

> "Behold, anent Art's palace, near a church
> Of most surpassing beauty, and amid
> Statues of kings, a pillar! no research
> Need peer it out, for it will *not* be hid:
> Up in the broad day's lustre doth it stand,
> A column raised to dear and dazzling fame,
> Mantling with pride the bosom of the land,
> And stamping glory there with Nelson's name."

Further westward, towering above the cupola of the Horse Guards, and dwarfing everything else around it, stands the York Column—a poor imitation of Trajan's Column—of which we shall have more to say when we shall have extended our perambulation to the neighbourhood of Carlton Gardens. The noble "banqueting house" of Whitehall, too, rears itself proudly on our right above the princely mansions and dwellings of the nobility which partly surround it, and whose gardens and lawns, before the formation of the Embankment, were washed by the "silver winding" Thames. All traces of the old Palace Stairs and the Privy Stairs of Whitehall which stood about here have long since disappeared; but its memory has been preserved in the pages of history. There the remains of many distinguished personages have been landed preparatory to interment. Those of Queen Elizabeth, of the poet Cowley, and of Lord Nelson, will occur at once to the reader of English history. When Elizabeth died at her palace at Sheen, or Richmond, in 1603, her coffin was brought in a barge with great state down the river to Whitehall, in order to be interred in the Abbey. The same was the case in 1667, with Abraham Cowley, on his death at Chertsey, where he spent the later years of his life, and where his house is still standing. To the latter occasion Pope gracefully alludes in the following lines:—

> "There the last numbers flow'd from Cowley's tongue.
> Oh! early lost! what tears the river shed
> When the sad pomp along his banks was led!
> His drooping swans on every note expire,
> And on his willows hung each Muse's lyre."

Cowley's funeral is thus mentioned under date July, 1667, by John Evelyn in his Diary:—"Went to Mr. Cowley's funeral, whose corpse lay at Wallingford House, and was thence conveyed to Westminster Abbey in a hearse with six horses and all funeral decency; near a hundred coaches of noblemen and persons of quality following; amongst these all the wits in the town, divers bishops and clergymen. He was interred next Geoffrey Chaucer and near Spenser."

A good story is told, the scene of which must have been not far from Westminster Bridge, of the popular divine, Dr. Sherlock, who was being ferried across before the bridge was built, and who was being carried, in spite of the efforts of the waterman, out of his course, either up or down the river. It is epigrammatically told in verse, in the last of which the reverend gentleman observes:—

> "With the tide we must swim;"

on which the wit who recounts the story adds, with a waggish humour—

> "To St. Paul's or to Lambeth was all one to him."

Still sailing up the stream, we shortly reach our landing-place by the arches of Westminster Bridge. The original structure, the second bridge built in London, was commenced in 1738 and finished in 1750. The Corporation of London had a notion that it would injure the trade of the City; and while the bill for its erection was under discussion in Parliament, they opposed it "tooth and nail." "For many years afterwards," writes Dr. C. Mackay in his "Thames and its Tributaries," with a playful and pardonable exaggeration, "London aldermen thought it a pollution to go over it, and passed it by with as much contempt as a dog would pass by a 'stinking brook.' So highly, however," he adds, "was the bridge esteemed by its proprietors that they procured the admission of a clause into the Act of Parliament by which the punishment of death without benefit of clergy was declared against any one who should wilfully deface and injure it. Dogs also were kept off it with as much rigour as that with which they are now excluded from Kensington Gardens." Of course this is mere badinage.

It cannot be too often impressed upon the reader that whenever mention is made in the writers of the Tudor or Stuart times of "bridges" existing in London, save and excepting London Bridge, they really mean only landing piers. From a very early date the citizens of London appear to have regarded the construction of a second bridge with intense jealousy, and from time to time any and every effort to construct a second one, though at a very remote distance, roused the fiercest opposition: an instance of which is to be found in the debate which occurred in Parliament in 1671 upon a proposal to erect a bridge at Putney, the rejection of the bill being effected by the influence of the Londoners.

The inconvenience which had been occasioned by the great resort of coaches, and other vehicles, passing and repassing at the Westminster side, induced Dr. Potter, Archbishop of Canterbury, and several noblemen, to procure an Act of Parliament in the year 1736, for building a bridge across the river Thames, from New Palace Yard, Westminster, to the opposite shore in the county of Surrey. This act, however, was not obtained without great opposition from the City of London, as well as from Southwark; and some fainter efforts in the same direction were used by the bargemen and watermen of the Thames. But private interest was obliged to give way to public advantage, and preparations were made for carrying on this great undertaking under the sanction of the Legislature. It should be mentioned here that the original design was for a wooden bridge, which idea was set aside after the severe frost of 1739-40, when the Thames was frozen over several weeks, and some of the piers for the wooden bridge were carried away. A stone bridge, from its greater durability, was then decided on, and the funds in aid of the expense were defrayed by public lotteries and Parliamentary grants.

The ballast-men of the Trinity House were employed to open a large hole for the foundation of the first pier, to the depth of five feet under the bed of the river; and this being finished and levelled at the bottom, it was kept clear by a proper inclosure of strong piles. In the meantime a strong caisson was prepared of the form and dimensions of the intended pier in the clear; this was made water-proof, and being brought over the place, was secured within the piles.

In this wooden case the first stone was laid on the 29th of January, 1738-9, by Henry, Earl of Pembroke. The caisson was above the high-water mark, and sinking gradually by the weight of the prodigious blocks of stone, the men could work below the level of the water as conveniently as on dry ground. Thus the middle pier was first formed, as were all the rest in the same manner; and when finished, the sides of the caisson being taken asunder, the stone-work appeared entire. The time occupied in building the bridge was eleven years and nine months; and the total expense, including the repairs of the piers, which sank during the erection, amounted to £389,500. The opening ceremony took place on the 17th of November, 1750.

Till the building of Westminster Bridge the only communication between Lambeth and Westminster was by the ferry-boat near the palace gate, which was the property of the Archbishop of Canterbury, and granted by patent under a rent of twenty pence. On opening Westminster Bridge, in 1750, it ceased, and £2,205 was given to the see as an equivalent. Previous to that time there were two considerable inns for the reception of travellers, who, arriving in the evening, did not choose to cross the water at such an hour, or, in case of bad weather, might prefer waiting for better.

On the 13th of November, 1750, the commissioners of the new bridge appointed a number of watchmen to guard it, and ordered thirty-two lamps of a particular size to be fixed on it. The treasurer of the bridge, we are told, "paid the rulers of the Watermen's Company, and the stewards of the chests at Westminster, £2,500, to be laid out in some of the funds secured by Parliament to maintain the poor of the said chests, instead of the money gained by the Sunday ferry for foot-passengers."

Old Westminster Bridge was long considered a triumph of engineering skill. Labelye, the architect, introduced a system of foundations which is stated to have answered very well in numerous cases, but which failed utterly here; namely, in sinking the caissons, as above stated, with the lower courses already built upon them. During the progress of the work some trifling disturbances of the bed of the river gave rise to settlements, which were easily repaired at the time. Upon the enlargement of the tideway, however, in consequence of the removal of Old London Bridge, the scouring action of the river soon carried away the substratum of several of the piers of the bridge; and, finally, after much discussion, many years' repair, great and constant expense, and occasional interruption of the carriage traffic, its demólition became a matter of necessity.

The old bridge was built of Portland stone; it was 1,223 feet in length by 44 feet in width, and there were thirteen large and two small semi-circular arches, springing about two feet above low-water mark. The centre arch was 76 feet span, the others decreasing on each side by regular intervals of 4 feet each, excepting the small arches, which were 25 feet span each. The parapet on each side was surmounted by an open balustrade. Between each arch was a semi-octagonal recess or turret, which afforded a covered shelter for foot-passengers. Owing to the sinking of the piers, however, and the generally unsafe condition of the bridge, these turrets were removed some years before the total demolition of the bridge, and some of them have been re-erected in Victoria Park, where they serve as alcoves. With regard to these turrets, Labelye, the architect, says they were not only built for their evident accommodation of passengers, desiring or obliged to stop without interfering with the roadway, or for the relief they afforded to the eye in breaking so long a line, but for the additional security they gave to the bridge, by strengthening the parts between the arches, and thereby affording so much more weight to repel the lateral pressure. Maitland, however, mentions a more serious purpose to which these recesses might have been put; he says "they might have served for places of ambush for robbers and cut-throats," but for the establishment of a guard of twelve watchmen specially appointed for the security of the passage during the night. The writer of the account of Westminster, in the "Beauties of England and Wales," mentions a peculiarity which these recesses possessed, somewhat analogous to the whispering gallery in St. Paul's Cathedral. He says, "So just are their proportions, and so complete and uniform their symmetry, that, if a person whispers against the wall on the one side of the way, he may be plainly heard on the opposite side; and parties may converse without being prevented by the interruption of the street or the noise of carriages."

The new bridge at Westminster, which occupies the place of the old one, but which is almost double the width, is a very handsome structure built chiefly of iron. It was commenced in 1855 by Mr. Page, and completed in 1862, the latter part of the work having been carried out under the direction of the late Sir Charles Barry, the well-known architect. The present bridge was constructed in two portions, the first half being erected at the western side of the original structure, and opened for traffic, after which the demolition of the old bridge was proceeded with; the remaining half —occupying the exact site of the old bridge—was added on the eastern side of the new structure. The bridge is 1,160 feet long by 85 feet wide, and is at once graceful and massive; it consists of seven arches (the centre one having a span of 120 feet), resting on granite piers, the parapet and ornamental portions having been designed to accord with the adjacent Houses of Parliament. The roadway is 53 feet wide, and each footway 15 feet; the former was divided into going and coming roads, and had tramways, or grooves, for the wheels of heavy vehicles. The cost of construction of the present bridge was £206,000.

It is well known that in 1688 the bed of the Thames between Westminster and Lambeth was made the depository of the Great Seal of England by James II. "He obtained possession of it," says Mr. Jesse, in his "London," "on the night of his flight from Whitehall, and purposely let it fall into the water as he passed across the river." Mr. Jesse adds that not long afterwards the seal was recovered by a fisherman and restored to the Government.

The following beautiful sonnet, composed by William Wordsworth in 1803, gives us a lifelike picture of London as seen from the river at Westminster at sunrise on a summer morning:—

"Earth has not anything to show more fair;
Dull would he be of soul who could pass by
A sight so touching in its majesty;
This city now doth like a garment wear
The beauty of the morning; silent, bare,
Ships, towers, domes, theatres, and temples lie,
Open unto the fields and to the sky,
All bright and glittering in the smokeless air.
Never did sun more beautifully steep
In his first splendour valley, rock, or hill;
Ne'er saw I—never felt—a calm so deep.
The river glideth at its own sweet will.
Dear God! the very houses seem asleep,
And all that mighty heart is lying still."

ALCOVE ON OLD WESTMINSTER BRIDGE.. (*See page* 299.)

CHAPTER XXXVIII.

THE RIVER THAMES (*continued*).

> "Such a stream doth run
> By lovely London as beneath the sun
> There's not the like."—*Old Ballad.*

Poetic Effusions in Honour of the Thames—"Swan-upping"—River Waifs and Dead Houses—Watermen and Wherrymen—Authorised Rates of Charges made by Watermen—Doggett's Coat and Badge—Thomas Doggett as an Actor—Miss Benger's Apostrophies of Taylor, the "Water-Poet"—The Thames as the Great Medium of Conveyance—State Processions—Amusements on the Thames—Bathing in the Thames—Condition of the River in 1874—Depredations from Merchant Vessels—Training-vessels for the Royal Navy and Merchant Service—Mercantile Importance of the Thames.

"Of the London and Westminster of Chaucer's time," writes Mr. Matthew Browne in his pleasant work, "Chaucer's England," "there is little which the poet, however forewarned, would recognise if he were to return. The Thames, certainly, he would scarcely know, with its many bridges. The London Bridge of Peter Colechurch, with its crypt and fishpond in one of the piers, and the drawbridge arch over which rushed the insurgent commons of England under Wat Tyler, he would surely miss. And John of Gaunt's London palace of the Savoy which the insurgents burnt; would he know it? or would he know Westminster Abbey? Not Henry the Seventh's chapel, of course; nor Sir Christopher Wren's clumsy towers. Not St. Paul's, which in his days had a spire. . . . . Not the streets; assuredly not the Strand, which in the days of the Plantagenets was really a strand sloping down to the river, with only a house here and there . . . . He would know the Tower, however, and Lambeth Palace, perhaps, and St. Mary's Overies, where his contemporary, Gower, was married by William of Wykeham."

But even the Thames has seen its changes. Three hundred years ago the river on both sides was fringed with trees and flowers to such an extent that Izaak Walton quotes the compliment of a German poet of his own time:—

> "So many gardens dress'd with curious care
> That Thames with royal Tiber may compare."

Indeed, this noble river has been a great theme for poets of all time, and deservedly. It is called by Pope the "silver Thames" and the "fruitful Thame;" by Spenser "the silver-streaming Thames," and by Herrick "the silver-footed Thamesis." Sir John Denham's charming lines, so descriptive of the English beauty of the Thames, often as they have been quoted, will bear being repeated here:—

THE THAMES AT LOW WATER.

"Oh! could I flow like thee, and make thy stream
My great example as it is my theme!
Though deep, yet clear; though gentle, yet not dull;
Strong without rage; without o'erflowing full."

Drayton, too, in a poem published in "England's Helicon" in 1600, thus eulogises the Thames and along with it Elizabeth under the fanciful name of "Beta:"—

"And oh! thou silver Thames, O dearest crystal flood!
Beta alone the phœnix is of all thy watery brood;
The queen of virgins only she,
And thou the queen of floods shalt be.
Range all thy swans, fair Thames, together in a rank,
And place them duly one by one upon thy stately bank."

But it is sadly to be feared that such poets were inspired less by a reverence for Father Thames than by a desire to stand well with the always vain but now aged queen, whom Horace Walpole, with his usual cynicism, describes at this period as being "an old woman with bare neck, black teeth, and false red hair."

The river and the metropolis, both so dear to Englishmen, are thus fantastically celebrated by Pope in his "Windsor Forest," from which we quote the following lines:—

"From his oozy bed
Old Father Thames advanced his reverend head;
His tresses dropp'd with dews, and o'er the stream
His shining horns diffused a golden gleam:
Grav'd on his arm appear'd the moon that guides
His swelling waters and alternate tides:
The figur'd streams in waves of silver roll'd,
And on her banks Augusta rose in gold."

In Drayton's poem, "Polyolbion," published in 1613, in "The Seventeenth Song," we read:—

"When Thames now understood what pains the Mole did take,
How far the loving nymph adventur'd for his sake;
Although with Medway matcht, yet never could remove
The often-quick'ning sparks of his more ancient love.
So that it comes to pass, when by great Nature's guide
The ocean doth return, and thrusteth in the tide

Up towards the place where first his much-loved Mole was seen,
He ever since doth flow beyond delightful Shene."

Pope, in his imitation of Spenser, has described the alleys on the banks of the river in and about London minutely and vividly, but in lines which will scarcely bear quotation. And the poet Gray describes in effect its quiet and peaceful character, when he asks in one of his letters to Warton, "Do you think that rivers which have lived in London and its neighbourhood all their days, will run roaring and tumbling about like your tramontane torrents in the North?"

The following charming verses on our much-loved river, from the first volume of *Once a Week*, based on the quaint expression of Leland, who speaks of London as "a praty town by Tamise ripe," are not so well known as they deserve to be:—

"Of Tamise ripe old Leland tells:
I read, and many a thought up-swells
Of Nature in her gentlest dress,
Of peaceful homes of happiness,
Deep-meadow'd farms, sheep-sprinkled downs,
Fair bridges with their 'praty towns
By Tamise ripe.'

* * * * * * *

"Fair Oxford with her crown of towers,
Fair Eton in her happy bowers,
The 'reach' by Henley broadly spread,
High Windsor, with her royal dead,
And Richmond's lawns and Hampton's glades;
What shore has memories and shades
Like 'Tamise ripe?'

"Not vine-clad Rhine, nor Danube's flood,
Nor sad Ticino, red with blood,
Not ice-born Rhone or laughing Seine,
Nor all the golden streams of Spain;
Far dearer to our English eyes
And bound with English destinies
Is 'Tamise ripe.'

"High up on Danesfield's guarded post
Great Alfred turn'd the heathen host;
Below the vaults of Hurley sent
A tyrant into banishment;
And still more sacred was the deed
Done on the isle by Runnymede
On 'Tamise ripe.'

"And down where commerce stains the tide
Lies London in her dusky pride,
Deep in dim wreaths of smoke enfurl'd,
The wonder of the modern world:
How much to love within the walls
That lie beneath the shade of Paul's
By 'Tamise ripe'!"

The romance of the river Thames, not in its sylvan, fishing, boating, and "swan-upping" aspect above bridge, but in its melodramatically maritime characteristics below bridge, was a theme which seemed to afford unflagging delight to Charles Dickens. Thames mud appeared to the great novelist redolent of mysterious interest, and the waterside scenes in "The Old Curiosity Shop," including the wharf where Mr. Quilp, the dwarf, broke up his ships, where Mr. Sampson Brass so nearly broke his shins, and where the immortal Tom Scott so continuously stood on his head, were rivalled in graphic vividness thirty years afterwards by the waterside scenes and characters pictured in "Our Mutual Friend." But with all this it is certain that the romance of the river between London Bridge and Greenwich has been for many years declining, and that civilisation is all the better for the disappearance of those picturesque features described in 1798—not, indeed, in a work of fiction, but in a most forcible, albeit prosaic manner by Mr. C. Colquhoun, one of the police magistrates of the metropolis. The lighter-buzzards, the "light horsemen," the sham "bummarees" and felonious "stevedores," the "tea-skippers," "whisky-runners," and "rough-scullers"—in other words, the robbers, pirates, smugglers, and murderers who formerly infested the Pool and the Port of London—are now but a feeble folk in comparison with the great flotilla of river desperadoes denounced by Mr. Colquhoun, whose work mainly led to the establishment of the Thames Police. Since then "Cuckold's Point" and "Execution Dock" have fallen out of the chart, and, with the exception of an annual proportion of lighter-robbing and tobacco-smuggling, the river Thames may, in the present day, be considered as quite respectable.

In Fitzstephen's time the Thames at London was indeed "a fishful river," and we read of the Thames fishermen presenting their tithe of salmon at the high altar of the abbey church of St. Peter, and claiming, on that occasion, the right to sit at the Prior of Westminster's own table. At this period the supply of fish materially contributed to the subsistence of the inhabitants of the metropolis, and the river below the site of the present London Bridge abounded with fish. In 1376–7 a law was passed in Parliament for the saving of salmon and other fry of fish; and in 1381-2 "swannes" that came through the bridge or beneath the bridge were the fees of the Constable of the Tower.

The regulations respecting the keeping of swans on the Thames have always been very strict, and from a very early date the privilege of being allowed to keep them has been very jealously guarded. For example, we find that in the twenty-second year of the reign of Edward IV., 1483, it was ordered that no person not possessing a freehold of the clear yearly value of five marks should be permitted to keep any swans; and in the eleventh year of Henry VII., 1496, it was ordained that any one stealing a swan's egg should have one year's imprisonment, and be fined at the king's will; and stealing, setting snares for, or driving grey or white swans, was punished still more severely. In the time of Henry VIII. no persons having swans could appoint a new swanherd without the licence of the king's swanherd; and every swanherd on the river was bound to attend upon the king's swanherd, on warning, or else pay a fine. The Royal swanherd was obliged to keep a book of swan marks, in which no new ones could be inserted without special licence. Cygnets received the mark found on the parent bird, but if the old swans had no mark at the time of the "upping" (or marking), then the old and young birds were seized for the king, and marked accordingly. No swanherd was allowed to mark a bird, except in the presence of the king's swanherd or his deputy. When the swan made her nest on the bank of the river, instead of on one of the islands, one young bird was given to the owner of the soil, in order to induce him to protect the nest. This was called the ground bird. The Dyers' and Vintners' Companies have for several hundred years enjoyed the privilege of preserving swans on the Thames from London to some miles above Windsor, and they still continue the old custom of going with their friends and guests with the Royal swanherdsman, and their own swanherds and assistants, in the month of July or August in every year, from Lambeth, on their swan voyage, for the purpose of catching and "upping" (or marking) all the cygnets of the year. The junior warden of the Vintner's Company is called the "swan-warden"; the appointment to the office of Royal swanherd being vested in the Lord Chamberlain for the time being. Eton College has also the privilege of keeping these birds. At one period the Vintners' Company possessed over 500 swans, but the number is now much less, as, since they have ceased to be served up at great banquets and entertainments, the value of them has greatly declined.

A correspondent in a weekly journal has pictured to us in vivid colours the sad story of the "River Waifs and Dead-houses," which we here quote, as a striking contrast to the poetic and romantic views of the Thames given above:—

"Very peaceful and beautiful does the river look as we push off from one of the queer old flights of steps to be found at intervals all along the riversides. The light of the afternoon sun is gleaming down through a soft luminous mist, beneath which the face of old Father Thames looks up so smiling and placid that the idea that beneath his heaving bosom he conceals hideous secrets of death and decay, seems well nigh incredible. But he does so, nevertheless. Rarely a day passes but some poor struggling wretch goes down into those mysterious depths beneath that shining, glittering surface, never to rise again, or, if to rise, only to find a brief resting-place in one of the grim, foul little 'dead-houses'—scarcely less repulsive—dotted here and there among the dense population along the shores on either side of the great silent highway.

"Of course they are not all found; but within the London portion of the river Thames—between Chelsea and Barking, that is—there are on an average three or four of these poor waifs of humanity picked up every week.

"Yonder goes one of them, covered over with a cloth, in that small boat, threading its way through the midst of the shipping towards the foot of a long narrow stair, leading up through quaint old blocks of building overhanging the river. Following in the track of it I am soon standing before a tall iron railing, shutting in from the busy world a dreary little patch of ground, planted with old moss-covered gravestones and overrun with weeds. In the middle of this plot stands the dead-house. The depository of the dead must, of course, under any circumstances, be a dismal and unpleasant place to visit; but about many of these river-side houses there is—or one fancies there is—something peculiarly oppressive and dejecting, and any one tempted to entertain the idea of evading the responsibilities and troubles of a troublesome world by a short cut over the parapet of Waterloo Bridge would do well to take a turn round to some of them. If the thought of being brought there, friendless and unknown, bundled unceremoniously down on to a bare floor damp and blood-stained, covered with filthy-looking cloths, and laid in a 'shell,' in which temporarily, perhaps, hundreds of other piteous objects have already awaited identification or consignment to a nameless grave—if the thought of that does not act as a powerful deterrent there must, one would think, be a natural *penchant* for suicide, with which it would be hopeless to contend. There is something unutterably sad in the idea of such a termination to all the hopes and fears, the struggles and strivings of a human life; and there is something hideously grotesque in the aspect of the grizzled, crinkly-faced old beadle, as he sets about his preparations for the coroner, and chuckles at the evident shrinking of his visitor from the long black box in which, as he rolls up his sleeves, he tells him he has rather a bad subject to deal with. It is clear that he is rather proud of the indifference which long familiarity with the dead has enabled him to acquire, and he evidently enjoys the shock which he conveys in reply to a question as to what it is he is sweeping out into a corner of the ground. 'What's them? Why, somebody's toes,' says the old man; and he adds, with a grim little smile, 'There's 'undreds o' toes down in that corner.'

"The body just brought in has been laid upon the slate shelf which runs along two sides of the building, and in the 'shell' on the floor are the remains of a young man, probably one of a score or so of poor fellows who lost their lives during the two or three days of dense fog some weeks ago, and the bodies of some of whom have ever since been floating about the still awful gloom of the bed of the river. No description of the contents of that shell can be attempted. Without some clear and specific object in doing so—such as we have here—even the mention of it would be unwarrantable. Only those who have seen a human body under such circumstances can form any conception of the duty which somebody has to perform before an inquest can be held, and they only are in a position to understand how inadequate and imperfect are the arrangements of the various metropolitan authorities for dealing with them.

"A story, which under other circumstances would be ludicrous, is told of a military officer who, some time ago, was called on to go to one of these places to identify one of his men who had been accidentally drowned in the summer time, and whose body had been recovered after many days' immersion. The officer had gone through some active service, and made light of the warning of those in charge of the mortuary as to the shock he might possibly receive. He would take just a sip of brandy if, as they said, the smell of the place was so very unpleasant; but as to the sight of a dead body—pooh, nonsense! He had seen too many of them. It had been necessary to place a heavy stone on the lid of the shell containing the poor fellow, and no sooner was this removed and the lid raised than, on the instant, this stout-hearted officer rushed from the place sick and pale as a ghost, and declaring that if his whole regiment were drowned he would never go near another such a sight.

"It is not surprising that the appearance of some of these melancholy objects on the river by night is often sufficient to unnerve men of the most dauntless character and whose familiarity with them would, it might be supposed, tend to render them comparatively indifferent. Veteran watermen are sometimes found to be the veriest children in dealing with them. There is an 'old stager' now on the river whose courage, under all ordinary circumstances, has been proved in a thousand different ways, but who yet dare not stay by himself for a few moments in charge of one of these stark, silent creatures. He and his comrades one night brought one to shore tied to the boat, which was left in his charge while his companions fetched a 'shell.' They had no sooner disappeared than he made his way to a neighbouring public-house, ostensibly to get a light for his lantern, but, as the joke goes, to let some of the folks there know that there was something to be seen down at his boat. His little *ruse* was successful, but his troubles were not quite over. His comrades returned with the shell, and all marched off with the body to the dead-house, which was reached by crossing a churchyard. On their arrival he was sent back to the boat, but with such terror had the sight of that object inspired this burly, really bold-hearted man, that he could not for the life of him open the gate of the churchyard, and stood inside fumbling at the handle and shaking with fear until a woman passed, and she, poor soul, took him for a ghost, and when he asked her the time of night took to her heels and ran off in frantic terror.

"It would be reasonable to suppose that with an average of some 150 to 200 of these bodies requiring attention every year there would, at proper intervals along the river-banks, and at no great distance from the river, be found not only mortuaries of the most complete and perfect construction, but every facility for conveying the bodies to them. Such, however, is by no means the case. Till within the past few months, the body of a person found drowned on the lower side of London Bridge should have been deposited in a kind of vault just between the church of St. Magnus the Martyr and the bridge. At the present time, no matter how sickening and dreadful the object found may be, it must be conveyed through the public streets to the mortuary in Golden Lane, a distance considerably over a mile. If found within that part of the river lying between the Equitable Gas Works and Chelsea College, it must be conveyed right away to Mount Street, in the neighbourhood of Hanover Square, a distance certainly not less than two miles. The idea of a corpse—it may be in an advanced stage of decomposition—being dragged from the river, laid in a filthy shell, and carried upon men's shoulders for a distance of two miles, and that, perhaps, in the height of summer, is something most revolting, and altogether discreditable to those who are responsible for it. In other cases the distance is not so great, but the accommodation for properly dealing with the dead is altogether wanting. The only dead-house for the river between Nine Elms and Waterloo Bridge is a kind of tool-house in one corner of Lambeth churchyard. Lower down the river another little tool-house, standing close under the windows of a row of cottages, is the only mortuary. Even where the places themselves are tolerably satisfactory their situations are, in some instances, most objectionable. There is a new mortuary in Pennyfields, Poplar. It is situated at the bottom of a close and narrow lane, between the workhouse on the one hand, and a densely-populated little street on the other. Often there are five or six bodies lying here at one time, and the surrounding inhabitants speak of the stench as at times something most unbearable.

"The discussion that has lately (1870) been going on as to the best method of disposing of the dead, is no doubt a very important one; but it is evident that in London at least we have not as yet given anything like sufficient attention to the disposal of the dead during the interval between death and the final solemnity, whatever it may be. This applies not only to the river district, but to all parts of London; but in no other part does it happen that bodies that have been practically buried for weeks or even months are dragged to the light of day, and have to be dealt with as in the case of an ordinary death. In no part, therefore, is it so important that mortuary accommodation of the most complete kind shall be easily accessible, and, it may be added, in no part is it so thoroughly defective. There is, of course, great difficulty in securing open spaces for these structures, and the cost would, in some cases, be very serious if provided on shore. Where this appears to be an insuperable difficulty, however, a very simple and inexpensive solution of it would be to set up a floating mortuary here and there. This would afford fresh air, plenty of water, and ready access. Something ought speedily to be done in this matter." Things have improved considerably since these words were written, but complaint is still made from time to time that the mortuary accommodation of the metropolis is inadequate.

Of the Thames watermen and wherrymen, a brief mention has been made in the second volume of this work (see pages 51 and 52): we may, however, add here a few more particulars concerning this once celebrated and now almost extinct body of men.

As may easily be imagined, they formed very much of a caste by themselves, and recognised their kinship in the craft by being ambitious of burial, when they died, in the southern side of the churchyard of St. Martin's-in-the-Fields. They were a rough, saucy, and independent lot, if we may judge from allusions to them which occur in the novels, comedies, farces, and popular songs of the last century. Their phraseology, too, was as peculiar as that of the cabmen and omnibus drivers of our own day. Peter Cunningham calls it "the water dialect or mob language," the use of which he reckons as "one of the privileges of the river assumed by the fraternity," a language of which Ned Ward and Tom Brown have both left us specimens, and of which Fielding complains so touchingly in his "Voyage to Lisbon;" and he quotes, in support of his statement, several passages from Ben Jonson, Samuel Pepys, and Wycherley. It will be remembered that in the *Spectator* (No. 383) Sir Roger de Coverley is "shocked" at the saucy language with which he is greeted by two or three young fellows, whilst taking his pleasure in a boat on the Thames; and Boswell, in his "Life of Johnson," records the fact that once when the learned doctor was in a similar situation, he gave back a wherryman raillery for raillery in terms which we can scarcely quote in these pages.

The Thames watermen received their licences from, and were directly amenable to, the Lord Mayor and the other members of the Thames Conservancy; and their fares were regulated by a published scale of charges a hundred years ago. A copy of the "Rates of Watermen plying on the River Thames, either with oars or skullers," dated 1770, gives a table of charges, showing that a fare could be carried with "oars" for a shilling from London Bridge to Limehouse, Shadwell Dock, or Ratcliff Cross; or from either side above London Bridge to Lambeth or Vauxhall. Eightpence was the charge for the same mode of conveyance from the Temple, Blackfriars, or Paul's Wharf to Lambeth; whilst sixpence would frank a voyager from London Bridge or St. Olave's, Tooley Street, to "Wapping Old Stairs" or Rotherhithe Church; or from Billingsgate and St. Olave's to St. Saviour's Mill, from any stairs below London Bridge and Westminster, or from Whitehall to Lambeth or Vauxhall; whilst any lady or gentleman could be ferried "over the water directly from any place between Vauxhall in the west, and Limehouse in the east, for fourpence." The charges for "skullers" for each of the above-named voyages were exactly half the sums here named. The authorised "rates of oars, down and up the river, as well for the whole fare as for company"—in other words, for a single voyager, or each person forming a party—are curious. From London to Greenwich or Deptford, the charge for a single individual was eighteenpence, to Blackwall two shillings, to Woolwich half-a-crown, to Purfleet or Erith three shillings, to Grays or Greenhithe four shillings, and to Gravesend four and sixpence. When persons made the voyage in parties, each of the "company," be the latter large or small, was to be charged about a sixth of the above rates. The same regulations held good "above bridge" also: you could be taken by "oars" to Chelsea, Battersea, or Wandsworth for eighteenpence; to Putney, Fulham, or Barnes for two shillings; to Hammersmith, Chiswick, or Mortlake for half-a-crown; to Brentford, Isleworth, or Richmond for three and sixpence; to Twickenham for four shillings; to Kingston for five; to Hampton Court for six; to Hampton town, Sunbury, or Walton for seven; to Weybridge or Chertsey for ten; to Staines for twelve; and all the way to Windsor for fourteen shillings. If a party was got up for the occasion the charge was a shilling for each individual for any distance beyond Kingston, even as far as Windsor.

OLD WHITEHALL STAIRS. (*See page* 297.)

To the above list the same little book gives in an appendix the "Rates authorised for carrying goods in the tilt-boat from London to Gravesend." For this passage the charge was for each single person, ninepence; for a hogshead of liquor, two shillings; for a firkin of goods, twopence; for half a firkin, a penny; for a hundredweight of dry goods, fourpence; for a sack of corn, salt, &c., sixpence; for an "ordinary hamper," sixpence; and it is added, for the information of those whom it may concern, that "the hire of the whole tilt-boat was £1 2s. 6d." By a "tilt" boat of course is meant a boat with a covering; the term still survives, as we need hardly remind our readers, in the term "tilt" cart. It is interesting to compare these rates of transit by oars and scullers along "the silent highway" of old Father Thames with the fares charged now a-days to voyagers along

OLD WHITEHALL PALACE FROM THE RIVER. (*See page* 297.)

the same route in penny steamboats, which, with all their faults, are a good deal cheaper and swifter than their precursors.

The olden recreations on "the noble Thames" are of great celebrity. Fitzstephen tells us of the ancient Londoners fighting "battles on Easter holidays on the water, by striking a shield with a lance." There was also a kind of water tournament, in which the combatants, standing on two wherries, rowed and ran against the other, fighting with staves and swords. In Gower's time the sovereign was rowed in his tapestried barge, probably the first royal barge upon the Thames; and upon this great highway Richard II., seeing the good old rhymer, called him on board the royal vessel, and there commanded him to "make a book after his hest," which was the origin of the "Confessio Amantis." At this period a portion of London Bridge was movable, so that vessels of burthen might pass up the river, to unload at Queenhithe and elsewhere; and stairs, watergates, and palaces studded both shores. At this time, too, we are informed, boats conveyed passengers, for the sum of twopence each, from London to Gravesend.

One of the most interesting annual events in the present day in connection with the Thames watermen, and not the least popular gala day in these times, though it may hardly be compared with the Derby Day at Epsom or with the Oxford and Cambridge boat-race, is the one afforded by Thomas Doggett, comedian, on the 1st of August, to commemorate the accession of the House of Brunswick. "This scene," says Mr. J. T. Smith in his "Book for a Rainy Day," "is sure to be picturesque and cheerful should it be lit up by the glorious sun 'that gems the sea and every land that blooms.' In 1715, the year after George I. came to the throne, Doggett, to quicken the industry and raise a laudable emulation in our young men of the Thames, whereby they not only may acquire a knowledge of the river but a skill in managing the oar with dexterity, gave an orange-coloured coat and silver badge, on which was sculptured the Hanoverian Horse, to the successful candidate of six young watermen just out of their apprenticeship, to be rowed for on the 1st of August, when the current was strongest against them, starting from the 'Old Swan,' London Bridge, to the 'Swan' at Chelsea." On the 1st of August, 1722, the year after Doggett's death, pursuant to the tenor of his will, the prize was first rowed for, and has been given annually ever since.

"They gripe their oars, and every panting breast
Is raised by turns with hope, by turns with fear depressed."

Charles Dibdin was so amused with the sight of the contest for Doggett's prize, that in 1774 he brought out at the Haymarket a ballad opera, entitled *The Waterman: or, the First of August*, the hero in which, "Tom Tug," sings the well-known song—

"And did you ne'er hear of a jolly young waterman,
Who at Blackfriars Bridge used for to ply?
He feather'd his oars with such skill and dexterity,
Winning each heart and delighting each eye;"

and another when he has resolved to cast away his cares and be off to sea:—

"Then, farewell, my trim-built wherry,
Oars and coat, and badge, farewell!
Never more at Chelsea ferry
Shall your Thomas take a spell," &c.

However, Tom rowed for Doggett's coat and badge, which he had an eye upon, in order to obtain his love if possible by his prowess. She was seated at the "Swan Inn," Chelsea, and admired the successful candidate before she discovered him to be her suitor Thomas, then "blushed an answer to his wooing tale," and it is to be hoped lived happily with him for ever afterwards.

The old "Swan Inn" at Chelsea, we may add, was swept away about the year 1873 to make room for the Thames Embankment; but the coat and badge is still rowed for, the destination of the race being the Cadogan Pier at Chelsea. The Fishmongers' Company, of which Thomas Doggett was a member, added six guineas to the first prize; and besides this there are several other prizes awarded to the different competitors in the race. The second and third prizes are respectively five guineas and three guineas, derived from a variety of sources, among others a bequest of South Sea stock under the will of Sir William Jolliffe. The prize for the fourth man is two guineas, and for the fifth and sixth men £1 11s. 6d. and £1 6s. respectively. There are also different sums occasionally given by private individuals to the winner, or to the first, second, and third in the race. The competition is between six watermen, each being in a boat by himself with short oars or sculls; and the competitors are those who have been first and second in three trial heats from Putney to Hammersmith. The barge-master of the Fishmongers' Company is ordinarily the umpire; and the race always excites much local interest, being one of those manly sports in which the English take much pleasure.

Thomas Doggett is stated to have been a native of Dublin, and to have been born about the middle of the seventeenth century. Colley Cibber, speaking of him, says, "As an actor he was a great observer of Nature; and as a singer he had no competitor." He was the author of the "Country Wake," a comedy published in 1696, and was a patentee of Drury Lane Theatre until 1712. He died in 1721. It may be added that Doggett was not the only actor who took an interest in the Thames watermen, for the proprietors of the old Vauxhall Gardens, and Astley the equestrian, gave wherries to be rowed for; as did also Edmund Kean, the tragedian.

Among the most celebrated of Thames watermen in bygone days was Taylor, "the water poet," of whom we have already spoken. Miss Benger thus apostrophises both the poet and the river at once:—

> "And thou, O Thames, his lonely sighs hast caught.
> When one, the rhyming Charon of his day,
> Who tugged the oar, yet conned a merry lay,
> Full oft unconscious of the freight he bore,
> Transferred the musing bard from shore to shore.
> Too careless *Taylor!* hadst thou well divined,
> The marvellous man to thy frail skiff consigned,
> Thou shouldst have craved one tributary line,
> To blend his glorious destiny with thine!
> Nor vain the prayer!—who generous homage pays
> To genius, wins the second meed of praise."

Down to about the middle of the seventeenth century, when not only coaches, but also sedan chairs, had become pretty general, the Thames had formed the great medium of metropolitan conveyance. Its banks on either side were studded thick, as far as London extended, with the quays and "stairs" of the nobles, and wharves of the commons, while its waters were peopled with every kind of vessel, from the bucentaur-like barge of royalty, to the nutshell skiff or wherry. In 1454, Sir John Norman, Lord Mayor elect, built a magnificent barge for the use and honour of his mayoralty; before his time it was usual for the chief magistrate and his train to go to Westminster Hall on horseback. The companies followed Norman's example, and constructed elegant vessels to accompany their mayors. The watermen were so elated by this circumstance that they caused a commemoration song to be composed on the occasion, beginning, "Row thy boat, Norman," &c.

Down to the time of the discontinuance of the "water pageant" as part of the Lord Mayor's state procession to Westminster, the officials connected with the state barge included the water-bailiff, one of his lordship's esquires, with a salary of £500 a year, a shallop, and eight men; and in the suite were a barge-master and thirty-two City watermen. The watermen, clad in livery and wearing the badge won in the match above mentioned, have been wont to take part in the Lord Mayor's Show on the 9th of November; and the trumpeters who formerly heralded his lordship's approach to Westminster from the prow of the gilded barge, now precede his lordship's state carriage on foot in all civic state ceremonies.

The remains of Anne of Bohemia, queen of Henry VII., who died at Richmond, were honoured with a state funeral by water, being brought with great pomp by the river to Westminster. In 1533 the mayor and citizens accompanied Anne Boleyn in their barges from Greenwich to the Tower, preparatory to her coronation at Westminster; and this was the highway along which that unfortunate lady and more than one other of the wives of Henry VIII. made their last journey. Along it also "the seven bishops" were conveyed from Westminster to the Tower in the reign of James II. Mr. Peter Cunningham briefly reminds us that State prisoners committed from the Council Chamber to the Tower or the Fleet were invariably taken by water.

Passing up the Thames on frequent occasions might be seen in mid-stream the royal barge of Queen Elizabeth with her Majesty on board in gayest trim, on her way up the stream along with the tide going to her palace at Westminster, and possibly to land at Whitehall Stairs, or at the Westminster Palace Water Gate, at that time known, as we learn from Ralph Aggas' map, as "The Queen's Stairs."

After the great civil war, however, the royal water processions dwindled into the paltry annual pageant of the Lord Mayor's Show; and even this, we need hardly say, has now died out. The state barge last in use by the Lord Mayor was built in 1816, and named the *Maria Wood* (from the then Lord Mayor's eldest daughter); it was very capacious, and richly carved and gilt.* A few of the City Companies had their own state barges, "to attend my Lord Mayor;" as the Fishmongers, Vintners, Dyers, Stationers, Skinners, and Watermen. The barge belonging to the Goldsmiths' Company was sold in 1850.

The river state barge of the Queen has not been used since the year 1849, when Her Majesty went by water to open the new Coal Exchange. The Lords of the Admiralty have likewise their state barge; but it is seldom or never now brought into use. Possibly water pageants may some day be revived.

The nobility, in imitation of royalty, laid aside their gilded barges; the fashionables who dwelt near the Thames, at St. Katharine's, Bankside, Lambeth Marsh, Westminster, Whitefriars, Cole-

* See also Vol. I., p. 447.

harbour, and other such convenient localities for a water fête, preferred an inland pic-nic among the gardens or forests, to which their carriages could waft them in an hour or two; while the busy Inns of Court, whose thousands of students and practitioners had hitherto used the facilities of the river alike for business or for pleasure, were now to be found flying along the streets with their books, briefs, and blue bags, six in a coach. The Thames, no longer the great highway of London, had become little better than a water conveyance, in the absence of bridges, between the City and the Borough; and the small clusters of ferrymen that now lingered on at the different crossing-places, looking out hungrily for a chance fare, were but the ghosts of a departed glory, as they uplifted their voices in supplication with, "Boat, your honour! boat, boat!"

The Thames was the usual road, and persons, a century ago, spoke of "taking the water" as we speak of taking a cab or omnibus. To quote an instance from the *Somerset House Gazette*:—"'You do me great honour, Mr. Handel,' said my great uncle. 'I take this early visit as a great kindness.' 'A delightful morning for the water,' said Colley Cibber. 'Pray, did you come with oars or scullers, Mr. Handel?' asked Pepusch, who had lately been setting the airs to the songs in the *Beggar's Opera*."

It may interest some readers, however, to learn that when George IV. came to the throne there were still 3,000 wherries plying on the Thames, while the hackney coaches could muster only a sorry 1,200 in the whole of London. As late as the year 1829, if not more recently still, a boat was the usual conveyance from the neighbourhood of Westminster to Vauxhall; and Mr. J. T. Smith, in his "Book for a Rainy Day," tells many anecdotes about the "Thames watermen," whose work was of course at an end as soon as new bridges were built and cheap steamboats put upon the river.

A couple of centuries ago the river was so clear and pure that the noblemen who lived upon its banks along the Strand used to bathe in it constantly. It is on record, for instance, that in the reign of Charles I. such was the practice of Lord Northampton; and Roger North tells us, in his "Lives of the Norths," that his relative, Dudley North, used to swim on the Thames so constantly —and "above bridge," too—that "he could live in the water an afternoon with as much ease as others walk upon land." Horace Walpole, too, tells Lady Craven in one of his letters that Lord Chesterfield waggishly addressed a letter to his friend the Earl of Pembroke, who was fond of swimming in these parts, "To the Earl of Pembroke, in the Thames, over against Whitehall." Lord Byron tells us in one of his letters, in 1807, that he took a swim from Lambeth through Westminster and Blackfriars Bridges down to London Bridge apparently, or even lower, for he reckons the length of his voyage as three miles.

That a very different state of things afterwards came about in the condition or the appearance of the Thames may be inferred when we state that from the Report of the Medical Officer of Health, submitted to the Corporation of London towards the close of 1874, it appears that during the month of September of that year 2,083 vessels had been inspected in the river and the docks between Vauxhall and Woolwich, 366 of which required cleansing, 93 sick sailors had been found afloat and referred to the Seamen's Hospital at Greenwich, and of 19 samples of drinking water taken from vessels in various parts of the port for purposes of analysis, seven were found unfit for human consumption. In this matter, however, it is to be hoped that we have made some advance since 1874. The practice of carrying Asiatic crews on board British ships has revived very much since 1872, and there are now always not fewer than from 500 to 700 Lascars about Limehouse.

Those who do not know what the state of things was in the Thames in the days when shipping discharged in the stream may be astonished to read of the doings little short of piractical which were a part of the established order of things, and prevailed into the reign of George IV., when the opening of the West India Docks enabled at least a portion of the shipping to discharge their cargoes with some safety. In 1798 the depredations from merchant vessels in the river Thames were estimated by Mr. Colquhoun to amount to £506,500 a year. "Scuffle-hunters," long-shore thieves, mudlarks, "Peterboatmen," river pirates, "light horsemen," and last, but not least, the captains and mates of the vessels and the revenue officers themselves preyed upon the shipping, and "one gigantic system of plunder seems to have prevailed throughout." Not only hogsheads of sugar and puncheons of rum, but anchors, cables, and other tackle were carried off by thieves; and mates and revenue officers seem to have had a regular scale of charges for retiring to their berths while robbery of the hold or deck was going on.

"Most of these infamous proceedings," says Mr. W. S. Lindsay, in his work on "Our Mercantile Marine," "were carried on according to a regular system, and in gangs, frequently composed of one or more receivers, together with coopers, watermen, and lumpers, who were all necessary in their different occupations to the accomplishment of the general design of wholesale plunder. They went on board the merchant vessel completely prepared with iron crows, adzes, and other implements to open and again head up the casks; with shovels to take out the sugar, and a number of bags made to contain 100 lb. each. These bags went by the name of 'black strap,' having been previously dyed black to prevent their being conspicuous in the night when stowed in the bottom of a river boat or wherry. In the course of judicial proceedings it has been shown that in the progress of the delivery of a large ship's cargo about ten to fifteen tons of sugar were on an average removed in these nocturnal expeditions, exclusive of what had been obtained by the lumpers during the day, which was frequently excessive and almost uncontrolled whenever night plunder had occurred. This indulgence was generally insisted on and granted to lumpers to prevent their making discoveries of what they called the 'drum hogsheads' found in the hold on going to work in the morning, by which were understood hogsheads out of which from one-sixth to one-fourth of the contents had been stolen the night preceding. In this manner one gang of plunderers was compelled to purchase the connivance of another to the ruinous loss of the merchant."

It was estimated that about 11,000 persons got a dishonest livelihood by taking part in the rascalities which received their first death-blow from the high walls of the West India Docks. On the manifold advantage of the dock and bonded warehouse system, which now extends to every shipping port in the kingdom, it is needless to dilate, though outsiders will thank Mr. Lindsay for the clear and interesting explanation of the course of shipping business as it is now conducted in his work above referred to.

In these days from four to five hundred boys are accommodated on the *Chichester* and *Arethusa* training ships, off Greenhithe. Other training-ships on the Thames are the *Warspite*, off Woolwich; the *Cornwall*, off Purfleet; the *Worcester*, off Greenhithe; and the *Shaftesbury* and the *Exmouth*, off Grays.

The mercantile importance of this noble stream is greater than that of any other river in the world. Its merchantmen visit the most distant parts of the globe; and the productions of every soil and of every clime are wafted home upon its bosom to answer the demands of British commerce. The frozen shores of the Baltic and North America, the sultry regions of both the Indies, and the arid coasts of Africa have alike resounded with its name; and there is not a single country, perhaps, in any quarter of the earth, bordering on the sea, that has not been visited by its sails.

CHAPTER XXXIX.

THE RIVER THAMES (*continued*).

"Cœlo gratissimus amnis."—*Virgil.*

Remarkable Frosts on the Thames—Frost Fair in 1683—Rhyming Description of "Blanket Fair."—Evelyn's Account of the Fair—Printing on the Ice—Charles II.'s Partiality to Frost Fair—The River again frozen over in 1709, 1715, 1739, 1767, 1788, and 1814—Curious Handbills printed on the Ice—Singular Feats performed on the Thames—Captain Boyton's Life-preserving Dress—Scott, the American Diver—Rise and Fall of the Tide—Projected Improvements for the Bed of the River.

Happily in our latitude winter is not often so severe as to "bind in frosty chains" the river which runs through the heart of our metropolis; but still, if the old annalists and historians are to be believed, the Thames from time to time has been frozen into ice-fields, and its surface has been made the scene of frost-fairs. To mention a few instances: we are told that in the reign of Stephen, in the year 1150, "after a very wet summer there was in December so great a frost that horses and carriages crossed it upon the ice as safely as upon the dry ground, and that the frost lasted till the following month of March." Again we read that in 1281 the Thames was frozen over, and that on the breaking up of the ice five of the arches of old London Bridge were carried away. "In 1434," says Northouck, "the Thames was so strongly frozen over, that merchandise and provisions brought into the mouth of the river were obliged to be unladen, and brought by land to the city." In 1515, too, carriages passed over on the ice from Lambeth to Westminster. At this time it is said the frost and snow were so severe that five arches of London Bridge were "borne downe and carried away with the streame." On the 21st of December, 1564, during the prevalence of a hard frost, we read of diversions on the Thames, some playing at football, and others "shooting at marks." The courtiers from the palace at Whitehall mixed with the citizens, and tradition reports that Queen Elizabeth herself walked upon the ice. On the night of the 3rd of January following, however, it began to thaw, and on the 5th there was no ice to be seen on the river. In 1620 a great frost enabled the Londoners to carry on all manner of sports and trades upon the river.

FROST FAIR ON THE THAMES IN 1683.

In a curious volume of London ballads and broadsides in the British Museum is one entitled "Great Britain's Wonder, or London's Admiration," being "a true representation of a prodigious frost which began about the beginning of December, 1683, and continued till the fourth day of February following. It held on the Thames with such violence that men and beasts, coaches and carts, went as frequently thereon as boats were wont to pass before. There was also" (continues the writer) "a street of booths built from the Temple to Southwark, where were sold all sorts of goods imaginable, namely, cloaths, plate, earthenware, meat, drink, brandy, tobacco, and a hundred sorts of commodities not here inserted: it being the wonder of this present age and a great consternation to all the spectators." The rude cut beneath the title shows the Middlesex shore, taken from the centre of the river, from Arundel House to the eastern end of the Temple; giving a view of Essex Buildings with its ugly round-headed arch, and the three groups of stairs belonging to Arundel House, Essex House, and the Temple. The street of booths holds out all sorts of signs, just like the houses in the Strand. There are men and boys making slides, skating, and sledging in all directions; some of the sledges are of the ordinary type, like the low brewer's dray drawn by heavy horses; some are more artistic, made up like gondolas; some are apparently genuine boats, with sails; in two places are carriages drawn by a single horse, and just opposite the Temple Stairs a bull is being baited. Gallants in the fashionable dresses of the day are promenading, with wigs and swords; while the ladies, true to the instinct of their sex, are "shopping" briskly. In a corner are five men playing at skittles; one of them is smoking a pipe. The doggerel verses below the cut tell how

"The Thames is now both fair and market too,
Where many thousands daily do resort.

* * * * *

There you may see the coaches swiftly run,
As if beneath the ice were waters none,
And shoals of people everywhere there be,
Just like the herrings in the brackish sea.
And there the quaking watermen will stand ye,
'Kind master, drink you beer, or ale, or brandy;
Walk in, kind sir, this booth it is the chief,
We'll entertain you with a slice of beef.'
Another cries, 'Here, master, they but scoff ye;
Here is a dish of famous new-made coffee.'

* * * * *

entitled "A True Description of Blanket Fair upon the River Thames in the Time of the Great Frost, in the Year of our Lord 1683," gives a representation of the ox being roasted, and also of the "hunting the fox," Reynard being pursued by two men with clubs and five queer-looking dogs: in this one of the carriages has two horses; the verses are just a shade above those already quoted, but running in the same descriptive vein, as will be seen from the following specimen:—

FROST ON THE THAMES, 1814.

There you may also this hard frosty winter
See on the rocky ice a WORKING-PRINTER,
Who hopes by his own art to reap some gain
Which he perchance does think he may obtain.
Here also is a lottery, music too,
Yea, a cheating, drunken, lewd, and debauch'd crew;
Hot codlins, pancakes, ducks, and goose, and sack,
Rabbit, capon, hen, turkey, and a wooden jack.

* * * * * *

There on a sign you may most plainly see 't,
Here's the first tavern built in Freezeland Street.
There is bull-baiting and bear-baiting too.

* * * * * *

There roasted was a great and well-fed ox
And there with dogs hunted the common fox."

Another rough print in the same collection, taken from almost the very same point of view,

"The art of printing there was to be seen,
Which in no former age had ever been;
And goldsmiths' shops well furnishèd with plate;
But they must dearly pay for 't that would ha' it,
And coffee-houses in great numbers were
Scattered about in this cold-freezing fair.
There might you sit down by a char-cole fire
And for your money have your heart's desire,
A dish of coffee, chocolate, or tea:
Could man desire more furnishèd to be?"

In the same collection is a ballad, of a few weeks' later date, "The Thames uncas'd; or, the Waterman's Song upon the Thaw;" the last stanza runs thus:—

"Meantime, if ought of honour you've got,
Let the printers have their due,

> Who printed your names on the river Thames,
> While their hands with the cold look'd blue;
> There's mine, there's thine, will for ages shine,
> Now the Thames again does flow;
> Then let's gang hence, to our boats' commence,
> For the frost is over now."

In another ballad, printed and sold on the ice about this time, entitled "Blanket Fair, or History of Temple Street, being a Relation of the Merry Pranks played on the River Thames during the Great Frost," we read—

> "I'll tell you a story as true as 'tis rare,
> Of a river turn'd into a Bartlemy Fair.
> Since old Christmas last,
> There has bin such a frost,
> That the Thames has by half the whole nation bin crost.
> O scullers! I pity your fate of extreams,
> Each landman is now become free of the Thames."

On the 1st of January, 1684, John Evelyn tells us that whole streets of booths were set out on the Thames, and that he crossed the river on the ice on foot upon the 9th in order to dine with the Archbishop of Canterbury at Lambeth, and again, in his coach, from Lambeth to the Horseferry at Millbank, upon the 5th of February. On the 6th he observes that the ice had "now become so thick as to beare not onely streetes of boothes in which they roasted meate, and had divers shops of wares quite acrosse as in a towne, but coaches, carts, and horses passed over. At this time there was a foot-passage quite over the river, from Lambeth-stairs to the Horse-ferry at Westminster; and hackney coaches began to carry fares from Somerset House and the Temple to Southwark. On January 23rd, the first day of Hilary Term, they were regularly employed in hire, where the watermen were accustomed to be found. In this arrangement the means of conveyance only, and not the ordinary way, was altered; since the use of boats to Westminster was almost universal at the period, as the rough paving of the streets rendered riding through them in coaches very uneasy." By the 16th the number of persons keeping shops on the ice had so greatly increased that Evelyn says, "the Thames was filled with people and tents selling all sorts of wares as in the City;" and by the 24th the varieties and festivities of a fair appear to have been completely established. "The frost," he states, "continuing more and more severe, the Thames before London was still planted with boothes in formal streets, all sorts of trades, and shops furnish'd and full of commodities, even to a printing presse, where the people and ladys tooke a fancy to have their names printed, and the day and yeare set down, when printed on the Thames. This humour took so universally, that 'twas estimated the printer gained about £5 a day for printing a line onely at sixpence a name, besides what he got by ballads, &c." In a poem commemorative of this frost, published at the time, there occurs the following passage relating to the printers; the concluding four lines of which have been used in some of the verses produced at every frost fair, from that in 1684 to the last in 1814:—

> "——— To the Print-house go,
> Where men the Art of Printing seem to know:
> Where, for a Teaster, you may have your name
> Printed, hereafter for to shew the same;
> And sure, in former ages, ne'er was found
> A Press to Print where men so oft were drown'd!"*

Evelyn also quaintly tells us how that "coaches plied from Westminster to the Temple, and from several other staires, to and fro, as in the streetes: sleds [sledges], sliding with skeetes [skates], a bull-baiting, horse and coach races, puppet-plays and interludes, cookes, tippling, and other lewd places; so that it seem'd to be a bacchanalian triumph, or carnival on the water." This traffic and festivity were continued until February 5th, when the same authority states that "it began to thaw, but froze again. My coach crossed from Lambeth to the horse-ferry at Millbank, Westminster. The booths were almost taken downe; but there was first a map or land-skip cut in copper, representing all the manner of the camp, and the several actions, sports and pastimes thereon, in memory of so signal a frost. . . . London, by reason of the excessive coldness of the aire hindering the ascent of the smoke, was so fill'd with this fuliginous steame of the sea-coale, that hardly could one see across the streetes; and this filling the lungs with its gross particles, exceedingly obstructed the breath, so as no one could scarcely breathe. There was no water to be had from the pipes and engines; nor could the brewers and divers other tradesmen work; and every moment was full of disastrous accidents." It was during the continuance of this fair that Evelyn saw a "human salamander," when he dined at Sir Stephen Fox's, and "after dinner came a fellow who ate live charcoal, glowingly ignited, quenching them in his mouth, and then champing and swallowing them down. There was also a dog which," Evelyn quaintly remarks, "seemed to do many rational actions."

The very curious original drawing of this fair, engraven on a reduced scale in Smith's "Antiquities of London," represents the Thames, looking

* "Thamesis's Advice to the Painter from her Frigid Zone; or, Wonders on the Water." London: Printed by G. Groom, on the River of Thames. Small folio half-sheet, 74 lines.

from the western side of the Temple Stairs, appearing on the left, towards London Bridge, which is faintly shown in the view at the back with all the various buildings standing upon it. "The time when the view was taken," says the author of that work, "was the day previous to the first thaw, as the original is dated in a contemporaneous hand at the top of the right-hand corner, 'Munday, February the 4th, 1683-4.' The drawing consists of a spirited though unfinished sketch, on stout and coarse paper in pencil, slightly shaded with Indian ink; which was the well-known style of an artist of the seventeenth century, peculiarly eminent for his views, namely, Thomas Wyck—usually called Old Wyck, to distinguish him from his son John—who spent the greater part of his life in England. This sketch is preserved in the 'Illustrated Pennant's London,' formerly belonging to Mr. John Charles Crowle, in the Print Room of the British Museum. On the right of the view is an oblique prospect of the double line of tents which extended across the centre of the river, called at the time Temple Street, consisting of taverns, toy shops, &c., which were generally distinguished by some title or sign, as the 'Duke of York's Coffee-house,' 'the Tory booth,' 'the booth with a phenix on it, and insured to last as long as the foundation stands,' 'the Half-way House,' 'the Bear Gardenshire Booth,' 'the Roast Beef Booth,' 'the Music Booth,' 'the Printing Booth,' 'the Lottery Booth,' and 'the Horn Tavern Booth,' which is indicated about the centre of the view by the antlers of a stag raised above it. On the outside of this street were pursued the various sports of the fair, some of which are also shown in the annexed plate; but in the nearer and larger figures introduced in the pictorial map mentioned by Evelyn, there appear extensive circles of spectators, surrounding a bull-baiting, and the rapid revolution of a whirling-chair or car, drawn by several men by a long rope fastened to a stake, fixed in the ice. Large boats covered with tilts, capable of containing a considerable number of passengers, and decorated with flags and streamers, are represented as being used for sledges, some of them being drawn by horses, and others by watermen, in want of their usual employment. Another sort of boat was mounted on wheels, and one vessel called the 'Drum-boat' was distinguished by a drummer placed at the prow. The pastimes of throwing at a cock, sliding and skating, roasting an ox, foot-ball, skittles, pigeon-holes, cups and balls, &c., are represented in a large print as being carried on in various parts of the river; whilst a sliding-hutch propelled by a stick, a chariot moved by a screw, and stately coaches, filled with visitors, appear to be rapidly moving in various directions, and sledges with coals and wood are passing between the London and Southwark shores. The gardens of the Temple and the river itself are both filled in the large plate with numerous spectators, as they are also shown in the present view; but, in addition to its originality, the drawing now engraved is, perhaps, more pictorially interesting than the print, from the prospect being considerably more spacious and carefully executed; as it exhibits the whole line of the Bankside to St. Saviour's Church, with the Tower, the Monument, finished in 1677, the Windmill near Queenhythe, the new Bow Church, and some others of the new churches, the vacant site and ruins of Bridewell Palace, and Old London Bridge."

With our copy of this interesting drawing is introduced another equally curious relic of the same Frost Fair, from the collection of Henry Hyde, second Earl of Clarendon, and formerly in the collection of Mr. William Upcott. It consists of an impression of the specimen of printing on the ice, executed for King Charles II. and the Royal Family who visited the fair with him. The names upon the paper are Charles, King; James, Duke (of York, his brother, subsequently King James II.); Katherine, Queen (Catharine, Infanta of Portugal, Queen of Charles II.); Mary, Duchess (Mary d'Este, sister of Francis, Duke of Modena, the second duchess of James); Anne, princess (the second daughter of the Duke of York, afterwards Queen Anne); George, prince (the princess's husband, George of Denmark). The concluding name, "Hans in Kelder," was no doubt dictated by the humour of the king; it literally signifies "Jack in the Cellar," and alludes to the interesting situation of the Princess Anne. The card, which was printed with a type border, was worded as follows:—

CHARLES, KING.	MARY, DUTCHESS.
KATHERINE, QUEEN.	ANNE, PRINCESS.
JAMES, DUKE.	GEORGE, PRINCE.

HANS IN KELDER.

London: Printed by G. Groom, on the Ice, on the River of Thames, January 31, 1684.

Charles II. seems to have been very partial to "Frost Fair." He is reported to have joined in a fox-hunt on the Thames; and a French traveller present in London at the time, states, in a small volume printed at Paris, that the king on one occasion passed a whole night upon the ice.

A contemporaneous notice of Frost Fair contained in a diary cited in *The Gentleman's Magazine* for 1814, states that on February 2nd, in 1684, an ox was roasted whole over against Whitehall, and that King Charles and the Queen ate a part of it. His Majesty appears to have taken much pleasure in viewing the lively scene from his palace, since in the poem also printed upon the ice, entitled "Thamesis's Advice to the Painter," there occur the following lines :—

> "Then draw the king, who on his leads doth stray
> To view the throng as on a Lord Mayor's day,
> And thus unto his nobles pleased to say :
> 'With these men on this ice I'd undertake
> To cause the Turk all Europe to forsake ;
> An army of these men, arm'd and complete,
> Would soon the Turk in Christendom defeat.' "

The print of Frost Fair, referred to in the diary of Evelyn, is entitled "An Exact and Lively Mapp or Representation of Boothes and all the varieties of Showes and Humours upon the Ice on the River of Thames by London, during that memorable Frost, in the 35th Yeare of the Reigne of His Sacred Majesty King Charles the Second, Anno Dm. MDCLXXXIII., with an Alphabetical Explanation of the most remarkable figures." It consists of a whole sheet copper-plate, the prospect being represented horizontally from the Temple Stairs and Bankside to London Bridge. In an oval cartouche at the top of the view, within the frame of the print, appears the title; and on the outside, below, are the alphabetical references with the words, "Printed and sold by William Warter, Stationer, at the signe of the Talbott under the Mitre Tavern in Fleete Street, London." An impression of this plate will be found in the Royal Collection of Topographical Prints and Drawings given by George IV. to the British Museum, vol. xxvii., art. 39. There is also a variation of the same engraving in the City Library at Guildhall, divided with common ink into compartments as if intended to be used as cards, and numbered in the margin in type with Roman numerals, in three series of ten each and two extra. A descriptive list of the other prints, printed papers, and tracts relating to the Frost Fair of 1683–1684, will be found in Wilkinson's "Londina Illustrata," vol. i., whence much of the preceding notices has been derived; another list is contained in the catalogue of the Sutherland collection of Prints and Drawings inserted as illustrations in Lord Clarendon's "Life" and "History of the Rebellion," and Burnet's "History of his Own Times."

Again the Duke of York (James II.) writes to his son-in-law—and destined supplanter—William of Orange, under date January 4, 1683–4 :—"The weather is so very sharp and the frost so great that the river here is quite frozen over, so that for these three days past people have gone over it in several places, and many booths are built on it between Lambeth and Westminster, where they roast meat and sell drink." During the continuance of the frost at this time, which lasted until the 4th of February, about forty coaches plied on the Thames as on dry land, and the scene enacted on the glassy surface of the river in its course through London was known as "Frost" or "Blanket" fair.

In 1709 the Thames was again frozen over, but the frost was not sufficiently permanent to allow of a repetition of Frost Fair, although several persons crossed over on the ice.

In the winter of 1715–16 the frost was again so intensely severe that the river Thames was frozen over during almost the space of three months. Booths were erected on the congealed river for the sale of all kinds of commodities, and all the fun of the fair of 1684 was revived. On the 19th of January, 1716, two large oxen were roasted whole on the ice; the vast quantities of snow which had fallen at different times in the season rendered the City almost impassable. The Prince of Wales was attracted to the fair, and a newspaper of the day intimates that the theatres were almost deserted.

The winter of the year 1739, generally known as "the hard winter," was a season of distress to the labouring part of the public. A most severe frost began on Christmas Day, and continued till the ensuing February. Its severity was beyond precedent, and the effect produced was long felt. Many persons who had lived in Hudson's Bay territory declared that they had never known it colder in that frozen region than it was in England during that winter. The Thames was soon covered with floating rocks and shoals of ice; and when these were fixed, the river represented a snowy field rising in many places in hillocks and huge heaps of icebergs, and many artists seized the opportunity of making sketches of the strange scene thus presented "above bridge." The river Thames was so solidly frozen that great numbers of people dwelt upon it in tents, and a variety of booths was erected on it for the entertainment of the populace. A few days after it began there arose a very high wind, which did considerable damage to the shipping, that happened at that time to be very numerous. Several vessels laden with corn, others with coals, &c., were sunk by the ice; many had holes beat in their sides by falling on their anchors: several lighters and boats were confined under the ice; in short, a more dismal scene presented itself on the river Thames than had ever been beheld by the oldest man living. The damage done between the Medway and London Bridge was computed at £100,000, and besides many persons lost their lives from the severity of the weather. The watermen and fishermen were entirely disabled from earning their livelihood, as were the lower classes of labourers from their employment in the open air; and the calamity was rendered more severe by coals and other necessaries being advanced in their price in proportion to the intenseness and continuance of the frost. Happily for the poor, the hand of charity was liberally extended; great benefactions were given by persons of opulent fortunes, and considerable collections were made in most of the parishes in London; and from this benevolent assistance many wretched families were preserved that otherwise must have inevitably perished. During the nine weeks' continuance of the frost coaches plied upon the Thames, and festivities and diversions of all kinds were enjoyed upon the ice. Little or no novelty, however, appears to have been introduced into the amusements of this fair, and the same things were done as on the former occasion, even to the roasting of the regulation ox on the ice, a feat which appears to have been accomplished with some little ceremony, for we read that "Mr. Hodgeson, a butcher of St. James's Market, claimed the privilege of knocking down the beast as a right inherent in his family, his father having knocked down the ox roasted in the river in 1684, as he himself did that roasted in 1715 near Hungerford Stairs." The beast was fixed to a stake in the open market, and Mr. Hodgeson "came dressed in a rich laced cambric apron, a silver steel, and a hat and feathers, to perform the office." Printing-booths were again set up on the ice, and at one of these establishments, bearing the sign of the "Golden King's Head," was sold "An Account of the principal Frosts for above a Hundred Years," with a frontispiece of London Bridge at the time of the frost, which purported to have been printed on the ice. Another popular publication was "The Humble Petition of the River Thames to the Venerable Sages of Westminster Hall," in which we read that "ministers of punishment have treated him with the utmost contempt and insolence, have even made a publick shew of him, have call'd in heaps of ragamuffins to trample upon him, and, what is worst of all, have forced a numerous family, which he used to provide for, to beg in the streets." In this fair "Doll the Pippin Woman," recorded in Gay's "Trivia," lost her life:—

"Doll every day had walk'd these treacherous roads;
Her neck grew warp'd beneath autumnal loads
Of various fruit: she now a basket bore;
That head, alas! shall basket bear no more.
* * * * *
The crackling crystal yields, she smiles, she dies;
Her head chopt off, from her lost shoulders flies;
'Pippins,' she cries, but Death her voice confounds;
And pip, pip, pip, along the ice resounds."

Towards the end of December, 1767, a violent frost began, which continued to increase, and was very severe till the 16th of January following. During its continuance, the sufferings of the poor in town and country were truly pitiable. Fuel and other necessaries of life were remarkably dear: the river Thames was frozen so hard, that the navigation was entirely stopped both above and below the bridge: many persons perished in boats and other craft that were jammed in by the ice; and the wherries in the river were wholly unemployed. Many accidents happened in the cities of London and Westminster, and several people perished by the cold in the streets. The severity of the frost was equally felt in the country; many persons were found dead in the snow, the roads were rendered quite impassable, and it was at the imminent hazard of their lives that the coachmen and mail-drivers performed their journeys. This was followed by a violent hurricane, by which damage was sustained, in the City and its neighbourhood, to the amount of £50,000.

Again there was a very severe frost in 1777–8, and the Thames was frozen over at Kingston. In the winter of 1788-9 the Thames was again frozen over, and a bear-hunt is stated to have taken place on the ice off Rotherhithe. During this frost the fair on the ice occupied a considerably larger space than on any previous occasion, extending as it did from Shadwell to Putney; it included, among other amusements, a travelling menagerie of beasts which moved about from place to place.

At the beginning of January, 1811, a very severe frost set in. On the 8th, the Thames was so much frozen, that there was only a narrow channel in the centre free from ice. The banks of the river were so firmly set with ice and snow that people could walk upon it from Battersea Bridge to Hungerford Stairs.

In Hughson's "London" we read that "the year 1814 began with an immense fog which lasted about a week, during which a number of accidents occurred. On the 8th of January, however, the fog disappeared, in consequence of a change of wind; and a frost then set in, almost as unexampled in its duration and severity as the fog had been for its density. The frost continued with little intermission till the 20th of March. On the 31st of January several persons walked across the Thames between London and Blackfriars Bridges; and on the 3rd of February a sheep was roasted on the ice on the same spot, and the whole space between the two bridges had become a complete fair. Thousands of persons were seen moving in all directions; about thirty booths were erected for the sale of porter, spirits, &c., as well as for skittles, dancing, and other diversions. Several printers had presses on the ice, and pulled off various impressions, for which they found a very rapid sale. So long a continuance of cold weather has seldom been experienced in our climate."

THE LONDON SCHOOL BOARD OFFICES, 1874. (*See page* 326.)

Cyrus Redding records in his "Fifty Years' Recollections" having spent this "bitter" winter in London, and having "walked from Blackfriars to London Bridge on the ice, dirty, and impure, and lumpy as it was." He describes it as "a dreary-looking scene." He adds, however, "The serpentine skaters, the promenading, the streets piled up with snow and ice, and the well and ill-clad spectators, as they were then combined, were amusing novelties."

A cotemporary account states, with minute precision, that on the morning of Sunday, the 30th of January, 1814, huge masses of ice quite blocked up the Thames between London and Blackfriars Bridges, and that no less than seventy persons walked across from Queenhithe to the opposite shore. On the same night the frost so welded the

THE EMBANKMENT, FROM CHARING CROSS BRIDGE, 1872.

vast mass together into one compact field as to render it almost immovable by the tide. On Tuesday the river presented a solid surface from Blackfriars Bridge to some distance below Three Crane Stairs, and "thousands perambulated the rugged plain, whereon a variety of amusements was provided. Among the more curious of these," continues the account, "was the ceremony of roasting a small sheep: for a view of this extraordinary spectacle sixpence was demanded and willingly paid. The delicate meat, when done, was sold at a shilling a slice, and termed 'Lapland mutton.' There were set up a great number of booths, ornamented with streamers, flags, and signs, and within them was a plentiful supply of favourite luxuries.

Near Blackfriars Bridge, however, a plumber named Davies, having ventured to cross with some lead in his hands, sank between two masses, and was seen no more. Two young women, too, nearly shared the same fate, but they were rescued from their perilous situation by the prompt efforts of some of the Thames watermen. From the solid obstruction the tide did not appear to ebb for some days more than half the usual mark. On Wednesday, the 2nd of February, the sports were repeated, and the Thames presented a complete 'frost fair' for a few days. The grand 'mall' or walk now extended, not as on former occasions across the river, but down the centre from Blackfriars to London Bridge; this was named the 'City Road,' and was lined on both sides by booths of all descriptions. Eight or ten printing-presses were erected, and numerous cards and broadsides were printed on the ice in commemoration of 'the great frost.' Some of these frost-fair typographers showed considerable taste in their handiwork. At one of the presses was hoisted an orange-coloured standard, with the watch-word 'Orange Boven' in large letters, in allusion to the recent restoration of the Stadtholder to the Government of Holland, which had been for several years under the dominion of the French. From this press, too, were issued such papers as this:—

FROST FAIR.

'Amidst the arts which on the Thames appear,
To tell the wonders of this icy year,
Printing demands first place, which at one view
Erects a monument of That and You.'

Another paper runs thus:—

'You that walk here and do design to tell
Your children's children what this year befell,
Come buy this print, and it will then be seen
That such a year as this hath seldom been.'"

A handbill printed and sold on the ice contains the following notice:—"Whereas, you, J. Frost, have by force and violence taken possession of the River Thames, I hereby give you warning to quit immediately.—A. THAW." Copies of the Lord's Prayer and several other pieces, both sacred and profane, were "worked off" at these icy printing-presses, and found many willing purchasers at high prices. On Thursday the number of booths and stalls, and also that of the visitors, was largely increased. Swings, book-stalls, skittles, dancing booths, merry-go-rounds, sliding barges, and all the other usual appendages of Greenwich and Bartlemy Fairs, now appeared in scores. The ice seemed to be a solid rock, and presented a truly picturesque appearance. Friday, the 4th, brought a fresh accession of booths and of pedlars to sell their wares, and the greatest rubbish that would have long remained unsold on the land was raked up from cellars and garrets and sold at double and treble its value. Books and toys labelled with the words "bought on the Thames" found purchasers on every side.

The Thames watermen, who it might have been supposed would have been ruined by the weather, reaped a considerable harvest; for every person was made to pay a toll of twopence or threepence before he was admitted into the precincts of "Frost Fair;" and some douceur was expected besides on quitting the scene. Indeed, some of them were said to have made as much in coppers as six pounds a day! On this afternoon, however, there occurred an incident which warned the most venturesome that the ice was not so solid, or at all events so safe, as it appeared; for three persons, a man and two lads, being on a piece of ice just above London Bridge, the latter suddenly became detached from the main body, and was carried by the tide through one of the arches. They laid themselves down at full length for safety, and happily were rescued by some Billingsgate fishermen. On the Wednesday, Thursday, and Friday "Frost Fair" was in full favour, and the grand walk between Blackfriars and London Bridges was crowded till after nightfall. Saturday, the 5th, augured but badly for the continuance of the "Frost Fair," for the wind veered round to the south, and there was a slight fall of snow and sleet. The visitors, however, were not to be deterred by trifles. Thousands again ventured on the surface, and still there was as much life and bustle as before on the frozen element; the footpath down the middle of the river was hard and secure, and amongst the crowd were some donkeys, which brought in to their owners considerable profit, as a donkey ride on the ice was charged a shilling.

These caused much merriment, as may very easily be supposed. Towards the evening the crowd thinned very much, for the rain began to fall and the ice to crack, threatening to float away and carry off booths, donkeys, printing-presses, and all the amusements of the last few days, to the no small dismay of stall-keepers, shop-keepers, typographers, and (unlicensed) publicans. The thaw, however, advanced rapidly, more rapidly indeed than heedlessness and indiscretion retreated. Two young men ventured on the ice above Blackfriars Bridge, notwithstanding the warnings of the watermen; the mass on which they stood was carried away, and they perished. On Sunday morning, February 6th, at an early hour the tide began to flow, and the thaw assisted the rising tide to break up the ice-field. On Monday, the thaw continuing, immense fragments of ice were in motion, floating up and down according to the set of the tide, carrying, of course, many of the barges and lighters from their moorings above bridge, and drifting them into positions where they speedily became wrecks and sunk. In two or three days more the frozen element again became fluid, and old Father Thames, under the bright rays of the sun, relaxed his "grim-visaged front," and very soon looked as cheerful and as busy as ever.

There can be little doubt, if reliance can be placed on the calculations of civil engineers, that the Thames would have been frozen over in 1838, in 1853, and again in 1894-5, if it had not been for the removal of old London Bridge, the narrow arches of which prevented the masses of ice from escaping seaward. The removal of this impediment has much increased what is called the "scour" of the river; and it is highly improbable that, however protracted, the frost will be able to coagulate the ice into one mass as it did, at all events, in the winters of 1564, 1608, 1634, 1683, 1715, 1739, 1789, and (as we have said above) in 1813-14.

The Thames "between bridges" in its normal and unfrozen state has been the scene of some curious experiments, wagers, &c. For instance, Mr. John Timbs, in his "Curiosities of London," states that in July, 1776, a man safely crossed the Thames in a butcher's tray from Somerset House for a wager; upon which feat depended £14,000. Again, towards the latter portion of his life, M. Lunardi, the first successful aëronaut in London, made several excursions on the Thames in a sort of tin life-buoy, which he named a water-balloon. This invention, however, has perhaps been improved on by Captain Paul Boyton, who, in the early part of the year of grace 1875, might have been seen making his way up and down the river between Westminster Bridge and Greenwich in a very novel manner. Dressed in an oil-skin or india-rubber suit of clothes, of sufficient capacity to allow of its being inflated, the captain could lie at full length on the surface of the water, or, placing himself partly in a sitting posture, propel himself comfortably along (canoe fashion) by means of a short paddle. Captain Boyton belonged to an American organisation, entitled the "Camden and Atlantic Life Guards," of which the mission was to save, not to slay; and he could boast that, armoured in the uniform of his invention, he had rescued seventy-one persons from the waves off the coast of New Jersey. The waterproof suit, which weighed about fifteen pounds, was in five separate parts—that is to say, head, breast, back, and two legs; and when all were inflated, it was capable of sustaining four men in addition to the wearer.

About the year 1841 an American diver, named Scott, created some sensation by leaping from the parapets of Southwark and Waterloo Bridges into the river beneath, which was nearly full of floating ice, but the poor fellow shortly afterwards killed himself by hanging from a scaffold upon the latter bridge. Now and then a theatrical clown navigates the river in a washing-tub drawn by geese; and occasionally there are wonderful stories of sharks, porpoises, and other strange things—all "very like a whale"—leaving their ocean sire and disporting themselves "above bridge."

Sometimes, by a freak of nature, the tide in the Thames falls very low; and by a very high wind from the south-west the river is occasionally *blown out*—or, in other words, the bed is left nearly dry from shore to shore—so that many an adventurous or frolicsome wight has been known to "walk across the Thames." As a rule, however, the tide in the Thames is generally regular in its ebb and flow, though a very strong wind from the north-west, if it comes at spring-tides, causes the river to rise higher on account of the volume of water which it forces up from the Northern Ocean. It is perhaps worthy of note that several times since the making of the Embankment, the tide in the Thames has risen many inches above Trinity mark, and inundated the south bank of the river along Lambeth, Bankside, and Rotherhithe, and even as far as Woolwich, causing a considerable loss of property.

Hunter in his "History of London" records the fact that in February, 1762, the tide overflowed the banks to such an extent that casks and other articles of merchandise were swept away from the wharves and quays, and the prison-yard of the Borough compter was some inches under water, and in the next month at spring-tide, the water rushed in a body into Westminster Hall. The same thing seems to have happened in the following September, when the water is said to have risen twelve feet perpendicular in five hours. The worst effects of this high tide, it appears, were felt below bridge; the cattle being carried away—so Hunter says—in the marshes about Stratford and Bow. "From the nearest computation, 70,000 pigs were supposed to have been lost. Several persons lost their lives on the high road, and many machines (*i.e.* carriages and wagons) were overturned. The houses from Bow Bridge to Stratford were all overflowed, and the inhabitants obliged to get out of their windows." The same thing appears to have recurred in the February of the following year, and again in September, 1764. He also tells us the tide in the Thames ebbed and flowed, in 1661, three times within seven hours, its waters being thrown into the most violent agitation.

In order to maintain the flow and "scour" of the Thames, an Act of Common Council was passed in 1538 to enforce an early statute of Henry VIII. forbidding persons to throw solid matter or refuse into the river, but allowing them to scoop out and carry away the shelves of sand, gravel, &c., as ballast, or for any other purpose, and compelling the owners to keep the banks on either side in a fit and proper state of repair. From time to time, we may here remark, a variety of projects have been put forward having for their immediate object the improvement of the bed and course of the river both below and above London Bridge, and more than once it has been seriously proposed to dig an entirely new course, in a direct line from Lambeth to Rotherhithe; but though these plans were canvassed and agitated from time to time, the vested interests which opposed them have succeeded in carrying the day, and for a brief period the subject has fallen through, only to be again and again brought forward and as often disposed of in a similar manner.

CHAPTER XL.

THE VICTORIA EMBANKMENT.

"I send, I send, here my supremest kiss
To thee, my silver-footed Tamasis;
No more shall I re-iterate thy Strand,
Whereon so many goodly structures stand."—*R. Herrick.*

The Thames Banks in the Early Ages—Sir Christopher Wren's Plan for embanking the River—Evelyn's Suggestion with the same View—The Subject brought before Parliament by Sir F. W. Trench—Mr. James Walker's Plan—The Victoria Embankment commenced—The Work described—Land reclaimed from the Thames—The Metropolitan District Railway—Quantities of Materials used in constructing the Embankment—Offices of the London School Board—Somerset House and the New Will Depository—Special Curiosities in the Will Office—Cleopatra's Needle—The Savoy Theatre—The Buckingham Water-gate—Statue of Sir James Outram—The Avenue Theatre—Public Garden and Promenade—St. Stephen's Club.

Many architects and geologists, from the days of Sir Christopher Wren, have been of opinion that the Thames was formerly not a river, but an estuary, the shores of which were the hills of Camberwell and Sydenham on the south, and of Highgate and Hampstead on the north, with a large sandy plain at low water, through which the river wound its tortuous way. Sir Christopher Wren especially considered that these sands being driven with the wind gradually formed sand-hills, which in the course of time, and by aid of Roman engineers, were embanked and so changed into meadows, or at all events into *terra firma*, the river being so reduced into its present channel, and wharves being built along the line of wall towards the river.

Considering that a large portion of what is commonly called London is lower in level than the high-water mark in the Thames, it is clear that the river must have been embanked from a very early period. Antiquaries have written to show that the river-walls of the Thames were the work of the native British before the advent of the Romans, who, no doubt, completed the work which was already begun; but it is certain that they were not completed until a date subsequent to the Norman Conquest.

The plan proposed by Sir Christopher Wren for rebuilding of London after the Great Fire included "a commodious quay on the whole bank of the river from the Tower to Blackfriars;" but unfortunately his idea was not adopted, and the opportunity was lost for ever. "The ingenious Mr. Evelyn," says Northouck, "suggested another plan with the same view, and besides lessening the most considerable declivities, he proposed further to employ the rubbish in filling up the shore of the Thames to low-water mark in a straight line from the Tower to the Temple, and form an ample quay, if it could be done without increasing the rapidity of the stream." But here again the old selfish objection of "vested interests" cropped up, and defeated the scheme, which it was reserved by Providence for Lord Palmerston, during his tenure of the Premiership, to carry through Parliament and enforce upon the citizens to their very great and manifest benefit.

During the reigns of George IV. and William IV., and in the early part of Victoria, the subject of an embankment for the river from London Bridge to Westminster was brought forward yearly in Parliament by the late Sir Frederick W. Trench, but still, as is too often the case, "nothing was done." Perhaps in the event London has been fortunate, for if the work of embanking the Thames had been taken in hand in the days of our fathers or our grandfathers, it is to be feared that it would not have been carried out upon the scale of magnificence which marks the work of Sir J. W. Bazalgette. It appears that in 1840 Mr. James Walker laid down for the Corporation a line of embankment, which has now in the main been followed.

This great work is in three divisions—namely, the "Victoria," extending from the northern end of Blackfriars Bridge to Westminster; the "Albert," from the Lambeth end of Westminster Bridge to Vauxhall; and a third section extending from Chelsea Bridge to the Cadogan Pier at Chelsea, close by Battersea Bridge.

The Victoria Embankment, of which alone we shall treat in this chapter, forms a wide and convenient line of communication between the City and the West End or more fashionable parts of London. It was commenced in February, 1864, and completed in July, 1870; and as a piece of engineering skill it is second to none of the great achievements that have marked the Victorian era. The river-side footway between Westminster Bridge and the Temple was opened to the public in 1868; but at that time the completion of the carriage-way was prevented by the unfinished condition of the Metropolitan District Railway between Westminster and Blackfriars, and this obstacle was not removed until the end of May, 1870. On the 30th of May the first passenger train passed under the Embankment to the then terminal station at Blackfriars, and within six weeks from that date the carriage-way of the Embankment was formed and the northern footway paved; and the whole was thrown open to the public on the 13th of July in that year. The "opening" ceremony was performed by the Prince of Wales, accompanied by the Princess Louise, on behalf of Her Majesty, after whom this noble thoroughfare is named, and of whom a statue, by C. B. Birch, A.R.A., was placed at the Blackfriars end in 1896.

Following in an even line the general curve of the river, the Embankment rises at each end by a gentle gradient to open upon Bridge Street, Westminster, opposite the Clock Tower of the Houses of Parliament, and upon Bridge Street, Blackfriars, opposite the station of the Metropolitan District Railway. It passes beneath the Charing Cross Railway Bridge at Hungerford, and the first arch on the Middlesex side of Waterloo Bridge. It is about a mile and a quarter in length, and is 100 feet in width throughout. The carriage-way is 64 feet wide; the footway on the land side 16 feet, and that on the river side 20 feet, each planted with trees 20 feet apart. On the river side the footway is bounded by a moulded granite parapet, 3 feet 6 inches in height, and on the land side partly by walls and partly by cast-iron railings.

The wall of the Embankment is a work of extraordinary magnitude and solidity. It is carried down to a depth of 32½ feet below Trinity high-water mark, and 14 feet below low water; and the level of the roadway is generally four feet above high water, rising at the extremities to twenty feet. The rising ground at each extremity is retained by the increased height of the wall, which is built throughout of brick, faced with granite, and founded in Portland cement concrete. The river front presents a slightly concave surface, which is plain from the base to mean high-water level, and is ornamented above that level by mouldings, stopped at intervals of about seventy feet by plain blocks of granite, bearing lamp standards of cast iron, and relieved on the river-face by bronze lions' heads, carrying mooring rings. The uniformity of line is broken at intervals by massive piers of granite (intended to be surmounted with groups of statuary), which flank recesses for steamboat landing-stages; and at other places by stairs projecting into the river, and designed as landing-places for small craft. The steamboat piers occur at Westminster, Charing Cross, and Waterloo Bridges, and those for small boats midway between Westminster and Charing Cross, and between Charing Cross and Waterloo Bridges, and both are united at the Temple Pier, opposite Essex Street.

Within the recesses for the steamboat landing-stages are placed admirably-contrived timber platforms, which rise and fall with the tide, and which carry the lower ends of gangways that are hinged to the masonry above. The gangways are formed of two wrought-iron girders, carrying a timber platform; and they move between granite walls parallel to the general line of the roadway. Upon the platforms there are waiting-rooms for passengers.

On the land side the Embankment is bounded from Westminster almost to Whitehall Place by four acres of recovered foreshore that were claimed by the Crown, but now belong to the City of Westminster. A broad and commodious approach to the Embankment occurs somewhat to the south-west of the Hungerford Railway Bridge, opening out of Whitehall Place. From there to Waterloo Bridge the Embankment is bounded by a similar foreshore, amounting to nearly eight acres, and becoming gradually narrowed from west to east. This portion is planted as an ornamental garden for the enjoyment of the public. To the east of Waterloo Bridge is what was once the river front of Somerset House, all marked and stained by water, and with huge mooring rings projecting from the masonry, but now quite inland. Next comes a space behind the Temple Railway Station, communicating with Surrey Street, Norfolk Street, and Arundel Street. Then another small portion of public ornamental garden, and then a piece added to the grounds of the Temple, but upon which the Templars are not able to build. Lastly, we come to a splendid site where stand the City of London Schools, Sion College, the offices of the Thames Conservancy, and the Guildhall School of Music.

To the east of Blackfriars Bridge the Embankment roadway is prolonged to the Mansion House by Queen Victoria Street, forming one grand thoroughfare between the Houses of Parliament and the City. The eastern portion of this thoroughfare, between Cannon Street and the Mansion House, was completed and opened for public traffic in October, 1869.

WHITEHALL GARDENS FROM THE RIVER. (*See page* 328.)

The total area of the land reclaimed from the river amounts to $37\frac{1}{4}$ acres. Of this, nineteen acres are occupied by the carriage and foot ways, eight acres are devoted to garden, and the rest has been conveyed to the Crown, the Templars, and other proprietors along the line. Within the Embankment wall, and forming a portion of its structure, is placed the Low Level Intercepting Sewer, which is an integral portion of the main drainage scheme. Above it is a subway for gas and water pipes, the dimensions of the subway being 7 feet 6 inches in height and 9 feet in width;

and the diameter of the sewer varying from 7 feet 9 inches to 8 feet 3 inches. These are both situate under the footway next the river. The footways are paved with York stone, with granite curbs.

To the east of the Temple the roadways are carried over a double covered way, originally belonging to the City Gas Company, and leading to a landing-wharf, by which coals might be conveyed from the river without interference with the traffic. At this point, moreover, the subterranean engineering was of extreme complexity, for the sewers, the Fleet ditch, the subways, the Gas Company's railroad, the public railway, and a variety of gas, water, and telegraph pipes had to be interlaced in a way that almost defies description.

In connection with the steamboat pier at Westminster Bridge a subway has been constructed, communicating with the subway already existing under Bridge Street, and affording an underground thoroughfare for foot passengers between the Houses of Parliament, the railway station, the steamboat pier, and the footways in Bridge Street and on the river and land sides of the Embankment.

The Metropolitan District Railway enters the land reclaimed by the Embankment at the point between Cannon Row and Westminster Bridge, and passes under the public road as far as Charing Cross steamboat pier, where it diverges to the land side of the roadway to the Charing Cross Station, the roof of which rises above the surface and is enclosed by screen walls of brickwork. Immediately east of the station are three openings for ventilation of the railway, which, together with the screen walls, are partially concealed by the mounds and shrubberies of the ornamental grounds. East of the openings, the railway is carried in a covered way under the ornamental grounds as far as the Waterloo steamboat pier, where it again passes under the roadway to the Temple Station, and is thence continued on the land side of the roadway to within a few feet of Blackfriars Bridge. From the east end of the Temple Gardens the concrete wall which retains the earth for the rising approach road to Blackfriars forms also the side wall of the railway. The level of the rails is generally $17\frac{1}{2}$ feet below the surface of the road, which is carried over the railway by cast-iron girders and brick arches, the upper surface of the arches being 18 inches below the surface of the road.

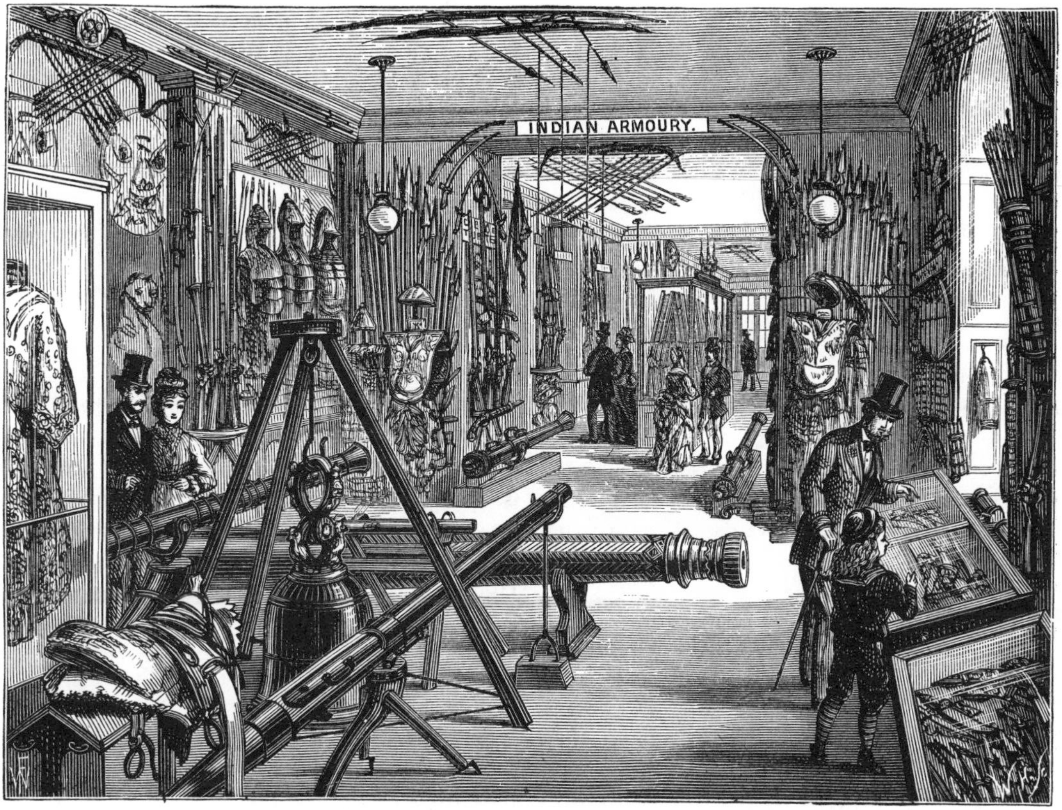

ROYAL UNITED SERVICE MUSEUM, 1876. (*See pages* 334, 335.)

Mr. Peter Cunningham, writing in 1850, remarks, "I cannot conclude this too brief account of our noble river without expressing a wish that the side sewer and terrace Embankment scheme (so long ago talked about and first projected by John Martin, the painter) may be carried out before many years are over. By narrowing the current," he adds, "we shall recover a large quantity of waste ground on either side, and escape from the huge unhealthy mud-banks that disfigure the river about Scotland Yard." What would he have said had he lived to see the completion of the gigantic undertaking which forms the subject of the present chapter?

It is not easy for persons unaccustomed to deal with such matters to form any clear conception of great quantities expressed in numerical statements; but it is, nevertheless, worth while to place on record the official accounts of the cost of the work, and of the amount of various kinds of material employed in its construction. The total cost is estimated at £1,260,000, and the purchase of property at £450,000. The quantities of materials are stated to have been as follows:—Granite, 650,000 cubic feet; brickwork, 80,000 cubic yards; concrete, 140,000 cubic yards; timber (for coffer-dam, &c.), 500,000 cubic feet; caissons (for ditto), 2,500 tons; earth filling, 1,000,000 cubic yards; excavation, 144,000 cubic yards; York paving, 125,000 superficial feet; broken granite, 50,000 superficial yards.

It is but right that, in describing a work of such grandeur and national importance as the Thames Embankment, we should mention the names, not only of the principal engineer—Sir Joseph W. Bazalgette—to whom, of course, it will be a monument of enduring fame, but also of those of the contractors and resident engineers; the former were Messrs. Furness, Ritson, and Webster, and the latter Messrs. Lovick and Cooper.

The Act of Parliament under which the Metropolitan Board of Works obtained powers for the formation of new streets in connection with the Thames Embankment contains in its preamble a curious reference to the Act of William and Mary "for the relief of the orphans and other creditors of the City of London." That piece of legislation provided for the raising of a fund by the imposition of a duty on coal and on wine; and subsequent enactments continued the levy, appropriating its benefit to other requirements of metropolitan improvement. The charges on the fund set apart for making new approaches to London Bridge having been satisfied, the residue was by this Act transferred to the purposes of the Thames Embankment. In 1889, however, a Bill was passed cancelling the duties. The Embankment answers a treble purpose: it serves as an effective relief to our overcrowded streets by the formation of a wide thoroughfare; it improves the navigation of the river; and it has also given an opportunity for making the low-level sewer without disturbing the Strand or Fleet Street. The importance of the improvement of the river is obvious to all, for not only has the Embankment added a handsome frontage to the side of the Thames which previously had been a public eyesore, but it has also been the means of getting rid of the unequal deposits of mud in its bed, assisting the removal of the scour of the river, and consequently improving the health of the inhabitants of London.

In those days it was difficult for the Metropolitan Board to raise capital at a less rate of interest than 4½ per cent. The importance of the work, however, had been impressed upon the ruling powers of the Government, and Parliament passed a bill by which the Board was greatly assisted in the undertaking.

Although that portion of the Embankment lying between Westminster and Waterloo Bridges is perhaps the most picturesque and varied of the whole line, that between Waterloo and Blackfriars is by no means wanting in interest and architectural effect. For the first time we have a land view of Sir W. Chambers' beautiful building, Somerset House; whilst the neighbouring Temple Gardens, "blooming in the midst of a nest of lawyers," have gained some 200 feet in depth, and thus become, on the whole, a really handsome pleasure-ground.

With this general view of the Victoria Embankment, we will at once proceed to point out some of the principal buildings that overlook it. As we pass from east to west we see, after De Keyser's Royal Hotel, the City of London School,* completed in 1882, and forming an admirable specimen of the Italian Renaissance, with an ornate front displaying polished columns of Aberdeen granite, and statues of Shakespeare, Milton, Newton, Bacon, and Sir Thomas More. A little way back from the Embankment is the Guildhall School of Music, opened in 1886, and behind this is the City of London School for Girls, dating from 1893. The next building on the Embankment is Sion College, a Perpendicular building with a parvised porch, flanked by the offices of the Thames Conservancy, in the same style. Of Sion College, formerly in London Wall, we have spoken before,† and all that need be added here

* See also Vol. I., p. 375. † See also Vol. II., pp. 168–70.

is that the present building was completed in 1886. Then come the Temple Gardens, and beyond these is one of the three Embankment Gardens, backed by the offices of the London School Board, a Renaissance building of Portland stone, with bands of red brick, which had to wait until 1895 for its completion. The original architects were Messrs. Bodley and Garner; the more recent works were carried out under the supervision of Colonel Edis. In the prettily laid out Garden in front of the building is most appropriately placed a statue of the late William Edward Forster, the founder of the School Board system. Here also is Woolner's sitting figure of John Stuart Mill; and at the eastern gate are replicas of the Herculaneum "Wrestlers," while at the western end is a statue of Isambard Kingdom Brunel.

Between the Temple and Somerset House the north side of the roadway is occupied in part by the Temple Station of the Metropolitan District Railway, by the back of which is a roadway skirting the lower ends of Howard and Norfolk Streets, thus opening up communication between the Embankment and the Strand.

We now pass the Thames front of Somerset House. Of this building we have spoken generally in a previous chapter. We may, however, add here that some of the rooms under the noble balustraded terrace, which for about 600 feet overlook the Embankment, are now set apart as the national depository of wills. These documents, amounting to some tons in weight, were removed hither from Doctors' Commons at the end of the year 1874. Nearly the whole of the southern front of Somerset House, having been vacated by the Admiralty, was fitted up for their accommodation, and a range of spacious apartments some two hundred feet in length, occupying the interior of the great terrace, and also a considerable portion of the basement of Somerset House itself, has been fitted up with miles of shelving, whereon are stowed away long rows of folio volumes of formidable dimensions. The fact that in the new office at Somerset House there is a depository for the executed wills of living persons (as, indeed, there was in Doctors' Commons) must be set down in the category of "things not generally known." Known, however, or not, it is true; for any man or woman in the kingdom not incapacitated from making a will may forthwith sign, seal, and deliver here, on payment of a fee of 12s. 6d., his or her last will and testament, to be kept safely and securely until his or her death makes it operative. While in the custody of the office it is kept in a fire-proof room, and can never again be seen by the testator or testatrix. Here the motto is plain and simple, "*Vestigia nulla retrorsum.*" It is, however, competent to the testator to annul it wholly or to vary it in part by making a fresh will or a codicil; and such fresh will or codicil he may either deposit at Somerset House or keep in his own custody. *Apropos* of this subject, what reader will not remember the Mr. Spenlow in "David Copperfield" moralising on the uncertainty of life and the duty of making a will, and then next day dying intestate?

As to the antiquity of the documents that have been brought from Doctors' Commons to Somerset House, they may be briefly summed up by saying that the original wills commence with the year 1483, the first of Edward V. The copies date from just a century earlier, viz., in the reign of Richard II. The latter are written on parchment, strongly bound, with brazen clasps. A very small volume suffices to contain the wills of a year or even of ten years before the Reformation. As we come down to more recent times the bulk of the volumes containing the wills steadily increases with the wealth and population of London and of the kingdom. Indeed, from about 1860 down to the present time the average number of volumes filled with the wills proved in the Prerogative Court of London amounts to nearly twenty a year. These wills themselves annually average, perhaps, 10,000 in the London district alone; while those of the rest of the kingdom may possibly be reckoned at 17,000 more.

It may be added that among the special curiosities of this storehouse of ancient documents are some wills which the nation, and, indeed, the world, would not willingly let perish. With a single exception, these have been transferred from Doctors' Commons to Somerset House. Here the visitor, if properly introduced, may see the wills of the painter Vandyck, of Dr. Johnson, of Lord Nelson, of William Pitt, of Edmund Burke, of Sir Isaac Newton, of Inigo Jones, of Izaak Walton, of the Duke of Wellington, of John Milton, and, above all, that of William Shakespeare. This, being of exceptional interest, has been exceptionally treated, and the three folio pages of which it consists are placed under an air-tight frame made of polished oak and plate glass. The will of the great Napoleon was to be seen for many years at old Doctors' Commons, but it was restored to the French nation in 1853, in compliance with the request of the Emperor Louis Napoleon.

It may, perhaps, be added here that in 1824 there was published a short-lived periodical, somewhat of the nature of the old *Tatlers* and *Spectators*, and partly a precursor of the *Pall Mall Gazette* and other light and chatty newspapers of our own day, called the *Somerset House Gazette*, edited by "Ephraim Hardcastle, Esq.,"—of course an assumed name.

Passing on under the northern arch of Waterloo Bridge, we enter upon the pleasantest portion of the Embankment. Here a considerable portion of land has been reclaimed from the Thames, the whole of which, except the roadway, is laid out as a garden. So high has the ground here been raised that it has fairly eclipsed Inigo Jones's water-gate, at the foot of Buckingham Street. A walk 16 feet in width is carried the entire length of the ground, both on the east and west sides, and from these several other walks are carried across the area at right angles, while others are circular in form. There are three circular mounds and two of oblong form, portions of which are planted with flowers and shrubs, and the remaining parts turfed over.

About midway between Waterloo and Charing Cross Bridges rises the tall obelisk known as Cleopatra's Needle. This object of Egyptian antiquity, which is set up on the outer margin of the Embankment, immediately overlooking the river, was brought from Alexandria to this country in 1878–9, mainly through the exertions of a private gentleman, the late Sir Erasmus Wilson, F.R.S. The obelisk, 60 feet in height, stands upon a massive granite pedestal, flanked on either side by a colossal bronze sphinx. On each side of the pedestal is affixed a bronze tablet; that which faces the river bears the following inscription:—

> "Through the patriotic zeal of Erasmus Wilson, F.R.S., this obelisk was brought from Alexandria in an iron cylinder; it was abandoned in the Bay of Biscay, recovered, and erected on this spot by John Dixon, C.E., in the 42nd year of the reign of Queen Victoria."

In another it is recorded that—

> "This obelisk, quarried at Syeni, was erected at Heliopolis by the Pharaoh Thothmes III., about 500 B.C.,"

with other details of the ancient history of the relic.

At the lower end of Beaufort Buildings, not far from the Thames Embankment, stands the Savoy Theatre. This structure, which was built in 1881, was intended to be specially devoted to the representation of comic or satirical opera, and was opened in October of the above year with the play of "Patience," transferred from the Opera Comique. The main frontage of the theatre looks towards the river, and is constructed of red brick and Portland stone, in the Italian style of architecture. The theatre possesses several features of a novel and distinctive character; it is isolated from other buildings, and every part of the house possesses two means of egress, there being entrances and exits on all four sides. From the Strand, or northern boundary of the theatre, there is a considerable descent in the roadway along Beaufort Buildings, and with the view of providing both stage and auditorium space, excavations have been made within the building over the entire area of the interior to the depth at the north end of almost the height of the external walls themselves from the street level, with proportionate excavation at the south end. This permits of a spacious stage and stage-dock beneath it at the north end, together with a large and convenient auditorium area, including pit, stalls, lower and upper circle, and gallery. The theatre, which was planned to seat nearly 1,300 persons, was built from the designs of Mr. Phipps. Between it and the Embankment stands the Savoy Hotel, and beside it, on the west, is the huge Hôtel Cecil, the largest establishment of the kind in the country. On the east is the Examination Hall of the Royal Colleges of Physicians and Surgeons, a featureless building of red brick faced with Portland stone.

Following the course of the Embankment, under the fan-shaped connection of Charing Cross Bridge with the railway station, we now emerge upon what may be considered historic ground. Extending almost in a direct line with that portion of the Embankment which we have so far traversed, the broad roadway is continued through into Whitehall Place. Between this roadway and the railway station is Scotland Yard, for many years the head-quarters of the Metropolitan Police, about which we shall have more to say in the following chapter; and to the right of this, till its demolition to form a new opening from Charing Cross to the Embankment, stood Northumberland House. Close by the railway station is the Avenue Theatre, erected in 1881; opposite the theatre, and in Northumberland Avenue, is the apex of the triangle formed by the Hotel Métropole; then as we proceed towards Westminster we see the gigantic National Liberal Club, with its magnificent frontage to the Embankment. In the garden beneath the Club is a statue of Sir Bartle Frere, flanked by one of Wm. Tyndall, and by another of General Sir James Outram, while in the garden mentioned above, are statues of Burns and Robert Raikes, and a fountain commemorating Henry Fawcett.

Just above the railway bridge, if we had gone up the river in a steamer thirty years ago, or as now, wending our way along Sir J. W. Bazalgette's Embankment, we should have come upon a green oasis amid the surrounding streets—we refer to Whitehall Gardens. "It is," writes Dr. C. Mackay in 1840, in his "Thames and its Tributaries," "a fair lawn, neatly trimmed, and divided into compartments by little walls. . . . Just behind the house with the bow-windows, inhabited by Sir Robert Peel, is the spot where Charles the First was beheaded. In a nook close by, as if purposely hidden from the view of the world, is a very good statue of a very bad king. Unknown to the thousands of London, James the Second rears his brazen head in a corner, ashamed apparently . . . . to affront the eyes of the nation which he misgoverned."

Beyond the gardens of Montagu House, the town residence of the Duke of Buccleuch, is New Scotland Yard, designed by Mr. Norman Shaw, R.A., and completed in 1891, when it became the headquarters of the Metropolitan Police. At the junction of the Victoria Embankment with Bridge Street, close by the foot of Westminster Bridge, and facing the Clock Tower of the Houses of Parliament, stands the St. Stephen's Club. It immediately adjoins Westminster Bridge Railway Station, to which, as well as to the Houses of Parliament, it has an access under the roadway, quite protected from wind and rain. The building, which is constructed of Bath stone, with grey polished granite columns, occupies a somewhat irregularly-shaped block of land; and it was erected in 1874, from the designs of Mr. J. Whichcord, F.S.A. The club-house, which rises from the lower basement to the full height of 100 feet, is in the Classical or Palladian style. The rooms are lofty and light. The house is well warmed throughout by an apparatus, the coils of which are cleverly concealed, and from top to bottom it is fitted up with electric bells of the newest pattern. At the top of the house is the culinary department —an arrangement by which the smell of the cooking escapes without entering the club. The attic floor contains, besides accommodation for servants, a large kitchen, superintended by a French *chef de cuisine*. On the floor next the attics are two billiard-rooms, two dining-rooms, with a similar arrangement, and an occasional room for breakfasts, &c. On the next—in other words, on the first floor—are a smoking-room, a card-room, and a dining-room for members only. On the ground floor the entrance from the Embankment opens into a lofty hall paved partially with encaustic tiles and partially with inlaid polished oak, the ceiling supported by red scagliola columns, and lighted with stained-glass windows. On the left of the entrance-hall there is a small reception-room for strangers, leading into the morning-room, a lofty apartment, lighted by five large windows looking on the river and the Houses of Parliament, the ground ceiling resting on verd antique columns. To the upper floor access is gained by a spiral staircase in the Jacobean style, in plan not unlike the great staircase in the rear of Devonshire House. The windows of this staircase look out on the roof of the railway station below, and, therefore, have been filled with painted glass, in diaper work. The staircase is so arranged as to be continued down into the basement, where it leads to the secretary's office, bath-rooms, lavatories, &c. And as we read of another place that shall be nameless that "in the lowest depths there is a lower still," so in what we may call the basement of the basement there are wine and beer cellars, and strong rooms for other stores, and a place for working the hydraulic lift, by which all the provisions are raised to the top of the house without passing up the staircase.

Let us now turn our steps landward, and investigate the neighbourhood more in detail.

CHAPTER XLI.

SCOTLAND YARD AND THE METROPOLITAN POLICE.

"Stands Scotland where it did?"—*Shakespeare.*

Situation and Extent—Originally the Residence of the Scottish Kings and Ambassadors when in England—Margaret Queen of Scots entertained here—Decay of the Palace—John Milton and "Beau" Fielding Residents here—Inigo Jones, Sir John Denham, and Sir Christopher Wren—Sir John Vanbrugh and his "Goose Pie"—Sir Joshua Reynolds' Encomiums on Vanbrugh's Merits—Rowe's Poetical Allusion to him—Josiah Wedgwood's Residence—The "Well's" Coffee House—Attack on Lord Herbert of Cherbury—The Palace Court or Marshalsea—The Metropolitan Police Force—Cabs and Hackney Coaches—Sedan Chairs—Care of "Tipplers"—Harrington House—"Man's" Coffee House—Whitehall Place—Middle Scotland Yard—Royal United Service Institution—Government Offices—Fife House—A "canny" Scotch Earl—Whitehall Stairs.

Having finished our "tour of the Thames" by way of the new Embankment, we must ask our readers to throw themselves in imagination back a century or so, and to step with ourselves mentally out of a Thames wherry alongside of the old Palace stairs at Whitehall, at the end abutting on Scotland Yard, which lies immediately on our right as we land. To this spot, most interesting on account of its old associations, it is our intention to devote the present chapter.

It was in 1829 that Scotland Yard became the headquarters of the Metropolitan Police, though, as we have seen (p. 329), it has now ceased to be so, more commodious premises having been erected on the Victoria Embankment, close to Westminster Bridge. It is bounded on the east by what was once the garden of Northumberland House, and is now divided into Great and Middle Scotland Yard, the latter division lying close to Whitehall Yard. Both yards together constitute a poor and mean space, which certainly is no credit to the city of which it forms so important a part. How few of our readers are aware that those mean buildings cover the site of what was once a magnificent palace, built by our Saxon sovereigns for the reception of the kings of Scotland, as often as they visited this country.

Old writers describe the locality as lying a little to the south of Charing Cross, on the eastern side of the highway leading thence to Whitehall, where there stood a "palace with large pleasure-grounds extending to the river;" and where, according to Stow, "great buildings have been, for the receipt of the kings of Scotland, and other estates of that country." The old chronicler speaks of the site as "a large plot of ground enclosed with brick [walls], and called 'Scotland.'" "This property," says Mr. Newton, in his "London in the Olden Time," "was given by the Saxon King Edgar to Kenneth III., King of Scotland, for his residence, upon his annual visit to London to do homage for his kingdom to the Crown of England. It continued afterwards to be the residence of the Scottish kings when they attended the English Parliament as barons of the realm. The last of the Scottish royal family who resided here," he adds, "was Margaret, Queen of Scots, and sister to King Henry VIII., who had her abiding there when she came to England after the death of her husband," James IV., who fell at the battle of Flodden Field. She was here entertained with great splendour by her brother, as soon as he was reconciled to her second marriage with the Earl of Arran; afterwards she lived here as became a widow, in privacy, keeping up little or no semblance of state. A note in Brayley's "Londoniana" states: "The Scottish kings appear to have been anciently regarded as members of the English Parliament; and there are instances among the Tower Records of the issuing of writs to summon their attendance at Westminster. Thus in Pinkerton's 'Iconographia Scotica' is an engraving of Edward I. sitting in Parliament, with Alexander King of Scots on his right, and Llewellyn Prince of Wales on his left; and this is said to have been taken from a copy of an ancient limning formerly in the English College of Arms." It may be added that it was for their fiefs in Cumberland and Westmoreland, and not for their dominions to the north of the Tweed, that the Scottish sovereigns did homage. Besides the Scottish kings, their ambassadors also were lodged here from time to time.

The situation and extent of the mansion and grounds which occupied this site are well known to the antiquary and topographer. Concerning the details of the palace, however, we are much in the dark. There is no print of it in existence, so far as we have been able to discover; and almost all that is known about it prior to the Reformation is that it was allowed to fall into decay by Henry VIII.—most probably on account of the part which James had taken in siding with the French in the wars between the two countries.

In the reign of Elizabeth the palace had become a ruin; and upon the union of the Scottish and English crowns the *raison d'être* of the palace had ceased to exist. It was therefore dismantled, and partly demolished, its site being devoted to some of the offices of the Government, for which its proximity to Whitehall fitted it admirably.

Here John Milton lived whilst serving the Government of the Commonwealth, and acting as Latin Secretary to Oliver Cromwell, and here he lost an infant son. Here died, in the early part of the last century, that mixture of Hercules and Adonis, the eccentric "Beau Fielding," divorced from the notorious Duchess of Cleveland on the ground of bigamy, as being already the husband of the Dowager Countess of Purbeck. A full account of the career of Beau Fielding will be found in Nos. 50 and 51 of the *Tatler*, drawn by the pen of Sir Richard Steele.

Part of the remains of the Palace was, for many years, the official residence of the Surveyor of Works to the Crown. "Here," writes Mr. Peter Cunningham, "lived Inigo Jones; here died his successor, Sir John Denham, the poet of Cooper's Hill, and his successor again, Sir Christopher Wren; and here, in a fantastic house, immortalised by Swift in some ludicrous lines, lived Sir John Vanbrugh. The house of the latter was designed and built by himself, from the ruins of Whitehall, destroyed by fire in 1697."

Mr. Cunningham, in his "Life of Inigo Jones," tells us an anecdote of the great architect connected with this place, illustrative of the insecurity of the times: "Near his house in Scotland Yard, Inigo Jones, uniting with Nicholas Stone, the sculptor, buried his money in a private place. The Parliament published an order encouraging servants to

SCOTLAND YARD, ABOUT 1720.

inform of such concealments, and as four of the workmen were privy to the deposit, Jones and his friends removed it privately, and with their own hands buried it in Lambeth Marsh."

Sir John Vanbrugh, who died in 1726, was celebrated in his day not merely as an architect, but also as a comic poet and an accomplished man of letters. He was Comptroller of the Royal Works and Palaces, and his house between Scotland Yard and Whitehall, which he built for himself, was remarkable for its tiny dimensions. His friends called it a "pill-box," and Swift compared it to a goose-pie. The small size of his own house certainly was a fair object of ridicule when contrasted with the ponderous dimensions of the palace at Blenheim, and other designs by him. The epitaph on his tomb is witty and well known—

"Lie heavy on him, earth, for he
Laid many a heavy load on thee."

When he was made Clarencieux King-at-Arms Swift said he might now "build houses." The secret of this ridicule was that Vanbrugh was a Whig. Sir Joshua Reynolds has left the following high encomium on his merits as an architect :—"In the buildings of Vanbrugh, who was a poet as well as an architect, there is a greater display of imagination than we shall find, perhaps, in any other; and this is the ground of the effect we feel in many of his works, notwithstanding the faults with which many of them are charged. For this purpose Vanbrugh appears to have had recourse to some principles of the Gothic architecture, which, though not so ancient as the Grecian, *is more so to our imagination*, with which the artist is more concerned than with absolute truth. "To speak of Vanbrugh," adds Sir Joshua, "in the language of a painter, he had originality of invention, he understood light and shadow, and had great skill in composition. To support his principal object he produced his second and third groups in masses. He perfectly understood, in his art, what is the most difficult in ours, the conduct of the background, by which the design and invention are set off to the greatest advantage. What the background is in painting, in architecture is the real ground on which the building is erected; and no architect took greater care that his work should not appear crude and hard—that is, that it did not abruptly start out of the ground without expectation or preparation.

"This is a tribute which a painter owes to an architect who composed like a painter, and was defrauded of the due reward of his merit by the wits of his time, *who did not understand the principles of composition in poetry better than he, and who knew little or nothing of what he understood perfectly—the general ruling principles of architecture and painting.* Vanbrugh's fate was that of the great Perrault. Both were the objects of the petulant sarcasms of factious men of letters, and both have left some of the fairest monuments which to this day decorate their several countries—the façade of the Louvre, Blenheim, and Castle Howard."

It need scarcely be remarked here, in explanation of the allusion of Sir Joshua Reynolds, that Vanbrugh was almost as celebrated for his comedies as for his architecture. Rowe thus mentions him :—

"I'm in with Captain Vanbrugh at the present,
A most sweet-mannered gentleman and pleasant;
He writes your comedies, draws schemes and models,
And builds dukes' houses upon very odd hills.
For him, so much I dote on him, that I,
If I was sure to go to heaven, would die."

There was, in 1767–8, at the corner of Scotland Yard, opposite the Admiralty, a large house for which Josiah Wedgwood was in treaty, in order to establish a show-room or gallery of his pottery and porcelain at the West End; but, from some reason or other, the negotiation dropped through.

Here, too, was a celebrated coffee-house named "Well's," as appears from the following advertisement in Salisbury's *Flying Post*, preserved in the first volume of Malcolm's "Manners and Customs of London :"—"Whereas, six gentlemen (all of the same honourable profession), having been more than ordinarily put to it for a little pocket-money, did, on the 14th instant, in the evening, near Kentish Town, borrow of two persons (in a coach) a certain sum of money, without staying to give bond for the repayment; and whereas, fancy was taken to the hat, peruke, cravat, sword, and cane of one of the creditors, which were all lent as freely as the money: these are therefore to desire the said six worthies, how fond soever they may be of the other loans, to un-fancy the cane again, and send it to 'Well's' Coffee-house, in Scotland Yard, it being too short for any such proper gentlemen as they are to walk with, and too small for any of their important uses, and, withal, only valuable as having been the gift of a friend."

It was in Scotland Yard that a knight, Sir John Ayres, with the aid of four retainers, in a fit of ungrounded jealousy, waylaid Lord Herbert of Cherbury, whom he attacked with swords and daggers, though he did not succeed in wounding him, as we learn from that noble lord's "Life.

Early in the present century the Palace Court or Marshalsea was held in Scotland Yard. The court had jurisdiction of all civil suits within twelve miles of the palace. The process was short and not expensive, judgment being obtained in three weeks.

In 1829, on the formation of the new police, introduced by Sir Robert Peel to supersede the ancient "Charlies," Scotland Yard was made, as we have said, the principal station of the Metropolitan Force. The area under their jurisdiction (which excludes the City of London proper) extends from Cheshunt in the north to Chipstead in the south, and from Chadwell Heath in the east to Staines in the west. The Metropolitan Police district contains the whole of the county of Middlesex, and those parishes in the counties of Surrey, Hertford, Essex, and Kent of which any part is not more than fifteen miles in a straight line from Charing Cross, except the City of London and the Liberties. The force is also employed in Her Majesty's dockyards and military stations situated beyond the Metropolitan Police district, as well as on the Thames.

In 1896 the Metropolitan Police Force consisted of 15,271 men, made up of the Chief Commissioner, three Assistant-Commissioners, four Chief Constables, 32 superintendents, 592 inspectors, 1,870 sergeants, and 12,777 constables. The cost of maintaining this enormous force is about £1,720,000 a year, of which nearly £1,270,000 is absorbed by salaries and wages. The Police district consists of twenty-two divisions, each of them under the oversight of a superintendent, and each of them comprising sub-divisions in charge of inspectors. There are about 260 mounted officers, who patrol the outer sub-divisions and are also available for special duty at large gatherings, processions, &c. One of the most important of the agencies at New Scotland Yard is that known as the Criminal Investigation Department, which was organised in 1878 under a Director, and is now presided over by Dr. Anderson.

The office for cab licences and regulations, before its removal to Scotland Yard—it is now, of course, at New Scotland Yard—had been for many years located in Essex Street, in the Strand. We learn from a letter addressed to the Earl of Strafford in 1634, that "The Maypole" in the Strand was the place where the first stand of hackney carriages was established in London; the enterprising gentleman who introduced them to the public was a Captain Bailey—the same, it is supposed, who had served under Raleigh in one of his expeditions to Guiana. The following is an extract from the letter:—"He hath erected, acc^{g} to his ability, some four hackney coaches, put his men in livery, and appointed them to stand at 'The Maypole,' in the Strand, giving them instructions at what rates to carry men into several parts of the town, where all day they may be had. Other hackney men seeing this way, they flocked to the same place, and perform their journeys at the same rate, so that sometimes there is twenty of them together, which disperse up and down, so that they and others are to be had everywhere, as watermen are to be had at the waterside. Everybody is much pleased with it, for whereas before coaches could not be had but at great rates, now a man may have one much cheaper." A strange contrast these four hackney coaches of 1634 make to the thousands of hansoms and four-wheeled cabs which now ply for hire in the great metropolis!

The use of hackney coaches was but very trifling in 1626; for among the many monopolies granted by the king was one which gave rise to the use of sedan chairs in London. This grant was made to Sir Sanders Duncombe, who had probably seen them at Sedan, in France, where they were first made; it is expressed in the following terms:—"Whereas the streets of our cities of London and Westminster, and their suburbs, are of late so much encumbered with the unnecessary multitude of coaches that many of our subjects are thereby exposed to great danger, and the necessary use of carts and carriages for provisions thereby much hindered; and Sir Sanders Duncombe's petition, representing that in many parts beyond sea people are much carried in chairs that are covered, whereby few coaches are used among them; wherefore we have granted to him the sole privilege to use, let, or hire a number of the said covered chairs for fourteen years."

This patent was soon followed by a proclamation against hackney coaches, strictly commanding, "That no hackney coach should be used in the City of London, or suburbs thereof, other than by carrying of people to and from their habitations in the country; and that no person should make use of a coach in the City except such persons as could keep four able horses fit for his Majesty's service, which were to be ready when called for under a severe penalty."

That sedan chairs were in use in the East long before they were known in France or in London is clear from the fact that one is introduced in Sir G. Staunton's Embassy to China. And if a classical origin be sought for them, it is on record that Pliny states that his own uncle was accustomed to be carried abroad in a chair.

At the end of the seventeenth, and throughout the greater part of the eighteenth century, the sedan chair was the vehicle almost always employed by "the quality" at the West End in going backwards and forwards between each other's houses, and to Court. Even at the coronation of

William III. the peers and peeresses who desire to be present are desired, in the official programme, to come in chairs, carriages and coaches not being allowed on that day to approach the Abbey. At the coronation of George I. and George II. both were allowed.

Hackney coaches, superseding as they did the old "sedans," were, at first, often called "hackney chairs," the word *chaise* being a sort of equivalent for a "chair," and also for a "carriage." Thus, in his "Book for a Rainy Day," Mr. Smith remarks that in 1766 "hackney chairs were so numerous that their stands extended round Covent Garden, and often down the adjacent streets." Not only was the sedan chair one of the necessary social appliances of the London people in the early part of the present century, but the same may be said of the good old lumbering hackney coach. This genteel vehicle, in the natural order of events, like the heavy stage-coaches, has long ago become a thing of history. It is a sorry thing to reflect upon how the cherished objects of our youth pass away, and are superseded by modern inventions, to be in their turn associated with notions of antiquity in the minds of a generation of beings having new ideas and new habits.

Apropos of cabs and the police—or, rather, parliamentary regulations for the suppression of drunkenness—we may be pardoned for giving the following curious piece of information relating to the "Jarveys" of old, for which we are indebted to Walker's "Original:"—"I will add one more instance of change. A retired hackney-coachman, giving an account of his life to a friend of mine, stated that his principal gains had been derived from cruising at late hours in particular quarters of the town to pick up drunken gentlemen. If they were able to tell their address, he conveyed them straight home; if not, he carried them to certain taverns, where the custom was to secure their property and put them to bed. In the morning he called to take them home, and was generally handsomely rewarded. He said there were other gentlemen who pursued the same course, and they all considered it their policy to be strictly honest. The same calling is said to have been pursued for many years in Paris. The tariff for taking the drunkard home is—or was—ten sous; and his conductor was known as *L'Ange Gardien*."

Instead of a few dozens of chairs and hackney coaches, the people of London, writes Mr. Diprose, in his "Book about London," "are now daily whisked about the town in upwards of three thousand cabs and twelve hundred omnibuses, besides a fleet of river steamers. These conveyances annually carry more passengers than three times the number of the whole population of the United Kingdom." Since Mr. Diprose's book was published the number of public conveyances has, of course, greatly increased. There are now upwards of two thousand omnibuses, in addition to 1,100 tram-cars.

Hard by the north side of Scotland Yard, in a blind alley called Craig's Court, opening out of Charing Cross and backing upon what was once the western side of the garden of Northumberland House, is Harrington House, a dull, heavy, and gloomy mansion, belonging to the Earls of Harrington. Close by used to stand the "Northumberland" Coffee-house, one of Sheridan's favourite haunts.

Between Scotland Yard and the river-side in the rear was "Man's," or as it was sometimes styled, "Old Man's" Coffee-house; and another, possibly a rival one, known as "Young Man's." The former is said by Mr. Peter Cunningham to have been so called after the first keeper—one Alexander Man—and to have dated from the reign of Charles II. Defoe, in his "Journey through England," mentions them among the lesser though favourite coffee-houses of the day. "The Scots," he writes, "go generally to the 'British,' and a mixture of all sorts to the 'Smyrna.' There are also other little coffee-houses much frequented in this neighbourhood—'Young Man's' for officers; 'Old Man's' for stock-jobbers, paymasters, and courtiers; and 'Little Man's' for sharpers."

Whitehall Place, which we cross on our way to Middle Scotland Yard, was formed about the year 1820. It is a broad thoroughfare now connecting the Embankment with Whitehall, opposite the Admiralty. Here several of the houses are used as Government offices—such as those of the Woods, Forests, and Land Revenues; the Ecclesiastical Commissioners for England, and Church Estates Commissioners; Parks, Palaces, and Public Buildings; and Commissioners in Lunacy. Here, too, is the National Liberal Club, with the fine block of flats known as Whitehall Court adjoining it, and forming part of the design; while opposite is one of the fronts of the huge caravanserai known as the Hôtel Métropole.

A portion of Middle Scotland Yard used to be occupied by the Royal United Service Institution Museum, transferred in 1895 to what was the Chapel Royal, Whitehall. This building we shall describe when we come to Whitehall, but we may here give some account of the Museum, which comprises a splendid collection of arms and accoutrements, and models illustrative of the naval architecture of various nations. Two of the models are particularly worthy of notice—that of "The Field and Battle of Waterloo," by Captain Siborne; and "The South of the Crimea and Siege of Sebastopol," by Colonel Hamilton. A smaller model, but one of equal interest to the above, gives the visitor a clear idea of Nelson's last and greatest victory, the battle of Trafalgar. There is also a Chinese cabinet, and a variety of naval and military curiosities. Here the curious visitor may see, among the articles exhibited, the jaws of a shark enclosing a tin box. The history of this tin box is thus told by Mr. John Timbs:—"A ship on her way to the West Indies fell in with and chased a suspicious-looking craft, which had all the appearance of a slaver. During the pursuit the chased vessel threw something overboard. She was subsequently captured, and taken into Port Royal to be tried as a slaver. In absence of the ship's papers and other proofs, the slaver was not only in a fair way to escape condemnation, but her captain was anticipating the recovery of pecuniary damages against his captor for illegal detention. While the subject was under discussion, a vessel came into port which had followed closely in the track in the chase above described. She had caught a shark; and in its stomach was found a tin box, which contained the slaver's papers. Upon the strength of this evidence the slaver was condemned. The written account is attached to the box." In the armoury sections are many remarkable relics, which associate us with the great and perilous events in the history of our own and other countries. From the savage's war-dress of skin and feathers to the latest improvement in armour-plated vessels—from clubs and bows and arrows to the modern quick-firing gun, the development of war material may be traced through almost every stage. There are trophies of the Crimean War and of the last campaign in China, as well as of our "little wars" with savage tribes on our frontiers; and among the most recent acquisitions under this head are some interesting objects brought back by the last Ashanti Expedition (1895–96). Here also one may see pistols which belonged to Sir Ralph Abercromby, Bolwar, and Tippo Sahib; and swords which were once wielded by Cromwell and General Wolfe. One interesting relic of a by-gone system of naval warfare may be discovered in a piece of clockwork which formed part of the paraphernalia of an old-fashioned fire-ship. This mechanism was so contrived that at the end of a given time it would set fire to the vessel as it bore down on the enemy. Another means of accomplishing a somewhat similar result, though without any reference to the enemy, is shown in the nest of a family of rats, discovered on board the *Revenge*. These frugal creatures had laid by a store of matches, which ignited and set fire to the nest, the burnt remnant of which shows what a very narrow escape the vessel had from destruction. The gradual development of the lifeboat into its present form is shown in a very interesting series of models running back to a very primitive type, and an old suggestion for lessening the danger of the Goodwin Sands is embodied in the model of a floating refuge. Here, too, are kept the sad relics of the unfortunate expedition to the Arctic regions conducted by Sir John Franklin, discovered by Sir Leopold M'Clintock, of H.M.S. *Fox*, in 1859, and equally melancholy mementoes of the *Royal George*, which sank at Spithead in 1782—an event which moved Cowper to write the fine poem, "Toll for the brave." There are also personal relics of Drake, Nelson, Captain Cook, and other naval heroes. Soldiers and sailors in uniform are admitted to the Museum free; the fee to the general public is sixpence.

The Royal United Service Institution was established in 1831 to promote naval and military art, science, and literature by means of a library, the delivery of lectures, the exhibition of inventions, the publication of a journal, and the formation of a museum; and in 1860 it received a royal charter. The annual subscription is one pound, with an entrance fee of the like amount, and the sum of ten pounds, which includes the entrance fee, constitutes a member for life. It is now housed in a new building adjoining the Museum on the south, the foundation-stone being laid by the Prince of Wales as "Admiral of the Fleet and Field Marshal" in 1893. The structure includes a large library, a commodious lecture-hall, with smoking-room, &c.

At No. 3 in Whitehall Yard (now demolished) was the office of the Comptroller-General of the Exchequer, where was formerly held "The Trial of the Pyx," a ceremony of late years performed at the Hall of the Goldsmiths' Company, as described in page 357 of the first volume of this work.

In the course of the last century the greater part of what had been the "Private" or "Privy" Gardens of Whitehall Palace became gradually covered by the houses of favoured nobles, who obtained leases from the Crown at easy rents. "Among the first of these," says Pennant, "on the site of the small beer-cellar [of which a view is preserved in No. 4 of Hollar's prints of Whitehall], is the house of the Earl of Fife." Scotch to the backbone, the noble earl who built it was resolved, it would appear, that even when in London he would never tread on other than Scottish soil; and, therefore, when he embanked the river to form a terrace commanding the water, he ordered that all the gravel necessary to form it should be brought up from his native Fifeshire. Fife House in the last century was rich in curious relics of the past, and must have been well worth a visit. Lord Fife used to show with pride a collection of Gobelin tapestry, which he had brought from Paris, and a small but select gallery of paintings, including a portrait of Charles I. when Prince of Wales, which was painted by Velasquez at Madrid. In one of the walls of this house was an archway of the Tudor style which had a direct communication with the Palace or Privy Stairs at Whitehall.

A SEDAN CHAIR (*see page* 333).

Fife House was for some years occupied by the Earl of Liverpool during his premiership; and it was within its walls that he breathed his last, in the month of December, 1828. The house was pulled down about the year 1862, to make room for improvements. It had for a few years been used as the receptacle of the collection forming the East India Museum, which was removed hither on the demolition of the East India House in Leadenhall street. The contents of this Museum were afterwards removed to the new India Office in Charles Street. Here, close by, in 1835, lived the Right Honourable James Abercromby, before he became Speaker of the House of Commons; the last Lord Liverpool at the same time occupying Fife House, where his half-brother, the Premier, had died some seven years before.

Leading from the palace down to the river were two pairs of stairs — the one public, the other known as the "privy" stairs, for the use of the Court. The first was still in use in Pennant's time; "the other," says that writer, "is made up in the old wall adjacent to the house of the Earl of Fife, where the arch of the portal remains entire." Henry and his daughter Elizabeth, as we know, made by water such of their journeys and progresses as they did not make on horseback, though on some occasions they went mounted on a litter carried on men's shoulders. "Coaches," says Pennant, "had been introduced into England by Henry Fitzalan, Earl of Arundel, one of Elizabeth's admirers, but the spirited princess seems to have disdained their use. The author of "An Estimate of the Manners of the Times," published in 1758, asks, with reference to the Sedan chairs, of which we have spoken above, "How would he have been laughed at in the days of Elizabeth, when a great queen rode on horseback to St. Paul's, who should have foretold that in less than two centuries no

COACHES: REIGN OF QUEEN ANNE.

man of fashion would cross the street at the west-end to dinner, without the effeminate covering and conveyance of an easy chair?"

The last occasion on which Her Majesty went by state upon the Thames was in 1849, when she opened the new Coal Exchange in the City. On that occasion she embarked and landed on her return at Whitehall Stairs, as her proud predecessor Elizabeth had often landed before her. Since that year we believe that the royal barge has been allowed to slumber in its dry-dock, and the royal bargemaster and watermen have enjoyed a sinecure.

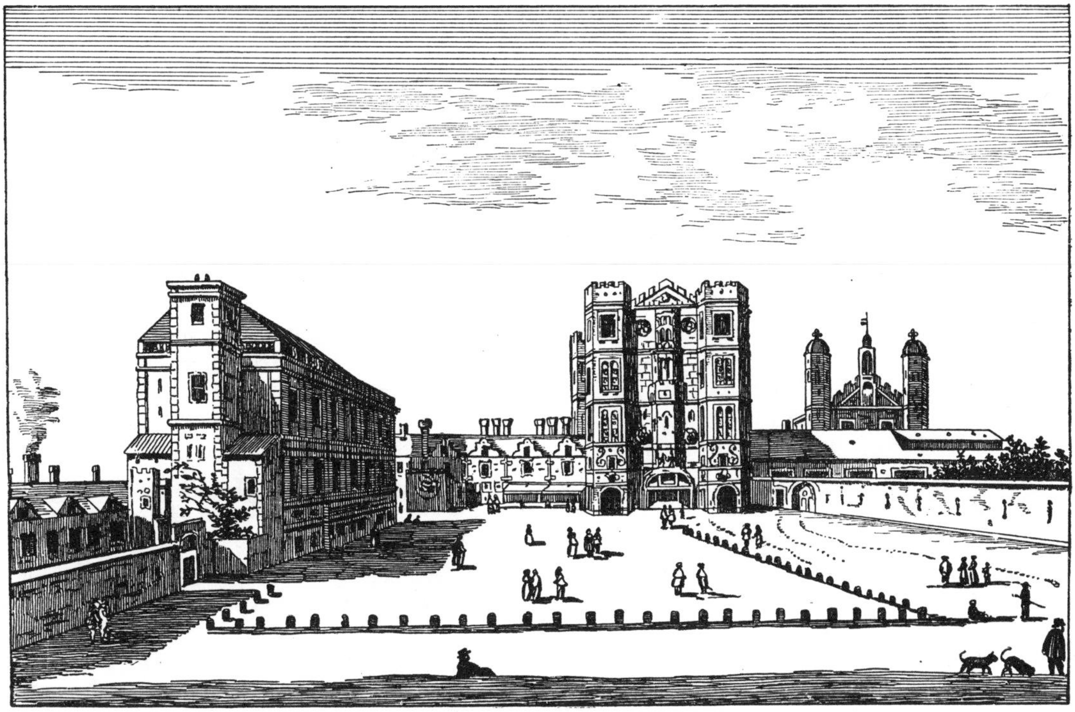

WHITEHALL ABOUT 1650. (*From a Copy by Smith of a Rare Print by Israel Silvestre.*)

CHAPTER XLII.

WHITEHALL.—HISTORICAL REMARKS.

"You must no more call it York Place—that is past;
For since the Cardinal fell that title's lost;
'Tis now the King's, and called Whitehall."
Shakespeare's Henry VIII., Act IV., sc. 1.

The most Polite Court in Europe—A School of Manners and Morals—Historical Account of Whitehall—Anciently called York Place—Name of York Place changed to Whitehall—Wolsey's Style of Living here—Visit of Henry VIII.—The Fall of Wolsey—Additions to the Palace by Henry VIII.—Queen Mary at Whitehall—The Palace attacked by Rioters—Tilting-Matches and Pageants—Queen Elizabeth's Library—The "Fortresse of Perfect Beautie"—Masques and Revels at Whitehall—The Office of "Master of the Revels"—The Tilt-yard—Charles Killigrew—Serving up the Queen's Dinner—Christian IV. of Denmark and James I.—The Gunpowder Plot—Library of James I. at Whitehall—George Villiers, Duke of Buckingham.

The moment that we pass out of the Strand, or make our way from the Victoria Embankment into Charing Cross, and wander either westwards through Spring Gardens into St. James's Park, or in a southerly direction past Whitehall towards the venerable Abbey of Westminster, we must feel, if we know anything of the history of our country under the Tudors and the Stuarts, that we are treading on ground which is most rich in historic memories. In fact, it may be said without fear of contradiction that the triangular space which lies between the new Palaces of Whitehall and St. James's, and the old Palace at Westminster, is holy ground, having been the scene of more important events in English history than all which have been witnessed by the rest of the two cities of London and Westminster together. It is to be hoped, therefore, that the following chapter will not be deficient in interest. Strange indeed would it be if it were, seeing that for all this part of

London, and for this period in the annals of Great Britain, we have the most abundant stores of material provided—not merely in the gossiping Diaries of Evelyn and Pepys, but in the memoirs and correspondence of scores of statesmen, courtiers, and writers, from the Augustan era of Queen Anne down to Sir Nathaniel Wraxall, the late Duke of Buckingham, and Lord William Lennox.

Nothing can be further from our purpose than to write a complete history—either topographical or biographical—of the Palace of Whitehall. To attempt to do so would be in effect to write the history of our Tudor and Stuart sovereigns; a task which has been so well done by Miss Lucy Aikin as to render it needless for us to attempt a rival account. Whitehall was, however, as Walpole tells us, "the most polite court in Europe;" and if it was not a school of morals, at all events it was a school of manners, such as would make a "fine gentleman" or "fine lady" of the age. And therefore a few brief sketches of the palace as Englishmen find it in the reigns of Henry VIII. and Elizabeth, of James I. and Charles I., may not be a task either impossible or unattractive to our readers. It is to be feared, however, that the standard of morality was not very high among the female part of the Court at Whitehall, at the close of the reign of Charles II. Macaulay, at all events, writes:—"In that court a maid of honour who dressed in such a manner as to do full justice to a white bosom, who ogled significantly, who danced voluptuously, who excelled in pert repartee, who was not ashamed to romp with lords of the bedchamber and captains of the guards, to sing sly verses with a sly expression, or to put on a page's dress for a frolic, was more likely to be followed and admired, more likely to be honoured with royal attentions, more likely to win a rich husband, than Jane Grey or Lucy Hutchinson would have been. In such circumstances the standard of female attainments was necessarily low, and it was more dangerous to be above that standard than to be beneath it. Extreme ignorance and frivolity were thought less unbecoming in a lady than the slightest tincture of pedantry. Of the too celebrated women whose faces we still admire on the walls of Hampton Court few indeed were in the habit of reading anything more valuable than acrostics, lampoons, and translations of the Clelia and the Grand Cyrus."

It is remarked in the "New View of London," published in 1708, that "heretofore there have been many courts of our kings and queens in London and Westminster, as the Tower of London, where some believe Julius Cæsar lodged, and William the Conqueror; in the Old Jewry, where Henry VI.; Baynard's Castle, where Henry VII.; Bridewell, where John and Henry VIII.; Tower Royal, where Richard II. and Stephen; the Wardrobe, in Great Carter Lane, where Richard III. [resided]; also at Somerset House, kept by Queen Elizabeth, and at Westminster, near the Hall, where Edward the Confessor, and several other kings, kept their courts. But of later times," continues the writer, "the place for the Court, when in town, was mostly Whitehall, a very pleasant and commodious situation, looking into St. James's Park, the canal, &c., on the west, and the noble river of Thames on the east; Privy Garden, with fountain, statues, &c., and an open prospect to the statue at Charing Cross on the north." With these few words of preface let us proceed.

Whitehall was known as York Place when in the possession of Cardinal Wolsey, with whose history the palace is so intimately connected. But long before that time it had been in lay hands. We read that it was erected on lands originally belonging to one Odo, a goldsmith, and that Hubert de Burgh, Lord Chief Justice of England under John and Henry III., and who gained himself a name in the Crusades, had a mansion on this very site; having purchased the latter from the Dean and Chapter of Westminster, to whom it had been previously given or bequeathed. He left his house, about the year 1240, to the monastery of Black Friars or Dominicans, whose principal abode at that time was in Holborn. They sold it to Walter de Grey, Archbishop of York, who settled it not on his family, but on his successors in that see, as their town residence, whence it was called York Place; and it was not until it passed out of their hands into those of King Henry—*how* is known to every reader of a child's first History of England—that it came to be known as Whitehall; a change of name which, if not duly "recorded at the Heralds' College," is, at all events, notified by Shakespeare in the lines quoted at the head of this chapter.

To give a detailed account of all the scenes which the Palace of Whitehall witnessed in its heyday and prime, when it was the favourite abode of our Tudor and Stuart sovereigns, would really be—as we have said—to write a history of the courts and cabinets of each successive monarch from the Reformation down to the Revolution—a task which would be impossible within the limits of this book, and foreign to the purpose which we have in view. But we cannot here, in justice to our subject, forbear the due encomium to Cardinal Wolsey. We do not attempt to defend his political character, or the arrogant means by which he supported it. But he made his greatness subservient to the improvement and decoration of his country. Christ Church, Oxford, and Hampton Court are existing monuments of his liberality; and the recollection that he exhibited at his palace at Whitehall of all that was exquisite in art, refined in taste, elegant in manners, and respectable in literature, should urge us, at the same time that we pity and regret the failings of this great minister, to applaud his public spirit, and give deserved honour to the greatness of his munificence.

The sumptuous style of living adopted by Wolsey here is known to every child who has read the History of England—how he formed his domestic establishment on the model of the royal court, ranging those under his roof under three classes, to each of which a separate table was assigned, including a company of young noblemen who were placed in his household in order to receive a polite education; how he was waited on by a *chef de cuisine* with a gold chain round his neck, by yeomen of the barge, by a master of the horse and sixteen grooms of the stable, and a tribe of secretaries, grooms, and yeomen of the chamber, amounting in all to nearly a hundred and fifty persons. Such was the proud state which "my Lord Cardinal of York" kept at Whitehall, and which in the end drew down upon him the envy and wrath of his sovereign.

Here Wolsey was visited by Henry not only privately, but also in state; and we find in Shakespeare graphic pictures of the ambitious cardinal, his sensual master, and the court manners of the period in which he lived. His gentleman usher, George Cavendish, also thus writes, in his "Life and Death of Thomas Woolsey," a work reprinted in the "Harleian Miscellany." The extract, though long, is worth preserving here as a picture complete in itself:—"He lived a long season ruling all appertaining to the King by his wisdom, and all other weighty matters of foreign regions with which the King of this realm had any occasion to intermeddle. All ambassadors of foreign potentates were always despatched by his discretion, to whom they had always access for their despatch. And when it pleased the King's Majesty, for his recreation, to repair unto the Cardinal's house, as he did at divers times in the year, at which times there wanted no preparations or goodly furniture, with viands of the finest sort that might be provided for money or friendship, such pleasures were then devised for the King's comfort and consolation as might be invented or by man's wit imagined. The banquets were set forth with masks and mummeries in so gorgeous a sort and costly manner that it was a heaven to behold. There wanted no dames or damsels meet or apt to dance with the maskers, or to garnish the place for the time with other goodly disports. Then was there all kind of music and harmony set forth, with excellent voices both of men and children. I have seen the King suddenly come in thither in a mask, with a dozen of other maskers, all in garments like shepherds, made of fine cloth of gold and fine crimson satin paned, and caps of the same, with vizors of good proportion of visnomy; their hairs and beards either of fine gold wire or else of silver, and some being of black silk: having sixteen torchbearers, besides their drums, and other persons attending upon them, with vizors, and clothed all in satin of the same colours. And at his coming, and before he came into the hall—ye shall understand that he came by water to the water-gate without any noise—where, against his coming, were laid charged many chambers, and at his landing they were all shot off, which made such a rumble in the air that it was like thunder. It made all the noblemen, ladies, and gentlemen to muse what it should mean coming so suddenly, they sitting quietly at a solemn banquet; under this sort:—First, ye shall perceive that the tables were set in the chamber of presence, banquet-wise covered, my Lord Cardinal sitting under the cloth of estate, and there having his service all alone; and then was there set a lady and a nobleman, or a gentleman and gentlewoman, throughout all the tables in the chamber on the one side, which were made and joined as it were but one table. All which order and device was done and devised by the Lord Sands, Lord Chamberlain to the King; and also by Sir Henry Guildford, Comptroller to the King. Then immediately after this great shot of guns the Cardinal desired the Lord Chamberlain and Comptroller to look what this sudden shot should mean, as though he knew nothing of the matter. They, thereupon looking out of the windows into Thames, returned again, and showed him that it seemed to them there should be some noblemen and strangers arrived at his bridge, as ambassadors from some foreign prince. With that quoth the Cardinal, 'I shall desire you, because ye can speak French, to take the pains to go down into the hall to encounter and to receive them according to their estates, and to conduct them into this chamber, where they shall see us, and all these noble personages, sitting merrily at our banquet, desiring them to sit down with us, and to take part of our fare and pastime.' Then they went incontinent down into the hall, where they received them with twenty new torches, and conveyed them up into the chamber, with such a number of drums and fifes as I have seldom seen together at one time in any masque. At their arrival into the chamber, two and two together, they went directly before the Cardinal, where he sat, saluting him very reverently; to whom the Lord Chamberlain for them said, 'Sir, forasmuch as they be strangers and can speak no English, they have desired me to declare unto your grace thus: they, having understanding of this your triumphant banquet, where was assembled such a number of excellent fair dames, could do no less, under the supportation of your good grace, but to repair hither, to view as well their incomparable beauty as for to accompany them at mumchance, and then after to dance with them, and so to have of them acquaintance. And, sir, they furthermore require of your grace license to accomplish the cause of their repair.' To whom the Cardinal answered that he was very well contented they should do so. Then the maskers went first and saluted all the dames as they sat, and then returned to the most worthiest, and there opened a cup full of gold with crowns and other pieces of coin, to whom they set divers pieces to cast at—thus perusing all the ladies and gentlemen; and some they lost, and of some they won. And thus done they returned unto the Cardinal with great reverence, pouring down all the crowns in the cup, which was about 200 crowns. 'At all,' quoth the Cardinal, and so cast the dice, and won them all at a cast, whereat was great joy made. Then quoth the Cardinal to my Lord Chamberlain, 'I pray you show them that it seemeth me that there should be amongst them some noble man, whom I suppose to be much more worthy of honour to sit and occupy this room and place than I; to whom I would gladly, if I knew him, surrender my place, according to my duty.' Then spake to them my Lord Chamberlain in French, declaring my Lord Cardinal's mind; and they, rounding him again in the ear, my Lord Chamberlain said to my Lord Cardinal, 'Sir, they confess that there is among them such a noble personage, whom, if your grace can appoint him from the other, he is content to disclose himself and to accept your place most worthily.' With that the Cardinal, taking a good advisement among them, at the last quoth he, 'Meseemeth the gentleman with the black beard should be even he.' And with that he arose out of his chair, and offered the same to the gentleman in the black beard with his cap in his hand. The person to whom he offered then his chair was Sir Edward Neville, a comely knight of a goodly personage, that much more resembled the King's person in that mask than any other. The King, hearing and perceiving the Cardinal so deceived in his estimation and choice, could not forbear laughing, but plucked down his vizor and Master Neville's also, and dashed out with such a pleasant countenance and cheer that all noble estates there assembled, seeing the King to be there amongst them, rejoiced very much. The Cardinal eftsoons desired his Highness to take the place of estate; to whom the King answered that he would go first and shift his apparel; and so departed and went straight into my Lord's bed-chamber, where was a great fire made and prepared for him, and there new apparelled him with rich and princely garments. And in the time of the King's absence the dishes of the banquet were clean taken up, and the tables spread again with new and sweet perfumed cloths, every man sitting still until the King and his maskers came in among them again, every man being newly apparelled. Then the King took his seat under the cloth of estate, commanding no man to remove, but sit still as they did before. Then in came a new banquet before the King's Majesty and to all the rest through the tables; wherein, I suppose, were served two hundred dishes or above, of wondrous costly meats and devices subtilly devised. Thus passed they forth the whole night with banqueting, dancing, and other triumphant devices, to the great comfort of the King and pleasant regard of the nobility there assembled."

It is hoped that this long quotation will be pardoned by the reader, on account of the graphic picture which it presents to his eyes of "the inner life of Whitehall" in the days of the eighth Henry.

It was at the "masque" above described that the fickle-minded monarch first cast his admiring eyes on the ill-fated Anne Boleyn. Within a few short months Whitehall Palace was the scene where Wolsey took a final leave of "all his greatness." The profusion of rich things—hangings of cloth of gold and of silver; thousands of pieces of fine holland; the quantities of plate, even of pure gold, which covered two great tables, all of which were seized by his cruel and rapacious master—are so many proofs of his amazing wealth, splendour, and pride. It was from Whitehall Stairs that the "great Lord Cardinal" entered his barge to be rowed to Esher, after his disgrace. As every reader of history knows, the Palace passed into the possession of the Crown upon the fall of Cardinal Wolsey. It was granted by Act of Parliament to Henry VIII. "because the old Palace nigh to the Monastery of

St. Peter is now, and has long before been in a state of ruin and decay."

Henry VIII. seems to have taken a delight in his buildings at Whitehall, to which he added many sumptuous apartments. He also formed a collection of pictures, to which considerable additions were made by the unfortunate Charles I. Henry, as a sovereign, shows a strange admixture of barbarity and culture; "his cruelty could not suppress his love of the arts; and his love of the arts could not soften his savage nature. The prince who, with the utmost *sang froid*, could burn Protestants and Catholics, take off the heads of the partners of his bed one day, and celebrate new nuptials on the next, had, notwithstanding, a strong taste for refined pleasures. He cultivated architecture and painting, and invited from abroad artists of the first merit." Accordingly he commissioned Holbein to build a new gate at Whitehall with bricks of two colours, light and dark alternately, and disposed in a tesselated fashion; but of this we shall have more to say in a future chapter.

In the reign of Edward VI., it appears, there was an outdoor pulpit or preaching-place in one of the court-yards of the palace; and here Bishop Latimer, after his release from the Tower, and also many others, were in the habit of preaching, "on Sundays and holidays, to the King and the Protector, while many of all ranks resorted thither." Owing to the delicate constitution of the young king, the Parliament was held at Whitehall on one occasion during his reign.

On the last day of September, 1553, soon after her accession, Queen Mary rode in great state from the Tower, through the City, to Westminster. "The citizens received her with such respect that on her alighting at the Palace at Whitehall she publicly thanked the Lord Mayor. On the following day she was crowned with the greatest magnificence. The Lord Mayor, attended by twelve of the chief citizens, officiated as chief butler; for which service the Mayor received a gold cup and cover, weighing seventeen ounces, as his fee."

Whitehall Palace was attacked by the rioters under Sir Thomas Wyatt, and from it Elizabeth was conveyed a prisoner to the Tower, by order of her sister Mary, who had kept her "in a kind of honourable custody."

Here Lord Brooke and Sir Philip Sidney took a chief part in the tilting-matches and other pageants by which the marriage of Queen Mary with Philip of Spain was enlivened. It was this Lord Brooke (see Vol. II., p. 549) who, though no mean scholar, and an able statesman, declared that he wished to be known to posterity only as Shakespeare's friend, Ben Jonson's master, and the patron of Lord Chancellor Egerton. In November, 1558, Elizabeth made the same royal progress in equal state, and amid even greater rejoicings than had ushered in the reign of her sister Mary.

In Elizabeth's time, it would appear, there were great doings at Whitehall on several occasions. Not only were tournaments instituted, but there were "revels and maskings, and various other mummeries." Queen Elizabeth, as every reader of history knows, was passionately fond of dancing; in this sport she would occupy herself on rainy days in her palace, dancing to the scraping of a tiny fiddle; and it is impossible not to admire her humour whenever a messenger came to her from her cousin, James VI. of Scotland; for Sir Roger Ashton assures us that, as often as he had to deliver any letters to her from his master, on lifting up the hangings he was sure to find her dancing, in order that he might be able to tell James, from his own observation, how little chance there was of his early succession to the throne.

Her library at Whitehall was well stored with books—not only in English and French, but in Greek and Italian; and her autographs show that she was skilful in penmanship. Among the other distinguished foreigners who visited her here was her lover, the Duc of Anjou, whom she received with every species of coquetry. On the 1st of January, 1581, was held in this yard "the most sumptuous tournament ever celebrated," in honour of the French commissioners sent over from France to propose the alliance. A banqueting-house, most superbly ornamented, was erected within its precincts, at the expense of more than fifteen hundred pounds. "The gallerie adjoining to Her Majestie's house at Whitehall," says Holinshed, in his "Chronicles," "whereat her person should be placed, was called, and not without cause, the Castell or fortresse of perfect Beautie!" "Romantic fooleries!" is the quiet remark of the antiquary Pennant; and it were well if every comment as terse as this were equally just. Though eight-and-forty years of age, the queen received every outward sign of flattery that the charms of fifteen could claim. The "fortresse of perfect Beautie" was assailed by Desire and his four foster-children. The combatants on both sides were persons of the first rank, and a regular summons was first sent to the possessor of the "Castell" with a song, of which this is a part:—

"Yield, yield, O yield, ye that this fort do hold,
Which seated is in Honour's spotless field:
Desire's great force no forces can withhold,
Then to Desire's desire, O yield, O yield!"

This ended, we are told that "two cannons were fired off, one with sweet powder, and the other with sweet water; and after these were stores of pretty scaling-ladders, and then the footmen threw floures and such fancies against the walls, with all such devices as might seem fit shot for Desire." In the end Desire was repulsed and forced to make submission; and thus ended an "amorous foolery" which the patient reader may find described at full length in Weldon's "Court of King James."

All Christmas plays were performed before the Court by the "children of the Chapel Royal;" and we read in Ben Jonson's Life that his *Cynthia's Revels* were put on this stage by those juvenile actors. We read also of a masque by Ben Jonson being performed at Whitehall by command of the Queen, who appeared in it herself, along with several of the ladies of her Court. Inigo Jones, it appears, contributed to the splendour of these masques, embellishing them with every grace and propriety of scenic decoration; at all events, Mr. Gerard writes to Lord Strafford: "Such a splendid scene built over the altar at Somerset House, 'The Glory of Heaven.' Inigo Jones never presented a more curious piece in any of the masques at Whitehall."

Whitehall, indeed, was the scene of many gorgeous entertainments, but none, perhaps, of its shows was more attractive than the magnificent masque got up by the Inns of Court, as "a mark of love and duty to their majesties," just at the time when Prynne, the sedition-monger, had published one of his scurrilous works. We read that in February, 1634, this masque was brought to Whitehall by the loyal barristers, who, as we know and have already explained, were of old addicted to such shows. Henry Lawes undertook the music; Inigo Jones was machinist; and Selden's antiquarian lore was called into request, in order to ensure accuracy in the costumes. The masque itself, entitled *The Triumph of Peace*, was from the courtly pen of Shirley. "At length the great day arrived. From Ely House, on Holborn Hill, the procession set forth down Chancery Lane. A hundred gentlemen of the Inns of Court, all splendidly mounted, were followed by an anti-masque of grotesque figures; then came four chariots, carrying in as many companies the masquers from the four inns. On their arrival at Whitehall *The Triumph of Peace* was acted at the Banqueting House. It was a comic allegory of the social pleasures of peace, ending with a gorgeous tableau, in which the other deities appeared, all grouped round the peaceful goddess Irene." The performance itself, which cost about £21,000, caused a perfect *furore*, and is often mentioned by writers of the time. A fortnight later Carew's masque, *The British Heaven*, was acted on the same boards at Whitehall—Lawes and Inigo Jones helping as before—by Charles I. himself, assisted by a dozen or so of his courtiers. In fact, the masque—as an intermediate step between the pastoral idyll, which is purely ideal, and the reality of the drama proper—at this time had become the favourite form which "private theatricals" assumed in the time of our last Tudor and our first Stuart sovereign, and its home was the Palace of White-

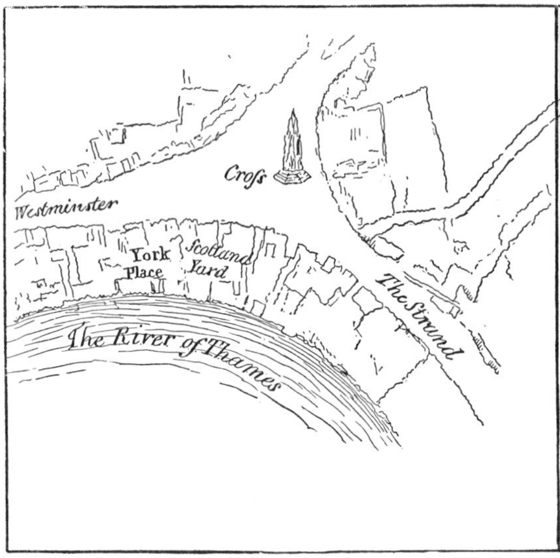

YORK PLACE.

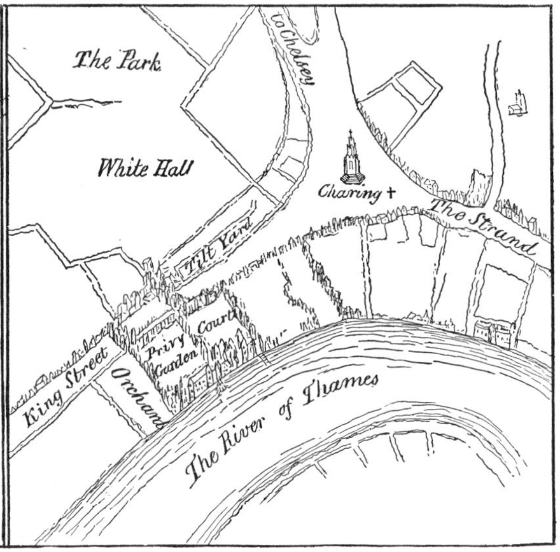

WHITEHALL IN THE REIGN OF HENRY VIII.

(*From two small Maps, printed with Fisher's Plan of Whitehall.*)

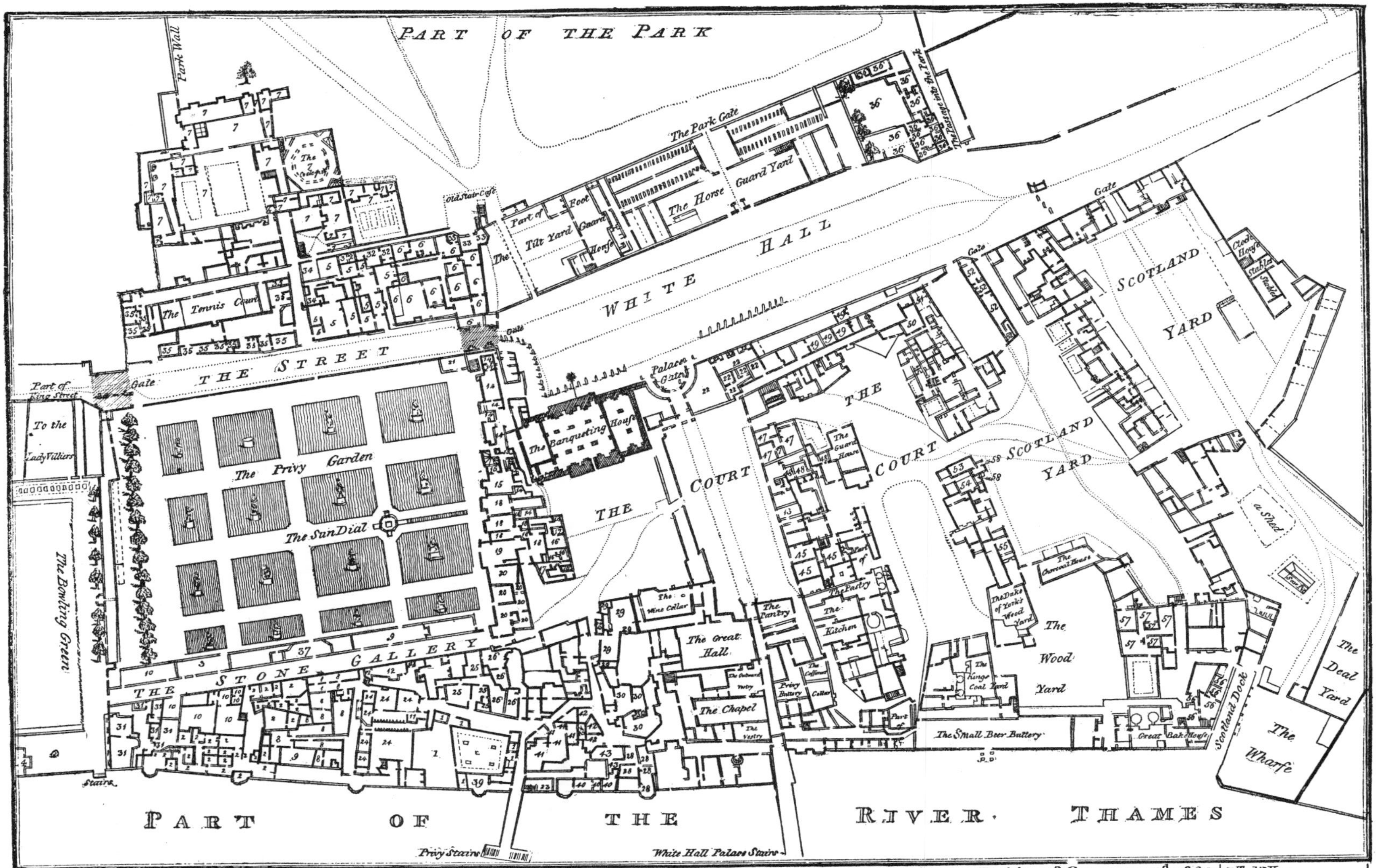

A reduced copy of FISHER'S GROUND PLAN of the *ROYAL PALACE of WHITEHALL*, taken in the Reign of CHARLES 2d. 1680.

1. Lodgings belon.g to his Majesty
2. To his Royal Highness.
3. His Highness Prince Rupert
4. The Duke of Richmond.
5. The Duke of Monmouth
6. The Duke of Ormond
7. The Duke of Albemarl
8. The Earl of Bath
9. The Earl of Lauderdale
10. The Lord Peterborough
11. The Lord Gerrard
12. The Lord Crofts
13. The Lord Belassis
14. The Lord Chamberlain
15. The Lord Keeper
16. The Council Office
17. Sir Edw.d Walker
18. The Treasury Chambers
19. The King's Laboratory & Bath
20. The Lord Arlington's Office
21. Sir Robert Murrey
22. The Wardrobe
23. Her Majesties Apartments
24. The Maids of Honor
25. The Countess of Suffolk
26. The Queen's Wardrobe
27. Mad.m Charlotte Killegrew
28. The Lady Arlington
29. The Lady Silvis
30. The Countess of Falmouth
31. M.rs Kirks.
32. Coun.ss of Castlemain's Kitchen
33. Colonel Darcy's
34. Sir Philip Killegrew
35. Captain Cook
36. M.rs Kirke
37. M.r Hyde
38. M.r Povey
39. M.r Chiffinch
40. Sir William Killegrew
41. Sir Francis Clinton
42. D.r Frazier
43. Father Patricks
44. To M.r Bryan
45. Sir Henry Wood
46. Sir George Carteret
47. The Officers of y.e Jewel Office
48. The Quarter Waiters
49. Sir John Trevors
50. To M.r Lightfoot
51. To M.r Vasse
52. To M.r Lisle
53. Sir Paul Neale
54. The King's Musick House
55. To M.r Early
56. To Sir Stephen Fox
57. To M.r Churchill

* The Spot where Charles I. was beheaded.

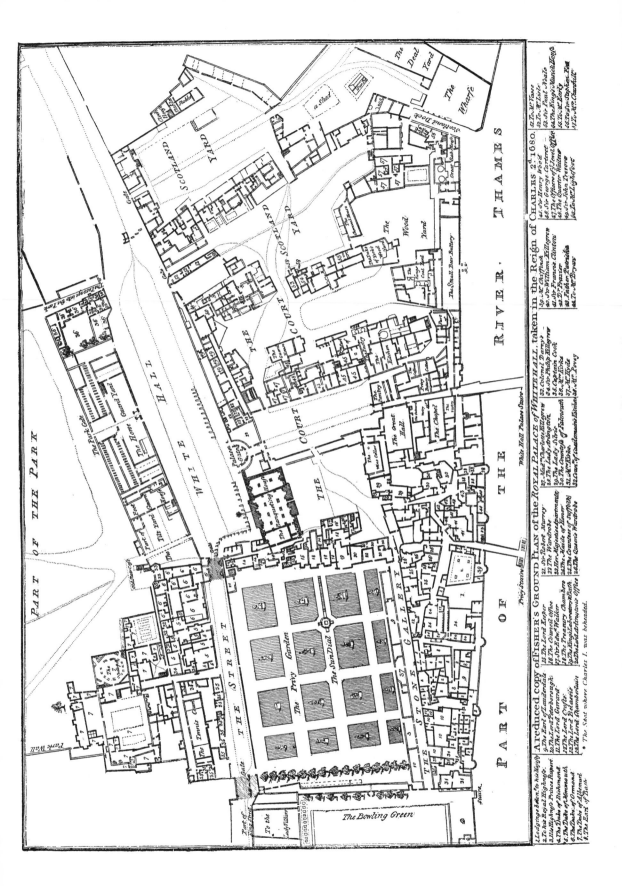

hall. The masque, as such, is styled by pleasant and witty Leigh Hunt "the only glory of King James' reign, and the greatest glory of Whitehall."

In the palace was a private theatre, with a little stage, the contrivance of Inigo Jones, whom Ephraim Hardcastle, in the *Somerset House Gazette*, does not hesitate to call "the father of scene-painting in England." Elegant masques were performed here by "his Majesty's servants," in the reign of James I. "These pieces," says Horace Walpole, "were sometimes composed at the command of the king in compliment to the nuptials of certain lords and ladies of the Court;" and he grows positively eloquent in their praise, as a "custom productive of much good, by encouraging marriage among the young nobility." Ben Jonson was the poet, Inigo Jones the inventor of the decorations, Laniere and Ferrabosco composed the symphonies, and the king, queen, and young nobility danced in the interludes. To such an extent was the splendour of these "shows" celebrated at the rival court of the Tuileries and Versailles that the same author asserts that they formed the model which was followed in the celebrated *fêtes* of Louis le Grand.

One of the officers of the Court was the "Master of the Revels," whose office was created in 1546, by Henry VIII.—a fitting compliment to the theory—we can hardly say the fiction—which made the stage-players of the date "his Majesty's servants." Mr. Frost, in his "Old Showmen of London," tells us that all the professors of the various arts of popular entertainment had to pay an annual licence duty to the Master of the Revels, whose jurisdiction extended over all wandering minstrels, and every one who blew a trumpet publicly, except (strangely enough) "the King's Players." The seal of his office, used under five sovereigns in succession, engraved on wood, was formerly in the possession of the late Mr. Francis Douce, by whose permission it was engraved for Smith's "Ancient Topography of London," where it may be seen. The legend round it was "SIGILL: OFFIC: *Jocor: Mascar: et: Revell: Dni: Regis.*

From the same authority (Frost's "Old Showmen of London") we learn that the office of Master of the Revels, which had been held by Thomas Killigrew, the Court jester, was conferred, at his death, on his son Charles. Concerning this son the *London Gazette* of 1682 has the following advertisement:—"Whereas, Mr. John Clarke, of London, bookseller, did rent of Charles Killigrew, Esq., the licensing of all ballad-singers for five years, which time is expired at Lady-day next; these are therefore to give notice to all ballad-singers that they take out licenses at the Office of the Revels, at Whitehall, for singing and selling of ballads and small books, according to ancient custom. And all persons concerned are hereby desired to take notice of and to suppress all mountebanks, rope-dancers, prize-players, ballad-singers, and such as make show of motions and strange sights, that have not a license in red and black letters, under the hand and seal of the said Charles Killigrew, Esq., Master of the Revels to His Majesty."

"The Tilt-yard adjoining the Palace," says Pennant, "was the delight of Queen Elizabeth, who was remarkable not only for the strength of her common sense and the violence of her disposition, but for her absurd and romantic vanity." Here, in her sixty-sixth year, "with wrinkled face, red periwig, little eyes, hooked nose, skinny lips, and black teeth," to use the phrase of Hentzner in his "Travels," she could drink in the flatteries of her favourite courtiers. Essex, by the lips of his "squire," here told her of her beauty and her worth; and a Dutch ambassador here assured her Majesty that he had undertaken the voyage to see her Majesty, who "for beauty and wisdom excelled all the other beauties in the world!"

In the collection of letters made by the late Mr. E. Lodge is one from Mr. Brackenbury to Lord Talbot, in which occurs the following passage, illustrative of Queen Elizabeth's love of her Tilt-yard:—"These sports were great, and done in costly sort, to Her Majesty's great lykinge . . . The nineteenth day, being St. Elizabeth's Day, the Erle of Cumberland, the Erle of Essex, and my Lord Burley dyd chaleng all comers, six courses apeace, which was very honourablye performed." The walls of the palace, however, if they had tongues, could tell some amusing stories of Elizabeth's passions and "tantarums;" for instance, in the same collection we read, in a letter from John Stanhope to Lord Talbot, "Thys night, God wylling, she [the queen] will go to Richmond, and on Saturday next to Somersett House; and yf she could overcome her passyon agst. my Lo. of Essex for his maryage no doubt she would be much the quyëter; yett she doth use ytt more temperately than was thought for, and (God be thanked) she *doth not strike all she thretes.*" Clearly she was a "hard hitter" when the Tudor blood within her was fairly roused.

The following account of the process of "serving up the queen's dinner" we take from Hentzner's "Travels in England," published in the reign of Elizabeth:—

"While the Queen was at prayers in the ante-chapel, a gentleman entered the room, having a rod, and along with him another who had a tablecloth, which, after they had both knelt three times with the utmost veneration, he spread upon the table, and after kneeling again, they both retired. Then came two others, one with the rod again, the other with a salt-cellar, a plate, and bread: when they had knelt as the others had done, and placed what was brought upon the table, they also retired, with the same ceremonies performed by the first. At last came an unmarried lady ('we,' says Hentzner, 'were told she was a countess'), and along with her a married one, bearing a tasting-knife; the former was dressed in white silk, who, when she had prostrated herself three times in the most graceful manner, approached the table, and rubbed the plates with bread and salt, with as much awe as if the Queen had been present. When they had waited there a little while, the yeomen of the guard entered, bare-headed, clothed in scarlet, with a golden rose upon their backs, bringing in at each turn a course of twenty-four dishes, served in plate, most of it gilt; these dishes were received by a gentleman in the same order they were brought, and placed upon the table, while the lady taster gave to each of the guard a mouthful to eat of the particular dish he had brought, for fear of any poison. During the time that this guard (which consists of the tallest and stoutest men that can be found in all England, being carefully selected for this purpose) were bringing dinner, twelve trumpets and two kettledrums made the hall ring for half an hour together. At the end of all this ceremonial, a number of unmarried ladies appeared, who, with particular solemnity, lifted the meat off the table, and conveyed it into the Queen's inner and more private chamber, where, after she had chosen for herself, the rest went to the ladies of the Court. The Queen dined and supped alone, with very few attendants, and it was very seldom that anybody, native or foreigner, was admitted at that time, and then only at the intercession of somebody in power."

Bishop Goodman, in his MS. "Memoirs of the Court of James I.," in the Bodleian Library at Oxford, tells us that it was Queen Elizabeth's constant custom, even to a late period of her reign, "a little before her coronation day," to come from Richmond to London, and to dine with the Lord Admiral (the Earl of Effingham), at his house at Chelsea, and then to set out from Chelsea, when it was "dark night," for Whitehall, where the Lord Mayor and aldermen met her. "All the way long from Chelsea to Whitehall," he adds, "was full of people to see her." The vain and silly queen appears to have liked to make these entries into London by night, because the torch-light did not reveal her wrinkles so clearly as the day. "In her yearly journeys," writes the bishop, "at her coming to London, you must understand that she did desire to be seen and to be magnified; but in her old age she had not only great wrinkles, but she had a goggle throat, with a great gullet hanging out, as her grandfather, Henry VII., is painted withal."

From and after the reign of Elizabeth the Court no longer oscillated between Greenwich, the Tower, and Westminster, moving about the goods and chattels of the Crown as occasion served. Though the Tower was still theoretically the seat of all the great attributes of royalty, and was sometimes occupied by the sovereign upon occasions of extraordinary solemnity, yet, from this time forth, Whitehall became the settled and fixed centre of courtly splendour and magnificence, so as soon to form a history of its own.

Lord Orrery, in a letter addressed to Dr. Birch, in November, 1741, observes, "I look upon anecdotes as debts due to the public, and which every man, when he has that kind of cash by him, ought to pay." It is with a strong feeling of the truth of this remark that we here introduce one or two anecdotes concerning the former occupants of Whitehall.

It is on record that in 1608, when Christian IV. of Denmark, brother of the queen of James I., came to London to visit his brother-in-law, both kings got drunk together, in order to celebrate their happy meeting. An account of their shameful debauch on this occasion, which may well make us blush for royalty, will be found in Mr. John Timbs's "Romance of London;" but, in mercy to the memory of James, we will not repeat its details here.

It was here that Lord Monteagle communicated to James I.'s ministers the singular letter which was the cause of the discovery of the Gunpowder Plot, and Guy Fawkes was examined in the king's bed-chamber.

John Evelyn describes the interior of the King's Library here with great minuteness:—"Sept. 2, 1680.—I had an opportunity, his Majesty being at Windsor, of seeing his private library at Whitehall at my full ease. I went with the expectation of finding some curiosities, but though there are about a thousand volumes, there were few of importance that I had not perused before. They consisted chiefly of such works as had been dedicated or presented to him, a few histories, some travels and French books, abundance of mapps and sea-chartes, entertainments, and pomps, buildings and pieces relating to the navy, and some mathematical instruments; but what was most rare were three or four Romish Breviaries, with a good deal of miniature and monkish painting and gilding, one of which is most excellently done, both as to the figures, grotesques, and compartments, to the utmost of that curious art. There is another, in which I find written by the hand of King Henry VII. his giving it to his deare daughter Margaret (afterwards Queen of Scots), in which he desires her to pray for his soule, subscribing his name at length. There is also the processe of the philosopher's great Elixir, represented in divers pieces of excellent miniature; but the discourse is in High Dutch, a MS. There is also another MS., in 4to, of above 300 yeares old, in French, being an 'Institution of Physicke,' and in the botanical parts the plants are curiously painted in miniature; also a folio MS. of good thicknesse, being the severall exercises, as Theames (*sic*), Orations, Translations, &c., of King Edward VI., all written and subscribed with his own hand very legible, and divers of the Greeke interleaved and corrected after the manner of schoolboys' exercises, and that exceedingly well and proper, and with some Epistles to his preceptor, which show'd that young prince to have been extraordinarily advanc'd in learning, and as Cardan (who had been in England) affirmed, stupendiously knowing for his age. There is likewise his Journal, no lesse testifying his early ripeness and care about affaires of state." A great part of this library, there is reason to fear, perished in the fire which destroyed the palace, as will be related in a following chapter.

Here George Villiers, afterwards Duke of Buckingham, came, when quite a young man, in the reign of James I., "to make his fortune at Court;" to which, it would seem, he brought nothing, if we may judge by what Lord Clarendon tells us, but good looks and personal graces. "He came to Whitehall," says his biographer, "in a reign when the Scots were as numerous there as the English," and was fortunate in finding a friend in Sir John Graham, who presented him to the king, in the hopes of so cutting out the other royal favourite, Somerset. In this he was successful, and young Villiers was made cupbearer to the king, and received the honour of knighthood "in the Queen's bed-chamber at Whitehall, with the Prince's rapier, and sworn one of the Gentlemen of His Majesty's Bedchamber." He next was promoted to the Mastership of the Horse, and other honours soon followed. Henceforth Villiers becomes the silly and pedantic king's "dear child and gossip, Steenie," and his Court history is interwoven with that of the walls of old Whitehall. The duke, it may be added, lived in greater pomp than any nobleman of his time, having six horses to his carriage, which, from its singularity, "made him the stare of the people, as did also his being carried about in a chair on men's shoulders;" the noise and exclamations against it were so great that the people would openly upbraid him in the streets, as the means of bringing men to so servile a condition as horses; but in a short time chairs became common, and the carrying of them was looked upon as a profitable employment—so various and fickle are the fancies of the time! In dress he was extravagant beyond precedent, for in a MS. in the Harleian library, quoted in Mr. Oldys' "Life of Raleigh," we read: "It was common with him at any ordinary dancing to have his cloaths trimmed with great diamond buttons, and to have diamond hatbands, cockades, and earrings, to be yoked with great and manifold knots of pearl—in short, to be manacled, fettered, and imprisoned in jewels, insomuch that at his going over to Paris, in 1625, he had twenty-seven suits of cloaths made, the richest that embroidery, lace, silk, velvet, gold, and gems could contribute; one of which was a white uncut velvet, set all over, both suit and cloak, with diamonds, valued at fourscore thousand pounds, besides a great feather stuck all over with diamonds; as were also his sword, girdle, hatband, and spurs." His entertainments to the king were also of the most sumptuous order; in them the good, easy James would take rather more than prudence dictated; for he was one of those who "never mixed water with his wine." When we mention Villiers travelling with six horses, we may as well add here that the "proud" Earl of Northumberland, Henry Percy, on his release from the Tower, where he had been confined after the conspiracy of Guido Fawkes, on hearing that Buckingham drove his coach and six —then a great novelty—ordered that if the king's favourite used six horses, eight should be put before his own, and drove these along the Strand to Westminster, passing, of course, along the fron of Whitehall.

CHAPTER XLIII.

WHITEHALL AND ITS HISTORICAL ASSOCIATIONS (*continued*).

"Parte aliâ lautas ædes, magna ātria regum
Cernere erit."

Charles I. and the Parliament—Cromwell and the Commonwealth—The King brought to Trial—Execution of Charles I.—The Site of the Execution—Andrew Marvell's Lines on the Occasion—Who was the Executioner of Charles I.?—The Actual Scene of the Execution—Pennant's Opinion—The King's Bearing—A Singular Coincidence—Who struck the Fatal Blow?—Varying Statements upon this Point.

When the Banqueting House of Whitehall was first erected, it was little thought that James was constructing a passage from it for his son and successor, Charles I., to the scaffold. It would be unpardonable to pass over an event of this magnitude slightly. Rapin has laid down what has been said for and against the proceedings of the Parliament in their quarrel with Charles I., which led to the establishment of the Commonwealth, and the whole question has been thoroughly investigated by more recent writers, with the impartiality that is characteristic of the new school of historians. Mr. Nightingale, in "The Beauties of England and Wales," describes the matter as follows, from a more partial point of view:—"The unfortunate monarch was evidently the prey of two contending parties: the Independents, whose descendants still survive in the various sects now called Calvinistic Methodists; and the Presbyterians, who are now risen or degenerated into the sects of Unitarians, Arians, and General Baptists. The first of these parties was bent on the king's destruction; the latter wished to save him, and eventually brought about the restoration of Charles II., though they could not succeed in saving the life of his father. The rebellious army had the support of the Independents; but it should not therefore be concluded that the king had the cordial support of the Presbyterians, whom nothing would satisfy but the abolition of the episcopacy, though they do not seem to have wished this at the expense of their monarch's life."

On the 28th of April, 1648, the House of Commons voted:—"1. That the government of the kingdom should be still by the King, Lords, and Commons. 2. That the groundwork for this government should be the propositions last presented to the king at Hampton Court. 3. That any member of the House should have leave to speak freely to any votes, ordinances, or declarations concerning the king, &c."

These votes did not at all accord with the designs of the Independents, who meant to abolish all kingly authority, and establish a Commonwealth; and who, although weak in the House, but strong in the field, contrived to prevent a reconciliation or treaty with the king till Cromwell should be sufficiently strong to allow them to act with the necessary vigour against their enemies—the Scots, the Royalists, and the Presbyterians. In the meanwhile Cromwell gained strength, and the Independents at length openly demanded "that the king be brought to justice, as the capital cause of all the evils in the kingdom, and of so much blood being shed." Every day gave new force to their designs, and new strength to their vengeance. They had possession of the king's person, and removed him, contrary to the instructions of the Parliament, to Hurst Castle, in Hampshire.

On the 19th of January, 1648-9, the king, who had in the meantime been removed from Hurst Castle to Windsor, was brought to St. James's. His trial was quickly hurried on, and on the 27th of January sentence of death was passed upon him. His Majesty was taken back to St. James's Palace, and the sentence was carried into effect three days afterwards upon a scaffold erected in front of the Banqueting House of Whitehall. Mr. J. H. Jesse thus minutely describes the last sad scene:—

"Colonel Hacker having knocked at his door and informed him that it was time to depart, Charles took Bishop Juxon by the hand, and bidding his faithful attendant Herbert to bring with him his silver clock, intimated to Hacker, with a cheerful countenance, that he was ready to accompany him. As he passed through the Palace Garden into the Park, he inquired of Herbert the hour of the day, bidding him at the same time keep the clock for *his* sake. The procession was a remarkable one. On each side of the king marched a line of soldiers, while before him and behind him were a guard of halberdiers, their drums beating and colours flying. On his right hand was Bishop Juxon, and on his left hand Colonel Tomlinson, both bareheaded. There is a tradition that during his walk he pointed out a tree, not far from the entrance to Spring Gardens, which he said had been planted by his brother Henry. He was subjected to more than one annoyance during his progress. On reaching the spot where the Horse Guards now stand, Charles ascended a staircase which then communicated with Whitehall Palace, and passing along the famous gallery which at that time ran across the street, was conducted to his usual bedchamber, where he remained till summoned by Hacker to the scaffold."

"This day," according to a contemporary MS., "his Majesty died upon a scaffold at Whitehall. His children were with him last night. To the Duke of Gloucester he gave his 'George;' to the Lady Elizabeth his ring off his finger. He told them his subjects had many things to give *their* children, but that was all he had to give them. This day, about one o'clock, he came from St. James's in a long black cloak and grey stockings. The Palsgrave came through the Park with him. He was faint, and was forced to sit down and rest in the Park. He went into Whitehall the usual way out of the Park, and so came out of the Banqueting House upon planks, made purposely to the scaffold. He was not long there, and what he spoke was to the two bishops, Dr. Juxon and Dr. Morton. To Dr. Juxon he gave his hat and cloak. He prayed with them, walked twice or thrice about the scaffold, and held out his hands to the people. His last words, as I am informed, were, 'To your power I must submit, but your authority I deny.' He pulled his doublet off, and kneeled down to the block himself. When some officer offered to unbutton him, or some such like thing, he thrust him from him. Two men, in vizards and false hair, were appointed to be his executioners. Who they were is not known. Some say he that did it was the common hangman; others, that it was one Captain Foxley, and that the hangman refused. The Bishop of London had been constantly with him since sentence was given. Since he died they

QUEEN ELIZABETH. (*From the Portrait by Zucchero*, 1575.)

have made proclamation that no man, upon pain of I know not what, shall presume to proclaim his son Prince Charles as King; and this is all I have yet heard of this sad day's work."

It has often been denied that the *front* of Whitehall was the actual scene of the execution of King Charles I. But the fact that the sad scene was witnessed by Archbishop Usher from the roof of Wallingford House, which stood on the spot now occupied by the Admiralty, establishes the precise locality. "The Archbishop," says his biographer, "lived at my Lady Peterborough's house, near Charing Cross; and on the day that King Charles was put to death he got upon the leads, at the desire of some of his friends, to see his beloved sovereign for the last time. When he came upon the leads the King was in his speech; he stood motionless for some time, and sighed, and then, lifting up his tears to heaven, seemed to pray very earnestly. But when his Majesty had done speaking, and had pulled off his cloak and doublet, and stood stripped in his waistcoat, and that the villains in vizards began to put up his hair, the good Bishop, no longer able to endure so horrible a sight, grew pale and began to faint; so that if he had not been observed by his own servant and others that stood near him, he had fainted away. So they presently carried him down and laid him upon his bed." The warrant for the execution, too, expressly commanded that the bloody deed should take place "in the open street before Whitehall." Mr. J. W. Croker denied that this was the actual scene, on the ground that "the street in front of the Banqueting House did not then exist." The contemporary prints, however, show that Croker was in error in this assertion, for the high road from Charing Cross to Westminster ran then, as now, under the very windows of the Banqueting Hall. Mr. J. H. Jesse confirms, by the evidence of his own eyes, the assertion of George Herbert (who attended the king to the last), that "a passage was broken through the wall by which the king passed unto the scaffold." He writes:—

OLD VIEW OF WHITEHALL YARD. (*See page* 335.)

"Having curiosity enough to visit the interior of the building, the walls of which were then [at the renovation of the Banqueting House] laid bare, a space was pointed out to the writer between the upper and lower centre windows, of about seven feet in height and four in breadth, the bricks of which presented a broken and jagged appearance, and the brickwork introduced was evidently of a different date from that of the rest of the building. There can be little doubt that it was through this passage that Charles walked to the fatal stage."

Pennant confirms the circumstantial account given above, stating that the passage broken in the wall in order to make a passage for Charles to the scaffold still remained when he wrote, forming the door to a small additional building of later date.

It is on record, and attested on all hands, that the king walked to the scaffold with a cheerful countenance and a firm and undaunted step, as one who was convinced that he died in a good cause and with a good conscience. Thus it comes to pass that one who certainly was no partisan of Charles I., or an advocate of the "divine right of kings," Andrew Marvell, penned such lines as these:

"While round the armèd bands
Did clasp their bloody hands,
He nothing common did, or mean,
Upon that memorable scene,
Nor called the gods, with vulgar spite,
To vindicate his hopeless right;
But with his keener eye
The axe's edge did try;
Then bowed his kingly head
Down, as upon a bed."

In a rare book, called "Gleanings," by R. Groves, published in 1651, we find noticed the following coincidence, which is certainly singular, if true:—"King Charles was beheaded in that very place where the first blood was shed in the beginning of our late troubles; for a company of the citizens returning from Westminster, where they had been petitioning quietly for justice, were set upon by some of the Court as they passed Whitehall: in the which tumult divers were hurt and one or more were slain just by the Banqueting House, in the place where stood the scaffold on which he suffered. 'Tis further remarkable," adds the writer, "that he should end his days in a tragedie at the Banqueting House, where he had seene and caused many a comedy to be acted on the Lord's Day."

"By a signal providence," says Wheatley, "the bloody rebels chose that day for murdering their king on which the history of our Saviour's sufferings (Matt. xxvii.) was appointed to be read as a lesson. The blessed martyr had forgot that it came in the ordinary course; and therefore, when Bishop Juxon (who read the morning office immediately before his martyrdom) named this chapter, the good prince asked him if he had singled it out as fit for the occasion: and when he was informed it was the lesson for the day, could not without a simple complacency and joy admire how suitably it concurred with his circumstances."

In this day, even those who hold that the execution of the king was unjustifiable are not likely to go so far as to endorse the exaggerated sentiments of the following epitaph, which we find in the "Eikon Basilike," published in 1648, when the irritation against the regicides was at its highest pitch:—

"So falls the stately cedar; while it stood,
That was the onely glory of the wood;
Great Charles, thou earthly god, celestial man,
Whose life, like others, though it were a span,
Yet in that span was comprehended more
Than earth hath waters, or the ocean shore;
Thy heavenly virtues angels should rehearse,
It is a theam too high for humane verse.
Hee that would know thee right, then let him look
Upon thy rare-incomparable book,
And read it or'e and or'e, which if he do,
Hee'll find thee king, and priest, and prophet too,
And sadly see our losse, and though in vain,
With fruitlesse wishes, call thee back again.
Nor shall oblivion sit upon thy herse,
Though there were neither monument nor verse.
Thy suff'rings and thy death let no man name;
It was thy glorie, but the kingdom's shame."

A question has often been asked, who was the executioner of Charles I.? We do not mean, who were the men at whose bidding the deed was done?—for their names have all come down to posterity as those of "the regicides"—but, whose hand actually dealt the blow? There are undoubtedly very strong reasons for believing that it was Richard Brandon, a resident in Rosemary Lane, the entry of whose death occurs in the register of St. Mary's, Whitechapel, under date June 21st, 1649.* To the entry is appended a note, evidently of about the same date, to the effect that "this R. Brandon is supposed to have cut off the head of Charles the First." This man is stated to have been the son of Gregory Brandon, who beheaded Lord Strafford, and may therefore be said to have claimed the gallows as his inheritance. Besides, in the "Confessions of Richard Brandon, the Hangman" (1649), we meet with the following passage:—"He [Brandon] likewise confessed that he had thirty pounds for his pains, all paid him in half-crowns within an hour after the blow was given, and that he had an orange stuck full of cloves and a handkercher out of the king's pocket, so soon as he was carried from the scaffold, for which orange he was proffered twenty shillings by a gentleman in Whitehall, but refused the same, and afterwards sold it for ten shillings in Rosemary Lane." If this indeed be true, it follows that the man who struck the fatal blow did not long survive the deed. He was buried in Whitechapel churchyard; and it was with

* See Vol. II., p. 143.

great difficulty that his interment was effected, so strong was the popular loathing against him. Various authorities, however, at different times, have charged with the deed Dun (styled in one of Butler's poems "Squire Dun"), Gregory Brandon, William Walker, Richard Brandon, Hugh Peters, Colonel Joyce, William Hewlett, and lastly, Lord Stair. Against some of these the accusation is utterly groundless. According to Sir Nathaniel Wraxall, George Selwyn, "that insatiable amateur of executions," told the story of King Charles's execution from information which he professed to have obtained from the Duchess of Portsmouth, who, he said, "always asserted, on the authority of Charles the Second, that the king, his father, was not beheaded by either Colonel Joyce or Colonel Pride, as was then commonly believed; but that the real name of the executioner was *Gregory* Brandon; that this man had worn a black crape stretched over his face, and had no sooner taken off the king's head than he was put into a boat at Whitehall Stairs, together with the block, the black cloth that covered it, the axe, and every other article that had been stained with the royal blood. Being conveyed to the Tower, all the implements used in the decapitation had been immediately reduced to ashes. A purse containing one hundred broad pieces of gold was then delivered to Brandon, and he was dismissed. He survived the transaction many years, but divulged it a short time before he died. This account," Wraxall adds, "as coming from the Duchess of Portsmouth, challenges great respect."

By Lilly's Life it would appear that the man who acted as the executioner of Charles I. was Lieut.-Colonel Joyce; but whether it was Joyce's or Brandon's hand that shed the king's blood, it is impossible to say with absolute certainty, and the question must be classed with the many that have to be regarded as insoluble.

CHAPTER XLIV.

WHITEHALL AND ITS HISTORICAL ASSOCIATIONS (*continued*).

"Lucent genialibus altis
Aurea fulcra toris, epulæque ante ora paratæ
Regifico luxo."—*Virg. Æn.* vi.

A Singular Prophecy—The Ill-fated Bust of Charles I.—Charles I. as a Patron of the Fine Arts—Relics of the "Martyr King"—"Touching" for the King's Evil—Anecdote of "Archy," the King's Jester, and Archbishop Laud—The Restoration of Charles II.—Charles II. and Lady Castlemaine—Loose Life of the Court—Catharine of Braganza—Dr. South and Lord Lauderdale—Visits of John Evelyn to Whitehall—Sir William Penn—The Duke of Monmouth—The Last Hours and Death of Charles II.—The Last of the Stuarts—Whitehall as the Focus of Political Intrigue, and the Chief Staple of News—Serious Conflagrations at Whitehall.

MANY are the tales and anecdotes to which the life and death of King Charles gave rise, but among them, perhaps, few are more singular than the subjoined "prophecy," referred to by Howell in a letter to Sir Edward Spencer, dated February 20th, 1647-8:—"Surely the witch of Endor is no fable; the burning Joan of Arc at Rouen, and the Marchioness d'Ancre, of late years, in Paris, are no fables: the execution of Nostradamus for a kind of witch, some fourscore years since, who, among other things, foretold that the '*Senate of London will kill their King.*'"

Mr. Timbs, in his "Romance of London," relates a strange story of the ill-fated bust of Charles I. carved by Bernini, on the authority of a pamphlet on the character of Charles I., by Zachary Grey, LL.D.:—"Vandyke having drawn the king in three different faces—a profile, three-quarters, and a full face—the picture was sent to Rome for Bernini to make a bust from it. He was unaccountably dilatory in the work; and upon this being complained of, he said that he had set about it several times, but there was something so unfortunate in the features of the face that he was shocked every time he examined it, and forced to leave off the work; and if there was any stress to be laid on physiognomy, he was sure the person whom the picture represented was destined to a violent end. The bust was at last finished, and sent to England. As soon as the ship that brought it arrived in the river, the king, who was very impatient to see the bust, ordered it to be carried immediately to Chelsea. It was conveyed thither, and placed upon a table in the garden, whither the king went with a train of nobility to inspect the bust. As they were viewing it, a hawk flew over their heads with a partridge in its claws which he had wounded to death. Some of the partridge's blood fell upon the neck of the bust, where it remained without being wiped off. This bust was placed over the door of the king's closet at Whitehall, and continued there until the palace was destroyed by fire."

It is generally stated that Charles I. showed him self a most liberal patron of the arts. That this may have been true to some extent, cannot be doubted; but it may be desirable here to record the fact that among the State Papers there is, or was some years ago, a long bill sent in by Vandyke, for work done, and docketed by the king's own hand. The picture of his Majesty dressed for the chase, for which Vandyke charged £200, is assessed by the King at £100 instead, and in many other instances there is even a greater reduction made. Other pictures the King marked with a cross, which is explained by a note at the back by Endymion Porter, to the effect that as they were to be paid for by the Queen, his Majesty had left them for his wife to reduce at her own pleasure.

It may be added that, in spite of having done so much work for royalty, Vandyke died poor, and that his daughter was allowed a small pension—which, by the way, was most irregularly paid—on account of sums owing to her father's estate by Charles I. We are accustomed to rank Charles II. with bad paymasters, but it is to be feared that his father obtained his reputation as an art patron at much too cheap a rate.

It is also stated that King Charles I. possessed numerous portraits, drawn by Holbein, of several personages of the Court of Henry VIII., from the highest down to Mrs. Jack or Jackson, the nurse of King Edward VI. These drawings, it is said, the King exchanged for a single picture; but how they came back into the possession of the Crown is not clear. Mr. J. T. Smith, in his "Book for a Rainy Day," says that they were discovered at Kensington Palace, and taken from their frames and bound in two volumes. It would be interesting to know whether they are still in existence.

A vignette of the Bible used by King Charles I. upon the scaffold, and presented by him to Dr. Juxon, the Bishop of London, who attended him in his last moments, will be found in Smith's "Historical and Literary Curiosities."

The shirt, stained on the wrist with some drops of blood, in which Charles I. was beheaded, also his watch, which he gave at the place of execution to Mr. John Ashburnham, his white silk drawers, and the sheet that was thrown over his body, were long preserved in the vestry of Ashburnham Church, in Sussex, having been, as the "Beauties of England and Wales" informs us, "bequeathed, in 1743, by Bertram Ashburnham, Esq., to the clerk of the parish and his successors for ever, to be exhibited as curiosities." These relics of the "martyr king," we may add, have somehow found their way back into the hands of the Ashburnham family, and are now very carefully preserved at Ashburnham Place, the seat of the earls of that name. This mansion was built by John Ashburnham, who was "page of the bed-chamber" to both Charles I. and Charles II., and who died in 1671. He attended his sovereign to the last, till he fell on the scaffold, and thus obtained possession of the articles worn by the king on that mournful occasion. Horsfield tells us that "the superstitious of the last, and even of the present age, have occasionally resorted to these relics for the cure of the king's evil."

With reference to the supposed efficacy of the touch of royalty in curing diseases, we may state that, under the Stuarts, there might be seen in the gazettes occasional advertisements announcing when and where a gracious king would next cure his subjects of scrofula by a touch of his royal finger. As may readily be supposed, the Palace at Whitehall was the place most frequently chosen for the "touching" or the "healing" Here is one of the notices issued by command of Charles I.:—"Whitehall, May 16, 1644.—His Sacred Majesty having declared it to be his Royal will and purpose to continue the healing of his people for the Evil during the month of May, and then to give over till Michaelmas next, I am commanded to give notice thereof, that the people may not come up to town in the interim, and lose their labour."

Charles II. is said to have "touched" 92,000 people for the king's evil—about twenty a day for his whole reign. The practice was continued by James II., for Evelyn, in his "Diary," under date of 1687, writes, "I saw his Majesty touch for the evil." The word "touching" gives us a most inadequate idea of the deliberate solemnity of this ceremonial in the days of the Stuarts. Imagine the king seated in a chair of state upon his throne, under a rich canopy, in a spacious hall of the palace. Each surgeon led his patients in turn to the foot of the throne, where they knelt, and while a chaplain in full canonicals intoned the words, "He put His hands upon them and healed them," the king stroked their faces with both hands at once. When all had been thus "touched," they came up to the throne again in the same order, and the king hung about the neck of each, by a blue ribbon, a golden coin, while the chaplain chanted, "This is the true Light who came into the world." And the whole concluded with the reading of the epistle for the day and prayers for the sick.

The following description of the process of "touching" for the king's evil we take from Oudert's MS. Diary:—"A young gentlewoman, Elizabeth Stephens, of the age of sixteen, came to the Presence Chamber in 1640, to be 'touched for the Evil,' with which she was so afflicted that, by her own and her mother's testimony, she had not seen with her left eye for above a month. After prayers read by Dr. Sanderson, she knelt down to be 'touched,' with the rest, by the King. His Majesty then touched her in the usual manner, and put a ribbon with a piece of money hanging to it about her neck. Which done, his Majesty turned to the Duke of Richmond, the Earl of Southampton, and the Earl of Lindsey, to discourse with them. And the young gentlewoman said of her own accord, openly, 'Now, God be praised, I can see of this sore eye,' and afterwards declared that she did see more and more by it, and could by degrees endure the light of the candle." The Bourbon kings of France were supposed to possess a like power of healing, in virtue of their descent from St. Louis. On the day after their coronation at Rheims they went in procession to the Abbey of St. Rémy, in that city, in the garden of which convent they touched all those afflicted with the evil that were brought to them, making the sign of the cross with their fingers on the forehead of the sick person, saying, "Le Roi vous touche; Dieu vous guérisse."

The form of prayer for the healing, we may add, is still to be seen in old Prayer-books, bound up with the rest of the occasional services. It was not dropped out till the reign of George I.

A capital story is told about "Archy," the king's fool, and Archbishop Laud, in connection with the Court of Whitehall. It is thus told in "The Book of Table Talk," published by Charles Knight:—"When news arrived from Scotland of the bad reception which the king's proclamation respecting the Book of Common Prayer had met with there, Archibald, the king's fool, happening to meet the Archbishop of Canterbury, who was going to the council-table, said to his grace, 'Wha's feule now? doth not your grace hear the news from Striveling about the Liturgy?" But the poor jester soon learned that Laud was not a person whom even his jester's coat and privileged folly permitted him to tamper with. The primate immediately laid his complaint before the Council. How far it was attended to, the following order of Council, issued the very day on which the offence was committed, will show:—'At Whitehall, the 11th of March, 1637. It is this day ordered by his Majesty, with the advice of the Board, that Archibald Armstrong, the King's Fool, for certain scandalous words of a high nature spoken by him against the Lord Archbishop of Canterbury his Grace, and proved to be uttered by him by two witnesses, shall have his coat pulled over his head and be discharged of the King's service and banished the Court; for which the Lord Chamberlain of the King's household is prayed and required to give order to be executed.' And immediately the same was put into execution." Thus was poor Archy degraded and dismissed from his Majesty's service. "What was this," asks Leigh Hunt, "but to say that the fool was fool no longer? 'Write me down an ass,' says 'Dogberry,' in the comedy. 'Write down that Archy is no fool,' says King Charles in Council. 'He has called the Archbishop one; and therefore we are all agreed, his Grace included, that the man has proved himself to be no longer entitled to the appellation.'" Archy, it appears, had on a previous occasion, when called upon to say grace before meat, incurred the displeasure of Archbishop Laud, by saying, "Great laud to the king, and little Laud to the devil."

In a pamphlet printed in 1641, entitled "Archy's Dream: sometime Jester to His Majestie, but exiled the Court by Canterburie's malice, with a relation for whom an odde chair stood void in hell," the following reason is given for Archy's banishment from Court:—"A certain nobleman asking him what he would do with his handsome daughters, he replied that he knew very well what to do with *them*, but he had sons whom he knew not what to do with; he would gladly make scholars of them, but that he feared the archbishop would cut off their ears."

In the "Strafford Letters" will be found, as Mr. Jesse reminds us in his work on "London," several interesting notices of Archbishop Laud passing between his palace at Lambeth and the royal palace at Whitehall. For example, in one of his letters to the earl, alluding to his health as not so good as it was formerly, he expresses a regret that "in consequence of his elevation to the see of Canterbury he has now simply to glide across the river in his barge, when on his way either to the Court or the Star Chamber; whereas, when Bishop of London, there were five miles of rough road between Fulham Palace and Whitehall, the jolting over which in his coach he describes as having been very beneficial to his health."

On his restoration, May 29th, 1660, King Charles II. was brought back hither "in military fashion" through London, by way of the Strand, "all the streetes and windows even to Whitehall being replenished with innumerable people of all conditions." It must have been indeed a gay sight to have seen the king returning to the palace of his ancestors, and the demonstrations of joy on the occasion are described as having been extravagant in the extreme. Space will not permit us to enter into the details of the enthusiastic reception on the part of the Londoners, or of the seven hours' ride through the streets to Whitehall; all this will be found described with picturesque minuteness in the pages of Sir Edward Walker's "Manner of the Most Happy Return in England of our most gracious Sovereign Lord, King Charles the Second," and also at page 702 of Whitelock's "Memorials."

notice of each other; only at first entry he put off his hat, and she made him a very civil salute; but afterwards they took no notice one of another; but both of them now and then would take their child, which the nurse held in her arms, and dandle it."

THE HOLBEIN GATEWAY, WHITEHALL. *From a Drawing by G. Vertue.* (*See page* 362.)

On the 23rd of August, 1662, the King and Queen came by water from Hampton Court, and landed at "Whitehall Bridge," as the Stairs were often called. On this occasion Pepys draws our attention to the presence of the celebrated Lady Castlemaine, and also of her husband. "But that which pleased me most was that my Lady Castlemaine stood over against us on a piece of Whitehall. But methought it was strange to see her lord and her upon the same place, walking up and down and taking no

Pepys tells us distinctly that the removal of Lord Clarendon from place and power was "certainly designed in my Lady Castlemaine's chamber," and he adds that he saw "several of the gallants of Whitehall" staying to see the Lord Chancellor pass by, and talking to her in her "birdcage."

The loose life led by the Court of Charles II. at Whitehall—or, indeed, wherever it may have been quartered—is a matter of historic notoriety. A good insight into these royal escapades is given by

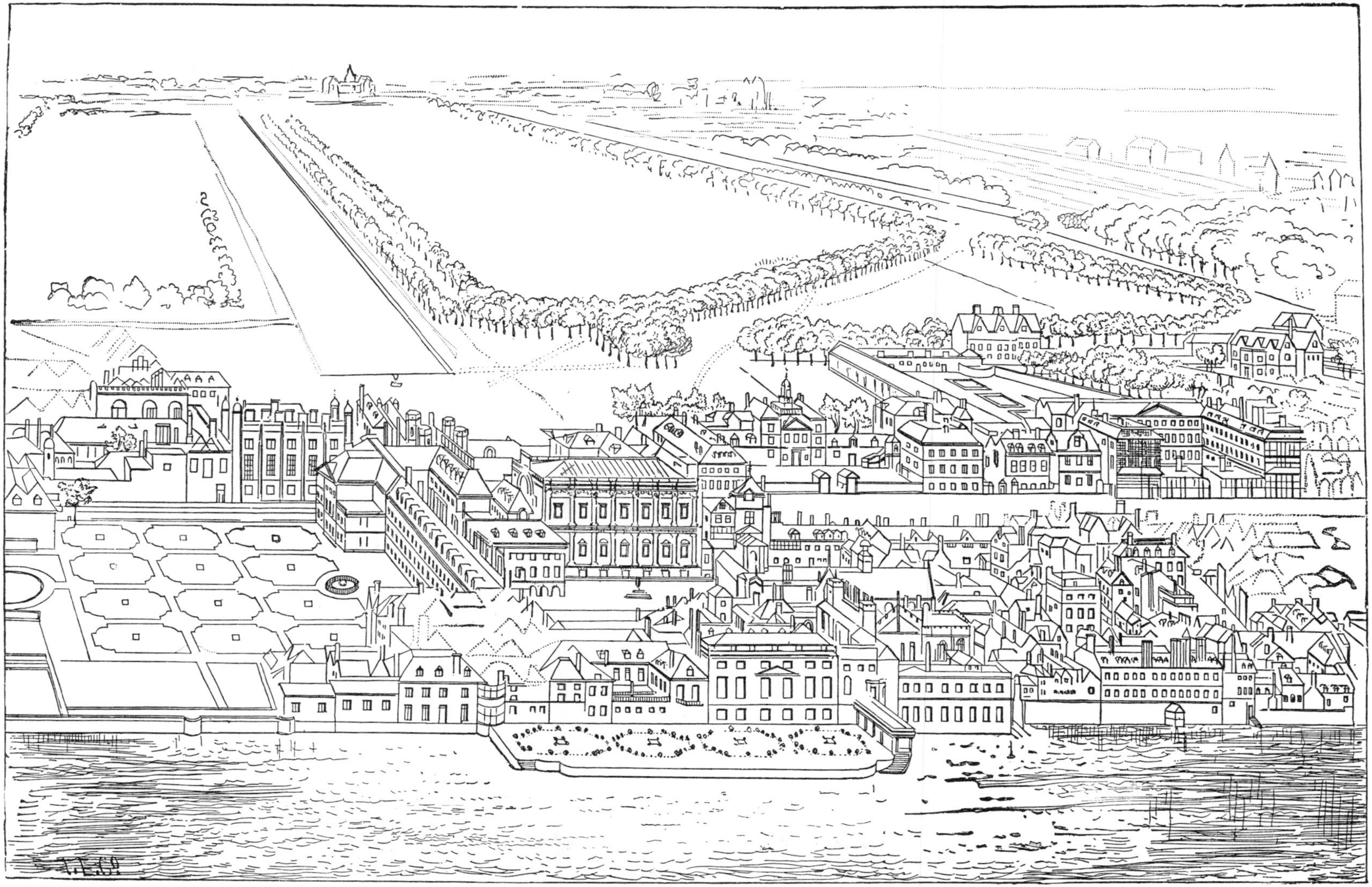

WHITEHALL, FROM THE RIVER. (*From a Copy by Smith of a View taken shortly after the Fire.*)

quaint old Pepys, who, writing in his "Diary" under date April 25th, 1663, says: "I did hear that the Queene is much grieved of late at the King's neglecting her, he not having supped with her once this quarter of a year, and almost every night with Lady Castlemaine, who hath been with him this St. George's Feast at Windsor." It is said by several retailers of Court gossip that the king spent in Lady Castlemaine's apartments the whole of the week previous to the arrival of his wife, Catherine of Braganza.

Here, probably, and not, as usually supposed, at the house of Sir Samuel Morland, at Vauxhall, Charles II. first spent his hours in dalliance with Barbara Palmer, afterwards Countess of Castlemaine and Duchess of Cleveland, of whom we shall have more to say anon, when we reach the neighbourhood of St. James's Palace. Her apartments, or lodgings, according to the privately-printed "Memoir" of the lady by Mr. G. S. Steinman, were on that part of Whitehall which bordered on the Holbein Gateway, on the south side of a detached pile of buildings leading to the Cock-pit, not far from the top of King Street.

Pepys, in his "Diary," notes the fact that on more than one Sunday he "observed how the Duke and Mrs. Palmer" (the subsequent Duchess) "did talk to one another very wantonly" in the chapel, during service-time, "through the hangings that part the king's closet and the closet where the ladies sit." Her presence here was indeed a standing insult to Charles's poor queen, Catharine of Braganza, to whom her ladyship must have caused many a heartfelt pang as a wife.

But if such was the case with Lady Castlemaine, it would seem, however, that the maids of honour and the other ladies of the Court of Whitehall were left very much to their own devices under the Stuart *régime*, and were not subject to any very strict control. "What mad freaks the mayds of honour at the Court do have!" writes Pepys in his "Diary." "That Mrs. Jennings, one of the Duchess's maids, the other day dressed herself up like an orange-wench, and went up and down and cried oranges, till, falling down by some accident, her fine shoes were discovered, and she put to a great deal of shame: so that such as these tricks and worse among them, thereby few will venture upon them for wives."

To the lax and immoral Court the Queen seems to have shown herself a marked exception. "To Whitehall," writes Pepys in his "Diary" in June, 1664, "where Mr. Pearce showed me the Queene's bed-chamber and her closet, where she had nothing but some pretty pious pictures, and books of devotion; and her holy water at her head as she sleeps; with a clock at her bedside, wherein burns a lamp that tells her the hour of the night at any time." Poor lonely Catherine of Braganza! it was probably at a very late hour of the night, or rather a very early hour of the morning, that the hands of her clock pointed to when Charles entered that room, after "supping with Lady Castlemaine" and other rivals of the Queen in his royal affections. No wonder that Charles did not find it compatible with his gallantries that his wife should be living at Whitehall, and, therefore, that he should have quietly disposed of her in lodgings at Somerset House, as we have seen in a previous chapter.

King Charles II., and his religious instructors, too, have been the theme of numerous *bon mots.* One of these has reference to Dr. South, who once, preaching before the king and his profligate Court at Whitehall, perceived in the middle of his sermon that sleep had taken possession of all his hearers. The doctor stopped, and changing his tone of voice, called three times to Lord Lauderdale, who, starting up, "My lord," said South, with great composure, "I am sorry to interrupt your repose, but I must beg you will not snore so loud, lest you awaken his Majesty."

In the year 1682 the Russian, Moroccan, and East Indian ambassadors all happened to be in London at the same time, and Evelyn, in his "Diary," gives us an amusing account of an evening which he spent in the company of those from Africa at the rooms of the Duchess of Portsmouth, in Whitehall.

It was at Whitehall, as Pepys tells us in his "Diary," that he found his friend Mr. Coventry chatting over a map of America with Sir William Penn.

In February, 1686, as he tells us in his "Diary," John Evelyn "came to lodge at Whitehall, in the Lord Privy Seal's lodgings."

Here James Walters, Duke of Monmouth, the natural son of Charles II., was allowed to assume the airs, and indeed all but the name, of royalty, and would stand with his hat on his head, as Macaulay remarks, when the Howards and the Seymours stood uncovered.

It was at the Court at Whitehall that Sidney, Lord Godolphin, the veteran statesman and courtier, was brought up as a page.

Having been the residence of so many of our English sovereigns in succession, the walls of Whitehall have witnessed many curious and interesting scenes, some also over which perhaps it would be well if a veil could be drawn. Foremost among such scenes may be reckoned the death of

Charles II., the details of which, gathered from Evelyn, and Burnet, and some other sources, have been worked up by Macaulay into a most effective picture, which has also employed the pencil of at least one modern painter of eminence.

"The palace," writes Macaulay, "had seldom presented a gayer or more scandalous appearance than on the evening of Sunday, the 1st of February, 1685. Some grave persons, who had gone thither, after the fashion of that age, to pay their duty to their sovereign, and who had expected that on such a day his Court would wear a decent aspect, were struck with astonishment and horror. The great gallery of Whitehall, an admirable relic of the magnificence of the Tudors, was crowded with revellers and gamblers. The king sat there chatting and toying with three women, whose charms were the boast and whose vices were the disgrace of three nations. Barbara Palmer, Duchess of Cleveland, was there, no longer young, but still retaining some traces of that superb and voluptuous loveliness which twenty years before overcame the hearts of all men. There, too, was the Duchess of Portsmouth, whose soft and infantine features were lighted up with the vivacity of France. Hortensia Mancini, Duchess of Mazarin, and niece of the great Cardinal, completed the group. . . . . While Charles flirted with his three sultanas, Hortensia's French page, a handsome boy, whose vocal performances were the delight of Whitehall, and were rewarded by numerous presents of rich clothes, ponies, and guineas, warbled some amatory verses. A party of twenty courtiers were seated at cards round a large table, on which gold was heaped in mountains. In the midst of this scene the king complained that he felt unwell; he was carried off to his chamber in a swoon, but recovered a little on being bled, or 'blooded,' as the phrase then went. He was laid on his bed, where, during a short time, the Duchess of Portsmouth hung over him with the familiarity of a wife. But the alarm had been given. The Queen and the Duchess of York were hastening to the room. The favourite concubine was forced to retire to her own apartments. Those apartments had been thrice pulled down and thrice rebuilt by her lover, to gratify her caprice. The very furniture of the chimney was massy silver. Several fine paintings, which properly belonged to the Queen, had been transferred to the dwelling of the mistress. The sideboards were piled with richly-wrought plate. In the niches stood cabinets, the masterpieces of Japanese art. On the hangings, fresh from the looms of Paris, were depicted, in tints which no English tapestry could rival, birds of gorgeous plumage, landscapes, hunting-matches, the lordly terrace of Saint Germains, the statues and fountains of Versailles. In the midst of this splendour, purchased by guilt and shame, the unhappy woman gave herself up to an agony of grief which, to do her justice, was not wholly selfish.

"And now the gates of Whitehall, which ordinarily stood open to all comers, were closed; but persons whose faces were known were still permitted to enter. The ante-chambers and galleries were soon filled to overflowing, and even the sick room was crowded with peers, privy councillors, and foreign ministers; all the medical men of note in London were summoned. The Queen was for a time assiduous in her attendance. The Duke of York scarcely left his brother's bedside. The primate and four other bishops were then in London; they remained in London all day, and took it by turns to sit up at night in the king's room."

The services of the bishops, however, were not required. Macaulay remarks of the Duchess of Portsmouth that "a life of frivolity and vice had not extinguished in her all sentiments of religion, or all that kindness which is the glory of her sex." It was by her suggestion that a Roman Catholic priest, Father Huddleston, the same who had aided Charles in his escape after the battle of Worcester, was sent for, to offer the consolations of religion. The courtiers were all ordered to withdraw, except Duras, Lord Feversham, and Granville, Earl of Bath, both of whom were Protestants, and faithful friends. The rest shall be told in Macaulay's words:—"Even the physicians withdrew. The back door was then opened, and Father Huddleston entered. A cloak had been thrown over his sacred vestments, and his shaven crown was concealed by a flowing wig. 'Sir,' said the Duke [of York], 'this good man once saved your life. He now comes to save your soul.' Charles faintly answered, 'He is welcome.' Huddleston went through his part better than had been expected. He knelt by the bed, listened to the confession, pronounced the absolution, and administered extreme unction. He asked if the king wished to receive the Lord's Supper. 'Surely,' said Charles, 'if I am not unworthy.' The host was brought in. Charles feebly strove to rise and kneel before it. The priest bade him lie still, and assured him that God would accept the humiliation of his soul, and would not require the humiliation of his body. The king found so much difficulty in swallowing that it was necessary to open the door and procure a glass of water. This rite ended, the monk held up a crucifix before the penitent, charged him to fix his last thoughts on the sufferings of the Redeemer, and withdrew. The whole ceremony had occupied about three quarters of an hour, and during that time the courtiers who filled the outer room had communicated their suspicions to each other by whispers and significant glances. The door was at length thrown open, and the crowd again filled the chamber of death.

"It was now late in the evening. The king seemed much relieved by what had passed. His natural children were brought to his bedside, the Dukes of Grafton, Southampton, and Northumberland, sons of the Duchess of Cleveland; the Duke of St. Albans, son of Eleanor Gwynn; and the Duke of Richmond, son of the Duchess of Portsmouth. Charles blessed them all, but spoke with peculiar tenderness to Richmond. One face which should have been there was wanting. The eldest and beloved child was an exile and a wanderer; his name was not once mentioned by his father.

"During the night Charles earnestly recommended the Duchess of Portsmouth and her boy to the care of James. 'And do not,' he good-naturedly added, 'let poor Nelly starve.' The Queen sent excuses for her absence by Halifax. She said that she was too much disordered to resume her post by the couch, and implored pardon for any offence she might unwittingly have given. 'She ask my pardon, poor woman!' cried Charles; 'I ask hers, with all my heart.'

"The morning light began to peep through the windows of Whitehall, and Charles desired the attendants to pull aside the curtains, that he might have one more look at the day. He remarked that it was time to wind up a clock which stood near his bed. These little circumstances were long remembered, because they proved beyond dispute that while he declared himself a Roman Catholic he was in full possession of his faculties. He apologised to those who had stood round him all night for the trouble which he had caused. He had been, he said, a most unconscionable time dying, but he hoped they would excuse it. This was the last glimpse of that exquisite urbanity so often found potent to charm away the resentment of a justly incensed nation. Soon after dawn the speech of the dying man failed. Before ten his senses were gone. Great numbers had repaired to the churches at the hour of morning service. When the prayer for the king was read, loud groans and sobs showed how deeply his people felt for him. At noon on Friday, the 6th of February, he passed away without a struggle."

Since the time of Œdipus no royal line has equalled that of the Stuarts in its calamities. The first James of Scotland, adorned with the graces of poetry and chivalry, a wise legislator, a sagacious and resolute king, perished in his forty-fourth year. His son, the second James, was killed, in his thirtieth year, at the siege of Roxburgh Castle, by the bursting of a cannon. The third James, after the battle of Sauchieburn, in which his rebellious subjects were countenanced and aided by his own son, was stabbed, in his thirty-sixth year, beneath a humble roof, by a pretended priest. That son, the chivalrous madman of Flodden, compassed his own death and that of the flower of his kingdom, while only forty years of age, by a foolish knight-errantry. At an age ten years younger, his only son, James V., died of a broken heart. Over the suffering and follies—if we may not say crimes—and over the mournful and unwarrantable doom of the beauteous Mary, the world will never cease to debate. Her grandson expiated at Whitehall, by a bloody death, the errors chiefly induced by his self-will and his pernicious education. The second Charles, the "Merry Monarch," had a fate as sad as any of his ancestors; for though he died in his bed, his life was that of a heartless voluptuary, who had found in his years of seeming prosperity neither truth in man nor fidelity in woman. His brother, the bigot James, lost three kingdoms, and disinherited the dynasty, for his blind adherence to a faith that failed to regulate his life. The Old Pretender was a cipher, and the Young Pretender, after a youthful flash of promise, passed a useless life, and ended it as a drunken dotard. The last of the race, Henry, Cardinal York, died in 1804, a spiritless old man, and a pensioner of that House of Hanover against which his father and brother had waged war with no advantage to themselves, and with the forfeiture of life and lands, of liberty and country, to many of the noblest and most chivalrous inhabitants of our island.

Happy had it been for Charles II. if he had demeaned himself as well in his prosperous as in his adverse fortune. The recorded facts are highly honourable to him and the companions of his exile; while Cromwell, as the Queen of Bohemia said, was like the beast in the Revelation, that all kings and nations worshipped. Charles's horses, and some of them were favourites, were sold at Brussels, because he could not pay for their keep; and during the two years that he resided at Cologne he never kept a coach. So straitened were the exiles for money that even the postage of letters between Sir Richard Browne and Hyde was no easy burthen; and there was a mutiny in the ambassador's kitchen, because the maid "might not be trusted with the government, and the buying the meat, in which she was thought too lavish." Hyde writes that he had not been master of a crown for many months; that he was cold for want of clothes and fire; and for all the meat which he had eaten for three months he was in debt to a poor woman who was no longer able to trust. "Our necessities," he says, "would be more insupportable, if we did not see the king reduced to greater distress than you can believe or imagine." Of Charles, in prosperity, a few days before his death, Evelyn draws a fearful picture. Writing on the day when James was proclaimed, he says, "I can never forget the inexpressible luxury and profaneness, gaming, and all dissoluteness and, as it were, total forgetfulness of God (it being Sunday evening), which this day se'nnight I was witness of; the King sitting and toying with his concubines, Portsmouth, Cleaveland, and Mazarine, &c.; a French boy singing love-songs in that glorious gallery; whilst about twenty of the great courtiers and other dissolute persons were at basset round a large table, a bank of at least £2,000 in gold before them, upon which two gentlemen who were with me made reflections with astonishment. Six days after, all was in the dust!"

Whitehall, when Charles II. dwelt there, was the focus of political intrigue as well as of gaiety. "Half the jobbing and half the flirting of the metropolis," writes Macaulay, "went on under his roof. Whoever could make himself agreeable to the prince, or could secure the good offices of the mistress, might hope to rise in the world without rendering any service to the Government, without being even known by sight to any minister of state. This courtier got a frigate, and that a company; a third, the pardon of a rich offender; a fourth, a lease of Crown land on easy terms. If the king notified his pleasure that a briefless lawyer should be made a judge, or that a libertine baronet should be made a peer, the gravest counsellors, after a little murmuring, submitted. Interest, therefore, drew a constant press of suitors to the gates of the palace, and those gates always stood wide. The king kept open house every day, and all day long, for the good society of London, the extreme Whigs only excepted. Hardly any gentleman had any difficulty in making his way to the royal presence. The "levee" was exactly what the word imports. Some men of quality came every morning to stand round their master, to chat with him while his wig was combed and his cravat tied, and to accompany him in his early walk through the Park. All persons who had been properly introduced might, without any special invitation, go to see him dine, sup, dance, and play at hazard, and might have the pleasure of hearing him tell stories, which indeed he told remarkably well, about his flight from Worcester, and about the misery which he had endured when he was a State prisoner in the hands of the canting meddling preachers of Scotland. Bystanders whom his Majesty recognised often came in for a courteous word. This proved a far more successful kingcraft than any that his father or grandfather had practised. It was not easy for the most austere republican of the school of Marvell to resist the fascination of so much good humour and affability; and many a veteran Cavalier in whose heart the remembrance of unrequited sacrifices and services had been festering during twenty years, was compensated in one moment for wounds and sequestrations by his sovereign's kind nod, and 'God bless you, my old friend!'

"Whitehall naturally became the chief staple of news. Whenever there was a rumour that anything important had happened or was about to happen, people hastened thither to obtain intelligence from the fountain-head. The galleries presented the appearance of a modern club-room at an anxious time. They were full of people inquiring whether the Dutch mail was in; what tidings the express from France had brought; whether John Sobiesky had beaten the Turks; whether the Doge of Genoa was really at Paris. These were matters about which it was safe to talk aloud. But there were subjects concerning which information was asked and given in whispers. Had Halifax got the better of Rochester? Was there to be a Parliament? Was the Duke of York really going to Scotland? Had Monmouth really been summoned from the Hague? Men tried to read the countenance of every minister as he went through the throng to and from the royal closet. All sorts of auguries were drawn from the tone in which his Majesty spoke to the Lord President, or from the laugh with which his Majesty honoured a jest of the Lord Privy Seal; and in a few hours the hopes and fears inspired by such slight indications had spread to all the coffee-houses from St. James's to the Tower."

Notwithstanding the thirst for news and love of Court gossip, the Stuart kings appear to have lived here very much in public; so much so, indeed, that, if we may trust Macaulay, the "newswriters" of the reign of Charles II. would occasionally obtain admission into the gallery at Whitehall Palace, in order to tell their country friends how the king and duke looked, and what games the courtiers played at.

The sources from which Macaulay drew his information about the state of the Court are too numerous to recapitulate. Among them are the Despatches of Barillon, Van Citters, Ronquillo, and Adda; the Travels of the Grand Duke Cosmo; the Works of Roger North, the Diaries of Pepys and Evelyn, and the Memoirs of Grammont.

THE KING STREET GATEWAY, WHITEHALL. (*See page* 363.)

The royal family of Stuart would seem to have been as unfortunate in their domestic servants as in their fate; for Northouck tells us that twice within a few years, in the reign of William and Mary, the Palace of Whitehall suffered serious damage by fire; firstly in April, 1691, when a large part of it was destroyed "through the negligence of a maid-servant, who, about eight o'clock at night," says the very circumstantial Northouck, "to save the labour of cutting a candle from a pound, burnt it off, and threw the rest carelessly by before the flame was out. It burnt violently till four next morning, and destroyed the Duchess of Portsmouth's lodgings, with all the stone gallery and buildings behind and down to the Thames." Six years later, we learn from the same authority, by "the carelessness of a laundress," all the body of the Palace, with the new gallery, council-chamber, and several adjoining apartments, shared the same fate. It was with the greatest difficulty that the Banqueting Hall was saved. "The king," adds Northouck, "sent message after message from Kensington, for its preservation;" though it is hard to see how even royal "messengers" could have been of as much use as a few rude fire-engines.

Another event connected with Whitehall in the reigns of the Stuarts, should be mentioned here—namely, that within its walls the devotion of the "Sacred Heart," devised by Sister Marguerite Mary Alacoque at Paray-le-Monial, in France, was first publicly preached and taught in England, by Father Colombiere, the confessor of the Duchess of York—Mary of Modena, afterwards queen of James II.

SIR HENRY LEE OF DITCHLEY. *From a Portrait by Basire.* (*See page* 364.)

CHAPTER XLV.

WHITEHALL.—THE BUILDINGS DESCRIBED.

"Donec templa refeceris."—*Horace.*

Description of the Old Palace—Additions made by Henry VIII.—The Holbein Gateway—Westminster Gate—Knights of the Tilt-yard—Inigo Jones' Design for a New Palace—Residence of the Ladies and Gentlemen of the Court—An Ingenious Design for Rebuilding Whitehall—Description of the Banqueting House—The Chapel Royal—Rubens' Painted Ceiling—"Maunday" Thursday—The Statue of James II.

Although the present remains of Whitehall are comparatively modern, not reaching farther back than the time of the Tudors, yet we know, as recorded above, that a stately palace stood on this spot as early as the reign of Henry III., when the Chief Justice of England, Hubert de Burgh, Earl of Kent, resided in it. At his death he left it to the "Black" Friars of Holborn, who sold it to the

Archbishop of York; and his successors in that metropolitan see made it their town residence for nearly three centuries. The last of the archbishops who tenanted it was Cardinal Wolsey, under whom it became one of the most sumptuous palaces in England.

The ancient palace of Whitehall, if we include its precincts, was of great extent, stretching from close to where now stands Westminster Bridge nearly up to Scotland Yard. It comprised a hall, chapel, banqueting-house, and other apartments, as "Henry VIII.'s Gallery," the "Boarded Gallery," the "Matted Gallery," the "Shield Gallery," the "Stone Gallery," the "Adam and Eve Gallery" (so named from the picture by Mabuse), and the "Vane Room." Some idea of the extent of the palace early in the sixteenth century may be formed from the following description of it, which occurs in the Act of Parliament by which it was given to the royal tyrant. Here it is styled "one great mansion-place and house, being a parcel of the possessions of the Archbishopric of York, situate in the town of Westminster, not much distant from the same ancient palace." And referring to Cardinal Wolsey, it adds that "he had lately, upon the soil of the said mansion-place and house, and upon ground thereunto belonging, most sumptuously and curiously built and edified many and distinct beautiful, costly, and pleasant lodgings, buildings, and mansions for his grace's singular pleasure, comfort, and commodity, to the honour of his highness and the realm; and thereunto adjoining had made a park, walled and environed with brick and stone; and then devised and ordained many and singular commodious things, pleasures, and other necessaries, apt and convenient to appertain to so noble a prince for his pastime and pleasure." And it must be owned that if the prints of the period are to be trusted, this description is not overdrawn. By the same Act of Parliament it was directed to be called "The King's Palace at Westminster" for ever. Its limits were defined on the one side by the "street leading from Charing Cross unto the Sanctuary Gate at Westminster," and on the other by "the water of the Thames." At this time it consisted of "a mansion with two gardens and three acres of land." Henry VIII., as we have shown in a preceding chapter, added very considerably to the buildings; and he likewise ordered a tennis-court, a cock-pit, and bowling-greens to be formed, "with other conveniences for various kinds of diversion." Here Holbein painted the portraits of Henry VII. and Henry VIII., with their queens, and also the "Dance of Death." Here, too—or, rather, across the roadway in front, leading from Charing Cross to Westminster—he built his famous gateway.

Holbein had been induced to come over to England through the reputation of the taste and generosity of Henry VIII. He was introduced to the king by the instrumentality of Sir Thomas More, at his house at Chelsea, where a number of the painter's works had been recently ranged round the walls. Taken immediately into the king's service, Holbein had apartments assigned to him in the old palace at Whitehall, for which he designed, at the king's request, in 1546, the gateway above alluded to. It stood in front of the palace, opposite the Tilt-yard, and was flanked on either side by a low brick building of a single storey in height. Its position was a little nearer to Westminster Abbey than the north-west corner of York House. The edifice was constructed of small square stones and flint boulders, of two distinct colours, "glazed and disposed in a tessellated manner." On each front there were four busts or medallions, "naturally coloured and gilt," which are stated to have resisted all influences of the weather. They were of terra-cotta, as large as life, or even a little larger, and represented some of the chief characters of the age. Among them were Henry VII., Henry VIII., and Bishop Fisher. These busts were believed by some persons to have been the work of an Italian artist named Torregiano; but Mr. Cunningham, in an article on the subject in the *Gentleman's Magazine* for June, 1866, inclines to the opinion that they were executed by John de Maiano, the sculptor of the medallions on Hampton Court Gateway. On either side of the archway were lofty embattled octagonal turrets, the faces of which, between the windows, were likewise ornamented with busts, &c. The rooms above the archway were long used as the State Paper Office.

The Holbein Gateway, as it was generally called, was removed in 1749-50, in order to widen the street and approaches to Westminster. After its demolition most of the glazed bricks and stone dressings of this historical building, rich in two centuries of associations with our kings, from Henry VIII. to William III., "were sold to repair the high roads."

Mr. J. T. Smith, in his "Antiquities of Westminster," in alluding to this gateway, says: "It is scarcely to be supposed that, in the time of Hubert de Burgh's residence here, there was anything like that noble space which the width of the street opposite Whitehall now (1807) affords. On the contrary, the probability seems to be that there was not, and it is far more likely that it did not at that time exceed the breadth of the present King Street.

Passing by Whitehall the street was continued along a street of this same width, which originally had on its eastern side the wall of part of the garden, or orchard, or other ground, if we may trust honest John Stow, belonging to Whitehall, as may be seen in the plan made in 1680, by John Fisher, a surveyor at that time, and which was afterwards engraved by Vertue. On the western side this street had the wall of that enclosure since converted into St. James's Park; but when Henry VIII. had acquired possession of Whitehall in 1531, by exchanging with the abbot and convent of Westminster, he procured to himself this enclosure, part of which he converted into the before-mentioned park, and on the rest he erected a tennis-court, a cock-pit, a bowling-alley, a long stone gallery—which was for some time occupied by the late Duke of Dorset, and subsequently by Lord Whitworth—and other buildings, many of which are wholly, or in part, still (1807) remaining."

This building, it appears, the king connected with the palace on the opposite side by two gateways across the street; one of them at about the middle of King Street, which was demolished in 1723; the other, nearer to Charing Cross, adjoining the north-east corner of the gallery above-mentioned, was the gateway designed by Hans Holbein. This latter gate, it is stated in the "New View of London" (1708), was termed "Cock-pit Gate," and it is said to have been "an extraordinarily beautiful gate." The writer thus describes it: "It is built of square stone, with small squares of flint boulder, very neatly set. It has also battlements, and four lofty towers; and the whole is enriched with busts, roses, portcullises, and queen's arms, both on the north and south sides. There are no gates hung at present, but the hinges show there have been. This is an aperture from the Cock-pit into the broad part of Charing Cross, before Whitehall Gate." We have given views of both these gates, copied from old prints published while they were standing. The Holbein Gateway is shown on page 354, and the King Street Gateway on page 360.

On the taking down of this latter gate it was begged and obtained by William, Duke of Cumberland, son of George II., and then Ranger of Windsor Park and Forest, with the view of re-erecting it at the end of the Long Walk, in the Great Park at Windsor. The stones were accordingly removed, but the re-building of it at Windsor appears to have been abandoned. Some of the material, however, we are told, was, by the Duke's direction, worked up in several different buildings erected by the Duke in the Great Park. "A medallion from it," adds Mr. J. T. Smith, "is in one of the fronts of a keeper's lodge, near Virginia Water. A similar medallion, part of it also, is in another cottage, built about the year 1790, in the Great Park, and accessible from the road from Peascod Street, by the barracks. Other stones form the basement as high as the dado or moulding, and also the cornice, of the inside of a chapel at the Great Lodge, which chapel was begun in the Duke's lifetime, but was unfinished at his death." The busts were, in number, four on each side; they had ornamented mouldings round them, and were of baked clay, in proper colours, and glazed in the manner of Delft ware, which had preserved them entire. Mr. Smith, in the "Antiquities of Westminster," says that after the gate was taken down three of the busts fell into the hands of a man who kept an old iron shop in Belton Street, St. Giles's, to whom, it is supposed, they had been sold after having been stolen when the gate was taken down. This man had them in his possession some three or four years, when they were bought, about the year 1765, by a Mr. Wright, who employed Flaxman, the sculptor, then a boy, to repair them. They were in terra cotta, coloured and gilt. The dress of one of the busts was painted dark red, and the ornaments gilt, among which were alternately the Rose and H, and the Crown and R, in gold. Mr. Wright resided at Hatfield Priory, near Witham, in Essex, and the above-mentioned busts, when Mr. Smith wrote, were in the possession of his great-grandson, Mr. John Wright, who, in a letter to "Sylvanus Urban," says, "I remember some years ago (after reading an account of the busts in the 'Antiquities of Westminster'), scraping off some of the paint, and I found them glazed and coloured. I suppose the reason they were painted over was that a good deal of the enamel had worn off, or was damaged in some way, so Flaxman thought it better to paint them."

Maitland, in his "History of London" (1739), speaks of Holbein's gateway as still standing. He calls it "the present stately gate, opposite the Banqueting House." He adds, that soon after becoming possessed of Whitehall, "Henry, for other diversions, erected, contiguous to the aforesaid gate, a tennis-court, cock-pit, and places to bowl in; the former of which only," he adds, "are now remaining, the rest being converted into dwelling-houses, and offices for the Privy Council, Treasury, and Secretaries of State."

The Cockpit gateway is described in the work above referred to as "an ancient piece of building, opening out of the Cock-pit into King Street, in the north part of Westminster," and is often styled

"Westminster Gate;" the writer adds that "the structure is old, with the remains of several figures, the queen's arms, roses, &c., whereby it was enriched. It hath four towers, and the south side is adorned with pilasters and entablature of the Ionic order." It was lower than the Holbein Gateway, and not anything like so handsome; its towers were semi-circular projections, pierced with semi-circular lights, and on the top of the towers were semi-circular domelets. Altogether, if we may judge from the prints of the gate published by Kip, and also in the "Vetusta Monumenta" by the Society of Antiquaries, it was one of the ugliest structures in the metropolis. This was removed in 1723, as it blocked up the road which was then the sole access from Charing Cross to the Houses of Parliament and the Courts of Law.

In this gateway were the lodgings of the beautiful and intriguing Countess of Buckingham, the mother of George Villiers, Duke of Buckingham. She died here in 1632, and her body was conveyed hence along King Street to the Abbey to be laid beside that of her murdered son. King's Gate was converted by Henry into a passage connecting Whitehall with the park, the tennis-court, bowling-green, and tilting-yard.

The Tilt-yard stood a little to the south of "the Horse Guard Yard," adjoining the north gate of King Street; having a gate into the park, close to which was an old staircase, used, no doubt, by Elizabeth and her courtiers on State occasions, and leading to the Royal gallery. In Sydney's "State Papers" there is to be found an amusing account of the diversions of Queen Bess, which shows that even when not far short of her seventieth year, she could pursue the pleasures of out-door sports among her courtiers with the energy of youth or of middle age. "Her Majesty says she is very well. This day she appoints a Frenchman to do feats upon a rope in the conduit court: to-morrow she hath commanded the bears, the bull, and the ape to be baited in the Tilt-yard. Upon Wednesday she will have 'solemne dauncing.'"

The chief heroes of the Tilt-yard were Sir Henry Lee, of Ditchley, Knight of the Garter, and "the faithful and devoted knight of this romantic Princess," and George, Earl of Cumberland. The former had made a vow to present himself at the Tilt-yard annually on the 27th of November, till disabled by age, and so gave rise to a school of knights of the Tilt-yard, embracing about twenty-five of the most celebrated members of the Court, including Sir Christopher Hatton, and Robert, Earl of Leicester. In due course of time Sir Henry resigned his post in favour of the Earl of Cumberland. In 1590, it is on record that "with much form and in the true spirit of chivalry and romance, in the presence of the Queen and of the whole Court, he armed the new champion with his own hands, and mounted him on his horse. He then offered his own armour at the foot of a crowned pillar near her Majesty's feet; after which he clothed himself in a coat of black velvet pointed under the arm, and instead of a helmet, covered his head with a buttoned cap of the country fashion," as Walpole tells us in his "Miscellaneous Antiquities." Sir Henry died at the age of eighty, and was buried at Quarendon, near Aylesbury, where the inscription on his tomb recorded the fact that—

> "In courtly jousts his sovereign's knight he was;
> Six princes did he serve."

In the reign of James I., the old Palace of Whitehall had become so ruinous, the greater part having been destroyed by fire in 1619, that it was determined to rebuild it. Dr. Mackay, in his "Thames and its Tributaries," says that the King "entrusted the design to Inigo Jones, who built the edifice now known as the Banqueting House, . . . which was intended as a part, and a very small one, of a more magnificent conception. The palace was to have consisted of four fronts, each with an entrance between two towers. Within these were to have been one large central court and five smaller ones, and between two of the latter a handsome circus, with an arcade below, supported by pillars in the form of caryatides. The whole length of the palace was to have been 1,152 feet, and its depth 872 feet; but the times which succeeded those of James were not favourable for such designs and expenses as these, and so the palace was never completed." The original drawings, bold in their conception, are preserved at Worcester College, Oxford; and the building, as designed by Inigo Jones, has been frequently engraved. The building was actually commenced, but in consequence of the civil wars, the Banqueting House was the only portion of the design completed. This splendid fragment, which exists before our eyes, has often excited lamentations that the design of Inigo Jones was never completed; yet Horace Walpole, an incomparable critic on all writings, characters, and buildings but his own, throws strong doubts on its probable excellence. "Several plates of the intended new Palace of Whitehall," he writes, "have been given, but, I believe, from no finished design of Inigo Jones. . . . The strange kind of cherubims on the towers at the end are preposterous ornaments; and, whether of Inigo's design or not, bear no relation to the rest. The great towers in the front are too near, and evidently borrowed from what he had seen in Gothic, than in Roman, buildings. The circular court is a picturesque thought, but without meaning or utility." It is true that he equally doubts the published design to be the final one; for he continues:—"The four great sheets are evidently made up from general hints; nor could such a source of invention and taste as the mind of Inigo Jones ever produce such sameness." On this passage Dr. Croly remarks in a note on Pope's "Windsor Forest:"—"Whether the design were regal or not, the situation showed a regal sense. The position on the Thames was fit for the sea-king; its command of the rising country in front gave it the brightness and the beauty of the English landscape, before that fine space was overrun with graceless buildings. The sovereign of England has now a new palace near the Thames, but without communication with it; and near the country, but without a prospect. Yet the architecture has been needlessly criticised; with some striking errors, it has many beauties. Blackened by smoke and buried in fog, what architecture can struggle against its location? A happier site would discover in it details of elegance, novelty, and grandeur."

"At the time of the execution of King Charles," says Pennant, "contiguous to the Banqueting House was a large building with a long roof and a small cupola rising out of the middle, which is shown in Hollar's etching. Under this cupola there was an entrance and an unsightly gateway."

Directly behind the Banqueting House, very near the river, was a chapel belonging to the Palace; but no engravings of it are known to exist; and all trace of its site has disappeared. It must have stood as nearly as possible on the site of Fife House. The screen of the Queen's Chapel here, we are told, was removed by Sir William Chambers to his residence at Whitton, near Hounslow, where he set it up as a summer-house in his garden.

The Stone Gallery ran along the east, between the garden and the river, following as nearly as possible the line of the terrace which afterwards formed "Privy Gardens." The "lodgings belonging to his Majesty" faced the river, close to the "Privy Stairs." Those of the Duke of York adjoined them on the south, commanding also a view of the river. Those of Prince Rupert, the Duke of Monmouth, the ladies of the Court, of the maids of honour, the "Countess of Castlemaine," and the "Countess of Suffolk" were situated between the river-side and the Stone Gallery. Nell Gwynne, not having the honour of belonging to the establishment of Catherine of Braganza, was obliged to keep to her apartments in Pall Mall.

"The intended Palace at Whitehall," says one writer, "if it had been carried out would have been the most truly magnificent and beautiful fabric of any of the kind in Europe. His Majesty did not send to Italy and Flanders for architects as he did for Albano and Vandyck; he had Inigo Jones. A higher compliment to both English royalty and English art could not well be paid." As it is, we can only regret that the same chance of leaving behind him a memorial worthy of his genius was not given to Inigo Jones that was given to Sir Christopher Wren.

It is not generally known that in the early part of the last century an ingenious speculator proposed to improve Westminster by carrying out the design of Inigo Jones for rebuilding Whitehall. The expense he estimated at little over half a million, and he proposed, as a means of raising that sum, that the city of Westminster should be incorporated, to consist of a mayor, recorder, and twenty-four aldermen; that the profits arising to the said corporation, after defraying its own necessary expenses, should, for seven years, be appropriated to carry on the intended new palace; that duties should be laid upon new improved rents within the city of Westminster; that all officers who held two or more offices above the annual value of £300, should pay a certain poundage, as should likewise all such as had any right or title to any house, office, or lodging within the said new projected Palace; and, lastly, that all improvements of any part of the ground of Whitehall, and the benefit arising to Her Majesty from all new inventions or forfeitures should for a term of years be appropriated to the same purpose. This plan, which might ultimately have much benefited the locality, it is superfluous to add, was never carried into effect.

The Banqueting House, so called from having been placed on the side of the apartments so called erected by Elizabeth, was begun in 1619, and finished in two years. It is divided into three storeys, of which the lowest or basement storey consists of a rustic wall, with small square windows. Above this springs a range of columns and pilasters of the Ionic order; between the columns are seven windows, with alternate arched and triangular pediments; over these is placed the proper entablature, on which is raised a second series of the Corinthian order, consisting also of columns and pilasters, their capitals being connected with festoons of flowers, with masks and other ornaments in the centre. From the entablature of this series rises a balustrade, with attic pedestals in their places crowning the whole. The building consists chiefly of one room, of an oblong form, a double cube of 55 feet. The stone for building it was drawn from the quarries at Portland, under authority of the sign-manual of James I.

INTERIOR OF THE OLD CHAPEL ROYAL (BANQUETING HOUSE), WHITEHALL (1876).

Charles I. commissioned Rubens to paint the ceiling, and by the agency of this great artist the King was enabled to secure the noble cartoons of Raffaelle, which are preserved at the South Kensington Museum. Charles also collected a considerable number of paintings by the best masters, but these were seized by order of Parliament, who sold many of the paintings and statues, and ordered the "superstitious pictures" to be burnt. After Sir P. Lely's death, his noble collection of drawings and pictures was exhibited in the Royal Banqueting House, and in consequence realised, when subsequently put up for auction, the very large sum of £26,000. Rubens's painted ceiling is divided by a rich framework of gilded mouldings into nine compartments, the subjects being what are called allegorical, the centre one representing the apotheosis of James I., or his supposed translation into the celestial regions. The king, supported by an eagle, is borne upwards, attended by figures as the representatives of Religion, Justice, &c. His Majesty appears seated on his throne, and turning with horror from War and other such-like deities, and resigning himself to Peace and her natural attendants, Commerce and the Fine Arts—a curious commentary on the Puritan age which followed so soon after the execution of the ceiling. On either side of this central compartment are oblong panels, on which the painter has endeavoured to express the peace and plenty, the harmony and happiness, which he presumed to have signalised the reign of its boldness and success. These paintings have been more than once re-touched, on one occasion by no less an artist than Cipriani; and though there is an immense distance between this artist and Rubens, there is no apparent injury done to the work. The Banqueting House cost £17,000.

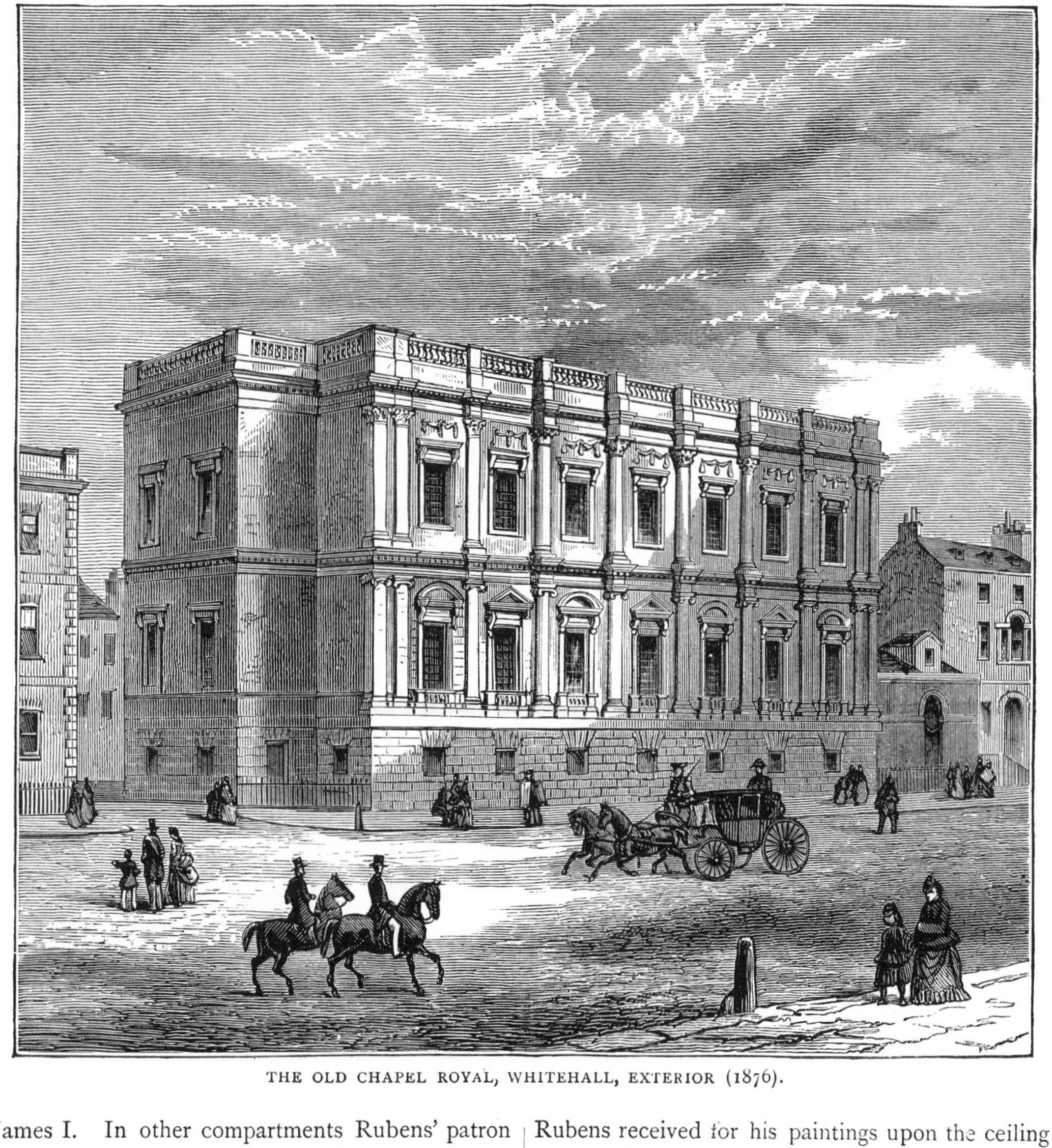

THE OLD CHAPEL ROYAL, WHITEHALL, EXTERIOR (1876).

James I. In other compartments Rubens' patron and employer, Charles, is introduced, in scenes intended to represent his birth, and as being crowned King of Scotland; while the oval compartments at the corners are intended, by allegorical figures, to show the triumph of the Virtues, such as Temperance, &c., over the Vices. Vandyck was to have painted the sides of the apartment with the history of the Order of the Garter. The execution of particular parts is to be admired for

Rubens received for his paintings upon the ceiling —about four hundred yards of work—the sum of four thousand pounds, or nearly ten pounds a yard; while Sir James Thornhill, three quarters of a century later, was paid only three pounds a yard for his decorations on the ceiling of Greenwich Hospital. Cipriani had two thousand pounds for his re-touching. This noble building was turned into a chapel by George I., and remained a Chapel Royal until 1890, when it was dismantled. Three years later it was handed over to the Royal United Service Institution for its Museum, of which we have already given some account (pp. 334-335). The clerical establishment of the Chapel Royal consisted of a Dean and Sub-Dean, a morning reader and two permanent preachers and readers, or chaplains; there were also two Select Preachers, chosen by the Bishop of London from the two chief Universities alternately. In 1812 five eagles and four other standards, captured from the French in the Peninsula, were publicly deposited in this chapel; and in January, 1816, the same ceremony was repeated in respect of the standards taken at the Battle of Waterloo, on the 18th of June preceding; but on the opening of the new military chapel in Birdcage Walk these trophies were removed thither. The front of the Banqueting House was largely repaired and beautified in 1829. The basement was until 1890 partly used for Government stores; it was then restored and furnished with a concrete floor, and now contains the heavy guns and shells, &c., belonging to the Institution to which the building has been transferred. The Banqueting Hall itself has not been altered structurally, and even the wood of the oak pews, which had, of course, to be removed when the place was converted into a Museum, was used as panelling for the bases of the walls and piers. The Banqueting House, although, as we have seen, converted into a chapel in the reign of George I., was never consecrated, which fact was mentioned in the House of Commons some years ago, when it was proposed to use the hall as a picture-gallery.

Evelyn in his "Diary" frequently mentions the service here, and on one occasion (at Easter, 1684), when the King received the communion, he adds, "Note, there was parfume burnt before the office began."

We must not omit to mention here an interesting ceremony which was performed in the Chapel Royal, Whitehall, from a remote period, namely, the distribution of the "Maundy," or royal alms, to the poor.

The custom of distributing the royal alms on "Maunday" Thursday—as the day before Good Friday is styled—has come down from the old Roman Catholic ages. Some such ceremony was performed by personages of the highest rank, both temporal and spiritual, from the Pope down to nobles and lords in their castles, in commemoration of our Redeemer, who "washed his disciples' feet" when He gave them that "new commandment," or "mandate," whence the day has its name. Queen Elizabeth performed this ceremony at her palace at Greenwich; and the last of our sovereigns who went through it in person was James II. After him, under the Hanoverian line, it was performed by the Royal Almoner. The following cotemporary account of the ceremony in the reign of George II. may possibly raise a smile:—"On the 5th of April, 1731, it being Maunday Thursday, the King being then in his forty-eighth year, there was distributed, at the Banqueting House, Whitehall, to forty-eight poor men, and forty-eight poor women, boiled beef and shoulders of mutton, and small bowls of ale, which is called dinner; after that, large wooden platters of fish and loaves, viz., undressed, one large ling and one large dried cod; twelve red herrings and twelve white herrings, and four half-quartern loaves. Each person had one platter of this provision; after which was distributed to them shoes, stockings, linen and woollen cloth, and leathern bags, with one penny, twopenny, threepenny, and fourpennypieces of silver, and shillings, to each about four pounds in value. His Grace the Lord Archbishop of York, Lord High Almoner, also performed the annual ceremony of washing the feet of the poor in the Royal Chapel, Whitehall, as was formerly done by the kings themselves."

Gradual changes, however, have taken place in the manner of performing this ceremony. The ceremony is thus described towards the close of the reign of George III., namely, in 1814:—"In the morning the Sub-Almoner, the Secretary of the Lord High Almoner, and others belonging to the Lord Chamberlain's Office, attended by a party of the Yeomen of the Guard, distributed to seventy-five poor women and seventy-five poor men, being as many as the King was years old, a quantity of salt fish, consisting of salmon, cod, and herrings, pieces of very fine beef, five loaves of bread, and some ale to drink the King's health. . . . A procession entered of those engaged in the ceremony, consisting of a party of the Yeomen of the Guard, one of them carrying on his head a large gold dish, containing one hundred and fifty bags, with seventy-five silver pennies in each, for the poor people, which was placed in the royal closet. They were followed by the Sub-Almoner, in his robes, with a sash of fine linen over his shoulder and crossing his waist. He was followed by two boys, two girls, the secretary, and other gentlemen, all carrying nosegays. The Church Evening Service was then performed, at the conclusion of which the silver pennies were distributed, and woollen cloth, linen, shoes and stockings, to the men and women, and a cup of wine to drink the King's health."

The royal alms now are dispensed in money and clothing, the payment in kind of fish and flesh having been practically commuted. A few years ago it was thought that the ceremony would have been allowed to die out; but such has not been the case, and the gifts are distributed by the Lord High Almoner to so many men, and the like number of women, as may correspond with the number of years in the age of Her Majesty.

Although the mandate, or Maunday, is now little more than an empty ceremony, yet it is one which enshrines a lesson of true Christian charity. So far from censuring or despising such acts of condescension on the part of the royal and noble towards their poorer brethren and sisters, we ought rather to regret that so few opportunities occur in a year for bringing into contact and contrast the squalid poverty of "St. Giles's" with the wealth and luxury of "St. James's," and so leading the inmates of the latter region, in the words of the poet—

"To learn the luxury of doing good."

We may, perhaps, be pardoned for reminding our readers here that the "Beef-eaters"—as the Yeomen of the Royal Guard who do duty on these occasions are called—are really *buffetiers*, that is, personal attendants of the sovereign, who, on high festivals, and on other state occasions, were ranged near the royal sideboard, or *buffet*.

In the open space in the rear, between the chapel and the houses in Whitehall Gardens, stands the celebrated statue of James II., which was set up in 1686, just two years before his abdication. It is of bronze, and represents the king as dressed in a Roman toga, and its elegant proportions have often been admired. It is the work of Grinling Gibbons. Indeed, it has been said to be nearly the only statue in the metropolis that will bear a rigid inspection as a work of art. It suffers, however, from the want of an open space around it sufficiently large to set it off to advantage.

As to the author of this statue, it is only fair to add that great doubts have prevailed. They would appear, however, to be negatived by the following passage in the "Autobiography of Sir John Bramston," published under the auspices of the Camden Society. "On New Year's Day, 1686," writes Sir John, "a statue in brass was to be seen, placed the day before in the yard at Whitehall, made by Gibbons at the charge of Toby Runstick, of the present king, James II." Horace Walpole, therefore, was correct in his surmise on the subject. "I am the rather inclined to attribute the statue at Whitehall to Gibbons, because I know of no other artist of that time capable of it." It is strange that so little should have been known for certain as to its author, considering that when it was first set up it was made the subject of numerous sets of verses and *jeux d'esprit*. "The figure, looking as it does towards the river," writes John Timbs, "was said to prognosticate the king's flight. This, however, is not more probable than that he is pointing to the spot where his father was executed, which is a vulgar error. It may be taken as a sign of the moderation of the Revolution of 1688 that after the accession of William III. the statue was still left standing." Possibly, however, this fact, so unlike what would have happened in Paris under like circumstances, may be ascribed to the new king being the son-in-law of James.

CHAPTER XLVI.

WHITEHALL, AND ITS HISTORICAL REMINISCENCES (*continued*).

"——— Non isto vivitur illic
Quo tu rere modo."—*Horace.*

Whitehall forsaken as a Royal Residence—Partial Restoration of the Palace—The Cock-pit—Cromwell and Sir Roger L'Estrange—Death of Oliver Cromwell—The Ultimate Fate of Cromwell's Body—The Exhumation discussed—Curious Record in an Old Parish Register—George Monk at the Cock-pit—Fashionable Life under the Stuarts—Cock-fighting—Defoe's Account—Its Prevalence in England.

In the "New View of London," published in 1708, we read, "This Palace being in the beginning of January, 1697, demolished by fire, except the Banqueting House and the Holbein Gateway, there has since been no reception of the Court in town but at St. James's Palace, . . . and Whitehall will doubtless be rebuilt in a short time, being designed one of the most famous palaces in Christendom." It was not rebuilt, however; and gradually the royal family removed from Whitehall to St. James's Palace, which thenceforward became known as the head-quarters of the English Court.

On page 355 there will be found a copy of a curious outline print giving a bird's-eye view of Whitehall Palace as it appeared after the fire of 1697. In this engraving a sort of lawn, divided into four parterres, projects into the river; while modern mansions of the classical style have taken the place of the old low semi-Gothic houses which previously figured in the foreground.

It is true that after the Restoration Charles II. had made a partial "restoration" at Whitehall. Horace Walpole, in his "Anecdotes of Painting," mentions, as a mark of Charles's taste, that he erected at Whitehall five curious sun-dials. He also collected again a considerable part of the treasures which had been dissipated, and added suites of apartments for the use of his abandoned favourites. James II., too, was occupying Whitehall at the time of the unexpected invasion by the Dutch. He is reported to have caused the weather-vane, which still remains, to be erected on the roof of the palace, in order that he might judge whether or not the elements were favourable to his enemies.

Whitehall Palace, nevertheless, now exists only as a fragment. "The present Banqueting House is, indeed," says Mr. Edward M. Barry, "not one-fortieth part of the original design. Had the latter been carried out, the question of our public offices would probably have been settled for ever, and a modern prime minister would not have had the opportunity of forcing his taste on a reluctant architect."

There were two "cock-pits" in the neighbourhood of this palace; the one on the site of the present Privy Council Office, and the other near the junction of Queen Street and Dartmouth Street with Bird-cage Walk. The two are often confounded together, but the former is the one most frequently mentioned in history in connection with distinguished persons. Philip Herbert, Earl of Pembroke, one of two brothers to whom Shakespeare's Works were dedicated, held the Cock-pit apartments at Whitehall under the Crown, and from a window of his apartment saw his sovereign, Charles I., walk from St. James's to the scaffold. At his death in January, 1649-50, Oliver Cromwell took possession of the rooms; and here, as Mr. Peter Cunningham tells us, he addressed his letter to his aged mother, Elizabeth Bourchier, giving an account of the battle of Dunbar. Here he was waited upon by a deputation from the Parliament, desiring him to "magnify himself with the title of king;" and here Milton and Andrew Marvell, his secretaries, and Waller and Dryden, were his frequent guests. Though averse, by principle, to dramatic entertainments, Oliver Cromwell liked the organ, and took John Hingston, the organist of Charles I., into his own employ. He used often to summon him to play before him at the Cock-pit in Whitehall, near which he resided. Hingston, it appears, used to have concerts at his own house, at which Cromwell would often be present. In one of these musical entertainments Sir Roger L'Estrange happened to be a performer. As he did not leave the room when the Protector entered, his cavalier friends gave him the name of "Oliver's Fiddler," and the name was so serious an annoyance to him after the Restoration, that in 1662 he published a pamphlet, entitled "Truth and Loyalty Vindicated," in which he clears himself from the charge of Republican tendencies, and relates the affair just as it happened:—"Concerning the story of the fiddle, this, I suppose, might be the rise of it. Being in St. James's Park I heard an organ touched in a little low room of one Mr. Hingston: I went in, and found a private company of five or six persons; they desired me to take a viole and bear a part. I did so, and that a part too not much to advance the reputation of my cunning. By-and-by, without the least colour of a design or expectation, in came Cromwell. He found us playing, and, as I remember, so he left us."

The great "Lord Protector" died at Whitehall on the 3rd of September, 1658, after a protracted illness, and amidst the raging of a terrific storm. During his last illness Cromwell became so depressed and debilitated that he would allow no barber to come near him; and his beard, instead of being cut in a certain fashion, grew all over his face. After his death the body lay in state at Somerset House, having been carefully embalmed, and was afterwards buried with more than regal honours in Henry VII.'s Chapel in Westminster Abbey. John Evelyn, in his "Diary," under date of October 2nd, tells us how that he "saw the superb funerall of the Lord Protector. He was carried from Somerset House in a velvet bed of State drawn by six horses, houss'd by the same; the pall held up by his new lords; Oliver lying in effigie in royal robes, and crown'd with a crown, sceptre, and globe, like a king. The pendants and guidions were carried by the officers of the army; and the imperial banner, acheivement, &c., by the heraulds in their coates; a rich compareason'd horse, embroider'd all over with gold; a knight of honor arm'd cap-a-pie, and after all, his guards, soldiers, and innumerable mourners. In this equipage they proceeded to Westminster; but it was the joyfullest funeral I ever saw, for there were none that cried but dogs, which the soldiers hooted away with a barbarous noise, drinking and taking tobacco in the streets as they went."

The ultimate fate of Cromwell's body has at different periods given rise to much controversy from the Restoration down to the present time. It is asserted that after the Restoration it was taken out of his grave, together with the bodies of Ireton (Cromwell's son-in-law) and Bradshaw; the latter, as President of the High Court of Justice, having pronounced sentence of death on Charles I. The three bodies are then said to have been taken in carts to the "Red Lion," in Holborn, and on the 30th of January, the anniversary of King Charles's death, to have been removed on sledges to Tyburn, where they were hanged until sunset, and then taken down and beheaded, their bodies buried in a deep pit under the gallows, and their heads stuck upon the top of Westminster Hall, where at that time sentinels walked.

A strong corroboration of the main incidents of this story is to be found in the "Fifty Years' Recollections, Literary and Personal," of the late Mr. Cyrus Redding, and resting on the authority of Horace Smith, one of the authors of "Rejected Addresses," &c. Redding writes under date about 1821 or 1822:—"Horace Smith was acquainted with a medical gentleman who had in his possession the head of Oliver Cromwell, and in order to gratify my curiosity he gave me a note (of introduction) to him. There accompanied the head a memorandum relating to its history. It had been torn from the tomb with the heads of Ireton and Bradshaw after the accession of Charles II., under a feeling of impotent vengeance. All three were fixed over the entrance of Westminster Hall, the other bones of those three distinguished men being interred at Tyburn under the gibbet—an act well befitting the Stuart character. During a stormy night," he adds, "the head in the centre, that of Cromwell, fell to the ground. The sentry on guard beneath having a natural respect for an heroic soldier, no matter of what party, took up the head and placed it under his cloak until he went off duty. He then carried it to the Russells, who were the nearest relations of Cromwell's family, and disposed of it to them. It belonged to a lady, a descendant of the Cromwells, who did not like to keep it in her house. There was a written minute extant along with it. The disappearance of the head (off Westminster Hall) is mentioned in some of the publications of the time. It had been carefully embalmed, as Cromwell's body is known to have been two years before its disinterment. The nostrils were filled with a substance like cotton. The brain had been extracted by dividing the scalp. The membranes within were perfect, but dried up and looked like parchment. The decapitation had evidently been performed after death, as the state of the flesh over the vertebræ of the neck plainly showed. It was hacked, and the severance had evidently been done by a hand not used to the work, for there were several other cuts beside that which actually separated the bone. The beard, of a chestnut colour, seemed to have grown after death. An ashen pole, pointed with iron, had received the head clumsily impaled upon its point, which came out an inch or so above the crown, rusty and time-worn. The wood of the staff and the skin itself had been perforated by the common wood-worm. I wrote to Horace Smith that I had seen the head, and deemed it genuine. Smith replied, 'I am gratified that you were pleased with Cromwell's head, as I was when I saw it, being fully persuaded of its identity.'" It remains, then, on record that two persons, both men of the world and of large experience, and yet so different from each other in character as Horace Smith and Cyrus Redding, were satisfied with the evidence brought before them to prove its being genuine three-quarters of a century ago. (See also *post*, pp. 539-542.)

In *Notes and Queries*, September, 1874, p. 205, we read that "Cromwell's body was dug up, his head put on a pike and exposed, and, after passing through several hands, was offered for sale to one of the Russells, who was a lineal descendant of Oliver Cromwell through his daughter, Lady Rich."

According to some authorities, the remains were privately conveyed from Whitehall and interred next to those of Mrs. Claypole, Oliver Cromwell's favourite daughter, in Northamptonshire, in accordance with his own wish, the funeral in Westminster Abbey being a mock ceremonial. According to others, the remains were conveyed to the field of Naseby, and interred at midnight in the very spot where he made his last victorious charge, the field being afterwards ploughed over that his enemies might not discover the spot. Another account, indorsed by Heath, the author of the "Flagellum"—who, by the way, contradicts himself, as he afterwards goes on to describe the exhumation in the abbey and the subsequent gibbeting—is that as the body was decomposed and corrupt to such an extent that it was impossible either to embalm or publicly bury it, it was encased in lead and flung into the Thames at midnight. Oldmixon adds that it was thrown into "the deepest part of the Thames." To say nothing of the intrinsic improbability of these accounts, of the fact that neither Cromwell nor his friends were likely to anticipate any indignity being offered to his remains, of the difficulty of secretly conveying the corpse either to Northamptonshire or to Naseby, of the physical impossibility of decomposition necessitating a hurried burial in the Thames—though this is certainly the best

WHITEHALL, LOOKING TOWARDS THE HOLBEIN GATEWAY. (*From a View by Maurer*, 1753.)

authenticated theory—there is, as we shall see, every reason to believe that he was actually interred near his mother and his daughter in the Abbey. First, there is the fact that none of the leading men of the day had any suspicion that the funeral procession, of which we have many elaborate accounts, was a mock ceremonial. Secondly, Cromwell would naturally desire to lie with his mother and daughter in the national mausoleum among those whom he must have looked on as his royal predecessors. Thirdly, Noble, a trustworthy and sensible historian, distinctly says, in his memoirs of the "Protectorate House of Cromwell," that the body was deposited in Westminster Abbey, under a magnificent hearse of wax, on the spot subsequently occupied by the tomb of the Duke of Buckingham, adding that at the Restoration "they found in a vault at the east end of the middle aisle a magnificent coffin which contained the body of the late Protector, upon whose breast was a copper plate double gilt, which upon one side had the arms of the Commonwealth impaling those of the deceased." Of this Noble gives a fac-simile. He then goes on to say that he saw the receipt of the money paid to one John Lewis, a mason, for exhuming the bodies of Cromwell, Ireton, and Bradshaw. This account is corroborated by the following passage in a work entitled "Oliver Cromwell and his Times," by Thomas Cromwell:—"When the coffin of Cromwell was broken into, a leaden canister was found lying on his breast, and within it a copper gilt plate with the arms of England impaling those of Cromwell," &c. "This copper plate is or was," says a writer in the *Gentleman's Magazine* for 1867, "in the possession of the Marquis of Ripon. There can be little doubt, therefore," he adds, "that the body of Cromwell was, after his death, veritably interred in the Abbey. It is perfectly certain, moreover, that after the exhumation it was conveyed to Red Lion Square. Noble tells us that the body lay at the Red Lion from Saturday, January 26, 1660, to the Monday following; and the question is, did it ever leave the Red Lion? It is quite conceivable that Cromwell's partisans bribed the officers who were placed to watch the body, and, like the Ephesian matron in Petronius, substituted another body in its place." On the opposite side, however, we have the testimony of those who actually inspected Cromwell's head on the spikes. "Saw the heads of Cromwell, Brad-

WHITEHALL GARDENS. (*See page* 376.)

shaw, and Ireton set up at the further end of the hall" (Westminster), writes Pepys; and in the diary of a M. Sainthill, a Spanish ambassador of the time, quoted in *Notes and Queries*, series 3, vol. iii., we find the following entry: "The odious carcases of Oliver Cromwell, Ireton, and Bradshawe were drawn on sledges to Tyburn, where they were hanged by the neck from the morning until four in the afternoon."

With reference to the above subject, it may be added that in the register-book of the parish of Deddington, in Oxfordshire, there is the following somewhat singular entry:—"His Majesty Charles II. came into London 29 day of May, 1660, which was 12 year of his raign, which was brought in without bloodshed, and his father was put to death the 30th January, 1648, by the tyrannical power of Oliver Cromwell, who died September 3d, 1658, and was taken up after he had been buried two years and above, and was hanged at Tiborne, and his head was sett up at Westminster; his body was buried underneath the Tyborne, 1661: which Oliver did governe for some years in England."

It may be remembered that in 1653 Cromwell returned from Westminster to Whitehall, with the keys of the House of Commons in his pocket, after having dissolved the "Long" Parliament, as he subsequently explained to the "Barebones" Parliament assembled in the Council Chamber here.

George Monk, Duke of Albemarle, was the next tenant of the Cock-pit at Whitehall, shortly before the Restoration. These apartments were confirmed to the Duke by Charles II., and he died here in 1670. We have already given our readers a good deal of information respecting the private relations of the Duke in our account of the Strand. Then came to reside here George Villiers, Duke of Buckingham, who died in 1687. After the disastrous fire in Whitehall, in 1697, the Cock-pit was converted into offices for the Privy Council; and in 1710, in the Council Chamber, Guiscard attempted to assassinate that noble collector of books and patron of men of letters—Robert Harley, Earl of Oxford. The Cock-pit retained its original name long after the change of its use, for the minutes of the Lords Commissioners of His Majesty's Treasury were dated from the "Cock-pit at Whitehall," as late as the year 1780, if not later. The "Picture of London" (1810) refers to the Council Chamber, as "commonly called the Cock-pit."

Here is a graphic description of Court life at Whitehall in the gay days of our Stuart kings:—"Hyde Park, in the reign of the second Charles," wrote Grace and Philip Wharton in their "Queens of Society," "was only a country drive, a field, in fact, belonging to a publican. Sometimes the Princess Anne might be seen driving there . . . in her coach, panelled only, and without glass windows—a luxury introduced by Charles II. There they encountered Lady Castlemaine and Miss Stuart, whose quarrel as to which should first use the famous coach presented by Grammont to the King was the theme of Whitehall. Sometimes from the groves and alleys of Spring Gardens they emerged perhaps into the broad walks of St. James's Park, between the alleys of which the gay and titled resorted to *cafés*, such as those permitted in the gardens of the Tuileries. Sometimes again the Princess Anne, accompanied by the haughty Freeman (Sarah, Duchess of Marlborough) in her hood and mantle, descended White Hall Stairs and took her pleasure in her barge on the then fresh and pure waters of the Thames, beyond which were green fields and shady trees. These were all inexpensive pleasures; and both 'Mrs. Freeman' and 'Mrs. Morley' (the Princess Anne) were economical. The Princess's allowance from the Privy Purse was small, and Lord Churchill's means were moderate. More frequently, however, the two friends sat in the Princess's boudoir, then termed her 'closet,' and in that sanctum discussed passing events with bitterness—the dramatic close of the days of Charles II., who begged pardon of his surrounding courtiers for 'being so long a dying;' the accession and unpopularity of his brother James, and afterwards the event which roused even Anne from her apathy and made her malicious—the birth of the Prince whom we southrons call the Pretender."

Some account of the "diversion" carried on at the Cock-pit in former times, and of cock-fighting in general, may not be out of place here. Fitz-stephen, who wrote the life of Archbishop Becket, in the reign of Henry II., is the first of our writers that mentions cock-fighting, describing it as the sport of school-boys on Shrove Tuesday. The Cock-pit, it appears, was the school, and the master was the comptroller and director of the sport. From this time, at least, the diversion, however absurd and even impious, was continued among us. It was followed, though disapproved and prohibited, in the 39th year of Edward III.; also in the reigns of Henry VIII. and Queen Elizabeth. It has been by some called a royal diversion, and, as every one knows, the Cock-pit at Whitehall was erected by a crowned head, for the more magnificent celebration of the sport. It was prohibited, however, by one of the Acts of Oliver Cromwell, March 31, 1654.

British cocks are mentioned by Cæsar; but the first actual notice of cock-fighting, as an established sport of the Londoners, occurs in Fitzstephen, who traces it back to the reign of Henry II. From Edward III. down to the days of the Regency—when the then Lord Lonsdale treated the allied sovereigns in 1814 to an exhibition of it—and, perhaps, we may say even to our own time, it has been a fashionable amusement with a certain set of individuals. Henry VIII., as everybody knows, added a cock-pit to his new palace at Whitehall; and even the learned pedant, James I., if we are correctly informed, used to go to witness the sport twice a week.

"A cock-fight," says Defoe, in his "Journey through England" (1724), "is the very model of an amphitheatre of the ancients. The cocks fight here in the area, as the beasts did formerly among the Romans, and round the circle above sit the spectators in their several rows. It is wonderful to see the courage of these little creatures, who always hold fighting on till one of them drops, and dies on the spot. I was at several of these matches, and never saw a cock run away. However, I must own it to be a remnant of the barbarous customs of this island, and too cruel for my entertainment. There is always a continued noise among the spectators in laying wagers upon every blow each cock gives, who, by the way, I must tell you, wear steel spurs (called gaffles) for their surer execution. And this noise runs, fluctuating backwards and forwards, during each battle, which is a great amusement, and I believe abundance of people get money by taking and laying odds on each stroke, and find their account at the end of the battle, but these are people that must nicely understand it. If an Italian, a German, or a Frenchman should by chance come into these cock-pits, without knowing beforehand what is meant by this clamour, he would certainly conclude the assembly to be all mad, by their continued outcries of 'six to four, ten pounds to a crown,' which is always repeated here, and with great earnestness, every spectator taking part with his favourite cock, as if it were a party cause."

That cock-fighting was the original appropriation of the pit of our theatres has been supposed by some who support their view by such quotations as the following:—

> "Let but Beatrice
> And Benedict be seen: Lo! in a trice,
> The cockpit, galleries, boxes, all are full."

In the *Gentleman's Journal*, 1692, is given an English epigram, "On a Cock at Rochester," by Sir Charles Sedley, wherein the following lines, which imply, as it would seem, as if the cock had suffered this annual barbarity by way of punishment for St. Peter's crime:—

> "May'st thou be punished for St. Peter's crime,
> And on Shrove Tuesday perish in thy prime."

Cock-fighting, it would appear, was peculiarly an English amusement in the seventeenth and eighteenth centuries. The characteristics of this brutal sport may be gathered from the remark of a contemporary writer, who, addressing a friend in Paris, tells him that it is worth while to come to England, if it be only to see an election and a cock-pit match. "There is a celestial spirit of anarchy and confusion in these two scenes that words cannot paint."

"Cocks of the game are yet cherished," says Stow, "by divers men for their pleasure, much money being laid on their heads, when they fight in pits, whereof some be costly made for that purpose."

It remains only to add that there were in the seventeenth century, in London and its suburbs, a variety of places where the sport of cock-fighting was practised: the best known were the Royal Cock-pit, in the Birdcage Walk; one in Bainbridge Street, St. Giles'; one "near Gray's Inn Lane;" one in "Pickled-egg Walk;" others at New Vauxhall Gardens, in St. George's-in-the-East, and in Old Gravel Lane, over Blackfriars Bridge. Cock-pits, therefore, in the good old Stuart times, must have been pretty evenly distributed among all classes of the community. The Royal Cock-pit, it will be remembered, afforded to Hogarth characters for what has been epigrammatically and wittily termed "one of his worst subjects, though best plates."

We have said that very little, indeed nothing, of old Whitehall remains. From the twenty-fifth volume of the "Archæologia" we learn that the last portion of it, an embattled doorway of the Tudor date and style, was removed in 1847. Fifteen years or so previously a stone apartment with a groined roof, no doubt a portion of the old palace, was discovered by Mr. Sidney Smirke, F.S.A., in the basement of Cromwell House, in Whitehall Yard; and it seems probable, on referring to Fisher's plan (of which we have given a copy on p. 343), that it formed part of the wine-cellar. Its identity was established by a doorway bearing in its spandrils the arms of Wolsey and of the see of York.

CHAPTER XLVII.

WHITEHALL:—ITS PRECINCT, GARDENS, &c.

"Magnos Senecæ prædivitis hortos."—*Juvenal.*

The Privy Gardens and King Charles's curious Sun-dials—Name changed to Whitehall Gardens—Lady Hervey and Sir Thomas Robinson—Sir Robert Peel's House—Pembroke House and Gwydyr House—The Local Government Board—The Duchess of Portland's Museum of Sculpture—Montagu House—Richmond House—The Duke of Richmond's Gallery of Art—Richmond Terrace—Beating the Bounds—Cannon Row—The Civil Service Commission—Derby Court—Manchester Buildings—A Touching Incident in connection with the Last Days of Charles I.—Parliament Street—Messrs. Nichols' Printing-office—Assassination of Mr. Drummond—The Residence of Charles James Fox—Whitehall Club—The *Whitehall Evening Post*—Curious House Signs.

THE gardens adjoining Whitehall Palace on the south and south-west were laid out in terraces, square and formal in plan, and adorned, after the fashion of the times, with statues of marble and bronze, many of which were subsequently removed to Hampton Court. "In the Privy Garden," says John Timbs, "was a dial, which was set up by Edward Gunter, Professor of Astronomy at Gresham College, and of which he published a description by command of James I., in 1624. A large stone pedestal bore four dials at the four corners, and the great horizontal concave in the centre; and, besides, east, west, north, and south dials at the sides." In the reign of Charles II. this dial was defaced by a nobleman of the court, when drunk; and Andrew Marvell wrote upon it the following epigram:—

"This place for a dial was too insecure,
Since a guard and a garden it could not defend;
For, so near to the court, they will never endure,
A witness to show how their time they mis-spend."

In the court-yard, facing the Banqueting House, was another curious dial, set up in 1669, by order of Charles II. It was invented by one Francis Hall, *alias* Lyne, a Jesuit and Professor of Mathematics at Liége. The dial consisted of five stages rising in a pyramidical form, and bearing several vertical and reclining dials, globes cut into planes, and glass bowls, showing besides "the houres of all kinds," and "many things also belonging to geography, astronomy, and astrology, by the sun's shadow made visible to the eye." Among the pictures were portraits of the King, the two Queens, the Duke of York, and Prince Rupert. Father Lyne published a description of this dial, which consisted of seventy-three parts, and was illustrated with seventeen plates. It would appear, from what the author of the "Curiosities of London" says, that it was subsequently set up at Buckingham House.

We read incidentally that the gardens were intersected by a brook or rivulet, which here ran into the Thames; for in 1667 there was an order made by the Court of Sewers, as to the "sluice near Sir Robert Pye's, and the outfall thereof into the river, near the old orchard at Whitehall, now the Bowling Green." This orchard dated back as far as the reign of Henry VIII.

The site of the old palace of Whitehall, which was made extra-parochial at an early date, formerly formed part of the parish of St. Margaret's, Westminster. In order to assert the extent of the parish, the authorities, in "beating the bounds," took a boat at Parliament Stairs and rowed to the centre arch of Westminster Bridge, where there was a mark, and then landing at Privy Garden Stairs, "passed before Montagu House to the house of the Earl of Lowden" (Loudoun), afterwards the Duke of Richmond's, of which we shall have more to say presently.

Down to a comparatively recent date, the gardens above mentioned were called by the old name of the "Privy Gardens," but this has now become changed to "Whitehall Gardens"—a name given to a row of houses in the rear of the Banqueting House, which, until the formation of the Victoria Embankment, had its gardens and lawns sloping to the Thames. Whitehall Gardens were very fashionable residences in the reign of William IV. In 1835, No. 1, the present home of the National Club, was the town residence of the Marquis of Ailsa, and afterwards of the Dowager Marchioness of Exeter; and further on were the houses of Lord Farnborough (better known as Sir Charles Long) and the Earl of Malmesbury. Here, too, lived, in the time of Pitt and Fox, old Lady Townshend, who in her early days had been one of the "queens of society" in the court of George II. Here used to drop in of an evening George Selwyn and the other wits of the age; and it was said of her by Sir N. W. Wraxall, that, "in the empire of mind, she had succeeded to the place left vacant by Mrs. Hervey and Lady Mary Wortley Montagu, in the previous generation." Mr. Disraeli (afterwards Earl of Beaconsfield) lived in the house, No. 2, from 1873 down to 1879.

Lady Townshend's house was celebrated for the *bon mots* of its mistress. Lady Lepel Hervey tells a good story of her and two Sir Thomas Robinsons, who had both offended her. The one was very tall and thin, the other very plump and short. "I can't bear them; and I can't imagine," remarked her ladyship, "why the one should be preferred to the other, one bit. I see but little difference between them; the one Sir Thomas is as broad as the other is long." Lady Townshend's pleasantry, however, it should be remarked here, was scarcely just. The "broad" Sir Thomas was a man of merit and ability, and for some time Secretary of State, and afterwards was created Lord Grantham. The "long" Sir Thomas was a celebrated bore and butt of the day. Lord Chesterfield used to bear with his dulness for the sake of laughing at him. "One day," adds Lady Hervey, "when Sir Thomas requested his lordship to honour him with some poetic mention, Lord Chesterfield qualified his whim by the following couplet:—

'Unlike my subject will I frame my song,
It *shall* be witty, and it *shan't* be long.'"

In No. 4, a house with a large bow window, the late Sir Robert Peel lived, before and during his premiership; and here he died, July 2nd, 1850, from the effects of a fall from his horse, a few days previously, on Constitution Hill. In this house, whilst occupied by the Peel family, there was a fine gallery of paintings by the old masters, and the best collection of modern portraits by Sir Thomas Lawrence. Those of Canning, Wellington, &c., were there, and a variety of others too many to enumerate here.

Among the other mansions built on the site of the old Privy Gardens two deserve to be mentioned here—viz., Pembroke House and Gwydyr House.

"Lord Pembroke's house at Whitehall," writes Lady Hervey, in 1762, "is taken for the Duc de Nivernois, the French Ambassador." His name will be remembered as one of the *Quarante* and an inveterate versifier; and it is said that not a sitting of that illustrious body took place at Paris which the duke did not enliven by reading out a fable. It is to be hoped that he was more merciful to West-end society here. The mansion known as Pembroke House was afterwards occupied by the late Earl of Harrington, and passed, in or about the year 1853, into the hands of the Government, who turned it into one of the departments of the State.

At Gwydyr House for many years were the offices of the Commissioners of Revenue Inquiry, the Commissioners for Promoting the Fine Arts, and the Commissioners of the Health of Towns. Within its walls is now carried on the business of the Charity Commission for England and Wales. The Local Government Board, established in 1873, has its offices in Whitehall. On the formation of this Board the Poor Law Board ceased to exist, and all the powers hitherto exercised by the Secretary of State and the Privy Council were transferred to this department. The powers exercised by the Local Government Board relate to the registration of births, deaths, and marriages, public health, drainage, public improvements, local government, &c., and also to the prevention of disease. Close by is one of the offices of the Board of Trade, and also that of the Commercial, Labour, and Statistical Departments of the Board.

One of the almost forgotten memories of the neighbourhood of Whitehall, is the celebrated Museum of Sculpture and Works of Art made by the Duchess of Portland. "Here," writes John Timbs, "Pennant was shown a rich pearl surmounted with a crown, which was taken out of the ear of Charles I., after his head was cut off. Here, also, was the Barberini or Portland Vase, purchased by the Duchess from Sir William Hamilton for 1,800 guineas, and subsequently deposited by the Duke of Portland in the British Museum."

Sir Christopher Wren was ordered by Queen Anne, in 1705, to erect a wall to enclose that part of the garden which contained the fountain, as a pleasure-ground to the house inhabited by the Scotch commissioners appointed to settle the terms of the union of the two kingdoms.

At the southern end of Whitehall Gardens is Montagu House, the town mansion of the Duke of Buccleuch, who inherited it from the noble family of Montagu. The old house was a low building, and, with the exception of the pictures it contained, had little or nothing to call for special remark. The building was demolished about the year 1860, when the present magnificent mansion, in the Italian style, was built upon its site, the architect being Mr. George Burn.

There is here a splendid gallery of pictures containing many examples of the first masters. One, having special reference to the locality, is Canaletti's fine view of Whitehall, showing Holbein's Gateway, Inigo Jones's Banqueting House, and the steeple of St. Martin's Church, with the scaffolding about it. Then there are a large number of portraits by Vandyck and others, formerly belonging to Sir Peter Lely, and purchased at the sale of his effects by Ralph, Duke of Montagu. There are also other fine pictures by Vandyck, and a series of family portraits.

On the site of what is now Richmond Terrace was formerly Richmond House, the town residence of the Dukes of Richmond. This mansion stood at the southern end of the Privy Gardens, and faced Whitehall and Charing Cross, on ground previously occupied by the apartments of the Duchess of Portsmouth, Louise Renée de Perrencourt, whose son by Charles II. was the first Duke of Richmond. The house was built for George, second Duke, by the famous architect Boyle, Earl of Burlington, concerning whom Pope asks, "Who builds like Boyle?"

Among those enlightened noblemen and gentle- generous invitation several young artists, whose names were afterwards known to the world, entered themselves as students. Cipriani, the painter, and Wilton, the sculptor, presided as instructors, till the students were sufficiently advanced to follow their bent unaided, and silver medals were occasionally awarded. This benefit was given to the rising school without fee or emolument. The gallery was opened in 1758, ten years before the

WESTMINSTER BRIDGE. *From Canaletti's View.* (*See page* 299.)

men who co-operated practically, and not merely by word of mouth, with George III. in his zeal for the promotion of the fine arts, Charles, the third Duke of Richmond, who held the title from 1750 down to 1806, claims a prominent notice. After his return from "the grand tour," the Duke munificently opened a school for the study of painting and sculpture at his house, at the end of Privy Gardens. Here a spacious gallery was provided, with every convenience and accommodation for the students, and a fine collection of casts, moulded from the most select antique and modern statues at Rome and Florence, was procured. These were set out as models, and young artists were invited, by public advertisement, to make the gallery a school for the study of art. In consequence of this foundation of the Royal Academy. In 1770 it contained upwards of twenty-five statues, and among them may be noted the Apollo Belvidere, the Gladiator, the Venus de Medici, the Dancing Faun, Group of Hercules and Antæus, the Rape of the Sabines, and a variety of casts from the Trajan Column, &c. The value of such a school in London, at a time when there were no railways or other facilities for foreign travel, can hardly be exaggerated. Among the artists who owed some of their early art-training to this school, the *Somerset House Gazette* mentions John Parker, a painter of historical portraits, long resident in Rome; John Hamilton Mortimer, the pupil of Robert Edge Pine (known to his friends as "Friar Pine"), who outstripped all his compeers in the drawing of the

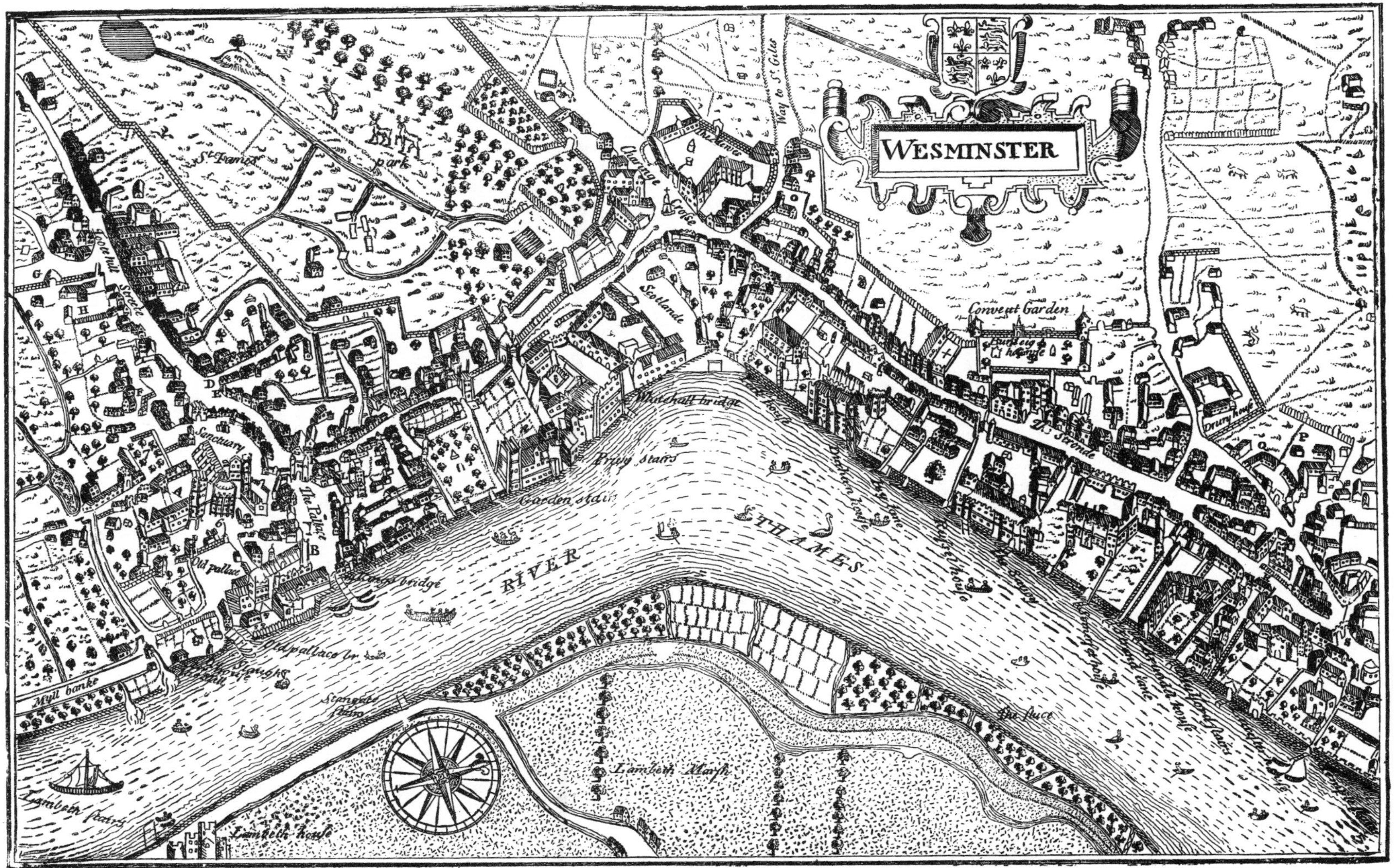

PLAN OF WESTMINSTER. (*From Norden's Survey, taken in Queen Elizabeth's Reign*, 1593.)

A. The Abbey. B. Westminster Hall. D. Long Ditch. E. Thieving Lane. F. The Amnerie. G. Way to Tothill Fields. H. The Lord Dacres. K. King Street. L. Round Woolstaple. M. The Park Lodgings. N. The Tilt Yard. O. St. Martin's-in-the-Fields. P. Clement's Lane. Q. New Inn. R. St Clement Danes. S. Temple Bar.

antique figure, and obtained several prizes from the Society of Arts for drawings made here; Richard Cosway, the miniature painter, and William Parrs, whose productions figured on the walls at the first exhibition of the Royal Academy. This artist was a great traveller, and much patronised by the Lord Palmerston of that day. Another was John A. Grosse, a native of Geneva, and a pupil of Cipriani; another was William Parry, son of a blind Welsh harpist, who obtained several prizes for drawings made in this gallery, and afterwards was a favourite pupil of Sir Joshua Reynolds. Parry made a drawing of the Duke's gallery itself, into which he introduced several portraits: to the curious the discovery of this representation of a place so memorable would be a prize indeed. The Duke of Richmond, too, was a liberal patron of the meritorious artists of his time, as is proved by their numerous works in the Gallery at Goodwood. In other respects the Duke was often attacked for a want of hospitality and liberality; but, possibly, if he had squandered his wealth in giving costly banquets at Whitehall the artists of a century ago would have been so much the more poorly off. It would be well indeed for art, and indeed for literature also, if there were amongst us more noblemen endowed with the same generous feelings as Charles, Duke of Richmond. There is a deep truth in the old line which says:—

"Sint Mæcenates, non deerunt, Flacce, Marones."

But the house has also yet another claim to be remembered, for it was here that the first meeting of the friends of Parliamentary Reform was held, in May, 1782, a week or two before the subject was brought forward by Mr. Pitt in the House of Commons.

The mansion was burnt to the ground in December, 1791. There is an engraving of the house by Boydell; and Edwards, in his "Anecdotes," mentions the drawing of the gallery by Parry, alluded to above, which he considered curious, as being "the only representation of the place." On the site of this mansion, as already stated, has risen Richmond Terrace, a noble row of houses overlooking Montagu House and Whitehall Gardens, standing at right angles to the Thames Embankment, and having an entrance from Parliament Street through handsome iron gates.

We read in Macaulay that in the panic arising out of the perjuries of Titus Oates patrols were marched up and down the streets, and that cannon were planted round Whitehall. The same, too, was the case during the agitation respecting the bill for excluding the Duke of York from the throne.

The house No. 3 in Richmond Terrace is rich in some historical traditions of the last generation. On the formation of Lord Grey's ministry, in 1830, it was occupied by the Premier's brother-in-law, the late Mr. Edward Ellice, M.P., who had a very extensive acquaintance and influence among the Liberal party. As it was near to the Treasury and to the House of Commons, it soon became the head-quarters of the Whigs, and the chief centre of communication between the friends of the intended Reform Bill which was engrossing the attention of the public, including not only the old Whigs and modern Liberals, but also the Radicals of Birmingham. When Parliament was dissolved, in 1831, this house again became the chief centre of action, where candidates came to make inquiries for vacant constituencies, and deputations from near and distant boroughs came in search after eligible candidates, a committee for that purpose sitting there *en permanence*, under the auspices of Mr. Ellice, who here gave Parliamentary dinners and Liberal *re-unions*. After the death of his wife, Lady Hannah Grey, the house passed into the hands of another leading Liberal, a son-in-law of Earl Grey, Sir Charles Wood, who, in the year 1866, was created Viscount Halifax in reward of his long official services.

It was conclusively shown, in the trial of Sir C. Burrell *v.* Nicholson, before Lord Denman, in December, 1833, that when the Palace of Whitehall was seized upon by Henry VIII., he added to its precincts the ground on the south, where Richmond Terrace now stands, the land originally being part of St. Margaret's parish, and belonging to the Abbot of Westminster. The two gardens and three acres of land which the king got from Wolsey were not enough for his Majesty.

At Richmond Terrace, on making the customary perambulation of the bounds of St. Margaret's parish every third year, a little parish apprentice usually was whipped soundly in order that the tradition might be kept up of the limits which marked off the precinct of Whitehall from the mother parish out of which it had been carved.

Extending from the back of Richmond Terrace to Bridge Street, Westminster, and about midway between the Thames and Parliament Street, is a narrow thoroughfare called Cannon (or Canon) Row, which has a little history of its own. We learn from Stow and from John Selden that Cannon Row—or, as it was often called, Channel Row—derived its name from being the residence allotted to the canons of St. Stephen's Chapel. Stow informs us that among its inhabitants in his time were "divers noblemen and gentlemen," as Sir Edward

Hobbes, John Thynne, Esq., Henry Clinton, Earl of Lincoln, and the Earl of Derby and the Duchess of Somerset, mother of the Earl of Hertford, who both occupied "stately" houses.

On the south side stands a dull and heavy building, erected in 1784 for the Ordnance Board, but soon after appropriated to the then newly-formed Board of Control. The architect was a Mr. W. Atkinson. It is now occupied by the Civil Service Commissioners.

In Cannon Row was the "Rhenish Wine House of good resort," to use Strype's quaint expression, and mentioned by Prior and Montague in terms which imply that it was well known in their day:—

"What wretch would nibble on a hanging shelf
When at Pontack's he may regale himself,
Or to the house of cleanly Rhenish go,
Or that at Charing Cross, or that in Channel Row?"

Here stood the "stately" house built by the termagant Anne Stanhope, wife of the Protector Somerset, whose dispute about some trifling point of female precedence is said to have contributed in some degree to her husband's fall. Here, too, was Manchester House, which appears to have been cut up into tenements in the reign of Queen Anne.

Leading out of this row on the east side was formerly Derby Court, so called from the town residence of the Earl of Derby, which it adjoined. Stow describes it, in 1598, as "a stately house," then in the course of erection. It was surrendered in the time of Charles I. to the use of the Parliament, who occupied it for meetings of committees. Here died Pym, and here, as we learn from Ludlow's "Memoirs," his body was publicly exposed after his death. After the Restoration, the Stanleys removed elsewhere, and the mansion was occupied as the office of the Lord High Admiral.

A view of Westminster Bridge, whilst in the course of erection, painted by Canaletti (see page 378), shows the Middlesex bank of the river about Cannon Row and Whitehall covered with handsome mansions, most of which rise perpendicularly out of the river, with stairs and landing-places.

Between Cannon Row and the river, extending in a southerly direction, was a double row of private houses, principally occupied by bachelor members of Parliament, and known as Manchester Buildings. Their site is now covered by the Metropolitan District Railway Station and the St. Stephen's Club. They were so called because they adjoined the town residence of the Earls of Manchester, with "a very fine court which hath a handsome freestone pavement," as we learn from Strype; and adjoining the houses of the Earls of Derby and Lincoln. According to Mr. Peter Cunningham, a gaming-house in these buildings was once occupied by Thurtell, who murdered Mr. Weare.

Cannon Row is of historic interest on account of its connection with the very last days of the life of King Charles I. In Wood's "Athenæ Oxoniensis," we find the following touching narrative told by the King's faithful attendant, Herbert:—

"The same evening [January 28th, 1648–9], two days before his execution, the King took a ring from his finger, having an emerald set therein between two diamonds, and gave it to Mr. Herbert, and commanded him, as late as 'twas, to go with it from St. James's to a lady living then in Canon Row, on the back side of King Street, in Westminster, and to give it to her without saying anything. The night was exceeding dark, and guards were set in several places; nevertheless, getting the word from Colonel Matthew Tomlinson, Mr. Herbert passed currently through in all places where sentinels were, but was bid stand till the corporal had the word from him. Being come to the lady's house, he delivered her the ring. 'Sir,' said she, 'give me leave to show you the way into the parlour;' where, being seated, she desired him to stay till she returned. In a little time after she came in and put into his hands a little cabinet, closed with three seals, two of which were the King's arms, and the third was the figure of a Roman; which done, she desired him to deliver it to the same hand that sent the ring; which ring was left with her; and afterwards, Mr. Herbert taking his leave, he gave the cabinet into the hands of his Majesty (at St. James's), who told him that he should see it opened next morning. Morning being over, the Bishop (Juxon) was early with the King, and, after prayers, his Majesty broke the seals, and showed them what was contained in the cabinet. There were diamonds and jewels—most part broken Georges and Garters. 'You see,' said he, 'all the wealth now in my power to give to my children.'"

Parliament Street, the line of thoroughfare which forms a direct communication between Whitehall and Westminster, was driven through the heart of the "Privy Garden" and the "Bowling Green," displacing the terraces, sun-dials, and statues, about the year 1732, in order to supersede the narrow road which led to Westminster from Charing Cross. Previously the only access from the one spot to the other was by King Street, a narrow way, muddy and ill paved, which ran parallel to Parliament Street from the corner of Downing Street to the Abbey. At the northern end it was spanned by the lofty and imposing gateway, called, from its designer, Holbein's Gate, of which we have already spoken. So bad was King Street as a thoroughfare that we are told that, when the King went to open Parliament in the winter in the early part of the eighteenth century, it was often found necessary to throw down a supply of fagots in the ruts in order to allow the royal coach to pass along. But of King Street we shall have more to say hereafter.

For thirty-six years, from 1820 down to 1856, the Messrs. Nichols issued the *Gentleman's Magazine* at their printing-office in this street. The work of editing and printing the *Gentleman's Magazine* had for many years previously been conducted by the Messrs. Nichols at their office in Red Lion Passage, Fleet Street. As far back as 1792, the writers in the *Gentleman's Magazine* were thus satirised—much to their own credit—by "Peter Pindar:"—

"And see the hacks of Nichols's Magazine
Rush loyal to berhyme a King and Queen."

It was in Parliament Street, on the 26th of January, 1843, that Mr. E. Drummond, private secretary to Sir Robert Peel, was shot by a man named Macnaghten, who mistook him for the Premier. No. 52 in this street was for many years the residence of Charles James Fox.

At the corner of Derby Street, the short thoroughfare leading out of Parliament Street into Cannon Row, stands the Whitehall Club, which was built about the year 1866. The building, Italian in style, is constructed of stone, and consists of three storeys, besides offices in the basement. It was built from the designs of the late Mr. Parnell, at a cost of about £25,000. Over the doorway and upon the cornice is some admirable sculpture executed by Mr. Tolmie. The rooms are spacious and lofty, and well adapted to the purposes to which they are devoted.

Close by stood a small public-house, of which Charles Dickens tells us, that when a very young boy, he lounged in there and asked for a glass of ale, which the kind-hearted landlady gave him, after sundry inquiries as to his name, age, and belongings, and into the bargain a kiss, "half-admiring, half-compassionate, but all womanly and good, I am sure."

With respect to this highly historical neighbourhood, Pope, as usual, minutely accurate in details, thus writes in a spirit of prophecy, which, it is needless to say, has never yet been quite fulfilled to the letter:—

"Behold! Augusta's glittering spires increase,
And temples rise, the beauteous works of peace.
I see, I see, where two fair cities bend
Their ample bow, a new Whitehall ascend;
There mighty nations shall enquire their doom,
The world's great oracle in times to come:
There kings shall sue, and suppliant states be seen
Once more to bend before a British Queen."

And yet, after all, the seer may be regarded as not so very wide of the mark, if we interpret a "new Whitehall" to mean the new Houses of Parliament, and the new Foreign, Indian, and Colonial Offices, which have lately risen on the Park side of Whitehall, and have well nigh effaced the narrow and close *cul de sac* of Downing Street.

Before closing our remarks on Whitehall, we may state that in September, 1718, De Foe, then busy in the midst of politics, secular and religious, started the *Whitehall Evening Post*, a newspaper consisting of two leaves, in small quarto, and published on Tuesdays, Thursdays, and Saturdays. De Foe was connected with it till June, 1720, but the paper continued to exist for many years after this date. Whether it was actually published at Whitehall, or near to it, is not known, but it is probable that it was connected with the courtly locality through some of its contributors.

It must be remembered that before the middle of the eighteenth century, nearly every house in the leading streets of London and Westminster had its sign. Thus an observer in the reign of James I. remarks: "On the way from Somerset House to Charing Cross we pass the 'White Hart,' the 'Red Lion,' the 'Mairmade,' the 'iii Tuns,' 'Salutation,' the 'Graihound,' the 'Bell,' and the 'Golden Lyon;' in sight of Charing Cross, the 'Garter,' the 'Crown,' the 'Bear and Ragged Staffe,' the 'Angel,' the 'King Harry (*sic*) Head.'" It is almost needless to add that all trace and nearly every record of these house signs have long since disappeared before the onward march of the prosaic spirit of modern progress. "The houses in the West-end, in 1685, were not numbered," writes Macaulay; "there would, indeed, have been very little advantage in numbering them, for of the coachmen, chairmen, porters, and errand-boys of London only a small proportion could read, and it was necessary to use marks which the most ignorant could understand. The shops were therefore distinguished by painted or sculptured signs, which gave a gay and grotesque aspect to the streets." If the walk from Charing Cross to Whitechapel lay through an "endless succession of 'Saracens' Heads,' 'Royal Oaks,' 'Blue Bears,' and 'Golden Lambs,' which disappeared when they were no longer required for the direction of the common people," the same, in a certain degree, must have been true of the walk from Charing Cross to Westminster Abbey.

CHAPTER XLVIII.

WHITEHALL.—THE WESTERN SIDE.

"A royal house, with learned Muses grac'd,
But by his death imperfect and defac'd."
Storer's Metrical History of Wolsey.

Wallingford House—Pope's Lines on the Death-bed Scene of Villiers, Duke of Buckingham—Wallingford House converted into the Admiralty Office—The Semaphore Telegraph—Authority and Jurisdiction of the Admiralty—Career of Lord Sandwich at the Admiralty—Funeral of Lord Nelson—Anecdote of Mr. Croker—The Horse Guards—The Commander-in-Chief's Department—Pennant's View of the Old Horse Guards—Dover House—The Treasury—Downing Street: its Political Associations, and Anecdotes of Former Occupants—The Old Foreign Office—The New Foreign, India, and Colonial Offices—Library of the India Office.

NEARLY the whole of the western side of Whitehall, between Charing Cross and Parliament Street, is occupied either by Government buildings or by other edifices of public importance. First of all we have, nearly opposite to Scotland Yard, the building known to all officers of Her Majesty's navy as the Admiralty. The present extensive building was erected in the reign of George II., from the designs of Ripley, on the site of Wallingford House, a fine mansion, built by William, Lord Knollys, Viscount Wallingford, and Earl of Banbury, in the second year of Charles I.

Wallingford House was subsequently used by the "Lord Protector" and his councillors for the purpose of holding consultations on public affairs. Here, too, was born the notorious and reprobate Villiers, Duke of Buckingham, the second of his line who bore that fatal title—the son of the royal favourite assassinated by Felton, and the man who, having squandered a princely fortune, and thrown away a splendid position, became the butt for Dryden's satire, while his death-bed served to "point a moral" for Pope:—

"In the worst inn's worst room, with mat half hung,
The floors of plaster and the walls of dung,
On once a flock-bed, but repaired with straw,
With tape-tied curtains never meant to draw,
The 'George' and 'Garter' dangling from that bed,
Where tawdry yellow strives with dirty red,
Great Villiers lies. Alas! how changed for him,
That life of pleasure and that soul of whim!
Gallant and gay in Cliefden's proud alcove—
The bower of wanton Shrewsbury and love;
Or just as gay at Council, in a ring
Of mimic statesmen and their merry King:
No wit to flatter left of all his store,
No fool to laugh at, which he valued more,
There, victor of his health, of fortune, friends,
And fame, this lord of useless thousands ends!"

Though the first line, as it has often been observed, embodies a poetical fiction, the picture as a whole is true, in spite of an error in topography. It was not at a paltry "inn" in Yorkshire, as commonly supposed, but at Kirby Mallory, in Leicestershire, at the house of one of his tenants, that Villiers, Duke of Buckingham, was suddenly struck with illness and died. From his biography by his retainer Fairfax, and from an account of his death-bed in the "Collection of Letters of Persons of Quality and Others," it is clear that, although he did not die in actual want of the necessaries of life, yet he died in comparative poverty, having wasted his fortune to a mere nothing—he who had been literally "the lord of thousands."

Wallingford House was purchased in the reign of William III., and appointed for the Admiralty Office, which had been removed thither from Duke Street, Westminster. The present edifice is very extensive. The front elevation, facing the street, has two deep wings, forming a court-yard, and in the centre is a portico formed of four lofty columns of the Ionic order; these support the pediment, within which are the Admiralty arms. The interior is very convenient, and comprises a large hall and numerous offices appropriated to the transacting of maritime concerns. The screen before the court, which was subsequently built by Robert Adam, has been much admired; it consists of a piazza of the Doric order supporting its entablature, and enriched with marine ornaments. It must be owned that the heavy structure, as a whole, is better adapted for use than for show; and it may be remarked that Pennant speaks of the Admiralty as "a clumsy pile, but properly veiled from the street by Mr. Adam's handsome screen."

During the great war against Napoleon, and subsequently, the Admiralty was surmounted by a "telegraph," as the semaphore was then called. By this "telegraph" a message could be sent, on fine days and in clear weather, to Portsmouth, and to one or two other stations, in an hour, or even in less time; and the semaphore stood on the top of the mansion until its use was entirely superseded by the electric telegraph. Hence it is that Leigh Hunt quaintly remarks, in the year 1835: "Where the poor archbishop sank down in horror at the sight of King Charles's execution, telegraphs now ply their dumb and far-seen discourses, like spirits in the guise of mechanism, and tell news of the spread of liberty and knowledge all over the world."

What would he have said if he could have looked forward only five short years and seen the machine on which he dwelt thus proudly laid quietly on the shelf, being superseded by a far more ingenious and subtle mechanism, the result of the scientific researches of Sir Charles Wheatstone and of Sir William Fothergill Cooke?

The interior of the Admiralty, although convenient and capacious, offers nothing remarkable; nor do any particular ceremonies take place within its walls; it is business, not ceremony, that is here the order of the day. It has been remarked with truth that, "without any very extravagant stretch of fancy, the Admiralty may be said to be the mighty steam-engine which sets in motion and gives energy to all the rest of the *matériel* and machinery of our naval power, and consequently contributes much to that of the whole empire."

The authority and jurisdiction now vested in the Admiralty was originally exercised by an individual, a high officer of state, called the Admiral of the King. The first upon actual record was William de Leybourne, "Admiral de la Mer du Roy d'Angleterre," in 1297. The office of High Admiral continued to be held by an individual until the early part of the seventeenth century; in 1632 it was, for the first time, "put into commission," or its duty and authority confided to a Board of Commissioners, consisting of all the chief officers of state. At the Restoration the Duke of York was appointed Lord High Admiral, and he retained the office till 1684, when Charles II. took it upon himself; but James resumed it in the following year, on becoming king. The Revolution caused it again to be put into commission, till 1707, when Prince George of Denmark became Lord High Admiral, with an assisting council of four members. On his death, in the following year, the Earl of Pembroke was appointed to succeed him, in similar form; but within about a twelvemonth he resigned, and from that time to the present the office has always been in commission, with the exception of a brief interval in 1827–8, during which the title of Lord High Admiral was again restored, in the person of the Duke of Clarence, afterwards William IV. The Admiralty Board consists of six members, styled the Lords (Commissioners) of the Admiralty, who are not, however, all of equal dignity and authority; for besides taking official precedence of the others, the First Lord of the Admiralty has higher privileges

THE HORSE GUARDS, FROM ST. JAMES'S PARK. *Temp. Charles II.* (*See page* 387.)

and emoluments than his colleagues, and he is, by virtue of his official position, a member of the Cabinet.

The Great Room used to be, during the last century, hung round with pictures of the South Sea Islands, and decorated with naval emblems and curiosities; and in the good old days, when Lord Sandwich held the office of First Lord of the Admiralty, it was the scene of many hospitable and frolicsome dinners, presided over by the elegant Miss Ray, whose murder by the Rev. Mr. Hackman, on the 7th of April, 1779, we have recorded at some length in our chapter on Covent Garden. (See *ante*, p. 260.)

Lord Sandwich, whose name is most intimately connected with the control of the Admiralty during the early part of the reign of George III., was a man of high ability as a statesman, and one to whom history has scarcely done justice. He died in April, 1792. He was educated at Eton and at Trinity College, Cambridge, and in early life had spent two years in a classical tour round the coasts of the Mediterranean, of which he published an illustrated account, at a time when "illustrated" works were less common than now. In Lord North's ministry, in 1770, he was Secretary for Foreign Affairs, but exchanged his portfolio for that of First Lord of the Admiralty—a post for which his knowledge of maritime affairs especially fitted him. Sir N. W. Wraxall writes: "I saw, in 1782, the furniture of Lord Sandwich being carried off from the Admiralty, of which Keppel, who had been named as his successor, was just taking possession." Lord Sandwich's public career ended with the year 1784, after which date he divided his time between London and his seat at Hinchinbrooke, in Huntingdonshire. He knew most ancient and modern languages, was a collector of coins, and an excellent musician. "Others," observes Mr. Cradock, who knew him well, "received great emoluments for what they performed; Lord Sandwich was always content to know that he had deserved them. He was also, in many ways, a great practical benefactor to Greenwich Hospital."

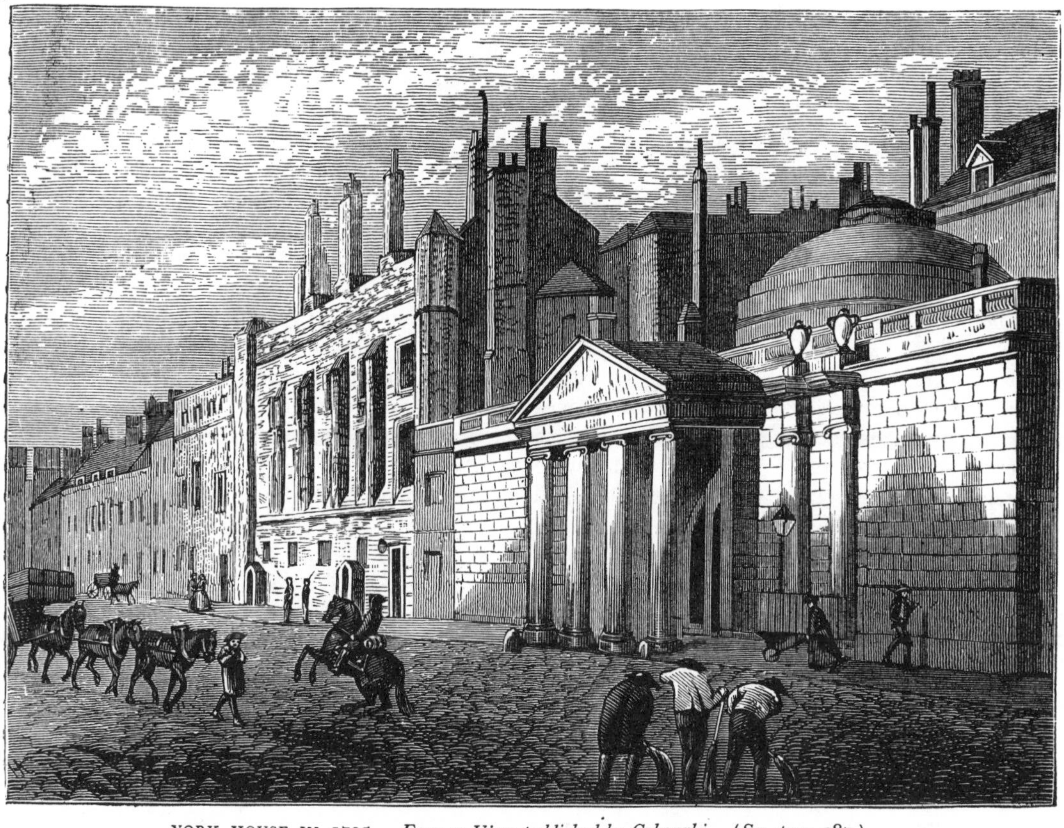

YORK HOUSE IN 1795. *From a View published by Colnaghi.* (*See page* 387.)

It was within the walls of Wallingford House that, in 1667, the body of the Court poet, Abraham Cowley, lay in state for a day before its interment in the Abbey hard by.

In the large room on the ground-floor, to the right as we enter, lay Nelson's body in state, on the night of January 8th, 1806, previous to its being buried the next day in St. Paul's. It had been brought from Greenwich by water to Whitehall, and thence carried to the Admiralty. The procession is described at full length in the *Gentleman's Magazine*, from which we abridge the following account:—It consisted of ten gun-boats, two and two; boats containing the River Fencibles; nine state barges, draped in black, containing the mourners, officials connected with the Admiralty, and also the Heralds of Arms, bearing the insignia of the deceased. The third barge, which contained the body, was covered with black velvet (the other barges being covered with black cloth), the top adorned with plumes of black feathers, and also with armorial bearings, and a viscount's coronet. The body was covered with a large sheet, and a pall of velvet adorned with six escutcheons. This part of the procession was flanked by eighteen row-boats of River Fencibles. Then came the state barges of eight of the City companies, flanked by the like number of row-boats with Harbour Marines. The funeral barge was rowed by sixteen seamen belonging to the *Victory;* the other barges by picked men from the Greenwich pensioners. As the procession passed the Tower minute-guns were here fired. The procession arrived at Whitehall Stairs about three o'clock, having been about three hours rowing up from Greenwich, when the King's, Admiralty, Lord Mayor's, and City barges drew up in two lines, through which the barge with the body passed, the bands at the same time playing the "Dead March" in "Saul," "with other dirgeful strains, with the most impressive effect, the gun-boats firing minute-guns all the time." During the time of disembarking there was a tremendous hail-storm. In the procession from Whitehall Stairs to the Admiralty the coffin was surmounted by a rich canopy, supported by six admirals. Every necessary preparation had been made at the Admiralty for receiving the body. The Captains' Room, in which it was placed, was hung with black cloth, and lighted with wax tapers placed in sconces on the sides. The body remained in the room, guarded by the officers of the house and the undertakers, till the ceremony of its removal to St. Paul's commenced. This took place on the following day, when the remains of Nelson were conveyed by the old sailors of the *Victory*, and a large military and naval procession, on a magnificent funeral car, or open hearse, decorated with a carved imitation of the head and stern of the *Victory*, surrounded with escutcheons of the arms of the deceased, and adorned with appropriate mottoes and emblematical devices; under an elevated canopy in the form of the upper part of an ancient sarcophagus, with six sable plumes and the coronet of a viscount in the centre, supported by four columns representing palm-trees, with wreaths of natural laurel and cypress entwining the shafts; the whole upon a four-wheeled carriage, drawn by six led horses, the caparisons adorned with armorial bearings.

Spacious as is the old Admiralty, it has been found, in these days of naval activity, utterly inadequate, and a large block of offices, in a modified form of the classic, with Anglo-Italian features, has been built in the rear, overlooking St. James's Park. This structure, completed in 1895, is to be supplemented by another on the north side, which will join the present buildings together at their northern extremities, and so will be formed three sides of a quadrangle enclosing the Admiralty Gardens.

A capital story in connection with the Admiralty is told by Mr. Cyrus Redding, in his "Fifty Years' Recollections:"—Mr. Croker, the Secretary of that department, happening to dine at the Pavilion at Brighton, under the Regency, entered into conversation with the Duke of Clarence. The latter liked nothing better than a sly cut at that department, and especially at Croker himself. In reply to some chance remark of the Secretary, the Duke said, "Ah! if ever I am king, I will be my own First Lord of the Admiralty." "Does your royal highness recollect," asked Croker, "what English king was his own First Lord the last time?" The duke shook his head, and replied in the negative. "It was James II., sir." There was a general laugh among the party, as well there might be; but the duke was taken aback, and the regent was greatly annoyed at the remark when repeated to him afterwards.

Adjoining the Admiralty, on the south side, is the extensive range of buildings known as the Horse Guards. The building, which is heavy and tasteless, is from the designs of Kent, and was erected about the year 1753, at a cost of £30,000. The clock in the turret which surmounts the centre of the building has always enjoyed a reputation for accuracy, and used to be the grand regulator of all the timepieces in its vicinity.

The open space at the back is the Parade Ground: here are two curious pieces of ordnance—one a large howitzer or mortar captured at the siege of Cadiz, in 1810, and the other a Turkish piece, taken at Alexandria, in 1801. Under two small pavilions in front, on either side of the entrance in Whitehall, sentinels, mounted, and in uniform, do duty from ten to four o'clock every day.

The Horse Guards is somewhat appropriately placed, occupying as it does the site of the Tilt-yard (or place for military exercises), of which we have already spoken. The origin of the name is this:—Soon after the Restoration Charles II. raised a body of troops, which he designated his "Horse Guards," to whom the special duty was assigned of protecting the king's person. For this troop stables and barracks were built in the Tilt-yard, but in 1751 these were pulled down to make way for the present edifice. Accommodation for the troops quartered here is provided by two lateral pavilions, which flank the east face of the main building. Here were for many years the head-quarters of the Commander-in-Chief, the Adjutant-General, and the Quartermaster-General, whose duties are now concentrated at the War Office, in Pall Mall. The Horse Guards now furnishes accommodation mainly for the Department of the Inspector-General of Fortifications. With the War Office we shall deal in our next volume, but of the Commander-in-Chief's department it may be said that it is solely devoted to the government, discipline, and movements of the military; and that to the Commander-in-Chief is unreservedly confided the rule and governance of the whole army. He is accessible not only to every commissioned officer of the British army, but to his immediate connections; and he or his deputy (the Military Secretary) holds a *levée* at intervals during the "season." Every person desirous of attending it previously sends a letter expressing that intention, and stating the object of his visit; and as these interviews are considered strictly confidential, by endorsing it "for the *levée*," he ensures its being opened and read by the great military authority addressed, and by him only. His (or her) name is then transferred to a list, against a number which regulates the order of the applicants' reception; the ladies being always, of course, admitted first. That number is copied upon the back of each visitor's letter, which is also endorsed with a memorandum, from which the answer is orally delivered at the interview. Thus the Commander-in-Chief is at no loss, and time is not wasted in discussion. During this *levée* there is an entire absence of ceremony of every description, and the Commander-in-Chief is the only personage who appears in regimentals. The suite of rooms, also, used for the purpose consists only of three—namely, a waiting-room, a vestibule (in which the ladies abide their turn), and the audience-chamber. The first of these is a good-sized apartment, and faces Whitehall; the walls are almost covered with maps, and the chairs surrounding the room are placed, with military precision, exactly equi-distant. The vestibule is a small circular hall, possessing nothing more remarkable than the boundary-line of the parishes of St. Martin's and St. Margaret's, Westminster, which is cut through its centre, and accompanied with suitable inscriptions. The audience-chamber, which overlooks the parade-ground in St. James's Park, partakes of the same degree of military formality that distinguishes the other rooms.

The ladies, as we have stated, are presented first. All being in readiness, the attendant in waiting, bearing a copy of the numbered list above mentioned, calls out the name of the visitor who is to be seen, and ushers her into the presence of the Commander-in-Chief. The confidential nature of the interview admits the presence of no other person—not even the private secretary. Thus there is every encouragement offered for the most minute and circumstantial detail of private interests and domestic matters, into which the head of the army fully enters, with a view to serving the applicant in proportion to the claims put forward. The ladies having all been received and dismissed, the gentlemen are then summoned, *seriatim*, in such a manner as to ensure that no moment of time shall be lost. Some of the visits are merely ceremonial; others—and by far the greater number—are made to follow up previously forwarded applications for some one or other of the few military appointments in the gift of the Commander-in-Chief.

Pennant gives an interesting view of the old Horse Guards from the Park, as the building must have appeared in 1660–70. In the background it shows the Banqueting House, the Holbein Gate, the Treasury in its ancient state, and the top of the Cock-pit adjoining. In the foreground is to be seen the "Merry Monarch," with his favourite dogs and an attendant train of courtiers. To the right of the spectator is the eastern end of the straight and formal "canal," which then almost bisected the Park. We have reproduced this print in a reduced form on page 384.

Between the Horse Guards and the Treasury stands Dover (formerly York) House, so called after the Hon. George Agar-Ellis, afterwards the accomplished Lord Dover. It is now the office of the Secretary of State for Scotland. It was built in 1774, by Payne, for Sir Matthew Fetherstonhaugh, who sold it to the first Lord Melbourne, father of the late Premier. In 1789 it was bought by the Duke of York, who added the domed entrance-hall and the grand staircase, and after whom it was called York House. A print of it was published by Colnaghi in 1795, dedicated to Lord Melbourne. Of this view we have given a copy on page 385. This mansion faces the Banqueting House of Whitehall at the point where Holbein's Gate once stood, and commands a front prospect of the broad and open thoroughfare from Charing Cross to Parliament Street.

The Treasury Buildings, which occupy some 300 feet of frontage to Whitehall extending from Dover House to Downing Street, were originally part of Cardinal Wolsey's Banqueting Hall, and were re-fronted by Sir John Soane, the architect and antiquary; and it is believed that the old buttresses are still *in situ.* A new façade, in the Corinthian style, was added by the late Sir Charles Barry, R.A., about the year 1850. By these alterations and additions, the whims and conceits of Sir John Soane have disappeared, and the order, which is a reduced and simplified model of that of the Temple of Jupiter Stator, has, by the enrichment of the frieze and the addition of considerable ornament above it, been brought more into harmony with the building (or rather the building with it), which would have been impossible with less enrichment. The building, which has a short return front towards Downing Street, also contains the office of the Privy Council, of the Education Department, and of the Board of Trade. *A propos* of the first-mentioned of these offices, we may here insert the text of the oath taken by the Clerk of Her Majesty's Privy Council, on appointment, which is as follows:—"You shall swear to be a true and faithful servant unto the Queen's Majesty, in the exercise of the functions of the Clerk of the Privy Council in ordinary. You shall not know or understand of any manner of thing to be attempted, done, or spoken against Her Majesty's person, honour, crown, or dignity royal; but you shall lett or withstand the same to the uttermost of your power, and either do or cause it to be revealed, either to Her Majesty herself, or to the Privy Council. You shall keep secret all matters committed and revealed unto you, or that shall be treated of secretly in council. And if any of the said treaties or councils shall touch any of the counsellors, you shall not reveal it unto him, but shall keep the same until such time as, by the consent of Her Majesty or by the Council, publication shall be made thereof. You shall to your uttermost bear faith and allegiance to the Queen's Majesty, and shall assist and defend all jurisdictions, pre-eminences, and authorities granted to Her Majesty, and annexed to the Crown by Act of Parliament or otherwise, against all foreign princes, persons, prelates, states, or potentates. And generally in all things you shall do as a faithful and true servant and subject ought to do to Her Majesty. So help you God, and the holy contents of this book."

The offices and official residence of the First Lord of the Treasury, where the Cabinets of Her Majesty's ministers have often been held, are, together with those of the Chancellor of the Exchequer, still located in Downing Street, in plainer buildings (partly erected for dwelling-houses), behind this handsome pile, and reaching to St. James's Park. The interior of the Treasury contains little or nothing very remarkable, excepting, perhaps, an old gilt state chair, or throne, which is placed at the head of the table in the Board-room.

Although all royal proclamations and diplomatic correspondence are dated "from our Palace at St. James's," yet for nearly the last two centuries the motive power, so to speak, of the administration of the country has had its head-quarters in Downing Street, a dull, narrow *cul de sac* running up westwards from the corner of the buildings of the Treasury. Almost the last of the houses which composed it disappeared in 1874, the work of demolition having been begun as far back as 1828; but its memory will long survive enshrined in the parliamentary history of the empire. Consequently, therefore, it must always be rich in its former associations; and probably no street in this metropolis, equally small in extent, can boast of having had such distinguished residents and tenants. Sir Robert Walpole, the Prime Minister of illustrious memory, made it his home during his long tenure of office; and he was the first Premier who did so. Lord North, as Premier, had his chambers here, occupying rooms on the first floor; and it is recorded of him that when he exchanged that post for the lesser responsibilities of a Secretary of State, he forgot that with the change of office came a change also of chambers, and walked mechanically into his old quarters instead of mounting another pair of stairs.

Different Prime Ministers have dealt differently with the official residence of the Premier in Downing Street. Some, like Pitt and Lord Grey, have made it really their home during their years of place and power; others, like Lord Melbourne and Sir Robert Peel, have used it only during the hours of business. Lord Grey took up his abode here; and it is here that R. B. Haydon has represented the earl pondering by his fireside after one of the great debates on the Reform Bill. Mr. Disraeli (afterwards Lord Beaconsfield) and Mr. Gladstone also took up their residence here as Premiers.

"Downing Street," says Mr. John Timbs, "has

a host of political associations, and anecdotes of its former occupants abound. When Sir Robert Walpole removed from his official residence here, he found an old account-book in which his father had set down his personal expenses. In three months and ten days, which he had spent in London one winter as a member of Parliament, he had expended but sixty-four pounds seven shillings and fivepence. There were in it many entries for 'Nottingham ale,' many eighteenpences for dinners, five shillings to 'Bob' Walpole, afterwards Earl of Orford, and one memorandum of 'six shillings given to Mr. Williams in exchange for a wig;' and yet this old man—the grandfather of Horace Walpole—had a rental of £2,000 a year. He little thought, poor penurious old man that he was, that a sum which maintained him for a whole parliamentary session, would scarcely serve for one of his grandsons to buy a pair of fans for a princess at Florence!"

Here, in 1763, was the hospitable house of Sir John Cust, Speaker of the House of Commons, often mentioned by Cradock in his "Memoirs;" and in this street Belzoni, the African explorer, and his wife lodged in 1820, on their return from Egypt and Nubia.

If we may believe Mr. Peter Cunningham, it was in this street that the Duke of Wellington and Lord Nelson met for the only time in their lives. It was at the Colonial Office, at that time "No. 14, Downing Street," in a small waiting-room on the right hand upon entering, that the two heroes—the former then plain Sir Arthur Wellesley—both wanting an interview with the Secretary of State—were accidentally brought into each other's presence. "The duke knew Nelson from his pictures: Lord Nelson, however, did not know the duke; but he was so struck with his conversation that he stepped out of the room to inquire who he was!" This *rencontre* has been made the subject of a picture, which is engraved.

The "heaven-born minister," William Pitt, lived in Downing Street; and here, as he tells us in Wraxall's "Memoirs," the first Marquis Cholmondeley waited on Pitt as head of the establishment of the Prince of Wales. "The affair," he writes, "related to a matter of accounts. I find it impossible to do justice to the perspicuity and rapidity of his (Pitt's) calculations. In the course of a few minutes he went through and settled every item, leaving me lost in admiration at his ability."

Pitt, during his tenure of office, not only kept up a house here, but made it his constant residence to such an extent that he was never willingly absent from its precincts. While his rival, Fox, could unbend himself in the society of his friends at Brooks's Club, or with his family at St. Anne's Hill, near Chertsey, Pitt could do nothing of the kind, and away from Downing Street he was miserable. When forced, from 1801 to 1804, to live in solitary grandeur at Walmer Castle, in the company of his niece, Lady Hester Stanhope, while Addington, whom he had raised to the highest posts from comparative obscurity, filled his place, he supported life only by the anticipation of a speedy return to Downing Street. His wishes were gratified. He resumed office after three years' exclusion, but in less than two more years he died, the victim of disappointed ambition.

> "Evertere domos totas optantibus ipsis
> Dî faciles."

Preliminaries of peace with France were signed at Lord Hawkesbury's office in Downing Street, on the 2nd of October, 1801; and on the 10th of the same month General Lauriston, Buonaparte's first aide-de-camp, arrived with the ratification. "On his arrival in town," we read, "he was greeted with immense cheering by the populace. On the same and following evening the metropolis was brilliantly illuminated."

Mr. Cyrus Redding tells an anecdote, the scene of which must have been laid in the house of the First Minister of the Crown, in the time of Earl Grey. A gentleman named Stuart, who had lately become proprietor of the *Courier* newspaper, and said to have made his money as a coal merchant in the City, waited on his lordship, and, without any circumlocution or "beating about the bush," offered for his acceptance the support of the paper—which up to then had been of Tory politics—in exchange for the Treasury patronage. Lord Grey looked at him with indignation, and quietly rang the bell, and when the footman entered, bade him "show that gentleman the door." It is probable that he did not know the right way to approach a minister, and that he was not worse or more corrupt than scores of members of Parliament and high-born individuals who have preferred similar requests. He merely mistook the way.

Another good story is told about Downing Street by Mr. T. Raikes, in his "Diary." In the early Reform riots, a mob ran violently into Downing Street and rushed up to the sentinel at the door of the Foreign Office, crying, "Liberty or death!" The soldier presented his musket, and said, "Hands off, you fellows! I know nothing about liberty; but if you come a step farther, I'll show you what death is!" It is to be hoped that the brave fellow was rewarded for his pluck and his wit too.

The general appearance of Downing Street as it was in the reign of George IV. or William IV. is thus hit off by Theodore Hook: "There is a fascination in that little *cul de sac;* an hour's inhalation of its atmosphere affects some men with giddiness, others with blindness, and very frequently with the most oblivious boastfulness." And possibly those who know anything of public life and politics will confess that the wit was not far from the mark.

THE NEW FOREIGN OFFICE. (*See page* 392.)

Between "The King's Printing-office" at Westminster and the various offices of State which centre in Downing Street, for many years there used daily to trudge a messenger or errand-carrier named John Smith, who was a favourite with several Premiers in succession, from Sir Robert Walpole down to William Pitt. What others accounted humble work became in his hands most important; and "the King's Messenger," as he styled himself, yielded to none of his Majesty's ministers in his idea of the dignity of his office, when entrusted with addresses, bills, royal speeches, and other State papers. At the offices of the Secretaries of State, when loaded with parcels of this description, he would throw open every chamber without ceremony; the Treasury and Exchequer doors could not oppose him, and even the study of archbishops has often been invaded by this important messenger of the press. His antiquated and greasy garb corresponded with his wizard-like shape, and his immense cocked hat was continually in motion, to assist him in the bows of the old school. The recognition and nods of great men were his especial delight; but he imagined that this courtesy was due to his character, as being identified with the State, and the Chancellor and the Speaker were considered by him in no other view than persons filling departments in common with himself, for the seals of the one and the mace of the other did not, in his estimation, distinguish them more than the bag used by himself in the transmission of the despatches entrusted to his care. The imperfect intellect given to him seemed only to fit

WESTMINSTER. FROM THE ROOF OF WHITEHALL. (*From a View published by Smith*, 1807.)

him for the situation he filled. Take him out of it, he was as helpless as a child, and easily became a dupe to any one who was disposed to impose upon him. With a high opinion of his own judgment, however, he diverted himself and others by mimicking the voice and manner of his superiors, when he thought he perceived any assumption of character. Poor old John Smith, who felt as if he carried the world on his shoulders, and was as important a part of the constitution, in his own conceit, as the Prime Minister himself, died in 1818, at the age of ninety.

Downing Street—though for a century and a half the name was almost synonymous with the existing administration—has become almost entirely a thing of the past; for though two or three of the houses which were so familiar to Spencer Perceval, George Canning, and Lord Liverpool are still standing at the farther end, yet most of them have been absorbed into the large block of new public buildings which have been erected on its southern side. The clearance of Downing Street, however, as we have already shown, has been long in progress, having been commenced as far back as the year 1828, when "The Cat and Bagpipes," at its south-eastern corner, disappeared. Here, in early life, George Rose, a clerk in a Government office, afterwards Secretary of the Treasury, used to dine on a plain mutton chop.

The old Foreign Office, which stood on the south side of the street, was a brick building, with no architectural pretensions. It consisted of a centre, with two slightly projecting wings, and presented—at all events, in its latter days—anything but a fitting appearance for the use to which it was applied. It was demolished about the year 1864, in order to clear a site for the new Government offices, of which we shall presently speak. The public business of the country had been for many years carried on in the double row of mean and unsightly houses which formed the old street, when, at length, an elaborate report was presented to both Houses of Parliament, containing recommendations for the erection of a suitable block of buildings on a uniform plan, for the accommodation of ministers in the transaction of the business of the State. Nothing, however, came of these recommendations; and although the subject was from time to time brought forward in Parliament, and inquiries were made and plans suggested, nothing was done except the extension and decoration of the Whitehall front of the Treasury Buildings by Sir Charles Barry. In the meantime the question was in the way of one settlement by the fact that some of the old barns in Downing Street, and the Foreign Office especially, were on the eve of tumbling down. By the elegant and decorative aid of beams and girders the walls were secured for a time; but at length even this standfast system was found insufficient to prevent the crumbling to pieces of the mortar and brickwork, in consequence of which the business of our diplomacy was temporarily transferred to Pembroke House, in Whitehall Gardens.

As soon as the old Foreign Office was levelled with the ground a new and stately edifice was commenced. The block of buildings extends from King Street (part of which has been merged in an enlargement of Parliament Street) on the east, to St. James's Park, near Storey's Gate, on the west; and from Downing Street on the north to Charles Street on the south. The buildings, which cover a large space of ground, surround two quadrangular courts, and are occupied by the Secretaries of State for Foreign Affairs, for India, for the Colonies, and for the Home Department. The whole exterior group of buildings was designed by Sir G. Gilbert Scott, R.A., the architect of the Foreign Office throughout; while the interior of the India Office, with the external work of the inner court belonging to that range of buildings, is the work of Sir M. Digby Wyatt, R.A.

The buildings are faced with Portland stone; granite is used for the window-columns, and granite, marble, and glass—mostly green and red—is largely employed in the decoration, in the shape of bosses and otherwise, in the friezes.

The various fronts display a large amount of carving, the execution of which was entrusted to several sculptors of eminence. The design for the buildings gave rise, from time to time, in the House of Commons, to some warm and animated discussions, which came to be familiarly called the "battles of the styles," and in which Lord Palmerston, the then Premier, vigorously defended the classical Italian or Palladian against the advocates of the Gothic. The result has been the erection of an edifice which may be said to belong to a style strictly "Palmerstonian," the architect—although chiefly celebrated for his Gothic designs—having, with a grim humour, adopted a plan which, it is stated, owed a good deal to the Premier, and which may be put down as broadly Italian, with an occasional infusion of Gothic. The Park front, as seen on approaching it from the Parade behind the Horse Guards, is at once bold and massive, the principal features being the lofty tower which separates the Foreign Office from that devoted to the Indian Department, and the grand semi-circular sweep which rounds off the angle of the building towards the Park. The niches at the angles on this side of the India Office are filled with statues of Indian statesmen. The tower on the Foreign Office side, though lower by a storey, is much more bulky than that belonging to the India Office.

In the stone-vaulted entrances through the India Office from Charles Street, and through the Foreign Office from Downing Street, are columns each of a single stone, eleven feet high; the vaulting in each case is handsome, and the groins show an incised ornament, filled in with red Parian cement. Across Downing Street, at the western end, a broad flight of steps gives access to St. James's Park; a flight of steps also leads from Charles Street into the Park.

The portion of the building which fronts Parliament Street is devoted to the Colonial and Home Departments. This part of the structure was only completed towards the commencement of the year 1875. It is adorned with statues of several eminent statesmen, including the late Lords Grenville, Liverpool, Melbourne, and Glenelg, Sir Robert Peel, Sir James Graham, Sir George Cornewall Lewis, Earl Russell, Sir George Grey, the late Earl of Derby, Earl Grey, and Sir William Molesworth.

The inner court of the Foreign Office, which is entered from Downing Street, is quite plain. Against the topmost storey, surrounding the quadrangle, stand, at certain intervals, a series of sculptured figures. Those on the Foreign Office front are emblematical of countries—Italy, France, and so on; whilst those on the other sides represent the Indian tribes—an Affghan, a Goorka, a Malay, a Mahratta, and so forth.

The principal apartments are on the first floor, and include the Cabinet-room, 70 feet long by 35 feet wide, and two spacious conference-rooms. All these rooms communicate, and afford accommodation for balls and other *réunions*. Over and below these rooms are libraries. The grand staircase occupies an area of 60 feet by 25 feet. On the India Office side there are four great staircases, but all much less in size than the Foreign Office staircase. One of these staircases has the walls ornamented with life-size statues of Indian statesmen, standing in arched niches; and upon the upper part of the wall is an oval-shaped allegorical painting brought from one of the ceilings of the old East India House in Leadenhall Street. The principal entrance to the India Office is in Charles Street. The court-yard occupies nearly a central position in the building, and affords means of light and air to a large number of the rooms on the north, east, and west sides, and to a portion of the main corridor on the south side. Above the windows of the upper storey, set within large escalop shells, are a series of busts—twenty-eight in number—of celebrated worthies, both civil and military, connected with our Indian empire, beginning with Admiral Watson and Lord Macartney, and including heroes of recent historical renown—as Havelock, Clyde, and Lawrence. At the four angles of the court are niches filled with statues; the four on the ground floor are of Lords Hastings, Minto, Amherst, and Wellesley, sculptured by Mr. Protat: those on the first floor, immediately above the others, are Cornwallis and Clive, by Mr. Nicholls; and Warren Hastings and Lord Teignmouth, by Mr. Phyffers, by whom also many of the panels have been elaborately carved.

This court is remarkable for the variety of materials employed for decorative purposes. The floor is composed of tiles, laid to a pattern. The main portion of the walling, plain and decorative, is of Portland stone. The bays of the ground floor and first storey are divided by piers faced with Doric columns of red Peterhead granite, with capitals of red Mansfield stone; whilst those on the second floor are of dark-grey Aberdeen granite, with stone capitals of the same colour; and the arches between the piers are filled with glass. In addition to these materials there are majolica and mosaic friezes and pateras, and tessellated floors and ceilings in the logias. The court is rectangular in plan, 115 feet long by 60 feet wide, and is covered by a roofing of iron and glass. Upon the floor of this court is the celebrated collection of antiquities known as the Elliott Marbles.

Some of the ceilings of the rooms in the India Office are handsomely worked in plaster, partly modelled from Indian fruits and flowers. In the committee-room there is a handsome fireplace of carved white marble, brought from the old East India House; and on the opposite wall hangs the life-size portrait of Warren Hastings which formerly occupied a conspicuous position in the old establishment. There is also a statue of Warren Hastings at the foot of the grand staircase.

In the basement floor of the building are a number of rooms and vaulted chambers. Some of these rooms are used for culinary purposes; others as engine-rooms in connection with the hot-water apparatus for heating the building, and also with the hydraulic lifts, tanks, and mains. A large part of the basement is made use of as workshops for carpenters and other branches of mechanical labour, a large number of hands being constantly employed. The space immediately beneath the pavement of the inner court of the India Office is entirely filled with racks in which are stowed away some thousands of volumes of the records from the old East India House.

At the top of this building, in a place by no means secure against fire, called the "Record Office," is a most valuable library of Oriental treasures, which contains Arabic manuscripts to the number of about 2,000; Persian to double that amount; while of Sanscrit there are not less than 4,500, and many of these are gorgeously illuminated. Besides these there are 50,000 printed volumes, the greater part of which are Oriental works. On the same floor, down to the beginning of the year 1875, a series of rooms connected with each other had been set apart as the India Museum. This valuable collection, which had previously (since its removal from Leadenhall Street) enjoyed a temporary retreat at Fife House, in Whitehall Yard, has now been transferred to South Kensington, where it has been permanently located in a part of the building occupied by the Industrial Exhibition of 1862.

The business of our Indian empire, as has been stated in a previous chapter (see Vol. II., p. 184), was formerly transacted to a very great extent at the old house of the East India Company, in Leadenhall Street. On the transfer, however, of the government of India to the Crown, in 1858, the old Board of Control in Cannon Row was abolished, and a Council of State for India was instituted. The official duties connected with the Indian Government were at the same time transferred to Westminster.

CHAPTER XLIX.

WESTMINSTER ABBEY.—ITS EARLY HISTORY.

"And they shall then behold the scene around
In wasted age, in antique beauty, faded;
Our great Cathedral fane in silence bound."

Whitehead's "Legends of London."

Etymology of Westminster—A Startling Proposition—The Legend of St. Peter's Dedication of the First Abbey—The Building burnt by the Danes and restored by King Edgar—Rebuilt by Edward the Confessor—Death of Edward the Confessor—Additions and Alterations to the Abbey by Henry III.—Translation of the Body of Edward the Confessor—The Abbey damaged by Fire in 1297—Violation of the Right of Sanctuary—Completion of the Building—Funeral of Henry VII.—Surrender of the Abbey to Henry VIII.—The Benedictine Rule restored by Queen Mary—The Abbey in the Days of its Glory under the Plantagenets.

It has been appositely remarked that whereas the City is the heart, Westminster is the head of our great metropolis; while the suburbs in general constitute its limbs and extremities. And this is true in so far as that, while the City is the centre of all commercial transactions, Westminster is the residence of the Court and the seat of the Legislature which directs and controls the political affairs of the nation.

In the first chapter of this volume we have endeavoured to set before the reader a general outline of the history and boundaries of the City of Westminster, together with some particulars of the foundation of its Abbey. It is stated by historians—and the statement is generally accepted as true—that Miletus, who was ordained Bishop of the East Saxons by St. Augustine, erected two cathedral churches; the one in London, dedicated to St. Paul; and the other in the island of Thorney, which he dedicated to St. Peter. This latter, which, in fact, was an abbey or minster, was situated to the westward of the City of London, and, according to one old annalist, was for that reason called "Westminster," to distinguish it from the Abbey of Grace on Tower Hill, called "Eastminster;" Maitland, however, proves this to be a mistake, by showing that this city was called Westminster in an undated "charter of sanctuary" granted by Edward the Confessor, who died in 1066, whilst the Abbey of Grace was not founded till the fourteenth century; he therefore supposes that the appellation of Westminster was given to distinguish it from St. Paul's Church, in the City of London.

Apropos of the origin or foundation of this locality, we may here state that we have heard of a startling proposition—namely, that the site of the ancient British city, Lun *Dîn*, or "the city of mud or clay," was Westminster, and that London as now known was that of the first Roman *castrum*. We can only exclaim, with the poet—

"This is the age of new inventions."

Froude says that the cathedral is, or rather was in the Middle Ages, the city, and that other institutions grouped themselves around it, and gradually grew up under its shadow. This is certainly true of Westminster. In course of time, round the monastery were erected a few houses, which at length grew into a small town, called in ancient writings "the town of Westminster." Another cause of its growth was the royal palace which for centuries nestled under the shadow of the noble Abbey; and, consequently, most of the chief nobility, as we have seen in our "progress" through the Strand and Whitehall, erected in its vicinity inns, or town houses, the sites of many of which still retain the names of their former owners. It may be added here that it was probably on account of the contiguity of the royal palace of Westminster to the monastery that the king was allowed the privilege of a separate entrance to the church.

In course of time Westminster became a place of high consideration; but it received its most distinguished honours from Henry VIII., who, on the dissolution of the Monastery of St. Peter, converted it into a bishopric, with a dean and twelve prebendaries, and appointed the whole county of Middlesex, except Fulham, which was to remain with the bishopric of London, to be its diocese. On this occasion Westminster became a city; for the making of which, according to Lord Chief Justice Coke, nothing more is required than for it to be the seat of episcopal power. It did not, however, as we have shown, long continue to enjoy this distinction, for it never had but one bishop, Thomas Thirleby, upon whose translation to Norwich, in 1550, Edward VI. dissolved the new bishopric, and its right to the epithet of city has been questioned. However, Westminster has ever since continued to be called a city, and is so styled in our statutes.

It is observed with justice by Mr. Wood, in his "Ecclesiastical Antiquities of London," that Sebert, who founded the Cathedral of St. Paul within the walls of the City of London, was no less the founder of the Benedictine church and monastery—our Rheims and St. Denis in one—outside the same. He apparently rejects the story of St. Peter being the actual founder of the first consecrated fabric that arose upon the island of Thorney; but he gives the following legend:—

"The night before the dedication, it is related that St. Peter, in an unknown garb, showed himself to a fisher on the Surrey side, and bade him carry him over, with promise of reward. The fisher complied, and saw his fare enter the new-built Church of Sebert, that suddenly seemed on fire, with a glow that enkindled the firmament. Meantime the heavenly host scattered sound and fragrance, the fisher of souls wrote upon the pavement the alphabet in Greek and Hebrew, in twelve places anointed the walls with the holy oil, lighted the tapers, sprinkled the water, and did all else needful for the dedication of a church.

"These circumstances, and the signs following, were pondered on by St. Edward, last but one of our Saxon kings, who earnestly desired to repair that ruined monastery, and restore it to honour and splendour. The Pope approved the plan, and one of the most magnificent fabrics in Christendom was the result."

The building of the Abbey is, indeed, involved in mists too dense for the sun of antiquarian research to penetrate. The period of its erection, previous to Edward the Confessor's days, will not probably ever be discovered. "In this venerable building," writes Mr. Allen, in his "History of London and Westminster," "lived Sulgardus, a monk who devoted his leisure hours to writing a history of it. He has, indeed, according to custom, used but little ceremony with St. Peter or the choir of heaven, for he pressed both into his service in order to make the consecration of this church hallowed and sublime."

Widmore, who, in writing his history, had access to every species of record belonging to the Abbey, fixed its foundation between the years 730 and 740, but is unable to say who was its founder. Allen, in his version of the legend of St. Peter and the fisherman who ferried him over the water, adds that some of the monastic writers improved upon the vision of Wulsinus by asserting that Peter rewarded the fisherman "with a miraculous draught of salmon," assuring him and his fellow-watermen that they should never want fish, "provided they would give one-tenth of what they caught to the newly-consecrated church." For several centuries, it is asserted, this tale was implicitly believed, and during that time the monks of Westminster doubtless fared sumptuously on the offerings of the Thames fishermen. "What was at first solicited as a benevolence in course of time was claimed as a right, so that in the year 1231 the monks brought an action at law against the priest of Rotherhithe, in which they compelled him to give up to them one-half of the tithe of all salmon caught in his parish."

Though nothing can with certainty be concluded from these fictions, it may nevertheless be presumed that both the ancient church dedicated to St. Paul in London, and this dedicated to St. Peter in Westminster, were among the earliest works of the first converts to Christianity in Britain. With their religion the Christians introduced a new manner of building, and "their great aim seems to have been, by affecting loftiness and ornament, to bring the plain simplicity of the Pagan architects into contempt." Sebert has been generally accredited with having superintended the building of the earliest church on this site, or, at all events, with having completed that part of it which now forms the eastern angle. From Sebert's death up to the time of Edward the Confessor, the Abbey, it appears, remained a monument of the sacrilegious fury of the times, and suffered greatly from the ravages of the Danes. King Edgar, through the influence of Dunstan, is said to have effected some restoration of the fabric, and to have appropriated it to the order of St. Benedict, establishing there twelve monks, with endowments sufficient for their maintenance.

About the middle of the eleventh century, Edward the Confessor resolved thoroughly to restore the building, or, as some authors state, to reconstruct it entirely, in the Saxon style. For this purpose large sums of money were given to the monks by the king; and his nobles, like true courtiers, copied his example. The plan of this building was that of a cross, which naturally was the pattern and type for church-building throughout the kingdom. On the completion of the church, Edward determined to have it consecrated in the most solemn and impressive manner, and with that intent summoned all the bishops and nobles in the kingdom to be witnesses of the ceremony, which took place on Holy Innocents' Day (December 28),

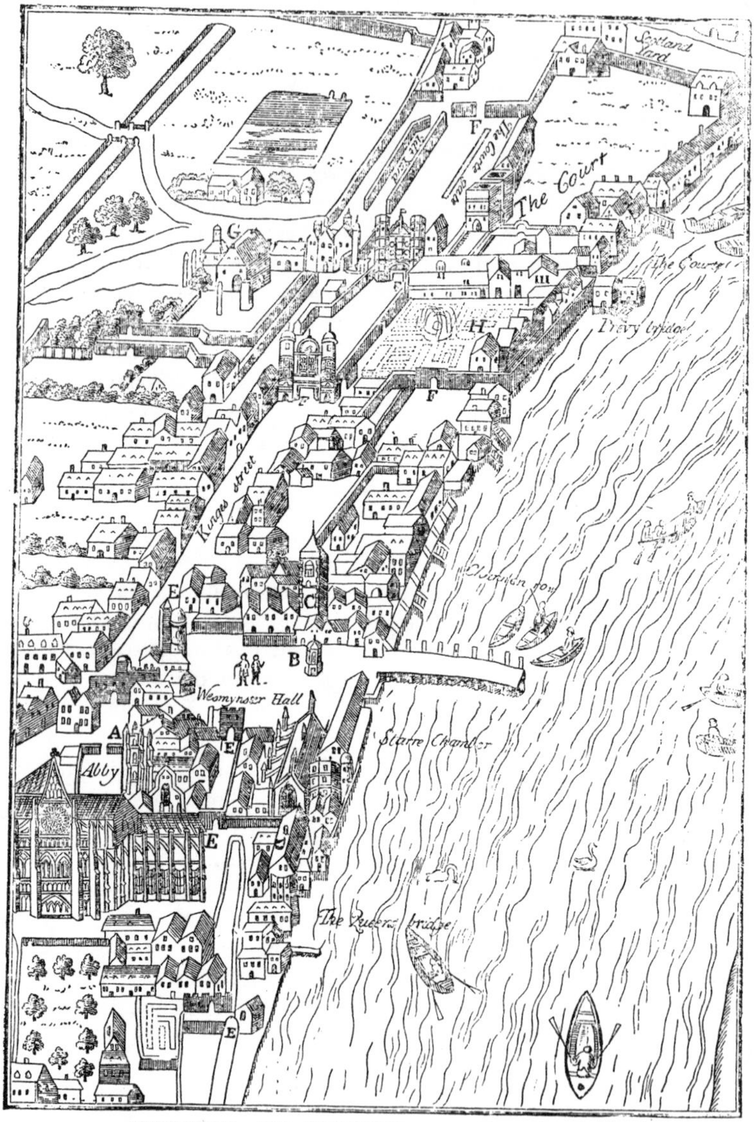

WHITEHALL AND WESTMINSTER. (*From Aggas' Map.*)

1065. Edward, in order to ingratiate himself with his clergy, not only confirmed to the monks all former endowments, but granted them a new charter, in which he recited the account of St. Peter's consecration, the ravages of the Danes, and the motives which prompted him to restore the sacred edifice to its former splendour, and endow it with more ample powers and privileges. This charter concluded with solemn imprecations against all who should, in time to come, dare to deface or to demolish any part of the building, or to infringe the rights of the priesthood. Within a few days after the consecration of the new Abbey Church, on the 4th or 5th of January, 1066, Edward the Confessor breathed his last, in the Palace hard by, and was buried before the high altar of the new structure.

During the time of Abbot Laurentius, about the year 1159, extensive repairs were made in the out-buildings of the monastery, which had been destroyed by fire. In 1220 Henry III. laid the first stone of a chapel, which was dedicated to the Blessed Virgin, and was called "The Lady Chapel." Its site was that whereon now stands Henry VII.'s Chapel. Queen Eleanor, wife of Henry III., was crowned here with much splendour and liberality on the part of the citizens of London, in spite of the discredit and unpopularity of her husband, who not long afterwards granted a large sum towards

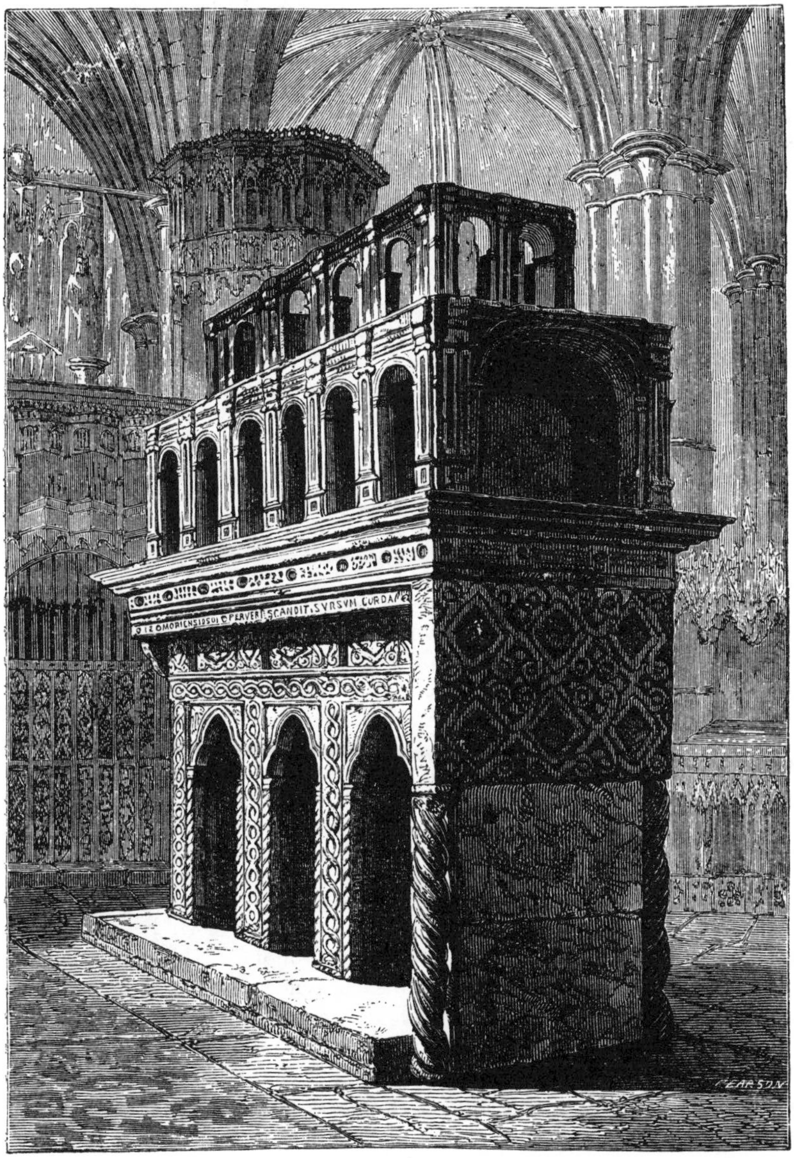

THE TOMB OF EDWARD THE CONFESSOR.

rebuilding the Abbey Church. This, according to Matthew Paris, was in 1245. Speaking of this sovereign, under that date, the old chronicler says:—"The king in the same year commanded that the Church of St. Peter, at Westminster, should be enlarged, and the tower with the eastern part overthrown, to be built anew and more handsome, at his own charge, and fitted to the residue or western part." For this purpose, Henry appropriated a considerable sum to the church, and in 1246 "the sum of £2,591, due from the widow of one David of Oxford, a Jew, was assigned by him to that use."

In 1247, if we may trust the statement of a writer in Neale and Brayley's "History of Westminster Abbey," "on the day of the translation of Edward the Confessor, a vessel of blood, which, in the preceding year, had been sent to the King by the Knights Templars and Hospitallers in the Holy Land, and was attested by Robert, the Patriarch of Jerusalem, to have trickled from our Saviour's wounds at His crucifixion, was presented with great ceremony to this church."

On the 13th of October, 1269, the new church, of which the eastern part, with the choir and transepts, appears to have been at that time completed, was first opened for divine service; and on the same day, writes Dart, from "Wyke's Chronicles," the body of Edward the Confessor, "that before laye in the syde of the quere, where the monkes nowe singe," was removed with great solemnity "into ye chapell, at the backe of the hygh aulter, and there layde in a ryche shryne."

It is impossible to ascertain how far the building had progressed at the time of Henry's death, in 1272. According to Fabian, the choir was not actually finished till some thirteen years later. A short time previous to the rebuilding of the church, Abbot Richard de Crokesley had erected a chapel near the north door, and dedicated it to St. Edmund. This was taken down with the rest by Henry III. Not long afterwards the beautiful mosaic pavement before the high altar was laid; it was the gift of Abbot Ware, who died in 1283, and was buried under it.

In 1297 the Abbey was considerably damaged by a fire which broke out in the lesser hall in the king's palace adjoining. In the succeeding century great additions were made to the fabric by Abbots Langham and Litlington; the latter, says Widmore, quoting from the records, "built the present college hall, the kitchen, the Jerusalem Chamber, the abbot's house (now the Deanery), the bailiff's, the cellarer's, the infirmarer's, and the sacrist's houses, the malt-house (afterwards used as a dormitory for the King's Scholars), and the adjoining tower, the wall of the infirmary garden, and also finished the south and west sides of the cloisters." Abbot Litlington died in the reign of Richard II. It is hardly necessary to add that the Edwardian era was the culminating period of Gothic or pointed architecture.

In 1378 the right of sanctuary possessed by the Abbey was for the first time violated, and the church itself made the scene of a most atrocious murder. It appears that, during one of the campaigns of the Black Prince, two esquires, Frank de Haule and John Schakell, had taken prisoner a Spanish (or, according to Pennant, a French) count. He had, however, a powerful friend at court, in the person of John of Gaunt. The two English captors refused to part with so valuable a prize; and John of Gaunt at once imprisoned them in the Tower, whence they made their escape, and took refuge at Westminster. They were pursued by Sir Allan Boxhull, Constable of the Tower, and Sir Ralph de Ferrers, with fifty armed men. De Haule and Schakell, it is supposed, had fled not merely into the Abbey, but into the choir of the church, while the mass was being celebrated. The deacon had just uttered the words of the Gospel of the day—"If the good man of the house had known what time the thief would come"—when the clash of arms was heard, and the pursuers, regardless of the time or the place, suddenly burst in upon the service. Schakell succeeded in escaping, but Haule was intercepted. He fled round the choir twice, with his enemies hacking at him as he ran; and, pierced with twelve wounds, he sank dead at the prior's stall, close by the north side of the entrance of the choir. His servant and one of the monks fell with him. He was regarded as a martyr to the injured right of the Abbey, and obtained the honour (at that time unusual) of burial within its walls—the first who was laid, so far as we know, in the south transept; to be followed a few years later by Geoffrey Chaucer, who was interred at his feet. A brass effigy and a long epitaph, till within the last century, marked the stone where he lay, and another inscription was engraved on the stone where he fell. The Abbey was shut up for four months. Even the sitting of the King's Parliament was suspended, lest its assembly should be polluted by sitting within the desecrated precincts; and the aggressors were excommunicated by the Archbishop of Canterbury.

During the reign of Richard II. the rebuilding of the western part of the church was carried out; and Abbot Esteney, who died in 1498, contributed largely towards finishing it, and made the great west window. Abbot Islip made many additions to the fabric, but the nave remained in an unfinished state till the year 1740, when the two western towers were completed from designs by Sir Christopher Wren, greatly modified, however, after his death.

The first stone of the magnificent Chapel of Henry VII., at the eastern end of the Abbey Church, was laid in 1502, during the government of Abbot Islip; it was erected on the site of two chapels, dedicated respectively to the Virgin Mary and to St. Erasmus, which had been pulled down to make room for the new fabric; and, like its predecessor, when completed, it was dedicated to the Blessed Virgin. It was designed by Henry VII. as a burying-place for himself and his successors, and he expressly enjoined in his will that none but those of the blood royal should be inhumed therein.

Henry VII. by his will left his funeral to the discretion of his executors, only charging them to avoid "dampnable pompe and outrageous superfluities." As he requests that the chapel should be finished as soon as possible after his decease, if not then completed, and particularly mentions that the windows were to be glazed with stories, images, arms, badges, and cognisances, according to the designs given by him to the prior of St. Bartholomew's—and that the walls, doors, windows, vaults, and statues, within and without, should be adorned with arms and badges—it may be concluded that much remained to be done in the year 1509, as he died within a month after the date of the will. He ordered that his body should be interred before the high altar, with that of his wife, and that the tomb should be made of touchstone, with niches, and statues of his guardian saints in copper gilt, the inscription to be confined merely to name and dates.

That his soul might rest in peace, Henry requested 10,000 masses should be said in the monastery, London and its neighbourhood, for its repose—"1,500 in honour of the Trinity, 2,500 in honour of the five wounds of our Lord Jesus Christ, 2,500 for the five joys of our Lady, 450 in honour of the nine orders of Angels, 150 in honour of the patriarchs, 600 to that of the twelve apostles, and 2,300 to the honour of all saints," and all these to be sung in one short month after his decease! He likewise directed that a statue of himself, kneeling, three feet in height from the knees, should be carved in wood, representing him in armour, with a sword and spurs, and holding the crown of Richard III. won by him at Bosworth Field. The figure was to be plated with fine gold, and the arms of England and France enamelled on it. A tablet of silver gilt supporting it, enamelled with black letters, "Rex Henricus Septimus," was to be placed on the shrine of St. Edward, to whom, with St. Mary and Almighty God, he dedicated the statue. He also gave in trust to the abbot and convent £2,000 to be distributed in charity, and 500 marks to the finishing of the church.

How far Henry's directions regarding his funeral were carried out may be gleaned from Malcolm's account of the ceremony. He says: "On the 9th of May, 1509, the body of Henry VII. was placed in a chariot, covered with black cloth of gold, which was drawn by five spirited horses, whose trappings were of black velvet, adorned with quishions of gold. The effigies of his Majesty lay upon the corpse, dressed in his regal habiliments. The carriage had suspended on it banners of arms, titles, and pedigrees. A number of prelates preceded the body, who were followed by the deceased king's servants; after it were nine mourners. Six hundred men bearing torches surrounded the chariot.

"The chariot was met in St. George's Fields [he died at Windsor] by all the priests and clergy of London and its neighbourhood; and at London Bridge by the Lord Mayor, aldermen, and common council, in black. To render this awful scene sublimely grand, the way was lined with children, who held burning tapers: those, with the flashes of great torches, whose red rays, darting in every direction upon glittering objects, and embroidered copes, showing the solemn pace, uplifted eyes, and mournful countenances, must have formed a noble picture. The slow, monotonous notes of the chaunt, mixed with the sonorous tones of the great bells, were not less grateful to the ear. When the body had arrived at St. Paul's, which was superbly illuminated, it was taken from the chariot and carried to the choir, where it was placed beneath a hearse arrayed with all the accompaniments of death. A solemn mass and dirge were then sung, and a sermon preached by the Bishop of Rochester. It rested all night in the church. On the following day the procession recommenced in the same manner, except that Sir Edward Howard rode before, on a fine charger, clothed with drapery on which was the king's arms.

"We will now suppose him removed by six lords from his chariot to the hearse prepared for him, formed by nine pillars, set full of burning tapers, enclosed by a double railing; view him placed under it, and his effigies on a rich pall of gold; close to him the nine mourners; near them knights bearing banners of saints, and surrounded by officers of arms. The prelates, abbot, prior, and convent, and priests, in measured paces, silently taking their places; when, breaking through the awful pause, Garter King-at-Arms cried, with an audible voice, 'Pray for the soul of the noble prince, Henry the Seventh, late king of this realm.' A deep peal from the organ and choir answers in a chaunt of *placebo* and the dirge; the sounds die away, and with them the whole assembly retires."

On the 16th of January, 1539–40, this Abbey was surrendered to Henry VIII. by Abbot Boston and twenty-four of the monks, and immediately dissolved. Here the king was married to Anne of Cleves, whom he soon afterwards divorced. After its short-lived career as a bishopric, under Dr. Thirleby, during the reigns of Henry VIII. and Edward VI., on the accession of Queen Mary the monastery was again restored to the order of St. Benedict, which was one of the most wealthy, powerful, and learned in England before the Reformation.

Westminster was the second mitred abbey in the kingdom, and its abbot, before the Reformation, had a seat among the peers of Parliament; but it would astonish most readers, even devout Roman Catholics, to learn that at this day there are in existence four "reverend" or "very reverend" gentlemen who style themselves the "Abbots" of Westminster, St. Albans, Bury St. Edmunds, and Glastonbury respectively! How amused Dean Bradley must be, while holding in his hands the keys of the Abbey of St. Peter's, Westminster, to know that he has a rival who would gladly relieve him of them!

Mr. Wood, in his "Ecclesiastical Antiquities of London," draws the following picture of the Abbey in the days of its glory and pride, in the age of the Plantagenets:—

"The abbot took his meals with the guests and strangers. When these were not numerous, the abbot might invite to his table any he pleased of the community. Some of the seniors were, however, left in the refectory to keep order. When a guest was announced, the abbot and brethren went to receive him. They first prayed with him, and then gave him the kiss of peace, and either inclined the head or made a protestation. The guests were then conducted into the church. After this the superior, or one to whom he gave authority, sat with the guests and read to them a portion of Scripture. The abbot sat at table with the guests, except on fast-days. He gave water to the guests for their hands, and, with the assistance of the community, washed their feet. Then was said, 'Suscepimus, Deus, misericordiam tuam in medio templi tui.' A kitchen was set apart for the abbot and the guests. Two of the community were appointed annually to serve in this kitchen. The apartment for the guests was furnished with a sufficient number of beds for their use, and was under the special charge of one of the community. None of the community, unless under a command to do so, spoke to or associated with the guests. If an encounter with them was unavoidable, they were passed with a salutation and a request for their prayers.

"The porter was the chief domestic of a Benedictine monastery. He had a cell near the gate, and, being himself chosen for years and discretion, had a younger man as his companion. The monks served weekly, by turns, in the kitchen and at table. On leaving this service, both those who relinquished and those who took up this task washed the feet of the community. On Saturdays all the plates were cleaned and given to the cellarer. After refection or dinner, which, from Easter till Holy Rood Day, was at twelve o'clock, the meridian or noon-sleep was permitted. From Holy Rood till Lent, there was reading from prime till eight o'clock, when tierce followed; and after that, labour till nones, when there was dinner. Even during the summer dinner was at nones (three o'clock) on Wednesdays and Fridays. There was silence during dinner, unbroken save by the reading of Scripture by one of the community appointed for a week for the purpose. There was a collation or spiritual lecture every evening before night-song, after which there was silence. The monks rose two hours after midnight to say office; and every week the Psalter was sung through. All left the church at a sign from the abbot. Lamps were kept burning in the dormitory. The community slept in their habits, with their girdles on."

The same writer also remarks: "The Abbey Church of Westminster was the house of prayer, and served no other purpose. Here, when the divine office was ended, the monks bowed to the altar and retired in profound silence, in order that the quiet of any of the community who desired to continue his devotions in private might be undisturbed. If any of them sought to devote his leisure to prayer he entered the church quietly, without pride or ostentation, not with a loud noise, but with tears and fervour of soul, as bidden by the rule of St. Benedict."

According to Tanner, Fosbrooke, and other writers on mediæval monasticism, the habit of the Benedictine monks was a black loose coat, or rather gown, of stuff reaching down to their heels, with a cowl or hood of the same, and a scapulary; and under that another habit of white flannel, equal in size. From the colour of their outer habits the Benedictines were generally known as the Black Monks.

CHAPTER L.

WESTMINSTER ABBEY.—HISTORICAL CEREMONIES, &c.

"From hence we may that antique pile behold
Where royal heads receive the sacred gold;
It gives them crowns, and does their ashes keep:
There made like gods, like mortals there they sleep
Making the circle of their reign complete,
Those suns of empire, where they rise they set."—*Waller.*

Coronation of William the Conqueror—Bad Auguries—Coronation of Richard I.—Outrage against the Jews—Coronation of Anne Boleyn—Revival of the "Old Religion" by Queen Mary—Relic of the True Cross—The present Collegiate Establishment founded by Queen Elizabeth—Funeral of James I.—Assaults on the Abbey—Coronation of Charles II.—Parliamentary Grants for the Repair of the Abbey—The Abbey damaged by an Earthquake—Coronation of George III. and Queen Charlotte—Humility of a King—The Handel Festivals—Origin of the National Anthem—Further Grants for the Repair of the Abbey—A Narrow Escape from Destruction by Fire—Coronation of George IV.—An Unfortunate Queen—Coronation of William IV. and Queen Adelaide—Coronation of Queen Victoria—A Singular Incident.

WESTMINSTER ABBEY has been for many centuries the scene of the coronations of our sovereigns. The first who was crowned here was Harold, in January, 1066, previous to which date most of the Saxon kings had been crowned at Kingston-on-Thames. Want of space prevents us from noticing many curious customs now disused in those imposing ceremonies; but our account of the Abbey would be incomplete were we to pass over some of the more exciting incidents attending some of them.

It was on Christmas Day, in the year 1066, that the new Abbey of Westminster, the last work of Edward the Confessor, was chosen as the place for the coronation of the first of our Norman kings, William the Conqueror. The suburbs, the streets of London, and all the approaches to the Abbey, we are told, were lined with double rows of soldiers, horse and foot. The Conqueror rode through the ranks, and entered the Abbey Church, attended by 260 of his warlike chiefs, by many priests and monks, and a considerable number of the English who had been gained over to act a part in the pageantry. At the opening of the ceremony one of William's prelates, Geoffrey, the Bishop of Coutances, asked the Normans, in the French language, if they were of opinion that their chief should take the title of King of England; and then the Archbishop of York asked the English if they would have William the Norman for their king. The reply on either side was given by acclamation in the affirmative, and the shouts and cheers thus raised were so loud that they startled the foreign cavalry stationed round the Abbey. The troops took the confused noise for a cry of alarm raised by their friends, and as they had received orders to be on the alert and ready to act in case of any seditious movement, they rushed to the English houses nearest the Abbey and set fire to them all. A few, thinking to succour their betrayed duke, and the nobles they served, ran to the church, where, at sight of their naked swords and the smoke and flames that were rising, the tumult soon became as great as that without its walls. The Normans fancied the whole population of London and its neighbourhood had risen against them; while the English imagined that they had been duped by a vain show, and drawn together, unarmed and defenceless, that they might be massacred. Both parties ran out of the Abbey, and the ceremony was interrupted, though William, left almost alone in the church, or with none but Archbishop Aldred and some terrified priests of both nations near to him at the altar, decidedly refused to postpone the celebration. The service was therefore completed amidst these bad auguries, but in the utmost hurry and confusion; and the Conqueror took the usual coronation oath of the Anglo-Saxon kings, making, as an addition of his own, the solemn promise that he would treat the English people as well as the best of their kings had done. Meanwhile the commotion without still continued, and it is not mentioned at what hour of the day or night the conflagration ended. The English who had been at the Abbey ran to extinguish the fire—the Normans, it is said, to plunder and otherwise profit by the disorder; but it appears that some of the latter exerted themselves to stop the progress of the flames, and to put an end to a riot peculiarly unpalatable to their master, whose anxious wish was certainly, at that time, to conciliate the two nations.

In 1189 the coronation of Richard I. at Westminster was characterised by even a worse tumult than that which served as an accompaniment to the coronation of the Conqueror. The festival in itself was held with unusual magnificence; the abbots and bishops, and most of the lay barons, attending on the occasion. The unction over, and the king being royally arrayed, he was led up to the altar, where the archbishop adjured him, in the name of Almighty God, not to assume the royal dignity unless he fully purposed to keep the oaths he had sworn. Richard repeated his solemn promises, and with his own hands taking the ponderous crown from off the altar, "in signification that he held it only from God," he delivered it to king's will), who, in a tumult raised by the multitude, were furiously murdered; which, though it was afterwards punished by the laws, might seem a presage that this lion-hearted king should be a

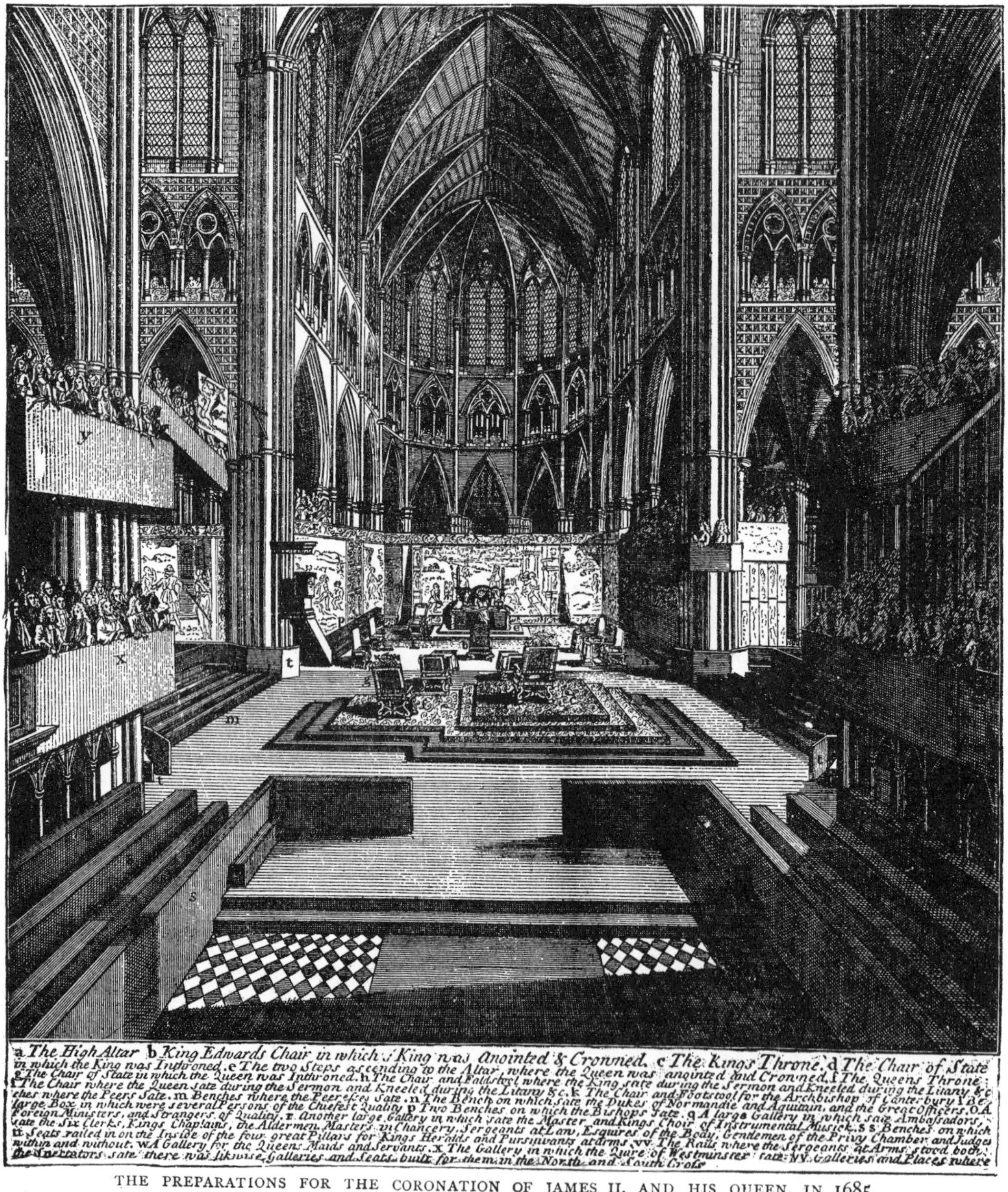

THE PREPARATIONS FOR THE CORONATION OF JAMES II. AND HIS QUEEN, IN 1685.
(*From Sandford's "History," published* 1687.)

the archbishop, who instantly put it on his head, and so completed all the ceremonies of the coronation. "Which act," says old Speed, with a coldbloodedness less excusable than his superstition, "was accidentally hanselled and auspicated by the blood of many Jews (though utterly against the special destroyer of the enemies of our Church." We abridge the following account from Hunter's "History of London:"—"Among the vast concourse which the coronation had attracted to the metropolis, many wealthy Jews had flocked from every part of the kingdom, to consult with their

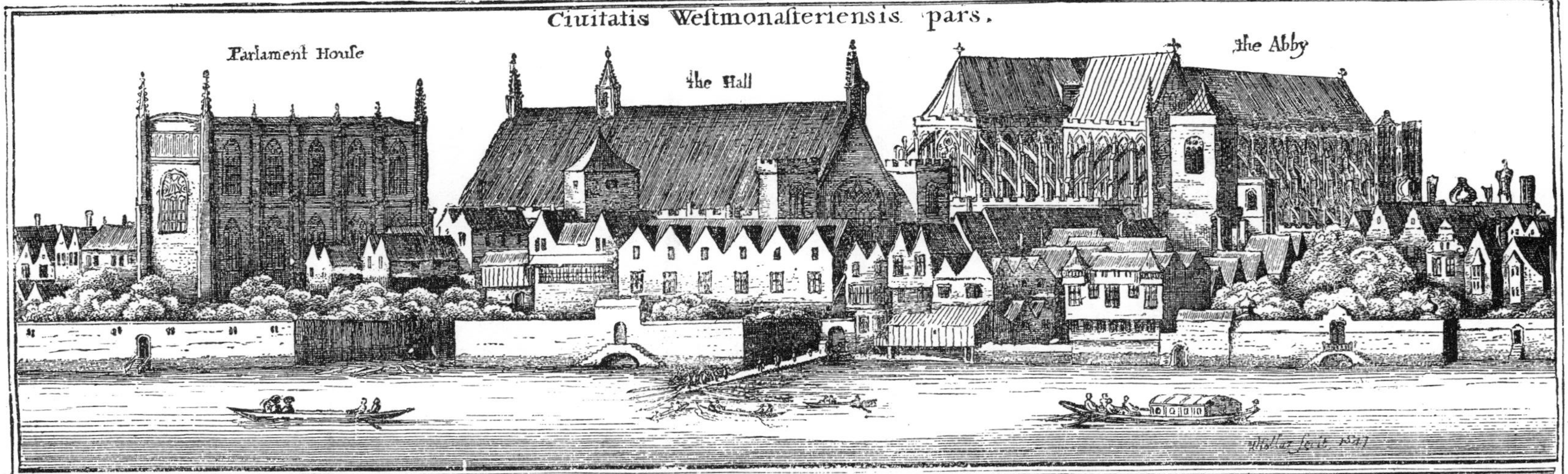

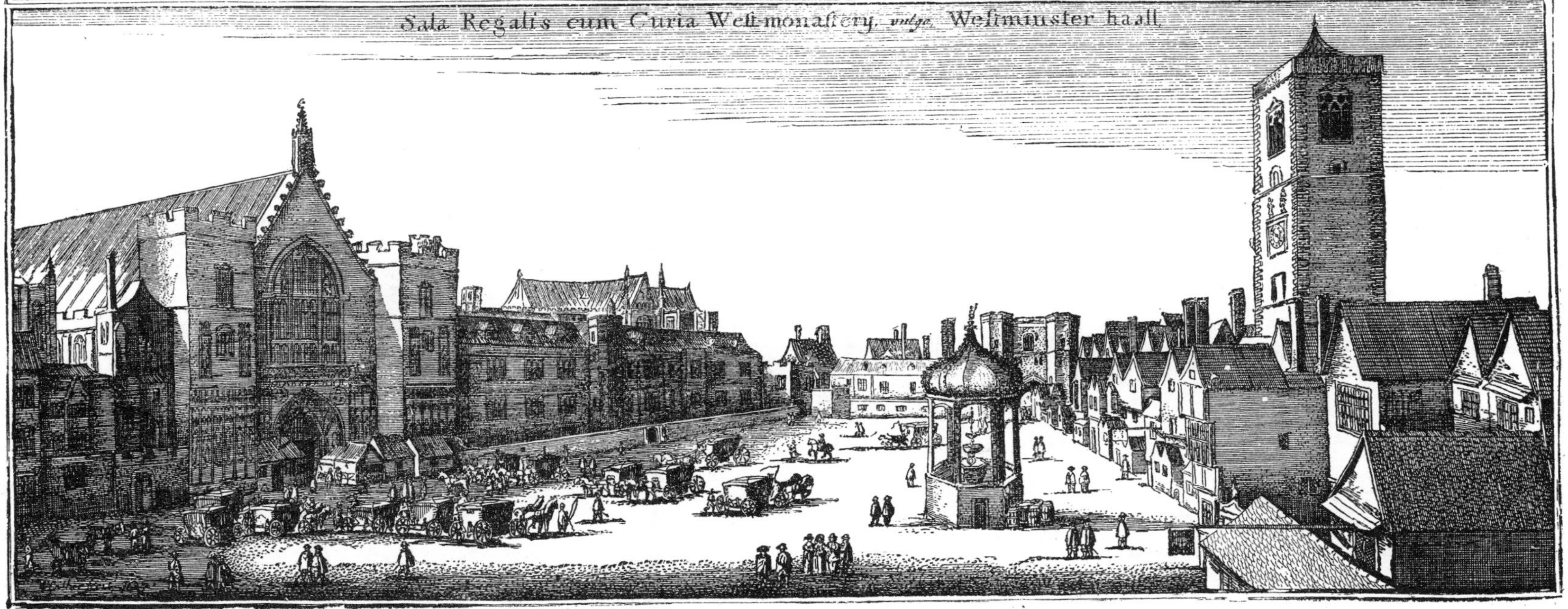

TWO VIEWS OF WESTMINSTER. (*From Original Etchings by Hollar*, 1647.)

friends in the City about presenting a liberal free-will offering to the king on his accession. Richard had issued a proclamation prohibiting all persons of that nation to enter the Abbey or Westminster Hall on the day that ceremony was performed. Some of them were, however, detected pressing among the crowd into the Hall. This brought upon them, at first, a torrent of abuse of language, which soon changed into the more formidable assaults of brickbats and bludgeons. Perceiving too late their imprudence, and the danger in which it had involved them, the poor Jews endeavoured to make good their retreat into the City, pursued and pelted by a furious multitude. In this state of fermentation it was easy to give out, and as easily believed, that the king had issued orders to destroy all Jews. Never were real orders more promptly and more ferociously executed. Many of those unhappy creatures were inhumanly massacred in the streets; such as were able to escape to their habitations, or had stayed at home, were not the more secure. The houses were either broken into and plundered or burnt over their heads. Those who were shut up perished in the flames; those who forced their way out fell by the sword."

"On the Sunday after her public entry into London," writes Miss Lucy Aikin, in her "Memoirs of the Court of Queen Elizabeth," . . . "Henry caused his new queen (Anna Boleyn) to be crowned at Westminster with great solemnity," an honour which that many-wived monarch never thought proper to confer on any of her successors.

On the revival of the "old religion," under Queen Mary, John Feckenham, late Dean of St. Paul's, was appointed Abbot of Westminster and Chaplain to her Majesty, and, with fourteen monks, took possession of the Abbey. Malcolm quotes a few lines from a proclamation issued in 1553, to show the probable state in which Feckenham found the Abbey. Speaking of the churches—"especially within the cittie of London, irreverently used, and by divers insolent rashe persones sundrie waies abused, soe farre forth, that many quarreles, riottes, frayes, and bloudshedinges have been made in some of the said churches, besides shotinge of hand-gonnes to doves, and the com'on bringinge of horses and mules into and throughe the said churches." He was indefatigable in restoring the building to its former state, and Mary, with great zeal, collected into it as many as she could of the rich habits and other insignia of its former splendid worship; but the death of his royal mistress put an end to his exertions, and his authority as abbot ceased on the 12th of July, 1559.

At the death of Queen Mary, Feckenham carefully removed from the Abbey the "relic of the true cross," which had been exposed there to the veneration of the faithful for centuries. It was carefully secreted during nearly two centuries, and found in 1822, in a box along with some antique vestments, at the house of a Roman Catholic gentleman in Holborn—Mr. Langdale. Having been duly authenticated, it was removed to the Benedictine College of St. Gregory, at Downside, near Bath, where it is still kept. It may be added that this particular relic is minutely described in the Chevalier Fleury's work on "Relics of the True Cross."

Pennant rightly, though no doubt sarcastically, observes that "an abbey is nothing without relics;" and he accordingly enumerates among those belonging to St. Peter's "the veil and some of the milk of the Virgin Mary, the blade-bone of St. Benedict, the finger of St. Alphage, the head of St. Maxilla, and half the jawbone of St. Anastatia."

Queen Elizabeth founded the present establishment, which is collegiate, consisting of a dean, six canons, and six minor canons; to which is attached a school for boys, who are denominated Queen's or King's Scholars, with a master and usher; and also twelve almsmen, an organist, and choristers.

The funeral of James I., as we learn from the "Calendar of State Papers," edited by the late Mr. John Bruce, was a most magnificent and costly pageant, the expense of carrying the royal body from Denmark House to the Abbey being set down at £50,000. And no wonder, considering that "blacks," or, in other words, mourning-cloaks, were given to nine thousand persons, and that the rest of the outlay was on the same lavish scale. Not only the members of the king's and queen's household—including the "sworn drummers" and "the keepers of his Majesty's cormorants"—but even the entire household of "Steenie," Duke of Buckingham, were put into mourning on this occasion; and the people had to pay the bill. No doubt, therefore, the great funeral of May 7th, 1625, was "the greatest ever known in England." The hearse was fashioned under the charge of Inigo Jones, and the sermon, preached by the Lord Keeper, John Williams, afterwards Archbishop of York, was two hours in length! No wonder that, only two months later, we find it recorded, in a royal message addressed to the House of Commons by Charles I., that "the ordinary revenue is clogged with debts, and exhausted with the late king's funeral and other expenses of necessity and honour."

In the reign of Charles I. the Abbey underwent

an assault from the mob, who took that means of showing their "zeal for the good old cause;" they were, however, beaten off, and a Sir Richard Wiseman, one of the number, was killed. Much injury was done to the building by the iconoclasts of that period; and, by order of the Parliament, the sacred vestments were seized and burnt.

In spite of the restoration of the king, and of episcopacy, and of the accustomed rites of the Established Church, it does not appear that the Abbey was very crowded when opened for service, or that the service itself was very satisfactorily performed. At all events, Pepys, in his "Diary," July 1, 1660, tells us he went "in the afternoon to the Abbey, where a good sermon by a stranger, but no Common Prayer yet." On the 7th of October, apparently matters have slightly improved, for on that day Pepys was at the Abbey, and tells us that he "heard them read the Church Service," though "very ridiculously." And again, a few days previously, the diarist writes—"To the Abbey to see them at vespers. There I found but a thin congregation."

The following particulars of the coronation of Charles II. are extracted from a brief narrative printed and published by authority in 1662 :—

"Upon the 23rd of April, being St. George's Day, about half an hour after seven in the morning, the King entered into his rich barge, took water from the Privy Stairs, at Whitehall, and landed at the Parliament Stairs; from whence he proceeded up to the room behind the Lords' House called the Prince's Lodgings, where, after he had reposed himself for a while, he was arrayed in his royal robes of crimson velvet furr'd with ermine. By which time the nobility, being assembled, robed themselves in the Lords' House and Painted Chamber. The Judges also, with those of the long robe, the Knights of the Bath, and Gentlemen of the Privy Chamber, met in the Court of Requests. After some space, the King's heralds and pursuivants began to set the proceeding in order, each of them taking his share assigned in chapter (held at the Heralds' Office the evening before), and thence directed all the before-mentioned degrees (except the nobility) down into Westminster Hall, where the rest of the proceeding attended, and from whence the march began.

"About half an hour after nine the nobility (having been first called over in the Painted Chamber) proceeded, each according to his rank and dignity, in their robes and coronets, before the King, through the Court of Requests into Westminster Hall, ascended up to the state platform, which was raised at the west end, and placed themselves upon each side thereof. His Majesty being set in his chair, under a rich cloth of state, first Sir Gilbert Talbot, the Master of the Jewel House, presented the Sword of State, as also Curtana, and two other swords, to the Lord High Constable, who took and delivered them to the Lord High Chamberlain, and he (having drawn the last) laid them upon the table before the King. Then the said Master of the Jewel House delivered likewise the spurs to the Lord High Constable, and he again the same to the Lord High Chamberlain, who also placed them upon the table.

"Immediately after the Dean and Prebends of Westminster (by whom the regalia had been brought in procession from the Abbey Church unto Westminster Hall), being vested in rich copes, proceeded from the lower end thereof in the manner following :—

"The Serjeant of the Vestry, in a scarlet mantle; the Children of the King's Chapel, being twelve in number, in scarlet mantles; the Quire of Westminster, in surplices; the Gentlemen of the King's Chapel, being thirty-three in number, in scarlet mantles; the Pursuivants, Heralds, and Provincial Kings; the Dean (Dr. Earle), carrying St. Edward's crown; Dr. Helyn, the sceptre with the cross; Dr. Heywood, the sceptre with the dove; Dr. Nicholas, the orb with the cross; Dr. Killegrew, King Edward's staff; Dr. Jones, the chalice and patena; Dr. Dowty, the spoon: and Dr. Busby, the ampulla.

"All standing towards the lower end of the Hall, ready to proceed, they made their first reverence together; then coming to the middle of the said Hall, they there made a second; and thence going a little further, both the quires fell off, and stood on either side, through which lane the pursuivants, heralds, and kings passing, fell likewise off on either side, the seniours still placing themselves uppermost towards the throne; after whom the Dean and Prebends proceeded, and arrived at the foot of the stone steps ascending to the throne, where they made another reverence. This being done, the Dean and Prebends, with Garter Principal King-of-Arms before them (he having waited their coming thither), ascended the steps, and approaching near to the table before the King, made their last reverence.

"The Dean first presented the crown, which was by the Lord High Constable and Lord Great Chamberlain set upon the table; who afterwards took from each of the prebends that part of the regalia which they carried, and laid them also by the crown; which done, they retired. Then the Lord Great Chamberlain, presenting the regalia severally to the King, his Majesty thereupon disposed of them unto the noblemen hereafter named, to be carried by them in the procession to the Abbey Church, viz.:

"St. Edward's staff, to the Earl of Sandwich; the spurs to the Earl of Pembroke and Montgomery; the sceptre with the cross to the Earl of Bedford; the pointed sword (borne on the left hand of Curtana) to the Earl of Derby; the pointed sword (borne on the right hand thereof) to the Earl of Shrewsbury; Curtana, to the Earl of Oxford; the sword of state to the Earl of Manchester; the sceptre with the dove to the Duke of Albemarle; the orb with the cross to the Duke of Buckingham; St. Edward's crown to the Duke of Ormond; the patena to the Bishop of Exeter; and, lastly, the chalice to the Bishop of London.

"And because the spoon and ampulla were not to be borne in the proceeding, and therefore ought not to have been brought thither, but left placed upon the high altar, in the Abbey Church, there to lye in readiness, they were not presented to the King, but commanded to be sent back thither, and laid thereon.

"All things being thus far prepared, and it being about ten a clock, the proceeding began from out the said Hall into the Palace Yard, through the Gate House and the end of King Street, thence along the Great Sanctuary, and so to the west end of the Abbey Church, all upon blew (*sic*) cloth, which was spread upon the ground from the throne in Westminster Hall to the great step in the Abbey Church by Sir George Carteret, Knt., Vice-Chamberlain, appointed by the King to be his almoner for this day."

Of the ceremony in the Abbey on this occasion we glean the following particulars from the amusing pages of Pepys. Under date of April 23, 1666, the witty diarist writes:—

"About four I arose and got to the Abbey, where I followed Sir J. Denham, the surveyor, with some company that he was leading in. And, with much ado, by the favour of Mr. Cooper, his man, did get up into a great scaffold, across the north end of the Abbey, where, with a great deal of patience, I sat from past four till eleven, before the King came in. And a great pleasure it was to see the Abbey raised in the middle, all covered with red, and a throne (that is, a chaire) and footstoole on the top of it; and all the officers of all kinds, so much as the very fidlers, in red vests. At last comes in the Dean and Prebends of Westminster, with the bishops (many of them in cloth of gold copes), and after them the nobility, all in their Parliament robes, which was a most magnificent sight. Then the Duke and the King, with a sceptre (carried by my Lord Sandwich) and sword and wand before him, and the crowne too. The King in his robes, bare-headed, which was very fine. And after all had placed themselves, there was a sermon and the service; and then in the quire at the high altar, the King passed through the ceremonies of the coronation, which, to my great grief, I and most in the Abbey could not see. The crowne having been put on his head, a great shout begun, and he came forth to the throne, and there passed through more ceremonies, as taking the oath, and having things read to him by the bishopp; and his lords (who put on their caps as soon as the King put on his crowne) and bishops came and kneeled before him. And three times the King-at-Arms went to the three open places on the scaffold, and proclaimed, that if any one could show any reason why Charles Stewart should not be King of England, that now he should come and speak. And a general pardon was also read by the Lord Chancellor, and meddalls flung up and down by my Lord Cornwallis, of silver, but I could not come by any. But so great a noise that I could make but little of the musique; and, indeed, it was lost to everybody. I went out a little while before the King had done all his ceremonies, and went round the Abbey to Westminster Hall, all the way within rayles, and 10,000 people, with the ground covered with blue cloth, and scaffolds all the way."

In the reign of William III. the House of Commons granted an annual sum for repairing the Abbey; and under Queen Anne an Act was passed allowing £4,000 a year towards the same purpose. The like sum was afforded by various Acts of George II., but in 1738 the works were at a standstill for want of money, and a petition was presented, which was referred to a committee of the whole House. The assistance, however, which was granted was inconsiderable, and even that was not paid till some time after.

In 1750 the top of one of the piers on the north side of the Abbey fell, through an earthquake, with the iron and lead that had fastened it. Several houses fell in, and many chimneys were damaged. Another shock had been felt during the preceding month.

On the occasion of the coronation of George III. and Queen Charlotte, on the 22nd of September, 1761, the Abbey was filled with galleries, and a platform was erected from the upper end of Westminster Hall, where the procession was to commence, and continued through New Palace Yard, Parliament Street, and Bridge Street, into King Street, and so on through the west door of the

Abbey to the choir. The following account of the ceremony we take from the *Gentleman's Magazine* of the above year:—"About half an hour after one, their Majesties entered the Abbey, and went to their seats on the east side of the throne. The Archbishop of Canterbury made the recognition, and then their Majesties made their first oblation, and took their seats on the south side of the altar. The Litany began, during which the regalia were severally presented at the altar, and the great officers retired to their seats.

"The Litany being ended, and part of the Communion Service being read by the Archbishop, Dr. Drummond, Bishop of Salisbury, preached the sermon, which being ended, his Majesty made the usual declaration, and took and subscribed the coronation oath.

"After *Veni Creator* his Majesty removed to St. Edward's chair, and the unction was performed by the Archbishop, four Knights of the Garter holding a pall over his Majesty during the anointing, viz., the Duke of Devonshire, Earl of Northumberland, Earl of Hertford, and Earl Waldegrave. The spurs were then presented, and his Majesty girt with the sword, which was afterwards offered and redeemed.

"His Majesty was then invested with the armill, the purple robe or imperial pall, and orb, and afterwards receiving the ring, returned the orb to the altar. The Marquis of Rockingham, deputy to the Duke of Norfolk, as Lord of the Manor of Worksop, presented a right-hand glove to his Majesty, who, putting it on, received from the Archbishop the sceptre with the cross, and afterwards the sceptre with the dove, with his left hand, and the Marquis did afterwards support his Majesty's right hand as occasion required. The Archbishop then set the crown upon his Majesty's head, about half an hour after three o'clock, amidst the acclamations of an infinite number of spectators; upon which the peers put on their coronets, the Dukes of Normandy and Aquitaine their hats, the bishops, Knights of the Bath, and judges their caps, and the kings of arms their crowns. Then the Archbishop presented the Bible, and pronounced the benediction, and his Majesty kissed the bishops kneeling before him.

"Whilst *Te Deum* was singing, his Majesty was enthroned, whereupon the bishops performed their homage, and then the temporal lords: first, his Royal Highness the Duke of York, and his Royal Highness the Duke of Cumberland, each for himself; then the Duke of Devonshire, Lord Chamberlain, pronounced the words of homage for all the dukes; the Marquis of Rockingham, for the marquises; Earl Talbot, Lord High Steward, for the earls; Viscount Saye and Sele, for the viscounts; and Lord Henley, Lord High Chancellor, for the barons. Every peer, likewise taking off his coronet, touched the King's crown, and kissed his left cheek.

"The coronation of his Majesty being finished, the Queen removed from her seat to the south side of the area, to a chair placed before the altar, and was anointed (four ladies holding a pall over her Majesty), and afterwards invested with the ring and crowned by the Archbishop, upon which the peeresses put on their coronets. The Archbishop then delivered the sceptre into her right hand, and the ivory rod into her left hand. Their Majesties then made their second oblation and received the communion, and the final prayers being read, they retired into St. Andrew's Chapel, where they were invested with their royal robes and crowns of state."

The following story, we may here remark, shows the religious feelings of George III. to great advantage:—"When the King approached the communion-table, in order to receive the sacrament, he inquired of the Archbishop, *whether he should not lay aside his crown?* The Archbishop asked the Bishop of Rochester, but neither of them could say what had been the usual form. The King determined within himself that humility best became such a solemn act of devotion, took off his crown and laid it down during the administration."

It may interest such of our readers as care for sacred music, to be reminded that the first of those Handel Festivals, which within our own day have become so popular at Exeter Hall, and at the Crystal Palace at Sydenham, was celebrated here on the 26th of May, 1784. The idea of holding these musical gatherings originated in a conversation at the house of a Mr. Joah Bate, between that gentleman, Lord Fitzwilliam, and Sir Watkin Williams Wynn, on the grand effect produced by large bands. That year had just completed a century from Handel's birth, and twenty-five years from his death. When the plan had assumed some degree of form, the Abbey was naturally thought of as the place best calculated for such a scene. The King offered his patronage, and the consent of the Dean and Chapter was readily obtained. The festival took place in the nave of the Abbey.

The following inscription on a tablet of white marble was (on Saturday, June 5th, 1784) placed over the monument of Handel in the south transept:—"Within these walls the memory of Handel was celebrated, under the patronage of his most gracious Majesty, George III., on the 24th and 29th of May, and on the 3rd and 5th of June, 1784. The music performed on this solemnity was selected from his own works, by the direction of Brownlow, Earl of Exeter; John, Earl of Sandwich; Henry, Earl of Uxbridge; Sir Watkin Williams Wynn, and Sir Richard Jebb, Baronets; and conducted by Joah Bate, Esq."

NORTH TRANSEPT OF WESTMINSTER ABBEY, 1830. (*See page* 424.)

The Handel Festivals continued to be held in the Abbey till the year 1790, when they were transferred to St. Margaret's Church, close by, for a year or two; and subsequently, on one occasion, the celebration was held in the Banqueting House at Whitehall.

Apropos of the Handel festivals, we may add that, on the authority of an entry in "Raikes's Journal," our National Anthem of "God save the King," composed in the time of George I., has always been considered of English origin; but from the "Memoirs of Madame de Crégn," it appears to have been almost a literal translation of the "cantique" which was always sung by the demoiselles de St. Cyr when Louis XIV. entered the chapel of that establishment to hear the morning prayer. The words were by M. de Brincse, and the music by the famous Sully :—

"Grand Dieu, sauve le Roi !
Grand Dieu, venge le Roi !
Vive le Roi !
Que toujours glorieux,
Louis victorieux
Voie ses ennemis,
Toujours soumis !
Grand Dieu, sauve le Roi !
Grand Dieu, venge le Roi !
Vive le Roi !"

It appears to have been translated and adapted to the House of Hanover by Handel.

The exterior of the Abbey had become in such a sad state of decay in the beginning of the present century, that a memorial on the subject was addressed to the Lords of the Treasury in 1806. The petition was immediately referred to a "committee of taste," in consequence of whose report it was laid before the House of Commons, and the sum of £2,000 was at once granted towards the projected repairs. From subsequent reports made to Parliament, it appears that upwards of £42,000 were granted for reparations between 1807 and 1822; and since that time further grants have been occasionally made by Parliament for the same purpose.

In July, 1803, the Abbey very narrowly escaped destruction, through the carelessness of some of the plumbers who were employed in repairing the lantern at the junction of the four long timber roofs. Fortunately the fire broke out in the day-time, or the consequences might have been very serious; as it was, the cost of repairing the damage done amounted to £3,500.

On the 19th of July, 1821, George IV. was crowned with the usual pomp and ceremony in the Abbey, the champion's duty being performed by Henry Dymoke, Esq. (afterwards Sir Henry Dymoke, Bart.), as deputy for his father, the Rev. John Dymoke, Hereditary Grand Champion of England, an office which is attached to the feudal manor of Scrivelsby, in Lincolnshire. We shall have more to say with reference to the champion's duties in our chapter on Westminster Hall. The procession from Westminster Hall was headed by the "King's Herbwoman, with her six maids," scattering flowers along the raised and carpeted platform, which was traversed by the king and the long line of nobles, and others who preceded him. The ceremony in the Abbey was, on this occasion, very similar to that which had been performed sixty years previously at the coronation of George III., which we have described above; but one touching incident towards its close should not be lost sight

SIR CHRISTOPHER WREN'S DESIGN FOR THE COMPLETION OF WESTMINSTER ABBEY.

of here. His unfortunate queen—Caroline of Brunswick—presenting herself for admission to the Abbey in order to be crowned as Queen Consort, was rudely repulsed from the doors, both at Poets' Corner and at the western entrance. Little more than a fortnight afterwards, on the 7th of August, she died at Brandenburg House, the victim of a broken heart.

On the 14th, when her remains were removed for interment at Brunswick, a shameful riot took place in the streets of London. For some reason or other, which was never explained, the queen's corpse was ordered to be carried into Essex *en route* for Harwich, not through the heart of the City, but by the circuitous route of the New Road. The people, who had made common cause with the injured lady, regarded this as an indignity, and in opposition to the orders of the king's ministers and of the authorities of the Horse Guards, they succeeded in forcing the funeral *cortège* to pass through Fleet Street and St. Paul's; in a conflict between the mob and the soldiers, two of the former were killed.

We learn incidentally from Mr. Raikes' "Journal" that the coronation of William IV. and Queen Adelaide (1831) cost only £37,000. "The Queen was so anxious that no expense should be incurred on her account, that she would not permit either the purchase or the hire of a crown from Rundell's for herself, but ordered that it should be composed of her own jewels and made up at her own expense." At the previous coronation, that of George IV., the charge of Messrs. Rundell, for the loan of jewels only, was £16,000, as interest on their value.

The coronation of Her Majesty Queen Victoria, on the 28th of June, 1838, was conducted in most respects after the *reformed* model of that of her immediate predecessor, the walking procession of "all the estates of the realm," and the banquet in Westminster Hall, with all the feudal services attendant thereon, being wholly dispensed with. There was, however, a State procession, which was attended by the foreign ministers and ambassadors, and which wound its way from Buckingham Palace by Constitution Hill, Piccadilly, St. James's Street, Pall Mall, Charing Cross, Whitehall, and Parliament Street, to the Abbey. Here the peers and peeresses, the great officers of state, and others who were to take part in the ceremony, had assembled some time before the arrival of Her Majesty. All being in readiness, the Queen, arrayed in her royal robe of crimson velvet, furred with ermine and bordered with gold lace, wearing the collars of the Orders of the Garter, Thistle, Bath, and St. Patrick, and having on her head a circlet of gold, was conducted, amidst a most magnificent procession, up the nave into the choir. The dresses worn by many of the nobles on this occasion are described as most superb, and Prince Esterhazy's uniform is stated to have been so gorgeous that he seemed to be quite encased in precious stones. The coronation ceremony was impressively performed. The first part of the service over, the Archbishop of Canterbury, standing before the altar, and having St. Edward's crown before him, took the same into his hands, consecrated and blessed it with the prayer, "O God, who crownest thy faithful servants, with mercy," &c. Then the Archbishop came from the altar, assisted by the Archbishops of York and Armagh, with the Bishops of London, Winchester, and other bishops, the Sub-dean of Westminster carrying the crown, which the Archbishop took and placed on Her Majesty's head; when the people, with loud and repeated cheers, cried, "God save the Queen." Immediately the peers and peeresses present put on their coronets, the bishops their caps, and the Deputy-Garter King-of-Arms his crown; the trumpets meanwhile sounding, the drums beating, and the Tower and Park guns firing by signal.

Mr. Rush, the American Minister, who was an eye-witness of the coronation, thus describes the scene at this moment:—"The beautiful and almost startling effect of the sudden gleams of the noonday sun, as they shot through the windows of the Abbey at the very instant at which the Archbishop of Canterbury placed the crown upon the head of the youthful female sovereign, falling directly where he stood and she knelt—which in old Rome would have been seized upon as the most auspicious of omens; the like simultaneous putting on of his coronet by each peer at a given moment as by enchantment; the beauty and grace of the Queen's train-bearers; and the scattering of the gold medals among the aristocratic throng as the ceremonies drew to a close, and good-humoured strife to catch them—all this will be long remembered by those who had the good fortune to witness that magnificent spectacle. But there was no banquet in the hall—no champion—no Duke of Wellington on horseback by his side."

Lady Clementina Davies, in her "Recollections of Society," gives the following sketch of the scene:—"I was present at Queen Victoria's coronation; when she knelt and the crown was placed on her brow, a ray of sunshine fell on her face; the day had been dull, but the sunlight on the diamonds made a kind of halo round her head. When she was conducted to King Edward's chair, to which the peers came to swear allegiance, the Duke of Wellington, having to back down the steps of the throne, threw his robe over his arm, and his great military boots became visible; still he made a safe and not ungraceful descent. When it came to Lord Rolle's turn to walk backward, he lost his footing and rolled down. He sustained no damage, but when he stumbled, the Queen started forward as though to save him!"

From the account of the coronation in the *Gentleman's Magazine*, it appears that the venerable Lord Rolle, from his feeble and infirm state, fell in *ascending* the steps; "whereupon Her Majesty rose from her seat, extended her hand to him to kiss, and expressed a hope that his lordship was not hurt. This act of royal and gracious kindness was instantly felt and appreciated by all the spectators, who loudly and zealously applauded it." "When the Peers had done their homage," continues the writer, "the House of Commons, determined not to be outdone in the manifestation of loyalty, immediately gave, every man, nine loud and hearty cheers, accompanied with reiterated cries of 'God save Queen Victoria!' The simultaneous burst of loyal feeling seemed as if it had been provided for in the programme. The assembled multitudes in the galleries and vaultings were not behind 'Her Majesty's faithful Commons' in their enthusiasm, but caught up and repeated the shouts until the vaulted roof and arches of the whole sacred edifice rang with one universal acclaim."

Mr. Rush gives the following description of the incident alluded to above, in his "Court of London:"—"It was feared, at first, that he [Lord Rolle] had injured himself, and all eyes were riveted to the spot. In an instant a dozen arms and hands were extended to assist him to rise; conspicuous among the number being those of the youthful maiden Queen herself, who quickly rose to go towards him as by a feminine instinct, the latter triumphing, at such a moment, over all the pageantry which surrounded her. When it was found that he was not hurt, a sprightly young lady—the daughter of a peer—in the box immediately adjoining that of the ambassadors and ministers, was heard to say, 'Oh, it's nothing; it's only part of his tenure to play the "roll" at the coronation.'"

The most memorable service held in the Abbey of recent years was that which commemorated the Jubilee of the Queen's reign, on the 21st of June, 1887. It was attended by many foreign princes, all the surviving members of Her Majesty's family, and representatives of the most important sections and interests of the empire. The service was repeated on the following day, when special care was taken to admit large bodies of working men and women.

CHAPTER LI.

WESTMINSTER ABBEY.—A SURVEY OF THE BUILDING.

"How reverend is the face of all this pile,
Whose ancient pillars rear their marble heads
To bear aloft its arch'd and ponderous roof
By its own weight made steadfast and immovable,
Looking tranquillity. It strikes an awe
And terror on my waking sight; the tombs
And monumental caves of death look cold."—*Wordsworth.*

Extent of the Abbey Possessions—Exterior Views of the Church—Dimensions of the Building—The West Front and Wren's Gothic Towers—The North Transept and "Solomon's Porch"—The Chapels—General Description of the South Side—Appearance of the Interior from the West Doorway—Churchill's Satirical Poem on the Tombs and Monuments—Pitt's Funeral—The Burial of Charles J. Fox, and his Monument—Vice-Admiral Tyrrell—Congreve, the Dramatist—Mrs. Oldfield—Secretary Craggs—The Poet Wordsworth—Robert Stephenson—Sir Charles Barry—George Peabody—David Livingstone—Other recent Interments—Sunday Evening Services.

OTHER cathedrals may surpass the Abbey of St. Peter's, Westminster, in the grandeur of their architecture; yet its situation and the varied character of its parts, and its completeness as a whole—combined with its national character as the place where our monarchs have been crowned, and where so many of them are buried, surrounded by the statesmen, courtiers, ecclesiastics, poets, and other illustrious persons of five centuries—make it a type of the British Constitution—the union of the Monarchy, the Church, and the State. The first subjects of the Crown interred here—except the members of the monastery itself—were the officers of Edward the Confessor, "thus," as Dean Stanley has touchingly observed, "reunited with him whom they had served in life." The custom was adopted, and the numbers greatly increased in subsequent reigns; and in the time of Elizabeth, the Abbey had become the place of sepulture of the most eminent persons in the empire—"the first-fruits of England's political, naval, and military glory."

Although the charge of the Abbey had been originally committed to a "college of priests," the fact that it contains the remains and memorials of persons of such varied professions, and of so many shades of political and religious opinion—the juxtaposition, as it were, of rivals in life, such as Queen Elizabeth and Mary Queen of Scots, Pitt and Fox, and others—prove that its keepers have in most cases risen to the greatness of their position, and have not been wholly influenced by a sectarian spirit of exclusiveness. Side by side with our sovereigns, Westminster Abbey enshrines the remains of politicians, warriors, judges, actors, philanthropists, physicians, until it has passed into a proverb. "Victory, or Westminster Abbey!" Nelson is reported to have exclaimed, when leading his ship into action at Trafalgar; though, as a matter of fact, he missed the latter alternative, being buried, as we have seen, in St. Paul's.

As St. Paul's has become the Pantheon for the reception of our naval and military heroes, so the Abbey has gradually become the last resting-place of those who have fought the battle of life in another way—the men who have added renown to their country as statesmen and as men of letters. There are, of course, a few exceptions, for do not Sir Christopher Wren, Sir Joshua Reynolds, Turner and Landseer, Leighton and Millais, lie in St. Paul's? whilst the Abbey covers the ashes of Lords Howe and Ligonier, Admiral Sir Peter Warren, Admiral Sir Cloudesley Shovel, Lieutenant-General Sir Eyre Coote, Vice-Admiral Sir Henry Blackwood, General Lawrence, and others in both branches of the service.

"The Abbey Church," says Mr. Bardwell, the architect, "formerly arose a magnificent apex to a royal palace, surrounded by its own greater and lesser sanctuaries and almonries; its bell-towers (the principal one 72 feet 6 inches square, with walls 20 feet thick), chapels, prisons, gatehouses, boundary-walls, and a train of other buildings, of which we can at the present day scarcely form an idea. In addition to all the land around it, extending from the Thames to Oxford Street, and from Vauxhall Bridge Road to the church of St. Mary-le-Strand, the Abbey possessed 97 towns and villages, 17 hamlets, and 216 manors. Its officers fed hundreds of persons daily, and one of its priests (not the abbot) entertained at his 'pavilion in Tothill,' the king and queen, with so large a party, that seven hundred dishes did not suffice for the first table; and even the Abbey butler, in the reign of Edward III., rebuilt at his own expense the stately gatehouse which gave entrance to Tothill Street."

With the exception of the Chapter House, the Jerusalem Chamber, the cloisters, and one or two fragments of buildings on the southern side, the Abbey Church is now all that remains of the ancient monastic edifice. The general aspect of this structure is grand in the extreme—perhaps not to be surpassed by any Gothic edifice in the kingdom; whilst in its details it presents a rich field of beautiful variety, almost every period of Gothic architecture being illustrated in one part or other.

The exterior view of the Abbey is best obtained from a distance, its exquisite proportions being, perhaps, better appreciated when seen from the high ground in the Green Park. For a nearer and more minute survey, the west front is seen to great advantage from Victoria Street, the north transept and aisle from the corner of King Street, and the south side from College Street. St. Margaret's Church, standing immediately beside the Abbey, has the effect of causing the proportions of the larger fabric to stand out in a bold and imposing relief.

The church consists of a nave, choir, aisles, transepts, and sacrarium; and at the east end are Edward the Confessor's, Henry VII.'s, and seven other chapels. Its dimensions are, from east to west, including Henry VII.'s Chapel, 375 feet; across the transepts it measures 200 feet; the height of the nave and choir is 101 feet; height to the roof of the lantern about 140 feet, and the height of the western towers 225 feet.

The west front of the Abbey, it must be owned, is poor enough, when compared with that of most English or foreign cathedrals. In fact, as we are told in the *Grub Street Journal* for March 6, 1735, it was never really finished at all, being "by Providence reserved for the able hand of the judicious Mr. Hawksmore." The English reader who knows anything of the beautiful symmetry of Gothic architecture will wish that Mr. Hawksmore's "judicious" work had been applied to some other and less noble edifice; and even Chamberlain's statement that the skill of Sir Christopher Wren in the two western towers is "thought to exceed in point of workmanship any part of the ancient building," will hardly be endorsed by the merest tyro in Gothic architecture.

It is generally said that the western towers of the Abbey were completed by Sir Christopher Wren; but this is not true, though he commenced the work, in apparent disdain of the rules of pointed architecture. Nevertheless, Sir Christopher would seem to have been opposed to any confusion of style in designing, for in a letter to Dr. Atterbury, Bishop of Rochester, he says, "I shall speedily prepare draughts and models, such as I conceive proper to agree with the original scheme of the architect, without any modern mixtures to show my own inventions." We have given on page 409 a reproduction of a design said to have been prepared by Wren for the completion of the work, which includes as a principal feature a spire rising from the low central tower.

Mr. A. Wood remarks with great justice here: "That many layers of classical cornice should appear on the face of Gothic towers will in time be felt to be a disgrace to our architecture; and we may ourselves, perhaps, see these towers rebuilt, from the roof of the church upwards, with Wren's proportions, but with pure and harmonious detail." Since the time of Sir Christopher the rules of Gothic art have been so deeply and accurately studied and mastered (thanks to the efforts of the Oxford and Cambridge Architectural Societies, and the labours of Pugin and Sir G. Gilbert Scott), that there can be no doubt of the capacity of the present generation to bring to perfection that one portion of this noble structure which has come down to our hands, as a legacy from the so-called 'Dark Ages,' in one respect, and in one only, incomplete."

The principal entrance is at the western end, and, taken as a whole, makes anything but an imposing appearance. The great doorway is of considerable depth, and contracts inwards. The sides are composed of panels, and the roof is intersected with numerous ribs. On each side of the door are pedestals in empty niches, with shields in quatrefoils beneath them. A cornice extends above the doorway, on which are ten canopied niches, separated by small buttresses; these niches are without statues, and their canopies are cones foliaged and pinnacled. Over these there is a cantilever cornice, of modern date, and above the cornice is a frieze adorned with armorial bearings. Hence arises the great painted window; it has a border of eight pointed enriched panels, and over it a large heavy cornice, with a frieze inscribed "A. R. GEORGII II. VIII. MDCCXXXV." The roof is pointed, and contains a small window, with tracery.

The towers on either side of the west front are strengthened by substantial buttresses, with two ranges of canopied niches on their fronts. The lower windows of the towers are pointed; those above them arches only, filled with quatrefoils and circles. It is from this part that the incongruity of the new design begins in a Tuscan cornice; above this is a Grecian pediment and enrichments over the dial of the clock, and in each face of the topmost storeys is a Gothic window of poor design; the whole being crowned with battlements and pinnacles.

The west front, as we have seen, was only finished in the reign of George II., from designs by Wren, considerably altered, however, by Hawksmoor, and by John James, the latter's successor. "It is evident," observes Sir Christopher in his architectural report addressed to Bishop Atterbury, "that the two towers were left imperfect, the one much higher than the other, though still too low for bells, which are stifled by the height of the roof above them; they ought certainly to be carried to an equal height, one storey above the ridge of the roof, still continuing the Gothic manner in the stone-work and tracery. Something," he adds, "must be done to strengthen the west window, which is crazy; the pediment is only boarded, but ought undoubtedly to be of stone."

The north side of the church is supported by nine buttresses, each of five gradations, with pointed windows between them; the buttresses are connected with the clerestory of the nave by slender arches, and the wall is finished with battlements.

"Time was," writes Mr. Charles Knight of the north transept, "when this front had its statues of the twelve apostles at full length, and a vast number of other saints and martyrs, intermixed with intaglios, devices, and abundance of fretwork; and when, on account of its extreme beauty, it was called 'Solomon's Porch;' and now, even injured as it is, the whole forms a rich and beautiful façade." Since Mr. Knight wrote, this front has been virtually rebuilt—"a work," to quote from Mrs. Murray Smith's sumptuous volume entitled "Annals of Westminster Abbey," published in 1895, "commenced by Sir Gilbert Scott, after whose designs the triple portico was finished in 1885. The upper part was undertaken by Mr. Pearson, under whose supervision the eighteenth century front of Wren's time was transformed back to the Early English style; and in 1890 the whole exterior end of the north transept was completed, and the scaffolding, which had concealed it for so many years, was at last removed." Between the colonnade and the roof is a beautiful rose window.

The south transept underwent considerable repairs at the beginning of the present century, and the great rose window on that side was rebuilt in the year 1814. Within the last twenty years more than a score of the windows of the Abbey have been enriched with stained glass.

All the chapels that project on the north-east and south-east are, in their designs, like the body of the church; but the chapel of Henry VII., for its elegant outline and lavish ornamentation, is, perhaps, the chief point of attraction to most visitors on a first inspection.

pointed windows on each side, and the angles are finished octagonally.

Entering by the great western door, the mind of the visitor is at once filled with awe and astonishment at the sublimity of the scene presented to the eye. The nave and choir are separated from the side-aisles by lofty cloistered columns, supporting pointed arches, above which are the triforium and the clerestory windows, some of which are filled with stained glass, and from the piers between them spring the intersecting arches of the vaulted ceiling. The pillars terminate towards the east by a sweep, thereby enclosing the chapel of Edward the Confessor in a kind of semicircle, and excluding all the rest. The long side-aisles are com-

POETS' CORNER, WESTMINSTER ABBEY. (*See page* 425.)

The front of the south transept is far less elegant than that of the north, but this is rendered of little consequence by the confined nature of its situation, the library, chapter-house, and cloisters being so immediately contiguous as to exclude all the lower part from public view. All the exterior walls are embattled, and the roof is covered with lead. The central tower, or rather lantern, has a dwarfish and unfinished aspect; it has two narrow,

pletely filled with monuments erected to the memory of illustrious personages.

"In what is called the open part of the Abbey," says Mr. Godwin, in his "Essay on Sepulchres," "are to be found the tombs of many of our great literary characters, mixed with those of others who have a very slight claim to such a distinction. In the enclosed part the spectator is much more struck with the capriciousness of the muse of monumental fame. Except the kings down to those of the House of Stuart, he looks in vain for the tombs of almost all the great men that have adorned our annals. Instead of Simon Montfort, Stephen Langton, and Wickliffe, and the Montacutes, and the Nevilles, and Cardinal Wolsey, and Cranmer, and Sir Philip Sidney, and Lord Chancellor Bacon, and multitudes of others that offer themselves to the memory, we find Sir John Pickering, and Sir Bernard Brocas, who lost his head in the cause of Richard II., and Colonel

WESTMINSTER ABBEY: THE CHOIR. (*See page* 422.)

Popham, and Thomas Thynne, who is immortalised for having been shot in his coach, and Mrs. Nightingale. There is good reason for the absence of most, if not all, of the worthies above mentioned."

We cannot, of course, in these pages give anything like a detailed description of all the monuments that grace—or rather disgrace—the walls of this sacred edifice: suffice it to say that most of them are vile, and tasteless, and barbarous bits of heathen sculpture, utterly out of keeping with the house of God. On some of these memorials there is a grim humour and dry sarcasm which, in spite of the solemn associations around, provokes an irresistible smile; as, for instance, when we read it recorded on the tomb of Samuel Butler, the author of "Hudibras," that it was erected by a Lord Mayor of London, "that he who was destitute of all things when alive might not want a monument when dead." One cannot help remarking of such a tribute,—

"Sed quæ tarda venit gratia, sera venit."

It was to satirise this heathen and pagan style of monuments in the Abbey that Churchill wrote as follows in the "Foundling Hospital for Wit" (1771):—

"In fam'd cathedral who 'd expect
  Pallas, a heathen goddess,
To lift her shield come to protect
  Lord Stanhope—this most odd is!

"Or to see Hercules, a son
  Of Jupiter (as fabled),
There hov'ring o'er an admiral's bust,
  As if by him enabled.

"What could they more in times of yore,
  Do, heroes to defend?
What could the stage exhibit more
  Than make the gods descend?

"Verger or beadle, who thou art
That hast the supervising part,
  Fain would I mace thee lay on;
For Dean's Yard boys* with much surprise,
Being thus greatly edified,
May throw their heathen gods aside,
And shortly there, I fear, see rise
  In stone the whole Pantheon."

Over the west door, and immediately under the great window, has been turned a stone arch, on which has been erected a monument to the Right Hon. William Pitt. The statue, the workmanship of Sir Richard Westmacott, represents the illustrious statesman habited in the robes of Chancellor of the Exchequer; at the base are figures representing History recording his speeches, and Anarchy writhing in chains. The inscription runs thus:—

"This monument is erected by Parliament to William Pitt, son of William Earl of Chatham, in testimony of gratitude for the eminent public services, and of regret for the irreparable loss of that great and disinterested minister. He died January 23, 1806, in the forty-seventh year of his age."

Though a public funeral was voted to Pitt, yet only three hundred spectators were admitted within the walls of the Abbey on the occasion. Cyrus Redding was one of the favoured few: he thus describes the funeral:—"The procession came in at the great west entrance, having crossed the way from the Painted Chamber in the House of Lords, where the body had lain in state. It passed between two lines of Foot Guards. The spectators were ranged on a scaffolding covered with black. Muffled drums, with fifes, announced the entrance of the procession, in which were a number of distinguished persons—princes of the blood, statesmen, and fellow-ministers of the deceased. . . . Beilby Porteus, Bishop of London, read the service, standing by the side of the vault. The princes were in their royal robes. When the service was over, many advanced to look into the vault. The Dukes of York and Cumberland were among the number, and Lord Hawkesbury (afterwards Liverpool) took a glance, standing on the opposite side to where I and my fair companion were similarly occupied. The procession re-formed and took its leave; we stayed some time longer. The scene was novel. I could not help fixing my eyes, as long as I remained, upon the coffin of Lord Chatham, beneath whose monument we were standing. I thought of the share he had filled in a brilliant part of our history, and the mighty events he had influenced, for he was a great favourite in my youthful reading. The son became lost in the recollection of the father. Lady Chatham and a daughter lay in the same vault, on the verge of which, at the funeral, sat, as the nearest relative to the deceased, Pitt's brother, the *late* Earl of Chatham, as he was called, a nickname acquired from his going into his office when half the business of the day was over, his nights being devoted to play. He now lies in the same vault, memorable alone for his incapacity in the command of the unfortunate Walcheren expedition. Pitt was colonel of the Cinque Ports Volunteers, and hence his military funeral. The crowd outside the Abbey bandied jokes. They said that he was buried in military array lest his remains should be insulted. Lord Chatham's coffin, so it was reported, was found on its side when the vault was opened. This was

* The "Dean's Yard boys" in the above lines are, of course, the Westminster scholars.

attributed by some to the influx of the Thames, which had covered the vault with slime, but could hardly have overturned a heavy leaden coffin."

Not far from the monument of Pitt sleeps his great rival and opponent in the House of Commons, Charles James Fox, a man of whom, with all his personal faults, the nation may well feel proud. Cyrus Redding, in his "Fifty Years' Reminiscences," thus describes the funeral of this distinguished statesman:—"I saw the obsequies of Fox, a walking funeral from the Stable Yard, St. James's, by Pall Mall and Charing Cross, lines of volunteers *en haye*, keeping the ground. I recollect the Whig Club among the followers, and a large body of the electors of Westminster, with the cabinet council, but no royalty, for which some kind of excuse was made. Literally the tears of the crowd incensed the bier of Fox. The affection displayed by the people was extraordinary; I saw men crying like children." The monument of Fox, which was also the work of Sir R. Westmacott, represents the great statesman on a mattress, falling into the arms of Liberty. Peace (with the olive-branch and dove) is reclining on his knee, whilst in the foreground is an African, kneeling, as if testifying his gratitude for the part which Fox took in the cause of freedom. He died in September, 1806, at the age of fifty-seven.

It is impossible not to be struck with the proximity of Pitt's monument to that of Fox, and not to call to mind the touching lines of Sir Walter Scott on these two eminent statesmen:—

> "The mighty chiefs sleep side by side;
> Drop upon Fox's grave the tear,
> 'Twill trickle to his rival's bier."

One of the most curious monuments, perhaps, in the Abbey is that near the cloister door, in the south aisle of the nave. It commemorates Vice-Admiral Richard Tyrrell, commander of the *Buckingham*, who died in 1766, whilst on his return to England from the Leeward Islands, after an engagement with the French. His body, the inscription informs us, "according to his own desire, was committed to the sea, with proper honours and ceremonies." "To comprehend this monument," says Mr. Malcolm, "the spectator must suppose himself in a diving-bell at the bottom of the sea. When he has shaken off the terrors of his situation he will find on his right hand the *Buckingham*, of sixty-six guns, jammed in a bed of coral. Directly before him he will perceive a figure pointing to a spot on a globe, either intending to show where the deceased body was committed to the deep, or the latitude where an action, mentioned in the inscription, was fought." The figures introduced into this piece of monumental composition are History, Navigation, and Hibernia; they are represented among the rocks, with the sea above their heads; above all is the Admiral himself, ascending amidst heavy clouds—the latter being highly suggestive of ill-made pancakes.

In the south aisle of the nave is the monument erected to William Congreve, the dramatist, by Henrietta, Duchess of Marlborough, his relations with whom while alive, coupled with the fact of his leaving her a legacy of £10,000, have been made the subject of many scandalous surmises. To this fact Horace Walpole alludes in one of his "Letters:" —"When the younger Duchess (of Marlborough) exposed herself by placing a monument and silly epitaph of her own composing and bad spelling to Congreve in Westminster Abbey, her mother, quoting the words, said, 'I know not what pleasure she might have had in his company, but I am sure it was no honour.'"

Near the monument of Congreve is buried the celebrated actress, Mrs. Oldfield, if we may believe her maid, "in a very fine Brussells' lace headdress, a Holland shift with a tucker and double ruffles of the same lace, a pair of new kid gloves, and her body wrapped up in a winding-sheet." It is to this funeral array that Pope alludes—

> "'Odious! in woollen! 'twould a saint provoke!'
> Were the last words that poor Narcissa spoke.
> 'No; let a charming chintz and Brussels' lace
> Wrap my cold limbs, and shade my lifeless face:
> One would not, sure, be frightful when one's dead,
> And—Betty, give this cheek a little red!'"

The accomplished actress, Mrs. Oldfield, died in October, 1730. She lies near the tomb of Craggs, as well as near that of Congreve, not far from the Consistory Court. It is said by Mr. J. H. Jesse that, at her burial, a bystander scribbled on paper and threw into her grave the following epigram:—

> "If penance in the Bishop's Court be feared,
> Congreve, and Craggs, and Oldfield will be scared
> To find that at the Resurrection Day
> They all so near the consistory lay."

The Craggs mentioned in this verse was a man of low extraction, being only a shoemaker's son; but he nevertheless rose to a high and honourable position in the State. He was made Secretary for War in 1717, and soon afterwards a member of the Privy Council. The epitaph on his monument, written by Pope, runs as follows:—

> "Statesman, yet friend to truth, of soul sincere,
> In action faithful, and in honour clear;
> Who broke no promise, served no private end,
> Who gain'd no title, and who lost no friend.
> Ennobled by himself, by all approved,
> Praised, wept, and honour'd by the muse he loved."

To any one who knows anything of the history of the South Sea scheme, and of Mr. Secretary Craggs' connection with it, we are afraid these lines will be considered as over-rating his merits.

In the north aisle of the choir is a monument to William Wilberforce, the philanthropist, who died in 1833, and whose remains were honoured with a public funeral.

Close by the south-west corner of the Abbey is a statue of William Wordsworth, placed here by the friends and admirers of the poet. Wordsworth died at Rydal Mount, Westmoreland, in April, 1850. The statue, executed by Thrupp, represents the poet in a meditative attitude; and the quiet and secluded spot in which it is placed, apart from the crowd, and in a peaceful retirement of its own, harmonise with, and are expressive of, the tranquil tenor of his life, and the thoughtful, sublime, and philosophic character of his works. The place which has been thus happily selected for the statue is the Baptistry, in the centre of which is the font. In allusion to this circumstance the following sonnet from Wordsworth's poems ("Ecclesiastical Sonnets," vol. iv., page 269) has been inscribed near the statue:—

HOLY BAPTISM.

"Blest be the Church, that watching o'er the needs
Of infancy, provides a timely shower
Whose virtue changes to a Christian flower
A growth from sinful Nature's bed of weeds!
Fitliest beneath the sacred roof proceeds
The ministration; while parental Love
Looks on, and grace descendeth from above,
As the high service pledges now, now pleads.
There, should vain thoughts outspread their wings and fly
To meet the coming hours of festal mirth,
The tombs—which hear and answer that brief cry,
The infant's notice of his second birth—
Recall the wandering soul to sympathy
With what man hopes from heaven yet fears from earth."

The gallery high up in the southern wall, near the Baptistry, was erected for the accommodation of the Royal Family to view the procession of the Knights of the Bath, on the occasions when their installation took place here. The procession entered at Poets' Corner, and proceeded round the west end, and up the north aisle, into Henry VII.'s Chapel, where the ceremony was performed; as we shall notice more particularly in speaking of that part of the building.

Robert Stephenson, the eminent engineer, who died in 1859, is commemorated by a brass figure of life-size, in the floor of the nave, in addition to which is an elaborate painted window illustrative of his fertile genius. Sir Charles Barry, the architect of the new Houses of Parliament, also lies in the centre of the nave; his grave is covered by a slab of black Irish marble, inlaid with brass, bearing his name and the date of his death, and appropriately engraved. Here, too, lie Sir Gilbert Scott and Mr. G. E. Street, two other well-known architects.

In the early spring of the year 1870 the body of Mr. George Peabody, the philanthropist, who bequeathed a large share of his wealth for the purpose of improving the homes of the working classes in this metropolis, was laid in a temporary resting-place in the nave, until arrangements could be made for its transfer to America. A suitable inscription marks the spot where the body rested. "He was a man," to use the apt expression of Mr. Gladstone within a few days after Mr. Peabody's death, "who taught us in this commercial age, which has witnessed the building up of so many colossal fortunes, at once the noblest and most needful of all lessons; he has shown us all how a man can be the master of his wealth instead of being its slave."

In the summer of 1874 a grave was opened in the centre of the nave of the venerable Abbey to receive the body of David Livingstone, the African explorer and missionary. He had died in the centre of that continent nearly a year before, but his body had been embalmed by friendly hands, and was brought back to England in order to receive the honour of a public funeral. Among more recent interments in the Abbey have been those of Sir Charles Lyell, the famous geologist; Lord Lawrence, some time Governor-General of India; Bishop Thirlwall; Sir Rowland Hill, the deviser of the penny post; George Grote, the historian of Greece; Field-Marshal Sir George Pollock; and Lady Augusta and Dean Stanley.

The pulpit in the nave is used only for the special Sunday evening services. It is composed of variegated marble, interspersed with rich foliage, and some very tasteful mosaic: around it are the figures of St. Paul, St. Peter, and the four Evangelists, and in front, in a medallion, is a head of the Saviour crowned with thorns. An inscription sets forth that "this pulpit is presented to the Dean and Chapter of Westminster by a few friends in grateful commemoration of the opening of the nave for public worship and preaching, in January, 1858." The Abbey, like most, if not all, of our cathedrals, was for many years very little used except on Sundays, and even then the nave was seldom, if ever, utilised for worship. In 1858, however, the then Dean, Archbishop Trench, instituted special services on Sunday evenings in the nave, and his successors, have also followed up the example. We may add that the House of Peers used to attend service here on "High Days and Holy Days," just as the Commons went to hear sermons in St. Margaret's Church close by.

We may perhaps be pardoned for ending this chapter by recording here the bitter sarcasm contained in Pope's well-known epitaph headed "One who would *not* be buried in the Abbey:"—

> "Heroes and kings, your distance keep!
> In peace let one poor poet sleep,
> Who never flattered folks like you!
> Let Horace blush, and Virgil too."

CHAPTER LII.

WESTMINSTER ABBEY.—THE CHOIR, TRANSEPTS, &c.

> "Where through the long-drawn aisle and fretted vault
> The pealing organ swells the notes of praise." —*Gray's Elegy.*

The Choir Screen—Monuments of Earl Stanhope and Sir Isaac Newton—Curious Monument of Thomas Thynne, and the Story of Thynne's Assassination—Admiral Sir Cloudesley Shovel—Major André—Sir Charles Carteret—The "Musicians' Corner"—The Choir—Dr. Busby's Pavement and his Wig—Abbot Ware's Mosaic Pavement—Portrait of Richard II.—The Reredos—Discovery of Fragments of the Original Church—Monuments to Eminent Statesmen—Memorial Windows—Poets' Corner—Ben Jonson—Dryden—Handel—Milton—Gray—Matthew Prior—Old Parr—Charles Dickens—Goldsmith, and Dr. Johnson's Inscription—Spenser—Chaucer—Isaac Barrow—Addison's Reflections on Poets' Corner.

We now pass on eastwards, turning our backs on the great western entrance, on our way to that portion of the sacred edifice which forms the cross, and find ourselves confronted by a screen. This screen, separating the nave from the choir, was designed by Mr. Blore, the architect to the Abbey, and erected in 1831. It serves as the organ-gallery; the organ itself, however, is so placed between the columns at the sides that the view of the interior from end to end is in no way obstructed. Four pilasters with decorated finials divide the screen into three compartments, the centre for the gate of entrance to the choir from the nave, the other two contain the monuments of Earl Stanhope and Sir Isaac Newton. On each of the pilasters are projecting pedestals, which support the figures of Henry III. and his queen, Edward the Confessor and his queen, and Edward I. and his queen.

Here the body of the great Sir Isaac Newton, having lain in state in the Jerusalem Chamber for two days previously, was deposited in March, 1727. "Every honour," says a contemporary account, "was paid to his remains; the pall was supported by six peers." The monument was executed by Rysbrack; it represents the great astronomer in a recumbent posture, leaning his right arm on four folio volumes, entitled "Divinity," "Chronology," "Optics," and "Phil. Prin. Math.," and pointing to a scroll supported by winged cherubs. Over him is a large globe, projecting from a pyramid behind, whereon is delineated the course of the comet in 1680, with the signs, constellations, and planets; on the globe is the figure of Astronomy with her book closed, and beneath the principal figure is a bas-relief, representing the various labours in which Sir Isaac Newton chiefly employed his time, such as discovering the causes of gravitation, settling the principles of light and colour, and reducing the coinage to a determined standard. The inscription, which is in Latin, terminates with the exclamation, "How much reason mortals have to pride themselves in the existence of such and so great an ornament to the human race!"

In the south aisle, close by the choir-screen, is a monument to Thomas Thynne, Esq., of Longleat, in the county of Wilts, who was barbarously murdered while riding in his coach, in Pall Mall, in February, 1682, by three hired assassins, at the instigation of an infamous foreigner, Count Königsmark, from motives of jealousy. The monument is of a very sensational character, considering the place in which it is erected, displaying a representation of the tragic scene, with its surroundings, in bold relief. The coach, the coachman, servants and their wigs, the horses, and the bystanders are apparently drawn to the very life.

The story of Thynne's assassination runs as follows:—The murder was stimulated by a desire on the count's part to obtain in marriage the Lady Elizabeth Percy, the rich heiress of the Earl of Northumberland. The lady in her infancy had been betrothed to the Earl of Ogle, only son of the second Duke of Newcastle, but was left a widow before the marriage was consummated. She was soon afterwards married to Mr. Thomas Thynne, who, from his large income, was called "Tom of Ten Thousand;" but being scarcely fifteen years of age, her husband, at the earnest entreaty of her mother, was prevailed upon to allow her to travel another year before entering fully upon her wedded life. During this period she is reported to have become acquainted with Königsmark, a Hanoverian count. Whether she had ever given him any countenance is uncertain; but having no grounds to hope to obtain her while her husband lived, he plotted his death in the villainous manner above described. Königsmark, however, did not succeed by this means in gaining the prize, for the lady—alarmed, doubtless, at his blood-stained hands—not long afterwards married the Duke of Somerset.

WEST FRONT OF WESTMINSTER ABBEY, FROM TOTHILL STREET, 1820.

The monument of Admiral Sir Cloudesley Shovel, in the south aisle of the choir, consists of a recumbent figure of the admiral lying under a tent, and beneath it, in bas-relief, is a representation of the wreck of the *Association*, in which he lost his life. The inscription tells us that "he was deservedly beloved by his country, and esteemed, though dreaded, by the enemy, who had often experienced his conduct and courage. Being shipwrecked on the rocks of Scilly, in his voyage from Toulon, October 22, 1707, at night, in the fifty-seventh year of his age, his fate was lamented by all, but especially by the seafaring part of the nation, to whom he was a generous patron and a worthy example. His body was flung on the shore, and buried with others in the sand; but being soon after taken up was placed under this monument, which his royal mistress had caused to be erected, to commemorate his steady loyalty and extraordinary virtues."

A story is told which illustrates the personal bravery of Sir Cloudesley Shovel. When a boy in the navy, under the patronage of Sir John Narborough, hearing that admiral express an earnest wish that some papers of consequence might be conveyed to the captain of a distant ship in action, he immediately undertook to swim through the line of the enemy's fire with the despatches in his mouth, a feat which he actually performed, reaching the ship in safety.

Occasionally epigrams and witticisms relating to current events have been wafered or pasted on to some of the monuments and statues in the Abbey, though the practice has never reached the dignity of a custom here, as in the case of the well-known Pasquin statue at Rome, which gave rise to the word "pasquinade." One such example, however, we are able to give here from a manuscript, apparently of about 1780, in the possession of a former verger:—

"The following lines were written and wafered up against Major André's monument, after its having been defaced, &c., by knocking off the hands and heads of some of the figures:—

"'Forbear rash mortals, nor with brutal rage
Deface this noble monumental page;
Let the just marble future ages tell
Britannia mourn'd when her brave hero fell.'"

Major André was buried in the south aisle, and the monument referred to in the above lines was erected at the express command of George III. On it is represented a soldier carrying a flag of truce, and presenting to George Washington a letter which André had addressed to his Excellency the night previous to his execution. It may be added here, in justification of the lines quoted above, that the present is the third head placed on the figure of General Washington, and that several of the others are new, the originals, which are stated to have been exceedingly well executed, having entirely disappeared.

Immediately beneath the organ-loft, in the north aisle, is the tomb of the last representative of the Carteret family—Sir Charles, who died in 1715.

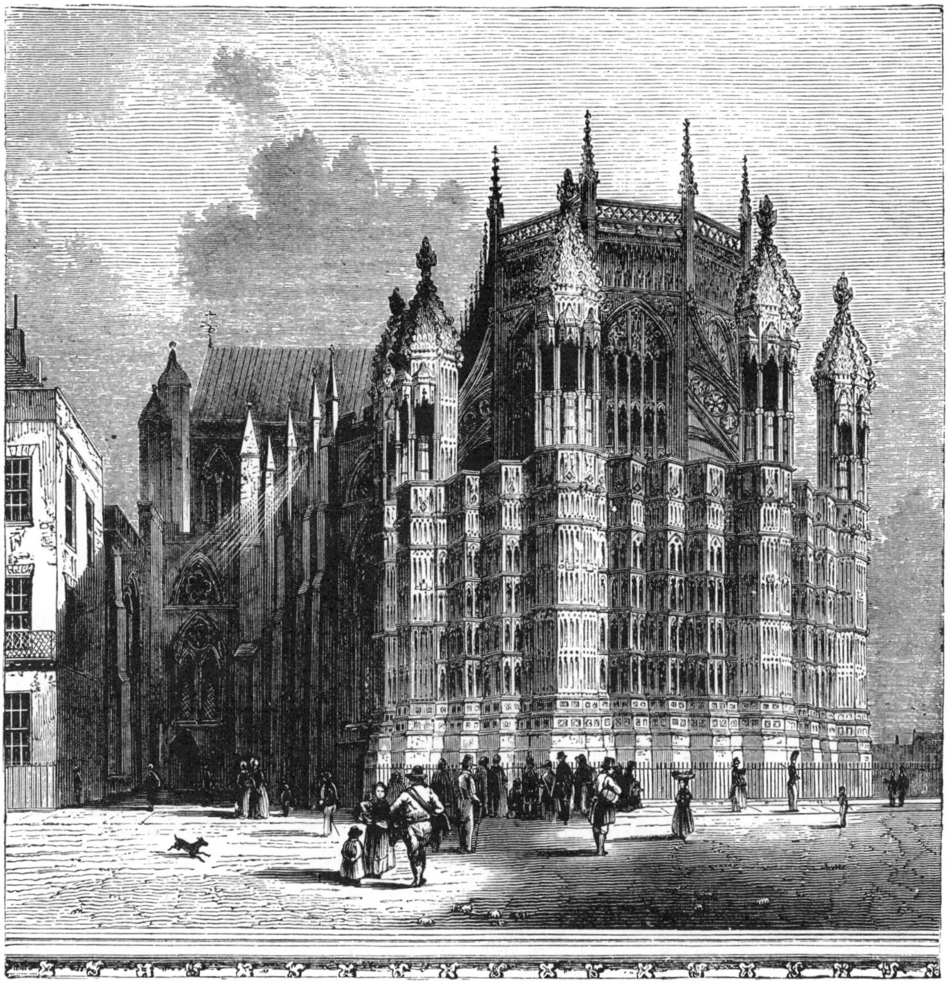

KING HENRY VII.'S CHAPEL, 1876. (*See page* 399.)

The tomb is a sarcophagus of marble, either built into the wall, or so executed as to represent such a position. To the right of the spectator a stout cherub leans on a diagonally disposed narrow slab of marble, probably intended to represent a sunbeam, on which are inscribed the names of several of the family. Above this quaint and ugly tomb, the whole of the wall-space between the soffit of the organ-loft, the door giving access to the stairs, and the end of the same—some nine feet square —is occupied by a new, bright, chromatic decoration. It is divided, by a light scroll-work, into four compartments, each containing the coat of arms of a peer or peeress, with supporters, coronet, and motto. The arms are those of Grace, Countess Granville, who died in 1744; John, Earl Granville, 1763; Martha, Viscountess Lansdown, 1689; and Frances, wife of the above-named Earl John. A short inscription of the name, distinctions, and date of the birth and of the death of each is clearly and distinctly painted beneath each blazon, and on a tablet extending under the whole is the following legend: "All the above lie buried in the vault of their relative, General George Monk, Duke of Albemarle, K.G.; and this record is inscribed by order of their descendant and inheritor, the sub-dean of this collegiate church, A.D. 1869." This sub-dean was Lord John Thynne.

In the north aisle of the choir are appropriately deposited the remains of several men, who in their time achieved celebrity as musicians or composers, many of whom were organists of this church; among them are Dr. Samuel Arnold, Dr. Burney, Dr. Blow, Dr. Croft, Henry Purcell, and, lastly, Sir William Sterndale Bennett.

We now pass into the choir, remarking only that the style of architecture adopted for its fittings, though of recent date, is a copy of that which prevailed in the reign of Edward III. It was designed by Mr. Blore, and executed in 1848. The dean's and sub-dean's stalls are on either side of the iron gate, in the centre of the screen, and are alike in general design; that of the dean, however, is more elaborately treated in its ornamental details. The canons' stalls have groined canopies springing from slender moulded shafts with carved capitals, and are separated by buttresses terminating in pinnacles. The fronts of the pews and the ornamental accessories of the stalls are carved to represent the foliage of vine, ivy, oak, willow, &c.

The organ formerly stood in the centre of the screen, and consequently obstructed the view down the whole length of the building, but this very objectionable arrangement was altered in the year 1848. It is now divided into three distinct portions, the principal of which are under the arches at the north and south ends of the screen. Each part of the organ, however, is so connected by a nice mechanical contrivance that they are all brought under the command of the performer.

The marble pavement of the floor, in lozenges of black and white, was given by Dr. Busby, who died in 1695, and whose tomb is in the south transept. Dr. Busby was the celebrated prebendary of Westminster, and master of the school, whose rigid discipline has, to a great extent, caused his name to be handed down to posterity.

But it was not only as a schoolmaster that Dr. Busby's name is celebrated; he has come down to modern times as associated with the wig which bore, and perhaps still bears, his name. But this derivation will hardly stand. A "busby," as our grandfathers used to style the large perukes of their day, half in jest, was but an elongation of the briefer and simpler "buzz"—a frizzled and bushy device for the covering of the head. As all the existing portraits of the reverend doctor represent him with a close cap, or at all events, without a wig, it is probable that the "busby" was so called in sport, *lucus a non lucendo*.

The sacrarium is reached by an ascent of four or five steps. Here the pavement is an elaborate piece of mosaic. It was the work of Abbot Ware, and was laid in 1260. The lower dais of the altar and sedilia is formed of stones of various colours, and laid in rich and varied patterns; and the steps are of Purbeck marble. On the south side hangs a whole-length portrait of Richard II. This picture hung for many years in the Jerusalem Chamber, and was exhibited at the National Portrait Exhibition at South Kensington. It has been discovered that the original portrait was subsequently covered by successive coatings of paint, so laid on as not only to obscure, but materially to alter the drawing, and to disguise the character of the original picture. This mask of paint was removed in 1866, and the real old picture painted in tempera, and apparently from the life, revealed underneath it in an almost perfect state of preservation. Mr. George Scharf, at the time Secretary of the National Portrait Gallery, in writing to the *Athenæum* respecting this discovery, observed:—"Instead of a large, coarse heavy-toned figure, with very dark, solid shadows, strongly-marked eyebrows, and a confident expression (almost amounting to a stare) about the dark-brown sparkling eyes, we now have a delicate, pale picture; carefully modelled forms, with a placid and almost sad expression of countenance; grey eyes, partially lost under heavy lids; pale yellow eyebrows, and golden-brown hair. These latter points fully agree with the king's profile, in the well-known little tempera Diptych at Wilton, belonging to the Earl of Pembroke. The long thin nose accords with the bronze effigy of the king in Westminster Abbey; whilst the mouth, hitherto smiling and ruddy, has become delicate, but weak, and drooping in a curve, as if drawn down by sorrowful anticipations even in the midst of pageantry. Upon the face there is a preponderance of shadow, composed of soft brown tones, such as are observable in early Italian paintings of the Umbrian and Sienese schools executed at a corresponding period. Indeed, the general appearance of the picture now forcibly recalls the productions of Simone Memmi, Taddeo Bartoli, Gritto da Fabriano, and Spinello Aretino; but more especially those of their works which have suffered under a similar infliction of coatings of whitewash or plasterings of modern paint. Many alterations seem to have been made by the restorer in various parts of this figure of King Richard, and well-devised folds of drapery quite destroyed through ignorance. The position of the little finger of his left hand, holding the sceptre, was found to have been materially altered. The letters R, surmounted by a crown, strewn over his blue robe, were changed in shape, and the dark spots on his broad ermine cape were distorted from their primitively simple tapering forms into strange twisted masses of heavy black paint. The globe held in his right hand, and covered with some very inappropriate acanthus leaves, was at once found to be false, and beneath it was laid bare a slightly convex disc of plain gold, very highly burnished. This, however, was not an original part of the picture. A plain flat globe with its delicate gilding was found still lower: and it was then ascertained that the head of the sceptre and the crown on his head had in like manner been loaded with gold and polished. Beneath these masses of solid burnished gilding, bearing false forms and ornaments unknown to the fourteenth century, was found the original Gothic work, traced with a free brush in beautiful foliage upon the genuine gold surface lying upon the gesso preparation spread over the panel itself, and constituting a perfectly different crown as well as heading to the sceptre from those hitherto seen. The singular device of a fir cone on the summit of the sceptre has disappeared entirely. The diaper, composed of a raised pattern, decorating the background, coated over with a coarse bronze powder, and not even gilded, was found to be a false addition. It was moulded in composition or cement, possibly as early as the reign of the Tudors. Not only did it stand condemned in itself by clumsiness of workmanship and a reckless fitting together of the component parts, but it was found to have extensively overlaid some of the most beautiful foliage and pieces of ornamentation. The picture is painted on oak, composed of six planks joined vertically, but so admirably bound together as to appear one solid mass. The back is quite plain."

From a MS. note in a copy of the authorised Guide belonging to a former verger, we glean the following particulars with regard to this historical portrait:—"There was formerly placed near the pulpit an ancient portrait of Richard II., sitting in a gilt chair, dressed in a green vest flowered with gold; with gold shoes ornamented with pearls. This piece, which is 6 feet 11 inches in length, and 3 feet 7 inches in breadth, was removed on the new fitting-up of the choir, to the Jerusalem Chamber, where the Dean, &c., meet to transact business. The lower part," adds the writer, "is somewhat defaced."

Of this picture Pennant, writing in 1790, observes that "after the test of near four hundred years it is in the highest preservation, and not less remarkable for the elegance of the colouring than for the excellent drawing, considering the early age of the performance. We must allow it has been repainted, but nothing seems altered, if we may collect from the print made by Vertue, excepting a correction of the site of the cross issuing out of the globe. The background is elevated above the figure, of an uneven surface, and gilt. The curious will find in the first volume of Mr. Walpole's 'Anecdotes,' an ingenious conjecture as to the method of painting in that early period, which has given such amazing duration to the labours of its artists."

On either side of the altar are the curious and interesting monuments of King Sebert; Ann of Cleves, wife of Henry VIII.; Aveline, Countess of Lancaster; Aymer de Valence; and Edmund Crouchback.

The reredos, which was put up in 1867, was designed and executed under the superintendence of Sir G. Gilbert Scott. It is chiefly composed of white and coloured alabaster, combined with a reddish spar. It consists of a façade occupying the whole space between two main pillars, having two doors, one on each side, giving access to the shrine of Edward the Confessor behind. The doorways are arched and richly moulded. On either side of each door is a large canopied niche with pedestal, and containing statues of Moses, St. Peter, St. Luke, and King David; and on the inner side of each large niche are two smaller ones, placed vertically. These niches are all most elaborately enriched with tabernacle work, groined and surrounded with pierced tracery and carved work, and terminated with pinnacles, flying buttresses, and spires, all profusely crocketed and finished. The whole is surmounted with a bold cornice, superbly carved and sculptured with subjects illustrative of the life of our Lord. In the space between the inner niches and above the communion-table is a recess, wherein is placed an elaborate and minutely finished picture of the Last Supper, in Venetian glass mosaic; the picture is 12 feet 6 inches by 5 feet 5 inches in size, and was executed from the cartoon of Mr. Clayton, by Salviati, at Venice.

During the exploration necessitated by laying the new flooring in front of the altar, there were discovered on the north side, about three feet below the pavement, the bases of three piers which formed part of the old abbey of Edward the Confessor. They are of early Norman character, and, from their position, it is presumed that that early structure was nearly equal in size to the present fabric. Means have been adopted by which these remains have been so covered with the pavement that they can be easily uncovered and exposed to view. Dugdale tells us, on the authority of one of the early writers, that the church, as rebuilt by Edward the Confessor, was finished in a few years, and that "it was supported by many pillars and arches." Camden, however, has left us a fuller description, translated from a manuscript of the very period. "The principal area or nave of the church stood on lofty arches of hewn stone, jointed together in the nicest manner, and the vault was covered with a strong double arched roof of stone on both sides. The cross which embraced the choir, and by its transept supported a high tower in the middle, rose first with a low strong arch, and then swelled out with several winding staircases, to the single wall, up to the wooden roof, which was carefully covered with lead."

The solemn office of crowning and enthroning the sovereigns of England takes place in the centre of the sacrarium; and beneath the lantern or central tower, on a raised dais, is placed the throne at which the peers do homage. The details of these interesting ceremonies we have already given (pages 401 to 409).

Passing into the north transept, we are forcibly reminded by many of the monuments we see around us of the truth of the remarks made by a writer in the *Literary World:* "From St. Stephen's to Westminster Abbey the distance is short, but the road is difficult; and those who have traced it gloriously, led on by genius, and supported by principle, sleep calmly the sleep of death, unmoved by all that could once animate their glowing souls, within a few paces of the scene of their past triumphs. What a contrast between the scene of turmoil and worldly cares before us—the passion-stirring harangues and the angry rejoinders—and the awful silence of the house of God, where reposes all that was earthly of those deathless souls!"

Here, almost side by side, rest the ashes of George Canning, Sir Robert Peel, Lord Palmerston, Sir G. Cornewall Lewis, Pitt, Fox, and Grattan. Richard Cobden, who was buried in 1865 at West Lavington, in Sussex, is here commemorated by a bust; as is also the late Earl of Aberdeen. The latter, which is said to be a faithful representation of the deceased statesman, was executed by Mr. Matthew Noble. The following is the inscription on the bust:—

"GEORGE GORDON, fourth Earl of Aberdeen, K.T., K.G. Born January 28, 1784; died December 14, 1860. Ambassador, Secretary of State, Prime Minister."

Near the north doorway is the monument to William Pitt, the first Earl of Chatham, who died on the 11th of May, 1778, a few weeks after being seized with a fit whilst speaking in his place as a peer in the House of Lords in reply to the Duke of Richmond on the inexpediency of carrying on the American war.

The statue to the Earl of Chatham was erected by a special vote of the public money, at the cost of £6,000. Cowper makes the following allusion to it in "The Task:"—

"Bacon there
Gives more than female beauty to a stone,
And Chatham's eloquence to marble lips."

The monument was designed by Bacon, who also erected the cenotaph to the same statesman in Guildhall. It is, of course, wholly out of keeping with the architecture of the building or with the character of a church, but it is a fine specimen of its kind, and simple in design, though embracing six figures. In a niche, in the upper part of a large pyramid, is the statue of the earl. On a sarcophagus underneath recline Prudence and Fortitude. A group still lower down consists of Britannia on a rock with the Ocean and the Earth at her feet, intended to exhibit Lord Chatham's wisdom and fortitude. The statue of the earl is in his parliamentary robes; he is in the action of speaking, the right hand thrown forward and elevated, and the whole attitude strongly expressive of that species of oratory for which his lordship was so deservedly celebrated. Prudence has her usual symbols, a serpent twisted round a mirror. Fortitude is characterised by the shaft of a column, and is clothed in a lion's skin. The energy of this figure strongly contrasts the repose and contemplative character of Prudence. Britannia, as mistress of the sea, holds in her right hand the trident of Neptune. Ocean is entirely naked, except that his symbol, the dolphin, is so managed, that decency is perfectly secured: the action of Ocean is agitated, and his countenance severe, which is opposed by the utmost ease in the figure of the Earth, who is leaning on a terrestrial globe, her head crowned with fruit, which also lies in some profusion at the foot of the pyramid. In the centre of the plinth is the following inscription :—

"Erected by the King and Parliament as a testimony to the virtues and abilities of WILLIAM PITT, Earl of Chatham, during whose administration Divine Providence exalted Great Britain to an height of prosperity and glory unknown to any former age."

Close by the statue of Canning are two magnificent monuments to the old Dukes of Newcastle. The first is that of William Cavendish, Duke of Newcastle, and his duchess, Margaret, youngest sister of Lord Lucas. This duchess, as we learn from the inscription, "was a wise, witty, and learned lady, which her many books do well testify; she was a most virtuous, loving, and careful wife, and was with her lord all the time of his banishment and miseries; and when he came home, never parted from him in his solitary retirements." The basement of the tomb is covered with armour, on which is a handsome pedestal; reposing on a mat under a circular pediment lie the figures of the duke and duchess. His Grace held many great offices of state, and died in 1676. The other monument is that of John Holles, Duke of Newcastle, who died in 1711. The monument was executed by Gibbs, and is a beautiful pile of architecture, of the Composite order. The basement, columns, and pediment are composed of richly-variegated marble; at the sides of the base are symbolical statues of Wisdom and Sincerity; angels and cherubs in somewhat meaningless attitudes appear on the upper part of the monument, whilst the armed duke reclines in a very awkward manner upon a sarcophagus, having in one hand a general's truncheon, and in the other a ducal coronet.

The six lancet windows in the north transept are filled with stained glass to the memory of Major-General Sir H. W. Barnard and others who "died in the service of the Queen and their country in India," in 1857 and 1858; and there is also a memorial window in the west aisle of this transept to Brigadier the Hon. Adrian Hope, C.B

Crossing to the south transept, or, as it is now popularly and most appropriately called, "Poets' Corner," we enter that part of the Abbey which has become the resting-place of the remains of most of England's greatest men in the field of literature and art. Here sleep in peace such celebrities as Chaucer, Dryden, Booth, Drayton, Edmund Spenser, Samuel Butler, Garrick, Camden, Nicholas Rowe, Isaac Casaubon, Handel, Addison, John Gay, Thomas Campbell, Matthew Prior, Cowley, Sir William Davenant, Lord Macaulay, George Grote, Charles Dickens, Robert Browning, and Lord Tennyson. With such an assemblage around us we can do no more than select a few of the monuments as deserving of special notice.

That to the memory of Garrick represents the great actor throwing aside a curtain, which reveals a medallion of Shakespeare, allegorically indicating the power he possessed of unveiling the beauties of the "bard of all time." Tragedy and Comedy are seen personified, with their appropriate emblems.

Mr. J. T. Smith, in his "Book for a Rainy Day," alluding to the death of Garrick, on the 20th of January, 1780, and his burial in Westminster Abbey, remarks that a facetious friend, with an ill-timed levity, lifted up the latch of Nollekens' studio, and said, "For the information of the sons of Phidias, I beg to observe that David Garrick is now on his way to pay his respects to the gentlemen in Poets' Corner; I left him just as he was quitting the boards of the Adelphi." Mr. Smith then adds: "I begged of my father, who then carved for Mr. Nollekens, to allow me to go to Charing Cross, to see the funeral of Garrick pass. There was a great crowd. I was there in a few minutes, followed him to the Abbey, heard the service, and saw him buried."

William Camden, the eminent antiquary, who died in 1623, is commemorated by a half-length figure, in the dress of his time, holding in his left hand a book, and in his right his gloves, resting on an altar, on the front of which is an inscription setting forth his "indefatigable industry in illustrating our British antiquities, and his candour, sincerity, and pleasant good humour in private life." He was for some time second master of Westminster School, where Ben Jonson—one of the noblest of English dramatists—was his pupil. Here is a marble monument to Jonson, finely executed by Rysbrack; it is ornamented with emblematical figures, "alluding, perhaps," it has been suggested, "to the malice and envy of his contemporaries." A writer in the *Athenæum* has pointed out that the bust of Ben Jonson shows a sculptural error of the kind referred to in the following verses, taken from "A Choice Collection of Poetry, most carefully collected from Original Manuscripts, by Joseph Yarrow, Comedian, York," and published in the year 1738.

INTERIOR OF KING HENRY VII.'S CHAPEL. (*See page* 434.)

house the politest men of that age, and among them Shakespeare is said to have been a frequent visitor. Upon Ben Jonson's death, Davenant succeeded him as Poet Laureate to Charles I., but having, as it is stated, lost his nose by an *accident*, he was cruelly bantered by the wits of the succeeding reign. He died in 1668.

Shakespeare himself does not lie here, as everybody knows; there is, nevertheless, a monument to him in Poets' Corner. Pericles has told us many centuries ago, that "the whole earth is a monument of men of genius;" and in a like spirit sings Ben Jonson:—

"My Shakespear, rise; I will not lodge thee by
Chaucer or Spenser, or bid Beaumont hie
A little further off to make thee room:
Thou art a monument without a tomb."

The monument to John Dryden was erected by Sheffield, Duke of Buckingham, who had refused to aid the poet in his lifetime, thereby giving point to the satiric assertion of Pope, that—

"He help'd to bury whom he help d to starve."

Bishop Atterbury thus writes to Pope on this subject:—"What do you think of some such short inscription as this in Latin, which may, in a few words, say all that is to be said of Dryden, and yet nothing more than he deserves?—'JOHANNI DRYDENO, cvi poesis Anglicana vim svam ac veneres debet, et siqva in posтervm avgebitvr lavde, est adhvc debitvra, honoris ergo,' &c. To show you that I am as much in earnest in the affair as you yourself, something I will send you too of this kind in English. If your design holds of fixing Dryden's name only below, and his busto above, may not lines like these be grav'd under the name?

'This Sheffield rais'd, to Dryden's ashes just;
Here fix'd his name, and there his laurel'd bust.
What else the Muse in marble might express,
Is known already; praise would make him less.'

Or thus:—

More needs not; where acknowledg'd merits reign,
Praise is impertinent, and censure vain.'"

Handel's monument is the last which Roubiliac lived to complete. It is affirmed that the sculptor first became conspicuous, and afterwards finished the exercise of his art, through working on the figure of this extraordinary musician. The statue of Handel upon his monument is considered very elegant and life-like. The left arm is resting on a group of musical instruments, and the attitude is expressive of great attention to the harmony of an angel playing on a harp in the clouds overhead.

Milton and Gray, though both are interred elsewhere, have each a monument here erected to their memory. That to the former was executed by Rysbrack, and has under the bust simply the name "Milton." On the front of the pedestal is the following inscription:—

"In the year of our Lord Christ one thousand seven hundred and thirty-seven, this bust of the author of 'Paradise Lost' was placed here by William Benson, Esq., one of the two auditors of the imprests to his Majesty King George II., formerly Surveyor-General of the Works to his Majesty King George I."

The monument erected to the memory of Gray consists of an alto-relievo of the Lyric Muse holding a medallion bust of the poet, and at the same time pointing a finger to the bust of Milton, which is immediately above it. The memorial, which was the work of John Bacon, the sculptor, bears the following lines:—

"No more the Grecian Muse unrivall'd reigns
To Britain let the nations homage pay;
She felt a Homer's fire in Milton's strains,
A Pindar's rapture in the lyre of Gray.
Died July 30, 1771, aged 54."

The stately monument of Matthew Prior, close by, is a sarcophagus surmounted by a bust and pediment. On one side of the pedestal stands the figure of Thalia, with a flute in her hand, and on the other side History, with her book shut. From the Latin inscription we learn that while Prior "was busied in writing the history of his own times, Death interposed and broke the thread of his discourse and of his life, September 18, 1721, in the fifty-seventh year of his age."

With reference to Prior's funeral Dr. Atterbury thus writes to Pope:—"I had not strength enough to attend Mr. Prior to his grave, else I would have done it, to have showed his friends that I had forgot and forgiven what he wrote on me. He is buried, as he desired, at the feet of Spenser, and I will take care to make good in every respect what I said to him when living, particularly as to the triplet he wrote for his own epitaph, which, while we were in good terms, I promised him should never appear on his tomb while I was Dean of Westminster."

It was Matthew Prior by whom the celebrated epigram and epitaph in one was written:—

"Nobles and heralds, by your leave,
Here lies what once was Matthew Prior,
The son of Adam and of Eve:—
Can Bourbon or Nassau go higher?"

"Old Parr," of whom we have spoken in a previous chapter (page 74), lies in Poets' Corner, near the door of St. Faith's—or, as it is often called, St. Blaize's—Chapel. He lived in the reigns of ten sovereigns, did penance for bastardy when above the age of 100, and died in November, 1635, aged 152 years. Near to him are the remains of Richard Brinsley Sheridan, Samuel Johnson, General Sir Archibald Campbell, John Duke of Argyll and Greenwich, and—though last, not least—Charles Dickens. His grave is covered by a slab of black marble, thus inscribed: "Charles Dickens, born February 7th, 1812, died June 9th, 1870." At his death passed away "the greatest instructor of the nineteenth century," and one of whom Caroline Norton some years previously had written:—

"Not merely thine the tribute praise
Which greets an author's progress here;
Not merely thine the fabled bays
Whose verdure brightens his career;
Thine the pure triumph to have taught
Thy brother-man a gentle part,
In every line of fervent thought
Which gushes from thy generous heart:
For thine are words which rouse up all
The dormant good among us found—
Like drops which from a fountain fall
To bless and fertilise the ground!"

It was at first intended that Charles Dickens should be buried in Rochester Cathedral, in accordance with the instructions contained in his will; but the voice of the nation was allowed to prevail over his own expressed wish, and very early on Tuesday, the 14th of June, 1870, he was laid to his rest in Poets' Corner. "Next to him lies Richard Cumberland; Mrs. Pritchard's monument looks down upon him, and immediately behind is David Garrick's. Nor is the actor's delightful art more worthily represented than the nobler genius of the author. Facing the grave, and on its right and left, are the monuments of Chaucer, Shakespeare, and Dryden, the three immortals who did most to create and settle the language to which Charles Dickens has given an undying name." So writes his friend, John Forster.

Apropos of this funeral we may add that Mr. B. Jerrold tells us that he met Charles Dickens about a month before his death at Charing Cross, and had a long chat with him about old friends, and Gustave Doré, and London—"a subject which no one ever knew half so well as himself, in all its highways and byways"—and that, on parting, Dickens "turned wearily towards the Abbey." "I never, however, for one moment, dreamed," he adds, "that within a month he would be resting there for ever, buried under flowers cast by loving hands, and that the whole civilised world would be lamenting the loss of the great and good Englishman."

Lord Shelburne, afterwards the first Marquis of Lansdowne, in a letter on sepulchral monuments in general, addressed to the committee for erecting a memorial to John Howard, the philanthropist, expresses a hope that St. Paul's may be preserved from becoming disfigured after the manner of Westminster Abbey by absurd and inappropriate sculpture. "It would be not only invidious," he writes, "but unfair to criticise the several monuments in Westminster Abbey; but let any person of the least feeling, not to mention taste or art, divest his mind of prejudice, and he must find himself more interested in viewing the single statue erected by Mr. Horace Walpole to his mother, Lady Orford, than with any of the piles erected to great men." The monument of Lady Orford is in the south aisle of Henry VII.'s Chapel, which we shall notice in our next chapter.

The fulsome expressions which are to be read upon most of the monuments here are enough to make one wish for a return to the simplicity of the old Roman inscriptions, and to provoke others besides children, as they look around, to ask, "But where are the bad people?" It is a fact that the Dean and Chapter refused to admit the body of Lord Byron into the Abbey; but with that single exception, we fear, the remark of Dr. King in "Anecdotes of his Own Times," is but too true:—"The dean and prebendaries of Westminster sell the sacred ground to any persons who think proper to purchase it; no objection is made to the quality or character of those to whom a monument is to be erected under this holy roof; the peer and the player, the chaste and the unchaste, are here deposited without distinction. But if you examine their characters here engraven on the monumental marble, you will not find one person amongst them all who, when living, had not been endowed with the most eminent qualities both of body and mind. General ———, who rose to his high post by such arts as are a disgrace to human nature, appears in Westminster Abbey to have possessed as great talents and as many virtues as Scipio Africanus."

It is to be hoped that, at all events, in recent times, so severe and caustic a remark has not been deserved by the Chapter of Westminster; indeed, we may safely say that the great and celebrated men who lately have been buried in the Abbey were men of whom England and English society may well be proud.

The monument to Goldsmith (who lies buried elsewhere) is of interest, on account of its connection with the name of Dr. Johnson. It was at first intended that this great essayist and master of the English tongue, who wanted but common prudence in order to have made one of the finest of characters, should have been buried in the Abbey, with a magnificent funeral; but the knowledge of his numerous debts unpaid caused the scheme to be withdrawn, and his body was interred in the churchyard of the Temple Church. It was decided, however, that a tablet should be raised to his memory in the Abbey. Sir Joshua Reynolds chose the spot, immediately over the doorway of St. Blaize's Chapel, and close to the memorial of Gay; and Dr. Johnson undertook to write the inscription. Johnson wrote this in Latin, and presented it to his friends for their approval. They wished that it had been written in the tongue which Goldsmith so excelled in writing; but the worthy doctor insisted that he would be no party to putting up English inscriptions in such a place as the Abbey, and by his persistency he gained the day. Thus it is that we have an inscription unintelligible to half at least of those who read and delight in his "Deserted Village" and his "Vicar of Wakefield," most of whom, it may be presumed, would also be interested in knowing what Dr. Johnson thought and said of him.*

Spenser lies here, not far from Chaucer. The short but beautiful inscription on his monument runs thus:—

> "Here lies, expecting the second coming of our Saviour Jesus Christ, the body of Edmund Spenser, the prince of poets in his time, whose divine spirit needs no other witness than the works which he left behind him."

It is recorded that at his funeral several of his poet brethren attended, and threw into his grave all sorts of epitaphs, elegies, and panegyrics. "'Gentle Willy' (as Spenser himself styles Shakespeare), we may be tolerably sure," says Charles Knight, "was among those mourners."

As for Chaucer, the same author observes with much justice and beauty, "like the fabled swan, he may be said to have literally died singing, for among his works we find 'A Ballad made by Geoffrey Chaucer upon his death-bed, *lying in his great anguish*.'"

Chaucer was buried in the cloisters of the Abbey, outside the building itself, but his remains were removed into the south transept in 1555. The tomb has been much defaced, but still exhibits traces of its former magnificence. It is an altar-tomb within a recess, and is surmounted by an elaborate canopy. In 1868 a memorial window was set up immediately above the tomb. The design is intended to embody his intellectual labours and his position amongst his contemporaries. At the base are the Canterbury Pilgrims, showing the setting out from London and the arrival at Canterbury. The medallions above represent Chaucer receiving a commission, with others, in 1372, from King Edward III. to the Doge of Genoa, and his reception by the latter. At the top the subjects are taken from the poem entitled "The Floure and the Leafe." On the right side, dressed in white, are the Lady of the Leafe, and attendants; on the left side is the Lady of the Floure, dressed in green. In the tracery above the portrait of Chaucer occupies the centre, between that of Edward III. and Philippa his wife; below them, Gower and John of Gaunt; and above are Wickliffe and Strode, his contemporaries. At the base of the window is the name "Geoffrey Chaucer, died A.D. 1400," and four lines selected from the poem entitled "Balade of Gode Counsaile:"—

> "Flee fro the prees, and dwell with soth-fastnesse,
> Suffise unto thy good though it be small;"
> * * * * *
> "That thee is sent receyve in buxomnesse;
> The wrestling for this world asketh a fall."

This window is a brilliant piece of colour, and an interesting addition to the attractions of the Abbey.

Poets' Corner, however, as our readers will already perhaps have noticed, is not confined to poets alone, but includes those who have courted other muses besides the muse of song. Divines, philosophers, actors, musicians, dramatists, architects, and critics, each and all have found a last resting-place in this part of the Abbey. Here, for instance, lies Dr. Isaac Barrow, whose life justifies the inscription which speaks of him as "a man almost divine and truly great, if greatness be comprised in piety, probity, and faith, the deepest learning, equal modesty and morals, in every respect sanctified and sweet." Dr. Barrow was master of Trinity College, Cambridge: he was so powerful and exhaustive in his sermons, that Charles II. wittily styled him the "unfair" preacher, because he left nothing for others to say on the subjects of his discourses.

Poets' Corner! "We could wish most heartily," writes Charles Knight, "we knew the name of him who first gave this appellation to the south transept of the old Abbey, and thus helped, most probably, to make it what it is, the richest little spot the earth possesses in its connection with the princes of song. Such a man ought himself to have a monument among them. Though he may never have written a line, we could almost venture to assert he must have had a kindred spirit to those who lie buried there, so exquisitely applicable is his phrase, so felicitously illustrative of the poet

* "Qui nullum fere scribendi genus non tetigit, nullum quod tetigit non ornavit."

who, with all his exhaustion of old worlds and creation of new, is generally most deeply attached to some of the smallest corners of that on which he moves. . . . In a word, we might have sought in vain for any other appellation that would have expressed with equal force the *home* feeling with which we desire, however unconsciously, to invest this abode of our dead poets, or that would have harmonised so finely with our mingled sentiments of affection and reverence for their memory."

It may be well here to quote the sober and touching reflections of Addison upon this sacred spot:—"When I look upon the tombs of the great, every emotion of envy dies in me; when I read the epitaphs of the beautiful, every inordinate desire goes out; when I meet with the grief of parents upon a tombstone, my heart melts with compassion; when I see the tombs of parents themselves, I consider the vanity of grieving for those whom we must quickly follow. When I see kings lying by those who deposed them, when I consider rival wits placed side by side, or the holy men that divided the world with their contests and disputes, I reflect with sorrow and astonishment on the little competitions, factions, and debates of mankind. When I read the several dates of the tombs, of some that died yesterday, and some six hundred years ago, I consider that great day when we shall all of us be contemporaries and make our appearance together."

CHAPTER LIII.

WESTMINSTER ABBEY.—THE CHAPELS AND ROYAL TOMBS.

"A feeling sad came o'er me as I trod the sacred ground
Where Tudors and Plantagenets were lying all around;
I stepp'd with noiseless foot, as though the sound of mortal tread
Might burst the bands of the dreamless sleep that wraps the mighty dead!"

Ingoldsby Legends.

Tomb of King Sebert—St. Benedict's Chapel—St. Edmund's Chapel—St. Nicholas's Chapel—Henry VII.'s Chapel—The Royal Vault—An Authentic Ghost Story—Monument to Edward VI.—The Five Chapels—Tomb of Henry VII. and Queen—"Steenie" and his Funeral—Cromwell's Last Resting-place—The Old Royal Vault—Monuments to Mary and Elizabeth—The Chapel of St. Paul—A Punning Epitaph—St. Edward's Chapel, or Chapel of the Kings—Chantry of Henry V.—Tomb of Edward III.—The Coronation Chairs—Opening a Royal Tomb—Shrine of Edward the Confessor—Islip's Chapel and "The Ragged Regiment"—The Chapels of St. John, St. Andrew, and St. Michael.

THE chapels at the east end of the Abbey Church are nine in number. Commencing on the south side by "Poets' Corner," and following the curve round to the north transept, we find them dedicated to the following saints:—St. Benedict, St. Edmund, St. Nicholas, St. Mary the Blessed Virgin (Henry VII.'s Chapel), St. Paul, St. Edward, St. John the Baptist, Abbot Islip's Chapel, St. John the Evangelist, St. Michael, and St. Andrew; but the three last named are now thrown into one. The kings buried in the Abbey are Sebert, Edward the Confessor, Henry III., Edward I., Edward III., Richard II., Henry V., Edward V., Henry VII., Edward VI., James I., Charles II., William III., and George II. Besides these there are fourteen queens, that is, five reigning sovereigns—Mary, Elizabeth, Mary Queen of Scots, Mary II., and Anne; the rest are the consorts of kings.

The tomb of Sebert, king of the East Saxons, who died in 616, and of Ethelgoda, his queen, is on the left of the gate of entrance to the chapels. The lower part of the tomb is covered by a plain arch forming a recess, and in the upper part seems to have been at one time richly adorned with paintings, of which there are slight traces left. Over the tomb, under a glass case, is preserved an elaborate work (measuring about eleven feet in length by three feet in height), which is supposed to have originally formed part of an altar decoration, and probably is of the fourteenth century.

"Henry III. performed two acts of pious respect to the remains of the founders of the Abbey, which," writes Pennant, "must not be omitted; he translated those of Sebert into a tomb of touchstone, beneath an arch made in the wall. Above this were paintings, long since defaced, done by order of the king, who was strongly imbued with a love of the arts." Horace Walpole has preserved, in his "Anecdotes of Painting," several of the royal instructions as to the number of mural decorations in this church. Among these is a direction for painting two cherubims "*cum vultu hilari et jocoso.*"

The Chapel of St. Benedict is separated from the south transept and the ambulatory, or chancel aisle, simply by a screen of monuments and their railings. At the east end, where stood the altar of St. Benedict, is the tomb of Frances, Countess of Hertford, whose effigy, as Malcolm states, "lies precisely where the candlesticks and host formerly stood." The oldest tomb in this chapel is that of Simon de Langham, who was a monk, prior, and afterwards Abbot of Westminster, Archbishop of Canterbury, and a cardinal. He died in 1376. The monument is of the altar form, with the sides adorned with quatrefoils and shields of arms, and on it lies an effigy of the archbishop, robed and mitred; it was formerly surmounted with a wooden canopy. In this chapel lie also several of the deans of Westminster.

Between the Chapel of St. Benedict and that of St. Edmund is a monument to the children of Henry III. Although it is now sadly defaced, this monument appears to have been a very elaborate one, richly adorned with mosaic work. In the state records there is the king's order for the erection of a monument in this place, "and for allowing Master Simon de Wells five marks and a half to defray his expenses, in bringing from the city a certain brass image, to set upon the tomb of his daughter Catherine; and for paying Simon de Gloucester, the king's goldsmith, seventy marks, for a silver image for the like purpose."

The Chapel of St. Edmund forms an hexagonal projection upon the passage leading from Palace Yard to "Poets' Corner." St. Edmund was Archbishop of Canterbury, and the anniversary held at his altar was on the 16th of November. An ancient wooden screen separates this chapel from the aisle. Here are several interesting tombs and monuments. On the east side of the doorway is the alabaster monument of John of Eltham, second son of Edward II., and so called from Eltham, in Kent, the place of his birth. The head of the statue is encircled in a coronet of large and small leaves,

TOMB OF HENRY III.

ON BEN JONSON'S BUST.

WITH THE BUTTONS ON THE WRONG SIDE.

"O rare *Ben Jonson!* what a turn-coat grown?
Thou ne'er wore such 'til thou wast clad in stone;
When Time thy coat, thy only coat impairs,
Thou'lt find a patron in an hundred years;
Let not then this mistake disturb thy sprite,
Another age shall set thy buttons right."

gravestone is explained by the fact that the coffin was deposited in an upright position, possibly . . . . to diminish the fee by economy of space. The tradition that Jonson had been interred in such a manner was generally discredited until the grave was opened a few years ago, when the remains of the poet were found in an erect posture."

HANDEL'S MONUMENT. (*See page* 428.)

This great dramatist and contemporary of Shakespeare was buried in the north aisle, and on a plain stone over his grave are to be seen the words "O! rare Ben Jonson"—an epitaph perhaps the more forcible for its quaint brevity. The words are said to have been cut by a mason for eighteenpence, paid him by a passer-by, "Jack Young." Mr. R. Bell, in his "Life of Ben Jonson," writes, "The smallness of the surface occupied by the

Allen, in his "History of London and Westminster," says that the epitaph on Jonson's gravestone was engraved by direction of Sir William Davenant, who has on his own tombstone, in the pavement on the west side of Poets' Corner, "O! rare Sir William Davenant." Sir William Davenant was the son of a vintner, and was born at Oxford in 1605; his mother, who was a woman of admirable wit and sprightly conversation, drew to her remarkable for being the earliest specimen of the kind. The details of plate-armour, surcoat, gorget, coroneted helmet, with other accessories, give great antiquarian interest to this work. It was formerly surmounted by a canopy, of which, however, no traces are now visible. Near it is a little altar-tomb of Petworth marble, with diminutive effigies of William of Windsor and Blanche of the Tower, children of Edward III., both of whom died young. west side of the doorway is the monument of William de Valence, Earl of Pembroke, half-brother to Henry III.; it is an altar-tomb of stone, surmounted by a broken sarcophagus, on which is a recumbent effigy of the earl. The figure is of wood, and was originally covered with copper-gilt, as was the chest on which it lies. The earl was treacherously slain at Bayonne, in France, in 1296, and his body was brought to England for interment in this chapel. "An indulgence of one hundred days was granted to all devout people who should offer up prayers for his soul."

ENTRANCE TO HENRY VII.'S CHAPEL. (*See page* 434.)

Close by is a slab of stained marble, that is perhaps less remarkable for its elegance than for the inscription it bears, which is as follows:—"In this chapel lies interred all that was mortal of the most illustrious and most benevolent John Paul Howard, Earl of Stafford, who, in 1738, married Elizabeth, daughter of A. Ewens, of the county of Somerset, Esq. His heart was as truly great and noble as his high descent; faithful to his God; a lover of his country; a relation to relations; a detester of detraction; a friend to mankind. Naturally generous and compassionate, his liberality and his charity to the poor were without bounds. Being snatched away suddenly by death, which he had long meditated and expected with constancy, he went to a better life the 1st of April, 1762, having lived sixty-one years, nine months, and six days." On the

Among the remaining monuments in St. Edmund's Chapel are those of Monck, Bishop of Hereford (1661); the Duchess of Suffolk (1558); Francis Holles, son of the Earl of Clare (1622); Lady Jane Seymour (1560); Sir Bernard Brocas (1400); Sir Humphrey Bourchier (1470); Eleanor de Bohun, Duchess of Gloucester (1399)—this is a monumental brass, representing the deceased in her conventual dress, as a nun of Barking Abbey; Robert Waldby, Archbishop of York (1397); and Mary, Countess of Stafford (1693).

Next in order is the Chapel of St. Nicholas, in the centre of which is an altar-tomb surmounted with the effigies of Sir George Villiers, who died in 1605, and of his lady, Mary Beaumont, created in 1618 Countess of Buckingham. Their son was advanced by James I. to the dukedom of Buckingham. Under this tomb were deposited, long after her decease, the remains of Katharine Valois, queen of Henry V., who died at Bermondsey Abbey, Southwark, in 1437, and was buried in the lady chapel at the east end of that abbey, where she remained till her grandson, Henry VII., built his chapel, after which her remains found a temporary resting-place in a chest placed near the tomb of her husband. That her remains were not allowed to rest undisturbed before their final consignment to the tomb in this chapel, may be gathered from the following entry in Pepys' diary, where, under date of March 23, 1667-8, we read:—"To Westminster Abbey, and there did see all the tombs very finely, having one with us alone; . . . and here we did see, by particular favour, the body of Queen Katharine of Valois; and I had the upper part of her body in my hands, and I did kiss her mouth, reflecting upon it that I did kiss a queen, and that this was my birthday, thirty-six years old, that I did kiss a queen." But what the particular point was which connected his thirty-sixth birthday with such an act, is more than we are told in his narrative.

The most stately monument in this chapel, and indeed one of the most magnificent in the Abbey, is that erected by Lord Burleigh to the memory of Mildred, his wife, and their eldest daughter Ann, Countess of Oxford. It rises to the height of twenty-four feet, and is constructed of various coloured marbles, after a design of the Corinthian order. The Latin inscriptions, which are very long, were written by Lord Burleigh himself, and set forth the varied accomplishments and the virtues of the two ladies who are represented in effigy in the lower part of the monument. The figure of Lord Burleigh, in his robes, and in a kneeling attitude, appears in the upper part of the monument.

Leaving the Chapel of St. Nicholas, we at once pass into the stately portico of the Chapel of the Blessed Virgin Mary, commonly called Henry VII.'s Chapel. The portico is beneath the oratory or chantry of Henry V., which forms an arch across the aisle directly east of his tomb. An ascent of twelve steps leads to the gates opening to the nave or body of the chapel; on the right and left are doors opening into the side aisles. The gates are of brass, most curiously wrought, forming a kind of framework, the panels of which are filled with the portcullis and crown, fleur-de-lis, the falcon and fetterlock, the thistle and crown, the united roses of York and Lancaster entwined in a crown, the initials R. H., the royal crown, and the three lions of England. The chapel itself forms the eastern extremity of the whole fabric, and is the most florid example of the perpendicular style of Gothic architecture that exists in this country; besides this, it is, in respect to its preservation, the most perfect example. We read that in the year 1502 Henry VII. took down the old and decayed "Lady Chapel," which hitherto stood here, and also a tavern that adjoined it, and erected on their site the splendid and elaborate structure which we now see before us. Leland calls this chapel "the miracle of the world;" and though his praise may well be pronounced extravagant, it is generally considered that the architectural splendour of this edifice is of the highest order. It has in England only one rival in the richness of its decoration, namely, King's College Chapel, at Cambridge. The roofs of both are among the glories of the later Gothic style. Externally the edifice is enriched with elaborate carvings and flying buttresses. The cost of Henry VII.'s chapel was 14,000 pounds: a large sum at that day.

The nave has five clustered columns on each side, the lower parts of which can be seen only in the side aisles, as they are hidden in the nave by the stalls of the Knights of the Bath, who were formerly installed here. The columns support four noble arches on each side, and the springing for the pendants of the roof; similar arches also divide the nave from the five small chapels at the east end. Immediately under the arches, and extending entirely round the chapel, is a range of demi-angels, projecting from the wall, in high relief. They support shields emblazoned with the devices of Henry VII.—the rose, portcullis, fleur-de-lis, &c. Over these angels are rows of octangular pedestals and niches containing statues of saints, martyrs, and other venerable personages. The chapel is lighted by two ranges of windows, of which there are fourteen in the upper, and nineteen in the lower; they were formerly of painted or diapered glass, having in every pane a white rose, the badge of Lancaster, or an 𝔥, the initial of the founder's name, but only a few of them are now remaining. In the upper window at the east end Henry VII. is represented in stained glass. Between the stone ceiling and the roof there is a spacious chamber lighted by Gothic openings through the walls.

The knights' stalls on either side of the nave are surmounted with canopies somewhat similar to those in the choir referred to in a preceding chapter; in them are fixed brass plates with the armorial bearings, &c., of the knights, and over them hang their banners, swords, and helmets. In front and below the stalls are seats for the esquires. The seats are so arranged as to form, when turned up, what are known as *misereres*. On these the monks and canons of former times, with the assistance of their elbows on the upper part of the stalls, half supported themselves during certain parts of their long services, and especially at the Miserere Psalm, so as not to be obliged always to stand or kneel. They are so contrived, that if the body became supine by sleep, they naturally fell down, and the unfortunate monk who rested upon it was thrown forward on to the pavement in front. The seats are fixed to the wall by hinges; when they are down nothing is to be seen, but upon turning them up we find those grotesque representations which were characteristics of the times in which they were carved. Many of them display an irresistible whimsicality of thought, often ludicrously coarsely and vulgarly expressed.

In the centre, between the knights' stalls, is the royal vault, wherein George II. and his queen, Caroline, are buried, together with the Prince and Princess of Wales, two Dukes of Cumberland, the Duke of York, Prince Frederick William, and the Princesses Amelia, Caroline, Elizabeth, Louisa, and Anne.

An amusing story with reference to the royal vault is told by Mr. J. Timbs, in his work on "London and Westminster," quoted from Sinclair's "Invisible World." The substance of the narrative is that five or six gentlemen who had dined together at a tavern afterwards paid a visit to the royal vault. Returning to the tavern, their conversation turned upon apparitions and a future state, when one among them, who was an infidel in such matters, took upon himself to rally the others, who seemed rather inclined to a contrary opinion. To end the contest, they proposed to him a wager of twenty guineas that he had not courage enough to go alone at midnight into the vault of Henry VII.'s Chapel. This he at once accepted; the money was forthwith deposited in the hands of the landlord of the house, and the party set out, after having engaged one of the vergers to attend the adventurous gentleman to the gate of the chapel, there to shut him in and to await his return. It had been arranged that the gentleman should stick the blade of his penknife in the earth of the vault, and leave it there, so that it might be found the next morning. It was agreed that his friends should remain for him at the door. Every step he took had its echo; and the lamp which the verger had left burning before the door of the chapel, by its faint glimmer, added to the solemnity of the scene. "At length," runs the narrative, "sometimes groping his way, and sometimes directed by the distant lamp, he reached the entrance of the vault. His inward tremor increased, yet, determined not to be overpowered by it, he descended, and having reached the last stair, stooped forward and stuck his penknife into the earth; but as he was rising to turn back and leave the vault, he felt something, as he thought, suddenly catch hold of him and pluck him forward. He lost in an instant everything that could support him, and fell into a swoon, with his head in the vault, and part of his body on the stairs."

His friends waited patiently till one o'clock, when, not making his appearance, they resolved to enter the Abbey with the verger, in search of him. On reaching the stairs of the vault and looking down, they saw the condition he was in. All attempts to restore him were in vain, till they got out of the Abbey, when the fresh air recovered him. He was afterwards taken to a tavern, when he related the circumstances as above described, adding that "he had neither seen nor heard anything, but that his reason might easily account for; but should have returned with the same sentiments he went with, had not this unseen hand convinced him of the injustice of his unbelief.

"One of the company now saw the penknife sticking through the fore-lappet of his coat, on which, presently conjecturing the truth, and finding how deeply affected his friend was by his mistake, as, indeed, were all the rest, not doubting but his return had been impeded by a supernatural hand, he plucked out the penknife before them all, and said, 'Here is the mystery discovered. In the attitude of stooping to stick this into the ground it happened, as you see, to pass through the coat; and on your attempting to rise, the terror you were in magnified this little obstruction into an imaginary impossibility of withdrawing yourself.'

"His friends now ridiculed his credulity, but the singularity of the accident did not shake his faith."

Near the slab marking the entrance to the royal vault, Edward VI., grandson of the founder of this chapel, was buried, in 1553. The site is now covered by a communion-table, on which is a Latin inscription to the following effect:—"In place of the ancient altar, destroyed in the Civil Wars, to the honour of God and in pious memory of Edward VI., who is buried beneath, this holy table, in a gentler age, was placed by Arthur Penrhyn Stanley, D.D., Dean of Westminster, 1870." The beautifully carved frieze of the lost altar was found, in 1869, in Edward VI.'s grave, and has been placed upon the marble slab which covers the new table.

The altar here alluded to was composed of a single piece of basaltic stone, known as touchstone. To this altar Henry in his will bequeathed "One grete piece of the holie crosse, which by the high provision of our Lord God was conveied, bought, and delivered to us from the isle of Cyo in Grece, set in gold and garnished with perles and precious stones; and also the preciouse relique of one of the legges of St. George, set in silver, parcel gilte, which came into the hands of our broder and cousyn Lewys of France, the time that he wan and recovered the citie of Millein, and given and sent to us by our cousyn the Cardinal of Amboise."

The first occasion on which the new communion-table was used was in 1870, when the Dean administered the holy sacrament to the revisers of the New Testament, preparatory to commencing their labours. The committee appointed by Convocation for the revision of the authorised version of the Scriptures had invited other scholars and divines to join them, many of whom accepted the invitation. "In front of this table, then, round the grave of the youthful Protestant king in whose reign the English Bible first received its acknowledged place in the coronation of the sovereign, as well as its free and general circulation throughout the people, knelt together the band of scholars and divines, consisting of representatives of almost every form of Christian belief in England. There were bishops, deans, doctors of the universities, clergymen of parishes in England and Scotland, members of the Free Church of Scotland, and of the chief denominations in England."

This was not the only religious ceremony that has taken place here, apart from the installation of the Knights of the Bath, since the time of the Reformation, for in Henry VII.'s Chapel, as we learn from John Evelyn, the nephew of the diarist, "John Evelyn of Wotton, Esq., was married by the Bishop of Rochester to the daughter and heyre (*sic*) of Mr. Eversfield, of Sussex; her fortune £8,000."

At the back of the table is the principal object of interest in this chapel, as well for antiquity as for fine workmanship—namely, the magnificent tomb of Henry VII. and Elizabeth his queen. The monument is enclosed within a curious brass screen, or "chantry," ornamented with statues; the royal pair, in their robes of state, lie on an elaborate tomb of black marble, at the corners of which are cherubs in a kneeling or sitting position. The statues, of bronze gilt, as well as the general accessories, were designed by the famous Italian sculptor, Torregiano, the contemporary and rival of Michael Angelo. Lord Bacon calls this monument "one of the stateliest and daintiest tombs in England."

Extending from the north to the south aisles, and forming the semi-circular termination of the fabric, are five deep recesses or "chapels." The first of these, on the north side, contains the monument of George Villiers, Duke of Buckingham—the "Steenie" and favourite of James I. and the companion of Charles I. The duke and his duchess, dressed in the costume of the time, are represented recumbent, side by side, on a table tomb, over a sarcophagus. The monument, which fills almost the entire recess, is carried at the back up to the top of the vaulting. At the four angles are figures in brass, above life-size, of Neptune, Mars, Minerva, and another, said to be emblematic of Benevolence; and the remainder of the work is composed of a variety of designs in arms, crests, mottoes, scrolls, &c. It will be remembered by every reader of history that the duke fell a victim to national resentment, in 1628, having perished at Portsmouth by the hand of the assassin Felton. In the next recess is the monument of John Sheffield, another Duke of Buckingham, where, on an altar of the finest-grained marble, lies, in a half-raised posture, his grace's effigy, in a Roman habit, with his duchess, Catherine, natural daughter of the Duke of York, afterwards King James II., sitting at his feet weeping. In the reign of Charles II., as the inscription sets forth, "he was General of the Dutch troop of horse, Governor of Kingston Castle upon Hull, and First Gentleman of the Bedchamber; in that of King James II., Lord Chamberlain; and in that of Queen Anne, Lord Privy Seal, and President of the Council. He was in his youth an excellent poet, and in his more advanced years a fine writer. His love of poetry is conspicuous, by the esteem and regard he had for the two great masters of it, who flourished in his own time, Dryden and Pope, to the first of whom he extended his friendship, even after death, by erecting a monument to his memory. To the latter he did honour, by writing a poem in his praise." Over his grace's effigy are inscribed, in Latin, sentences to the following import:—

"I liv'd doubtful, not dissolute,
I die unresolv'd, not unresign'd.
Ignorance and error are incident to human nature.
I trust in an almighty and all-good God.
O! thou Being of Beings, have compassion on me!"

And underneath it—

"For my King often, for my Country ever."

His grace died in the seventy-fourth year of his age, February 24th, 1720. He was the patron of Dryden, and his monument here bears the well-known line, "Dubius, sed non improbus, vixi." This inscription suggested to Matthew Prior his epigram on the duke's burial here, at which Bishop Atterbury, as Dean of Westminster, was the officiating minister :—

"'I have no hope,' the duke he says, and dies;
'In sure and certain hope,' the prelate cries;
Of these two learned peers, I prythee, say man,
Who is the lying knave, the priest or layman ?
The duke he stands an infidel confest,
'He's our "dear brother,"' quoth the lordly priest;
The duke, though knave, still 'brother dear,' he cries,
And who can say the reverend prelate lies ?"

The ceremony of the duke's state funeral was pompous enough ; but it is not a little strange to find Dr. Atterbury writing on the subject to Pope in terms which imply that he thought it a sham and unreality. "To-morrow I go to the deanery, and I believe I shall stay there till I have said 'dust to dust,' and shut up that last scene of pompous vanity." Pope, in writing back to his friend, simply says that "at the time of the duke's funeral he means to lie at the deanery" too, and to "moralise one evening with his clerical friend on the vanity of human glory."

The remains of James I. are interred in the tomb of Henry VII., whilst those of his queen, Anne of Denmark, repose in a tomb in front of the monument of Sheffield, Duke of Buckingham. The central recess is empty, but the one next to it, on the south side, contains the tomb of Anthony Philip, Duke de Montpensier, who died in 1807. He was second son of the Duke of Orleans, and brother of Louis Philippe, afterwards king of the French. The marble effigy of the duke, by Sir Richard Westmacott, lies extended on a low altar-tomb ; he is represented with ducal coronet and robes, and the expression is altogether one of dignity and repose.

The fifth recess, forming the east end of the south aisle, is almost filled with the enormous quadrangular tomb of Lewis, Duke of Richmond, and Frances, his wife. They are represented as lying on a marble table, under a canopy of brass, curiously wrought, and supported by the figures of Faith, Hope, Charity, and Prudence. On the top is a figure of Fame taking her flight, and resting only on her toe. This illustrious nobleman was son of Esmé Stuart, Duke of Lenox, and grandson of James, nephew of King James I., to whom he was first Gentleman of the Bedchamber and Privy Councillor, a Knight of the Garter, and Ambassador to France in behalf of Scotland. He died February the 16th, 1623. His lady was daughter of Thomas Lord Howard, of Bindon, son of the Duke of Norfolk, by Elizabeth, daughter of the Duke of Buckingham. She died October 8th, 1639. The east side of the chapel is defaced by a clumsy pyramid of black and white marble supporting a small urn containing the heart of Esmé Stuart, son of the Duke of Richmond and Lenox, by the Lady Mary, daughter of the Duke of Buckingham.

In the *Gentleman's Magazine* for the year 1784, it is remarked that "much has been said about the Spanish ambassadors in one of the chapels of Westminster Abbey, who are said to have been kept above ground for debt, but this story also, we have no doubt, may be classed among the vulgar errors." It is certain that one ambassador was kept unburied from 1691 to 1708, the date of the "New View," in which Hatton mentions that "in a feretory in the Duke of Richmond's little chapel, by his tomb, lieth visibly a coffin covered with red leather, and unburied, wherein is the corpse of Don Pedro de Ronquillo, Conde de Grenado, del con Sexo de Estado, &c., Ambassador Extra-ordinary from Spain to King James II., and to King William and Mary, ob. 1691" (ii. 514). "It is not improbable," observes Mr. Mackenzie Walcott, "that there was some difficulty raised about the burial service by the friends of the departed ambassador."

The body of Oliver Cromwell, together with those of four of his family, and six officers, was buried in the vault at the end of Henry VII.'s Chapel ; but their remains were removed with every possible indignity at the Restoration. There has always existed a lurking tradition that when Cromwell's body was dug up from its grave here, and thrown into a ditch at Tyburn, it was not allowed to remain there by his followers, but that they carried it away, and secretly gave it the rites of a decent sepulture. It has often been said that the place where it was laid is the centre of Red Lion Square, Bloomsbury. Others state that, for greater security, it was thrown into the Thames. The secret of his last resting-place will not be known till the last great day of all.

We now pass into the south aisle, which contains, besides five handsome monuments, the old royal vault, wherein are buried Charles II., William III., and Mary his consort, Queen Anne, and Prince George of Denmark. The first monument is that to Lady Margaret Douglas, daughter of Margaret, Queen of Scots, by the Earl of Angus. This lady, as the English inscription states, "had to her great-grandfather King Edward IV., to her grandfather King Henry VII., to her uncle King Henry VIII., to her cousin-german King Edward VI., to her brother King James V. of Scotland, to her son King Henry I. of Scotland, to her grandson King James VI., having to her great-grandmother and grandmother two queens, both named Elizabeth; to her mother, Margaret, Queen of Scots; to her after married to Matthew, Earl of Lenox, and became the mother of Lord Darnley, who, having married Mary Queen of Scots, was the father of King James I.

Next is the magnificent monument of Mary Queen of Scots, which was erected by her son,

CHANTRY OF HENRY V. (*See page* 441.)

aunt, Mary, the French queen; to her cousins-german, Mary and Elizabeth, Queens of England; to her niece and daughter-in-law, Mary, Queen of Scots." This lady, who is said to have been very beautiful, was privately married, in the year 1537, to Thomas Howard, son of the Duke of Norfolk, upon which account both of them were committed to the Tower by King Henry VIII., her uncle, for affiancing without his consent, and he died in prison; but Margaret, being released, was soon

James I., soon after his accession to the English throne. The unfortunate queen was beheaded in the hall of Fotheringay Castle, in Northamptonshire, in 1587, and her remains were first buried in Peterborough Cathedral; but James had her body privately removed to this church in 1612, under the superintendence of Dr. Neile, then Dean of Westminster, and buried in a vault beneath this monument. This tomb contains also the remains of the children of James I., Charles I., and James II.

We now come to another of the monumental works of Torregiano—namely, that of Margaret, Countess of Richmond, the mother of Henry VII. The aged and noble lady, whose effigy is in bronze gilt, is represented in what looks like the dress of a nun or recluse, with a mantle thrown or worn over all. She was married, in 1455, to Edmund Tudor, Earl of Richmond, but in the following year was left a widow, with one son (afterwards Henry VII.). She next became the wife of Sir Henry Stafford, who died in 1481; and in the following year she married Thomas Lord Stanley. In 1505 she founded Christ College, Cambridge, and she died in 1509. St. John's College, Cambridge, was founded in pursuance with her will.

ELIZABETH, WIFE OF HENRY VII. (*See page* 436.)

Overlooking this monument is a beautiful piece of sculpture, also the work of an Italian artist named Valory, to the memory of Catherine, Lady Walpole. The statue stands upon a square pedestal, upon which is an inscription which states that she was the first wife of Sir Robert Walpole, afterwards Earl of Orford, and that "'Horace, her youngest son,' consecrated this monument," as we have said above. The inscription further sets forth that "she had beauty and wit, without vice or vanity, and cultivated the arts without affectation: she was devout, though without bigotry to any sect; and was without prejudice to any party, though the wife of a minister, whose power she esteemed but when she could employ it to benefit the miserable, or to reward the meritorious; she loved a private life, though born to shine in public; and was an ornament to courts, untainted by them. She died August the 20th, 1737."

The only other monument in this aisle is to the memories of George Monk and Christopher, his son, both Dukes of Albemarle, and also of Elizabeth Duchess Dowager of Albemarle, relict of the latter.

The principal monument in the north aisle of Henry VII.'s Chapel is that of Queen Elizabeth. This is a sumptuous and lofty pile, of the Corinthian order, though of far less grandeur than that of her rival and victim, Mary Queen of Scots, in the south aisle. It consists of a low basement, panelled, with projecting pedestals, on which stand ten columns of black marble, with bases of white marble, and gilt capitals; the whole is crowned with a semi-circular canopy. In the recess is a thick slab, supported by four couchant lions, in which is a recumbent figure of the queen, executed in white marble. The inscription, which is in Latin, sets forth "her character, high descent, and the memorable acts of her glorious reign." This monument was erected by James I., at a cost of nearly £1,000.

Queen Mary, side by side with her Protestant sister Elizabeth, rests in the Abbey Church at Westminster, but no storied monument, no costly tomb, has been raised to her memory. She was interred with all the solemn funeral rites used by the Roman Church, and a mass of requiem, on the north side of the Chapel of Henry VII. During the reign of her successor not the slightest mark of respect was shown to her memory by the erection of a monument; and even at the present day no other memorial remains to point out the spot where she lies, except two small black tablets at the west base of the sumptuous tomb erected by order of King James I. over the ashes of Elizabeth, and her less fortunate sister. On them we read as follows:—

REGNO CONSORTES ET VRNA HIC OBDORMIMUS ELIZABETHA	ET MARIA SORORES IN SPE RESVRRECTIONIS

The little recess at the end of the north aisle, where the altar stood, contains a memorial erected by Charles II. to the memory of Edward V. and his brother Richard, Duke of York, who were suffocated in the Tower by order of their usurping uncle, the Duke of Gloucester, afterwards Richard III. The bones of the two princes, after lying there for nearly two hundred years, were discovered in 1674, buried beneath the stairs in the White Tower. It is remarkable that Edward was born within the precincts of Westminster Abbey, whither his mother had fled for sanctuary, in 1471, during the contest between the houses of York and Lancaster. At eleven years of age, upon the death of his father, in 1483, he was proclaimed king, and on the 23rd of June, in the same year, he was murdered in the manner above related. Richard, his brother, was born in May, 1474, and was married while a child to Ann Mowbray.

The spot, it would seem, is peculiarly appropriated for children, for here lie Sophia and Mary, daughters of James I. The former is commemorated by a child in a cradle, and the latter by a pretty little altar-tomb, on which reposes the effigy of an infant. This aisle contains also two other tombs, an exceedingly heavy one to George Saville, Marquis of Halifax, and another to Charles Montague, Earl of Halifax. In front of the latter monument Joseph Addison is buried, and to mark the spot a slab of white marble, inlaid with brass letters and devices, was placed here by the late Earl of Ellesmere, in 1849.

The Chapel of St. Paul, which is first on the north side of the Abbey after leaving that of Henry VII., contains a few monuments of interest or singularity, but space does not admit of our mentioning more than one or two. One of these is to the memory of Charles Holmes, Esq., Rear Admiral of the White, and commander of his Majesty's fleet stationed in Jamaica. It consists of a great statue of the admiral encased in Roman armour, and resting against an English eighteen-pounder mounted on a sea-carriage. Under a plain arch in the wall are the effigies of Sir John Fullerton and his lady, with an inscription stating that his "remnant" lies here. The epitaph tells us further that Sir John Fullerton was "a generous rewarder of all virtue, a severe reprover of all vice, a professed renouncer of all vanity. He was a firm pillar to the Commonwealth, a faithful patron to the Catholic Church, a fair pattern to the British Court. He lived to the welfare of his country, to the honour of his prince, to the glory of his God. He died *fuller* of faith than of fear, *fuller* of consolation than of pains, *fuller* of honour than of days." In this chapel is buried the learned Archbishop Ussher, whose funeral was celebrated with great pomp, partly—but only in part—at the cost of the Lord Protector Cromwell. This chapel contains also a monument by Chantrey to James Watt, the inventor of the steam-engine, "who" (to adopt the language of the inscription placed here by Lord Brougham), "directing the force of an original genius early exercised in philosophical research to the improvement of the steam-engine, enlarged the resources of his country, increased the power of man, and rose to an eminent place among the most illustrious followers of science, and the real benefactors of the world. Born at Greenock in 1736, he died at Heathfield, in Staffordshire, in 1819." This monument was erected in 1824 by public subscription, and is generally regarded as one of Chantrey's most successful works.

We now pass into the Chapel of Edward the Confessor—or, as it is sometimes called, the Chapel of the Kings—where we find the first regal monument, in point of date, having an effigy on it. It is that of the founder of the present fabric, Henry III., who died in 1272–3. The tomb is on the north side of the chapel, and was erected a few years after his death by his son and successor, Edward I. The workmanship and materials of this tomb are remarkable. The panels at the sides are of polished porphyry, surrounded by a framework of mosaic, with gilding and coloured stones. At each corner are twisted columns of variously-coloured marbles. On the top is a recumbent figure of the king, crowned, and habited in regal costume; it is of bronze gilt, and finely executed. This effigy is said by Walpole (who, by the way, does not mention his authority) to be considered the first example of metal-casting in England. The monument immediately adjoining is that of Queen Eleanor, the wife of Edward I., and merits attention for the extraordinary elegance and beauty displayed in its details.

Occupying the space between the two easternmost pillars of this chapel, is the chantry of the gallant prince, Henry V., the hero of Agincourt, on each side of which are images as large as life, guarding, as it were, the staircases ascending to it. Beneath is the tomb of the king, with his effigy, or, rather, what now remains of it. It is of oak, much mutilated, and headless. It is said originally to have been plated with silver gilt, and that the head was solid silver. Nothing is now left of the work but the rude wooden form upon which the "fine embroydered and gilded plates" were fastened. According to Camden, the head was gone when he wrote his "Britannia," in the reign of Elizabeth; it is said to have been stolen at the Reformation. Above the chantry are preserved the saddle, helmet, and shield of Henry V., supposed to have been used at Agincourt, and brought hither at his interment. This tomb was built by Henry VII., in compliment to his illustrious predecessor. "His Queen Catharine," writes Pennant, "had before erected his monument, and placed his image, cut in heart of oak and covered over with silver, on an altar-tomb. The head, as the guide tells us, was of solid silver, and was sacrilegiously stolen away in the reign of Henry VIII. The headless trunk of wood remains. On each side of this royal chapel is a winding staircase, enclosing a turret of open ironwork, which leads up into a chantry founded for the purpose of masses for the repose of the soul of that great prince. . . . . Here is kept a parcel of human figures, which in old times were dressed out and carried at funeral processions, but at present have very deservedly got the name of 'the ragged regiment.'" The collection of figures here alluded to, we may add, are now preserved over Islip's Chapel, where we shall presently find them.

"In the chapel of Henry V.," says Pennant, "among the other statues, is one of St. Denis of France, 'most composedly carrying his head in his hand.'" On the south side of the chantry is a representation of his coronation, and the figure of Henry himself is distinguished by a wen under his chin, which no doubt was taken from the life.

But little respect was paid by Henry VII. to his grandmother, Catharine, the consort of Henry V., who had sunk from being the queen-consort of the conqueror of France to the wife of a plain gentleman. Though she gave to England a long line of sovereigns, her grandson, on pulling down the old Lady Chapel, where she was buried, ungratefully neglected to honour her remains, but suffered them, as we are told, to be carelessly flung into a wooden chest, and they are now interred near the tomb of her husband.

The next monuments particularly worthy of remark are in memory of the glorious warrior, Edward III., his Queen Philippa, and two of their children. Edward died in 1377, and his effigy, of bronze, lies on a table of the same metal, and the whole has been richly gilt. In the statue, says Professor Westmacott, "there is evidence of great care in the portraiture of the deceased monarch. The face is long, and there is a remarkable fall in the lower lip; the hair is also, doubtless, represented as worn by the king; it is long, and slightly curling, and the beard is ample and flowing. Altogether, it is an interesting example of attention to nature in transmitting to posterity the likeness of one of England's greatest sovereigns. . . . . Among the careful details, it will be observed the shoes are what are now termed 'rights and lefts,' erroneously believed to be a very modern fashion of shoemaking." This tomb, like all others in the Abbey, has suffered greatly from neglect and ill treatment; much of its enrichment has disappeared, together with many of the numerous small brazen statues that decorated it. Six of these small statues remain, however, on the south side of the tomb—namely, those representing Edward, Joan de la Tour, Lionel, Edmund, Mary, and William. The tomb of Edward III. is thus mentioned by Addison, in the *Spectator:* "Sir Roger (de Coverley) in the next place laid his head upon Edward III.'s sword, and leaning upon the pommel of it, gave the history of the Black Prince, concluding that in Sir Richard Baker's opinion Edward III. was one of the greatest princes that ever sate on the English throne."

"His figure at full length, made of copper once gilt," writes Pennant, "lies beneath a rich Gothic shrine of the same material. His hair is dishevelled, his beard long and flowing. The figures of his children surround the altar-tomb. His worthy queen, Philippa, was interred at his feet, and her figure in alabaster represents her as a most masculine woman. The latter end of the king was marked by misfortunes, by the death of his son the Black Prince, by a raging pestilence, and, above all, by his unseasonable love in the years of his dotage." How finely does the poet Gray paint the scene of his death, and the gay entrance of his successor into power, in the bitter taunt which he puts into the mouth of a British bard:—

"Mighty victor! mighty lord,
Low on his funeral couch he lies;
No pitying heart nor eye afford
A tear to grace his obsequies.
Is the sable warrior fled?
Thy son is gone: he rests among the dead!
The swarm that in thy noontide beam were born?
Gone to salute the rising morn.
Fair laughs the morn, and soft the zephyr blows,
While, proudly riding o'er the azure realm,
In gallant trim the gilded vessel goes,
Youth on the prow, and pleasure at the helm,
Regardless of the sweeping whirlwind's sway
That, hush'd in grim repose, expects his evening prey."

The tomb is covered with a Gothic canopy, as is also that adjoining, which covers the remains of Queen Philippa, the consort of Edward III. She was the third daughter of William Earl of Hainault; and Harding tells us that when an embassy was sent by Edward to choose one of the earl's daughters, a certain English bishop advised him to select the lady of the largest frame, as promising a numerous progeny. The good bishop seems to have been a good judge, for she died in 1369, having borne to her sovereign lord a family of no less than fourteen children. The effigy on her tomb, though injured, is still in a condition to afford a good idea of her person, as well as of the art of the day; and the costume, especially the cushioned headdress, "gives great antiquarian value to this monument."

The tomb at the south-western corner of the chapel is that of Richard II. and Anne, his queen. Over it is a wooden canopy, remarkable for a curious painting of the Virgin Mary and our Saviour, remains of which are still visible upon it. His figure, and that of his first consort, Anne, daughter of the King of Bohemia, are of copper, and were once richly gilt. We are told that the king ordered these to be made in his lifetime by one of the goldsmiths in Wood Street, and that the expense of gilding them alone was 400 marks. Pennant draws attention to the fact that the king's countenance here is very unlike that shown in his portrait painted, of which we have spoken elsewhere.

Close by the screen separating this chapel from the sacrarium of the Abbey are the coronation chairs, together with the shield and sword of state carried before Edward III. in France. The more ancient of the coronation chairs was made by Edward I., in 1297. An oblong rough stone, brought from Scone, in Perthshire, by the king, with the Scottish regalia, and offered at St. Edward's shrine, is placed underneath it. In this chair all the reigning sovereigns of England have been crowned since Edward I. The old legend of the origin of the chair of King Edward cannot be better told than in the words of Addison, in the *Spectator*, though somewhat comically put together:—"We were then conveyed to the two coronation chairs, where my old friend (Sir Roger de Coverley), after having heard that the stone underneath the most ancient of them, which was brought from Scotland, was called Jacob's Pillow, sate himself down in the chair, and, looking like the figure of an old Gothic king, asked our interpreter what authority they had to say that Jacob had ever been in Scotland? The fellow, instead of returning him an answer, told him that he hoped his honour would pay the forfeit. I could observe Sir Roger a little ruffled at being thus trepanned; but our guide not insisting upon his demand, the knight soon recovered his good humour, and whispered in my ear that if Will Wimble were with us, and saw these two chairs, it would go hard but he would get a tobacco-stopper out of one or t'other of them."

Both chairs are of architectural design; the ancient one is supported upon four lions, but otherwise they are somewhat similar in appearance. The more modern of the two coronation chairs was made for the use of Mary II., when crowned along with her consort, William III. It may be added here that at the coronations of our kings and queens one or both, as circumstances may require, are richly covered with gold-beaten tissue, cushioned, and are placed in front of the altar.

The following we take from a manuscript account

of St. Edward's Chapel inserted in the note-book of one of the vergers of the Abbey :—

"In May, 1774, the Society of Antiquaries having found it mentioned in Rymer's 'Fœdera,' that King Edward I., surnamed 'Long Shanks,' was interred in a stone coffin, inclosed in a stone tomb, in the above chapel, and that he was done over with wax, and a sum of money allowed to preserve the tomb, determined to gratify their curiosity by endeavouring to discover the truth of it. Accordingly, they applied to the Dean of Westminster for leave to have the tomb opened. The dean, being desirous to give all encouragement to curious researches, readily complied with their request. At the time appointed for opening the tomb, the dean, with about fifteen of the society, attended, when, to their great astonishment, they found the royal corpse to appear as represented by the historian (*sic*). He had on a gold and silver tissue robe, over which was a very handsome one of crimson velvet, both of them quite fresh, and the jewels that were about him appeared exceedingly bright. He had in one hand a sceptre and dove, and in the other a sceptre and cross, which measured near five feet in length. The crown on his head being raised, the skull appeared bare; but the face and hands seemed perfectly entire. He measured in length 6 feet 2 inches. The king died on the 7th of July, 1307."

There is extant a minute description of the tomb and its contents, by Sir Joseph Ayloffe, an antiquary, who was present. "On lifting up the lid of the tomb the royal body was found wrapped in a strong and thick linen cloth, waxed on the inside: the head and face were covered with a sudarium or face-cloth of crimson sarsinet wrapped to three folds, conformable to the napkin used by our Saviour in his way to crucifixion . . . . On flinging open the external mantle, the corpse was discovered in all the ensigns of majesty, richly habited. The body was wrapped in a fine linen cere-cloth, closely fitted to every part of the body, even to the very fingers and face. The writs ordering the renewal of the waxen covering of the body of King Edward I. being extant, gave rise to this search. (They will be found in the third volume of the 'Archæologia'). Over the cere-cloth was a tunic of red silk damask; above that a stole of thick white tissue crossed the breast, and on this, at six inches distant from each other, quatrefoils of filigree-work of gilt metal set with stones, imitating rubies, sapphires, amethysts, &c.; and the intervals between the quatrefoils on the stole powdered with minute white beads, tacked down into a most elegant embroidery, in form not unlike what is called the 'true lovers' knot.' Above these habits was the royal mantle of rich crimson satin, fastened on the left shoulder with a magnificent fibula, of gilt metal richly chased, and ornamented with four pieces of red and four of blue transparent paste, and twenty-four more pearls. The corpse from the waist downwards was covered with a rich cloth of figured gold, which fell down to the feet and was tucked beneath them. On the back of each hand was a quatrefoil, like those on the stole. In the king's right hand was a sceptre with a cross of copper gilt, and of elegant workmanship, reaching to the right shoulder. In the left hand was the rod and dove, which passed over the shoulder and reached to the ear. The dove stood on a ball placed on three ranges of oak-leaves of enamelled green; the dove was of white enamel. On the head was a crown chased with trefoils made of gilt metal. The head itself was lodged in the cavity of the stone coffin, always observable in those receptacles of the dead. . . . . The corpse was dressed in conformity with ancient usage even as early as the time of the Saxon Sebert." It may be added that the dress is represented with tolerable accuracy on a seal of Edward himself, to be seen in Sandford's "Genealogy."

This tomb, which is very plain, and has, apparently, sustained very little injury, is in the north-western corner of the chapel. It bears the following apposite inscription :—

"Edvardus primus, Scotorum malleus, hic est."

Along the frieze of the screen of this chapel are fourteen sculptures, respecting the legend of the Confessor. The first is the trial of Queen Emma; the next the birth of Edward; another is his coronation; the fourth tells us how our saint was frightened into the abolition of the Dane-gelt, by his seeing the devil dance upon the money-casks; the fifth is the story of his winking at the thief who was robbing his treasure; the sixth is meant to relate the appearance of our Saviour to him; the seventh shows how the invasion of England was frustrated by the drowning of the Danish king; in the eighth is seen the quarrel between the boys Tosti and Harold, predicting their respective fates; in the ninth sculpture is the Confessor's vision of the seven sleepers; the tenth shows how he met St. John the Evangelist in the guise of a pilgrim; the eleventh, how the blind were cured by their eyes being washed in his dirty water; the twelfth, how St. John delivered to the pilgrims a ring; in the thirteenth they deliver the ring to the king, which he had unknowingly given to St. John as an alms, when he met him in the form of a pilgrim; this was attended with a message from the saint, foretelling the death of the king; and the fourteenth shows the consequential haste made by him to complete his pious foundation.

The following, according to Dugdale, is the story of the benefactions of Edward the Confessor to the Abbey:—The king, while in exile during the usurpation of the Danes, made a vow that if it should please God to restore him to the throne of his father, he would go in pilgrimage to Rome. Soon after his coronation, he made his intention known to the principal nobility, who, partly fearing disturbances in the absence of the king, and partly dreading a contest for the succession should he die upon the journey, endeavoured to dissuade him from it. Aelred, Archbishop of York, and Harman, Bishop of Winchester, with two abbots of monasteries, are stated to have been sent on an embassy to Rome, to procure the Pope's absolution from the vow; they returned with a rescript from Pope Leo IX., enjoining the king, by way of commutation, to expend the sums of money intended for his journey in the foundation or repair of some religious house dedicated to St. Peter. A revelation made to one Wolfine, or Wulsina, a monk of Worcester, is said to have determined the king to bestow his benefactions at Westminster.

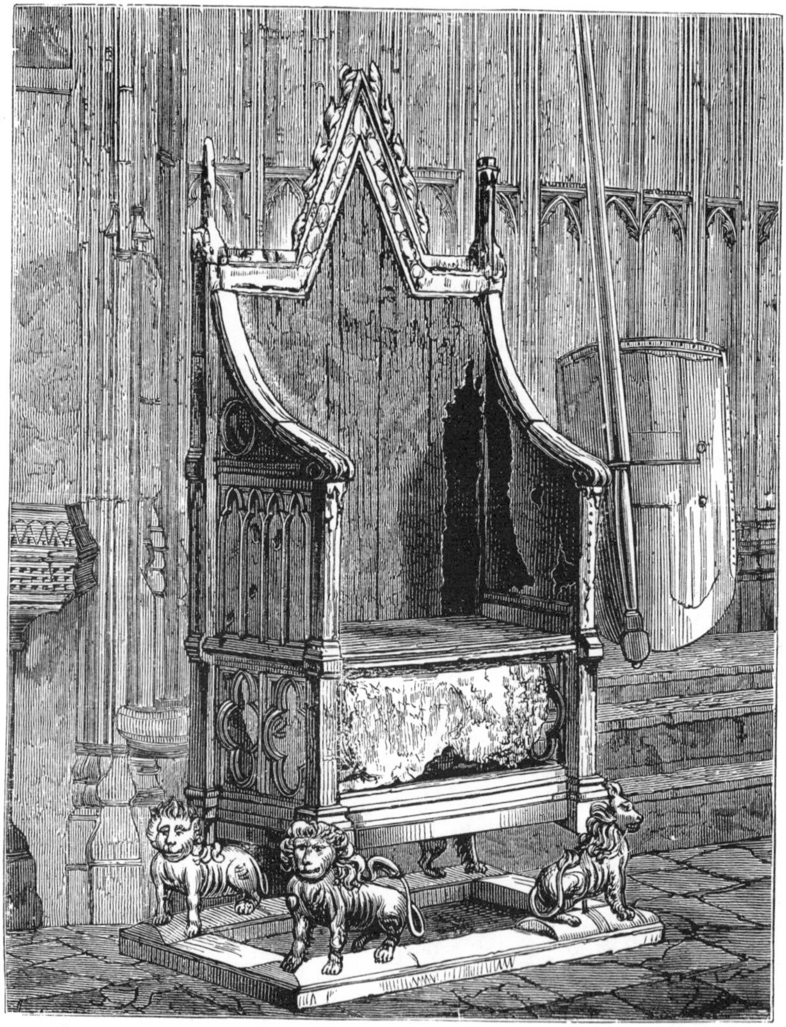

THE CORONATION CHAIR. (*See page* 442)

In the centre of this chapel stands the shrine of Edward the Confessor. This venerable curiosity, though now much mutilated, still enables us to form an opinion of its former richness and beauty. It was erected by Henry III. on the canonising of Edward, King of England, by Pope Alexander III., who caused his name to be placed in the catalogue of saints, and issued his bull to the Abbot Laurence and Convent of Westminster, enjoining "that his body be honoured here on earth, as his soul is glorified in heaven." The shrine was the work of the Italian artist Cavallini. Before this shrine was formerly kept a lamp continually burning, on one side of which stood a figure of the Virgin, wrought in silver, which, with two jewels of immense value, were presented as an offering by Queen Eleanor. On the other side stood another image of the Virgin, wrought in ivory, presented by Thomas à Becket, Archbishop of Canterbury. At this shrine Edward I. offered the Scottish regalia, and the coronation chair, which is still preserved. Alphonso, about the year 1280, offered here the golden coronet of Llewellyn, Prince of Wales, and other jewels. It is painful to witness the damage which has been done to this and several of the surrounding monuments, which were originally enriched with so much cost and art.

The stonework of Edward the Confessor's shrine is hollow within, and now encloses a large chest, which, soon after the coronation of James II., was found to contain the remains of St. Edward; for being broken (it is said) by accident, upon turning up the bones, a crucifix, richly ornamented and enamelled, was discovered, together with a gold chain twenty inches long, both of which were presented to his Majesty, who ordered the bones to be replaced in the old coffin and enclosed in a new one, made very strong. The coffin containing the king's remains is suspended by iron rods, firmly

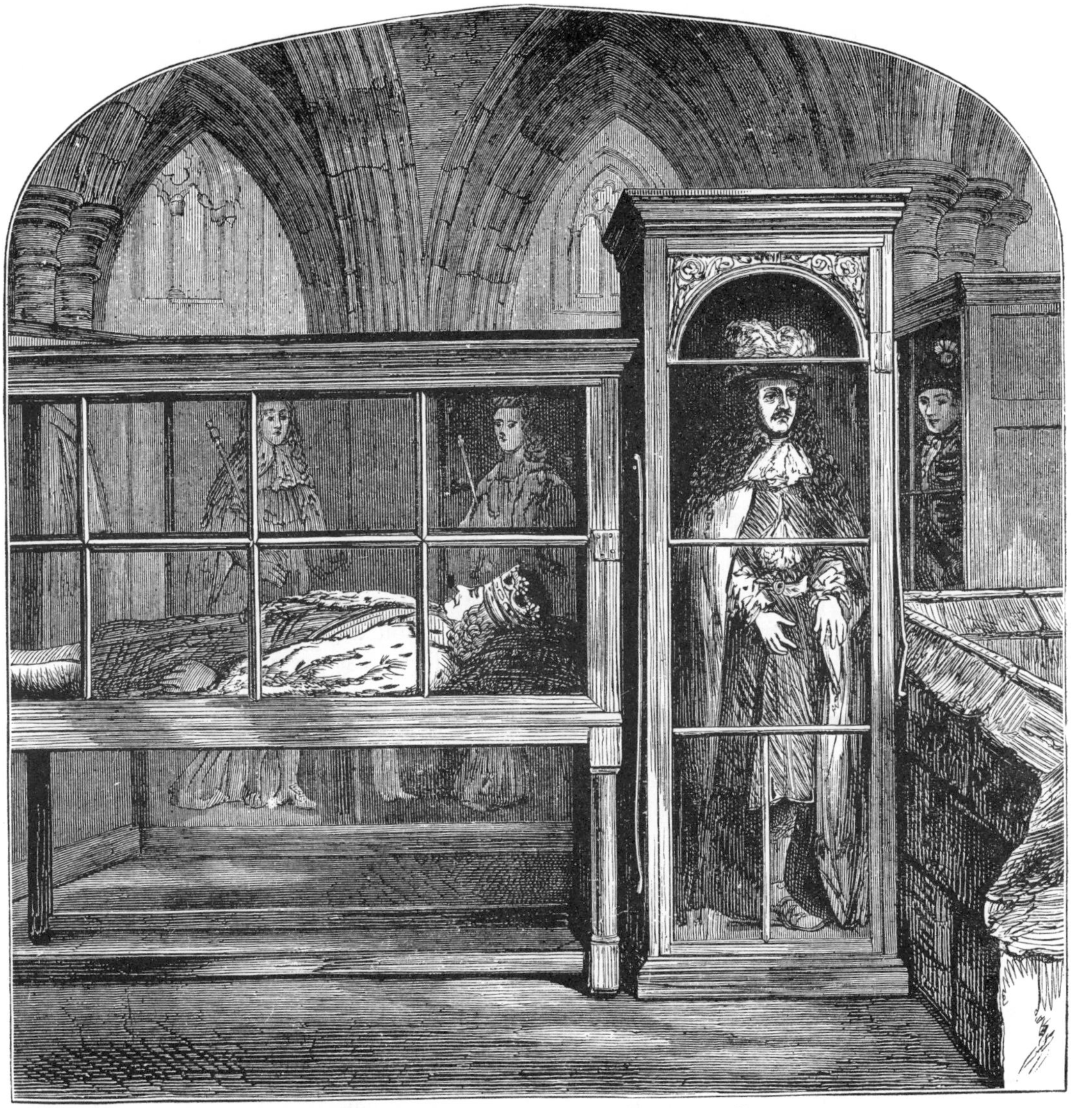

WAX FIGURES IN THE ABBEY. (*See page* 446.)

inserted in the stonework, at about half the depth of the shrine; and may be seen from the parapet of Henry VII.'s Chapel. On the south side of the shrine lies interred Editha, daughter of Goodwyn, Earl of Kent, and consort of St. Edward.

It is almost superfluous to state that the shrine of St. Edward, all through the Middle Ages, was a constant object of pilgrimages from all parts of England, though his tomb was never so popular as that of St. Thomas of Canterbury; and even since the Reformation it is frequently visited by Roman Catholics, who make it a matter of conscience to offer up a prayer at the foot of the coffin which still holds the saint's bones.

The Chapel of St. John the Baptist, which we next enter, contains little to call for particular mention here beyond monuments to the memory of Henry Carey; of Lord Hunsdon, first cousin and also chamberlain to Queen Elizabeth; and of Thomas Cecil, Earl of Exeter. The tomb of the Earl of Exeter is in the middle of the chapel; on it is his effigy, with a lady on his right side and a vacant space on his left for another; the lady is his first wife, Dorothy Nevil, daughter and co-heiress of Lord Latimer. The vacant space was intended for an effigy of his second wife, Frances Bridget, of the noble family of Chandos; but as the right side was taken up, she gave express orders by her will that her effigy should not be placed on his left. They are all three, nevertheless, buried together in one vault, as the inscription expresses.

The small chapel to which we now come, commonly known as Islip's Chapel, formerly contained a monument of Abbot Islip; but almost its only occupants now are the effigies of Sir Christopher Hatton and his lady, who are seen in reclining attitudes on cushions upon a sumptuous tomb of the seventeenth century. In the Islip Chapel is buried also William Pulteney, Earl of Bath. Outside the chapel is his monument, close to that of General Wolfe, the hero of Quebec. Islip's Chapel, we may here remark, is constantly used at the present day; for the bishops who are to be consecrated in the Abbey usually retire to it to put on their "rochets" and the other episcopal vestments.

In a chamber or gallery over Islip's Chapel, not ordinarily accessible to the public, is an exhibition of, perhaps, equal interest to the monuments interspersed throughout the sacred edifice, or rivalling in interest the famous exhibition of a somewhat similar character at Marylebone, that of Madame Tussaud. The collection has received the name of the "Ragged Regiment," and also "the Play of the Dead Volks." For many centuries preceding the present a curious custom prevailed at State funerals—namely, having exposed to view in the funeral car, or carried in the procession, a waxen effigy of the individual whose remains were about to be consigned to the tomb. The head of the defunct monarch, statesman, or warrior was modelled in wax, an effigy was built up, and clad in the actual garments worn by the deceased in his lifetime, but embellished with false gems. When the coffin had been deposited in the vault, the waxen effigy was either placed over the tomb as a sort of temporary substitute for a stone monument, or in some other convenient spot. Several of these effigies are preserved in glass cases like zoological specimens in the narrow chamber above referred to. Taking them in chronological order, the first is a striking effigy of Queen Elizabeth; the pale hawk-like features are deeply cut by sharp lines, the head is surmounted by a diadem, and the whole costume is profusely adorned with gems. Her Majesty is attired in that extravagantly long-waisted dress with which her portraits have made us familiar, and springing from the bodice is a pair of immense panniers which support a ponderous velvet robe, covered with gold embroidery, and trimmed with miniver; around the neck is a curious spreading ruff, stiffened with wire, and from this descends the long, straight, stiff bodice, made stiffer and heavier by a mass of rich silver embroidery.

At a respectful distance from the "Virgin Queen," stands a life-like figure of the "Merry Monarch," Charles II. A more distinct gleam of humour, however, is perceptible in this old waxen version of the founder of the Royal Society than in the portrait, by Lely, hanging in the reception-room of that learned body; but the main characteristics of the portrait and the image—the dark brow, the soft, melancholy eye, the disproportionately-long, straight nose, and the heavy under lip—are identical. The king is clad in a curious raiment of red and blue velvet, sorely faded from its ancient splendour, and the royal head is topped by a limp-looking hat and a tawdry feather.

Space does not admit of our giving a detailed account of this curious and interesting collection of wax figures; suffice it to say that it is not strictly confined to royal personages, for—apart from King William III. and his buxom queen Mary, and another effigy, superb in robes and strings of false jewellery, the counterfeit presentment of Queen Anne—we have here a recumbent figure of John Sheffield, Duke of Buckingham, and near him are his duchess and child. The lady is attired in a curiously long-waisted bodice much bejewelled, and wears a robe of remarkable brocade, wherein may be distinguished bridges, rivers, and verdant lawns, all coloured, as the heralds say, "proper." Then there are a Duchess of Richmond, and the elder Pitt, Lord Chatham, erect in his scarlet robes. Lastly, one more figure attracts attention. It is but a frail figure at best, but represents one "whose little body held a mighty mind." A huge cocked hat overshadows a pale, worn face of sweet expression; the lower limbs are slender and clad in white kerseymere and silk; a strange-looking blue coat, adorned with an immense quantity of gold lace and curious flat buttons, covers the superior part of the body, and is, on the left breast, marked by a galaxy of stars; the right sleeve of the quaint coat is armless;—the reader will hardly need be told that this is the effigy of a mighty man of valour—Lord Nelson.

Facing the entrance to the chapels we have just quitted, and occupying the north side of the sacrarium, are three tombs which form admirable illustrations of the elegant and yet rich style of monumental art of their time; they are those of Edmund Crouchback, Earl of Lancaster, son of Edward II.; of Aveline, his wife (1275); and that of Aymer de Valence, Earl of Pembroke (1323). There is so much similarity in the general design, that, as Professor Westmacott remarks, "it might fairly be imagined that the same artists were employed on all three works." In each case the monument consists of an altar-tomb, upon which reposes a recumbent figure of the deceased, and they are surmounted by lofty enriched canopies, tapering upwards with every variety of accessorial decoration. The following is Flaxman's criticism on two of these monuments:—"The monuments of Aymer de Valence and Edmund Crouchback are specimens of the magnificence of our sculpture in the reigns of our two first Edwards. The loftiness of the work, the number of arches and pinnacles, the lightness of the spires, the richness and profusion of foliage and crockets, the solemn repose of the principal statue, the delicacy of thought in the group of angels bearing the soul, and the tender sentiment of concern variously expressed in the relations ranged in order round the basement, forcibly arrest the attention, and carry the thoughts not only to other ages, but to other states of existence."

On the floor, near the above monuments, is a slab curiously inlaid with brass, representing John de Eastney, Abbot of Westminster, who died in 1498. In 1706 the grave was opened, and the body of the abbot discovered in a coffin quilted with yellow satin, having on him a gown of crimson silk, with a black girdle round the waist. On his legs were white silk stockings, and over his face a clean napkin, doubled up and laid corner-ways. The face, we are told, was in some degree discoloured, but the legs and arms were firm.

In the united Chapels of St. John the Evangelist, St. Michael, and St. Andrew are two or three particularly striking monuments. The first is to Lord and Lady Norris, who died in 1600. The effigies of both, in alabaster, lie recumbent on a raised tomb, above which is a canopy. On each side of the composition, at the base, are three kneeling figures, life-size, dressed in the armour of the period, representing the six sons of the deceased. Professor Westmacott has remarked with regard to this monument, that although the sculpture is not fine, the motive of the design is good and appropriate. "The effigies of the heads of the family reposing in death, with their sons kneeling and praying around them, are a touching and beautiful subject, well fitted for a mortuary chapel."

The next monument in this chapel to which we shall refer is that of Sir Francis Vere, one of the eminent worthies and warriors of the Elizabethan era. The effigy of the gallant soldier, habited in a loose gown, is recumbent on a low bed or table-tomb. At each corner is a knight, in full armour, kneeling, and supporting on his shoulders a large slab, which forms a canopy over the principal figure. On this are placed various pieces of armour, supposed to have belonged to the great general lying beneath.

On the east side of this chapel is a large monument of later date, by Roubiliac. It is in memory of Joseph Gascoigne Nightingale, Esq., of Minehead, Somerset, who died in 1752, and the Lady Elizabeth, his wife, eldest daughter and co-heiress of Washington, second Earl Ferrers, who died soon after marriage. In the upper part of the pyramidal composition, the lady is represented expiring in the arms of her husband; whilst in the lower part, a skeleton, partially draped, issues from the gates of a dark tomb, and appears in the act of hurling a dart at the female above. The husband, leaning forward, endeavours to ward off the fatal stroke, with the energy of despair, and extends his hand as a shield or guard between the sinking lady and the weapon of death.

Concerning these two monuments, Mr. Peter Cunningham tells a story in his "Hand-book of London." "When Roubiliac was erecting this monument, he was found one day by Gayfere, the Abbey mason, standing with his arms folded, and his looks fixed on one of the knightly figures which support the canopy over the statue of Sir Francis Vere. As Gayfere approached, the enthusiastic

Frenchman laid his hand upon his arm, pointed to the figure, and said, in a whisper, 'Hush! hush! sir, he vill speak presently.'"

On the opposite side of the aisle, on leaving this chapel, we see the monument to the memory of Field-Marshal Lord Ligonier. The inscription is only a recital of his titles and places, his age (92), and the date of his death in April, 1770. On the monument is a likeness of his lordship, in profile, and the medallions of Queen Anne, George I., II., and III., under whom his lordship served. On a scroll held by a figure symbolic of History, is the following list of battles in which he bore a part:—Schellenberg, Blenheim, Ramillies, Oudenarde, Taniere, Malplaquet, Dettingen, Fontenoy, Rocoux, and Laffeldt. He was the first Commander-in-Chief at the Horse Guards. Lord Ligonier, however, was not only a gallant officer, but a wit of no small ability. His regiment (the Fourth Horse) being reviewed by George II. before it was sent on foreign service, the king remarked to him, "Colonel, your men have the air of soldiers, but their horses look poor. How is that?" "Sir," replied Ligonier, "the men are Irish, and gentlemen too; but the horses are English."

Apart from the chapels above spoken of, there is still one more to which we must refer, namely, that dedicated to St. Faith—or, as it is more commonly designated, the Chapel of St. Blaize—at the end of the south transept. The doorway to this ancient chapel is close by the grave of Charles Dickens, and under the great rose window. It is a small oblong chamber, and served for many years as a vestry for the choristers. It is lighted on the south side by two windows in the vestibule of the Chapter House, and by the partially glazed door opening into the transept. For the dedication of the altar, writes Sir G. Gilbert Scott, we are indebted to Abbot Ware's "Customs of the Abbey," a work written in the thirteenth century, which narrowly escaped destruction at the burning of the Cottonian Library. The figure painted over the altar had long been said to represent no other than St. Faith; but till the discovery of the entry in Ware's volume, we had no record of such an altar. In that work, however, the altar of St. Faith is stated to be committed to the care of the *revestiarius*.

Scarcely any of the works executed since Roubiliac's time, however remarkable for other qualities, preserve any of the characteristics appropriate to church monuments. Again, quoting the words of Professor Westmacott, we might add that "it is rare that allusion is made to death, the hope of a future state, or the prayerful last moments of a Christian. The statues have a mere portrait character. The action of the figures has reference only to their worldly business and occupation, and the inscriptions record personal virtues, abilities, and prowess. The compositions are crowded with allegorical figures more or less good, as they are founded on or copied from the antique, and the recondite classical allusions can only be understood by the few. Such scenic designs as those representing Mr. Thynne attacked and murdered in his carriage; of the shipwrecked Admiral Tyrrell ascending out of the sea to heaven, amidst masses of clouds, while on all sides are the most preposterous accessories, including several life-size allegorical figures, prove the low character of monumental design, though they may, and undoubtedly do, show considerable artistic power or ingenuity. Truthfulness and individuality were first sacrificed to the absurd fancy of introducing classical details in the monuments. From ornamental the artist proceeded to personal *pseudo*-classical decoration, and we find the deceased English nobleman, statesman, or soldier dressed in a Roman cuirass, or toga, or paludamentum, mixed up with modern costume. Sheffield, Duke of Buckingham, in the costume of a Roman emperor, attended by his duchess in a court-dress of the time of George I.; the English admiral, Sir Cloudesley Shovel, in a Roman cuirass, sandals, and a full-bottomed wig, in his monument in the south aisle; and many others, equally inconsistent in time and place, show the extent to which this absurd fancy was carried."

With reference to the Gothic or Mediæval monuments in Westminster Abbey, the above writer remarks that, "judged as productions of fine art, it need scarcely be said that they fall far short of the excellence that the remains of sculpture of a much older date show the art was capable of attaining. They have, however, their own peculiar merit, arising out of the sentiment which pervades them, as expressive of certain feelings, and for its appropriateness both to place and object. There is a serious and religious character in the *motive* of these works which subdues and tranquillises the feelings of those who contemplate them, carrying the reflections of the thoughtful to objects beyond the present. In this respect, however deficient they may be in technical qualities, they fulfil a great purpose, and they stamp the monumental design of the fourteenth and fifteenth centuries with a principle which must be admitted to be one of high value, and well worthy of attention."

Pennant's remarks on the general character of the sculpture exhibited in the tombs throughout the Abbey are so just and true, that they may well be quoted by us:—"Here may be read an instructive lecture on the progress of these efforts of human skill, from the simple altar-tomb to the most ostentatious products of human vanity. The humble recumbent figure, with uplifted hands, as if deprecating the justice of Heaven for the offences of this mortal state; or the proper kneeling attitude, supplicating that mercy of which the purest must stand in need, may be seen here in various degrees of elegance. The careless lolling attitude of heroes in long gowns and flowing periwigs next succeeds; and, after them, busts or statues vaunting their merits, and attended with such a train of pagan deities as would almost lead us to suppose ourselves in a heathen Pantheon, rather than in a Christian church.

"In the ancient tombs there is a dull uniformity; the sides of the tombs are often embellished with the figures of the offspring of the deceased, often with figures of mourners and weepers, frequently in monastic habits. . . . In the reigns of Queen Elizabeth and James I. begins to appear a ray of taste in the sculptors." He means, of course, that their works begin to show an individuality which we seek in vain in the earlier productions of the chisel. He instances the sons of Henry Lord Norris, and the monument of Sir Francis Vere, in the chapel of St. Andrew; and that of Francis Holles, son of the Earl of Clare, dressed as a Grecian warrior. "The figure," he adds, "of Dr. Busby, Master of Westminster School, who died in 1695, is elegant and spirited. He lies resting on one arm, a pen in one hand and a book in the other, his countenance looking up. His loose dress is very favourable to the sculptor, who has given to it the most graceful flow: the close cap alone is inimical to his art."

Mr. W. Godwin complains, in his "Essay on Sepulchres," published in 1809, of the neglected state of the monuments. He writes: "The tomb of our renowned conqueror, Edward I., in the Abbey, is merely a rude vast pile of stones, with no inscription or record upon it, and which is known only by tradition to cover his ashes. The shrine of Edward the Confessor, erected at a vast expense by Henry III., is robbed and defaced by every comer. How Henry V. came by the loss of his head I do not pretend to explain. Every sort of indecorum has been practised on this venerable pile. The noses of a considerable part of the figures are broken off; and the last time that I was there, I found a little pebble placed by some wanton boy on the tip of the nose of the recumbent figure of Catharine, wife of George Villiers, first Duke of Buckingham, which no one had thought it worth his while to remove." Such complaints, fortunately, are no longer true; for although the chapels and royal tombs are freely open to the inspection of the public one day in each week, the utmost care is now taken by the visitors to preserve and protect them.

As Chamberlain remarks, in his "History of London," "The ravages made within this sacred building by Henry VIII., and the havoc without it, as well as within, during the unhappy civil commotions that defaced the ancient beauty of all the religious houses in the kingdom, can never be recovered."

The following quaint verses on the royal tombs in Westminster Abbey are taken from a work about two centuries and a half old; but the sentiments, though the author of the lines is unknown, belong to all ages:—

"Mortality, behold and fear;
What a change of flesh is here!
Think how many royal bones
Rest within this heap of stones!
Here, remov'd from beds of ease,
Dainty fare and what might please,
Fretted roofs and costly showes,
To a roof that flats the nose,
Which proclaims 'All flesh is grass!'
How the world's fair glories pass!
That there is no trust in health,
Youth or greatness, age or wealth;
For if such could have reprieved,
Those had been immortal lived.
Know from this the world's a snare;
How that greatness is but care;
How all pleasures are but pain,
And how short they do remain:.
For here they lie, had realms and lands,
That now want strength to stir their hands,
Where from their pulpits, ceiled with dust,
They preach, 'In greatness is no trust!'
Here's an acre sown indeed
With the richest royal seed
That the earth did e'er suck in
Since the first man dyed for sin.
Here the bones of birth have cried,
Though gods they were, as men they dyed.
Here are sands, ignoble things!
Dropt from the ruined sides of kings,
With whom the poor man's earth being shown,
The difference is not easy known.
Here's a world of pomp and state
Forgotten, dead, disconsolate!
Think, then, this scithe that mows down kings
Exempts no meaner mortal things.
Then bid the wanton lady tread
Amid the mazes of the dead;
And then, these truly understood,
More shall cool and quench the blood
Than her many sports a day
And her nightly wanton play.
Bid her paint till day of doom,
To this favour she must come.

Bid the merchant gather wealth,
The usurer exact by stealth,
The proud man beat it from his thought;
Yet to this shape must all be brought."

We may conclude this chapter with the remark that whilst London was confined within Temple Bar as its western limits, the glorious old Abbey of Westminster stood surrounded with green fields, and held a position towards the metropolis almost analogous to that of St. Denis, near Paris, in which the Bourbon kings and their immediate relatives for centuries lay buried, till the wild fury of the first French Revolution scattered their ashes to the winds of heaven. Let us hope that no such disaster may happen to the royal dust that lies within these consecrated walls.

THE CHAPEL OF THE PYX. (*See page* 454)

CHAPTER LIV.

WESTMINSTER ABBEY.—THE CHAPTER HOUSE, CLOISTERS, DEANERY, &c.

"There was the Chapter-house, wrought as a church,
Carved and covered and quaintly entayled;
With seemly selure y'set aloft,
As a parliament-house ypainted about."—*Piers Ploughman.*

A Benedictine Monastery—The Chapter House—Its former uses—Its Restoration—The Chapel of "The Pyx"—Robbing of the Treasury—Littlington Tower—St. Catharine's Chapel—The Little Cloister—The King's Jewel House—The Great Cloister—Burial-place of the Abbots—Ashburnham House—The Deanery—Jerusalem Chamber—Henry IV.'s Death—Restoration of the Jerusalem Chamber—The Building used as a Chapter House and Convocation House—Biographies of the Principal Deans—Precautions against Fire.

It has been observed by Mr. Spalding, in his work on "Italy," that "a mediæval monastery with its courts and cloister, its several buildings announcing their destination by their position—this of the superior, that of the dependent; this public and accessible, that private, with its garden, and its environing wall—was the successor of the Roman *villa urbana.*" But such a statement as this would argue gross ignorance, and a mind incapable of appreciating the real theory of the monastic life.

It is scarcely necessary to do more than state here that the "religious life," in some shape or other, dates from the first century of the Christian faith. It was only by degrees, however, that it developed itself in the Church, the hermits and recluses of the earlier ages abounding in Egypt and the countries nearest to the Holy Land. St. Benedict, who founded the noble monastery of Monte Casino in Italy in A.D. 530–32, is generally regarded as the founder—though in reality he was only the re-founder and reformer—of the monastic system in the Western or Latin Church. His rule was brought into England by St. Augustine; and if not before, at all events soon after, the Norman Conquest, the chief and wealthiest abbeys in our country were those of the Benedictines—Glastonbury, St. Albans, Abingdon, Canterbury, Westminster, &c. In fact, in a certain sense, nearly all the well-known monasteries followed the rule of St. Benedict, whether they were Cistercians, Carthusians, Cluniacs, or whatever the name of their discipline; it is said that all our cathedral priories, except Carlisle, were of the Benedictine order, and that the revenues of the Benedictine abbeys exceeded those of all the rest of the religious bodies put together.

THE CHAPTER HOUSE PREVIOUS TO ITS RESTORATION. (*See page* 454.)

"Water, a mill, a garden, an oven, &c.," writes Mr. Wood, in his "Ecclesiastical Antiquities," "were provided within the precincts of a Benedictine monastery to prevent necessity arising for the monks going abroad. When any of the monks were about to start on a journey, they obtained the prayers of the community; on their return, the wayfarers sought pardon for anything of which they had been guilty on their way, by neglecting the custody of their eyes, or ears, or by indulging in idle conversation."

Although most of the buildings appertaining to the "inner life" of the monastery at Westminster have disappeared, there is still much left that is interesting; for, besides the church itself, which is substantially the same now as it was before the Reformation, many of the other ancient parts of the Abbey still remain. For instance, the Chapter House and the Cloisters are both entire; and the same may be said of the Jerusalem Chamber.

Leaving the abbey church by a doorway at the east end of the south aisle, we are led by a descent of several steps to the north-eastern corner of the cloisters. Passing along the east walk, a doorway on the left will be found opening into the outer vestibule of the Chapter House.

"The chapter house in England," writes the Rev. Mackenzie Walcott, "was almost essentially a national peculiarity, unlike the alleys or oblong rooms which take their place on the Continent, forming the conventual or capitular Parliament House, and a distinctive and splendid building. That of Westminster is of considerable architectural history; firstly, because it replaces the round Chapter House erected by Edward the Confessor, and is of a polygonal form, like that of Worcester, these two being the only exceptions to the Benedictine rule of building rectangular chapter houses; and secondly, because it is built (almost exceptionally) over a crypt, the only other instance being at Wells, that of St. Paul's having perished in the Great Fire; and this crypt embodies the original structure of the Confessor."

Sir G. Gilbert Scott, in writing on the Chapter House at Westminster, says it "singles itself out from other beautiful works as a structure perfect in itself, of a purely English type as to its plan and outline, and as carrying out the principle of window tracery in a fuller and grander degree than any part of the church." It is evident from the actual building accounts which have been preserved that the Chapter House was erected in A.D. 1250–53, so that it formed part and parcel of the original plan of the church, though a separate structure; and this date agrees with that of "La Sainte Chapelle" at Paris, the windows of which are of a similar style; "thus showing that our English architecture was running a pretty parallel course with that of France."

The shape of the previous Chapter House, on the same spot, cannot be precisely determined. The present building stands over a crypt which may or may not have belonged to its predecessor. It is approached from the outer cloister by an outer and an inner vestibule; the former of limited height, owing to its passing under the dormitory; the latter lofty, and containing the flight of steps by which the raised level of the Chapter House is reached. The outer vestibule is divided into two walks by small columns of Purbeck marble, and the arch in the cloister by which we enter it is exquisitely carved. The bosses in this vestibule are also elaborate. The inner vestibule is divided into two unequal bays, pierced on both sides with windows; those on the northern side, however, look not into the open air, but towards the altar of St. Faith in the revestry.

The building is an octagon, the diagonals of which measure sixty feet; in other words, it is an octagon, inscribed in a circle of that diameter; it is loftier than most other buildings of the same kind. The central pillar is of Purbeck marble, consisting of a column surrounded by eight detached shafts: it is lofty and light, and the groining which shot up from it has been restored according to the original pattern by Sir G. G. Scott. Each side of the building is occupied by a spacious window, which fills nearly the whole width between the corner shafts. These windows are generally of four lights; the mullions are of Purbeck marble, and the heads filled with large circles and quatrefoils. The spaces beneath the windows are arcaded, with five arches in each, of a trefoil form and richly moulded. The five arches against the eastern wall are much richer and more deeply set than the others. They probably formed the seats of the five greater dignitaries of the Abbey—namely, the abbot in the centre; the prior and subprior, and the third and fourth priors. The seats all round are of stone, and on the backs of these is a series of paintings of religious subjects, of the 14th and 15th centuries; but as they are fully described by Sir Charles Eastlake in his work on oil paintings we need not pause on them in detail. The entire building, although loftier than the Chapter House at Salisbury Cathedral, is less rich in ornament, and probably a little earlier in date of erection; the two, however, are so like that no doubt the one suggested the general plan of the other. There is an excellent description of the building in a volume of papers read by Sir G. G. Scott at the London Congress of the Archæological Institute in July, 1866, and published by Mr. John Murray under the title of "Old London." In that paper the great architect expressed his doubt as to the possibility of "any approach being made to the correct restoration of the Chapter House." But since that date all difficulties have been surmounted; and although the rich painted glass which once threw its tints upon the tessellated pavement below has not been replaced as yet, still the groining of the lofty roof has been renewed, and the exterior has been freed from the wooden and stone encumbrances which for so long a period of vandalism and ignorance obscured the beauty of its Gothic details, and mutilated its fair proportions. The crypt below is comparatively plain, and of no great height; and there can be little doubt that it was formerly used as a chapel.

The chapter-house, as is well known, was the place where the monks and other dignitaries of monastic buildings met to transact the general business of their order; but that at Westminster has its political as well as its religious associations. Here, by consent of the then abbot, in 1377, the Commons of England first held their meetings, as part of the King's Parliament; and here they continued to hold their sittings until 1547, when Edward VI. granted them instead the use of St. Stephen's Chapel.

It appears that in the reign of James I., if not sooner, the records of the King's Bench and the Common Pleas were deposited in this place, and from that time down to the close of the year 1859 the records continued to increase. It is said that much damage was done to the Chapter House in the time of the Civil Wars. The old groined roof was standing in 1740. Remonstrances had been made to the Government, who were the custodians of the place, in consequence of its dangerous condition, some time before. At the above date certain surveyors reported that it was necessary to pull the structure down, and put up a new one. This report was, fortunately, not acted upon; and in the year 1744 upwards of £600 were expended on those repairs, which destroyed in a great measure the ancient appearance of the building. In 1862 the Dean and Chapter of Westminster called a meeting to take into consideration the steps which were desirable in order to call public attention to the ruinous condition of the Chapter House, with a view to its restoration; nothing, however, seems to have resulted from this meeting, and in 1865 another meeting for the same object was convened by the Society of Antiquaries. Dean Stanley, who was voted to the chair, having related the early history of the Chapter House, and alluded to the fact that it was the place of meeting of the first House of Commons, said: "I shall not go through the history of the House of Commons, during the 300 years that it sat in this Chapter House, but still it is impossible not for a moment to recall the extraordinary interest of the Chapter House in that connection, and to remember that almost all the struggles for liberty against the Crown must have taken place within these walls. There is one instance in which they met in the refectory to impeach Piers Gaveston, in the time of Edward II., but as a general rule we may feel satisfied that here took place those early struggles; and as the Commons sat here down to the time of Henry VIII., one may also figure to oneself that here also took place all the memorable acts of the first epoch of the Reformation. It is perhaps worthy of note that the last occasion on which the Commons sat in this house was the last day of the life of Henry VIII., and that their last act here was the attainder of the Duke of Norfolk. In 1547 the Commons moved to the Chapel of St. Stephen, within the walls of Westminster Palace, which had become vacant by the suppression of the Collegiate Chapel of St. Stephen's, Westminster. During the previous 300 years the Abbey must have exercised a kind of divided control over the Chapter House, for no doubt the chapter of the monks met here when the House of Commons was not sitting. But in 1547 the jurisdiction passed entirely away from the Chapter, and came exclusively into the possession of the Crown. In 1540, when the Abbey was dissolved, the Chapter House became absolute public and national property, and the Dean and Chapter that were created on their present footing by Queen Elizabeth never could have entered this Chapter House by right for the performance of any of their business. I believe," continued the Dean, "it is not quite clear where they held their chapter meetings from their first foundation, but it was probably in the Jerusalem Chamber, which is called in legal documents 'our Chapter House.' In 1547, therefore, we enter upon the third stage of its history. In the reign of Edward VI., or of Elizabeth—it is not quite clear which—the building was appropriated for the public records. Then commenced a course of ruin and dilapidation for which the Government must be considered responsible, and which it is the object of this meeting to press them to repair. No doubt these frightful cupboards are nothing but deformities; but, nevertheless, they once contained everything most interesting in English history. Up to the present day there is a board in Poets' Corner, outside the building, bearing this inscription—'All parcels and letters addressed to Sir Francis Palgrave at the Chapter House are to be forwarded to the Rolls' Court.' And here I may relate a story which Sir Francis himself told me. On the night of the great fire at the Houses of Parliament he and Dean Ireland were standing on the roof of the Chapter House, looking at the flames, when a sudden gust of wind seemed to bring the flames in that direction. Sir Francis implored the Dean to allow him to carry 'Domesday Book' and other valuable records into the Abbey, but the Dean answered that he could not think of doing so without first applying to Lord Melbourne. And this leads me to the fourth period. Three or four years ago the records were finally removed to the Rolls Court, and from that time the Chapter House has been left in the state in which you behold it. It is national property, but it has not been put to any national use. Now, it is obvious that before anything can be done with it it must be restored, not by the Dean and Chapter, for it never belonged to us, though if the Government will undertake to give it to us we will endeavour to preserve it as best we can. But, in the first instance, it must be restored to its original magnificence, and to the nation. That is the request we have to urge, and I now appear before you not as claiming anything for ourselves, but as demanding, in the name of the Dean and Chapter of Westminster and of the people of England, that the Chapter House should be restored to the state in which it was during the period when the House of Commons occupied it, and that it should be freed from the incumbrances no longer necessary now that the records have been deposited elsewhere. This, the 800th anniversary of the foundation of the Chapter House, and the 600th of the foundation of the House of Commons, is the very time to make the request, and the Government, I hope and believe, are not indisposed to lend a willing hand to a request coming from so venerable and important a body as the Society of Antiquaries. Mr. Gilbert Scott is willing to set before you the manner in which the restoration of the building is to be accomplished; so, with all these convergences of times, persons, and dispositions, I trust this meeting will not have been held in vain."

Early in the following year the sum of £7,000 was voted by Parliament for the restoration of the Chapter House; the work was placed in the hands of Sir G. Gilbert Scott, and the result of his labours, it need hardly be added, has fully justified the appointment. In January, 1882, a meeting was held in the Chapter House, when it was proposed to fill the windows with stained glass, as a memorial of the late Dean Stanley, and this work is now nearly completed.

Among the contents of the Chapter House whilst it was used as a repository for the Public Records was the original "Domesday Book," so familiar to every child who has read the history of our Saxon and Norman kings. "Though above seven hundred years old," wrote Pennant in 1790, "it is still in as fine preservation as if it was the work of yesterday."

This great work, together with the other public records that encumbered the place, was removed in the year 1863, to the Record Office in Fetter Lane. For many years this portion of Westminster Abbey had been allowed to fall into decay; it was filled from the floor to the ceiling with presses and galleries in which the deeds and other documents were stowed away. The old encaustic pavement was boarded over, and to this cause we are, perhaps, indebted for its preservation. The central pillar, from which sprung the groined roof, remained; but in other parts of this octagonal building terrible mischief had been done. The original windows, the same in size and general arrangement as they now appear, had been in some instances removed, and the space filled up with brickwork.

Close by the Chapter House is the Chapel of "the Pyx," an ancient vaulted chamber, formerly the depository of the regalia of the Scottish kings, including the Holy Cross of Holyrood. Dean Stanley thus writes concerning it: "In the eastern cloister is an ancient double door, which can never be opened, except by the officers of the Government or their representatives, bearing seven keys, some of them of large dimensions, that alone could admit to the chamber within. That chamber, which belongs to the Norman substructures beneath the dormitory, is no less than the Treasury of England. Hither were brought the most cherished possessions of the State."*

This chamber, as Mr. J. Timbs tells us in his "Romance of London," was once "the scene of a glorious haul by way of the robbery of about two millions of our money by certain folks, amongst whom the abbot and forty of his monks fell under suspicion, and were sent to the Tower. This money (£100,000) had been laid up for the Scotch wars by Edward I."

At the time of the Commonwealth, the Pyx Chamber seems to have been in the occupation of the Dean and Chapter, and upon their refusing to deliver up the keys to the officers of the House of Commons, the doors were forced open, and an inventory of the regalia was made. These were afterwards sold, and though subsequently recovered

---

* Stanley's "Memorials," &c., p. 427.

by the Crown, they were never restored to the custody of the Abbey, but at the time of the Restoration they were transferred to the Tower. The Pyx Chamber still remains in the exclusive occupation of the Crown. In this chamber is a stone altar that seems to have escaped destruction by the fanatics at the time of the Reformation and in the great Civil War. The groined roof is supported by Romanesque or semi-circular arches, and thick, short, round shafts. The keys of its double doors are now deposited with seven distinct officers of the Exchequer.

The gloomy-looking passage which extends southward by the door of the Pyx Chamber is known as the "dark cloisters," and leads to a small enclosure called the "Little Cloister." Here is the Littlington Tower, which was built by Abbot Littlington, and originally the bell-tower of the church. In it were four bells, which were rung when great meetings or prayers took place in St. Catherine's Chapel; a small flag being at the same time hoisted on the summit of the tower, as appears in Hollar's view. A writer of the fourteenth century says:—"At the Abbey of St. Peter's, Westminster, are two bells, which over all the bells in the world obtain the precedence in wonderful size and tone." We also read that "in the monasterye of Westminster ther was a fayr yong man which was blynde, whom the monks hadde ordeyned to rynge the bellys." St. Catharine's Chapel was in part pulled down in the year 1571; the bells (one dated as early as 1430) were taken down, and, with two new bells, were hung in one of the western towers of the Abbey Church. In Littlington Tower lived the noted Emma Lady Hamilton, when servant to Mr. Dare. The building, we are told by Mr. Timbs, "was restored by its tenant, Mr. R. Clark, one of the choir, who also erected in its front the original Gothic entrance to the Star Chamber Court, and its ancient bell-pull."

The Little Cloister is a square enclosure, having a fountain in the centre, surrounded by an arcade supported by plain semi-circular arches. At the south-eastern corner are the remains of St. Catharine's Chapel in the form of several arches, which are to be found in the garden of the Receiver's house. According to Dean Stanley, St. Catherine's Chapel, which was part of the monks' infirmary in ancient times, was on several occasions before the Reformation used for episcopal consecrations, and also as the meeting-place of the principal Councils of Westminster.

Not far from this interesting remnant of the old monastery, and near the south-eastern corner of the Abbey precincts, is an ancient square tower, which, as we learn from Dean Stanley's "Historical Memorials," is supposed to have served the purposes of a monastic prison, but which was sold by the Abbey to the Crown in the last year of Edward III. It bears in its architecture a striking resemblance to those parts of the Abbey which are known to have been built by Abbot Littlington, and no doubt dates from the same period. Close by the Chapter House is a little structure which for many years bore the name of the King's Jewel House. It then became the Parliament Office, and was used as a depository for Acts of Parliament. In 1864 these Acts were removed to the Victoria Tower, in the new Houses of Parliament, where they are still preserved; but the King's Jewel House still remains, a link connecting the English State and Church with the venerable past. It is now used as the depository of the standards of weights and measures, both old and new, in connection with the "Trial of the Pyx" (see Vol. I., page 357).

The Great Cloister is immediately contiguous to the south side of the nave of the Abbey Church. The northern and western sides of the cloisters were built by Abbot Littlington, who died in 1386. He also built the granary, which afterwards became the dormitory of the King's Scholars. By the Benedictine rule the monks were required to spend much of their time in the seclusion of the cloisters; and there the day of the month was proclaimed every morning after "prime" by the boys attached to the monastery. The old grey cloisters, with groined arches of the fourteenth century, surround a grassy area—"monastic solitude in contrast with the scene on the opposite side of the church."

The north walk of the cloisters is spanned by the buttresses of the nave, and at either end are entrances to the church. In the south walk are the remains of a lavatory, and towards the east end of this walk are the graves of some of the early abbots, but the memorials of only four are visible, namely, Vitalis, who died in 1082; Gilbert Crispin (1114); Lawrence, said to have been the first who obtained from the Pope the privilege of using the mitre, ring, and glove, and who died in 1175; the fourth slab is of black marble, called Long Meg, from its extraordinary length of eleven feet, and covers the ashes of Gervase de Blois, a natural son of King Stephen, who was appointed abbot in 1140 and deposed in 1159. In 1349, twenty-six of the monks of this abbey fell victims to a plague which was then raging, and they are reported by old Fuller to have been buried all in one grave in the south cloister, under the slab above alluded to. The humbler brethren of the monastery were mostly buried under the central plot of grass in the cloisters.

A small wooden door in the south walk leads to Ashburnham House, one of Inigo Jones's few remaining works. Close by the entrance to Ashburnham House is a monument to Peter Francis Courayer, a Roman Catholic clergyman, librarian and canon of the Abbey of Ste. Geneviève, at Paris. He translated and published several very valuable works on the validity of English orders; but his

THE WESTERN TOWERS AND THE CLOISTERS OF WESTMINSTER ABBEY, 1840. (*See page* 455.)

writings not being favourably received by members of his own Church, he took refuge in England in 1727, and was warmly received by the University of Oxford, who conferred upon him the degree of D.D. He died in 1776, at the age of ninety-five. There is in the east walk a monument to Sir Edmundbury Godfrey, who was murdered in the reign of Charles II., and a tablet to Lieutenant-General Withers, with an epitaph said to be by Pope. In the north walk lie buried Dr. Markham, Archbishop of York, who died in 1807, and also a former Bishop of St. David's; and there are here a few memorial tablets of no particular interest, unless perhaps we select one dated in 1621, remarkable for its quaintness, and inscribed to the memory of William Laurence, in these lines—

"With diligence and truth most exemplary,
Did William Laurence serve a Prebendary;
And for his pains, now past, before not lost,
Gain'd this remembrance at his master's cost.
Oh! read these lines again!—you seldom find
A servant faithful, and a master kind.
Short-hand he wrote, his flower in prime did fade,
And hasty Death short-hand of him hath made.
Well couth he numbers, and well measur'd land;
Thus doth he now that ground whereon you stand,
Wherein he lies so geometrical;
Art maketh some, but thus will Nature all."

About the year 1630, Dean Williams, afterwards Archbishop of York, spent a considerable sum in repairing the most decayed parts of the church; he also, says Dugdale, converted a room in the east part of the cloisters, which had been the monks' parlour, into a library which he furnished with books.

In the west walk is a monument to George Vertue, the antiquary and engraver, and also one, by Banks, to Woollett, another eminent engraver of the last century.

It does not appear that the nave and cloisters, though the last resting-places of so many eminent persons, were treated with due respect in the reign of Queen Anne. At all events the following occurs in the Acts of the Dean and Chapter, under date May 6th, 1710: "Whereas several butchers and other persons have of late, especially on market days, carried meat and other burdens through the church, and that in time of Divine service, to the great scandal and offence of all sober persons; and whereas divers disorderly beggars are daily walking and begging in the Abbey and cloisters;

and do fill the same with nastiness, whereby great offence is caused to all people going through the church and cloisters; and whereas many idle boys come into the cloisters daily, and there play at cards and other plays for money, and are often heard to curse and swear: Charles Baldwell is appointed beadel to restrain this, and to complain of offenders, if necessary, to a justice of the peace. And it is further ordered that if any boys that go to the grammar school, or are choristers of the church, do play there, the beadel do forthwith give in the names of such boys to one of the masters, that they may be punished according to their fault."

Ashburnham House, in Little Dean's Yard, as stated above, was built by Inigo Jones. Its chief beauty is a magnificent staircase. In this house was deposited the Cottonian Library (now in the British Museum), which had a narrow escape of being destroyed by fire here in 1731. One of the most important works in this library was the Customs Book of the Abbey, written by Abbot Ware in the thirteenth century. This volume has always been said to have been destroyed in the fire above alluded to, but its parched and shrivelled leaves have been preserved in the British Museum, and a few years ago underwent a restoring process by means of which the whole has become legible. Dean Stanley had a copy made, which is deposited in the Abbey Library.

In the garden is an alcove, also attributed to Inigo Jones, in imitation of part of a small Roman temple. In the coal-cellar are some remains of the vaults of the old conventual buildings, and in one of the walls may be seen a capital of the Early Norman period. The house, however, contains nothing else striking or important, and is chiefly memorable as having been at different times inhabited by Dean Milman and Dean Ireland. The garden between the house and the cloister occupies the site of what once was a hall or refectory or dormitory, as is shown by the deeply-splayed windows which are still to be seen in the wall rising far above the spring of the arches of the cloister roof. The house was in 1881-2 fitted up for the purposes of the Westminster School.

THE DEANERY.

The present Deanery, a substantial building of stone, occupies part of the site, and, indeed, is formed partly out of the ancient abbot's house, which enclosed a small court or garden lying to the west of the cloisters. It is one of the most curious buildings in the Abbey precincts. Over the doorway is a stone shield carved with the arms of the Deanery, namely—*Azure*, a cross patoncé between five martlets, four in the cantons of the cross, and one in base, *or;* on a chief of the last, a pale quarterly of France and England, between two roses, *gules*. Dart, in his "Lives of the Abbots of Westminster," says that Abbot Islip built the Dean's House and offices to the monastery; Dean Stanley, however, in his "Historical Memorials of Westminster," ascribes its erection to Abbot Littlington, with a slight addition by Abbot Islip. The doorway is close by the entrance to the cloisters from Dean's Yard. It stands round a small court, into which for the most part its windows look. Only from the grand dining-hall and its parlour there were originally windows into the open space before the Sanctuary. It was commonly called "Cheyney Gate Manor," from the conspicuous chain which was drawn across the entrance of the cloisters. Skirting the west side of the cloister are a suite of modern apartments and the dining-room. On the south side was the Abbot's long chamber, now the Dean's library; this is immediately above the entrance to the cloisters. The kitchen occupied the south-west corner, and extending thence to the Jerusalem Chamber was the abbot's refectory, now the college hall. Till Dean Buckland introduced a modern stove, this noble apartment was warmed by a huge brazier, of which the smoke escaped through a "louvre" in the roof.

The Jerusalem Chamber, to which we now make our way, was built by Abbot Littlington, towards the latter end of the fourteenth century; and it is supposed to have been either the "Guesten hall" or the abbot's withdrawing-room. It is known to every reader of English history and of Shakespeare, that in this chamber died King Henry IV., soon after an attack of illness which seized him whilst paying his devotions at the shrine of Edward the Confessor. It is scarcely necessary to repeat here the well-known lines of Shakespeare, and yet their omission would be unpardonable :—

> "*Henry*. Doth any name particular belong
> Unto the lodging where I first did swoon?
> *Warwick*. 'Tis call'd Jerusalem, my noble lord.
> *Henry*. Laud be to God! ev'n there my life must end.
> It hath been prophesied me many a year
> I shall not die but in Jerusalem;
> Which vainly I suppos'd the Holy Land.
> But bear me to that chamber: there I'll lie;
> In that Jerusalem shall Harry die."

With reference to the death of Henry IV. in this chamber, Pennant remarks, on the authority of Brown's "Fasciculus," that "the devil is said to have practised such a delusion on Pope Silvester II., having assured his Holiness that he should 'die in Jerusalem,' and kept his word, by taking him off in 1003, as he was saying mass in a church of that name in Rome."

In 1719 the body of Joseph Addison lay in state in the Jerusalem Chamber, before its burial in Henry VII.'s Chapel, as pictured in Tickell's elegy :—

> "Can I forget the dismal night that gave
> My soul's best part for ever to the grave?
> How silent did his old companions tread,
> By midnight lamps, the mansions of the dead:
> Through breathing statues, then unheeded things;
> Through rows of warriors, and through walks of kings."

Here, too, Congreve lay in state, before his pompous funeral, at which noblemen bore the pall; and here, also, a similar honour was paid to the body of Matthew Prior, for we are told in the *Daily Post* of September 24, 1721, that "the same evening the remains of Matthew Prior, Esquire, were carried to the Jerusalem Chamber, and splendidly interred in Westminster Abbey.

The portrait of Richard II., now in the chancel of the Abbey Church, hung for some time on the walls of this chamber, as already mentioned in a preceding chapter.

The exterior of the Jerusalem Chamber is not particularly attractive, and with its dwarf proportions it seems a sort of excrescence on the west front of the Abbey, from which it leads in a southward direction towards the Deanery. Between the years 1871 and 1874 the interior underwent a thorough restoration. Its walls are covered with ancient tapestry, and with cedar panelling; the fireplace is fitted with an antique grate, and the surrounding surface is covered with very handsome tiles, ornamented with a pattern combining roses and lilies, with the briars and the stems of each respectively, while around, in mediæval characters, are the three texts: "O pray for the peace of Jerusalem," "Build thou the walls of Jerusalem," and "Jerusalem which is above is free." The old Jacobean carving on the wall over the fireplace is retained; at the top is an admirably executed painting of the death of Henry IV. in this very chamber, with the line from the above quotation, "In that Jerusalem shall Harry die."

The Jerusalem Chamber began to be used as the Chapter House, probably, when the Abbey gave up its proper Chapter House to the Crown. Here, then, it may not be out of place to make some mention of the "staff" of the Abbey—or, rather, cathedral—for, as we have shown in a previous chapter, its duties are performed in all respects similar to any other cathedral body. The deanery is in the gift of the Crown; the Dean, whose power is absolute within the walls, has a salary of £2,000 per annum; he is also Dean of the Order of the Bath. There are, as we have already said, six canons, six minor canons, a chapter clerk, and an organist, besides vergers and choristers. The patronage which is vested in the Dean and Chapter of Westminster embraces the minor canonries, and extends over twenty-four benefices. Under the charge of the Dean and Chapter of the Abbey, and forming part of their especial charge, is Westminster School, or, to speak technically, "the College of St. Peter." As a school for the young was always a leading feature in every monastery, and especially in those of the Benedictine order, there can be no doubt that there was a school attached to the Abbey of Westminster in the old Saxon times. It was re-founded by Queen Elizabeth, and dates its precedence among the public schools of England from 1560. This school, however, will form the subject of our next chapter.

Besides being the place for the transaction of business by the Dean and Chapter, the Jerusalem Chamber was, until 1896, when the Great Hall of the Church House was opened (see Vol. IV., p. 38), the place of meeting for the Upper House of Convocation of the Province of Canterbury. In theory, the Church of England is governed by means of its Convocation of Bishops and Clergy; but, practically, Convocation is at present little more than a merely deliberative body. Still its moral influence is great, and no wise minister would venture to disregard its deliberately expressed opinion. There is a House of Convocation for each province, Canterbury and York. That of Canterbury consists of two Houses: the upper is confined to the bishops; the lower is composed of the deans of every cathedral, the archdeacons, with proctors elected from every cathedral chapter, and two more elected by the clergy of every diocese. In York there are two Houses, but the bishops, deans, archdeacons, and proctors sit together. A fresh election of proctors is made with every new Parliament.

The Jerusalem Chamber is also to be remembered as the scene of the labours of the committee appointed by Convocation in 1870 to revise the "authorised version" of the English Bible—labours which occupied several years.

On the suppression of the bishopric of Westminster, in the year 1550, the diocese was re-united to the see of London. "The lands of this bishopric," says Widmore, "were several of them exchanged with Ridley, just then made Bishop of London, for some belonging to that bishopric. Ridley had also the convicts' prison, a house between the west end of the Abbey and the gate-house; the bishop's palace, formerly the abbot's house, was given to the Lord Wentworth; a small parcel of lands was sold to Bishop Thirleby; several granted to one Sir Thomas Wroth, and others, said to be applied to the repair of St. Paul's, and to occasion the saying of 'robbing Peter to pay Paul.'" Bishop Thirleby is reported to have impoverished his bishopric very much by granting long leases of the estates. He was, immediately after his surrender, translated to Norwich, and thence, some years afterwards, to Ely.

We may add here, with reference to the suppression of the bishopric, that, under date of 1550, Strype, in his "Ecclesiastical Memorials," says that "the Church of Westminster, nearer to the King's house than any other, was not yet freed from its superstitions, both in apparel and books, which were still preserved there, which occasioned a letter, dated in February, from the King and his Council to the members of that church, 'that, in the presence of Mr. Vice-Chamberlain and Sir Anthony Aucher, all manner of garnishments and apparel of silver and gold, such as altar-cloths, copes, &c., should be taken away, and delivered to the said Sir Anthony; and to deface and carry out of the library at Westminster all books of superstition, such as missals, breviaries, processionals, &c.'" Widmore, too, informs us that "in May, 1553, the commissioners for gathering ecclesiastical goods carried away from hence all the plate and furniture of the church, except a silver pot, two gilt cups with covers, three herse cloths, twelve cushions, one carpet, eight stall cloths for the choir, three pulpit cloths, a little carpet for the dean's stall, and two table cloths."

Between the abolition of Westminster as a cathedral city by Henry VIII. and its return to monastic rule by order of Queen Mary—that is, from 1550 to 1556—no less than three deans were appointed; and from the restoration of the deanery in 1560, down to the present time, there have been upwards of twenty. Of these, some have held high preferment in the Church, or have had their names handed down to posterity through the share they have taken in political events or other matters of history. Space does not permit of our speaking of more than a few of the most important.

Lancelot Andrews, who held the deanery of Westminster when James I. came to the throne, was appointed to the bishopric of Chester in 1605, and afterwards translated to the see of Ely. In

1618 he was advanced to the bishopric of Winchester, and made Dean of the Chapel Royal. He was the author of several literary works; but that by which he is best known is his "Manual of Private Devotions and Meditations for Every Day in the Week," and a "Manual of Directions for the Visitation of the Sick." Bishop Andrews has the reputation of having been the most learned of his English contemporaries, excepting Usher, in the Fathers, ecclesiastical antiquities, and canon law. He was also celebrated for his talent at repartee, of which an instance is told in page 29, Vol. II., of this work. The good bishop is buried in St. Saviour's Church, Southwark.

Thomas Sprat, who became Dean of Westminster in 1683, was one of the original Fellows of the Royal Society, and in 1667 published its history. In 1684 he was consecrated Bishop of Rochester, and in return for the royal favours which had been conferred upon him he published a history of the Rye House Plot, entitled "A True Account and Declaration of the Horrid Conspiracy against the late King, his present Majesty, and the present Government." After the abdication of James II. an attempt was made to implicate the bishop in a pretended plot for restoring him, his signature having been fraudulently obtained; but he succeeded in establishing his innocence, after which he lived in retirement at Bromley, in Kent, till his death in 1713. Dr. Sprat was the author of a few short poems, and some other works of no great merit.

Francis Atterbury, who succeeded Dr. Sprat in the deanery, and also in the bishopric of Rochester, was a great controversialist in the reigns of Queen Anne and George I. He was a native of Milton, near Newport Pagnell, in Buckinghamshire, and was educated at Westminster School, and Christ Church, Oxford. Having taken orders, he was elected lecturer of St. Bride's, and soon afterwards nominated minister of Bridewell, where his pulpit eloquence attracted general attention. In the year 1700 he became engaged in a long controversy with Dr. Wake, afterwards Archbishop of Canterbury, and others, concerning the rights, powers, and privileges of Convocation, Atterbury denying the authority of the civil power over ecclesiastical synods; and the zeal with which he upheld his views secured for him the thanks of the Lower House of Convocation, and the degree of Doctor in Divinity from the University of Oxford. In 1704 he was appointed to the deanery of Carlisle, but shortly afterwards transferred to a canonry in Exeter Cathedral. In 1712 he was made Dean of Christ Church, Oxford, and in the following year was advanced to the bishopric of Rochester and the deanery of Westminster. On the death of Queen Anne Dr. Atterbury assumed a position of hostility to the House of Hanover, and all his energies were directed to bring about the restoration of the Stuart dynasty. This, perhaps, is the one great blot on his character, and it was the one which led to his downfall. On the breaking out of the rebellion in 1715 the other prelates published a declaration of abhorrence to it, but Atterbury refused his signature, and not long afterwards he incurred the suspicion of being deeply concerned in a succession of plots for the restoration of the ejected family. He was charged by a committee of the House of Commons with a treasonable correspondence, and the evidence against him being considered conclusive, he was committed to the Tower. The bill of pains and penalties which was passed against him by both the Upper and the Lower House "condemned him to deprivation from all his ecclesiastical preferments, incapacitated him from performing any spiritual functions, or holding any civil appointment, and sentenced him to perpetual exile." He accordingly quitted England for France in June, 1723, and after several changes of residence eventually died at Paris in 1732, in the seventieth year of his age. He was buried privately in Westminster Abbey, and no monument has been erected to his memory.

Samuel Horsley, who was installed in the deanery in 1793, was a distinguished prelate of the English Church, successively Bishop of St. David's, Rochester, and St. Asaph. He was a powerful theological controversialist, and the person against whom he chiefly directed his attack was Dr. Joseph Priestley. His published writings are very numerous, and a complete list of them is given in Nichols' "Literary Anecdotes of the Eighteenth Century." His "Seventeen Letters to Dr. Priestley" was regarded by the friends of the Church as "a masterly defence of the orthodox faith, and as the secure foundation of a high and lasting theological reputation." Soon after the publication of this work, Lord Thurlow, who was then chancellor, presented him with a prebendal stall in Gloucester Cathedral, his lordship, it is said, at the same time observing, that "those who defended the Church ought to be supported by the Church." Bishop Horsley vacated the deanery of Westminster in the year 1802, on his translation to the bishopric of St. Asaph.

John Ireland, who was appointed to the deanery in 1816, sprang from very humble parentage, and was born at Ashburton, in Devonshire, in the neighbourhood of which place he held his first curacy. He was afterwards vicar of Croydon, and promoted to a prebendal stall in Westminster Abbey. On his advancement to the deanery he was also nominated to the rectory of Islip, Oxon, which, however, he resigned some years before his death, which took place in 1842. Dr. Ireland was always distinguished by his warm patronage of learning. The University of Oxford is indebted to him for the scholarships bearing his name—four in number, of £30 per annum each, founded in 1825; and to be elected on his foundation is one of the greatest classical honours which the University can confer.

Dr. Samuel Wilberforce was next in succession to Dr. Ireland. He was the third son of the celebrated philanthropist, William Wilberforce, and was born in 1805. He was ordained as curate of Checkendon, in Oxfordshire, and his subsequent preferments were the rectory of Brightstone, archdeaconry of Surrey, the rectory of Alverstoke, a canonry of Winchester, a chaplaincy to the late Prince Consort, the Deanery of Westminster, and the post of Lord High Almoner. He was consecrated Bishop of Oxford in 1845, and translated to Winchester in 1869. Bishop Wilberforce took a prominent part in the debates in the House of Lords, and also in the Upper House of Convocation; and he was also well known as a most eloquent speaker at public meetings of a religious character. Bishop Wilberforce was accidentally killed, on the 19th of July, 1873, by being thrown from his horse.

William Buckland was nominated by Sir Robert Peel to the deanery, on the elevation of Dr. Wilberforce to the bishopric of Oxford, in 1845. In early life Dr. Buckland exhibited a marked tendency for the study of natural and physical science, and in 1813 we find him appointed to the Readership of Mineralogy, and in 1818 to the Readership of Geology, in the University of Oxford. His contributions to the "Proceedings" of the Geological Society were very numerous, and in the first volume of the "Bibliographia Geologiæ et Zoologiæ," published by the Ray Society, in 1848, there are references to no less than sixty-one distinct works and memoirs. In the year 1825 Dr. Buckland accepted the living of Stoke Charity, in Hampshire, and was promoted to a canonry in the Cathedral of Christ Church, Oxford. He twice filled the presidential chair of the Geological Society, and he also took a lively interest in the foundation of the British Association for the Advancement of Science. In 1847 he was appointed a trustee of the British Museum, and took an active part in the development of that department more especially devoted to geology and palæontology. Dr. Buckland seems not to have devoted himself to questions of technical theology. His views on this subject are chiefly contained in his "Bridgewater Treatise" and the "Vindiciæ." Amongst the list of his published works will be found but one sermon, and that devoted to the subject of death; it was published at Oxford in 1839.

Richard Chenevix Trench, who succeeded to the deanery on the death of Dr. Buckland, in 1856, was a nephew of the first Lord Ashtown, in the Irish peerage, and was born in Dublin in 1807. He graduated at Trinity College, Cambridge, and was soon afterwards ordained, and engaged upon a country curacy. It was not, however, as a scholar or a divine, but as a poet, that his name first became known. He is also the author of a large number of essays and treatises. In 1845 and 1846 he was Hulsean Lecturer at Cambridge, and for a short time one of the Select Preachers. About the year 1847 he became Theological Professor and Examiner at King's College, London, and continued to hold that appointment till his promotion to the Deanery of Westminster. He was consecrated Archbishop of Dublin in 1864, on the death of Dr. Whately, and died in 1886.

Arthur Penrhyn Stanley, D.D., who, in 1864, succeeded Archbishop Trench in the Deanery of Westminster, was the son of the late Right Rev. Edward Stanley, Bishop of Norwich. Educated under Dr. Arnold at Rugby, and having passed a very distinguished university career, he was for many years tutor of his college, and secretary of the Oxford University Commission. He was canon of Canterbury from 1851 to 1858; Regius Professor of Ecclesiastical History at Oxford, and canon of Christ Church; and also chaplain to the Bishop of London from 1858 to 1864. Dean Stanley first became known to the literary world by his admirable "Life of Dr. Arnold," published in 1844; among his most popular works after that date were his "Historical Memorials of Canterbury," "Sinai and Palestine," and his "Memorials of Westminster Abbey," a work to which we have to acknowledge our obligations. Dean Stanley died in 1881, and was succeeded by the Rev. George Granville Bradley, D.D., formerly Head Master of Marlborough College, and subsequently Master of University College, Oxford, and Canon of Worcester.

We may add here that every precaution is taken to ensure the protection of the Abbey from fire, the Dean and Chapter having caused to be erected in the south-west tower, at an altitude of 160 feet from the ground, a huge tank, capable of containing 6,000 gallons of water. The entire cost of these works amounted to £2,000.

It is not generally known that soon after the Reformation the Abbey very nearly shared the fate of Tintern, Glastonbury, Reading, Kirkstall, and Malmesbury. Pennant writes, "When the Protector, Somerset, ruled in the fulness of power, this sacred pile narrowly escaped a total demolition. It was his design to have pulled it down to the ground, and to have applied the materials towards the palace which he was then erecting in the Strand, known by the name of Somerset House. He was diverted from his design by a bribe of not fewer than fourteen manors!"

THE JERUSALEM CHAMBER. (*See page* 458.)

CHAPTER LV.

WESTMINSTER SCHOOL.

"Dear the schoolboy spot
We ne'er forget, though there we are forgot."—*Byron.*

Abbot Ingulph and Queen Edgitha—A Monastic School in the "Dark Ages"—The Beginning of Westminster School—Henry VIII.'s Additions to the Foundation—The School as founded by Queen Elizabeth—Election of Queen's Scholars—"Challenges"—Proposed removal of the School—Dr. Goodman's House at Chiswick—The College Hall—The School-room—Latin Prayers still said—The Dormitory—The Westminster Play—Edmund Curll's Piracy of a School Oration—The Prince Regent and the Marquis of Anglesey—The College Gardens—The Accommodation for Queen's Scholars—Rivalry between Westminster and Eton Boys—"Fagging."

UNDER the wing of almost every abbey and monastery in England there grew up a school for the education of the young; and Westminster formed no exception to the general rule. Tanner, in his "Notitia," tells us that there would appear to have been a school attached to the Abbey of St. Peter's from its first foundation. Under the system which prevailed throughout Christendom in the Middle Ages, whenever a bishop's see or a large abbey was founded, a school for the instruction of boys in religious and useful learning was sure to spring up, under the shadow of the church, after the example of the "schools of the prophets," of which mention is so often made in the Old Testament. This was the case not only at Canterbury, at Winchester, and in other cathedral cities, but in such abbey churches as those of Glastonbury, St. Albans, and Westminster. Accordingly we find that the Abbey of St. Peter's had not been very long in existence before provision was made for the instruction of the youth of the neighbourhood. At all events, it is an ascertained fact that even in the reign of Edward the Confessor, and probably at an earlier date, there was a school attached to it, for Ingulph, the abbot and historian of Croyland Abbey, states that he himself received his education there, adding that, in his way back from school, he would meet Edgitha, the queen, who would ask him as to his lessons, and "falling from grammar to the brighter studies of logic, wherein she had much skill and knowledge, she would subtilely catch him in the threads of argument, and afterwards send him home with cakes and money, which was counted out to him by her handmaidens," and then, like a good kind woman and queen as she was, she would "send him to the royal larder to refresh himself." The chronicle of Ingulph, we are aware, has been impeached as to its genuineness; but, at all events, genuine or not, it bears testimony to the tradition of an old monastic school here before the Conquest. Very few trustworthy notices, however, remain to show us the character of this early institution. Fitz-Stephen, in his "Life of Thomas à Becket," confirms the fact of a school being attached to the Abbey; and from other sources we know that a salary was paid by the almoner of the monastery to a schoolmaster for teaching boys grammar. This salary continued to be paid down to the time of the dissolution of the monasteries.

THE COLLEGE HALL. (*See page* 467.)

A school for the young being thus as necessary an adjunct to a monastery as were its cloisters and its mill, the three chief homes of the monks of London and its suburbs soon after the Norman Conquest—St. Paul's in the City, St. Mary Overy in Southwark, and the Abbey at Westminster—were no exceptions to the rule. It is clear from Fitz-Stephen (and from other writers too) that the attainments of many of the boy-scholars in those "dark ages" were of no mean order, and it is by no means certain that any London schoolmaster of our own enlightened age could afford a more creditable or amusing programme for his Prize Day, or "apposition," than one or two mentioned by that author. "On festival days the scholars held dialectic contests, in which the most straightforward disputants, whose object was the attainment of truth, fought with the legitimate weapons of syllogism and enthymeme. The more subtle and sophistical geniuses used the side-blows of paralogism and 'verbal inundation.' . . . . These exhibitions, we may believe, were confined to the elder scholars, who would more resemble the undergraduates of our universities at the present day. But the younger pupils were not without their trials of strength, for we learn that the boys of the different schools had 'sets-to with verses on the rudiments of grammar and the rules of preterites and supines.' But lest the spectators should fancy these feats, however improving, to be somewhat dull, a more lively entertainment was provided to follow on. Logical subtleties and grammatical puzzles were discarded, and a sort of Fescennine licence prevailed. Under fictitious names the foibles of their fellow-pupils, and even of the authorities, were lashed with a Socratic wit, and invectives of a fiercer kind took vent in bold dithyrambics." Possibly, in the annual "hits" at current events in the epilogue to the "Westminster Play" we have the remnant of this old playful satire preserved to us unchanged. But of one thing we may be sure, namely, that by such exercises as we have described above "sound and solid learning" was as much encouraged as by all our modern system of cramming and of competitive examinations.

Dean Stanley, in his "Memorials of Westminster Abbey," after describing the cloisters, adds, "In the north cloister, close by the entrance of the church, where the monks usually walked, sate the prior. In the western cloister sate the 'Master of the Novices,' with his disciples. This was the first beginning of Westminster School."

When he remodelled the Abbey and made it into a bishop's see, Henry VIII. added to the foundation two masters to teach forty grammar scholars. In the reign of Edward VI. we find one of the Reformers—Alexander Nowell—taking an active part in the instruction of the youths in "the new doctrines." During the reign of Queen Mary, when the monastic character of the church at Westminster was restored, we hear little or nothing about the school attached to it; but on the accession of Queen Elizabeth the Abbey underwent yet another change in 1560, being re-founded as a collegiate church, comprising besides a dean and twelve prebendaries and twelve almsmen, an upper and under master, and forty scholars; this arrangement has remained substantially the same down to the present time. The college as established by Elizabeth, and attached by her to the collegiate church, is described in books of the time as "A publique schoole for Grammar, Rhethorick, Poetrie, and for the Latin and Greek Languages." It was designed at first for not more than 120 boys, including the "Queen's Scholars," who were to be chosen in preference from among the choristers or from the sons of the chapter tenants.

Widmore tells us that on the surrender of the monastery to Henry VIII., the King included the school in his draft of the new establishment for the see of Westminster, which is still preserved in the archives of the chapter. "Queen Elizabeth," he adds, "did only continue her father's appointment: that princess made indeed a statute ordering the manner in which the scholars were to be elected upon the foundation in this school, and from thence to a college in each of the two Universities, as likewise the number so to be removed every year. Against this part of the order, both the Deans of Christ Church and the Masters of Trinity College struggled for a long time, but without good reason; some supposed advantage to such places by another scheme being not to be set against the express directions of the founders, they were at length obliged to acquiesce." In fact here, as elsewhere, the "Virgin Queen" contrived pretty effectively to have her own way. It was by her foresight that, in order to prevent family cliques obtaining possession of the school, a statute was added forbidding more than two youths from any one county being chosen in one year.

The right of election to Christ Church and Trinity College being such an important element in the constitution of Westminster as it now is, Elizabeth has always been considered to have a just claim to be looked upon as the royal foundress of the college. The foundation, then, as she left it, consisted of a head master, a second master or "usher," and forty "Queen's Scholars," who were maintained and educated free of cost and charge, with the privilege of election annually to three studentships at Christ Church, Oxford, and the same number of scholarships at Trinity College, Cambridge—six in all. This was to be the number elected each year *at the least*—"ad minimum;" but she adds "plures optamus:" so that (as there were, on the average, ten admitted each year to the college at Westminster) she seems to have meant that, if possible, all who were once thus admitted to her foundation should be provided for at one of the Universities. There was to be an annual election to supply the places of those thus drafted off to Oxford and Cambridge, each boy remaining four years in the college before presenting himself for the latter election, and if then rejected, leaving.

The resident Queen's Scholars live together, and are distinguished by cap and gown and white neck-cloth; in the Abbey they wear white surplices, as being part of the foundation of the collegiate church. The Governing body are the guardians of the college, and administer its revenues. Among the muniments of the Chapter, there are, doubtless, many curious items which would show the manner in which its domestic arrangements have been carried out. In 1606 an "Act of the Dean and Chapter" enacts that "trial be made of the burning of sea-coals in the kitchen for one year." The foundation now consists of 60 boys, 40 resident and 20 non-resident.

Since 1874 the studentships at Oxford and the scholarships at Cambridge have been thrown open to competition among the whole school. In addition to the studentships at Christ Church, Oxford, already mentioned, there are three exhibitions at the same college, and also two or more exhibitions from a bequest of Dr. Triplett, tenable for three years at any college of Oxford or Cambridge.

The Queen's Scholars hold their scholarships subject to an annual examination, in which any scholar failing to satisfy the examiners of his industry and progress in study, may forfeit his place on the foundation. The fixed expenses of a resident Queen's Scholar are £30 annually, which includes maintenance, as well as tuition in all branches of study. The tuition fees of boys, not Queen's Scholars, are thirty guineas a year, with an entrance fee of five guineas, while the fees for boarding, apart from tuition, are sixty-five guineas, with five guineas as an entrance fee. The examination for the Foundation takes place at the same time as that for exhibitions.

"Town Boys," or boys not on the foundation, are admitted ordinarily at ages ranging from ten to fourteen years. No boy is eligible for admission unless he is sufficiently advanced, in proportion to his age, to profit by the teaching of the school. Candidates are examined by the head master orally, and, if necessary, also on paper. The ordinary instruction in the school includes Scriptural teaching, classics, mathematics, and natural science, history, geography, English, French (or sometimes German for advanced pupils), together with drawing, singing, or writing, at the discretion of the head master.

The competition for nomination of boys to the college as Queen's Scholars was formerly conducted by an examination in Latin and Greek construing, parsing, and grammar, in a manner known as "challenges," which went on for about six weeks during the preceding winter. This system of examination has been thus described by Dean Liddell, who was formerly head master of Westminster School:—"It partakes somewhat of the nature of the old academic disputations. All the candidates for vacant places in college are presented to the master in the order of their forms. . . . The two lowest boys come up before the head master, having prepared a certain portion of Greek Epigrams and Ovid's Metamorphoses, which has been set to them a certain number of hours before. In preparing these passages they have the assistance of certain senior boys, who are called their 'helps.' With these boys, too, it should be remarked, they have been working for weeks or months beforehand in preparation for the struggle. The lower of the two boys is the challenger. He calls on the boy whom he challenges to translate the passage set them, and if he can correct any fault in translating he takes his place. The upper boy now becomes the challenger, and proceeds in the same way. When the translation is finished, the challenger—whichever of the two boys happens to be left in that position—has the right of putting questions in grammar, and if the challeng*ee* cannot answer them and the challenger answers them correctly, the former loses his place. In this way they attack each other until their stock of questions is exhausted. The 'helps' stand by during the challenge, and act as council to their 'men' in case there be any doubt as to the correctness of a question or an answer. The head master sits by as Moderator and decides the point at issue. The boy who, at the end of the challenge or contest between the two boys, is found to have finally retained his place, has subsequently the opportunity of challenging the boy next above him in the list of candidates for admission, and of thus fighting his way up through the list of competitors. The struggle ordinarily lasts from six to eight weeks; the ten who are highest at its close obtain admission to the foundation in the order in which they stand."

The school is at present divided into Forms, as follows:—Classical Side: Seventh, Sixth, Mathematical Sixth, Shell, Under Shell, Upper Fifth, Under Fifth, Upper Remove, Under Remove, Fourth; Modern Side: Modern Sixth, Modern Shells, University Matriculation Class, Modern Fifth, Modern Remove, Modern Fourth. On the classical side there are about 170 boys; on the modern, 70; and the number in each Form averages about 20. Since boys are no longer admitted at a very tender age, the lower Forms have disappeared.

Six exhibitions, tenable at the school, are

offered annually for competition to candidates (whether previously in the school or not) of ages between twelve and fourteen. Two are of the value of £30 and four of £20, raised to £50 or £30 respectively in the case of boarders. These "Exhibitions" are all tenable for two years, or until the holder is elected upon the foundation. A power is reserved of re-electing deserving candidates. The examination is held on Tuesday and Wednesday in Easter Week. No entrance fee is charged for exhibitioners. Some foundation vacancies are thrown open to competition at the same time.

The chief school prizes are:—The Mure scholarship, value about £40. This is awarded in October, for classical proficiency chiefly. The Marshal prizes for classics and divinity; the Dean's Greek Testament prizes, and Junior Prizes for Scripture knowledge; the Phillimore Prizes, for English Essay, and for Translation; the Gumbleton Prize, for English verse; the Ireland Prizes, for Greek and Latin composition; the Master's Prize, for mathematics; and the Cheyne Prizes for arithmetic.

It may be stated that Westminster is now almost wholly a school for the sons of the professional classes. Under the Public Schools Act (1868), Westminster School became entitled to three houses adjacent to the buildings, and Ashburnham House was a few years ago fitted up for school purposes.

The school has fluctuated considerably in its numbers. It appears to have been at its height in 1729, when it had 439 scholars. Two years later there were 377, and in 1771 only 248. The numbers stood about that ratio, now a little higher and then again lower, till 1818, when they reached a maximum of 324. They decreased rapidly from that date down to 1841, when they were only 67, from which date they have risen again steadily and gradually up to about 250.

In this present period of change, it will not be a matter of surprise to our readers to hear that it has been more than once proposed to remove Westminster School into the country, and that other proposals have been made for abolishing the college as a separate institution and house, and to turn its funds into exhibitions open to competition and tenable by boys in any of the boarding houses. The masters of the school, however, have almost one and all condemned the latter change, and the other has been forbidden by the Public Schools Act, under penalty of forfeiture of the entire property of the school. It must be allowed that the connection with the abbey could not be transplanted.

With regard to the removal of the college into the country, we may here remark that the second dean of Queen Elizabeth's nomination, Dr. Goodman, took one useful measure of precaution against the plague on behalf of the school and scholars. Happening to hold the prebend of Chiswick, he obtained for his church the privilege of being tenant in perpetuity of the prebendal estate, in order that it might afford a place of refuge for both masters and scholars, in case of an outbreak of that epidemic, setting apart for their use his house at Chiswick. According to the Lansdowne MSS., the house or "hospital" at Chiswick was built at the cost of £500. We shall probably have an opportunity of describing it hereafter, when we reach Chiswick. It may be interesting to learn that this ancient structure was often used by the scholars in former times, and that it was not pulled down until about the year 1870. The fund raised by its sale is set aside by the Governing Body to be applied to the payment of expenses incurred for the medical care and maintenance of the Queen's Scholars in time of sickness.

In Elizabeth's time it appears that the invalid scholars were sent down to Whethamstead, near St. Albans, under the charge of one of the prebendaries, who was to be paid twenty pence a week for his expenses.

On one occasion, in Elizabeth's reign, the school was removed to Putney, from June till Michaelmas, no doubt on account of some fever or plague breaking out. In 1569 the school was dispersed on account of the plague, from September 23 till the eve of All Saints' Day. The same occurred again in 1603.

Dean Goodman appears to have benefited the school in other ways also, collecting the scholars into one spacious chamber, and making regulations for their support and maintenance. During the rebellion, and the rule of the Puritan fanatics, the school appears to have been dispersed for a time, though subsequently, in 1649, provision was made by Act of Parliament for its continuance.

Westminster School is not separately endowed with lands and possessions, but is attached to the general foundation of the collegiate church, so far as it relates to the support of its "Queen's Scholars," as the boys on the foundation are called. These Queen's Scholars—those of them who are resident—sleep in a large dormitory, which is now cut up into little cells, or cubicula, by wooden partitions. The school, it may here be mentioned, is often called, in formal documents of the last century, "the King's School in Westminster."

Dean Stanley says that, as one not bred at

Westminster, he had forborne to enter into the history of the school. This is a serious loss, and he merely refers to the "Census Alumnorum Westmonasteriensium," and "Lusus Alteri Westmonasterienses," and to articles in *Blackwood's Magazine* for July and September, 1866. He expressly says, however, that "to Elizabeth, as to a second foundress, is ascribed the independent formation of the chapter with the school under the new title, which it has borne ever since, of the 'Collegiate Church of St. Peter, Westminster.'" Henceforth the institution became, strictly speaking, a great academical as well as an ecclesiastical body. The old dormitory of the monks was divided into two compartments, each destined to serve a distinct collegiate purpose. "The smaller portion was devoted to the library," as Dean Stanley states, "and the larger part to the schoolroom, which, though rebuilt almost from the floor in modern times, still covers the same space. . . . . The monastic granary which, under Dean Benson, had still been retained for the corn of the chapter, now became, and continued for nearly two hundred years, the college dormitory."

The following is an extract from "the Acts of the Dean and Chapter," 1599, May 7:—"It is decreed by Mr. Dean and the Prebendaries present, that in respect that the now school-house is too low, and too little to receive the number of scholars, that the old dorter (dormitory) of late years being to be made a larger school, shall be with all convenient speed turned to this good use for the benefit of the scholars, by such charitable contributions as shall be gathered for the finishing thereof."

The College Hall, which serves as a refectory for the Queen's Scholars, was originally the refectory of the abbot's house, and dates from the reign of Edward III. From the archives of the church it appears that it was built by Nicholas Littlington, the same to whom the Jerusalem Chamber and a large part of the Deanery are ascribed. It is a very handsome Gothic building, adjoining the Jerusalem Chamber, and has still the ancient louvre of five centuries ago. On each side are two long and massive tables of chestnut-wood, said to have been taken from the wreck of one of the vessels belonging to the Spanish Armada. In the "election" week there is a dinner in this hall, given by the governing body to the electors, the masters of the school, and as many old "Westminsters" as the hall will hold, on which occasion Latin epigrams are recited by the "King's Scholars."

The schoolroom is a spacious but gloomy apartment, extending behind the lower end of the eastern cloister, and above some of the most ancient parts of the Abbey, the chief of which is the Pyx Chamber. It was originally the dormitory of the monks, and it still retains much of its original character. It has a very handsome Gothic roof of wood, but the windows are modern insertions. The roof is secured by iron bars, the centre one of which formerly divided the upper from the lower school. Of this bar, however, we shall have more to say presently. Its walls on every side bear, carved in stone, the names of "Old Westminsters," with the dates of their leaving. The schoolroom is thus described by a writer in the *Gentleman's Magazine*, in the year 1739:—

"Fast by, an old but noble fabric stands,
No vulgar work, but raised by princely hands;
Which, grateful to Eliza's memory, pays,
In living monuments, an endless praise.
High, placed above, two royal lions stand,
The certain sign of courage and command.
If to the right you then your steps pursue,
An honour'd room employs and charms your view:
There Busby's awful picture decks the place,
Shining where once he shone a living grace.
Beneath the frame, in decent order placed,
The walls by various authors' works are graced.
Fixed to the roof, some curious laurels show
What they obtained who wrote the sheets below.
Fixed to support the roof above, to brave,
To stem the tide of Time's tempestuous wave,
Nine stately beams their spacious arches show,
And add a lustre to the school below."

The writer, who appears to have been a pupil at Westminster in the mastership of Dr. Freind, goes on to describe as follows the different classes of the school:—

"Ranged into seven distinct, the classes lie,
Which with the Pleiades in lustre vie.
Next to the door the first and least appears,
Designed for seeds of youth and tender years;
The second next your willing notice claims,
Her members more extensive, more her aims.
Thence a step nearer to Parnassus' height,
Look 'cross the school, the third employs your sight;
There Martial sings, there Justin's works appear,
And banish'd Ovid finds protection there.
From Ovid's tales transferr'd, the fourth pursues
Books more sublimely penn'd, more noble views:
Here Virgil shines; here youth is taught to speak
In different accents of the hoarser Greek.
Fifth: these more skill'd and deeper read in Greek,
From various books can various beauties seek.
The sixth, in every learned classic skill'd,
With nobler thoughts and brighter notions fill'd,
From day to day with learned youth supplies
And honours both the Universities.
Near these the *Shell's* * high concave walls appear,
Where Freind in state sits pleasingly severe:
Him as our ruler and our king we own;
His rod his sceptre, and his chair his throne."

* A sort of apse in which the schoolroom terminated. The class sitting there was named the "shell" form.

Many old customs have been, and still are, kept up in the school. For instance, Latin prayers, including the "Pater Noster" and the "Gratia Domini Nostri," are still said at the beginning and end of school, both in the morning and afternoon. The prayers are said by the captain of the school at his first appointment, afterwards by the three monitors in turn, each taking a week. The monitor of the week kneels in the centre of the school, with his face turned to the east; the head master and the other masters kneeling in file behind him. There can be little doubt that these customs were derived, and have been handed down unchanged, from the old days before the Reformation.

The dormitory, already mentioned, is a lofty but dreary-looking room, first erected for the King's Scholars by the Earl of Burlington, at the time when the celebrated Bishop Atterbury was Dean of Westminster. A thousand pounds had been left for this purpose by Sir Edward Hannes, one of the physicians in ordinary to Queen Anne, who had received his education at this school. But this legacy was not sufficient to meet the estimated expense, and the dormitory, in consequence, remained unexecuted until Atterbury revived the project, and procured a memorial to be presented by the Chapter to George I., running thus: "The Bishop of Rochester, Dean of Westminster, and the Chapter of that church, humbly represent to your Majesty, that Queen Elizabeth, of glorious memory, founded the college of Westminster, which has in all times since been highly favoured

THE SCHOOLROOM IN 1846. (*See page* 467.)

by your Majesty's royal ancestors, and has bred up great numbers of men, useful both in Church and State; among whom are several who have the honour to serve your Majesty in high stations: that the dormitory of the said college is in so ruinous a condition that it must of necessity be Majesty's royal example. The said Bishop and Chapter therefore humbly hope that your Majesty will, as an encouragement to learning, be pleased to bestow your royal bounty on this occasion in such measure as to your Majesty's high wisdom shall seem proper."

THE OLD DORMITORY IN 1840. (*See page* 468.)

forthwith rebuilt, the expenses of which building (besides other charges that may thereby be occasioned) will, according to the plan now humbly presented to your Majesty, amount to upwards of £5,000. As a foundation for raising this sum, a legacy has been left by one who was a member of this college; and there is good reason to believe that divers persons of quality, who owe their education to this place, may be disposed to favour this design, if they shall be incited by your

The king was pleased to respond to this memorial by the gift of £1,000 towards the desired object; the Prince of Wales contributed £500; the Parliament voted £1,200, and William Maurice, Esq., gave £500. The new building was at length commenced, on the west side of the college gardens, from the design of Boyle, Earl of Burlington, who personally superintended the works, but it was not erected until after a long Chancery suit as to the site, which came to an end in 1723. It is in a portion of this building, fitted up for the occasion as a theatre, that the Latin plays are annually represented by the King's Scholars.

We find that in nearly all the large schools which grew up under the shadow of the mediæval Church, it was customary at Christmas to perform plays of one kind or another, partly illustrative of the mysteries of the Christian religion, including "miracle plays" from the Bible, and legends of the early saints, and partly others of a purely secular and classical kind. At Westminster School it is a custom which dates from the foundation of the school itself, and is, indeed, prescribed by the royal foundress in the statutes. Before Christmas, yearly, three nights are set apart for the performance of a play from Terence or Plautus, the youthful actors being dressed up in the conventional costume of Athenian or Roman citizens, slaves, &c., and some sustaining the female parts. There are added to the performance a prologue and epilogue, also in Latin; the former recounting the events of interest to the school during the past twelve months, the latter satirising almost all the political and social subjects of the day. One end of the old dormitory is temporarily converted into a stage, and some admirable scenery, suited to the rather limited list of plays which are performed by the boys, is brought into use. The former scenery, contrived under Garrick's directions, was the gift of a master of the school, Dr. Markham, afterwards Archbishop of York, and of a late Dean of Westminster, Dr. Vincent. The present scenery was designed for Westminster School by the late eminent artist and architect, Mr. C. R. Cockerell, R.A. In 1873 the theatrical apparatus and scenery was repaired, and a new stage and auditorium added, by subscription among "Old Westminsters," at the cost of nearly £500. Large crowds of visitors flock to see the "Westminster Play," a spacious side box being reserved for the ladies.

Those who have followed the course of the Westminster Plays for something like half a century may have observed how curiously they reflect the change that has taken place in the taste and feelings of the general public. When correctness of costume was but little regarded on the English stage, and in farces supposed to represent the manners of (say) 1825, elderly gentlemen were attired after the fashion of Hogarth's pictures. The stage here was the scene of still more violent incongruities—Simo and Chremes, responsible Attic citizens, appeared in wigs and long waistcoats, as elders of the time of George II.; Davus was a smart footman, with red plush breeches and gold lace; Pamphilus exulted in his satin breeches and crescent-shaped opera hat; while Charinus, more modest, was content with a frock-coat and trousers. When the tunic and the chlamys took the place of habiliments that were inconsistent not only with the period represented by the fable, but likewise with each other, the reform of the Westminster Play might almost have been called a revolution.

However, for many years after they had put on the proper clothes, the Athenians, old and young, of St. Peter's, continued to disport themselves before the shabbiest of scenes, while their intervals of repose were marked by the shabbiest of drop-curtains, and two unsightly busts, intended for Terence and Plautus, seemed grimly to superintend the entertainment.

It has been more than once proposed to abolish the Westminster Play; but the suggestion has always called forth so much opposition that the reformers on this point have been completely overpowered by the conservative element, which is strong both in old and in present "Westminsters."

We may add here that it was as a Westminster school-boy, under Dr. Busby, that Barton Booth, the distinguished actor and contemporary of Betterton, earned his first laurels by his acting in a Latin play at this school. About to proceed to the University, he absconded and joined the company of Mr. Ashbury, the manager of the Dublin Theatre.

An almost complete collection of the Prologues and Epilogues of the plays from 1704 to 1868 has been printed in two volumes under the title of "Lusus Westmonasterienses," to which the editor has prefixed what may be called a literary history of such performances, not only at Westminster but at Oxford and Cambridge, and in our Inns of Court. Along with these are printed a variety of Latin, Greek, and English verses and epigrams recited from time to time in the "Declamations" at the annual Whitsuntide elections. The Prologues, as a series, are chiefly interesting to "Old Westminsters," since they dwell chiefly on the leading events connected with the life of the school and the minster to which it is an adjunct. The Epilogues, on the other hand, are of wider and more general interest; being for the most part mirrors of the manners and customs of the times, and touching in a humorous way on such subjects as divorces, duels, balloons, dress, Gretna Green unions, the Marriage Act passed in the year 1753, quack auctions, public amusements, civic banquets, doctors, lottery jobbers, railway frauds, Parliamentary debates, and indeed almost every conceivable subject. From these volumes we learn one or two curious facts about the Play; such as that in 1745 it was omitted on account of the panic caused by the Scottish Rebellion, and in 1782 on account of the death of Prince Alfred; and that it was Dr. Williamson who, in the second year of Her Majesty's reign, introduced the youthful actors upon the stage in Greek and Roman dresses instead of in the comparatively modern costume of the Georgian era. In 1726 the Prologue bewails the ruinous state of the old dormitory, whilst those of other years celebrate the accession of George III.; the birth of his eldest son, afterwards George IV.; the deaths of Harley, Earl of Oxford, and of the Dukes of Cumberland and Newcastle; the burning of the first Opera House; and the death of Nelson.

A school oration, probably a prologue or epilogue to one of the Plays, was pirated in 1716 by the notorious Edmund Curll, and printed by him with all sorts of blunders in the Latin. The boys accordingly invited him to the school to receive a corrected copy, but instead of giving it to him they treacherously whipped him and then put him under the pump.

We have said that the dormitory is made to serve as a theatre every Christmas for the Westminster Play; and half a century ago it was a dreary, comfortless chamber, not cut up, as now, into small and comfortable cubicles. It is said that the Prince of Wales, when Prince Regent, soon after the battle of Waterloo, attended "the Play" one evening, and was shown by the Marquis of Anglesey the simple and homely beds in the dormitory. "You don't mean to tell me," was his remark, "that Henry Paget ever slept in such a bed as that!" As the marquis, when plain Henry Paget, was not one of the King's Scholars, he did not actually sleep in the dormitory, but in one of the boarding-houses; but his brother Arthur did; and there is no reason to believe that at that date there was much difference between the college and the private boarding-houses in respect of creature comforts. The Duke of Wellington, with his known love of simplicity, would have thought those beds a good nursery for soldiers not of the "feather-bed" stamp.

Under the dormitory are sitting-rooms and studies for the boys; and a house attached serves as a sanatorium for invalids, superintended by a resident matron. Although built only in the early part of the last century, the building has a much more venerable aspect. The "College Gardens," which the dormitory now faces, were originally the Infirmary Garden of the Monastery. They then became the Garden of the Collegiate Body, of which the Dean is the head, and the "College" boys were those who, being in the school, were also of the foundation. It was never used as a playground by the scholars.

As late as the seventeenth century the College Garden contained fruit-trees and an orchard, which was carefully tended. The fruit-trees were ordered to be cut down and superseded by lime-trees in 1708.

In 1751, some persons having improperly got possession of keys admitting into the Garden of the Abbey or College Garden, it was ordered by an "Act of the Dean and Chapter," under date November 9, "that the lock thereof be altered, and that no key be allowed but to the gardener only, excepting that the Dean may lend his key to his Excellency, Count Zinzendorf, who lives over against the said gate, whilst his mansion-house at Chelsea is preparing for him, and that for his excellency's private use only."

The old dormitory was a Gothic building with a high-pitched roof, and a row of pointed double-lancet windows; the entrance being under a lofty gateway, also of the pointed style. Good prints of the old and new dormitories, showing the costume of the scholars in the middle of the eighteenth century, will be found prefixed to the "Alumni Westmonasterienses," published in 1852. The first of these dormitories, as we learn from the preface to the book, was originally built as a granary for the monks. The Earl of Burlington presented the model, and condescended to survey the building, thus realising the words of Pope, "Who builds like Boyle?" The spare vaults situated beneath the old dormitory were let for wine-cellars.

The accommodation provided for the resident Queen's Scholars, as we learn from the report of the Public Schools Commission, used to be very imperfect. No breakfast was provided, and they, therefore, had recourse for that meal to the boarding-house to which they had belonged formerly. The one large dormitory was their sitting-room by day and their sleeping-room by night. Under the new arrangements, this monastic room is now divided into forty sleeping places, ranged on either side of a central passage, and closed in by curtains and wooden partitions. Some sitting-rooms and private studies were at the same time made below. The Queen's Scholars now not only dine, but breakfast and sup in the College Hall.

At present the Governing Body defrays the

main cost of the maintenance and tuition of the resident Queen's Scholars, each of whom, however, has to pay £30 a year towards maintenance. The total school expenses of a boarder may be set down at £100 a year.

We learn from Bentley's "Correspondence" that, in the earlier days of his mastership of Trinity College, Cambridge, "the Westminster scholars got the major part of the fellowships" in that distinguished seat of learning, but he complains that subsequently the school did not quite maintain its character.

Evelyn has the following entry in his "Diary," under date 1661, May 13th:—"I heard and saw such exercises at the election of scholars at Westminster Schools to be sent to the University, in Latin and Greek, Hebrew and Arabic, in themes and extempry verses, as wonderfully astonished me in such youths, with such readiness and wit, some of whom not above twelve or thirteen years of age. Pity it is that what they attaine here so ripely, they either not retain or do not improve more considerably when they come to be men, though many of them do; and no less is to be blamed their odd pronouncing of Latin, so that none were able to understand or endure it. The examinants or 'Posers' were Dr. Duport, Greek Professor at Cambridge; Dr. Fell, Deane of Christ Church, Oxon; Dr. Pierson, Dr. Allestree, Deane of Westminster, and any that would." It is much to be regretted that our insular mode of pronouncing Latin, so censured by Evelyn, is still kept up not only at Westminster, but at all the rest of our chief public schools.

"Hereupon," writes Pope to the Earl of Burlington, in 1714, "I inquired of his son. The lad," says he, "has fine parts. . . . I spare for nothing in his education at Westminster. Pray, don't you think Westminster to be the best school in England? Most of the late Ministry came out of it, so did many of this Ministry."

A good story is told, illustrating the rivalry which has existed for three centuries between Westminster and Eton Schools. It is said that the Etonians on one occasion sent the Westminster boys a hexameter verse composed of only two words, challenging them to produce a pentameter also in two words so as to complete the sense. The Eton line ran thus:—

"Conturbabantur Constantinopolitani."

The Westminster boys replied to the challenge "by return of post:"—

"Innumerabilibus sollicitudinibus."

As the Eton line contains an obvious false quantity, the Westminster boys, who contrived to steer clear of mistakes, may be allowed to have had the best of it.

In the last century the education here, as at most of our public schools, was almost wholly confined to the dead languages. Mrs. Piozzi, in her "Johnsoniana," quotes the words of Dr. Johnson on this subject. "A boy should never be sent to Eton or Westminster before he is twelve years old at the least; for if in the years of his babyhood he escapes that general and transcendent knowledge without which life is perpetually put to a stand, he will never get it at a public school, where, if he does not learn Latin and Greek, he learns nothing."

In the last century, as we learn by constant allusions in Horace Walpole's letters, most of the young nobility who were not sent to Eton, were brought up at Westminster; and in the last generation Westminster was the school of such great families as the Russells, Petties, Dundases, and Pagets. In this respect, however, during the last half century it has been entirely superseded by Harrow; and the fact that it is situated in the heart of the metropolis has operated to its disadvantage so far as the accession of boarders or "oppidans" is concerned. Whilst the Charterhouse has doubled and even trebled its numbers by effecting a removal into the country, Westminster is confined by Act of Parliament to the ancient spot which has been the home of the school for eight centuries, and cannot exchange it for "fresh woods and pastures new." The result is, as might have been expected, that its numbers remain, and must remain, at a low ebb—comparatively low, that is, with reference to other large public schools.

The new arrangements under the Public Schools' Act have not made any alteration in the number of the resident "Queen's Scholars": they are still forty; they are, however, elected wholly instead of partly by merit; their merit being ascertained by an examination on paper and *viva voce*, combined with a system of "challenges," of which we have spoken above. In order to be elected "into college," a boy must be under fourteen years of age, unless he has previously attended the school as an oppidan, when the limit is raised to fifteen. To compete for the university scholarships, &c., for which, as we have seen, both Queen's Scholars and oppidans are eligible, it is necessary that the boys should have been at least three years in the school.

Until the college was thrown open to competition, the numbers of the school stood usually at about one hundred and fifty, but since that time they have largely increased, both as respects day scholars and boarders. There are several boarding-houses kept by various masters, and the total of the school now averages, as we have said, about 250 boys—a very satisfactory number, in all the circumstances.

The monitorial system and its co-relative, the "fagging" system, still prevail in the school, and are found to work satisfactorily, as the limits within which "fagging" is allowed are strictly defined; and in case of any abuse of power by the senior boys there is a right of appeal to the head-master open to the aggrieved party. It seems to be agreed on all hands that this twofold practice is an essential part of the system of an English public school, and it certainly bears the very strictest analogy to the facts of after-life, whatever be the calling or profession that is chosen on reaching manhood.

CHAPTER LVI.

WESTMINSTER SCHOOL (*continued*).

"At Westminster, where little poets strive
To set a distich upon six and five,
Where discipline helps opening buds of sense,
And makes his pupils proud with silver pence,
I was a poet too."—*Cowper.*

Noted Scholars and Eminent Masters—Cowper and the "Silver Pence" for the Best Writers of Latin Verse—"Glorious" John Dryden—Cowley—Hackluyt, the Divine and Geographer—Sir Francis Burdett's Expulsion from School—Warren Hastings, and the Cup given to the King's Scholars—Dr. Busby—A "Skit" on the School—The *Trifler*—Collection of Ancient and Modern Coins—The "Elizabethan" Club—Special Privileges enjoyed by the King's Scholars—Throwing the Pancake on Shrove Tuesday—A Generous Return for a Schoolfellow's Kindness—Athletic Sports—Aquatic Contests—Strange Origin of School Slang—Dean's Yard—"Mother Beakley's"—The Noble Art of Self-defence—Window-gardening—Discovery of Ancient Architectural Remains—Distinguished Residents in Dean's Yard—Queen Anne's Bounty—Henry Purcell.

Among the most eminent of "Old Westminsters" are reckoned the antiquary, William Camden; the Latin verse writer, Vincent (or, as he was termed by his contemporaries, Vinny) Bourne, the best of modern Latin poets except Milton; and Dr. Busby—all three of whom were masters as well.

Here, too, was educated Dr. Hinchcliffe, afterwards head-master of the school, and eventually Bishop of Peterborough. Bishop Cary and Dean Liddell were likewise formerly head-masters here.

Westminster can show a goodly list of scholars against its rival public schools, as will be seen when we mention the names of Cowley, Dryden, George Herbert, William Cartwright, Nathaniel Lee, Prior, Cowley, Rowe, Giles Fletcher, Jasper Mayne, Churchill, Dyer, Cowper, Southey, and Richard Cumberland, in the world of letters; Sir Harry Vane; the third Marquis of Lansdowne, Sir James Graham, the first Lord Colchester, and Earl Russell, among statesmen; Sir Christopher Wren; the eloquent and witty preacher, Dr. South; Bishop Atterbury; the celebrated divine and geographer, Hackluyt; the historians Gibbon, Camden, and Froude; the elder Colman; John Locke, the philosopher; Bunbury, whose prints of the early part of George III.'s reign are now so much in demand; John Horne Tooke; Brown Willis, the antiquary; Montagu, Earl of Halifax; Pulteney, Earl of Bath; Murray, Earl of Mansfield; Chief Justice Eardley Wilmot; Archdeacon Nares; Sir George Rose, the wit; and last not least, the first Governor-General of India, Warren Hastings. To come to more recent times, the first Lord Combermere and the first Marquis of Anglesey—both Field-Marshals in the army—were brought up at Westminster School: so also were the second Marquis of Westminster, Dr. Longley, Archbishop of Canterbury, Dr. T. V. Short, Bishop of St. Asaph, and Dr. G. E. L. Cotton, some time Master of Marlborough College, and afterwards Bishop of Calcutta.

It is well known that Ben Jonson was a scholar here; but it is not equally known that he was sent there by the friendship of Camden, at that time second master or usher. "The obligation," as Mr. Robert Bell tells us in his biography of the poet, "was never forgotten by Jonson, who retained to the end of his life the most affectionate regard for his early benefactor and instructor." He therefore thus apostrophises him:—

"Camden! most reverend head, to whom I owe
All that I am in arts, all that I know."

Here Ben Jonson "wrote all his verses," says the author of "Biographiana," first in prose, as his master taught him to do; saying that verses stood by sense without either colours or accent"

—meaning doubtless that the goodness of verses must be judged by their sense and meaning, not by their sound.

As will be seen by the names mentioned above, Westminster School has been particularly rich in poets. Cowper was a pupil here in the same boarding-house, as he informs us, with Richard Cumberland the author. In explanation of the motto from Cowper which heads this chapter, it should be said that, in the school-days of that poet, it was customary to receive a silver groat for a good exercise of Latin verses. An extraordinarily good set of verses sometimes had the further honour of being sent round the school to be read. "The other day," writes Cowper, "I sent my imagination upon a trip thirty years behind me. She was very obedient, and at last set me down on the sixth form at Westminster. Accordingly I was a schoolboy in high favour with the master, received a silver groat for my exercise, and had the pleasure of seeing it sent from form to form for the admiration of all who were able to understand it." Southey, who entered Westminster a little later, tells us that this latter custom was no longer observed in his day, but that "sweet remuneration was still dispensed in silver pence," and that his own "first literary profits were thus obtained"—namely, by his English verse exercises. We learn, however, that the custom is still retained—though only once a year—of reciting verses composed by the boys on themes previously chosen by the head-master, and announced to the school. The composers of the best lines on these occasions are still rewarded with silver pennies or silver three-penny pieces, according to their merit.

DR. BUSBY. (*See page* 476.)

"Glorious" John Dryden was admitted a King's

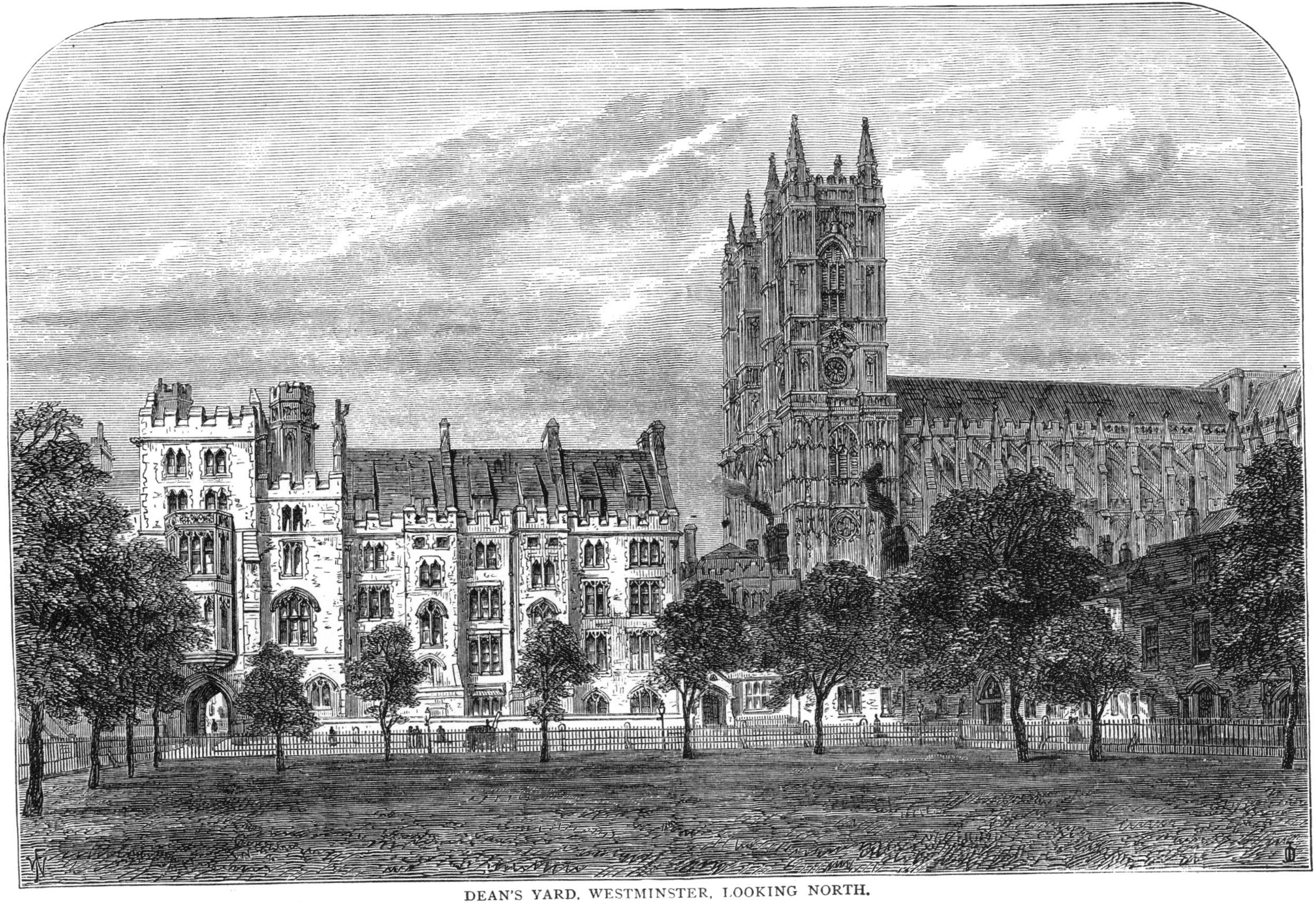

DEAN'S YARD, WESTMINSTER, LOOKING NORTH.

Scholar under the head-mastership of Dr. Busby, though the exact dates of his entry and of his leaving school are not known. The wooden form with his name cut upon it still remains in the school-room. Sir Walter Scott, in his "Life of Dryden," tells us that whilst a boy at school he translated the third Satire of Persius into English verse, and that many similar exercises composed by him before he was seventeen were in the hands of Dr. Busby, whom he always treated with great and heartfelt respect, addressing him in his letters, long after he ceased to be his pupil, as "honoured sir." Another of his poetical productions here was an elegy on the death of Henry Lord Hastings, one of his schoolfellows, which was printed in the "Lacrymæ Musarum."

Cowley's memory is connected with Westminster in quite another way; for he was precocious enough to publish a volume of poems whilst a boy at the school.

Hackluyt, the divine and geographer, expressly tells us in the dedication of his great work to Walsingham how much he owed to his early training at Westminster. He tells us that his love of maritime discovery and the researches of naval science first displayed itself when he was a Queen's Scholar in "that fruitfull nurserie," during his occasional visits to a cousin in the Middle Temple, where he delighted to pore over and to ask questions respecting the maps and books of geographical science which were scattered about his kinsman's chamber. His taste was happily fostered at school by a thoughtful and sympathetic master, and at Oxford he was able to follow up the subject by more extended study, reading over by degrees "whatsoever printed or written discoveries and voyages he found extant either in Greeke, Latine, Italian, Spanish, Portugall, French, or Englishe languages." He died in 1616, aged sixty-three, and was buried in the Abbey.

We may also name among the scholars here, Drs. Fell and Cyril Jackson, both Deans of Christ Church; Philip Henry, the Nonconformist; and the eccentric Edward Wortley Montagu. Of Montagu the story is told that he ran away from the school, and served for more than a year as apprentice to a fisherman at Blackwall; then went back to Westminster, but ran away again, this time effecting his escape to Oporto. He was in after life M.P. for Huntingdonshire and for Bossiney; he died in 1776.

Sir Francis Burdett, the future popular member for the City of Westminster, was educated at Westminster School, and used to tell in after life how he too had run away from it in company with another youngster of his own age; it is, however, on record that he was sent away for taking part in a rebellion against the head-master, Dr. Smith. Such is the goodly roll of those poets, theologians, scholars, warriors and statesmen who, when young, were here first qualified to serve God and their country, in Church and in State.

We have mentioned above, amongst the more celebrated scholars educated here, the name of Warren Hastings, the able, energetic, and successful Governor-General of India, whose impeachment before the House of Commons in Westminster Hall occupied seven years, and ended in a virtual acquittal. He went into college as head of his election in 1746. At Westminster he became a great friend of the future Lord Mansfield, whose friendship lasted through life. On leaving Westminster he was destined at first for Oxford; but the offer of a writership in Bengal coming at the moment turned his ambition in another channel, and his splendid Indian career was the result. If any of our readers desire to form a general opinion on the vexed question of Warren Hastings' conduct in India, they had better read Lord Thurlow's summing up of the evidence brought forward against him: it will be found in the Lords' Debates for February, March, and April, 1795.

It may not be out of place here to allude to the famous "Warren Hastings' Cup," which was given to the King's Scholars. It bears the following inscription:—"*Alumnis Regiis Scholæ Westmin. ipsi plerique Alumni d. d. d.* Warren Hastings, Elijah Impey, George Templer," &c., twenty-two names in all. During the dinners given in College Hall in election week, and on other great occasions, this cup, it is perhaps needless to say, is brought into use.

Of the celebrated Dr. Busby, head-master here in the reigns of Charles II. and James II., many anecdotes are told. Amongst others it is said that when the king one day came to see the school, he persisted in keeping his hat on his head in the royal presence. One of the lords or gentlemen in waiting remonstrated with him on this breach of courtly etiquette; but the worthy doctor replied that he had done it on purpose, for "it would never do for his boys to think that there was anybody superior to himself." Dr. Busby used to boast that out of the then bishops sixteen had been educated by him. Strange to say, Dr. Busby enjoyed the reputation of being fonder of the cane than any previous head-master, and we find a certain gentleman saying, "Dr. Busby was a great man! he whipped my grandfather, a very great man! I should have gone to him myself, if

I had not been a blockhead; a very great man!" One would almost like to inquire whether the use of the cane and the making of bishops have elsewhere gone hand in hand. "A wonderful fruit-bearing rod was that of Busby's," sarcastically observes Thackeray, as he recounts the public appointments which in the good old days of Queen Anne were bestowed on that reverend doctor's distinguished pupils. Dr. Busby, whose name and wig have both passed into proverbs, died in 1695, and was buried in the Abbey.

The Rev. Mr. Mason, in one of his letters to Horace Walpole, tells an anecdote which shows to how great an extent Westminster School was regarded during the last century as a school for dignitaries of the Church. He says, "There was a bishop—I think it was Sprat—who thanked God that he became a bishop, though he was *not* educated at Westminster." He adds, "I, on the contrary, would not have been educated there for the best pair of lawn sleeves in the kingdom. But *de gustibus non disputandum*."

The list of boys admitted into the College, as far as is known, goes no further back than 1762.

In the *Craftman*, published in 1727, is the following advertisement, put in without note or comment, but clearly a "skit" on the school:—"This is to give notice to all noblemen with large families and small estates, decay'd gentlemen, gamesters and others, that in the great school in Westminster boys are thoroughly instructed in all parts of useful learning. The said school is furnish'd with a master and one usher, who does all the business himself, and keeps his scholars in such order that the master never attends till upon some great occasion. This school is of a more excellent foundation than any that are yet known; for the scholars, instead of paying for their learning, are rewarded by every lesson that the usher gives them, provided they are perfect in it, and have it at their fingers' ends. N.B. This is no free school."

Like many public schools of the present day, Westminster School would seem formerly to have had a publication of its own, for we find that the *Trifler*, a new "periodical miscellany by Timothy Touchstone, of St. Peter's College, Westminster," was published by Robinson, of Paternoster Row, in 1788. It seems to have been short-lived, as it was completed in twenty-five parts, forming a single volume.

Thanks to the liberality of Sir David Dundas and Mr. C. W. Williams-Wynn, the college is in possession of a fine collection of ancient and modern coins, which has been further increased by purchases from the duplicates of the British Museum, and elsewhere.

That Westminster as a school is proud of its royal foundress may be inferred from the fact that a club of old Westminster men was established in the year 1863, called the "Elizabethan," and that the same name is given to a college magazine (not unlike the *Etonian* and the *Carthusian* of a former generation) edited by the scholars themselves. The object of the Elizabethan Club is to keep up the *religio loci* in every way, and maintain the *esprit de corps* by celebrating an annual Westminster dinner, by encouraging the college athletic sports, and other games, rowing, cricket, racquets, football, &c., and by collecting portraits, biographies, and other memorials of former scholars of the school.

In 1870, the Crimean Memorial in the Broad Sanctuary having become somewhat dilapidated, a sum of £30 towards its repair was voted by the Elizabethan Club.

The boys of St. Peter's College have enjoyed one or two special privileges on account of their close connection with the Abbey and Palace of Westminster, and of being a royal foundation. For instance, they have had the right of being present in the Speaker's Gallery at the debates in the House of Commons—a privilege, as we know, highly valued by such men as Lord John Russell and Sir James Graham—and also that of having seats in the Abbey at the coronation of the sovereign. Thus in an elaborate "Account of the Ceremonies observed in the Coronation of King James II. and his Consort," published in 1760, we find it mentioned that, "when the Queen entered the choir, the King's Scholars of Westminster School, in number forty, all in surplices, being placed in a gallery adjoining to the great organ, entertained her Majesty with this short prayer or salutation, 'Vivat Regina' (naming her Majesty's name); which they continued to sing until his Majesty entered the choir, whom they entertained in like manner with this prayer or salutation, 'Vivat Rex' (naming his Majesty's name); which they continued to sing until his Majesty ascended the throne."

We have alluded in the previous chapter to the bar of iron which still divides the "upper" from the "lower" school. Over this bar, on Shrove Tuesday, the ceremony of "throwing the pancake" takes place. This curious custom is a very old one, but we have no account of its origin; and Brand mentions a similar custom as prevailing at Eton. On that day shortly before nine o'clock (if we may trust the statement of a writer in the *Queen* newspaper), the college cook, attired in the insignia of his office, white cap and apron, preceded by one of the vergers of the Abbey, enters the school-room with due form, bearing in a frying-pan a very solid pancake, which, if he succeeds in pitching it over the bar, is scrambled for by the whole school assembled on the other side, the boy who catches it receiving a guinea from the Dean. However successful the cook may be in accomplishing his part of the performance, it may easily be inferred that it is only on rare occasions that the pancake is fairly caught and conveyed off whole and entire. On one occasion we learn that the cook failed to send the fritter over the bar, and that it was caught on the wrong side. Whether the Dean felt bound to pay to the cook his *honorarium* of a guinea in consequence of this misfortune, we know not. The boy who caught it, we are further informed, "hid it in his clothes, as the Spartan boy hid the fox, and courageously retained it in spite of the fierce assaults of which he was the object. He conveyed it at last to the Deanery, where the Dean, no doubt, was sitting in full canonicals and in breathless anxiety to await the issue of the cook's performance. Mr. H—— was, however, refused payment of the guinea, on the plea that the cook had not thrown the pancake over the bar, and the affair was therefore null and void. Quick as had been Mr. H——'s movements, it would seem that those of the master were not less so, for that gentleman, with a laudable regard for the economical distribution of the Abbey funds, had despatched a trusty messenger intimating that, in consequence of the cook's misfortune, the guinea might be saved."

The bar above mentioned originally had attached to it a curtain whereby "hangs a tale," related in the *Spectator*, No. 313. A boy is said to have saved his schoolfellow from Dr. Busby for having torn the curtain, by taking the blame upon himself. This boy, William Wake (the father of Archbishop Wake), was afterwards a colonel in the service of the King during the Civil War, and was a great sufferer in the royal cause. He joined in Penruddock's rebellion in 1665, and during his trial at Exeter was recognised by the commissioner who tried him as his old schoolfellow who had rendered the above service to him. Upon this the commissioner started off for London, and by his influence with the Protector succeeded in obtaining a pardon for his friend. The name of this man, who made so generous a return for his schoolfellow's kindness, is not known, but he is supposed to have been Serjeant Glynne, who took the most active part in the trial, and passed sentence on the prisoners.

Although situated in the metropolis, the Westminster School affords every opportunity for athletic sports. The playground for the younger boys is in Dean's Yard; the older boys disport themselves in the large enclosure in Vincent Square, consisting of some ten acres, originally an open common forming part of what were called "Tothill Fields." A favourite Westminster amusement has always been boating, which is still continued with no lack of zest on the upper reaches of the stream, where there is less danger than in the more crowded parts of the royal river, where barges and penny steamboats have to be reckoned with.

There was formerly an annual eight-oared match with Eton, which was Westminster's only rival on the water—no other of the public schools having the advantage of a river within reach. This match used to be looked forward to with the most intense interest and excitement during the whole rowing season.

It would be, of course, beyond our province to tell of the honours once won by Westminster boys as oarsmen, or at football; but to their prowess in the stern art of war the column in the Broad Sanctuary, facing the entrance to Dean's Yard, amply testifies; and the late Duke of Wellington always affirmed that the best officers on his staff had been public school boys.

In former days, when the river at Millbank was pure, the Westminster boys were able to practise rowing at their will; and so great was their aquatic prowess that at Oxford about the year 1827 the "Old Westminsters" made seven out of a crew of eight in the Christ Church boat when that boat was at the head of the river. In 1829, 1831, 1836, 1837, 1842, 1843, 1845, 1846, 1847, 1860, 1861, 1862, and 1864, the school contested the palm of the river with the Etonians, and not without frequent success. No race has taken place since the last-named date, the embankment of the Thames having effectually crippled the Westminster boys by depriving them of their boating quarters. A full account of these races will be found by the curious in the "Annual Report of the Elizabethan Club for 1871."

From the same source of information we learn that in a long summer day in 1825 a crew of Westminster boys rowed an eight-oared boat from the Horseferry to Windsor Bridge and back, about eighty-six miles, completing the distance in about twenty hours, including a stoppage for luncheon at Eton. This is a feat of which any school might surely be proud!

As an instance of the strange origin of the slang which is handed down by tradition from generation to generation in our public schools, we remark that the work "sky," which at Westminster denotes a boy or *gamin* of the streets, is derived from the classic "Volsci." It appears that in the feuds between the "town and gown" at Westminster in olden days the latter—as the *gens togata*, we suppose—styled themselves "Romans," and their foes "Volscians." With this explanation the abbreviation of "Volsci" into "sci" or "sky" becomes quite intelligible.

It may be added that in one of the volumes of the "British Essayists" there is a very excellent ghost story connected with the school, but want of space forbids our giving it here.

So many of the buildings in Dean's Yard are, or have been at some former period, closely connected with Westminster School, that no apology is needed for speaking of that ancient enclosure in this present chapter.

The ordinary public entrance to Dean's Yard is under a Gothic archway, which opens into the Broad Sanctuary. This archway is in the centre of a lofty range of stone-built mansions, of modern construction, but erected in a mediæval style of architecture, from the designs of Sir G. Gilbert Scott, in keeping with the venerable Abbey close by. The Broad Sanctuary (the name of which commemorates the right of sanctuary, of which we shall have more to say in our next chapter) adjoins the Jerusalem Chamber on the west, and forms the north side of Dean's Yard. The alterations and transformations that have been effected in this locality in recent years have been so great that, as a writer in the *Builder* of December, 1874, says, "when passing into the north-west angle of Dean's Yard, one finds his ingenuity somewhat taxed in attempting to identify the old with the present site."

Here, in former years, the time-worn mouldings of a broad arch, filled in with rubble and brickwork, indicated a remnant of the Gate House Prison, memorable as having been that from which the gallant Sir Walter Raleigh was taken to execution. Beside this prison, and in its rear, ran a small narrow lane leading down to the Almonry, with a hatch and wicket-gate on the left leading into Dean's Yard. On the right were a stonemason's yard, and several small but neatly-built tenements, in which lodgings for gentlemen were advertised by the small card in the window; and these, with a public-house, terminated the length of Flood Street, and occupied the ground on which now stand the modern mediæval block of buildings above mentioned. "It was," says the writer already referred to, "a retired and quiet nook, the silence of which was only broken by the clink on the anvil of the neighbouring forge, and the noise of the mason's saw."

Immediately before us, in the angle made by Flood Street and Little Dean Street, stood the quaint old tart-shop so well known to "Westminsters" as "Mother Beakley's," and in describing this shop we cannot do better than quote the words of the *Builder* :—

"It was a little square tower of timber, lath, and plaster, pierced with several lights of leaden casements; but the lower, or shop window, was a curiosity of stout cross-beam and upright framing, the superficial contents of which more than equalled that of the yellow time-stained and discoloured glass which filled the spaces.

"Here the morning draught of milk was vended to the early scholar, for it was partly dairy, partly early breakfast-house, a place whence messages were taken, or to which they were brought, and parcels delivered. The descent to this primitive Temple of Diana was by several stone steps, for the pavement of the street was about level with the window-sill, and the paved kitchen presented a heterogeneous assemblage of caps, straps of books, hockey-sticks, rolls, cricket-balls, and milk-cans, the presiding genius over which attended to the minor domestic requirements of the Westminster boy.

"Many a generation must have passed away during the existence of this relic, which had probably formed some portion of the eleemosynary buildings, and must have been a familiar object with the earliest scholars of the foundation. The primitive club-room must have been known to every boy that filled a place in Westminster School, from the days of Dr. Busby to those of Dr. Goodenough.

"But as great a change has taken place in the habits and manners of the boys as in the locality, and the regulations in connection with them are now considerably improved.

"What Old Westminster boy but would remember the battles of the Scholars' Green?

"In the old days there existed but a post and rail fence around it, and a short cut across it was frequently a temptation to the pedestrian; but woe to the trespasser if the boys were there. At that time, when the *noble* art of self-defence was fashionable, the Westminster boy was proud of displaying his prowess on any such occasion. There were no police then, and the population of the town could not have been one-half if a third of the present. A street-keeper or Bow-Street officer generally contrived to keep out of the way, and so the fight went on uninterruptedly until satisfaction had been obtained.

"On some such occasions an obstinate 'coaly' has been known to exercise the active muscular powers of a King's Scholar for an hour or more. If Greek met not Greek, he nevertheless objected neither to coaly, baker, dustman, sweep, nor other if trespasser, without further fear of the disgrace save that of being worsted in the encounter.

"A considerable amount of Vandalism mingled itself with what then passed for manly independent spirit. Within a quarter of a mile of the spot there existed a cock-pit, at which matches were fought at frequent intervals; and many a 'green coat and tops,' whilst betting on the barbarous sport of the time, would remember the locality in associations of his boyhood with his college experiences of the immediate neighbourhood.

"In passing through the Dean's Yard toward the cloisters you seem shut away from the noise and bustle of the world, and the Scholars' playground, so frequently the scene of dispute, is surrounded by an iron railing. Latterly, in the summer of each year the specimens of the window gardening in the neighbourhood are exhibited here, and prizes are awarded to the successful competitors in this humble but painstaking horticulture.

ENTRANCE TO WESTMINSTER SCHOOL.

"The old watchman's box under the College wall has disappeared, and his lanthorn long since been extinguished. The street-keeper has been supplanted by the helmeted policeman, in whose belted tunic we trace no resemblance to the square and long-tailed skirts and chimney-pot hat of his antecedent brother in 1832.

"If many of our old relics have disappeared, much of coarseness and rudeness of manners has been swept away with them; and in the recollection of an 'old site' and comparing it with the present we feel that there has been a slow but vast change in the habits, feelings, and manners of the population; . . . but, as in the human constitution the too rapid or the too slow circulation will be found equally detrimental to health, we can only desire that the boon of progress may never disturb the good which lies at the bottom of many of our institutions, although much of the rubbish which has accumulated in and about them may with advantage be got rid of."

That Dean's Yard was the chief playground of the boys before they obtained their ten acres in Vincent Square, is evident from a "Declamation" by Dean Vincent, dated 1800, and published in the "Lusus Westmonasterienses." It shows, moreover, that at that time there were tall and umbrageous elms, under the shade of which the boys could play, within the Abbey precincts.

THIEVING LANE. *From a Drawing by J. T. Smith*, 1808. (*See page* 483.)

"Has ædes juxta nostris patet area ludis,
Ulmorumque vetus protegit umbra locum.
Hic pueri, quoties Musæ gravis interruptum,
Haud indignanti Pallade, pendet opus,
Se fundunt apibus similes, quas vere Calymne
Nascenti multo pascit odora thymo:
Hic ludunt, volucrum ritu."

"During the progress of certain improvements

carried out in 1815," says the Rev. Mackenzie Walcott, "some very ancient architectural remains were discovered in Dean's Yard, portions, according to long tradition, of an old granary converted into a dormitory; at right angles to it were the brewhouse and bakehouse." From the same authority we learn that Camden the antiquary lodged in the Gate House, by the Queen's Scholars' Chambers; and we are also told that he "kept a Welsh servant, to improve him in that language, for the understanding of our antiquities."

According to Alexander Nowell, the Archbishop of Canterbury, in the reign of Richard I., lived in a house opposite the school. Here, in 1673, was born Joseph Wilcocks, Dean of Westminster, and successively Bishop of Gloucester and Rochester, whom Pope Clement VIII. called "the blessed heretic." William Wake, Bishop of Lincoln (who was subsequently Primate), and Thomas Sprat, Bishop of Rochester, both resided in Dean's Yard in the early part of last century. Here, too, lived Thomas Carte, the historian; and also Samuel, the elder brother and master of Charles Wesley, when usher in Westminster School. The house of Samuel Wesley was his brother's resort when in town. When occupied by the Huttons, it was the scene of Mr. Wesley's memorable declaration of conversion and "becoming a Christian." "What?" cried a lady present, "Mr. Wesley, what a hypocrite you must be! we believed you to be a Christian years ago."

Charles Wesley, like his more celebrated brother John, was a very able preacher, and "possessed," say Messrs. Coke and Moore, in the Life of his brother, "a remarkable talent of uttering the most striking truths with simplicity and brevity." At an early period of his life he showed a talent and turn for writing verse; and most of the new hymns published by John Wesley in his various collections were of Charles's composition. "In these hymns," observes his brother, in one of his prefaces, "there is no doggerel, no botches, nothing put in to patch up the rhyme; no feeble expletives. Here are (allow me to say) both the purity, the strength, and the elegance of the English language, and at the same time the utmost simplicity and plainness, suited to every capacity."

Great alteration has been made in the appearance of Dean's Yard within the last half century, particularly on the north and west sides; and the central space, which, as above stated, formerly served as the playground for the boys, and is now known as "The Elms," has been covered with grass and railed round. We have given a view of it, looking towards the Abbey, on page 475. The old well, too, which was once remarkable for its spring of clear and never-failing water, was suddenly dried up in 1865 during the construction of the Metropolitan District Railway, which runs near the northern side of Westminster Abbey.

No. 3 in Dean's Yard is the office of Queen Anne's Bounty. This institution, which is not, perhaps, a charity in the ordinary sense of the word, was established by Act of Parliament in 1704, for the augmentation of poor livings. The name "Queen Anne's Bounty," therefore, is given to a fund appropriated to increase the incomes of the poorer clergy of England, created out of the first-fruits and tenths, which, before the Reformation, formed part of the Papal exactions from the clergy. "The first-fruits" are defined by a writer in "Chambers's Encyclopædia" as "the first whole year's profit of all spiritual preferments," and the "tenths" as "one-tenth of their annual profits, both chargeable according to the ancient declared value of the benefice; but the poorer livings are now exempted from the tax." Henry VIII., on abolishing the Papal authority, annexed both first-fruits and tenths to the Crown; but Queen Anne first formed them into a fund for the augmentation of poor livings. The Archbishops, Bishops, Deans, Speaker of the House of Commons, Master of the Rolls, Privy Councillors, lieutenants and *custodes rotulorum* of the counties, the Judges, Queen's Serjeants-at-law, Attorney and Solicitor-General, Advocate-General, Chancellors and Vice-Chancellors of the two Universities, Lord Mayor and Aldermen of London, and mayors of the several cities; and by supplemental charter, the officers of the Board of Green Cloth, the Queen's Counsel, and the four clerks of the Privy Council, were made a corporation by the name of "The Governors of the Bounty of Queen Anne, for the Augmentation of the Maintenance of the Poor Clergy," and to this corporation was granted the revenue of first-fruits and tenths. The income is appropriated from year to year in capital sums, either to increase, by the accruing interest, the income of the incumbents, to purchase land for their benefit, to erect or rebuild parsonage-houses, to restore chancels when the incumbent is liable, to provide outhouses, but not to build or rebuild churches. The governors have also had the distribution of eleven sums of £100,000 each, voted by Parliament from 1809 to 1820, to augment the incomes of the poorer clergy. They present annually an account of their receipts and expenditure to Parliament.

In a house, now demolished, between Dean's Yard and the Almonry, lived and died, in 1695, the greatest of English composers, Henry Purcell. Born, it is generally supposed, in the city of Westminster, young Purcell was remarkable for precocity of talent, and seconded the liberality of Nature by his zeal and diligence. While yet a boy chorister in the Abbey he composed more than one anthem; and in 1676, though only eighteen years of age, was chosen to succeed Dr. Gibbons as the organist of Westminster Abbey. In 1682 he became one of the organists of the Chapel Royal, and there, as well as at the Abbey, produced his numerous anthems. Purcell was also the composer of several secular pieces, among them being the duet and chorus, "To Arms!" and the air, "Britons, Strike Home!" both of which will ever retain a place in our national *répertoire*. Part of the back wall of Purcell's house is still standing. The bicentenary of this great composer was celebrated in 1895.

The Rev. Joseph Nightingale, in the tenth volume of the "Beauties of England and Wales," in discoursing on this interesting locality, in the beginning of the present century, says: "Dean's Yard is certainly an odd mixture of decayed grandeur, modern ruins, strong old flinty walls, and crumbling new bricks. Even the very trees nod in unison with falling structures and broken rails, and the earth, in many a rise and fall, shows some remote effects of Henry VIII.'s dissolution of monasteries. There is a silent monastic air in the small court from which is the entrance to the Jerusalem Chamber, now extremely different from its ancient state, having undergone various alterations from the Reformation to the present time."

CHAPTER LVII.

THE SANCTUARY AND THE ALMONRY.

"I pray you, let us satisfy our eyes
With the memorials and the things of fame
That do renown this city."—*Shakespeare*, "*Twelfth Night.*"

The Right of Sanctuary—Benefit of the Clergy—Prohibition of Sanctuary—The Westminster Sanctuary becomes a Sink of Iniquity—Distinguished Personages who have fled hither for Refuge—Birth of Edward V. in the Sanctuary—Restraint on the Privileges of Sanctuary—Death of Skelton, the Poet—Abolition of the Privileges of Sanctuary—Cities of Refuge among the Ancient Jews—The Sanctuary in the Middle Ages—Amusing Description of a Procession of Sanctuary Men—The Buildings of the Sanctuary described—The "Quaker" Tavern—The Almonry—St. Anne's Chapel—The Gate House Prison, and its Distinguished Inmates—The Bishop of London's Prison—Caxton, and the first Printing-press in England—List of Works issued from Caxton's Press—Caxton's Accuracy as a Printer—Caxton's House near the Almonry.

"Not far from the Abbey," writes Pennant, "stood the Sanctuary, the place of refuge absurdly indulgenced in old times to criminals of certain descriptions. The church belonging to it was in the form of a cross, and double; one (chapel) being built over the other. Such is the account that Dr. Stukely gives of it, for he remembered it standing, as we are told in the first volume of the 'Archæologia;' it was of vast strength, and only with much labour was it demolished. It is supposed to have been the work of the Confessor." The right of sanctuary, Stow tells us, extended not only to the church itself, but to the churchyard and close adjoining, and even to a considerable distance. "At the entrance of the Close," he writes, "there is a lane that leadeth towards the west, called Thieving Lane, for that thieves were led that way to the Gate House while the Sanctuary was in force." This lane is now absorbed in Prince's Street, between Storey's Gate and the Broad Sanctuary.

A short account of the privilege of sanctuary may be of interest here. It appears that under our Norman kings this privilege was of a twofold character, protecting both debtors and criminals from arrest—the one general, and belonging to all churches; the other peculiar and particular, granted to sundry places by royal charter. Among such places in London were the Minories and St. Katharine's Hospital, near the Tower; Fulwood's Rents and Baldwin's Gardens, near Gray's Inn; Whitefriars, between Fleet Street and the Thames; the old Mint in Southwark; and the neighbourhood of Westminster Abbey.

"The *general* sanctuary afforded a refuge to those only who had been guilty of *capital* felonies. On reaching it, the felon was bound to declare that he had committed felony, and came to save his life. By the common law of England, if a person guilty of felony (excepting sacrilege) fled to a parish church or churchyard for sanctuary, he might, within forty days afterwards, go clothed in sackcloth before the coroner, confess the full particulars of his guilt, and take an oath to abjure the kingdom for ever; swearing not to return unless the king's licence were granted him to do so. Upon making his confession and taking his oath, he became attainted of the felony; he had forty days, from the day of his appearance before the coroner, allowed him to prepare for his departure, and the coroner assigned him such port as he chose for his embarkation, whither the felon was bound to repair immediately, with a cross in his hand, and to embark with all convenient speed. If he did not go directly out of the kingdom, or if he afterwards returned into England without licence, he was condemned to be hanged, unless he happened to be a clerk, in which case he was allowed the benefit of clergy."

A *peculiar* sanctuary might (if such privilege were granted by the king's charter) afford a place of refuge even to those who had committed high or petty treason; and a person escaping thither might, if he chose, remain undisturbed for life. He still, however, had the option of taking the oath of abjuration and quitting the realm for ever. Sanctuary, however, seems in neither case to have been allowed as a protection to those who escaped from the sheriff after having been delivered to him for execution.

"The right of sanctuary," says John Timbs, "was retained by Westminster even after the dissolution of the monasteries, &c., in 1540. Sanctuary men were allowed to use a whittle only at their meals, and compelled to wear a badge. They could not leave the precinct, without the Dean's licence, between sunset and sunrise."

Formerly, as we learn from Blackstone's "Common Laws of England," "the benefit of the clergy used to be pleaded before trial or conviction, and was called a declinatory plea, which was the name given also to that of sanctuary. But as the prisoner upon trial had an opportunity of being acquitted and totally discharged, and, if convicted of a clergyable felony, was entitled equally to his clergy after as before his conviction, this course was deemed extremely disadvantageous; and therefore the benefit of the clergy was rarely pleaded, excepting it was prayed by the convict before judgment was passed upon him."

Henry VII. wrote to Pope Alexander, desiring him to exercise his authority in prohibiting sanctuary to all such as had once enjoyed it; and to adjudge all Englishmen who fled to the sanctuary for the offence of treason, to be enemies to the Christian faith. "This request," as Baker in his "Chronicles" tells us, "was granted by the Pope, to the great contentment of the king and quiet of the realm."

The Westminster Sanctuary is thus noticed in Capgrave's "Chronicles of England" in 1409:—

"In this tyme Jon Prendigest, Knyte, and William Longe, kepte the se so weel, that no Englichman had harm. But many of the kyngis hous had envye with him, that he was compelled to take Westminster; and there so streytid, that he dwelled in the porch of the cherch both nyte and day. William Longe kepte stille the se, onto [the time that the] Chaunceler sent for him, and hite him he schuld no harm have; but whan he had him he sent him to the Toure."

Whatever may have been the advantages and benefits resulting from the right of sanctuary to the weaker classes in a rude and lawless age, it must be owned that in the course of time the charitable charter of Edward the Confessor became a curse to the metropolis; the sanctuary at Westminster becoming the home and head-quarters of all that was low and disreputable, and indeed a very sink of iniquity. It grew into an asylum for vagabonds, debtors, thieves, highwaymen, coiners, and felons, who could defy the law as long as they remained within its precincts. Here they formed a community of their own, adopted a common language and a code of habits, and demoralised each other and their neighbours as well.

Dean Stanley observes, respecting the right of sanctuary at Westminster, that it "was shared by the Abbey with at least thirty other English monasteries, but probably in none did the building occupy so prominent a position, and in none did it play so great a part." The grim old fortress, which was still standing in the seventeenth century, is itself a proof that the right reached back, if not to the time of Edward the Confessor, at least to the period when additional sanctity was imparted to the whole Abbey by his canonisation in 1198; and the right professed to be founded on charters by King Lucius.

Some instances of its use may be of interest here. To the Sanctuary at Westminster Judge Tresilian (*temp.* Richard II.) fled for refuge, but was dragged thence to Tyburn, where he was hanged. In 1441 the Duchess of Gloucester fled thither, being accused of witchcraft and high treason, but the wonted privilege was denied to her; and the same lot shortly afterwards befell one Thomas Barret, a gallant soldier who had served under the Duke of Bedford in the French wars, for he was "barbarously taken hence to death." In 1456 the Protector (the Duke of York), the Earl of Warwick, and others, "were noted with an execrable offence of the Abbot of Westminster and his monks, for that they took out of Sanctuarie at Westminster John Holland, Duke of Excester, and conveyed him to the Castle of

Pontfracte." In 1460 Lord de Scales, as he was on his way to seek shelter at Westminster, was killed in crossing the Thames. It is known to every reader of history how Elizabeth Woodville, the Queen of Edward IV., in the year 1471, escaped from the Tower, and registered herself and her companions here as "Sanctuary women;" and how here, "in great penury, and forsaken of all her friends," she gave birth to Edward V., who was "born in sorrow and baptised like a poor man's child." She is described by Sir Thomas More as sitting here "alow in the rushes," in her grief and distress. Here the unhappy queen was induced by the Duke of Buckingham and the Archbishop of York to surrender her little son, Edward V., to his uncle Richard, who carried him to the Tower, where the two children shared a common fate.

In the year 1487, during the pontificate of Innocent VIII., a bull was issued, by which a little restraint was laid on the privileges of sanctuary here. It provided that if thieves, murderers, or robbers, registered as sanctuary men, should sally out, and commit fresh crimes, which they frequently did, and enter again, in such cases they might be taken out of their sanctuaries by the king's officers; and also, that as for debtors, who had taken sanctuary to defraud their creditors, their persons only should be protected; but that their goods out of sanctuary should be liable to seizure. As for traitors, the king was allowed to appoint keepers for them in their sanctuaries to prevent their escape.

Long before this these privileged places had become great evils, and Henry VII. had applied to the Pope for a reformation of the abuses connected with them, but he could obtain only the concession here recorded, a concession which was confirmed by Pope Alexander VI. in 1493.

In the Sanctuary died the poet Skelton, tutor and poet Laureate to Henry VIII. He had fled thither to escape the vengeance of Cardinal Wolsey, whom he had lampooned in verses which show more dulness than malice.

The old sanctuaries and "spitals" continued in full force till the dissolution of the religious houses under Henry VIII., when several statutes were passed regulating, limiting, and partly abolishing the privilege of refuge, though it was not until the 21st of James I. that the latter was wholly swept away—in theory at least. The change introduced by Henry, as we learn from history, was followed by what has been termed the "age of beggars and thieves;" for when the poorer classes, who had grown up in dependence on the old abbeys and monasteries, came to be suddenly deprived of the means of subsistence by the stoppage of their alms, society had to suffer—not altogether undeservedly—for the change which the tyrannical king had brought about. It became necessary, therefore, to enact further laws for the punishment of sturdy and wilful beggars, and ultimately to bring in sundry "poor laws" to meet the case of the other large population which had been reduced to poverty by the stoppage of the alms on which they had lived. How far these measures tended to the happiness and social improvement of the lower orders it is not difficult for any reader of history to judge.

At the Reformation these places of sanctuary began to sink into disrepute. They were, however, still preserved, and, though none but the most abandoned resorted to them, the dread of innovation, or some other cause, preserved them from demolition, till, in the year 1697, the evils arising from them had grown so enormous that it became absolutely necessary to take some legislative measures for their destruction.

The privilege of sanctuary caused the houses within the precinct to let for high rents, but this privilege was totally abolished by James I., though the bulk of the houses which composed the precinct was not taken down till 1750.

It may be questioned how far it was politic to invest any place with such sanctity as that it should shelter a murderer against the strong hand of the law; for it will be remembered that the "cities of refuge" in the Old Testament were appointed for the benefit of none but those who had killed a neighbour by mischance (see Deut. iv. 42). Taking sanctuary was well understood among the ancient Jews. There were three cities of refuge on the east and three on the west side of Jordan. The Rabbins say that the high roads leading to these cities were kept free and in good repair, that finger-posts pointed in the direction leading to them, and that every facility was given to the refugee to make his escape from the hands of the avenger of blood. The Rev. Mr. Nightingale, in the "Beauties of England and Wales," says, "It is certain that among the Hebrews, with whom the practice originated, these privileged places were not designed to thwart or obstruct the ends of justice, but merely to protect the offender against the revenge of the friends of the slain."

As a proof of the extent to which the privilege of sanctuary was used in the Middle Ages, it may be mentioned here that the Rev. A. G. L'Estrange, the author of the work "From the Thames to the Tamar," states that at Beaulieu Abbey, near Southampton, in the year 1539, there were no less than "thirty-two sanctuary men for debt, felony, and murder." He adds that the sanctuary at Beaulieu was held in such reverence that even monarchs dared not violate it. "The greatest criminal or most obnoxious rebel who gained its gates and registered himself upon its books, was safe from his pursuers." It is said that after the rough work of the Reformation had been carried out in London the great church in the royal city of Lancaster was specially reserved by Henry VIII. as conferring that privilege on murderers.

In Machyn's "Diary" (written in 1556) is the following amusing description of a procession of Sanctuary men:—"The vj. day of December the Abbot of Westminster went a procession with his convent. Before him went all the Santuary men, with crosse keys upon their garments, and after whent iij for murder; on was the Lord Dacre's sone of the North, was wypyd with a shett abowt him for kyllyng of on Master West squyre dwellyng besyd . . .; and anodur theyff that dyd long to one of Master Comtroller . . . dyd kylle Recherd Eggylston, the Comtroller's tayller, and kylled him in the Long Acurs, the bak-syd Charyng Crosse; and a boy that kyld a byge boye that sold papers and prynted bokes with horlying of a stone, and yt hym under the ere in Westmynster Hall; the boy was one of the chylderyn that was at the sckoll ther in the Abbey; the boy ys a hossear sune aboyff London-stone."

We have given at the commencement of this chapter Dr. Stukeley's description of the Sanctuary. There were, however, here really two sanctuaries, the Great and tne Little; or rather, perhaps, two branches of the same institution. At the west end of the latter, in the time of Maitland, towards the end of the reign of George II., there were remains of "a prodigious strong stone building, of two hundred and ninety feet square, or seventy-two feet and a half the length of each side; and the walls in thickness no less than twenty-five feet." This fabric originally had but one entrance or door below, and that in the east side, with a window hard by, which seems to have been the only one below the height of twenty-two feet of the building, where the walls were reduced to three feet in thickness, and contained four windows on the south side. "The area of this exceedingly strong tower," continues Maitland,

OLD HOUSES IN TOTHILL STREET, WESTMINSTER, 1870. *From an Original Sketch.* (*See page* 488.)

THE LITTLE SANCTUARY. *From a Drawing by J. T. Smith,* 1808. (*See page* 488.)

"(exclusive of the arched cavities in the walls), by a wall from east to west, three feet in thickness, was divided into two spaces, about eleven feet each in width, representing a frame for bells, which plainly evinces it to have been the strong Bell Tower that was erected in the Little Sanctuary, by Edward III., for the use of the collegiate church of St. Stephen, and not, as Strype imagines it to have been, the church of the Holy Innocents, for that was the church of St. Mary-le-Strand." The walls of this building, says Mr. Mackenzie Walcott, were of Kentish rag-stone, cemented with mortar made of the same material. "Three angles of the lower church were built solid, sixteen feet square. In the upper church square rooms were made over these corners: probably one was the sacristan's parvise, and another the revestry. The principal gate was covered with plates of stout iron, while the esplanade at the top was paved with flat stones, and built upon with many little houses. The little circular staircase towards the east, and upon the outside near the principal entrance, led to the upper church, and may have been the work of King Edward III., when the larger staircase on the south-east angle was appropriated to his new clochard; it contained seventeen stairs, built in large blocks of stone."

Stow, in his description of Westminster, says, with reference to this ancient structure, "He [*i.e.* King Edward III.] also builded to the use of this chappell (though out of the Palace Court), some distance west, in the Little Sanctuarie, a strong clochard of stone and timber, covered with lead, and placed therein three great bels, since usually rung at coronations, triumphs, funerals of princes, and their obits. Of those bels, men fabuled that their ringing sowred all the drinke in the towne."

This strong tower, or a part of it, was afterwards converted into a tavern, which bore the sign of the "Three Tuns;" and its vaults served the purposes of a wine-cellar. The church was demolished about the year 1750, and on part of its site a meat-market was subsequently built. The market was removed early in the present century, and in its place was erected the present Guildhall or Sessions House, of which we shall have more to say when dealing with the modern memories of Westminster.

In the Great Sanctuary was formerly a tavern called the "Quaker." Pepys, on the 3rd of August, 1660, informs us that he dined at an ordinary called the "Quaker"—a somewhat unusual godfather for a sinful tavern. This house was pulled down only in the beginning of the present century to make way for an extension of the market-place, which in its turn has made room for a new Sessions House, as above mentioned. The last landlord opened a new public-house in Thieving Lane, and adorned the doorway of this house with twisted pillars decorated with vine-leaves, brought from the old "Quaker" tavern. Mr. J. T. Smith has given a view of this house in the additional plates to his "Antiquities of Westminster."

Close to the Sanctuary, and indeed adjoining its western side, was the Eleemosynary or Almonry, where the alms of the Abbey were daily doled out to the poor and needy. But it is far more memorable on quite another account—namely, as the first place in which a printing-press was set up in England. This was, says Pennant, in the year 1474, when William Caxton, encouraged by the learned Thomas Milling, then abbot, produced here "The Game and Play of the Chesse," "the first book ever printed in these kingdoms. There is," he adds, "a slight difference about the exact spot where it was printed; but all agree that it was within the precincts of this religious house."

The Almonry was a building, analogous to our more prosaic modern alms-houses, erected by King Henry VII. and his mother, the Lady Margaret, to the glory of God, for twelve poor men and poor women. The building was afterwards converted into lodgings for the choir-men of the Abbey, and called Choristers' Rents. These were pulled down at the beginning of the present century. Hard by stood the Chapel of St. Anne, now commemorated by St. Anne's Lane. This lane occupies part of the ground which was covered by the orchard and fruit-gardens of the Abbey, though it is difficult to realise the fact. Across the court ran the granary, parallel with what was the prior's lodging.

We have already stated that the Almonry was divided into two parts; and from Mr. Mackenzie Walcott's "Westminster" we learn that "the Great Almonry consisted of two oblong portions, parallel to the two Tothill Streets, and connected by a narrow lane (the entrance being from Dean's Yard); and that the Little Almonry, running southward, stood at its eastern end.

The Gate House, of which we have spoken in the preceding chapter as opening into Dean's Yard, adjoined the Almonry, and was once the principal approach to the Monastery itself. It stood at the western entrance of Tothill Street, and dated from the time of Edward III. Walter Warfield, "butler to the Abbey Church of Westminster," is stated to have been its builder. Many distinguished prisoners have been immured within its walls. Many of the royalists during the Civil Wars were confined here; among them was Colonel Richard Lovelace, the gay and gallant cavalier poet, who presented the petition of the Kentish men to the House of Commons for the restoration of the king to his rights. He is reported to have been a sort of "admirable Crichton" of his day, and, in the language of one of his friends, "the most beautiful and amiable person that the eye ever beheld." Be this, however, an exaggeration or not, it is certain that here, in the long tedious hours of his "durance vile," he wrote that exquisite poem, entitled "To Althea from Prison," in which occurs the stanza :—

"Stone walls do not a prison make,
Nor iron bars a cage ;
Minds innocent and quiet take
That for an hermitage."

It is sad to learn that the writer of such lines should have died in poverty, or, at all events, in dependence on the bounty of others, in the neighbourhood of Shoe Lane.

Dr. Goodman, Bishop of Gloucester, was another inmate of this prison in the seventeenth century, being committed by the Primate on his refusal to sign the Canons of the Church of England. In 1663, a notorious impostor, called the "German Princess," was incarcerated here, for having enticed a citizen's son into marriage ; she afterwards became an actress, and in the end was hanged at Tyburn for a robbery. After the Restoration, the famous Court dwarf, Jeffrey Hudson, here ended his days, having, after a life of continued misfortune, been imprisoned for his presumed complicity in the "Popish Plot." Sir Walter Scott has made his readers familiar with "Sir" Jeffrey Hudson in his "Peveril of the Peak ;" the brush of Vandyck has immortalised his dwarfish appearance ; and his clothes were long preserved as articles of curiosity in Sir Hans Sloane's Museum.

Once more, in 1701, the Kentish men sent to Westminster five representatives, deputy-lieutenants of the county, to remonstrate against the proceedings of the House of Commons. This petition being considered "scandalous and seditious," these gentlemen were entrusted to the custody of the Serjeant-at-Arms ; and we are told that they were confined in the Gate House Prison until the close of the session.

In 1716, Mr. Harley, uncle of the Earl of Oxford, and Ambassador at Hanover, was imprisoned here for prevarication in certain answers about his foreign negotiations ; here too, was incarcerated Jeremy Collier, the author of a valuable Ecclesiastical History ; and Richard Savage, the poet, who lodged in Westminster, was committed to this gaol for taking part in a lamentable street quarrel in which Mr. James Sinclair was killed. Among state prisoners, however, there were none sent hither more illustrious than Sir Walter Raleigh, who passed within its walls the night preceding his execution. Here his loving wife took her sad farewell of him, at the same time telling him that his judges had granted to her his body. "Well mayst thou, Bess," said he, smiling, "dispose of that when dead, which thou hadst not ever the disposing of when alive." At midnight, after her departure, he calmly sat down and wrote these lines :—

"E'en such is Time ! that takes on trust
Our youth, our joys, our all we have,
And pays us but with age and dust ;
Who in the dark and silent grave,
When we have wandered all our ways,
Shuts up the story of our days."

The old Gate House Prison was held by lease, under the Dean and Chapter, as a speculation ; the keeper obtaining fees, but being responsible for the safe keeping of his prisoners, and also for the good behaviour of his warders. In the middle of the last century, the building had fallen into such a dangerous state of decay, that it was shored up completely from the bottom to the top ; and in 1776 an order was made by the Dean and Chapter, directing its demolition, with the adjacent almshouses, and the lead and iron to be sold by direction of the surveyor of the church. The building in its latter years was used almost wholly as a debtors' prison : as we learn from Mr. Mackenzie Walcott's "Memorials of Westminster," the debtors "used to let down an alms-box, extended on a pole forty feet long, in order to collect the benevolences of the passers-by. They were allowed to purchase ardent spirits ; and the keeper used to go and shout from the window to the barman of the neighbouring tavern, the 'Angel,' by the not very gentle or complimentary appellation of 'Jack-ass, jack-ass,' thereby to signify the thirst of the prisoners."

Adjoining to the Gate House, on the east side, was another building of about the same age, which was used for "the Bishop of London's prison for clerks convicts ;" and close by this prison was "the long ditch," over which Queen Maud, the consort of Henry I., erected a bridge leading to Tothill Street and the Broadway.

As we have stated above, the constant tradition is that it was in the Almonry where William Caxton set up the first printing-press in England, under the auspices of the then abbot, Thomas Milling. Caxton was a native of the Weald of Kent, and born about the year 1412. He came to London, and resided in Westminster, being apprenticed to a mercer, and supporting his parents in his house until their death. He was left by his master a legacy of twenty marks, and spent some years abroad engaged in mercantile and diplomatic business. In 1464 he was employed by Edward IV. to negotiate a treaty with Philip, Duke of Burgundy. At Cologne he had printed and published one or two books, now so rare that scarcely a copy is known even to German bibliographers; and returning to England about 1472, set up a printing-press, as already mentioned, within the precincts of the Abbey. By some writers it has been thought not wholly improbable that at first he erected his press near one of the little chapels attached to the aisles of the Abbey, or in the ancient Scriptorium. There is some little doubt as to which was the first of the books that he printed here, whether "The Game of Chess," or "The Romance of Jason;" the first of these works Caxton himself had translated from the French, and the copies of it bore date 1474. In Timbs' "Things not Generally Known," we find that "Bartholomæus de Glanville, who flourished about the middle of the fourteenth century, wrote 'De Proprietatibus rerum,' which was first printed in folio by Caxton, in 1480. It was translated into English by Trevisa, and printed by Wynkyn de Worde in 1507. Dr. Dibdin, in his 'Typographical Antiquities,' styles this 'a volume of extraordinary typographical beauty and rarity.' It is the first book printed on paper made in England." It is, however, certain that Caxton soon found patrons of his new craft in Henry VII. and the royal family and many of the nobility. One or two of his works, including "The Wise Sayings and Dictes of Philosophers," were translated for his press by Anthony, Earl Rivers, under-governor to the Prince of Wales. It would be impossible to give here a full list of the works which in their turn came from Caxton's press. "The Moral Proverbs of Christina of Pisa," "A 'Chronicle,' with a Description of Britain subjoined to it," "The Mirror of the World," "Reynard the Fox," "Tully on Old Age and Friendship" (both translated by Tiptoft, Earl of Worcester), "Godfrey of Boulogne," the "Polychronicon," the "Confessio Amantis," "Order of Chivalry," "Picture of London," "Morte d'Arthur," "History of Charlemagne," "Book of Travellers," "The Fait of Armes and Chivalry," and Chaucer's "Canterbury Tales." For Chaucer's memory Caxton had a special veneration, as he showed by ordering a long epitaph to be written on the poet at his own expense, and inscribed on one of the pillars near his grave in the south aisle of the Abbey.

Stow, in his "Survey of London," says that "in the Eleemosynary, or Almonry (at Westminster Abbey), now corruptly called the Ambry, for that the alms of the Abbey were there distributed to the poor, John Islip, Abbot of Westminster, erected the first press for book-printing that ever was in England, and that Caxton was the first that practised it *in the said Abbey.*" Whether Caxton's press was at first actually within the walls of the Abbey Church, or merely in a small chapel near the Abbey, has always been a doubtful point; but be that as it may, we may state, for the benefit of the uninitiated, that the word "chapel" is to this day known in connection with printing-offices, and that the chief officer is called the "father of the chapel," and each member of it a "chapelonian." Thomas Milling was Abbot of Westminster in 1472, at the time when Caxton is stated to have established the art of printing in Westminster, and Islip did not succeed to the abbacy till some ten years *after Caxton's death;* so it is clear, judging from the above quotation, that Stow, wonderfully accurate as he was, still was not infallible.

Caxton appears to have carried on his business as a master printer to the very last, and to have taken also an active part as a parishioner of St. Margaret's, in the churchwardens' books of which parish his name occurs constantly as an auditor of the accounts. He died at his house in the Almonry, or (as he spells it) the "Almonestrye," in 1490-1, and was buried in St. Margaret's Church, to which he left by will a bequest of books, long since lost and dispersed. Though his work was confessedly not equal to the printing executed on the Continent during the same period, yet there was at the time when he lived no one whose talents, habits, and character were so well fitted to introduce and establish the art of printing in England. To record the fact that he succeeded in such an enterprise, the benefits of which we are all still enjoying, is praise enough, for it is an assertion of his claim to be regarded as one of the greatest benefactors of his country. It may here be remarked, in passing, that until the year 1642 it was never doubted that Caxton was the introducer of printing into this kingdom; but at that time a dispute happening to arise between the Stationers' Company and some private persons respecting a patent for printing, the case was formally argued in a court of law, and in the course of the pleadings the credit was proved incontestably to belong to William Caxton.

The following testimony to Caxton's character as both editor and printer is borne by Mr. Thomas Wright, F.S.A.:—"The art of printing had been invented and exercised for a considerable time, in most countries of Europe, before the art of criticism was called in to superintend and direct its operations. It is therefore much more to the honour of our meritorious countryman, William Caxton, that he chose to make the 'Canterbury Tales' one of the earliest productions of his press, than it can be to his discredit that he printed them very incorrectly. He probably took the first MS. that he could procure to print from, and, as it happened, changed it for the better, always giving the original reading in a foot-note."

The art of printing speedily gained high repute, and found followers accordingly; for previous to Caxton's death we find Wynkyn de Worde and three other foreigners, and another Englishman, one Thomas Hunt, established as printers in the metropolis.

We have already mentioned the tradition that it was "in or near the Abbey" that the first printing-press in England was set up by Caxton; but a placard printed in Caxton's largest type, and preserved in the library of Brasenose College, Oxford, fixes the Almonry as the scene of his labours; for in this placard Caxton invites customers to "come to Westmonester into the Almonestrye, at the 'Reed Pale,'" the name by which, as Mr. John Timbs tells us in his "Curiosities of London," was known the house in which Caxton is said to have lived. It stood in Little Dean Street, on the north side of the Almonry, with its back against that of a house on the south side of Tothill Street, or what is now the space between Tothill Street and the Westminster Palace Hotel. Bagford describes this house as of brick, with the sign of the "King's Head;" it was pulled down in November, 1845, before the removal of the other buildings in the Almonry. The house had a somewhat picturesque appearance: it was built partly of brick, and partly of timber and plaster; it was three storeys in height, the last storey having a wooden gallery or balcony resting on the projecting windows below, and doors leading out of it. The illustration given on page 492, copied from an engraving published in 1827, shows the house as it stood in the first half of the present century.

CHAPTER LVIII.

THE ROYAL PALACE OF WESTMINSTER.

"But that which makes her name through earth to ring,
She is the chamber to our gracious King,
The place in which the Parliament doth sit
For to determine things most requisite."—*Old Ballad.*

Extent and Boundaries of the Ancient Royal Palace—Edward the Confessor and the Thief—Death of Edward the Confessor—William the Conqueror—William Rufus builds the Great Hall—St. Stephen's Chapel—Birth of Edward I.—The Palace partially burnt—The Palace pillaged by the Earl of Gloucester's Soldiers—Stew-ponds—The Quintain—Henry VI. presented to the Lords of the Parliament—Death of Edward IV.—Henry VIII and Catharine of Arragon—Jousts and Tournaments—The Gradual Growth of the British Parliament—The Old House of Lords—The Prince's Chamber—The Painted Chamber—Charles I. and Oliver Cromwell—The Old House of Commons—Cotton's Gardens—Parliament Stairs—The Star Chamber—Great Accumulation of "Tallies"—"Bellamy's Coffee House."

THE ancient Royal Palace of Westminster was a magnificent and extensive pile, in part covering the ground now occupied by the two large areas or courts known as Old Palace Yard and New Palace Yard, and it consisted of a great number of buildings destined to various purposes. The two courts were bounded on the east by the river Thames, and on the west by the Abbey of St. Peter, St. Margaret's Church, the Great and Little Sanctuaries, &c., and were entered on the north and south by gates, which we shall presently describe more in detail. The original palace in which King Canute the Dane had lived is said to have been burnt down to the ground some thirty years before the Conquest. It was rebuilt by Edward the Confessor, and, as we learn from Fitz-Stephen, was a structure of great strength. Here, as Ingulphus tells us, Edward the Confessor held his court, and entertained the high and mighty Duke of Normandy—his own destined successor—when on a visit to England; and here, doubtless, was enacted the incident depicted in the fifth compartment of the historical frieze in the chapel of Edward the Confessor, in Westminster Abbey. "One day," so runs the legend, "as the king lay silent in one of the chambers of his palace, a young page, unconscious of his master's presence, entered the door; and finding a chest filled with treasures standing open, he filled his purse and departed. Avarice prompted a return; again the little thief came, and began to plunder anew. 'Hold, boy!' cried the gentle king, 'you had better be even content with that you have; for if Hugoline, my chamberlain, should come, you will certainly lose all, and be soundly whipped to boot.'"

The particulars of the death of Edward the Confessor, which occurred here, are thus touchingly told in Mr. Walcott's "Westminster," on the authority of Ailred, Abbot of Rievaulx :—"Upon the Eve of Christmas, 1065, the king was seized with a fever; and for three days, superior to nature, and When it was past, he laid his head down upon the couch, and began to be sorely pained. While he lay sick, he forbade his attendants to weep; and seeing his queen mourning and wailing, 'Mourn not, my daughter,' said he; 'I shall not die, but live; and passing from the country of the dead,

CAXTON'S HOUSE, WESTMINSTER. *From an Engraving published in* 1827. (*See page* 490.)

triumphing over the sickness, he bare the ornaments of majesty, and at the solemn banqueting sat amidst his bishops and nobles with what cheerfulness he might. But on the third day, perceiving that the time of his call was come, he bade that the church [of St. Peter] should be dedicated on the morrow. The joyous festival of the Holy Innocents was dawning, and with the assembled prelates and all the nobles of the king the solemnity began. verily I hope to behold the good things of the Lord in the land of the living.' So having commended himself wholly unto God, in the faith of Christ, and the hope of His promise, old and full of days, he departed from the world."

William the Conqueror, who was crowned at Westminster with his queen, Matilda, says Stow, "it is not to be doubted, builded much at this palace, for he found it farre inferiour to the building of princely palaces in France." Here the Norman kings occasionally resided when they could be enticed away from Winchester and the pleasures of the chase in the New Forest.

As far back as the reign of William Rufus, if we may trust the somewhat poetical statements of Fitz-Stephen, the buildings of the metropolis were grand in the extreme; at all events, he describes the king's palace as an incomparable edifice, connected with the City by suburbs two miles in length, and adds that the bishops, abbots, and noblemen of the kingdom resorted thither in large numbers, living in beautiful houses and maintaining magnificent establishments. The citizens too, no doubt, were initiated in the luxury of good living; for in the neighbourhood of the palace and of the Thames they had a large cooking establishment, at which dainties of every kind could be obtained. They had also in the same neighbourhood public and private schools of philosophy and polite literature; the drama, too, was cultivated; and Fitz-Stephen, who was himself a monk, writes in high terms of praise concerning the frequent exhibitions here of the miracles and martyrdoms of the saints.

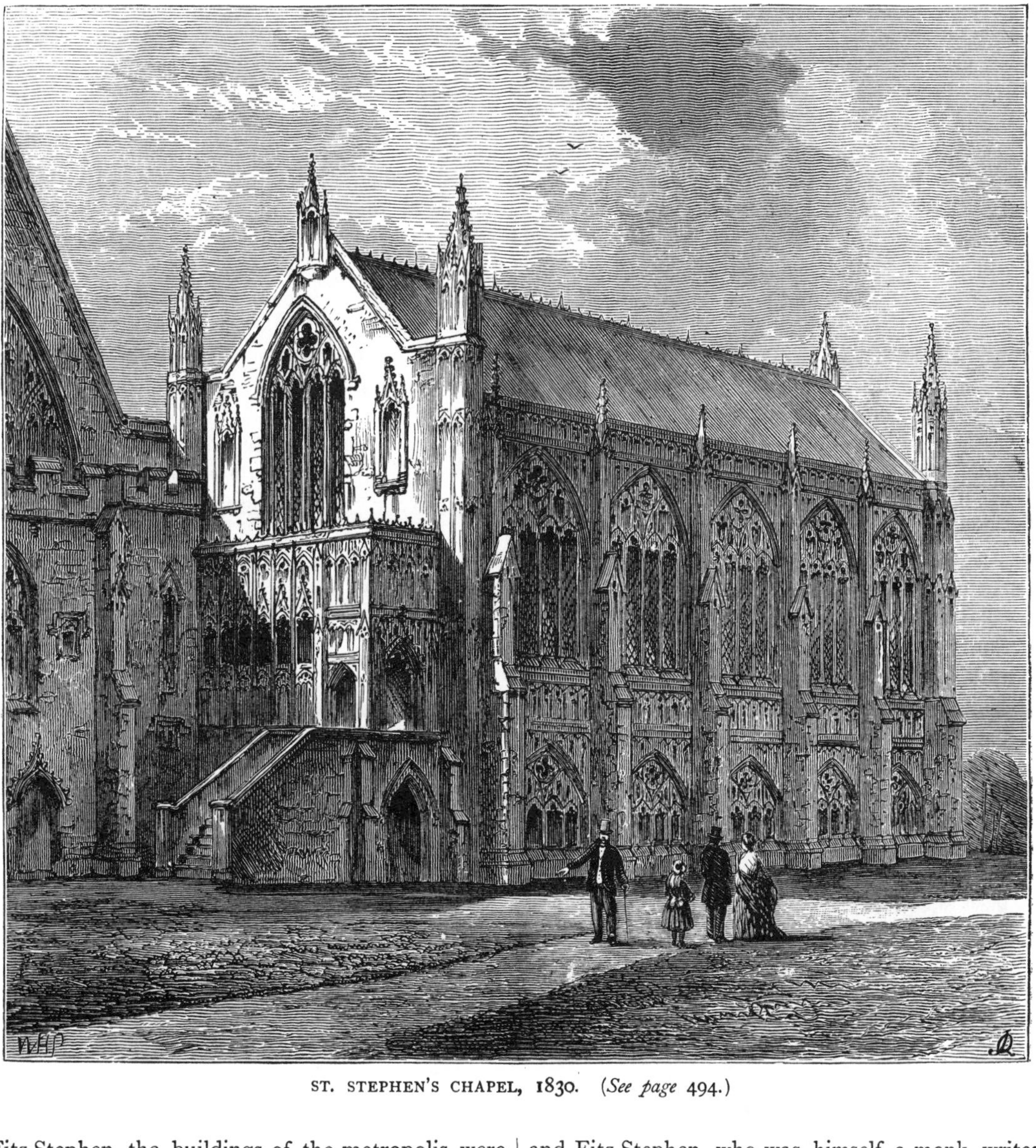

ST. STEPHEN'S CHAPEL, 1830. (*See page* 494.)

Roger of Wendover and Matthew Paris tell us that soon after he had built the great hall, William Rufus, keeping the festival of Whitsuntide here with royal splendour, and hearing his guests admiring its grandeur, boastfully exclaimed, "This hall is not big enough by half, and is but a bed-chamber in comparison of that which I mean to make." Notwithstanding this boast of William, it would appear that the palace soon afterwards was allowed to fall into decay; for early in the reign of Henry II., as Fitz-Stephen tells us, the Chancellor, Thomas à Becket, found it almost a ruin, and repaired it in an incredibly short space of time, namely, between Easter and Whitsuntide. With an amusing detail, which may serve to remind us that carpenters and masons are the same in all ages, he tells us that the workmen employed upon it made such a clatter that the good people who were near could scarcely hear each other speak. King Stephen had a few years earlier added to the royal palace a magnificent chapel, which was dedicated to the proto-martyr whose name he bore. This chapel, though now no longer in existence, has retained its memory; the name, by a sort of fiction and figure of speech, being used as synonymous for the Houses of Parliament themselves. It was rebuilt by Edward I., but having been burnt down in 1298 was restored, or rather built again *de novo*, under Edward II. and III., in the best and most perfect style of the Decorated Gothic; and it certainly must have formed one of the most elegant additions to the architecture of Westminster. Its walls were exquisitely painted in fresco work with a variety of subjects. When the chapel was fitted up for the use of the House of Commons in the reign of Edward VI., these mural paintings were covered over with wainscoting. They were, however, brought to light in the course of some repairs and alterations in the year 1800, when it was necessary to enlarge the apartment in order to accommodate the Irish members, just a hundred in number, who were added to the House of Commons by the Act of Union. At this time the paintings were in such a perfect state as to admit of their being copied and engraven. St. Stephen's Chapel was reduced to a ruin by the great fire in October, 1834.

In 1206, King John granted to Baldwin de London, clerk of his exchequer, the chapelship of St. Stephen's, at Westminster. At that time, therefore—or before it had been already dedicated to St. Stephen—it was probably intended to serve as a chapel for the palace, instead of a small one used by Edward the Confessor, which stood near the west side of Westminster Hall, and occupied a part of the spot where Cotton House afterwards stood; but which might have been thought or found too small or inelegant to suit with a royal residence, of which the present Westminster Hall was intended but as one room. That there was a chapel in use here before the erection of this, is clear, as it is on record that Hugo Flory was confirmed abbot of Canterbury in the king's chapel at Westminster in the time of William Rufus. As a chapel of the palace, and therefore to be maintained at the king's expense from time to time, it does not appear to have originally had any endowment; neither does there seem to have been any kind of property belonging to it until the time of its re-foundation—or, more properly speaking, its first foundation—and endowment by Edward III.

In 1239, this palace was the birthplace of the warrior king, Edward I. In 1263, the building suffered greatly by fire; and four years later, during the rupture between the king (Henry III.) and the Earl of Gloucester, "the soldiers lying at Southwark rowed over to Westminster, made havoc in the king's palace, drank up his wine, and broke the glass of the windows, and all other necessaries belonging to that palace they destroyed and wasted."

In the reign of Edward I. (1299) another fire destroyed or very much injured this ancient palace, and many houses adjoining; indeed, it received so much damage that the Parliament—which was at that time holding its sittings there—was held in the ensuing year at the house of the Archbishop of York in Whitehall.

Somewhere near the palace there were extensive stew-ponds in the reign of Henry III.; for, towards the end of that king's life, we find an order for the purchase of six hundred luces or pikes, a hundred of which were to be put into the king's ponds at Westminster.

Matthew Paris informs us that during the reign of Henry III. "the young Londoners, who were expert horsemen, assembled together to run at the quintain, setting up a peacock as the reward of the best player." The king happening then to be holding his court at Westminster, "some of his domestics came to see the pastime, and treated the Londoners with much insolence, calling them cowardly knaves and rascally clowns;" insults which, we may be sure, the Londoners were not slow to resent. In fact, if the truth must be told, the Londoners gave the king's domestics a sound drubbing. "The king, however," says Matthew Paris, "was incensed at the indignity thus laid upon his servants, and not taking into consideration the provocation which the Londoners had received, he fined the city a thousand marks."

The quintain, according to Strutt's "Sports and Pastimes," was originally a military exercise. It is of great antiquity, and was formerly much practised by the youths of London and Westminster. The sport is said to have been named after its inventor, one Quintus, possibly one of the Roman legions quartered in London sixteen hundred years ago; though who he was or when he lived is uncertain. Long anterior in date to the jousts and tournaments of the Middle Ages, the "quintain" would appear to have been originally nothing more than the trunk of a tree or a post, set up for the practice of tyros in chivalry with their spears. Subsequently, it became a more complicated sport, and one which required much skill and nerve. "A staff or spear was fixed in the earth, and a shield being hung upon it was the mark to strike at; the dexterity of the performer consisted in striking the shield in such a manner as to break its fastenings and bear it off. In process of time this diversion was improved, and instead of the staff and the shield, the resemblance of a human figure carved in wood was introduced. To render the appearance of this figure more formidable, it was generally made in the likeness of a Turk or Saracen armed at all points, bearing a shield on his left arm, and brandishing a club or sabre in his right. The quintain thus fashioned was placed on a pivot, and so contrived as to move round with facility. In running at this figure it was necessary for the horseman to direct his lance with great adroitness, and to make his stroke upon the forehead between the eyes, or else upon the nose; for, if he struck wide of those parts, especially upon the shield, the quintain turned round with much velocity, and in case he was not extremely careful, it would give him a severe blow upon the back with the wooden sabre held in the right hand, which was considered as highly disgraceful to the performer, while it excited the laughter and ridicule of the spectators."

THE SPEAKER'S HOUSE FROM THE RIVER, IN 1830. (*See page* 496.)

In 1422, Henry VI., an infant of eight months at his accession to the throne, was carried in his mother's lap in an open carriage from the City to Westminster, to be presented to the Lords of the Parliament, which was then holding its sitting; and we read that after his coronation, at ten years old, he was presented at Westminster with £1,000, by the Lord Mayor and citizens of London.

At his palace here, on the 9th of April, 1483, died King Edward IV. He was succeeded by his son Edward V., whose uncle Richard, Duke of Gloucester, acted as his guardian and Protector of the realm; and it was to the precincts of the Abbey that the young king's mother fled for refuge on hearing that Richard had ordered the Lords Rivers and Grey, and the other friends of her son, to be imprisoned in Pomfret Castle.

To the Abbey and Palace of Westminster went in solemn procession the young, and at that time promising king, Henry VIII., accompanied by his first wife, Catharine of Arragon, on his accession to the throne, the streets and public buildings on that occasion being enlivened with the gayest of decorations in honour of the royal visitors. Here the same monarch, in the days of his youth and popularity, reviewed the largest muster of the citizens of London that had ever been seen. They consisted of three divisions, each of 5,000 men, exclusive of pioneers and other attendants; and the king much approved of their appearance.

Westminster had long been the seat of the Royal Palace, of the High Court of Parliament, and of our legal tribunals; most of our sovereigns, since the Conquest at least, had been crowned and buried in the Abbey; and it was not until the ancient palace had been almost wholly destroyed by fire that Henry VIII., in 1530, bought Whitehall from Cardinal Wolsey—a purchase which put an end to most of the royal glories of Westminster proper.

This palace, indeed, was partially deserted by royalty in 1512, when part of it was burnt; but the grounds belonging to it seem to have been occasionally used for State purposes in later years; for in honour of the marriage of Henry VIII. with Anne of Cleves, we read that on May Day, 1540, unusually splendid "jousts" were opened at the palace, the challengers being headed by Sir John Dudley, and the defenders by the gallant and accomplished Earl of Surrey. "This entertainment," says Miss Lucy Aikin, "was continued for several successive days, during which the challengers, according to the costly fashion of ancient hospitality, kept open house at their common charge, and feasted the king and queen, the members of both Houses of Parliament, and the Lord Mayor and Aldermen of London with their wives."

All that now remains of the ancient palace is the Great Hall (of which we shall speak in a subsequent chapter) and the crypt under the Chapel of St. Stephen. Such parts of the rest of the structure as remained to our days—namely, the Star Chamber, the Painted Chamber, and the chapel itself with its cloisters, and the tapestry representing the Spanish Armada—were all destroyed in the fire which burnt down the Houses of Parliament on the 16th of October, 1834.

Previous to this fire, the Parliament had been in the habit of assembling here for nearly three centuries. Macaulay reminds us in his "History," that since the days of the Plantagenets the Houses of Parliament had regularly sat at Westminster, except when the plague was raging in the capital. He must have forgotten, however, the assembling of a Parliament at Oxford in the reign of Charles I.

The old house and the lobby belonging to it formed a building at right angles to the Hall, to which it joined on at the south-eastern corner. The building extended towards the river, being divided from it at the east end by a part of the Speaker's Garden. The length and breadth of the old house, with its lobby, were about half of those of the Hall, occupying about a fourth part of its area.

It is often said that the first assembling of the House of Commons originated from the battle of Evesham. It is true that the earliest instance on record of the representatives of the people assembling in Parliament occurred in the same year with the battle of Evesham; but it had no connection whatever with the event of that engagement, since the Parliament (to which for the first time citizens and burgesses were summoned) was assembled through the influence of the Earl of Leicester, who then held the king under his control; and the meeting took place in the beginning of the year 1265, the writs of summons having been issued in November, 1264; while the battle of Evesham, in which the Earl of Leicester was killed, did not happen till August 4, 1265, or between five and six months after the conclusion of the Parliament. From that period to the death of Henry III., in 1272, it does not appear that any election of citizens or burgesses, to attend Parliament, occurred. The next instance of such elections seems to have happened in the 18th of Edward I.; and the first returns to such writs of summons extant are dated the 23rd of the same reign, since which, with a few intermissions, they have been regularly continued. The correctness of these statements will appear from a reference to the 4th and 5th chapters of Sir W. Betham's work on "Dignities Feudal and Parliamentary," or to Sir James Mackintosh's History of England.

The assembly met on the 22nd of January, 1265, according to writs still extant directing the sheriffs to elect and return two knights for each county, two citizens for each city, and two burgesses for every borough or burgh in the country.

Sir William Blackstone says that we find the first record of any writ for summoning knights, citizens, and burgesses to Parliament towards the reign of Henry III.; but in another place he is more particular, and affirms that this constitution has subsisted, in fact, at least from the year 1266, the forty-ninth of Henry III. Sir Edward Coke has remarked that anciently the two houses sat together; and this appears to have been the case at least so late as the sixth year of Edward III. The surest mark of the division of the Parliament into two houses dates, as he says, from the time when the House of Commons first elected a permanent Speaker, as at the present day. After this division, he adds, the Commons assembled in the chapter-house of the abbot of Westminster, citing as his authority the parliament roll of the 50th Edward III., No. 8, which, consequently, proves the division to have taken place before this date.

Blackstone likewise says that the Parliament is supposed most probably to have assumed its present form during the reign of Edward III., by a separation of the Commons from the Lords; and that the statute for defining and ascertaining treasons was one of the first productions of this new-modelled assembly, and the translation of the law proceedings from French into Latin another. The statute of treasons was passed in the 20th year of Edward III., and that for the translation of law proceedings into Latin in the 36th year of the same king.

Inconvenience in the dispatch of public business must, no doubt, have been found to arise from the distance between the two houses, so long as the Commons continued to sit in the chapter-house of the Abbey; no wonder, therefore, that some more conveniently-situated building should have been thought of for that purpose; and that, on the surrender of St. Stephen's Chapel to the Crown, that edifice was assigned to the Commons as a place of meeting.

The old House of Lords, as it stood prior to the fire in 1834, was an oblong chamber, formed out of an ancient building long known as the Court of Requests. It was decorated with pinnacles on the side next to Abingdon Street, but had little in the way of architectural beauty to recommend it to particular notice. The interior was ornamented with tapestry hangings, consisting of historical figures, representing the defeat of the Spanish Armada in 1588. They were the gift of the States of Holland to Queen Elizabeth. The tapestry was divided into compartments by a framework of stained wood, and each design was surrounded by a border containing portraits of the several gallant officers who commanded in the English fleet at that important period. The throne was an arm-chair, elegantly carved and gilt, ornamented with crimson velvet. Above it was a canopy of crimson velvet, supported by two gilt Corinthian columns, and surmounted by the imperial crown.

The House of Lords did not occupy the whole of the old Court of Requests, part of the north end being formed into a lobby, by which the Commons passed to the Upper House. The royal approach to the old House of Lords was at the south-east corner of Old Palace Yard; it consisted of an enclosed Gothic corridor, with a porch of the same character, leading to a noble flight of stairs. It previously led to the Prince's Chamber and other apartments of the ancient palace, which had been taken down in 1823, when the foundations were laid for the royal gallery. Part of the ancient site was appropriated for a library and committee-rooms for the House of Lords and the House of Commons. Adjoining the ancient building known as the Prince's Chamber was the room which had long served as the House of Lords, in the cellars of which the celebrated "gunpowder treason" was intended to have taken effect. All this was destroyed towards the close of the last century, and some mean brick edifices were erected in their stead. The royal staircase of the late House of Lords was in two flights; on the top were recesses; to the right and left were arched openings to a decorated vestibule which was adorned by eight scagliola columns supporting four galleries; to the left, between four columns, was a large opening to the royal gallery. This chamber was divided into three compartments, each of which had a lantern dome filled with stained glass, and the whole surface of the ceiling and parts of the wall were extravagantly adorned with carvings of flowers and scrolls, whilst the lantern lights were vaulted, highly enriched, supported by columns, and additionally decorated by candelabra.

Adjoining the old House of Lords, and separating it from the House of Commons, was the ancient building called the Painted Chamber. This was an apartment in the old Royal Palace, and was often used as a place of meeting for the Lords and Commons when they held a conference. The chamber was small. When, in consequence of increased accommodation being required in the House of Commons, the tapestry and wainscoting were taken down, it was discovered that the interior had been originally painted with single figures and historical subjects, arranged round the chamber in a succession of subjects in six bands, somewhat similar to the Bayeux tapestry. Careful drawings were made at the time by Mr. J. T. Smith for his book on Westminster, and they have since been engraved in the "Vetusta Monumenta," from drawings made in 1819 by Charles Stothard.

The subjects represented were chiefly battle

scenes. We learn from Walpole's "Anecdotes of Painting" that they "were certainly as old as 1322, and perhaps much older, since in the twenty-first year of the reign of Henry III. a mandate occurs for paying to Odo the goldsmith, clerk of the works at Westminster, 'four pounds and eleven shillings for pictures to be done in the King's chamber there.'" It was from these mural paintings that the apartment came to be called the faces while engaged in signing the death-warrant of their king. Here the last remains of the gentle Elizabeth Claypole, and, in more recent times, the eloquent Earl of Chatham, and his son, William Pitt, successively lay in state. Here, also, on the night of February 14, 1685, was the last resting-place of the embalmed body of King Charles II. before it was finally laid within the royal vaults of the Abbey."

THE PAINTED CHAMBER, 1830. (*See page* 497.)

Painted Chamber. In this room the Parliaments were at one time opened, and it is said to have been the bed-chamber of Edward the Confessor. Howel relates a tradition that that monarch died in it. That Edward the Confessor died at Westminster, and consequently in his palace there, is an historical fact; but whether this identical chamber was the scene of his decease is a point open to speculation. On the third, fourth, and fifth days of the trial of Charles I., the examination of witnesses was carried on in the Painted Chamber, whither the court had adjourned from Westminster Hall. In this chamber, says Mr. Walcott, in his "Westminster," "occurred the ill-timed buffoonery between Oliver Cromwell and Henry Martin, when they inked each other's

We may here add that in the library of the House of Lords is the original warrant for the execution of Charles I., signed by Oliver Cromwell and the other Parliamentary leaders. It was found shortly after the Restoration in the possession of an old lady in Berkshire, and its fatal autographs formed the ground of the prosecution of the regicides. It is framed and glazed, and preserved here as a most curious and valuable document. It was lost for a time in the confusion consequent on the burning of the House of Lords in 1834, but was again found and replaced. To some minds it seemed as if the element of fire was averse to blotting out the memory of regicide names.

The old building used by the House of Commons for their sittings occupied the site of the present St. Stephen's Hall (p. 508), and, as already stated, was originally the chapel of the ancient palace. Being a free chapel, it was included in the statute of 1st Edward VI., and being transferred from the Church to the Crown, fell into the king's House of Commons. The lower storey, which was level with the pavement of the street, was formerly known as the Chapel of St. Mary in the Vaults; but part of it was latterly enclosed to contain a stove for warming the chamber above,

ENTRANCE TO THE HOUSE OF LORDS, 1780. (*See page* 497.)

hands, by whom it was assigned for the sittings of the representatives of the people.

The building was of an oblong shape, about ninety feet in length by thirty in width, and had externally at each corner an octagonal tower. It was lighted by five windows on each side, and its walls were supported by substantial buttresses between each window on the outside. It consisted of two storeys, the upper one being used as the and another portion served as the Speaker's state dining-room. The whole front, next to the street, was rebuilt in the Gothic style and cased with stucco at the beginning of the present century. The building is described by Mr. Allen in his "History of London" as "a confused and ill-formed assemblage of towers, turrets, and pinnacles, jumbled together without taste or judgment; rendered the more offensive from the proximity of the

Abbey and the Hall, and certainly not improved by the poverty-struck cloister subsequently appended to its basement."

In what manner the House of Commons was at first fitted up is not definitely known. In the seal for the Court of King's Bench at Westminster (1648), that for the Common Pleas for the county palatine of Lancaster (1648), the Parliament seal (1649), and the Dunbar medal (1650), the walls are represented as having only a plain wainscoting. However, it appears about the year 1651 they were covered with tapestry hangings, probably to conceal this wainscoting, for they are so given in the perspective view of the House of Commons, on the back of the Great Seal of the Commonwealth (1651), and in this manner they continued to be decorated down to the time of Queen Anne, in whose reign Sir Christopher Wren was employed to repair the building, and to fit the interior with galleries.

The House in itself had nothing very striking to recommend it; convenience, not ornament, appears to have been the principal object of those who enlarged this ancient chapel and applied it to the use of the Legislature. The galleries, which ran along the sides and west end, for the accommodation of members and strangers, were supported by slender iron pillars, crowned with gilt Corinthian capitals, and the walls were wainscoted to the ceiling. The Speaker's chair stood at some distance from the wall; it was highly ornamented with gilding, and bore the royal arms above. Before the chair was a table at which sat the Clerks of the Parliament. In the centre of the room, between the table and the bar, was a capacious area. The seats for the members occupied each side and both ends of the room, with the exception of the passages. There were five rows of seats, rising in gradation above each other, with short backs, and green morocco cushions. The usual entrance for members of Parliament to the old House of Commons was through Westminster Hall.

The Speaker's House, of which we have given a view on page 495, adjoined St. Stephen's Chapel, and there, in the days of Sir C. Manners Sutton, Theodore Hook, as a clever and witty Tory writer, had often been agreeably entertained. Paying his last visit to the Speaker's House after the fire of 1834, he was received, it seems, in an apartment which had escaped, but exhibited sad marks of the surrounding devastation. It was the break-up of many kind and grateful associations. In his diary-book, he says, "I turned after leaving them and kissed the threshold. I shall be there no more." His prophecy was true; for with the new year Sir C. Manners Sutton was superseded by Mr. Abercromby as Speaker.

On the south side of St. Stephen's Chapel were Cotton's Gardens, so called because they formed part of the residence of Sir Robert Cotton, the founder of the Cottonian Library, which forms such a valuable part of the British Museum. They are now partly covered over by the new House of Lords and the Peers' Court. Strype thus mentions Cotton House: "In the passage out of Westminster Hall into Old Palace Yard, a little beyond the stairs going up to St. Stephen's Chapel, now the Parliament House" (that is, the present St. Stephen's Hall), "is the house belonging to the ancient and noble family of the Cottons, wherein is kept a most inestimable library of manuscript volumes found both at home and abroad." Sir Christopher Wren describes the house in his time as in "a very ruinous condition." Charles I. stayed at Cotton House during part of his trial in Westminster Hall. On the side of Cotton's Gardens there was formerly an ancient chapel dedicated to "Our Lady de la Pieu;" though the name is variously spelt, in all probability it is a corruption of *les puits*, "the wells."

Between the Houses of Lords and Commons and the river were "Parliament Stairs." These stairs were open for the accommodation of the Westminster Scholars for rowing. Such, at all events, was the case as lately as 1801, when, as we learn from that matter-of-fact antiquary, Mr. J. T. Smith, "the key was held by Mr. Tyrwhitt, whose servants regularly opened and closed the gates morning and night."

Standing parallel with the river, on the eastern side of New Palace Yard, was the ancient council chamber of the royal palace, where the king sat in extraordinary causes. It was for some time used as the Lottery Office, and had been for centuries known as the "Star Chamber." The origin of the name of the Star Chamber has been much disputed; but "the most satisfactory explanation," says the author of "Things Not Generally Known," "appears to be that given by Mr. Caley in the third volume of the 'Archæologia,' namely, from the ceiling of the chamber being anciently ornamented with gilded stars." The occupation of the "Chambre des Estoyers" or "Estoilles," by the king's council, in the Palace at Westminster, can be traced to the reign of Edward III.; but no specific mention of the Star Chamber as a court of justice is found earlier than the reign of Henry VII., about which time the old title-deeds of "the Lords sitting in the Star Chamber," and "the council in the Star Chamber," says the author above referred to, seemed to have merged in this one distinguishing appellation. After the sittings, the Lords dined in the inner Star Chamber at the public expense. The mode of the proceedings was twofold: one *ore tenus*, or by the mouth; the other, by bill and answer. The proceeding *ore tenus*, usually adopted in political cases, originated in "soden reporte," which Mr. John Bruce, writing in the eighth volume of "Archæologia," considers to mean private and probably secret information given to the council. The person accused or suspected was immediately apprehended, and privately examined. If he confessed any offence, or if the cunning of his examiners drew from him, or his own simplicity let fall, any expressions which suited their purpose, he was at once brought to the bar, his confession or examination was read, he was convicted *ex ore suo* (out of his own mouth), and judgment was immediately pronounced against him. Imagination can scarcely picture a more terrible judicature. This tribunal was bound by no law, but created and defined the offences it punished; the judges were in point of fact the prosecutors; and every mixture of those two characters is inconsistent with impartial justice. Crimes of the greatest magnitude were tried in this court, but solely punished as trespasses, the council not having dared to usurp the power of inflicting death. Among the many abuses of the process was that, in the time of Queen Elizabeth, "many solicitors who lived in Wales, Cornwall, or the farthest parts of the North, did make a trade to sue forth a multitude of subpœnas to vex their neighbours, who, rather than they would travel to London, would give them any composition, though there were no colour of complaint against them." The process might anciently be served in any place: in the pre-Reformation times it was usually served in the market or church. The largest number of the council who attended the court in the reigns of Henry VII. and VIII. was nearly forty, of whom seven or eight were prelates; in the reign of Elizabeth the number was nearly thirty, but it subsequently declined. The chancellor was the supreme judge, and alone sat with his head uncovered. Upon important occasions, persons who wished "to get convenient places and standing" went there by three o'clock in the morning. The counsel were confined to a "laconical brevity;" the examinations of the witnesses were read, and the members of the court delivered their opinions in order from the inferior upwards, the archbishop preceding the chancellor. Every punishment, except death, was assumed to be within the power of the Star Chamber Court. Pillory, fine and imprisonment, and whipping, wearing of papers through Westminster Hall, and letters "seared in the face with hot irons," were ordinary punishments inflicted by this court.

Henry VII. had a fondness for sitting in the Star Chamber: the court was the great instrument for his "extort doynge;" and "the king took the matter into his own hands," was a Star-Chamber phrase; while "my attorney must speak to you," was a sure prelude to a heavy fine. Wolsey made a great display of his magnificence in the Star Chamber: he proceeded to the sittings of the court in great state, his mace and seal being carried before him; "he spared neither high nor low, but judged every estate according to their merits and deserts." After his fall, with the exception of occasional interference in religious matters and matters of police, we seldom hear of the Star Chamber.

The proceedings in the Star Chamber, being taken under ecclesiastical instead of royal authority, have always been regarded by Englishmen with extreme dislike and aversion. And it may be added that the severity of its sentences in proportion to the importance of the offences has given good reason for its unpopularity. Thus we read that "one Bennet was fined a thousand pounds to the king, and another thousand to the Earl of Marlborough, for saying that he dealt basely with him for not paying him thirty pounds, ... and laying to his lordship's charge that he was a common drunkard." Dr. Osbaldiston, too, a prebendary of Westminster, and formerly a master of Westminster School, and Dr. Williams, Bishop of Lincoln, were here found guilty of *scandalum magnatum* for defaming the great men of the day, by calling Archbishop Laud "the great Leviathan." The bishop was sentenced to pay a fine of £5,000, and Osbaldiston to have his ears tacked to the pillory in Palace Yard, a punishment which he escaped by going beyond the sea.

In the Star Chamber, in the year 1587, Philip Earl of Arundel was fined £10,000. In 1636, John Lilburne, being here convicted of publishing seditious libels, was sentenced to pay £5,000, to stand in the pillory, and be whipped at a cart's tail from Fleet Prison to the gate of Westminster Hall. About this time a more celebrated character figures in its annals. William Prynne, a barrister of Lincoln's Inn, was cited to appear in the Star Chamber for having published an attack upon the stage in the shape of a quarto volume of more than a thousand pages, entitled, "Histrio-Mastix: the Player's Scourge, or Actor's Tragedy;" he was also charged with having railed not only against all stage-plays and players, dancing, &c., but against all who thought fit to attend such performances, while he knew that the queen, the lords of council, &c., were oftentimes spectators of masques and dances. It was urged against him that he had thus cast aspersions upon the queen, spoken censoriously and uncharitably against all Christian people, and, in addition, had made use of infamous terms against the king. He was sentenced to stand twice in the pillory, to lose both his ears, to pay a heavy fine, and to be imprisoned for life. Mr. Gerard says, in one of his letters to Lord Strafford, "No mercy was showed to Prynne: he lost his first ear in the pillory in the Palace at Westminster, in full term; the other in Cheapside; where, whilst he stood, his volumes were burnt under his nose, which had almost suffocated him."

The Star Chamber, at the final abolition of the court by Parliament in 1641, was still holding its sittings in the buildings on the eastern side of New Palace Yard; these buildings appear to have been restored by Queen Elizabeth, as they bore the date 1602, and "E. R.," and an open rose on a star; they corresponded with the "Starre Chamber" in Aggas' plan of London (1570). The last of the buildings were taken down in 1836; drawings were then made of the court, which had an enriched ceiling, but there were no remains of the *star* ornamentations behind the Elizabethan panelling; the style of the chamber was Tudor-Gothic. A view of the building will be found on page 504. The remains were sold by auction and purchased by the late Sir Edward Cust, the walls of whose dining room at Leasowe Castle, Cheshire, they now decorate. They consist chiefly of oak-panelling, and a handsome chimney-piece of the Renaissance style, together with a single length of an earlier date, which stood at the end furthest removed from the chimney-piece, and was thought to have formed a background for the king's chair of state, if ever he chose to be present in the Council. The rose, the fleur de lys, the portcullis, and the pomegranate, which adorned parts of these remains, show their date conclusively—namely, the period of the first marriage of Henry VIII. The Star Chamber, it may be added, on the suppression of the Court which sat in it, became a depository for rubbish; and when the fire in which the Houses of Parliament were destroyed was extinguished, it was found that one side of it was full of the old "tallies," which were used—though it is difficult to believe the fact—down to the end of the Georgian era, to keep the national accounts!

Adjoining the old House of Commons was a coffee and chop house of great celebrity—indeed, it may be said of Parliamentary fame—known among the veterans of St. Stephen's Chapel as "Bellamy's." Englishmen, as we all know, can do nothing without a dinner, or a luncheon, at the least; and so to "Bellamy's," day after day during the Parliamentary session, would repair the members of committees, witnesses, lawyers and their clients, and in the evening many of the leading M.P.'s lounged in during dull debates, making it serve the purpose of a club. "Nothing is more common," observse a writer of the last generation, "than to adjourn upon occasions of triumphs in the Committee Rooms to 'Bellamy's,' where some of the best wine that can be drank in London, and some ot the best chops and steaks that were ever sought to be cooked, almost console even a country member or a stranger for an hour or two's imprisonment in a close room or crowded gallery. A man with eyes to see and a nose to smell, or a tongue to taste, perforce acknowledges that not even the houris in Paradise could serve up a better steak to the most devout Mohammedan that finds his way thither. . . . . The steaks are so hot, and so tender, and so accurately dressed, the old Nankin China is so inviting, and the port, the sherry, and the madeira so unexceptionable, and so excellently *bodied* for an Englishman's palate, that really now and then a man would rather dine at 'Bellamy's' than at home. And then it is so pleasant to watch the magical skill with which grave and learned members who have just alighted from their carriages and commenced an apology for their dinner or supper, as the case may be, jump up from their seats on hearing the 'division bell' ring, and run downstairs headlong into 'the House' in order to give their votes. True, they may not have heard a word of the debate, they may not know who has spoken, or what has been said in their absence; but I presume that in the House of Commons gentlemen come to vote by instinct. On many occasions have I been sipping my port in that coffee-room, and have heard the charmed bell rung, and have seen twenty members rise up, like Macbeth's guests, in most admired disorder." The "Family Joe Miller," published in the year 1848, writes—of course in fun—"The Bellamy privilege of feeding the House of Commons with beef is to be withdrawn, unless the honourable gentlemen are regularly crammed with wit for our volume before each debate." But "Bellamy's" time-honoured chop house has passed away, having been superseded by cooking "done on the premises" under the surveillance of a committee of "the House" itself: and so *stat nominis umbra.*

CHAPTER LIX.

THE NEW PALACE, WESTMINSTER.

"The echoes of its vaults are eloquent,
The stones have voices, and the walls do live;
It is the house of memory."—*Maturin.*

Extent and Dimensions of the New Palace—Plans and Suggestions for Enlarging and Improving the Old House before its Destruction by Fire—Selection of the Design for the New Building—Description of the Exterior—The Victoria Tower—The Fresco Paintings—The House of Lords—Site of the Old House of Commons—The New House of Commons—The Speaker's Residence—The Clock Tower, and Vicissitudes of "Big Ben."

THE site of the old Royal Palace at Westminster is now occupied by the Houses of Parliament, or, to speak more correctly, by the New Palace. This forms one of the most magnificent buildings ever erected in a single decade in Europe—probably the largest Gothic edifice in the world. The reader who has not yet had the good fortune to make a survey of this great temple of legislation may glean some idea of its vast proportions when we state that it covers an area of nearly nine acres; that to the eastward it presents a frontage of nearly 1,000 feet; that the great tower at the south-western extremity reaches the gigantic elevation of nearly 350 feet; that towers of lesser magnitude crown other portions of the building; that fourteen halls, galleries, vestibules, and other apartments of great capacity and noble proportions are contained within it; that it comprises several official residences, each a first-rate mansion, fit to receive families of distinction; that twenty corridors and lobbies are required to serve as the great roadways through this aggregation of edifices; that thirty-two noble apartments facing the river are occupied as committee-rooms; that libraries, waiting-rooms, dining-rooms, and clerks' offices, exist in a superabundant measure; that eleven greater courts and a score of minor openings give light and air to the interior of this superb fabric; that its cubic contents exceed 15,000,000 feet, being one-half more than St. Paul's; and that the structure contains not less than between 500 and 600 distinct apartments, amongst which is a chapel for Divine worship, formed out of the crypt of old St. Stephen's.

For some years previous to the destruction of the old Houses of Parliament by fire, on the 16th of October, 1834, various plans had been suggested for enlarging and improving the buildings, especially the House of Commons, which, besides not affording adequate accommodation for its numerous members, was ill ventilated and unwholesome, and negotiations for building a new House of Commons were at that time in progress. Indeed, it was not only the House of Commons which was felt to be too incommodious and ill suited for its purposes, but the same might also be said of the "Upper House;" for, at various times between 1790 and 1825, the late Sir John Soane was instructed to prepare plans and designs for the rebuilding of, or at all events, for making most extensive alterations and improvements in the existing House of Lords; and drawings of these designs, dated in 1794 and 1796, are to be seen in the Soane Museum, in Lincoln's Inn Fields. By their side is a view of a design for the Royal Gallery, erected by the same architect, in the House of Lords, in 1823-24. In the same year he almost wholly re-modelled the Court of Chancery, at Westminster, and the Court of King's Bench, close by, in 1826.

After the fire in 1834, commissioners were appointed to take into consideration whether it would be practicable to restore any part of the old building for the future meetings of the Parliament; or if that were not possible, on what plan an edifice more suited for the assembly of the Legislature should be erected. The latter course being at last decided on, as many as ninety-seven sets of designs were sent in, many of them of complicated and elaborate detail, showing great skill and talent on the part of the architects who exhibited them. The designs of Mr. (afterwards Sir) Charles Barry, R.A., were at last selected, in 1836; but it was not until 1839 that preparations for the new building were actually commenced. The "first stone" was laid on the 27th of April, 1840. In the details of the building he was largely assisted by the late Mr. A. W. Pugin, whose familiarity with Gothic architecture was probably unequalled since the Middle Ages.

A vignette showing the first design of Sir Charles Barry, with the Clock and Victoria Towers at either end, as at present, but with great variation in the details of the main body of the structure, may be seen in the first volume of Dr. C. Mackay's "Thames and its Tributaries."

Viewed from the river, the building presents a frontage of nearly a thousand feet, and consists of a centre portion with towers, two wings, and wing-towers at each end. The wings have two storeys above the basement; the centre and wing-towers three storeys. The wings and centre portions are divided into thirty-five bays by hexagonal buttresses, with sunk tracery and pinnacles to each. The bays between the principal windows contain the arms and supporters of all the sovereigns of England, richly carved, from William the Conqueror to her present Majesty, Queen Victoria; and on each side are panels, with sceptres, labels, and appropriate foliage. In bands underneath each window are the names of the several sovereigns, with the time of their reign and the date of their decease.

THE STAR CHAMBER. *From a Drawing taken in 1836.* (*See page* 500.)

The parapets to each bay are filled with rich tracery, in the centre of which is a niche, with the figure of an angel holding a shield, bearing the monogram "V.R." The towers have bold oriel windows, with armorial bearings on each, and panels containing the insignia of the present reign, with octagon turrets at the angles, and surmounted by an iron roof. Between the towers, at each end, are three bays, divided by smaller buttresses and bays, within which are windows and panels, containing the arms of the three kingdoms, with the rose, shamrock, and thistle entwined. The flanks of the wing-towers are divided into two bays by a square buttress, containing six niches, with statues of St. George, St. Andrew, St. Patrick, and St. David (the patron saints of the four kingdoms), and St. Peter and St. Paul. Between the windows are panels containing angels supporting an imperial crown over the royal arms. In bands over the windows of the second storey are panels, with the devices assumed by each sovereign since the Conquest, with mottoes and foliage. In the parapet in front of the towers, supported by an angel corbel, is a niche containing a statue of her Majesty; and the parapets at the back of each have a niche with a statue of Edward the Confessor, the founder of the first Royal Palace at Westminster.

The north and south returns of the river front are also divided into bays by hexagonal buttresses. Each bay is divided into two parts by niches, containing the statues of the Saxon kings and queens, from Vortigern (first king of the Heptarchy) down to Harold.

The exterior of the edifice is built of magnesian limestone, from Anston, in Yorkshire, and the interior of Caen stone; all the beams and girders are of iron, with brick arches between the floors, making the building entirely fire-proof. The commission recommended the magnesian limestone of

Bolsover Moor and its neighbourhood as the fittest and most durable material; but the quarry would not produce the quantity required, and the stone from Anston was used instead.

The residence for the Speaker is situated at the north end, the corresponding terminal towards the south containing the residence of the Peers' Librarian. Between the two extremes, and comprising what are called the curtain portions, are the library of the House of Peers and the library of the House of Commons; in the immediate centre is the conference-room for the two Houses. All this is on the principal floor, which is some fifteen feet above the terrace, or high-water mark. The whole of the floor above the libraries, and overlooking the river, is appropriated to committee-rooms for the purposes of Parliament, the Peers occupying about one-third towards the south, and the Commons two-thirds towards the north. The House of Peers and the House of Commons are situated in the rear of the front next the river, and are inclosed also towards the west, so as to be entirely surrounded by Parliamentary offices.

The Royal or Victoria Tower, at the south-west angle, is one of the most stupendous works of the kind ever conceived. It is seventy-five feet square, and rises to the height of 345 feet. "Compared with this magnificent altitude," says a writer in the *Illustrated London News*, "all other towers that we know of shrink into insignificance. There are spires enough, undoubtedly, of greater height, but no towers: even that noble one at Mechlin, half spire, half tower, and which, perhaps, comes nearest to that at Westminster, is but 348 feet to the top of the vane; while to the top of the vane of the Victoria Tower is no less than 420, more than double the height of the Monument, more than sixty feet higher than the top of the cross of St. Paul's, and within a few feet of three times the height of the famous tower of Pisa. The visitor who wishes to ascend the tower passes at once to the south octagon turret, which he enters through a low iron door. At the first moment all seems wrapped in darkness, but after a while the eye, growing accustomed to the obscurity, discerns the last step of a well-staircase of iron, which winds up and up in apparently endless spirals, till the circling balustrade is merged together in the long perspective, terminating at a dim bluish spot no bigger than your hand, which marks the outlet on

ST. STEPHEN'S CRYPT—INTERIOR. (*See page* 503.)

to the tower roof, nearly 350 feet above you. This tremendous flight of steps—the longest unbroken spiral staircase in the world—is illuminated only by the distant ray we have mentioned, and it is curious to note the solemn effect produced by the receding twilight as it penetrates deeper and deeper down the well till lost in almost total darkness. A dozen weary turns up this stair conduct the visitor by a passage to the first and largest floor in the tower—one which occupies the whole extent of the building over the great entrance archway. It is an apartment fifty-one feet square and seventeen feet six inches high, and this gives the visitor the best notion of the interior construction.

"The tower is constructed from top to bottom of brick, stone, and iron, without any admixture of combustible materials, being thus entirely fire-proof from base to summit. It was erected as a grand repository for State papers, records, and muniments of the nation; and for this purpose it is divided into eleven storeys, each of which, with the exception of the basement storey and the first floor immediately over it, contains sixteen fire-proof rooms. All these floors are made to communicate by means of a most singularly-constructed flying spiral staircase of iron, which passes through an octagonal aperture in all the floors, with each of which it joins by means of a short landing. The well of this beautiful staircase is about ten feet in diameter, and a similar aperture is made in the groined roof of the royal archway, but this is kept closed by means of a sliding iron door. When, however, it is drawn back, a person standing on the ground under the centre of the tower can see up at a glance, as through a telescope, from the bottom to the top.

"The roof of the tower is sloping, reaching sixteen feet above the parapet, and surrounded with a gilt railing six feet high. The four corners are guarded by four stone lions, twenty feet high, and from the base of the corners spring four cast-iron flying arched buttresses, which are formed in the centre in a kind of crown about thirty feet above the roof. The upper edges of these buttresses are decorated with a richly-gilt wrought-iron railing, which makes them, when united, still more resemble a coronet, and in keeping with the regal aspect of the tower. Seen from the outside, the great general features we have attempted to describe look bolder and more striking still; and though the ornaments are so numerous, the tracery so multiplied, and the height of the whole mass from the eye so great, there is still no confusion of parts. The mind fixes its massive and just proportions without distraction; and as the eye glances down its sculptured records of our line of kings, with all their bright historical associations connected with the very Parliament to which it marks the entrance, the visitor feels that it is more than a mere tower; it is a sculptured monument of our great history as a nation."

The royal entrance beneath this tower is probably one of the most striking and effective portions of the new Palace of Westminster. The loftiness of the vaulted groining, the rich and varied bosses at its intersections, the canopied niches over the doors, and the exquisite variety of the details, all unite in producing a charming whole. There are two lofty arches on the south and west sides, as entrances. Entering beneath the tower, the royal gateway is on the north side, and consists of a beautiful archway deeply recessed, having within it a lesser archway, serving as the doorway. Over this is a panel containing the royal arms, supported by angels, very elaborately sculptured. Above the outer arch the wall is panelled into five divisions, the three central ones having in them very beautiful niches, containing figures of the Queen, Justice, and Mercy, standing on short pedestals, bearing shields charged with devices, and further enriched with labels, &c.; and the two outer divisions are filled with angels holding labels. Round the outer edge of the arch is a peculiarly rich cresting of roses and leaves. On the eastern side the wall is divided, similarly to the northern, into a lofty arch containing a dwarf arch deeply recessed, which leads into a long and narrow passage communicating with the Royal Court, where the state carriages wait during the Queen's stay in the House of Lords. Over this dwarf archway the royal arms and the crest of the Prince of Wales are the decoration. There are five divisions on the main portion of the wall exactly corresponding to those on the north wall, three of them containing figures of St. George, St. Patrick, and St. Andrew, standing on pedestals bearing the respective crosses used as their symbols; and the remaining two, angels holding shields bearing the royal arms. The rose cresting adorns this as well as the other arch, and bosses of the utmost variety of design fill the hollow of the jambs in both the great arches. This stately tower (supplying what Wren considered Westminster so much to need) was finished, by slow degrees, in 1857, the architect deeming it of importance that the works should not proceed, for fear of settlement, at a greater rate than thirty feet a year.

The royal staircase is entered from the Victoria Tower, and is very beautiful in design. There are three flights of eight stairs each, leading to a vestibule of exquisite beauty, having clustered columns, supporting a very elegantly-groined roof, with bosses of great variety of design at the intersections of the ribs. Groups of pedestals, with statues, are at the bases of the columns. In this vestibule there are doors of entrance into a guard-room and into the Queen's Robing-room.

The Robing-room, a lofty and spacious apartment, with a canopied throne at the further end, is adorned with carvings and with Dyce's frescoes from the "Legend of King Arthur." There are two doors to this room, one close upon the porch, the other nearer the throne; and Her Majesty, entering at the former, comes forth at the latter into a noble hall, 110 feet long, 45 wide, and 45 high. This is called the Royal Gallery, and is decorated with frescoes illustrative of the "Death of Nelson at the Battle of Trafalgar," and the "Meeting of Wellington and Blucher at Waterloo," by Daniel Maclise, R.A. The windows are filled with stained glass, and the ceiling is richly adorned with gilding and heraldry.

Passing from the Royal Gallery we enter the Prince's Chamber. This apartment is decorated with equal splendour to that just described; it contains a noble marble group, by Gibson, of the Queen, supported by Justice and Mercy.

The House of Lords, which we now enter, is nearly 100 feet long by 45 feet wide, and the same in height. The chamber presents a *coup d'œil* of the utmost magnificence, no expense having been spared to make it one of the richest in the world. The ceiling first attracts attention. It is not arched, but perfectly horizontal; massive ribs, carved and gilt, divide it into eighteen compartments, and each of these is subdivided into five minor compartments, or panels, the ground of the panels being azure, enriched with heraldic devices. The ribs are, of course, supported by corbels and by spandrils, perforated. At each point in the ceiling where the ribs intersect each other, there are pendants, which greatly enhance the beauty of that portion of the building; but there are no depending lights—no lustres, no chandeliers swinging from the roof, to conceal elegance or cover deformity. The length of the House of Lords extends from north to south, and during the day it is lighted by twelve windows—six on either side —which reach nearly to the ceiling, but do not approach within twenty feet of the floor. These apertures are double glazed, the inner portion being of stained glass. Upon the same level with the windows, but on the northern and southern walls, are six compartments, three on each extremity of the house, filled with fresco paintings. The first of these frescoes, immediately over the throne, is the "Baptism of Ethelbert," painted by Mr. Dyce, R.A., and on either side are "Edward III. conferring the Order of the Garter on Edward the Black Prince," and "Henry, Prince of Wales, committed to Prison for assaulting Judge Gascoigne," both by Mr. Cope, R.A.; at the opposite end of the chamber are the "Spirit of Religion," by Mr. Horsley, R.A.; in the centre compartment, over the Strangers' Gallery, on either side are the "Spirit of Chivalry" and the "Spirit of Law," both by Daniel Maclise. Between the windows and at either end of the House, are eighteen niches, containing statues of the Magna Charta barons.

Having now surveyed the upper portion of the House, we descend to the galleries. That which is for strangers bearing peers' orders occupies the north wall, and contains accommodation for about one hundred and fifty persons. The throne and the reporters' gallery fill spaces of pretty nearly equal extent, but at opposite ends of the House. With the exception of those spaces, there is carried round the entire apartment a light gallery, consisting of only one line of seats, and capable of containing nearly two hundred persons. The railing which protects these seats is a very beautiful specimen of brass-work and enamel. The reporters' gallery is placed in front of the strangers' gallery, but considerably nearer to the floor, and immediately over the bar.

The floor of the House presents to the eye of the spectator three principal divisions, which extend transversely, viz., from east to west, each occupying the full breadth of the apartment, but unequal parts of its length. In the upper or southern division is the throne, together with spaces on either side assigned to distinguished foreigners and the eldest sons of peers. Next comes the central region, or "body of the House," the table and woolsack occupying the middle portion of the floor. On each side of these are placed, on ascending steps, five lines of benches, covered with scarlet morocco leather, which are reserved for the exclusive use of the peers. The northern or lower boundary of this division is called the "bar:" here the Speaker, accompanied by the assembly over which he presides, stands when summoned to attend Her Majesty or the Royal Commissioners. From that place gentlemen of the long robe address the House in its judicial capacity; witnesses are also there examined, and culprits are arraigned. The space below the bar affords standing room for two or three hundred persons who are entitled to admission there.

The throne is distinguished by an airy, light, and graceful character, which harmonises at once with the building and its surroundings. The platform on which Her Majesty's chair stands is ascended by four steps, and constitutes a sort of central compartment, on either side of which, forming as it were two wings, are minor elevations, where stand two other chairs of state, one for the Prince of Wales, and the other was placed for the late Prince Consort; the former is on the right of the throne, and the latter on the left. The framework of Her Majesty's chair of state is carved in gilt, and studded with crystals. In other respects the structure of these seats is conformable with the established fashion of such furniture, being cushioned with velvet and gold embroidery. The royal arms are emblazoned on the central chair, those of the heir-apparent on the chair appropriated to the Prince of Wales; the other chair is adorned with the shield of the late Prince Consort, surmounted by the multitudinous crests which Germans of noble blood are usually entitled to display. In the most elevated and conspicuous part of the throne are five niches, in which are placed statuettes, fully armed, each in the costume of one of the chief British orders of knighthood.

It was customary a century and a half ago, as now, for strangers, including ladies, to gain admission to hear the debates in the House of Peers, and probably in the House of Commons also. But in 1738 it was resolved to exclude the fair sex; and the attempt to enforce their exclusion led to an amusing scene which is described by Lady Mary Wortley Montague in one of her "Letters."

Passing northward, through the Peers' lobby and corridor, we reach the grand central octagon hall, above which rises the central tower. The exquisitely-groined stone roof of this hall is supported without a central pillar, and contains a long series of elaborately-carved bosses. Here are statues of Earl (Lord John) Russell, the Earl of Iddesleigh, and Earl Granville. One of Mr. John Bright, which was added in 1896, failed to give satisfaction, and has been removed.

The central hall gives access on the left to St. Stephen's Hall, which occupies the same space as St. Stephen's Chapel of the ancient Palace. Ranged along either side of St. Stephen's Hall are "statues of men who rose to eminence by the eloquence and abilities they displayed in the House of Commons"—Hampden, Falkland, Clarendon, Selden, Somers, Sir Robert Walpole, Lord Mansfield, Lord Chatham, Pitt, Fox, Burke, and Grattan. Visitors to the Houses of Parliament passing through St. Stephen's Hall and halting under the west doorway, see before them the area occupied by the "old" House of Commons and its lobby—the latter serving both as an outer hall and as a division-lobby. "About one-third of the pavement before us," says Mr. R. Palgrave in his "Notes to Lectures on the House of Commons," "was given to the lobby, for the partition that divided it from the House stood on the line between the statues of Chatham and Mansfield. The Speaker sat at the east end of the Hall, the one furthest from our station, as his chair was placed a few paces in front of the steps ascending to the Octagon Hall, and these steps cover the site of the little lobby at the back of the old House, called 'Solomon's Porch.'" On the left side of the entrance to St. Stephen's Hall is the Private Bill Office; the doorway leading to it is modern; so is a winding corkscrew staircase that leads thence down into the cloisters, as also a doorway that opens from those stairs into Westminster Hall; but both the doorway and the stairs are stated to occupy the same position as those which gave access to members to the House between the years 1547 and 1680—that is, from the time the Commons left the Abbey Chapter-house hard by, until the formation of a doorway in the south end wall of Westminster Hall, that led into a passage communicating with the west end of the Commons' Lobby. Here it was that Mr. Perceval passed along, on the 11th of May, 1812; for on the very spot where Burke's statue stands, by the left side of this very door into St. Stephen's Hall, stood, pistol in hand, the madman Bellingham, watching for his victim.

The walls of the corridor leading from the House of Peers to the grand central hall, and also the one leading thence to the House of Commons, are covered with fresco paintings in compartments, the subjects being historical, such as the "Last Sleep of Argyll," the "Execution of Montrose," the "Departure of the Pilgrim Fathers," &c. These frescoes were painted by Cope, Ward, Herbert, and other Royal Academicians.

The Lobby of the House of Commons itself is a very fine apartment, square in plan, about forty-five feet each way, and having a doorway in each side. It forms the chief vestibule to the House of Commons, and by a short corridor communicates with the great octagonal hall in the centre of the Palace, which, in fact, forms the only entrance to the Lobby. Each side of the Lobby is alike in its general features, being divided into three equal parts—the central portion containing a deeply-recessed and lofty doorway, and the others being divided into two storeys. In this hall the messengers of the House sit waiting to be dispatched either to Government offices for documents, or, in the event of a division, to hunt out for members, however late it may be, or, rather, however early in the morning. In connection with this lobby an amusing story is told in Diprose's "Book about London," in which an Irish M.P. figured as the principal personage concerned. "He had taken—his custom always of an afternoon'—some powerful potations of brandy, and falling soundly asleep in his seat in the House, was 'left alone in his glory.' Awaking about two o'clock in the morning, and finding his dormitory more capacious and costly in its fittings than his back attic in Manchester Buildings, he rushed out of the House into the Lobby, when two firemen immediately laid hold of the alarmed and half-sleeping M.P., and sternly demanded what brought him there. He good-humouredly answered, that was what he wanted to ascertain himself; but of one thing the firemen might be certain, that he was not Guy Faux. The worthy guardians against fire and thieves assured the M.P. that he could not leave the House, so that he must rest contented until the morning. 'Well, then,' said the son of Erin, I will go back into the House of Commons, and sleep in the Speaker's chair; far better than a police cell. Some people have a difficulty in getting into this House: my difficulty consists in getting out of it.'"

In this lobby the "Whip"—or whipper-in of his party—spends most of his time, rarely entering the House, but "button-holing" every doubtful and recusant member preparatory to a division, and making as many promises within any given hour as would take him any given seven years to accomplish. The electric bell, which gives notice of a division, rings simultaneously in every department of the vast building, and then comes a schoolboy rush of the members, many of whom, perhaps, have never heard one word of the debate, and know as much about the merits of the question upon which the division is about to take place as does the bell which has summoned them to vote.

The House of Commons, which was first used for the sittings of members in 1850, is of the same height and width as the House of Lords, but little more than sixty feet long, being reduced to the smallest possible size for the sake of hearing. So far as decoration goes, this chamber, compared with the House of Lords, may be considered plain and unpretending. It is surrounded by galleries, which diminish its apparent size. The height of the House and the form of the roof are materially altered from the original design; but, though shorn of its loftiness, it is a magnificent and imposing apartment. The ceiling is divided longitudinally into three parts, the centre division being horizontal, the others inclined downwards; and these longitudinal sections are divided by massive ribs, resting on corbels, into square compartments, which are again subdivided, the horizontal into sixteen, and the other compartments into twenty, small square panels; and on these are painted alternately a rose and a portcullis within floreated circles. The massive ribs are carved along the sides with a very elaborate and beautiful label pattern. The corbels rest on elegantly enriched shafts, springing from brackets having shields supported by lions sculptured upon them; and these are placed on the level of the lower part of the windows. The walls from beneath the windows to the galleries are panelled, the panelling being crested with a very beautiful brattishing.

On the east and west sides of the House there are six windows, and at the north and south ends there are three compartments to correspond with the fenestral arrangement of the sides; these spaces are filled with a very pretty lattice-work of wrought brass, forming a screen to the ladies' galleries. The windows are filled with rich stained glass, displaying the armorial insignia of twenty-four of the English boroughs.

The galleries are particularly effective specimens of design in Gothic wood-work; and, with their hand-rails and trefoil ornament of wrought brass, are extremely fine. The side galleries are for the use of members of the House, and each contains two rows of seats. The northern gallery is for the use of the reporters, and to it there is a separate staircase with retiring-rooms. The southern gallery is divided into three portions, one for peers and other distinguished visitors, the second for those who have orders from the Speaker, the third for those who have orders from members of the House. The galleries are supported by pillars, and underneath, towards the wall, they are coved; which parts we hope will, at no distant day, bear on their gilded surfaces the achievements of the different speakers of the House of Commons, in similar style to the coved soffits of the galleries to the House of Lords. The fronts of the galleries, we should observe, bear on small shields the badges and monograms of the various Sovereigns of England. The Speaker's chair, at the north end of the House, is of very fine design. There are several rows of seats in the body of the House; and all being of ample dimensions, and covered with green morocco leather, harmonising delightfully with the warm brown tints of the oak panelling and framing to the seats, produce an air of repose and comfort. The clerks' table is panelled beneath with elaborately-carved work, and at its southern end are brass scrolls for the Speaker's mace to rest in while the Speaker is in the chair; underneath there are wrought brackets for it to rest on whilst the House is in committee.

The seat of the Serjeant-at-Arms is near the bar, at the southern end of the House. There are two doors on either side of the House, to lead into ceiling into an air-shaft, its exit being provided for by the panels of the ceiling not being made to rest on the intersecting ribs, thus allowing a space of about three-quarters of an inch between the ribs and the panels.

Experiments were made in lighting the House

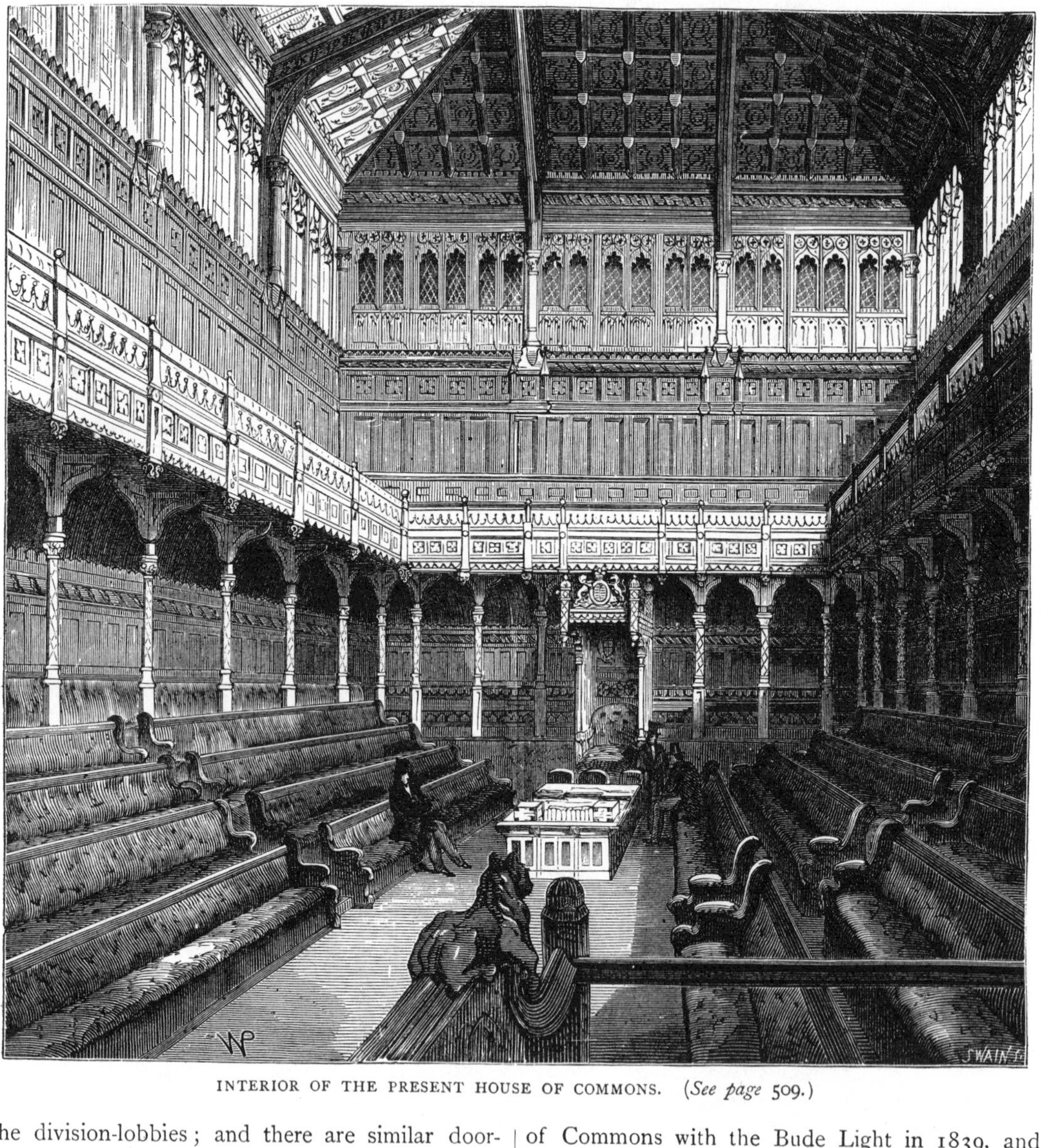

INTERIOR OF THE PRESENT HOUSE OF COMMONS. (*See page* 509.)

the division-lobbies; and there are similar doorways as entrances into the galleries. Behind the Speaker's chair is a doorway leading to retiring-rooms for the Speaker, and communicating with corridors which give access to the Speaker's official residence.

The ventilation of the House of Commons is carried out in a very elaborate fashion; the fresh warm air passing upwards through the perforated floor, and the vitiated air escaping through the

of Commons with the Bude Light in 1839, and the plan was adopted in the following year, to be itself superseded before long by a system which rendered unnecessary the massive chandeliers which were originally suspended from pendants at the intersections of the great beams of the ceiling. The House is now illuminated by gas jets placed above the ceiling. the result being that the light is at once softened and evenly diffused. In other parts of the Palace of Westminster the electric light has

INTERIOR OF THE HOUSE OF COMMONS, 1834. (*See page* 520.)

been installed, and it is by an electric lamp placed above the clock-tower that indication is given to the outside world that Parliament is sitting. During the day the fact is indicated by the Union Jack, which floats above the Victoria Tower.

On building the temporary House of Commons after the fire in 1834, a little gallery for newspaper reporters was erected over the Speaker's chair. What would Woodfall and Perry have given to be thus accommodated in the infancy of reporting? Is the reader aware of the particulars of the struggle of the press with the privileges of the House? They have been frequently recorded. A century and a half ago, when the *Gentleman's Magazine*—that most venerable of periodicals—was in its infancy, the editor, Edmund Cave, ventured to peep into the House and give the public some brief hints of what was said and done. But this was soon put a stop to. The public, however, beginning to relish periodical news, and especially having acquired a slight taste of Parliamentary reporting, were willing to receive more. Their conductors ran risks to supply the demand, but were obliged to offer their contraband goods under fictitious names.

What we to-day think of as journalism began when young Samuel Johnson first composed Parliamentary speeches for Cave's magazine, in 1740, which is equivalent to saying that it began in systematic deception. Johnson avowed the fact a few years later at Foote's table, and avowed it with feeling that seemed nearer akin to exultation than shame. A certain speech, attributed to the elder Pitt, being highly commended, one of the guests took down the magazine and read it aloud. When the company had given full vent to their admiration, Johnson, who had sat silent during the scene, startled them all by saying, "That speech I wrote in a garret in Exeter Street." Responding to their amazement, he explained—"I never was in the gallery of the House of Commons but once in my life. Cave had interest with the doorkeepers. He and the persons employed under him had admittance. They brought away the subject of discussion, the names of the speakers, the side they took, and the order in which they rose, together with notes of the various arguments adduced in the course of debate. The whole was afterwards communicated to me, and I composed the speeches in the form they now have." Here, perhaps, we have the origin of Dr. Johnson's aversion to newspapers, for we all abhor our sins when another commits them. He wrote in one of his *Idlers* for 1758, that if an ambassador may be defined as "a person who lies abroad for his country's good," an editor is one "who lies at home for his own." Towards the end of 1770 a daring effort was made by a number of printers to break through the privilege of the House, and boldly publish its proceedings. This created a great storm. The subject was taken up by the House in the beginning of the year 1771, and a squabble ensued which we have described elsewhere (Vol. I., p. 409). From that period the proceedings of the House have been regularly published. The reporters' gallery of the present House occupies a similar position to that above mentioned, over the Speaker's chair, but is, of course, more commodious, and furnished with suitable retiring-rooms, &c.

The system of reporting, as it now stands, is as follows:—The daily papers, both the metropolitan and provincial, have each a staff of gentlemen trained by long experience, by the aid of shorthand, to take down verbatim reports of the speeches delivered in Parliament. Each member of the staff connected with these papers takes his "turn" of about twenty minutes in the gallery, and on being relieved by his successor, hastily writes out a full or condensed report of the speech from his shorthand notes, and dispatches it by a messenger to his respective journal.

Occasionally the reporters, together with other "strangers," have been ordered to withdraw, by some obnoxious member drawing attention to their presence. But in the session of 1875, one evening the "gallery" was ordered to be cleared when the Prince of Wales was among the "strangers present;" and this was felt to be so outrageous a proceeding that, after much controversy, it was agreed by Mr. Disraeli and Lord Hartington, and definitely laid down for the future, "that if, at any sitting of the House, or in committee, any member shall take notice that strangers are present, Mr. Speaker, or the Chairman (as the case may be), shall forthwith put the question that strangers be ordered to withdraw, without permitting any debate or amendment; provided that Mr. Speaker and the Chairman may, whenever he think fit, order the withdrawal of strangers from the House."

À propos of the above subject, we may add that the late Mr. Luke Hansard, who made a fortune by his business as printer to the House of Commons and editor of the "Debates," several hundred volumes of which bear his name, came to London from Norwich in 1752, a poor friendless boy.

Sick of the drudgery of a solicitor's office, young Charles Dickens was placed, at sixteen or seventeen years old, with Messrs. Gurney, of Abingdon Street, the Parliamentary shorthand writers, where he soon learnt the use of his pen. He was a reporter in the gallery of the House of Commons at the age of eighteen.

The subject of taking oaths by members of Parliament previously to their being entitled to vote on any question has assumed considerable prominence within recent years—firstly, on account of the succession of attempts which have been made to modify the form of oath administered so as to admit of its reception by persons of the Jewish faith and others; and secondly, because of the wholesale performance of the ceremony which the election of a new Parliament necessarily causes. Apart from the religio-political view of the matter, it must be confessed that the proceeding is not very dignified or imposing. In the case of swearing-in of the members of a new Parliament, members present themselves at a long drawn out table, and range themselves, schoolboy fashion, along its sides. A number of pieces of cardboard, on which are printed forms of the oath, are then produced, and one of these is handed to each member. A corresponding number of Testaments are then distributed; after which the clerk, in a more or less audible voice, reads aloud the form of words constituting the oath, and the book is kissed, the only object, apparently, being to get the ceremony over with the least expenditure of time, and to allow it to convey as little meaning to the mind and heart of the ministrant as possible. When the oath is taken by members whom circumstances have caused to be elected in the beginning or in the course of a session, as contradistinguished from the opening of a new Parliament, the Speaker, as soon as questions are over, calls on members desiring to be sworn to come to the table. This the new member does; advancing up the floor of the House between two other members, who are styled his "introducers," and making bows at intervals as he passes along, he goes through the same course as above described. In one single case the above rule was relaxed, and the newly-elected member was allowed to take his seat without the usual introduction. An indispensable part of the ceremony is the production, by the member, of the documentary proof of his election, and the signing of the Parliamentary roll. At the end of it he is presented to the Speaker by the clerk, receives a shake of the hand and a few words of welcome from the right honourable gentleman, and afterwards takes his seat.

Down to the year 1858 it was necessary that every new member on taking his seat should take the oaths prescribed "on the faith of a Christian." But the election of the late Baron Rothschild for the City of London, and of Sir David Salomons for Greenwich, necessitated a departure from these words, and at last, after many delays, in 1860 the obnoxious words were omitted, and members of the Jewish body have since been sworn on the Old Testament only. Long before this, Quakers, Moravians, and others who objected on religious grounds to the taking of an oath, had been allowed to make affirmation, and since 1888 members generally, whatever their creed, have been permitted to choose between the two forms. The Act under which this change was effected was passed at the instance of the late Mr. Bradlaugh, one of the members for Northampton, who during the whole of the Parliament of 1880–85 was involved in conflict with the House of Commons on the subject. The House refused to allow him either to affirm, as he first claimed the right to do, or to take the oath, and he was violently expelled, and more than once his seat was declared vacant. But after the General Election of 1885 the House allowed him to take the oath, and in 1891, as he lay dying, the resolution of 1880 forbidding him either to be sworn or to affirm was expunged.

Connected with our legislative assemblies there are certain odd forms of proceeding, of which it may be presumed that very few but those acquainted with the details of Parliamentary business have any notion. Many persons, for instance, may have seen, while standing in the lobby of the House of Commons, the Speaker in his robes enter, preceded by a gentleman with a bag-wig and a sword by his side, carrying on his shoulder a heavy gilt club, surmounted by a crown—in short, a *mace;* but few people are cognisant how important this toy is to the legislative duties of their representatives. Be it known, then, that without it the House of Commons does not exist; and that it is as essential that the mace should be present at the deliberations of our senate, as that Mr. Speaker should be there himself: without a Speaker the House never proceeds to business, and without his mace the Speaker cannot take the chair. At the commencement of a new Parliament, and before the election of a Speaker, this valuable emblem of his dignity is hidden under the table of the House, and the clerk of the table presides during the election; but no sooner is the Speaker elected, than it is drawn from its hiding-place and deposited on the table, where it ever after remains during the sitting of the House; at its rising, Mr. Speaker carries it away with him, and never trusts it out of his keeping. This important question of the Speaker's duty in retaining constant possession of this, which may be called his gilt walking-stick, was most gravely decided in the year 1763, as appears by the "Journals of the House of Commons." On that occasion, Sir John Cust, the Speaker, being taken ill, sent to tell the House by the clerk at the table, that he could not take the chair. It appears that there was considerable discussion whether the mace ought not to have been in the House when this important communication was made. No one, however, presumed to say that it ought to have been on the table; but many maintained that it ought, for the dignity of the House, to have been underneath it. It was decided, however, that Mr. Speaker had done quite right not to part with his "bauble," and the House accordingly, as the "Journals" inform us, "adjourned themselves without the mace."

Down to the year 1853 it was not possible for the House to continue its sittings without the Speaker's presence; but in that year it was ordered that the Chairman of the Committee of Ways and Means do take the chair in the unavoidable absence of Mr. Speaker.

For a member to cross between the chair and the mace when it is taken from the table by the Serjeant-at-Arms, is an offence which it is the Speaker's duty to reprimand. If, however, a person is brought to the bar to give evidence or receive judgment, he is attended by the Serjeant-at-Arms with the mace on his shoulder; and however desirous any member may be to put a question to the person so standing at the bar, he cannot do so, because the mace is not *on* the table; he must, therefore, write down his questions before the prisoner appears, and propose them through the Speaker, who is the only person allowed to speak when his "bauble" is away.

If the House resolve itself into a committee, the mace is thrust *under* the table, and Mr. Speaker leaves his chair. In short, much of the deliberative proceedings of this branch of the Legislature is regulated by the position in which this important piece of furniture is placed: to use the words of the learned Hatsell, "When the mace lies *upon* the table, it is a *House;* when *under*, it is a *Committee.* When the mace is *out* of the House, no business can be done; when *from* the table and *upon* the Serjeant's shoulder, the Speaker alone manages."

It is a popular error that the mace now borne before the Speaker is the self-same "bauble" that Cromwell ordered away when he dismissed the "rump" of the Long Parliament in April, 1653. The Speaker's mace of the reign of Charles I. doubtless perished when the Crown plate was sold, in 1649. The Commonwealth mace, which came into use in that year, was ornamented "with flowers instead of the cross and ball at the top, and with the arms of England and Ireland, instead of the late king's." This was the "bauble" that Cromwell treated so disrespectfully; and it soon disappeared altogether, for the Restoration supplanted it with a new mace, "with the cross and his Majesty's arms, as they formerly were." The mace that now lies on the table of the House bears neither date, inscription, nor maker's name; but the initials "C.R." and the appearance of the workmanship, coupled with the order for a new mace in 1660, which appears in the "Journals of the House of Commons," fixes the date of its origin.

Considering the very limited area of the House of Commons, a fair proportion of accommodation is afforded to spectators of the proceedings of the Third Estate of the realm. On the floor of the House, but technically outside it, are seats which are appropriated to members of the Corps Diplomatique and other distinguished strangers. Overhead, as we have seen, is a gallery for such of the peers as may be interested in what is going on in the "lower House." The Speaker's Gallery, just behind, has two rows of seats, and will hold about 150 persons. Next to this, but entirely apart from it, access being gained to it by a totally different way, is the Strangers' Gallery.

Admission to the Strangers' Gallery is obtained by means of a written order from a member. There are three rows of seats, each accommodating about seventy persons, who, in common with all the occupants of the places devoted to the public, are subjected to very stringent rules of behaviour. No one is allowed to rise from his seat, except for the purpose of leaving, it is unlawful to glance at a newspaper, and silence as nearly absolute as possible must be observed. The privilege of entering the Strangers' Gallery is one which is very much sought after by enthusiastic constituents, who hunt after the "orders" of their members with considerable assiduity; and specimens of every class of the British elector and non-elector may be seen at times undergoing the rigid pleasure of seeing how things are done in Parliament.

In the course of the Crimean war in 1854-5, a military member of the House raised the question, and the Speaker decided that, although some such custom as the exclusion of officers or soldiers in uniform to the Strangers' Gallery had obtained, he knew of no order of the House to that effect; and now it is by no means an uncommon thing to see non-commissioned officers and privates in their regimentals listening with the prescribed gravity of demeanour to the emanations of the collected representative wisdom of the country.

Several amusing anecdotes are related with

reference to the presence of strangers in the Houses of Parliament during the sittings of the members. In 1833, a Scotch Highlander, in full costume, seated himself to the right of the Speaker's Chair, with as much equanimity as if he were reposing among the heather of his native hills. In 1834, a lady entered by mistake, and "caught the eye of the Speaker," who continued to gaze on her with apparent admiration and satisfaction, quite inattentive to the discourse in progress from a masculine orator, till the fair intruder suddenly vanished. And it is said that in April, 1833, a young Scotchman, finding his seat under the gallery unfavourable for hearing the speech of a countryman, proceeded to establish himself on the back benches, and remained there for two hours, and even till the House adjourned, in spite of the glaring eyes of Mr. Joseph Hume, fixed on him all the time with scrutinising suspicion.

Writing of the Skinners' Company, in his "Survey of the Cities of London and Westminster," Stow says:—"I cannot pass over a passage of one of this Company by reason of the novelty of it. In the year 1584, a new Parliament sat in November, when one Robinson, a lewd fellow, born in Stamford, and a Skinner, had the confidence to sit in the House all the day, though no member, and heard all the speeches, wherein many weighty matters were uttered relating to the concernments of the Queen and the kingdom; which contained such notable passages of State that Fleetwood, the Recorder of London, and then a member, called them *Magnalia Regni* in a letter to the Lord Treasurer. One of these speeches was made by Mr. Chancellor of the Exchequer, Sir Walter Mildmay, which tended to a generality upon the safety of the Queen, whose life was then in danger by a discontented party. Another speech was made by Mr. Vice-Chancellor Sir Christopher Hatton, which lasted two hours. His speech tended to particular and special actions, and concluded with the Queen's safety. When this fellow was discovered he was searched, and nothing found about him. Mr. Fleetwood, the Recorder, Mr. Beal, and other Parliament men and Papist-finders, were sent to search his lodgings, but found nothing. He remained for some time in the Serjeant's custody, and so, as it seems, was dismist."

A correspondent of the *Times* relates a curious incident which occurred to a country clergyman when the late illustrious Duke of Wellington was Prime Minister. "The said clergyman was a very plain country gentleman, the Rev. H. A. Hervey, of Bridekirk, in Cumberland. He walked very innocently into the House of Lords while their lordships were in debate, was not asked a question by any one; he took his seat among their lordships, having put down his hat near one that he saw lying in the neighbourhood where he was sitting; he felt himself very much at his ease, he did not for one moment think that he was out of his proper place there; and having remained until he thought it was time all good people who wished to keep good hours ought to be at home, he rose and went for his hat, but it was gone, and the one left in its place had written inside of it the word 'Wellington.' He was compelled to take it or go without one; and this he took down to his parish with him, and used to have great pleasure in showing it as the great Duke of Wellington's hat, which he was obliged to take, as, he said, 'no doubt the noble Duke had taken his hat by mistake.'"

Similar mishaps have occurred since, and will probably continue to happen. In 1875 an instance occurred in the House of Commons, of which the *Times* gives the following description:—"During the debate on Mr. Pease's motion, two strangers entered the House by the members' doorway, and passing unchallenged, took their seats in the body of the House, on the Liberal side, close by the chair of the Serjeant-at-Arms. There they sat, according to their own story, for over half an hour. How they passed the policemen and doorkeepers, by whom the entrance is so jealously guarded, it is hard to say. Probably they were helped by the easy unconsciousness which comes from ignorance of wrong doing. As they saw the gentlemen around them with their hats on, the two strangers observed what they thought was the etiquette of the place, and kept their hats on too. They had comfortable benches, were not at all crowded, and must have been charmed with the accommodation so thoughtfully provided by Parliament for visitors. At length a division was called. The Speaker's wonted emphatic warning, 'Strangers must withdraw,' fell upon deaf ears, for the two strangers did not understand the summons, and remained in their places. When the doors were locked and tellers were appointed, and members passed leisurely into the division lobbies, the two visitors must have begun to feel uncomfortable, and see that they were not quite where they ought to be. By this time Captain Gosset's attention had been called to them, and the first order they received was, 'Take your hats off.' As the doors were locked the intruders could not be turned out; and it would have been against all Parliamentary precedent to unlock the doors for any purpose. They were therefore led upstairs into the gallery reserved for distinguished strangers, and after the division was over were severely taken to task by Captain Gosset, Colonel Forester, and the officials of the House. Their explanation was simple: they had orders for the Strangers' Gallery, signed, oddly enough, by Colonel Forester himself. They were told by a policeman in the Central Hall to walk 'straight on,' and having done so only too literally, they found themselves in the body of the House, where they sat down, knowing no better. By one of the Standing Orders of the Commons, the Serjeant-at-Arms is directed 'from time to time to take into his custody any stranger or strangers he shall see, or who may be reported to him to be, in any part of the House or gallery appropriated to the members of this House, and also any stranger who, having been admitted into any other part of the House or gallery, shall misconduct himself, or shall not withdraw when strangers are directed to withdraw while the House or any Committee of the whole House is sitting; and that no person so taken into custody be discharged out of custody without the special order of the House.' It was thought, on the whole, inexpedient to make too much of this incident by taking the delinquents into custody, as they really appeared to have erred through ignorance, and therefore no notice was taken by the House of their intrusion. But they were severely admonished, and, it is to be hoped, were duly scared by the representation of the penalties they might have incurred, and the serious breach of the Standing Orders they had committed."

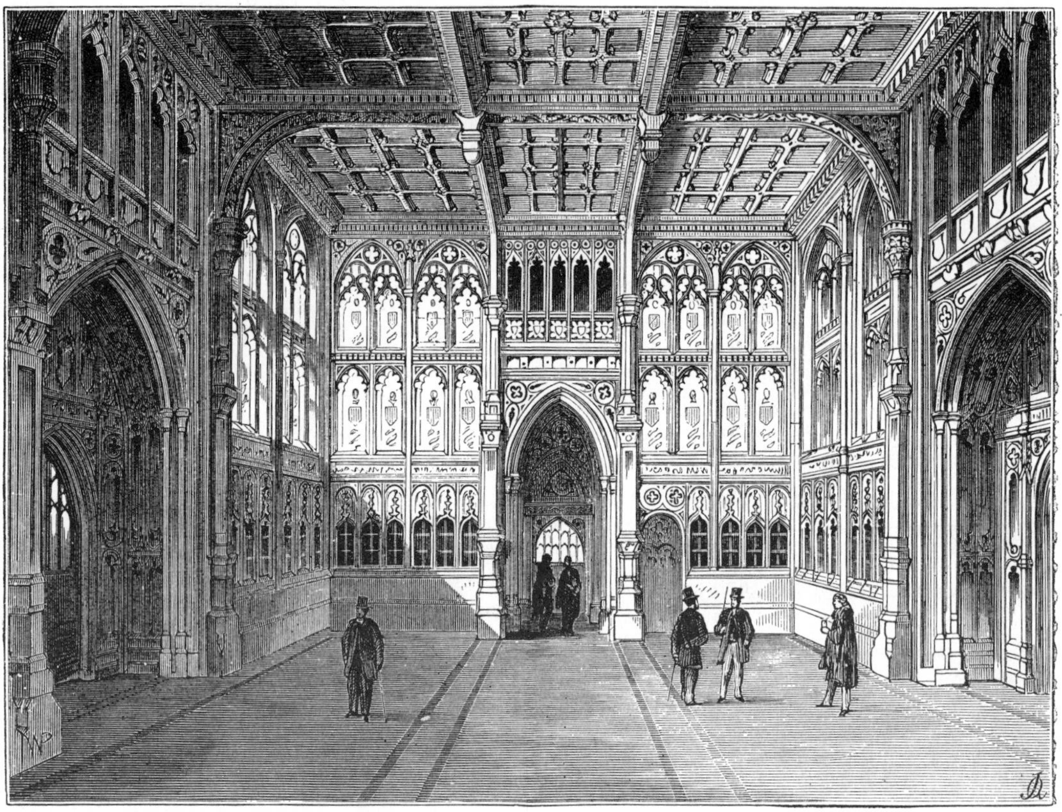

THE LOBBY OF THE HOUSE OF COMMONS. (*See page* 508.)

We have already spoken of the frescoes with which the walls of the Houses of Parliament are decorated; but we may here observe that their apparently decaying condition, after having been painted scarcely ten years, gave rise to considerable discussion and uneasiness. The "decay," in the case of Maclise's famous water-glass picture of the "Meeting of Wellington and Blucher," showed itself by an efflorescence which spread itself over the whole surface of the picture; but under the superintendence at first of the late Mr. Richmond, R.A., and more recently of Professor Church, this and others of the frescoes have been "restored."

The "division" lobbies are situated on the east and west sides of the House: herein is actually performed the act of governing this country, for, practically, the recording of the votes of members of the House decides every question of policy and administration. A "division" in the House of Commons is managed with great simplicity and adequate completeness. As soon as the moment arrives when it is the pleasure of the House to try the question before them by this test, the signal is given by the Speaker calling out, "Strangers must withdraw!" This order is obeyed only by the occupants of seats below the bar and the gallery just over the clock, both of which are actually within the House. The occupants of the Strangers' Gallery proper are now permitted to remain. As soon as the order to withdraw is given, a two-minute glass is turned by one of the clerks, in order to give time to members dispersed all over the purlieus of the House—the library, refreshment-room, &c.—to come in, and notice is given to them by the ringing of bells all over the building, which is effected simultaneously by means of electricity. As soon as the sand has run out, the doors are closed and locked by the Serjeant-at-Arms, and all late comers are excluded. The Speaker then puts the question, and, having declared which side in his opinion has the majority of voices, his decision is questioned by some member, and he then gives the direction, "The 'ayes' to the right, the 'noes' to the left," and the former file out of the door at the back of the chair; the latter pass up the gangway on the Opposition side, and out at a small door at the lower end of the House, at the left side, under the gallery. The Speaker then orders two "tellers" to each door, and one of them reports to him that "the House is clear." The members thus driven out of the body of the House find themselves in a long corridor, represented in the engraving on the opposite page; and at the end of the corridor is a railing and a desk, between which sufficient space is allowed for one person to pass at a time, after the manner of pay-places at the theatres. On one side of these stand two "tellers" (one of each of the parties then voting against the other), and two clerks, both of whom are provided with printed lists of the names of all the members of the House. As each member passes through the teller counts him—he himself usually calls out his name—and the clerks tick it off on the list, with a view to its being inserted in due course in the division lists which are printed every morning with the orders of the day. The members then return one by one into

THE REFRESHMENT-ROOM OF THE HOUSE OF LORDS. (*See page* 519.)

the body of the House, the ayes entering at the principal door below the bar, and the noes by the door at the back of the Speaker's chair. When all have passed, the tellers make up the figures, and, all four advancing to the table, one of those on the winning side, in a loud voice, declares the respective numbers. Although in description this may appear a cumbrous mode of collecting votes, it is in practice remarkably expeditious and very precise; and it gives the members only the trouble of taking a short walk through the lobby—a far less tedious operation than any process of counting or registering within the House would prove to be.

That the ventilation of the Houses of Parliament was far from satisfactory not many years ago may be gathered from an extract from the *Lancet*, and even now it can hardly be said that finality has been reached:—"Just now, as we all know, the purlieus of Westminster and Whitehall swarm with distinguished and undistinguished persons from the provinces, more or less concerned in private bills that are before committees of one or other House of Parliament. These persons pervade the hall, throng the lobbies and passages, and even crowd to suffocation the committee-rooms in which the actual business of the day is being transacted. As they pass by, diminishing gradations of space from the outermost to the innermost regions, the superlatively bucolic individual and the hardest-worked country lawyer alike become conscious not only of the absence of anything like fresh, but of the existence of positively foul air. And when the committee-room is reached, and the regulation five hours have been spent therein, we may fairly surmise that our country cousins, be they agriculturists, solicitors, agents, promoters, or oppositionists, go away to dinner with headache, indifferent appetite, and a profound contempt for sanitary legislation as indicated by the ventilating arrangements of the Palace at Westminster. A great deal has been said and written about a similar state of things in our law courts, both in the east and west of the metropolis; but any one who cares to penetrate into the innermost parts of the Houses of Parliament, and force his way into one of the rooms above quoted, will find that, though flanked by the Thames on one side, its stuffiness and odoriferous nastiness are really appalling, rivalling in these conditions the Old Bailey and an East-end police-court in their worst days. The Lords, perhaps. in these respects suffer more than the Commons; but in either case there is a grim irony in taking evidence relative to some sanitary bill in an atmosphere utterly unfit for healthy respiration or for any sort of continuous mental exertion."

The Speaker's House occupies part of the two pavilions, if we may so term them, forming the north end of the river-front of the Westminster Palace, next Westminster Bridge, and is approached by archways from New Palace Yard. It is of considerable extent, comprising from sixty to seventy rooms, and is finished throughout in the style of the structure generally. The staircase, with its carvings, tile-paving, and brass-work, is exceedingly effective and elegant, and everywhere there is a large amount of painted and gilded decoration. Cloisters, approached from the House, surround a court, about twenty feet square; the window-openings in the cloisters are filled with stained glass, containing the arms of all the Speakers, with the dates of their elections.

The first Speaker actually mentioned by that title in legal documents is Sir Wm. Hungerford, elected in 1377, in the reign of Edward III. We meet with the old name and armorial bearings of a Waldegrave as Speaker as early as 1382; in 1400, Sir John Tiptoft was elected, and he was the first Speaker elevated to the peerage, being created by Henry IV. of Lancaster, in 1406, Baron de Tiptoft, in return for certain "courtly compliances," which in those days meant a great deal. The Beauchamps are found as early as 1415, while the Baynards of Castle Baynard, in the City, where kings once stayed, and where the Duke of Buckingham offered the crown to Richard III., are seen no more after 1421. John Russell was Speaker in 1423 and 1432. From this date the election of Speakers seems to have occurred with each meeting of Parliament about once a year, till the time of Queen Elizabeth, when that arbitrary sovereign refused to ratify the election of Sir John Popham; afterwards, the great Edward Coke filled the chair. The year 1641 gives us the next name of great note—viz., William Lenthal, of Charles I.'s disordered Parliament—the man who refused to answer Charles's questions when he came to seize the members, and in that ill-advised act began the war in which he lost both crown and head. Sir Harbottle Grimston, chosen in the year 1660, whose arms are surmounted with the bloody hand of the Ulster knights, was the first Speaker whose election was never ratified by Charles II., though he still retained his Speakership. The haughty Edward Seymour, who used to speak of the Duke of Somerset as the younger branch of his family, followed the example of Sir Harbottle, though in a different way. Instead of asking Charles to ratify his election, which he knew the monarch never would do, he contented himself with announcing simply that he had been elected and was the

Speaker—a statement which left no course open to the irritated king but to add sharply, in reply, "Very well." The House that was summoned in 1689, after the abdication of James II., elected its own Speaker, Henry Powle; this election, also, was never confirmed by William of Orange. Mr. Wyndham Grenville, also, was elected without the royal sanction, in the year 1789, at a time when George III. was mentally incapable of attending to any business.

The name and arms of Sir John Trevor are to be seen in the Gothic windows, though Sir John was expelled the House for taking bribes. Of the whole 134 Speakers only eighteen have been raised to the peerage—by the titles of Baron Tiptoft, Lord Hungerford, Lord Audley, Earl of Oxford and Mortimer, Lord Onslow, Earl of Wilmington, Lord Grantley, Lord Grenville, Viscount Sidmouth, Lord Redesdale, Lord Colchester, Viscount Canterbury, Lord Dunfermline, Viscounts Eversley, Ossington, Hampden, and Peel.

The Refreshment-rooms of the House of Lords are the most luxurious apartments imaginable—the beautiful ceiling, the richly-carved doors, screens, and panelling, the fittings-up, the crimson and green paper-hangings, and the general decorations, being extremely striking and harmonious. The Refreshment-rooms are situated in the river-front of the Palace, behind the Lords' Library, and are approached from the House of Peers by the Bishops' Corridor, which communicates with the Victoria Lobby. These rooms are divided from each other by an elaborately-carved screen, or bar, at which the refreshments are served by means of lifts from the kitchens below; and every modern appliance in the management of the cuisine has been carefully studied. The rooms are lighted by windows on one side only, which look into the Peers' Court; on the opposite side, the walls are panelled, and have fireplaces of rich and beautiful design, the stone chimney-pieces being highly decorated with bosses and foliage.

The clock-tower, situated at the south-east end of the building, and closely abutting on Westminster Bridge, is forty feet square, surmounted by a richly-decorated belfry, and spire rising to the height of about 320 feet. The tower occupies as nearly as possible the site of the great clock-tower erected by Edward I. on the north side of New Palace Yard. That tower was built out of a fine imposed on a certain Chief Justice, who is said to have taken a bribe. At first it contained only a bell, "Great Tom of Westminster," which summoned Parliament and the four Courts of Law to their respective duties. In due time a clock was added, which, every time the bell told the hour, reminded the judges and legislators below of the words on its face, "Discite justitiam moniti et non temnere divos." Of this, the original clock-tower, we shall have more to say in our chapter on New Palace Yard. The clock of the present tower has four dials, and was constructed under the direction of Sir G. B. Airy, K.C.B., late Astronomer Royal. It may be added that most of the wheels are of cast iron; the hands and their appendages weigh about a ton and a half, and the pendulum 6 cwt. The dials are 22½ feet in diameter, or 400 superficial feet each, and are said to have cost more than the clock itself.

The first bell, which received the name of "Big Ben," was cast in 1856 at Norton, near Stockton-on-Tees, by Messrs. Warner, and weighed nearly 16 tons, with a clapper of 12 cwt. It bore the following inscription:—"Cast in the twentieth year of the reign of Her Majesty Queen Victoria, and in the year of our Lord 1856, from the design of Edmund Beckett Denison, Q.C.; Sir Benjamin Hall, Bart., M.P., Chief Commissioner of Works." On the waist or middle of the bell were the royal arms, and the names of the founders and patentees of the mode of casting which had been adopted for it, "John Warner and Sons, Crescent Foundry, Cripplegate, London." From the first, the fates seemed to be against the success of this bell, for on the voyage up to Westminster it was tossed about for several days at sea, and at the very starting stood a narrow chance of sending the vessel containing it to the bottom of the ocean. Arrived at Westminster, "Big Ben" found temporary shelter at the foot of the clock-tower, within hoarding and tarpaulin, and under a huge pair of cat-gallows; and here its sonorous tone was tested before it was finally hoisted to its lofty destination. Whatever may have been the opinion formed of its tone and quality at the trials to which it was subjected, certain it is that it had hung but a few months before it gave strong evidence of being cracked. Its real state was at once investigated by Dr. Percy, who reported that it was "porous, unhomogeneous, unsound, and a defective casting." Its doom was thus sealed. "Big Ben" was forthwith brought to the hammer, broken up and done for, and a new bell was at once cast in the foundry of Messrs. Mears, in Whitechapel. About this new bell there is no mistake. It is simply perfect as a casting in shape and in tone—the latter being E, which the late "Ben" was intended to produce, but which good intention was entirely frustrated by an undue thickness of metal in the waist of the monster. Of the former "Big Ben" it is not necessary to say more than that his successor is formed of the same metal. Unlike his predecessor, however, the present occupant of the loftiest belfry in London is tastefully ornamented with Gothic figures and tracery in low relief. On one side of his waist is the portcullis of Westminster; on the other are the arms of England, sharp and clear, as if chased by the hand. Round the outer lip is cast in Gothic letters: "This bell was cast by George Mears, of Whitechapel, for the clock of the Houses of Parliament, under the direction of Edmund Beckett Denison, Q.C., in the 21st year of the reign of Queen Victoria, and in the year of our Lord MDCCCLVIII."

This bell is estimated as being as nearly as possible fourteen tons, or about two tons lighter than the old bell. But though its form is somewhat different, and though there is less metal, its dimensions are the same as those of its predecessor. The head is more rounded, and the waist more sloped in. The sound-bow, or the place on which the clapper strikes, is also a trifle less in thickness than that of the old bell.

The work of getting the new bell into position took several days. On the 8th of October, 1858, it was placed upon its side upon a cradle, was run into the basement of the clock-tower, and placed under the shaft extending to the summit of the tower, up which it was afterwards hoisted by pulleys. The shaft is eleven feet by eight feet; it is intended for the descent of the clock-weights. Its sides were lined with timber and friction-wheels, to guide the passage of the bell upwards. The chain used in lifting the bell was 1,600 feet in length; it was made by Messrs. Crawshay, of Newcastle, and each link was separately tested. The beam on which the bell is hung is formed of oak and plates of iron, firmly bolted and riveted together, and it is fixed in the open lantern over the clock; it is twenty-five inches wide by nineteen thick, and is capable of sustaining a weight of 100 tons. Besides "Big Ben" there are four smaller bells, upon which the quarters are chimed.

"Who," asks Townsend in his "History of the House of Commons," "that has sat in the gallery of the old House—that venerable building which the calamitous fire of October 16th, 1834, reduced to ashes—can fail to recollect his first feeling of disappointment as he gazed with a sense of wounded pride around the dark and narrow room, and looked in astonishment at the honourable members grouped in various attitudes of carelessness and indifference? Yet such as it was, decked only with a new coating of paint and whitewash, destitute of all architectural pomp, unadorned by a single monument of sculpture or art—into that building what intelligent stranger was ever ushered for the first time without a throbbing heart and heightened pulse! Who but has lowered his voice on first entering that room as he felt the genius of the place compelling awe, the deep inspiration of the past! Mighty memories, sublime associations, breathe their subduing spells around the stranger. For not less than ten generations—ever since the gentle Edward VI. allotted that consecrated chamber to the great council of Parliament—the genius and virtue, the dignity and rank, the wisdom and eloquence, of the nation have been there represented. There blushed the chivalry of Raleigh. There wept the servile patriotism of Coke. There recorded its protest the faithful loyalty of Hyde. Its floor was once profaned by the hasty step of the unhappy Charles, who left his guards at the door as he faltered into the Speaker's chair, once far more basely desecrated by the stamp of Cromwell, as he crowded the benches of a truckling assembly with the myrmidons of a usurper. There, with an eye glowing fire, eloquent as his voice, Chatham spoke for immortality, and triumphing over physical weakness and bodily decay, made his very crutch an instrument of oratory. On the floor the mighty Burke—great even in his failures—threw down the dagger, a specimen of the presents which French fraternity was preparing for his countrymen. There Castlereagh walked proudly up the House, amid loud huzzas, with the treaty of peace, signed at Paris, in his hand. There Canning called the new world into existence, that he might redress the balance of the old. There the noblest sons of genius, Bacon, and Newton, and Wren, Addison, Gibbon, Mitford, have sat, 'mute, but not inglorious.' There Oglethorpe taught the lesson of humanity to inspect our prisons, and Meredith and Romilly pleaded against capital punishments that criminals were still men. Peals of laughter have awakened the echoes of that chamber to generations of wits—Martin, and Coventry, Charles Townshend, and Sheridan, and Canning. The hollow murmurs of sympathy have there rung back the funeral tribute to the elder and younger Pitt; to Grenville and Horner; to that eloquent orator, conspicuous among his countrymen, Grattan, who in his dying hour there poured forth his soul. What exhilarating cheers, the only rewards to St. John, for those lost orations which have perished for ever, have there rewarded the efforts of Pitt and Fox as they sank back exhausted! The forgotten oratory of that chamber would more than balance all that is recorded. Magnificent as the new building may be, adorned with paintings and embellished with trophies of our progress in the arts, far more convenient than the old chamber, in splendour not to be compared, can it ever rival, in the mind's eye, that humbler room empanelled with living memories, and blazoned with illustrations of the past?"

In closing this chapter, we cannot do better than quote the words of a writer in the *Illustrated London News*, when describing the progress of the new building:—"We cannot but think that its locality is most fitly chosen; the stream that bears on its bosom the commerce of a world flows before it, while close beside it are the venerable Hall and Abbey, rich with the recollections and associations of departed centuries. The very spirit of antiquity seems to hover over the walls and buttresses yet fresh from the hand of the artificer, shedding something of its venerable influence over that which dates but from yesterday. So is it with all the works and deeds of man; the present springs and takes its hue and character from the past, and both bear within them the seeds of the future. And with the future as it lies before us, how much will be linked with the edifice now springing into existence, under the eyes of the generation that saw its predecessor pass away like a dream! It may be long ere such recollections gather round the new Senate House, as hallowed the old Houses of Parliament, for in them the constitution of England was worked out through all the changes it has undergone since the first institution of Parliament as a recognised body. Much of evil, much of error, of passion and prejudice, found voice within those old walls; great and grievous was the wrong inflicted by many of the deeds there acted. But much also issued from thence of which we may be proud and thankful; wisdom, and eloquence, and patriotism, have spoke and wrought within them in troubled and dangerous times. May men of equal powers be found to meet the evil days which the brightest and most hopeful spirit must acknowledge are rising before us! But let those to whose hands Providence may commit the charge of this mighty empire, draw courage from the struggles of the past, and look back steadily to the recollections of the days of old—those imperishable associations which neither fire, nor storm, nor convulsion can sweep away!"

The destruction of the old Houses of Parliament, with a great part of the Speaker's official residence adjoining, occurred on the 16th of October, 1834. Mr. Raikes thus comments on the fire in his "Journal":—"The origin of this public misfortune is not known, but it appears to have been caused by some negligence in the House of Lords. The reports are very vague and uncertain. There may be something ominous in such a catastrophe at such a moment; the two contending bodies of the State, just arrayed in dire opposition to each other—the one insolent and overbearing in aggression, the other strict and obstinate in defence of its privileges—both buried in one common ruin. It appears that many of the archives of both Houses have been preserved, but not without considerable damage. The tapestry in the House of Lords, representing the defeat of the Spanish Armada, which was generally admired, has been a prey to the flames. Mr. Hume, during the last session, had been proposing, without success, a vote to build a larger House of Commons; a wag in the crowd, watching the progress of the conflagration, exclaimed, 'There is Mr. Hume's motion being carried without a division!' The old walls of St. Stephen's have witnessed a long career of British glory and prosperity: may it not have perished with them! Time will show that mystery; but if the character, talent, and honour of these public men who in years gone by have distinguished themselves within these walls contributed to support that career of glory, then may we own that they have not crumbled over the heads of men who are utterly incompetent, and incapable of maintaining it."

"Great," writes Dr. C. Mackay, "was the sorrow of every lover of his country, when the ancient seats of the British Legislature were destroyed; for, though they were but stones, and bricks and mortar, and wood, they were hallowed in the hearts of Englishmen. Who could help regretting that the very boards on which Chatham, and Pitt, and Fox, and Burke, and Canning trod would never more be trodden by the admirers of their worth; and that the walls that re-echoed to their words, and to the approving cheers of their delighted auditory, had crumbled in the flames? Not one who had a heart to feel, or a thought to bestow upon the matter."

The story of the burning of the Houses of Parliament has never been more truthfully or more comically told than by Charles Dickens, though we quote only from a humorous speech once made by him in Drury Lane Theatre, when the establishment of an Administrative Reform Association was publicly resolved upon, on account of the mismanagement of our army in the East. On that occasion he said:—"Ages ago, a savage mode of keeping accounts on notched sticks was introduced into the Court of Exchequer, and the accounts were kept much as Robinson Crusoe kept his calendar on the desert island. In the course of considerable revolutions of time, the celebrated Cocker was born and died; Walkinghame, of the 'Tutor's Assistant,' and well versed in figures, was also born and died; and a multitude of accountants, book-keepers, and actuaries were born and died. Still official routine inclined to these notched sticks, as if they were pillars of the Constitution, and still the Exchequer accounts continued to be kept on certain splints of elm-wood called *tallies*. In the reign of George III. an inquiry was made by some revolutionary spirit whether—pens, ink, and paper, slates and pencils, being in existence—this obstinate adherence to an obsolete custom ought to be continued, and whether a change ought not to be effected. All the red-tape in the country grew redder at the bare mention of this bold and original conception, and it took till 1826 to get these sticks abolished. In 1834 it was found that there was a considerable accumulation of them; and the question then arose —what was to be done with such worn-out, worm-eaten, rotten old bits of wood? The sticks were housed at Westminster, and it would naturally occur to any intelligent person that nothing could be easier than to allow them to be carried away for firewood by the miserable people who live in that neighbourhood. However, they never had been useful, and official routine required that they never should be, and so the order went forth that they were to be privately and confidentially burnt. It came to pass that they were burnt in a stove in the House of Lords. The stove, overgorged with these preposterous sticks, set fire to the panelling; the panelling set fire to the House of Lords; the House of Lords set fire to the House of Commons; the two houses were reduced to ashes; architects were called in to build others; and we are now in the second million of the cost thereof; the national pig is not nearly over the stile yet; and the little old woman, Britannia, hasn't got home to-night."

THE HOUSES OF PARLIAMENT AFTER THE FIRE, IN 1834.

The table of the old House of Commons, saved from the fire, was transferred to the office of the Board of Works, Whitehall. It was, it seems, part of the fittings of the House of Commons provided by Sir Christopher Wren, in 1706. The existence of this relic is generally unknown, and it has not yet been figured in any notice of the House of Commons.

After the fire of 1834, the two Houses of Parliament assembled in a temporary building, not unlike a barn, which was speedily run up, in order to accommodate the Imperial Legislature.

RUINS OF THE HOUSES OF PARLIAMENT.

1. Interior of St. Stephen's Chapel. 2. The Library. 3. Cloisters. 4. House of Lords.

CHAPTER LX.

HISTORICAL REMINISCENCES OF THE HOUSES OF PARLIAMENT.

"Jura magistratusque legunt, sanctumque senatum."—*Virgil*, "*Æn.*" i. 426.

The Origin of the Parliaments—Ladies summoned to Parliament by Proxy—Ratification of Magna Charta by Henry III.—The King gives an Unconditional Assent to the Demands of the Barons—The Mad Parliament—The Parliament of Batts—Queen Elizabeth in Parliament—The Committal of Members to the Tower—The Long Parliament—Catching the Speaker's Eye—"Pride's Purge"—The "Rump"—Cromwell dissolves the Long Parliament—The "Little Parliament"—William Lilly, the Astrologer—The Wilkes Riots—Death of the Earl of Chatham—Lord North and the American War—Lord North's Retirement—Robbery at Lord Nugent's House—The Crown in Danger—Assassination of Mr. Spencer Perceval—The Casting Vote of the Speaker—Mr. Pitt and Lord Melville—Canning and Sir Robert Peel—The Trial of Queen Caroline—Mr. Disraeli's Maiden Speech—The First Opening of Parliament by Queen Victoria.

Having thus described the buildings of the old and the new Palace, we venture to devote a chapter to a few scattered notes on subjects relating to the inner life of the Houses of Parliament, as likely to be of interest to English readers, because they will throw light on our national history; and if they are fragmentary, it must be remembered that a regular chapter on the history of the English Parliament would be foreign to the plan and scope of the present work.

There is nothing in our history more uncertain than the birth of our Parliaments and the extent of their power in their early days. Blackstone says that "the original, or first, institution of Parliaments is one of those matters which lie so far hidden in the dark ages of antiquity, that the tracing of it out is a thing equally difficult and uncertain;" and how members were returned to the "Michel-Synoth," or Michel-Gemote, or Wittenagemote, of our Saxon ancestors, it would, doubtless, puzzle the learning of modern Anglo-Saxon scholars to ascertain with precision. "In the simple days of good King Alfred," observes a writer in *Blackwood's Magazine*, "Parliaments were not summoned 'for the dispatch of business'—that is, to discuss regulations concerning the taxes and the public debt, bank affairs, East Indian and West Indian affairs, and a thousand other concerns of national moment, then lying unborn in the womb of time. In those days the Great Council was ordained to meet twice in the year, or oftener if need be, to treat of the government of God's people, how they should keep themselves from sin, should live in quiet, and should receive right." If this be so, no wonder that the early Norman kings should have summoned the bishops and the leading abbots of monasteries to aid their lay nobles in their deliberations for the good of the nation at large.

In these early days it would appear that the government of this country was not altogether in the hands of the sterner sex, for we read that in the reigns of Henry III. and Edward I., four abbesses, if no more, were summoned to Parliament—namely, those of Shaftesbury, Barking, Winchester, and Wilton. In the 35th of Edward III. there were summoned, by writ, to Parliament, by their proxies, Mary, Countess of Norfolk, Eleanor, Countess of Ormonde, Anne, Lady de Spenser, Phillippe, Countess of March, Joanna, Lady Fitzwalter, Agneta and Mary, Countesses of Pembroke, Margaret, Lady de Roos, Matilda, Countess of Oxford, and Catherine, Countess of Athol. These ladies were called "Ad colloquium tractandum" by their proxies, it being a privilege of the peerage to appear by such representation.

Gurdon, in his "Antiquities of Parliament," goes even farther back than this, for he says that "ladies of birth and quality sat in council with the Saxon Witas. The Abbess Hilda (says Bede) presided in an ecclesiastical synod. In Wighfred's great council at Becconfeld, A.D. 694, the abbesses sat and deliberated; and five of them signed decrees of that council along with the king, bishops, and nobles. King Edgar's charter to the Abbey of Crowland, A.D. 961, was with the consent of the nobles and abbesses, who signed the charter."

In 1225, Henry III. summoned a Parliament to meet at Westminster; and there Hubert de Burgh, having opened the proceedings by an explanatory speech, asked for money "to enable the king to recover his own." At first the assembly refused to make any grant, but it was finally agreed that a fifteenth of all movable property should be given, on the express condition, however, that the king should ratify the two charters. Henry, accordingly, gave a third ratification of Magna Charta, together with a ratification of the Charter of Forests, and sent fresh orders to some of his officers, who had hitherto treated them with little respect, to enforce all their provisions.

On the 2nd of May, 1258, another Parliament was summoned by the above monarch in the same place. At this time a scarcity of provisions, combined with the growing weakness and misgovernment of the king, had disposed the people to desperate measures. The barons, who had formed a new confederacy, went to Westminster Hall in complete armour. "As the king entered, there was a rattling of swords: his eye glanced timidly along the mailed ranks; and he said, with a faltering voice, 'What means this? Am I a prisoner?' 'Not so,' replied Roger Bigod; 'but your foreign favourites and your own extravagance have involved this realm in great wretchedness; wherefore we demand that the powers of government be entrusted and made over to a committee of bishops and barons, that the same may root up abuses and exact good laws.' The king could do nothing else than give an unconditional assent to the demands of the barons; and with promises on their part to help him pay his debts, and prosecute the claims of his son in Italy, the Parliament was dissolved, to meet again at an early date at Oxford. On the 11th of the following month, the Parliament, which the royalists called the 'Mad Parliament,' accordingly met at Oxford. Here a committee of government was appointed, and it was enacted 'that four knights should be chosen by the votes of the freeholders in each county, to lay before the Parliament all breaches of law and justice that might occur; that a new sheriff should be annually chosen by the freeholders in each county; and that three sessions of Parliament should be held regularly every year.'"

At the commencement of the fifteenth century the Parliament of England had come to be a more important element in the State than heretofore, the people being more fully and equitably represented. It consisted of the three estates—the nobility, the clergy, and the commons, while the last of these classes consisted of between two and three hundred members, composed partly of knights, citizens, and burgesses. In this way, every grade of rank in the commonalty, and every trade and profession, could find its representative and advocate in the great legislative assembly of the kingdom.

In the reign of Henry VI., on Parliament being summoned to meet, orders were sent to the members that they should not wear swords; so they came to Parliament (like modern butchers) with long staves, whence the Parliament got the name of "The Parliament of Batts;" and when the batts were prohibited, the members had recourse to stones and leaden bullets. This Parliament was opened with the Confirmation of Liberties.

Whenever she appeared in public, as we learn from Bohun's "Character of Elizabeth," the great Tudor queen was always richly decked out with costly clothes, and adorned with gold and jewels. "On such occasions," he writes, "she ever wore high shoes that she might seem taller than indeed she was. The first day of the Parliament she would appear in a robe embroidered with pearls, the royal crown on her head, the golden ball in her left hand, and the sceptre in her right; and as she then never failed of the loud acclamations of her people, so she was ever pleased with it, and went along in a kind of triumph with all the ensigns of majesty."

The closing scene of the third Parliament of Charles I. was marked by the committal to the Tower of some eight or nine members of the House of Commons for their opposition to the king's will and pleasure, and an indirect intimation by Charles of his intention of dispensing with Parliaments altogether.

The celebrated assembly known as the Long Parliament, which met for the first time at Westminster, on the 3rd of November, 1640, commenced its proceedings at eight in the morning; but after some time the attendance of members being found slack and irregular, sundry devices were resorted to, with the view of counteracting a movement which gave too much favour to early risers. At one time a roll was called; and at another it was ordered that whoever did not come at eight o'clock and be at prayers, should pay a fine of one shilling. On the first morning after this order was made, there was an excellent attendance. The House was full, but prayers could not be said. Mr. Speaker himself was not there—at a quarter before nine, in he walked. Prayers being over, Sir Harry Mildmay congratulated the House upon the good effect of the order made on the previous day; and said to the Speaker, that "he did hope that hereafter he would come in time;" which made the Speaker "throw down twelve pence upon the table." Other members coming in afterwards paid their respective shillings to the Serjeant. This shilling fine seems to have occasioned no little quibbling and contention, and it was accordingly soon relinquished. Another rule adopted in this Parliament, however, attained a firmer footing. On the 26th of November, in the same year, there was a long dispute as to who should speak; many members stood up at one time, each claiming precedence, and each backed by his friends. The confusion became intolerable. The passing of some rule preventing such discord in future was indispensable; and at last, as Sir Simonds D'Ewes tells us, "the House determined for Mr. White, and '*the Speaker's eye*' was adjudged to be evermore the rule;" and so it has remained down to the present day.

Towards the close of the year 1648, while the Commons were debating upon a treaty with King Charles, who was then in the hands of Cromwell, the House was surrounded by the regiment of horse of Colonel Rich and the foot regiment of Colonel Pride. These measures were taken with the view of ridding, or "purging the House of," its Presbyterian majority. Colonel Pride, from whose active part in it the operation has been called "Pride's Purge," posted himself in the lobby, and arrested forty-one of the leading Presbyterian members as they arrived, and sent them to prison. The "purge" was continued on the following day. Not a few of the obnoxious members fled into the country, or hid themselves in the city; so that in a few days all that were left in the House of Commons were some fifty Independents, who were afterwards styled the "Rump." Cromwell, who had in the meantime arrived in London, then went into the "purged" House, and received their "hearty thanks" for his "great services."

As might naturally be expected, there has been no lack of "scenes" in the Lower House of Parliament from the day when Oliver Cromwell, attended by Lambert and a few other officers, and a file of musketeers, came into the Chamber of the Commons, and pointing to the Speaker's mace, surmounted with the crown, told Harrison—a religious enthusiast, who had been as active in bringing the Long Parliament to an end as Pride had been in purging it—to "take away that bauble." The scene is familiar to most educated readers, thanks to the engraver's art. One by one, it would appear, the members quickly left the House, and thus a clearance was soon effected, and the "Long Parliament" dissolved. Cromwell issued proclamations containing the grounds and reasons for dissolving the late Parliament and calling a new one; the latter consisted of some 120 "known persons, fearing God, and of approved integrity." The most noted of these members was Barbone, a dealer in leather, whose name, converted into "Barebones," was afterwards applied to the whole Parliament, though the more common appellation for that assembly was the "Little Parliament."

One would like to have been present, even as a little mouse, at that sitting in 1666, when the House sent for the astrologer, William Lilly, and called on him then and there to explain one of his hieroglyphics, which seemed to foretell the Great Fire of London. We suspect, however, if the truth must be told, that it was not so much as an astrologer that he was consulted, as with a view of discovering if he had been made the depositary of any information or rumours which might have led him to expect such a catastrophe.

In the riots which arose out of the publication of No. 45 of the *North Briton*, by John Wilkes, the mob showed an amount of violence which had been unheard of for a century, within the very precincts of "our Palace of Westminster," and they were all but taking the life of Lord Mansfield. Indeed, if we may believe an eye-witness—Mr. Cradock—they proceeded to even greater lengths; at all events he writes in his "Memoirs:"—"Confusion might then be said to be at its height, for the mob had broke into the passage that leads to the throne; his Majesty was just robed, and was proceeding from the closet, when many of us were pressed directly forwards, and with our clothes torn were absolutely thrown into the House." Such scenes have not often happened either before or since.

The death of the Earl of Chatham, painted by Copley, has been made so well known by the engraving that it is scarcely necessary to do more than just mention it here in connection with the old House of Peers. On the 7th of April, 1779, the Duke of Richmond, as Principal Secretary of State, moved an address to the King, urging, in strong terms, the necessity of immediately recognising the independence of our North American colonies. America, he said, was lost, and her independence established; further struggles against the *de facto* state of things were useless. Lord Chatham came down to the House, very feeble, and bowed down with bodily infirmity. He wore his court dress of black velvet, but from his knees downward he was wrapped in flannel. He was led into the House leaning on the arms of two of his brother peers, when all the House rose through respect for him. He was pale and thin, but his eye sparkled with all its original fire and lustre. When the Duke had ended, Lord Chatham rose, and, lamenting that his ailments had prevented his attendance on the duties of his station, he declared that he had now made an effort beyond his powers, and that he was probably in his place for the last time in his life. In the strongest terms, however, he objected to the disgrace of surrendering the rights of the mother-country, and of abandoning its fairest possessions; and concluded his speech by urging that England should make one more effort to recover the revolted states, or to fall in the effort like men. In reply, the Duke of Richmond said that he knew of no means by which England could resist the combined forces of America and France, adding that if Lord Chatham could not point out those means, no man living could do so. Much agitated, Lord Chatham made another effort to address the House, but before he could articulate more than a word or two, he fell down suddenly in a convulsive fit. The Duke of

Cumberland, Lord Temple, and other peers who were near him, caught him in their arms; the House was cleared, and the debate adjourned. His lordship was taken off in his carriage to his favourite seat at Hayes, near Bromley, in Kent, where he lingered in an almost speechless state for a month, and died early in May. On the news of his death reaching the House of Commons, it was voted that a monument should be erected to his memory in Westminster Abbey; that £20,000 should be granted towards the payment of his debts; and that a provision should be made for his family in the shape of a pension of £4,000 a year, payable out of the Civil List, to be settled on the earldom. The title, however, became extinct on the death of his son and successor, in 1835. It is said—though, probably, with some little exaggeration—of the eloquence of the Earl of Chatham, that "his voice, even when it sank to a whisper, was heard to the remotest benches; when he strained it to its full strength, the sound rose like the swell of an organ of a great cathedral, shook the House with its peal, and was heard through lobbies and down staircases to the Court of Requests and the precincts of Westminster Hall."

When Lord North was Premier, in November, 1781, he was waited on in the House by Lord George Germain and Lord Stormont, with the intelligence of the defeat and surrender of the British forces in America under Lord Cornwallis. His subordinates arrived between one and two o'clock in the morning, were admitted, and told the sad news. "The First Minister's firmness," says Sir N. W. Wraxall, "and even his presence of mind, gave way for a short time under this awful disaster. I asked Lord George afterwards how he took the communication? As he would have taken a ball in his breast, replied Lord George; for he opened his arms, exclaiming wildly, as he paced up and down the apartment, 'O God! it is all over'— words which he repeated many times, in the deepest agitation and distress."

In the March following, Lord North, having been defeated on the American War, and "entering in his full-dress suit, and with the blue riband of the Order of the Garter over his coat," proceeded leisurely up the House, amidst the cries of "Order," and "Place," to announce his retirement from office. The scene inside and outside the House on this occasion has been well described by Sir N. W. Wraxall, who was then present. It appears, from his narrative, that to the very end Lord North retained that serenity and tranquillity which he had shown when he had behind his back a triumphant majority of supporters. "On that evening he had ordered his coach to remain at the House in waiting. In consequence of so unexpected an event as his resignation, and the House breaking up at an early hour, the housekeeper's room became crowded to the greatest degree, few members having ordered their carriages to be ready before midnight. In the midst of this confusion, Lord North's coach drove up to the door, and as he prepared to step into it, he said, turning to those who stood near him, with that unalterable equanimity and good temper which never forsook him, 'Good night, gentlemen; you see what it is to be in the secret!'"

His lordship was accustomed to sleep during the Parliamentary harangues of his adversaries, leaving Sir Grey Cooper to note down anything remarkable. During a debate on ship-building, some tedious speaker entered on an historical detail, in which, commencing with Noah's ark, he traced the progress of the art regularly downwards. When he came to mention the Spanish Armada, Sir Grey inadvertently awoke the slumbering Premier, who inquired at what era the honourable gentleman had arrived. Being answered, "We are now in the reign of Queen Elizabeth," "Dear Sir Grey," said he, "why not let me sleep a century or two more?"

Lord North, corpulent, easy, and good-natured, was most popular in the House of Commons; he was, however, very awkward in his gait, so awkward indeed that, if we may believe the gossiping Sir N. W. Wraxall, on one occasion when the House was full, he took off on the point of his sword the wig of his right-hand neighbour, Mr. Welbore Ellis, and carried it across a considerable part of the floor without ever suspecting or perceiving his mistake.

If our readers would gain a view of the inside of the House of Commons as it was in the good old days, "when George the Third was king," they should go to the pleasant and gossiping pages of Sir N. W. Wraxall, who thus describes that august chamber on the first night after Lord North's ministry had given place to the coalition under Lords Rockingham and Shelburne:—"Never was a more total change of costume beheld than the House of Commons presented to the eye when that assembly met for the dispatch of business after the Easter recess of 1782. The Treasury Bench, as well as the places behind it, had been for so many years occupied by Lord North and his friends, that it became difficult to recognise them again in their new seats, dispersed over the Opposition Benches, in great coats, frocks and boots. Mr. Ellis himself appeared for the first time in his life in an undress. To contemplate the ministers, their successors, emerged from their obscure lodgings, or from 'Brookes's,' having thrown off their blue and buff uniforms, now ornamented with the appendages of dress, or returning from Court, decorated with swords, lace, and hair-powder, excited still more astonishment. Even some degree of ridicule attached to this extraordinary and sudden metamorphosis, which afforded subject for conversation no less than food for mirth. It happened that just at the time when the change of administration took place, Lord Nugent's house in Great George Street having been broken open, was robbed of a variety of articles; among others, of a number of pairs of lace ruffles. He caused the particulars of the effects stolen to be advertised in some of the daily newspapers, where they were minutely specified with great precision. Coming down to the House of Commons immediately after the recess, a gentleman who accidentally sat next to him asked his lordship if he had yet made any discovery of the articles recently lost. 'I can't say that I have,' answered he, 'but I shrewdly suspect that I have seen some of my laced ruffles on the hands of the gentlemen who now occupy the Treasury Bench.' This reply, the effect of which was infinitely increased by the presence of Fox and Burke in their court dresses, soon obtained general circulation, and occasioned no little laughter."

LORD NORTH. (*See page* 527.)

Sir Nathanael Wraxall also tells the following good story, under the date 1782, showing that even at that period the circumlocution office and its red tape virtually existed:—"On the occasion of his Majesty going to Westminster, to prorogue the two Houses, it became indispensable to convey thither the royal crown and the sceptre, together with various other articles of the state regalia. The

Master of the Jewel Office being suppressed, in whose department these dispositions previously lay, application was made to the Lord Steward and the Lord Chamberlain, praying that orders might be issued to the keeper of the jewels in the Tower, for bringing them to Westminster on the day of the coaches being provided, in which the various articles were placed, with a view to render the transportation of them more private, the procession set out circuitously from the Tower, by the New Road, entering London again at Portland Street, and so proceeded down to Westminster. The blinds were

WILLIAM PITT. *From the Portrait by Hoppner.* (*See page* 531.)

prorogation. But these great officers of State not conceiving themselves to possess a power of interference, directions were at once dispatched for the purpose from the Home Secretary of State's office. After some consultation held relative to the safest mode of conveying these royal ornaments, none of the King's carriages being sent to receive them, application was next made to the magistrates at Bow Street, who detached four or five stout agents of the police for their protection. Two hackney- kept up the whole way; and after the prorogation they returned by the same road, without experiencing any accident. But it is unquestionable that eight or ten desperate fellows, had they been apprised of the circumstance, might have easily overpowered the persons employed, and carried off the jewels. The memorable enterprise of Colonel Blood, in the time of Charles II., who got possession of the crown and sceptre, though he ultimately failed, was, in fact, a far more hazardous undertaking, as he actually entered the Tower; whereas, in the present instance, the attempt might have been made in the street, or in the New Road. Any accident of the kind would necessarily have thrown some degree of ridicule, as well as of blame, on a system of economy productive of such consequences in its outset."

In the lobby of the old House, as stated above, Mr. Perceval, Prime Minister and Chancellor of the Exchequer, was assassinated by a pistol discharged at him by a disappointed Russia merchant, named John Bellingham, on Monday, the 11th of May, 1812. The following particulars of this tragic event are condensed from the evidence given at the inquest:—Bellingham had lived as a merchant in Liverpool, and, some three weeks previous to the murder, had called on General Gascoyne, M.P. for that borough, and requested his assistance to assert his claims upon Parliament, alleging that he had been falsely arrested at St. Petersburg, and that he had applied without effect to the then resident ambassador. The general recommended him to memorialise the minister. Nothing more appears to have been heard or seen of him till the afternoon of the above day, when, at about five o'clock, as Mr. Perceval was entering the lobby of the House of Commons, he was suddenly fired at by Bellingham, who was at once recognised by General Gascoyne, who happened to be in the House at the time. On the following Friday, the prisoner was brought to trial at the Old Bailey; he was found guilty, and condemned to death. His execution took place on the Monday morning after, in front of Newgate; so that the whole proceedings connected with this lamentable affair took place within one short week.

Connected with this event, there happened a circumstance so extraordinary and unaccountable, that, as it is probably very little known, we recount it for the benefit of our readers. It was first narrated in the principal newspapers at the time of the murder, and some years afterwards, the late Dr. Abercrombie was enabled, by the kindness of a medical friend, to obtain an account of it from the gentleman to whom the circumstance occurred. It was afterwards published by Dr. Abercrombie in his "Observations on the Intellectual Powers." The facts are simply as follow:—In the night of the 11th of May, 1812, Mr. Williams, of Scorrier House, Redruth, Cornwall, dreamed that he was standing in the lobby of the House of Commons, when a short gentleman entered, dressed in a blue coat and white waistcoat; immediately afterwards he saw a man, in a brown coat with yellow basket-metal buttons, draw a pistol from under his coat and discharge it at the former, who instantly fell, the blood issuing from a wound a little below the left breast. He saw the murderer seized by some gentlemen who were standing by, and dreamed that he was told that the murdered man was the Chancellor.

He awoke in great terror, and, rousing his wife, related the dream to her. She, however, made light of it, and he went to sleep again. Twice again, however, during the night were the same dreadful events presented to his imagination.

In the morning Mr. Williams made his strange dream known to all his acquaintances, and so great was the impression it made on his own mind that it was with much difficulty his friends dissuaded him from travelling to London to make it known to the Chancellor himself.

After being the talk of the neighbourhood for some few days, the matter rested, until the news was received that on that very day Mr. Perceval was shot in the lobby of the House of Commons, by a man named Bellingham. Some time afterwards Mr. Williams went to London, where he was shown the pictures of the murder (which were then published), and also the scene of the event itself. And it was found that the whole of the details of the dream corresponded with those of the real occurrence. The dresses of the murderer and his victim, the scene of the event, the title of the victim, the position occupied by the principal actors in the terrible tragedy, all agreed in the most startling manner with Mr. Williams's dream, which was thus entirely fulfilled.

It is not given to every one to "gain the ear of the House of Commons;" nor is it easy to say what are the precise qualifications for Parliamentary success in that line. Mr. Rae tells us, in his noble work on "The Opposition under George III.:"—"Erskine, who could mould a jury at his pleasure, and whose seductive voice could almost exorcise prejudice from a hostile court, could never influence a single division in the House of Commons, nor could he always gain an appreciative hearing. Flood, who came from Ireland, with the fame of a Demosthenes, failed to gain the ear of the House. The greatest glories of O'Connell are not enshrined in our Parliamentary annals. Lord Jeffrey, whose eminence as a critical writer was undisputed by any contemporary, was heard with bare courtesy when he addressed the House of Commons. Sir James Mackintosh, who entered Parliament with the lustre of a powerful forensic display undimmed, and with the reputation of being most fascinating in conversation, could seldom command the attention of his audience. Macaulay's spoken essays in the

House of Commons were as gorgeous and finished pieces of rhetoric as the essays he contributed to the *Edinburgh Review*, yet Macaulay never gained high honours as a Parliamentary debater. Bulwer Lytton delivered many polished orations in the House of Commons, but he did not equal as a speaker the fame he acquired as a novelist. . . . Though John Stuart Mill gave utterance to some things which it required great moral courage to express, yet his Parliamentary career did not increase his world-wide fame as a thinker. In addition to his extraordinary popularity as a novelist, Mr. Disraeli has risen to the first place in the estimation of Parliament; and in this respect he divides with Sheridan the crown of victory over almost insuperable obstacles."

Mr. Mark Boyd, in his "Fifty Years' Reminiscences," when speaking of the casting vote of the Speaker, relates a circumstance which bears upon the death of Mr. Pitt. He says: "A Speaker once was driven into the corner; he found that 'aye' or 'no,' guilty or not guilty, must be settled by his casting vote. For the question he had to decide was, whether or no Lord Melville, as Treasurer to the Navy, had been guilty of official misconduct. It was in the year 1805 (the impeachment was in 1804) that this accusation was brought before the Commons, and it provoked, you may suppose, the utmost zeal and heat. Much was proved against Lord Melville; much, however, of the desire to prove his guilt sprang from party hate. His accusers may have loved justice, but they certainly, also, loved to plague an antagonist. Mr. Pitt, the Prime Minister, was strong on Lord Melville's side, his friend and colleague, but the opposing party was zealous and powerful. The fierce debate ended with an even vote—216 members declared for Lord Melville; 216 voted for his guilt. Lord Melville's fate was thus placed in the Speaker's hands, to be decided by that one vote. Yet it was long before the Speaker could give his vote; agitation overcame him; his face grew white as a sheet. Terrible as was the distress to all who awaited the decision from the chair; terrible as was the Speaker's distress, this moment of suspense lasted ten long minutes. There the Speaker sat in silence: all were silent. At length his voice was heard; he gave his vote, and he condemned Lord Melville. One man, at least, that evening was overcome. Mr. Pitt was overcome; his friend was ruined. At the sound of the Speaker's voice, the Prime Minister crushed his hat over his brows to hide his streaming tears that poured over his cheeks; he pushed in haste out of the House. Some of his opponents, I am ashamed to say, thrust themselves near, 'to see how Billy looked.' His friends gathered in defence around, and screened him from rude glances. During a quarter of a century, indeed almost ever since he had been a boy, Mr. Pitt had battled it in Parliament. His experience there was not victory only, but often defeat. This defeat, however, he sank under; it was his last—he died ere many months had passed. The death of that great man was hastened by Speaker Abbot's casting vote." Lord Melville was afterwards tried by his peers, and acquitted.

Pitt was remarkable for the neatness and precision of his dress, and for the attention which he paid to the Graces. Fox, on the other hand, was always careless and untidy in his person. To such an extent did he carry this peculiarity, that one day an Opposition paper gravely announced, as a piece of fashionable news, that he had "appeared in St. Stephen's in a clean waistcoat."

It is not a little singular that the attainment of place and power by the Pitts was due to an accident. Thomas Pitt, of Blandford, Dorsetshire, Governor of Fort St. George in the East Indies, in the reign of Queen Anne, by a trifling purchase became the possessor of a diamond weighing 127 carats, which he sold to the King of France for £135,000. It was styled the "Pitt Diamond," and out of the purchase-money the family became so opulent that Mr. Pitt was enabled to send his son at an early age into the House of Commons.

We are told by those who were present on the happy occasion, that when, in the year 1814, Lord Castlereagh returned to England after concluding the negotiations of peace with France, the whole House rose up and cheered him as he entered. And it is almost needless to add that no less an honour was paid to the Duke of Wellington, in 1814, when he appeared at the bar of the House to return his acknowledgments for an address which had been presented to him at his private residence.

It was within the walls of this House that, during the first quarter of the present century, Canning, with all his fervid and brilliant rhetoric, would uphold the monarchical and aristocratical character of the English constitution, and scathe Hobhouse and Burdett, Mackintosh and Brougham, with his sarcasms, as often as they started the subject of a reform in the representation of the people. Here, at a later date, Sir Robert Peel, in opposition, would, night after night, enlighten and charm his audience with his ready and well-disciplined harangues, couched in flowing periods, and illustrated with the most varied resources of his gifted and classical mind.

In May, 1806, was instituted a royal commission, consisting of the Lords Erskine, Grenville, Spencer, and Ellenborough, all then members of the cabinet, to inquire into the charges brought against the Princess Caroline Amelia (afterwards Queen Caroline), the consort of George IV. Within a few months after her marriage with the Prince of Wales, domestic differences arose; and these unhappy differences, from whatever cause they sprang, terminated in a separation within three months after the birth of her only child, the Princess Charlotte. The Princess of Wales became the inhabitant of a separate establishment, and resided for some years at Blackheath, but in 1814 she retired to Italy. Of the life she had been leading during her exile there was many an unfavourable, and even foul, report; and although the "delicate investigation"—as the above commission came to be called—had been extinguished, a new one had followed her in her wanderings, and all the reports that were multiplying against her were collected and sent to London as fresh matters of accusation, should circumstances compel such a step. On her return to England, in 1820, the Government pressed proceedings against her. A secret inquiry was first held, against which the Queen vehemently protested, demanding time to bring witnesses from abroad, and requesting to be heard by counsel. Messrs. Brougham, Denman, and Williams, being allowed to present themselves at the bar of the House, dwelt eloquently upon the hardships of the Queen's case, and on the necessity of delay. On the day after the secret committee had given in its report, the Earl of Liverpool, in pursuance of it, brought in a Bill of Pains and Penalties, intituled "An Act to deprive her Majesty Queen Caroline Amelia Elizabeth of the title, prerogatives, rights, privileges, and exemptions of Queen-consort of this realm, and to dissolve the marriage between his Majesty and the said Caroline Amelia Elizabeth." The statement of the Attorney-General in support of the bill occupied two days in delivery. As he was finishing, the shoutings of a tremendous multitude announced the approach of her Majesty. She entered the House of Lords, and then the examination of witnesses was commenced. Upon hearing the clerk of the House call the name of Teodoro Majocchi, the third witness, the Queen started from her seat with a faint cry, and rushed out of the House. This man had been her servant, and a close eye-witness of most of her proceedings for a long time. It was assumed by some that her emotion and her cry proceeded from conscious guilt, taken by surprise at the production of such a witness; by others it was reasoned that she might have been excited only by disgust and indignation at the ingratitude and treachery of an old servant. The trial having lasted from the 19th of August to the 7th of September, the case against the Queen closed, and an adjournment took place to allow time for her counsel to prepare her defence. On the 3rd of October, Mr. Brougham delivered his speech for the defence at great length, and with astonishing eloquence and effect. He was ably followed by Mr. Williams; and the examination of the Queen's witnesses continued until the 24th of October. When it finished, Mr. Denman went over the whole case with vast ability and with equal boldness. "The witnesses against the Queen," we are told, "had in some instances prevaricated; and although a good deal of their testimony was perfectly convincing, the case, in the apprehension of what was perhaps the majority of the nation, was left in that state which Scotch lawyers call 'not proven.'" The Bill of Pains and Penalties afterwards passed the second and third reading, the latter, however, being carried by such a few votes, that Lord Liverpool declared that, looking at this small majority, and at the state of the public feeling, he and his colleagues abandoned the bill. The session of Parliament was in consequence unexpectedly prorogued by his Majesty. "Thus ended, in defeat and disgrace to the King, an indecent, obscene contest, which had filled right-minded men with unutterable disgust, and which had made every Englishman residing or travelling on the Continent hold down his head and blush for his sovereign and his country."

Mr. Rush, in his "Court of London," draws a vivid picture of one scene in the above drama:—"On November 23rd, 1820, an unusual sight," he writes, "was witnessed in the House of Commons. The Queen having applied to the ministry for a place to reside in since the Bill of Pains and Penalties against her was withdrawn, and her application being refused on the ground that it rested with Parliament to provide an establishment of that kind, Mr. Denman, as one of her counsel and also a member of the House, rose and endeavoured to read a message from her Majesty before the usual forms of prorogation were gone through; but he could obtain no hearing. Uproar and confusion followed, making it difficult to get through the forms. The prorogation, however, was duly effected in the end. The very fact of the Queen sending a message to the House may be considered as in character with the speech she was said to have made after the bill against her had passed to a second reading. Her counsel drew up a protest against it, which was taken to her to sign. This she did with a hearty good-will, exclaiming, as she threw down the pen, 'There! *Regina* still, in spite of them all!'"

As stated in "The Random Recollections of the House of Commons," Mr. Disraeli's own private friends looked forward to his introduction into the House of Commons as a circumstance which would be immediately followed by his obtaining for himself an oratorical reputation equal to that enjoyed by the most popular speakers in that assembly. "They thought that he would produce an extraordinary sensation, both in the House and in the country, by the power and splendour of his eloquence. But the result differed from the anticipation. It was known for some days previously that he was to make his maiden speech in the course of the discussion respecting the Spottiswoode combination. . . When he rose, which he did immediately after Mr. O'Connell had concluded his speech, all eyes were fixed upon him, and all ears were open to listen to his eloquence; but, before he had proceeded far, he furnished a striking illustration of the hazard that attends on highly-wrought expectations. After the first few minutes he met with every possible manifestation of opposition and ridicule from the Ministerial benches, and was, on the other hand, cheered in the loudest and most earnest manner by his Tory friends. At one time, in consequence of the extraordinary interruptions he met with, Mr. Disraeli intimated his willingness to resume his seat, if the House wished him to do so. He proceeded, however, for a short time longer, but was still assailed by groans and under-growls in all their varieties; the uproar, indeed, often became so great as completely to drown his voice. At last, losing all temper, which until now he had preserved in a wonderful manner, he paused in the midst of a sentence, and looking the Liberals indignantly in the face, raised his hands, and opening his mouth as wide as its dimensions would permit, said, in remarkably loud and almost terrific tones, 'Though I sit down now, the time will come when you will hear me!'" And come it did. But it was more than fourteen years before the clever novelist, having won his spurs as a debater, came to hold office as Chancellor of the Exchequer, and thirty before he took his seat at the head of the Treasury Bench as Premier.

We have not space to enumerate all the "scenes" that have taken place in the House of Commons since the accession of Her Majesty to the throne; we may, however, briefly mention those caused by Mr. Feargus O'Connor, in 1852, when his conduct on various occasions was so extravagant and violent that he was committed by the Speaker to the custody of the Serjeant-at-Arms; the rupture between O'Connell and Lord Maidstone, in 1838, which nearly ended in a duel; the attempts to "obstruct" the proceedings of the House made by Mr. Parnell and other Irish Home Rulers; the committal to the Clock Tower, and afterwards the expulsion from the precincts of the House, during the Parliament of 1880-5, of Mr. Charles Bradlaugh (see *ante*, p. 513); and the more recent occasion when members actually came to fisticuffs on the floor of the House.

The opening of a new Parliament by the sovereign in person is at any time an interesting circumstance, and has never failed to attract a large concourse of persons, not only to the vicinity of the Houses of Parliament, but to every part of the line of procession. The interest of such an occurrence on the occasion of the first opening of Parliament by Queen Victoria, after her accession to the throne in 1837, was greatly heightened by her Majesty being an amiable lady of the tender age of eighteen. Loyalty and gallantry, therefore, both combined to draw out the population of London to witness the ceremony. Lady Mary Montagu gives a graphic description of the siege which a troop of duchesses, countesses, and other titled ladies, laid to the door of the gallery of the House of Lords, when, in her time, some interesting debate was expected; and how, when they found, after a ten hours' assault, that the gallery was not to be taken by storm, they succeeded in effecting an entrance by stratagem. The ladies in the present case were not under the necessity of attempting an entrance into the gallery by sheer physical force, for they had in most cases procured a Lord Chamberlain's order of admission.

On the entry of her Majesty into the House, the peeresses and all present simultaneously rose, "while every breast throbbed with exultation at the sight of their sovereign." An eye-witness of the scene tells us that "her Majesty, having taken her seat on the throne, desired the peers to be seated. The intimation was known to be equally meant for the ladies. The Commons were then summoned into the royal presence. The summons was forthwith followed by a scene which strongly contrasted with that hitherto presented. There is a proverb, which is current in certain districts of the country, that some people are to be heard when they are not to be seen. The adage received a remarkable illustration in the case of the representatives of the people on this occasion. No sooner had the door been opened (in obedience to the mandate of the Queen) which leads into the passage through which they had to pass on their way to the bar of the House of Lords, than you heard a pattering of feet, as if it had been of the hoofs of some three or four score of quadrupeds. This, however, was only one of the classes of sounds which broke on the ears of all in the House of Lords, and even of those who were standing in the passages leading to it. There were loud exclamations of 'Ah! ah!' and a stentorian utterance of other sounds, which denoted nearest to the bar, and thereby obtain the best place for seeing and hearing. . . . Her Majesty having taken the oath against Popery," continues our informant, "which she did in a slow, serious, and audible manner, proceeded to read the royal speech, and a specimen of more tasteful and effective elocution it has never been my fortune to hear. The most perfect stillness reigned through the place while her Majesty was reading her speech. Her self-possession was the theme of

OLD PALACE YARD IN 1796. *From a Drawing by Miller.* (*See page* 536.)

that the parties from whom they proceeded had been suddenly subjected to some painful visitation. All eyes—not even excepting the eyes of her Majesty—were instantly turned towards the door of the passage whence the sounds proceeded. Out rushed, towards the bar of the House of Lords, a torrent of members of the Lower House, just as if the place which they had quitted had been on fire, and they had been escaping for their lives. The cause of the strange, if not alarming, sounds which had been heard a moment or two before, was now sufficiently intelligible to all. They arose from what Mr. O'Connell would call the mighty struggle among the members, as to who should reach the House of Lords first, and by that means get the universal admiration. Nothing could have been more complete."

A far different sight from that now witnessed must have been presented by either House of Parliament a century ago, when members wore their stars and their court dress, when wigs had not been laid aside, and when those who did not wear wigs would as soon have omitted to eat their dinner as to powder their hair. The bishops wore their wigs, at all events in their place in Parliament, down to her present Majesty's reign; and it is recorded that the first Duke of Cleveland, who died in 1842, was the last member of the House of Lords who appeared in that august assembly with a "pigtail" and powder.

WESTMINSTER HALL. *From a View published by J. T. Smith, 1808.* (*See page 539.*)

CHAPTER LXI.

NEW PALACE YARD AND WESTMINSTER HALL.

"I can re-people with the Past; and of
The Present there is still, for eye and thought,
And meditation chasten'd down, enough."—*Childe Harold.*

New Palace Yard in the Seventeenth Century—The High Gate—"Paradise" and the "Constabulary"—The Fountain—The Ancient Clock-tower and "Old Tom"—An Old Tale re-told—A King's Lamentation—Perkin Warbeck in the Stocks—Punishments for Libel—Leighton and Prynne in the Pillory—Execution of the Earl of Holland, the Duke of Hamilton, and Lord Capel—Titus Oates—The "Turk's Head" and the Rota Club—Statues of Lord Derby and George Canning—William Godwin, the Novelist—Westminster Hall—Heads of the Regicides exposed on the Top of Westminster Hall—The Fate of Cromwell's Head—Old Views of the Hall—Shops there—The Timber Roof—The First Day of Term—London Lickpenny—Peter the Great and his Lawyers.

FORTUNATELY we are not unacquainted with the general appearance of Westminster in the reign of Charles I., for among the etchings of Hollar, known as "the Long London Views," are sketches of the Parliament House, Westminster Hall, and the Abbey. Two of them are given on page 403. They were worked at Antwerp, in 1647, and show the whole river frontage, with wherries and covered boats. St. Stephen's Chapel stands well out, over a garden covered with trees, but it has lost the high-pitched roof which once surmounted it. Between Westminster Hall and the river is a row of low houses, from which stairs lead down to the river; and there is another garden, with stairs, near the present site of Cannon Row.

At the northern end of Westminster Hall is an open square, with a tower near where now is the entrance to King Street; there are a quantity of sheds against the chief entrance, which is continued on either side by wings of the Tudor style of architecture. At the north-west corner of the square is an entrance into St. James's Park under a gateway, standing as nearly as possible where now is Storey's Gate. In the foreground, almost in the centre, stands a conduit in the classical style, and the centre of the square is filled with heavy rumbling carriages, pedestrians, and market-women.

Such was the appearance, in the middle of the seventeenth century, of the open space fronting the principal entrance to Westminster Hall, and known as New Palace Yard, so called from its having been the great yard or court in which William Rufus intended to build a new palace, of which Westminster Hall was to have formed no mean part. Indeed, the Abbey, the Church of St. Margaret, and the Hall, which now stand almost in isolation, were at one time far more closely connected with each other and St. Stephen's Chapel, and formed part of one harmonious group. Smith writes, in his "Antiquities of Westminster:"—"A stone wall, with some houses and a clock-house, and also a gate towards the Woolstaple, occupied, in the time of Richard II., the north side of New Palace Yard; and a similar stone wall, with a gate at the end of Union Street, enclosed it on the west. This wall, by a gate at the north end of what is now St. Margaret Street, was connected with another like stone wall, extending westwards from the west side of Westminster Hall, so that New Palace Yard was completely enclosed; and lastly, at the south end of St. Margaret Street, across the north end of the present Abingdon Street, were in like manner stone walls with gates in them. By these means, with the Old Palace on the east and south sides, and a close adjoining Westminster Abbey, and the Abbey itself on the west, the close having a stone wall round it, Old Palace Yard, like the New, was completely enclosed." St. Margaret Street has long since vanished. It formed a continuation northwards of Old Palace Yard.

The gate on the west side was called the High Gate, from its stateliness and beauty. It was commenced by Richard II., on the east side of Union Street, and at the entrance of Broad Sanctuary, and was demolished in the reign of Queen Anne. The gateway on the south side, opening into a lane which led to St. Margaret's Church, was taken down a quarter of a century later, as "obstructing the passage of members on their way to Parliament." Upon the east side stood portions of the palace, which likewise had a gate beyond the Star Chamber, close to the King's Stairs, upon the bank of the Thames, and leading to the stairs. This water-gate was pulled down, to make room for the south-west abutment of the new bridge, at its erection.

"Of all the remarkable places in England," writes Dr. Mackay, in his Book on the Thames, "this and its neighbourhood is perhaps the most remarkable; and no other place upon the Thames—not even the princely towers and purlieus of Windsor itself—can vie with these in the recollections which they recall or the emotions which they excite. There stands yet—survivor amid calamity*—the elegant Hall of Westminster, with its entrances into the Chief Courts of Justice of this kingdom: courts in which Gascoigne, More, Hale, Bacon,

* These words were written shortly after the fire in which the Houses of Parliament were destroyed in 1834.

Camden, Holt, Coke, Mansfield, Eldon, Brougham, and a host of other eminent and learned men, have presided. There also are the remains of the Houses of Lords and Commons, where the liberties of England were gained gradually but surely, through long centuries of doubt and darkness. There began the struggle for freedom, which never ceased till its object was won; there was heard the eloquence of all the patriots that have arisen in our land since the days of Pym, Hollis, and Hampden; there was tyranny resisted by the tongue and the vote, stronger weapons in a right cause than the glaive or the gun; there was the right established, the wrong cast down, civilisation extended, and slavery abolished. There in former days were to be seen and heard a Cranmer, a Strafford, a Laud, and a Cromwell. Nearer our own age, a Marlborough, a Harley, a Walpole, a Bolingbroke, and a Chatham. Nearer still, a Pitt, a Fox, a Burke, a Grattan, and a Sheridan; a Canning, a Mackintosh, a Wilberforce and a Romilly; with many others who have written their names for good or for evil on the pages of history. And here too, in our own day, walking and breathing among us are to be seen, in their appointed season, a Wellington, a Brougham, a Denman, a Melbourne, a Russell, a Durham, a Peel, and an O'Connell, with hundreds more of great yet lesser note, whose names are inscribed already in the book of history, but whose deeds are not yet ended, and who are destined, perhaps, hereafter to make a still greater figure in the annals of the mightiest empire that the world ever saw."

From Mr. Mackenzie Walcott's "Memorials of Westminster," we learn that in Palace Yard were anciently pales about five feet high, put up to protect foot-passengers from mud and from danger also. Within these rails, close to St. Stephen's Chapel and the private Palace, were two messuages called "Paradise" and the "Constabulary," both of which were granted by Henry VI. to John, Duke of Bedford. Towards the north-west corner of the court stood an ornamental fountain, the water of which fell in large cascades, and on the occasion of special state ceremonies was made to run with streams of choice wine. King Henry VI. granted permission to the parish to make use of the surplus water which flowed from the conduit; and under the date 1524 there is the following note in the churchwardens' accounts:—"Mem^m. The King's Charter for the Condett at the Pales'-gate remayneth in the custody of the Churchwardens." The fountain was removed in the reign of Charles II.

On the front of a house which formerly stood exactly opposite the entrance into Westminster Hall was a dial inscribed with the line from Virgil, "Discite justitiam moniti," an inscription which is said to refer to a fine on a certain Chief Justice, named Ralph de Hingham, or De Hengham, in the reign of Henry III., for erasing or tampering with the Court Roll. The fine was employed, as we have stated in a previous chapter, in the construction of a bell-tower containing a clock, which, as it struck the hours, was intended to remind the ermined judges, as they sat in the Hall, of the fate of their "brother" and predecessor. The clock-tower remained here till 1698, when the great bell, called "Old Tom," was granted to the new cathedral of St. Paul's, whither it was removed, and stood under a shed in the churchyard until the turret was prepared for its reception.

From the fact that, previous to the grant of "Old Tom," St. Paul's was destitute of any heavy bell, it has been conjectured that this must have been the distant clock which the sentinel on duty at Windsor Castle, during the reign of William III., declared struck thirteen instead of twelve times at midnight, in order to prove that he could not have been guilty of sleeping upon his post, as he was accused by the guard who relieved him after the due time. The story is thus recorded in the *Public Advertiser*, Friday, June 22, 1770:—"Mr. John Hatfield, who died last Monday, at his house in Glasshouse Yard, Aldersgate, aged 102 years, was a soldier in the reign of William and Mary, and the person who was tried and condemned by a court-martial for falling asleep on his duty upon the Terrace at Windsor. He absolutely denied the charge against him, and solemnly declared that he heard St. Paul's clock strike thirteen; the truth of which was much doubted by the court, because of the great distance. But whilst he was under sentence of death, an affidavit was made by several persons that the clock actually did strike thirteen instead of twelve; whereupon he received his Majesty's pardon. The above his friends caused to be engraved on his plate, to satisfy the world of the truth of a story which has been much doubted, though he had often confirmed it to many gentlemen, and a few days before his death told it to several of his neighbours. He enjoyed his sight and memory to the day of his death."

Palace Yard in its day has witnessed strange scenes. Here, in 1297, when deserted by the Constable and Marshal of England, Edward I., with his son Edward, the Primate, and the Earl of Warwick, "mounting a platform erected against the front of Westminster Hall, lamented the burdensome taxes which his wars had laid upon England, and assuring the assemblage that he was proceeding to Flanders for the sake of his people, commended his son to their love." The air was rent with the outburst of unanimous loyalty which responded to his appeal.

Towards the close of the year 1497, Perkin Warbeck was brought from the Tower to Westminster; and in the following year he was taken, while attempting to make his escape out of England, and was set for a whole day in the stocks upon a scaffold before the entrance to Westminster Hall, where he read his confession, written with his own hand, "not without innumerable reproaches, mocks, and scornings."

John Stubs, the Puritan attorney, and Robert Page his servant, had their hands cut off in New Palace Yard, in 1580, for a libel against Queen Elizabeth; and a few years later, William Parry, a prisoner drawn from the Tower, was here hung and quartered for high treason. Here, in 1587, Thomas Lovelace, by a sentence of the Star Chamber, inflicted for "false accusations of his kinsmen," was "carried on horseback about the Hall, with his face to the taile;" he was then pilloried, and had one of his ears cut off. In 1612, Robert Creighton, Lord Sanquire, a Scotch nobleman, was hanged for murder in front of the Hall. (See Vol. I., page 184.)

In Palace Yard the pillory was frequently set up in the days of the Stuarts, and even of our Hanoverian sovereigns. Thus we read that in 1630, Alexander Leighton, the father of the Archbishop, was put into the pillory, after a public whipping, for "a fanatical and rude libel on the queen and bishops." Four years later, William Prynne, the irrepressible assailant of the clergy, being found guilty in the Star Chamber Court of being both a schismatic and a libeller, was sentenced to be branded on both cheeks with the letters S. L., to lose his ear in the pillory in Palace Yard, and to be imprisoned for life; the letters S. L., meaning "schismatical libeller," but which he wittily declared must stand for "Stigmata Laudis," the brands of Archbishop Laud. Fortune, however, stood his friend; his own party came into power, and he was not only released from prison, but got a seat in Parliament in 1640.

Amongst those who have suffered by the headsman's axe in front of Westminster Hall was Henry Rich, first Earl of Holland. He had been employed by Charles I. in various posts, and amongst other offices had negotiated the marriage between the King and Henrietta Maria. But afterwards he changed sides repeatedly, and was "faithful to neither cause, fighting at one time for the King, and at another for the Parliament." At last he was captured by the stern Roundheads, who, tired of his never-ending changes, put an end to him by beheading him, in company with the Duke of Hamilton and Lord Capel, in 1649. "Hamilton and Capel," writes Mr. Larwood, "died with dignity; but Lord Holland, after having petitioned for his life, thought fit to die like a coxcomb, and appeared on the scaffold dressed in white satin trimmed with silver, which made Bishop Warburton say that he 'lived like a knave and died like a fool.'"

In the year 1685 Titus Oates was stripped o his ecclesiastical habit, and led round Westminster Hall with a placard set upon him declaring his iniquity; and he afterwards stood a narrow chance of being torn to pieces in the pillory. A wag of the day, speaking of Titus Oates, wittily said—if we may take "Joe Miller's Jest Book" for truth—"that he was a rogue in grain, and deserved to be well threshed."

In 1764, "a libel on the laws of the land," in the shape of a pamphlet published under the title of "Le Droit du Roy," a "dangerous essay, and condemned by both Houses of Parliament," says Hunter, was burnt by the common hangman before the gate of Westminster Hall; and in the next year John Williams was pilloried here for having published the celebrated No. 45 of Wilkes' *North Briton*.

In New Palace Yard, near the Palace Stairs, was the "Turk's Head," otherwise known as "Miles' Coffee House," where the noted Rota Club met. This club was founded by James Harrington, in 1659, as a kind of debating society, for the dissemination of republican opinions, which he had glorified in the "Oceana." The design of this club was to promote the changing of certain members of Parliament annually by rotation.

On the formation of Bridge Street the dimensions of New Palace Yard were somewhat contracted by the building of new houses on the north side; but on their removal, in 1864, the Government decided upon leaving the space unencumbered with buildings, and have erected in their place simply an ornamental railing. The eastern side of the enclosure is formed by part of the new Houses of Parliament and by the southern side of the front of Westminster Hall, the old Law Courts having lately been pulled down. Westward, and extending as far as the Sessions Houses, the ground has been laid out as an ornamental garden, intersected by broad carriage-drives and footpaths. The various divisions are formed with grass-plots bordered with flowers, and a low ornamental railing. Here are statues of George Canning, by Westmacott; Sir Robert Peel and Lord Derby, by Noble; Palmerston, by Woolner; and Beaconsfield, by Raggi.

At his official residence in New Palace Yard, close by the entrance to Westminster Hall, died in the year 1836, William Godwin, the novelist. He was a native of Wisbeach, in Cambridgeshire, and the son of a Dissenting minister. Beginning life as a Nonconformist minister, he afterwards associated with the violent and democratic politicians of the day, and ultimately became an avowed free-thinker and despiser of religion, and the companion and friend of a party amongst whom were Holcroft, Thelwall, Hardy, and Horne Tooke, whom he defended when afterwards arraigned for high treason. Godwin then courted and frequented the society of Lauderdale, Fox, and Sheridan. He married the celebrated Miss Mary Wolstonecraft, authoress of "A Vindication of the Rights of Women," by whom he had a daughter who married the poet Shelley, and who was herself an authoress of some note. Godwin wrote and published the "Memoirs of Mary Wolstonecraft," "An Essay on Population," in opposition to Malthus, "A History of the Commonwealth of England," and other political works. He is, however, best known as a novelist, by his story of "Caleb Williams," &c.

With the exception of the great door and window facing Palace Yard, Westminster Hall, which we are now about to enter, has not a very commanding aspect in its exterior; indeed, nearly all that strikes the eye from the outside is of comparatively modern construction. The front is bounded on each side by projecting square embattled towers. The towers are pierced with pointed windows, and beneath are niches with canopies, which still show traces of their original carved work; in these niches is a series of statues of the kings of England, from the time of Stephen, standing in rows above each other. Between the towers is the body of the Hall, rising with a high pointed roof, and terminated by a pinnacle; and above the spacious porch is a large and magnificent window. In the spandrels of the doorway are the arms of Edward the Confessor and Richard II., together with other sculptures.

Some time after the Restoration, the head of Oliver Cromwell, whose remains had been dug up from their burial-place at Tyburn, was set up on the top of Westminster Hall along with those of the regicides, Ireton and Bradshaw. The following authentic account of the subsequent fate of the head we take from a letter, signed "Senex," in the *Times* of December 31, 1874:—

"Ireton's head was in the middle, and Cromwell's and Bradshaw's on either side. Cromwell's head, being embalmed, remained exposed to the atmosphere for twenty-five years, and then one stormy night it was blown down, and picked up by the sentry, who, hiding it under his cloak, took it home and secreted it in the chimney corner, and, as inquiries were constantly being made about it by the Government, it was only on his death-bed that he revealed where he had hidden it. His family sold the head to one of the Cambridgeshire Russells, and, in the same box in which it still is, it descended to a certain Samuel Russell, who being a needy and careless man, exhibited it in a place near Clare Market. There it was seen by James Cox, who then owned a famous museum. He tried in vain to buy the head from Russell; for, poor as he was, nothing would at first tempt him to part with the relic, but after a time Cox assisted him with money, and eventually, to clear himself from debt, he made the head over to Cox. When Cox at last parted with his museum he sold the head of Cromwell for £230 to three men, who bought it about the time of the French Revolution to exhibit in Mead Court, Bond Street, at half-a-crown a head. Curiously enough, it happened that each of these three gentlemen died a sudden death, and the head came into the possession of the three nieces of the last man who died. These young ladies, nervous at keeping it in the house, asked Mr. Wilkinson, their medical man, to take care of it for them, and they subsequently sold it to him. For the next fifteen or twenty years Mr. Wilkinson was in the habit of showing it to all the distinguished men of that day, and the head, much treasured, yet remains in his family.

"The circumstantial evidence is very curious. It is the only head in history which is known to have been embalmed and afterwards beheaded. On the back of the neck, above the vertebræ, is the mark of the cut of an axe where the executioner, having, perhaps, no proper block, had struck too high, and, laying the head in its soft, embalmed state on the block, flattened the nose on one side, making it adhere to the face. The hair grows promiscuously about the face, and the beard, stained to exactly the same colour by the embalming liquor, is tucked up under the chin, with the oaken staff of the spear with which the head was stuck upon Westminster Hall, which staff is perforated by a worm that never attacks oak until it has been for many years exposed to the weather.

"The iron spear-head, where it protrudes above the skull, is rusted away by the action of the atmosphere. The jagged way in which the top of the skull is removed throws us back to a time when surgery was in its infancy, while the embalming is so beautifully done that the cellular process of the gums and the membrane of the tongue are still to be seen. Several teeth are yet in the mouth; the membranes of the eyelids remain, the pia-mater and the dura-mater, thin membranes, which I believe lie over the brain, may be seen clinging to the inner and upper part of the skull. The brain was, of course, removed, but the compartments are very distinct. When the great sculptor, Flaxman, went to see it he said at once, 'You will not mind my expressing any disappointment I may feel on seeing the head?' 'Oh, no!' said Mr. Wilkinson, 'but will you tell me what are the characteristics by which the head might be recognised?' 'Well,' replied Flaxman, 'I know a great deal about the configuration of the head of Oliver Cromwell. He had a low, broad forehead, large orbits to the eyes, a high septum to the nose, and high cheek-bones; but there is one feature which will be with me a crucial test, and that is, that, instead of having the lower jaw-bone somewhat curved, it was particularly short and straight, but set out at angle, which gave him a jowlish appearance.' The head exactly answered to the description, and Flaxman went away expressing himself as convinced and delighted.

"The head has also a length from the forehead to the back of the head which is quite extraordinary, and one day, before Mr. Wilkinson retired from practice, his assistant called him into the surgery to point out to him how exactly the shaven head of a lad who was there as a patient resembled the embalmed head of Cromwell upstairs, and more particularly in the extreme length between the forehead and the occiput.

PALACE YARD, FROM THE SOUTH. *From a View by Canaletti.* (*See page* 536.)

"Mr. Wilkinson mentioned the circumstance to the gentleman who brought the lad to him. 'No wonder,' said the gentleman, 'for this lad is a direct descendant of Oliver Cromwell, whose name, like this boy's, was Williams before they changed it to Cromwell.' It was curious that this type should re-appear or remain after so many years.

"When the head was in the possession of Samuel Russell he was frequently intoxicated when he showed it to his friends, and they cut off pieces of the hair, until the head was closely cropped.

"A correspondent in the *Globe* of September, 1874, believed that the body of Cromwell, after removal from the Abbey, was buried in Red Lion

INTERIOR OF OLD WESTMINSTER HALL. *From a Print Published in* 1797. (*See page* 542.)

Square, and another body substituted and sent on to Tyburn with Ireton and Bradshaw. But it is not probable they could have obtained an embalmed body for the purpose. The embalmed head is now in the possession of Mr. Horace Wilkinson, Sevenoaks, Kent. There is a small hole where the wart was on his forehead, and the eyebrows met in the middle. The head has the appearance of hard, dry leather."

Formerly there stood several old buildings in the front, almost before the gate of the Hall; but these have been long since pulled down, and the whole of this part is now exposed to view. But it was not only on the outside of the building that the space was encroached upon; for a large part of the inside also was occupied by the stalls of sempstresses, milliners, law stationers, and second-hand booksellers, and even publishers. There is an old engraving of the Hall by Gravelot, representing these bookstalls as they were in his time, and Mr. Cunningham tells us that the duodecimo edition of the remains of Sir Walter Raleigh was printed for Henry Mortlock at the "Phœnix" in St. Paul's Churchyard, and at the "White Hart in Westminster Hall." Pepys tells us in his Diary, under date 20th January, 1659–60, that he had been "at Westminster Hall, where Mrs. Lane and the rest of the maids had their white scarfs [*i.e.* bought them], all having been at the burial of a young bookseller in the Hall." Laud also in his Diary records the fact that in February, 1630–1, the Hall itself had a narrow escape of being burnt down, through some of the little stalls and shops taking fire. And in like manner we read in "Tom Brown's Amusements," published in 1700:—"We entered into a great hall, where my Indian was surprised to see in the same place, men on the one side with baubles and toys, and on the other taken up with the fear of judgment, on which depends their inevitable destiny. In this shop are to be sold ribbons and gloves, towers and commodes by word of mouth; in another shop land and tenements are disposed of by decree. On your left hand you hear a nimble-tongued painted sempstress with her charming treble invite you to buy some of her knick-knacks, and on your right a deep-mouthed cryer, commanding impossibilities, viz., silence to be kept among women and lawyers."

In the "New View of London," published in 1708, this noble apartment is thus described:—"This hall was formerly made use of by the kings, &c., for feasting, and also as a room to relieve the poor; but for many years past—viz., since the ninth year of Henry III.—it has been the place where these Courts of Judicature sit. 1. The High Court of Chancery near the south-west angle. 2. That of the Queen's Bench near the south-east angle. 3. The Court of Common Pleas near the north door on the west side; and on that side above the steps is the Exchequer Court. . . . The sides are also used for shops, chiefly booksellers and milliners, and the feasts of our coronations are here kept. The length of this Hall is 228 feet, breadth 66, and height 90 feet. Contiguously to the south-east part of this Hall, up thirty-two steps, are the House of Commons and Speaker's Chamber, Court of Requests, Painted Chamber (said to have been Edward the Confessor's bedchamber, and now at the upper end fitted with a table and seats, where the Lords and Commons meet at a free conference between the two Houses about amendments to Bills, &c.), the House of Lords, Princes' Chamber (where the Queen is robed and unrobed on her coming to Parliament), and some others."

"It is very probably," continues the author of the above-mentioned work, "the most capacious room in Christendom, without pillars, taking it in all its dimensions of length, breadth, and height. It is situated on the south side of New Palace Yard, whence is a passage through this fabric to the Abbey, College, and School of Westminster. This room was first built by William Rufus in the year of our Lord 1097, as several authors affirm: the walls are of stone (partly boulder), the windows of the Gothic order, the floor paved with stone; but that which is most of curiosity is the roof covered with lead. It is made of Irish oak, so that it is always clean and free from that filth which is occasioned by vermin. There are no pillars to support the roof, notwithstanding its great altitude; but that is very artfully done by neat buttresses of the said timber, adorned and enriched with angels, &c. Under them are, however, much more noble ornaments of guidons, colours, and standards, ensigns and trophies of victory obtained most completely by the confederates under the command of his Grace the Duke of Marlborough." This is followed by a minute description of the "colours and standards" in detail with their mottoes and inscriptions. There is no doubt these are the same standards which afterwards were hung in Whitehall Chapel, and which now decorate the military chapel in Birdcage Walk. The "colours," adds the "New View," are a hundred and thirty-eight, and there are thirty-four "standards."

We get a pretty correct view of the inside of Westminster Hall as it must have appeared in the early part of the reign of George III., from a print published in the year 1797, entitled "The First

Day of Term." It shows the centre of the Hall filled with a motley throng, while on either side are the rows of banners mentioned in the above extract, beneath which on the east are rows of bookstalls, and on the west side sundry stalls of milliners, with ladies making purchases at the counter. At the further end of the Hall, upon the steps, are two large boxes or pews, in which are seated six officials in wigs and gowns, and looking as grave as judges. Below the print are the following Hudibrastic lines :—

"When Fools fall out, for every Flaw
They run horn-mad to go to Law.
A Hedge awry, a wrong-plac'd Gate,
Will serve to spend a whole estate ;
Your case the Lawyer says is good,
And Justice cannot be withstood ;
By tedious Process from above
From office they to office move,
Through Pleas, Demurrers, Dev'l and all,
At length they bring it to the Hall :
The dreadful Hall by Rufus rais'd
For lofty Gothic arches prais'd.
The First of Term, the fatal Day,
Doth various Images convey ;
First from the Courts with clam'rous call
The Criers their Attorneys call ;
One of the Gown, discreet and wise,
By proper means his Witness tries,
From Wreathcock's gang, not Right nor Laws,
It assures his trembling Client's cause,
This gnaws his Handkerchief, whilst that
Gives the kind ogling Nymph his Hat ;
Here one in love with Choristers
Minds singing more than Love's affairs ;
A Serjeant, limping on behind,
Shows Justice lame as well as blind.
To gain new clients some dispute ;
Others protract an ancient Suit.
Jargon and Noise alone prevail,
While Sense and Reason 's sure to fail
At Babel thus Law Term 's begun,
And now at W——tm——r go on."

It will be seen from the copy of this print, which we engrave on page 541, that the interior of the Hall was not wholly occupied by the lawyers and the Law Courts, but, as stated above, was made to accommodate an array of stalls of booksellers, law stationers, and milliners. We learn from the Diary of Laud and from Strype that the rents paid by these tenants belonged to the Warden of the Fleet. To this Wycherley alludes, in the Epilogue to the *Plain Dealer* :—

"In Hall of Westminster
Sleek sempstress vends amid the Courts her ware."

There is, or rather there was, published, a companion print to the above, entitled "The Last Day of Term," representing the lawyers going out of Court, with their clients grouped around them, some chuckling with delight over their gains and buttoning up their breeches pockets with an air of conscious pride, whilst others—a far larger tribe—are wailing and gnashing their teeth with disappointment. A copy of this print, said to be unique, is in the Gardner collection.

Westminster Hall is mentioned in "London Lickpenny," a ballad by John Lydgate, the Benedictine monk of Bury St. Edmunds, about the end of the fourteenth or the beginning of the sixteenth century, whose verses are placed by Gray next to those of Chaucer ; the lines show, at all events, that the lawyers of that day were very like those of the present time. The countryman from Kent, a veritable "Johnny Raw," on reaching Westminster Hall, finds "clerkes a great rout," and is much surprised on hearing an officer of the Court stand up and cry out, "Richard, Robert, and John of Kent." The sound of the word "Kent" is music to his ears ; but he finds—strange to say—that he can do nothing in London without money. It is the same as with the Eternal City two thousand years ago, "Omnia Romæ cum pretio." He tries the Common Law Courts and Chancery Courts, always with the same result, namely, that justice must be paid for :—

"In Westminster Hall I found out one
Which went in a long gown of raye ;
I crouched and kneelèd before him anon,
For Mary's love, of help I him pray,
'I wot not what thou meanest,' 'gan he say :
To get me hence he did me bede ,
For lack of money I could not speed.

"Within this Hall, neither rich nor yet poor
Would do for me aught, although I should die ;
Which seeing, I got me out of the door,
Where Flemynges began on me for to cry,
'Master, what will you coppen or buy ?
Fyne felt hats, or spectacles to read ?
Lay down your silver, and here you may speed.'"

The same fate again befalls poor "Lickpenny" outside the Hall :—

"When to Westminster-gate I presently went ;
When the sun was at hyghe prime ;
Cooks to me they took good intent,
And proffered me bread, with ale and wine,
Ribs of beef, both fat and full fine,
A fair cloth they began for to spread ;
But wanting money, I might not there speed."

In making his way through the crowd at Westminster Hall he has lost his hood. On reaching Cornhill he sees his own hood hanging up for sale —a sort of joke which has been a hundred times repeated in farces and tales of country bumpkins. The end is that he goes back into Kent just as he left it, or perhaps a little poorer and perhaps a little wiser, exclaiming—

"Now Jesus that in Bethlehem was born
Save London, and send lawyers true their meed,
For who wants money with them shall not speed."

Even as far back as the reign of Charles II. Westminster Hall appears to have been a great place for booksellers' stalls: thus Pepys tells us, under date September 4, 1663—"To Westminster Hall, and there bought the first news-booke of L'Estrange's writing." This L'Estrange was the author of numerous pamphlets and periodical publications, and afterwards Licenser of the Public Press to the King. Again we find Pepys writing in his Diary, October 26, 1660: "To Westminster Hall, and bought, among other books, one of the Life of our Queen, which I read at home to my wife; but it was so sillily writ that we did nothing but laugh at it." We get another glimpse of the appearance of the Hall a few months later, for in May, 1661, the inimitable Pepys writes: "I went to Westminster: where it was very pleasant to see the Hall in the condition it is in now, with the Judges on the benches at the further end of it."

With reference to Westminster Hall, Barrow tells an excellent story in his "Life of Peter the Great." When that sovereign was in London, and was taken to Westminster Hall, he very naturally asked who were those gentlemen in wig and gown whom he saw there in such numbers. In reply he was told that they were lawyers. "Lawyers!" he exclaimed in utter amazement; "why, I have but two lawyers in the whole of my dominions, and I mean to hang one of them the moment that I return home."

CHAPTER LXII.

WESTMINSTER HALL.—INCIDENTS IN ITS PAST HISTORY.

"—— The Great Hall of Westminster, the field
Where mutual frauds are fought, and no side yield."—*Ben Jonson.*

Law Students residing in the King's Court—The Hall built by William Rufus—The Poor regaled here by Henry III.—Prince Henry crowned in his Father's Lifetime—Sir John Dymoke, the King's Champion—The Hall rebuilt by Richard II.—Rejoicings for the Victory at Agincourt—Trial of 480 Persons concerned in the Riots on "Evil May-day"—Edward Stafford, Duke of Buckingham—Anne Boleyn in her Glory—A Touching Episode at the Trial of Sir Thomas More—Bishop Fisher—A Batch of State Trials—The Hall flooded—More Memorable Trials—An Incident in the Trial of Charles I.—Coronation Banquet of Charles II.—Trial of Lord Stafford—A Curious Trial for Murder—The Trial of the "Seven Bishops"—Lords Cromartie, Balmerino, and Kilmarnock—Attempt to blow up Westminster Hall—More State Trials—Coronation Banquets—St. Stephen's Crypt—Curiously-named Public Houses.

If William the Conqueror erected the Tower of London, at all events it was his son, William Rufus, who was the founder of Westminster Hall; not, it is true, as we now see it; for the Hall has since been rebuilt, as stated above.

The Law Courts, it appears, had been held in the Palace during the reign of William the Conqueror; and it is said that the law students had their residence in the King's Court. But this proving a great annoyance to his son, Westminster Hall was built by William Rufus in 1097. Two years afterwards that king held his court and kept his Whitsuntide festivities in the new Hall. "The attendants," so runs the story, to which we have already referred, "marvelling at its great size (270 feet in length and 74 in breadth), observed that it was 'too vast a fabric for such common use.' 'Nay,' said the doomed sovereign, with an insolent pride, 'it is but a bed-chamber to the palace that I will ere long raise up.'" Camden says that the foundations, which were visible in the time of Matthew Paris, stretched from the river to the highway pointing east and west; but the size of the original Hall may be better estimated when we are told that Henry III. entertained here, on New Year's Day, 1236, 6,000 poor men, women, and children.

It was here, in 1170, the young Prince Henry was crowned in his father's lifetime; "and the king upon that day served his son at the table as server, bringing up the boar's head, with trumpets before it. Whereupon that young man, conceiving a pride in his heart, beheld the standers-by with a more stately countenance than he had wont. The Archbishop of York, who sat by him, marking his behaviour, turned unto him and said: 'Be glad, my good son; there is not another prince in the world that hath such a server at his table.' To this the new king answered, as it were disdainfully, thus: 'Why dost marvel at that? my father doing it thinketh it not more than becometh him; he, being born of princely blood only on the mother's side, serveth me that am a king born.'"

In 1377, at the coronation of Richard II. (who was so wearied with the pageant that he was borne from the Abbey exhausted on a litter), history first informs us that Sir John Dymock, as successor of the Marmions who came over to England with the Conqueror, and in right of his wife Margaret de Ludlow, claiming the privilege by virtue of his tenure of the manor of Scrivelsby in Lincolnshire, having chosen the best charger save one in the king's stables, and the best suit of harness save one in the royal armoury, rode in armed to the teeth, and challenged as the King's Champion all opposers of the boy-monarch's title to the crown. In 1396 Richard celebrated here his nuptials with his child-queen, Isabella of France.

In the following year, the Hall having become decayed and ruinous, the king built a temporary structure, tiled, and of timber-work, open at the sides, in the midst of the Palace Court, between the Clochard and the Hall gate, for his Parliament to assemble in; this he surrounded with 4,000 archers, "malefactors of the county of Chester," with bended bows ready to shoot in case of need, as in that session he intended to try several captive noblemen—Lord Cobham and the Earls of Arundel and Warwick. "Wherever he lay," we are told, "his person was guarded by 200 Cheshire men." Thirteen bishops were in his train, "besides barons, knights, esquires, and others more than needed;" and 10,000 guests were invited every day, "under his household roof," to a lavishly-spread banquet. Twenty-eight oxen, three hundred sheep, and fowls without number, were daily consumed here on this occasion. We need not wonder then that Richard kept two thousand cooks.

Richard II. rebuilt Westminster Hall in its present form in 1397; and two years later, on the completion of the building, he kept his Christmas in it, with his characteristic magnificence.

Westminster Hall for many centuries was the scene of the state banquets given at the coronations of our monarchs, and also the place wherein the most important state trials have taken place. Besides these, many other curious incidents have taken place here; but space does not allow of our giving more than a cursory glance at a few of these historical events.

It is recorded that it was whilst the Lord Mayor was on his way to Westminster Hall, in November, 1415, in order to be sworn in, that the news of the victory of Agincourt was brought to the citizens and the Court. On the return of the king from France in triumph, soon afterwards, he was received with every outward manifestation of joy; tapestry being hung along the streets, and the conduits being made to run with wine. The Lord Mayor, aldermen, and citizens went in state to Westminster, where they presented the king with two basons of gold, in which was the then large sum of £1,000.

Here, in 1517, Henry VIII. appeared in person, with the Dukes of Norfolk and Suffolk, and other noblemen, the Lord Mayor, and the chief citizens, at the trial of 480 men and eleven women, with ropes about their necks, for being concerned in the rising of the 'prentices on Evil May-day, in a riot and assault upon foreigners. However, at the intercession of Cardinal Wolsey and others of rank (while three queens—Katharine, Mary of France, and Margaret of Scotland—"long on their knees begged pardon"), the king frankly forgave them; whereat the prisoners gave a "mighty shout for joy, throwing their halters toward the top of the Hall."

Edward Stafford, Duke of Buckingham, "the infatuated victim of an astrologer's promise to the throne," who in his rashness had affronted Wolsey, and even threatened the king, was tried in this Hall, in 1522; his own relative, the Duke of Norfolk, presiding on the occasion. With his death the hereditary office of High Constable of England was forfeited, and has never been revived.

In 1533, says Stow, Anne Boleyn "came to Westminster Hall, which was richly hanged with cloth of arras, and newlie glazed; and in the middest of the Hall shee was taken out of hir litter, and so led up to the high deske under the cloth of estate, on whose left hand was a cupboard of x. stages high, marveylous rich and beautifull to behold; and within a little season was brought to the Queen with a solemn service, in great standing spice-plates, a voyde of spice, and subtleties, with Ipocrasse and other wines, which shee sent downe to her ladies; and when the ladies had drunke, shee gave hearty thanks to the lords and ladies, and to the Mayor, and other that had given their attendance on hir. . . . . On Whit Sondaie shee came into the Hall, and stood under the cloth of estate, and then came into the King's Chappell, and the monks of Westminster, all in rich coapes, and many Bishops and Abbots in coapes and miters, which went into the middest of the Hall, and there stood a season; then was there a ray-cloth spreade from the Quene's standing in the Hall, through the Pallace and Sanctuary, which was rayled on both sides, to the high altar."

Two years later Westminster Hall was the scene of another incident in which Anne Boleyn appears to have again played a part. The event is thus touchingly described by Mr. Mackenzie Walcott:—"On May 7th, 1535, the learned Sir Thomas More was arraigned here, bearing the marks of his stern prison-house. As the fallen Chancellor was being led out from the Hall to the Tower, his broken-hearted son burst through the files of soldiery, and, throwing his arms about his father's neck and kissing his lips, implored the armed keepers that they would suffer him to share his parent's fate. Well did he deserve such tokens of filial love; for Sir Thomas, even when proceeding to the Superior Bench of the Chancery, never passed his father, then a Puisne judge of King's Bench, without kneeling down and imploring his blessing. When tidings of his death were brought to the king, while he played at the game of tables, Henry looked moodily upon Anne Boleyn, who stood by his chair, and said, 'Thou art the cause of this man's death!' and leaving his play, shut himself up to mourn alone in his chamber."

WARREN HASTINGS. (*See page* 554.)

That same year witnessed another victim of Henry's caprice doomed to the block in Westminster Hall, in the person of John Fisher, Bishop of Rochester, who had inflexibly opposed the divorce of the king, and his assumption of spiritual supremacy.

In July, 1535, William Lord Dacre of the North was accused of high treason; he was the only state prisoner in the reign of Henry VIII. who was declared not guilty. Upon the verdict "Not guilty" being returned by his peers, there was in the Hall "the greatest shout and cry of joy that the like no man living may remember that ever he heard."

Here, at the fatal bar, the Protector Somerset, "once all-powerful in the state, and the darling of the people," was brought to trial, in 1551, to be followed shortly afterwards by the Earl of Warwick, the Marquis of Northampton, the Protector's rival, Northumberland, and Henry Grey, Duke of Suffolk, father of the unhappy Lady Jane Grey. In 1554, Sir Thomas Wyatt was arraigned here for high treason.

Another peer of the realm, Lord Stourton, was

OLD ST. MARGARET STREET, WESTMINSTER (*page* 536). *From a Sketch made in* 1820.

publicly tried in Westminster Hall, as far back as the year 1556, for the murder of a Mr. Hartgyll and his son in Wiltshire, under very aggravated circumstances. The commission for trying his lordship was directed to the judges and to certain members of the Privy Council. At first Lord Stourton refused to plead, but the chief justice informed him that, if he persisted in his refusal, his high rank should not excuse him from being pressed to death. Upon this he confessed himself guilty, and was hanged at Salisbury, with a silken halter. There is a monument to his memory in Salisbury Cathedral, where some years ago the silken cord with which he was executed was to be seen suspended.

A curious incident occurred in the year 1555, on the occasion of the Lord Mayor presenting the sheriffs to the Barons of the Exchequer. The rain, it appears, fell in such torrents that the Hall was filled with water, and boats were rowed into King Street from the landing-place—a timber stage raised on piles, called the "King's Stairs." This, however, was not the first time that Westminster Hall had been inundated, for in 1236 "wherries were rowed in the midst of the Hall;" and eight years after "men took their horses, because the water ran over all." In 1579, after a flood, "fishes were left upon the floor of the Hall by the subsiding stream."

On the 26th of January, 1571, Thomas Howard, Duke of Norfolk, here received his death-warrant for his dangerous attachment to the fallen fortunes of Mary, Queen of Scots; Sir Henry Gates and Sir Thomas Palmer being condemned on a like charge the following day.

In 1589 Philip, Earl of Arundel, an ancestor of the present ducal house of Norfolk, was arraigned in the Hall upon a charge of "conspiring with certain priests of the Order of Jesus to change the religion and succession of these realms." Being asked if he had "anything further to say why sentence of death should not pass upon him, he only said the same words which his father had done before him in the same place, 'God's will be done.'" After languishing for four weary years in a dungeon, "death released him from his durance."

Robert Devereux, Earl of Essex, and Henry Wriothesley, Earl of Southampton, in the year 1600, passed from the bar in Westminster Hall to dungeons in the Tower.

In January, 1606, took place here, "the king being secretly present," the trial of Guido Faux, Sir Everard Digby, Winter, and the other conspirators in the Gunpowder Plot, of which we shall speak in a subsequent chapter.

For eighteen days, in 1640, a memorable trial was held here, before both Houses of Parliament—the one as accusers, the other as judges. "Beside the chair of state a dark cabinet, hung with arras, was erected for the King and Queen, who attended throughout that important time. Before the throne were the seats for the Peers, and in front of the woolsacks were nine stages of benches for the Commons. At the other end was the desk for the prisoner, who was brought hither, attended to the 'Bridge' by six barges rowed by fifty pair of oars, and manned by troops; the entries of Whitehall and King Street and Palace Yard being lined with guards." The trial in question was that of Thomas Wentworth, Earl of Strafford, "who had generously written to his master (Charles I.), to yield him up a sacrifice to save himself from the discontented clamours of the people." There is extant an extremely rare print, by Hollar, of the "True Manner of the Trial and Execution of Thomas, Earl of Strafford," representing the interior of Westminster Hall, which was fitted up for the occasion. This print shows the king, queen, and peers of several degrees all wearing their robes and hats, and the officials, clerks, &c.; the prisoner stands at the bar, attended by the Keeper of the Tower. The eloquent and pathetic defence of the earl is a matter of history. His children stood beside him. Pointing to them, "My lords," said he, "I have now delayed your lordships longer than I should else have done but for the interest of these dear pledges, which a departed saint in heaven has left me. I should be loth"—but here a flood of tears checked his utterance. "What I forfeit for myself, it is nothing; but I confess, that my indiscretion should forfeit for them, it wounds me very deeply. You will be pleased to pardon my infirmity. Something I should have said, but I see I shall not be able, and therefore I leave it. And now, my lords, I thank God that I have been, by His blessing, sufficiently instructed in the extreme vanity of all temporary enjoyments compared to the importance of our eternal duration. And so, my lords, even so with all humility, and with all tranquillity of mind, I submit, clearly and freely, to your judgments: and whether that righteous doom shall be to life or death, I shall repose myself, full of gratitude and confidence, in the arms of the great Author of my existence. *Te Deum laudamus.*"

The men of Surrey marched through London to Westminster to petition for the restoration of episcopacy, and also the king, their own lawful sovereign, to his due honours. They marched down Whitehall with trumpets, pipes, and fiddles, bearing ribbons of white and green, and crying out

"For God and King Charles!" and insulting the Puritan soldiery under Colonel Baxter. A fray arose, some of the party attacking the sentinels, whom they knocked down and disarmed, and one of whom they killed at the entrance of Westminster Hall. Lilly the astrologer, it appears, foretold this visit of the men of Surrey.

In January, 1648-9, Charles himself was brought to judgment in Westminster Hall. None, however, were found to bear witness but those who had usurped the seats of the lawful judges; while the courageous Lady Fairfax protested against the charge being brought "in the name of the people of England." The King entered the hall under the guard of Colonel Hacker and thirty-two officers, and seated himself, covered, in a chair of velvet provided for him, and "with a stern countenance surveyed the commissioners for the mock trial, amidst a total hush." When the Attorney-General rose to recite the charges, the King put out his cane, and touched him on the shoulder, bidding him "be silent:" the gold head fell heavily from the walking-stick to the ground; and his Majesty, who was not free from superstitious foreboding, we are told, picked up the ornament deeply affected, and spoke no more. On this occasion the astrologer Lilly was present, and he records how he "saw the silver top fall from off the King's staff." Exposed to the brutal insolence of his guards, who filled every avenue, and unawed by the approach of death, the royal prisoner sustained to the last, by his dignified demeanour and denial of the authority of the court, the majesty of a king. "On the last day of the trial, January 27, as the king passed, one of the soldiers, touched with respect and sympathy, exclaimed, 'God bless you, sire!' upon which the colonel, with savage insolence, struck the poor man sharply with his cane. 'Methinks, sir,' was King Charles' mild reproof, 'the punishment exceeds the offence.'"

On the 6th of May, 1660, Charles II. was proclaimed king at the gate of Westminster Hall, and just a twelvemonth afterwards the Act for the late king's trial was burned by the common hangman in the Hall while the courts were sitting.

Pepys, in his Diary, under date of April 21, 1661, after describing the scene in the Abbey at the coronation of Charles II., which we have quoted in a previous chapter, gives us the following particulars of the concluding part of the ceremony, which took place here:—"Into the Hall I got, where it was very fine with hangings and scaffolds one upon another, full of brave ladies; and my wife in one little one on the right hand. Here I staid walking up and down, and at last upon one of the side stalls I stood and saw the King come in with all the persons (but the soldiers) that were yesterday in the cavalcade; and a most pleasant sight it was to see them in their several robes. And the King come in with his crowne on, and his sceptre in his hand, under a canopy borne up by six silver staves, carried by Barons of the Cinque Ports, and little bells at every end. And after a long time, he got up to the farther end, and all set themselves down at their several tables; and that was also a brave sight: and the King's first course carried up by Knights of the Bath. And many fine ceremonies there was of the Heralds leading up people before him, and bowing, and my Lord of Albemarle's going to the kitchen and eating a bit of the first dish that was to go to the King's table. But, above all, was these three Lords, Northumberland, and Suffolke,* and the Duke of Ormond, coming before the courses on horseback, and staying so all dinner-time, and at last bringing up (Dymock) the King's Champion, all in armour, on horseback, with his spear and target carried before him. And a Herald proclaims, "That if any dare deny Charles Stewart to be lawful King of England, here was a Champion that would fight with him;' and with these words the Champion flings down his gauntlet, and all this he do three times in his going towards the King's table. To which when he is come, the King drinks to him, and then sends him the cup, which is of gold, and he drinks it off, and then rides back again with the cup in his hand. I went from the table to see the Bishops at dinner, and was infinitely pleased with it. And at the Lords' table I met with William Howe, and he spoke to my Lord for me, and he did give him four rabbits and a pullet, and so Mr. Creed and I got Mr. Minshell to give us some bread, and so we at a stall ate it, as everybody else did what they could get. I took a great deal of pleasure to go up and down and look upon the ladies, and to hear the musique of all sorts, but above all the 24 violins. About six o'clock at night they had dined, and I went up to my wife. And strange it is to think, that these two days have held up fair till all is done, and the King gone out of the Hall, and then it fell a-raining and thundering and lightning as I have not seen it do for some years: which people did take great notice of. God's blessing of the works of these two days, which is a foolery to take too much notice of such things. I observed little disorder in all this, only the King's Footmen had got hold of the canopy, and would keep it from the Barons of the Cinque Ports, which they endeavoured to force from them again, but could not

* James Howard, third Earl of Suffolk.

do it till my Lord Duke of Albemarle caused it to be put into Sir R. Pye's hand till to-morrow to be decided. At Mr. Bowyer's; a great deal of company; some I knew, others I did not. Here we stand upon the leads and below till it was late, expecting to see the fireworks, but they were not performed to-night: only the city had a light like a glory round about it with bonfires. At last I went to King Streete, and there sent Crockford to my father's and to my house, to tell them that I could not come home to-night because of the dirt, and a coach could not be had. And so I took my wife and Mrs. Frankleyn to Axe Yard; in which, at the further end, were three great bonfires, and great many gallants, men and women; and they laid hold of us, and would have us drink the King's health on our knees, kneeling upon a faggot; which we all did, they drinking to us one after another, which we thought a strange frolique. . . . Thus did the day end with joy everywhere; and blessed be God I have not heard of any mischance to any body through it all but only to Serjeant Glynne, whose horse fell upon him yesterday, and is like to kill him, which people do please themselves to see how just God is to punish the rogue at such a time as this, he being now one of the King's Serjeants, and rode in the cavalcade with Maynard, to whom people wish the same fortune. There was also this night in King Streete a woman had her eye put out by a boy's flinging a firebrand into the coach. Now, after all this, I can say that, besides the pleasure of the sight of these glorious things, I may now shut my eyes against any other object, nor for the future trouble myself to see things of state and showe, as being sure never to see the like again in this world."

In 1680 Viscount Stafford was condemned, in this Hall, for alleged participation, with four Roman Catholic noblemen, in a plot, the fabrication of the infamous Titus Oates. He defended himself with great composure and resolution, protesting his innocence, to the block; indeed, Lord Stafford's eloquence was proverbial. Rushworth remarks, "I need say little of his eloquence and ability in speech. Both Houses of Parliament in England, and the Star Chamber and the Council Table there, . . . and as much as any his last defence at his trial in Westminster Hall before the King, Queen, Lords, House of Commons, and a multitude of auditors of all sorts, are most full and abundant witnesses thereof."

A curious case, connected at once with the Peerage and the Court, arose towards the close of the reign of Charles II., when two persons, Thatcher and Waller, footmen to Lord Cornwallis, assaulted and murdered one Robert Clerk, in the parish of St. Margaret's, Westminster, "within 200 feet of the Palace of Whitehall." The footmen were found not guilty, on the ground that they were "waiting upon their lord," and Lord Cornwallis himself was put upon trial for the same offence, as principal. The trial is thus minutely narrated in "Reports of several Special Cases adjudged in the Courts of King's Bench and Common Pleas at Westminster," published in 1729; and, on account of the curious nature of its details, we here print it:—

"The Lord C. having been indicted for the murder of Robert Clerk mentioned in the case next preceding, the king for his trial constituted Heneage, Lord Finch, then High Chancellor of England, to be Lord High Steward, *hac vice tantum*. The trial was upon the 30th day of June, after Trinity Term, in the 28th year of the king. The proceedings were such as are described by Lord Coke in his Book of Pleas of the Crown, chap. 'Treason, of the Trial of Peers,' as to the summons of the Peers' Triers, the *certiorari* to the Lord Chief Justice for the indictment, and precept to the Constable of the Tower of London, and other formalities there mentioned. The Steward was attended from his house on the day of the trial quite to Westminster by the judges in their coaches. Sir Edward Walker, then Garter King-at-Arms, going before him in his coat with the serjeants-at-arms: when he was at the great door of the Hall he tarried till the judges were alighted out of their coaches, and then, the chief justices first, and the rest according to their seniority, passed by him, and advanced into the Court, which was a large tribunal erected for this purpose (the whole structure extended almost from the stairs leading to the Courts of King's Bench and Chancery to the Court of Common Pleas, but the Court itself was not so large by much). The cloth of state was placed aloft in the middle of both sides of it, but a little behind were built two small boxes. On the right were the King, the Queen, the Duke and Dutchess; the others were filled with persons of honour. The Peers' Triers were seated on both sides the chair of state, but at the distance of about five paces from it, and a step lower, on benches covered with green cloth, with which the whole Court was likewise covered. At the Peers' feet sat the judges, some on one side and some on the other, their seats being of the same height with the floor of the Court. In the middle was a place cut for the Clerk of the Crown of the King's Bench, and for his deputy, in the lower part. The King's Council—viz., his senior serjeant, attorney, and sollicitor—were placed. The prisoner was at the bar behind them, but raised about six feet, and directly over against the chair of state.

"After the Court was thus disposed, Chernoke, Serjeant-at-Arms, made proclamation three times, and command was made that all persons, except the Lords the Triers, and other peers of the realm, and the privy councellors and the judges, should be uncovered. Then the Clerk of the Crown read the indictment, and arraigned the prisoner, who pleaded 'Not guilty,' and put himself upon his peers, who were thirty-six, the greatest part of them of the most noble, of the greatest estate, and the wisest of the realm. Before any evidence was given, the Lord Steward made an elegant speech to the triers, and exhorted the prisoner to be of good courage and without fear, and to summon all the faculties of his soul to his assistance. Then the evidence was first opened by the Sollicitor-General, seconded by the Attorney, and concluded by Serjeant Maynard; the prisoner all the while behaving himself with humility, modesty, and prudence. After the evidence was concluded, the Lords went to consider and consult together in the Court of Wards, as I believe, and during their absence bisket and wine were distributed in the Court. After two hours or more, the lords returned, and the Lord Treasurer, in the name of his fellows, prayed the advice of the Lord Steward and the judges on this point, whether a person's presence at and abetting of a manslaughter committed by another made him guilty, as it was in the case of murder. To which the judges speaking—viz., those of the same side for themselves, and not all together—all agreed that the law was the same in case of manslaughter as of murder. Then the Lords went back, and in half an hour returned to give their verdict. And being seated in their places, the Lord Steward spoke first to the youngest lord, in this manner, 'My Lord A., is my Lord C. guilty, or not?' and so to every one, ascending from the youngest to the first; and each answered, in his order, 'Guilty,' or 'Not guilty, upon my honour.' And six of them pronounced him guilty of manslaughter, and the rest not guilty. This being recorded, the Lord Steward broke the white rod (which was held before him during the whole trial) over his head, and then the Court broke up."

Here, on the 15th of June, 1688, took place the trial of the "Seven Bishops" who had refused to accept King James's "Indulgence in Matters of Religion." They were: the Primate, Sancroft; Lloyd, of St. Asaph; Trelawney, of Bristol; White, of Peterborough; Turner, of Ely; Ken, of Bath and Wells; and Lake, of Chichester. The bishops, who had already undergone imprisonment in the Tower, were, as every reader of history knows, acquitted by their judges—an event which told the king that the days of his dynasty were numbered.

In 1699 Edward, Earl of Warwick, was publicly tried and convicted here of the manslaughter of Richard Coote, in a coffee-house in the Strand. Standing beside him, in the self-same dock, was a memorable criminal, Lord Mohun, who a few years previously had been charged with the murder of Mountford the actor, but acquitted. Again he escaped, on this occasion, but a little while after he fell mortally wounded by the Duke of Hamilton, in a duel fatal to both.

Passing over the trial of Dr. Sacheverell, we come to the year 1716, when were held the trials of Viscount Kenmure and the Earl of Derwentwater, who soon after died headless on the scaffold; the Earl of Carnwath and the Lords Widdrington and Nairn, each sentenced to a year's imprisonment, with forfeited titles and estates; and Nithsdale, who soon after owed his romantic escape to the affection of his wife, disguising him in a woman's dress and riding-hood, and herself remaining a prisoner in his gloomy cell in the Tower.

In 1746 sentence of death for high treason was here passed upon the Lords Cromartie, Balmerino, and Kilmarnock; to be followed within a few months by a like sentence being passed on the aged Lord Lovat, who upon leaving the Hall, called out to his judges, "Good day, my lords; you and I shall never meet again in the same place." The notorious Lawrence Shirley, Earl Ferrers, was arraigned here, in 1760, for the murder of his steward, found guilty, and sentenced to be executed at Tyburn.

In the "British Chronologist," under date July 14th, 1736, we read that—"When the courts were sitting in Westminster Hall, between one and two in the afternoon, a large bundle of brown paper was laid near the Chancery Court, with several crackers and parcels of gunpowder enclosed, which burst, and terrified the people that were attending the Courts of Chancery and King's Bench: and the explosion threw out several printed bills, which gave notice that, this being the last day of Term, the five following libels would be burnt in Westminster Hall, between the hours of 12 and 2—viz., the Gin Act, the Mortmain Act, the Westminster Bridge Act, the Smuggler's Act, and the Act for borrowing £600,000 on the sinking fund. One of these printed bills being carried to the Court of King's Bench, the grand jury presented it as a wicked, false, and scandalous libel; and a proclamation was issued on the 17th for discovering the persons concerned in this wicked and audacious outrage.

and a reward of £200 was offered for taking the author, printer, and publisher of the said false, malicious, and treasonable libel." Under date of December 7th of the same year we read that Mr. Nixon, a "Nonjuring" clergyman, was tried at the King's Bench before Lord Hardwicke, for a misdemeanour in making and publishing the above libel. He was found guilty, condemned to pay 200 marks, to suffer five years' imprisonment, and to be brought before the courts at Westminster, with a parchment round his head declaring his offence.

In April, 1776, Elizabeth Chudleigh was tried here for having married Evelyn Pierrepoint, Duke of Kingston, during the lifetime of her husband, Captain Hervey, Earl of Bristol. "Her beauty and her tears, however," says Mr. Mackenzie Walcott, "with the plea of the privilege of peerage, so wrought upon her judges, that they avoided the enactment of the penalty of her crime—the branding of her right hand upon the block. She was found guilty, advised 'not to do it again,' and discharged on payment of the fees." The whole scene, by the caprice of a morbid fashion, was converted into the semblance of a gala-day. Soldiers were posted at the gates, to regulate the entrance of the crowds that pressed in; and even ladies in full Court-dress attended to witness so rare a circumstance." Horace Walpole records the incidents of this trial day by day, in his letters to Sir Horace Mann.

MR. DYMOKE, THE KING'S CHAMPION.

(*From "An Authentic History of the Coronation of His Majesty King George the Fourth," by Robert Huish, Esq.* 1821.)

CORONATION OF GEORGE IV. IN WESTMINSTER HALL: THE CHAMPION'S CHALLENGE

From a Contemporary Engraving in the "Gentleman's Magazine." (*See page* 554.)

In February, 1788, was commenced the trial of Warren Hastings, the famous Indian administrator, before the House of Commons, in Westminster Hall. This trial, it is well known, lasted nearly as long as the siege of Troy, having lingered out through seven years, and having ended in his acquittal, in September, 1795. An acute criminal said that if it had been held in the court where he himself was tried, it would have been over in less than ten days. In his essay on Warren Hastings, Macaulay gives a vivid account of this remarkable prosecution.

The agitation produced by Burke's speech at this memorable trial was such that the whole audience appeared to have felt one convulsive emotion; and when it was over, it was some time before Mr. Fox could obtain a hearing. Amidst the assemblage of concurring praises which this speech excited, none was more remarkable than the tribute of Mr. Hastings himself. "For half an hour," said that gentleman, "I looked up at the orator in a reverie of wonder; and during that space I actually felt myself the most culpable man on earth." Had the sentiment concluded here, our readers would not believe that it was in the language or manner of Mr. Hastings. "But," continued he, "I recurred to my own bosom, and there found a consciousness which consoled me under all I heard and all I suffered." Sheridan's speech on the occasion was perhaps one of the finest rhetorical displays on record.

Lord Thurlow presided on this occasion, as Lord High Chancellor. During the progress of the trial, Fox, struck by the solemnity of Lord Thurlow's appearance, remarked to a friend, "I wonder whether any one ever *was* so wise as Thurlow *looks*."

The interior of the Hall on one memorable occasion is thus sketched by Lady Brownlow, in her "Reminiscences of a Septuagenarian:"—"My sister and I were taken one day by my grandmother to see Lord Melville's trial, in the early part of 1806. . . . It was a striking sight, and made a great impression on me. The Lord Chancellor (Erskine), the judges, the peers, all in their robes, the House of Commons, and the Speaker; at the bar, Lord Melville, who was seated, surrounded by the counsel for and against him; and in a sort of box near, the members of the House of Commons, who were the managers of the trial. Amongst them were Sheridan, Whitbread, and Fox, whom I saw then for the first and only time. His form, features, and bushy eyebrows I knew well, from prints and caricatures; but his complexion struck me as very peculiar, and, as I said when I returned home, it was the colour that yellow crape would have if stretched over black. He was then, probably, ill, for he died some weeks after—I think, before the termination of the trial."

Mrs. Somerville was present at the coronation banquet of George IV. in Westminster Hall, on the 19th of July, 1821, and has described the scene in her "Life." Another writer who was present at the ceremony has given a description of the scene in the *London Magazine*, from which we learn that after the return of the King and his gorgeous *cortége* from the Abbey, and everything being in readiness in the Hall, "the doors at the end of the Hall were opened, the clarions and trumpets sounding bravely at the time, and the Duke of Wellington, as Lord High Constable, the Marquis of Anglesey, as Lord High Steward, and Lord Howard of Effingham, as Deputy Earl Marshal, entered upon the floor on horseback. The Marquis of Anglesey's horse was a beautiful cream-coloured Arabian; Lord Howard's was a dun; and the Duke's a white steed. After a short pause, they rode gracefully up to the royal table, followed by the gentlemen with the first course. When the dishes were placed on the board, the bearers first retired, with their faces towards the king; and then the noble horsemen retreated, by backing their steeds down the Hall and out at the archway. Their noiseless steps on the blue cloth conveyed the idea that the horses had been shod with felt, according to Lear's invention. The Duke of Wellington's white charger 'walked away with himself' in the aptest manner; but the Marquis of Anglesey had great difficulty in persuading his Arabian to retire tailwise. The company could hardly be restrained from applauding, although it was evident that a shout would have settled the mind of this steed in a second, and have made him resolute against completing his unpleasant retreat. The pages soothed him before and behind; but he shook his head and tail, and paused occasionally, as if he had considerable doubts upon the subject.

"Before the dishes were uncovered, the Lord Great Chamberlain presented the bason and ewer, to bathe his Majesty's hands; and the Lord of the Manor of Heydon attended with a rich towel. The dishes were then bared; and his Majesty was helped, by the carvers, to some soup. He tasted it! This was a source of endless wonder to a lady near me.

"At the end of this course, the gates of the Hall were again thrown open, and a noble flourish of trumpets announced to all eager hearts that the Champion was about to enter. He advanced under the gateway, on a fine piebald charger (an ill colour), and clad in complete steel. The plumes on his head were tri-coloured, and extremely magnificent; and he bore in his hand the loose steel gauntlet, ready for the challenge. The Duke of Wellington was on his right hand; the Marquis of Anglesey on his left. When he had come within the limits of the Hall, he was about to throw down his glove at once, so eager was he for the fray; but the Herald distinctly said, 'Wait till I have read the Challenge,' and read it accordingly—the Champion husbanding his valour for a few minutes :—

"'If any person, of what degree soever, high or low, shall deny or gainsay our Sovereign Lord King George the Fourth of the United Kingdom of Great Britain and Ireland, Defender of the Faith, son and next heir to our Sovereign Lord King George the Third, the last King deceased, to be right heir to the Imperial Crown of this United Kingdom, or that he ought not to enjoy the same, here is his Champion, who saith that he lieth, and is a false traitor; being ready in person to combat with him, and in this quarrel will adventure his life against him on what day soever he shall be appointed.'

"At the conclusion of this 'awful challenge,' as a gentleman near me termed it, the Champion hurled down his gauntlet, which fell with a solemn clash upon the floor. It rang in most hearts! He then struck his wrist against his steeled side, as though to show how indifferent he was to the consequence of his challenge. This certainly had a very pleasing and gallant effect. The Herald, in a few seconds, took up the glove, delivered it to the Squire, who kissed it, and handed it to the Champion. In the middle of the Hall the same ceremony was performed; and at the foot of the royal platform it was a third time gone through. The King then drank his health, and, methinks, with real pleasure, for the Champion had right gallantly conducted himself. His Majesty then sent the cup to him; and he, taking it, drank to the King, but in so low a tone that I could only catch the meaning by the tumultuous shouts of the people. The noise seemed to awaken the courage of his horse; but he mastered his steed admirably. The ceremony of backing out of the Hall was then again performed, and successfully, with the exception of the Marquis of Anglesey's Arabian, whose doubts were not yet satisfied, and he was literally shown out by the pages.

"In Hall's Account of the Coronation of Henry VIII. and Katharine of Arragon, there is a very quaint and interesting account of the challenge, which, as I think it will aptly illustrate this part of my letter, and serve to amuse you, I shall take leave to copy :—

"'The seconde course beyng served, in at the Haule doore entered a Knyhte armed at al poyntes, his bases rich tissue embroudered, a great plume and a sumpteous of oistriche fethers on his helmet, sittyng on a great courser trapped in tissue and embroudered with tharmes of England and of Fraunce, and an herauld of armes before hym. And passyng through the Haule, presented hymself with humble reverence before the Kynge's Majestie, to whom Garter Kynge of Heraulds cried and said with a loude voyce, 'Sir Knyhte, from whence come you, and what is your pretence?' This Knyhtes name was Sir Robert Dimmoke, Champion to the Kynge by tenour of his enheritaunce, who answered the said Kynge of armes in effecte after this manner: 'Sir, the place that I come from is not materiall, nor the cause of my repaire hyther is not concernyng any matter of any place or countrey, but onely this.' And therewithal commanded his herauld to make an *O yes*. Then said the Knyhte to the Kynge of armes, 'Now shal ye hear the cause of my comynge and pretence.' Then he commanded his own herauld by proclamacion to saye: 'If there be any persone, of what estate or degree soever he be, that will saie or prove that King Henry the Eight is not the rightful enheritor and Kynge of this realm, I, Sir Robert Dimmoke, here his Champion, offre my glove, to fight in his querell with any persone to thutterance.'

"The Champions appear to have been more familiar in the olden time, and to have discoursed more freely with those about them; but perhaps the less that is said the better amongst fighting-men; so I shall not differ with our present Sir Knight on account of his solemn taciturnity. The same old writer from whom I have given you the above description speaks curiously of the pageants which were had to enliven the procession of Anne Boleyn from the Tower to Westminster. The Three Graces, he tells us, took their stand on Cornhill, and the Cardinal Virtues in Fleet Street; a fountain of Helicon ran Rhenish wine; and the conduit in Cheap, with a laudable courtesy, spouted claret. But I must not lose myself amongst books.

"On the Champion retiring, the second course was served up as before; the marquis's horse becoming more and more unmannerly. It was not amiss that his duties were over."

The health of the King having been duly proposed and drunk with great acclamations, the national air of "God save the King" was sung; and his Majesty shortly afterwards retired, amidst the joyous clamours of the company assembled to witness the ceremony.

The banquet in Westminster Hall at the coronation of George IV., we need hardly state, was of the most magnificent description; and as it may interest some of our readers to learn something of the nature of the viands and the quantity of the wines provided—and, we may add, consumed, for when the persons who took part in the coronation ceremonies had retired, the visitors in the galleries, who had been so long confined without victuals, finished what remained—we append the

BILL OF FARE.

Sufficient for a siege the bill of fare;
Denuded of their tribes, earth, sea, and air
Must all contribute to the banquet's zest.

Hot Dishes.—160 tureens of soup, 80 of turtle, 40 of rice, and 40 vermicelli; 160 dishes of fish, comprising 80 of turbot, 40 of trout, 40 of salmon; 160 hot joints, including 80 of venison, 40 of roast beef, with three barons, 40 of mutton and veal; 160 dishes of vegetables, including potatoes, peas, and cauliflowers; 480 sauce-boats, 240 of lobsters, 120 butter, 120 mint.

Cold Dishes.—80 dishes of braized ham; 80 savory pies; 80 dishes of daubed geese, two in each; 80 dishes of savory cakes; 80 pieces of beef braized; 80 dishes of capons braized, two in each; 1,190 side-dishes of various sorts; 320 dishes of mounted pastry; 320 dishes of small pastry; 400 dishes of jellies and creams; 160 dishes of shell-fish, 80 of lobster, and 80 of crayfish; 161 dishes of cold roast fowls; 80 dishes of cold house-lamb.

Total Quantities.—7,442 lbs. of beef; 7,133 lbs. of veal; 2,474 lbs. of mutton; 20 quarters of house-lamb; 20 legs of house-lamb; 5 saddles of lamb; 55 quarters of grass-lamb; 160 lambs' sweetbreads; 389 cow-heels; 400 calves' feet; 250 lbs. of suet; 160 geese; 720 pullets and capons; 1,610 chickens; 520 fowls for stock (hens); 1,730 lbs. of bacon; 550 lbs. of lard; 912 lbs. of butter; 84 hundred of eggs.

All these are independent of the eggs, butter, flour, and necessary articles in the pastry and confectionery departments—such as sugar, isinglass, fruits, &c.

WINES.

The choicest wines brought from fair Gallia's strand;
Burgundian nectar, sparkling Malvoisie,
The source of wit and gay hilarity.

The quantities ordered for the banquet were:—Champagne, 100 dozen; Burgundy, 20 dozen; claret, upwards of 200 dozen; hock, 50 dozen; Moselle, 50 dozen; Madeira, 50 dozen; sherry and port, about 350 dozen; iced punch, 100 gallons. The champagne, hock, and Moselle were iced before they went to table; and the whole of the wines were spoken of as being excellent by the thousands who had an opportunity of tasting them.

Of *ale*, 100 barrels were ordered for the use of the kitchen. The *porcelain* consisted of 6,794 dinner plates, 1,406 soup-plates, 1,499 dessert-plates, and 288 large pitchers for ale and beer. There were 240 yards of damask table-cloths for the Hall, and about 1,000 yards more laid on the tables in the other suites of rooms. The cutlery included 16,000 knives and forks, and 612 pairs of carvers.

Respecting the origin of the office of the King's Champion in England during the Saxon period we have no authentic account; but Sir William Dugdale asserts, both in his "Baronage of England" and his "History of Warwickshire," that William the Conqueror, to reward the services of those followers who aided him in subduing the kingdom, bestowed on them sundry manors and lands in various counties, subject to many curious feudal services. Among the most distinguished of the Conqueror's followers was Robert de Marmyon, on whom the Norman king, among other gifts, conferred the castle of Tamworth, in Warwickshire, to hold by knight's service, and also the manor of Scrivelsby, near Horncastle, in the north of Lincolnshire, to hold *per baroniam;* and his peculiar service and duty was to perform the office of Champion to the Kings of England on the days of their coronation. From this time the Marmyons of Scrivelsby became barons of the realm *per tenuram*, and they continued to flourish among the greater nobles for several generations, with much lustre and renown, intermarrying at each descent with the heiress of some of the most powerful barons of the age. But about the twentieth year of Edward I., Philip de Marmyon, fifth from the companion of the Conqueror, died, leaving only female issue; and thus the great inheritance of the family came to be divided; the Castle of Tamworth falling to the Frevilles, and the manor of Scrivelsby to the Ludlows, by the marriage of whose daughter and heiress, Margaret, with Sir John Dymoke, Knight, it came into that ancient and honourable house. From that period to the coronation of George IV., the office was executed by the Dymoke family. Since the accession of George IV. no coronation banquet has been held in Westminster Hall.

A capital story—we fear almost too good to be true—is told respecting the Champion at the coronation of William and Mary, in 1689. It will be found in the "Gazetteer" for August, 1784, nearly a century afterwards, and is therefore open to some suspicion. It runs as follows:—

"The Champion of England (Dymoke), dressed in armour of complete and glittering steel, his horse richly caparisoned, and his beaver finely capped with plumes of feathers, entered Westminster Hall, according to ancient custom, while the king and queen were at dinner. And, at his giving the usual challenge to any one that disputed their majesties' right to the crown of England, ... after he had flung down his gauntlet on the pavement, an old woman, who entered the Hall on crutches, ... took it up, and made off with great celerity, leaving her own glove with a challenge in it to meet her the next day, at an appointed hour, in Hyde Park. This occasioned some mirth at the lower end of the Hall, and it was remarked that every one was too well engaged to pursue her. A person in the same dress appeared the next day at the place appointed, though it was generally supposed to be a good swordsman in that disguise. However, the Champion of England politely declined any contest of that nature with one of the fair sex, and never made his appearance."

Westminster Hall has a connection, though only a momentary one, with the alchemist and astrologer, Count Cagliostro. His pretensions having been exposed by a Frenchman in the *Courrier de l'Europe*, then published in London, he was recognised and denounced before his face in this Hall, in 1785, as Joseph Balsamo, the swindler of Palermo. Such a disgrace, so publicly cast upon him, was not to be borne: it was "the last pound that broke the camel's back." The "count" and his "countess" at once packed up their traps, and left England, to prosecute their fraudulent career in Belgium, France, and Italy.

Westminster Hall has also its literary reminiscences, some of them small and trivial, yet not the less worth recording here on that account. Charles Dickens has told us how, on finding that his first contribution had been accepted and printed in the *Monthly Magazine*, he bought a copy in the Strand, and "walked with it into Westminster Hall, and turned in there for half an hour, because his eyes were so dimmed with joy and pride that they could not bear the street, and were not fit to be seen there."

It may be interesting to some of our readers to learn that when, in 1820, the roof of the famous old Hall was thoroughly repaired and completed towards the north, forty loads of oak, the remains of old men-of-war, which were broken up in Portsmouth Dockyard, were employed as materials. It may be added that the Hall was nearly involved in the destruction of the Houses of Parliament, for it was only by the utmost exertions that the flames, which at one time nearly burst through the south windows at the upper end, were checked in that direction. A few minutes more, and no human efforts could have rescued the Hall from the general conflagration, because, had the roof once caught fire, the flames would have swept through that forest of timber with uncontrollable fury.

In 1843, and again in the following year, Westminster Hall was used for the exhibition of a collection of works of art which had been made for the purpose of assisting the Commissioners on the Fine Arts in the selection of the persons to be employed in the decoration of the new Palace.

The Hall used to be open to the public daily, but a few years ago, when the Irish question was in an acute stage, an attempt was made to blow it up with dynamite, and now it is accessible on Saturdays only. Against the east wall are statues of several of our sovereigns—James I., Charles I., Charles II., William III. and Mary, George IV., and William IV. After the opening of the Royal Palace of Justice in the Strand, Soane's Law Courts, which formed an irritating excrescence on the west side of the Hall, were demolished, disclosing to view the original Norman wall and flying buttresses. These have been restored, and a cloister with gallery constructed, under the supervision of Mr. J. L. Pearson, R.A.

A modern doorway on the east side of Westminster Hall leads into St. Stephen's Cloisters. These were restored when the Palace was rebuilt. The existing fabric was the work of John Chambers, the last Dean of St. Stephen's, who lived to see his Chapel and Cloister both seized by the Crown. The lower tier is vaulted throughout; the vaulting being richest on the west side.

In the south-east corner of the Hall, a flight of steps leads to the beautiful little chapel of St. Stephen's, originally the crypt of the ancient building. This chapel, of which a view is given on page 505, has undergone a thorough restoration, and is a perfect gem of florid Gothic architecture. Its walls and groined ceiling are literally one blaze of gold and colours; the flooring is paved with highly-polished encaustic tiles of a rich pattern, and its windows are filled with stained glass. The ornamentation of this edifice is in the best style of the fourteenth century, and the bosses are remarkably fine. It is now fitted up as a place of worship for residents of the Palace.

In 1854, the body of an ecclesiastic, presumed to have been of some eminence from the position in which the corpse was found, was discovered by the workmen who were employed in removing part of the north wall of the crypt, necessary to the restoration of the edifice.

The remarkable feature in this discovery consists in the circumstance of the body having been literally built into the masonry of the wall, without coffin or any enclosure except the linen shroud in which it was wrapped; and by this it would appear to have been there deposited at the erection of the edifice; but whether translated to this situation or originally so buried, cannot be conjectured. Lying diagonally across the body from the left shoulder to the outer side of the right foot was an elaborately-carved wooden crozier. The remains were afterwards placed in an elm coffin and re-interred near the place where they were discovered.

A correspondent of the *Globe* newspaper, at the time of the discovery, suggested that the body was that of William Lyndwoode, Bishop of St. David's and Keeper of the Privy Seal, who founded a chantry in the Chapel of St. Stephen by deed, and died in 1446; as on reference to the patent-roll of 32 Henry III., M. 4, there will be found an entry of a licence, dated 19th of July, from the King to "Robert Pyke, clerk, and Adrian Grenebough, executors of William Lyndwoode, lately Bishop of St. David's and Keeper of the Privy Seal, for the foundation of a perpetual chantry in the Under-Chapel of St. Stephen, within the King's Palace of Westminster, for two perpetual chaplains, or at least for one perpetual chaplain, to celebrate divine service daily in the aforesaid Chapel, or one of them in the Under-Chapel (St. Mary's), and the other at the Chapel of St. Mary de la Pewe, situated near the King's said Chapel of St. Stephen, for the healthful estate of the King and his consort Margaret, Queen of England, and their souls when they shall die; and also for the soul of the afore-said bishop whose body lies buried in the said Under-Chapel," &c.

Close by Westminster Hall was a noted coffee-house, known alike to ears polite and not polite by the name of "Hell"—very much (it has been wittily remarked) "as the 'Devil' Tavern adjoined the Temple."

It is comically recorded in the *Somerset House Gazette*:—"First day of Term opens with a furious hurricane; . . a dozen country attorneys break-fast in 'Hell.'" There was apparently another coffee-house hard by, called the "Bell," much frequented by those who attended the Law Courts; for in the same work we read: "Juries swallow their claret in the afternoon at the 'Bell' at Westminster, as they swallowed their oaths in the morning; and get drunk by eight."

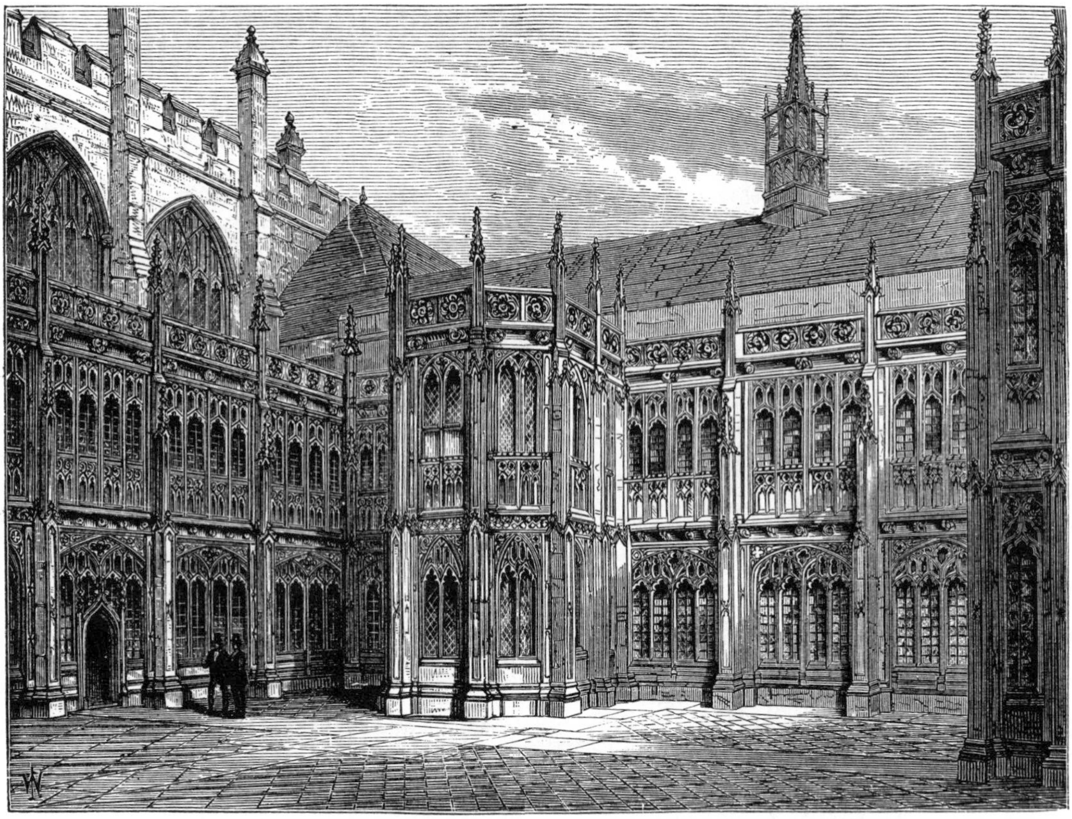

ST. STEPHEN'S CLOISTERS. (*See page* 557.)

One cannot help reading with a smile a statement made in Smith's "Antiquities of Westminster," that in the year 1550 the king "had taken into his own hands the house called 'Hell,' of the annual value of £4; the house called 'Purgatory,' of the annual value of £1 6s. 8d., and also five other houses adjoining the Exchequer, for the purpose of depositing and preserving the ducking-stool, or cucking-stool, employed by the good burgesses of Westminster for the punishment of scolds. The punishment is thus described in the *Mirror*, in the year 1830:—"The angry lady was strapped in a chair, fastened by an iron pin to one end of a long pole, suspended in the middle by a lofty trestle, which, being placed on the shore of the Thames, allowed the terrified culprit to be immersed in the river; when the lady's temper was supposed to be cooled by a few plunges, she was exposed, dripping and humbled, to the laugh of her neighbours."

Close to the Houses of Parliament stood another public-house, which appears to have enjoyed some little reputation in the last century. A writer in an early number of the *Spectator*, after observing that "all dependents run in some measure into the measures and behaviour of those whom they serve," thus humorously narrates his visit to the house in question:—"Falling in the other day at a victualling-house near the House of Peers, I heard the maid come down and tell the landlady at the bar that my lord bishop swore he would throw her out at window if she did not bring up more mild beer, and that my lord duke would have a double mug of purl. My surprise was increased in hearing loud and rustic voices speak and answer to each other upon the public affairs by the names of the most illustrious of our nobility; till of a sudden one came running in, and cried the House was rising. Down came all the company together, and away: the ale-house was immediately filled with clamour, and scoring one mug to the marquis of such a place, oil and vinegar to such an earl, three quarts to my new lord for wetting his title, and so forth. It is a thing too notorious to mention the crowds of servants, and their insolence, near the courts of justice, and the stairs towards the supreme assembly, where there is a universal mockery of all order, such riotous clamour and confusion, that one would think the whole nation lived in jest." A similar instance of "high life below stairs" has existed in the reign of Victoria.

Cotton House, we learn from Strype, "in the passage out of Westminster Hall into the Old Palace Yard (between the Abbey and the Houses of Parliament), a little below the stairs going up to St. Stephen's Chapel, now the Parliament House, on the left hand, is the house belonging to the ancient and noble family of the Cottons, wherein is kept a most inestimable library of manuscript volumes, found both at home and abroad."

To the south of St. Stephen's Chapel probably stood the Chapel of our Lady de la Pieu, on the site of what was known afterwards as Cotton's Garden. This garden belonged to the town house of Sir Robert Cotton, the founder of the Cottonian Library, and its site is at the present day covered by the House of Lords and the Peers' Court. The Chapel is supposed to have derived its name from the wells (*les puits*) hard by, one of which was in the Speaker's Court-yard, and another near the river, at the east end of New Palace Yard, where the Star Chamber stood, and another was in the south cloister of St. Stephen's Chapel. In this chapel knelt Richard II., with a retinue of two hundred persons, before he went out to meet Wat Tyler, at Smithfield, in June, 1381. The Chapel, along with Our Lady's altar, was burnt down in 1452, by the carelessness of a Westminster scholar, who had been sent to put out the lights. The Chapel was rebuilt by Anthony Widville, Earl Rivers, who by his will bequeathed his heart to be buried there, and left an endowment for a priest to offer mass in it for the repose of his soul. The date when this chapel was pulled down is not known.

CHAPTER LXIII.

THE OLD LAW COURTS AND OLD PALACE YARD.

"*M.*—I hate this place worse than a man who has inherited a Chancery-suit.
"*F.*—Why, you need not be afraid of this place; for a man without money needs no more fear a crowd of lawyers than a crowd of pickpockets."—*Wycherley.*

The Courts of Law first established in Westminster Hall—Ancient Mode of conferring Knighthood on the Judges—Henry III. and Henry de Bath—The Old Law Courts—Curious Custom observed at the Presentation of the Sheriffs in the Court of Exchequer—The Great Tichborne Imposture—The Court of Augmentations—Old Palace Yard—Geoffrey Chaucer—The "Gunpowder Plot"—Execution of Sir Walter Raleigh—Statue of Richard Cœur de Lion.

THE seats of justice, or courts of common law and chancery, which both before and after the Norman Conquest followed the sovereign, were in the reign of Henry III. made stationary, and appointed to be held in Westminster Hall. "In the King's Bench, or principal court, anciently called *Curia Domini Regis*, the king himself usually presided, and in his absence the *justiciarius Angliæ*, an officer of great trust, styled by our Saxon ancestors *Alderman*, or *totius Angliæ Aldermannus.*

The judges of the Court usually received the honour of knighthood, which degree was anciently conferred by bathing and other ceremonies; and the materials for their robes, &c., were furnished by the king. Walter de Clopton and Robert de Cherleton, made justices of the King's Bench and Common Pleas by Richard II., about to receive the order of knighthood 'as Bannerets at Wyndsore, on the feast of St. George,' had among other things allowed them, to keep their *vigils*, six ells of russet cloth long, and for their bath 'two cloths of gold *sigaston*, and one piece of green silk,' &c." John Whiddon, a justice of this Court, in the reign of Queen Mary, is said to have been the first judge who rode to Westminster Hall on a horse or gelding, before which time the judges rode on mules.

At the upper end of the new Hall stood the statues of the kings of England, from Edward the Confessor to Stephen, and also, on the south-east side, a marble bench, nineteen feet long and three feet broad, upon which the king sat at his coronation feast, and at other times the Lord Chancellor. This was the King's Bench for pleas of the Crown. In the south-west angle sat the Lord Chancellor, the Master of the Rolls, and eleven men learned in the civil law, called Masters of the Chancery. "It derived its name," says Mr. Mackenzie Walcott, "from the bar of open timber-work (*cancelli*), which separated this court (in the last century completely shutting it out from sight) from the lower part of the Hall." This screen was taken down before the coronation of George IV. Near the King's Bench, in front of the large chamber called the White Hall, was the Court of Wards and Liveries. In this chamber, originally called the Treasury, were kept many valuable state papers. Adjoining the Chancery was the Equity Court of Requests or Conscience, for trying suits made by way of petition to the sovereign; it was sometimes called the Poor Man's Court, "because he could there have right without paying for it." It is difficult to accept this statement literally.

In 1234, Henry III. sat in person in the King's Court, and in 1256 in the Court of Exchequer. Not long after, Henry de Bath, one of the judges, was accused of sedition; but he, "forewarned, forearmed," summoned his friends, and so went attended into the Hall. No sooner had he entered than the king, in a transport of disappointed rage, cried out, "My free pardon to him that strikes dead Henry of Bath!" The more prudent Council, however, we are told, dissuaded the angry monarch from so perilous a venture.

The old Law Courts were situated on the west side of the Hall, and were all contained in an Italian-fronted building erected from the designs of Sir John Soane. They each had an entrance from the Hall, and also from the street. The various courts harboured here were the Court of Queen's Bench, the Bail Court, the Court for Crown Cases Reserved, the Court of Common Pleas, the Court of Exchequer, the Rolls Court, the Arches Court, the High Court of Admiralty, the Vice-Chancellor's Court, and the Court of Probate and Divorce.

Of the courts of law adjoining the Hall, the author of "A New Critical Review of the Public Buildings," 1810, speaks as presenting a slovenly appearance, and utterly wanting in that pomp and magnificence which is necessary to enforce the respect which should ever attend on the administration of justice. In this observation most competent persons will agree with the writer, and at the same time regret that he did not live to see the old Law Courts pulled down and the new Law Courts rise in their place in the Strand.

Previously to the year 1859, when it was discontinued, a curious ancient tenure custom had been for centuries performed, on the occasion of the presentation of the sheriffs of London and Middlesex in the Court of Exchequer. After the ceremony of presentation, proclamation was made by the Crier of the Court for the service as follows:—"Oyez! oyez! oyez! Tenants and occupiers of a piece of waste ground called 'The Moors,' in the county of Salop, come forth and do your service, upon pain and peril that shall fall thereon!" The senior alderman below the chair then cut one fagot (small twigs) with a hatchet, and another with a billhook. The Crier then made this proclamation:—"Oyez! oyez! oyez! Tenants and occupiers of a certain tenement called 'The Forge,' in the parish of St. Clement Danes, in the county of Middlesex, come forth and do your service." The alderman then counted certain horseshoes and hobnails, and was questioned by the Queen's Remembrancer thus:—"How many have you?" "Six shoes." Then the alderman counted the nails. "How many have you?" "Sixty-one nails—good number." And so the ceremony ended.

Mr. Nichols, in the *Gentleman's Magazine* for October, 1804, describes the custom as performed in that year, and adds this explanation:—"The ceremony on this occasion, in the Court of Exchequer, which vulgar error supposed to be an unmeaning farce, is solemn and impressive; nor have the new sheriffs the least connection either with chopping of sticks or counting of hobnails.

The tenants of a manor in Shropshire are directed to come forth and do their suit and service; on which the senior alderman below the chair steps forward and chops a single stick, in token of its having been customary for the tenants of that manor to supply their lord with fuel. The owners of a forge in the parish of St. Clement (which formerly belonged to the City, and stood in the high road from the Temple to Westminster, but now no longer exists) are then called forth to do their suit and service; when an officer of the Court, in the presence of the senior alderman, produces six horseshoes and sixty-one hobnails, which he counts over in form before the Cursitor Baron, who on this particular occasion is the immediate representative of the sovereign."

Mr. Sheriff Hoare, in the journal of his shrievalty, 1640-41, in his own autograph writes:—"The senior alderman present cut one twig in two, and bent another, and the officers of the Court counted six horseshoes and hobnails. This formality, it is said, is passed through each year, by way of suit and service for the citizens holding some tenements in St. Clement Danes, as also some other lands; but *where they are situated no one knows, nor doth the City receive any rents or profits thereby.*"

The Court of Exchequer, be it observed, is the legal court of accounts; and, moreover, pursuant to the charter 32 Henry III., the high officers of the City are, on their appointment, to be presented to the sovereign, or, in the absence of majesty, to the sovereign's Justices or Barons of the Royal Exchequer.

In the Court of Common Pleas came on for hearing, on the 11th of May, 1871, the celebrated "Tichborne case"—so called. The lawsuit was technically an action for the purpose of ejecting Colonel Lushington from Tichborne House, Hampshire, which had been let to him, and was instituted by a person named Orton or Castro, who some time previously had arrived in England from Australia, and who represented himself to be Sir Roger Charles Doughty-Tichborne, Bart.; the latter having been lost at sea in the *Bella*, in 1854. Tichborne House still remained the property of the Tichborne family, and the action at once raised the question whether the "Claimant" was or was not identical with the young man who was so long believed to have perished in the *Bella*. The case was heard before Lord Chief Justice Bovill; Mr. Serjeant Ballantine and Mr. Giffard were retained as counsel for the "Claimant;" and on the side of the defendant was Lord Coleridge, then Solicitor-General, supported by Mr. Hawkins. Owing to frequent adjournments it was not until the 6th of March, 1872, that the trial was concluded, the proceedings having extended to 103 days. The "Claimant's" advisers, to avoid an inevitable verdict for their opponents, elected to be nonsuited, and thus the case came to a somewhat abrupt termination. This, however, was not to be the last the public were to hear of it, for the Lord Chief Justice at once committed the "Claimant" to Newgate on a charge of wilful and corrupt perjury and forgery.

After a few weeks' delay the "Claimant" was released from Newgate on bail, in the sum of £10,000, the sureties being Lord Rivers, Mr. Guildford Onslow, M.P., Mr. Whalley, M.P., and Mr. Attwood, a medical man residing at Bayswater. From this time till the commencement of the criminal trial—a period of thirteen months—a systematic agitation on the "Claimant's" behalf was kept up throughout the country, and public appeals were made for subscriptions to defray the expenses of his defence. The great trial itself commenced in the Court of Queen's Bench, at Westminster, on the 23rd of April, 1873, the proceedings being conducted under what is called a "trial at bar," and by that means were invested with some show of pomp and ceremony, and a dignity which they could not rightly claim, for it is only a trial of that nature before three judges that can be continued without regard to the ordinary periods of sessions or legal terms. The trial was presided over by Sir Alexander Cockburn, Lord Chief Justice of the Queen's Bench, Mr. Justice Mellor, and Mr. Justice Lush. On the side of the Crown were Mr. Hawkins and Mr. Serjeant Parry; on that of the defendant, Dr. Kenealy and Mr. MacMahon, M.P. The defendant was indicted under the name of "Arthur Orton, *alias* Thomas Castro;" and the trial ended on the 28th of February, 1874—a period of 188 days having been occupied in the proceedings. Throughout this extraordinary trial—so great had become the public excitement and curiosity in connection with the case—the arrival and departure of the "Claimant" in the carriage provided for him by his supporters were witnessed by thousands of persons, shouting lustily for "Sir Roger," while the object of their attentions, bowing to right and left, gracefully acknowledged these tokens of popularity. The number of witnesses examined amounted to 212, and the trial ended with a verdict of "Guilty," and a sentence of fourteen years' penal servitude. The foreman of the jury publicly declared that there was no doubt in the mind of any of the jurymen that the man who had for eight years assumed the name and title of the gentleman in whose unhappy fate the majority of the family had long believed was an impostor, who had added slander of the wickedest kind to his many other crimes. But not only were they satisfied of this; they were equally agreed that he was Arthur Orton, the son of a butcher at Wapping! And so ended another chapter in the history of great popular delusions. There were, however, especially among the uneducated classes, not a few who continued to believe in the impostor. In 1895, in a series of articles in the *People*, he confessed his guilt.

The Court of Augmentations was formerly held in a portion of the Old Palace, upon or near the site of the old Law Courts. It was founded by Henry VIII., for the purpose of surveying and governing all the forfeited ecclesiastical property secularised to the use of the king. Queen Mary dissolved this court, by letters patent, in 1554. All the deeds and resignations of abbeys, priories, and lands, and their valuations, were kept here. The judicial proceedings of the Courts of Augmentation and Surveys-General, which lasted for a short period after their creation by Henry VIII., and those of the Parliamentary Survey made under the Commonwealth, were also preserved here. These records were exposed to great danger at the burning of the Houses of Parliament in 1834.

At the southern end of Westminster Hall, and occupying the space between the Houses of Parliament and the Abbey, is Old Palace Yard. It was anciently bounded on the north by the south gate in St. Margaret's Lane; on the west by the Abbey; on the east by some of the inferior offices of the Palace, with a little court, in which, in 1732, was the king's fishmonger's house; and on the south by a gateway at the north end of the present Abingdon Street, then called Lindsay Lane. At the south-west end of this lane was Lindsay House, afterwards the residence of the Earl of Abingdon (from whom the present street received its name), and in 1708 the residence of Dormer, Earl of Carnarvon.

In the year 1399, Geoffrey Chaucer, "the first illuminer of the English language," entered into an agreement for the lease of a house adjoining the "White Rose" Tavern, which abutted on the old Lady Chapel of the Abbey. Chaucer held the office of Clerk of the King's Works, and was robbed (more than once) by Richard Brerelay and others, probably as he was going to or returning from Eltham. Brerelay, though he escaped punishment on this occasion, was afterwards tried for another highway robbery, pleaded "Not guilty," and "declared that he was ready to defend himself by his body against the approver (Clerk)," as Mr. W. Selby tells us in the Introduction to his "Life Records of Chaucer," thus demanding "the wager of battle." A duel was accordingly fought between Brerelay and Clerk (the said "approver") at Tothill on the 21st of April, 1391; the result being that the "approver" was vanquished, and forthwith received judgment to be hanged.

It is probable that it was in his house at Westminster that Chaucer ended his days. His house, the tavern, and St. Mary's Chapel were demolished in 1502, to give place to Henry VII.'s Chapel.

In a house which stood between the churchyard and the old Palace, lived "rare Ben Jonson," and here he died; so that two of the greatest of England's poets breathed their last almost upon the same spot. Nearly all the houses in Old Palace Yard, as well as the block known as Poets' Corner, have recently been demolished.

In the south-east corner of Old Palace Yard was a house which was at one time occupied as the Ordnance Office, and afterwards served as the entrance to the House of Lords. This house was hired by Percy, a gentleman-pensioner of the Court, and through it the conspirators in the "Gunpowder Plot" carried their barrels into a vault which formed part of the kitchens of the Old Palace.

This is perhaps a proper place for putting on record a correct account of the famous "Gunpowder Plot," which for nearly three centuries has made the name of Guido or Guy Fawkes a "household word" through the length and breadth of England: we will therefore condense it from the authentic pages of Dodd's "Church History," an acknowledged authority with the Roman Catholic body. It appears that, on the accession of James I., rightly or wrongly, the hopes of the Roman Catholics in England were raised by Cecil's assurance that the persecutions with which Elizabeth had visited them as rebels and traitors would be discontinued. In this hope, however, they were disappointed, and the discontent of some members of their body soon found means to express itself. "It broke out," says Dodd, "in the Gunpowder Plot, the contrivance of half-a-dozen persons of desperate fortunes, who by that means have brought an odium upon the body of Catholics, who have ever since laboured under the weight of that calumny, though nowise concerned. Now," he continues, "for the particulars of this horrid design, as I find them recorded by our historians. They tell us Mr. Catesby was the first contriver of the plot for blowing up the Parliament House, which, for a considerable time, he kept for himself, till he could meet with associates as desperate as himself to engage in it. At length he found those that were fit for his purpose—viz., Thomas Percy, Guy Faux, Thomas Winter, Robert Keyes, and Thomas Bates. To these he communicated his

EXECUTION OF THE CONSPIRATORS IN THE GUNPOWDER PLOT IN THE YEAR 1606. (*From a Print published in 1795.*)

design, who approved of it, and, as it is said, mutually joined in an oath of secrecy. Now the manner of carrying on the contrivance was this: Percy being well acquainted at Court, where he enjoyed a place, and upon this account was less order to fill it with fuel for a winter's provision. The care thereof was committed to Guy Faux, who took the name of John Johnston, and passed for Mr. Percy's servant. Hitherto the contrivance was kept a secret among the persons above men-

ST. MARGARET'S CHURCH, 1870. (*See page* 567.)

suspected, hired lodgings near the Parliament House, whereby the conspirators had the convenience of digging for a subterraneous passage. They laboured at this work for some months till, meeting with a very thick wall, which had a deep foundation, the work became tedious, and obliged them to desist. Meanwhile, Mr. Percy informed himself of a cellar directly under the Parliament House, which he immediately hired, as he gave out, in tioned. Yet they had scattered a report privately, among several Catholics, that something was in agitation in their favour; and people of that communion began to entertain thoughts that in a little time they should be made easy, though they neither knew when, nor by what means, it was to be effected. It appeared, indeed, afterwards, that some few were let further into the secret (though never acquainted with the blackest part of the records and rolls of that court." In explanation of this statement we may be pardoned for quoting Strype (Book vi.), who says that under Westminster Hall are certain subterraneous apartments, which are called the one "Paradise" and the other "Hell," which were given by the King to Sir Andrew Dudley, brother of the great Duke of Northumberland. A range of houses of red brick, extending from west to east, opposite the end of Henry VII.'s Chapel, at the same time was called "Heaven." Both the "Heaven" and the "Hell" here mentioned would seem to have been public-houses in the time of James I., and were probably frequented by low company, lawyers' clerks, &c. At all events, Ben Jonson, in the *Alchemist*, introduces "Doll Common" as personating the Queen of Fairies, and forbidding "Dapper" the lawyer's clerk, who is persuaded to believe himself her nephew, to break his fast in "Heaven" or "Hell," as not worthy of so distinguished a guest. Butler, moreover, in his "Hudibras" speaks of—

"False Heaven at the end of th' Hall."

GUY FAWKES'S CELLAR. (*See page* 563.)

It is stated, too, in an anonymous note on "Hudibras," that at the Restoration the body of Oliver Cromwell was dug up, and his head set up at one end of Westminster Hall, "near which place there is a house of entertainment commonly known by the name of 'Heaven.'" And it may be added that in the "History of Independency" there is mention made of a "victualling-house" in Westminster called "Hell."

Not far from this place was long preserved the

design), and had received private orders from Percy to be up in arms the 6th of November, 1605, which was the day after the plot was discovered. The only persons to whom these orders were directed were, Sir Everard Digby, Mr. Francis Tresham, Mr. John Grant, Mr. Ambrose Rookwood, Mr. Robert Winter, two Mr. Knights—John and Christopher. About ten days before the Parliament was to meet, which was on the 5th of November, a letter from an unknown hand was delivered to Lord Monteagle, a Catholic, admonishing him to be absent in Parliament on the day of their first meeting, for that a sudden judgment would fall upon the nation by an invisible hand, or to that purpose. The confusedness of style, with the ambiguity of expressions, both startled and puzzled his lordship; wherefore, having made Secretary Cecil acquainted with it, and the letter being canvassed several days before the king and council, they at length found out the sense and true meaning of it—viz., that the suddenness of the stratagem spoke gunpowder, and by the *nation* must be understood the *Parliament*. Upon this surmise Sir Thomas Knevet, by order of council, was deputed to make strict search in all the places and apartments near the Parliament House, which he did the day before the House was to meet, when he happened to spy out a person standing at a cellar door, ready booted and spurred, who, upon examination, confessed he had a design to set fire to a train of gunpowder which was to blow up the Parliament House; in confirmation whereof, upon a further scrutiny, thirty-six barrels of gunpowder were found in the cellar, concealed under billets and other fuel."

It is added by Winwood, more circumstantially, that "Sir Thomas Knevet, on going thither about midnight, unlooked for, into the vault, found that fellow Johnston newly come out of the vault, and, without asking any more questions, stayed him; and having no sooner removed the wood, he perceived the barrels, and so bound the caitiff fast, who made no difficulty to acknowledge the act, nor to confess clearly that the morrow following it should have been effected."

The rest of the story is well known. The conspirators, finding that their designs were suspected, quitted London, and made their rendezvous at Dunchurch, in Warwickshire; driven thence, they beat a retreat towards Stourbridge, where Catesby, Percy, and two more of their comrades were killed in defending the house where they took shelter; the rest, including Fawkes, were captured, brought to London, tried for treason, and executed in Old Palace Yard. We need scarcely add that the old custom of examining the cellars underneath the House of Lords, a few hours before the opening of Parliament, still continues to be observed, or that the custom had its origin in the infamous Gunpowder Plot.

A good story of the Gunpowder Plot is told in the "Railway Anecdote Book," but we cannot undertake to pledge ourselves to its truth. A former Lord Chamberlain was sent to examine the vaults under the Parliament House, and, returning with his report, said that "he had found five-and-twenty barrels of gunpowder; that he had removed ten of them, and hoped the other fifteen would do no harm."

It was in Old Palace Yard that, on a chill October morning in the year 1618, Sir Walter Raleigh was led forth to die by the headsman's axe. On the morning of Raleigh's execution his keeper brought a cup of sack to him, and inquired how he was pleased with it. "As well as he who drank of St. Giles's bowl as he rode to Tyburn," answered the knight, and said, "it was good drink if a man might but tarry by it." "Prithee, never fear, Ceeston," cried he to his old friend Sir Hugh, who was repulsed from the scaffold by the sheriff, "I shall have a place!" A man bald from extreme age pressed forward "to see him," he said, "and pray God for him." Raleigh took a richly embroidered cap from his own head, and placing it on that of the old man, said, "Take this, good friend, to remember me, for you have more need of it than I." "Farewell, my lords," was his cheerful parting to a courtly group who affectionately took their leave of him, "I have a long journey before me, and I must e'en say good-bye." "Now I am going to God," said that heroic spirit, as he trod the scaffold; and, gently touching the axe, added, "This is a sharp medicine, but it will cure all diseases." The very headsman shrank from beheading one so illustrious and brave, until the unquailing soldier addressed him, "What dost thou fear? Strike, man!" In another moment the mighty soul had fled from its mangled tenement. Cayley, after describing Sir Walter's execution, adds, "The head, after being shown on either side of the scaffold, was put into a leather bag, over which Sir Walter's gown was thrown, and the whole conveyed away in a mourning coach by Lady Raleigh. It was preserved by her in a case during the twenty-nine years which she survived her husband, and afterwards with no less piety by their affectionate son Carew, with whom it is supposed to have been buried at West Horsley, in Surrey. The body was interred in the chancel near the altar of St. Margaret's, Westminster."

In the Pepysian Collection at Magdalen College, Cambridge, is a ballad with this title, "Sir Walter Raleigh, his Lamentation, who was Beheaded in the Old Pallace of Westminster, the 29th of October, 1618. To the tune of 'Welladay.'"

In Old Palace Yard, about half way between Westminster Hall and the Peers' Entrance, is the statue of Richard Cœur de Lion, by the late Baron Marochetti, somewhat hastily pronounced by the *Edinburgh Review*, "the noblest equestrian statue in England." It stands on a pedestal a little over eight feet in height, with bassi-relievi on its panels. The king is seated on the back of a charger; but both the rider and the horse are open to grave criticism. The following critique may be taken, on the whole, as fair and just: "The group is picturesque; but the hind-quarters of the horse, and the fatiguing attitude of the man, are unsuccessful. The king appears to be sitting on his horse quietly, just as a groom does when without a saddle; whereas, since the attitude is supposed to be a momentary one, the figure should, with uplifted arm, have been raised in the stirrups. This would have given life to the figure, and would have connected it better with the horse. No man on a prancing charger would be lifting up his sword in a supposed dignified position with his feet dangling carelessly in the stirrups."

CHAPTER LXIV.

WESTMINSTER.—ST. MARGARET'S CHURCH.

"London and Westminster are two twin-sister cities, as joyned by one street, so watered by one stream; the first a breeder of grave magistrates; the second the burial-place of great monarchs."—*Heywood's "Porta Pietatis."*

Early History of St. Margaret's—The Present Church described—A Singular Bequest—Interesting Monuments—"State Services" before the Speaker and Members of the House of Commons—Eminent Puritan Divines—Lecturers and Curates since the Commonwealth—Extracts from the Churchwarden's Accounts—Edmund Waller and the Parliament—The "Solemn League and Covenant"—Pulpit Buffoonery—Long Sermons in Former Times—The "State's Arms"—"Humming" in Church—A Forçible Possession of the Pulpit—Performance of Oratorios—Electioneering Piety—John Milton's Marriage—Memorial Windows—Disgraceful Condition of the Churchyard—Alterations and Improvements—A Unique Relic.

The "City" of Westminster, properly speaking, consists of only two parishes—St. Margaret's and St. John's; but the "Liberties" of Westminster, as we have shown in a previous chapter, are far more extensive, comprising also those of St. Clement Danes, St. Mary-le-Strand, St. Martin's-in-the-Fields, St. Anne's, Soho, St. James's, Piccadilly, St. Paul's, Covent Garden, and St. George's, Hanover Square; besides the Precincts of the Savoy, the Abbey Precincts, and the Royal Palaces of Whitehall and St. James's.

Although the present Church of St. Margaret retains no traces of details earlier than the reigns of the Plantagenets, yet, writes Mr. Mackenzie Walcott, "there is, with the exception of the Abbey of St. Peter and St. Paul's Cathedral, no other ecclesiastical edifice throughout London and Westminster which can boast a greater antiquity, or more interesting foundation."

The original structure dated from a few years before the Conquest. We are told that Edward the Confessor, finding, as was natural, that a population was growing up around the Abbey walls, and was continually increased further by a miscellaneous crowd of persons who, for good or for bad reasons, sought the shelter of the Sanctuary, raised here a church in the round arched Saxon style, and dedicated it to St. Margaret. Another account represents the king as simply intending to benefit the respectable inhabitants of the neighbourhood. Whichever account is true, at all events one thing is certain—namely, that Edward was the great friend of the monks of St. Peter's, and he was naturally anxious that their spiritual meditations should not be broken in upon by parochial duties or secular cares.

This edifice appears to have stood until the reign of Edward I., when it was almost wholly taken down and rebuilt. Very extensive alterations were made again in the reign of Edward IV., at which time, according to Mr. Timbs, the surrounding level of the ground was nine feet lower than now, and a flight of stone steps led up to the nave.

The present building is a plain and handsome Gothic structure, with a panelled roof, slightly curved. In the old days, before the parishioners began to repair and restore it, the church must have been really handsome in its details, as it still is in its proportions, which are much admired for their harmony. In the tower is a peal of ten bells; these, however, are seldom rung, as on Sundays they would interfere with the services in the Abbey, close by. Formerly the bells had chime-hammers annexed to them, and tunes were played upon them at regular intervals.

The entrance-porch of the nave forms the framework to a beautiful picture. Lofty arches, of a very light and elegant character, with spandrils enriched with quatrefoils and trefoils springing from twelve clustered columns, divide the nave from the aisles. In 1878 the interior underwent a thorough restoration; the galleries being removed, and the old-fashioned "pews" superseded by open benches. The pulpit is considered the most richly ornamented in the metropolis.

The edifice is lighted by a series of large windows; that at the east end is very large and beautiful, and is filled with painted glass. It was made by order of the magistrates of Dort, in Holland, and designed by them as a present to Henry VII., for his new chapel in Westminster Abbey; but that monarch dying before it was finished, it was set up in the private chapel of the Abbot of Waltham, at Copt Hall, near Epping, in Essex. There it remained till the Dissolution, when it was removed to New Hall, in the same county, and on General Monk coming into possession of that place, he preserved the window from demolition. In 1758, the window was purchased by the inhabitants of the parish.

The subject is the Crucifixion, with numerous subordinate figures, all which are of admirable execution. On the one side is King Henry VII., and on the other his queen, both kneeling. Their portraits are stated to have been taken from original pictures, sent to Dort for that purpose. Over the king is the figure of St. George, his patron saint, and above that a white rose and a red one; over the figure of the queen is a representation of St. Catherine of Alexandria, with the instruments of her martyrdom, and above the saint are the arms of the kingdom of Granada. The window occasioned a considerable agitation in the parish, and gave rise to some religious controversy at the time of its insertion. Among the accessory parts, there is a representation of a devil carrying off the soul of the impenitent thief, and an angel performing the same office for that of the penitent one. It was determined by some pious Protestants that this was downright Popery, if not blasphemy, and that such "superstitious allegories" were not proper to be admitted into a church set apart by law for the reformed worship. Even some members of the Chapter of Westminster Abbey, in whose gift the living is, expressed their discontent on the subject, as incompatible with the spirit of the Prayer Book. Through the firmness of the rector, Dr. Wilson, the window was happily preserved and maintained in its position; and the Society of Antiquaries caused a fine engraving of it to be made at their own expense.

The putting up of this splendid window gave rise to a serious and tedious law-suit against the churchwardens, which was brought forward under an old dormant statute of Edward VI., namely, "An Act for abolishing and putting away divers Books and Images," the ground of offence being the representation of the Crucifixion of our Blessed Lord, which the prosecution were pleased to term a "superstitious image or picture;" and a further grievance, that the churchwardens had not first obtained a faculty or licence from the Ordinary. However, this Act was made against actual images, not paintings or delineations upon walls or in windows. The prosecution was instituted in the name of Daniel Gell, the Registrar of the Ecclesiastical Court of the Dean and Chapter, who was in consequence struck off the list of vestrymen. The suit lasted seven years, and its conclusion is thus mentioned in the "Annual Register:"—"An appeal came lately before the Court of Delegates, between the Dean and Chapter of Westminster Abbey and the parishioners of St. Margaret's, concerning the painted window in the church: the bill was ordered to be dismissed, each side being condemned to pay its own costs."

The memory of the successful issue of this trial is perpetuated in a very beautiful and richly-chased cup, stand, and cover, silver-gilt, weighing upwards of ninety-three ounces, which Mr. Samuel Pierson, who had been churchwarden for seven successive years, presented during the time as a gift for ever to the churchwardens of the parish. It is the "loving cup" of St. Margaret's, and is produced with especial ceremony at the chief parochial entertainments.

Close by the north-west porch of the church is an ancient and massive carved seat, evidently of the fifteenth century; on it every Sunday, after morning prayers, six pence and a loaf of bread are given away to each of sixteen poor widows belonging to the parish, the bequest of Mrs. Joyce Goddard, in 1621.

In various parts of the church are monuments, more or less sumptuous and tasteful, to Mr. James Palmer, the founder of Palmer's Almshouses, and a native of the parish; to Thomas Arneway, and to Cornelius Vandan, both large benefactors of St. Margaret's parish; the latter monument bears the date 1577.

At the eastern corner of the south aisle, in an enclosure forming a vestibule to both the vestry and the church, are some very interesting monuments.

The largest and finest of these is one in the Jacobean style, to Marie, Lady Dudley, a daughter of the Lord High Admiral, Lord Howard of Effingham, and grand-daughter of Thomas, second Duke of Norfolk. She died in the year 1600, having married first Edward Sutton, Lord Dudley, and secondly Richard Montpesson, Esq., who erected the tomb. The husband is represented in a kneeling attitude, the lady recumbent. The monument, which bears a striking resemblance to the "Founder's Tomb" in the Charter House Chapel, is adorned with colour and armorial bearings.

Opposite to it is a mural tablet, erected by the Roxburghe Club in 1820, in memory of Caxton, "who, as early as the year 1477, set up a printing-press in the Abbey," as mentioned in our account of the Almonry. The window above it was filled with stained glass in honour of Caxton in 1882.

Another mural tablet, close by, records the fact of Sir Walter Raleigh's body having been buried here on the day of his execution in Palace Yard. On it are inscribed the following words:—"Reader, should you reflect on his errors, remember his many virtues, and that he was mortal;" words which, perhaps, would have been better addressed to King James, when they might have altered his fate. The west window has been filled with stained glass, the gift of Americans, as a memorial of Raleigh.

The question has more than once been started as to the burial-place of Wenceslaus Hollar. In the introduction to the catalogue of the exhibition of his etchings at the Burlington Fine Arts Club, Vertue is quoted by the compiler as having found the register of his death at St. Margaret's Church, which agrees with the account of Aubrey. But in Mr. Jesse's "Memorials of London"—a very trustworthy book—we are told that his remains lie in the burying-ground attached to the "New Chapel" in "Petty France." It does not, of course, follow that because the name of Hollar is to be found in the register of St. Margaret's Church, therefore his body was buried in that church, or even in the churchyard; but Aubrey happens to mention the very spot—"near the north-west corner of the tower"—and he is followed by another painstaking antiquary, Mr. Peter Cunningham. An interesting notice of Hollar's life will be found in Aubrey, who tells us that his father was ruined on account of adopting the Protestant religion, but that the artist died a Catholic; "of which religion," he quaintly adds, "I suppose he might be ever since he came to Arundel House."

In the ambulatory, near the door of the porch under the tower, is a mural monument to Mrs. Elizabeth Corbett, which is of considerable interest on account of its inscription, consisting of ten lines of verse from the pen of Pope. The literature of tombstones is not always of a first-rate order; but it deserves to be noted that Dr. Johnson, in his "Lives of the Poets," mentions this inscription as perhaps the happiest and best specimen of such poetry. The verses run as follows:—

"Here rests a woman, good without pretence,
Blest with plain reason, and with sober sense:
No conquest she but her own self desired,
No arts essayed, but not to be admired:
Passion and pride were to her soul unknown;
Convinced that virtue only is our own:
So unaffected, so composed a mind,
So firm, yet soft, so strong, yet so refined,
Heaven, as its purest gold, by tortures tried;—
The saint sustain'd it, but the woman died."

"I have always," says Dr. Johnson, "considered this as the most valuable of all Pope's epitaphs: the subject of it is a character not discriminated by any shining or eminent peculiarities; yet that which really makes, though not the splendour, the felicity of life, and that which every wise man will choose for his final and lasting companion in the languor of age, in the quiet of privacy, when he departs weary and disgusted from the ostentatious, the volatile and the vain. Of such a character, which the dull overlook, and the gay despise, it was fit that the value should be made known, and the dignity established. Domestic virtue, as it is exerted without great occasions, or conspicuous consequences, in an even unnoted tenor, required the genius of Pope to display it in such a manner as might attract regard and enforce reverence. Who can forbear to lament that this amiable woman has no name in the verses? If the particular lines of this inscription be examined, it will appear less faulty than the rest. There is scarcely one line taken from commonplaces, unless it be that in which *virtue only* is said to be *our own*. I once heard a lady of great beauty and excellence object to the fourth line, that it contained an unnatural and incredible panegyric. Of this let the ladies judge." Those who are inclined to be hyper-critical might possibly object to the third line, as not being quite in strict accordance with the grammatical rule which objects to the omission of words which are necessary to express the whole meaning of the writer. But a little licence must be allowed to poets, and they must not be tied down too closely to literal accuracy and exact expressions.

St. Margaret's Church contains also the remains of Skelton, the merry poet-laureate of Henry VIII., and of James Harrington, author of "Oceana." Over Skelton's tomb is this whimsical inscription:—

"Come, Alecto, lend me thy torch,
To find a churchyard in a church porch;
Poverty and poetry this tomb doth enclose:
Therefore, gentlemen, be merry in prose."

On the walls of the vestry hang two old and curious prints giving views of the interior of the several monuments now removed, as well as the original pew of the Speaker—on the epistle side of the chancel—and the old pulpit and reading-desk, which are different in character and position from those in use at the present day. We give a copy of this engraving below.

INTERIOR OF ST. MARGARET'S CHURCH. (*From Crockhall and Hodges' Prayer Book*, 1695.)

church in the reigns of Charles II. and of William and Mary, with the House of Commons in state attending the service. The latter engraving is a copy of the print by Brook, prefixed to Warner's edition of the "Book of Common Prayer," printed for Crockhall and Hodges, in 1695. It shows the old east window with the date 1692 (upwards of half a century before the erection of the present window), the communion-table before the erection of the basso-relievo modelled by Van Nost, and

Down to a very recent date, the Speaker and the House of Commons used to attend this church in state upon the days of what were known as the "State Services," such as the 30th of January (King Charles' Martyrdom), the 5th of November (Gunpowder Plot), the day of the King's or Queen's Accession, and the 29th of May (the Restoration of King Charles II.), when the sermon was always delivered by the Speaker's chaplain. Of late years the attendance of members of the Lower House

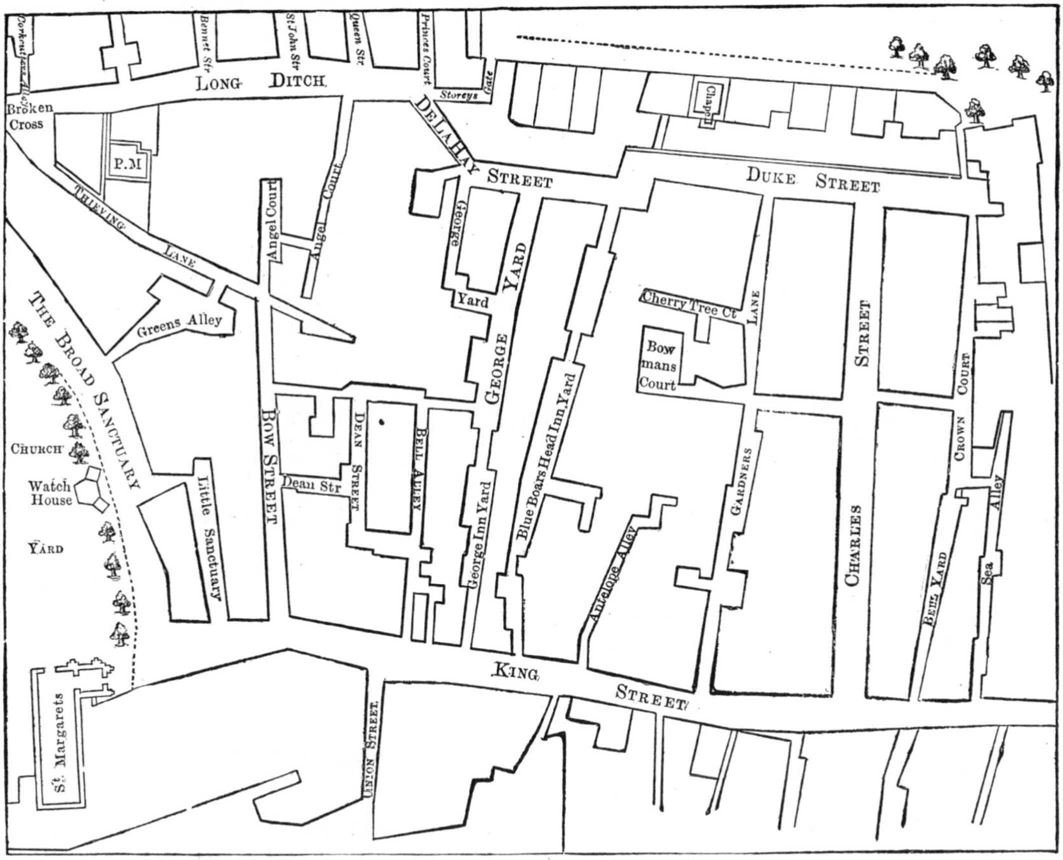

1. Before the Erection of Great George Street.

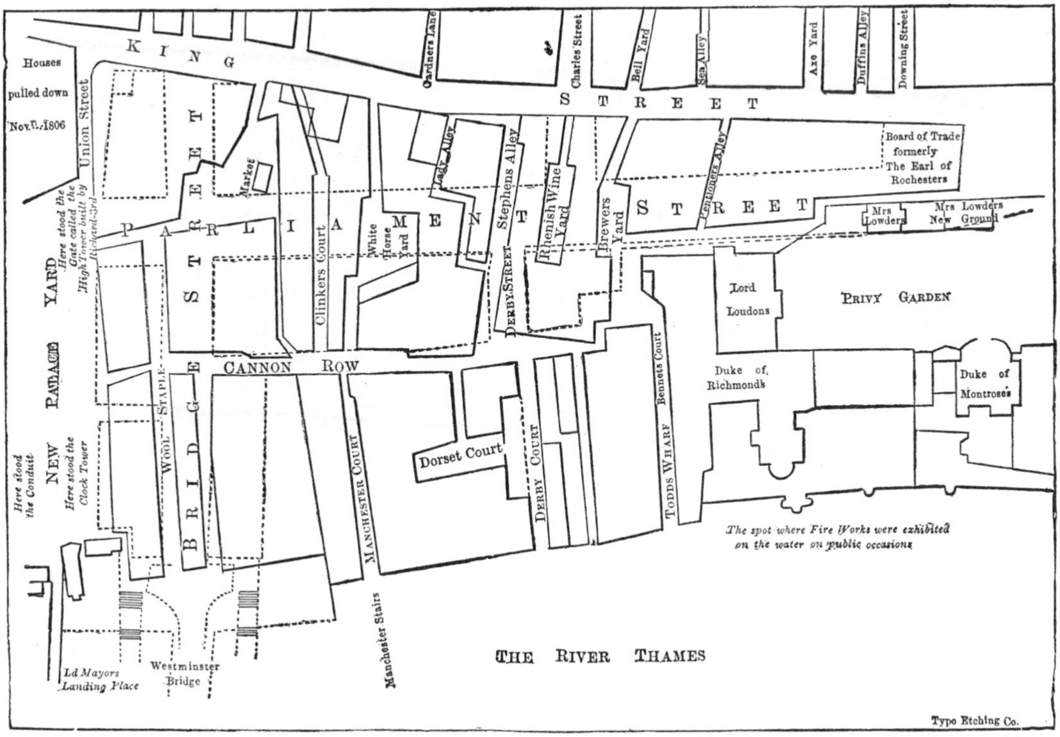

2. Before the Erection of Parliament Street.

PLAN OF A PORTION OF WESTMINSTER BETWEEN 1734 AND 1748.

had dwindled down to some seven or eight individuals, besides the Speaker himself, the Serjeant-at-Arms, and a sprinkling of clerks of the House. The State services were struck out of the Book of Common Prayer by an order in Council in the year 1858, and from that day "Mr. Speaker" has not appeared here in his wig and gown upon a week-day.

Mr. Mackenzie Walcott enumerates the following names in a list of the most eminent Puritan divines who have occupied the pulpit of St. Margaret's Church:—Calamy, Vines, Nye, Manton, Marshall, Gauden, Owen, Burgess, Newcomen, Reynolds, Cheynell, Baxter, the "critical" Lightfoot, the "illuminated" Doctor Taylor; Goodwyn, the "windmill with a weathercock atop;" and Case, who censured Oliver Cromwell to his face, and who, when discoursing before General Monk, cried out, "There are some who will betray three kingdoms for filthy lucre's sake," and threw his handkerchief into the General's face, suiting the action to the word.

This church has had several distinguished clergymen as lecturers and curates since the time of the Commonwealth, among whom we may name Dr. Outram, the accomplished Oriental scholar, and author of "De Sacrificiis;" Dr. Sprat, afterwards Dean of Westminster and Bishop of Rochester; Richard Widmore, the historian of the Abbey; Dr. Wilson, who received a sharp reprimand from George III., soon after his accession, for his fulsome flattery of the King in the pulpit—his Majesty informing Dr. Wilson that he went to church "to hear God praised, and not himself;" Dr. Taylor, the friend of Dr. Johnson, and who performed the burial service at the funeral of the great lexicographer; Dr. Stevens, afterwards Dean of Rochester; Dr. Webber, who became Dean of Ripon; Dr. Henry Hart Milman, afterwards Dean of St. Paul's; and Dr. Farrar, now Dean of Canterbury. The present rector is Canon Eyton.

As might be expected, the church does not now possess all that it could boast of in the way of accessories and ornaments before the Reformation. Besides its nave, it once had a choir, now almost wholly removed; and in its side aisles were chapels with altars dedicated to St. Margaret, St. George, St. Katharine, St. Cornelius, St. Erasmus, St. John, and two to St. Nicholas and St. Christopher. The churchwardens' accounts, still existing, serve to show with how much of zeal and devotion these altars were maintained down to the time of their dismantling by order of Henry VIII.

Some idea may be formed as to the rapidity with which ecclesiastical changes were wrought in the system of the English Church when we add that whereas in 1556 the sum of 11s. was paid to one Clerke "for making thymage (*sic*) of St. Margaret," in 1559 we find entries of 2s. 8d., of 1s., and of 1s. to John Rial for "taking down the Roode Mary and John," for "taking down the tabil (*sic*), or the high altar," and for "cleaving and sawing the Rood Mary and John." It may be noted also that the large sum of 1s. was charged and paid "for ringing at the beheading of the Queen of Scotts." In 1563, a plague similar to the influenza visited Westminster, and the inhabitants were compelled to perform quarantine. Under this year there is an entry as follows:—"1563. *Item.*—To the paynter of Totehill Street for payntinge of certeyn blew crosses to be fyxed upon sundrie houses infected, vj."

A century later, a *red* cross was the mark of an infected house. Thirty years afterwards the dogs were supposed to carry the plague about in their coats, on which the inhabitants commenced a crusade against them, and resolved to abide in their filth and carelessness. In the next ten years the persecution was renewed, and in 1603 a plague devastated the parish, when among the entries is the following:—"Payd for the graves of CCCCLI. poore folk xxxvij^s. vij^d."—doubtless a *contract* job. There are also items for "pitch and tarre for the visited houses, 12^d.," and for "papers with 'Lord, have mercy upon us!' 12^d." The dogs were again assailed, and 500 were slaughtered as a propitiation to the demon of pestilence. In the above year one Robert Wells of this parish was paid the sum of 6s. 8d. "for killing of fourscore dogs." The same individual appears to have received 10s. for "ringing at the time when the Parliament-house should have been blown up." The more recent entries refer for the most part to such prosaic matters as loads of gravel, work done about the hospital, the making of petticoats, beds, bolsters, &c., for the children, and the erection and repair of the "Butts" in "Tuthill Fields."

In May, 1642, the plot of Edmund Waller, the poet, designed to resist the violent councils of the Parliament, was first made known in St. Margaret's. "At a solemn fast, when they were listening to the sermon, a messenger entered the church, and communicated his errand to Pym, who whispered it to others who were placed near him, and then went with them out of the church, leaving the rest in solicitude and amazement. They immediately sent guards to the proper places, and that night apprehended Tompkyns and Waller, having yet traced nothing, but that letters had been intercepted, from which it appeared that the Parliament and the Cit were soon to be delivered into the hands of the Cavaliers."

In September of the same year the Solemn League and Covenant was taken in this church by both Houses of Parliament, the Assembly of Divines, and the Scottish Commissioners. "Mr. Nye read the Covenant from the pulpit, all signifying their assent to it by holding up their hands; and the members afterwards signed the parchment-roll, and then Dr. Gouge implored a blessing upon their act."

In the general spoliation of the churches which took place after the "martyrdom" of Charles I., St. Margaret's did not escape the ruthless storm, for we learn that "the font was broken down, and replaced by a miserable pewter basin, the organ was sold to a Puritan brazier, the altar destroyed, the beautiful chancel-screen hewn down, monumental brasses were torn from the graves of the sleeping departed, monuments and inscriptions were r eparably defaced."

"One scene," writes Mr. Mackenzie Walcott, "is preserved to us of those troublous times, which is a memorable example of 'Religion turned into Rebellion and Faith into Faction.' On December 20, 1648, the notorious Hugh Peters, the 'pulpit-buffoon,' as he is styled by Dugdale, preached his memorable sermon before the House of Commons; and the following description of it forms part of the evidence upon which he was condemned, and made to suffer the recompense of his guilt on October 16, 1660, presenting a memorable spectacle of meanness and a thorough coward's heart." The evidence of an eye-witness (Mr. Beaver) thus describes the scene:—"I passed through St. Margaret's Churchyard to go on my way home again. . . . I perceived all the churchyard full of musquets and pikes upon the ground, and asked some of the soldiers who were there guarding the Parliament, that were keeping a fast at St. Margaret's. 'Who preaches?' said I. They told me, 'Mr. Peters is just now gone up into the pulpit.' Said I, 'Well, I must needs have the curiosity to hear that man,' having already heard many stories about his preaching, though God knows I did not do it out of any matter of devotion. I crowded near the pulpit, and came near the Speaker's pew, . . . and I saw a great many members there whom I knew well." He then proceeds to record at length the vile blasphemy of this fierce-minded fanatic, who drew a shocking parallel between the events of those times and the circumstances of the condemnation of our Lord and Saviour, calling King Charles "the great Barabbas, the murderer, the tyrant, and the traitor." For two or three hours' time that he spent, he (Mr. Peters) did nothing but rake up all the reasons, arguments, and examples that he could in order to persuade them to bring the king to a condign, speedy, and capital punishment.

The first notice of any parliamentary assistance being granted to St. Margaret's Church occurs in the year 1650, under the Commonwealth. "It is most probable," writes Mr. Mackenzie Walcott, "that soon after the ancient chapel of St. Stephen had been yielded up by King Edward VI. to be a place no more of prayer, but for the deliberations of the House of Commons, the members of the lower House of Parliament attended divine service in St. Margaret's Church while the Lords went to the Abbey. In the reign of King James I., how ever, we have certain proof of their partaking of the Holy Sacrament in St. Margaret's."

Long sermons, it is well known, were the rule of the day under the Puritan *régime*. Thus we read that "on Tuesday, November 17, 1640, was the Fast Day, which was kept piously and devoutly. Dr. Burgess and Mr. Marshall preached before the House, at least seven hours between them, taking their texts from Jeremiah i. 5 and 2 Chronicles ii. 2," respectively.

In 1660, "the State's Arms," which had been painted up in various parts of the church and vestry were removed, and an order was made by the vestry "that the churchwardens prepare the King's Majesty's arms, to be richly carved, made, and gilded, after the best manner that can be invented with as much grace as may be, to be set up in the parish church of St. Margaret, and to be as fair and beautiful in every respect as the King's Arms are set up in and about the City of London." They are now preserved in the vestry.

The first gallery in the church was built in the north aisle in 1641, and in 1681 it was determined to build another over the south aisle, "exclusively for persons of quality." On this occasion we are told incidentally that Sir Christopher Wren himself attended in the vestry, and promised to lend his assistance in its design and erection. We learn from Mr. Mackenzie Walcott that the ill-advised gentleman who presented this cumbrous gift to the church was a certain civic knight, a loyalist and a miser, Sir John Cutler, the same who is immortalised by Pope's cutting satire. It must be remembered in his excuse that Wren knew little about the theory and principles of the Gothic or Pointed architecture, though so skilled in all that was connected with every variety of the Classical or Italian school.

About the sermons of the time and the demeanour of the congregation Dr. Johnson relates a singular anecdote. "Burnet and Spratt were old rivals. On some public occasion they both preached before the House of Commons. There prevailed in those days an indecent custom: when the preacher touched any favourite topic in a manner that delighted his audiences, their approbation was expressed by a loud hum, continued in proportion to their zeal or pleasure. When Burnet preached, part of his congregation hummed so loudly and so long, that he sat down to enjoy it, and rubbed his face with his handkerchief. When Spratt preached, he likewise was honoured with a like animating hum, but he stretched out his hand to the congregation, and cried, 'Peace, peace; I pray you, peace!'" "Burnet's sermon," says Salmon, "was remarkable for sedition, and Spratt's for loyalty. Burnet had the thanks of the House; Spratt had no thanks, but a good living from the King, which he said was of as much value as the thanks of the Commons." It is said that one day when preaching here before the House of Commons, Bishop Burnet turned his hour-glass, in order to show that he was about to continue his discourse, and that he was nearly interrupted by the applauding murmurs of his hearers—a strong testimony to his eloquence, or their power of endurance.

A curious traditionary custom had been preserved here, to commemorate the restoration of the Royal Family. A triumphal arch was raised every year in the church; but early in the last century a portion of it, happening to fall, killed a carpenter, whereupon the vestry directed that "the triumphal arch behind the pulpit should be taken down, erected by Sir William Playters, Knt."

In 1735 the church was repaired, and its tower cased, the expense of the undertaking being defrayed by a Parliamentary grant, in consideration of its being the church where the members of the House of Commons attended divine service on stated holidays.

The celebrated Whitefield, too, preached one of his extraordinary discourses in this church one Sunday evening in February, 1739, "having actually seized possession of the pulpit by violence; and then was locked up in it by the sexton, and kept there guarded by six lusty fellows, to the great confusion of the bewildered congregation."

In June, 1742, the House of Commons formally renewed a resolution which had been passed in 1699, but had gradually come to be neglected, to the effect "that for the future no person, except the chaplain, who was under the dignity of a Dean or the Degree of Doctor of Divinity, be recommended to preach before this House." The original order, it appears, was made in consequence of a comment made by one of the Puritan preachers, Stephen Marshall, on the death of King Charles I., saying that "it should be a lesson to all kings lest they should come to the same end."

In 1763 the vestry directed that "the figures of St. Peter and St. Paul should be painted, in imitation of statuary, by Mr. Cassali, and placed in niches on each side of the altar of the church." This was done at the cost of nearly £40, which was part of a gift of the Duke of Northumberland to the parish.

In May, 1792–93, and again in June, 1794, there was a performance of sacred music in this church, the oratorio of the "Messiah" being sung, for the benefit of the Royal Society of British Musicians, under the patronage of George III. In 1795, however, an objection was raised to a repetition of these musical festivals, on the ground that for a considerable length of time the church had to be closed, in order to be prepared with seats sufficiently numerous to accommodate the large audience meeting for such a purpose; and, accordingly, that year witnessed the last of these performances in St. Margaret's Church.

An anecdote illustrative of what may be styled electioneering piety, is told about this church. In the year 1768 a printed notice was stuck upon the doors and walls of the church, one Sunday morning, to the effect that "The prayers of the congregation are earnestly desired for the restoration of liberty, depending on the election of Mr. Wilkes."

In St. Margaret's Church, in 1656, John Milton was married to his second wife, Katherine Woodcocke, who, with her infant child, is buried here. In 1888 a memorial window was unveiled in the north aisle. It was the gift of an American gentleman, and bears an inscription by Whittier. Another stained-glass window is in memory of Admiral Blake, who was buried in the churchyard; and yet others commemorate Lord Frederick Cavendish, Lord and Lady Hatherley, Sir Thomas Erskine May, Mr. W. H. Smith, and Mr. Edward Lloyd, printer and publisher. In 1887 one of those in the south aisle was filled with stained glass in honour of Queen Victoria's Jubilee; to this there is an inscription by Browning. Viscount Sherbrooke (Robert Lowe) is commemorated by an elegant new porch, built at the cost of Lady Sherbrooke.

In St. Margaret's Thomas Campbell was married; and here Barbara Villiers, afterwards Duchess of Cleveland, was baptised in November, 1640.

Mr. Wood, in his "Ecclesiastical Antiquities of London," says there was a "scala cœli" in this church; but in all probability he has mistaken St.

Margaret's Chapel for that of St. Marie de la Pieu, which stood close to St. Stephen's Chapel. Tradition says that a stone cross and pulpit stood here, but no picture of it is known to exist now.

For many years, down to the time when Parliament came to a decision on the subject of intramural interment, the churchyard of St. Margaret's had been a standing disgrace to the parish, in consequence of its overcrowded condition. In 1850 Dr. Reid reported that "the state of the burying-ground was prejudicial to the air supplied at the Houses of Parliament, and also to the whole neighbourhood; that offensive emanations had been noticed at all hours of the night and morning;" and that even "fresh meat was frequently tainted by the deleterious gases issuing from this churchyard." A new burial-ground for the parish was at length obtained in the neighbourhood of the Fulham Road, and the churchyard was levelled and paved over with grave-stones.

It has frequently been proposed to remove even the church itself, as obstructing the view of the Abbey. Many persons, however, are of opinion that it serves to set off the larger edifice, whose grandeur is all the more clearly seen when placed in close contrast with the humble parochial edifice. Canon Conway remarks that—"It may be questioned whether the removal of the church would greatly improve the view of the Abbey from the northern approach, inasmuch as the great length of the Abbey when seen in full flank (as may be noticed from Vauxhall Bridge) must awkwardly expose the defect occasioned by the absence of the central tower."

The alterations and improvements in the neighbourhood of the Abbey date from about the year 1806. Hunter, writing in 1811, congratulates his readers on the fact that at the cost of nearly half a million "the whole of the buildings which obscured St. Margaret's Church, between King Street and Palace Yard, have been removed, and also those in the Broad Sanctuary east and west of the new Sessions House." Although much that was old and dirty was swept away, it is to be feared that many relics of antiquity perished. In 1881–82 a great improvement was made in the appearance of the Churchyard by converting it into green turf, so as to form a better approach to the Abbey.

A unique relic connected with this parish is the tobacco-box belonging to the Past Overseers' Society. It is an object of antiquarian curiosity, and an article of considerable intrinsic value. Its history is curious and interesting. The original oval-shaped box, made of common horn, and of a portable size for the pocket, was purchased by a Mr. Monck at "Horn Fair," in the village of Charlton, near Woolwich, for the trifling sum of fourpence, and from it he often replenished his neighbour's pipe at the meetings of his predecessors and companions in the office of overseers of the poor. In 1713 he presented it to the Society of Past Overseers, and in 1720 this body of worthies ornamented the lid with a silver rim, in commemoration of the donor. The next addition was a silver side-case and bottom, in 1726. In 1740 an embossed border was placed upon the lid, and the bottom enriched with an emblem of Charity. In 1746 Hogarth engraved inside the lid a bust of the Duke of Cumberland, with allegorical figures and scroll, commemorating the Battle of Culloden. In 1765 an interwoven scroll was added to the lid, enclosing a plate with the arms of the City of Westminster, and an inscription to the following effect:—"This box to be delivered to every succeeding set of overseers, on penalty of five guineas."

The original horn box being thus ornamented, an additional case of silver, lined with crimson velvet, was provided for it, and this, in its turn, became enveloped in a third, fourth, fifth, and sixth case, each bearing proofs of the liberality of its several custodians—the senior overseer for the time being—silver plates engraved with emblematical and historical subjects, portraits, and inscriptions. The outer case, which was added in 1878, is octagonal in shape, about 3 feet in height, formed of panelled oak, and was presented by Mr. G. T. Miller, J.P. The plate recording this fact is engraved with a representation of Cleopatra's Needle, and is also inscribed with the names of the churchwardens and overseers for the time being of the combined parishes of St. Margaret and St. John, Westminster, together with the records of the following historical events:—"The War between Russia and Turkey;" "Loss of H.M.S. *Eurydice* with 326 lives off the Isle of Wight, 24th March, 1878;" "Opening of the New Infirmary, Fulham;" "St. Margaret's Church closed for Restoration;" and "The Needle was safely towed into the East India Docks, January, 1878." Another plate was added to the box in April, 1882, and bears upon it three finely-engraved portraits, with dates of the deaths of Lord Beaconsfield, Lord Hatherley, and Dean Stanley. The historical event recorded upon this plate is the laying of the foundation stone of the New Town Hall by the Baroness Burdett-Coutts in 1882. Other plates have been added year by year since 1882, and in 1887, Jubilee year, the outermost case was surmounted by a silver statuette of the Queen.

Among the historical subjects engraved on the inner cases are, a view of the fireworks in St. James's Park, to celebrate the Peace of Aix-la-Chapelle, in 1749; Admiral Keppel's Action off Ushant, and his acquittal after a court-martial; the Battle of the Nile; the Battle of Trafalgar, 1805; the Battle of Waterloo, 1815; the Bombardment of Algiers, 1816; the interior of the old House of Lords at the Trial of Queen Caroline, 1820; and the Coronation of George IV. and his visit to Scotland, in 1822. The whole of these subjects are beautifully engraved, as also are the portraits, of which there are several, embracing among others, John Wilkes, churchwarden in 1759, and afterwards Lord Mayor of London; Nelson, Duncan, Howe, Vincent, Fox, and Pitt; George IV. as Prince Regent, the Princess Charlotte, and Queen Charlotte. The most interesting engravings, perhaps, are those of local subjects, such as the "View of the North Front of Westminster Hall;" the "Interior of Westminster Hall, with the Volunteers of the City of Westminster attending Divine Service at the Drum-head on a Fast Day, 1803;" the "Old Sessions' House;" a "View of St. Margaret's, from the North-west," and also views of the west front, the tower, and the altar-piece. In 1813 a large silver plate was added to the then outer case, with a portrait of the Duke of Wellington, commemorating the cenenary of the box.

The top of the second case has a representation of the Guardians of the Poor in the Board-room, and an inscription, which runs as follows:—"The original box and cases to be given to every succeeding set of overseers, on penalty of fifty guineas, 1783." It will be observed from this last inscription that the fine imposed was now multiplied by ten.

In 1793, Mr. Read, a past overseer, detained the box in revenge, because his accounts had not been passed. An action was brought against the offender, which was long delayed, owing to two members of the society giving him a release, which he successfully pleaded in bar to the action. This rendered it necessary to take proceedings in Equity; and accordingly a bill was filed in the Court of Chancery against all three, and Mr. Read was compelled to deposit the box with Master Leeds until the end of the suit. Three long years of litigation ensued. Eventually the Chancellor directed the box to be restored to the Overseers' Society, and Mr. Read paid in costs £300. The extra costs amounted to £76 13s. 11d., owing to the illegal proceedings of Mr. Read. Some £90 were at once raised, and the surplus spent upon adding a third case, of an octagon shape. The top records the triumph—Justice trampling upon a prostrate man, from whose face a mask falls upon a writhing serpent. A second plate, on the outside of the fly-lid, represents the Lord Chancellor, Lord Loughborough, pronouncing his decree for the restoration of the box, March 5, 1796.

On the fourth case is an engraving of the Anniversary Meeting of the Past Overseers' Society, with the churchwarden giving the charge previous to delivering the box to the succeeding overseer, who is bound to produce it at certain parochial entertainments, with three pipes of tobacco at the least. under the penalty of six bottles of claret, and to return the whole, with some addition, safe and sound, under a penalty of 200 guineas. One plate on the outer case records the royal command for the box to be taken to Buckingham Palace, and the fact of its inspection by Her Majesty, the Prince Consort, and the royal family. A tobacco-stopper of mother-of-pearl, with a silver chain, enclosed within the box, completes this unique memorial of the kindly feeling which perpetuates year by year the old ceremonies of this most united parish, and renders this traditionary piece of plate of great price, far outweighing its own intrinsic value.

The parish of St. Margaret's in olden time extended as far as Charing Cross, and even up the Strand as far as the western boundary of the houses in St. Clement's Danes. Though the site of the old palace of Whitehall, to the extent of about three acres, was made extra-parochial at an early date, yet the registers of this parish contain records of a great number of baptisms and burials from almost every part of it which can be identified by name—the Palace itself, the Queen's House, the Pantry, the Laundry, the Chapel, the Tilt-Yard, the Privy Garden, the Tennis Court, and lastly the Cock-pit.

It may be well to conclude this chapter by remarking that St. Margaret's Church is dedicated not to the holy Queen of Scotland, as most persons imagine, but to St. Margaret, "Virgin and Martyr of Antioch," on whose well-known legend Dean Milman founded the story of the poem which first made his name known to the world, "The Martyr of Antioch."

END OF VOL. III.